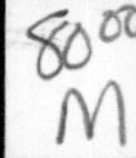
80.00
M

EVANSTON PUBLIC LIBRARY
W9-BJM-577

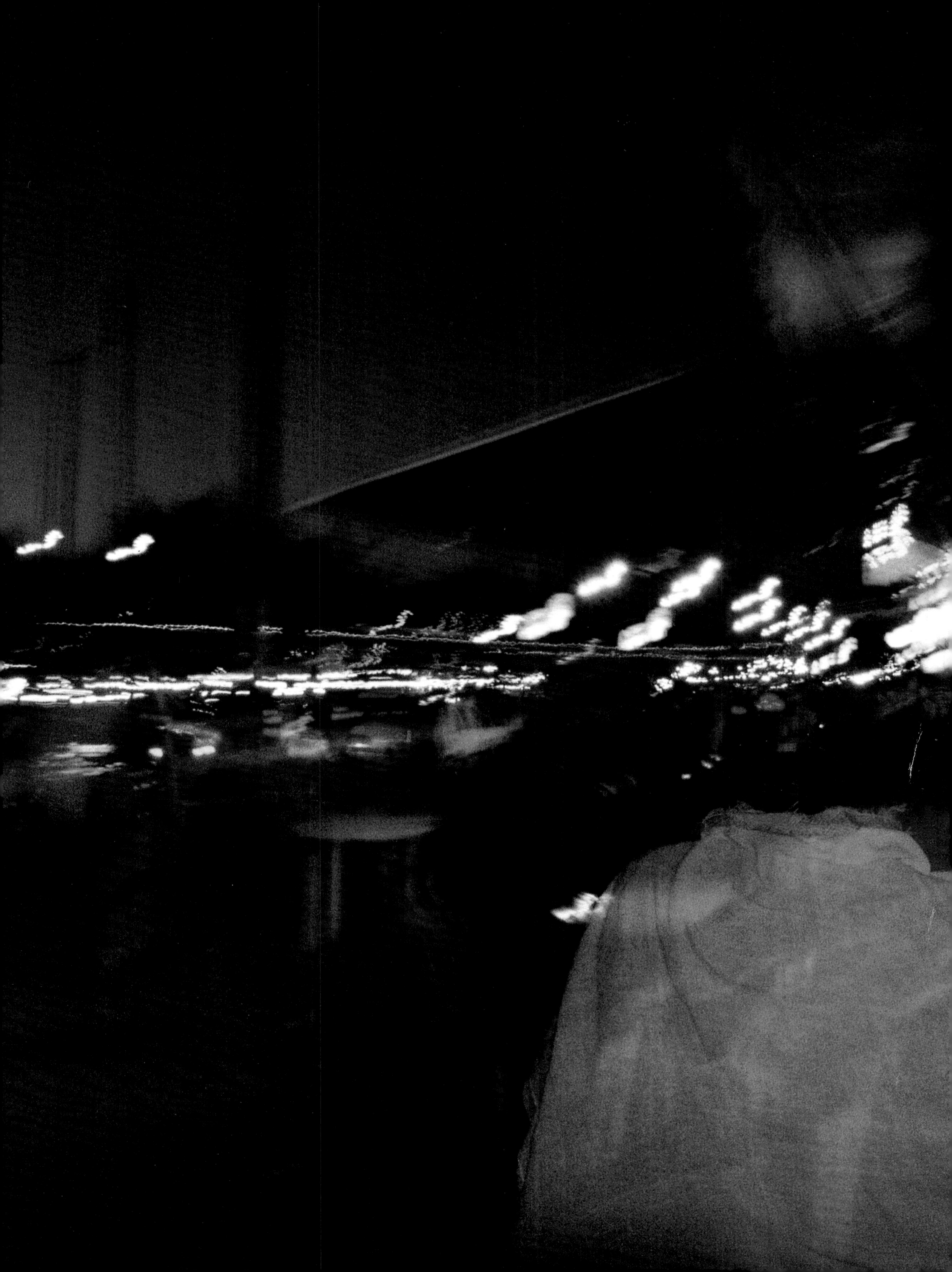

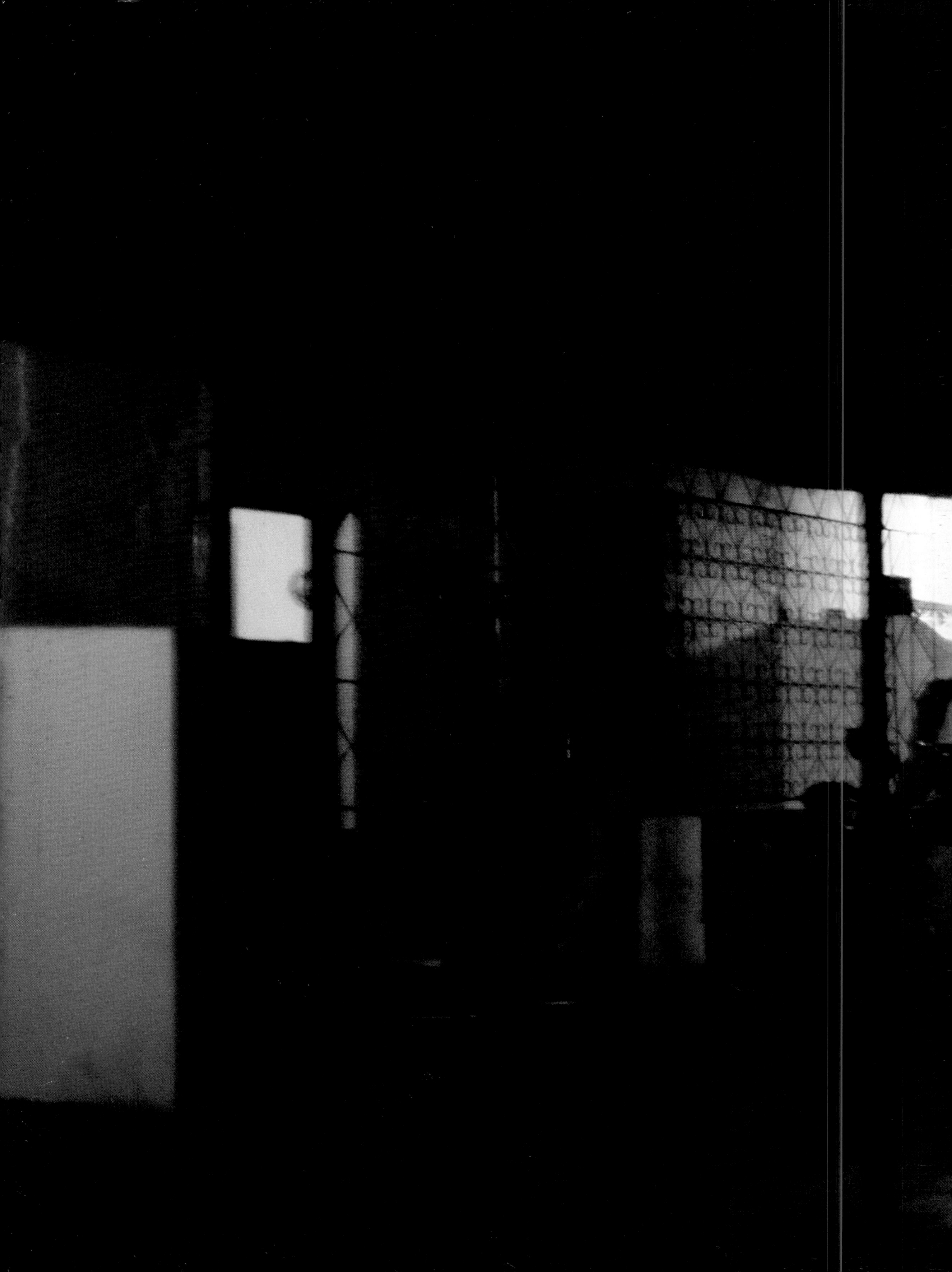

An Anthology of African Art
The Twentieth Century

Edited by N'Goné Fall and Jean Loup Pivin

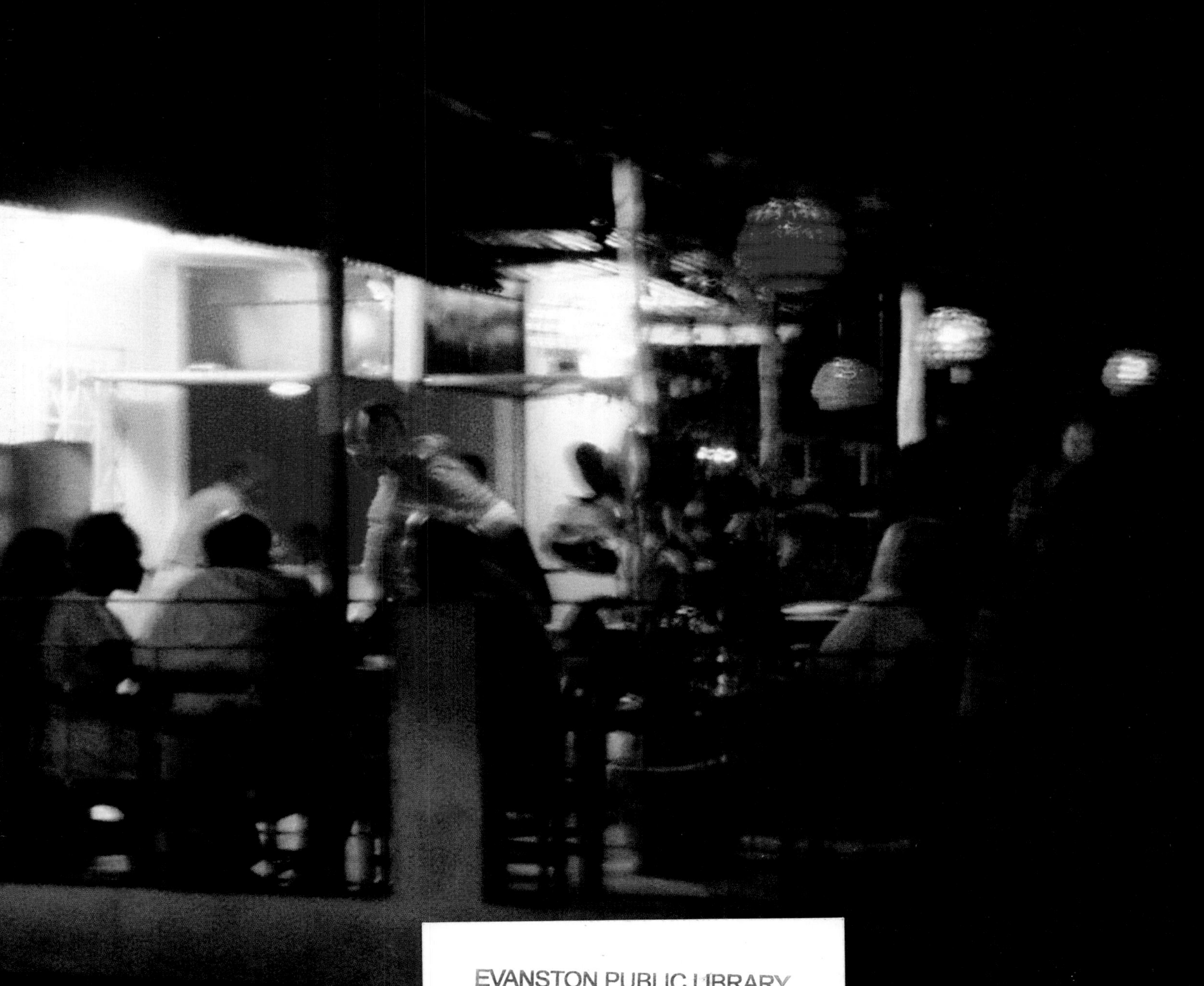

D.A.P./Distributed Art Publishers, Inc., New York
Revue Noire Éditions, African Contemporary Art, Paris

An Anthology of African Art:
The Twentieth Century

Managing Editor Lori Waxman
Translation All Languages Ltd., Toronto
Typesetting Steven Mosier/THING
Cover design goodesignny.com
Printing Eurografica, Vicenza, Italy
Type Akzidenz Grotesque Berthold

Published by
D.A.P./Distributed Art Publishers, Inc.
155 Sixth Avenue, 2nd floor, New York NY 10013
T (212) 627-1999 F(212) 627-9484
www.artbook.com

ISBN 1-891024-38-8

Library of Congress Cataloging-in-Publication Data

Anthologie de l'art africain du XXe siècle. English
An anthology of african art : the twentieth century / edited by N'Goné Fall and Jean Loup Pivin.-- English language ed.
p. cm.
Includes bibliographical references and index.
ISBN 1-891024-38-8 (hardcover)
1. Art, African--Africa, Sub-Saharan--20th century. I. Fall, N'Goné. II. Pivin, Jean Loup.
N7391.65 A5713 2002001449
2002001449

Editors N'Goné Fall and Jean Loup Pivin
Coordinator N'Goné Fall
Art Director Pascal Martin Saint Léon
Documentation and Illustrations Farid Abdelouahab
Creative Design Loïc Le Gall

Translations:
English texts Solange Schnall, Pierre-Richard Rouillon
German texts Edith Vielle
Spanish texts Frédérique Fau

Acknowledgements:
Elsbeth Court, Célestin Badibanga ne Mwine, Culture et Développement/France, Amirou Diallo, les Éditions de l'Oeil, Heidi Ernst-Luseno, Florence Fofana Denis Gérard, Johannesburg Art Gallery/South Africa, Sidney Littlefield Kasfir, Odile Meyer, Musée des Arts Africains et Océaniens/France, Musée des Beaux-Arts d'Angoulême/France, Musée d'Histoire Naturelle de La Rochelle/France, Musée Royal de l'Afrique Centrale/Belgium, Sandra Nagel, National Gallery of Zimbabwe, National Museum of Accra/Ghana, National Museum of Lagos/Nigeria, Prof. Joseph Nkrumah, Amadou Njoya, Chica Okeke, Jean-Dominique Penel, South African National Gallery/South Africa, Amadou Sow, Stephen Friedman Gallery/United Kingdom, Nancy Vanderlinden, the authors and artists whose works are reproduced in this book.

First published by :
Éditions Revue Noire
8 rue Cels, 75014 Paris
tél.: 33 (0)1 43 20 92 00
fax: 33 (0)1 43 22 92 60
redaction@revuenoire.com
http://www.revuenoire.com

First French edition : ISBN 2-909571-34-3, à Paris, octobre 2001.

With the assistance of the Institute for Cultural Enterprise, a New York Foundation for the Arts program, thanks to the generous support of the Ford Foundation.

With the assistance of the Centre National du Livre.

And the Prince Claus Fund for Culture and Development.

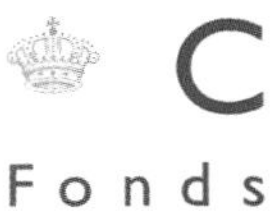

C
Fonds
Fondation Prince Claus *pour la* Culture et le Développement

Table of contents

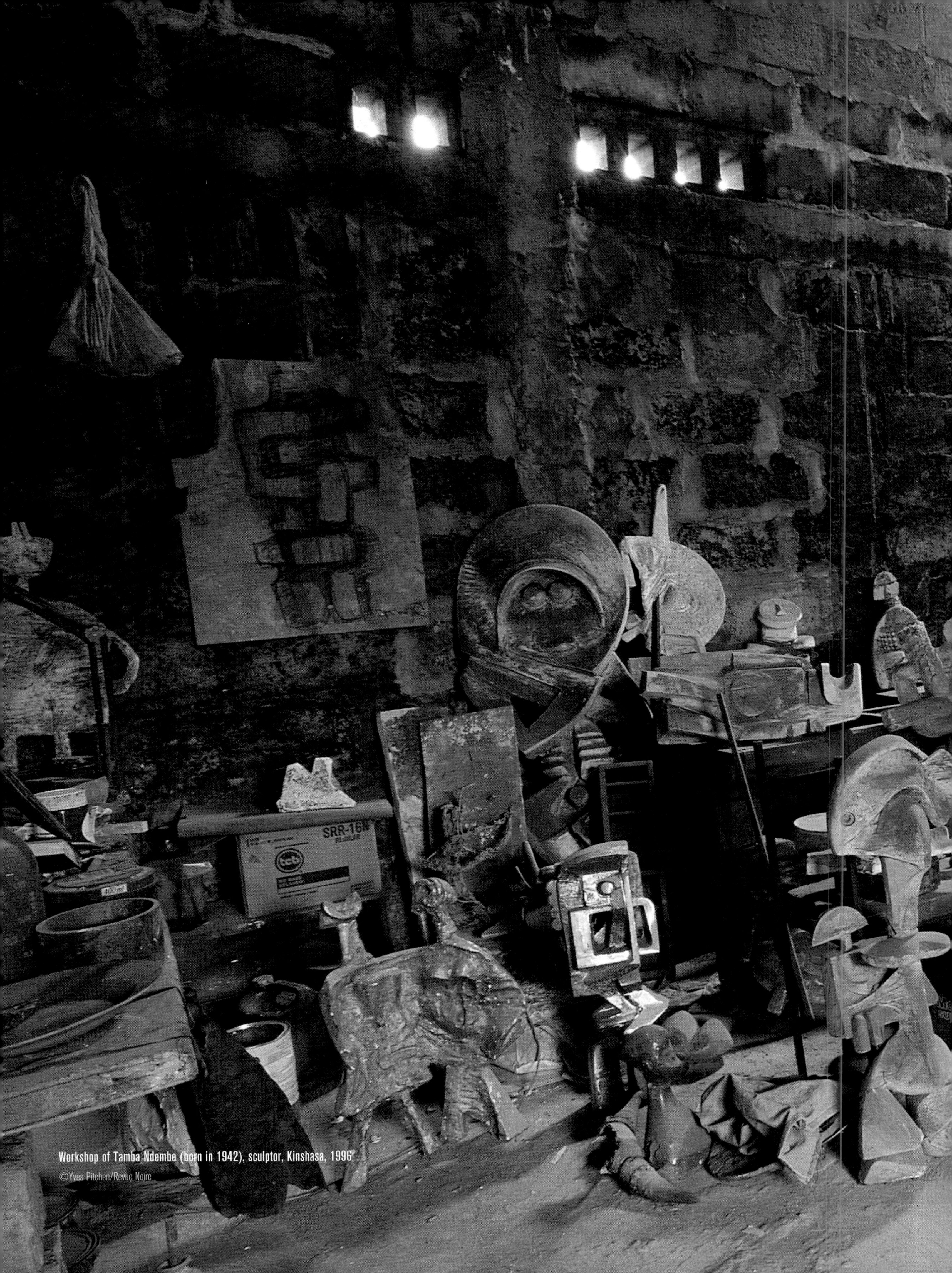

Workshop of Tamba Ndembe (born in 1942), sculptor, Kinshasa, 1996

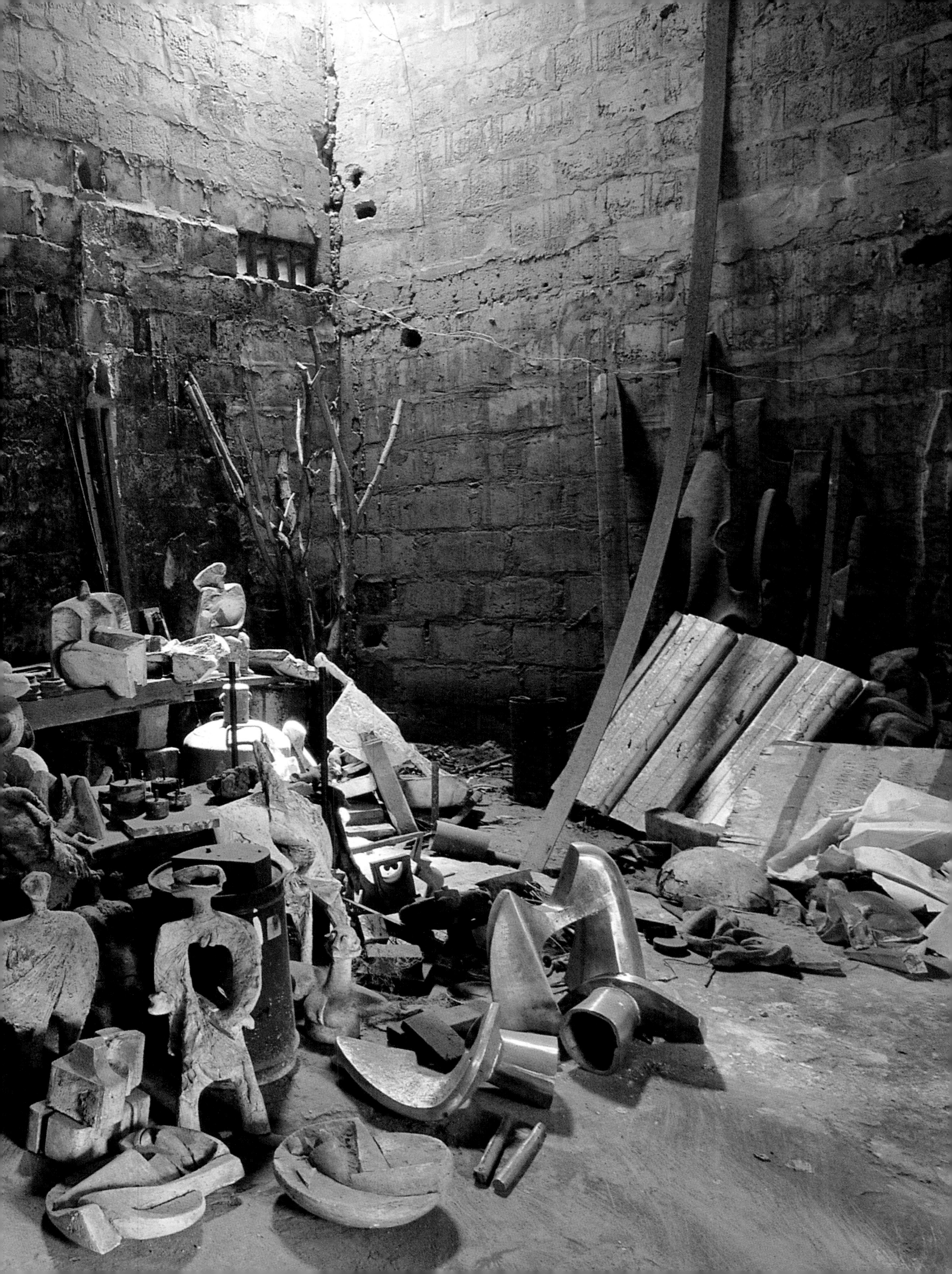

POSTULATES AND CONVICTIONS

Jean Loup Pivin

Although, over the past ten years, Revue Noire has attempted to expand people's understanding of Africa's contemporary expressions and of its Diaspora, our intention was not necessarily to write, publication after publication, a history of Africa, but simply to portray the continent's present reality.

The goal of this work is actually to put the contemporary into perspective in relation to the past and thereby take the first steps towards defining the continent's art history. We have not included Mediterranean Africa and the Indian Ocean, but have instead concentrated on 20th century Africa, when the artist, in the modern sense of the word, was born.

Putting together a synthesis of multiple historical works would have been a useful exercise. However, considering the example of Senegal alone, our own searches have revealed that although there have been numerous texts written on its recent history, nothing exists between the end of the 19th century and the 1950s, except in popular form, which may seem unbelievable. However, it is mainly on the English-speaking countries that in-depth research has been done in this field.

Although we were able to expand the field of knowledge by gathering theories and perspectives on specific experiences and countries, in order to try to open up our field of vision with respect to African art, we never sought to provide ONE truth, ONE single image of contemporary African creation. This is why we have gathered the opinions of historians, anthropologists and also of relevant everyday observers (African, whenever possible), without any reverse ostracism. As is always the case with the Revue Noire approach, we study a subject by gathering scattered contributions in order to establish an open, not closed, vision and knowledge. This explains why some texts may at times appear dissonant, at the very least, and contradictory, at the very most.

As we attempted to show with the Anthology of African Photography, this work is meant to be ambitious, but remains genuinely humble and conscious of its limits. We hope that this book will entice each African region and country to create its own history of forms. Let us meet again in ten years to take stock and enhance these initial comments, this initial desire to gain some insight into the art produced on the African continent.

A certain number of convictions overlap these presuppositions, which are intended to be objective.

Cultural evolutions and revolutions are inevitable

The presence of colonists, the military and European modernity have painted African modernity. But the transportation, knowledge, economic and communications revolutions that fueled the West would have nonetheless reached the African continent, with or without military colonization. These revolutions would have given rise, in any case, to phenomena of international urbanization, deculturation or superimposition of several cultural models, as has been currently happening since the waves of independence. Appropriation would have occurred, in any event, but probably in a less tense cosmopolitan environment. We are not saying this to rewrite history, but simply to assert that military colonialism brings about cultural colonialism or "natural" cultural exchanges, whether or not one wants to underestimate the natural abilities of each culture to feed itself off the culture of others. Everyone is aware of what the neighbor is thinking and producing. This cultural colonial fact is partially related to the vision of the colonizer, who prevents, to a certain extent, the free integration of Western revolutions at its pace and within its ability, as was probably the dream of Sultan Njoya of Cameroon at the beginning of the 20th century.

The cultural, economic, technological and scientific revolutions that have traumatized even the West, as though it could not control the tools it had created, would have, in any circumstance, been integrated either harmoniously or tragically.

There is no simple answer to the issue of the transparency of the new techniques imported. One of the current problems involves knowing whether a technique can be used without espousing its esthetic and cultural consequences, or the knowledge and contexts existing beforehand. The answer is complex, but not opaque.

African photography is the best evidence of this. It brings to life millions of images using technical criteria, but applies them to their cultural and formal (namely, artistic) contexts, thereby transforming photography into an original expression. Besides photography, we can find other expressions that use the techniques of Western art and even certain esthetic principles, while avoiding its content and meanings; however, these remain marginal in relation to the majority of what has been revealed in African art in the 20th century. Unlike photography, which lives off of its domestic market, most of the "modern" expression of African arts is based on a European market – of the colonial administrator, the colonist, as well as of the visitor or the traveler – giving the purchaser of a piece of art some type of right to violate the inspiration. A somewhat sympathetic, but not quite cultivated market, which sees in the painting or sculpture an ornament for the home or palace. Artists are seen as artisans (the best proof of this is seen in the first craft, and not art, schools, even if they could sometimes share the same name). Modern African art will take decades to free itself from this image. Is it still free from Western demand, as pure as it may be?

Modern african art is not an abuse of language

Content

When we speak of modern African art, the words used refer to the notion of art, a notion of Africanness and modernity. These words are referenced in European art history, but when they are used together in this way, have no content for Africa. Modern Western art is based on the artist's autonomy in relation to the order placed. The artist steps back from society in order to better portray it, to better interpret the spiritual side or to better communicate with nature, with the "natural order of things." Contrary to African civilizations, we speak of the death of the individual outside society. The individual does not exist, only society does. The individual cannot be alone, isolated in the face of his fate and social integration. Every individual is the child of his mother, of his family, and of his culture. He is not alone. If he steps outside this circle, it is because he wants to die. If in fact these references can also be applied to the notion of artist, a notion that breaks away from the notion of blacksmith, of assistant to the divine (priest), or of sculptor of ancestral African societies and civilizations, the African artist living in the city or countryside becomes, once again, alone and "one" when he produces his work with or without any order. Henceforth, the African artist's fate takes the same turn as the Western artist's, and he simply becomes an artist whose geographical origin is only important to him. His work alone can be viewed and judged without any contextualization of origin or race. This last point is the claim made by most contemporary artists in Africa. Thus, instead of speaking of the African artist, we will speak, more correctly, of the artist of Africa.

Form

The black continent has never actually received the media attention and praise for its talents to which Europe and America have been privy, despite a few fairly brilliant attempts. National authorities have been too concerned with political and economic emergencies and with meeting the population's basic needs. Before them, the colonial authorities were not quite convinced of the need for education at all, let alone the need for artistic education. As a result, they only carried out very few, isolated actions during the last decades of their occupation, as we will see in this book. We will also be speaking about African plastic arts, or plastic arts in Africa, without necessarily trying to create a style, school or a specifically African approach, even though, in certain cases, such an approach exists.
The purpose of this book is to touch upon generations of artists in all genres, and not a specific territory or fertile land. These are not traditional ritual artists, but rather multiple artistic forms that cannot be viewed from the angle of relentless African uniqueness, even though the subject matter imposed on the first generations of artists was the image of a deliberately grotesque Africa. This did not, however, take away from the talent of those who had to respond to this.

The need to include time – a historical perspective – in how African art is viewed

To include time in african productions has also become essential. We progressively discover that African civilizations are not fossilized and monolithic, but rather engraved in time like all other civilizations. Modern art in Africa was not born in the 1950s. It evolved not only from the colonial process, but also from the maturation and development of the forms of its very culture and civilizations. Africa is braving new social, economic and political modes as it always has, in the same way other civilizations do, including Europe, namely with its own history and values. It is perhaps in this sense that we can speak of an African modernity, without necessarily evoking ONE TYPE of African art.

We should not be satisfied with the mere utterance of false facts, such as those included in copying or the absence of writing

Copying

All initiatory education focuses on the conscious and unconscious reproduction of a model, which does not involve copying in the sense of industrial copy or tracing paper, but rather perpetuating in a close form espousing the essential elements to be reproduced. This characteristic has remained a staple of all "self-taught" expressions, and even of "erudite" expressions, to use the language of Pierre Gaudibert in his work on contemporary African art. However, it is important not to reduce copying to the "imbecile" level. If every artist from whatever corner of the world were to admit that ex nihilo "creation" does not exist and that everything involves appropriation and influence, then every artist would appreciate the non-induced, "non-copied" portion of his work. The appreciation of this personal part, which is proper to the individual, did not initially exist in Africa, which does not mean that it cannot exist to the same extent as any other "manufacturer" of form, including the traditional sculptor of ritual art. This absence of inhibition, absence of problems with difference is probably part of what will be observed in all of Africa's artistic currents in the 20th century. Whereas the historian of Western art focuses his observations mainly on breaking away, on change, on what creates the individuality, novelty or originality of a work, the same critic's observations on African art will be on the permanence, the connection with the timelessness of a creation, and will give this criterion supremacy. This reinforces a predisposition to creation based on a model, which corroborates our previous comment, namely the need to put time into how one looks at African art. Although it is important to show permanence, it is even more essential to show invention and renewal, which are at the heart of artistic production in Africa, behind a façade of permanence and continuity. Each reader must understand that an African artist is the same as a European, American or Asian artist, that he is more than a product of his past and of his future.

Absence of writing
In order to battle the a priori absence of writing in Africa, most people have sought, and seek still, to retort that everything is writing, as will sometimes be seen in certain texts in this book. This would lead us to a semiological analysis of forms, as if the process for manufacturing forms was based on a writing style with a verb, subject and object, with invariant terms and language. The notion of language recognized by all African societies and civilizations did not result in most of them being written. Also, for thousands of years, all of the civilizations of the world considered language and the different components of the universe of forms – painting, sculpture, architecture, dance, music, singing and words – to be sufficiently rich to portray a reality and its abstraction. Somebody's word was worth his signature on paper, a story told had the same value as a written text. Moreover, digital technology, which has become a full-fledged form of information and communication transcription between humans, can be called a new expression without the people and cultures who have not possessed it for thousands of years being uncultivated and unrefined beings and civilizations, lacking knowledge and know-how.
The materialistic evolutionism that has set into Western thought since the 19th century can no longer be removed from modern thought. Progress in the field of humanity and spirituality hardly makes sense anymore. Although social cohesion and the connection to nature and the cosmos when reflecting upon death (whether or not in a religious context) take precedence, in certain societies and civilizations, over mastering subject-matter, these societies and civilizations cannot be judged based on the material development of Western societies, which contribute nothing to the fundamental questions of man and social values. The current problem of social breakdown in all cities around the world is a prime example of this.
Trying to find writing where none exists, namely in the universe of forms, is due simply to the unfortunate fluency of language, i.e. an error. However, finding one or more meanings therein remains one of our main concerns: "meaning" should be construed as signification and sensations.

"Good contemporary African art" does not exist
The debate surrounding modern art in Africa has been all the rage both inside Africa and outside the continent from the beginning of the century until the last decade of the 20th century. From one coast to the other, words ring out: Black Identity, African Identity, the trap of mimicry, the trap of academism, the trap of the international market (we'll get to this later), the forced marriage of tradition and modernity, the political desire for social art with a social vocation before and after the independence movement. Mixing genres is frequent between still living ritual art, popular art, urban art, recovery art and the art that certain people would like to call sophisticated. Social anthropologists fight with too few art critics to assert a solely contextual reading. All speeches are good and accompany varied productions of varied talents. Contempt for artists who are conscious of their work has long resulted in their being seen as "sexual psychopaths sacrificed on the altar of acculturation." Attempts have even been made to portray these artists as merely "bastard" products of an impossible synthesis between Africa and the West. People want something that is authentic, true and pure, even if they have to invent it. Artists wishing to paint, sculpt or produce as they see fit have been tossed around, knocked down, and mostly ignored because they only partially participate in the debate from which they are the first to be excluded.

This battle against such received ideas is part of our preliminary discussion
Critics, exhibit commissioners, chance specialists of development, non-African artists, collectors, merchants, Africa enthusiasts, and Africanists have been trying for decades to define "good contemporary African art," art which, not including Western "mimicry" and "empty repetition of traditional arts," has been asserting itself. Revue Noire has been trying to cut itself out of all of these discussions since 1990 in order to give an image, a simple image of the multiplicity of contemporary creation everywhere and in all of its disciplines, without seeking to espouse any type of doctrine of "good modern art." Pierre Verger – the expert, the "babalao," the photographer, the free man – used to tell us not to try to interpret reality, but just to see it and listen to it and wait for the meaning to make sense, if our poor minds can find any. What may come of this exercise, by looking at tens of thousands of published and exhibited images, is that there is not one, but multiple forms of expression for contemporary African art, as is the case everywhere else in the world. There is, sometimes, a "technological" lag because the means and the "observers" are less numerous than elsewhere (even though everything is changing at a fast pace).

The international market, or the pseudo exteriority imposed, must be put into perspective
Similarly, the "international market" is often mentioned, without truly knowing what it involves, and demonized in reviews and newspaper articles as an agent that destroys African "authenticity." Unfortunately, the international market has only recently developed a marginal interest in African artists living in Africa. We can assert that hardly any African artists have penetrated the international market in 2001. This is simply because the international market looks at the work and the artist, and not their origins. And the truly international market, which is a speculative tool connected to an artist's starification and the rarity of the work, can only integrate a few artists from the entire planet per year. This is why, in the 1990s, only twenty African artists gained international recognition without all of them entering the "international market." That is just twenty artists per decade for an entire continent! However, it is true that the purchasing model and criteria are linked to the international market, itself a mirror of current artistic and social trends. Nevertheless, can we truly reduce an artist's production solely to a market's goal, whatever that market? If, for example, the current criteria for purchasing plastic art works are "White" because buyers have been historically, and continue to be predominantly White, does that mean that there are paintings for Whites and paintings for Blacks, or paintings done by Blacks and paintings done by Whites? This wording, which is quite easy to understand and to transform into an ideological slogan, is blasphemous, with

respect to the artistic creation itself, and insulting, with respect to the entire production of a continent.

There are local micro markets sustained over the past two generations by genuine African collectors in the large regional African capitals, on the one hand, and, on the other hand, by enthusiasts, collectors, travelers, Western-origin expatriates, all of whom are little concerned with racial criteria. As for the artists themselves, they work as they like, without worrying about races and nations, which some ideologists would like to state as being their source of inspiration. No artist in the world paints thinking about his country's borders. He works for the world and cares little about the origin of the person who will be admiring his work. We will, therefore, be speaking less about the "international market" than about the movement of forms and ideas that the world is spreading throughout the continents.

In concluding with this notion of imposed exteriority, let us mention the fate of the artist, which is controlled both inside and outside his country. The desire to meet people, the allure of exhibits, of markets, of recognition and of a standard of living are found in the large capital cities of rich countries more so than in most African countries. This is not a value judgment, but simply a fact that invalidates, more than ever, the lucky or actual talent that exists outside their countries. As for other talents, certain artists hope to travel, others are convinced that their place is in their country and continent. There are thousands of them, who are, at times, tired of being judged by dubious criteria.

This notion of an international market, established specifically for plastic arts, is not taken as seriously by most other African artistic expressions, such as music, dance, architecture, photography, textile creation, and fashion, simply because the domestic market is strong. Yet, is there necessarily more "authenticity" and less foreign influences? Of course not. We must drop these simple economic and political terms, without, however, ignoring them, in order to better tackle this global phenomenon of reciprocal "influences."

Note In order to make things easier, we will speak of the West when referring to Europe and North America, which invented a model of thought for human development. In this book, at least in the parts written by the Revue Noire team, we will consciously try to avoid speaking about ethnic groups and clans, terms used to enable the West and its human sciences to speak about archaic "others." We will be speaking about peoples and cultures, societies and civilizations.

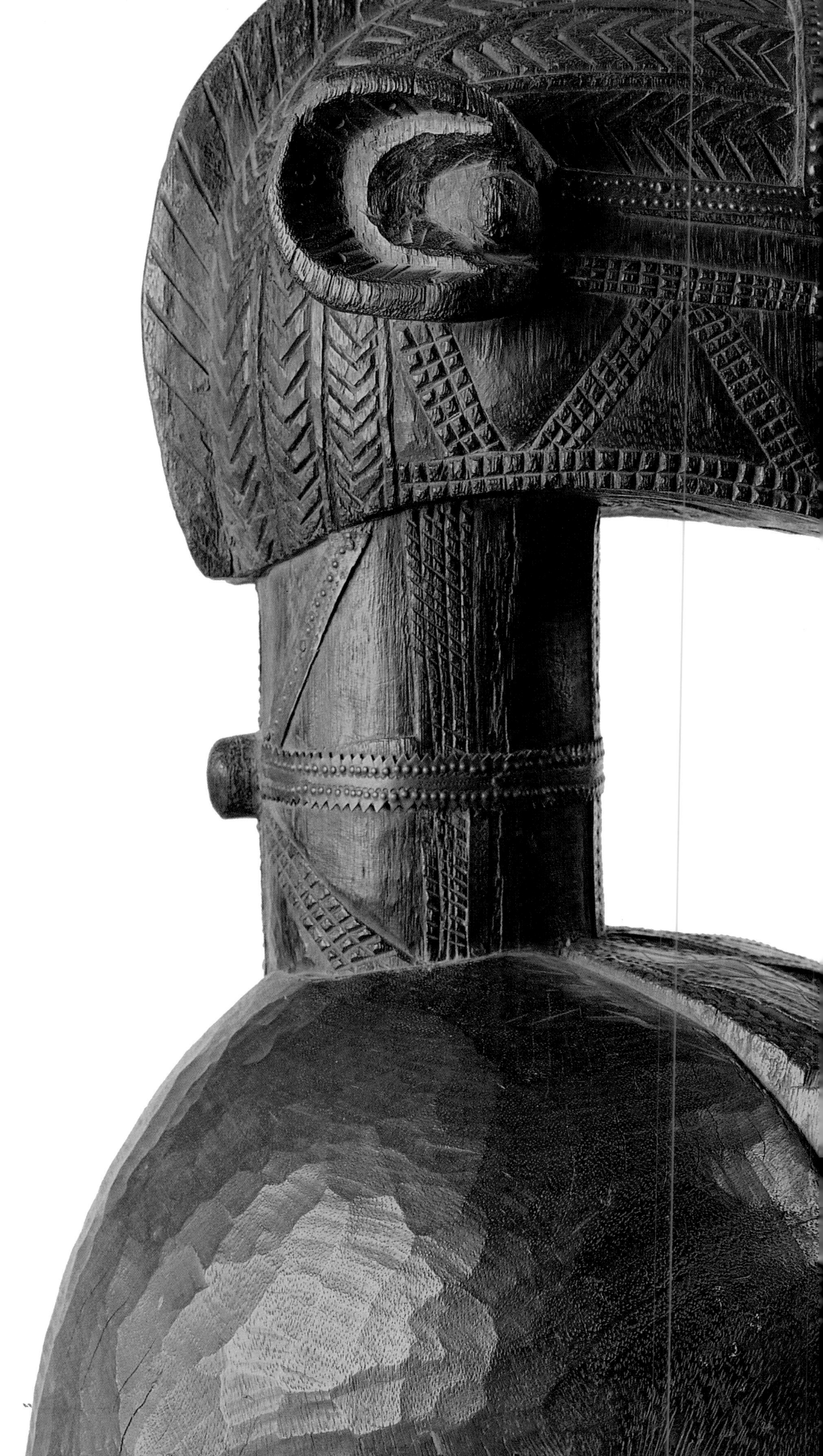

Guinea, Baga, late 19th Century
Nimba Mask
Wood, metal. H. 102 cm. Paris, MAAO
(legs Georges Salles) ©Photo Labat/CFAO

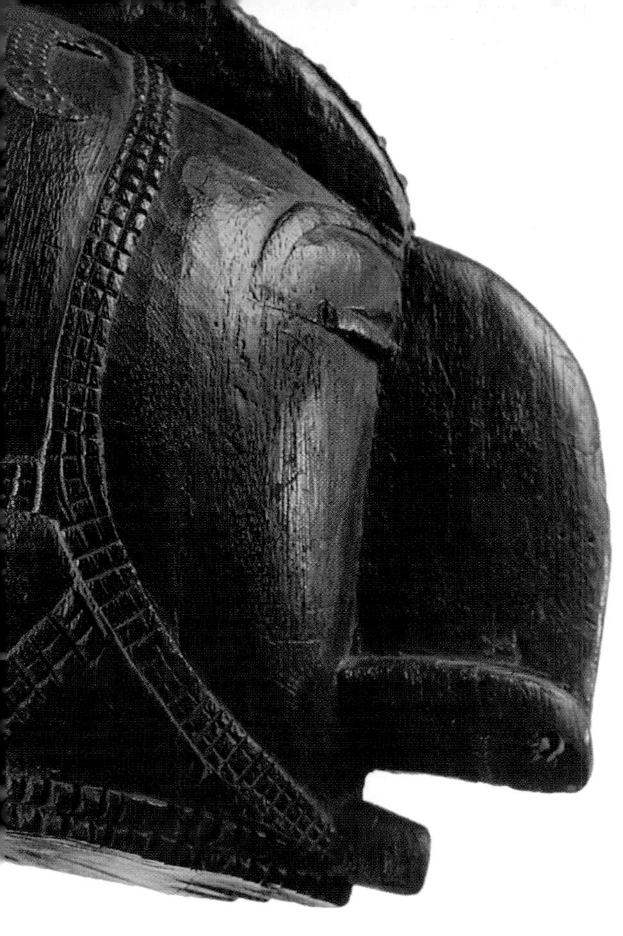

Permanence

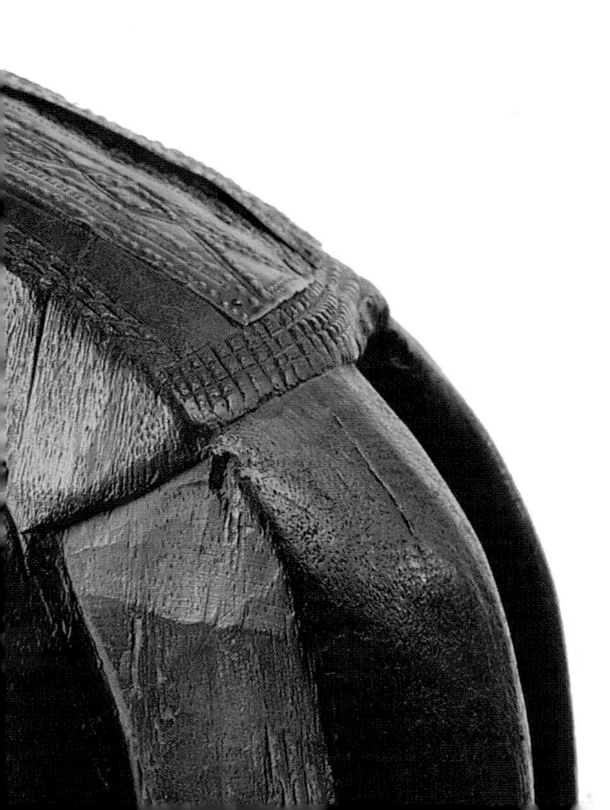

GEOGRAPHICAL AND CULTURAL AREAS
Elikia M'Bokolo

Africa: a cultural area or cultural areas? Considering this concept as a singular or plural reality is not just a mere intellectual exercise. It is based on conflicting phenomena seen in this land in the practices of the social players. This concept also deals with internal and external queries regarding the trends and outlooks of the future of Africa at the end of the 20th century and the beginning of the 21st century.

As soon as we mention the word "Africa," we run the risk of having thrown in our faces, as examples of "proof" of Africa's plurality, a series of "facts" and concrete "immediate data," whether this data is static, permanent or transient. We are reminded that this is an immense continent, stretching over more than 7,000 km from West to East and from North to South. Its peoples, if we consider its recent history alone, have experienced multiple and various types of colonization over a relatively long period of time: almost five hundred years for the Portuguese colonies; over three centuries (from the 17th century to the 20th century) for South Africa; less than a decade for Ethiopia (1935-1941); about a century (from 1880-1890 to 1960-1970) for most of the current States. Regaining its sovereignty in the second half of the 20th century did not prevent strongly contrasting policies and undertakings to arise on the economic and political levels, as can indeed be witnessed by the numerous conflicts that have been shaking the continent since the 1990s.

Despite the strength of the evidence that seems to accompany them, these facts and data are not entirely convincing.

Africa today: a cultural area

Everybody is willing to subscribe to the idea that Africa is a single unit, provided, however, that the bases and content of this unit are specified. In actual fact, it is, quite paradoxically, a multiple unit.
It is a unit of condition, first and foremost. In all of human memory, no continent has had a fate quite like Africa's. On the negative side, this fate is a long succession of hardships, from the slave trade, to colonial domination, to post-colonial abuses. On the positive side, it is a sort of ongoing success story, in which the continent constantly gets up after being knocked down, overcomes the gravest of crises, each time regaining an autonomy that is unceasingly threatened. That is why these issues of memory are so important in today's African communities, as can be seen in its storybook, film, musical and, of course, scientific productions. The message is the same in all of its languages: restoring the greatness of "Africa, the cradle of Humanity" and land of notorious empires and glorious heroes, from Soundiata Keita to Shaka, King of the Zulus, and Samory Toure; re-establishing the central place of Africa in the history of the world; emphasizing the West's responsibilities for its current decline.

This unit is, secondly, a unit of perception: friendly or hostile, captivated or horrified, optimistic or pessimistic, the glance cast by the others, the non-Africans, over its fate, gives Africa a sort of homogeneity that provides positive or, most often, negative reinforcement of Africans' own perception. They are attentive to the complex dynamics of Africa today and worried about showing the positive potentialities...

It is, finally, a unit of will, founder of Pan-Africanism. This will is strengthened by the contemporary evolution of Africa over the past one hundred years. Africans from all walks of life, from Abeokuta to Addis Ababa, from Dakar to Durban, from Kinshasa to N'Djamena and Bulawayo, have continued to rise up with the same goals in mind, goals which have been reaffirmed over the past decades, with the same force they had a century or more ago: the inevitable "regeneration" of the continent, its necessary and possible "rebirth," its unity. This theme appeared relatively early, in the mid 19th century, when European imperialism had not yet set its heart on the African continent. It was starting in 1868 that a doctor from Sierra Leone, Africanus Horton, popularized the notion of vindication of the African race. The will to "rehabilitate" Africa in its entirely or just the "black race" in view of a past deemed ignominious, and in view of a visibly promising future, gave impetus to social African forces throughout the 20th century.

All of this is indeed true. But, what about the other data that support a definitely plural Africa?

The Africans' Africa: an accepted and managed plurality

As an immediately perceptible reality, this plural Africa is not, however, reduced to insurmountable contradictions or eternal antagonisms between a handful of "ethnic groups," between "peoples" considered as permanent, or, even less, between "races." The question here is, rather, how African societies have built great groups of civilization, making the most of multiple opportunities offered by circumstances and created by these societies. Faced with the successive shocks of a history increasingly imposed from the outside, these groups did not remain insensitive, impermeable or rigid. They did not entirely fold, either, to unreservedly conform to new standards, in other words, to alienate themselves. In this land that has been inhabited since time immemorial, African cultural areas are open groups, bearers of multiple dynamics and in constant negotiation with forces acting from within and from without.

An observer today taking the time to examine the profound and unwieldy characteristics of African societies, would see emerge, from ancient times, long before the carvings made by modern colonialism, a half dozen groups that originally combined the optimal exploitation of resources, the linking of social relationships with forms of political organization and with the symbolic order of representations and beliefs.

The ancient geography of Arab travelers had a good understanding of one of these groups, perhaps the best known one, and, without giving it much thought, hastily called it Bilad al-

Sudan (the Country of the Blacks). From the coast of Senegal to today's Chad, at the crossroads of the Sahara and the Sahel, extends a vast space, whose main traits become well ingrained from the 8th century at the latest: multi-colored people; early diversification and dynamic economic activities in production and exchange; an opening up towards the outside world; the vitality of Islam; the general implementation of state forms as a means of political organization; dissemination of the written word at the same time as the strength of the oral word continued to flourish. Ancient anthropological approaches, which still have some disciples today, sought to classify these populations into "races" and "mixtures of races": "Negroes," which constituted the base population, "white" nomads who came from the desert and from northern Africa, Berbers, then Arabs, and Fulas, whose origins and identity remain a topic of controversy. However, another classification may be preferred, based, instead, on societies and political structures, which the first European travelers describe from the middle of the 14th century and who appear as they do today: Serer, Wolof, Balant, Bambara, etc. Undoubtedly, of greater importance is the expansion, beyond subsistence activities, of a truly merchant economy, connecting the Sudanese countries with the countries of the forest, towards the south, and, towards the north, to the Mediterranean shore, and based primarily on the salt, gold, cola nut and slave routes. Of course, colonization disrupted the commercial relationships between the Sudanese countries and those on the Mediterranean, but left intact, willy-nilly, the other relationships. It was on these routes that Islam penetrated western Africa beginning in the 8th century. Although the penetration was peaceful, the subsequent expansion of Islam was more violent. The first version of Islam had been that of the elite populations, princes and merchants. The conversion of the masses began slowly, then sped up starting in the 17th century thanks to preachers who encouraged the jihad (the holy war). Long-distance trade and the existence of active merchant groups gave rise, very early on, to the advent of an urban civilization equaled only in eastern Africa: Awdaghost, Timbuktu, Walata, Wadane, Gao, Agades, Dienne, Kano, Katsina, etc. There are numerous examples of cities that were intellectual pockets, commercial metropolises or political capitals. Without abolishing the village and lineage base of the local societies, it was here that States flourished: some small, like the Haussa city-states, and others quite extensive, like the Mali or Songhai empires. These empires did not cease to haunt the political memory of Africans, as can be seen from the Leopold Sedar Senghor and Modibo Keita joint venture to create a Mali Federation at the time of independence.

To the south of the great forest, from the Congolese and Angolan coasts to the coast of Mozambique, emerged another group, which was also noteworthy due to the strength of its state forms, although the kingdoms and the empires had different bases. Until the 15th century, contacts with the outside world remained very limited here, despite the activity of the Indian and Arab merchants in the Indian Ocean. However, besides a connection between the languages (subsequently qualified as "Bantu" by specialists), internal exchanges seem to have been very intense: product exchanges (especially salt, copper and gold); population shifts; circulation of political models that borrowed identical myths based on the pagan concept of sacred royalty, in which the king, symbol of perfection right down to his body, obtained his legitimacy from his role as intercessor between his subjects, the ancestors and the gods. This shows the central role of the religions in these societies. Although the Sudanese countries became essential links for African Islam, the savannahs in the south appear as the cradle of a rebellious animism and, at the same time, the hearth of an original and vigorous Christianity. Very visible today, the dynamics of Christianity, which now embraces all of central and southern Africa, began in the 15th century and intensified in the 18th century. At this time, it was attacked by the ravages of the slave trade and troubled by seeing Christian missionaries assist the slave traders, people sought their salvation in a renewed Christianity, both iconoclastic and "African" in nature, spreading a message of equality between humans, fraternity between peoples and individual freedom. This same message was used in the 20th century, first to fight against the colonizers, then to forge communities in response to the misfortunes of the times.

Between these two savannah regions, the forest was never the self-contained and inhospitable world to which allusion is often made. Although the region has always been known for its scarce population, numerous waterways facilitated population shifts and the dissemination of techniques and forms of social and political organization that offer a great number of relationships: occupational specialization and integration, through exchanges, between hunters-gatherers and farmers; adoption of the Bantu languages by the various groups present; the central village square as a place and as an institution for establishing the social structure; the progressive drop within the villages of consanguinity in favor of more heterogeneous social relationships founded on the predominance of a "great man" surrounded by his close family and numerous "youngsters," free men, "protégés," "clients" and "dependents"; development of the chieftainship; strength of beliefs, religious practices and rites of the land.

The axis of the highlands, which runs from Ethiopia to the Great Lakes, also constitutes a separate and unique area. Of course, we must not believe everything we read in contemporary mythologies, which emerged in the 19th century with colonization and was re-appropriated by the social players. Obsessed by the issue of the origins and identity of individuals, and laden with reckonings regarding battles for power, these mythologies describe origins, migration routes, and filiations without any regard to the facts established by historians. Even though the presence of pastoral activities, rendered possible by climatic conditions and the existence of ancient States, give this space a particular profile, we can discern at least two sub-groups.

The first is the "Horn of Africa," centered around Ethiopia. Although it was the successor of the ancient Axum kingdom, whose apogee ran from the 3rd to the 6th century, and whose territory constitutes the heart of modern-day Ethiopia, this country still tried to create for itself a more glorious origin. Written in the 14th century, The History of the Kings, by Tarike

Negast, and The Glory of the Kings, by Kebra Negast, are two books with a lasting influence that sought to and succeeded in giving credence to the story according to which the Axum and Ethiopian kings were descendents of the love between Solomon and the Queen of Saba. Revived in the 19th century, this myth granted Menelik II (the first Menelik was apparently the son of Solomon and the Queen of Saba) and Haile Selassie an unprecedented prestige among Africans, which can be seen, in particular, in music, and gave Menelik II a decisive role in the birth of the Organization for African Unity.

From Uganda to Burundi, on either side of the Great Lakes, the oral stories passed on by the official traditionalists of the pre-colonial States establish the relationship between these various States (Kitara, Bunyoro, Buganda, Busoga, Ankole, Rwanda, Burundi), all the while legitimizing the royalty and justifying the social divides, especially between breeders and farmers. In reality, this region is not characterized by these myths, whose political exploitation in the 20th century would generate atrocious dramas, culminating in the Rwandan genocide in 1994, and would make the Great Lakes one of the most unstable regions on the continent. It is, rather, the intensity of the exchanges between the different parties that make up the region, the exceptionally high density of its population, the early and prolonged existence of States concerned with integrating their populations into true nations, and the frequent recourse to civil war or to outside war as a way to manage politics.

What remains is those very extensive peripheries, which run from Senegal to Mogadishu by the Cape of Good Hope, privileged areas of contact with the outside world, where, through conflicts and exchanges, cultures with a high degree of interbreeding have developed. It is true that all civilizations are mixed races, created by borrowing from and tinkering with indigenous bases and outside contributions. The interbreeding that developed on the African coasts is not any less unique.

From Senegal to Mozambique, it actually appears as the paradoxical outcome of the destructive enterprise created by the slave trade. Thrown by force into the vicious trade circle, many African societies sought to meet the challenge either by head-on resistance, by drawing from the resources of religion (Islam and Christianity), or, as in the Gulf of Guinea, by forming or by reinforcing States such as Benin and Dahomey, capable of better negotiating their insertion into the new order imposed by Europe. In Senegambia, on the "Slave Coast," in Angola, in Cape Town and in Mozambique, the presence of European forts and trading posts gave this process a particular intensity and led to the creation of a group with a relatively high number of people of mixed-race. On the social and cultural levels, a sort of "Creole" civilization began to emerge, based on an original language (in which one could notice, depending on the regions, bits of English, Danish, Dutch, French and Portuguese), on ways of living, doing things and believing, coexisting more or less with European elements and an African foundation. In the 19th century, this process took on a new scope, first in Angola and in Dahomey, with the influx of black, mixed or white immigrants from Brazil, then on the Gold Coast and in Nigeria, due to the influence of people from Sierra Leone and from Liberia. In these two countries, an original social group emerged, formed by "Africans" returning from the United States (to Liberia), expelled from Canada, Great Britain, or forced off slave traders' boats (Sierra Leone). Although "acculturated" to the West, they shared this passion for Africa, which made them the best supporters of pan-Africanism and of this completely new and still current idea of "modernity," according to which, contrary to the colonialist vision of the Westerners, Africans themselves would choose what, if anything, they wanted to retain from the West, instead of having a foreign culture imposed on them. It was also up to them to decide how they would integrate these outside contributions and their local heritages.

Only South Africa, due to the racism instituted by the authorities, failed, early on, to be part of this group evolution. It is not that racism and racial tensions were absent elsewhere. This ideology affected every place where the slave trade had been practiced. But in South Africa, biological interbreeding, evidenced from the time the Dutch settled there in 1652, and the intense acculturation to which the Boers were subjected, did not prevent the early formalization of a racism (prohibition of "mixed marriages" in 1685). This was reinforced over the following centuries and would mark South African society up to the current date.

On the coast of the Indian Ocean, the cultural confrontation did not occur because, unlike the Atlantic coast, where trade was the foundation for the Euro-African relationship, the merchant relationships on the east coast were, first and foremost, exchanges of products, with the slave trade only taking off in the 19th century. Very early on, individuals and groups of very diverse origins settled there: Iranians from Shiraz, persecuted for their Islamic faith, Indians attracted by the commerce, and especially Arabs, whose families had settled there well before the arrival of the Europeans in the 15th century and whose number suddenly grew in the 19th century following the transfer, in 1840, of the Sultan capital from Oman to Zanzibar. Under these conditions, the cultural syntheses here were both earlier and more intense, as can be seen on a linguistic and literary level. In one of the most ancient Swahili writings, the History of Kilwa (16th century), the language and writing are in Arabic and only a few words are in Bantu. But, while written in Arabic script, the History of Mombasa, dating back to the end of the 18th century and the beginning of the 19th century, is entirely in Bantu. If Swahili is today, more so than English, the most used language of administration, knowledge and communication in Tanzania, this is not only due to President Julius Nyerere's decision to make Swahili the official language of Tanzania; it is also due to a long-standing cultural and social dynamic.

Imperialistic Africa: incomplete reconstructions
We mistakenly speak exclusively of European imperialism when we mention imperialistic action in Africa. Other imperial ambitions were also present, such as the advances stopped by the European powers, and set in motion profound dynamics that continue to act in Africa today.

These dynamics came from the north and east of the continent. Between Sudanese Africa and Mediterranean Africa, the essentially pre-19th century trade and religious relationships changed in nature starting in the 1800s, when the Nile Valley began to grow larger than the axes that connected the Sudanese countries to the Maghreb. At the instigation of Muhammad Ali, the Ruler of Egypt from 1805 to 1848, and of his successors, this country devised an imperial policy that progressively extended its influence towards the south, first in the Sudan (in its current state), then towards the regions that are today part of Chad, Central Africa, Uganda and Congo. It was in the name of a type of humanitarianism, that claimed to free the "Blacks" from "Arab" slavery, that the various colonizers rushed to the Great Lakes region of Africa. In the 1950s, the same colonizers would denounce, under Nasser's anti-colonial policy, the pursuit of this old imperial dream. However, the impact of Nasser's policy was considerable in transforming pan-Africanism. Pan-Africanism was long confined to a sort of pan-Blackism, according to which Africa was exclusively the continent of the Blacks and the solidarity to be built involved only the Blacks of Africa and their descendants in the American and European Diaspora. It then took on a new content and, under the supervision of Kwame Nkrumah and of Nasser, set itself the goal of liberating and unifying the entire African continent. It is out of this expansion of horizons that the Organization for African Unity was born, with all the projects that have accompanied it since the 1960s.

Towards the east, Zanzibar itself became, as of the 1840s, the seat of an imperial dream that threw the Arabs and Swahilis, in search of a place to provide them with supplies of ivory and slaves, into a sort of long march towards the west. In about 1880, when the colonizers decided to share Africa amongst themselves, they had reached the territories located, today, in eastern Congo. Although colonization succeeded in eliminating them as a leading group, it was unable to prevent the persistence of the prestige of "ustaarabu" – the Arab civilization and way of being, including the practice of Islam – and it resigned itself to granting Swahili, and three other languages, the status of mandatory common language of the natives. It is clear that, besides the crises and conflicts that are tearing up the Africa of the Great Lakes today, we are in the presence of a vast group whose resilience dates far back into the past.

What must be retained from colonization is the long-term effects that, from the point of view of spatial organization, make this period in African history a long-lasting abrupt transition.

First of all, there are the State borders, which, it is well recognized, do not correspond to any of the ancient dynamics of Africa. But, these borders have also ultimately defined a referential horizon and a policy framework for Africans as citizens, not only because the international community, beginning with the OAF, recognizes their legitimacy and their role as guarantors of stability for the continent, but also because this territorial framework has produced, in turn, a feeling of community, with risks of identity-related tensions noticed here and there.

Then there are these numerous inheritances of linguistic, administrative, cultural and, sometimes, financial divisions. The reality of these divisions is reinforced by the desire of former colonial powers to maintain privileged links with their former possessions, through the Commonwealth, the Francophonie, the "Franco-African Summits," the institutionalization of the PALOPs (African Countries with Portuguese as the Official Language), through more or less secret agreements, and through multiple efficient and discrete networks.

The Africa of tomorrow: official and dynamic trans-border groupings
Based on these inheritances and this situation, what tomorrow will bring is open to speculation, given the way the world is evolving, the place assigned to Africa and the images that designate it. Although globalization-related phenomena appear to blur the relationships that have ensued from colonization, the feeling – whether or not legitimate – of the marginalization of the continent is associated with all types of movements, specific to the continent, that will engage Africa on the road to new reconstructions.

First of all, we have noticed that the States do not remain inert. The great ambitions of the 1950s and 1960s, aimed at creating a great continental State, appear, today, to be permanently shelved. However, small-scale grouping projects, which bring a few States together for modest development programs, do not appear to muster up any greater enthusiasm. What emerge and become established are intermediate strategies focused either on managing problems or structural conflicts (such as the Tuareg issue, the civil wars in Angola, Sierra Leone, Liberia and Congo, the recurring conflicts of the Great Lakes) or on a desire to build, on a large-scale, a long-term development, centered around the permanent interests of the local societies, which is illustrated, in particular, by the ECWAS (Economic Community of Western African States), the SADC (Southern African Development Community), and the COMESA (Common Market of Eastern and Southern Africa). One could believe that we are speaking of economics and geopolitics, but it is known that, everywhere in the world, these are the bases that are now used to build solidarities and identities.

On the other hand, what has been called "the African crisis" for a quarter century has affected the reconstruction of the Africans' spaces and support systems.

The "crisis" actually refers to a very heterogeneous set of phenomena: divestiture by the State in social and cultural programs and privatization of certain State functions; the widespread implementation of war as a method of political management, as a method of extracting riches and as a method of socializing youth; massive rural exodus making urban macrocephaly a characteristic of all regions and of all African countries, and making the cities privileged places for the production of forms of cosmopolitan life and transnational cultures; intra-African, individual and collective migrations, whether voluntary or forced, caused by these wars, which have resulted in these types of migrations outweighing migrations towards other continents despite their growing number. There has also been a proliferation of enclaves, which may be related (in the case of gold and diamonds) or not related (in the case of oil) to civil wars, a rise in the number of people with an illegal status, whether illegal immigrants or unauthorized occupants of lands in rural and urban areas; diffusion of the administrative and political model of decentralization which, while reinforcing the power of the usual authorities, transforms part of the urban elites, especially youths and women, into "development brokers" and into forced intermediaries of the money lenders and of foreign partners; development of individualism and, at the same time, of new forms of solidarity based on exclusion (the ideologies of the original people and the practices of ethnic or national autochthony) or integration (religious fraternities, merchant and financial networks, etc.).

In this new context, the processes that we are witnessing continue to disturb us through their contradictions. Although they remain frameworks, the various frontiers of African society, the borders of States, ethnic groups, local communities and of larger groups developed by colonization, are now being questioned. While this is happening, interest in and the credibility of the issue of an African rebirth, an issue that is dear to these new African leaders who came to power in the 1990s, continues to grow. This issue is particular in that it takes into account both the glorious and unsettling past of Africa, the battles that the continent continues to wage in the present, and the rather optimistic perspectives that Africans believe they can set for their future. This last potentiality, which is pan-African in essence, is what most mobilizes specialists of the spirit and of taste, intellectuals, writers, musicians and artists.

This is why we can bet that the Africa of tomorrow will be, in people's consciousness and in fact, both a cultural area and a plurality of cultural areas.

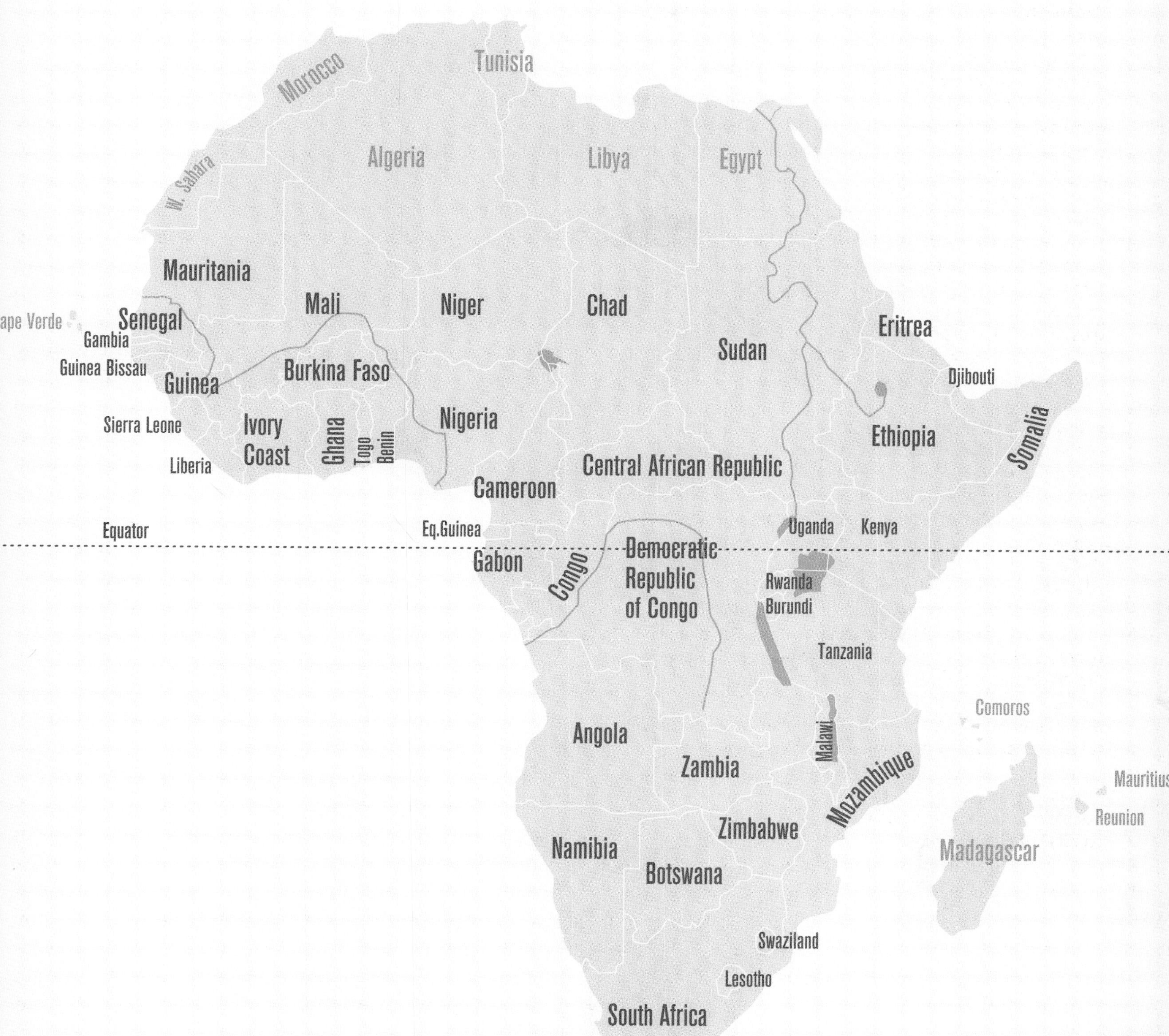
Morocco
Tunisia
Algeria
Libya
Egypt
W. Sahara
Mauritania
Mali
Niger
Chad
Cape Verde
Senegal
Gambia
Guinea Bissau
Guinea
Burkina Faso
Sudan
Eritrea
Djibouti
Sierra Leone
Ivory Coast
Ghana
Togo
Benin
Nigeria
Ethiopia
Somalia
Liberia
Central African Republic
Cameroon
Equator
Eq.Guinea
Uganda
Kenya
Gabon
Congo
Democratic Republic of Congo
Rwanda
Burundi
Tanzania
Comoros
Angola
Malawi
Zambia
Mozambique
Mauritius
Reunion
Zimbabwe
Namibia
Madagascar
Botswana
Swaziland
Lesotho
South Africa

Territory of forms

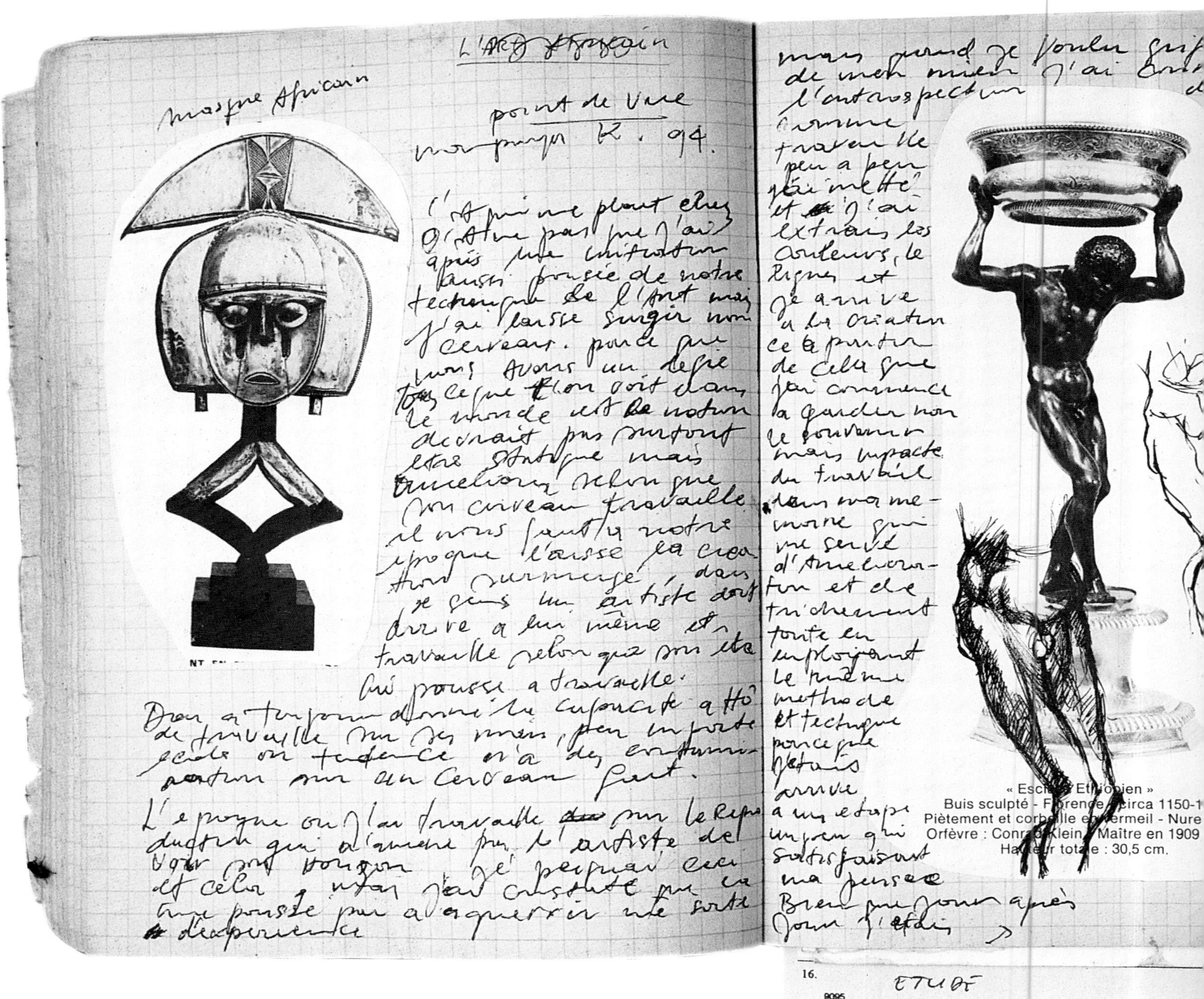

Pages from an Art History notebook of Francis Mampuya (born in 1967), DRC

ART WITHOUT HISTORY, EVEN IF....

Jean Loup Pivin

No general work has been done to give the African continent's traditional ritual arts a perspective throughout time and geographical areas. The result: illegal or scientific collections mostly obtained during the time of colonization, that are today found in all the museums around the world and Africa, only portray a suspended moment in the history of the production of forms from the various African cultures and civilizations, primarily the 19th and 20th centuries. It is as if we were only to retain, from Europe, the Italian Renaissance between 1470 and 1490, a Roman fresco in Spain, and the 19th century impressionist works in France.

This, combined with the profoundly fixed idea that "eternal Africa" continues to tirelessly reproduce forms that have been based on the same model since the dawn of time, keeps the belief alive that Africa's human evolution has come to a standstill, whereas the industrial and post-industrial Western world has moved on. Africa has thus become our Middle Ages, not to mention "our living Neolithic Age." It is difficult for the West to conceive that all civilizations follow a path that differs from its own. It cannot imagine other forms of autonomy. Its own definition of evolution of the human race depends on it. The reason there is no history of African art, even if, here and there, certain works try to create the first links between eras, is because of this evolutionist pattern. The basic principle of the rarity of the material traces of certain non-materialistic African civilizations is not enough.

Of course, if this history of expressions were to exist in Africa, it should not try to forget the history of Western art, but rather try to avoid basing itself entirely on it, since most expressions refer to each other and take root in another definition of the world, of humanity, of nature and of the cosmos.
The history of African art is constantly coming up against the history of architecture, textile, dance, music and song. This occurs because in the African production of forms, there were no masks without paint, without being worn by people wearing face paint and in costume, acting out roles in ritualized dramatic art, with dance and with songs containing words that were sung or chanted as psalms, in a non-neutral natural or architectural décor. The challenge of simultaneously writing the histories of all the expressions becomes difficult, but, at the same time, indispensable. This is one of the reasons for renewing the actual form of this writing. It is also a way to render accessible the different disciplines and the different separations between the arts the West has established.

One of the constant difficulties for the person looking at a piece of art (be it a statue in the great door of a French gothic cathedral or a small Malian Tellem statue) is not avoiding putting the work before us in a sociological and contextualized setting – getting to know it, so to speak – but rather penetrating its meanings without anything more than one's own intuition and the receptivity of one's senses. Wondering about art is like wondering about the indomitable side that lies outside everyone's intellect, i.e. desire, repulsion, life and death wishes, and vital enthusiasm. And is like returning from this experience fed, filled and perhaps transformed, without any other possible analysis, with the silly hope of a powerful encounter with art, with another person, with other reasons for living. And moving on. Why do we need to know, to experience the art of things and of life? Why do we need to go behind the mirror of a reality that industrial and post-industrial civilization constantly wants to objectify? Because it does not seek, at any moment, to be any type of mirror of reality – it does not copy reality – African art is a mirror of the meaning and of the spirit of reality. This search is explicitly shared by all modern movements of Western culture.

Territory of forms

NOTES BY ÉTIENNE FÉAU

Mali, Bamana, 20th Century
Cimier tyi wara
Darkened wood, traces of red pigments.
H. 58.5 cm. Paris, MAAO ©Photo Labat/CFAO

The Bambara (or Bamana) are the heirs of the great Mali empire (11th-15th century) and of two later kingdoms, the kingdoms of Segou and of Kaarta. Long ago, knowledge was passed on, from childhood to adulthood, through the Djo initiation. Six societies gradually took over this initiation in the following order: the Ndomo, the Komo, the Nama, the Kono, the Tyi Wara and the Korè. The societies used various objects, especially masks made by sculptors-blacksmiths. Primitively attached to a wicker headpiece, this sculpture is like a mask and is used for agrarian rites, generated by a society of initiates called Tyi Wara ("champion of the cultures"). The sculpture has an audacious style and portrays three animals combined as one. The antelope, whose horns symbolize growth. The pangolin symbolizes strength and determination. The anteater, whose burrowing muzzle extends the antelope's head, refers here to the special way the peanut grows, which is replanted, after it flowers, to produce its fruit underground.

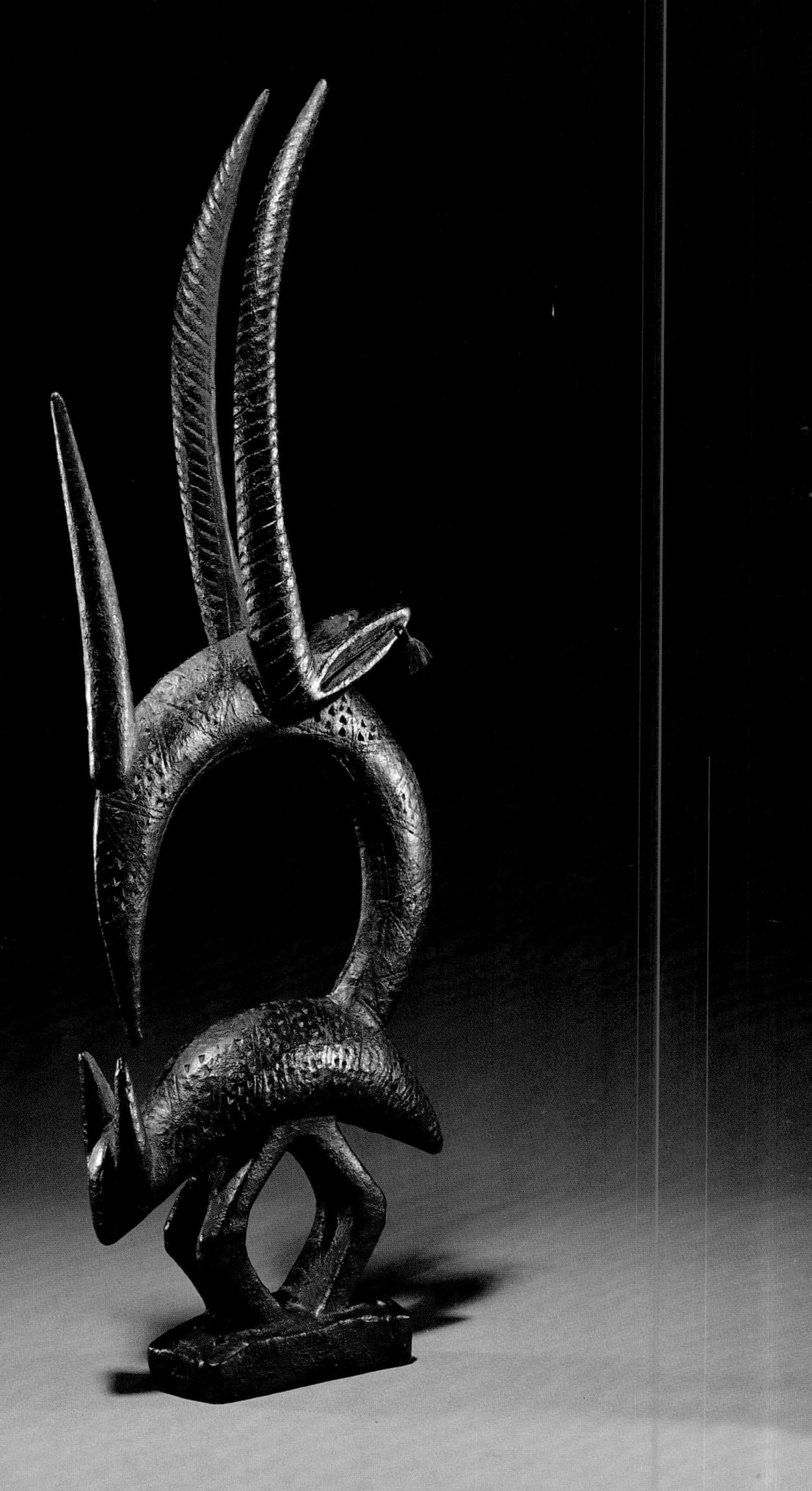

page on right:
Mali, Dogon, 20th Century
Mask of a ground-feeding bird – The Dyodyomini
Bois, H. 81 cm. Paris, MAAO (dépôt IFAN, Dakar) ©RMN

These masks, maintained by the Awa, a secret society that brings together all circumcised men, appear essentially during ceremonies ending a period of mourning and give form to the great spirits who participated in the various stages of the Earth's creation. Among these masks is the ground-feeding bird whose long beak refers to the fertility of men and of the Earth.

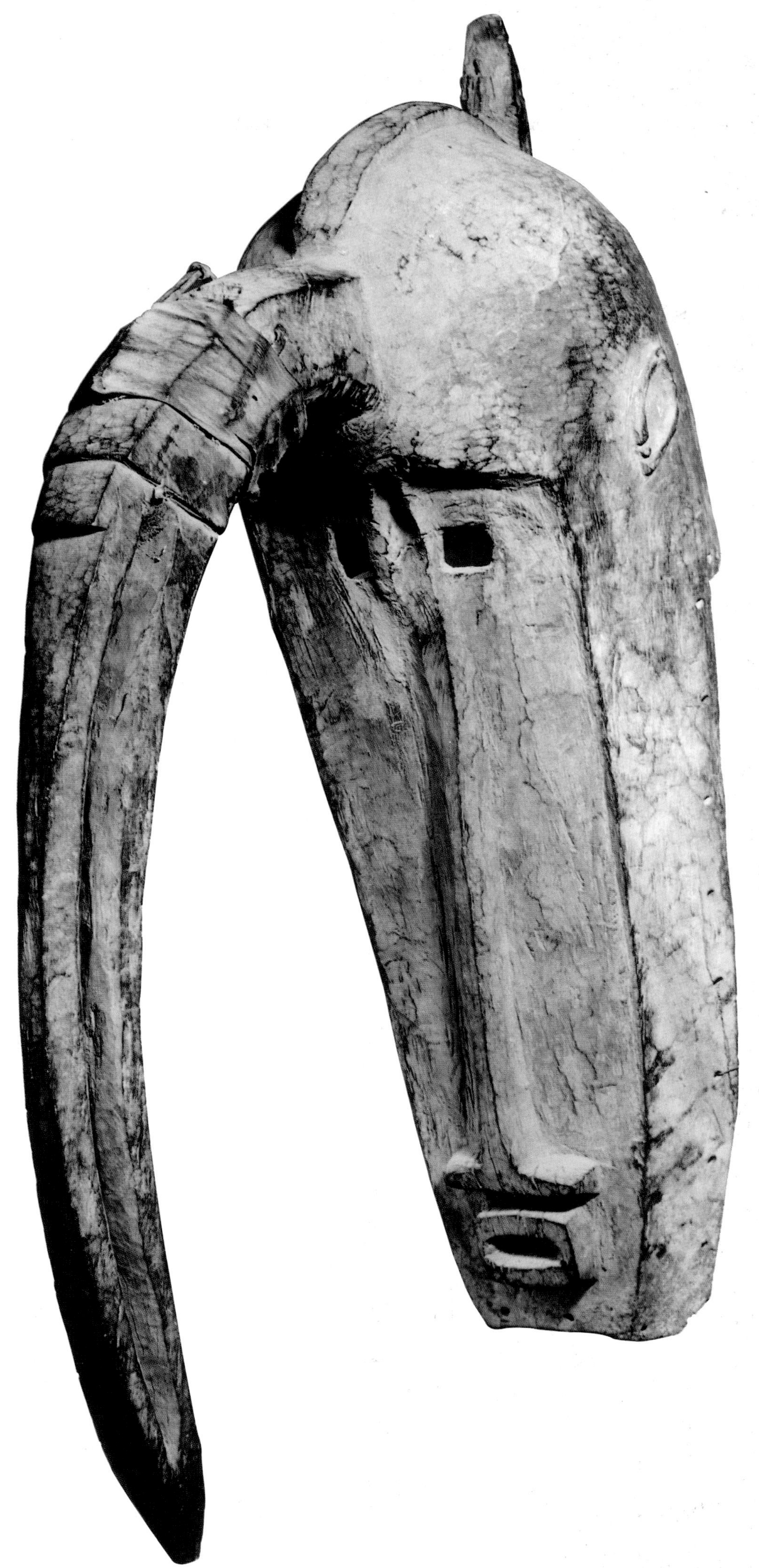

Ivory Coast, Senufo-Ligbi, early 20th Century
Do Mask
Wood. H. 41 cm. Paris, MAAO (former Bediat collection)
©Photo Labat/CFAO

Senufo farmers occupy a vast territory spanning over three countries, northern Ivory Coast, Mali and Burkina Faso. Most of the works of art produced by the Senufo sculptors are the accessories of an initiatory society, the Poro tribe. This institution, once very powerful, governed the community life of individuals of both sexes. Initiation begins at about seven years of age and continues until death in seven-year cycles. Thus, in levels, the child, adolescent, then the adult, progresses through different stages of initiatory knowledge until they reach supreme wisdom and the highest Poro rank. Among the Poro accessories, the Senufo use several types of masks, of which the best known are the kponiugo ("Poro head"), a zoomorphic helmet combining the traits of various mythical animals such as the hyena, crocodile, antelope or chameleon, and the kpelye, a small facial mask with feminine traits, topped with horns and with side ornaments.

Burkina Faso, Bobo, 20th Century
Blacksmith's Molo Mask
Polychrome wood. H. 140 cm. Paris, MAAO
©RMN

The Bobo tribe occupies the southwest region of Burkina Faso and the regions bordering on Mali, where they live primarily from farming timothy grass and sorghum. The initiatory ceremonies, New Year's festivities and funerals of the Bobo tribe are occasions for portraying spectacular masks made of leaves and fibers, as well as very stylized wooden painted masks of a human or animal head. They also use their own rituals with heavy wooden masks called Molos. These most often represent a large antelope symbolizing Dwo, a spiritual being born out of a pact between men and the supreme god Wuro. These masks were sculpted in absolute secrecy far from the village and consecrated by various sacrifices.

page on right:
Burkina Faso, Gurunsi, mid 20th Century
Blade Mask
Polychrome Wood. H. 210 cm. Paris, MAAO
©Photo Labat/CFAO

Sculpted from softwood, the Doyo or Nwo mask are used primarily for the initiation of youths and also during everyday (market dances) and ritual (funeral) ceremonies. Topped with a high blade with engraved and pierced patterns, it portrays a round face, with eyes designed as two concentric circles, and combines animal references (an owl's face, a hornbill's beak) with geometric figures (checked diamond shapes, chevrons painted in black and white). Enhanced with red paint, the bird's beak suggests the man's genitals, whereas the round or diamond-shaped mouth suggests the woman's. This spectacular mask is apparently a creation that is proper to the Gurunsi tribe, a generic term that means diverse populations, such as the Nuna, Nunuma and Winiama, who live southwest of the Mossi plateau.

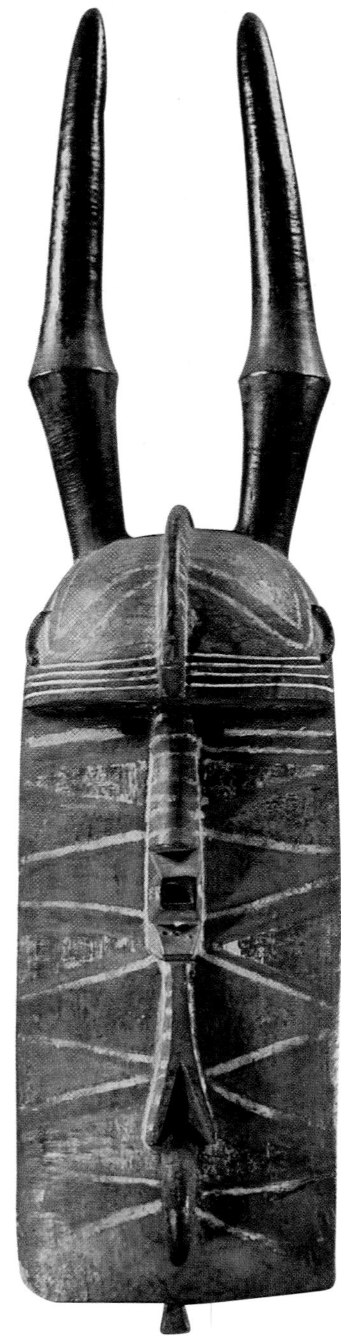

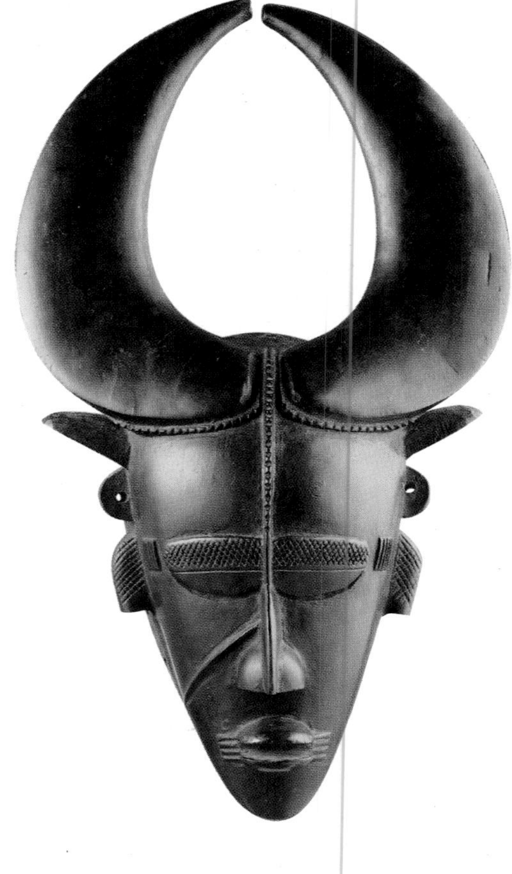

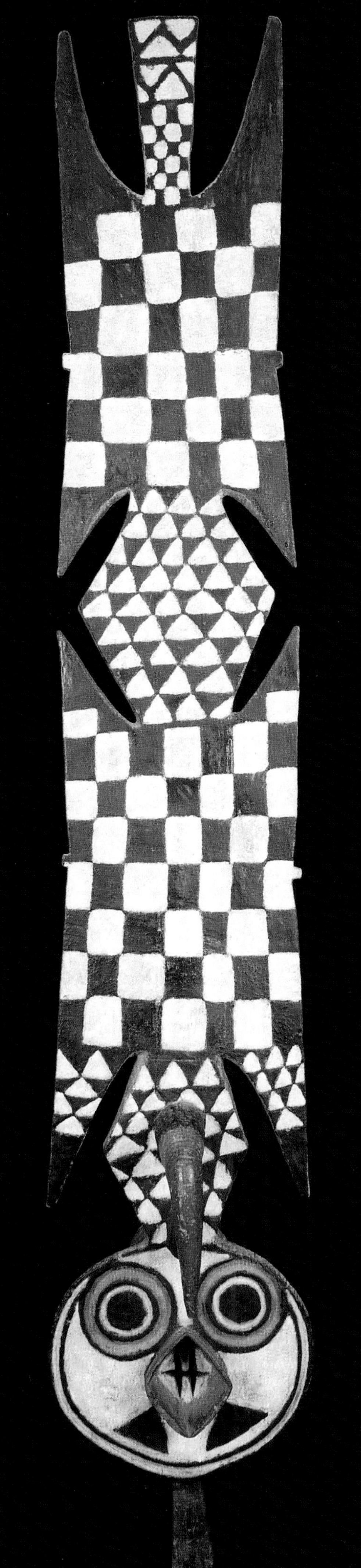

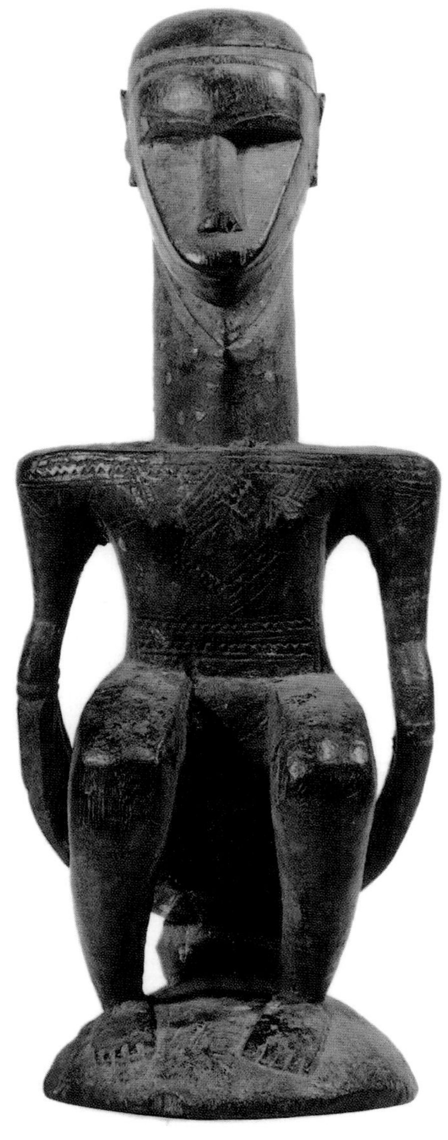

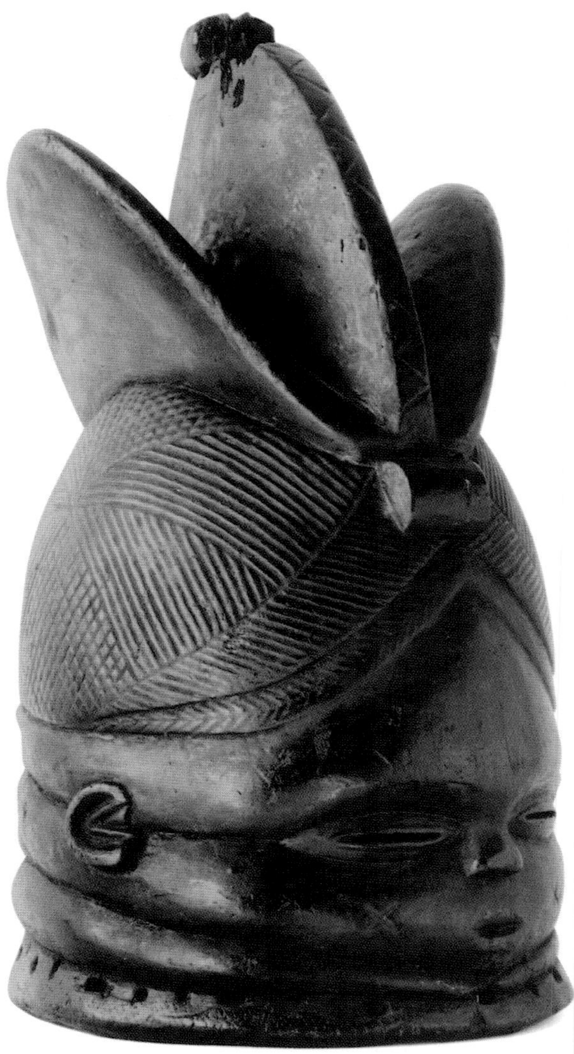

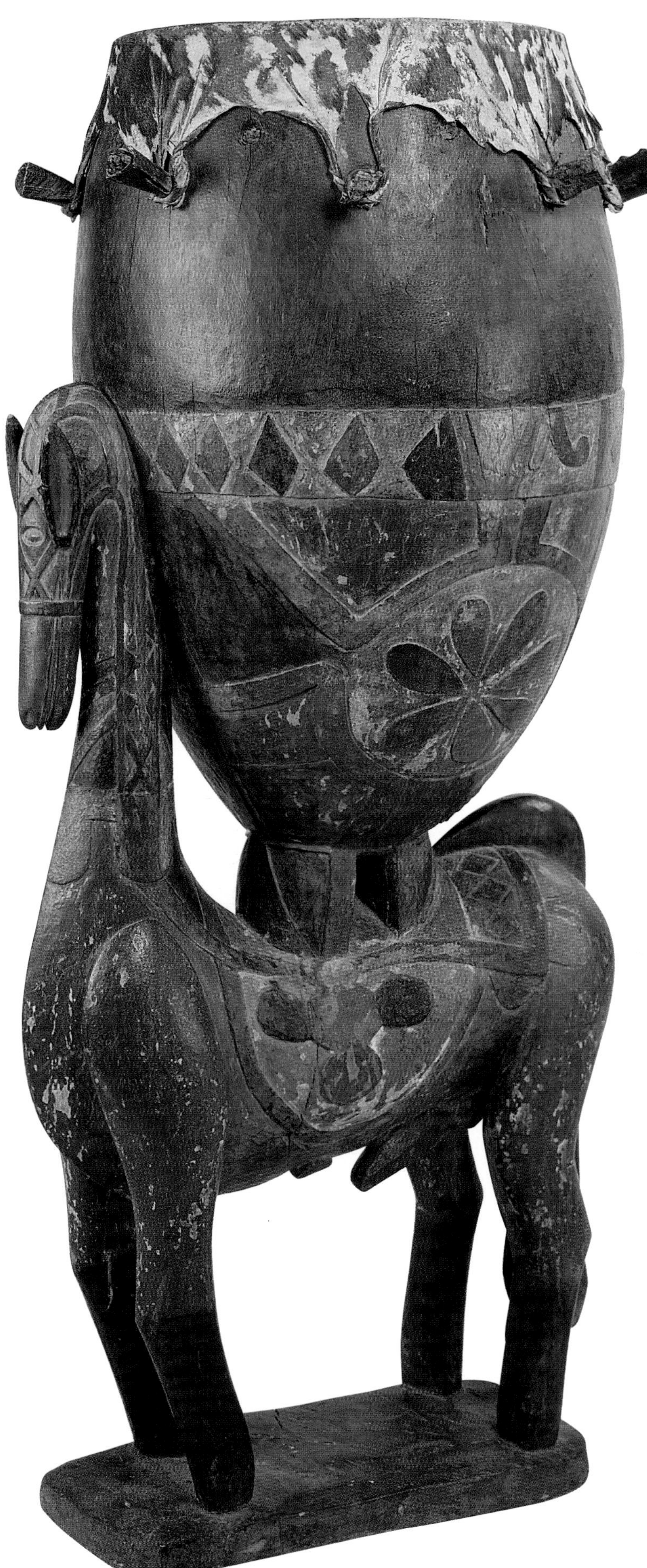

facing page, on left:
Bissagos Islands, Bidyogo, late 19th Century
Iran Statuette
Wood, H. 38.5 cm. Paris, MAAO ©RMN

The Bissagos archipelago was discovered off Guinea-Bissau in 1456 by the Portuguese, who reported the presence of wooden idols early on. For the Bidyogo, all sacred things bear the creole name of Iran and provoke fear and respect. At the top of the hierarchy sits the "iran grande do chão," possessor of the Earth, intermediary between the great divinity Nindu and humans, before each important community activity: initiation, accession of a new chief, funeral, the sowing or harvest seasons. Then come the inferior irans, to whom one prays, in a clan or privately, for health, maternity, rain, etc. Most often, iran statues are representations of a man sitting or standing, in a hierarchical position: the head prognathic, looking towards the sky, and the eyes closed or set in lead, expressing an interior vision.

facing page, on right:
Sierra Leone, Mende, 20th Century
Sowei Mask
Wood, H. 39.5 cm. Angoulême, MBA ©Marie Fagué

In all of Africa, the mask represents an exclusively male institution. There are, however, a few exceptions such as the Mende of Sierra Leone. A large part of the social life of the Mende is governed by two associations: one masculine, the Poro, and the other feminine, the Sande, still called Bundu. The sowei mask appears when the young women formally step out of the sacred forest where they have stayed for three months, during which they have learned the rules of life and have undergone excision. These masks are, however, sculpted by men. They are accompanied by a cotton costume and a loose-fitting raffia ruff.
A helmet sculpted from softwood portrays the thin face of a young woman with slanting eyes and a domed forehead, topped with a hairstyle, often with three loops. This is the idealized feminine spirit Nowo, whose neck folds are always well defined, an absolute criteria of human beauty and reminiscent of the chrysalis.

Guinea, Baga, late 19th Century
Caryatid Drum
Polychrome Wood, duiker hide, horns,. H. 132 cm.
Paris, MAAO ©Photo Labat/CFAO

The Baga, who live on the coast of Guinea, used to draw their social cohesion from a very powerful secret society, the Simo. The Simo rites, which took place in the height of the dry season, revealed, during the end-of-initiation ceremonies, a wide variety of realistic and polychrome sculptures, masks and puppets made of crafted wood. The Simo accessories also included tall membrane drums in polychrome wood, supported by spectacular female or equestrian caryatids. The horse, which was once unknown in Baga country, is a motif inspired by colonial officers on horseback. Its proud, delicately stylized silhouette emphasizes the social value of the instrument.

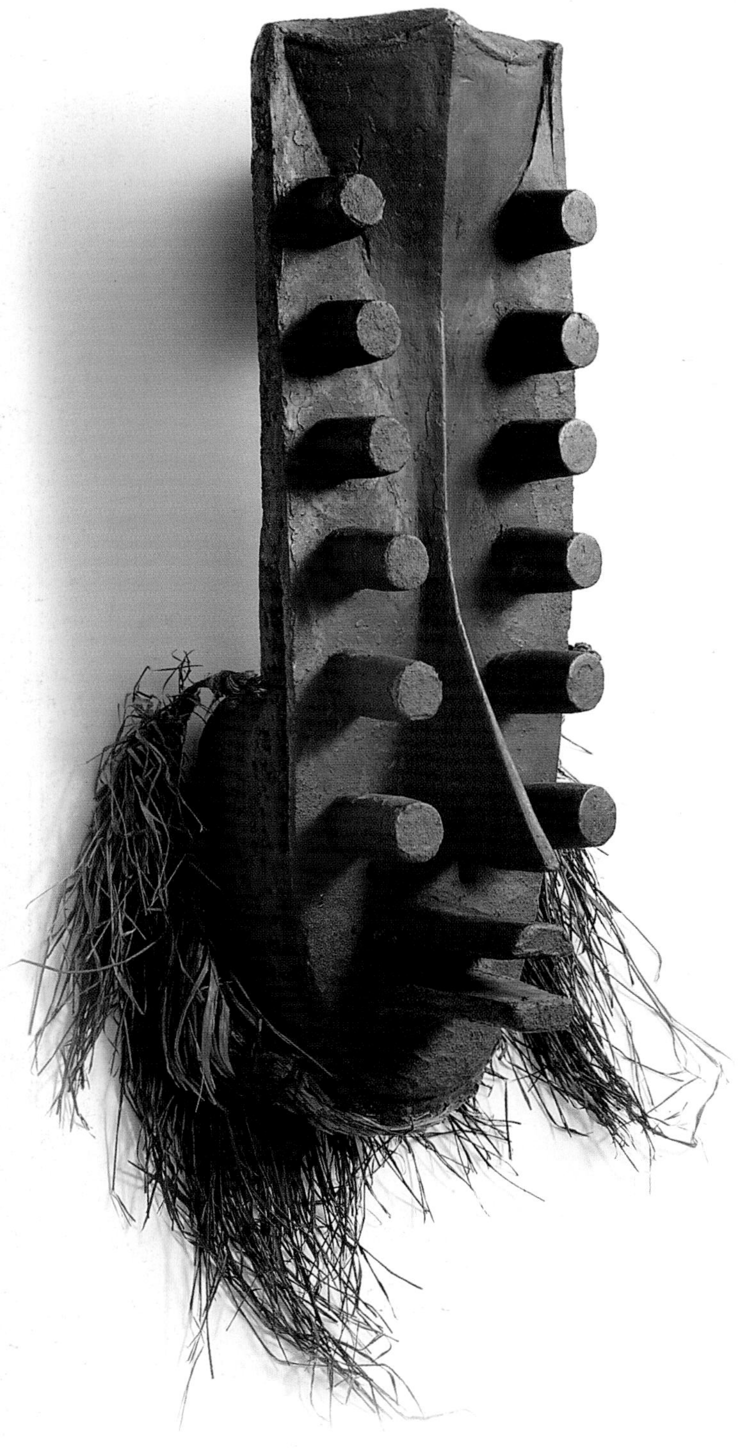

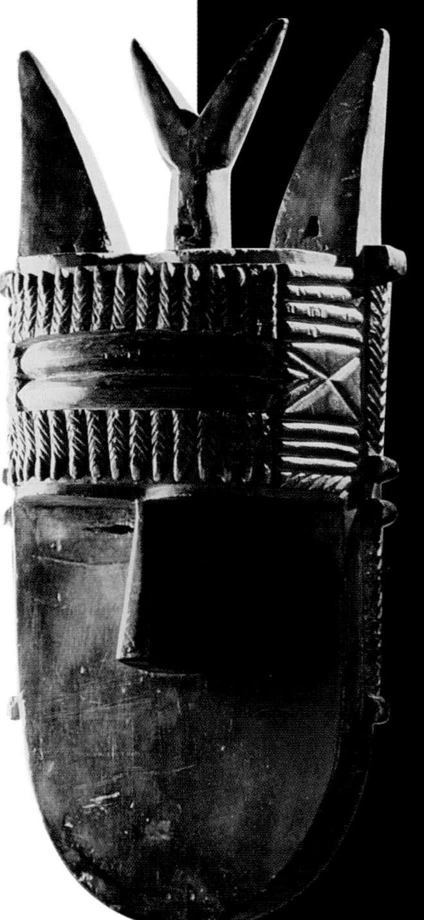

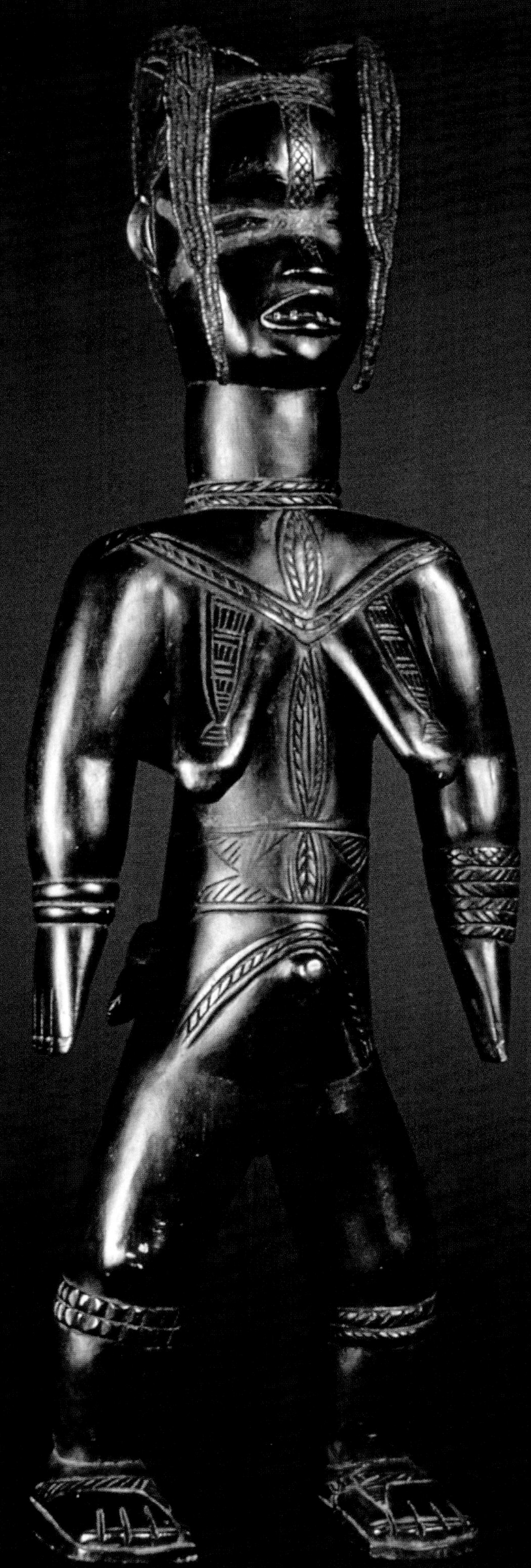

Guinea, Toma, late 19th Century
Simogui Mask
Darkened wood, H. 57 cm. Angoulême, MBA (Dr Lhomme)
©Photo Thierry Blais

Located at the border of Liberia and Guinea, in the heart of the forest zone, the Toma have organized their political and religious life around the Poro society, which is in charge of initiating young men. Among the masks that are part of the Poro rights, the bakrogui mask, still called angbai or simogui, depending on the authors, represents the stylized features of an ancestor, with a protruding nose and forehead on a flat face, topped with horns, making it a very bold sculpture.

Ivory Coast, Oubi, mid 20th Century
Mask
Wood, vegetable fibers. H. 42 cm.
Paris, MAAO (MIFAN warehouse, Dakar) ©Photo Labat/CFAO

Located in southwestern Ivory Coast, in the region tracing the border with Liberia, the Krou made spectacular masks with a flat face, domed forehead and tubular, often polychrome eyes. The best known of these masks, kept at the Musée de l'Homme, has a precubist design, and inspired Picasso's Guitar (1913) sculpture, in which all of the volumes are reversed. With its six rows of eyes, this mask was obtained from the Oubi, a section of the Bakwe group living in the Tai region.

Ivory Coast, Dan, Zlan work, circa 1950
Statue of a Woman with Child
Wood, vegetable fibers. H. 63 cm. Paris, MAAO
©Photo Pierre Reimbold

The Dan are of Mande origin and occupy a region in Ivory Coast, on the border of Liberia and Guinea. The Dan are well known for the quality of their sculptures, for their masks with very gentle faces, covered with beautiful dark and shiny patinas, and for their rich, cast brass finery made using the lost-wax process. This statue represents a woman carrying a child on her back and has naturalist features, typical of the forest region. It is the work of a well-known sculptor called Zlan, who worked circa 1960 in the Ivory Coast and Liberia border regions for a large number of sponsors. This work is not related to a particular rite or myth, as is often the case with statues in western Africa. It is simply the portrait of a deceased woman, whose memory the husband and family wished to keep alive.

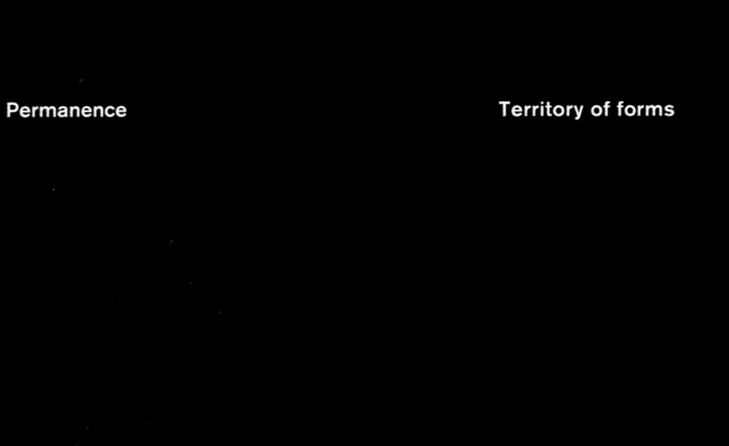

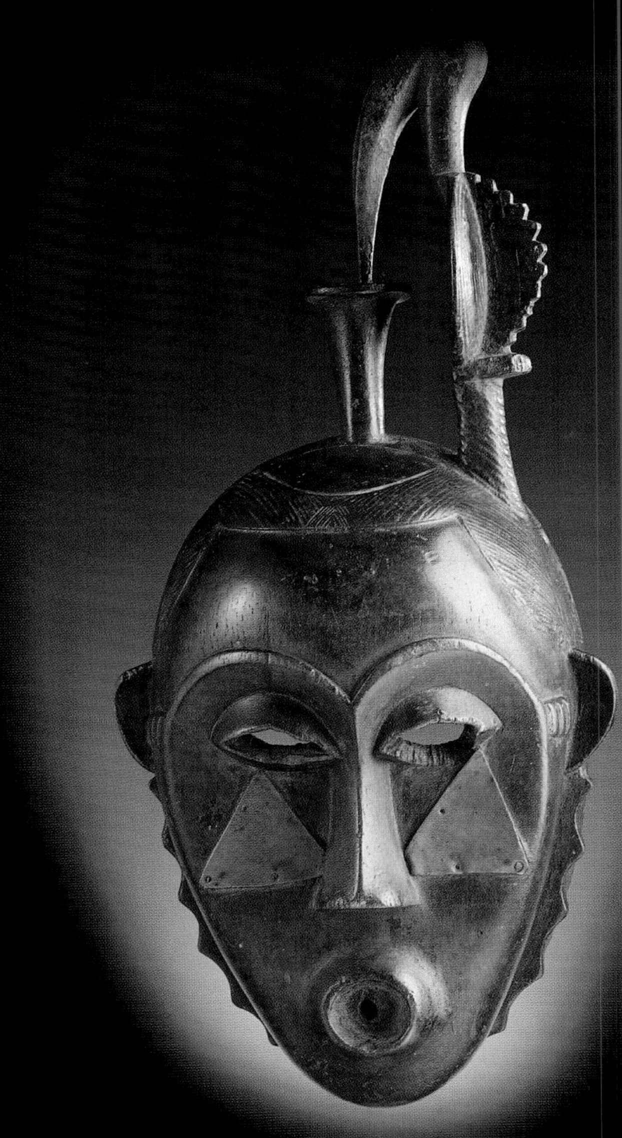

facing page:
Ivory Coast, Gouro, late 19th Century
Gye Mask
Wood, vegetable fibers. H. 34 cm. Paris, MAAO
©Photo Labat/CFAO

Living in the heart of Ivory Coast, in the Zuenoula region, the Gouro farmers, use different masks that come out during spectacular dances. The most well known are the gou, an anthropomorphic mask with a delicate, female face; the zamble, with a leopard's head, topped with antelope horns; and, finally the zahouli, considered as the ancestor, with a female face surrounded by a serpent. This mask, located to the north of the Gouro country, towards Bouafle, and known among the Yaoure neighbors, represents the Gye or Dye spirit, who is worshipped in the men's sacred woods and who cannot be looked upon by women.

Ivory Coast, Yaoure, late 19th Century
Bird Mask
Hardwood with black patina, brass pieces. H. 40 cm.
Paris, MAAO (former Paul Guillaume collection)
©Photo Labat/CFAO

The Yaoure, of Akan origin, live in the Bouafle region, at the crossroads of the Gouro and Baule territories. Characterized by a face with harmonious features and a jagged beard, their masks are among the most sophisticated sculptures in Ivory Coast. Yaoure masks are often topped with allegoric figures, in this case a bird (a second, positioned symmetrically, has been lost). This bird is the hornbill, whose long beak is in a mortar, probably an allusion to the sexual act.

Ivory Coast, Baule, mid 20th Century
Blolo Bla Statue
Wood with brown patina, beads in glass paste. H. 54 cm.
Paris, MAAO ©Photo Labat/CFAO

Living in central Ivory Coast, the Baule are one of the numerous Akan groups who emigrated from the former Gold Coast between the 15th and the 18th centuries. Baule statuary is used for divination and psychiatry, and not for the worship of ancestors, as it was long believed. For the Baule, bloblo represents the hereafter. Existence actually follows a perpetual rotation from the world of the living to the world of the dead. In the previous world, the individual left his wife and children, a family that he only recalls later on, in adolescence or adulthood, when psychological problems begin to surface. The Komienfwe soothsayer is then consulted and he establishes the origin of the illness, which is attributed to the jealously of the husband (bloblo bian) or of the wife (bloblo bla) in the afterworld towards the living spouse. He then asks the patient to have a professional sculptor produce a statuette, for which very specific physical indications are provided (hairstyle, clothing, scarifications). Once the statuette is completed, it is received as if the husband or wife in the afterworld had come down to Earth to be with his/her spouse. A small marriage and reconciliation ceremony is then performed. This statuette is carefully kept in the patient's room, looked after and fed each day.

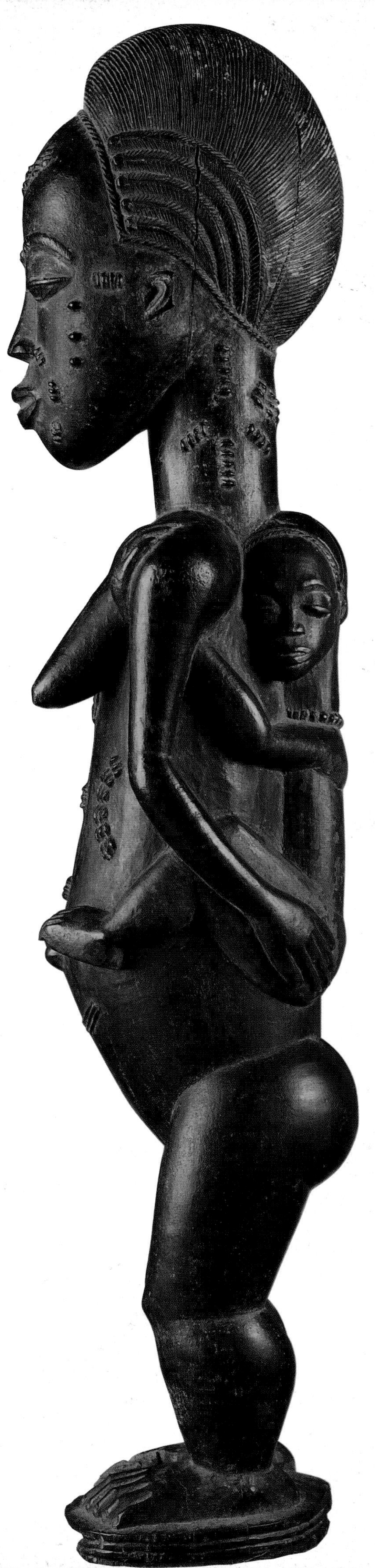

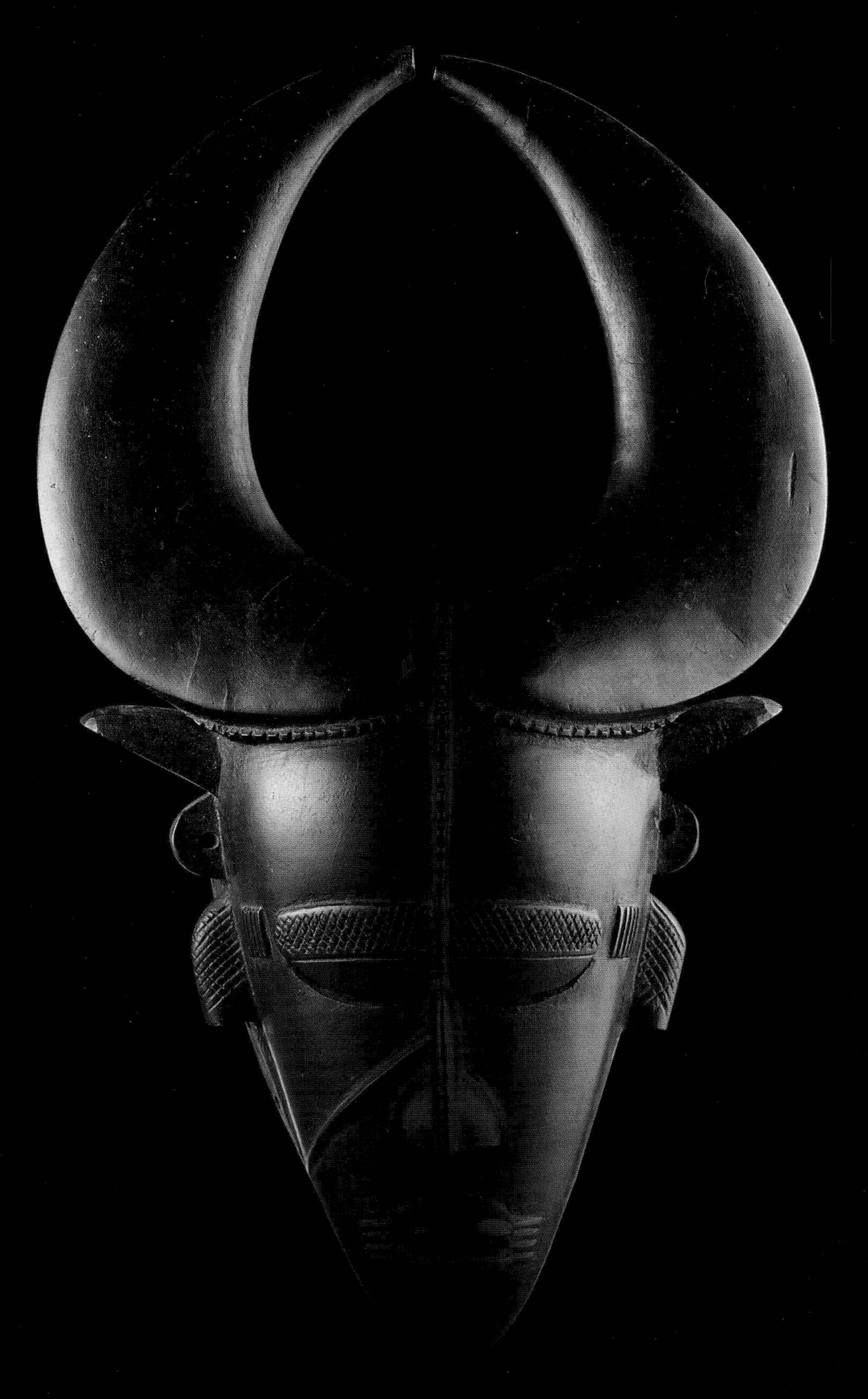

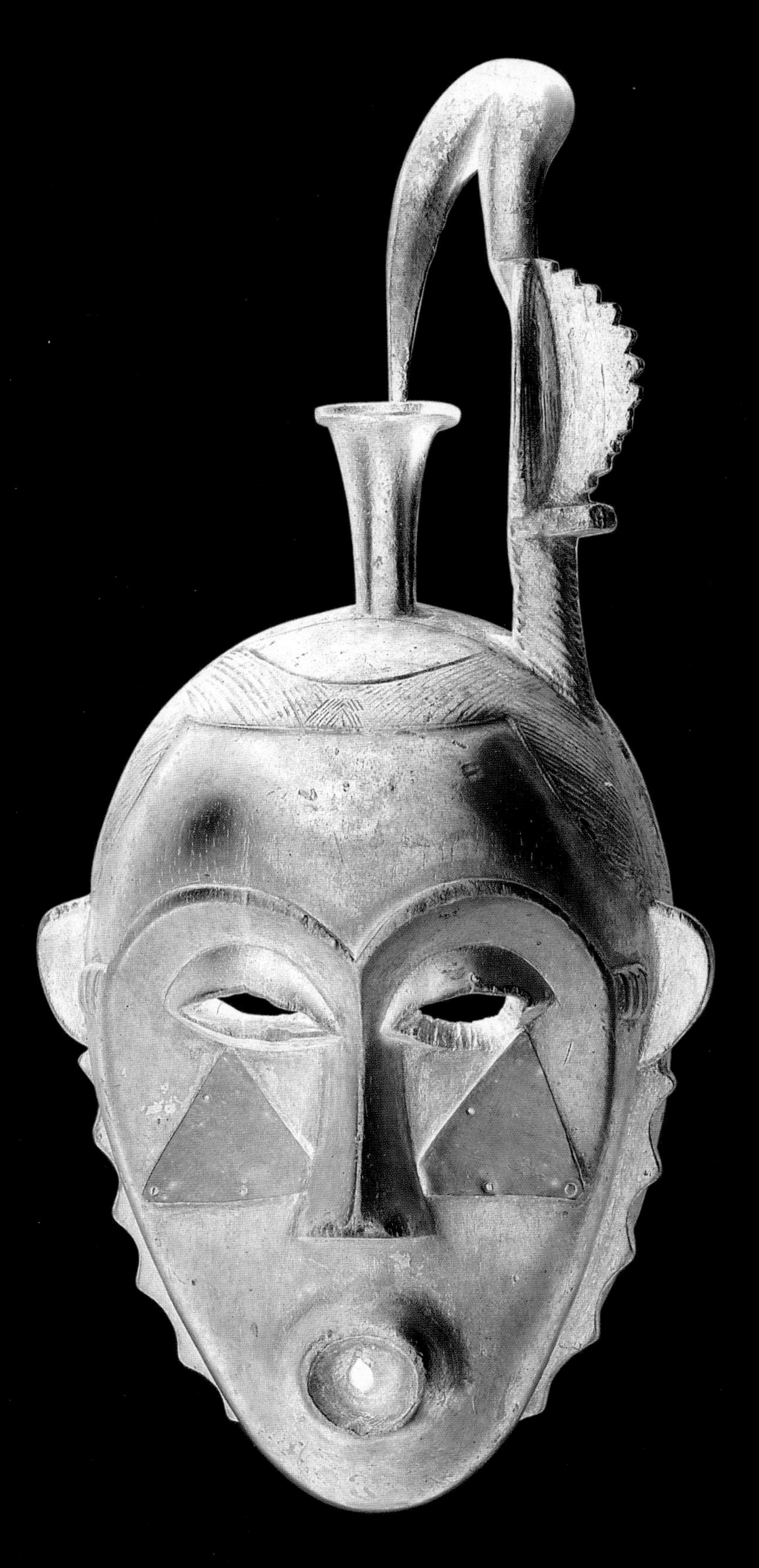

Ivory Coast or Ghana, Akan, early 20th Century
Figurative weight: hunting scene
Brass. H. 4 cm
Paris, MAAO (donated by Alexandre Ignatieff) ©Labat/CFAO

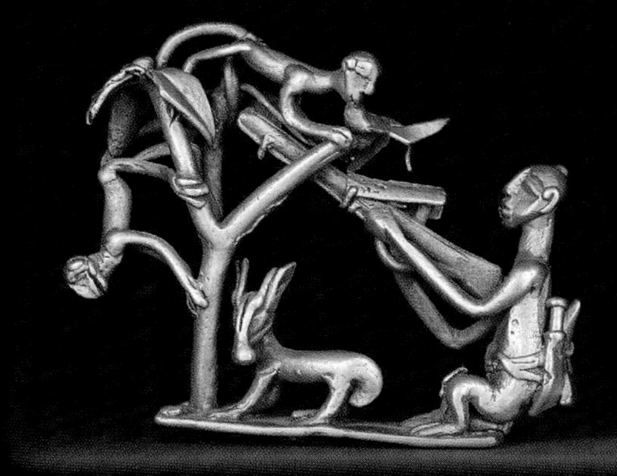

Countless in number and in form, cast brass weights made using the lost-wax process were once used by the Akan to weigh gold. Each of them actually corresponded to a certain quantity of gold powder, which served as currency on the Gold Coast until 1889. A set of weights constituted the dya, that is the inheritance for an individual or a family. There were two types:
- the geometric weights, whose hollow or raised symbols corresponded to a certain numeric value.
- the figurative weights, representing small, scenes of everyday life, people, animals, chiefdom symbols, etc., that always illustrate a proverb, were used for special transactions, such as settling a debt, tax, fine or the costs of a ceremony. This is actually a very complicated system (with male and female weights) that eludes Cartesian reasoning. These weights disappeared almost a century ago and were very poorly studied. An Anyi king used to say that these weights actually enabled the counter, the expert, to illustrate legendary stories or to pass along a moral code. While today they have lost their economic value, they continue to represent a treasure of reference signs and shapes for the entire Akan cultural world and even for western Africa.

Ghana, Ashanti, 20th Century
Akua Ba Statuette
Wood, H. 19.8 cm. Angoulême, MBA
(donated by Hervé Belkiri-Deluen)
©D.R.

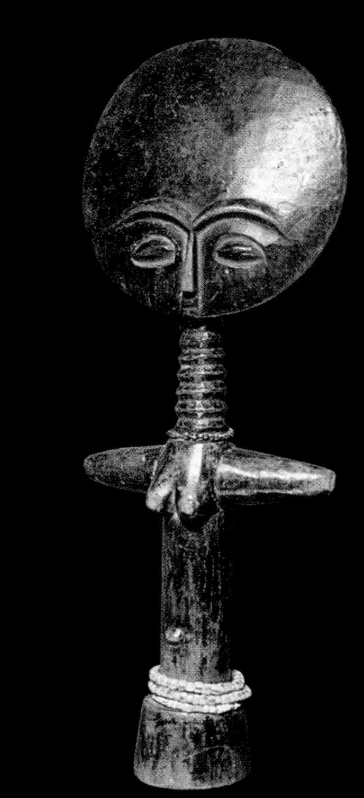

Among the Ashanti, who do not have any statuary, we find stylized, flat-headed dolls, with an annulated neck, called akua ba (little women). They were used by young girls and also by young mothers, who would keep them clenched in their pagne to protect their pregnancy and to preside over the birth of a beautiful child.

facing page:
Benin, Fon of Abomey, late 19th Century
Behanzin's Recade
Wood, iron, leather. Lg. 53.8 cm. La Rochelle, MHN
©Museum d'Histoire Naturelle, La Rochelle

The recade of the Fon kings of Abomey derives its name from the Portuguese word recado, meaning messenger. These curved wooden rods adorned with royal emblems in iron or clipped brass (Ghezo's buffalo, Glele's lion, Behanzin's shark), were the safe-conducts of ambassadors and war chiefs. When he appeared in public, the king himself carried one on his shoulder, with the angled part facing the ground. The motifs on these recades illustrate genuine proverbial discourses. Here, the notorious shark of Behanzin (1889-1893) recalls the motto of he who dared stand up to increasingly indiscrete Western incursions: "the furious shark has disturbed the bar."

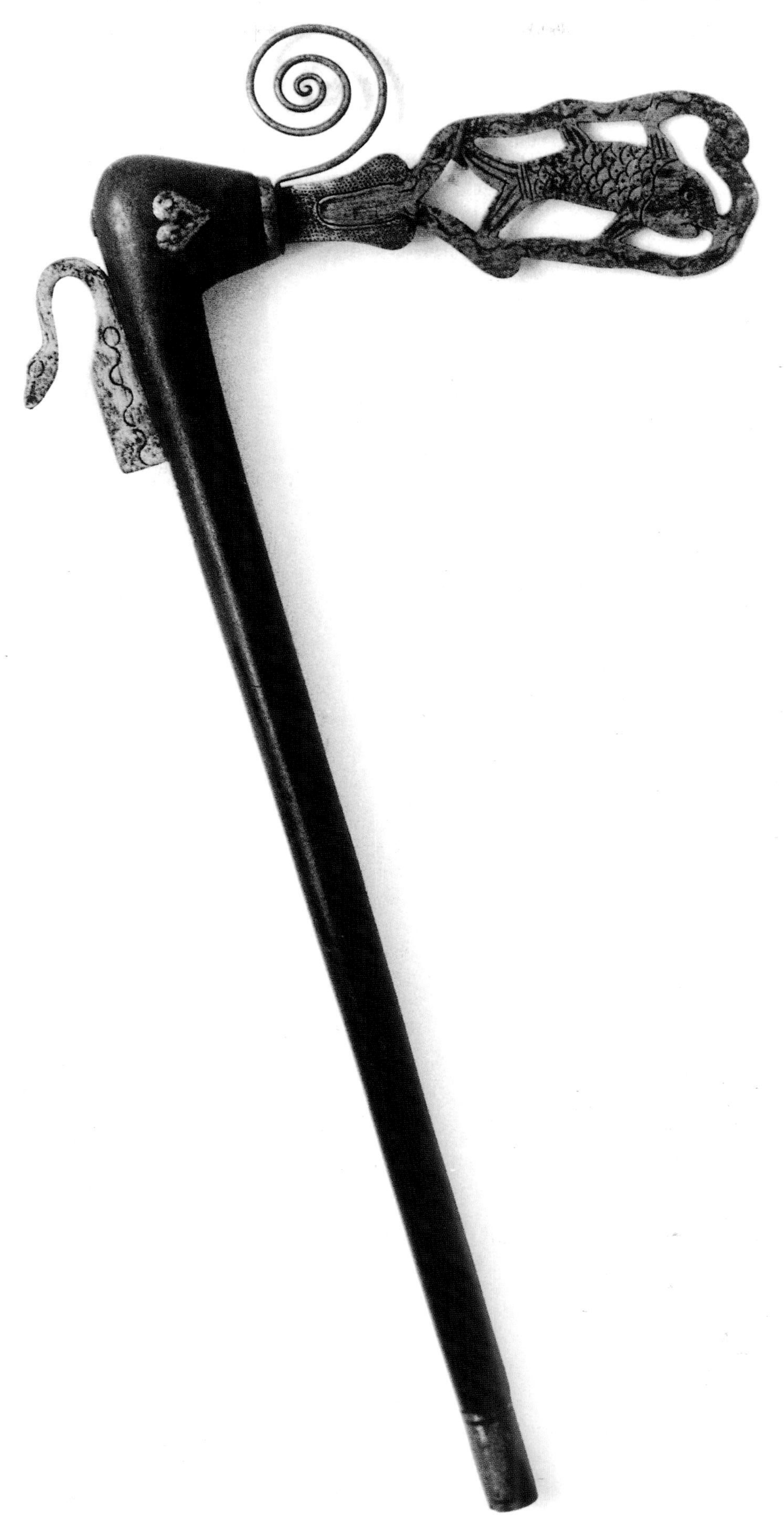

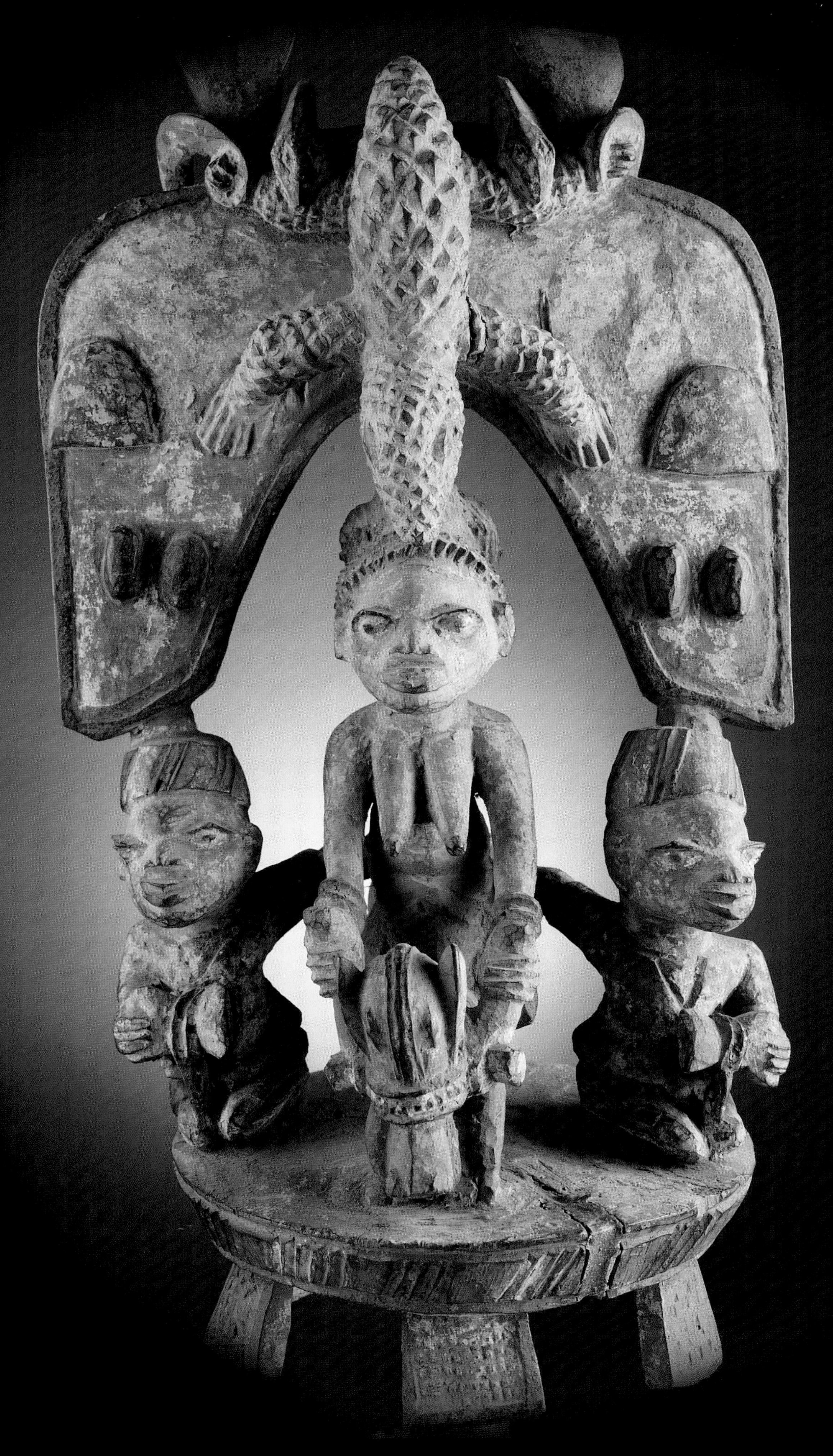

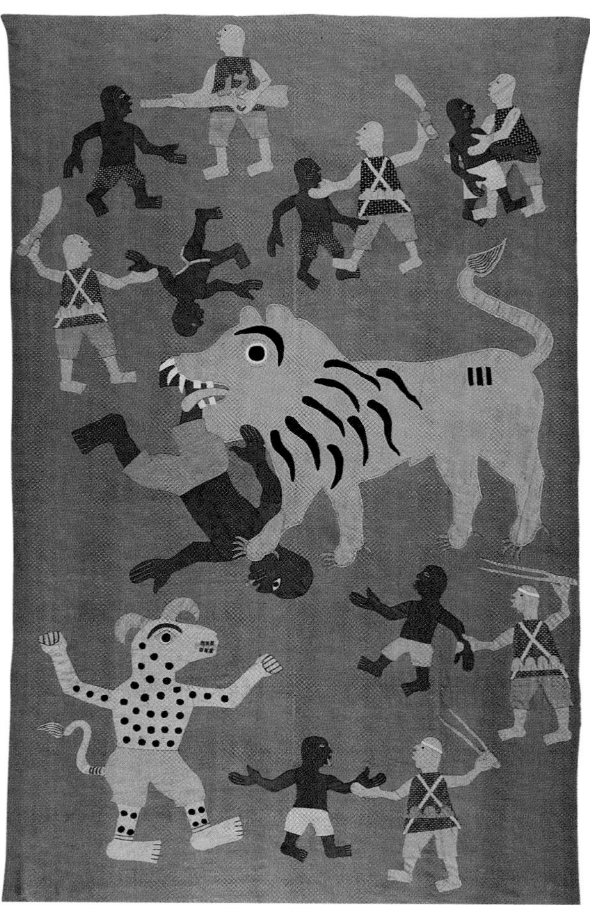

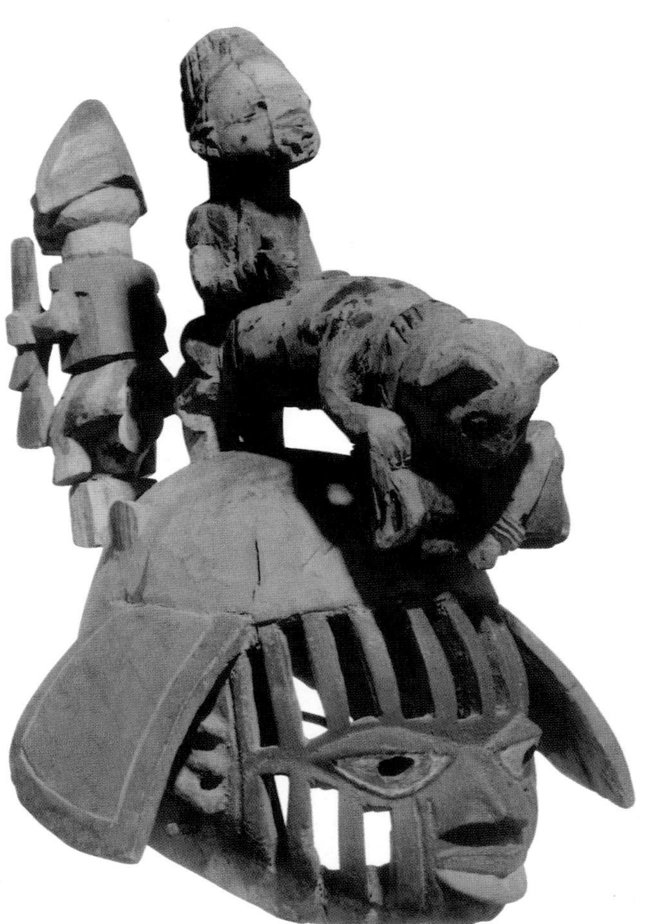

facing page:
Benin, Yoruba, mid 20th Century
Shango Emblem
Polychrome wood. H. 50 cm. Paris, MAAO (IFAN warehouse, Dakar)

As an allusion to the "thunderbolts" that have fallen from the sky, which farmers gather in their fields, the double axe that tops this rod symbolizes Shango, the god of thunder honored by the Yoruba of Nigeria and of Benin. Generally representing a kneeling woman holding twins to her breast, this type of rod was kept by the priest or priestess of the divinity. Shango, who is among the most effective Orishas from the Yoruba pantheon, recalls the legendary figure of an ancient Oyo king, a great fetisher, revered for his powers and beauty, who disappeared during a violent storm. This is why he is considered the protector of children and presides, in particular, over the worship of the Ibeji twins.

Benin, Fon of Abomey, late 19th Century
Glele's Wall Covering
Cotton. H. 220 cm. Paris, MAAO

Founded in the 17th century, the Fon kingdom of Abomey extended to the Ouidah and devoted itself very early on to the slave trade with the Europeans. In the next century, the Fon kingdom became the vassal of the Yoruba empire of Oyo. In 1851, King Ghezo (1818-1858) was able to free himself from the Yoruba, who he crushed in the Abeokuta battle in 1851. His successor, King Glele (1858-1889), the last independent Dahomey sovereign, also did battle against his Yoruba neighbors, the Nago, a conflict that is shown on this wall covering made from cut and sewn European fabrics. In the center, the lion-headed king and his light-skinned soldiers cut off the heads of their Nago enemies, who we can recognize from their black skin and their facial scarifications (three gashes on each cheek).

Nigeria, Yoruba, early 20th Century
Gelede Mask
Wood. H. 43 cm Angoulême, MBA
(Châtellerault Museum warehouse)

The Yoruba from Benin and Nigeria have a large range of masks. The most famous are handled by the Gelede society, which derived its name from worship dedicated to Mothers, i.e. older women who are the most influential members of this society and who are in charge of fighting against all the harmful forces. Once per year, in the spring, a large masquerade brings out in public several dozen spectacular masks worn not only by adults, but also by children. These masks are comprised of a heavy costume of multicolored fabrics and a sculpted wooden helmet representing the different social levels. Here, we have a hunting scene that is short-lived by the hunter, who is devoured by a furious panther. The brightly colored calm and beautiful faces of the Gelede masks are supposed to appease evil influences from the afterworld and thwart the criminal actions of sorcerers.

Nigeria, Ibo-Izi, mid 20th Century
Elephant Mask
Wood. Lg. 54.5 cm. Paris, MAAO
©Photo Labat/CFAO

Several Ibo groups in the northeast are familiar with the Ogbodo enyi ("elephant spirit") mask, a spectacular mask with a flowing raffia robe and a heavy wooden mask combining human and the pachyderm's traits. A human head called Ntekpe is added to the back. It is not known if the head is a portrait of a notable or of one of the "spirit's children." A copy of this essentially male mask has been exceptionally worn several times a year by a woman in the Izzi village since 1975, when an oracle ordered her, that year, to ward off an epidemic that was killing children.

Nigeria, Ijo, mid 20th Century
Fish Mask
Wood. Lg. 155 cm. Paris, MAAO
©RMN-J.G. Berizzi

In the Port-Harcourt region, shark-shaped crests are very popular at masquerades. The shark masks (Ofurumo) have a grand reputation among the populations along the delta, where fishermen are often faced with these dangerous fish as they cross the bar of their long, slender boats. Their dance can lead to a genuine pantomime of the fishermen hunting and capturing the shark or sharks. Attached to a wicker headpiece, this long shark with an aerodynamic shape comes with a mobile jaw that contains terrifying teeth.

facing page:
Nigeria, Mumuye, 20th Century
Mask
Wood. H. 33.5 cm. Paris, MAAO
©Photo Labat/CFAO

The Mumuye, who live in eastern Nigeria, close to the Cameroon border, are especially known for their stylized-shaped statuary, discovered in the 1970s. These statues represent protective ancestors who are supposed to oversee the well-being of individuals and families. They are often sculpted using large adz strokes with bold triangle shapes. The arms cover the abdomen, the earlobes, pierced with a hole, are often exaggerated, and the eyes are outlined with kaolin. The Mumuye masks are less known, yet this strange, alien-looking face, which was first attributed to the neighboring Mambila on the Cameroon border, was recently returned to the Nigerian Mumuye.

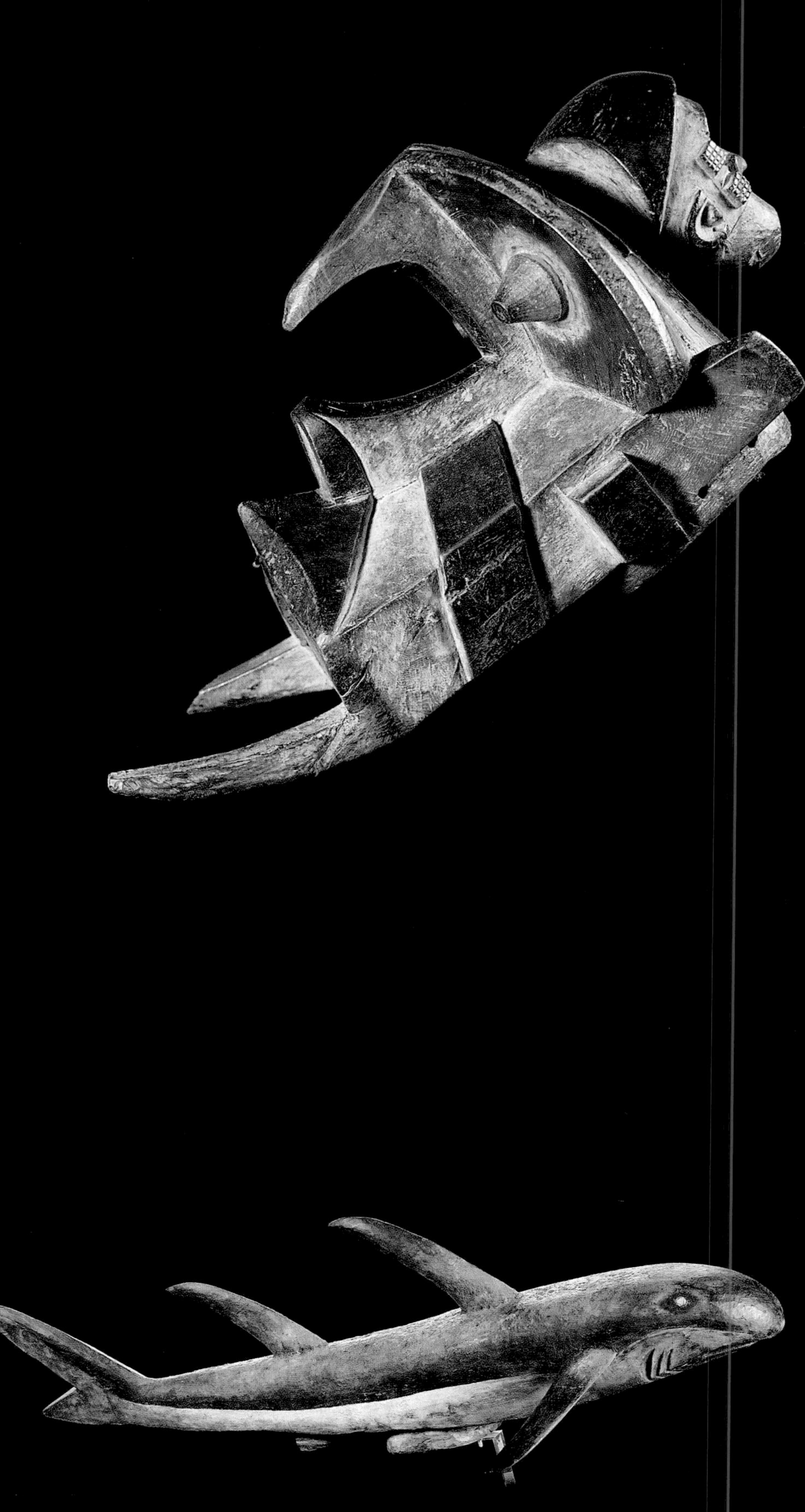

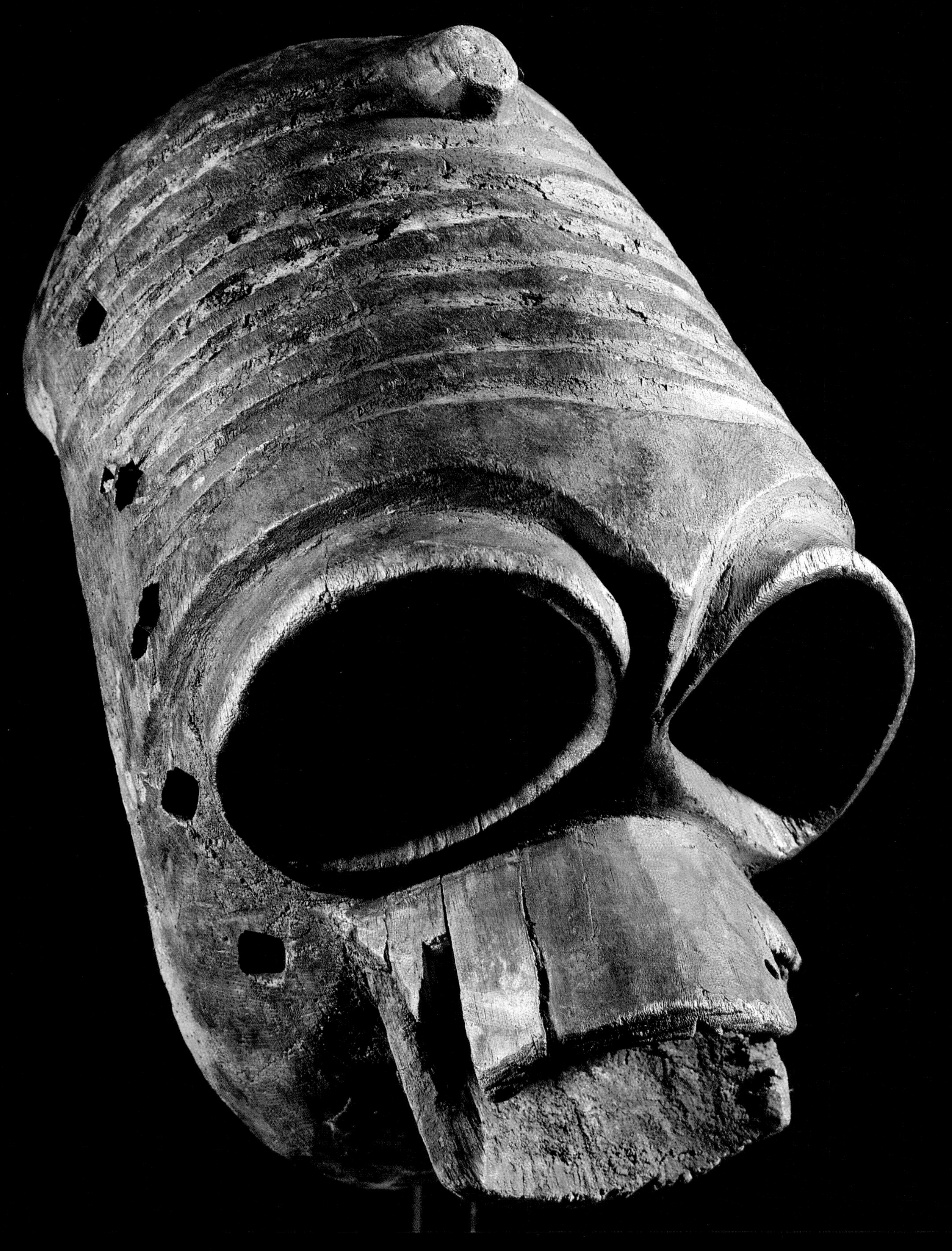

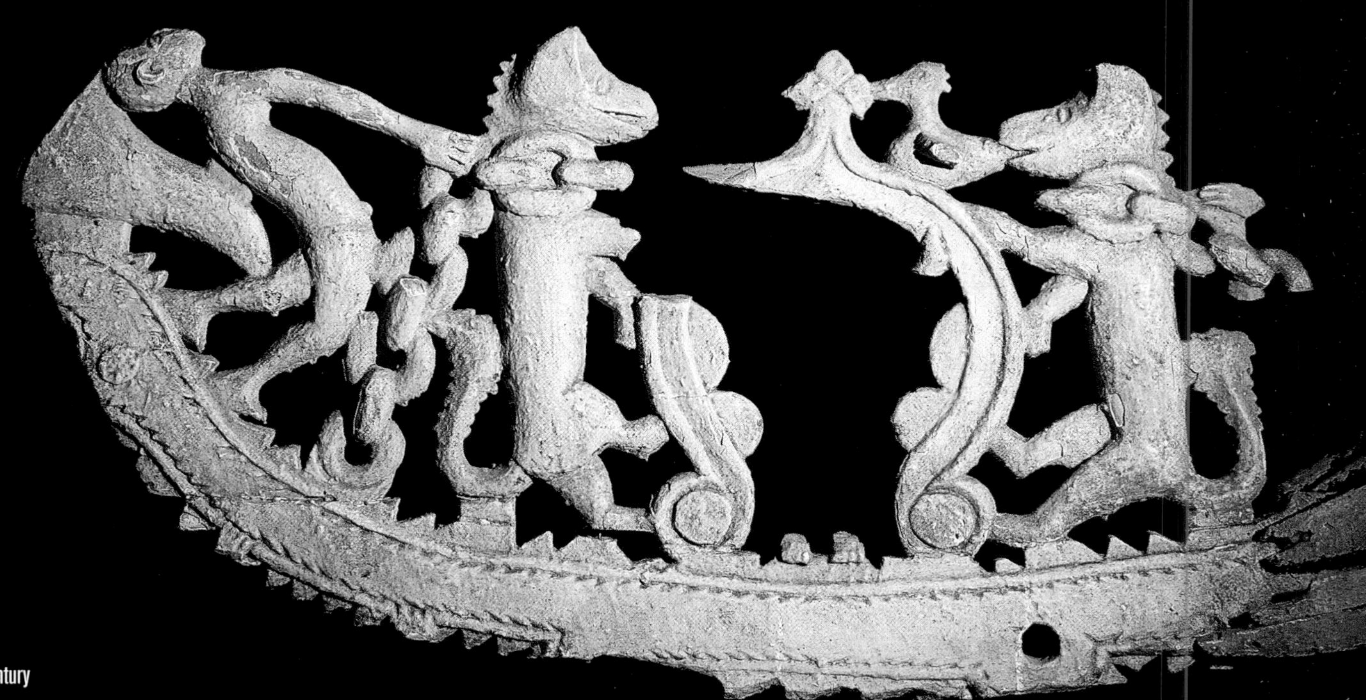

Cameroon, Duala, early 20th Century
Tange Pirogue Bow
Wood, Kaoli. Lg. 220 cm Paris, MH
©Musée de l'Homme, Paris/photo D. Destable

At the beginning of the century, the Duala had a very rich folklore, characterized, among other things, by pirogue races and by the use of large polychrome wood buffalo masks. Today, spectacular regattas are still organized during Independence Day (July 12) activities. Taking part in these regattas are long pirogues (myolos) measuring 20 to 30 meters in length and mounted by 40 to 80 paddlers. The long, slender bows (tange) on these pirogues are sculpted with magnificent grid-type scenes that are polychrome in nature. These scenes often represent animals and these bows are deemed an indispensable ornament to winning the race.

Cameroon, Bamileke, late 19th Century
Queen of Bansoa
Wood, beads in glass paste. H. 111.5 cm
Paris, MAAO (Harter bequest)
©Photo RMN-Mathéus

This wooden statue, sculpted from one single piece and entirely covered with small red, white and black beads in glass plate, portrays a Bamileke queen sitting with dignity on a caryatid seat (the royal panther) and holding a cup in her hands. In most of the Bamileke chiefdoms in the Cameroon Grassland, these statues, monumental by nature, are displayed during large royal ceremonies such as the funeral of a king or the investiture of his successor. These statues are called tutuo, akukuo or fuon-toh and represent the royal ancestors. The beading technique is specific to the Grassland. The wooden statue is covered with a raffia cloth on which a series of European-made glass beads, obtained from the slave trade, have been sewn in lines.

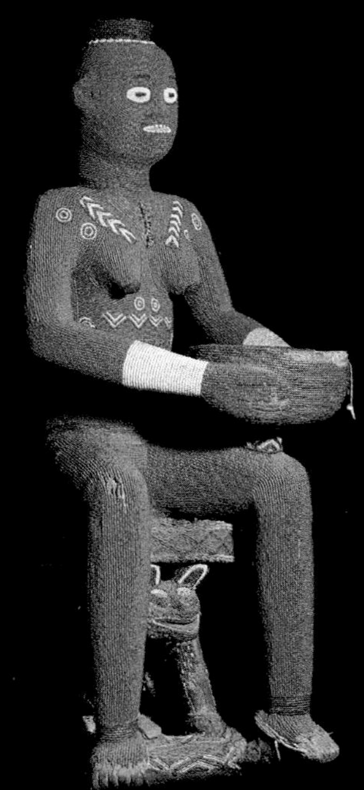

Cameroon, Bamoum, 1st half of the 20th Century
Nsoro Society Mask
Wood, vegetable fibers. H. 70 cm. Paris, MAAO (Harter bequest)
©RMN-Mathéus

The Bamoum kingdom forms the vastest traditional political entity in the Cameroon Grassland. This mask is comprised of a heavy solid wood head with big eyes and an aggressive mouth set on a rattan headpiece and surrounded by a vast ruff of vegetable fibers. It belonged to the secrete Nsoro society, an association for the most valiant warriors in the royal army and was used during the funerals of chiefs or elders of the society.

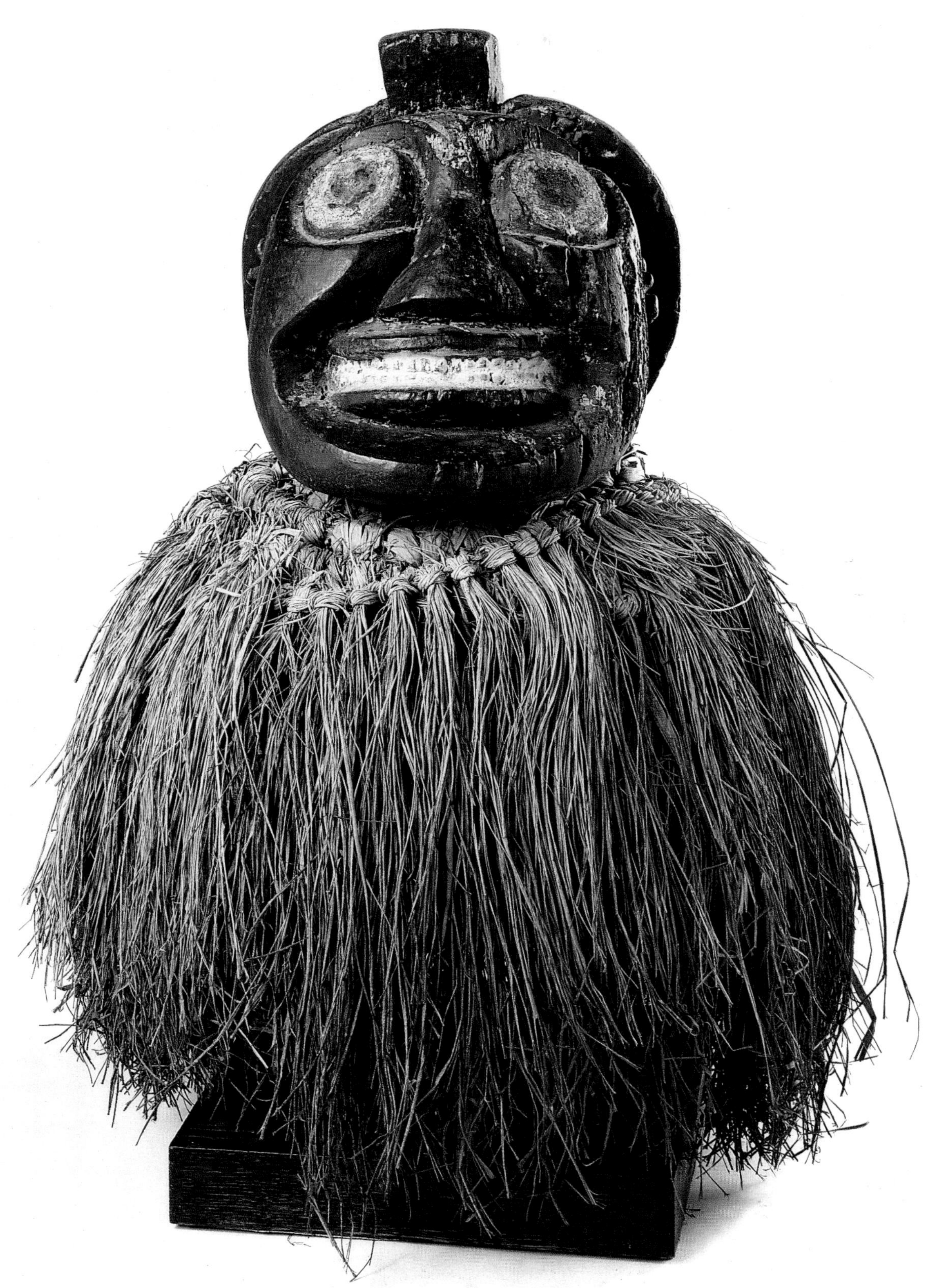

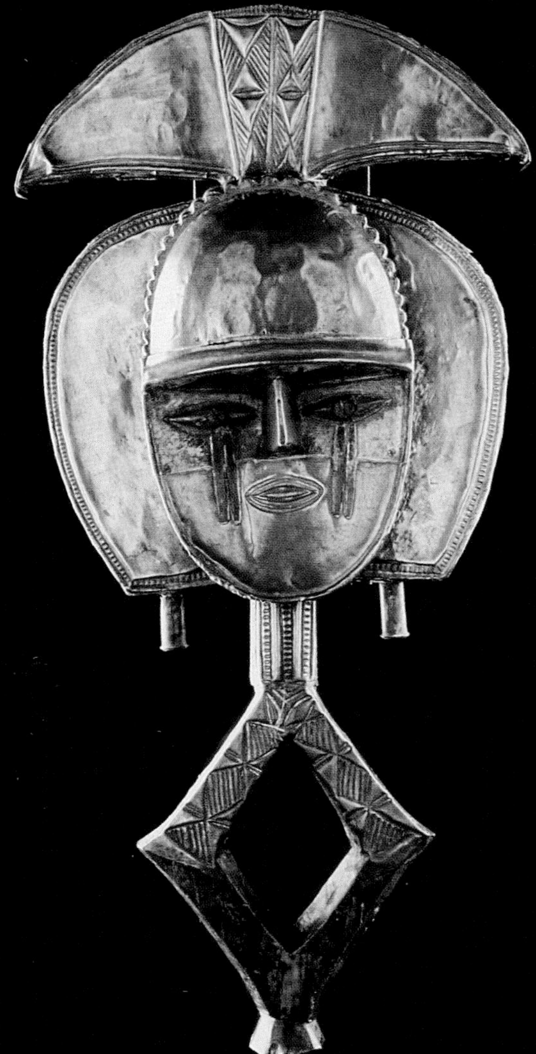

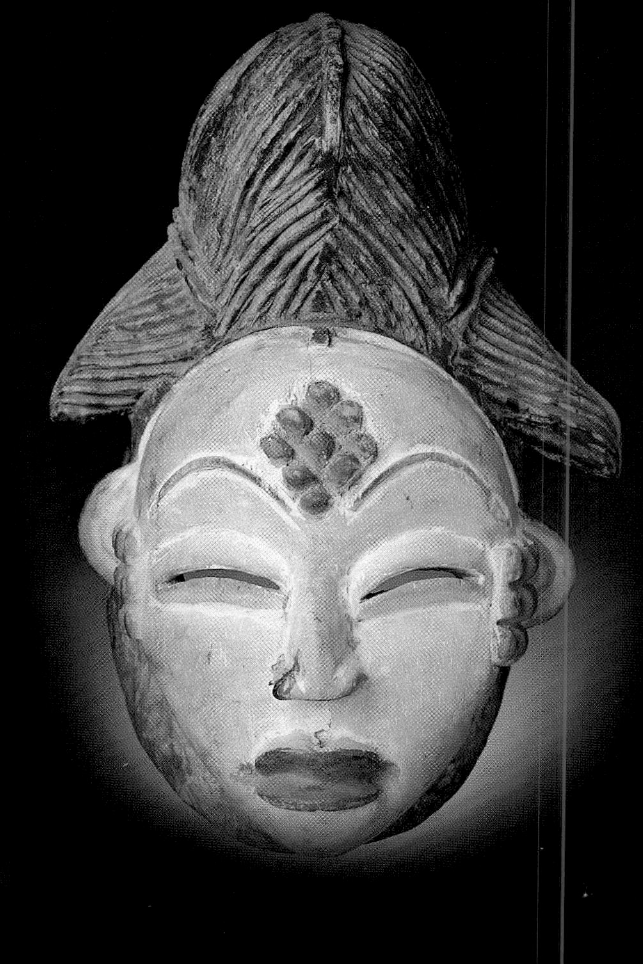

Gabon, Kota, late 20th Century
Reliquary Figure
Wood, copper, brass. H. 60 cm. Angouleme, MBA
(Dr. Lhomme bequest)

This stylized wooden figure, covered with repoussé and riveted brass leaves, copper strips and iron nails, originally topped a box made of tree bark or wicker containing the bones of an ancestor from the lineage. This reliquary, called a mbulu ngulu, was supposed to lock away the deceased's vital breath and, under the Bwiti worship, was consulted for all types of matters.

Gabon, Pounou, early 20th Century
Mask
Polychrome Wood. H. 37 cm. Paris, MAAO

Coincidentally resembling a Japanese theater mask, this mask portrays a face whitened with kaolin, slanting eyes and a triple-looped hairstyle. Beneath the features of a beautiful girl from the afterworld, this mask falls under the Okuyi white mask category, well known in Gabon among the Pounou and their Loumbo or Eshira neighbors, who, often raised on stilts, appear in initiation ceremonies and funeral rituals.

facing page:
Gabon, Fang, 1st half of the 20th Century
Mask
Wood, feathers, H. 18 cm. Paris, MAAO

The Fang use numerous masks as part of their initiation ceremonies and during funerals. These masks are often handled by secret societies (like the So or the Ngil) and portray long faces whitened with kaolin. One recurring mask is the nlo ngon tnân mask (head of the young white girl), which represents the spirit of an ancestor, typical with its pallid, heart-shaped face and slanting eyes, topped here with a tiara of feathers from a large black bird, either a hornbill or a bird of prey.

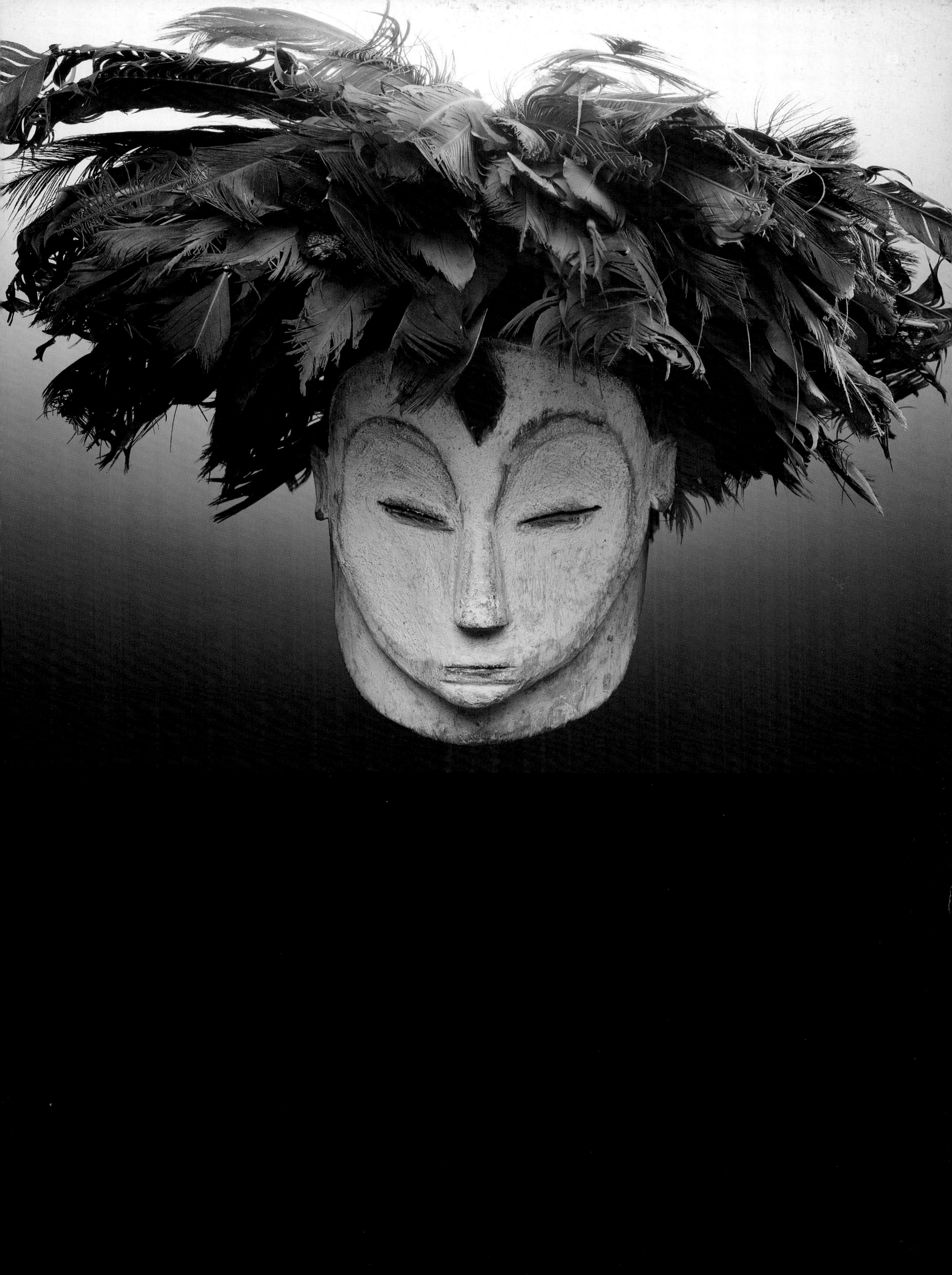

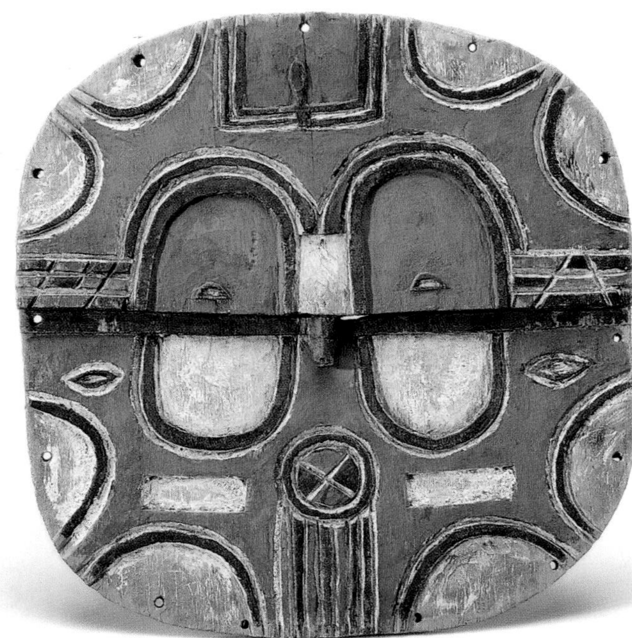

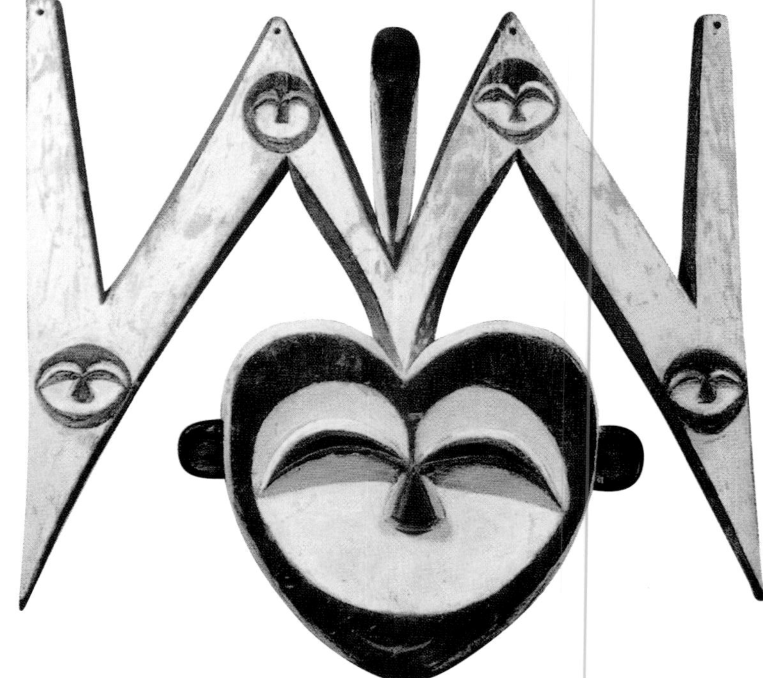

Congo, Teke-Tsayi, early 20th Century
Kidoumou Mask
Wood, pigments. H. 32.7 cm. Paris, MH

The Tsayi form a faction of the Teke on the border between Gabon and Congo-Brazza. They are known for their abstract, two-dimensional and polychrome art, which is fairly rare in African art. This art can be seen on the solar side of the kidoumou, a mask sculpted from a piece of carved softwood and covered with pigments, accompanied by a crown of black feathers and a raffia body stocking. Used in the past for the initiation of boys, this mask disappeared with colonization, and was then reintroduced, after independence, in Congo folklore as an emblematic form of the Teke culture.

Congo, Kwele, early 20th Century
Mask
Wood, pigments. H. 63 cm. La Rochelle, MHN

Found in the region between Congo and Gabon, the Kwele made very beautiful heart-shaped anthropomorphic masks, with a concave face painted white. These masks are called pipibuze and represent spirits from the afterworld. They have half-closed eyes and a serene expression. Generically called gon, the Kwele masks were used during youth initiation rites.

facing page:
Congo, Bembe, early 20th Century
Muziri Reliquary Mannequin
Wood, bone, iron, brass, red cotton cloth. H. 63.7 cm.
La Rochelle, MHN (don Briaud)

The Bembe attach great importance to the worship of ancestors. One of the supports used by this worship is the muziri ("fetish"), an anthropomorphic mannequin always dressed in red cloth and containing the relics of a sage or a chief reputed for his justice. Always portrayed sitting, the figure raises one arm towards the sky and lowers the other towards the Earth (allusions to the cosmogonic beliefs). Replicas of the deceased's tegumentary scarifications are marked on the torso and face with chalk. The muziri worship has been persecuted by imported religions and is, thus, on the road to complete disappearance. It used to be headed by a notable or a clan elder, or possibly by the nganga, the healing soothsayer.

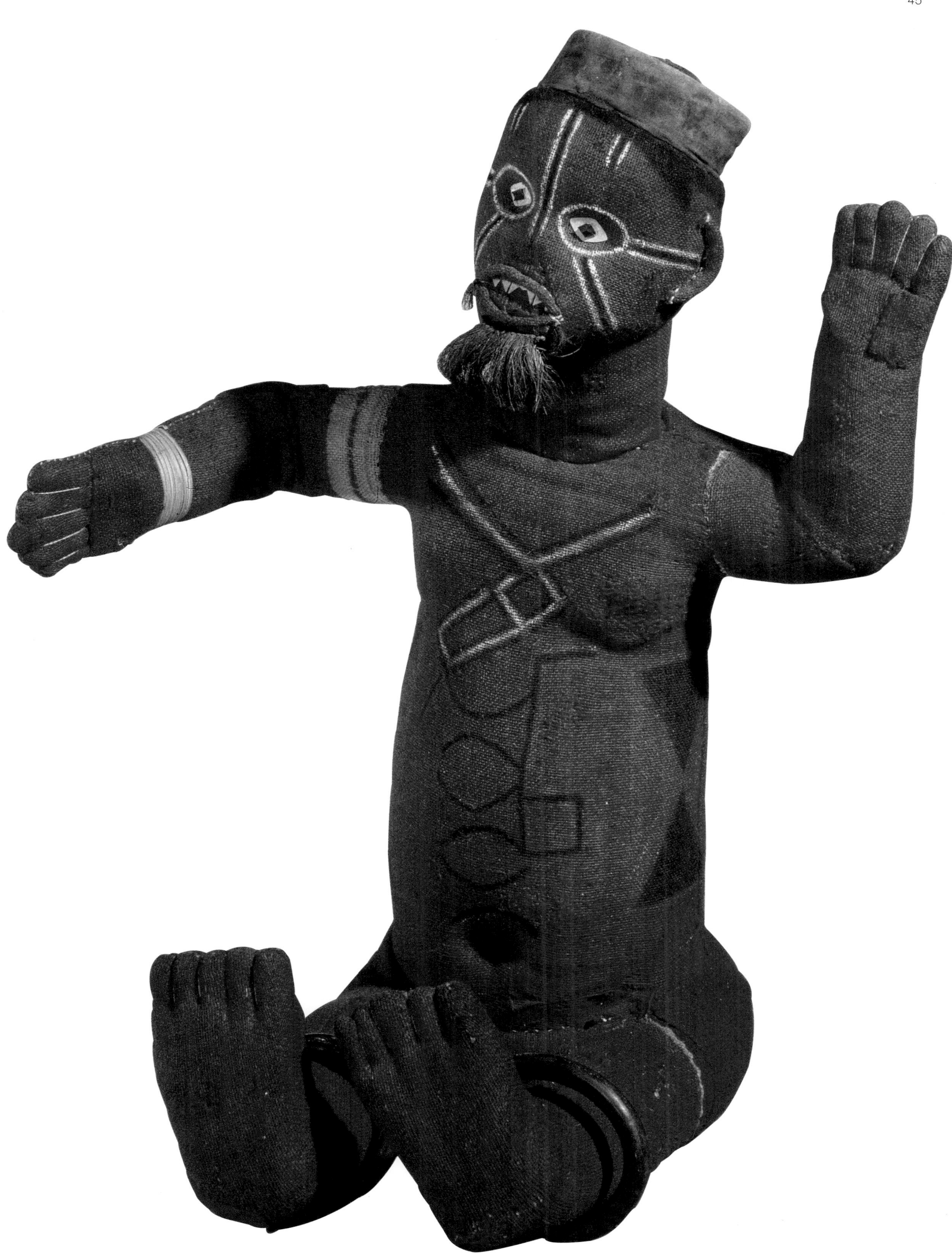

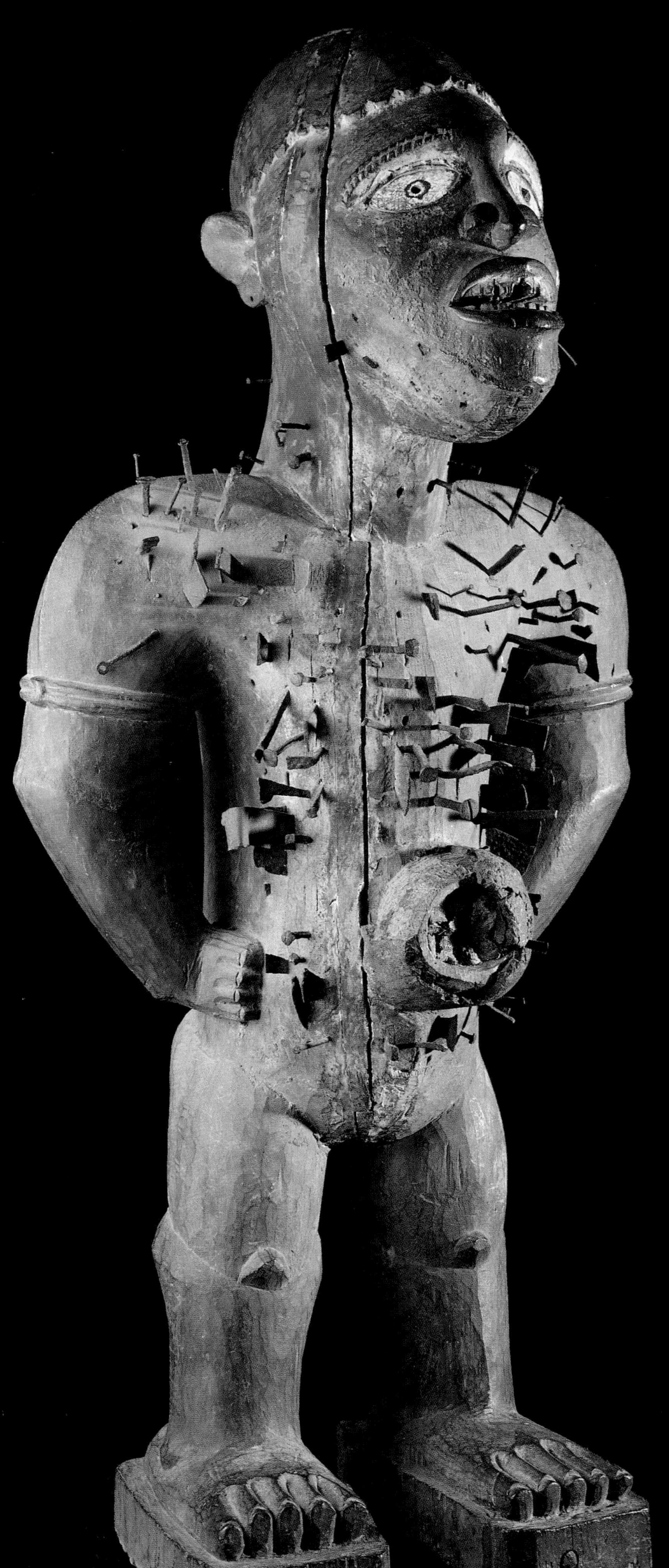

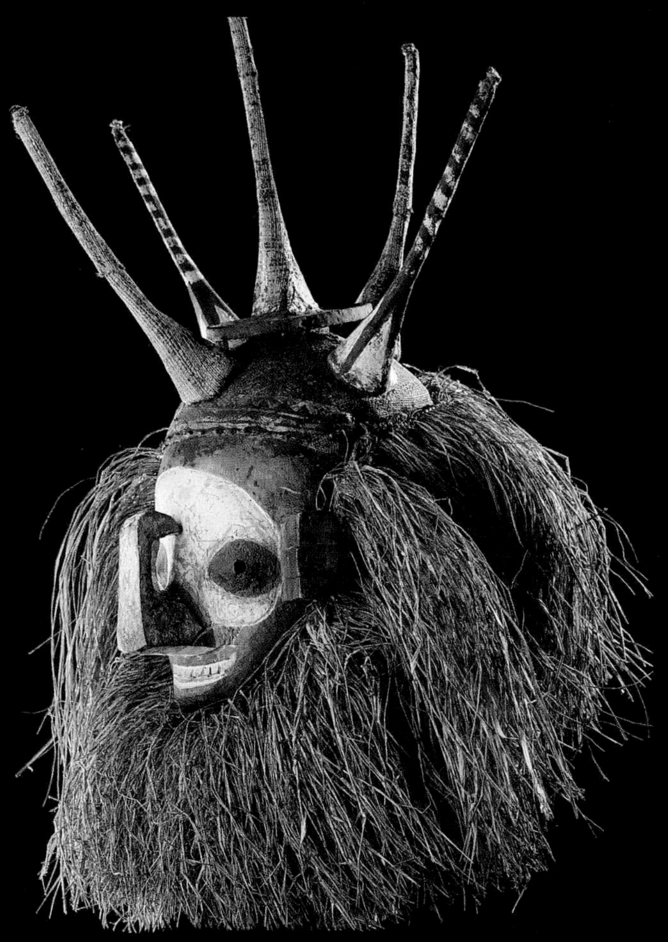

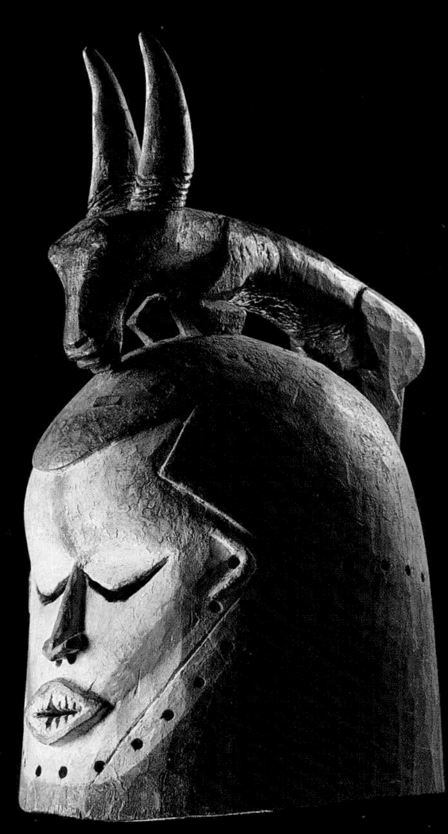

facing page:
DRC, Vili, late 19th Century
Nkondi Statue
Wood, iron nails. H. 108 cm. Paris, MAAO

Among the Kongo, the nganga or healing soothsayer is consulted for all problems affecting an individual or a group. Among all of the nganga's accessories, the main one is the nkondi, which represents a figure whose right arm is raised, brandishing a spear or a dagger, and carrying on its stomach a container of magical objects, which is often closed by a piece of mirror. It is barbed with nails and iron objects, which are prayers addressed to the spirit of the fetish, which is supposed to ward off and catalyze evil, or at least keep it at a distance. The nkondi can also be a dog or a leopard. The tradition of using nails came from superstitious European customs brought to the Congo by the Portuguese.

DRC, Yaka, early 20th Century
Mask
Wood. H. 70 cm. Paris, MAAO

The Yaka style is easy to recognize: the statues and masks have odd-looking trumpet-shaped noses. Their very colorful masks are used during the circumcision closure ceremony (nkhanda). Made and then worn by young Tundansi initiates to the sound of shrill voices, ndemba masks are comprised of a softwood wolf, an esparto superstructure and a raffia fabric, coated with a blackish resin, often with multiple braids vertically raised, as well as with a vast ruff and a raffia body stocking. The kholula, the mask of the group's chief, is often topped with an animal, figure or spectacular group.

DRC, Suku, early 20th Century
Mask
Polychrome Wood. H. 49 cm. Paris, MAAO

The Suku have institutions that resemble those of the Yaka and their neighbors from the Kwango Kwilu in the Congo. At the youth initiation ceremony, they use helmet masks called hemba, which represent the faces of elders, whitened with kaolin. These are often topped with figures or animals with an allegoric function, such as here with the antelope, the symbol of agility.

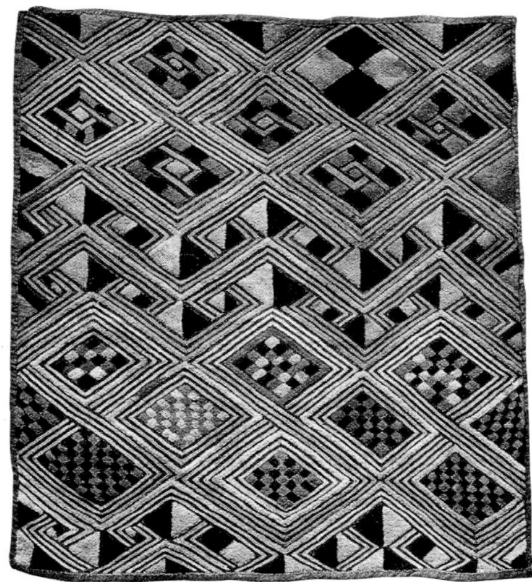

DRC, Kuba, 20th Century
Embroidered Raffia Matting
Raffia. Paris, MAAO
©D.R.

Among the Kuba arts, what stands out is the exceptional quality of the decorative arts, in particular the textiles and the raffia matting woven by the men and embroidered by the women. Certain parts of the embroidery are sheared using the velvet technique. The inventiveness, infinite variations of simple patterns such as the cross or royal interlace, and the refusal of any controlled symmetry, preferring instead syncopation, all make these embroideries striking. Collected by families as works of art, these textiles were rarely worn.

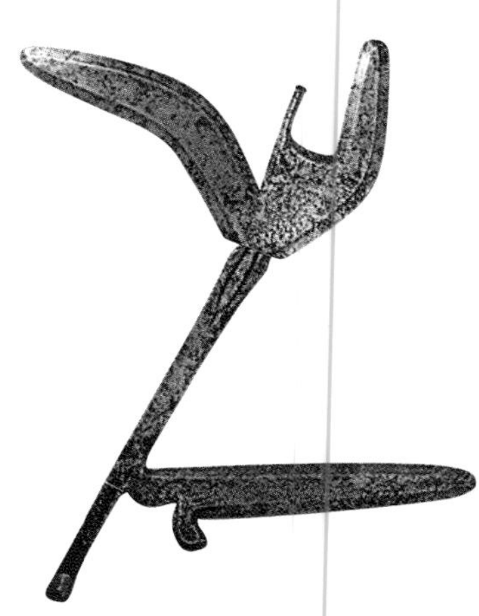

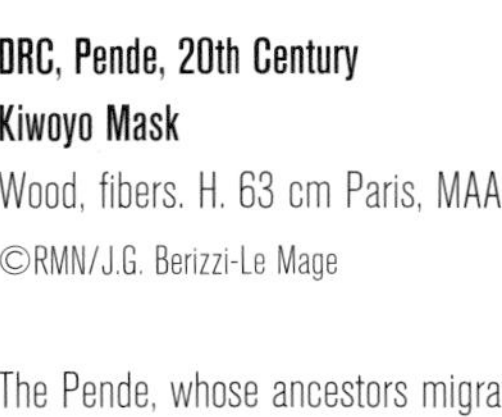

DRC, Pende, 20th Century
Kiwoyo Mask
Wood, fibers. H. 63 cm Paris, MAAO
©RMN/J.G. Berizzi-Le Mage

The Pende, whose ancestors migrated from Angola in the 18th Century, use numerous masks in the Mukanda initiation rites (especially during circumcision) and at other times in community life. The mbuya masks represent various typical characters in society, such as the chief, the soothsayer, the fool or the epileptic with the twisted mouth, the hunter, the widow, the lover, the executioner, etc. whose farcical attitudes amuse the public. This copy represents the kiwoyo or giwoyo, the face of the victorious hunter. Its chin is elongated into a type of beard adorned with champlevé and painted geometric patterns, which recalls both an elder's long beard and the pangolin. Dancing with a fly-killer in each hand.

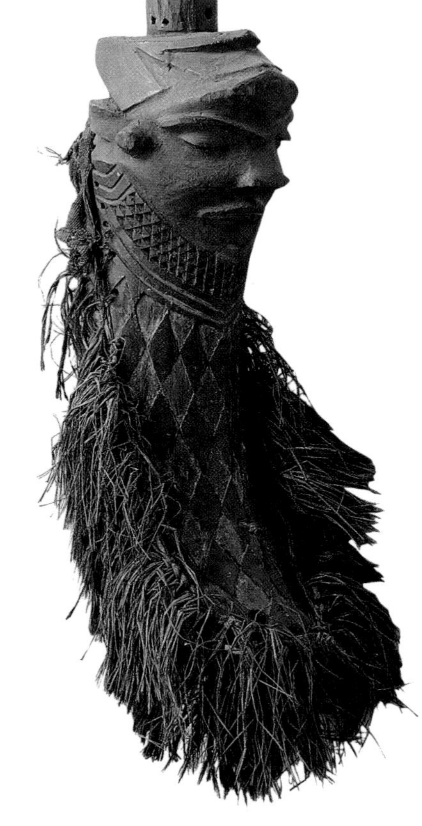

Central African Republic, Nzakara, late 19th Century
Throwing Knife
Wrought iron. H. 37 cm. Angouleme, MBA (Dr. Lhomme bequest)
©D.R.

Among the people of Upper Oubangui, edged weapons, double-edged swords, daggers, throwing knives, lances, harpoons, offensive and ceremonial weapons reached, in the late 19th century, a high degree of technical and formal perfection and almost replaced the statuary, which was barely developed in this region. Of these weapons, the throwing knives are the most incredible. These multi-shaped knives were not always functional and were often used as money of exchange between the groups.

Angola, Chokwe,
Chair
Wood. H. 58.5 cm. Paris, MAAO
©Photo Labat/CFAO

The Chokwe are known for the sophistication and stylistic unity of their sculpture. These great mask sculptors have also produced a wealth of furniture, whose caryatid monoxylic seats and upright chairs are inspired by the European model introduced by the Portuguese in the 16th century. These little thrones, called Chitwamo, are abundantly sculpted with proverbs and morals. The central theme here is the couple, a man and a woman nursing her child, both seated with dignity atop the back of the chair or speaking face to face on the front rung, or a man and a woman huddled together on the back rung. There are also allusions to the Mukanda initiation. On the back of the chair are two examples of the Chihongo mask with winglets, whereas on the side rungs, fans out a procession of small stylized figures walking or dancing in a straight line, with their hands on their shoulders. . .

DRC, Mangbetou, mid 20th Century
Pagne
Beaten bark and pigments. H. 168 cm.
Paris, MAAO (former Croisière Noire Citroën collection)
©Photo Labat/CFAO

Before the colonial age, the pagne, made with the beaten bark of a fig tree flattened and softened using an ivory beater, was one of the main pieces of clothing in Central Africa. This mangbetou pagne is made from three pieces sewn together and is decorated with graphic patterns using a black stroke. These patterns recall those found nearby on the barks painted by Pygmy, Sua and Mbuti women. Magbetou art has greatly impressed the members of the Croisière Noire Citroën. This discovery had repercussions on decorative art in the 1930s.

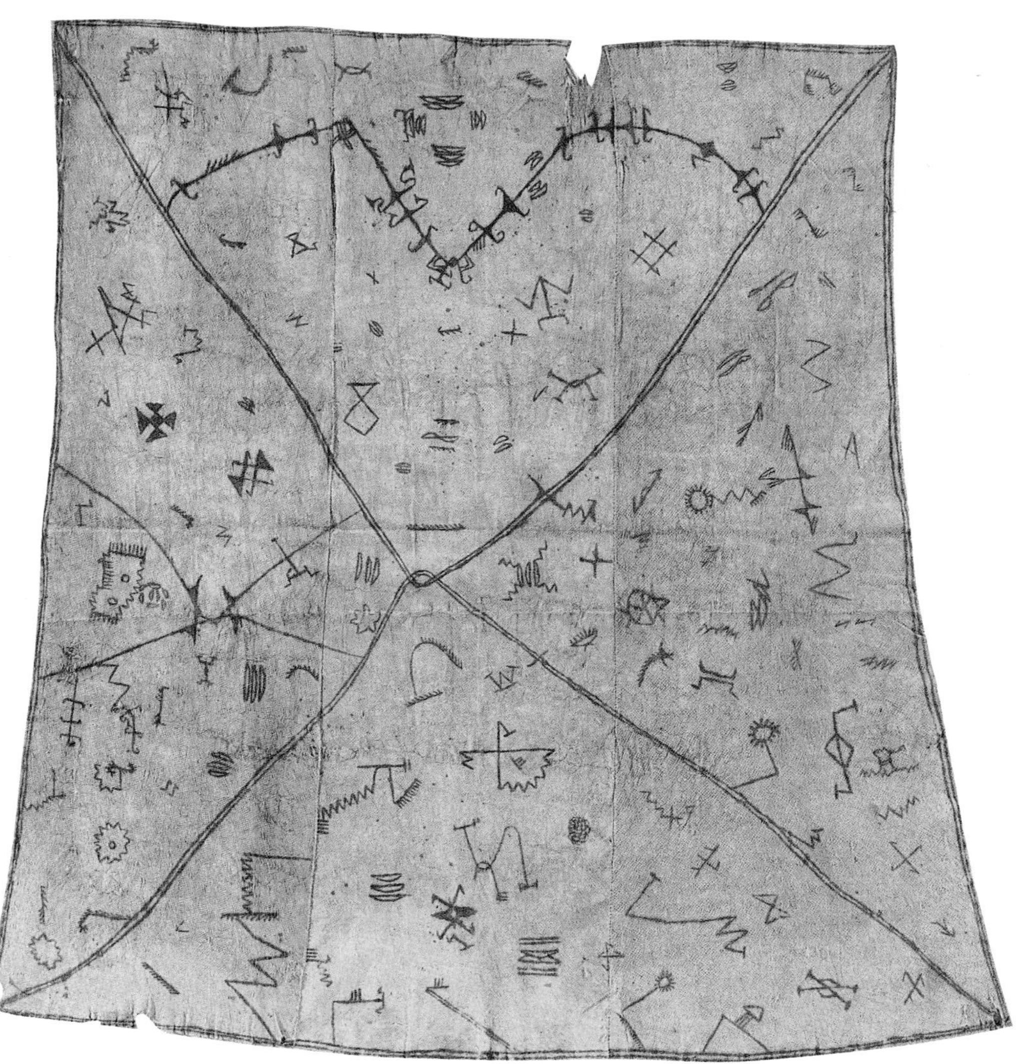

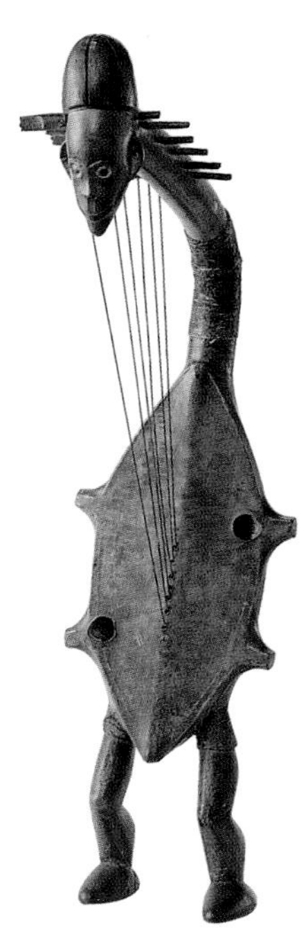

Central African Republic, Ngbaka, late 19th Century
Harp
Wood, hide. H. 87 cm. Paris, MAAO
©RMN/J.G. Berizzi-Le Mage

This type of harp, called a ngombi, with a boat-shaped case, is typical of the Ngbaka region in Lobaye, Central Africa. Here the sculptor delved into his imagination and gave his instrument the shape of the human body. The ngombi is used to accompany epic stories and songs.

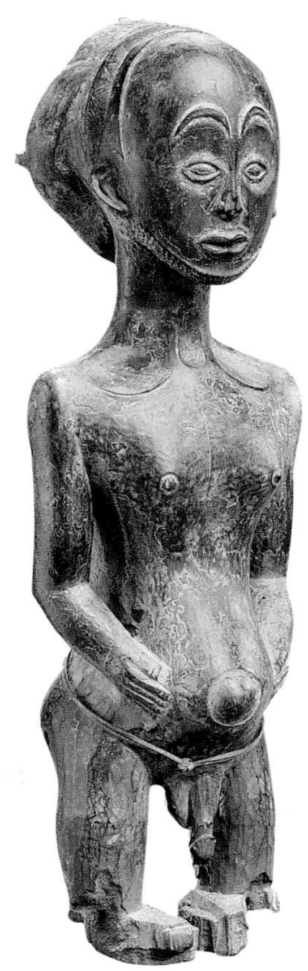

DRC, Luba-Hemba, late 19th Century
Statue of an Ancestor
Wood. H. 20 cm Tervuren, MRAC
©Africa-Museum Tervuren (Belgium)/Photo R. Asselberghs

The Hemba are known for their hierarchical and sophisticated statuary. The singiti statues are effigies of deceased chiefs from the families of princes. Each statue bears the name of a deceased sovereign. The lanky torso, face with gentle features, hair pulled back in a bun and fine beard, place this statue among the classic, niembo style.

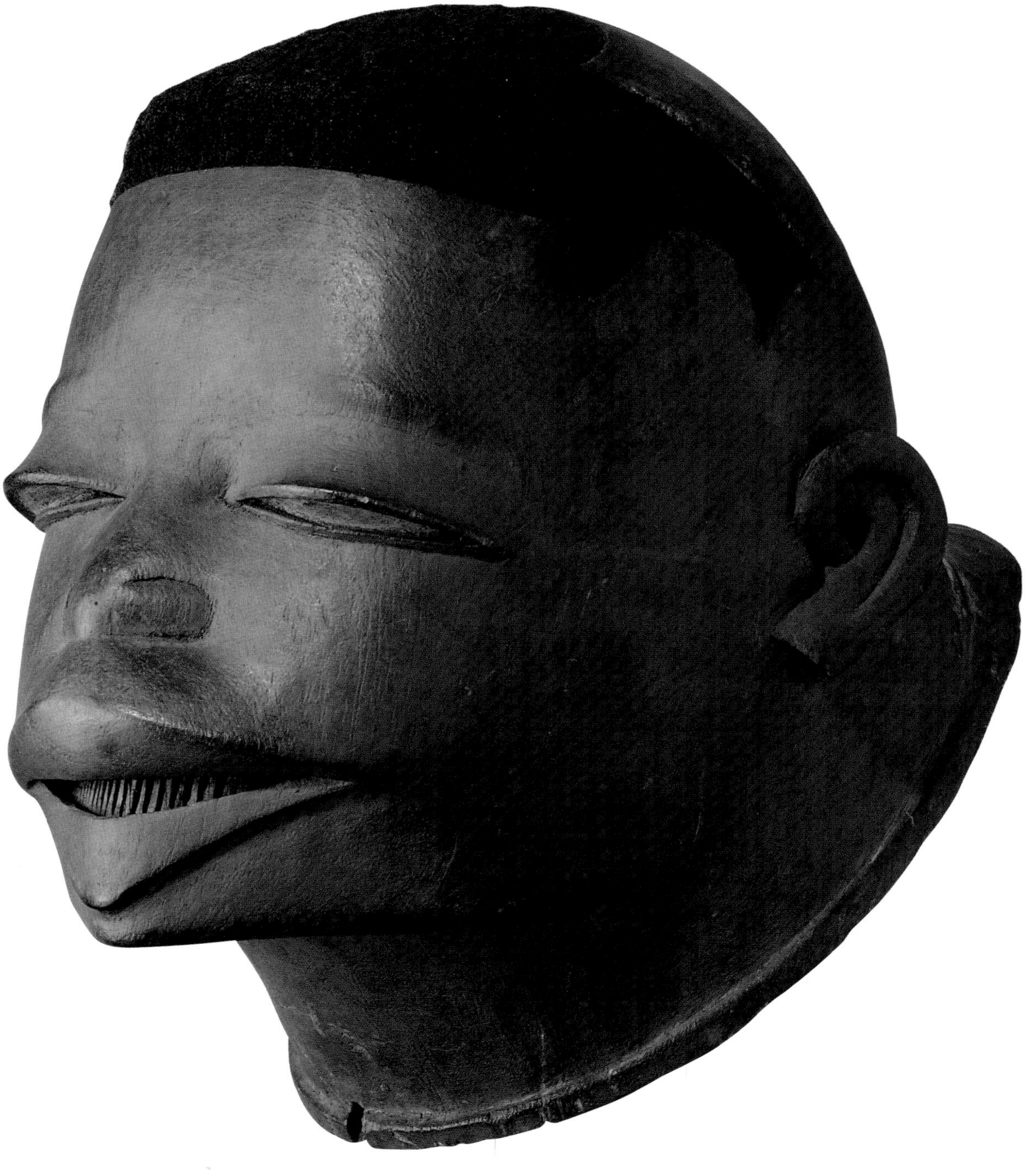

Tanzania, Makonde, mid 20th Century
Lipico Mask
Wood, human hair, aluminum. H. 25 cm.
Paris, MAAO (Monbrison gift)

The Makonde rites of passage, apply different masks, the best known of which is the lipico mask (plural: mapico). It is in the shape of a helmet and is adorned with scarifications made from applied wax. Human hair is glued to the skull. A discoid labret is often inserted into the upper lip. The mapico masks represent the ancestors who return masked to express their joy with the completion of the initiation. Some masks must inspire terror in women, who can only attend their apparition bent at the waist and with their heads bowed towards the ground.

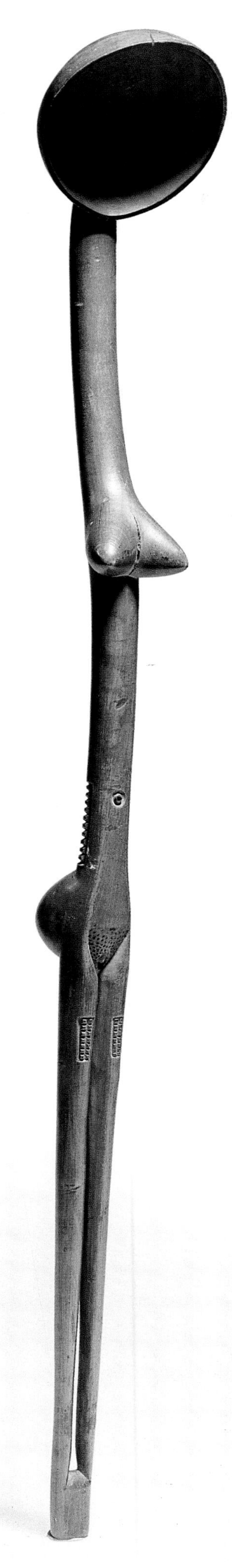

South Africa, Zulu, mid 20th Century
Anthropomorphic Spoon
Wood. H. 57 cm. Paris, LGAP (former MH collection)
©Destable et Lemzaouda

The Zulu, who hardly have a statuary, have developed quality craftsmanship that has gone unnoticed: furniture, milk jugs and meat plates in sculpted wood, pottery for beer and other objects of daily life, with elegant shapes, such as this rare spoon, whose handle recalls the gracious shapes of the female body.

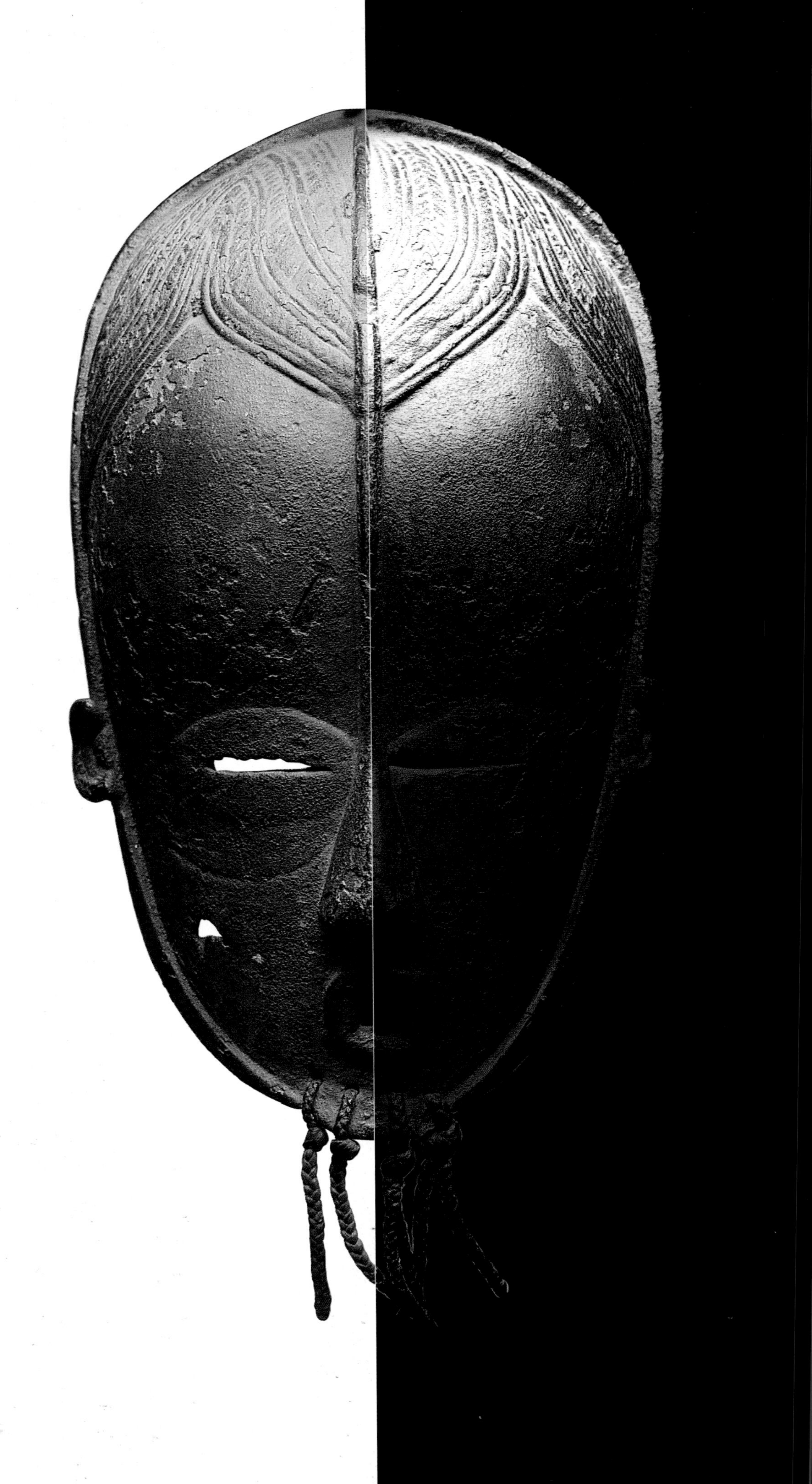

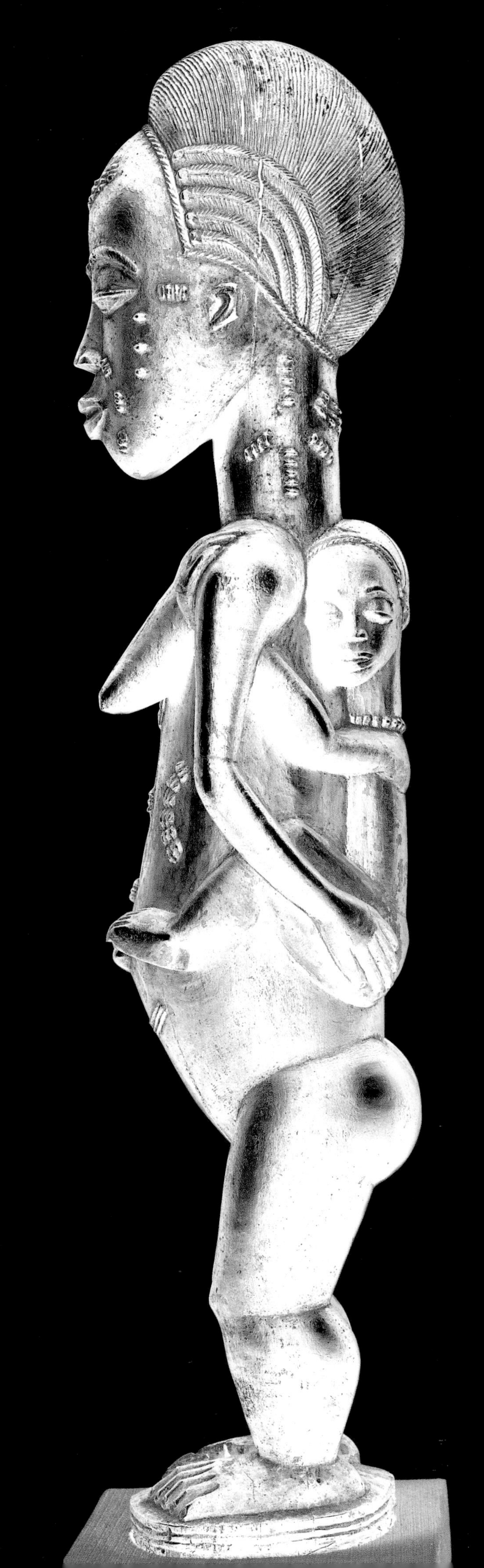

Abjuration of Jao I, King of Congo, 1491,
Engraving of Théodore de Bry, 1598
©D.R.

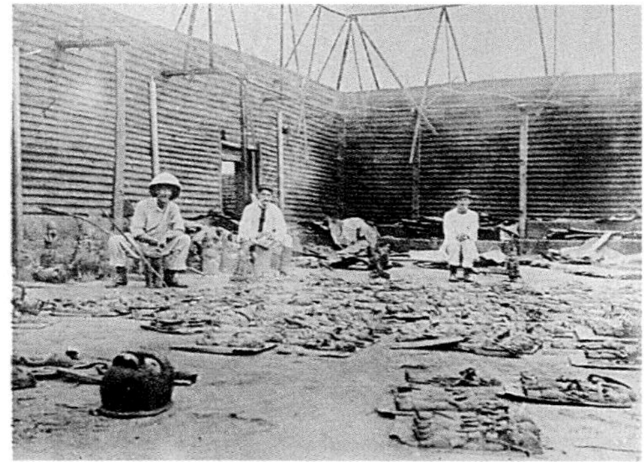

The sacking of Benin City during the punitive British expedition, 1897
©D.R.

TERRITORY OF FORMS
Étienne Féau

One century after being "discovered" by the West, nobody disputes the value and universality of African art. However, there is still a great deal of ignorance and misunderstanding surrounding an art that continues to be described as "first" or "distant," terms that anthropologists and art historians wholeheartedly refute. Today, we know much more about the forms and contents and cannot continue to hold onto just one Western point of view. We have indeed noticed an incredible hiatus between what the West draws from Africa's art, through lavish exhibits or beautiful books with images, and African reality. It is time to return to Africa, to the men and societies, to current expressions, to the point of view of the users or the authorized representatives of the cultures concerned.

Europe established the first contacts with coastal societies from sub-Saharan Africa in the 15th century. Although fiendish-looking wooden "idols" or "fetishes" disappeared with the first auto-da-fes of the Christian missionaries, trunks and saltshakers sculpted from ivory quickly made it into the curious offices of the great merchants and princes of the Renaissance. Qualified as Afro-Portuguese, this ordered art closely corresponds to the work of African Sherbro, Bini and Kongo sculptors. One would have to wait until the late 19th century to see, in great numbers, more typical and diversified objects among the first trophies of the colonial conquest – statues, masks, furniture – initially considered to be summary productions testifying to the feeble technological and artistic level of people urgently requiring civilization! However, an unexpected exception occurred with the bronze and ivory aulic art objects that the English took back in 1897 from their punitive expedition against the kingdom of Benin, and which the great British, German and Austrian museums would later fight to obtain.

In the first decade of the 20th century, in Paris, Berlin, Prague and Saint Petersburg, a certain number of intellectuals and artists discovered "Negro art" in museums of ethnography or in the pavilions of the first colonial fairs, through a few key pieces that they were the first to recognize as works of art. This type of art then came into vogue. Its impact was felt in the artistic creation of the 20th century, which also led to many intellectual and financial speculations.
From 1930-50, material art and cultures from sub-Saharan Africa finally became a study unit in social studies: ethnology with Marcel Mauss and Marcel Griaule; archeology with Bernard Fagg, Frank Willett and Raymond Mauny; art history of African art with its pioneers Karl Kjersmeier and Frans Olbrechts; and, finally, a new subject, ethno-esthetics, which did not reach the development desired by its initiator Jean Laude.

There are currently two waves:
- on the one hand, ethnologists who, jealous of their "terrain" often have a fragmented vision of the old continent; as champions of the myth or of blood relations systems, they misunderstand African art, and many of them even refute the notion of art or esthetics;
- on the other hand, collectors, merchants, artists or enthusiasts, who sustain a fantastical vision of African art, and for whom the "first" work of art is perceived as being all the more beautiful, all the more expensive from a market point of view as well, that we know nothing, or we do not want to know anything about it, freezing it in its pseudo mystery and non-history.

A trait common to all of Africa is animism, the oldest religious fundamental. This belief gives a soul to everything in the world and preaches a special relationship between man and nature. As if to prepare the groundwork for the monotheistic religions that would subsequently arrive, most myths make mention of one single god, a supreme creator that is not represented, but who is addressed through spirits or secondary deities, with the ancestors acting as the privileged ambassadors of the afterworld. Prayers, offerings, sacrifices, even trances and possessions are necessary in animist worship and easily set works of art in motion. Although African artists have long been familiar with working with clay, ivory, sometimes stone, and

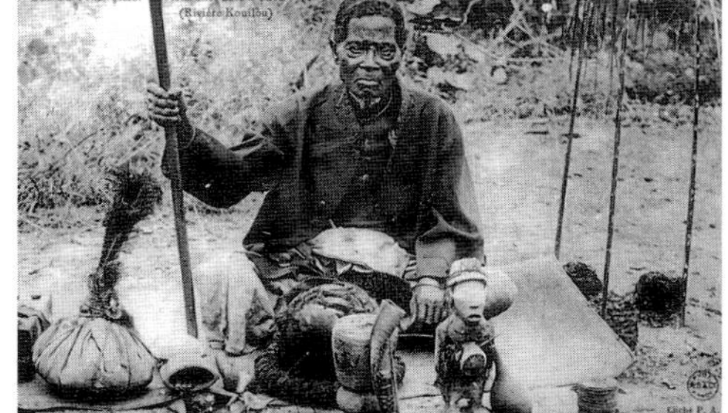

Nganga healing soothsayer before his nkissi fetishes, Congo, Early 20th Century

metal alloy, wood remains the material of choice for essentially religious reasons. They use the softest wood (bombax) to the hardest (ironwood, ebony) and all types of clear or dark wood in between, carved with an adz or a gouge.

The backers of the works of art are almost always professionals, priests, soothsayers, healers or fetishers, like the Baule komien or the Congolese nganga. Through their knowledge of the afterworld, the latter foresee the rites and forms that will please the spirits. Although some of them are able to make the objects required for the ritual themselves, they prefer to call upon a professional artist to ensure that the work is properly done. However, once produced by the sculptor, the object is validated, made sacred and "taken over" by the fetisher alone. The sponsor may also be someone similar to the fetisher, such as a family, a village association or even an initiation society.

As for the artists, blacksmiths or sculptors, their status varies depending on the regions: they may either be caste-classified, like the populations from northern Ivory Coast, Mali or Burkina, where the trade and the esthetic canons are passed down from generation to generation, or not, like other more southern populations, such as the Baule, where sculpture is a personal vocation. Although caste artists are often discredited in West Africa from a social point of view, in Central Africa the situation is otherwise for the same magical and religious reasons (fear of fire and ritual objects). Wood sculpting, forging and casting metals are an aristocratic privilege. In the Cameroon Grassland, artists have a high social status, near the throne, since art and power are permanently bound. Thus, Kings Bamoum and Bamileke claimed, as their own work, the sculptures produced by the artisans working for them. It is said that certain Fons (kings) enjoyed sculpting and producing bead art themselves. There are also examples of sculptors who ascended to the throne. In the Congolese regions, oral tradition tells tales of the heroic deeds of the blacksmith kings who alone knew how to forge the weapons that would push the invader back or conquer new territories. Today still, the anvil is the first symbol of power among the Kuba kings in the Democratic Republic of Congo.

Also, each culture, at a given time during its history, developed very specific formal canons that differ from those of neighboring populations, thereby quashing, for example, any confusion between the Senufo and Baule, Yoruba and Igbo, Bembe or Teke styles. Also rejected is any evolutionary postulate of a first, second or last art, which has become definitively obsolete. Let us look at this striking example: does Yoruba art fall under "first art" when, in fact, we can measure over two thousand years of history and artistic creation in this cultural sector, from Nok to Ife, from Ife to Ila or Ibadan! We can also see, in certain cultures, the coexistence of naturalist and abstract forms without any inhibitions, as is the case with the Nigerian Igbo. In concluding, although they have reached us unsigned, the works are never anonymous in the environment where they are used: following the work of Frans Olbrechts and of William Fagg, specialists have been endeavoring to find workshops, to determine styles and influences, to attribute works back to their owners, as was done in the second half of the 19th century for the Flemish or Italian Primitives.

The statuary

One thing should first be noted: there is no known individualized representation of a living man or woman, a "portrait" as we understand it in the West, in traditional African art. Except, however, for certain "fetishes" used by healers – like the Kongo nkisis – which basically represent a sick person, and which contain neuralgic "medications." These are pathological and not physiological portraits on which the entire nganga science is carried out and concentrated. Whether in the form of statuettes or masks, in wood, stone, terracotta or metal, the anthropomorphic representations of African art are:

- those of anthropomorphic or zoomorphic spirits or genies from nature,
- most often those of deceased people who, through their moral qualities or

social ranking (chiefs, kings, elders) have reached the status of Ancestors during a last rite of passage.

Spirits, genies and gods

The belief in two parallel worlds (the world of men and the world of spirits, the world of the village and the world of the bush) prevails in a large number of African cultures. Here, positive or negative spirits or genies evolve and their good graces are sought through prayer and sacrifice. This has resulted in the bateba statuettes, used by the Lobi soothsayers to ward off the thila or bad genies, and even in the nkisi or butti fetishes, which the Congolese Kongo and Teke shower with particular devotion between divination and medicine. Let us mention in particular the blolo bla and blolo bian statuettes of the Baule in Ivory Coast, which are used in divination and psychiatry and not in the worship of ancestors, as was long believed. For the Baule, blolo represents the other world, a duplicate of our own, the place of our origin and our end. Existence actually perpetually rotates from one space to another. In the first, the individual has left behind his wife and children and he only recalls this previous family later on, during adolescence or adulthood, when psychological disorders appear. The komienfwe soothsayer is then consulted to establish the source of the evil sent by the husband (blolo bian) or the wife (blolo bla) out of jealousy towards the terrestrial spouse. He asks the patient to have a professional sculptor produce a statuette with very specific physical traits (attitude, hairstyle, clothing, scarifications). Once completed, this statuette is welcomed as if the husband or wife from the afterworld had descended to Earth to be with his/her spouse, and a brief marriage and reconciliation ceremony is actually conducted. This statuette is carefully kept in the patient's room, where it is cared for and fed each day.

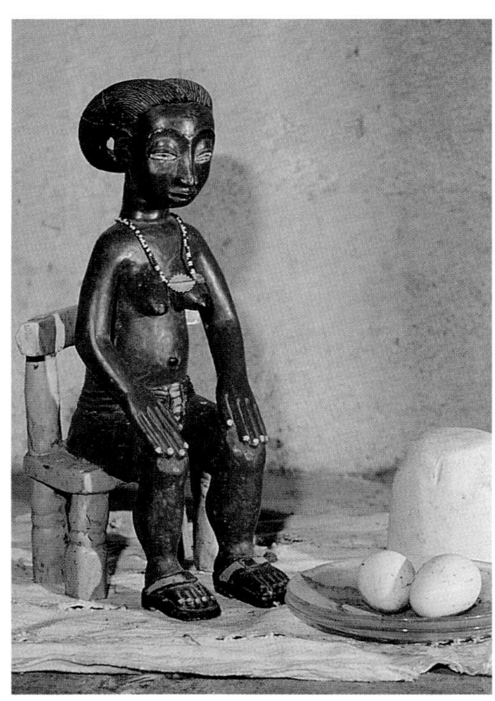

Baule statuette in use, Ivory Coast

The ancestors

The worship of Ancestors is a common practice in all of Africa. According to this belief, after physical death, the individual enters the world of the spirits, which is neither heaven nor hell, but a space parallel to the space of the living, where the soul continues to evolve, according to its good or bad qualities. What is important is that it not be forgotten by the world of the living and that it reach the rank of Ancestors of the family or clan.
In many regions, Ancestors are represented as plastic figures in order to immortalize their memory. We can date the genealogy of the Congolese Kuba kings back to the 16th century thanks to a series of highly artistic wooden statues called ndops, which are now shared by the Kinshasa, Tervuren and London museums. Among other peoples whose funeral practices may last several years, artwork replaces the body of the deceased, which could not be kept. This is the case of the prestigious bronze or terracotta heads of the Ife Oni in Nigeria, primitively set on wooden mannequins ... Elsewhere, commemorative portraits, like the heavy bronze heads of the Benin Oba, were originally topped with ivory tusks adorned with sculpted bas-reliefs, recalling the Prince's heroic deeds, and religiously kept on the royal altars. Reliquaries were also kept, which contained the bones of ancestors from the lineage, sometimes topped with very beautiful figures, such as the ones honoring the Fang and the Kota in Gabon, as part of Bwete or Byeri worship.
In other sectors, all of the deceased are automatically represented in the form of terracotta statuettes, briefly modeled by potters, and gathered in sanctuaries, places of sacrifice, such as the mma of the Anyi of lower Ivory Coast. Seen as privileged intermediaries between the living and the gods, the ancestors also intervene in the form of masks, such as those of the Ogooue population of Gabon, which are painted white, the color of the afterworld.

The woman

There are numerous representations of ancestor-Mothers portrayed in all of the beauty and dignity of fertile women: the opulent bust and the stomach, the promise of future generations, are particularly highlighted, a constant reminder of Fertility, the fundamental theme of African art and philosophies.
Representations of women in labor are rarer than those of pregnant women. However, a few ivory sculptures portraying a birth exist among the Igbo and the Kongo peoples.

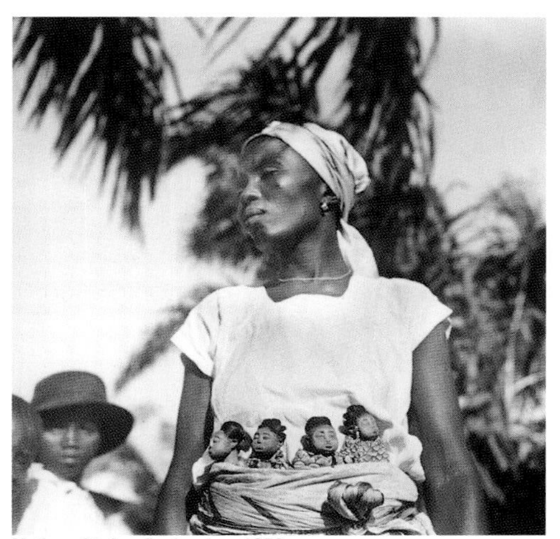
Mother of twins, Benin, circa 1950
©Pierre Verger

The child

Numerous sculptures exist of women nursing, with the child on their knees or back, among the Baule and Anyi in Ivory Coast, among the Yoruba in Benin and Nigeria, the Bamileke in Cameroon, the Yombe in Congo and the Chokwe in Angola. But the subject represented is less the child than the mother. In African art, the child is never represented for itself because it is a socially incomplete being. If a child dies, it cannot have the rank of an ancestor because it has not procreated and has not scaled the echelons of knowledge. One exception, however, is the akua ba dolls of the Ashanti in Ghana, or the venanvi and ibeji statuettes of the Fon and Yoruba in Benin and Nigeria who worship the Twins. Among these peoples, twins are considered to be donated by heaven and become a genuine cult. Should, by some misfortune, one or both of the twins die at a young age, small statuettes, called ere ibeji by the Yoruba, are sculpted in their image (they are actually in the image of the adult they should have become). The mother (or the surviving spouse) must feed, dress, protect and honor them for as long as she lives, as though they were living.

The couple

It is the union of the couple that secures the perpetuation of the species. Prior to the introduction of photography, there did not appear to be in Africa any anecdotal representation of the living couple. However, there are numerous representations of ancestor couples. They often relate to the great myths of origin and of the first human couple. The Dogon in Mali and the Senufo in Ivory Coast have produced very beautiful images of the first civilizing human couple. The man and the woman are seated next to each other, as equals, with the man carrying on his shoulder the farmer's hoe, or holding in his hand the calabash containing precious seeds...
In other cases, the first couple is replaced by a hermaphrodite figure, which, alone, summarizes the origins of man. We will see further on how masks also enjoy portraying the first couple and are produced in pairs, male and female. The male mask is more frightening and aggressive, and the female mask has a more delicate and gentle face, as is the case among the peoples in southwestern Ivory Coast. Still other types of objects recall the First Couple, especially drums, often visibly sexed, that have dialogues like a husband and wife do at crucial moments in their social and religious life.

Representations of the sexual act itself are much rarer. There are, however, a few examples among the statuettes used by the Lobi soothsayers. These are "weights-proverbs" once used by the Akan from Ivory Coast and Ghana to weigh gold, hut doors and trays for the divination of Fa among the Yoruba in Benin and Nigeria, as well as Chokwe thrones in Angola. These representations have, in any case, a religious value, which is to summon Fertility.

We have seen the figurative side of African art, which is easy to decipher upon first view. Let us now look at the abstract and symbolic side, which has been poorly studied to date (only Father Engelbert Mveng, Jean Gabus, Frédéric Bouabré-Bruly and, more recently, Clémentine Faïk-Nzuji have tried) and about which there is much to be said ...
In African societies deemed to be without writing, the slightest form, the slightest sign have specific meanings that often escape the unknowing eye.

Cosmogonic symbols

The two major cosmogonic entities are Heaven and Earth, often seen as husband and wife, with creation being the fruit of their union. Thus, among the Baule in Ivory Coast, heaven and earth have a dimension other than the purely physical or cosmogonic one. In representations, especially on masks, Nyamye, god of Heaven, and Assie, his wife, a chthonic goddess, are represented only by the animals that are related to them mythologically: the buffalo and the ram, for the one, the serpent, crocodile or chimpanzee, for the other...

Animals

In mythologies, as in artistic representations, animals play a preponderant role. According to numerous myths, the Divinity created animals before Man, and it is they ("the primordial animals of creation") who, upon the appearance of the first man on earth, taught him the rules of life... To these are added or superimposed the animal-symbols of a divinity, as well as the totemic or heraldic animals that are closely tied into the history or life of a family or clan. Therefore, man must revere or protect the animal claimed by his family as a mascot and never eat its flesh. Let us not forget that the animal encountered in the bush may contain the spirit of a grandparent or of an individual who fell prey to sorcery. Some animals, which are quite commonly represented in African art, have this problem.

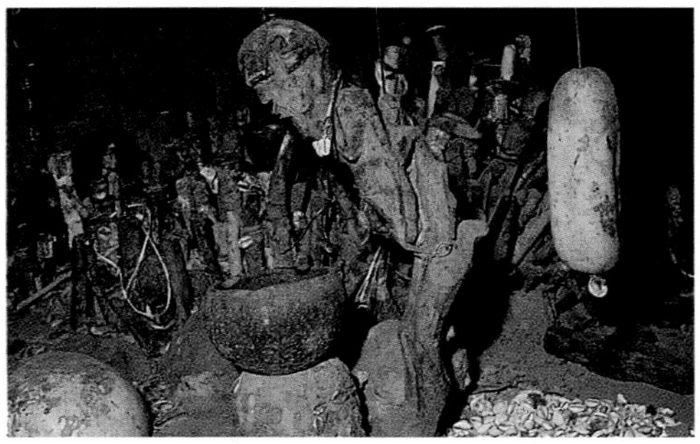

The snake: by its shape, it recalls the man's genitals and its wave-like movement recalls running water. It is the symbol of longevity and of immortality. By sloughing its skin, it gives the impression that it incessantly regenerates. As it comes from the depths of the earth, it is also the messenger of the dead, which is why it has been particularly protected and revered in Africa since the dawn of time. It is found, coiled upon itself or in a sinusoidal movement, on the Senufo and Baule hut doors, on seat edges or on divinatory cups of the Yoruba, on the figureheads of Duala pirogues in Cameroon and in the sculptures of many other African peoples. But the most impressive serpent figure is surely Bandjoni of the Baga and Nalou of Guinea. This sinuous figure, made of monoxylic wood decorated with brightly colored geometric patterns, can reach up to two meters in height. Bandjoni is said to be born of the eggs of the female python Ninkinanka, a genie of the water, of the spring, of the rainbow and of the earthquake. It is consulted on many occasions. It is the snake that detects criminals and sorcerers; it sets the day of the circumcision and makes, on this occasion, its sole public outing from the sacred woods.

Lobi soothsayer altar, Ivory Coast

Because of its horns, the antelope is also related to fertility. The antelope or oryx are used as models for many Mali, Burkina Faso and northern Ivory Coast masks. The Tyi Wara antelope of the Mali Bambara is a well known figure in African art and is, in fact, a mask, but the limit between mask, crest and sculpture worn on the head or at arm's length is unclear. It is worn on the heads of dancers belonging to the brotherhood with the same name during agrarian rites, its long horns symbolizing the growth and fertility of the fields ...

The bird: depending on the region, it can be the hornbill or the turaco. The first is omnipresent in Senufo statuary: doors, drums, mortars, masks, weaving loom pulleys. A spectacular sculpture, placed in the sacred Poro enclosure and often standing over a meter high, represents this bird with its wings spread out and its long beak resting on its rounded stomach. Initiates are well aware that the beak symbolizes the male genitals and that the stomach represents a pregnant woman, a promise of generations to come... The heavy nimba mask, the goddess of fertility among the Guinea Baga, offers, in the same spirit, an abundant bust and a composite face with a hornbill beak.

Other animals are recurring features in myths and in certain cultures' sculptures: the catfish, crocodile, ram, buffalo or elephant among the Albino Baule; the chameleon, tortoise or hyena among their Senufo neighbors; the panther, spider or frog in the chiefdoms of the Cameroon Grassland, etc.

We should not overlook the numerous two-dimensional signs that can be read on house walls, on mask decorations, on pottery, in the weft of fabrics, in paints or in body scarifications, which also reveal that Africans give of themselves. African art is a genuine mine of signs that actually constitute a written language. According to Father Mveng, "language and written language: African art only actually has meaning for those who know how to read. A statuette, a mask and also the design on a piece of pottery or a simple plant ligature (it is known that the Bidyogo from the Bissagos Islands have a genuine writing system based on plant knots) contain many hidden messages for the informed user...

Masks

The mask is a very old institution, and pre-historic paintings (in Tassili, Algeria, in Tibesti or Ennedi, Chad) prove that it existed in an ancient era when the fertile Sahara plains were still inhabited by black populations. Today, in most traditional societies, the institution of the mask is associated with agrarian, funeral and initiatory rites. It appears, above all, in geographically stable agricultural societies and never, at least in the sculpted form, in societies of nomad shepherds.

The mask is widely scattered from the north to the south of the continent. Despite its many uses and forms, its deep meaning has three dimensions:

- a religious dimension, in the literal sense of the word: "which connects" two worlds, the world of the living and the spirit world (white masks of the Ogoue peoples); and a secular meaning (race masks in the Dan country). Masks are exhibited most often to recall the remarkable events that occurred when the world was born and which led to the organization of the world and of society. They refer either to the divine Creation and the cosmogonies, or to the facts and actions of the founding heroes of clans or kingdoms.
- a spiritual dimension: the mask does not represent a man, but a spirit, an unchanging and exemplary model that cannot be affected by time and into which the individual cannot slip. It is the mask, not the bearer, that is important. "The African mask," writes Malraux, "does not portray a human expression. It is an apparition. The sculptor does not carve into it an unknown ghost. Instead it arouses it through its geometry. Its mask is not made to look like a man, but rather not to. Animal masks are not animals. The antelope mask is not an antelope, but the antelope spirit, and it is the sculptor's style that makes it a spirit."
- finally, a social dimension: masks are often the guarantors, the guardians of social institutions. They appear to retell the great founding myths and also to ensure that everything goes well during a ceremony or a celebration, to ward off anything that could disrupt order in the village and in the family. They even police certain rites: armed with whips, they hold back children, spoilsports or women, who are often prohibited from looking upon the masks. On other occasions, they are used to protect society from malefactors and sorcerers. They are kept by members of secret societies who often use them as instruments of political pressure (in Congo or in the Cameroon Grassland).

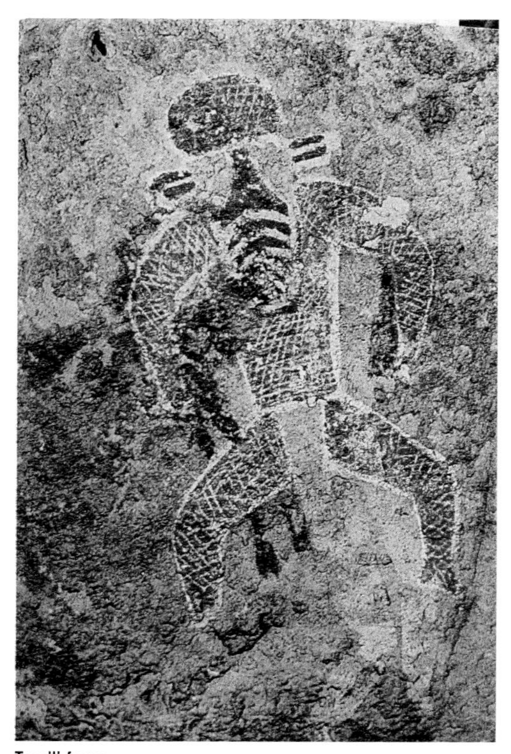

Tassili fresco

Black Africa has produced an infinite number of masks, remarkable for their:

- morphological diversity: the mask is not only a sculpted wooden object. It is not limited to the wooden wolf placed over the face. It is a complex entity that should be considered part of the dancer's body. From the simplest to the most complex form, masks are most often made from very codified and detailed models, which does not in the least prevent the sculptor from being inventive. Certain masks are functional replicas and others are unique and strong creations.

There are several types: leaf, fiber, wicker or fabric masks; face masks, portraying a wooden, bone or metal wolf; helmet masks, covering the entire head, or half helmets, falling over the brow ridge (Senufo, Yoruba, Fang); helmet covers, topped with horns or crests; blade masks (Dogon, Bobo, Mossi); masks topped with sculptures (the Bambara tyi wara); monumental masks worn by several dancers (such as the Senufo nasolo); puppets or fools' baubles held at arm's length (the Kuyu kyebe-kyebe). Face painting is also based on the extensive definition of the mask (see face paintings of the Nigerian Bororo or the Sudanese Nouba).

- technological diversity: wood, fibers, metal, ivory, bone, etc. Wood may be left rough, glazed or painted, adorned with repoussé metal leaves, fragments of mirrors, or beads (such as certain Bamileke masks in Cameroon or the Congolese and Zambian tabwa masks).
- iconographic diversity: anthropomorphic (deceased people, divinities, mythical characters); zoomorphic (mythical or totemic animals), fantastic or composite figures (human heads with horns, etc.); there are also masks topped with group figures (among the Yoruba and the Nigerian Igbo), and even with all sorts of objects, such as houses, motorcycles and sewing machines.

- numeric disparity, depending on the culture: some use a large number of masks (such as the We from southwestern Ivory Coast or the Bwa from Burkina Faso), others only have a single model (the adone with an antelope's head used when ending the mourning period among the Kurumba of Burkina Faso).

The mask does not end with the sculpted part. The costume and the accessories that accompany it (hood, feathers, fiber ruff, strips of fabric and bells) are also important. It cannot be cut off from its movement, from the dance, the accompanying music or the participation of onlookers. It cannot be cut off, in particular, from the rite or institution with which it is connected. It is an error only to consider this single piece of wood, as beautiful as it may be, and despite its message and its deep meaning. It is like reducing an opera to the baritone's suit or to any stage accessory!

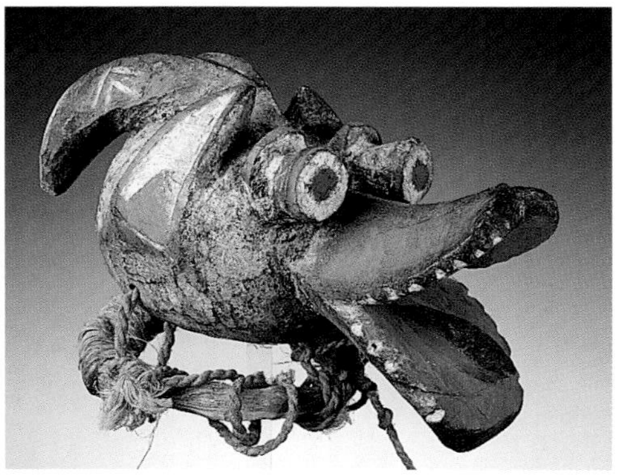

There are three essential levels to the African mask:
- a material level, on which the mask is perceived with its constituent elements and with all of the adornments and accessories it has lost in our museum display cases;
- a thematic and scenographic level that restores the mask to the myth that is at its origin and to all of the gestures and sounds that accompany it (drums, whistles, mask's voice, etc.);
- a social and structural level that replaces the mask in the game of social relationships within which it has a representative and often regulating role: initiations of youths or the performances of associations in charge within the building society and the public exhibit of the masks.

Mambila mask, Nigeria, mid 20th Century

Finery and objects of power

This category of objects is an equally rich field of African art. It includes: finery and insignia of power, clothing, weapons, pieces of furniture and musical instruments, which have produced, according to the sectors and eras, genuine works of art. The boundary between art and craftsmanship is indeed sometimes difficult to establish. A great number of delicately adorned functional objects, sometimes sculpted by great masters, have been found, such as spoons, seats, drums or weaving loom pulleys. Unlike masks or statues, these objects could be made in a rougher manner, with the artistic quality disappearing in view of their more immediate functional role.

Jewels and clothing

Since the dawn of time in Africa, a wide variety of tegumentary scarifications, jewelry made of stone, fibers, leather, glass, cast or peened metal have constituted a fully fledged art form, and their extension into statuary can also be studied. Along the same line, textile represents one of the most precious victories of man over matter. The first articles of clothing, made of bark or vegetable fibers, were later replaced by raffia matting or cotton cloths woven by often caste-classified weavers using vertical or horizontal looms, and later dyed or embroidered by their wives. From the simple loincloth to the more elaborate ceremonial costume, the art of dressing oneself varies throughout the continent and is always of great social importance. What is important here is the high artistic value of certain textiles and the rich source of two-dimensional signs that they represent. Among the best-known examples in West Africa are the wool and cotton tellem fabrics discovered in 1971 by Dutch archeologists in the Bandiagara cliffs in Mali, which dated back to the 11th and 12th centuries; the cotton or silk pagnes adorned with heraldic patterns worn for a full two centuries by aristocratic Akan families in Ivory Coast and Ghana, called kita or kente; in Central Africa, more precisely in the Democratic Republic of Congo, the beaten bark of the Mbuti or Mangbetou women, adorned with constantly changing abstract painting; and, finally, the velvet embroidered raffia matting and the large pagnes with cut out patterns of the Kuba and their Kasai neighbors, whose subtle geometric variations are testimony of a previous cynetic art.

Insignia of power

In all of Africa, walking sticks, scepters, leading-staffs and other symbols of power, used not only by representatives of temporal or religious power, but also

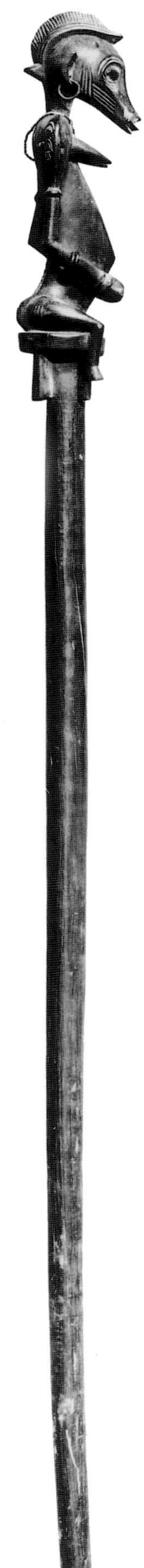

Senoufo tefalipithia cane, Ivory Coast, MAAO

by representatives of a given social or professional class, were sculpted with the greatest of care. In this section, we should mention the multi-form regalia of the Akan in Ghana and Ivory Coast, which include the bia seat with a curved tablet, speaking-staffs, ceremonial sabers, sumptuous gold jewelry that accompany the brightly colored Kente pagnes; the Tefalipithia culture's cane, topped with a "beautiful girl," given each year to a young deserving farmer among the Senufo in northern Ivory Coast, or even among the Dan in the southwestern forest region; the large wake mia spoon, an ostentatious insignia of the organizer of the banquet on festival or masquerade days; the "recades" or symbols of the "messengers," carved wooden staffs, adorned with pieces of metal representing the symbols of the Fon kings of Abomey, and even, further south in Angola, staffs adorned with a delicate sculpted head of the Chokwe, Lunda or Mbundo chiefs. We should point out not only the beauty, but also the social and monetary value of edged weapons, especially in Central Africa, between Chad, the Central African Republic and the Democratic Republic of Congo, whose bold shapes are evidence of the high degree of technical expertise and formal inventiveness of the blacksmiths. In addition to the edged weapons, double-edged swords and multi-pointed Kipinga throwing knives, we also find very beautiful wicker shields adorned with bold geometric patterns, which are earmarks.

What we retain at the end of this quick presentation is the very intense intentional and emotional charge of African art, whether it be statues, masks or sculpted staffs, and its very particular connection to the incantatory, mythical or proverbial Word. One of the most pressing missions of anthropology and art history is to restore to objects of African art this speech, without which we could not understand them.

Ritual practices in movement

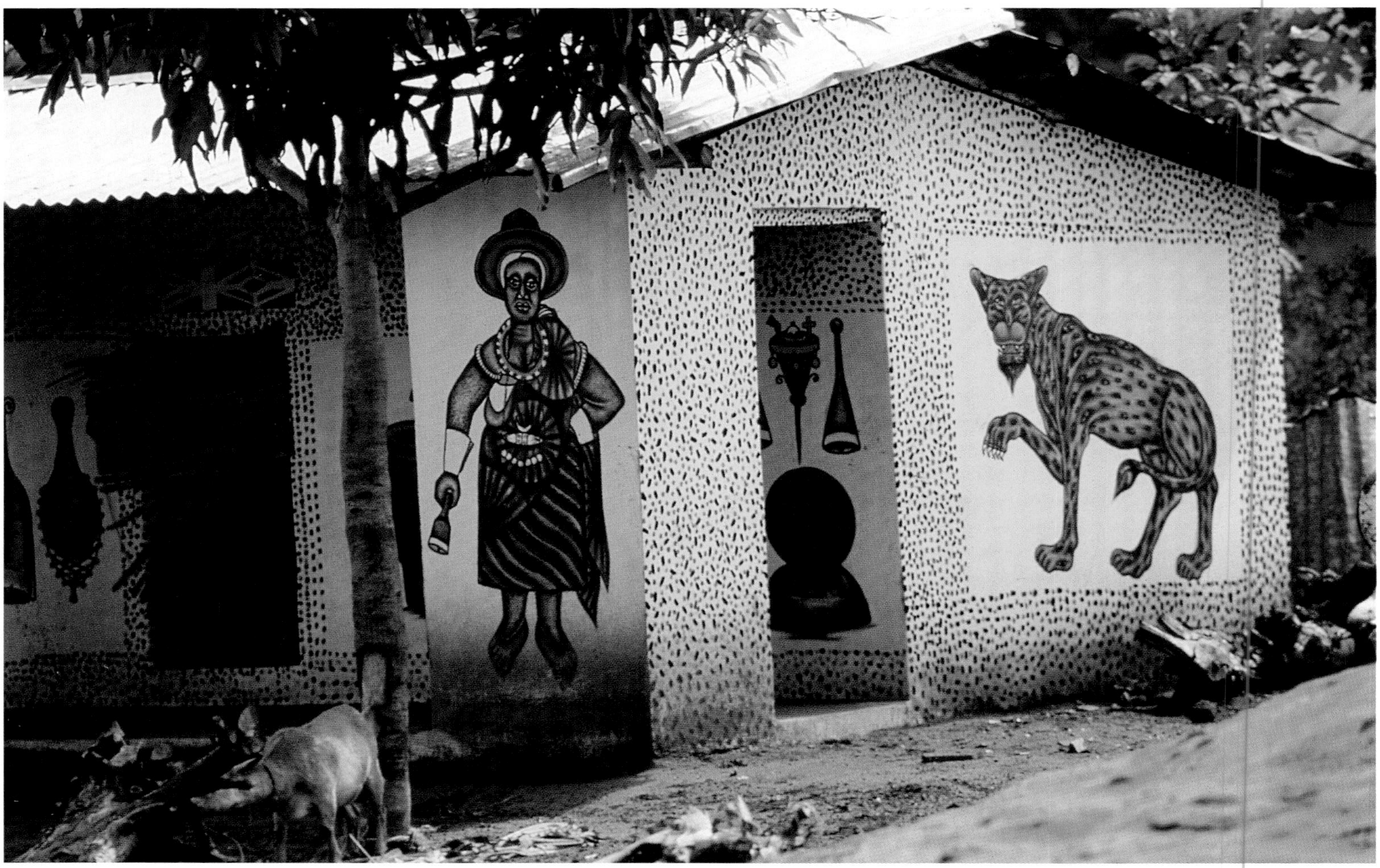

©Henry Chauvin/Revue Noire

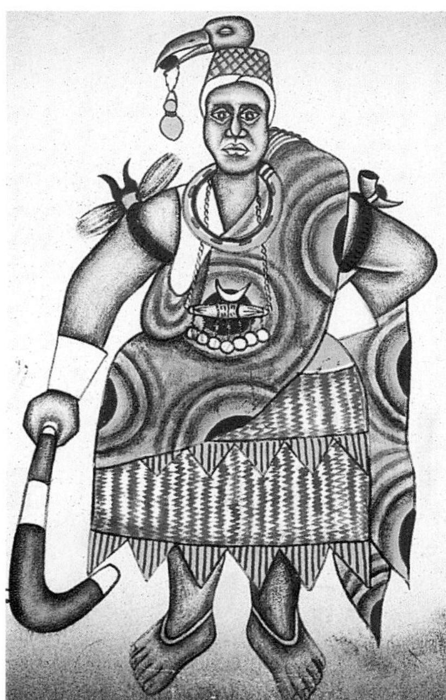

©Érick Ahounou/Revue Noire

Although the original form of the rite is in the process of disappearing as the century wears on, it still remains present in the soul of artists and producers of forms, regardless of the period in which they evolve. Despite the advent of the city and its new models, the rite, like the gods, does not die. J.L.P.

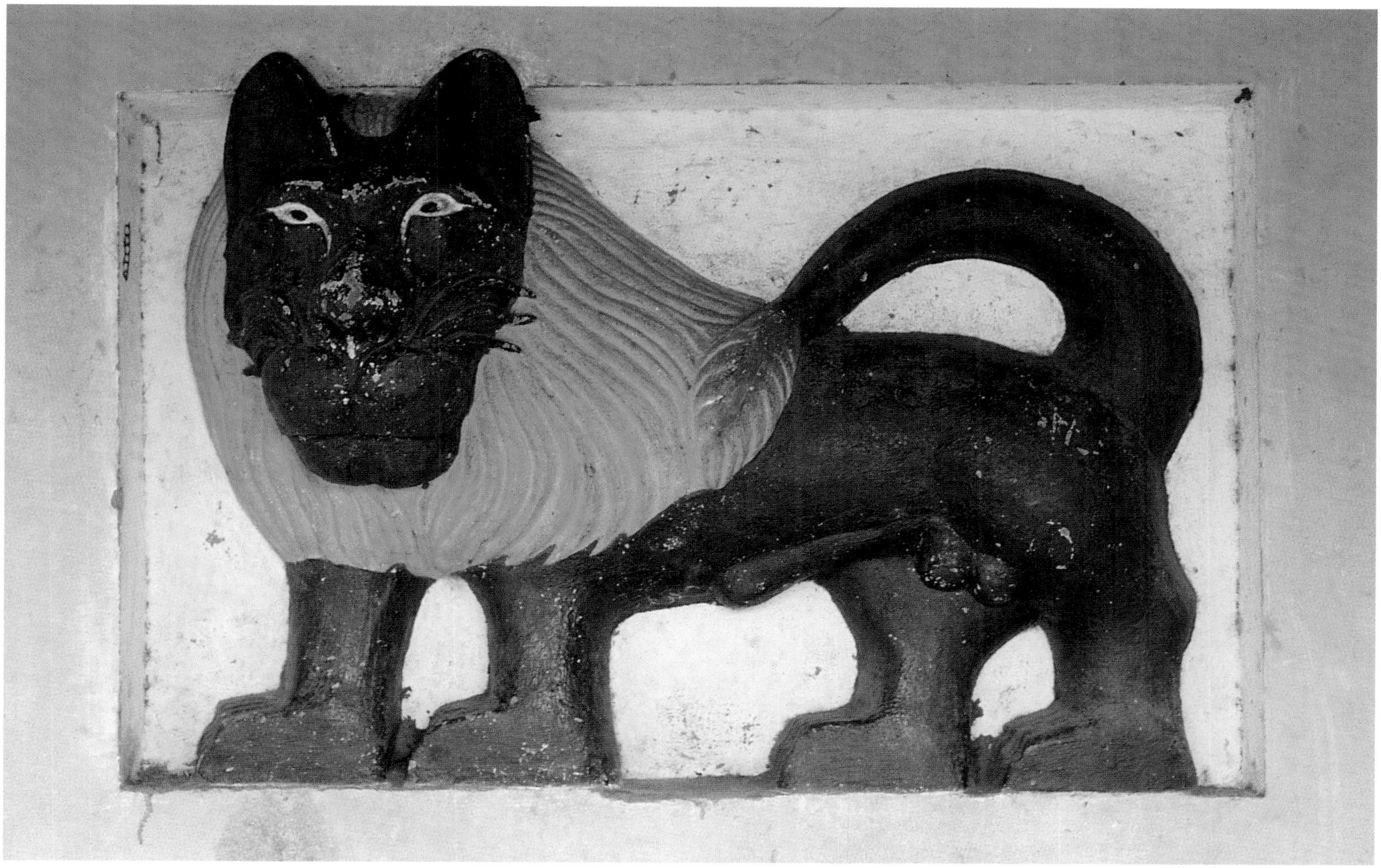

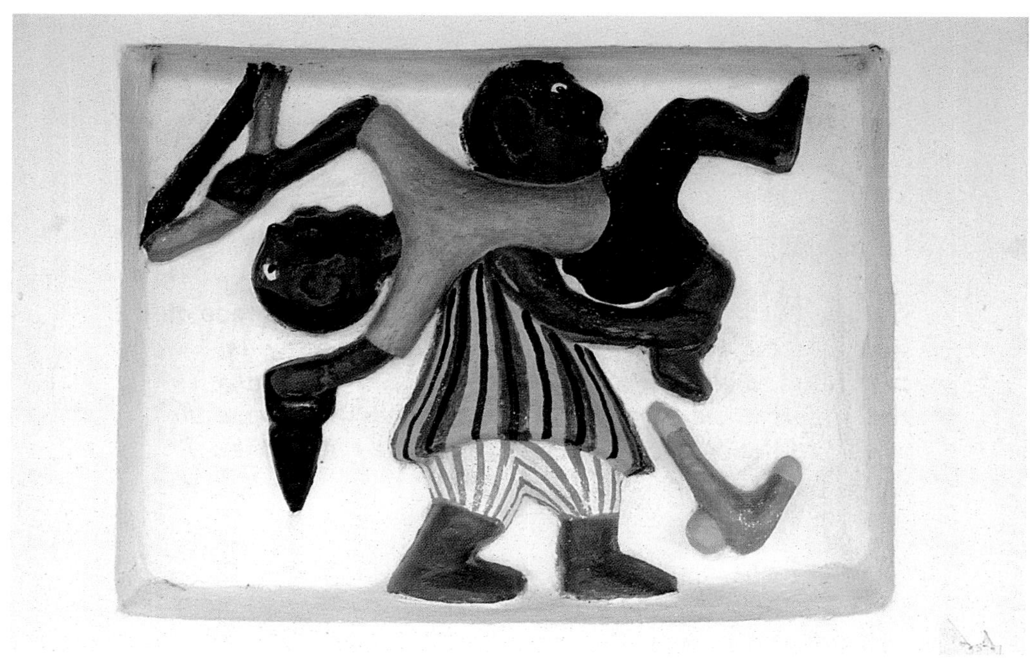

Cyprien Tokoudagba (born in 1939), Benin
facing page:
Voodoo temple

above:
bas-reliefs
©Érick Ahounou/Revue Noire

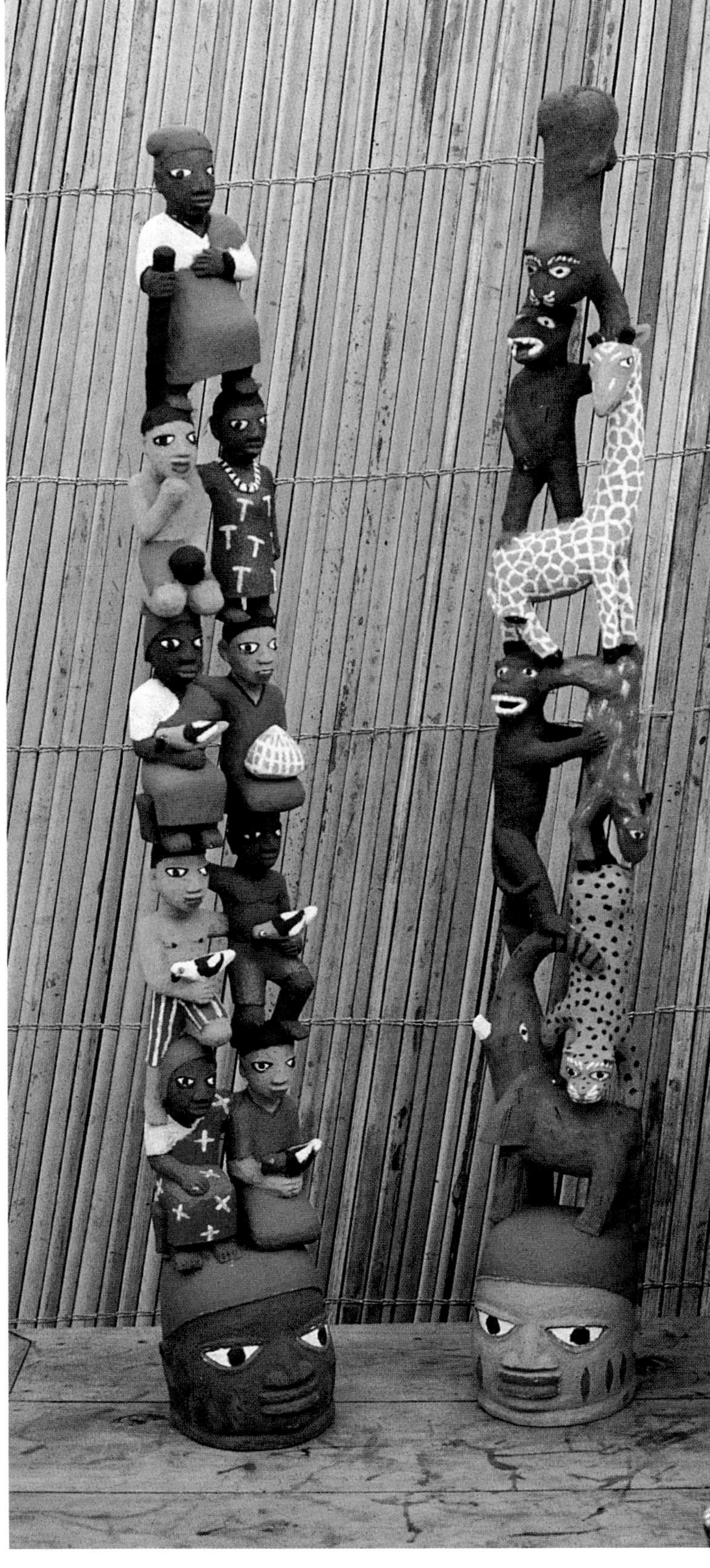

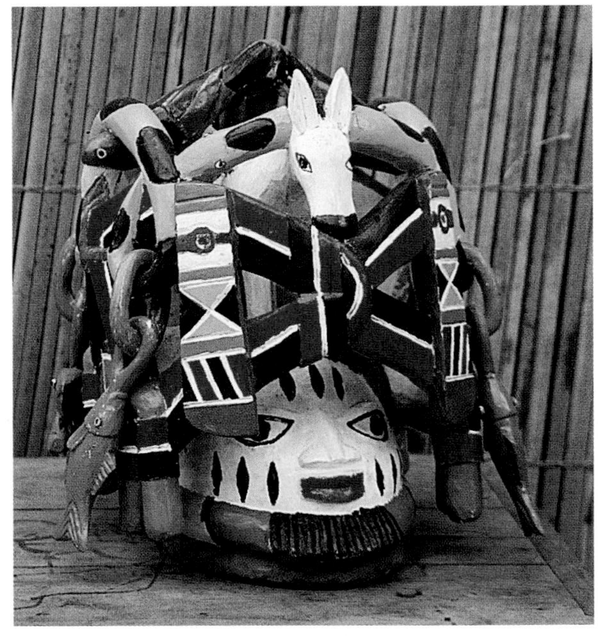

Eloi Lokossou, Benin, 1995
Masks

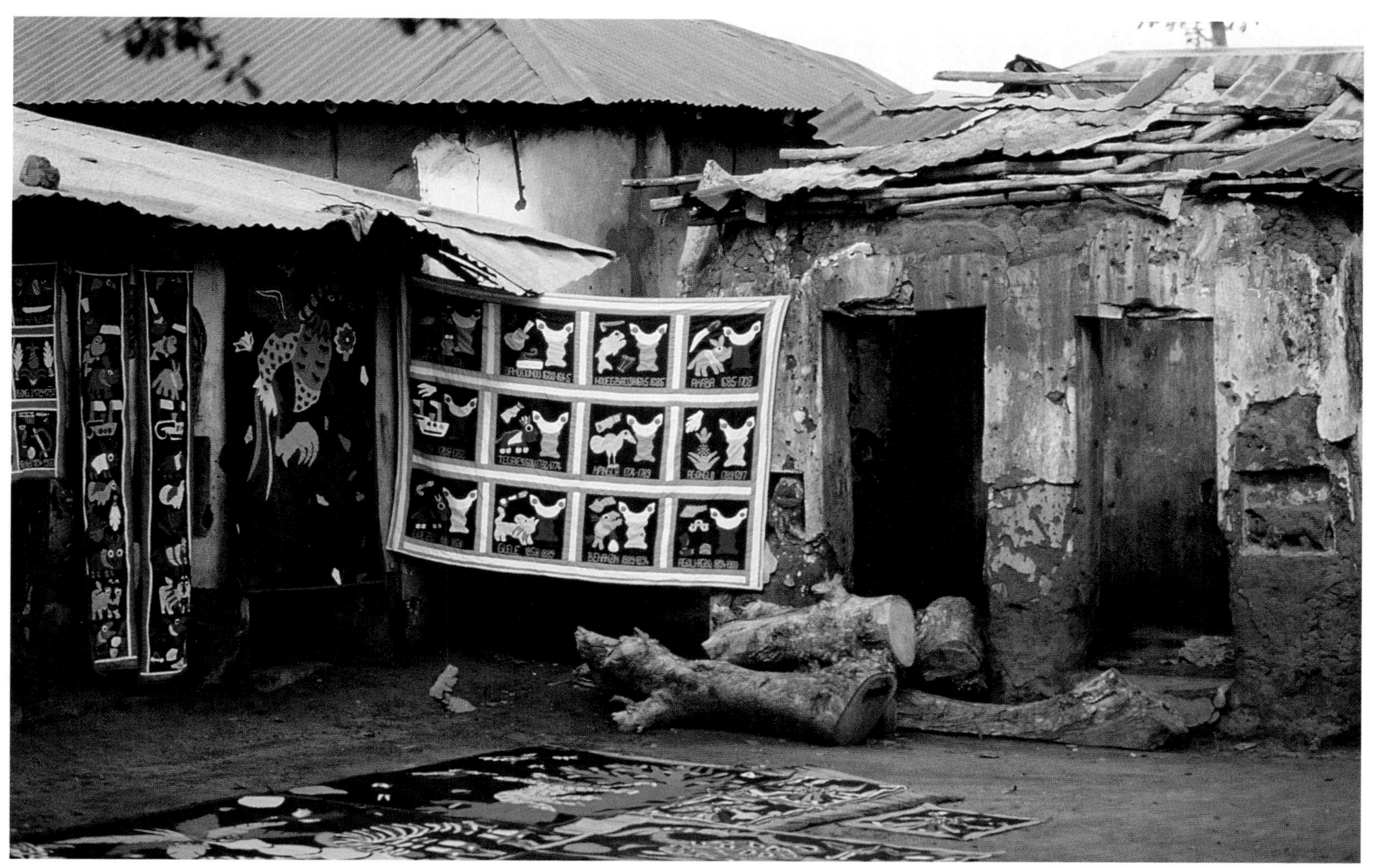

Alphonse Yemadje (born in 1934), Benin, 1995
Appliqués

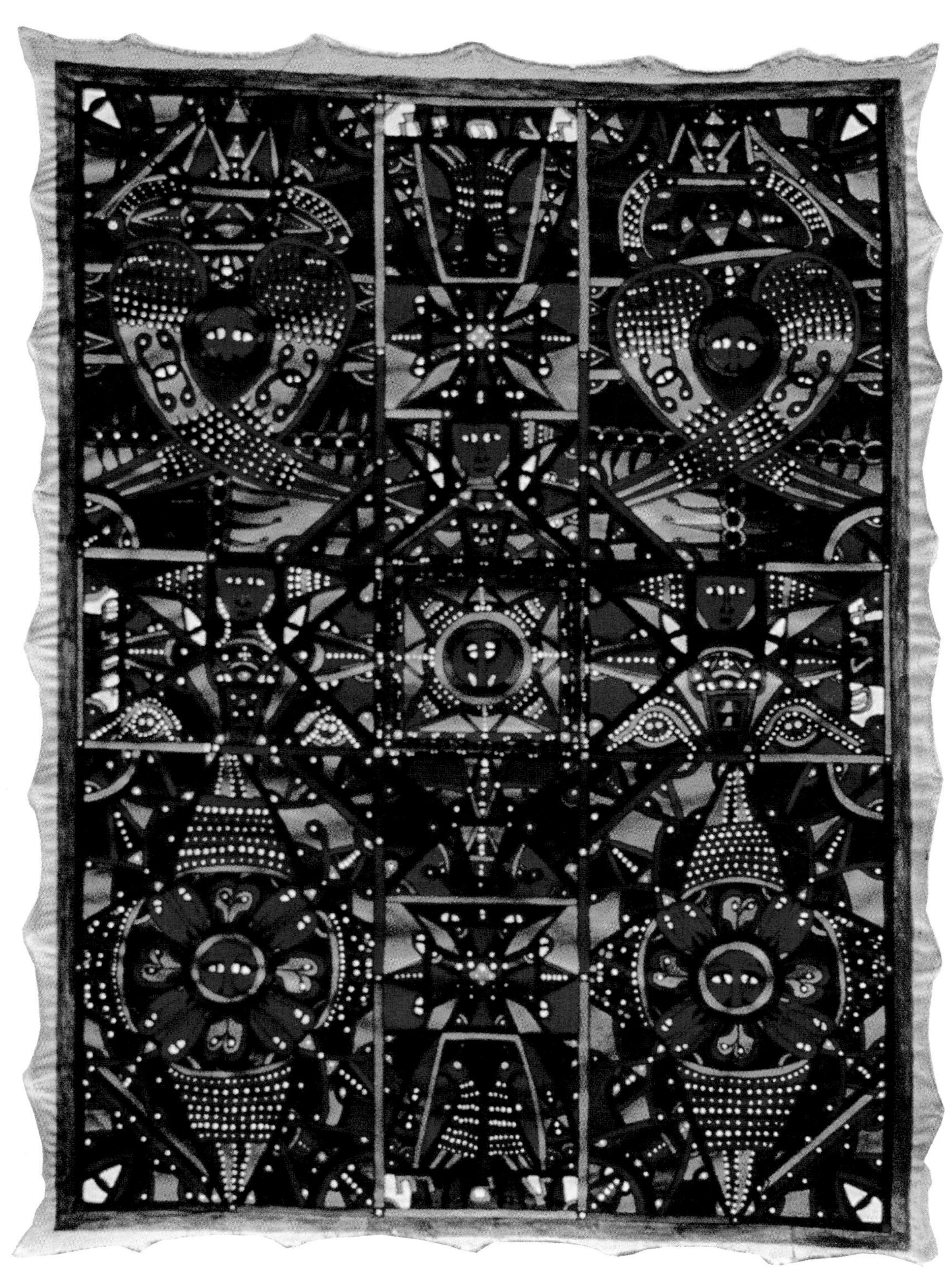

Gera (born in 1941),
"Wisdom," Ethiopia, 1992
©D.R.

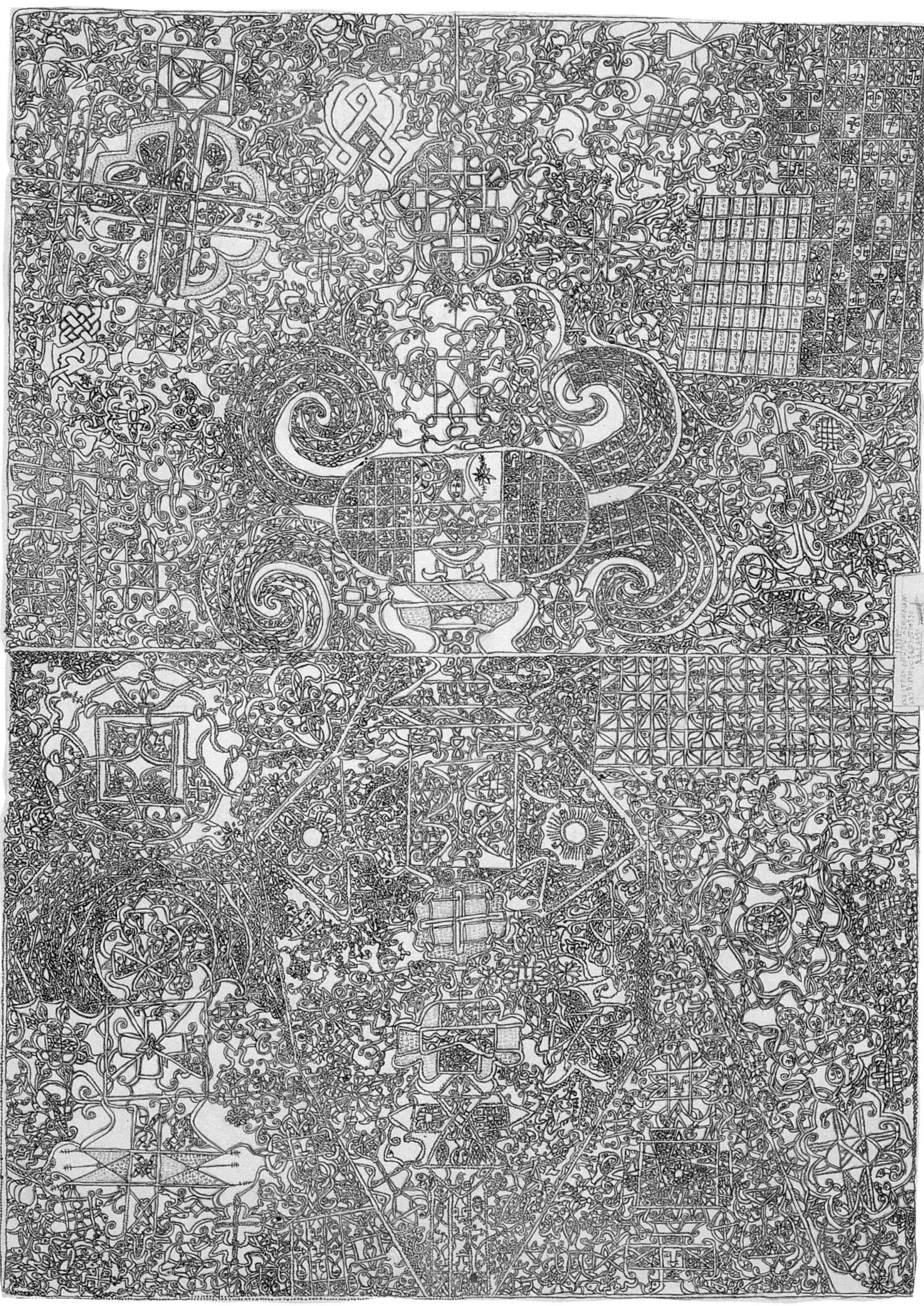

Gedeon Makonnen (1939-2000), Ethiopia

RITUAL PRACTICES IN MOVEMENT

Étienne Féau & Patrick Breton

The 20th Century will have seen an extraordinary acceleration of History. From one decade to the next, anthropologists and historians alike have observed the evolution and dynamism of religious and social institutions. One of the countries where artistic expression is both the most deeply rooted and the most up-to-date is Nigeria. In this melting pot of civilizations, religious beliefs have remained quite enduring, despite the changes brought about by the major monotheistic religions. Creation remains surprisingly fertile and varied in a large number of cultural sectors, such as the masquerades of the Yoruba and Igbo, and of their Igala or Idoma neighbors on the other side of the Niger River. Although Benin has lost its kingdoms, there is a perpetual court art, which has been reinvented by the descendants of the artists working for the royal families. And in modern-day Ethiopia, with its enduring and solidly established beliefs, priests continue to produce magical rolls and talismans to cure the ill and protect against the evil eye.

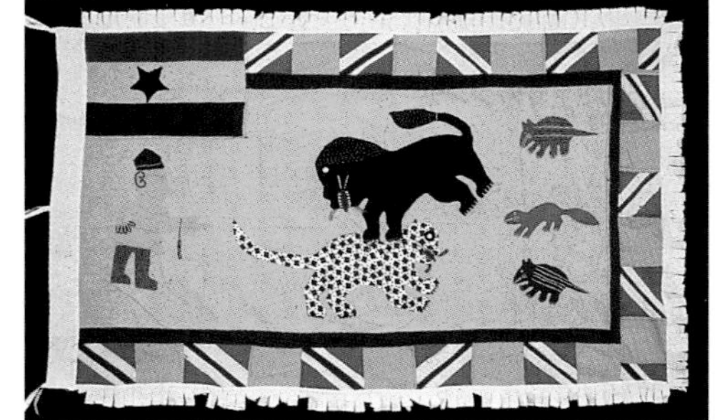

Kwelu Kakanu, flag, Ghana

©Revue Noire

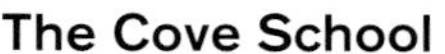

The Cove School

Half-way between the rival Abomey and Ketou kingdoms, Cove sleeps beneath the sun. The workshop of Eloi Lokossou is filled with children, goats, masks, columns and Vespa parts. A type of miraculous site. This wood craftsman, who wears his name well (the name of the Iroko cult) makes both traditional Gelede and educational masks: a doctor with moveable parts vaccinates a patient, a motorcyclist perched on his bike dashes towards eternity with his beautiful scarified face. With the Gelede, everything is possible. It makes novelty a vital principle. With his column masks, Lokossou has continued to use ancient techniques that give his sculptures a grainy dullness that resembles terracotta. Column masks that stand about a meter tall tell the tales of the Fon. In a schoolbook, Lokossou has recorded fifty stories to sculpt: defending the chiefdoms, stories of ceremonies, and animals. There is no limit to man's imagination. Neither ritual nor functional, these column masks keep watch, like lookout posts and wooden griots, over the survival of the eternal word.

Court Art

The history of the royal courts of the Golf of Benin is no secret: glory and fortune obtained from the black slave trade and exchanges with the devil. But this dubious glory was accompanied by an artistic boom, whose heritage is still very much alive: court art devoted to fairly powerful monarchs to maintain dynasties of palace artisans. Blacksmiths, bronze and brass casters, sculptors, weavers and dyers, each trade has its prestigious families. These generations of royal artisans were actually born in the 18th century. Less than a century later, the Yemadje family was offering its services to King Agonglo. It is said that the first tapestries were used as strategic maps for military operations. These patterns, applied as a rebus, also boasted of warrior victories and court scenes. Although the color code was slowly lost as the clientele became more concerned with the decorative rather than the authentic aspect, the symbolism of the characters, the hierarchy of their height, done without any perspective, has, however, remained until the present day. Alphonse Yemadje (born in 1934) revived this tradition in the 80s. Weaving by himself large pieces of cotton fabric sewn in strips, this former Indochina farmhand tells tales of cruel and very ancient combats. Julien Yemadje, teacher and dyer, works in the centuries-old royal Abomey workshop. The two cousins produced thirty paintings in 1994 to illustrate the Fables of La Fontaine. Wherever the tale is king, La Fontaine must naturally be mentioned. Alphonse and Julien Yemadje have lent their art to the universal soul.

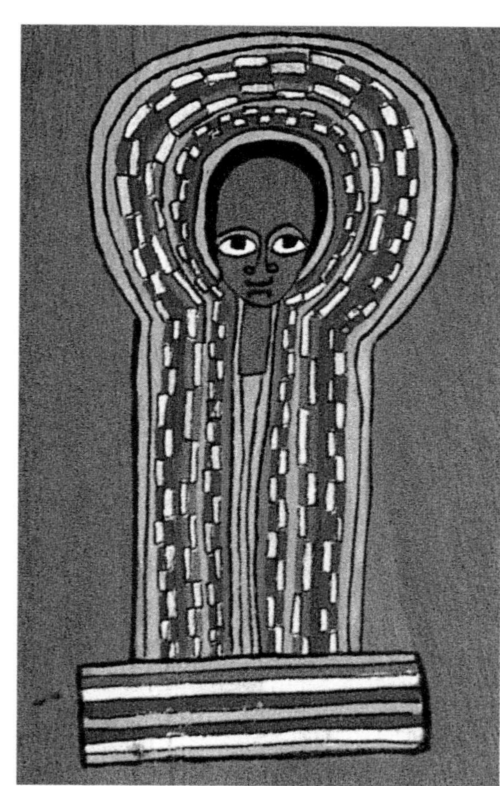

Naomi Tesfaye (born in 1967), Ethiopia

©Revue Noire

Ritual Art

Customary artists succeeded in adapting their mediums to European demand. One of these artists is Cyprien Tokoudagba (born in 1954) from Benin, who currently paints figurative or abstract patterns on canvas, inspired by the décor of the Abomey voodoo temples. But Toloudagba is not at all a naïve painter. Brought up with the voodoo worship, he has reinvented ancient techniques on new mediums. His first work as an artisan was with terracotta, which he learned to model using the bas-relief techniques of the Abomey palace. But his elegant and pure style was truly revealed in his paintings of convents and temples and in his models with shaded relief. Today he is a known and courted master. We can find among his ancestors a minister of King Glele, a weaver who hunted wild animals, and great artisans. Tokoudagba knows his origins. Admittedly, although he is a perfect master of his art, there is a constant repetition of sacred figures. Working alternatively with terracotta, reinforced concrete or mural frescos, he has succeeded in popularizing all of the images of the invisible without folklore.

Sacred Art

In Ethiopia, the "magic roll" is used for people suffering from serious disorders or to protect them from the evil eye. It is comprised of strips of parchment containing the sick person's name and can only be made by a debtera (priest or cleric), who has written up the appropriate prayers. Texts and images are chosen by the debtera based on the patient's symptoms: figures of angels, characters, geometric patterns and omnipresence of pairs of eyes. As for the text, it is written in the Amharic language or in secret characters accessible only to initiates. This tradition is passed on from debtera to debtera. Only a man of letters may prepare a talisman and use this autonomous pictorial tradition. Gera (born in 1941) is a scholar of the Ethiopian church. He has a degree in rhetorical poetry and also excels in the science of the talismans he reinterprets. Following an order for 140 illustrations for the Book of the Mystery of Heaven and Earth, Gera declared himself to be a painter and an artist. Since then, he has joined the world of Western public and private collections. This was also the case with Gedeon (1939-2000) esteemed for his science of medicine and talismans, whose classical themes he masters. More so than Gera, his work is very close to the traditional and complex lines of the architecture of interlaced letters, which became, over the centuries, mysterious and inaccessible to the layperson.

With access to canvas or paper following a Western "suggestion," these artists enter the art market with a strange status. And perhaps with a misunderstanding. Far from being self-taught, primitive artists who throw to the world a handful of troubling issues or their personal quest, are first and foremost healing priests, talented artisans, invested with the knowledge and powers of their community. We understand the temptation to make them cross the bridge that leads to self-expression. But on a blank page, their universe, as surprising and strong as it may appear to the layperson, remains sometimes a dead letter. With bold solid colors, and identically repeated shapes, we lose the magic of time, the small cracks, the laterite graduations that the rain and the wind inflict on the temple walls. And the roll no longer has either magical or healing powers. Thus, the prayers and sacrifices represented take on slightly acidic nuances, the temples appear pockmarked and everyone speaks secretly of a world that cannot easily suffer museum picture rails.

For Africa, as for the rest of the world, the 20th century was a century of upheaval and ruptures. Although it has evolved towards new forms and new mediums, African art maintains its dynamism and thousand-year-old qualities of expression, invention and adaptation. Its art is well engrained in a historical setting that it continues to create and that does not stop on an arbitrarily set date at the beginning or end of the colonial era, as is claimed by supporters of neoprimitivism, clouded by so-called pure forms from the "precontact" period.

[1] Jacques Mercier, Le roi Salomon et les maîtres du regard, Ed. RMN, Paris 1992

Popular Neo-Christian art in Ethiopia

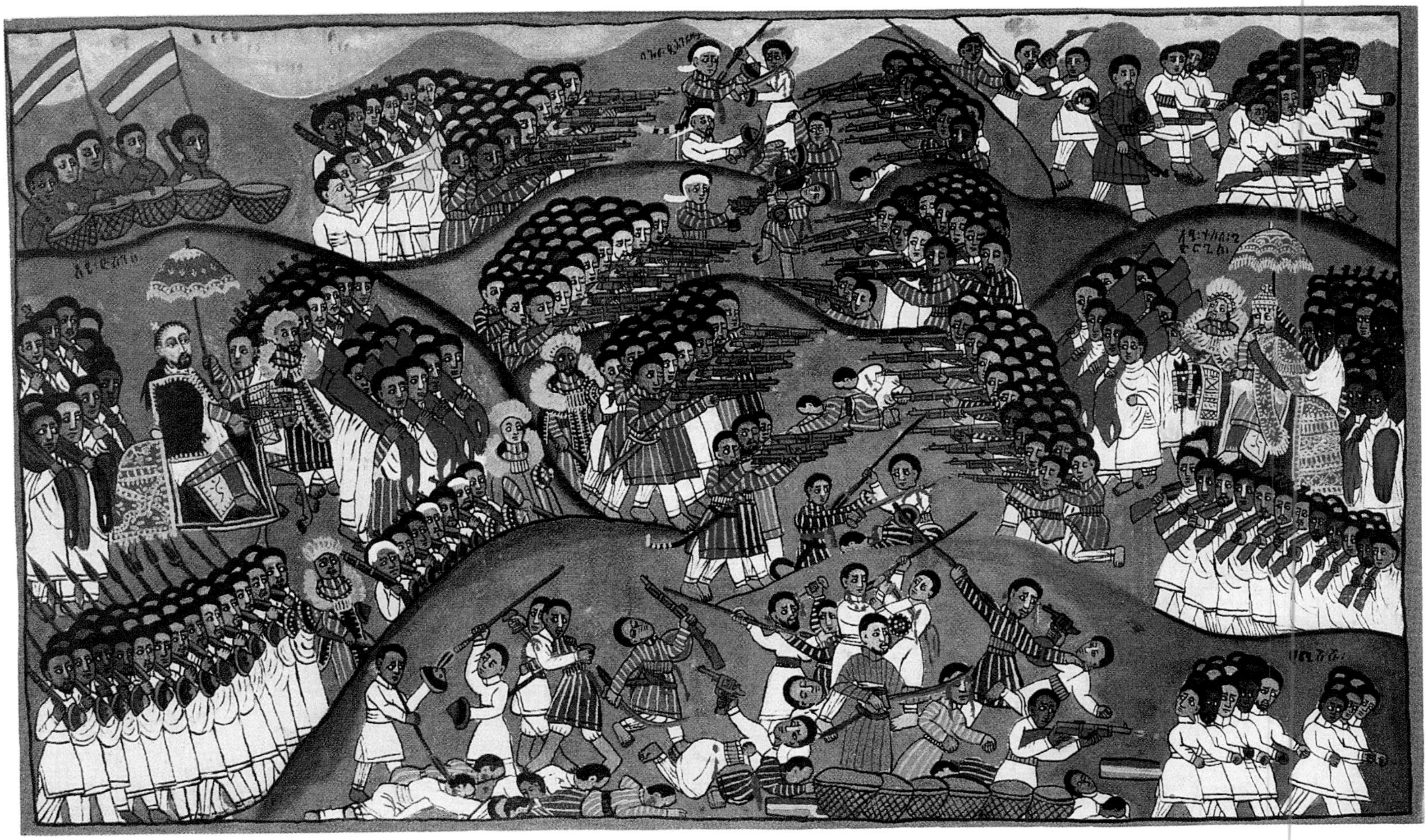

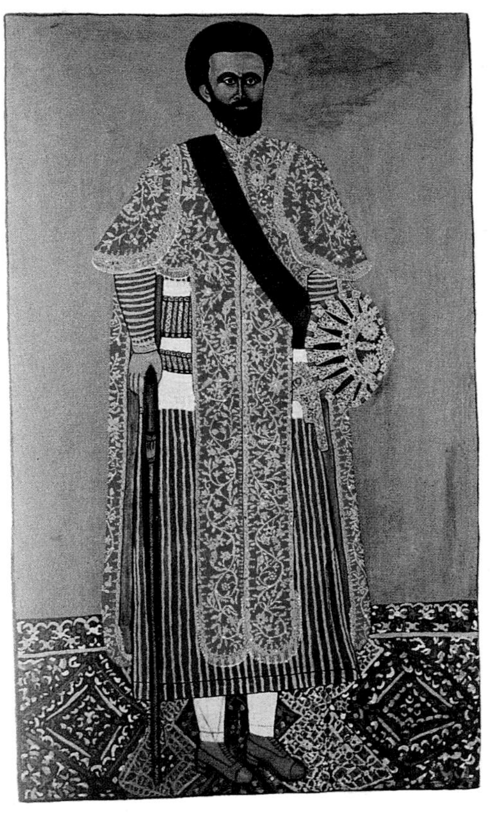

While this scan of the universe of African forms remains an exercise in style that leaves very little place for special cases, it is, however, difficult to ignore the very particular art of Ethiopia, which dates back to the Middle Ages (13th century) with an original production of icons, miniatures, illumination of manuscripts, then of frescoes, all of Christian inspiration. It is difficult to measure its influence, but it is hardly likely that any one part of Africa may be unaware of this autonomous expression. This Ethiopian exception is not truly unique and is found among others that will probably be revealed over the course of time and research.

top:
Alaqa Eleyas (c. 1961-?),
"The Battle of Adwa, 1896,"
On the left, Emperor Menelik under the royal canopy, at the head of his army. On the right, Italian troops.
©Denis Gérard

left:
Bahaylu Gabra Maryam (early 20th century),
"Sultan Khogole of Beni Shangul"
©Denis Gérard

facing page:
Belachew Yimer (1894-?),
"The Battle of Maqdala, 1868,"
Emperor Tewodros commits suicide beneath the royal tent.
©Denis Gérard

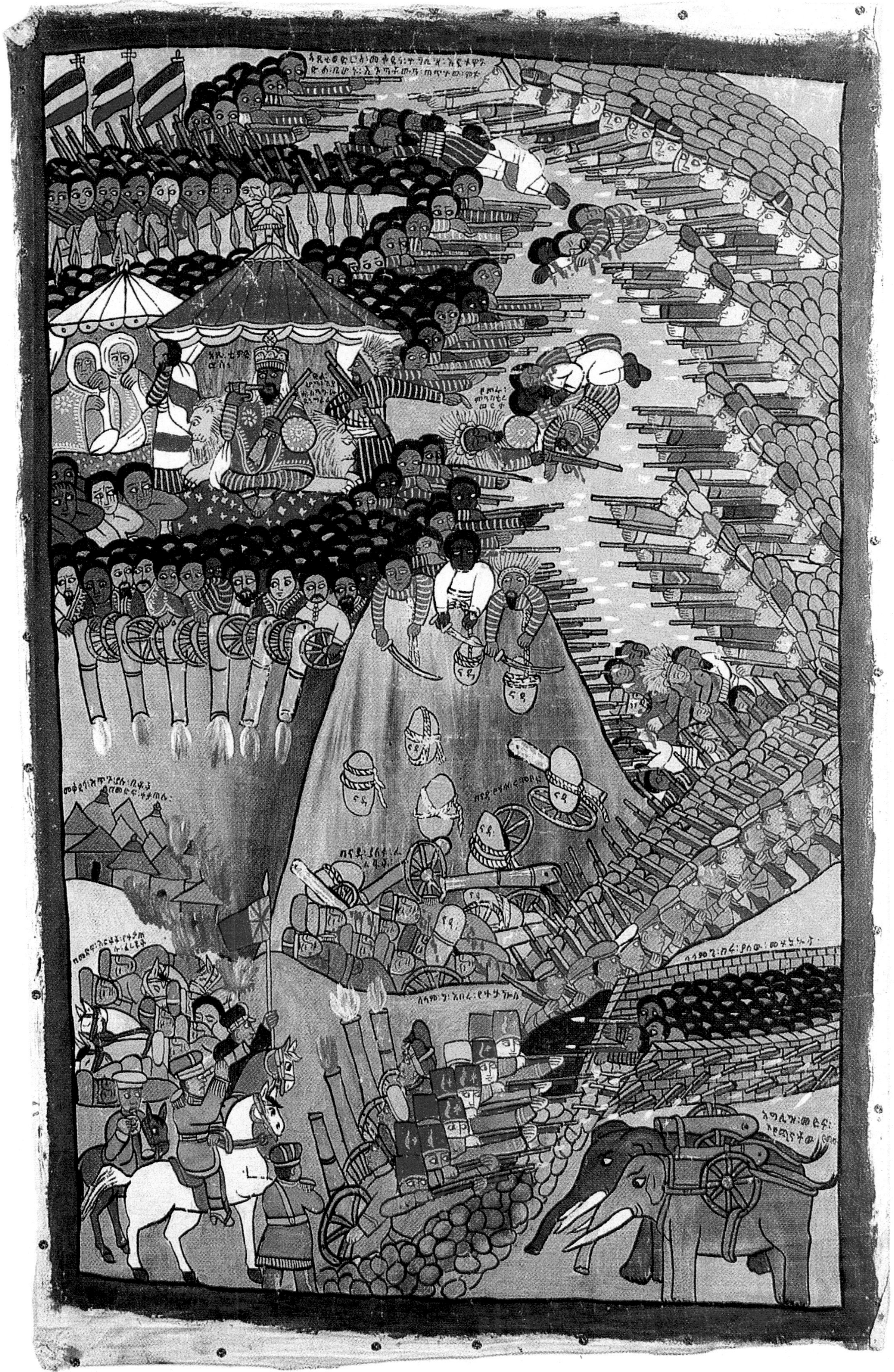

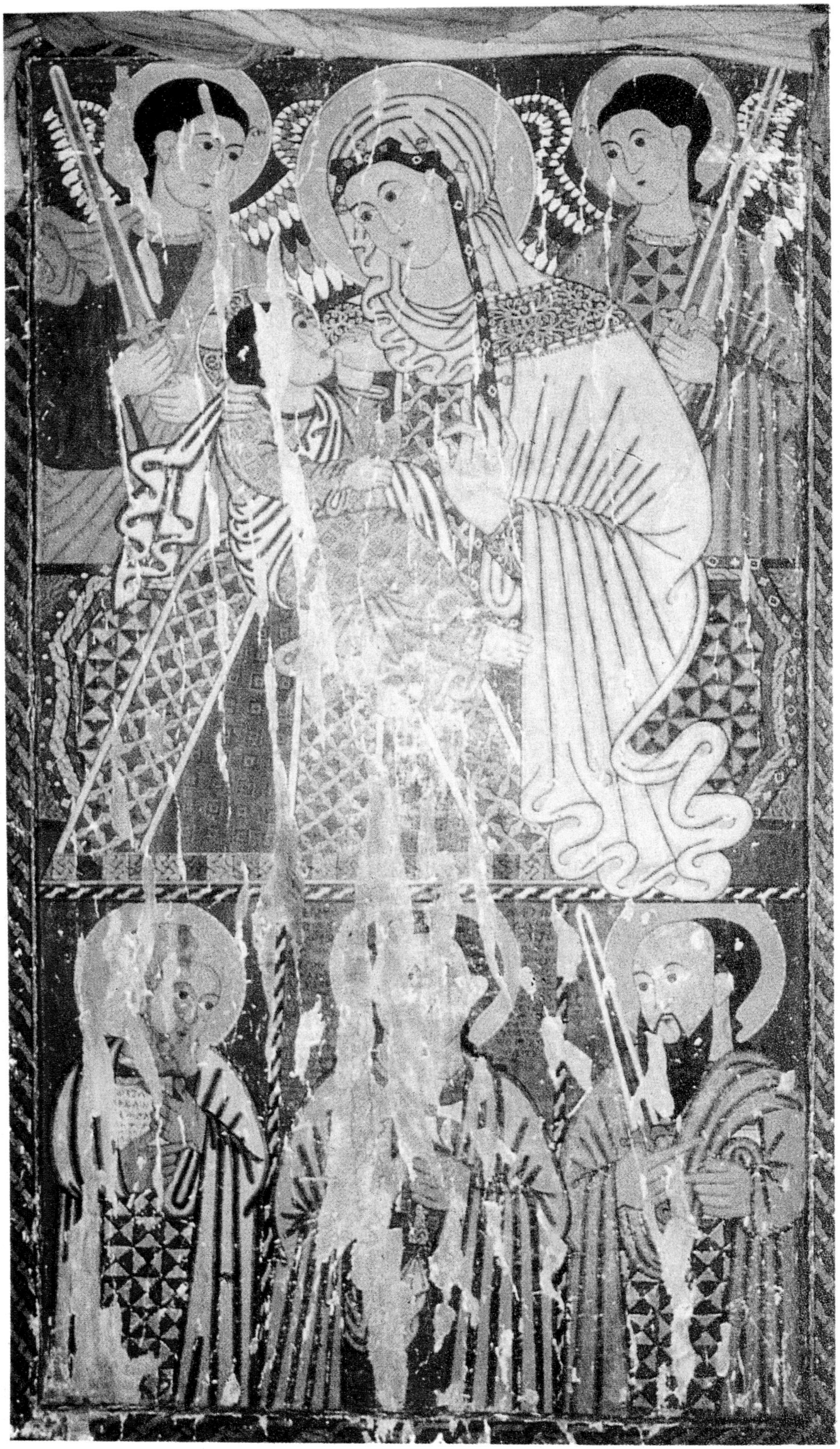

Fere Seyon, Virgin with Child, late 15th, early 16th century
Daga Estefanos Church, Lake Tana, Ethiopia

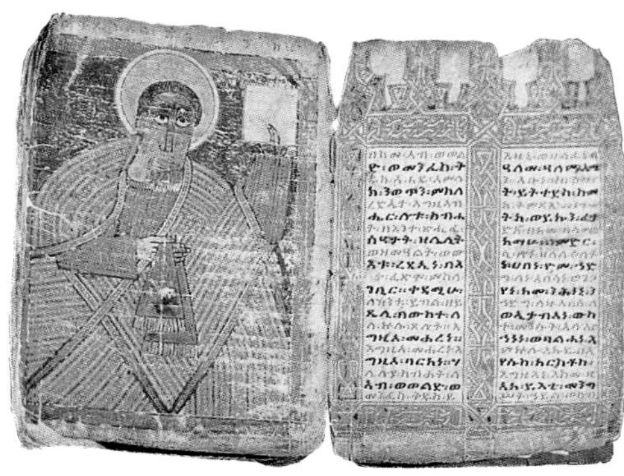

Psautier, "Hymn of Hymns and Evening Prayers," 15th Century

ETHIOPIAN CHRISTIAN ART: ITS ORIGINS AND EVOLUTION

Richard Pankhurst

Ethiopia, because of its North-East African location, adopted Christianity close on two millennia before most other parts of the continent, Egypt and Nubia excepted. Though Christianity came to Ethiopia in the early fourth century, there are virtually no extant Ethiopian paintings prior to the 13th century. The Ethiopians translated the Bible into the country's classical (and ecclesiastical language) Ge'ez, and copied the illustrations from the religious manuscripts they encountered. Some of this copying was done in Jerusalem, where the Ethiopian community in the early fourteenth century had a scriptorium for the production of manuscripts, but most would have been carried out in the country itself. Ethiopian artists, when copying foreign models, invariably transformed them. By emphasising the features they felt important, and omitting details that appeared to them irrelevant, they Ethiopianised such works almost out of all recognition.
The earliest Ethiopian paintings, dated from Medieval Times, which are as unique as they are beautiful, were deeply influenced by Byzantine art, so much so indeed that Ethiopian art has been described as Byzantine art produced on African soil. It has, however, undoubted African characteristics, which should not be ignored.

Art with a didactic purpose

Ethiopian art, which had an essentially didactic purpose, was highly stylised, and indeed often captioned. It found expression in imaginary portraits of the four Evangelists, at the beginning of each of the Gospels - often depicted seated with a pen in hand, and one or two horn inkwells. There were also pictures illustrating important events in the life of Christ, the Virgin Mary, and sundry Saints. Such pictures, many of which reached great heights of splendour, were painted, to European eyes, in a remarkably limited range of colours: red, yellow, green, and blue, with a single background colour. Colours were in many cases made from local stone, earth, plants, and especially flowers. The use of imported paints nevertheless in due course became increasingly common in the more important settlements. Paintings lacked moreover any shading, let alone perspective.

Painters, who passed on their knowledge from father to son or from master to disciple, were concerned primarily with telling the Bible story. Pictures, which were at times almost abstract, schematic, or diagrammatic, and in some instances charmingly geometrical, boldly disregarded the laws of visual proportion. The size in which any individual was depicted was likewise a function of his or her importance rather of distance from the viewer. Similarly, if useful for telling the story, it was not considered wrong to paint a finger longer than an arm, or an eye larger than a mouth. An even more characteristic aspect of Ethiopian stylisation, then and later, was that Biblical personalities, and the good in general, had to be depicted in full face, with two eyes, while the evil were depicted in profile, with one. This was, it should be emphasised, by no means, however, a hard and fast rule, for there were often many exceptions. Ethiopian painters, like artists elsewhere in Christendom in those days, worked essentially in the service of God, and for the most part would have felt it presumptuous to sign their paintings. A few painters, such as the fifteenth century artist Fere Seyon[1], did, however, record their identity on their pictures. This was done on both wall paintings and manuscripts.

Gondarine art

Ethiopian painting evolved significantly in the seventeenth and eighteenth centuries. These witnessed the foundation and growth of the city of Gondar, which became the capital of the realm in 1636, during the reign of Emperor Fasiladas. Two successive phases are discerned, known respectively as the First and Second Gondarine periods.

The first, which coincided with the seventeenth century, and the reigns of Emperor Fasiladas and of his son Yohannes I, reached a high level of visual perfection, and has been spoken of as the Golden Age of Ethiopian art. Such art - invariably religious - maintained the basic features, and conventions, of earlier,

[1] Feré Seyon was an Ethiopian artist who lived during the reign of Emperor Zar'a Ya'qob (1433-68). A monk at the monastery of Guben, Feré Seyon is known as the author of the only signed Ethiopian picture of this period. It is a large and exquisitely produced panel painting, with a richly framed border, and is preserved in the monastery of Daga Estifanos in Lake Tana. The upper half of the painting depicts the Virgin and Child, the latter holding a spotted pigeon, while the lower depicts three personages: St Peter, with a copy of the Gospels, St Paul with a sword and a book, and St Stephen raising his right hand in blessing.

Medieval Ethiopian art, but was to some extent influenced by European Renaissance models, among them Biblical engravings imported by the Jesuits. One of the most remarkable new literary works to be illustrated in this period was the Miracles of the Virgin Mary, whose Ethiopian image was based on that in the Church of Santa Maria Maggiore in Rome. These Miracles were artistically important in that they were illustrated with many features of everyday Ethiopian life. The range of stories depicted was, however, significantly wider. Ethiopian painters of this period delineated figures with dark lines, and filled in the area marked out with a flat clear colour, once more usually red, yellow, green, and blue. Good examples can be seen for example in the British Library, i.e. among the manuscripts looted from Emperor Tewodros's capital at Maqdala (the return of which is currently demanded in Ethiopia). Pictures, though softer than in earlier times, were still often schematic. The background was also flat, but often divided horizontally into two or three bands of red, yellow and green (which were later to be chosen as the Ethiopian national colours). Figures were in many instances elongated, with relatively small pear-shaped heads, and large almond eyes. Faces were often modeled, with red wash, to accentuate the cheeks. Hair was depicted in solid black, with rounded curls. Robes were not infrequently painted in yellow, decorated with parallel lines in red interspersed with small lines and dots, likewise in red.

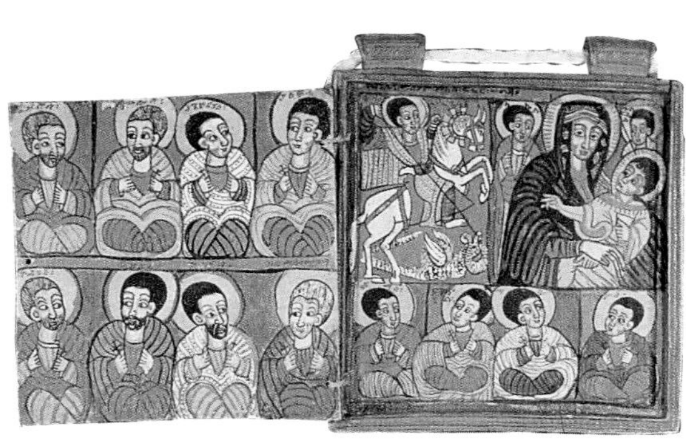

"Our Mother Mary and her Beloved Son, Gabriel, Michael and the Saints," late 17th Century, Gondar

The Second Gondarine period, which developed largely in the eighteenth century, differs from the First, in that the painters were much more concerned to depict the real world, to express movement, and to make the figures appear alive. This was in part achieved by slight modeling, to give them a more rounded appearance. Hair is depicted with greater care than in the past, sometimes indicating waves. There was also some indication of shadows, which produced an impression almost of perspective. The background was often occupied with representations of trees, plants, birds and other animals, albeit conceived in generalised rather than specific terms. Such plants and creatures tended to be only incidental to the story, and were therefore treated in a merely cursory manner. The clothing of this period was distinctive. Often gorgeous and multicoloured, and beautifully executed, it in many instances fell into carefully drawn folds. Second Gondarine art tended moreover to have richer, deeper and more sombre colours than were earlier in use, and employed a more extensive variety of shades. Personalities depicted included the principal rulers of the time: Emperors Iyasu I – one of the greatest of Ethiopian emperors, Iyasu II and the redoubtable Empress Mentewab, one of the country's most renowned women rulers, who served as Regent first for her son, and later for her grandson. There were also frequent representations of the donors of paintings, who were often shown in a prone, and subordinate, position at the foot of the work. They tended to be much smaller and less impressive than those in some European paintings of the time.

Paintings in Gondarine times tended to be both Ethiopianised, and secularised. We thus see representations of typical Ethiopian clothing, hair-styles, and crowns; horse and mule decorations; spears, shields and other weapons (including seventeenth century muskets anachronistically carried by the Pharaoh's soldiers seen drowning frantically in the Red Sea!); drinking, cooking and other such-like vessels. Agriculture is depicted with typical zebu cattle, and with oxen pulling the typical Ethiopian plough. All this, it should be emphasised, is invaluable for the economic and social historian no less than the art historian, as it gives us invaluable glimpses into Ethiopian life of the past. With this in view the present writer is currently engaged in the cataloguing Ethiopian secular artifacts displayed in ecclesiastical manuscripts.

A popular art

The closing years of the nineteenth century, after the battle of Adwa of 1896 – an historic event which preserved Ethiopia's age-old independence throughout the European Scramble for Africa – witnessed interesting new artistic developments. The coming of foreign diplomats, and other visitors from abroad, created an entirely new, commercial, demand for Ethiopian art. Painters, for the most part churchmen, had formerly worked almost entirely for the church, with the consequence that manuscript, icon and wall paintings were, as we have seen, virtually all religious. Foreign visitors, on the other hand, were more interested in art which was exotic, and characteristically Ethiopian. The old Ethiopian church artists – or in many cases their sons, using new powers of invention, therefore evolved a new form of popular – or tourist – art, which they often signed.

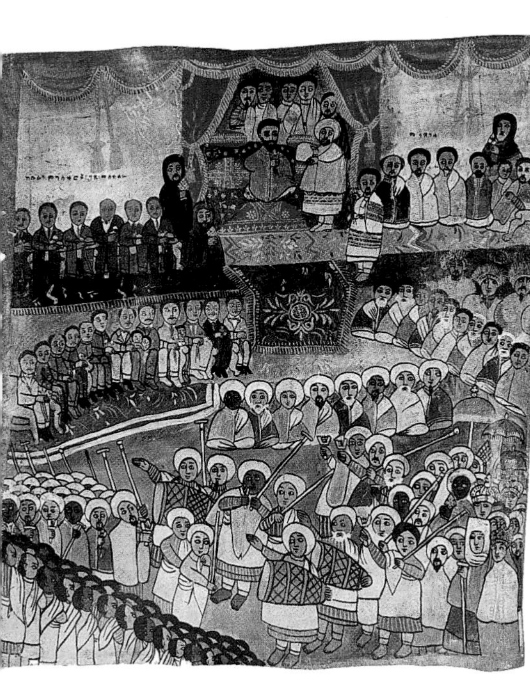

Belachew Yimer (born c. 1894-?), "Reception at the Palace of Emperor Haile Selassie"
©Denis Gérard

Building on the Ethiopianisation and securalisation of traditional Christian art in Gondarine times, these artists carried it one stage further, by turning out increasing numbers of paintings depicting such quintessentially Ethiopian themes. This art, which may be termed Ethiopian neo-Christian art, included the event of the Queen of Sheba's visit to King Solomon. This is usually presented as a strip cartoon chronicling the story. Other popular pictures include farming activity, arranged in twelve squares, one for each month of the year (with ploughing for example already depicted, as we have seen, in Gondarine art); hunting scenes, depicting the slaughter of elephants, and other animals; and, perhaps most popular of all, stylised, representations of the hundred-and-four-year- old battle of Adwa referred to above. Though new these popular post-Gondarine paintings, which are of no small historical and cultural interest, maintained many of the old conventions of Ethiopian Christian art. Lacking perspective, like the paintings of the past, they are for example largely schematic in form, and are in many instances captioned. It is worthy of note that in the Battle of Adwa paintings (which are reminiscent of battle scenes earlier painted in Gondarine times) Menilek's army is depicted full face, while the Italians are in profile. (Readers, tell us why!) The engagement having been fought on St George's Day, the Saint is often depicted in the sky, immediately above the two armies, sometimes in a rainbow, fighting heroically on the Ethiopian side.

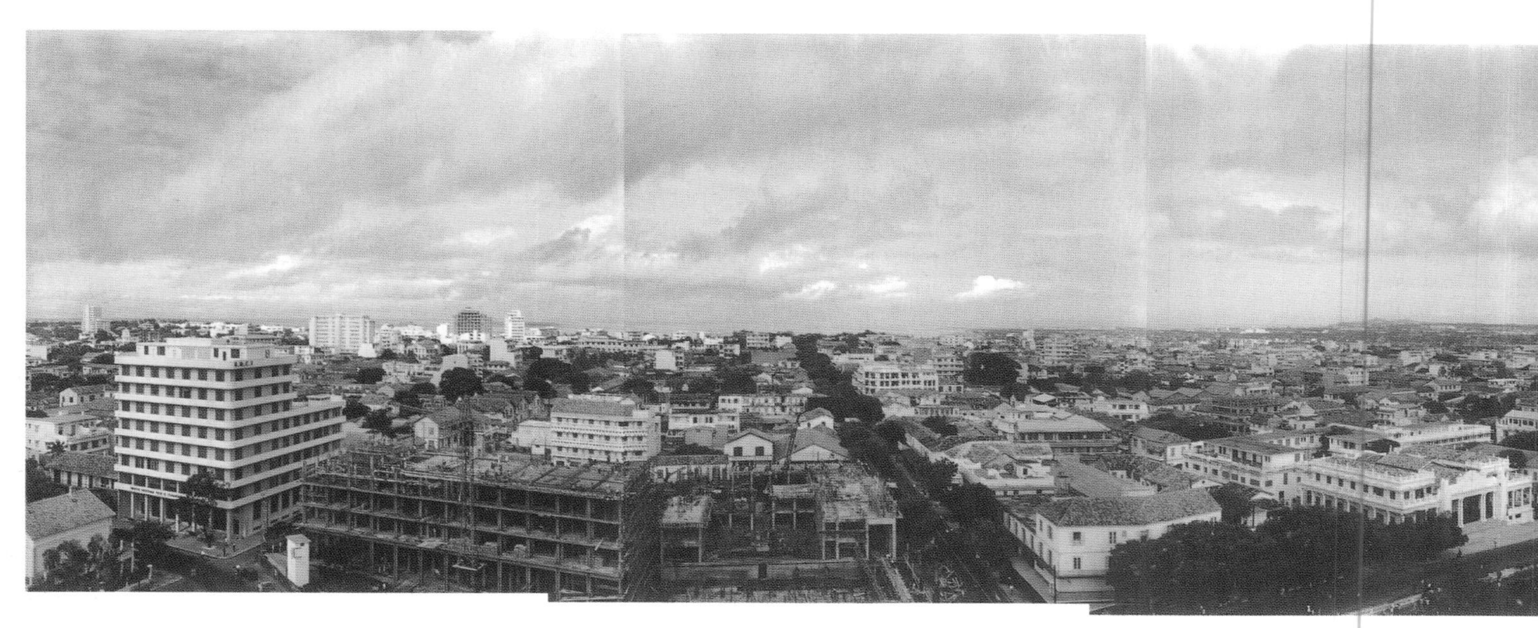

Aerial view of Dakar, Senegal, 1954 ©D.R.

The modern city

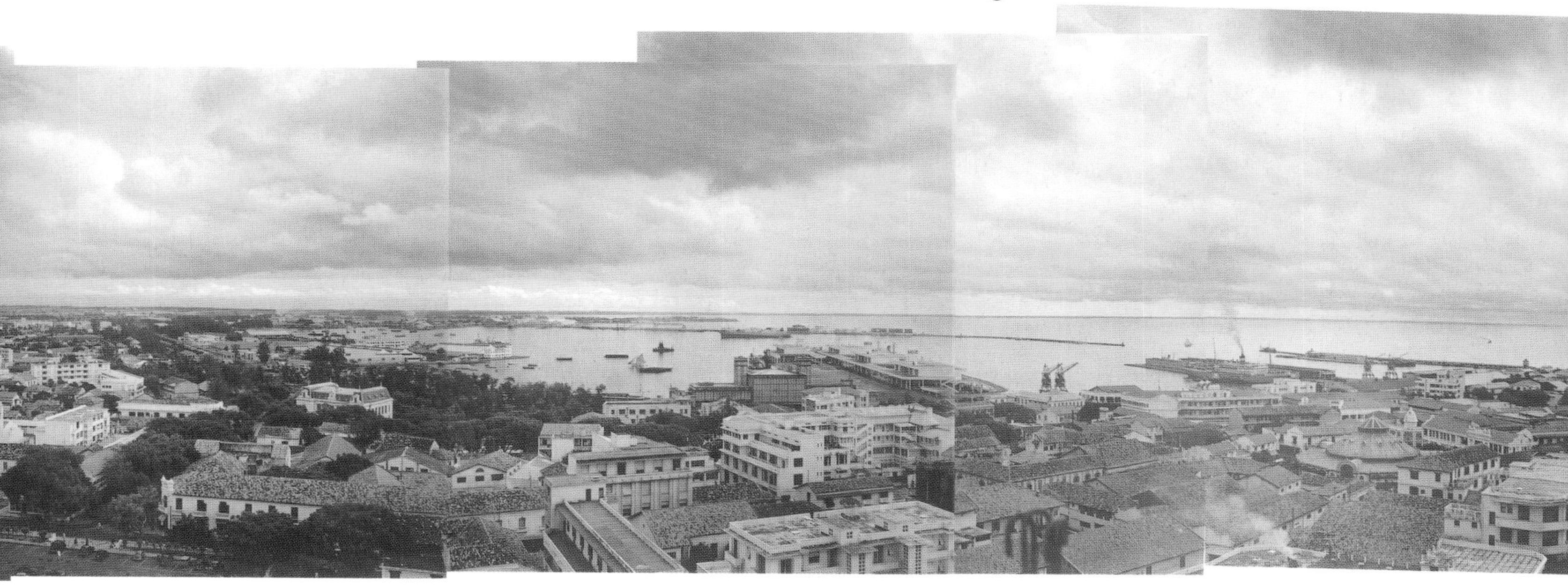

A city of boundless expressions

Jean Loup Pivin

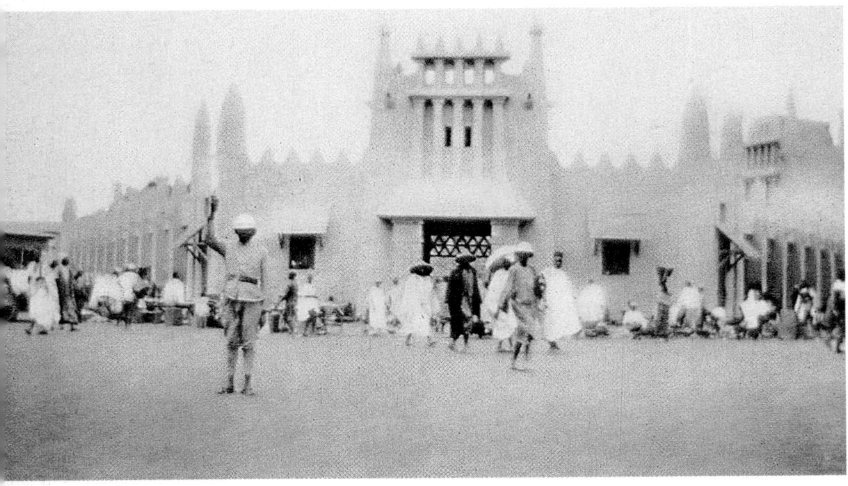

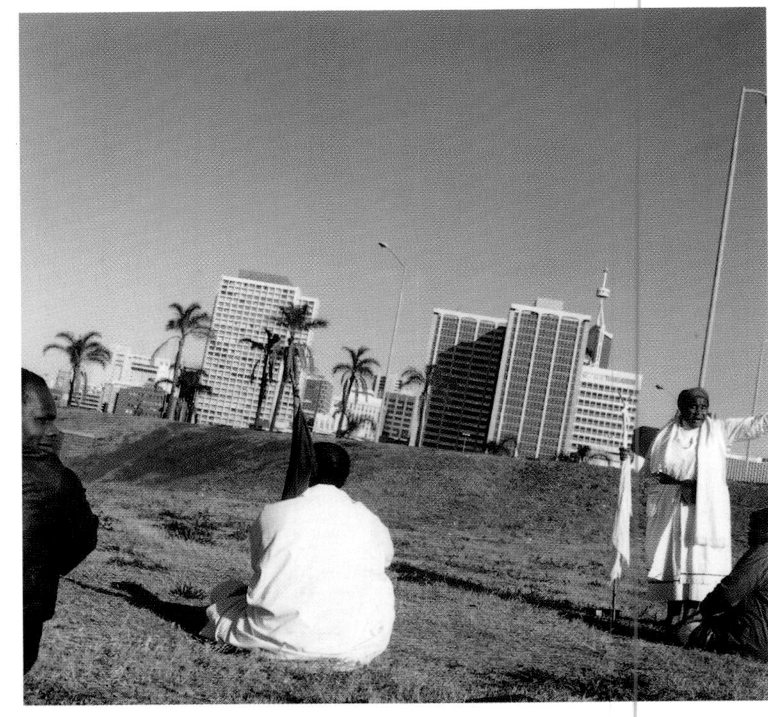

above:
The marketplace in Bamako, Mali, 1930
©D.R.

right:
Lagos, Nigeria ©Akinbode Akinbiyi

facing page:
Aerial view of Bamako, Mali, 1950 ©D.R. coll.particulière

Fog

The modern city imposes its model. Lifestyles, thought and ways of life in a society change, as do formal productions. Photography fills homes, buildings and objects leave behind their rituality to take on other forms and functions that change the face of traditional social values. The different traditional objects adorn themselves with new or salvaged materials. Images and their esthetic quality are jostled by the thousands of magazines that change hands, by the initial advertisements and by the notables, especially those from the coast, who, for several centuries, own numerous objects coming from the West, the East and the Far East. They actually own many more objects than the modern schools, which, at the beginning of the 20th century, were totally non-existent. From Senegalese glass frames to Ghanaian coffins, new popular syncretic forms flourished all over the continent. There are the syncretic forms from Europe and Africa – a confrontation of spiritual and social values and forms – the autonomous forms emerging directly from the cultural forge of the continually bustling city. And then there are, of course, forms of individuality that enrich theoretical, divine, dreamed and illuminated universes, thereby producing messages to a universe and society under construction. More than ever, this chapter cuts across all of the visual arts disciplines, such as living arts, and expressions, such as architecture, film or literature, because the modern city builds its own expressions based on all of these aspects. We will attempt, nonetheless, to refocus our approach on the visual arts as entities or as a part of larger entities.

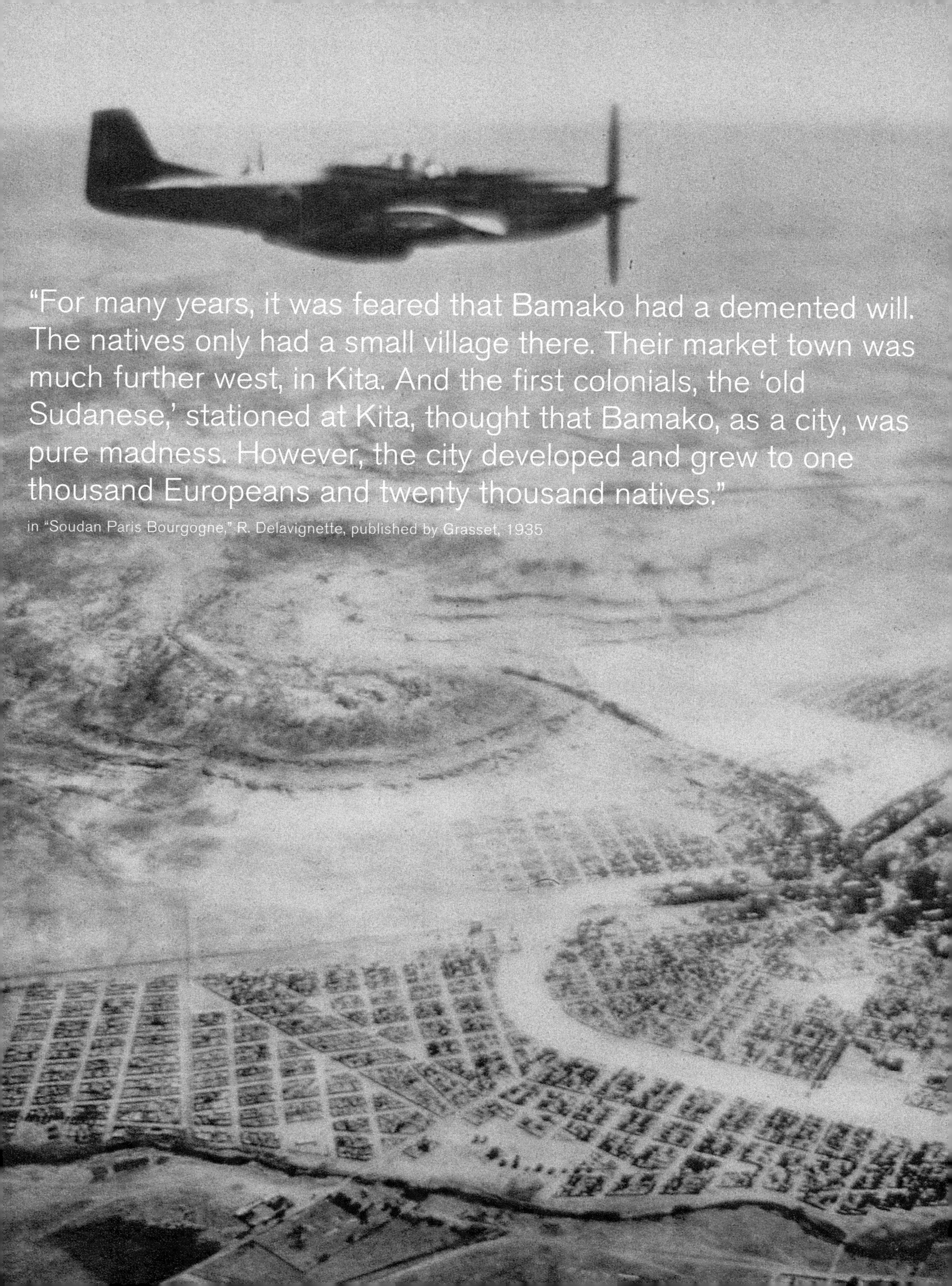

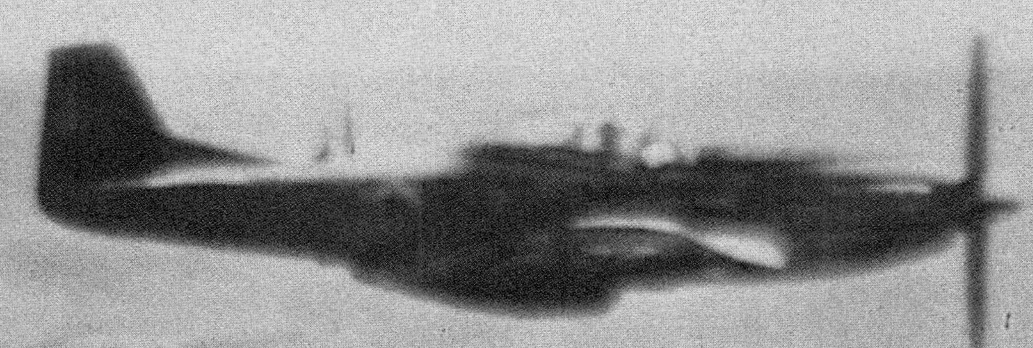

"For many years, it was feared that Bamako had a demented will. The natives only had a small village there. Their market town was much further west, in Kita. And the first colonials, the 'old Sudanese,' stationed at Kita, thought that Bamako, as a city, was pure madness. However, the city developed and grew to one thousand Europeans and twenty thousand natives."

in "Soudan Paris Bourgogne," R. Delavignette, published by Grasset, 1935

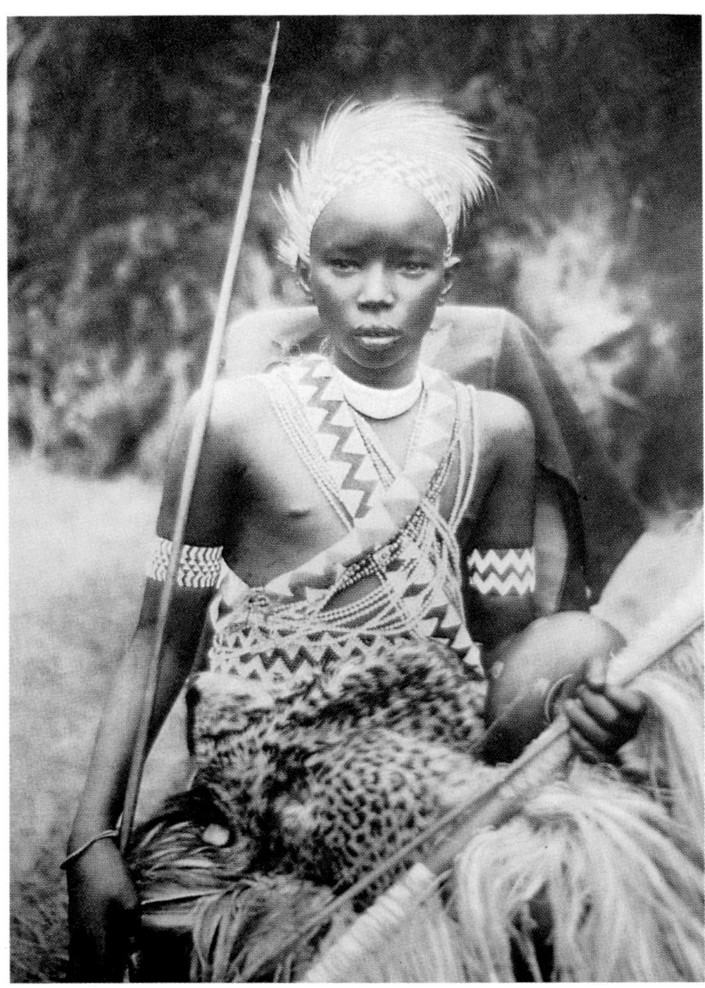

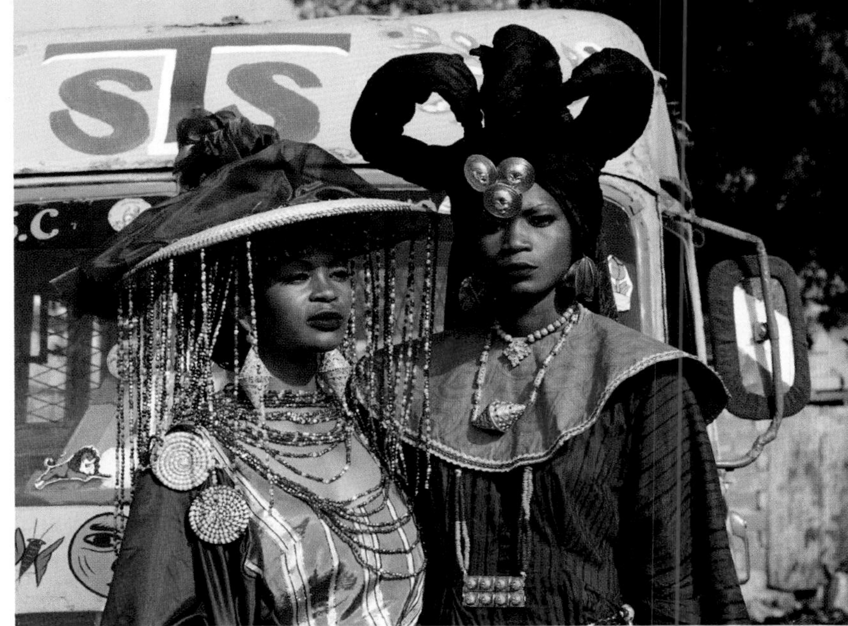

left:
Mwanbutsa, king of Urundi, Burundi, 1929 ©D.R.

right:
Creations by Oumou Sy, Senegal, 1997 ©Mamadou Touré Béhan/Revue Noire

In the beginning there was perfume, clothing and jewelry

Trying to integrate everything into the formal production of a continent could lead to aberrations and a dilution of our subject. Yet one of the first plastic expressions of African cultures is directly related to the body. Body painting, scarification, costumes and hairstyles will always be present in the modern city and enhanced by make-up, hairstyles, costumes and jewelry. Continually renewed traditional or industrial textile, trend-setting designs, jewelry and bags all form the first activity manufactured in Africa, whether as part of production, an economic and commercial activity, or as an artistic creation. Although numerous items are imported, with, at times, exclusive productions for Africa, such as Wax, most items are designed and made in Africa. Hand weaving, dyes (which are, admittedly, chemical and mostly imported), industrial fabrics, and sewing work are constantly being renewed and reinvented. The patterns and colors on the dyed pagnes are renewed several times a year by genuine diva dyers, whose reputation stretches beyond country borders. Make-up, creams and perfumes remain partially traditional and are mostly imported. Nevertheless, they are an intrinsic part of African cultures. All of these body-related material elements demonstrate, more than any other art, including ritual, the importance granted to this first expression of African culture. We could throw away the mask as we throw away the fabric, both of which are related to the moment they are worn on the body of an individual and a society. It does not really matter if the mask is picked up by a merchant or if the fabric ends up as a rag. Its time has passed.
Conversely, the folly of the individual, of the person who physically withdraws from society, will expose the body, without any hairstyle or body finery.

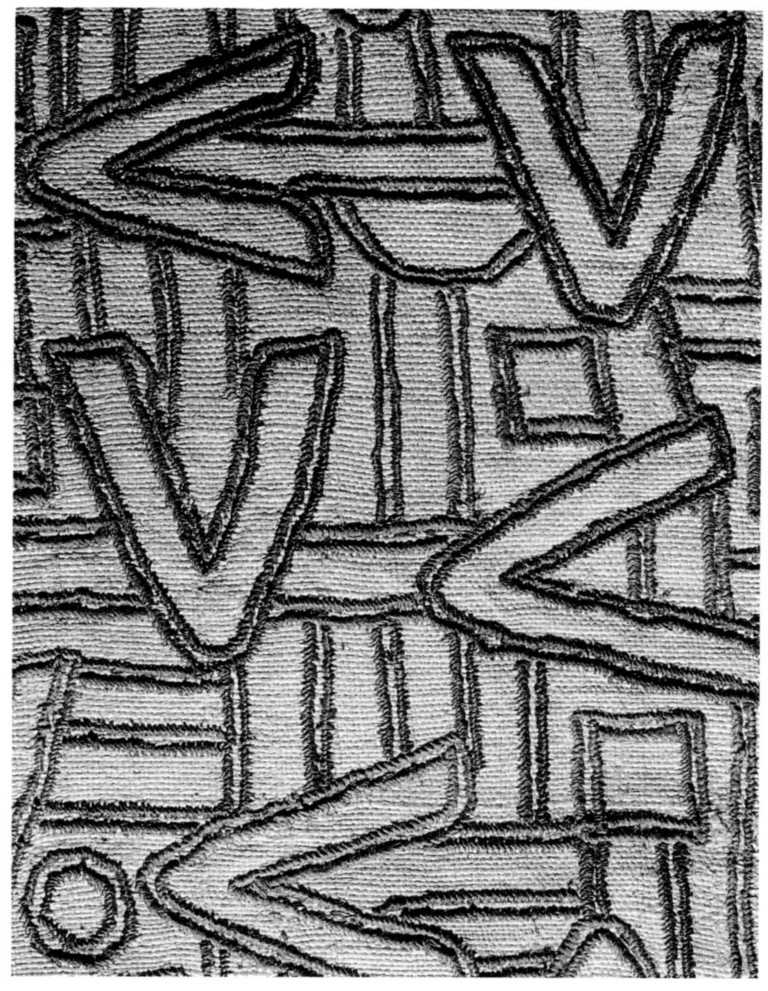

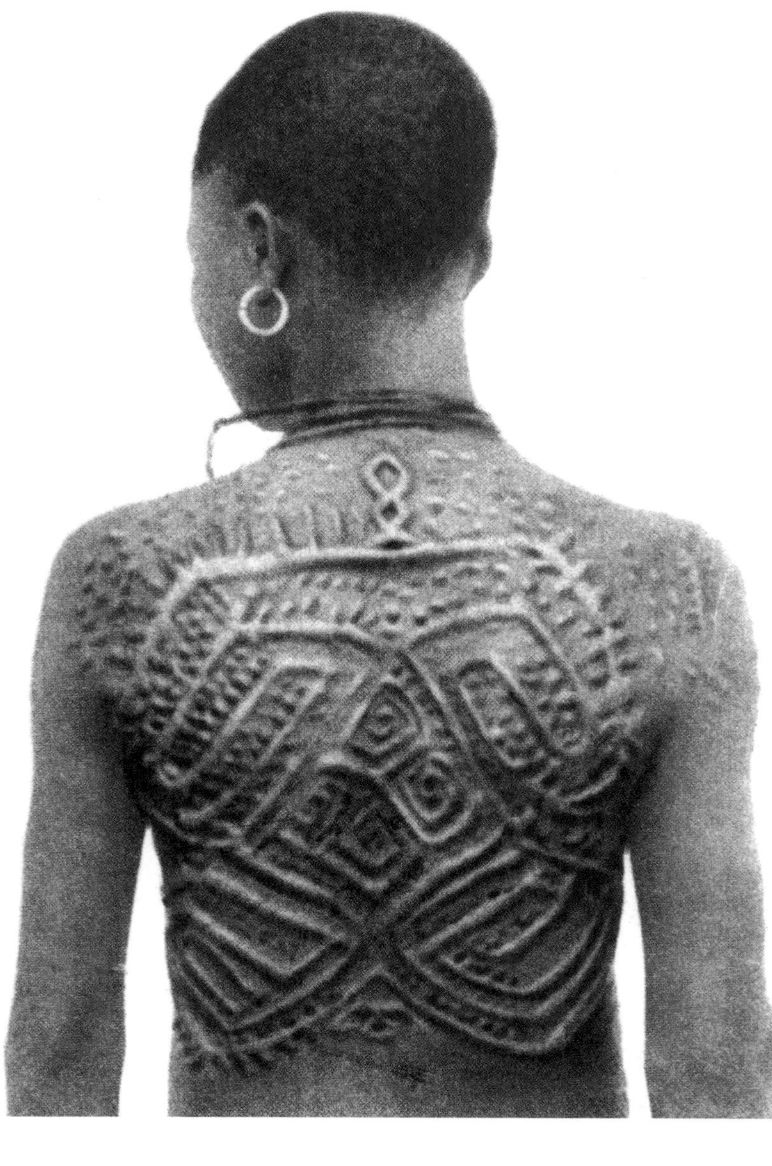

above:
Kuba fabric, RDC ©Revue Noire

right:
Mayumbe scarification, c. 1920 ©D.R.

From the frock to the "sape" (extravagant dressing)

The first photographs taken in Saint-Louis, Bassam or Lagos, dating from the end of the 19th century and the beginning of the 20th century, reveal a dandy-like sophistication in the clothing, in the completely European suits that are a far cry from the image of Tintin in the Congo. The extreme care given to the art of dressing remains one of the fundamental traditional aspects of urban living, regardless of whether the outfit falls under local, European or international fashions. Even the rapper will adhere to the most minute details of the image. Whether for holidays, ceremonies, outings or a studio photograph sitting, perfumed and neatly dressed princes and princesses all look the same, regardless of whether they are stepping out of bourgeois or miserable homes: they remain princesses and princes all the same. The clothing and jewelry will be rented, borrowed or purchased, such that the mason, saleswoman, secretary or entrepreneur will each find his/her own underlying identity. It is the jewels and embroidery that make the social difference. As a result, in many African countries, although the foreigner sees only the underlying misery, this misery is counterbalanced by these moments that transcend a reality sometimes experienced with difficulty: the "true" reality is the one lived during these moments, and not the reverse. In Kinshasa or Brazzaville, the "Sapeurs" (a young man, often in Zaire or Congo, who is a kind of dandy, dressing elegantly and organizing great parties and galas in order to present his elegance and to compete with others), not only make an art of dressing, but also turn it into a piece of theatrical art. This art becomes part of the concert, in an attempt to steal the limelight away, even for a moment, from the biggest singers or musical groups, who are also wearing monstrous outfits.

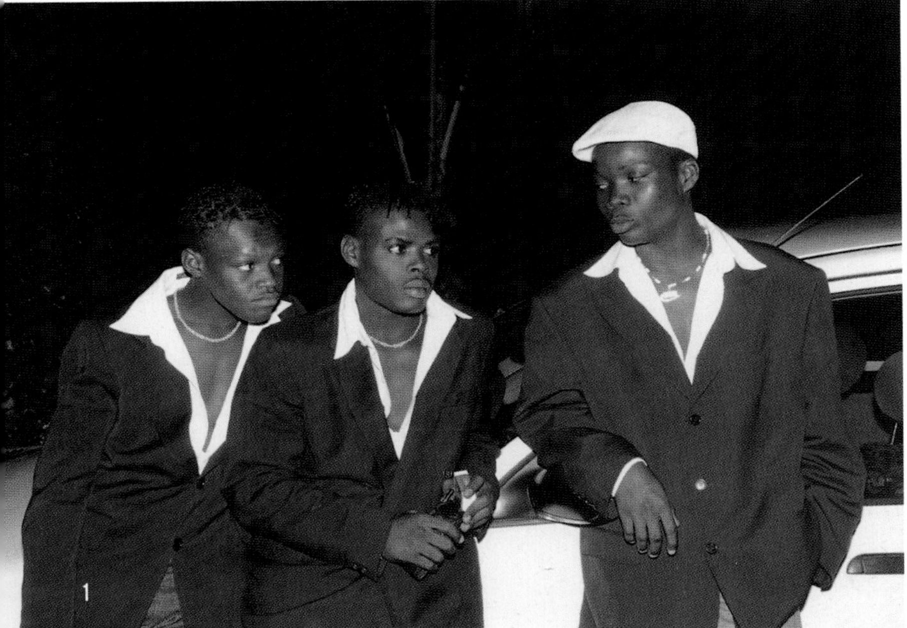
1

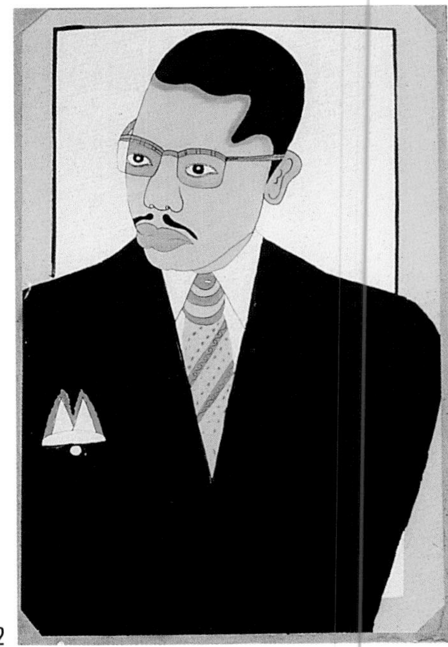
2

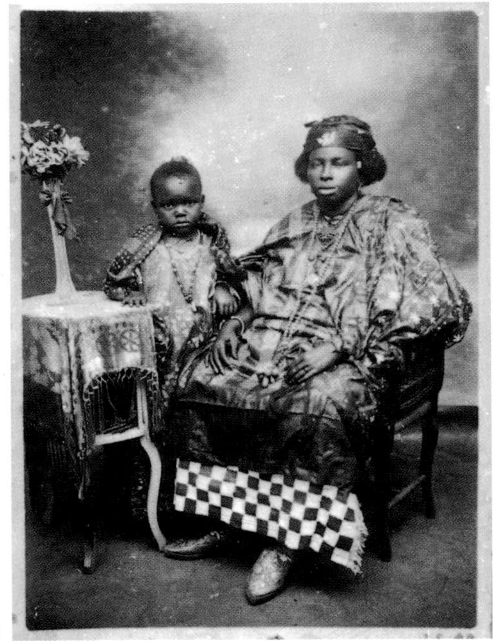
3

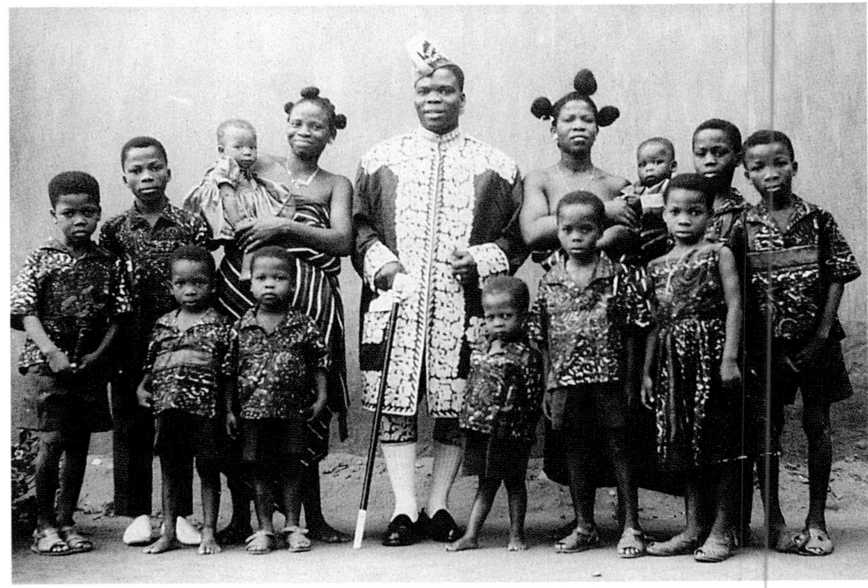
4

Could this be considered visual arts? This is probably the heart of African visual arts, with this artistic cross-cutting that is at the basis of the originality of African cultures. When dressing up, the clothing does not have to be new or original; however, it must, according to a given code, be the most spectacular, the most perfect, the most fitting according to a collective mental image, to an idea shared by all, and not the individual. The way one walks and one's facial expression is as important as how one is dressed and made up. This "sape" phenomenon can be found in the African Diasporas around the world, from New York to Bahia. Owning is being, or being is owning: a new relationship with material culture difficult for a Westerner to grasp. The wearer of the outfit does not have to have the house and material lifestyle that go along with it. It does not matter whether home is a small, comfortless room or a plush house.

Photography

It is now easier to understand why photographic studies proliferate in Africa more so than photographic reporters and invent, for each person photographed, a universe that transforms reality into a series of meanings and codes, most of which the mere onlooker cannot understand. The approach taken by the person manufacturing the photographic image is not unlike the approach taken by the manufacturer of a ritual statuette: no copying from reality, but rather a sublimation, transcendence or immanence of reality. Photography, the royal tool for objectifying reality, was created for this purpose, and is thus used to transform reality and to show another reality. This takes us back to one of the first comments we made in this work on the transparency of the techniques and technologies of others. One gets dressed up for a photograph, to send a message to the family and the village, with flowers, silver notes on the forehead, an entire

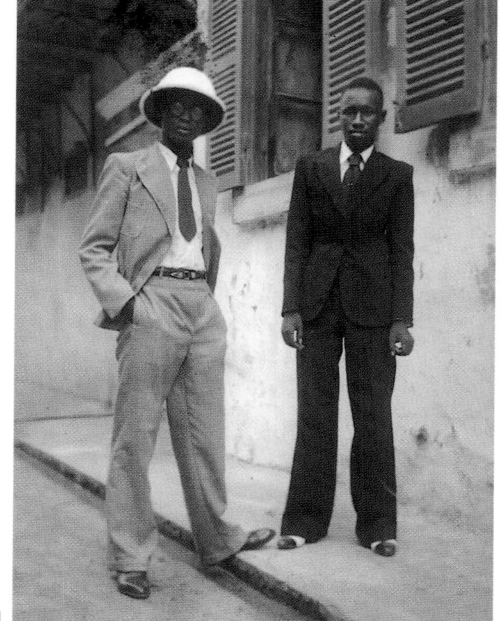
4

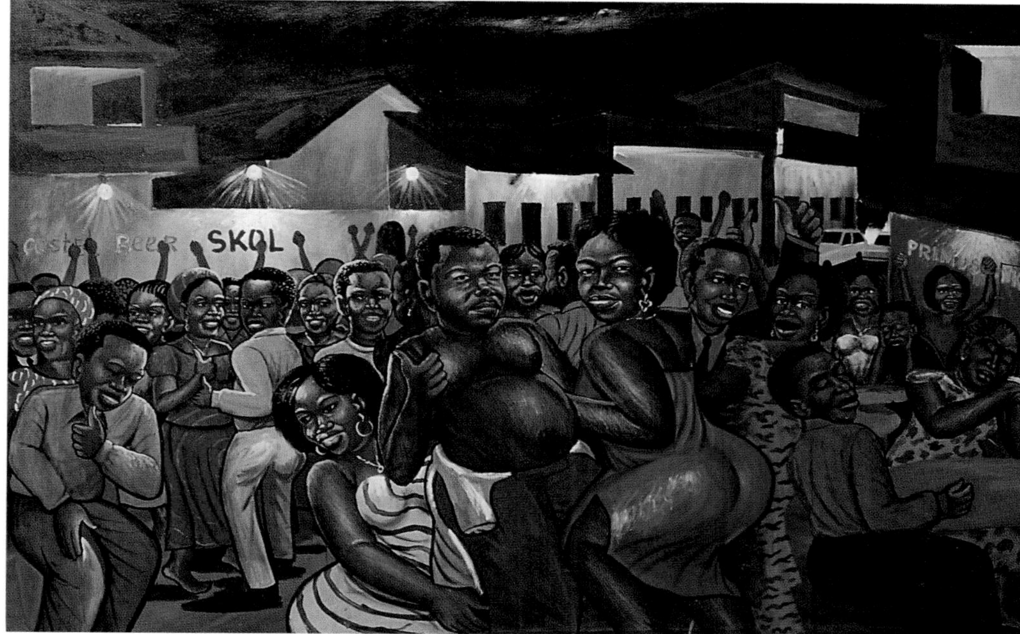

5

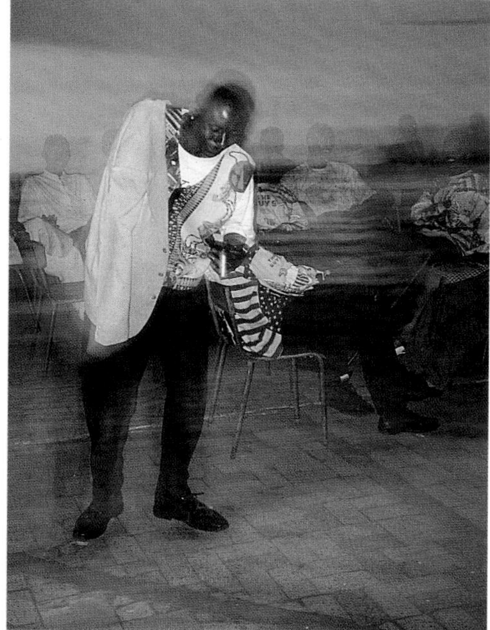
6

left page:
1. **Abidjan, 1998** ©Bruno de Medeiros
2. **Anonymous, Senegal,** "Portrait of Cheikh Tidjane Sy" ©MAAO
3. **Saint-Louis, Senegal, c.a. 1930,** unknown photographer, ©Revue Noire
4. **Benin, c.a. 1950** ©Joseph Moïse Agbodjelou

right page:
4. **Saint-Louis, Senegal, c.a. 1930,** unknown photographer ©Revue Noire
5. **Moké (born in 1950), RDC, 1996** ©Yves Pitchen/Revue Noire
6. **A Kinshasa 'firefighter', RDC, 1996** ©Yves Pitchen/Revue Noire

series of codes that can be read by the person or persons receiving it. The outfit, make-up and body posture will be a series of signs that appear, as such, in line with the relationship that traditional cultures have with reality, that urban men and women maintain. The décor is as important as the outfit and the pose, and the photographer is chosen for his décor. This is not a solely African phenomenon. The studio photographer's backdrop is always painted as a cyclorama. An illusion that does not seek to copy reality, but to represent it, the painting, like the outfit or the statuette, suggests the meaning of reality. Without being too caricatural or allusive, the illusion does not cheat. It states, through the subject used – almost always a rich and modern house, a modern city with modern buildings, or, at least, trendy fabrics, whether draped or spread out – the individual's projection, his social desire, his concern with others. The real house does not exist. Only the one in the studio is of any importance.

The house

The brick or mud house does, however, exist. Whatever the size, it must correspond not only to a functional need, but also, probably, to a more complex image, because the house itself is connected to the life that unfolds within. Aside from the larger bourgeois homes, most popular homes in divided or "spontaneous" neighborhoods (not to say, squatted neighborhoods) follow, on the one hand, a representation of the city's social and physical entity, where the façade may or may not be of any importance, depending on the country and culture, and, on the other hand, the notion of a somewhat big family, once again depending on the culture (even if the house has a room to rent out to strangers). People live both inside and outside, and often more outside than in. Therefore, the house exists, above all, to establish and delimit a closed exterior social space.

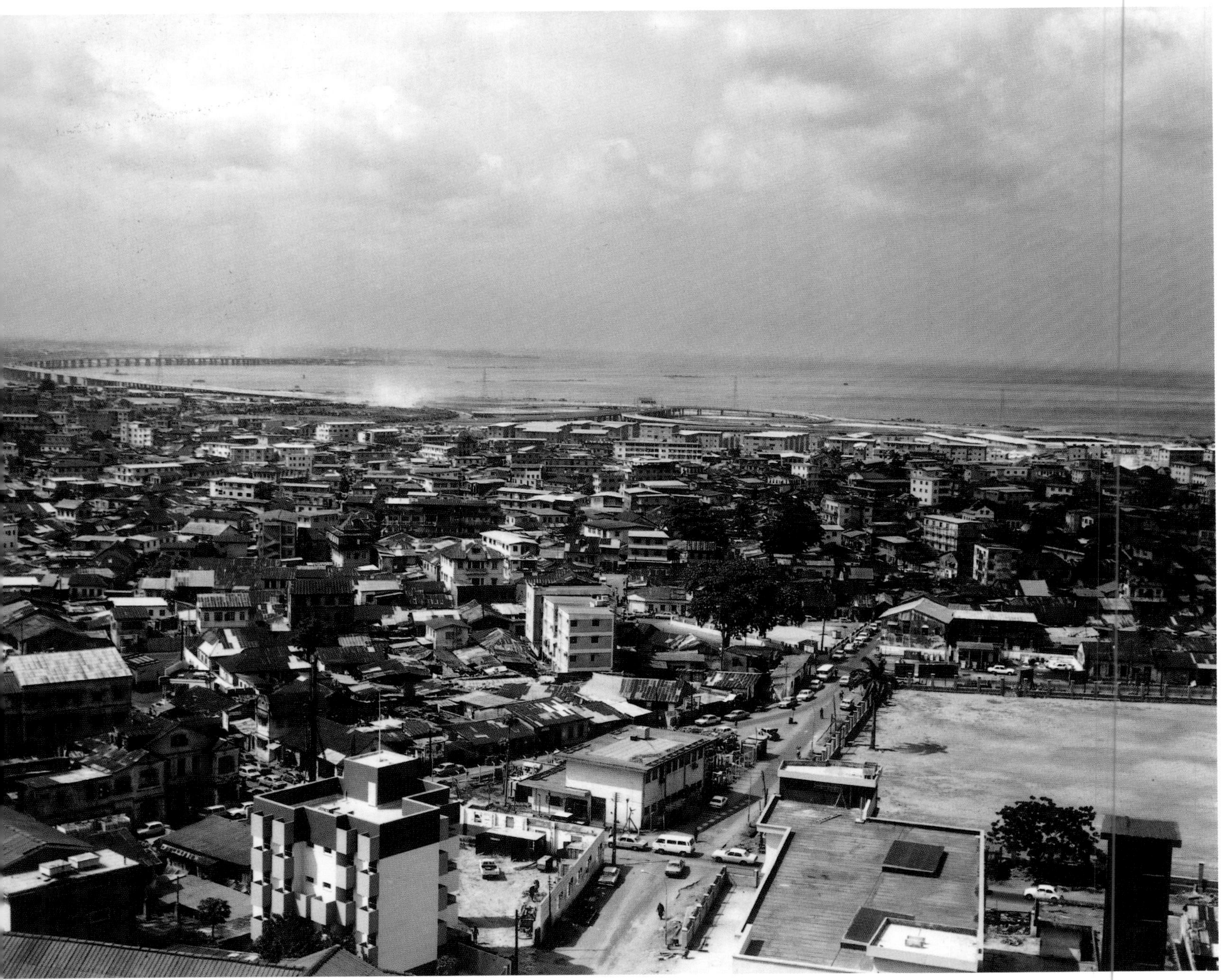

The built portion is used to harbor objects, provide intimacy for intimate moments, and to take shelter during storms. The size and configuration of the yard are essential, whereas the actual built house may be reduced to its simplest form: an enclosure. The enclosure is indicative of the dwelling. Respecting the city's life consists in building elements that reproduce what forms the city, what represents it. Thus, it is more important to conform than to identify oneself. This explains all the types of houses that strike a balance between colonial architectures (a square house, with a separate story, porch, cloth roofs) and an international style with traditional architectural references, of which the yard is the major element.

Urban Africa

Architecture is rarely an object isolated in a context. It (almost) becomes systematically integrated in an urban environment that it helps build. Reinforcing the comment made by Elikia M'Bekolo on cities and African urban tradition, the notion of urbanity is closely tied into the different historical African societies (even nomadic societies with temporary dwellings). They are federated around the housing development (village, borough or city), with concrete and physical markings of all symbolic elements forming the social, economic, spiritual and cultural cohesion. More so than today, the African housing development is a formal urban model resulting from the organization of each society. Nevertheless, the transformations of the housing development resulting from the invasion of the international city's political, economic and cultural model, initially embodied by the colonial city, have taken over today's African city. The materialism of money, the solitude of the individual, and social violence have made African cities not unlike other cities. Even though

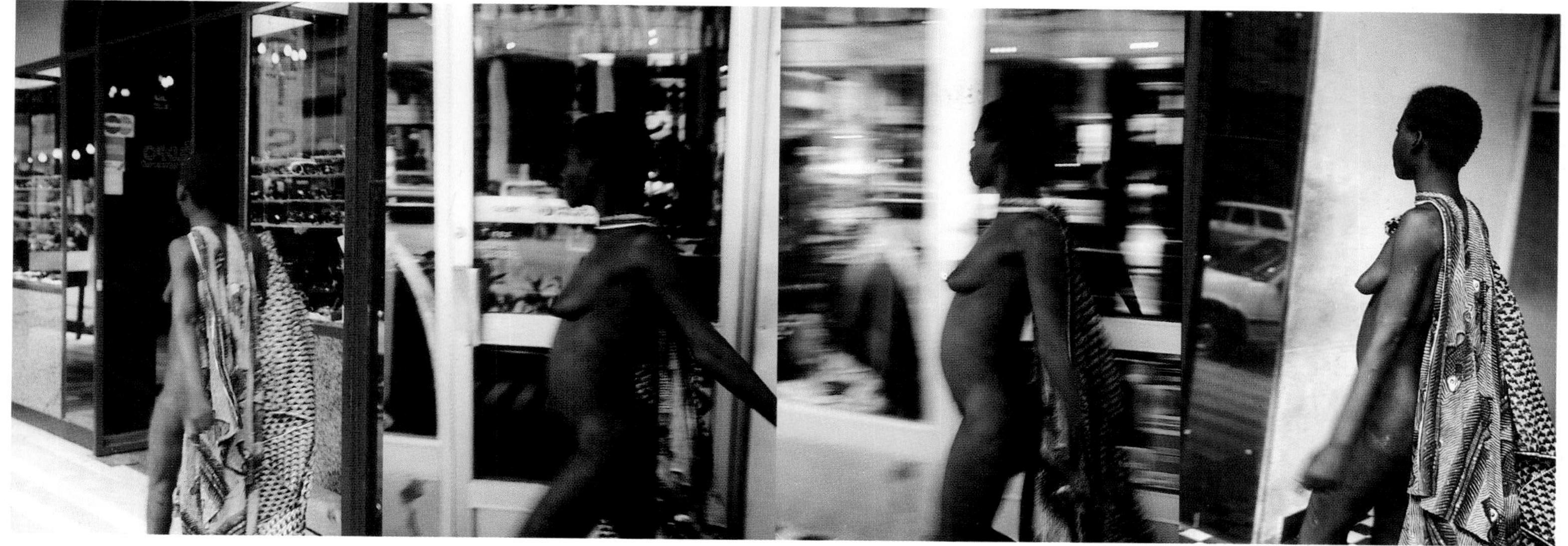

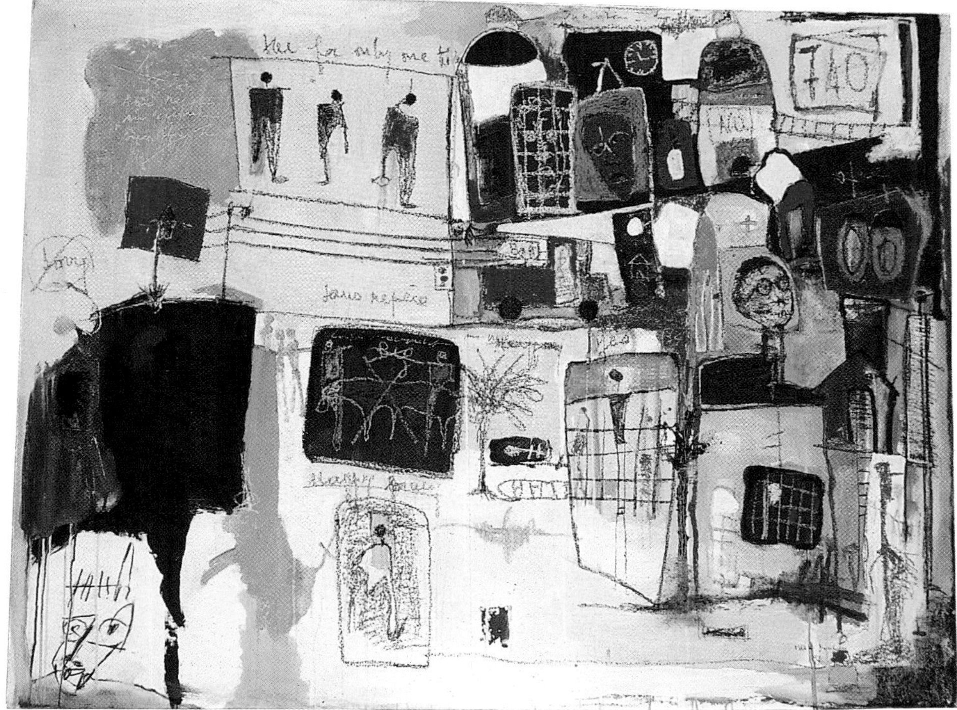

facing page:
Lagos, Nigeria ©Akinbode Akinbiyi

top:
Abidjan, Ivory Coast, 1992 ©Dorris Haron Kasco

bottom:
Joël Mpah Dooh (born 1956), Cameroon, 1997
©Galerie Mam

the "rurality" of most of the populations of each nation could be mentioned, the cultural referent of the modern city has become overwhelming. This referent includes "a vast process of individualization containing as many lows (fracture of ancient solidarities) as highs (emancipation of the dominated classes)," says Elikia M'Bekolo in the following text. How much longer and for how many generations will the urban and rural traditional cultural and social content still remain the backdrop of modern urban African identity?
This is the framework that has been harboring, for several generations, all of the new cultural and artistic expressions, including plastic arts.

Typology of demand

Although, in the field of music, dance and textile creation, symbioses gave form and dimension to a modern and varied African production, integrated within its own demand, and, therefore, its own market, the expression of demand in plastic arts was more subtle and sometimes ambiguous.
There are different types, namely:
- a new popular art for advertising and décor aimed at the population (houses, popular public places, such as night clubs, rotisseries, and maquis), which includes photography.
- a syncretic art related to ancestral traditions tinged with Western influences, such as Senegalese glass frames or colonist statuary, and also to the works of artists "inhabited" by messages and destinies, such as Bruly Bouabré.
- a "fine art," related to the birth of the artist, as we will see in the following chapter, aimed at travelers, foreign residents, and "cultured" colonists who want artistic work resembling Western canons, but with an African subject.

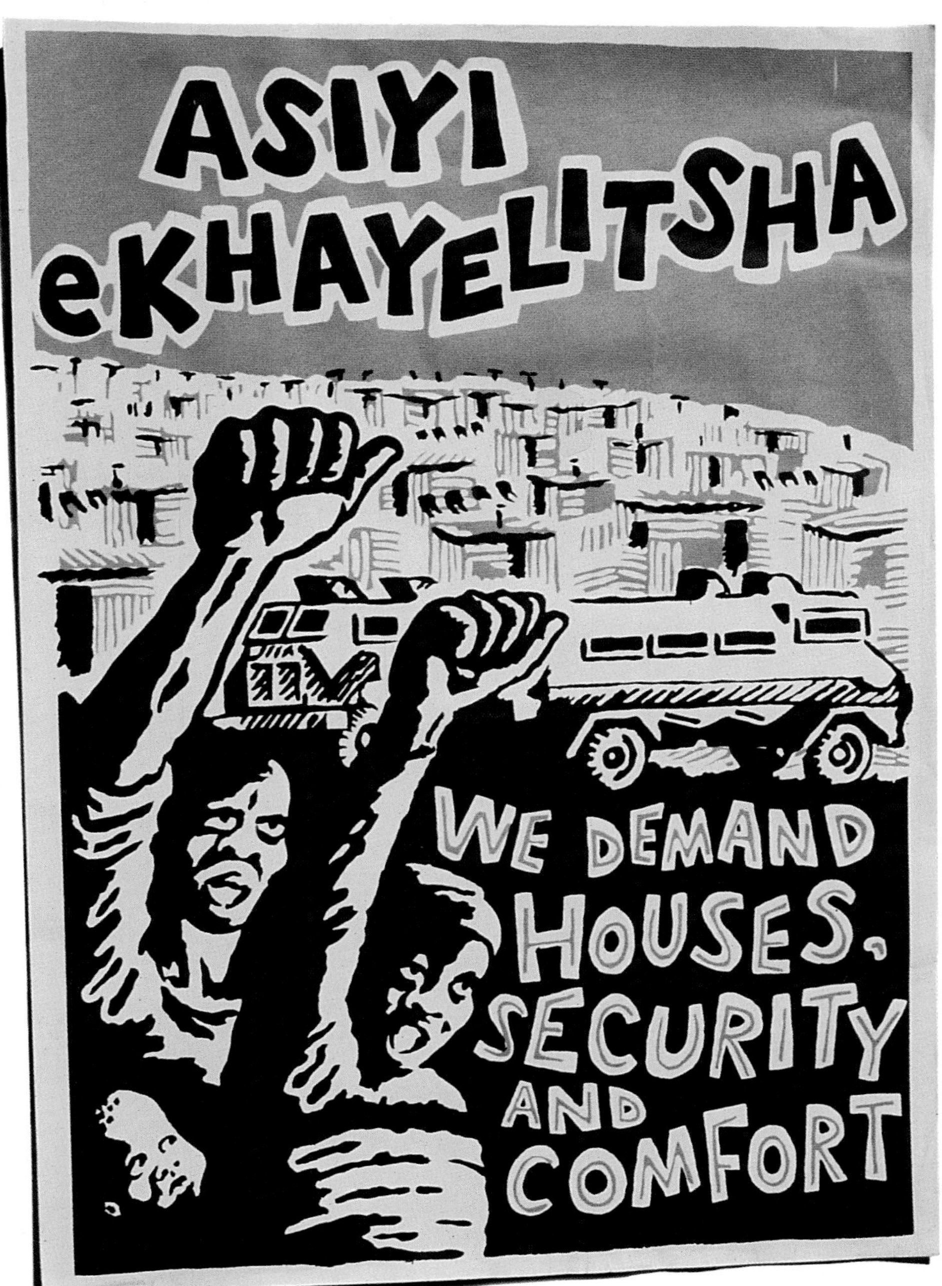

- airport art: souvenirs, a caricature of the image of an ideal Africa, aimed at the same types of people, but not cultured.

This breakdown is based on an analysis of demand, even if many creations are not produced based on demand alone. However, demand influences form, and vice versa, in cities undergoing constant evolution, when different types of disorders do not undermine the minimum amount of stability required for new practices and new markets to flourish. With the double phenomenon of increasingly poor populations and a wealthier bourgeoisie that is increasingly open to the world, the vitality of survival, related, for certain artists, to a revival in creativity, is in line with a continuously insurrectional context. Elikia M'Bekolo will be speaking about the typical African city-dweller, who, through a "passionate attitude," will foster the "coexistence of individualism, submission and a spirit of rebellion." The African artist does not escape from this. It is in this context that he will express, often through metaphors, his different types of anger, weariness and hope. There are few or no direct meanings. The art of litotes and metaphors prevails. Thus, a singer will more readily sing about the wounds of Africa than about those of his own country in order to avoid censure or political disgrace, but everyone understands. In painting, we find the compulsory subject of South African apartheid being painted by generations who did not experience any in their countries, in order to be able to express the political violence that occurs in their homelands. The fight against apartheid becomes the fight against all violence carried out by arbitrary powers.

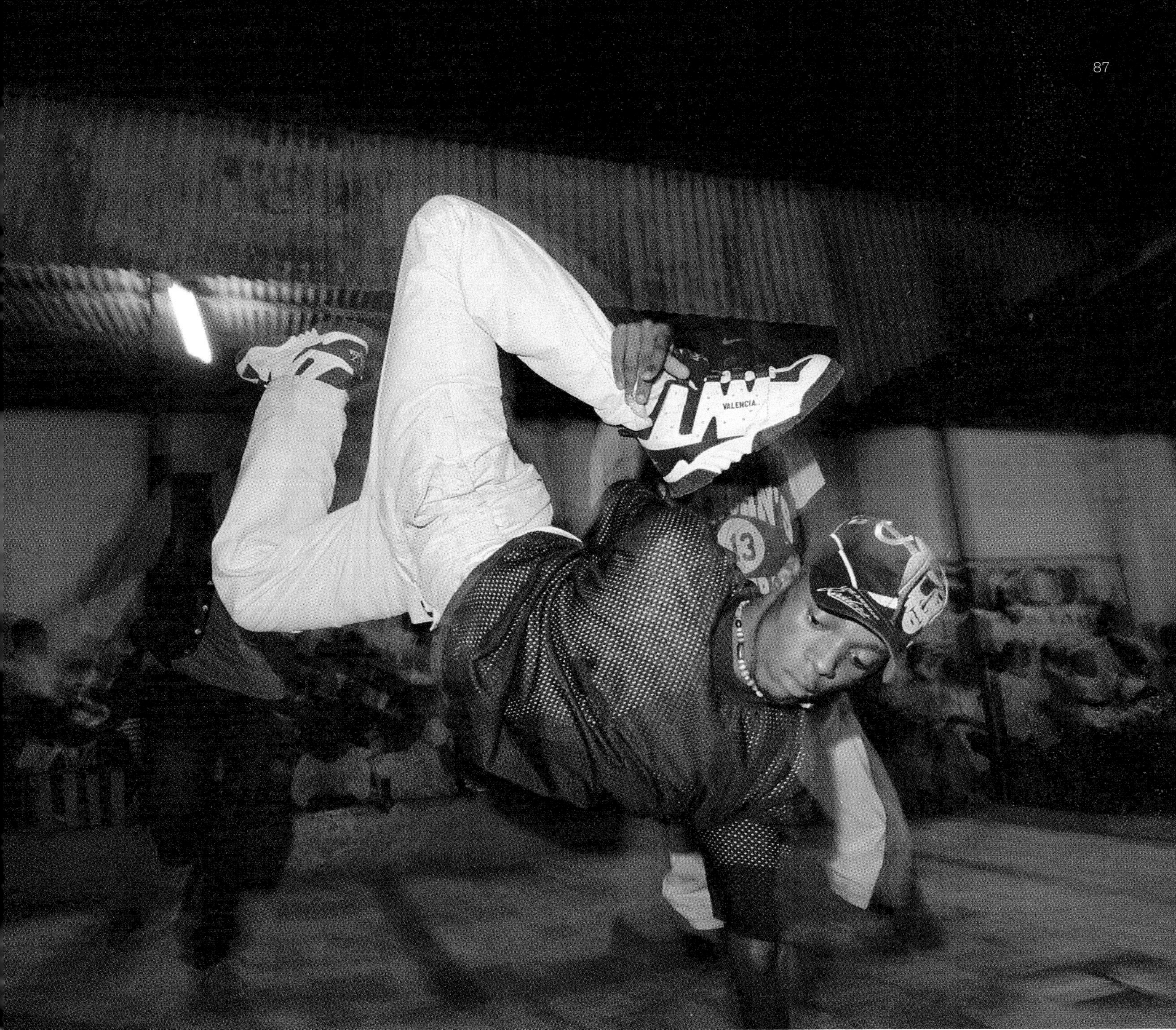

above:
Poster "Community Arts Project,"
Cape Town, South Africa ©Sue Willimason

facing page:
Dancer from the TNM group, Kinshasa, RDC, 1996
©Yves Pitchen/Revue Noire

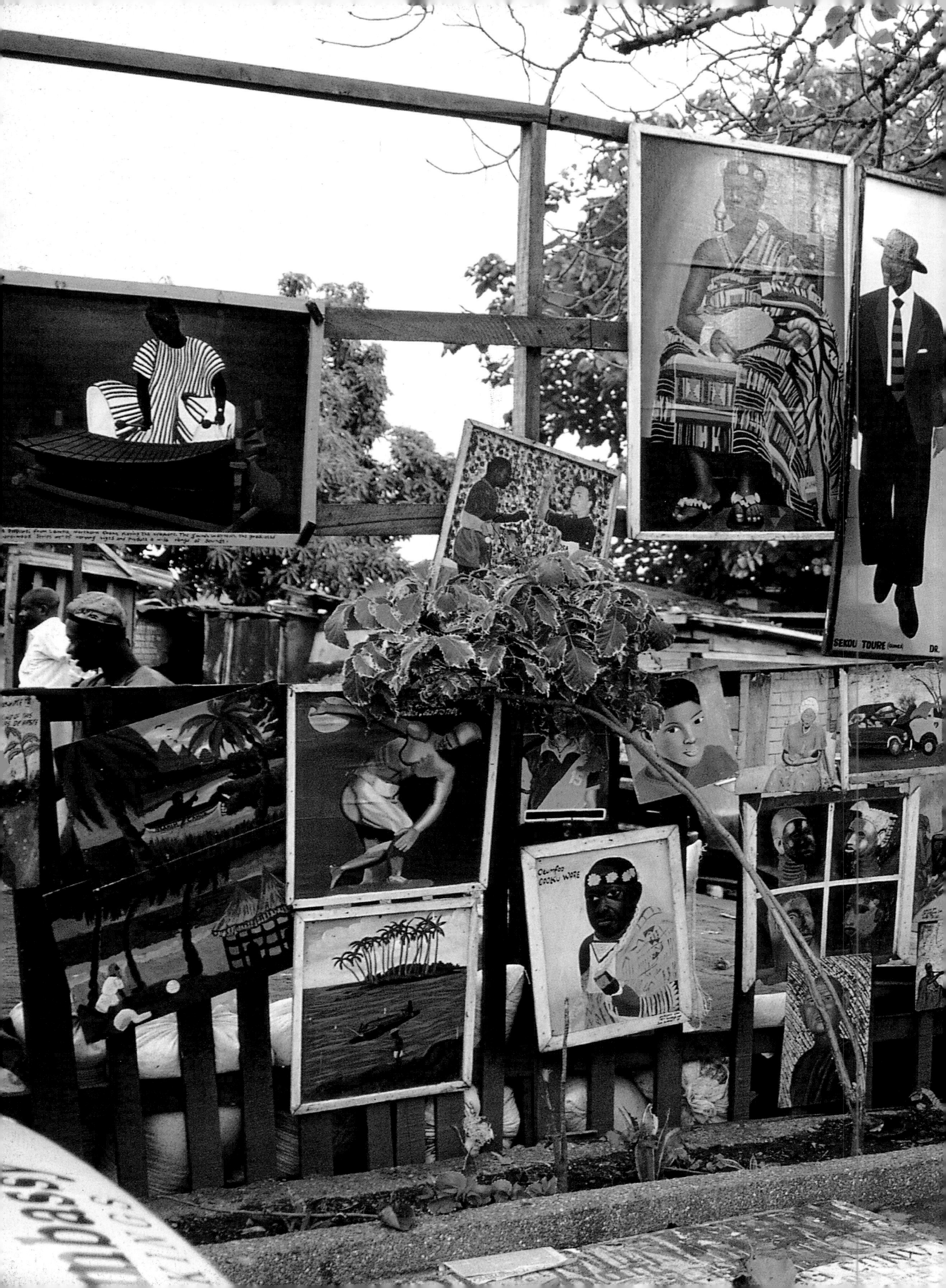
SEKOU TOURE

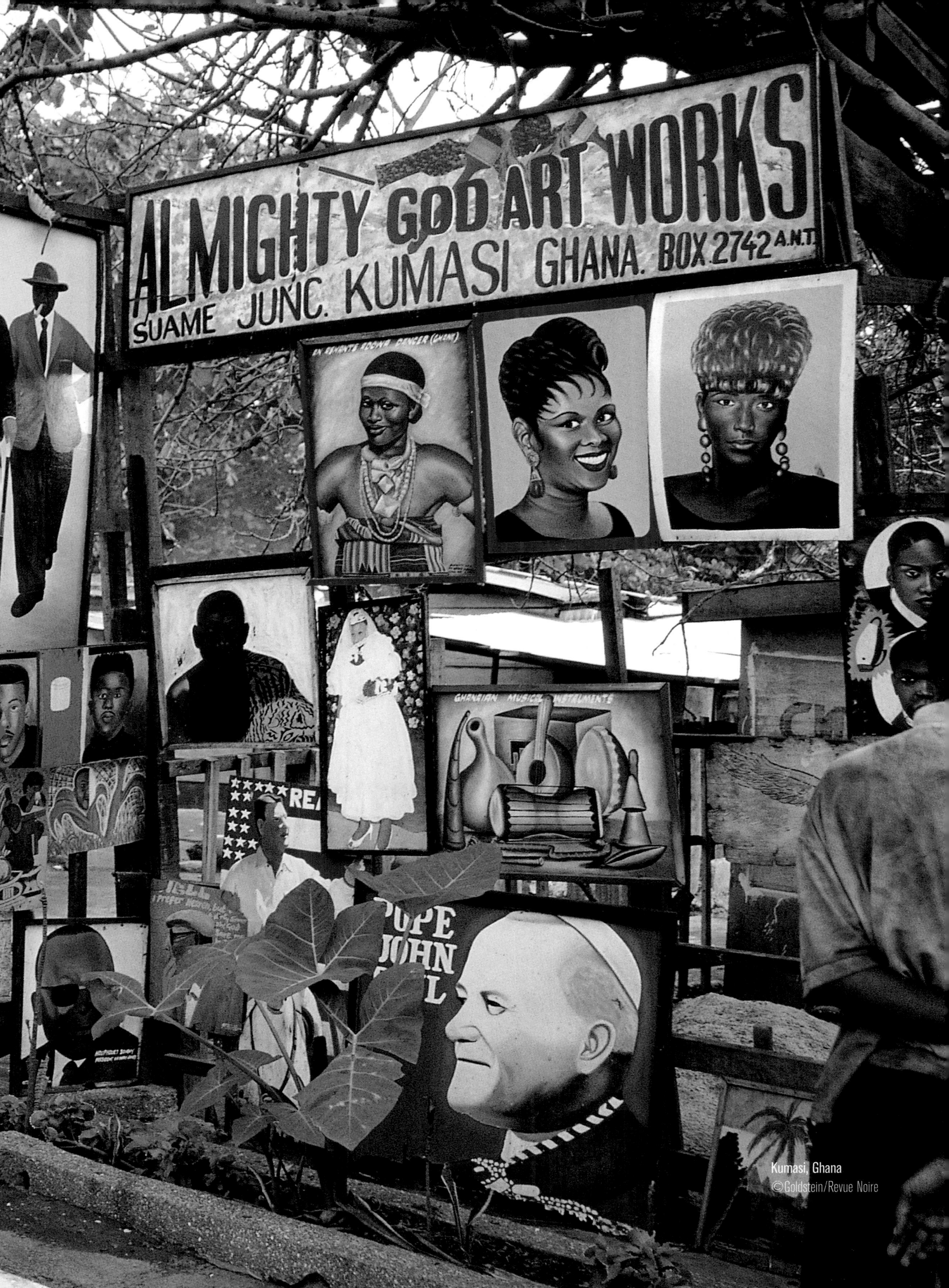

Kumasi, Ghana
©Goldstein/Revue Noire

Birth of the colonial cities

Elikia M'Bokolo

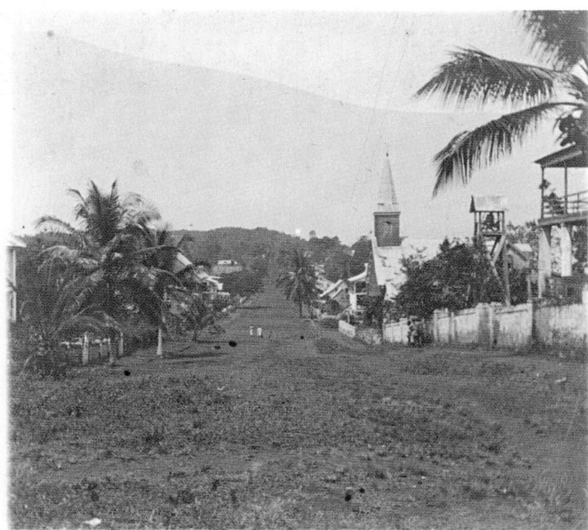

Moravia, Liberia, c.a. 1890 ©D.R.

Considered to be the sign par excellence of modernity and to be the privileged place of the modernization process, the African cities we know today were long seen, and are often still seen, as exclusive and unilateral ex nihilo creations of colonization. In reality, the formation of African cities under colonization observed very complex mechanisms, which, when taken into consideration, casts doubt on the antagonistic couple "Rural African" – "Urban Africa" that was supposed to express the change brought about with colonization. We should highlight that, in the evolution of contemporary Africa, the chronology of its political history (that of colonization) and the chronology of its social history (that of urbanization) are relatively autonomous. In its political history, the ruptures corresponding to the height of colonization were sometimes brutal. Conversely, in its social history, unquestionable ruptures coexist with numerous, often misunderstood continuities.

If we are looking to date the urban phenomenon in Africa, it is quite clear that it was not colonization that created African cities. When the Europeans began the process of dismantling and dividing up Africa at the Berlin Conference (1884-1885), the continent already had numerous cities and genuine urban civilization in certain regions. Far from rejecting them all, the colonizers tried to capture some of these urban dynamics before the African societies could take them back again.

Some of these ancient cities were purely African and stood, depending on the regions, as political capitals, commercial metropolises, religious cities or even military forts.

Dakar, Senegal, subdivision plan from 1871

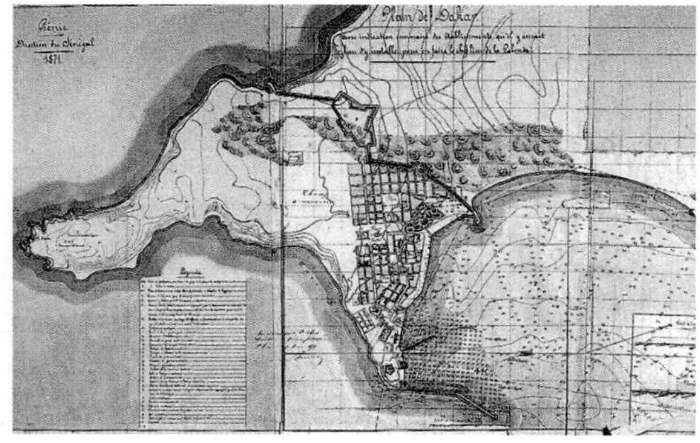

Rich in urban civilizations dating to the Middle Ages, western, Sahelian and Sudanese Africa is home to a great number of them. The old trans-Saharan trade "terminals," such as Oualatta, Timbuktu, Agades, Kuka and Abeche, continue to thrive, despite the growth of trade on the Atlantic, which provides benefits to coastal cities to the detriment of those in the interior. However, not everything is collapsing within the continent. Thus, next to the Haussa cities, which are trying to remain stable, the political and religious revolution started by Ousman Dan Fodio at the beginning of the 19th century led to the creation or development of housing developments such as Sokoto, a religious capital, and Kano, a trade metropolis. During the travels of the German explorer Heinrich Barth (1848-1853), Kano was a large city whose "great advantage was that trade and industry stood hand in hand, providing work for almost every family." The activities that created the fortune of Kano today were already popular at this time, namely textile craftsmanship and industry, hide and leather work, the money trade and banking. Political and economic evolution, characterized by the reinforcement of state structures, as in Ashanti and Dahomey, and by the dynamism of commercial activities, produced the same effects. Kumasi, the capital city of the Ashanti kingdom (modern day Ghana) is credited with 30,000 inhabitants in the mid-19th century. Further east, in Yoruba country (Nigeria), following wars that accompanied political restructuring, new cities were initially formed as places of refuge, before becoming dynamic through the growth of exchanges and the arrival of the "Saros," former slaves who settled in Sierra-Leone and who became the perfect example of "cultural intermediaries." In about 1850-1860, Ibadan had about 60,000 inhabitants and Abeokuta 100,000.

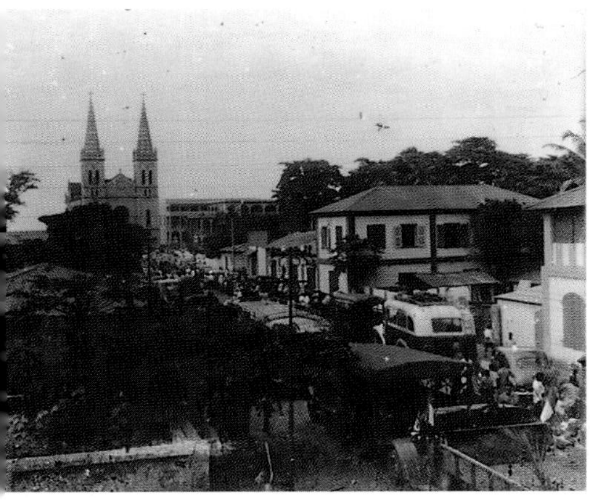
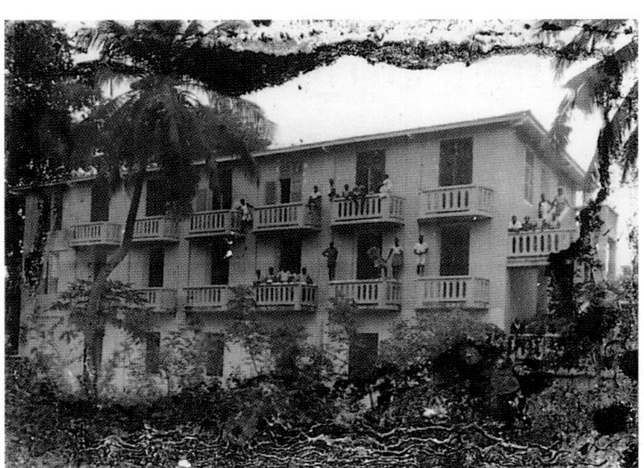
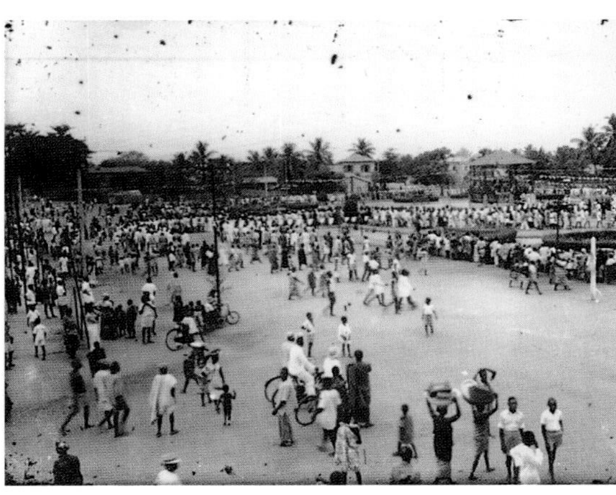
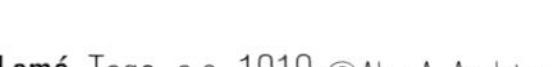

Lomé, Togo, c.a. 1910 ©Alex A. Acolatse

Central and southern Africa are traditionally considered not to have undergone similar urban formations. These ideas, however, should be reviewed. Although, due to building materials, the African cities in this region often did not leave behind any durable traces, they did, however, exist. As commercial crossroads or political capitals, some of them still exist today, despite the changes imposed by colonization. It is not by chance that the two rival colonizing states, Belgium and France, ended up establishing their respective capitals, Leopoldville (Kinshasa) and Brazzaville, face to face. Pool Malebo, where these two metropolises are found, had always been the primary location for bulk breaking in the "great Congolese trade" network between the land routes (on the Pool side) and the water routes (north of the Pool, where the river becomes navigable). It was here that very dense and long-standing human settlements were established. There, in the 19th century, four administratively independent groups shared the same activities, the same very elaborate social organization and the same cultural practices and conceptions: Mfwa and Mpila on the right bank; Kinshasa and Ntamo on the left bank. Similarly, the Arab-Swahili and Luso-African trade networks that spread throughout the continent from Zanzibar and Luanda, respectively, gave rise to a series of large trade centers. Some of these centers, such as Tabora and Ujiji (Tanzania) or Kisangani (Democratic Republic of Congo) survived colonial control.

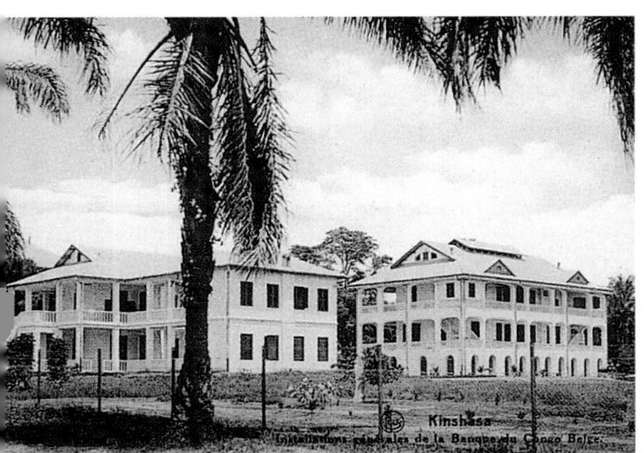

Léopoldville (Kinshasa), DRC
©D.R.

Cities of foreign origin existed on the coasts and were the beginnings of the modern colonial cities.

Very early on, Arab emigrants esta-blished trading posts on the Indian Ocean in Zanzibar, Mogadishu, Mom-basa, Pangani and Kilwa. These posts experienced an incredible boom in the 19th century, after the Sultan of Oman transferred the capital of his States to Zanzibar and built a genuine commercial empire from the island. While maintaining their essentially commercial functions, these cities experienced considerable growth in their populations, which changed into societies dominated by class structures rather than lineage structures. As masters of political power who were also involved in trade activities, the Arabs saw a bourgeoisie of bankers (almost exclusively of Indian origin) and planters (Arabs and Swahilis) form at their side. A widespread proletariat, which included household and plantation slaves, as well as precarious workers, with the main group being the porters, developed below them.

Saint-Louis, Senegal, c. 1930, unknown photographer ©Revue Noire

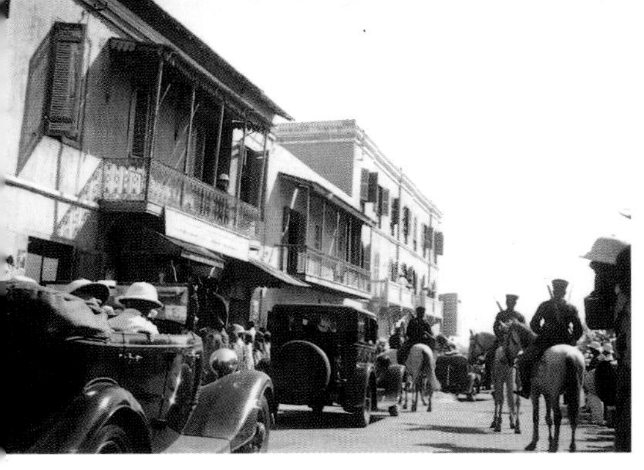

From the coast of Mozambique, to Saint-Louis in Senegal, passing through the Cape of Good Hope, flourished Euro-pean trading posts that had either been strategic forts (Cape Town, Goree), administrative capitals (Dakar), or, most often, hubs of the slave trade, such as Luanda, Saint-Louis, Gold Coast forts (Ghana), and the sadly notorious "Slave Coast," from Togo to Nigeria (such as Ouidah and Porto-Novo in modern day Benin). In the 19th century, former slave colonies were transformed into cosmo-politan cities: English Freetown, first populated by slaves repatriated from Great Britain and Nova Scotia, then slaves pulled off slave ships; Libreville, its French counterpart, where slaves cap-tured by the French Navy were mixed with the inhabitants of the Gabon estuary villages.

Djenne, Mali ©D.R.

Colonial urbanization, both continuous and violent, developed in this urban framework. The colonizers abandoned only very few existing urban centers, whether they were prestigious centers such as Timbuktu and Djenne in central Sudan, or Goree and Abomey in western Africa, the river cities and land crossroads of central Africa. Colonial urbanization actually developed using different formulas. In certain cases, ancient sites were re-inhabited and restructured based on the needs of the colonial administration and, especially, of European trade. In other cases, new cities were established, sometimes ex nihilo, but most often on previously known sites.

The role of the State was decisive throughout the continent in creating, stabilizing and promoting the colonial cities. All of the colonial regimes had fortified posts and colonization posts used as administrative centers for the territory, warehouse cities or capitals. The choice of capitals always helped the quick development of cities, as evidenced by many examples, such as Dakar and Brazzaville, respective capitals of the federations of French West Africa and French Equatorial Africa; Leopoldville (Kinshasa) in Belgian Congo (D.R.C.); Dar es Salaam in Tanganyika; Yaounde and Ouagadougou instead and in place of Duala and Bobo-Dioulasso. It was also the public powers that established innumerable regulations concerning access to land ownership, urban planning and architectural standards, health and hygiene rules used as the basis for segregating Blacks from Whites. But the economy also played a sometimes decisive role where colonial capitalism was able to flourish through the development of mining resources, as in southern and central Africa.

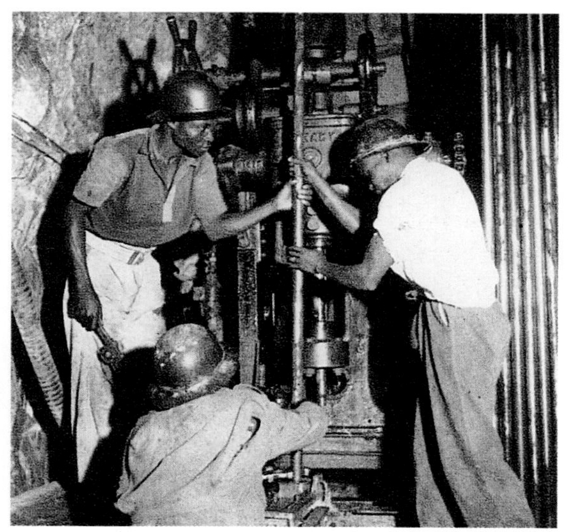

Miners in Belgian Congo ©D.R.

South Africa was the first to see mining towns erected. These were initially mushroom towns, the largest of which still exist today. It is not that Africans did not know how to mine underground metals. Copper and gold had been worked for centuries and had led to internal exchanges and a very active and very beneficial international trade. However, things began to change with the discovery of the Griqualand diamond in 1867, and, especially, with the discovery of the Rand gold in 1886. Overnight, there was a real rush on South Africa. Gold diggers, poor wretches dreaming of making a quick fortune, and money buccaneers, who gained control of everything, flocked here from every corner of the earth, and especially from Great Britain. However, the mushroom towns ended up becoming permanent fixtures on the landscape dating to the pre-colonial times, thanks, in part, to the Blacks. The first miners were, in fact, proletarianized Blacks who, after fiercely resisting the Boers and the English, yielded before firearms during the second half of the 19th century, and who, in the new industrial economy, had nothing more to offer than the strength of their arms. Urban growth occurred at a dizzying pace in this region. In less than a generation, the so-called Langlaagte, where gold had been discovered, had become Johannesburg, and was more populated, more cosmopolitan and richer than the capital Pretoria.

Similar phenomena occurred at the beginning of the 20th century, in the Katanga and Northern Rhodesia (Zambia) copperbelt. This region's development would pick up from the 1920s with the growing demand for copper caused by the development of the electrical industry and the automobile industry in western Europe and in the United States. The mining of Katanga copper posed, among others, a problem with labor in a region that was both under-populated and rebellious to colonial domination. The Union Minière du Haut-Katanga (Mining Union of Upper Katanga), formed in 1906, had to undertake greater prospecting in other provinces of the Congo (DRC) and in neighboring colonies, such as Angola, Northern Rhodesia, Nyassaland (Malawi) and Mozambique. This is why, in the late 1950s, the "copper capital," Elizabethville (Lubumbashi), still had a very colorful population, only 39% of which came from Katanga. The other city dwellers came or were the descendents of people coming primarily from the neighboring Kasai (54%), Kivu and Rwanda-Urundi. The experience of Katanga, where many workers from Northern Rhodesia came to work, facilitated the recruiting of a labor force for the copper mines of this country from the 1920s.

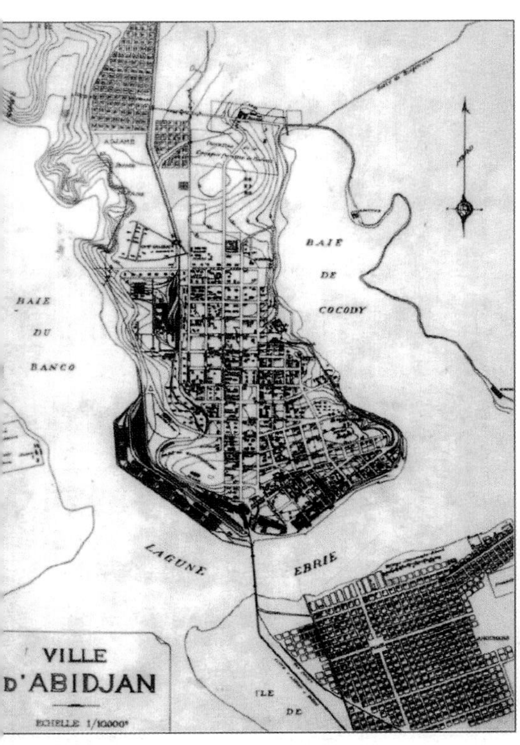

Map of Abidjan, Ivory Coast, c. 1933

The mining economy in central and southern Africa required the development of a network of both vast and relatively dense railways. The railways would, in turn, become privileged axes of the urban network.

Regardless of the formulas or conditions used to form and develop the colonial cities, the pace of this transformation was, overall, similar in all cases.

During the first decades of colonization growth was slow, except in a few mining enclaves and along certain axes of communication. At this time, the urban population was far from being "stabilized," to use a colonial concept. Lacking in qualifications, poorly paid and poorly staffed by the colonial administration, and thereby generally escaping the control of the authorities, the city dwellers were, in reality, migrants going from mine to mine, from one town to the next, without excluding a temporary or definitive return to the village. The fear of death played a major role in the displacement of this work force ridden with disease and threatened by a soaring mortality rate. Up until World War I, the mortality rate in the Katanga mines was between 70 and 140 per thousand, a high level due to poor living conditions, malnutrition and new diseases, including pneumonia. The colonizers, therefore, had to implement whatever measures were necessary to keep the new city dwellers in place, while keeping them at a respectable distance from the Europeans.

During this initial phase, the colonial cities maintained durable characteristics: a strict division of the urban space between the European and African neighborhoods, and the prison environment of the African towns. The segregation of Whites and Blacks, which began at the end of the 19th century, was not particular to southern Africa. All African cities tried out the color bar with an intensity that varied depending on the era. This bar is based first and foremost on sanitary considerations, justified, in the eyes of the colonizers, by the frequency of epidemics, including yellow fever and the plague. Africans were then cleared out of the urban centers and thrown to the peripheries, whereas the Europeans settled on the plateaus and well-ventilated areas deemed healthy. Taught by history that "all empires will fall" and that all colonization will eventually collapse, the colonial States were not only concerned with separating Whites from Blacks, but also took care to protect Whites from any possible rioters and other criminals, whether collective or isolated. This is why there was almost always an empty space between the European city and the African neighborhoods, ostensibly occupied by a military camp. To this was often added an array of regulations, obligations and prohibitions (requirement to constantly wear a pass, prohibition from walking around the "white city" at night, etc.), the most complete set of which were offered by South Africa and the Belgian Congo.

After World War I, urban growth began to progressively quicken and its pace began to closely resemble that of the fluctuations in the global economy. But this was merely an impression, albeit probably true, which could not be backed up due to a lack of figures.

The "Roaring Twenties" witnessed relatively strong growth, related to the consolidation of the colonial hold, to the proliferation of voluntary migrations towards the cities and a semblance of economic prosperity. During the 1930s, the decade of the Great Depression, the continent experienced a combination of two reverse quantitative movements prolonged by World War II. First of all, due to the sudden increase in unemployment, there were considerably fewer people living in the cities. Secondly, encouraged by the crisis in export farming, there was a flow of "illegal" people moving to the cities, who were not registered in the official census logs. Thus, in South Africa, although the growth rate slowed down, overall flow was up: 25.1% of the population in 1921, 31.4% in 1935 and 38.4% in 1946. However, on the qualitative level, movements criticizing and opposing the colonial order spread.

The "Glorious Thirties," which corresponded to the years of political emancipation on the continent, was also a period of high urban growth, in quantitative terms, and of urban crisis, in qualitative terms. African urban growth corresponds to a general movement throughout all non-industrialized countries.

At the same time, the urbanization rate varied greatly from one region of Africa to the next, in obvious relation to the degree of integration in the global capitalist economy. It is not an exaggeration to say that this regional variation in rates goes hand in hand with the types of integration in the global economy: relatively high rates in mining economies (southern and central Africa), low rates in primarily agricultural economies.

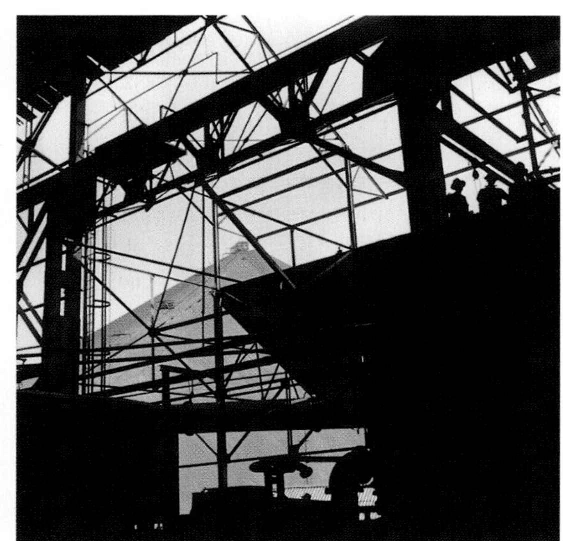

Belgian Congo, 1951 ©Pierre Verger

Although the numbers show that there was certain growth in the urban population, the same held true for what some people consider the "urban crisis." With the requirement for professional qualification, many jobs were created during the "Glorious Thirties," yet there was no supply of work for the growing demand from rural emigrants and young city dwellers without qualifications. Lacking in the means needed to obtain urban real estate, pay rising rents or build housing in compliance with the urban planning rules imposed by the colonizers ("hard" construction; the adoption of certain materials, such as cement, bricks, sheet metal and tiles; proper space ratios between the size of the family and the inhabitable surface), these unqualified youths took over urban areas that had not been provided with mains services, that were not properly equipped, but that were still beyond the reach of the public powers, and built dwellings in these areas using precarious materials. Although the word "bidonville" (shantytown), coined by Dr. Materi, first appeared in 1931 with respect to Tunis, this phenomenon was already somewhat widespread at this time and merely became worse subsequently. The South African townships, regulated by the Native Urban Areas Act of 1923, were an extreme case. While the Native Tryst and Land Act of 1913 had only left 7.3% of the land to "native reserves," thereby forcing Africans to work for Whites, the public authorities deemed that "by nature, Africans are not city dwellers and have not yet successfully adapted to urban life." Whereas the law recognized that certain classes of Africans were entitled to live in "townships," they were, however, prohibited from owning any property there. But the law was unable to withstand the pressure of a forced rural exodus: in Orlando, Sophiatown, the Eastern and Western "Native Townships," Alexandra, Soweto (South West Township), the native housing developments expanded around Johannesburg with catastrophic overpopulation and living conditions.

City life? Whether controlled or created by the Europeans, the urban environment always appeared as a hostile space for Africans. Well before the novel "Ville cruelle" (Cruel City) was written by the Cameroonian Eza Boto (Mongo Beti), published in 1954, numerous artists from southern and central Africa, and in particular musicians, had already illustrated the relevance of a theme found later on, in the 1980s, among sociologists, urbanists and politicians, which included notions of "urban pathology," "urban misery" and "urban evil," coined by, among others, Jean-Marc Ela (African Cities, Paris, Karthala, 1983). From the beginning of the 20th century, popular songs rejecting the hardships of urban life and glorifying, with nostalgia, the charms of village life, were coming from mining towns in South Africa.

However, over time, things began to slowly change. In the 1940s and 1950s, middle-of-the-road popular music, flourishing in the big South African, Ghanaian, Nigerian and Congolese cities, glorified, instead, the theme of the "happy city," a space of freedom, a place filled with all sorts of opportunities.

This complexity of urban life and its contradictions were felt by all city dwellers and by the most perceptive observers of African societies. "In Black Africa," states the Cameroonian sociologist Jean-Marc Ela, "the mass poverty of city dwellers can be felt on all street corners, masked by the music coming from the bars and the stream of conversations on

[1] Jean-Marc Ela, "African Cities," Paris, Khartala, p. 84

the last soccer game. The working-class districts are dens of misery unheard of in traditional society."[1]

There is undoubtedly no reason to compare disastrous "sociological realities" and the "social conscious" that is blind to these realities. For, in the picture of urban life, areas of darkness and light are constantly mingling. On the dark side, certain long-term traits are dominant: the weight of foreign domination, subsequently replaced by the ostentation and harshness of post-colonial authorities; unemployment, employment-related uncertainties and pressures; the anonymity of relationships between people; loss of connection with one's roots and misery. On the light side, the city does indeed offer many opportunities, the bulk of which may lie in the social relationships, in the rupture of old social structures benefiting certain groups that had been, until then, contained and controlled by the complex network of "traditional" obligations. Women, first and foremost, became freed from the control of ancient lineages and men, and undoubtedly gained freedom: the freedom to choose a companion, or perhaps a spouse, especially in the first half of the 20th century, when cities were mostly occupied by males and women were rare; the increasing freedom to choose a job, to keep one's wages and, based on their skills, to compete with men. Youths then progressively became genuine social actors and would be the ones to set out, without restraint, on the paths of cultural and artistic innovation. Finally, the "social juniors" – the slaves, caste-classified individuals and dependants of any type – acquired, in turn, previously unheard of independence. In general, what occurred was a vast process of individualization with as many lows (rupture of former solidarities) as highs (emancipation of dominated classes).

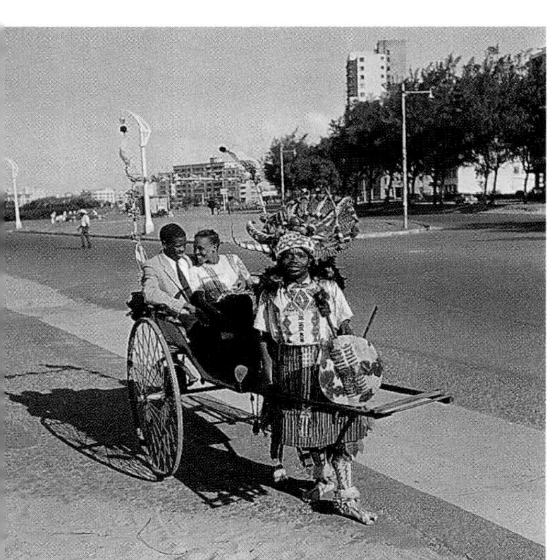

Cape Town, South Africa, 1954, in *Drum* ©Bob Gosani

The reconstructions that affected the social fabric were no less complex. Perhaps most striking were the new types of urban solidarities and brotherhoods providing an informative example of this creativity. There were, of course, initially, the "tribal" and "ethnic" brotherhoods that drew and delighted specialists. These "associations of natives" were often exclusive and intolerant, and led to bloody confrontations in African cities, as can be seen from the most dramatic example, Brazzaville, in 1959. Then there were the "integrating brotherhoods," which, over time, appeared to prevail over the "ethnic brotherhoods." These "integrating brotherhoods" had very diverse bases, all of which took into account new situations and aspirations generated by the urban environment:
- residence,
- educational past,
- occupation,
- mutual assistance, such as in the form of economic solidarity, illustrated by the "tontines,"
- urban worship, city pleasures and elegance, of which the most striking examples probably originated in Brazzaville and Kinshasa, as can still be seen today from the upsurge of the "Sapeur" groups,
- sharing of common values, in particular faith, belief and identical religious values, the past and present strength of which can be seen in the number of "prayer groups" and other religious, Christian, Muslim and Pagan fraternities.

After all is said and done, these facts still question the originality of African "urban sociabilities." It is perhaps in the field of social relationships and forms of creativity that African cities stand out most in relation to both other cities in developing countries and cities in industrialized states. In an old essay that remains relevant, devoted to "mentalities" in urban metropolises, Georg Simmel defined the "typical city dweller," a product of the monetary economy, as having two distinctive traits. On the one hand, "intellectuality," "recognized as protection of subjective life against the violence of the big city." On the other hand, a "blasé attitude," defined as "indifference to the difference of things"[2]. While African cities apparently reproduced the first trait, the same cannot be said for the second. One could, conversely, characterize the "typical African city dweller" as having a "passionate attitude," in which coexists individualism, submission and a spirit of rebellion…

[2] Simmel, G. "Metropolises and Mentalities" (1903), quoted by Roncayolo, M. and Paquot, T. eds. Cities and Urban Civilization, 18th-20th Century, Paris, Larousse, 1992, pp. 300-310

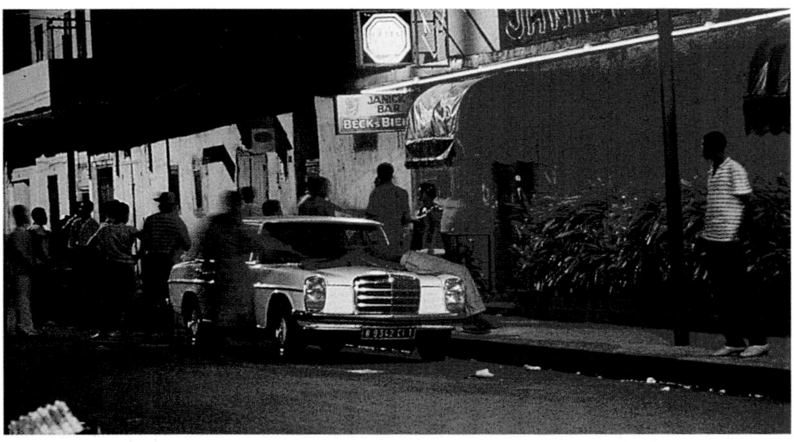

Bissau, Guinea Bissau ©Revue Noire

As a place of confrontation, turmoil and creativity, cities occupied a central place in the overall history of colonization. It was actually through the cities that colonization was established in Africa, by conquering or destroying ancient cities and founding their own urban centers. But it was also through the cities that colonization was driven out of Africa, thanks to the combined action of these social forces, which the cities themselves had actually liberated. There were the women who rebelled early on (Lomé in 1931, Grand Bassam in 1949); the youths, such as the small boys and verandah boys from Accra mobilized by Kwame Nkrumah; the "new men" who, opposed both to the traditional elites and the colonial authorities, provided the nationalist parties with their most ardent militants.

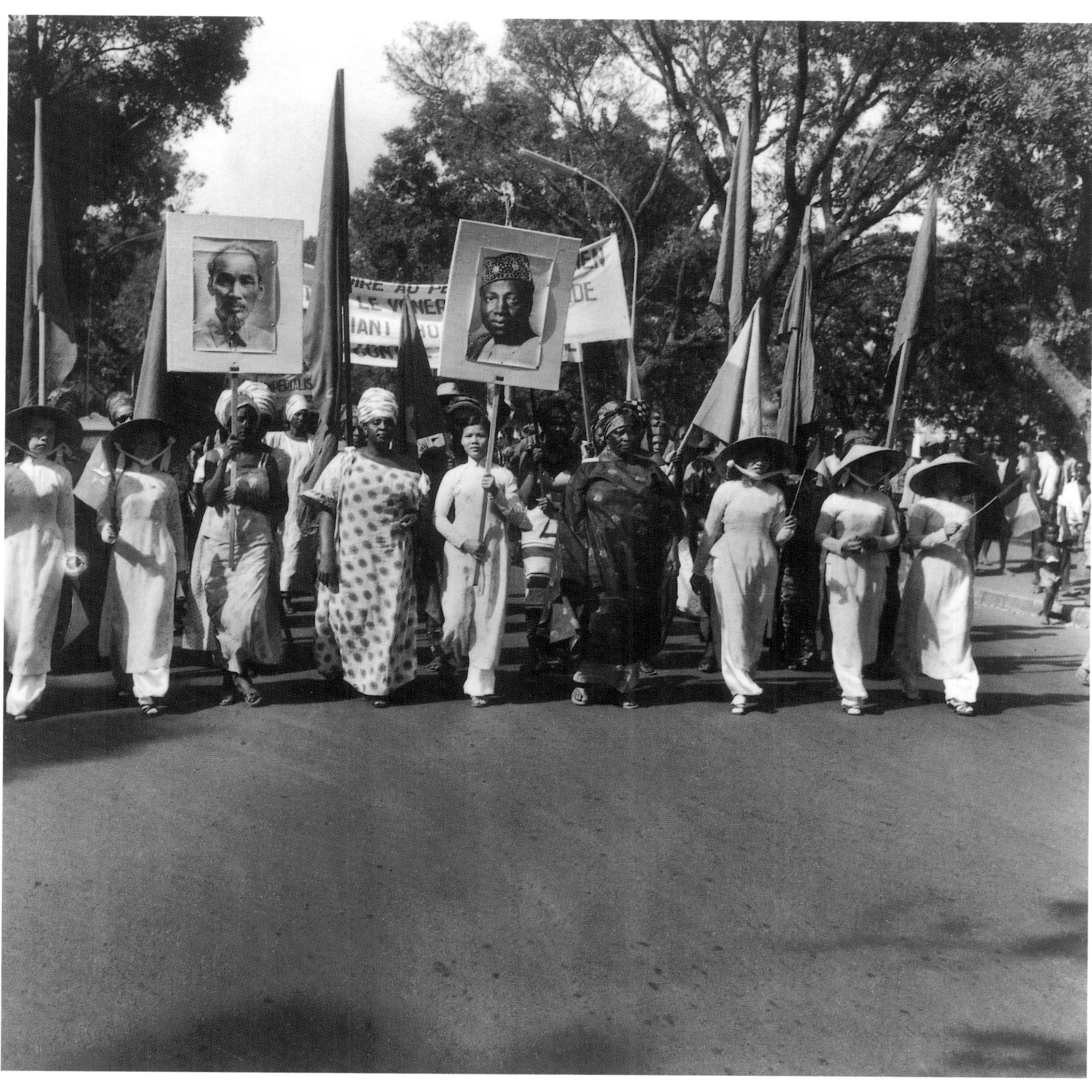

Bamako, Mali, c.a. 1965 ©AMAP

Neo-traditional sculpture in Nigeria

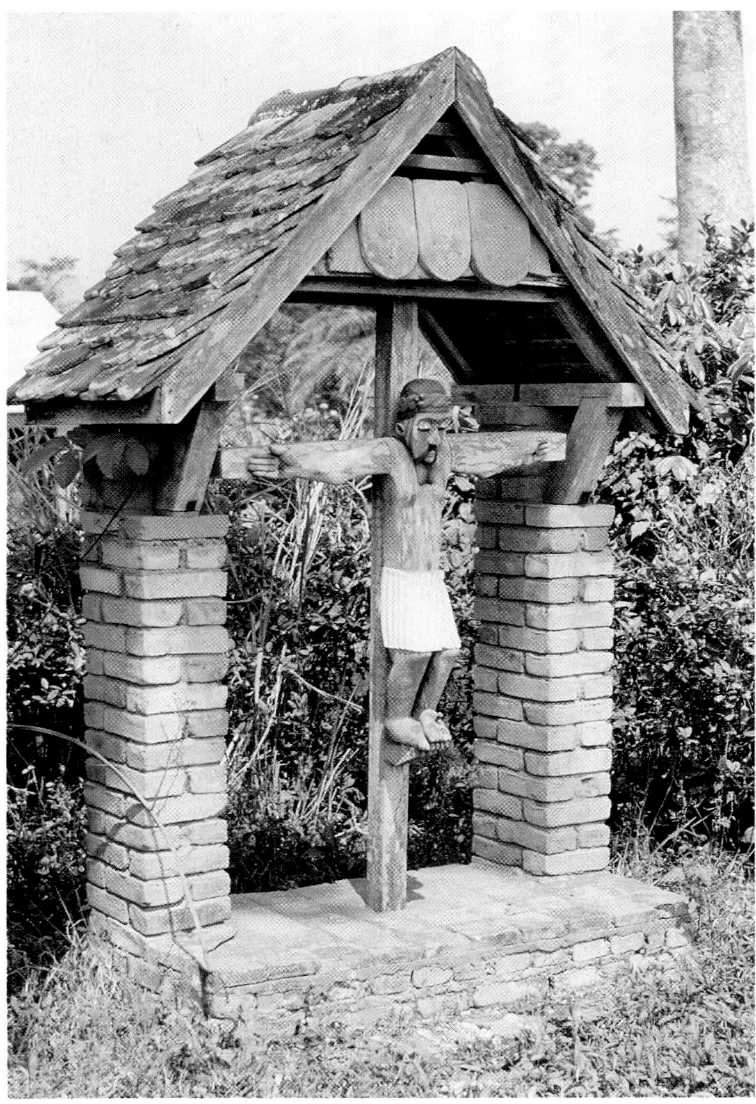

The notion of "neo-traditional" to describe a practice and a traditional cottage inspiration adapted to the aspirations and market of the modern city is a phenomenon that can be observed throughout Africa. Based on John Picton's analysis of the specific history of neo-traditional Yoruba sculpture in Nigeria, keys emerge, thereby allowing this practice to be seen in other geographical and cultural areas. The practice/thought, tradition/modernity debate is fueled here by a popular synthesis.

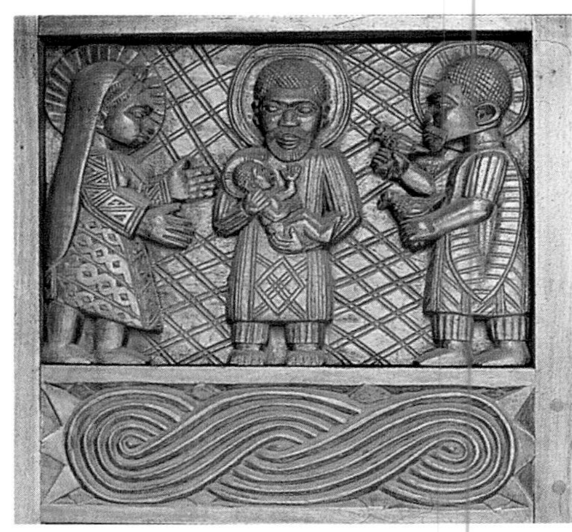

George Bandele, 1950
Cross in Oye-Ekiti
wood sculpture
©John Picton, 1965

Lamidi Fakeye (born in 1925), 1956
Detail of a door of the Ibadan Cathedral
wood sculpture
©John Picton, 1990

facing page:
George Bandele, 1950
Catholic church in Oye-Ekiti, wood sculpture
©John Picton, 1965

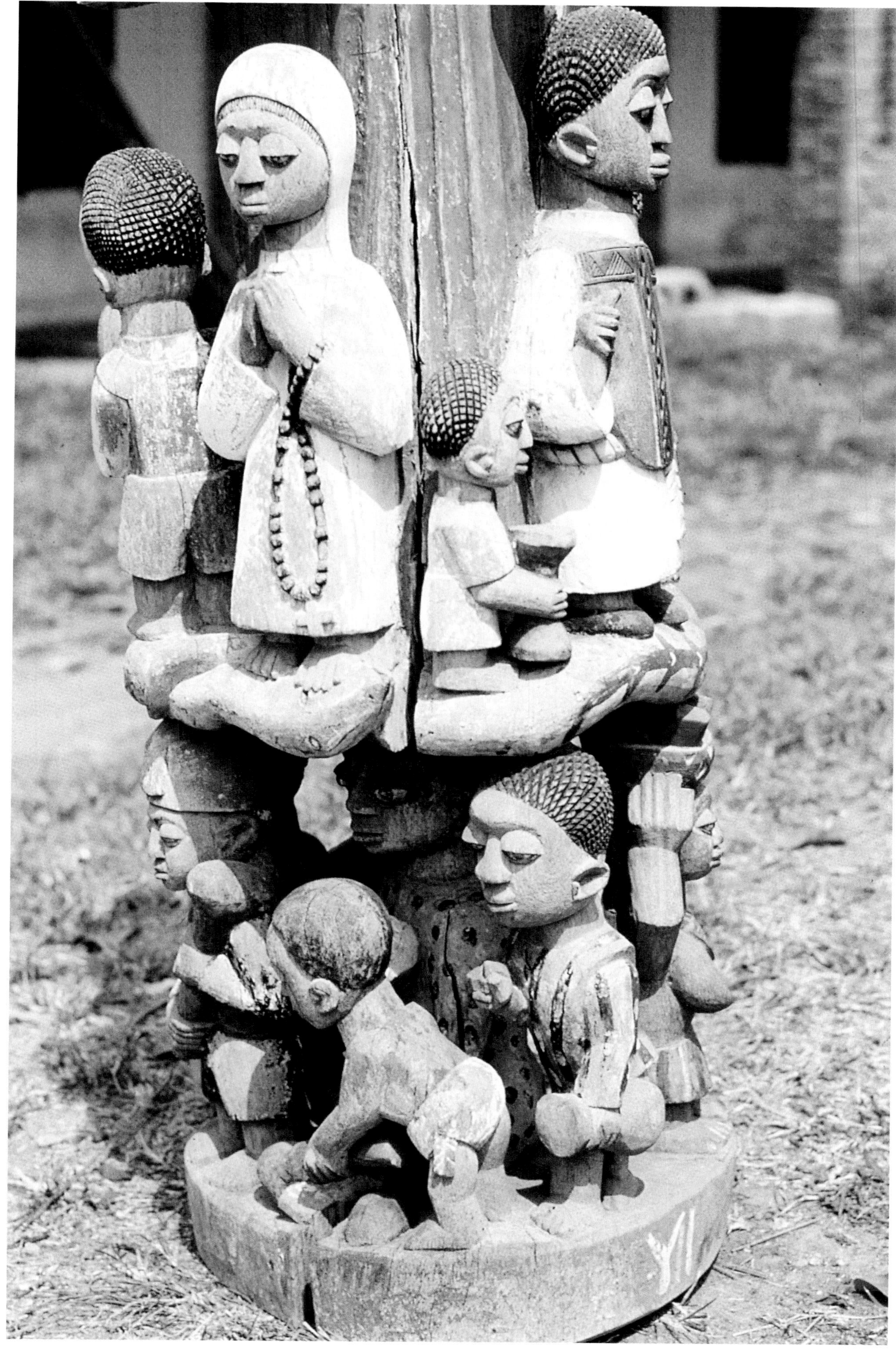

NEO-TRADITIONAL SCULPTURE IN NIGERIA
John Picton

As one might expect in a continent as large and diverse as Africa, there is no one modernity. The patterns of development are as diverse as the locations and languages, the traditions and trading patterns, and the diverse requirements of missionary religions, Islam as well as Christianity. In Nigeria, for example, Protestant missionaries pioneered the liturgical use of local language and musical forms, whereas the Catholics initiated developments in the visual arts and material culture of Christianity; and it is here that the best-documented example of the movement now designated Neo-Traditional begins.

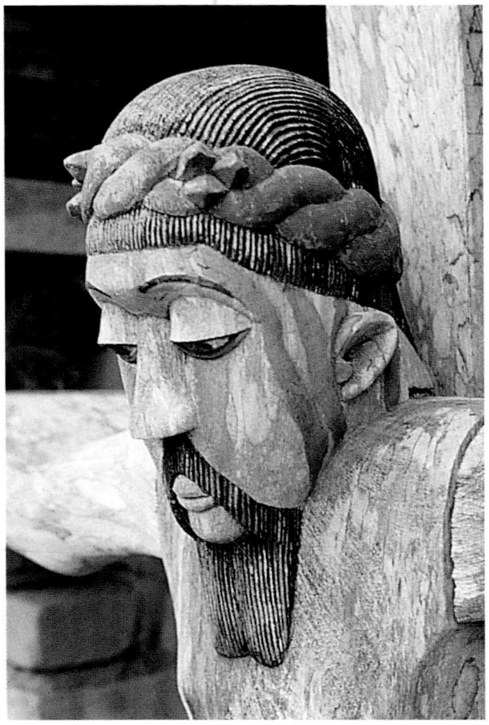

In 1946 the African Missions Society decided to study the uses of African visual culture in a Christian liturgical context, and two young priests, Kevin Carroll and Sean O'Mahoney, were sent to Oye-Ekiti in north-east Yoruba a region well known for its monumental sculpture, masquerade, textiles, pottery and beaded embroidery. Early in 1947 they began to recruit local women and men with skills in these arts and George Bandele soon presented himself for employment as a sculptor. He was the son of Areogun of Osi-Ilorin (circa 1880-1954), one of the greatest masters of the pre-modern tradition of the area, and Bandele had been trained by one of his father's assistants. Bandele was an accomplished artist whose work could be found in the temples to deities and the houses of the local nobility; but fashions were changing, in house building as in religion, and he had found himself without commissions: his sculpture found no place in the new Brazillian architecture.

George Bandele, 1950
Detail of a Oye-Ekiti cross
wood sculpture
©John Picton, 1965

Now working for the Catholic church, Bandele continued carving in the tradition in which he has been trained, bringing images of Jesus, Mary, and so forth, into his repetoire. He also had to reckon with hitherto unfamiliar technical difficulties, eg the use of seasoned wood, or the making of door panels to fit carpentered frames. (There is no objective reason why this could not have happened in a Brazillian context but for the fact that in Lagos there was no tradition of monumental decorative sculpture.) Bandele's sculptural self-confidence was restored and he was now in a position to train apprentices. The most significant of these was Lamidi Fakeye, who came from a carving household in another town but accepeted Carrroll's invitation to retrain under Bandele. It is also worth noting that Lamidi was a Muslim, while as far as one can tell Bandele's Catholicism was more-or-less nominal. Carrroll took the view that as much of the sculpture of the region was not overtly religious in either context or content, what mattered was the skill of the artist not the quality of his religious devotion.

In 1953 the project came to an end. Carroll and O'Mahoney were each sent to separate parishes and told to apply what they had learned. Bandele moved with Carroll and continued working under his patronage on and off for another fifteen years. Fakeye moved with O'Mahoney and received significant commission from non-ecclesiastical patronage, in 1956 for the furniture of the Western Region parliament, and in 1960 for doors for the Ibadan University hospital. About this time Fakeye set himself up as an independent studio master in the city of Ibadan, taking apprentices and extending his field of patronage to include (initially expatriate) university and government service personnel, who would purchase from him genre figures, mothers and children and so forth, as ornaments for the dining room. By the mid-60s Lamidi made his first visit to Europe, and soon established himself as part of an American lecture circuit. In due course he accepted a teaching appointment at Ife University in the Fine Art Department, to work alongside such overt modernists as Agbo Folarin and Moyo Okediji.

By this time many of Bandele's and Lamidi's former apprentices, often family members were themselves working as independent sculptors, mostly carving decorative figure sculptures for Nigerian middle-class households (teachers, doctors, administrators, etc), and it is in this

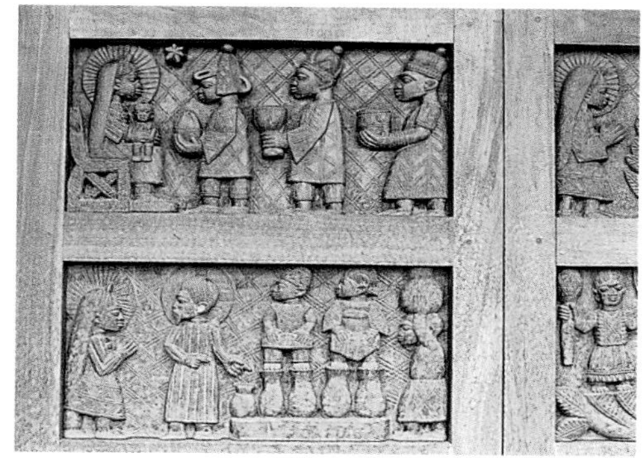

Lamidi Fakeye (born in 1925), 1956
Detail of a door of the Ibadan Cathedral
wood sculpture
©John Picton, 1990

Areogun (1880-1954), 1953
This figure, commissioned by Father Kevin Caroll in 1953 to represent one of the three Wise Men, was fashioned not from the likeness of a Yoruba King, but from a traditional representation of the God, Eshu.
wood sculpture
©John Picton, 1965

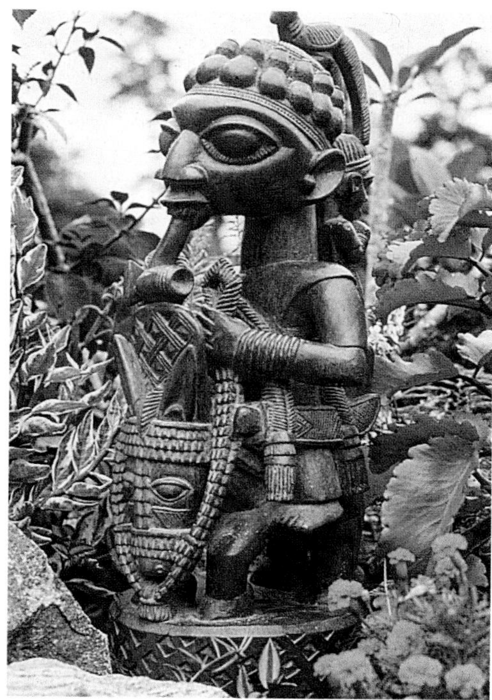

context that their work became known as Neo-Traditional. Shortly before his death in Nigeria in 1993 Father Carroll estimated that some 25 sculptors were now active full-time sculptors as a result of their project. However, the initial reaction to this work was sometimes mixed. Magnificent doors were carved for the Cathedral in Ibadan as for many churches, whereas sculptures purchased for the Cathedral in Lagos were removed by members of a congregation dominated by the descendants of Brazillian repatriates. Nevertheless, by setting himself up independently and successfully widening the field of patronage Lamidi capitalised on his ability and opportunity to render a sense of tradition in the modern world, notwithstanding that the location of patronage had shifted from palace and temple to the middle-class sitting room and church.

Perhaps it was ironic that one of the great sculptural traditions of a "pagan" pre-modern era was transformed through a Catholic policy of dressing the liturgy up in local culture; or perhaps it was entirely appropriate! It is also worth noting that while Brazillian architecture and Neo-Traditional sculpture had their origins in very different contexts, they nevetheless came together, co-incidentally maybe, as significant elements in a modern Yoruba identity as marked in the visual arts. Therein, the Neo-Traditional movement highlights almost as nothing else can that African modernity, even Nigerian modernity, even Yoruba modernity, is neither a simple nor a unified thing; and that it can take directions (eg via Islam and the various Christianities) that would seem abberant in a Euro-American context.

The Yoruba Neo-Traditional movement is by no means unique, even though it is the best documented. In Benin City, for example, brass casting continues as much in the service of middle-class patronage as in the service of the king and the chiefly nobility. In the Igbo-speaking region village-based mask carvers have sometimes developed their forms in response to a modern urban requirement for things to hang on the wall. In all these cases a cultural link with the past is preserved in ways that support modern definitions of ethnicity. In contrast, in a university fine art department that sense of tradition, together with the forms and practices of the past, becomes part of one's subject matter. Ethnicity may well be within the grid of experience an artist brings to bear on his or her work, and yet the work itself will transcend the relevance of ethnic categorisation.

Ibrahim Njoya, master of Bamoun drawing

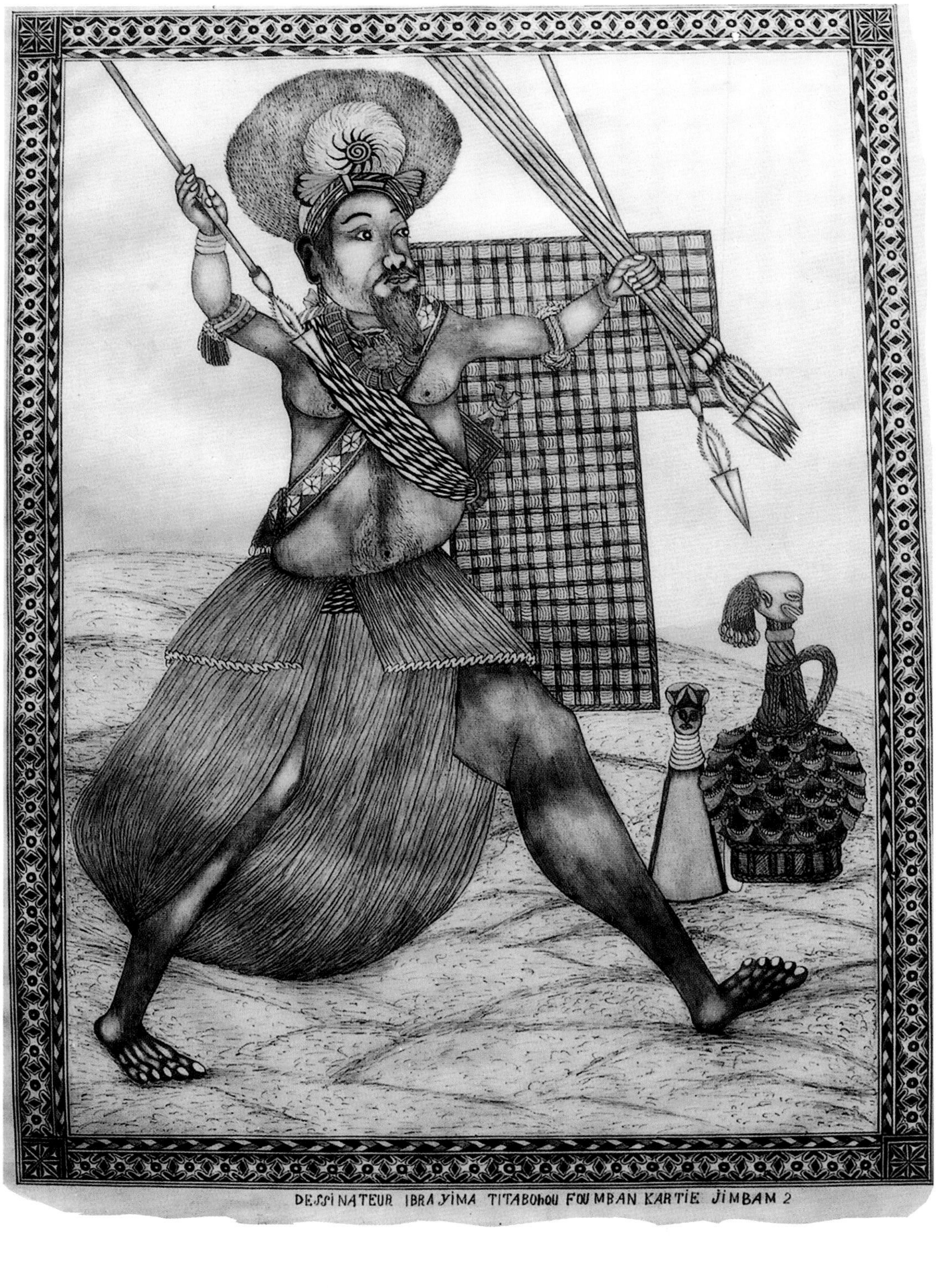

DESSINATEUR IBRA YIMA TITABOHOU FOUMBAN KARTIE JIMBAM 2

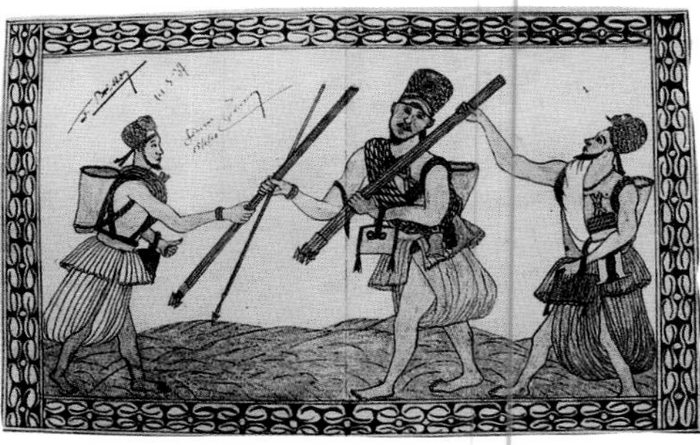

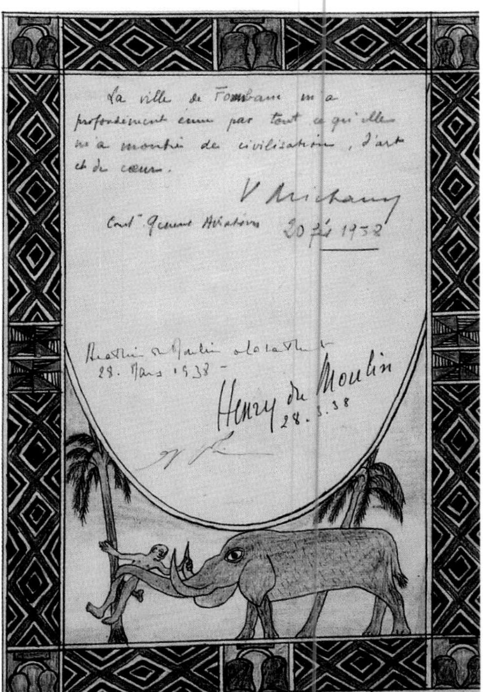

Drawings from the gold book of the ATB (1934-1960) ©Alexandra Loumpet-Galitzine

IBRAHIM NJOYA (c. 1890-1966), MASTER OF BAMOUN DRAWING

Alexandra Loumpet-Galitzine

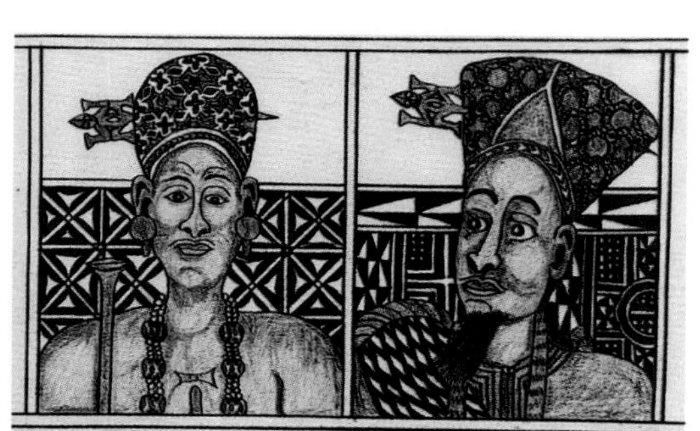

Drawing is a relatively recent pictorial mode in the Bamoun kingdom, an ancient centralized state of the Western Cameroon Grassfields. Appearing in the 1920s through the work of a single man, Ibrahim Njoya, this technique revitalized the traditional style of forms and also led to an historical rupture. This was a hagiographic and narrative distanced art, the function of which was to legitimize a secular sovereignty destabilized by the colonial order.

The work of Ibrahim Njoya is closely related to the irreversible transformation of the emblematic reign of Njoya, the seventeenth Mfon of the Bamoun. This exceptional young sovereign, an innovator in many fields, acceded to the throne in about 1890. In 1896, he devised an original and unique script that, in less than fifteen years, changed from an ideographic version to a syllabic and phonetic form. This major invention paved the way for a linear and spatial system and fostered the emergence of new skills.

The first Europeans who entered Foumban, the kingdom's capital, in 1902, introduced the use of new materials (paper, ink, pencils) and visual codes, spread through newspapers, illustrated Bibles and photographs. In 1916, the Germans were replaced by the English, and then by the French. For ten years, the French pursued a policy of decentralizing the royal power, which led to lifting of prohibitions on materials and patterns reserved for the court, the creation of a craft district far from the palace, and the public exhibition of royal symbols.

There are two evident periods in the work of Ibrahim Njoya.
The first phase began circa 1925, when the first known figurative drawings were made on paper, and ended in 1933 upon the death in exile of King Njoya.

Born at the beginning of the king's reign and instructed at the royal Bamoun writing school, the sovereign's namesake was noticed early on for his fleeting drawings in sand, and his talents as a scribe and decorator. Ibrahim Njoya became the king's secretary when the latter began to write the history of the kingdom. He progressively developed a representation on a flat medium using topographical maps, sculpted panels, and then illustrations.

The drawings of this period were part of a policy of reaffirming sovereignty using vehicles borrowed from the Europeans. We are thus able to show that, from 1927, most drawings were directly inspired by photographs taken by the Germans between 1906 and 1912.

This use of photographs highlighted the role of King Njoya in the appearance of drawings. The monarch's interest in this new technique, studied by Geary, shows that frames quickly acquired a status with rank. From 1912, the king composed and took the frames himself, thereby controlling a personalized representation of himself. In 1920, he acquired his own camera. The political use of portrayals was reinforced by the production of drawings idealizing the successive kings and major episodes in the history of Bamoun (gesture of the founding hero, victorious battles, etc.).

Ibrahim Njoya's second phase of production corresponds to the fall of the traditional kingdom. Voided of their military substance, the drawings changed from a style of participation to a style of expression of a plastic Bamoun identity. In other words, the referential and emotional functions became masked by the esthetic function alone, thereby meeting the implicit wishes of "French peace."

From 1933, Ibrahim Njoya filled mainly European orders, including orders from the Museum of Bamoun Arts and Traditions, founded by the French Institute of Black Africa (IFAN Center of Cameroon). Under the influence of this ethnographic museum, the artist illustrated craftsmanship, scenes of every day life, pre-colonial architecture, and drew portraits of superior leaders appointed by the French. Unlike some of his students, the most illustrious of whom was Tita Mbohu, Ibrahim Njoya did not represent scenes related to colonization.

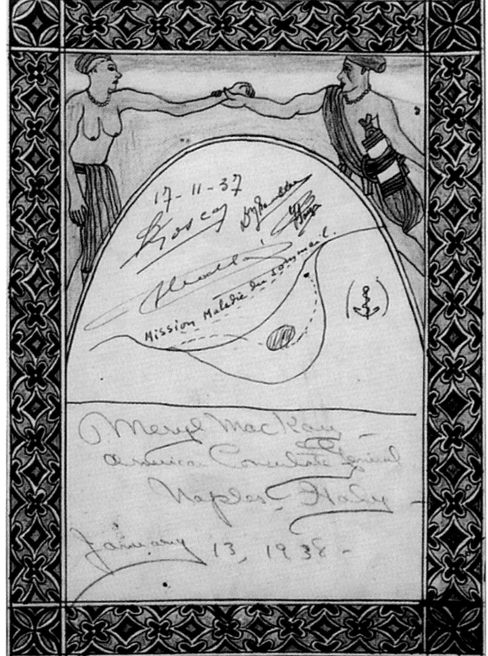

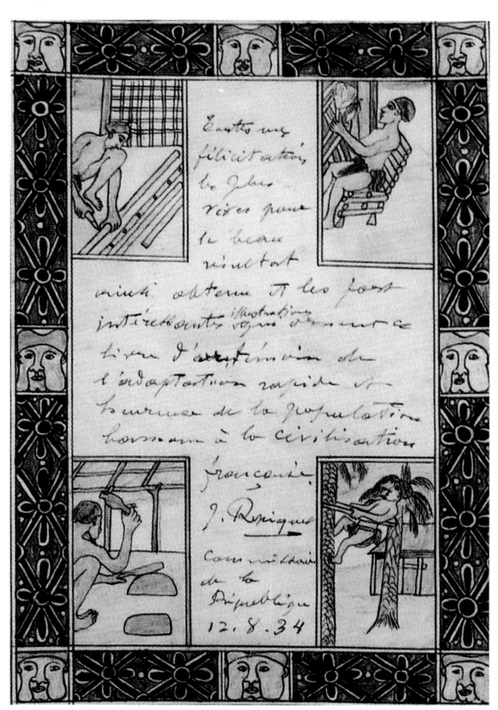

From World War II to his death on August 9, 1966, the artist multiplied his illustrations and mural decorations by making replicas, creating composite drawings and portraits of kings in the form of genealogical paintings. The effigies of the new sultan, Njimoluh, which conventionally rendered his face and the details of his clothing, were essentially destined for a foreign clientele.

Ibrahim Njoya's often-imitated style remains, nevertheless, easily recognizable. The some one hundred polychrome drawings listed today, made with native or imported ink and pencils, use two separate techniques. The freely inspired freehand drawings integrate all of the representations of the pre-colonial kingdom. They highlight a chronologically undetermined period, characterized by the conventional way in which costumes were treated and the great diversity in the positions of the subjects.

The scenes are identified by the selection of significant historical elements, such as the presence of horsemen, and by the addition of inscriptions in Bamoun writing. In the illustration of tales, the factual chronology is organized by the internal division of the drawing into boxes.

The full-length portraits of the first sovereigns form a specific category, affirming the importance afforded to the individualization of the people and the graphic solutions developed in the absence of information. The characters are differentiated by how faces, not bodies, are treated. The latter appear unusually stiff and not quite natural. This differentiation gradually disappears as bust portraits emerge. The age, sex and royal symbols (hairstyles, finery) actually foster an identification that is highlighted by the association of objects and symbols, scenes or landscapes (Nshare Yen with a pirogue, Mbuembue dancing the Nja). These combinations eventually stabilized and still represent, today, the canons of the monarchs.

The care given to friezes, demarcations of space that re-work old royal patterns, is another constituent of Ibrahim Njoya's style. Once exclusively reserved to drawings of kings, friezes became both an identifying factor of the subject and an independent code of interpretation. Subsequently extended to all drawings, they became exclusively ornamental.

The colors used by the artist are part of a polychrome tradition that surfaced at the beginning of the 19th century in the mottling of objects. Indigo blue, the color of the royal batiks and of sought-after oblong beads, and red, were the preferred colors used in drawings of kings. The characters were filled by pencil fading on paper. Drawings based on photographs concern mainly portraits of Ibrahim Njoya's contemporaries. The photographs were either faithfully reproduced (portrait of Chief Njikam based on a 1935 Labouret frame) or slightly altered in order to accentuate a hierarchical position. In this perspective, friezes of Islamic and native inspiration reinforce social status and are inspired by official colonial photographs (framed portraits of William II).

The effigies of recent kings (Mbuembue, Nsangu) were done using an intermediary technique, in which elements of photographs of King Njoya were integrated into a freer composition.

The use of photographic frames became more widespread in the 1950s, and contributed to introducing an absent perspective in drawings in the initial period. The portraits of King Njimoluh and of the current sultan, Mbombo Njoya, include turbans and modern accessories (watches, glasses, etc.).

In general, current Bamoun drawings reflect two main waves: a production of themes reduced in number, destined for foreigners, made using ink or felt-tip pens and based on photographs and replicas; and original creations presented by young artists and characterized either by a realistic style, or by working on symbolic backgrounds and patterns, as well as a return to traditional materials (vegetable and mineral dyes, additions of fibers and raised elements). Finally, realistic portraits painted based on photographs, supplemented by traditional Bamoun patterns, are an extension of the first representational drawings.

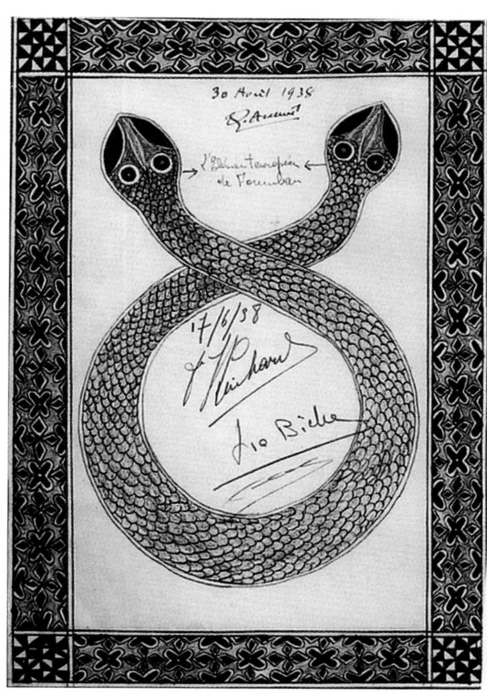

Ibrahim Njoya remains the reference in Bamoun drawing according to artists who tend to claim to be direct descendants of the master or of his best heirs. They thus use both an individual model of pictorial creation and a solidly rooted pattern of corporal organization. Finally, the originality of Bamoun drawings resides in their capacity to form a new plastic expression, integrated in a general formal style, based on borrowings and adaptations of outside techniques. This recovery and re-creation phenomenon, present since the foundation of the kingdom in many areas, contributes to differentiating Bamoun cultural identity. In this framework, the artist Ibrahim Njoya has devised a secularized version of court art that is now used by the entire kingdom.

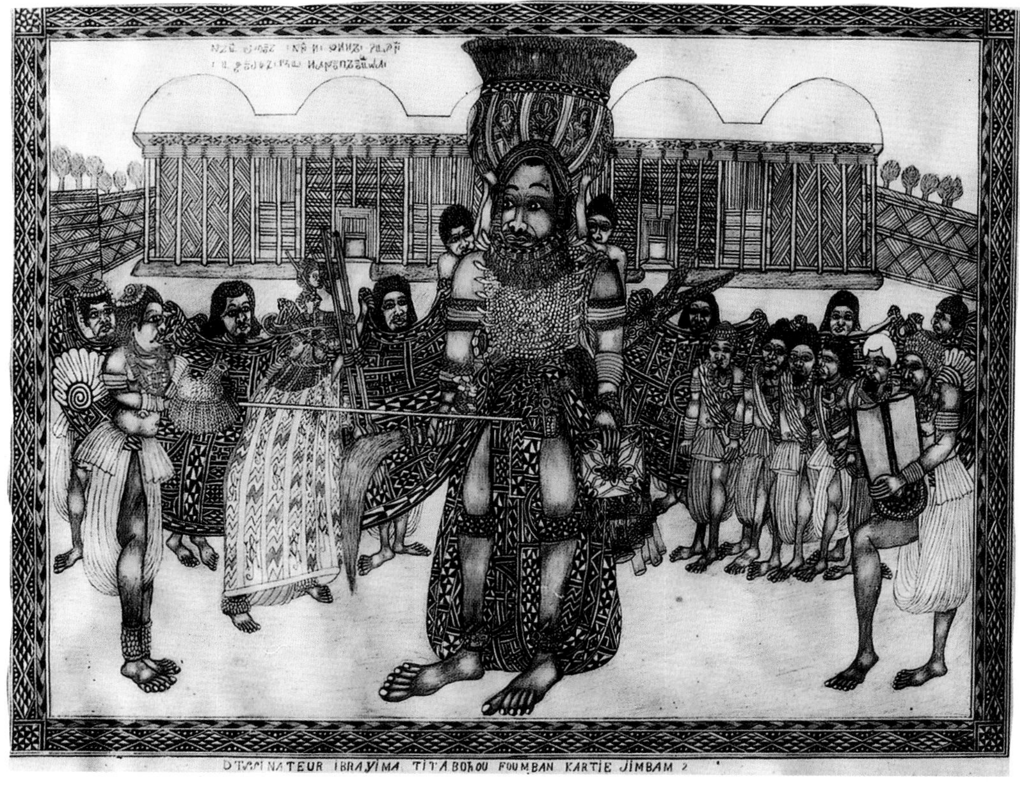

Drawings from the gold book of the ATB (1934-1960)
©Alexandra Loumpet-Galitzine

Representation and advertising

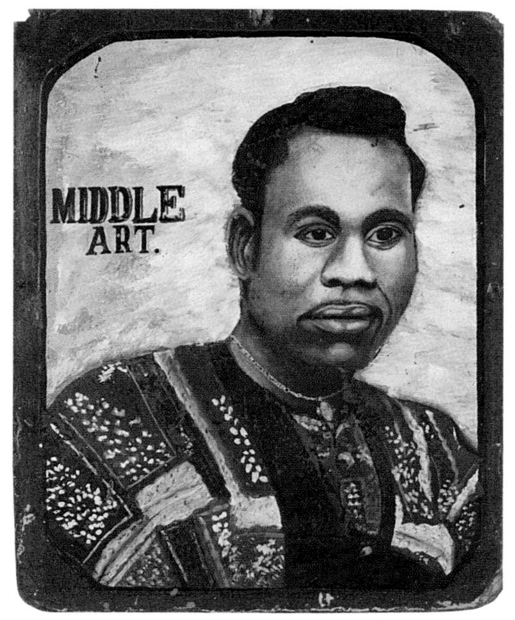

No country can escape the imagery of the painted frescoes on rotisserie houses and maquis, on the showcards of small and big stores, and on postcards. These images and their artists are ageless and are replaced as the fashions and beliefs of the time change. The signature itself is as much an advertisement as recognition of full-fledged status as an artist. "I am a great artist. Do you want a modern or classical painting?" These phrases, often slipped in during lulls in conversation, are more indicative of the doubt than the certainty of the artist's work. However, the artist works without hesitating, obeying the laws of demand. This does not, however, prevent him from having his secret garden, from painting for the love of painting, even if, while painting, he asks himself if he will be able to sell a work not ordered.

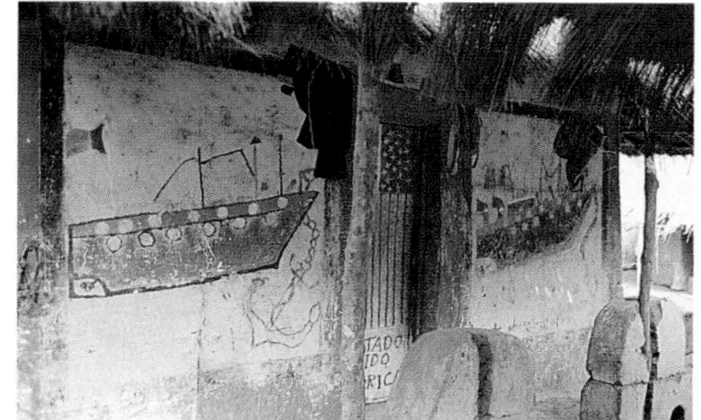

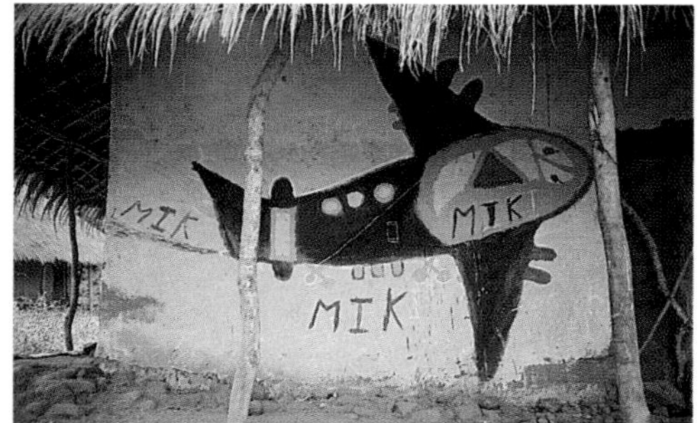

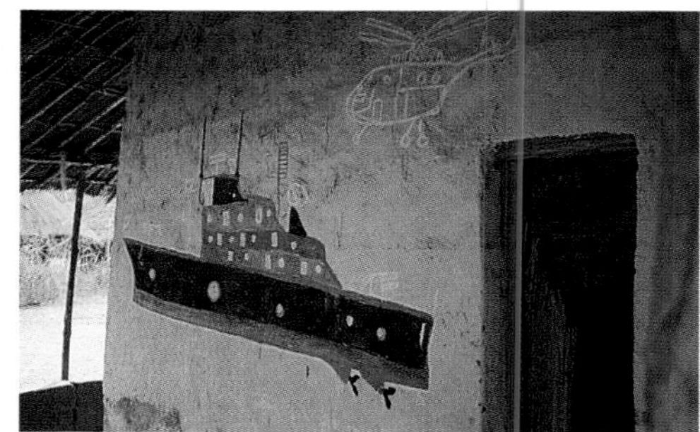

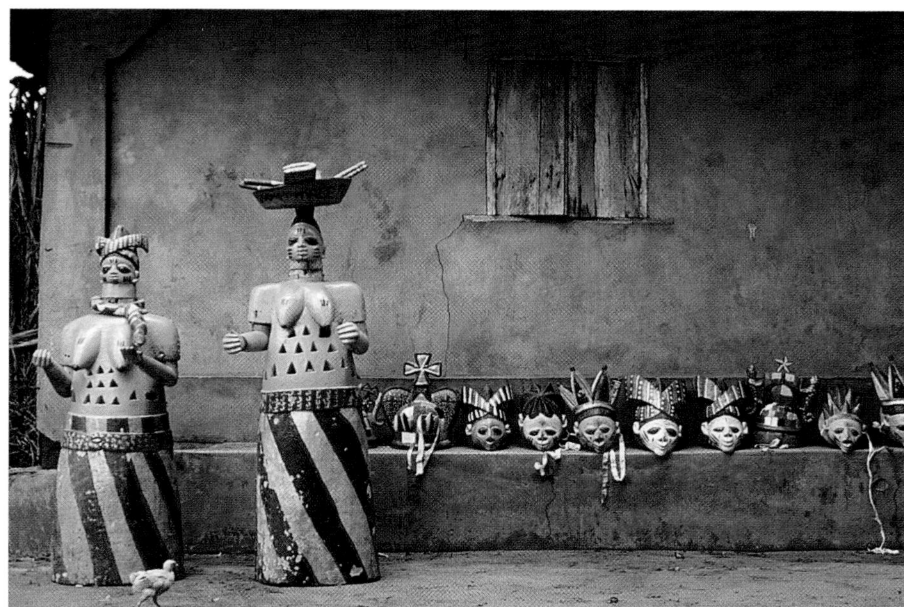

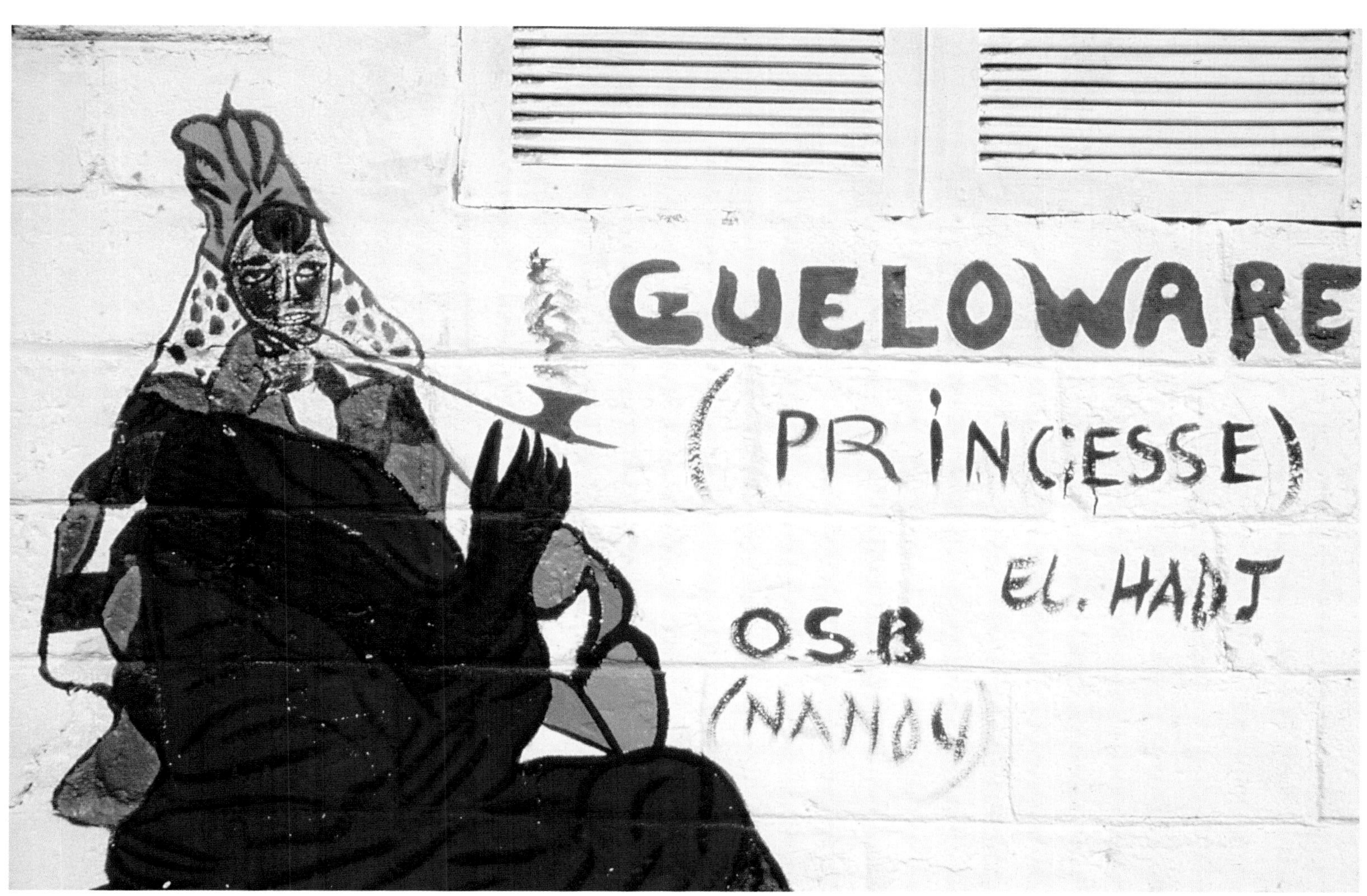

facing page:
Middle Art (born in 1936), Nigeria, towards 1960
self-portrait, painting on plywood
©Maison Iwalewa, Université de Bayreuth

Mural paintings, Guinea Bissau
©Revue Noire

Eloi Lokossou, Benin, 1995
©Henry Chauvin/Revue Noire

above:
Mur Set Setal, end of the 1980's
©Bouna Medoune Seye/Revue Noire

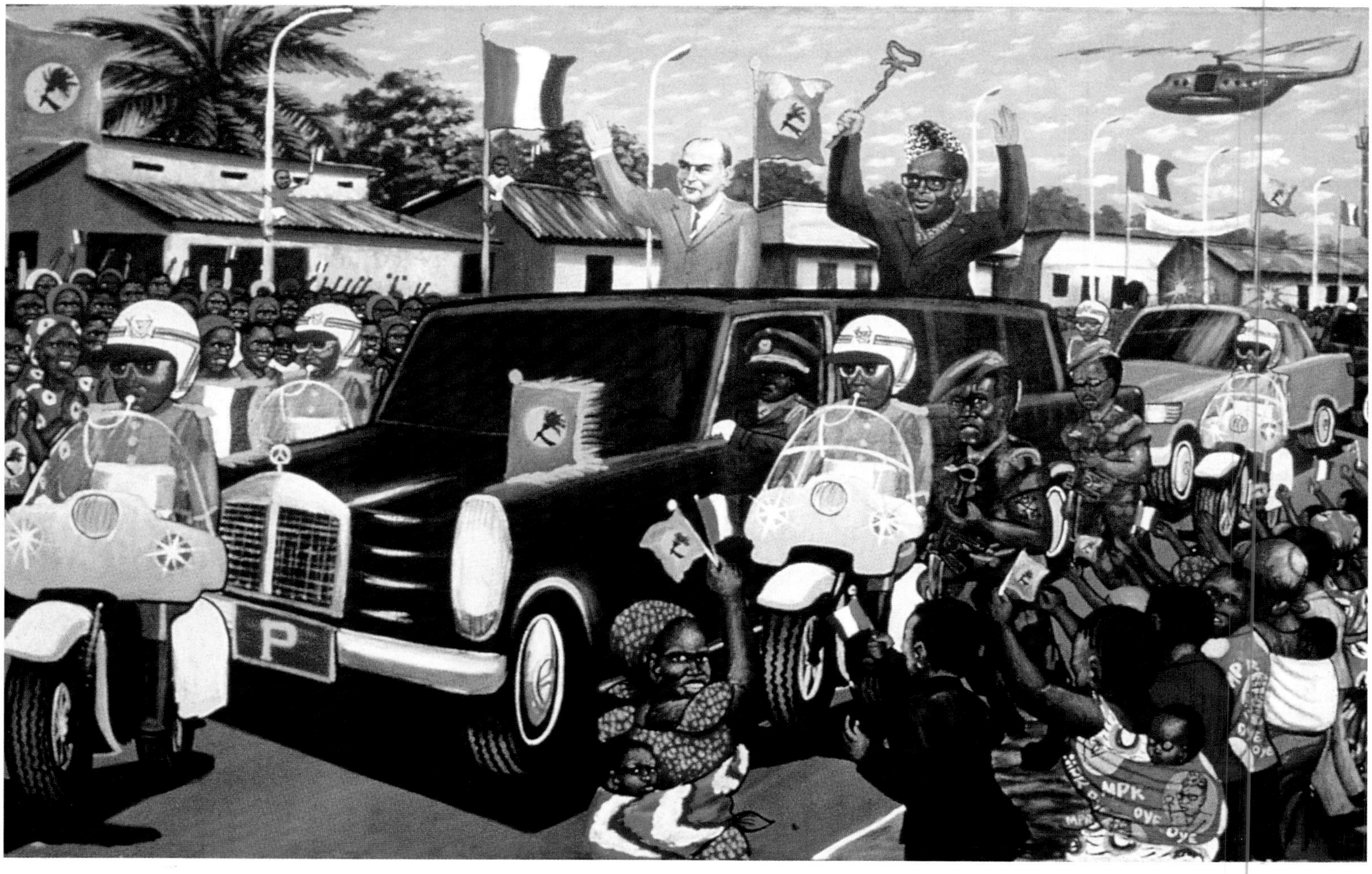

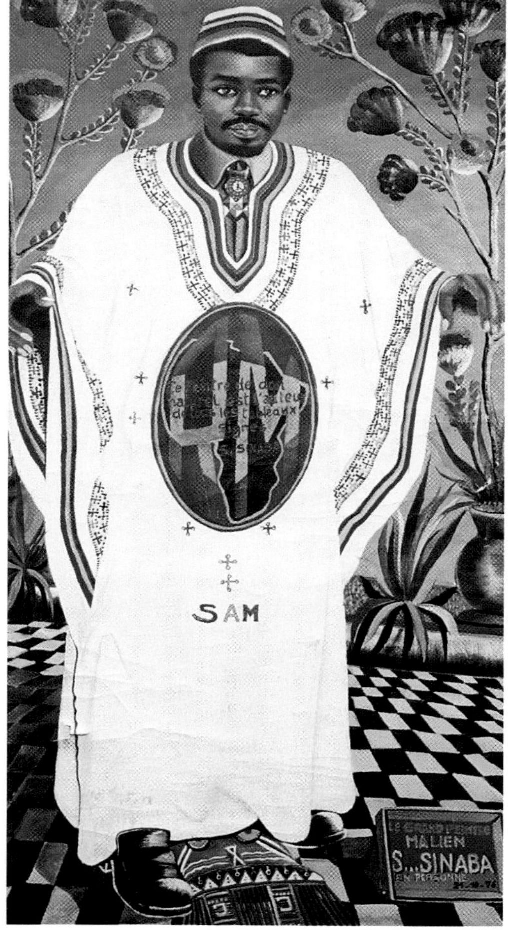
SAM
MALIEN
S...SINABA

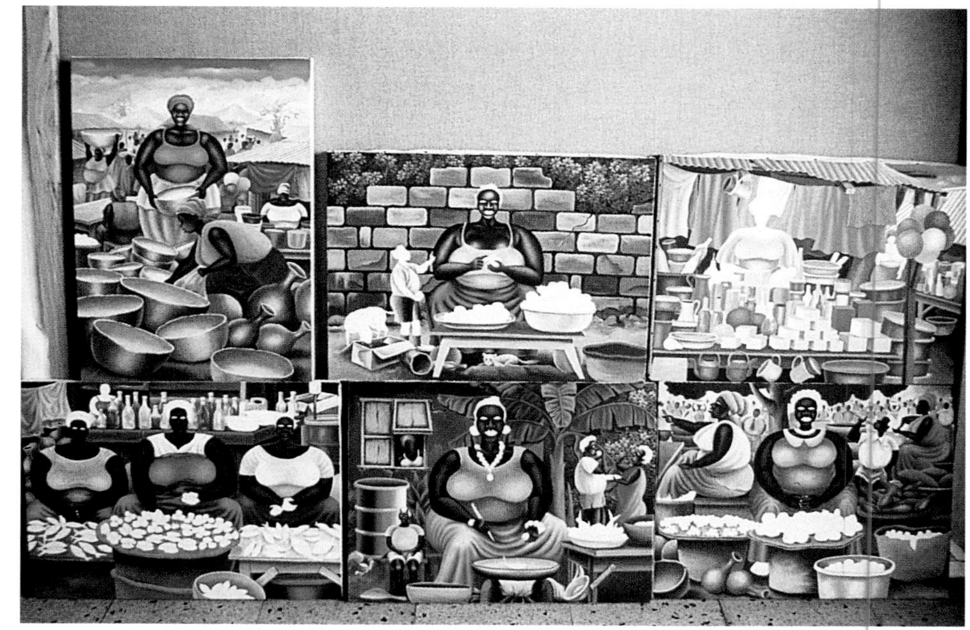

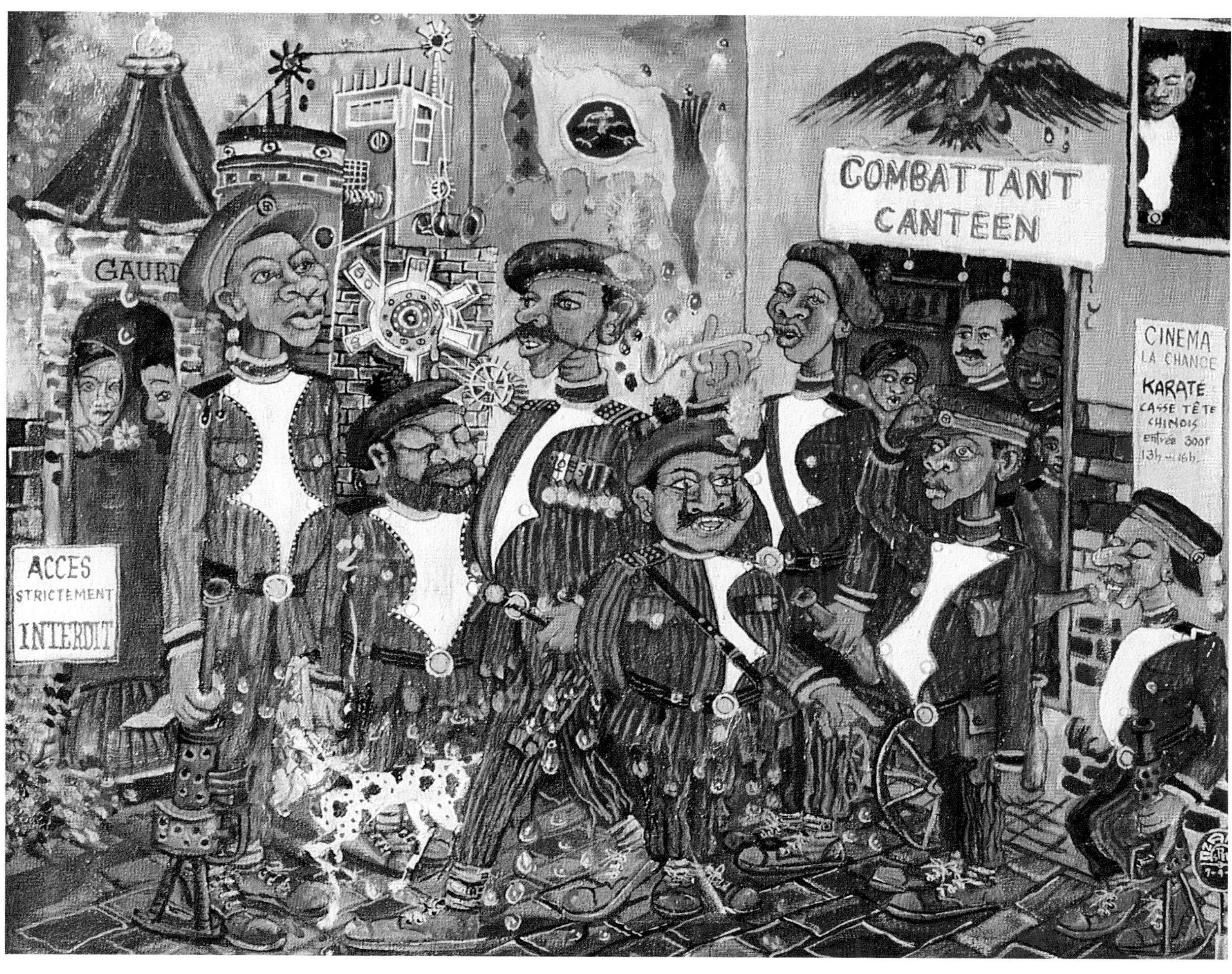

facing page, above:
Moké (1950-2001), RDC, "Mitterrand and Mobutu," 1990
112x180 cm.
©Revue Noire

facing page, below:
Sinaba, Mali, 1976
©Revue Noire

Augustin Aka Kassi (born in 1966), Ivory Coast, 1991
©Revue Noire

above:
Nzante Spee (born in 1951), Cameroon
©Revue Noire

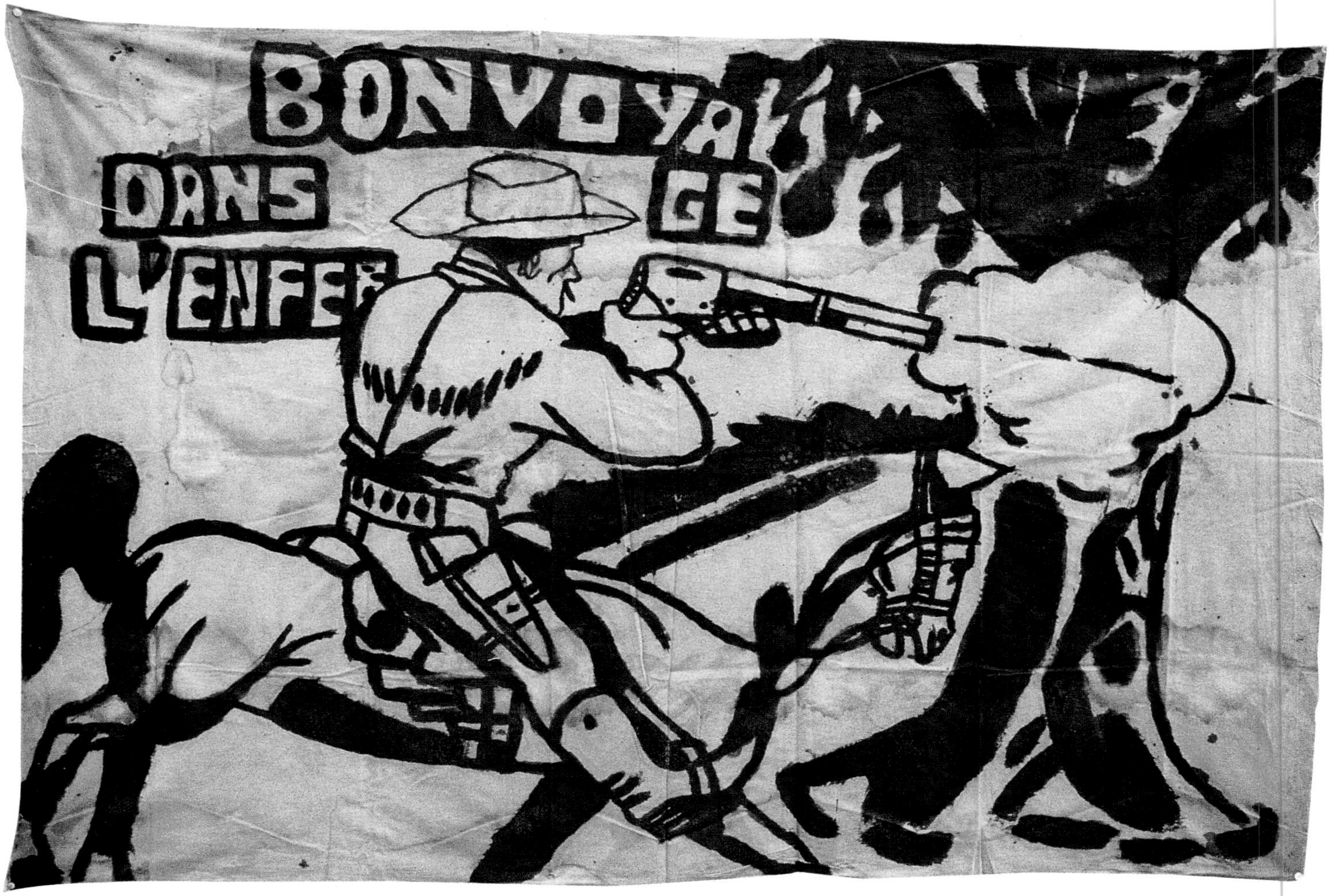

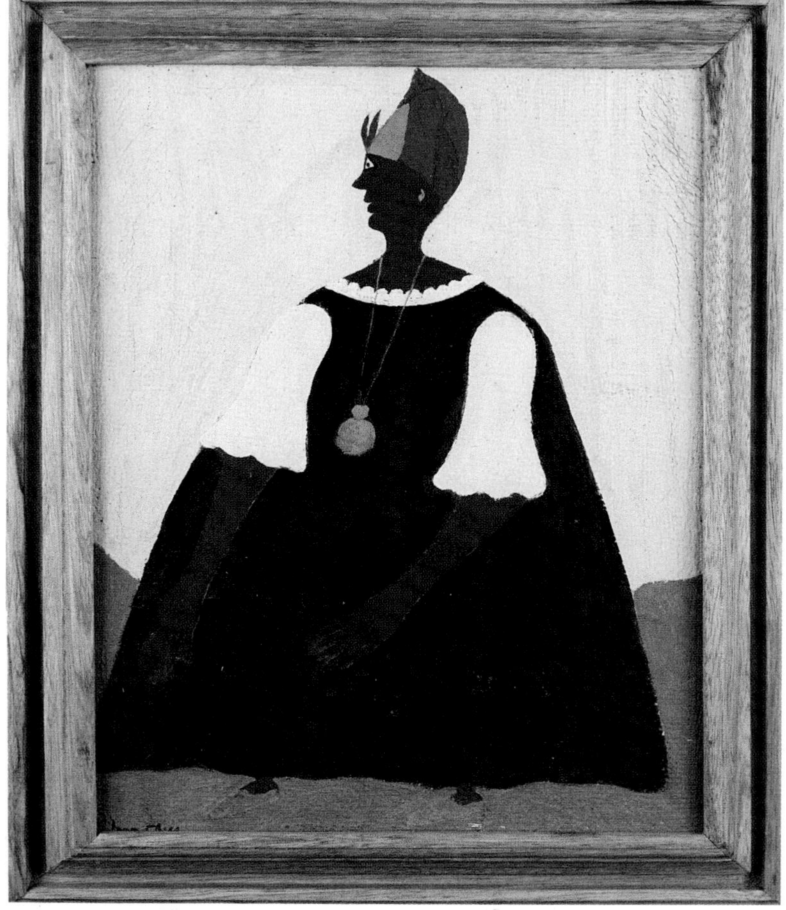

above:
Bogolan, San, Mali, 1977
160x100
©Revue Noire

right:
M'Bor Faye (1900-1984), Senegal, "Lahia Diarra," 1974,
oil on canvas, 38,5x48 cm.
©Revue Noire

facing page:
Sunday Jack Akpan (born in 1940), Nigeria,
"Portrait of a Man in Uniform," 1989
acrylic on cement, h. 184,5 cm.
©Musée d'Art contemporain de Lyon

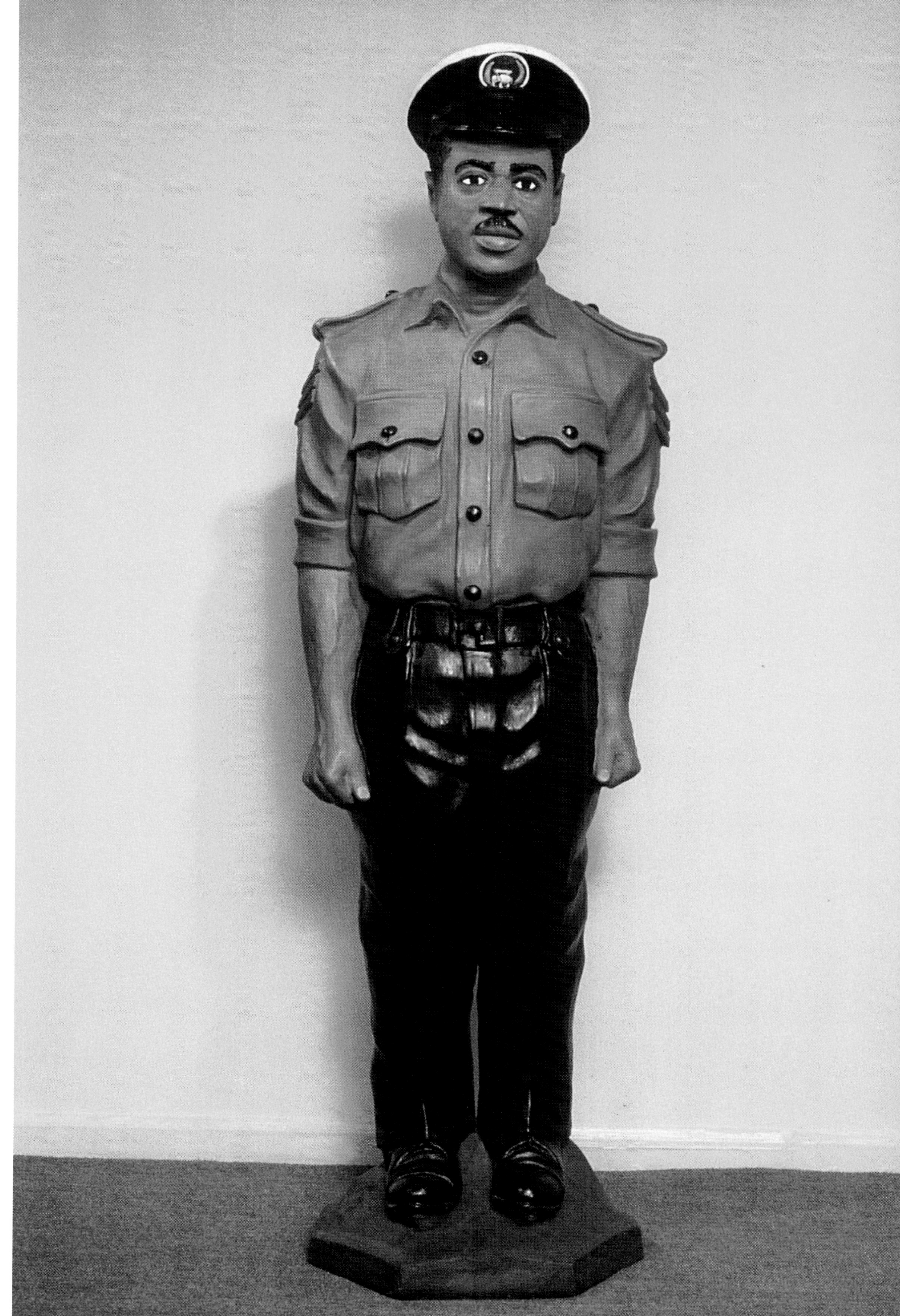

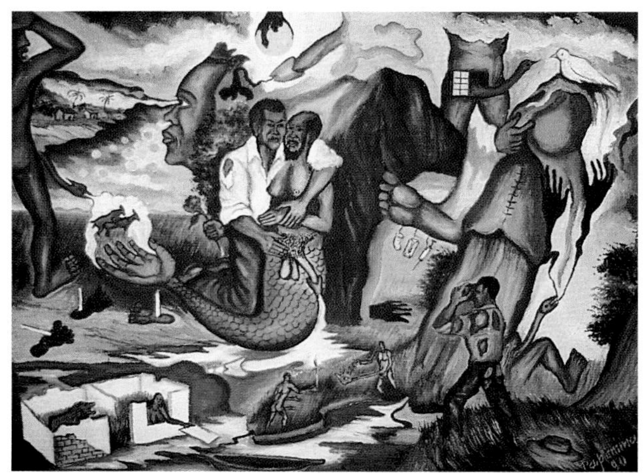

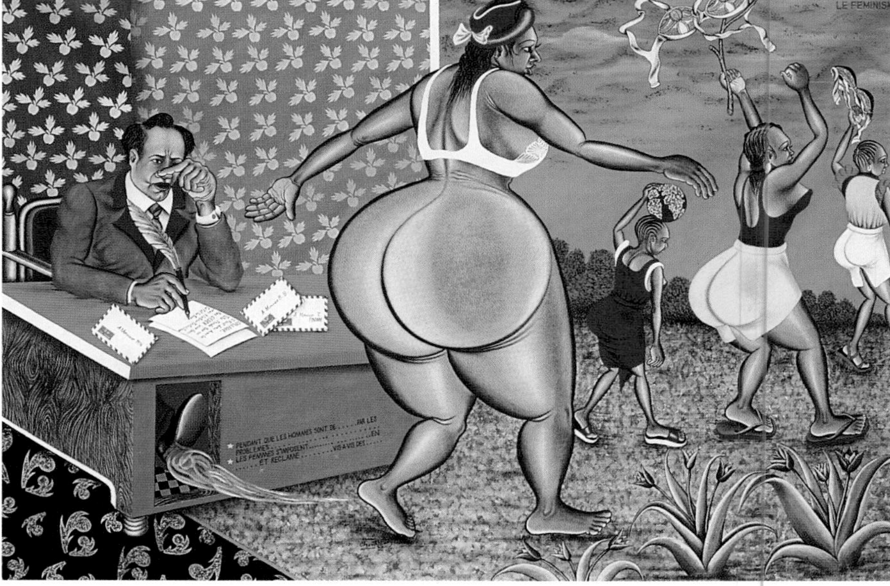

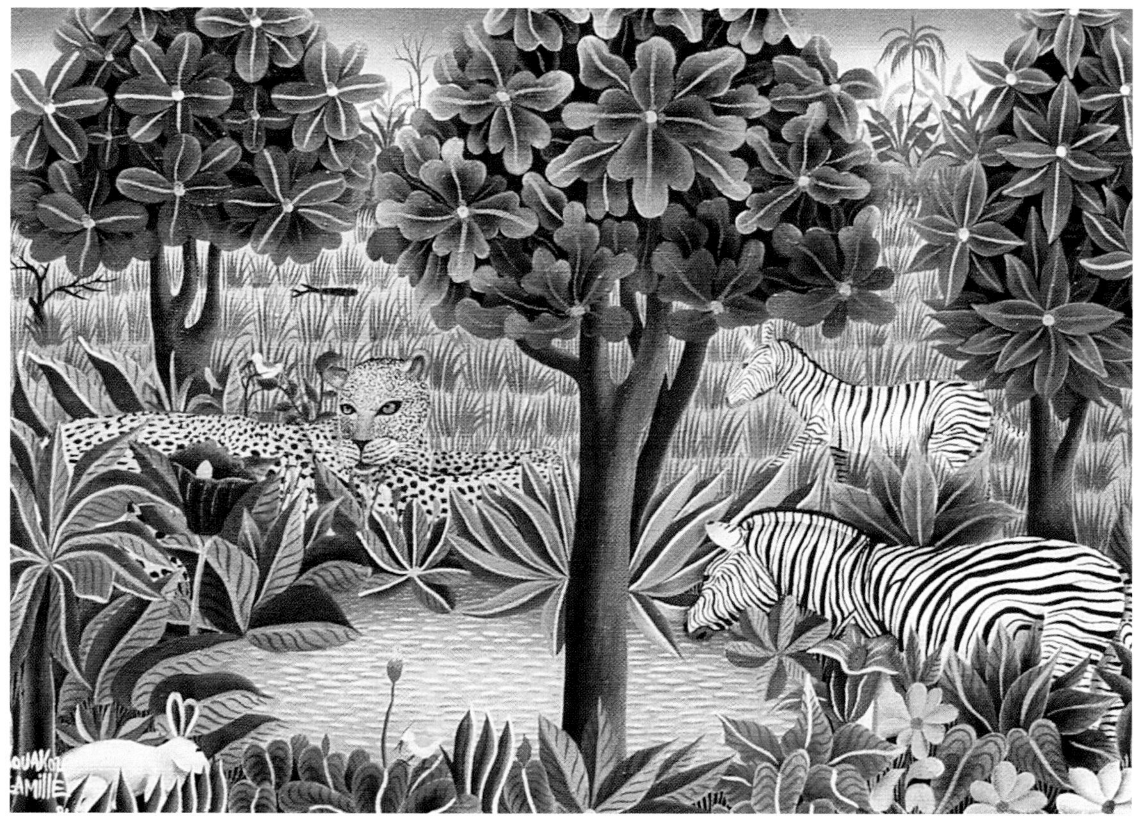

above, on left:
Pap'Emma, DRC, "Flower of Paradise"
oil on canvas, 30x25 cm
©Revue Noire

above, on right:
Cheik Ledy (born in 1962), DRC
©Yves Pitchen/Revue Noire

left:
Camille Kouakou (born in 1965), Ivory Coast, 1991
©Revue Noire

facing page:
Trigo Paula (born in 1950), Congo, "Maternity," 1984
oil on canvas, 122x88 cm.
©Revue Noire

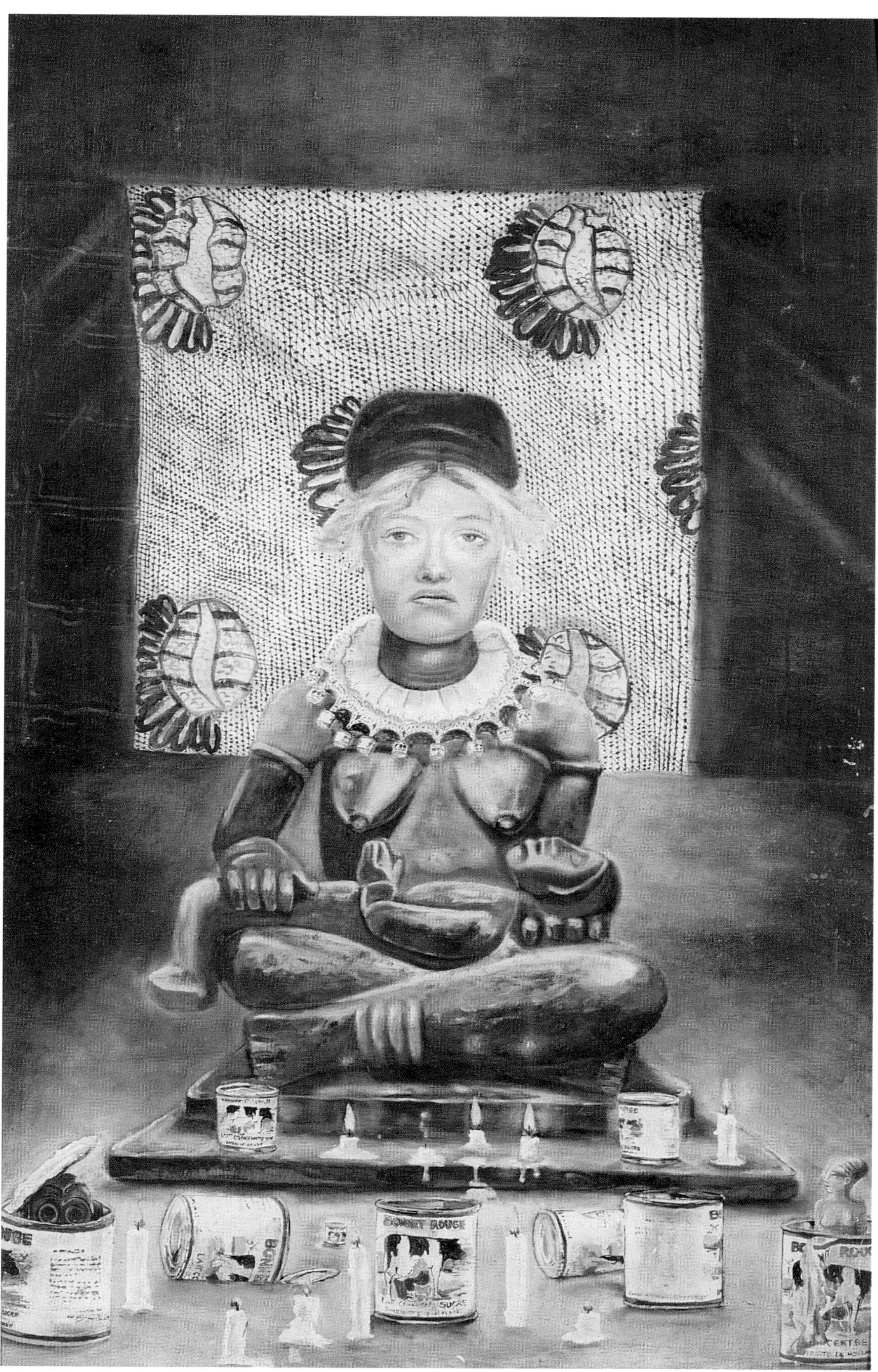
BONNET ROUGE

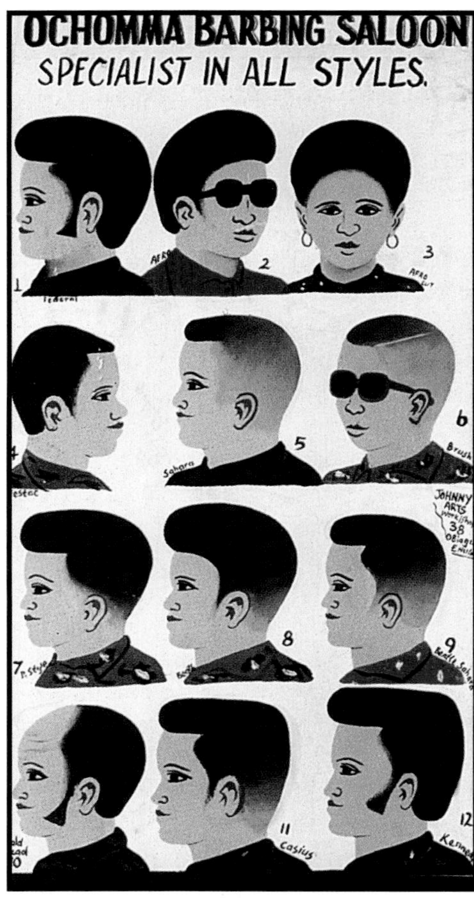

Johnny Art, Sign for Barber, circa 1962, Nigeria
oil on board, 41 x 122 cm.
©Maison Iwalewa, Université de Bayreuth

REPRESENTATION AND ADVERTISING SIGNS

Till Förster

In the mid-20th century, large African cities were a fascinating place. Following the war and the restrictions it also imposed on colonial Africa, a period of economic recovery began, accompanied by political independence movements. Bearers of promises and hopes, the cities became attractive sites. Modern life in the metropolises, from which the African countryside was largely cut off, appeared to hold great possibilities. Those who were not employed by a big company or by the (post) colonial administration often created their own small business. Economic and cultural exchanges with Europe changed and intensified in the 50s and 60s. The visual world of African cities transformed rapidly. New media became an integral part of daily life and contributed to the onset of a new form of representational art. Illustrations in newspapers and magazines, photography and films, cinema, and later on television and advertising images spread messages of modernity and new visual and figurative habits[1].

Sometimes, this new representational art could form a link with former local visual habits, or transform them. This was how the concrete sculptures of Aniedi Okon Akpan and Sunday Jack Akpan[2] took on the close-to-nature style of some of the Ibibio masks and of the representations of Mami Wata, long spread throughout the western coast of Africa. Many life-size figures ordered by relatives represented a deceased person. Other clients were merchants who ordered concrete sculptures for advertising purposes. The Akpans produced what the market was asking of them: lions, eagles and other heraldic animals. They also sculpted police officers, soldiers, soccer players, angels and preachers. They were entrepreneurs who ran their workshops like advertising agencies.

Yet, the figures produced for advertising purposes in the Akpan workshops were an exception found essentially in south-eastern Nigeria, and in a similar form in Ghana today. As a general rule, the artisans of this growing informal art used another new technique: painting. First of all, it was known, according to its definition, as the "painting of signs," then as "popular painting" or "urban art." Hotels, motorcycle and car repair shops, bars, restaurants and, naturally, the best known hairstylists, all needed signs on which to boast the merits of their craftsmanship or of their products. Many public administrations also displayed large-size images in front of their establishments and regional offices.

Today, we find advertising signs in almost all African cities. Their emergence is closely linked to the advent of the new representational art. In fact, the two are indivisible. This new art has different aspects. However, oil painting is governed, first and foremost, by a two-dimensional representation of man, which, even if it already existed in a scattered manner, was, in general, a new form of artistic expression, whose appearance was linked to the colonization of Africa. The growing presence of signs, photographs, illustrated newspapers and magazines made it possible to become familiar with these representational forms, especially in the cities. Since the end of World War II, at the latest, a number of these media had become accessible to the new bourgeois classes who knew how to read and write.

Excluding paintings for administrations, written and figurative elements are almost always found in advertising signs. On hairstylists' signs, the hairstyles are laid out by type and include the name of the style. This specific combination of the written word and images is characteristic of African sign painting and was only partially influenced by the comic strips that developed later on. It has advantages in that the images are aimed at all of the city's passersby. They can be understood both by clients who know how to read and those who cannot read, or who read only poorly. Moreover, it has recently been observed that the portion of urban African images covered by writing has increased. This change is an obvious indication of the increased literacy rates among modern African societies.

[1] This does not mean that just anyone could buy an illustrated magazine or a movie ticket. The printed matter passed through many hands before being thrown out. Nigeria is an exception. It had an abundant and varied press in the 50s and 60s, prior to the military coup of 1966. In the former French colonies, however, until the 1980s, often only one newspaper supporting the State existed.

[2] Anledi Okon Akpan (born in 1916) and Sunday Jack Akpan (born in 1940) are not related and each manage workshops (Nicklini 1974, Ruprecht 1993).

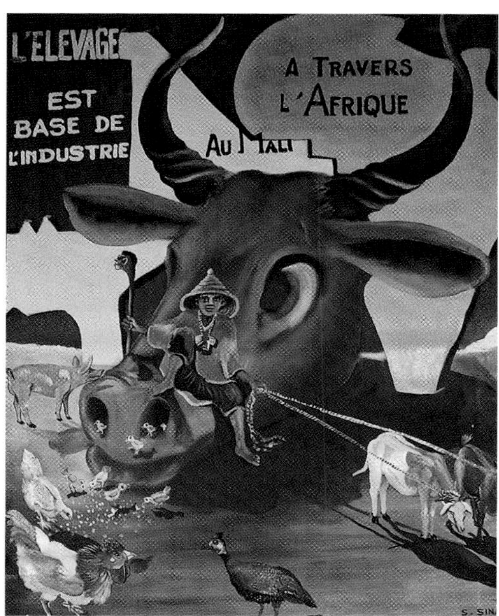

Sinaba, Mali, 1977

©Revue Noire

Sign painters must know how to read and write in order to do their job. Of course, they probably come from an agricultural milieu, but, in general, they have been living for a long time in large boroughs or even in a city where they have been able to get an education. The city is the only place where they can acquire a clientele, because in the small villages, the links that shape human networks are still so close that advertising aimed at a third anonymous person would be superfluous. Everyone knows who does what and who offers what product. Things are different in the city. The advertising sign assumes that there are social differences. Without it, and without the rapid growth of African cities during and after the colonial period, sign painting would not exist.

Painting is, above all, a craft industry and not art, in the modern sense of the word. Many duties are shared. Workshops are sufficiently big and are not comprised of one man alone. Several painters may work on one painting. The price depends on the surface area of the image, as well as on the number and quality of the colors used. As usual, the price is negotiated in advance, and, when it is set, the esthetic value is hardly ever questioned.

Most workshops bear the name of their founder. If the founder is the only person working there, the workshop's name would be referred to as the artist's name. However, most of the time there are several painters working in the same place, as was the case with the workshop of Sunny Arts in Jos, a merchant town located on one of the largest south-north national roads in Nigeria. As a result, most of the orders placed with the Sunny Arts workshop were for the decoration of trucks. But, if so desired, advertising posters could also be made, such as hairstylists' signs. One of the painters specialized in kung-fu and cowboy sculptures. They were driven around the entire northern part of Nigeria on board trucks. And so their author became known for his qualities and his work became "Adullahi O."[3]

Portraits of family members are another area of sign painting. They were rarely painted from live subjects. In general, the painters used photographs, which became widespread after World War II. In the 50s, there were essentially small studios in all big cities in western Africa.[4] These were generally decorated with accessories recalling local art or aimed at discovering the vast world, such as the metropolis of the country or a large mosque in northern Africa or the Middle East. Black and white film was used. The people being photographed had to prepare themselves by putting on beautiful clothing and posing.

Inhabitants of African cities were familiar with the technique of photography and its art in the 50s.[5] The proofs were also used to commemorate loved ones or, more rarely, friends. They were framed using two pieces of glass on which a brightly colored frame was painted. In many bourgeois homes, they were hung on the ceiling, from where the family's grandmother, so to speak, could observe her descendants. In hot and humid climates, the gelatin layer on photographic paper between the two pieces of glass would sometimes be quickly destroyed by bacteria. Numerous photographs that had often been worked well beyond the author's recommendations would eventually fade or become covered with spots. One solution was to have the photograph taken again, but this was not always possible if the person photographed had died in the meantime. In such cases, photographs were replaced with paintings. This technique was also used to obtain enlargements or durable reproductions. Unlike in Europe, photography was not the poor relative of painting. Painting and the portrait were indebted to photography. A stylistic comparison of these two genres could reveal this kinship in many regions of Africa, especially in the case of glass paintings.

[3] Kasfir 2000, page 38

[4] Guggenheim Museum, 1996. Revue Noire, 1998. Wendl & Behnrend, 1998.

[5] However, this knowledge of photographic technology only developed much later in the countryside. It should be noted that women acquired it much later than men.

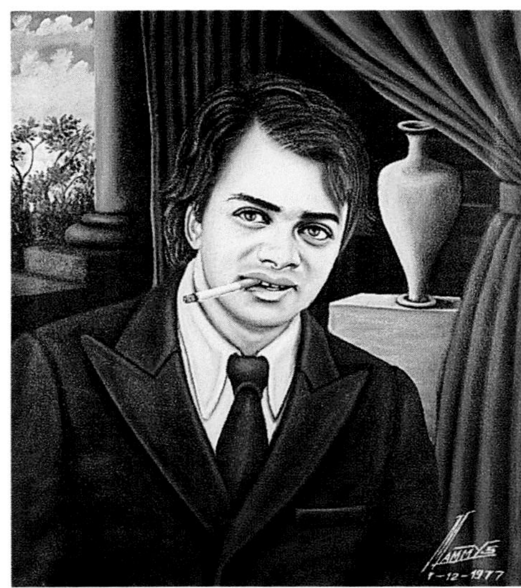

Mamy Soumbourou aka Mammys, "Portrait of Jean Loup Pivin"
Mali, 1977
©Revue Noire

Middle Art

Few of these painters are known in the international art world. Most of the time, their work was collected as an expression of "naïve folk art." Augustin Okoye, who called himself Middle Art, is an exception. Born in 1936 and a native of the Nri region in the Ibo region of southwestern Nigeria, he went to Onitsha, one of the Ibo economic centers, to learn the art of painting signs. After an apprenticeship period in two workshops, he opened his own and called it Middle Art, a widespread name in the region.[6]
Most orders came from local merchants and were used for advertising. During this period, Middle Art painted a few signs to promote his own business and show off his skills. This is how his most well known works were created. These include a self-portrait painted on the door to this workshop and another representation of himself with the Sardauna of Sokoto, the most influential political man in the country at the time.[7]

The first creations of Middle Art may be used to illustrate the relationship between painting and photography. He considers his self-portrait painted with oil on a hard fiber plate as his first painting. With its almost square format, it resembles, down to the smallest details, the traditional photographic portrait of the time in western Africa. Since photographers almost always used a twin-lens reflex, without any particular accessory, it was only possible to take bust shots. Close-ups would have required equipment too expensive for the photographer. With the negatives, they could make enlargements using an identity photograph shot. In this case, perspective was necessary: the ears had to be bare and well visible, which required the person photographed to look at the camera sidelong. The proofs were given to the client in a small folder that covered the corners.

It is a sure bet that Middle Art used this type of photograph as a model for his first self-portrait. The painter's face contains gray shades that correspond to the technique used in photography. His posture closely resembles the one he would have had in this type of photograph. However, his clothing and the background are without relief. Middle Art's signature appears in the top left corner. A red border frames the painting and covers the corners.

The same holds true for the self-portrait of Middle Art on his workshop door and for the representation of the Sardauna of Sokoto. Another photographic genre was used as a model. The full body photograph represents, in addition to the portrait, a local photographic tradition. Even today, cutting the body would be seen as an attack on human integrity. It would be unthinkable to do a "cut" work in the strict sense of the word when commemorating a family member. This is also the case for clothing. The photograph must show the model from his/her best angle. In southern Nigeria, which is a rather Christian area and includes the Ibo region, European clothing must be worn, namely a suit, a white shirt and a tie. In the Muslim north, the richly decorated clothing of devout Muslims must be worn. This is how Middle Art and the Sardauna are represented. Such pomp and ceremony would not be needed to illustrate the fictitious awarding of a gold prize.

It should be noted that the content of the painting goes beyond art itself. Ulli Beier, who discovered Middle Art, sees in the first painting a "touching dream,"[8] because the highly placed politician would never have paid any attention to a sign painter from Ibo, especially since he came from another part of the country and represented another religion. Yet, the representation becomes more meaningful when it is not merely seen from a personal perspective. Middle Art painted politicians to promote his own business.[9] The latter would draw clients to his workshop. The Hausa in the northern part of the country were among the most prosperous businesses and merchants in Nigeria, and in the Ibo region. The Hausa, therefore, represented potential clients and informing them of his opening in this manner was not pointless.

Middle Art, who suffered greatly during the Biafra war, is currently living as a sign painter in Onitsha. However, the great era of sign painting already seems

[6] The two apprenticeship workshops were called Young Art and Gills Art. These were also typical names used at all times (Middle Art 1990, page 26).

[7] The Sardauna of Sokoto was the legitimate successor of the Caliph of Sokoto, the biggest pre-colonial empire in the land that would become Nigeria. He was assassinated by gunfire during the first military coup in 1966.

[8] Beier, 1990, page 21.

[9] Bender, 1990, page 180-183.

to be part of the past in some African countries. In many cities, advertising signs are being replaced more and more by large prints, provided by international firms. The domain of sign painting belongs to the small, even very small businesses, small crafts that proliferate on the street corners of working-class districts.

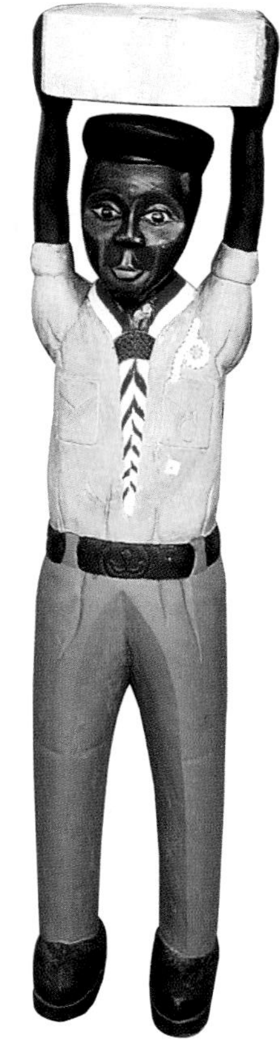

Komi Sokemawou (born in 1960), planter, Togo, 1990
h. 55 cm.
©Revue Noire

Middle Art (Augustin Okoye, born in 1936), Nigeria
Middle Art receives a prize from the hands of Sardauna de Sokoto.
Oil on fibreboard, circa 1966, 119 x 73 cm.
©Maison Iwalewa, Université de Bayreuth

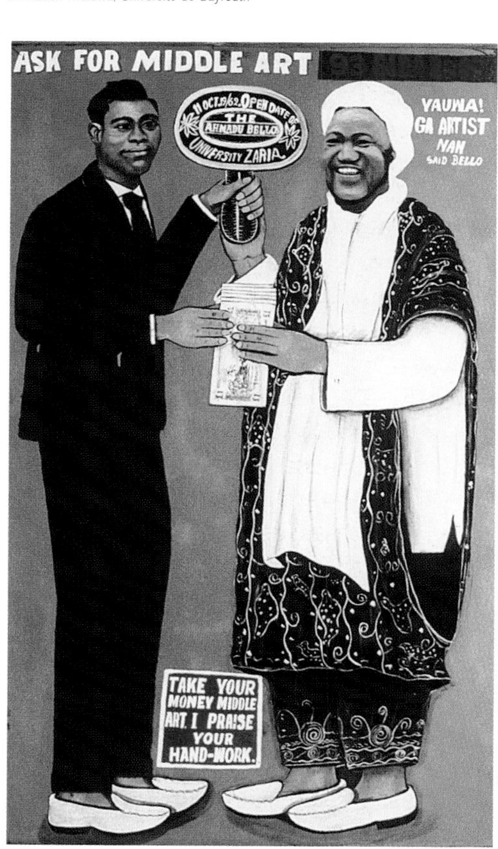

Mamy Soumbourou aka Mammys, Mali
Diana huntress, oil.
©Revue Noire

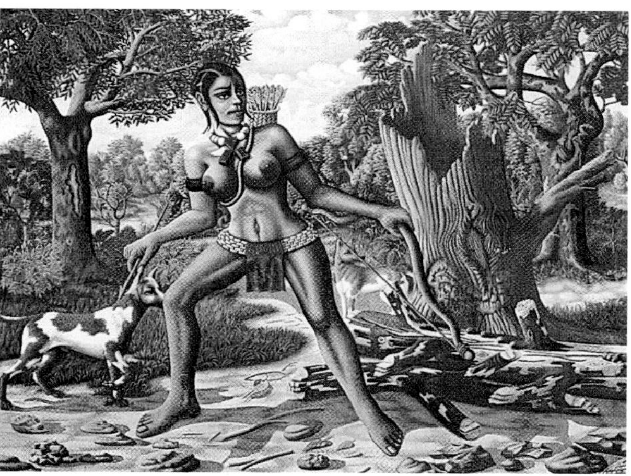

Middle Art (Augustin Okoye, born in 1936), self-portrait, Nigeria, circa 1970
Oil on plate, 186,5 x 61 cm
©Maison Iwalewa, Université de Bayreuth

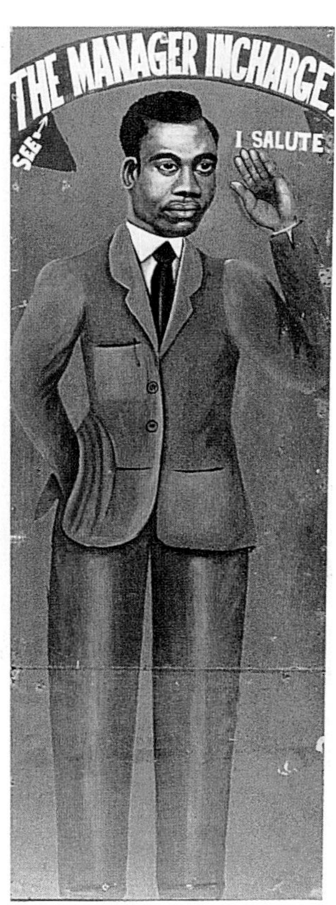

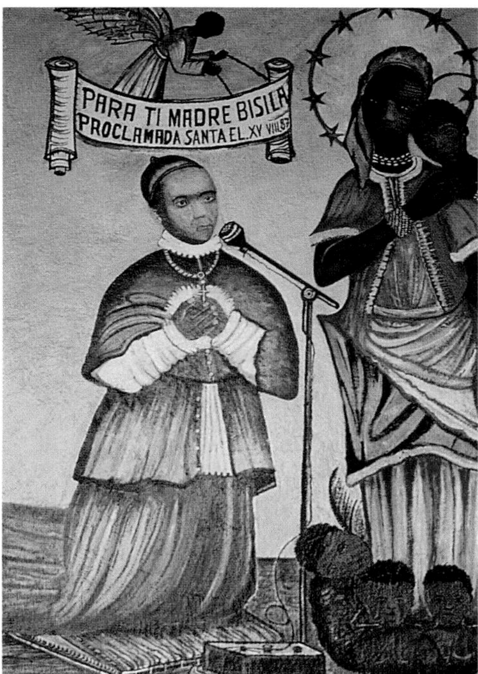

Candido Buna, Guinea Bissau

©Revue Noire

AIRPORT ART

Bennetta Jules-Rosette

As the crossroads of international travel, the airport becomes the metonym for local art produced for sale to outsiders. A liminal space, the airport erases and suspends cultures in moments of border crossing. Over the past two decades, airport art, which is a type of tourist art, has assumed an increasingly important position in the works of art historians, anthropologists, and collectors because of its challenge to tradition in a postmodern universe of rapidity and rupture. No longer viewed as a mere aberration of mass culture, airport and tourist art may be seen as reflections of culture contact and change that subvert the canons of non-Western art history. Airport art is based on the permeability of apparently simple and transparent images and codes. Artists manipulate these familiar images for both their commercial and aesthetic effects by playing upon the paradoxes and illusions that arise at moments of border crossing.

History of tourist art

Although contact art has long existed on the African continent, from the Portuguese ivories of West Africa to early nineteenth-century carved images of Europeans, contemporary tourist art has its roots in the colonial art schools and academies of the mid-twentieth century. Sponsors and brokers such as Pierre Romain-Desfossés in Kinshasa, Pierre Lods in Brazzaville, Ulli Beier in Lagos, and Frank McEwen in Harare provided instruction and work space for artists, and generated with their protégés the foundational images that have become the hallmarks of tourist and airport art - the idyllic landscape (with its numerous variations), the portrait, and the curio reproduction.

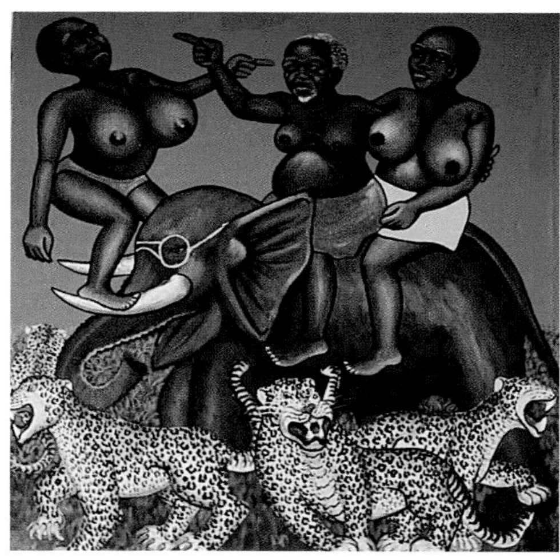

Moké (born in 1950), DRC

©Revue Noire

While much early tourist art was anonymous, the postcolonial era has witnessed the rise of individual artists, cooperatives, and collectives producing art works with definite signatures, growing reputations, and distinctive styles. Noteworthy among these collective enterprises are the Kamba carving cooperatives of Kenya, the Bini carvers of Benin City, the sculptors of Grand Bassam, Côte d'Ivoire, the Kinshasa painters' studios, and the textile cooperatives of northern Côte d'Ivoire and Burkina Faso.

Aesthetics of communication

In tourist art, the audience sets the stage on which new objects are received. Tourist art involves a process that anthropologist David MacDougall has described as "the simultaneous perception of different frames of reference, in boundaries crossed." Artists respond to perceived audience demand, but this response is indirect and mediated by the border crossings of culture brokers and fluctuations in the tourist art market. When Kamba carvers in Nairobi produced red-and-black theatrical-style masks and Masai carvings, they responded to what they perceived as the tastes of Japanese consumers. Some representations of technology in tourist art, such as sculptor Koffi Kouakou's carved computers in Côte d'Ivoire or miniature airplane carvings by Kamba carver Joseph Muli in Kenya, were direct responses to orders subsequently reproduced in large quantities. Often individual image creators such as Kouakou and Muli generate new designs that are copied and reproduced based on their commercial viability. This process of reproduction gluts the tourist art market and creates the effect of standardization. In fact, the artists themselves often apply standards of mechanical quality control to repetitive reproductions in order to assure that genres and forms remain stable and saleable. This process results in an aesthetics of communication in which image production and styles are controlled by direct and indirect interactions with consumer audiences. Successful innovations occurring in this cycle of communication and exchange are rapidly reproduced.

Issues of authenticity

The debate over authenticity is critical to discussions of tourist art. While some critics seek to justify the authenticity of tourist art by placing it on a continuum with other forms of contemporary African art, such as folk art and urban art , others

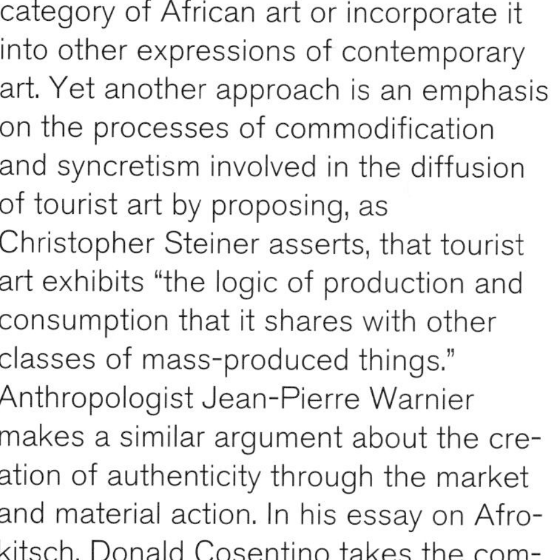

question any inclusion of tourist art in the category of African art or incorporate it into other expressions of contemporary art. Yet another approach is an emphasis on the processes of commodification and syncretism involved in the diffusion of tourist art by proposing, as Christopher Steiner asserts, that tourist art exhibits "the logic of production and consumption that it shares with other classes of mass-produced things." Anthropologist Jean-Pierre Warnier makes a similar argument about the creation of authenticity through the market and material action. In his essay on Afro-kitsch, Donald Cosentino takes the commodification approach a step further by demonstrating how African leaders have reappropriated tourist art by marketing wax prints, T-shirts, boubous, and watches sporting their images.

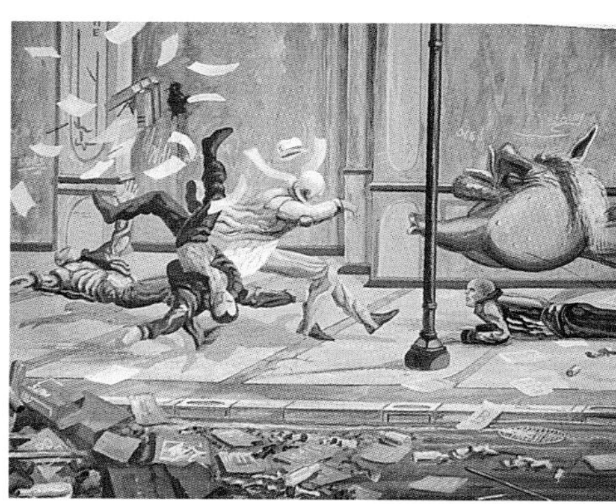

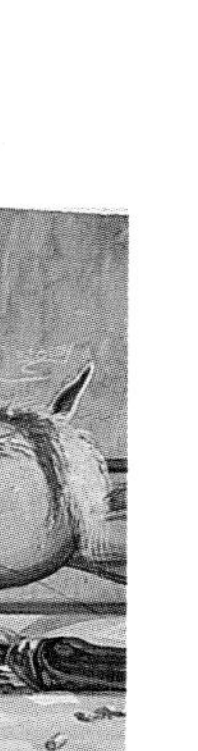

Mandengué Dinh, Cameroon, 1990

©Revue Noire

The impact of tourist art: innovation or inertia?

In spite of scholarly and institutional debates over whether tourist art is an empty category, redundant for research and display, the art continues to be produced with vitality across the African continent. One of the distinguishing features of tourist art and a primary motivation for its commodification, is its strong reliance on culture brokers for the distribution and the modification of images. The "cash-credit-ordering system," through which brokers and clients influence styles in direct orders, leads to the creation of new images, such as Kouakou's carved computer. In addition, innovative international brokers such as Giovanni Franco Scanzi, who developed a collector's market for Baoulé slingshots, are able to transfer folk, utilitarian, and tourist pieces into the gallery trade. Similar transpositions take place with idyllic landscape paintings and portraiture as artists and brokers open up new local and international audiences for these works. When art works crisscross competing markets, artists (often the same individuals) alter the content and genres of their products with stylized representations of place, space, and time. This protean quality of tourist art is the key to understanding its vibrancy and the challenge it poses for art criticism and classification.

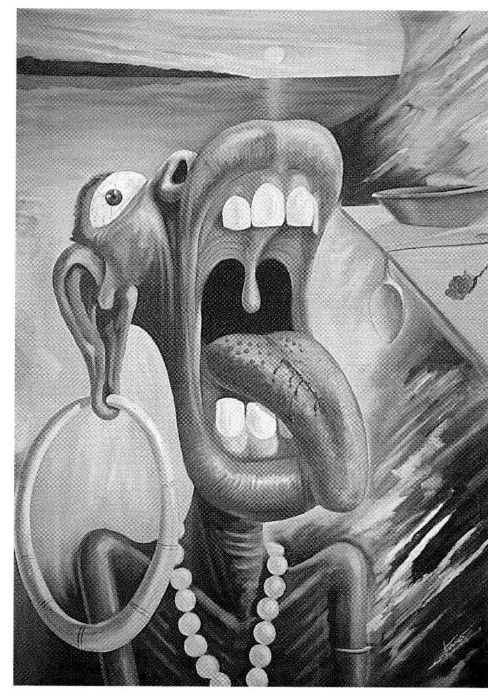

Guilhermo Semedo Tavares (born in 1964), Guinea Bissau, 1992

©Revue Noire

Tourist art is a hybridized product of intercultural communication arising from the commercial milieux in which it is fashioned. Yet, the new genres and styles also reflect the innovations and talents of image creators by combining the reprise of cultural and artistic traditions with the logic of mass commodification in the international art market.

The "souwères"

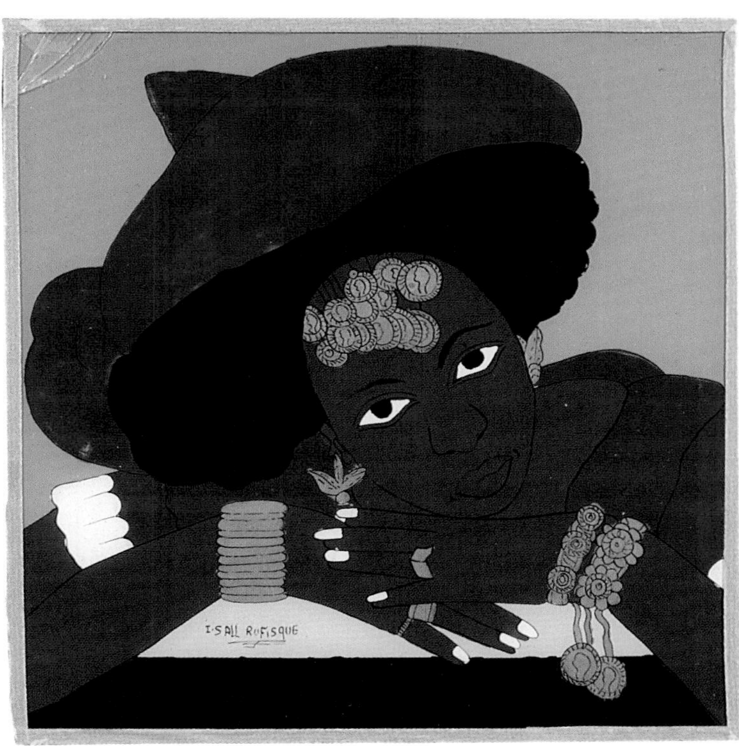

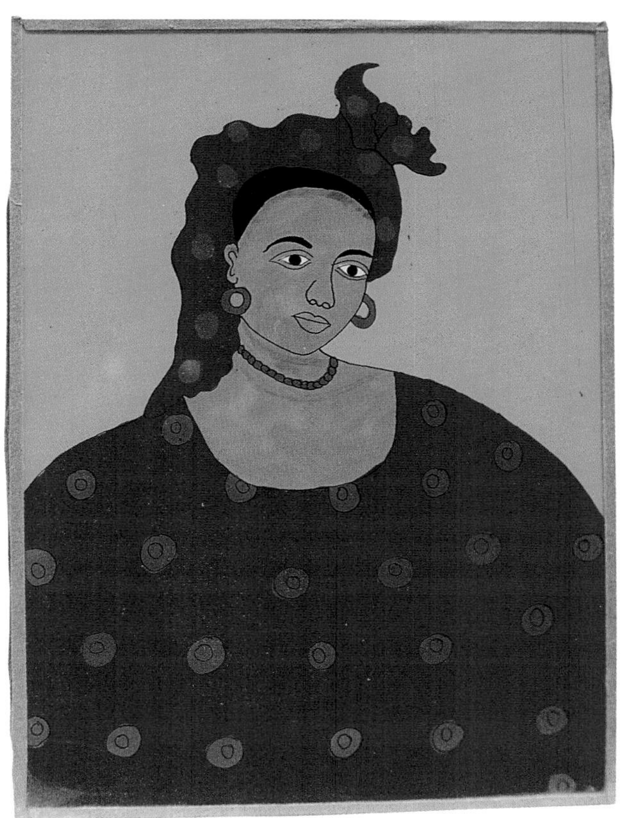

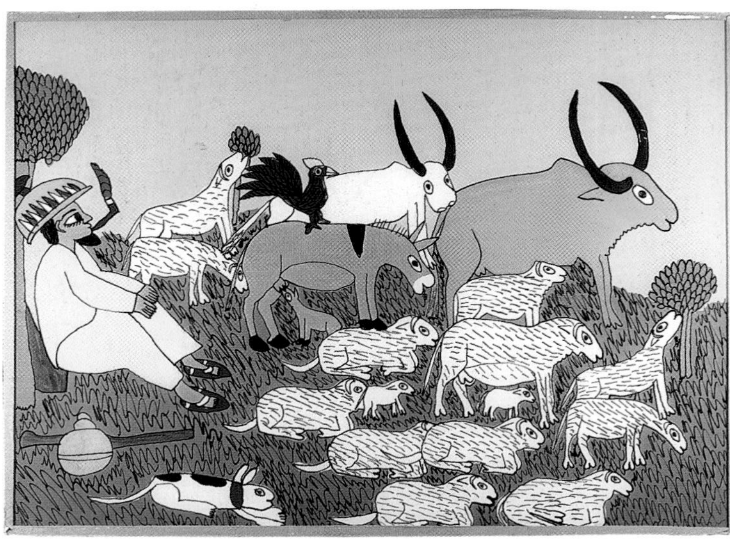

The production of "souwères" (glass paintings) is rooted in the trade that, for centuries has marked the coastal cultural identity of Senegal. Trade took place not only with merchant Europe, but also, and more so, with the Arab world of the south and the east, which was in turn supplied by the Orient and the Far East. All of Sahelian Africa was privy to the circulation of products, thoughts and cultures coming from the desert, which was as much an East/West as a North/South boulevard. The surprising discovery of Manufrance rifles by René Caillé, the first European to penetrate Djenne and Timbuktu, is a perfect example of this.

The current tourist destination of the souwères brings to mind this intimate relationship between the souwère and the Senegalese. The relationship between the souwère and photography is a wonderful example: the souwère, a painted frame containing a photograph, may also deliberately draw its inspiration from photographs, such as those of Mama Casset. In the 50s, 60s and 70s, Mama Casset was an elegant and sensual image of Senegalese women. Famous names came up in this circle, such as the painter Gora Mbengue. A reverse phenomenon is thus created, whereby the photograph serves as a reference for the painting, as John Picton emphasizes with respect to funeral sculptures, and Till Forster, with respect to advertising painting in Ghana and Nigeria.

all glass paintings: ©Revue Noire

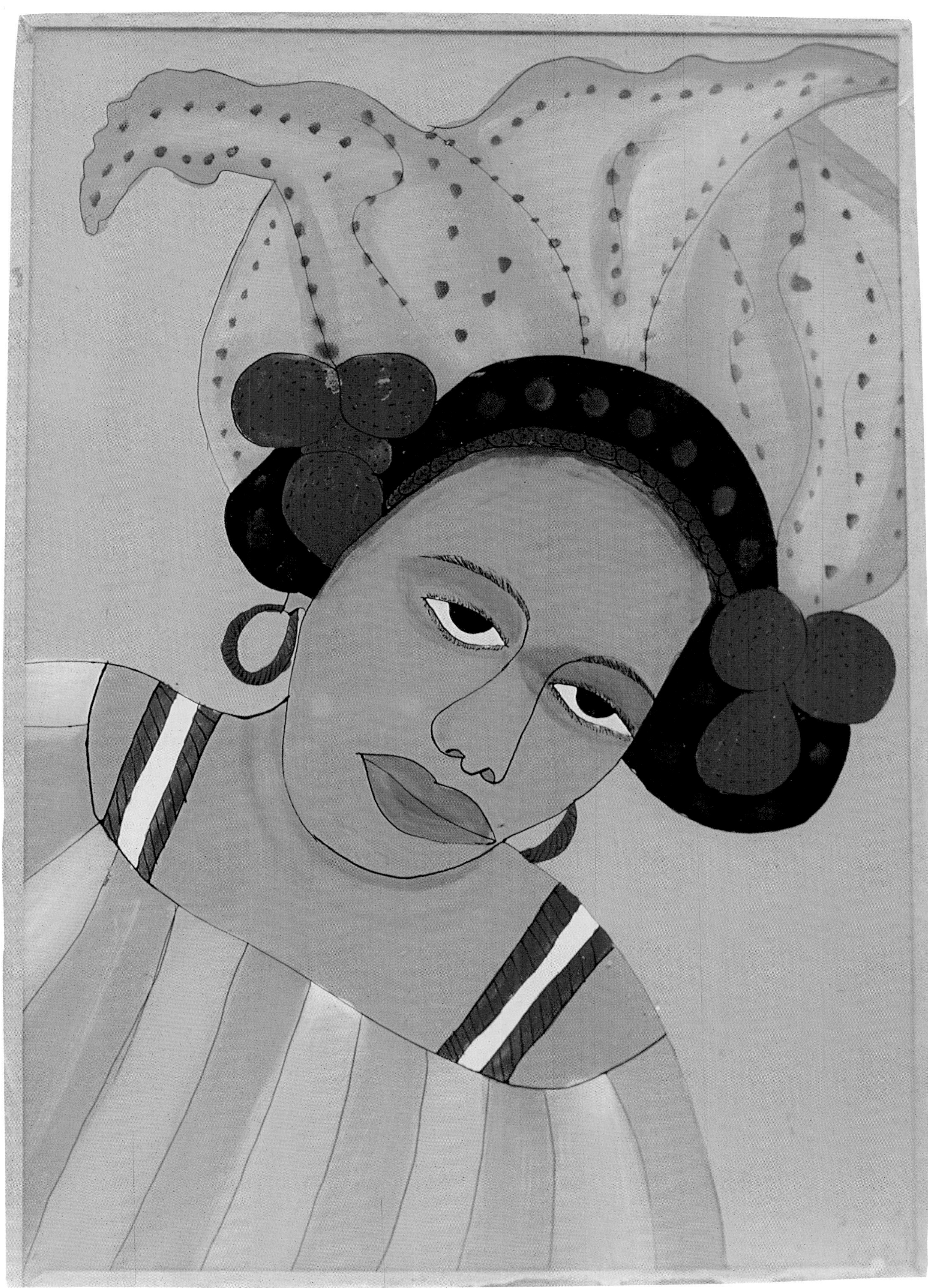

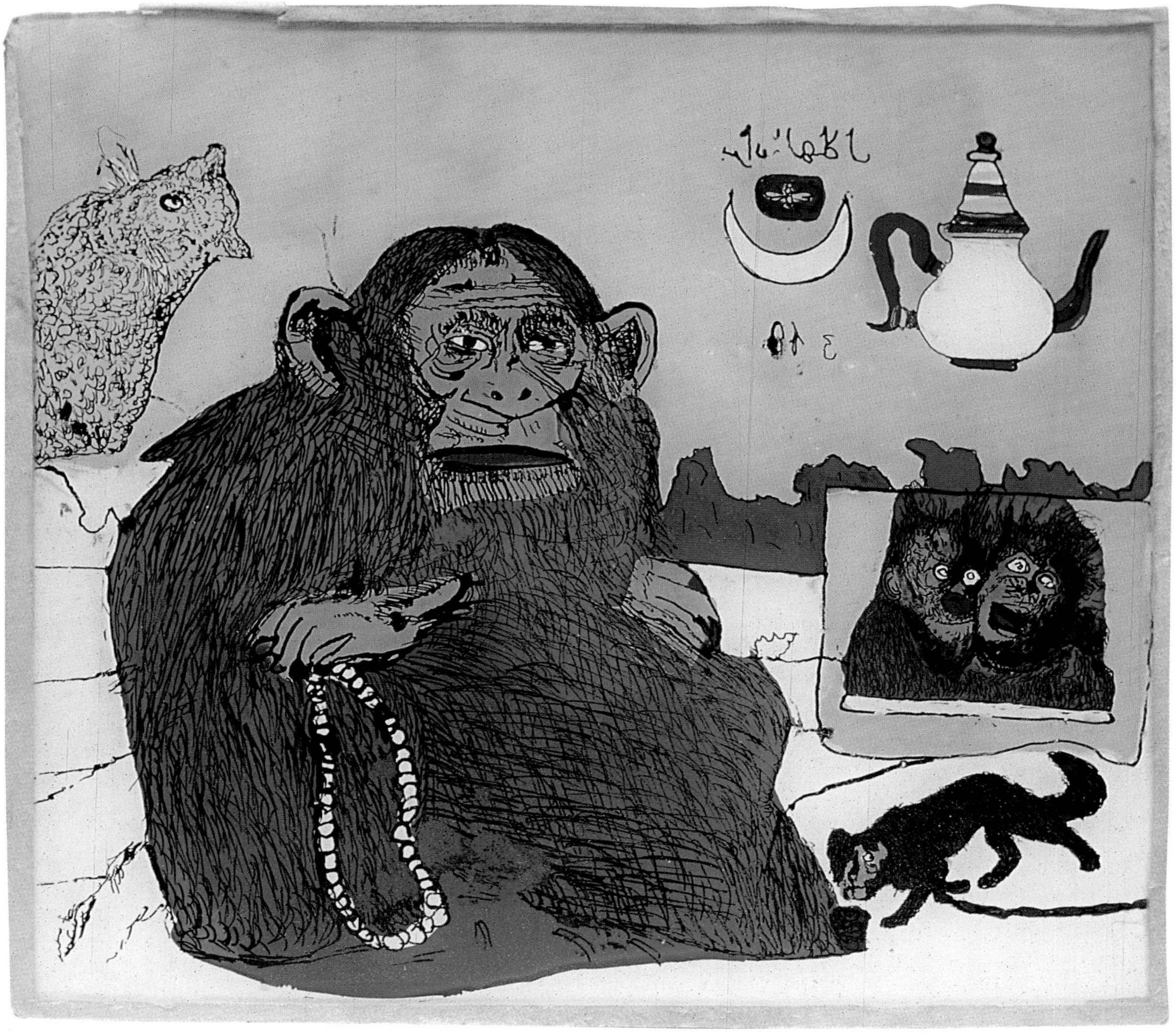

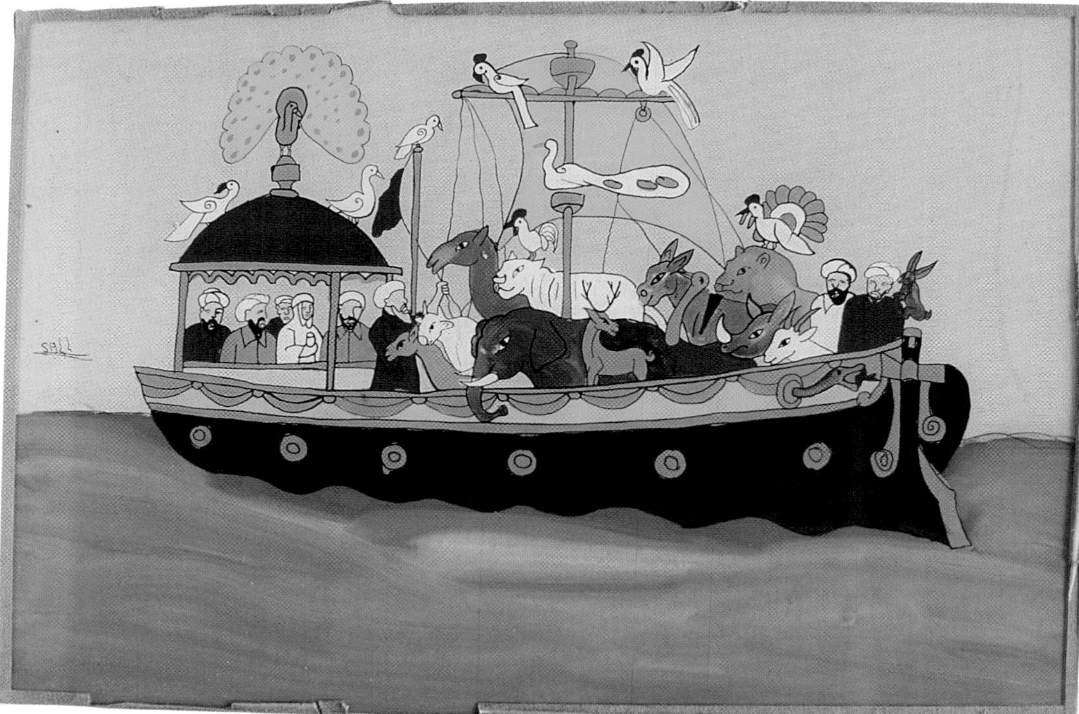

this page:
Mali underwater

GLASS PAINTING IN SENEGAL
Marie-Hélène Boisdur de Toffol

Glass paintings appeared in western Africa at about the end of the 19th century. They were quite numerous in Senegal, Ivory Coast, Mali and Nigeria at the beginning of the 20th century. Other pockets also developed in Niger, Zaire and Somalia. The paintings were done using a constant process: the subject was painted in reverse on one side of the glass, then the plate was turned over and applied to a sheet of wood or cardboard, depending on when it was manufactured, and framed. The technique used was actually a painting on the back of the piece of glass. The glass gave the range of colors a particular brilliance because it eliminated the air space that formed between a framed painting and the glass.

The different layers of colors were applied in reverse succession in relation to the usual painting. The image developed in several distinct phases and left no room for error. The first phase consisted in drawing the subject's outline using dark and accurate lines, thereby creating a network of perfectly defined small surfaces. Then, the inner drawings were done and the details painted. The flat surfaces were then filled with color. Depending on the era and the glass painter, gilding was sometimes added to this color scheme.

Urban art

The art of painting on glass is specifically urban, as are signs, advertisements, painting of bars or trucks, and pleasure paintings done on other mediums. Its birth is contemporaneous with the creation of the "modern day" large African cities. Its propagation and evolution made it into a living art, an image of the new Africa of the big cities, crossroads and melting pots of influence, of peoples and cultures. Glass painting portrays the concerns and daily habits of city populations, their dreams, deep aspirations, religious beliefs, attachment to certain myths and legends or the partially lost village lifestyle. The works produced by glass painters give rise to a mythology where the traditional and modern world mixes with the profane and religious world. In fact, Islamic themes, a historical cycle, a repertoire of major political and religious events in the 20th century and portraits are added to these themes emerging from a certain vision of traditional Africa. As a result, the impact of the African, Arab-Islamic and Western cultures are, to varying degrees, constantly recorded as images by glass painters.

Scenes from everyday life

The urban world is described with humor through street scenes and portraits of typical people. For example, the thief and the police officer are often represented in their antagonism (pursuits, arrests, etc.).

However, the source of inspiration and nostalgia is life in the village. Hairstyling sessions, tending to the herds, fields of crops, preparing meals, portraits of men and women in traditional garb, are all repeated themes. The privileged activities of each ethnic group are pretexts for pictorial compositions. The Fula are represented leading their herds. The activities of the Moors are symbolized by traveling caravans. The traditional cultures of the different regions are portrayed by scenes of life in the fields. The structure and architecture of the villages of each ethnic group are respected. Portraits most often represent various aspects of female elegance and thus recall the criteria for beauty and the features of the clothing worn by the Senegalese people. The sumptuousness of the female Wolof costume or the legendary elegance of the Saint-Louis "Signares" in days of old are described.

Tales, legends and myths

The religious and mythical beliefs, the legends of the countries of western Africa are also illustrated at times. There are numerous versions of the exploits of "Samba Gueladio Diegui," a wise man, a valorous hero, a competent king, whose legendary figure appears in the oral tradition of the Fula, Bambara, Toucouleur and Wolof ethnic groups. A certain number of old or contemporary glass paintings are representations of the female genie of the waters of Nigeria, called Mami Wata.

Serpents, symbols of the fluidity of the waters, twist around her arms and neck. Some glass paintings portray tales with morals. These tales are fairly short stories that, beneath pleasant exteriors, are used to enlighten and socialize. What often remains of these stories are proverbs to slip into conversations, and paintings filled with imagination and humor. Many of these paintings are variants on the theme of the hunted hunter, the jealous spouse, the gullible person and the trickster. Like the storyteller, the glass painter is the guardian of oral literature. Like the sculptor of old, he creates, on order, works that reflect a culture, with its manifestations, activities and values.

Historic cycle

The painter is also a griot. As a chronicler and poet, his role is to memorize the history of the country, of its chiefs, of its ethnic groups and of its families. Thus, a certain number of glass paintings constitute a sort of historical cycle where one can see representations of battles, soldiers and war-chiefs. The protagonists of the colonial wars are especially portrayed. The repeated representations of the large faces of those who resisted colonization, such as Lat Dior, Alboury N'Diaye, and Ba Diakhou, reveal a latent feeling of patriotism and national conscious. The success of glass painting at the beginning of the 20th century relates to colonization. This folk art was something of a response to colonialism. It helped to ensure the survival of certain values that participate in the symbiosis of composite cultural elements. The same phenomenon can actually be found in Tunisian glass paintings in the 20s. Masmoudi, in *La Peinture sur verre en Tunisie* (Tunis 1972), states that, in the 1880s, when the city of Gabes was putting up great resistance to the French, the representations of heroes and horsemen of the past multiplied in Tunisian glass frames.

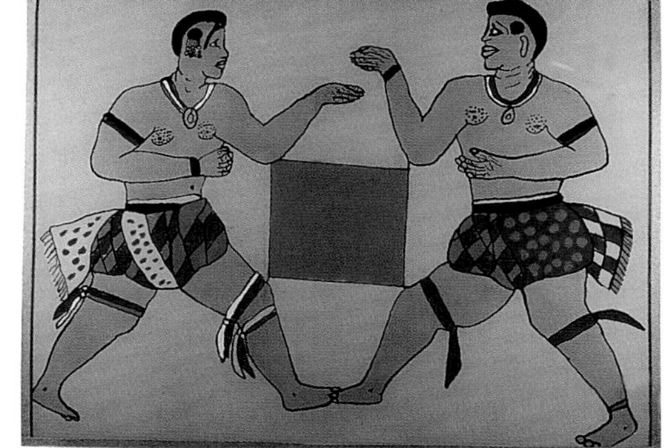

Fighters

©Revue Noire

Glass painting and Islam

Islam also has a very important role in the production and dissemination of glass paintings. Several accounts agree and confirm that the first glass painters in western Africa were calligraphers and illuminators of the Koran. Glass painting in Senegal, for example, was apparently born out of both urbanization and Islamization in the 19th century. As a result, it developed an extremely rich iconography portraying both images of the Shiite representational repertoire and scenes of local marabout Islam. We also find calligraphy or pictograms quoting words or verses from the Koran. Signs, which, in the way they are laid out, create the shape of a bird, read in Arabic "My success comes from God alone. It is to God that I return." With Islam being the third Abrahamic Religion, certain paintings portray Adam, Eve, Abraham, Noah, etc., thereby illustrating verse 78 of the third Sura "We believe in God, in what he revealed to us, to Abraham, Ismael, Jacob, Jesus and in what the prophets received from heaven. We do not make any difference between them. We are resigned to the will of God."
To these representations are added those of the main themes of Shiite imagery: Al Buraq, the prophet's winged beast, similar to the portrayal of the main episodes that mark the Alide epic. Of particular importance are glass paintings representing the "Companions of the Prophet," the four "al Rashidûn," or "well-guided," caliphs (Abubakar, Umar, Uthman and Ali), the battle between Ali and Ras Al Ghoul, the monstrous Yemenite prince, Ali and his two sons, Hassan and Husayn, the battles of the first days of Islam, such as the battle of Badar. Finally, the religiously inspired glass frames may also be devoted to specific aspects of the propagation of the Islamic religion in Africa. Aside from the scenes related to daily religious life (a person returning from the mosque, men in prayer etc.), there are numerous glass paintings of chiefs of the marabout brotherhood: chiefs of the Quadria brotherhood, el Hadj Malick Sy, founder of the Tijania brotherhood, Limamou Laye, founder of the Layennes brotherhood, Cheick Amadou Bamba M'Backé (1859-1927), founder of the Mourides brotherhood. More narrative glass paintings illustrate the life of some of these religious leaders. The body of work devoted to the stages of the life of Amadou Bamba is an example of this in its richness and variety.

Decorative frames and photographs

Decorative frames complete this section. They portray birds, roosters usually in a confrontational pose, geometric or floral patterns. A photograph often appears at the heart of these frames, such as the photograph of a religious leader, a grandparent, a child, evidence of one's belonging to a genealogy, family, secular or religious community.

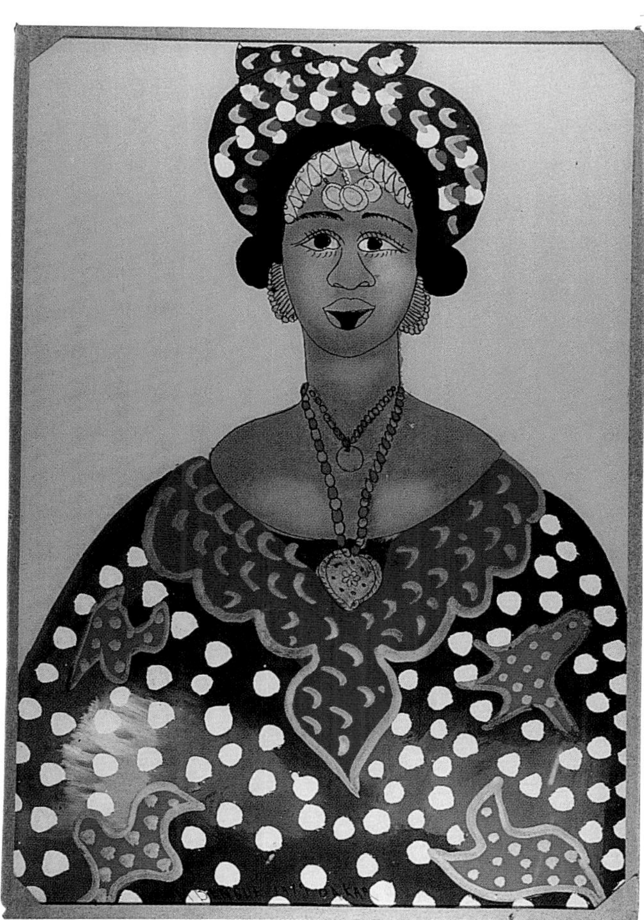

A Saint-Lousie woman

©Revue Noire

An example of popular cultural dynamism

Glass painters have, therefore, created original works. They have rejected the archetypes of the past, but have maintained links with traditions. They have adopted imported techniques, but have been subject to their messages, such that they have worked on a new form of art adapted to their era and public, to which they have maintained the ties, despite social mutations. This approach is an example of real popular cultural dynamism. We are in the presence of real work on plastic and thematic elements, of a genuine pictorial quest. The glass frames are not only partial testimonies of the creative experiences of the men of our era. They are also a link between a long-gone cultural past and a future African plastic production. As such, they are potential materials that provide reflection on the evolution of African art.

Cheikh Amadou Bamba

©Revue Noire

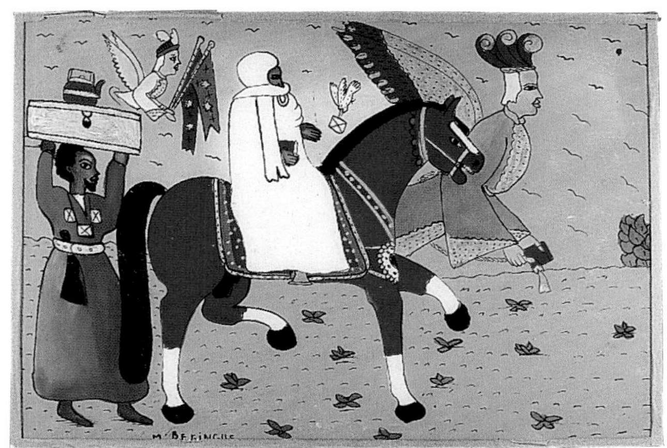

Cheikh Amadou Bamba meeting French troops

©Revue Noire

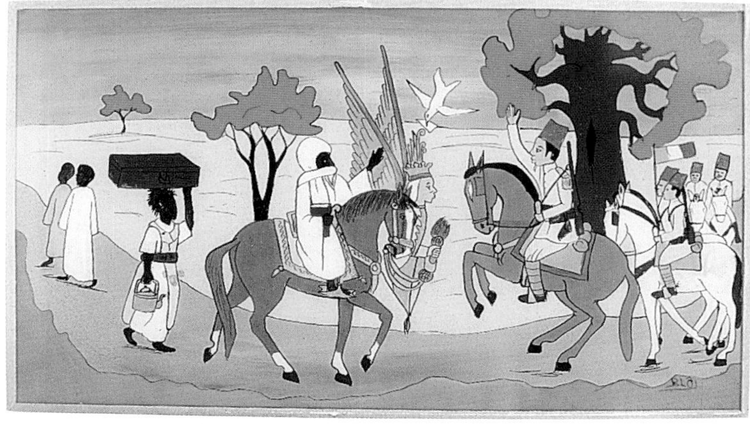

Coffins and funeral art

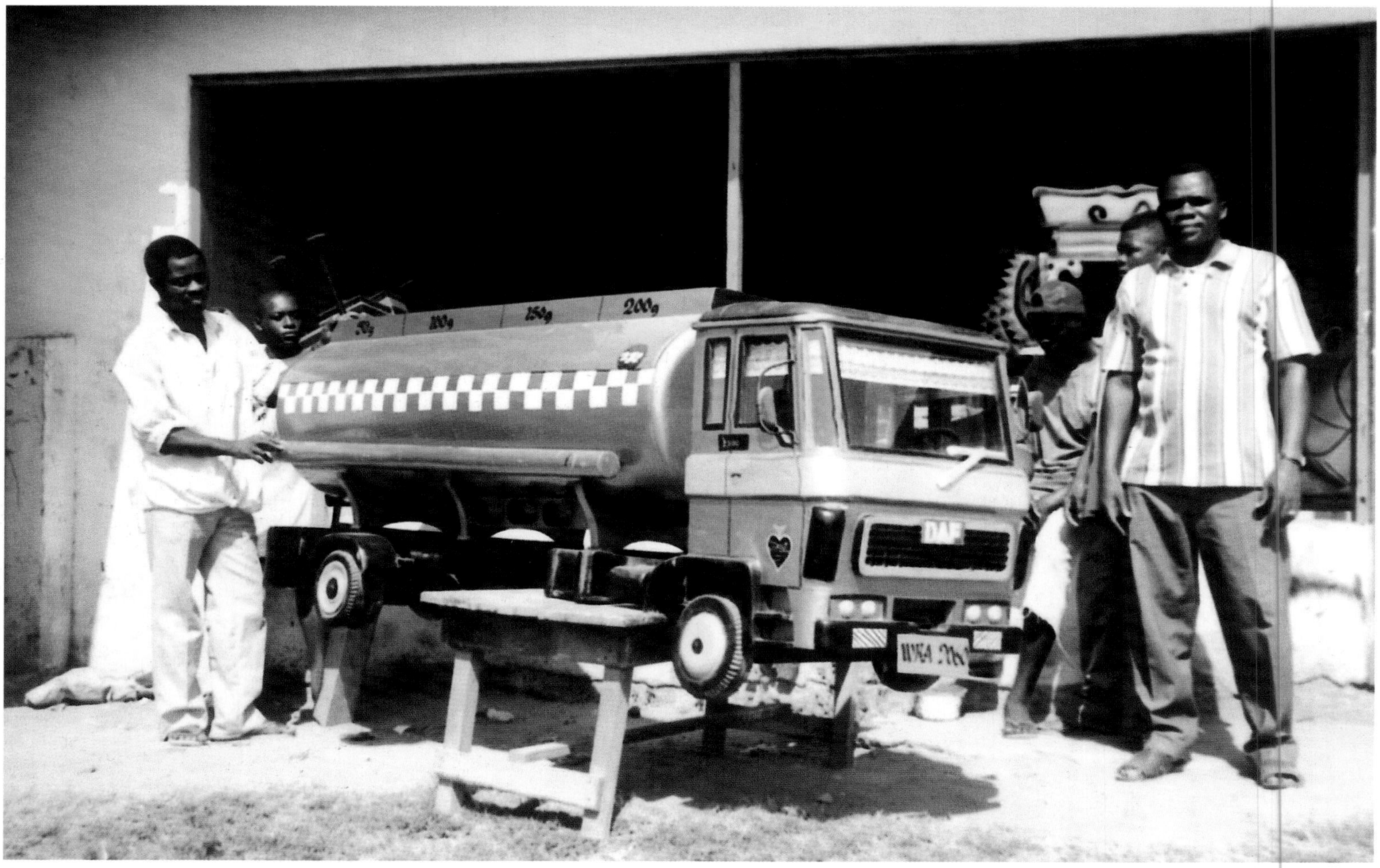

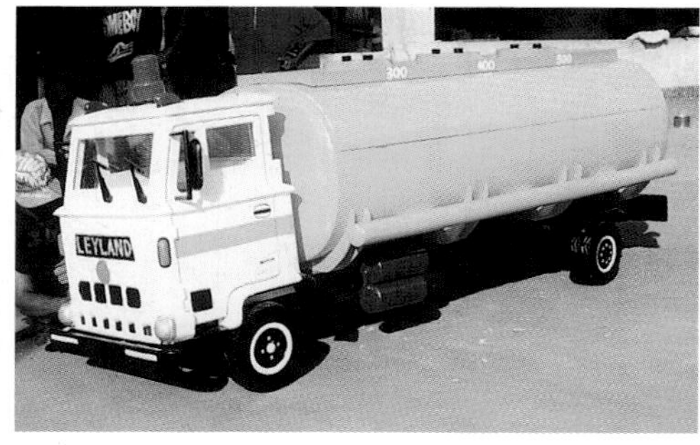

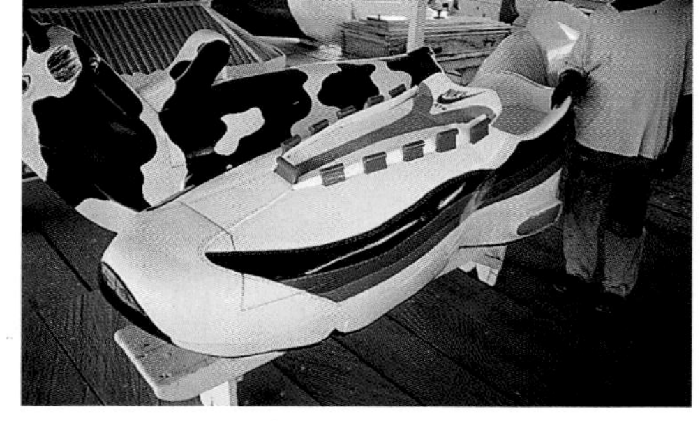

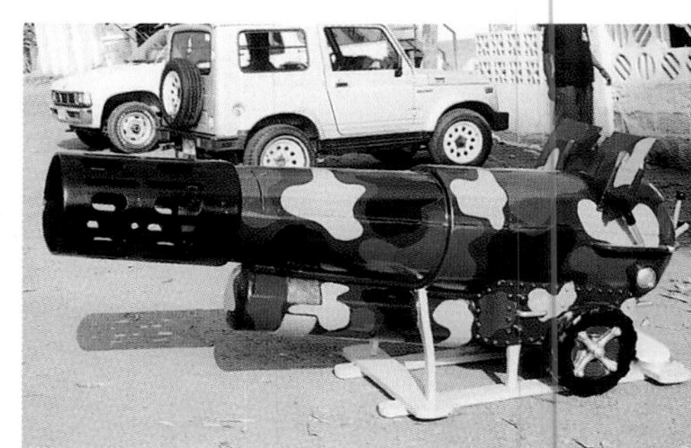

above:
Kane Kwei (1922-1992), Ghana, coffins
©Revue Noire

below:
Paa Joe (born in 1945), Ghana, coffins
©Revue Noire

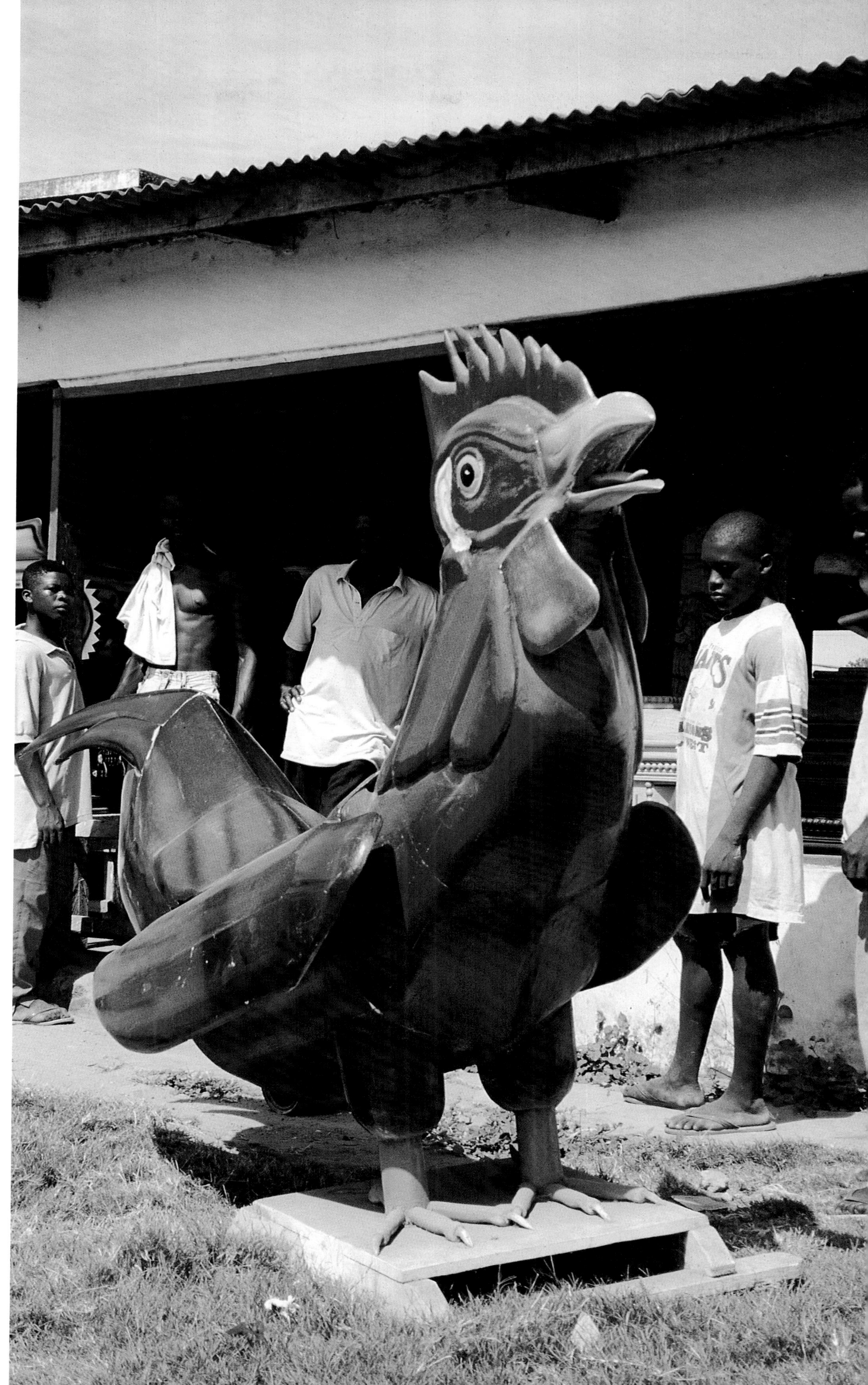

Kane Kwei (1922-1992), Ghana, coffin
©Revue Noire

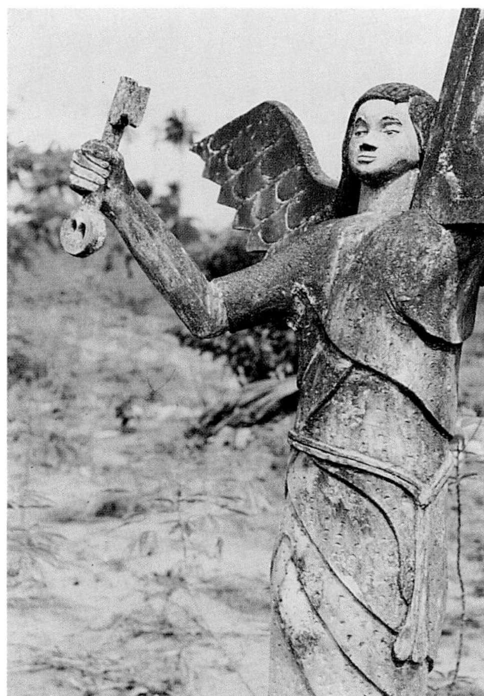
Angel, cement, Nigeria
©John Picton

Stephen Zanoo, c.a. 1990, mausoleum, Nigeria
©John Picton

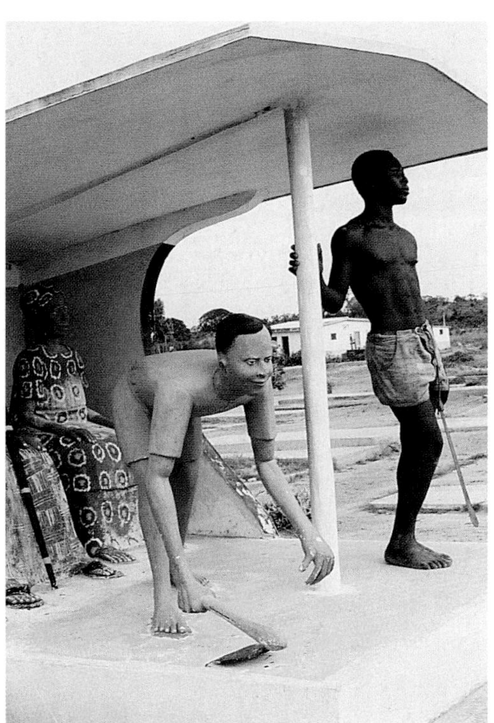

CEMENT SCULPTURES AND FANTASY COFFINS
John Picton

One of the many areas of 20th-century visual practice still in need of research is the development of funerary and related arts. These include sculpture in cement, figurative portrait painting and fantasy-coffin making. The published examples of sculptured and painted funerary monuments suggest a distribution from Akan peoples of southern Ivory Coast (Domowitz & Mandirola 1984) to Calabar in south-east Nigeria. The earliest evidence known to me for the use of cement in making of monumental funerary sculpture comes from inscriptions on south-east Nigerian examples giving dates in the second decade of the 20th century (Beier 1960, Butler 1963); and on this basis it would seem likely that this art has its origins in the late 19th-century import of commemorative monumental sculpture for the graves of leading traders and city state rulers in the coastal ports in this region. However, this is not a single tradition, for the range of forms and intentions differ from region to region. Anang monuments around Ikot Ekpene in south-east Nigeria are often built in tiered form with figures at each level. Southern Akan and Ewe monuments are rather more like single-storey houses with the figures placed within. Moreover, in Fante communities in southern Ghana, cement sculptures adorn the asafo (military company) houses (Cole & Ross 1977).

At the present time, the best-known exponents of this art are Sunday Jack Akpan, who works in the Anang region of south-east Nigeria (Vogel 1991, 101) and Stephen Zanoo in the Anlo region of south-east Ghana (Wendl & du Plessis 1998). Both of them work from photographs. Akpan is known for both portrait statues and genre figures; while Zanoo has developed the practice of showing something of the life history of the deceased in his sculpture. Graves with painted portraits of the deceased are also popular in the Anlo region, but little is yet known beyond the location of some of the painters in Aflao (on the border with Togo). What is clear is that both painters and sculptors rely upon photography for their imagery; and the inter-relationship between these three mediums of representation remains yet one more subject for research.

It is has been though that the making of fantasy coffins was initiated by Kane Kwei (1922-1992), a carpenter in the Ga-speaking village of Teshie, east of Accra; but according Secretan (1995) it is not quite that simple. After the end of World War II in 1945 it seems that the chief of Teshie had commissioned a palanquin in the shape of an eagle from the workshop of Ata Owoo (1904-1976), the leading master-carpenter in Teshie, and a man with a reputation for ornamental woodwork. The chief would be carried in the palanquin at appropriate festival occasions. The chief of a neighbouring community was so impressd by this that he commissioned a palanquin in the shape of a cocoa pod; but he died before its completion so he was buried in it instead. This was what gave Kane Kwei and his elder brother, also a carpenter, the idea of making an aeroplane-shaped coffin for their grandmother when she died in 1951 as she had said she used to dream of flying. With the public admiration for the aeroplane and the encouragement of Ata Owoo, Kane Kwei that same year set himself up with one apprentice in his own worshop to concentrate of coffin-making. The next one he made was for a fisherman, and was made in the shape of a fishing canoe; and thereafter, all manner of subjects were employed in coffin imagery, sometimes chosen to denote the occupation of the deceased, and sometimes to denote other qualities: the hen, for example, for a mother with many children. Although now occasionally commissioned by individuals and museums from Europe and America, the patrons of this art are the families of well-to-do men and women in the Ga-speaking communities to the east of Accra. By the time of his death in 1992, Kane Kwei's annual turnover of coffins was around thirty.

There are now three or four coffin workshops along the Accra-Teshie-Nungwa Road.

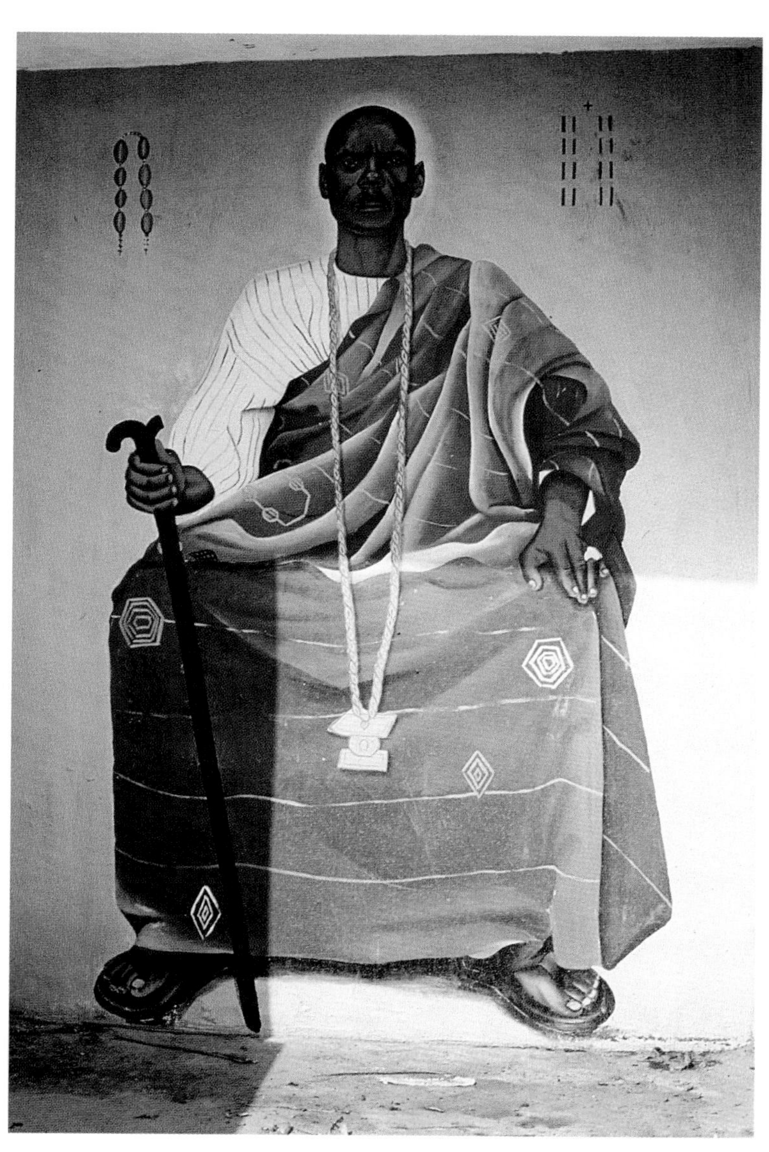

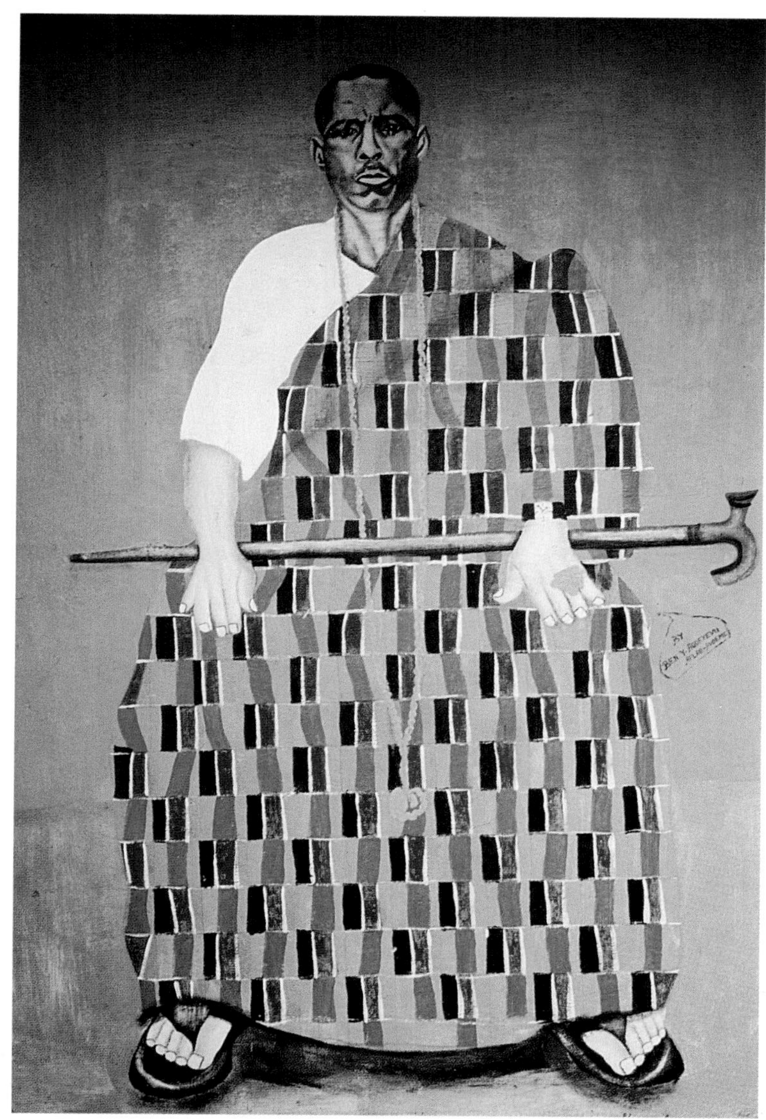

Anonymous, 1990, Ghana

Messenger artists

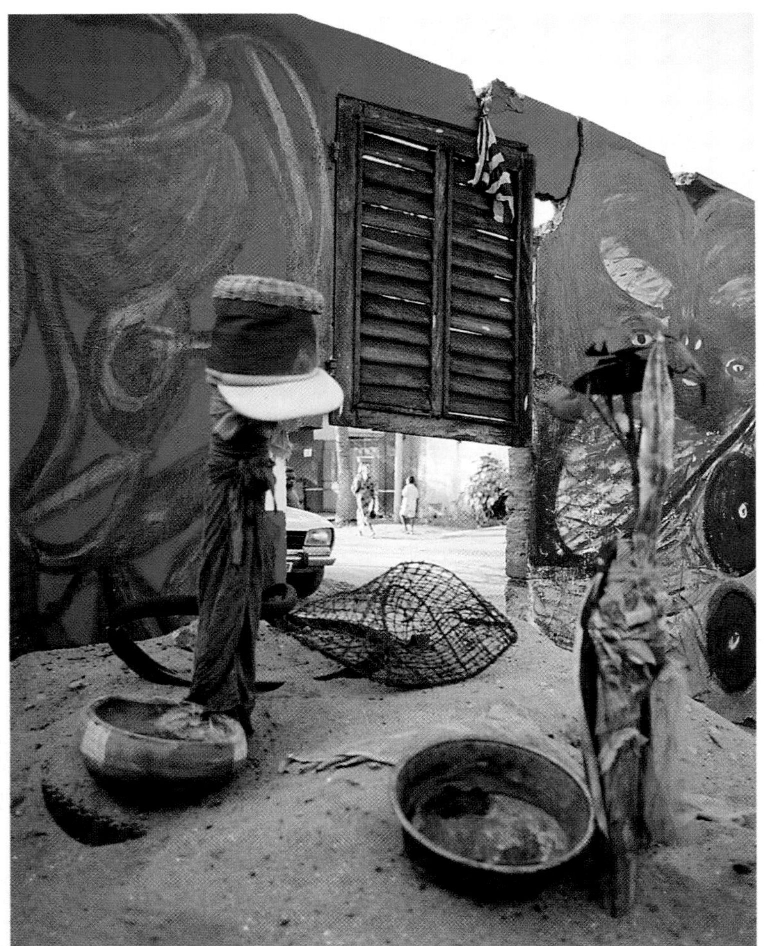

Zinsou, Benin,1995

©Érick Ahounou/Revue Noire

Not concerned with making art a career or with seeking recognition and an audience, there exists a type of artist who does not, or will not, acknowledge that he is an artist. This is probably because this type of artist does not want to lose his pleasure in his work or does not want to confront the judgement of other people, preferring to keep his work solitary, reserved to a restricted circle, away from the world and its constraints. It is as though they do not want to sully their communication movement with the stars, men, the history of men, the belief of men, nature and animals.

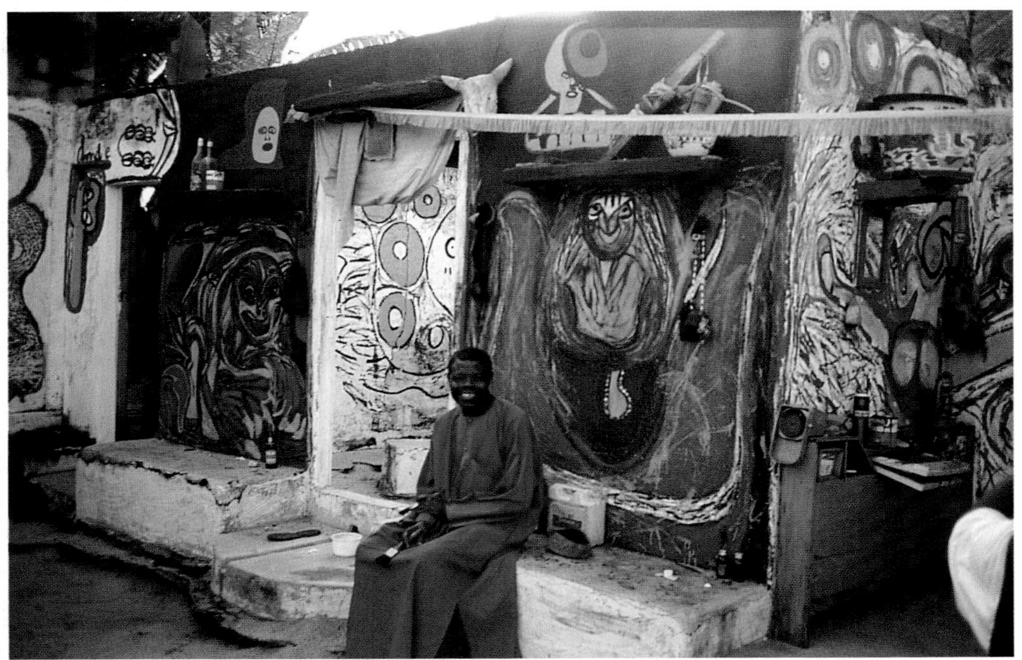

Zinsou

Deep within one of the most underprivileged districts of Cotonou, a man decided to make his house into a work of art. The house had been destroyed by fire. But Zinsou began to rebuild a private space, to which he keeps the key around his neck. Besides this landmark, all that remains are roofless walls, all brightly colored with both abstract and representational patterns, marking out spaces that are like so many alcoves dedicated to prayer. A pagan prayer, because Zinsou states that he is not religious. A shoe here, a talisman or key hooked on a wall there, intended to open some imaginary paradise, a dressing table, a tinplate plate. Zinsou seems to evolve in another world, marginalized by the inhabitants of the district, who think he is crazy. He passes in silence through our era, brush in hand, erecting what appears to be a monument to his own glory. He was born in Benin in 1958 and changed his name to "It's the Future." The past is of no concern to him.

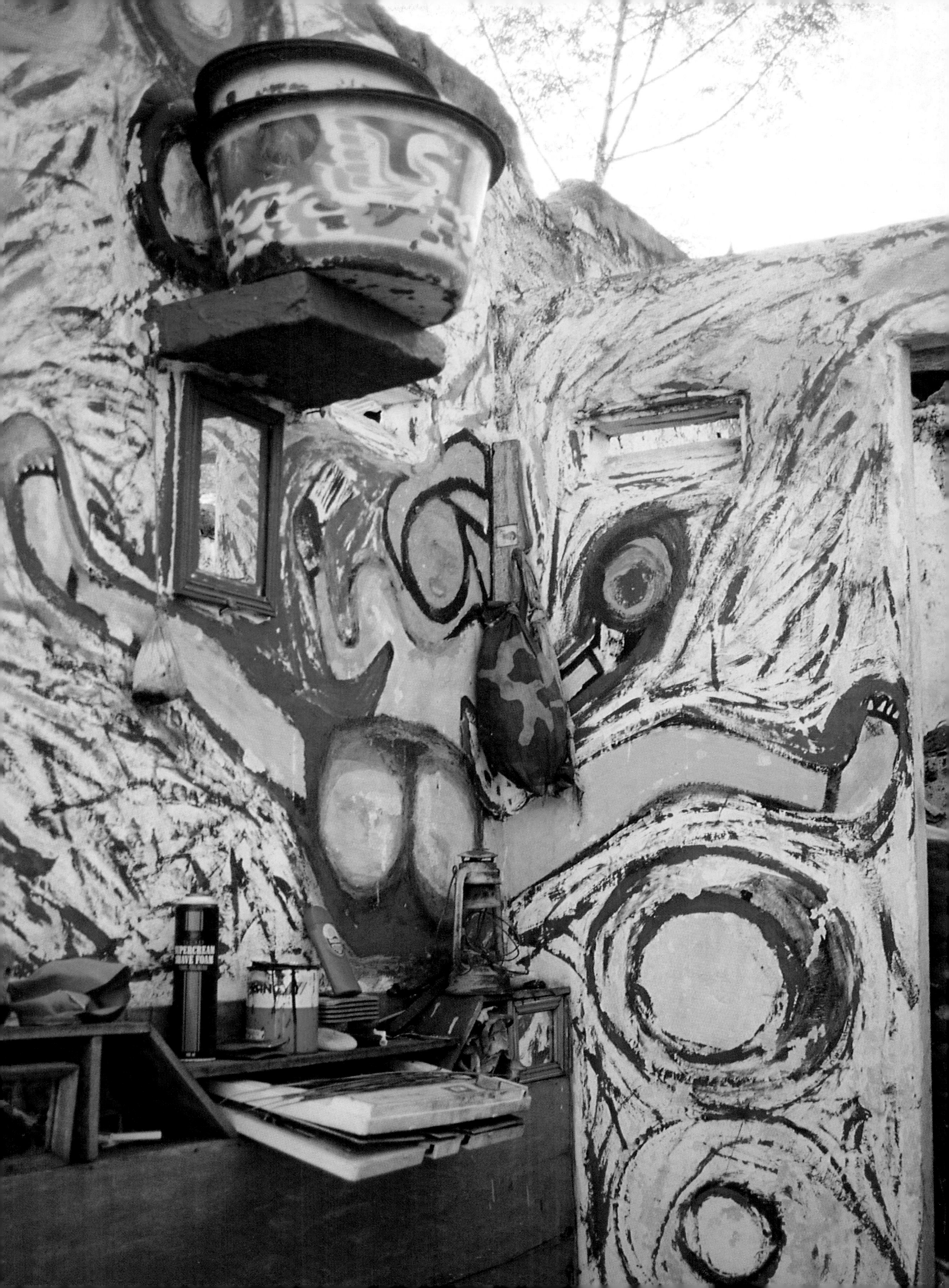

Frédéric Bruly Bouabré

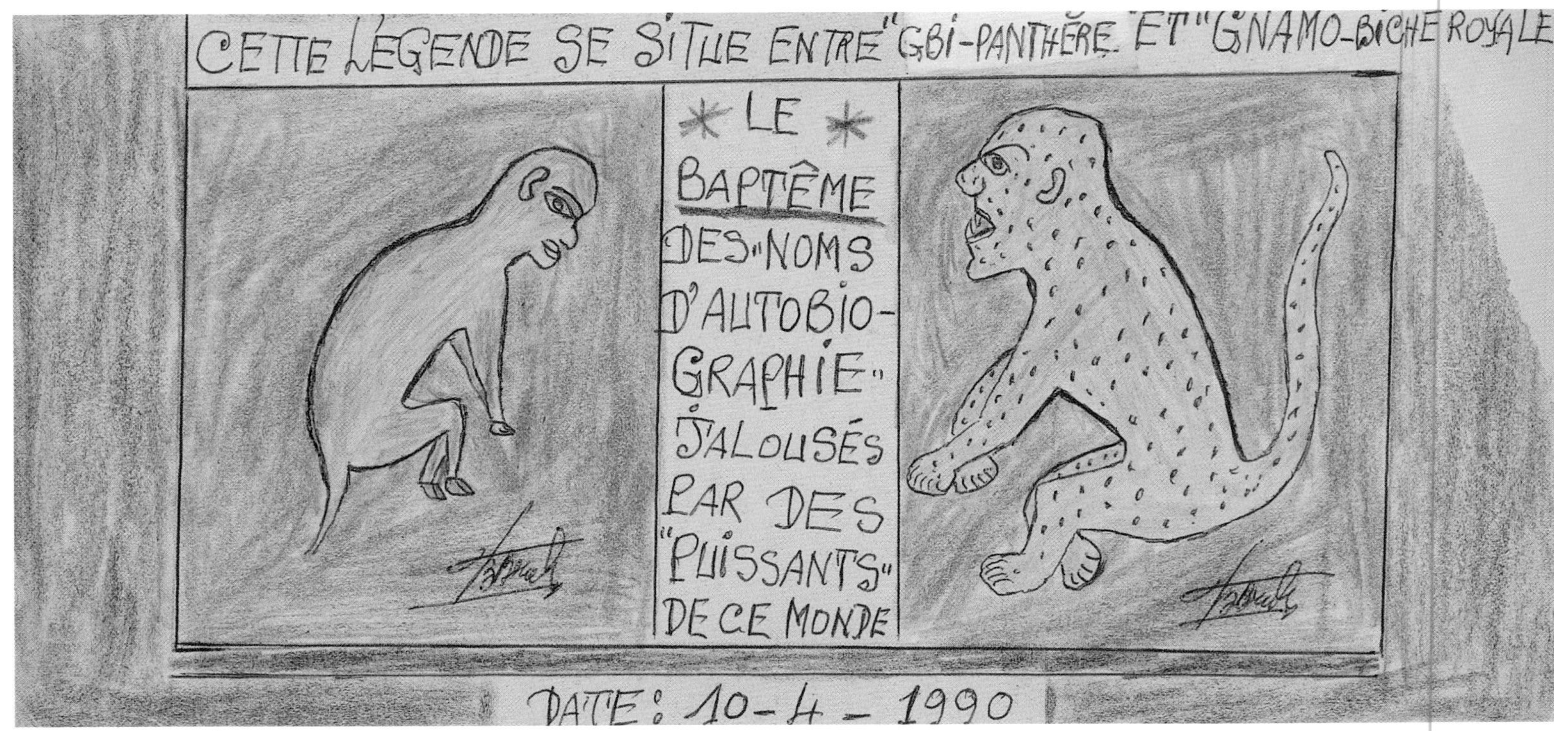

The drawings of Bruly Bouabré, combined with texts, are an accident in his inspired adventure. They are the notebook of his thoughts during the day and night. Bruly Bouabré is a philosopher and a writer. He has written thousands of pages about his Bete people, his inventions and research. He is a storyteller, who, through his metaphoric stories, shows the power of a philosophy.

In his opinion, he has created two essential works. First of all, a universal African alphabet developed in 1956 from small stones gathered in his village. This meteor dust, or gifts from the sky, are sacred objects. His second work is the creation of a religion, "the Order of the Victims of Persecution," resulting from a revelation from the sun one March 11, 1948. The son of a fetisher who spoke to the Earth and the Moon, Bruly Bouabré is a loner educated during the colonial era, which forced a cohabitation between innate Bete teachings and public and Catholic teachings. The independence of Ivory Coast has not, however, granted him his place. Bruly Bouabré, born in Ivory Coast in 1923, has been waiting, since the West's recognition, for the recognition of his Ivorian and African brothers, to whom he has devoted his life and work.

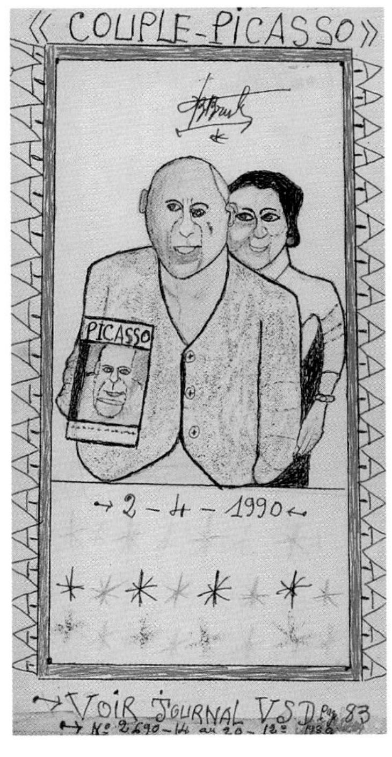

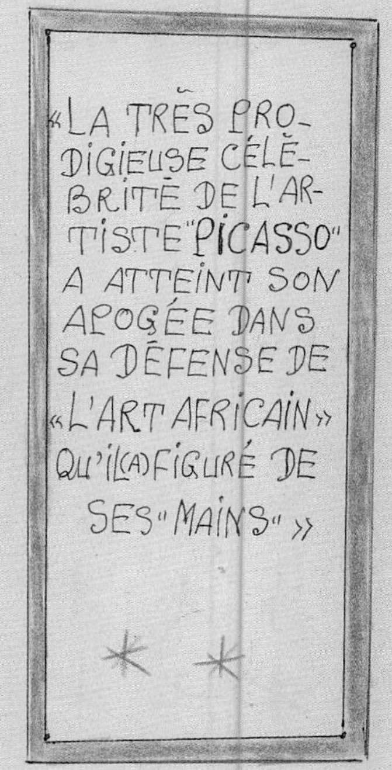

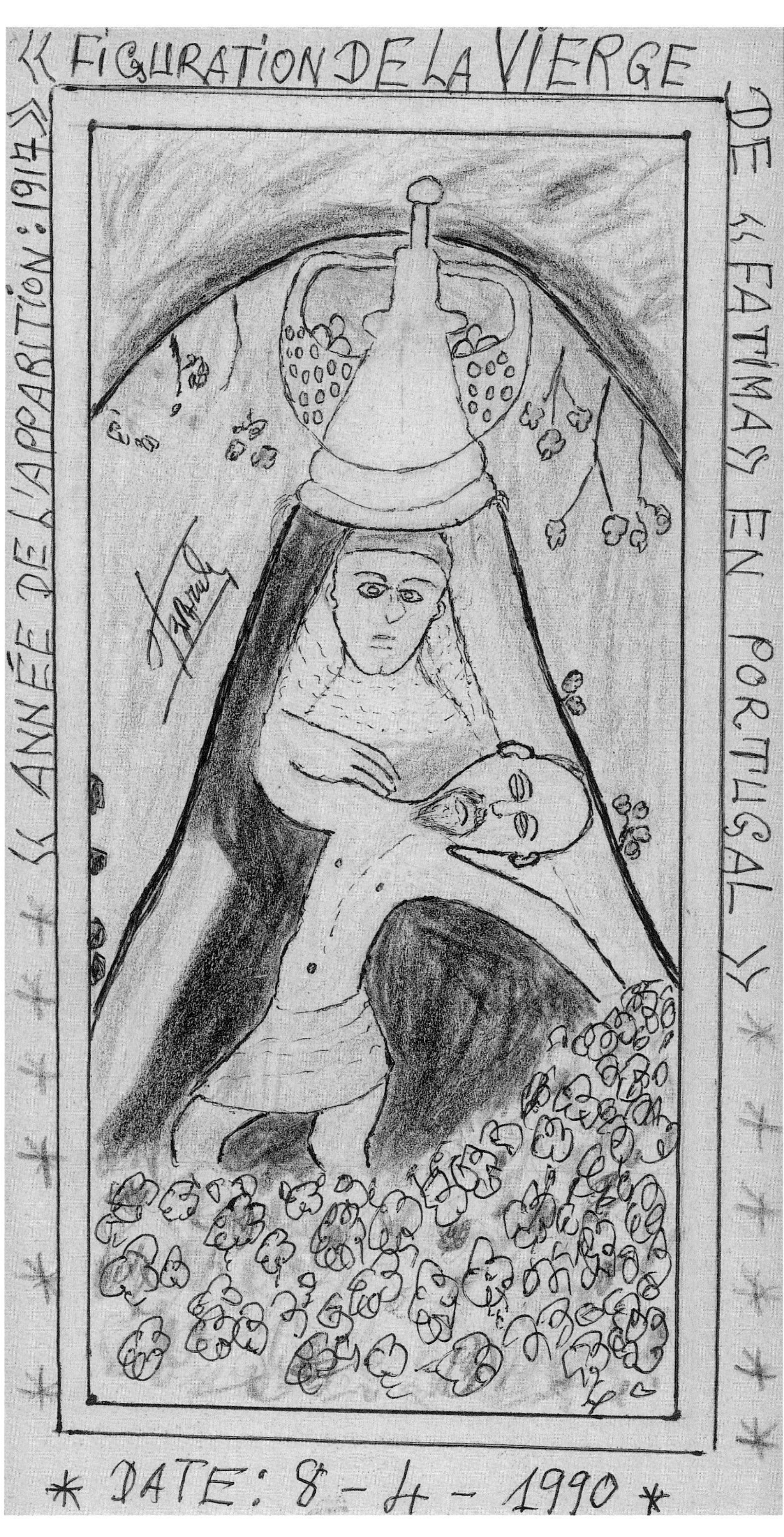

facing page:
"The Baptism," Ivory Coast, 1990
colored pencils and ballpoint pen on paper, 33 x 16 cm

"The Picasso couple," Ivory Coast, 1990
colored pencils and ballpoint pen on paper, 16 x 33 cm

right:
"Representation of the Virgin," Ivory Coast, 1990
colored pencils and ballpoint pen on paper, 33 x 16 cm

Malam Zabeirou

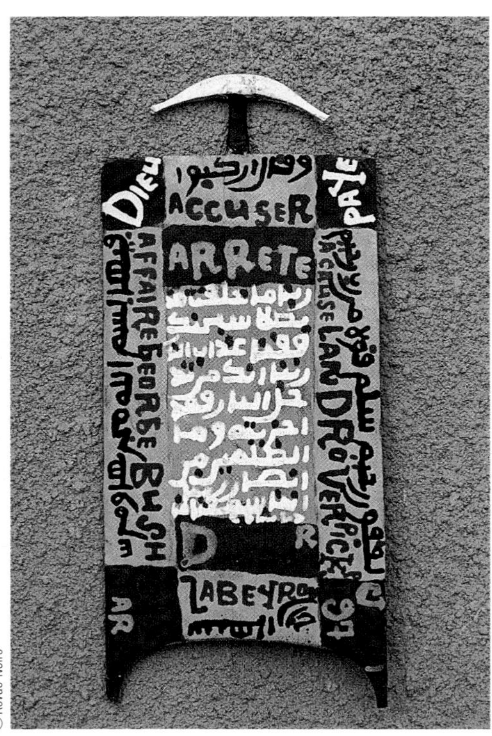

©Revue Noire

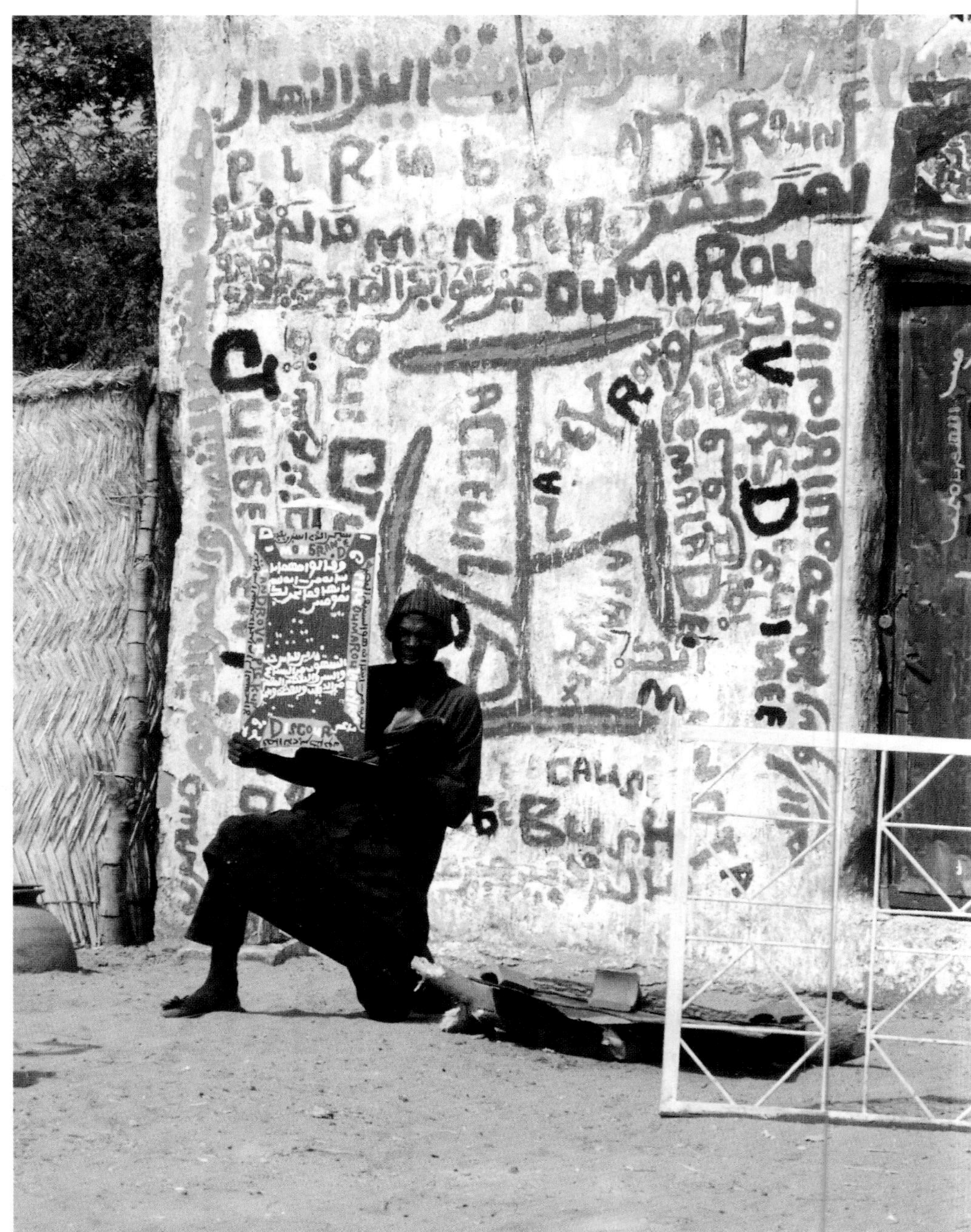

Malam Zabeirou records all of his town's and his life's memorable events on the walls of his franchise and in annals of the Koran. This journalist, historian and preacher has meticulously archived his annals and makes his neighbors, who think he is crazy, smile. This self-educated man lives in Maradi, in southern Niger.

Amadou Moctar M'Baye

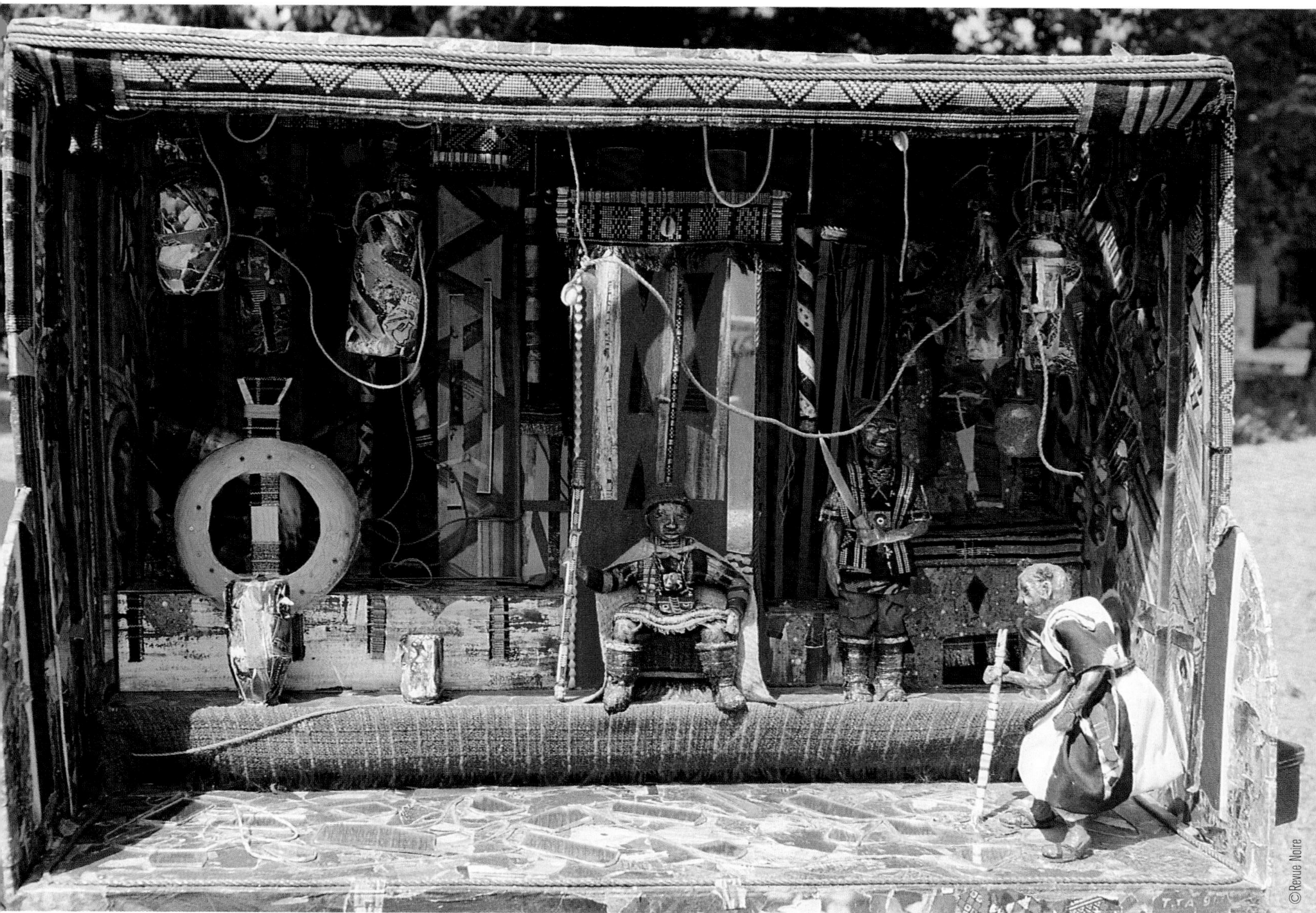

Born in Senegal in 1945, Amadou Moctar Mbaye had a career as a teacher before entering the Regular Superior School of Artistic Education in 1986. His passion for the theater and history could never be denied. "When I got the idea to tackle the history of Senegal, an operating environment had to be created and I confess that, at that precise moment, all reality had to offer me was something as mundane as a box." Battles, princesses, warriors, kings, sorcerers, were staged in these miniature theaters, placed on a pedestal, veiled in black and covered with a lid. All of these are examples that show that Moctar M'Baye is an educational visual artist who is proud of his country's history.

Jackson Hlungwani

Jackson Hlungwani was born in South Africa in 1923. He was ordained a priest of the African Zionist Church (asynchretism combining Christianity with traditional South African beliefs and customs) prior to founding his own church. Near his home, on the side of a hill, is a site with building remains dating back to the Iron Age. On divine order, he has spent 30 years embellishing the site by adding wooden sculptures to it. The fish, fauna, biblical characters and angels constitute a complex unity that he has named New Jerusalem, the new Nation of God and Christ, where he organizes religious ceremonies. Hlungwani has a vision of the world that recognizes the existence of opposed dualities: God and the devil, male and female, black and white, old and new. The history of South Africa and its contradictions are omnipresent. New Jerusalem was shown, exhibited in galleries, and most of the pieces were sold. What remains is a permanent facility commissioned by the Johannesburg Art Gallery in 1991.

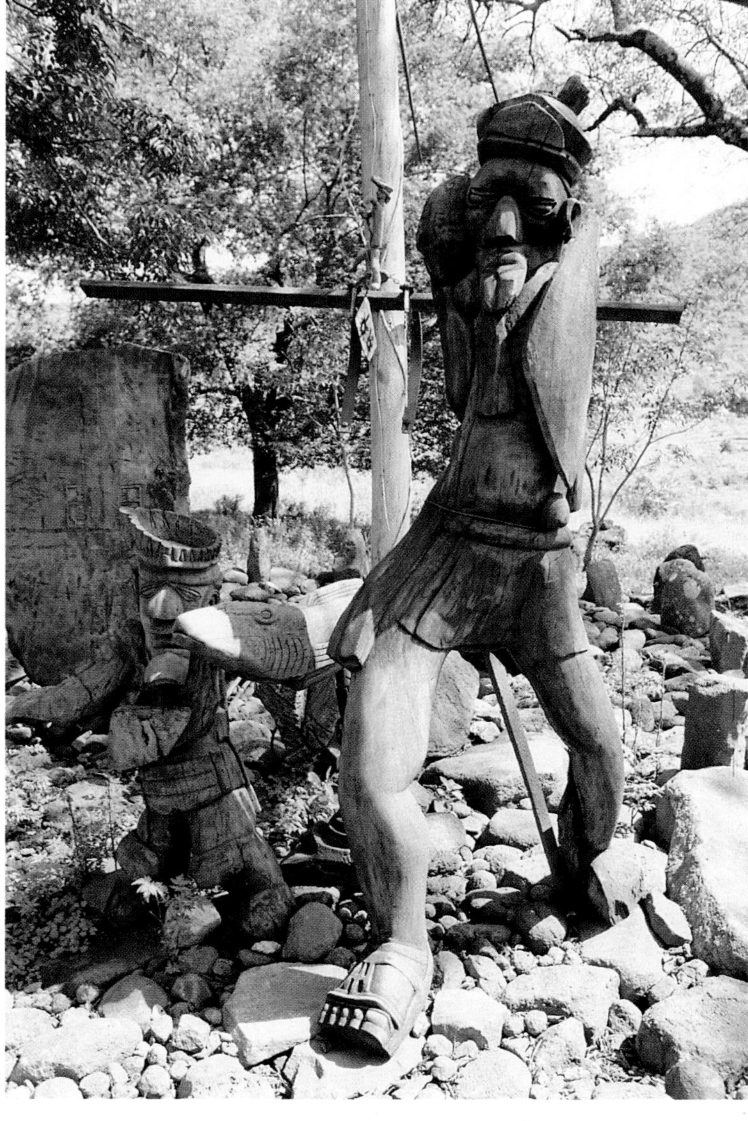

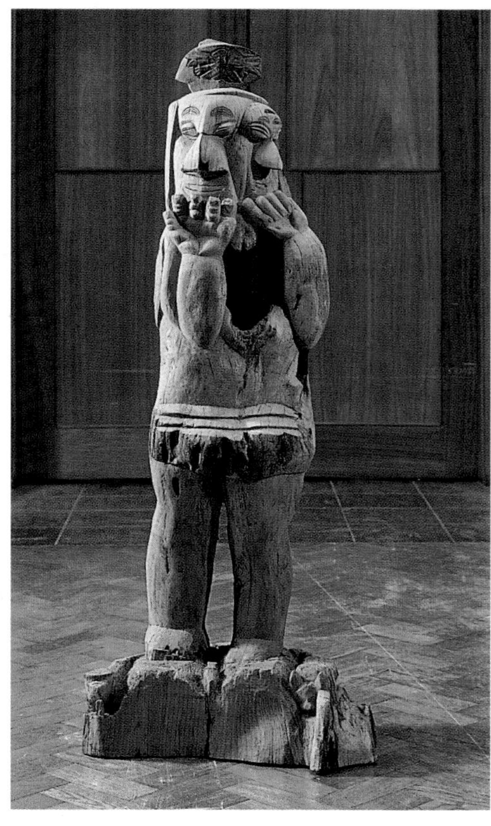

left:
"Cane," South Africa, 1983
©Gavin Younge

above:
"God and Christ," South Africa
©Johannesburg Art Gallery

facing page:
"Large Crucifix," South Africa
©Johannesburg Art Gallery

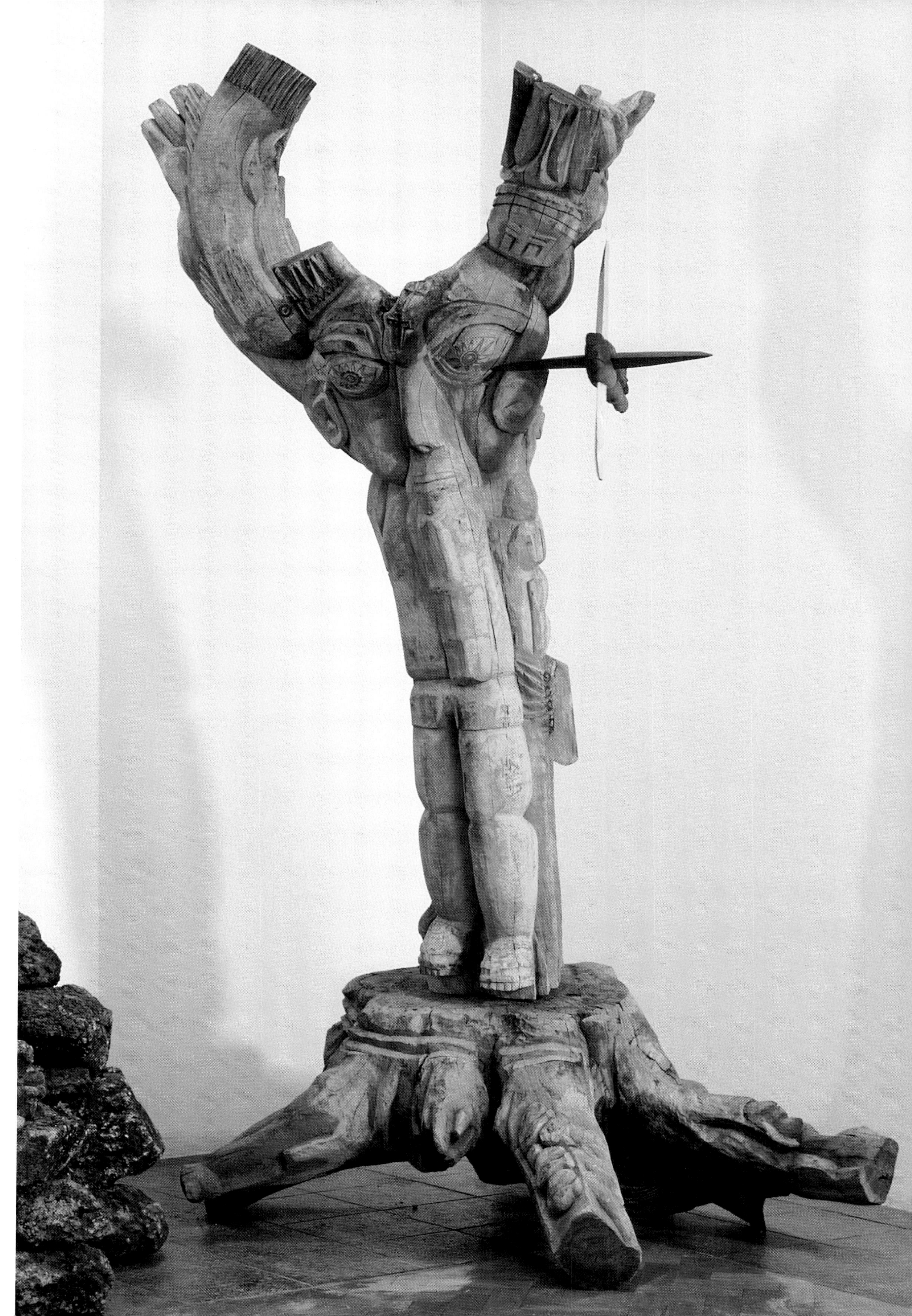

Dialiba Konaté

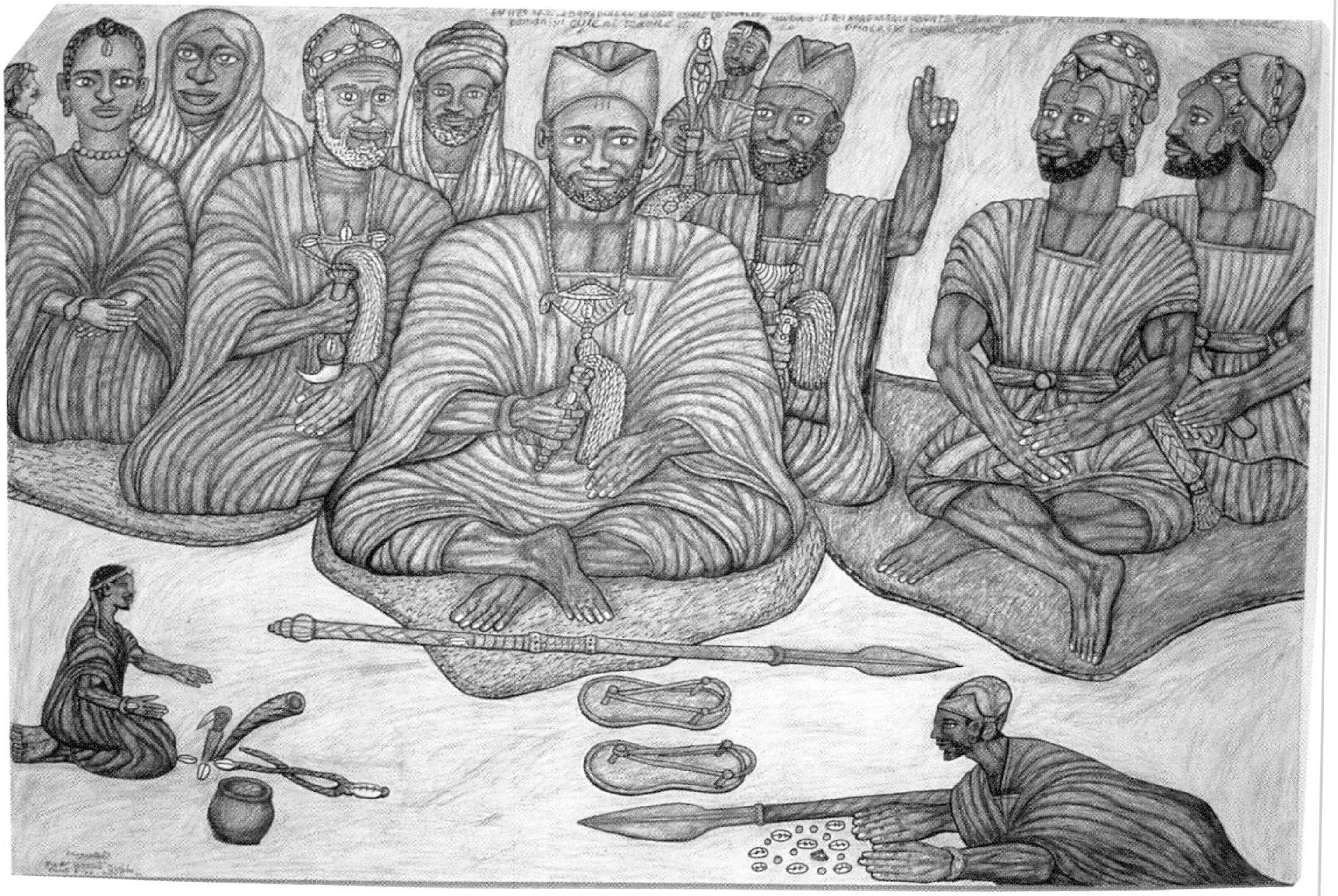

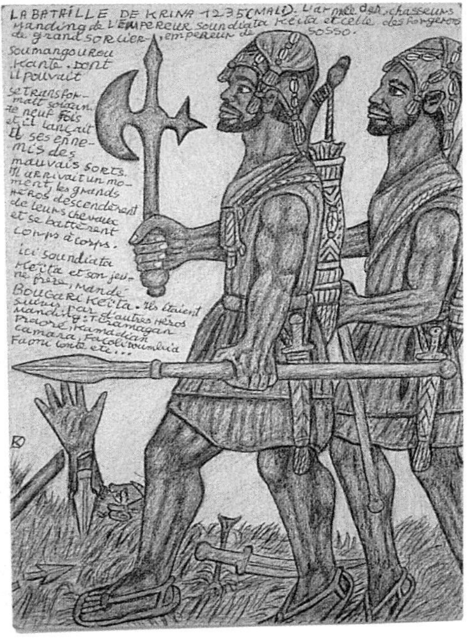

Dialiba Konaté was born in Senegal in 1942. He settled in France in 1965 and worked as a ledger keeper at FINA-France. A passionate artist during his free time and an eminent scholar of Malinke traditions, in the early 80s Konaté enrolled at the Université de Paris VIII - Saint-Denis, where, in 1983, he obtained a post-master's degree in plastic arts, after obtaining a BA and a master's degree. His passion for African history led him to translate, into images, what the griots have been repeating for centuries in words and songs. His neatly documented color drawings and the legends that accompany them remain unpublished and have only rarely had the opportunity to be shown to the public.

"At the court of Naré Magan Konaté, King of Manding, father of Soundiata Keïta," Mali, 2000
ballpoint pen and colored pencils on paper, 45 x 64.5 cm
©D.R.

"Soundiata Keïta at the battle of Kirina," Mali, 1999
ballpoint pen and colored pencils on gray cardboard, 37.7 x 24 cm
©D.R.

Alpha Woualid Diallo

Alpha Woualid Diallo was born in Senegal in 1927. This sales representative devoted himself to historical painting starting in 1966. He produced many series of paintings on all of the decisive battles and of the major symbolic figures of Senegal during the colonial era. His paintings have a harsh realism to them and have also been used as illustrations in history books, on postage stamps and in television series. Woualid Diallo sees himself first and foremost as a researcher who retranscribes the oral and written history of his country as faithfully as possible.

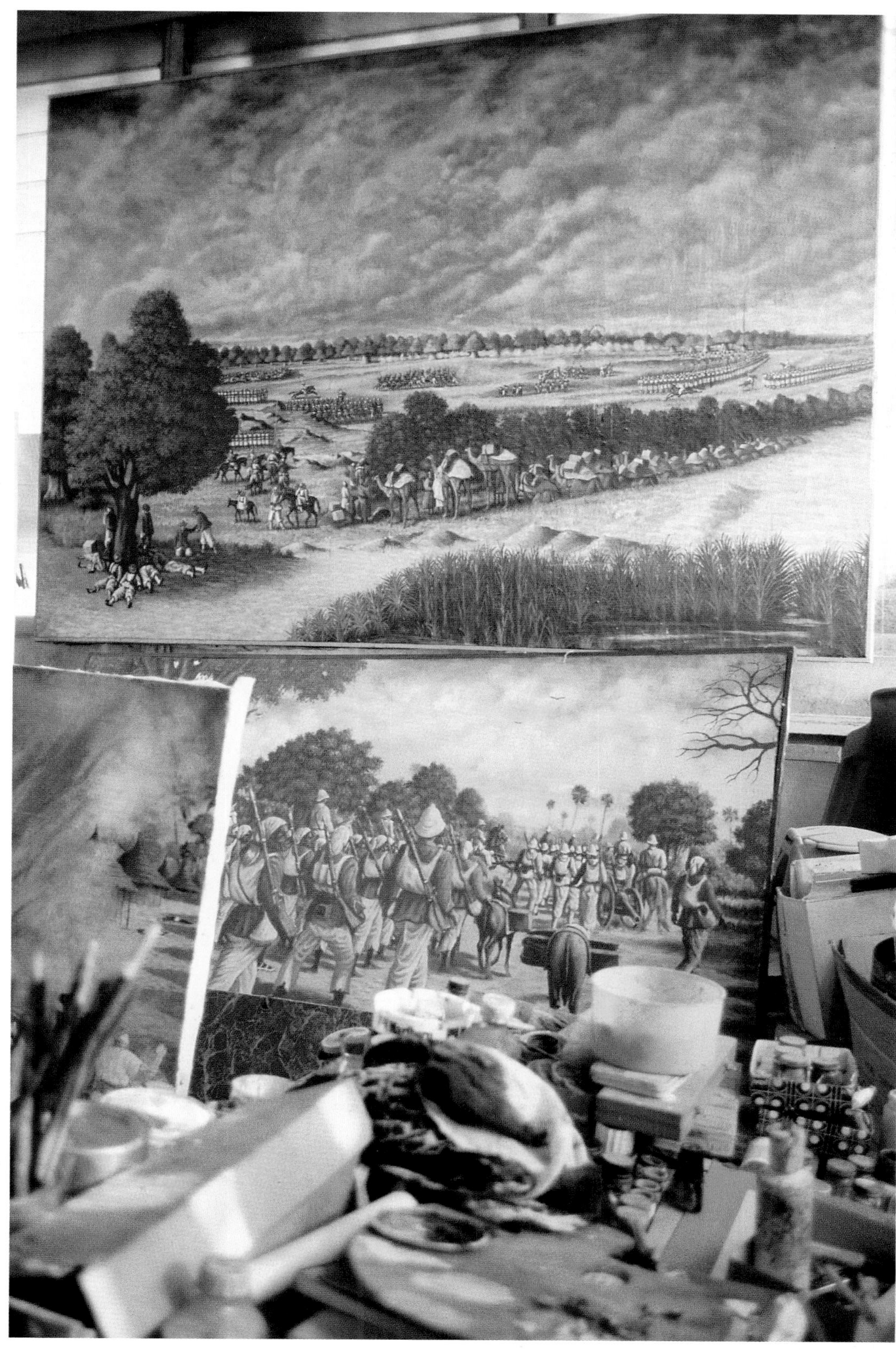

Workshop of Alpha Wallid Diallo in Dakar, Senegal, 1992

©Revue Noire

Georges Adeagbo, Benin

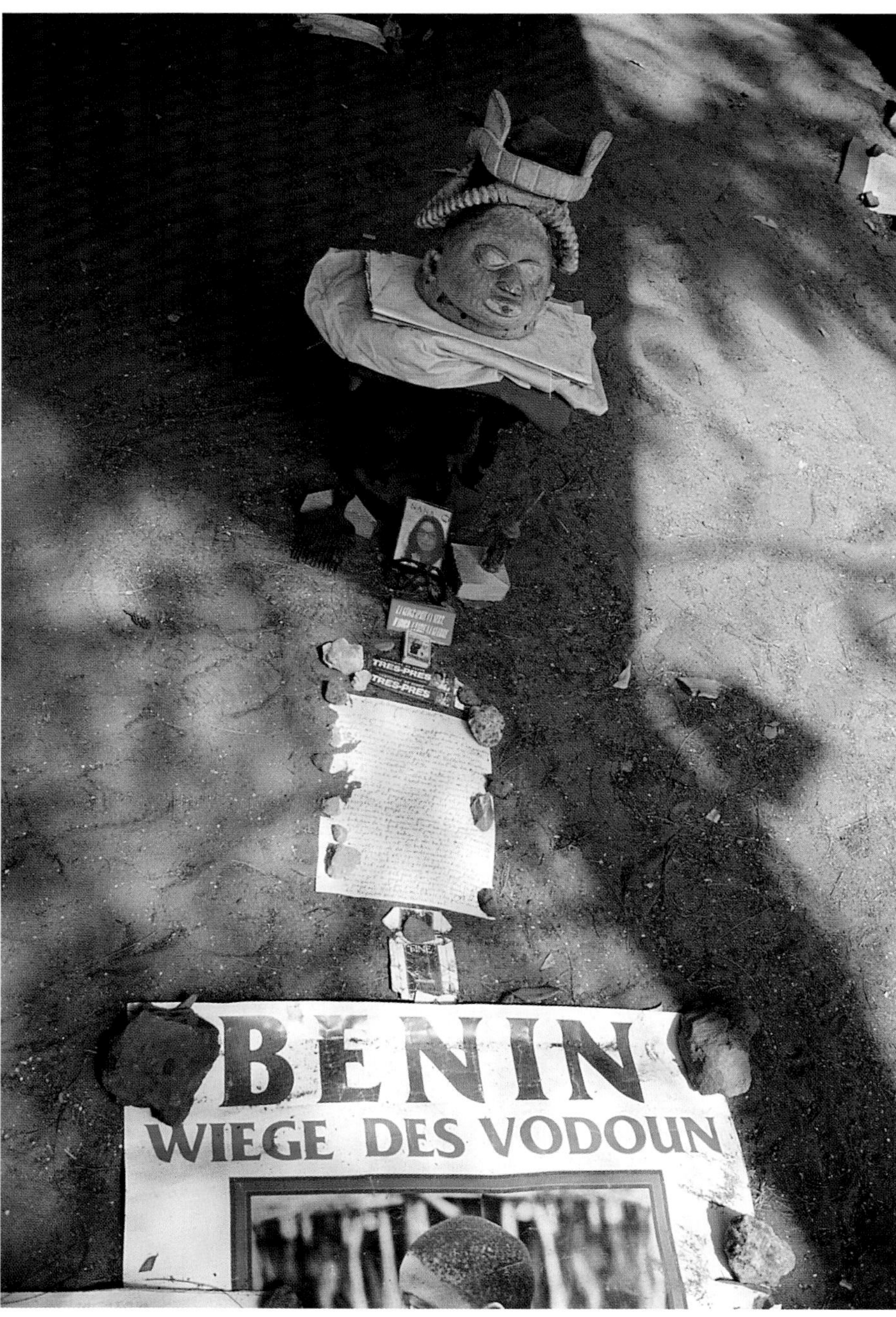

Georges Adeagbo was born in Benin in 1942. He returned to Benin in 1971 after completing law studies in France and dedicated himself entirely to his art. This self-taught artist has been leading a passionate battle, against all odds, to be able to express himself. The fierce opposition of his friends and family has led him to the psychiatric hospital almost ten times, but has not succeeded in diverting him from his vocation.
His uniqueness resides in the fact that he is able to integrate the elements that he has doggedly selected in ever-changing places, at specific moments. These include statuettes, newspaper clippings, personal notes and broken toys. The objects are never placed haphazardly. The long line produced refers to his vision of the history of the world. He creates, in this manner, installations that he calls "exhibits," telling himself that perhaps one day he will be understood.

The Dakar Biennial, 1996

©collection Revue Noire

facing page:
The Dakar Biennial, 1996

©collection Revue Noire

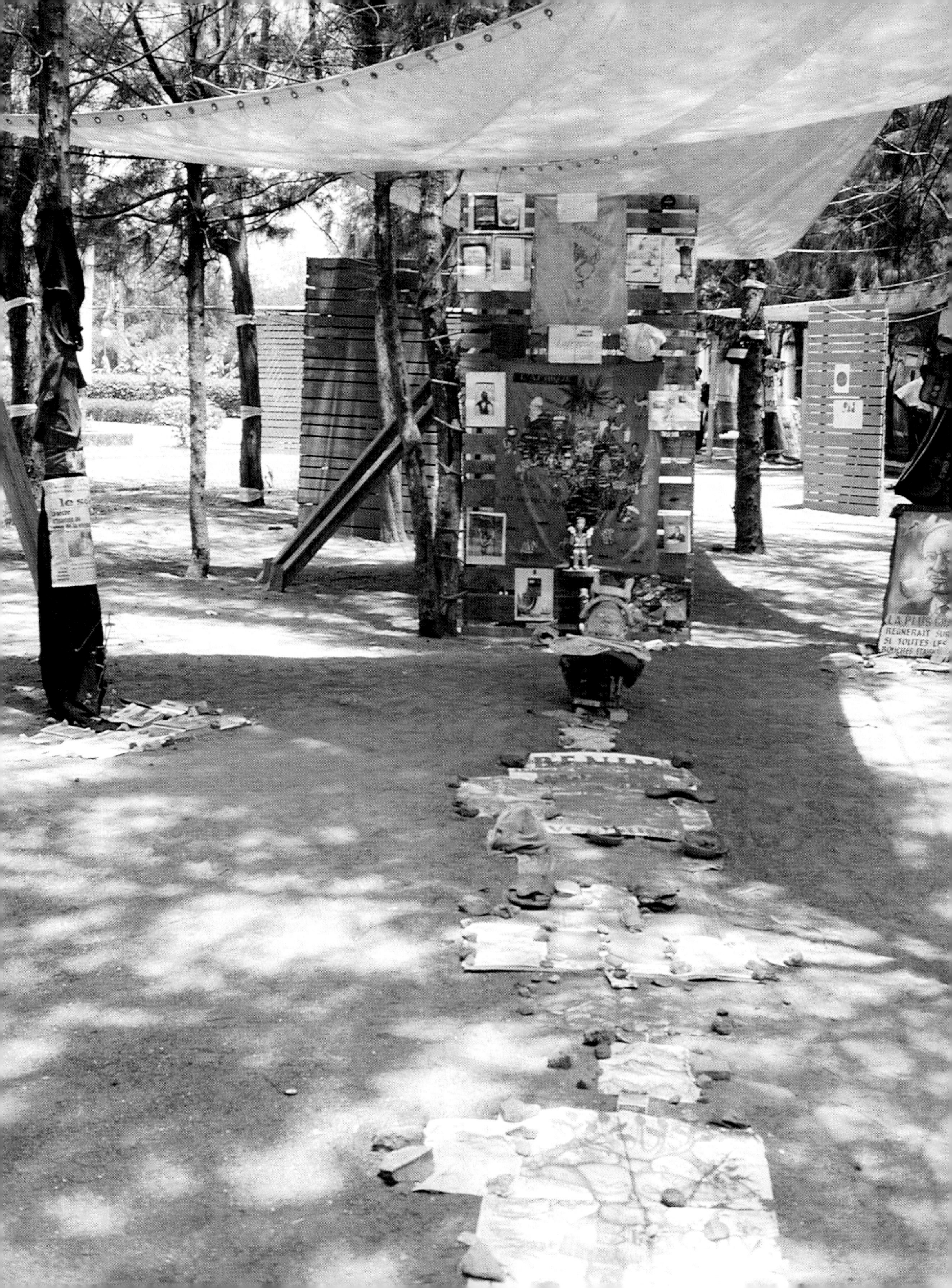
SI TOUTES LES

Clément-Marie Biazin

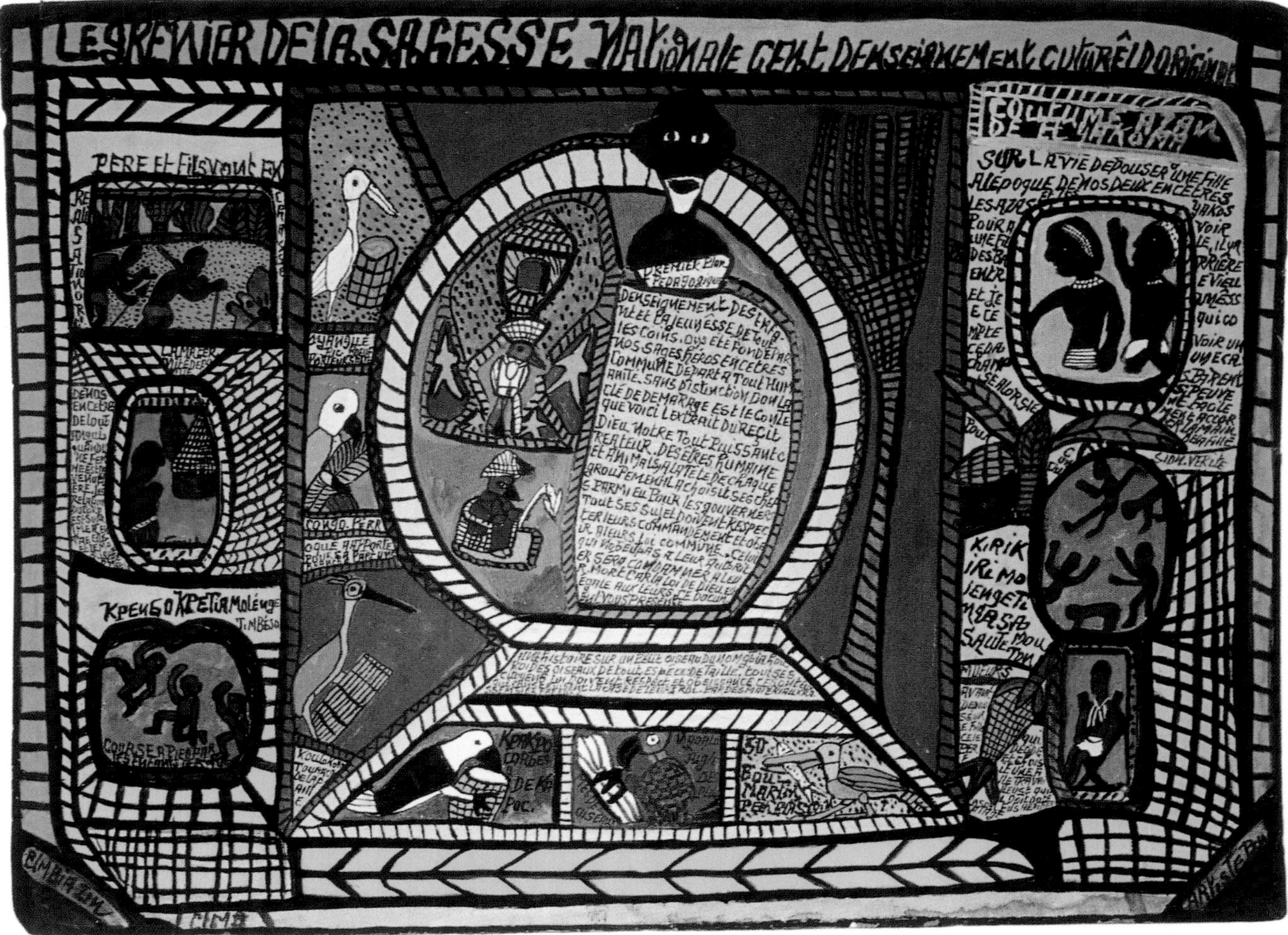

Born to a bricklayer father and farmer mother in 1924, Clément-Marie Biazin is part of the group of artists commonly referred to as self-taught. Twenty years of travelling (between 1946 and 1966) took him to live in the countries of central Africa, living by his wits and accepting whatever was offered to him to survive. Biazin was not just an ordinary traveler. He was a bit more curious than the others and always a foreigner. Biazin began to paint and draw. To make his message understood, he added comments to his works that act as ethnographic notes on this continent where it is believed that all men are alike. This is how he became a historian, pedagogue and memoralist. He chronicled his time without any apparent hierarchy. An event from everyday life was just as important as any international event. Biazin did not live to see the fruit of his teachings. This humanist, who worked to elevate Africans, died in 1981 from leprosy, in the most dire of poverty.

"The Granary of National Wisdom," Central African Republic, 1976

Mbezele Solo Aloys

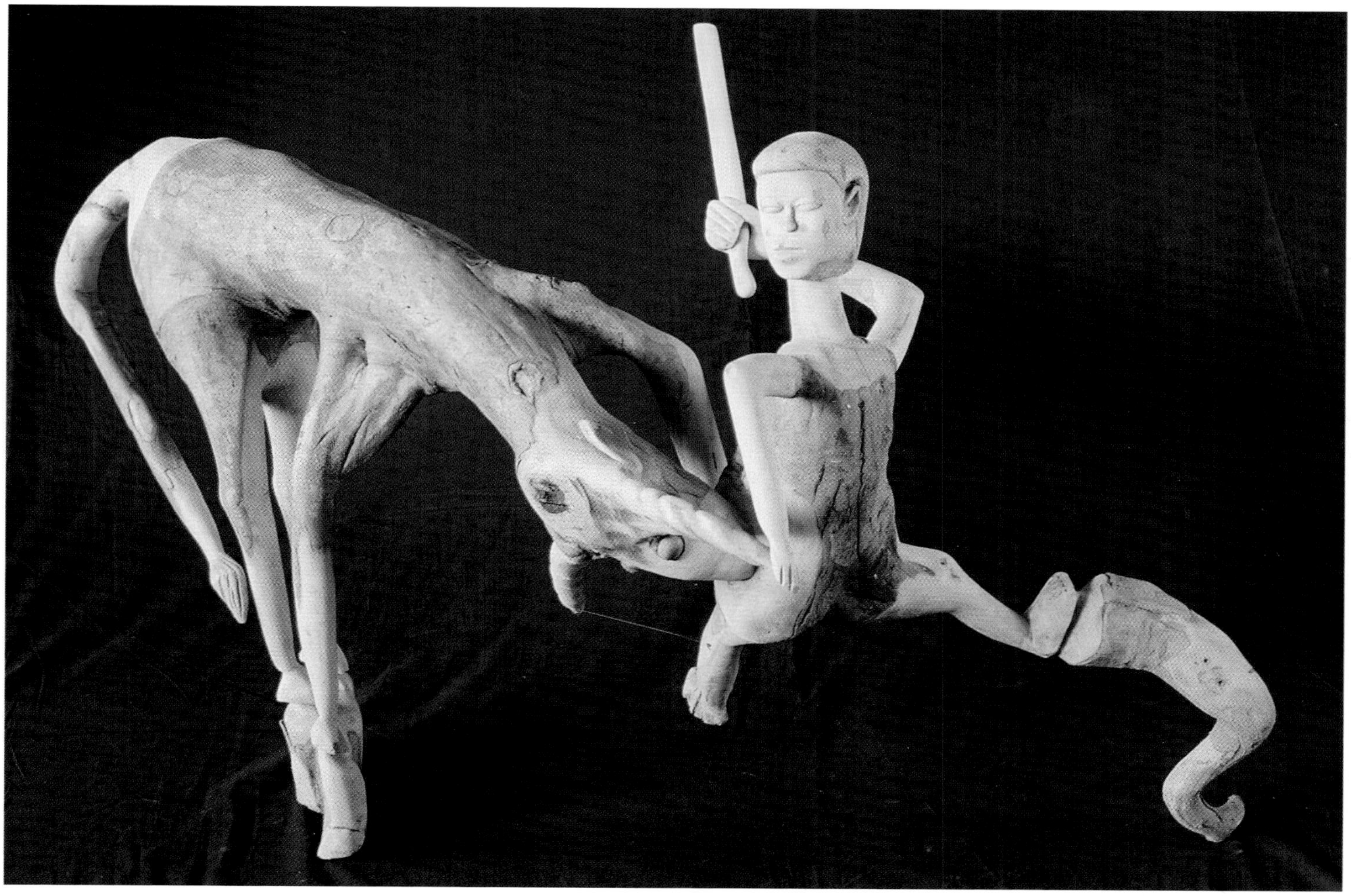

An entire mysterious world can be seen through Nature's unpredictable forms, enriched by Mbezele Solo Aloys's imagination. Scenes from everyday life, zombies, animals, battles, and couples all reveal both the transparency of the real and a fertile artistic creation, deeply rooted in a rough poetic form.

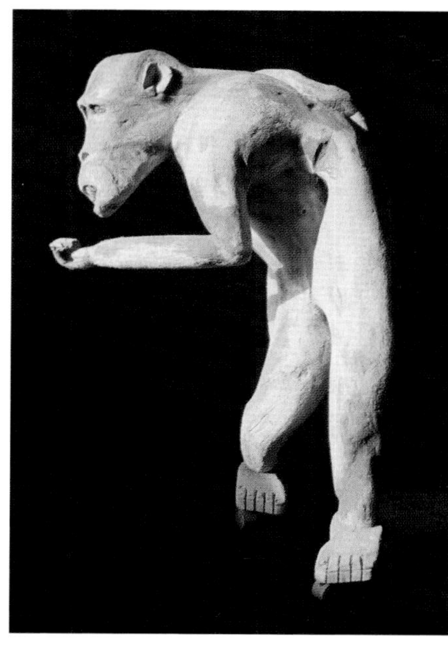

Paulo Capela

Paulo Capela, a self-taught man born in Angola in 1947, began drawing in 1960. This fervent Catholic has spent hours interpreting the Bible and recording his "conversations with the Holy Spirit" on the walls. His mystical productions about Christ, sacred texts and cultural Angolan actors fill the large room used as a workshop, a dwelling, a temple. An unusual place where the gods of the Book coexist with ancient sculptures, it also includes a portrait of the first president of Angola with a flag of the USA, an advertising slogan faces a portrait of Lenin, and Che Guevara looks at three Coca-Cola cans. These private altars have, above all, a symbolic function: an ideal representation of the world where communism calmly walks alongside capitalist icons. Because, although the cold war is over, Angola has not yet gotten over its contradictions.

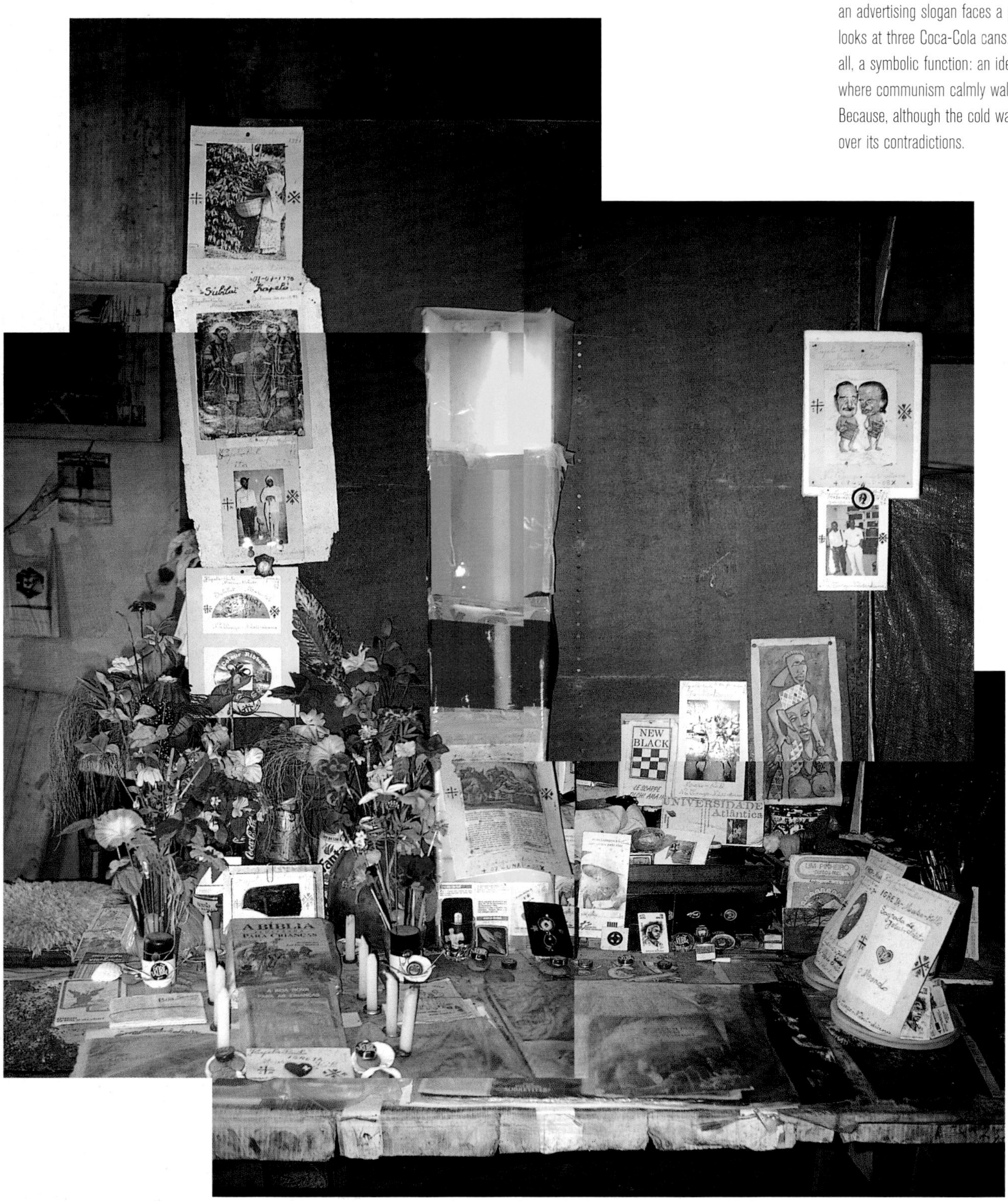

Workshop of Paulo Capela in Luanda, Angola, 1998

©Revue Noire

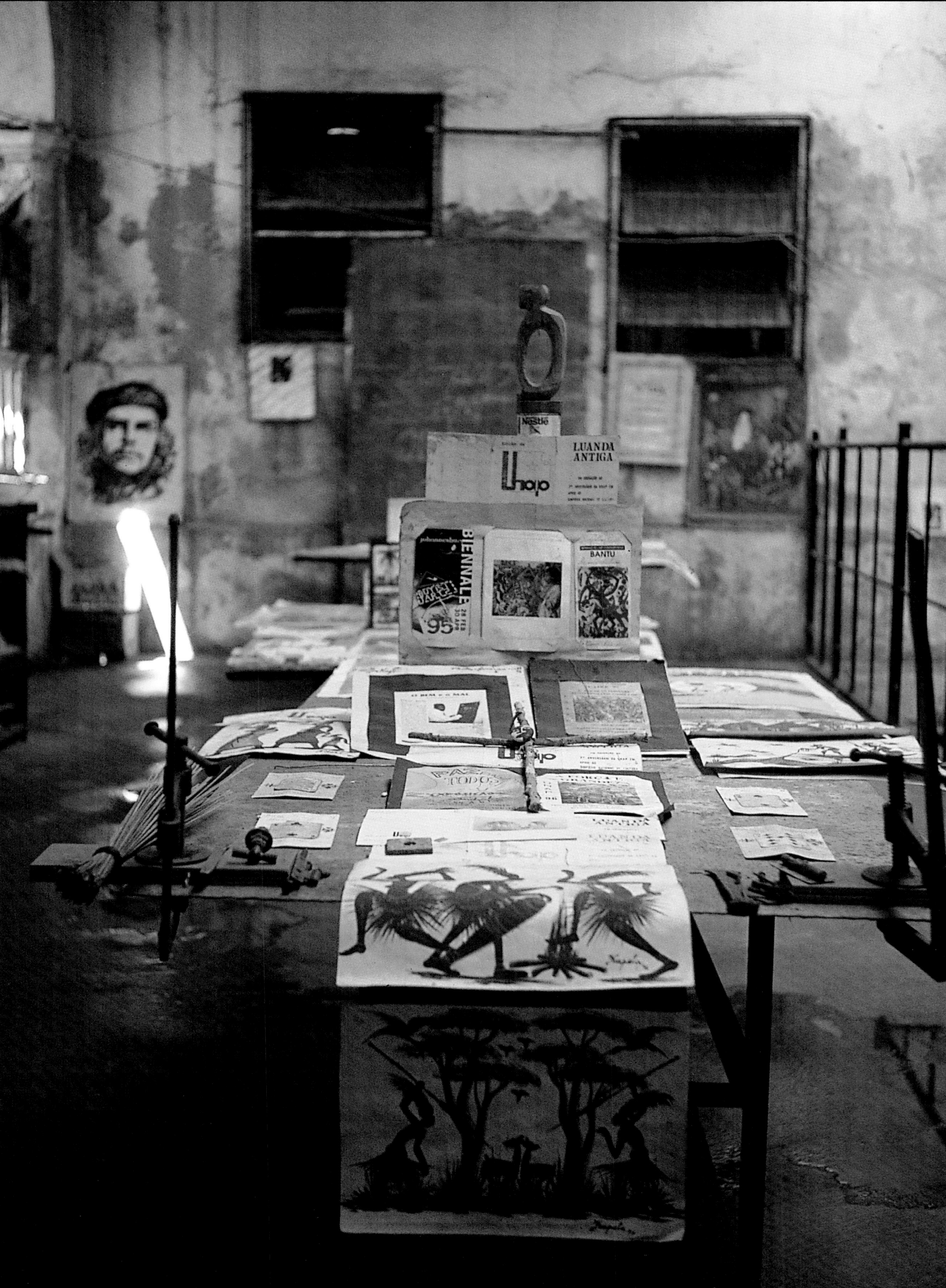

Nestlé
LUANDA
ANTIGA
BIENNALE
95
BANTU

Gabriel Tatsinkou

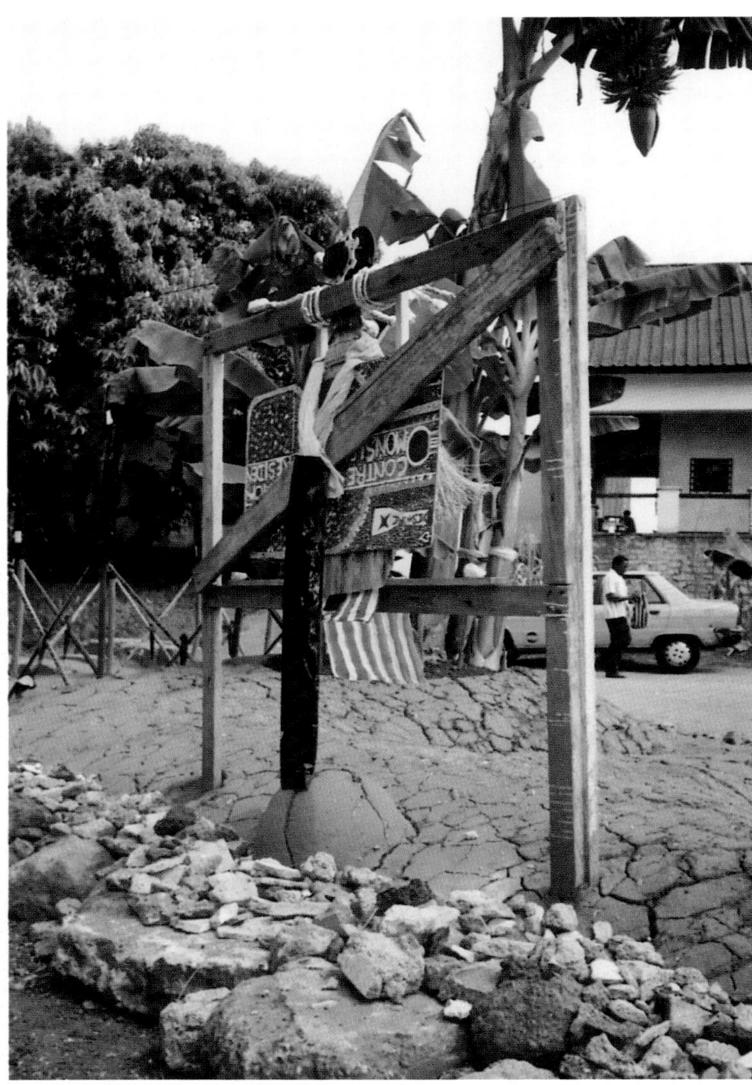

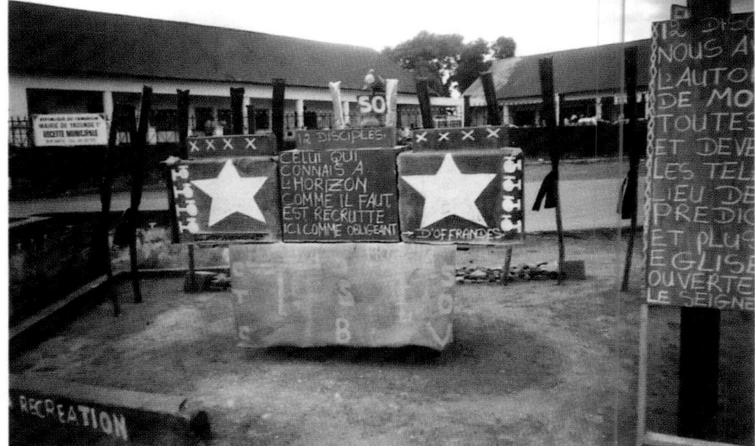

"God is in the midst of writing up a report, because the time of the event has come." It is with this solemn phrase that Gabriel Tatsinkou, "the thirteenth disciple and plastic arts researcher" presents his work, orchestrated around the idea of divine order. Tatsinkou, who set himself up in a public place, intends to fight the deterioration of the urban environment, the idolatry of capitalism and to "push people onto the road of modernism." Squares become "temples" for remarks, the presidents of the Republic and pop stars are represented by potted plants that he regularly waters, and Christ or the Cross are always omnipresent. Born in 1961 in Cameroon, he practiced plastic arts for two years before "shifting" towards a formal and plastic personal search.

Cameroon, 1998

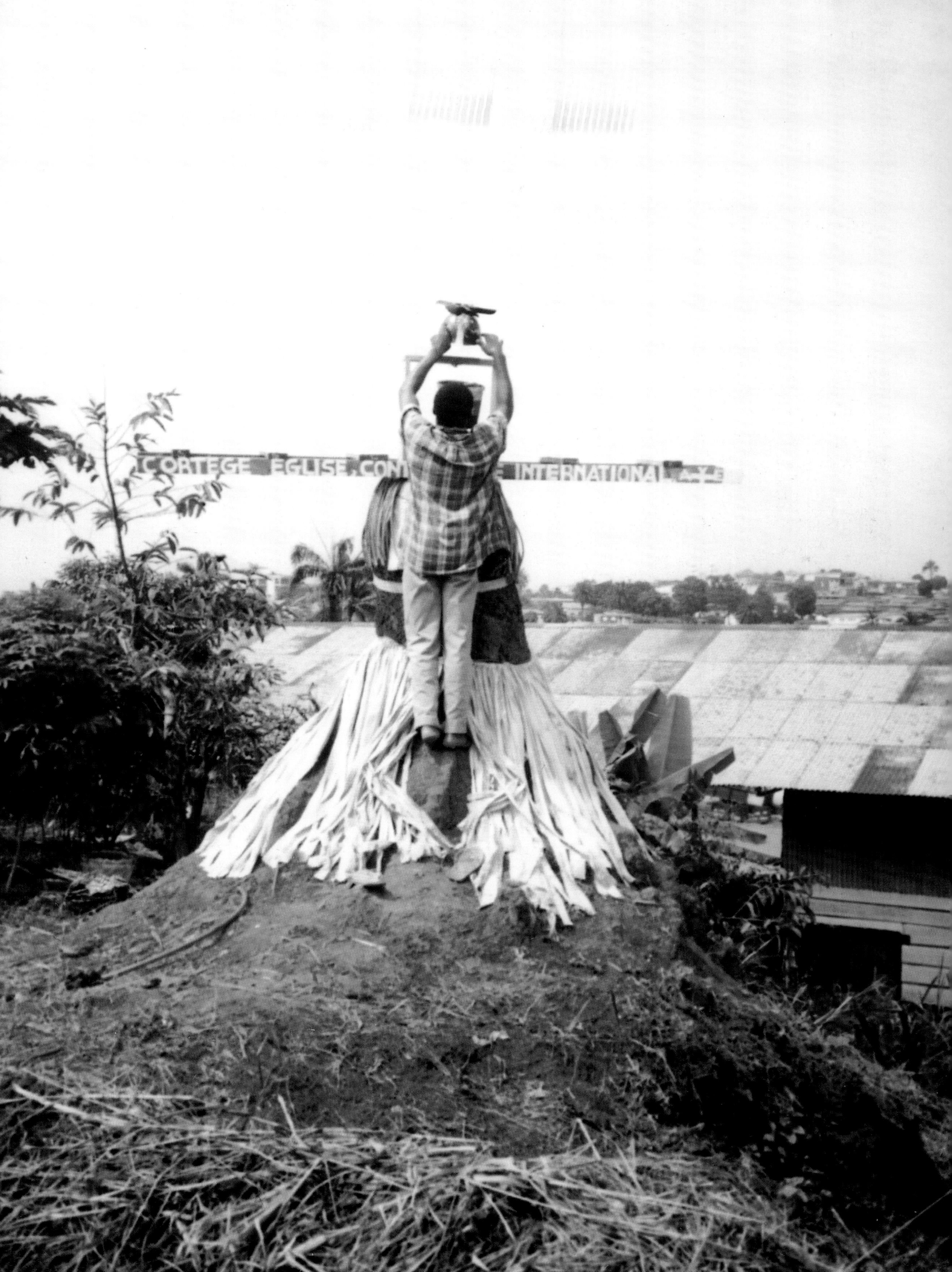
CORTEGE EGLISE CON
INTERNATIONAL

MESSENGER ARTISTS
Jean Loup Pivin

Frédéric Bruly Bouabré and Jackson Hlungwani: one from a French-speaking country, Ivory Coast, and the other from English-speaking South Africa. These two men have reinvented the world in which they live by designing it and giving it a form. They see themselves as prophets of a new, better and happy humanity with love for one's neighbor and from a God comprised of many Gods, a plural God that is the synthesis of those surrounding them. Bruly has written hundreds of pages of theories, metaphorical tales, has reinvented a style, a rite and illustrates them for certain people. Jackson Hlungwani spreads the word of this plural God and has set himself up among nature, on a hill near his home. He marks his space with pieces of wood gathered nearby, leaves some of them as they are and sculpts others, all the while respecting the initial form. He has created a place for himself, void of any structures, where he officiates: a sacred temple of nature in nature. Other, more humble artists are doing this just for their pleasure, without any other search for prophecy. Perhaps they see themselves as bearers of a memory, such as Biazin, Zinsou, Dialiba Konaté or Alpha Wallid Diallo, messengers for their nearest and dearest, for a society that they consider a family, their family.

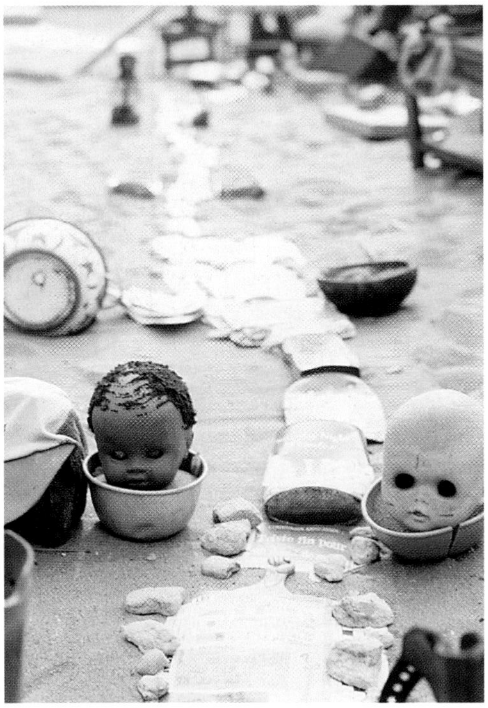

Georges Adeagbo (born in 1942), Cotonou, 1995
©D.R.

We could associate them with what in the Euro-American culture is called Rough Art, a type of art that falls outside the criteria of esthetic trends and the history of Western art. A type of art created by people who have an "impassioned need" to create. Whether they keep or erase their work, show it or hide it, what is most important to them is to be able to create. As self-taught artists, they do not seek to compare themselves to anyone. Instead they draw consciously or subconsciously, as their hand, skill and desire dictate, from universes of eclectic forms to create their own original form, making it intimate, without seeking to do so. They are unquestionably of their time, of their landscape, of their society. They inadvertently create an unthinkable synthesis for scientists, an intuitive and considered, sincere and bold synthesis, not necessarily for others, but for themselves first and foremost. It is their secret garden to be shared with close friends and family.

Ousmane Sow would also fit into this category of secret artists. For decades, he created his sculptures for himself, without seeking recognition, without displaying his sculptures, merely with the happiness of his hands to model forms and increasingly big bodies, and to create scenes of a humanity into which he is slipping.

Had nobody come to find them, these people would have continued to live with their pleasure or pain of creating. But then, one day, curious, enthusiastic and professional people took a closer look and were surprised, fascinated and conquered by these great silent works, and conquered by the humility or illumination of the men who invent them. The magic falls away, the great works are scattered among streams of fans and merchants, rare funds become less rare, the media, who they thought were unaware of them, opened up to them. For the humble, refusing so many honors would not be a humble gesture. For the re-founders of humanity, religion and societies, one would think that they would develop delusions of grandeur and overwhelming pride, when all they seek is to find solutions to the evils they identify, to offer and share paths other than those set out before us each day as new realities dictate. They accept the changes in their society and see in them the opportunity to introduce therein their universe, questions and answers.

These artists' works often fulfill a need for an immediacy of perception, for a sympathy from the public, from all publics, whether cultured or not, African or non-African, as if the most accessible and sensitive part of the art, for all, were just that. There is no underlying intellectual nuance or reference to a movement or esthetic aspect; it is just simply sincere in its awkwardness, and emotional because it is existential for the person creating it and for the person looking at it. Escaping one's own folly and the folly of reality, and building another reality,

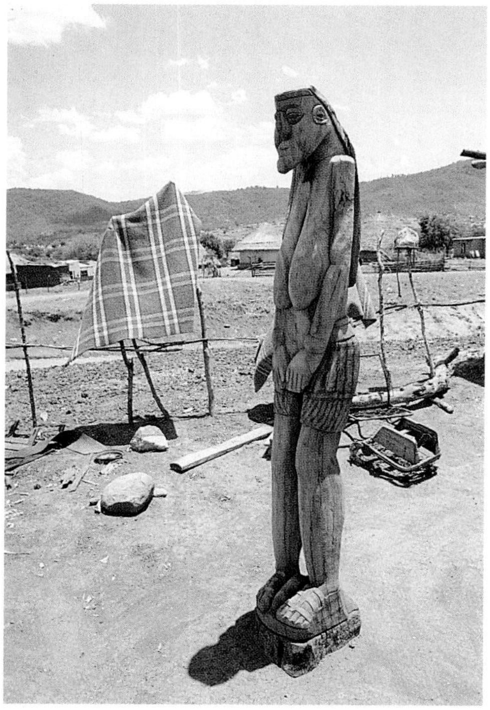

Jackson Hlungwani (born in 1923), South Africa, 1983

©Gavin Younge

either mentally or on a reduced scale, as a model, a work of fiction, is what remains. Georges Adeagbo reconstructs using newspapers with significant words, copies of ritual art and objects from all of the ports around the world, a sort of ephemeral path to thought, just to advance by a few steps everyday into the real world. No type of art can escape this without truly knowing if, one day, provisional and reduced forms will need to be produced on the scale that current daily life has provided.

But who knows what the scale or true size of tomorrow's projects will be? Modernity has continued to quash the relationship of man with the objects built by him. The most majestic palaces of the history of all civilizations are much more trivial than the slightest industrial construction. The new reference points include all things huge and fast. There are no more links with those that were long the reference. They prevent the scales of tomorrow from being defined. Thus, it will always be easy to look at the past of African or European trees, houses or villages and to shed the tear that will permit pit owners and merchants of certitude to configure the artistic landscape of our towns.

The utopian factory, a poem. Inventing a language and wanting to spread it through a leaflet also written in the universal language invented but only understood by absolutely no one is the best evidence of the graphic, solely formal communicability of this new language. This is a simply poetic act performed by Bruly Bouabré. The process of imprisonment that creates a world free of outside influences and soiling, gives a utopian value to almost all artistic projects. After all, what workshop does not look like a secret cave, closed in upon itself? At Chéri Samba's place, the cave is, moreover, preceded by a labyrinth. At Bruly Bouabré's place, the Zeprégühé chapel-library resembles an initiatory site. At Jackson Hlungwani's place, with its Bruly-type mystical realism, the natural site is inhabited by thousands of little nothings and bits of sculpted wood transformed into works of art.
This poetic utopia has little opportunity to come out of its form, to become a reality and enter into the great totalitarian utopias: poetic thought of survival. Reason becomes the mathematical grid of the art work, as is the case with Pume, who takes control of each form of his small black and white squares. The process of creation replaces art as a purpose and as a matter transformed into merchandise, whereas Pume steps back from art by inventing the reproducibility of his works as an industrial product. No work is original, even if more than one prototype has never been made or sold, or only sold to the rare purchaser. Pume became Bylex, the code name of the utopian project, the trademark of an improbable industrial product. When Pume invented a shoe that grows with age, it matters little that, in reality, the shoe becomes worn or the user must throw it out because he/she does not like it any more, because the idea of wearing the same object immobilizes time and man in a style, a frozen form, like someone chasing after ideas who catches an unchanging and eternal concept in his nets. The shoe is nothing more than this, a victorious man's odd quest for time. The time arrow is reduced to an adjusting knob used to expand reality to its own size.

With the purest desire for artistic experience, these African artists, almost all undertaking several spiritual and cultural practices of form, escape the marginal fate of rough art, even if, in fact, the need is the same. If Georges Adeagbo continues along his paths in Europe any old how, he does so at the Venice Biennale or in a gallery, but not in the street as he does in Cotonou, because that would resemble a contemporary art facility, when this is not at all what he seeks. It would also be highly unlikely to see such a facility belonging to a mere inhabitant on a Parisian street corner.

As magical or social mediums of speech, these artists' works appear to be one of the political and spiritual hearts of modern African creation, transcending eras, trends, races and civilizations by holding on to the basics.

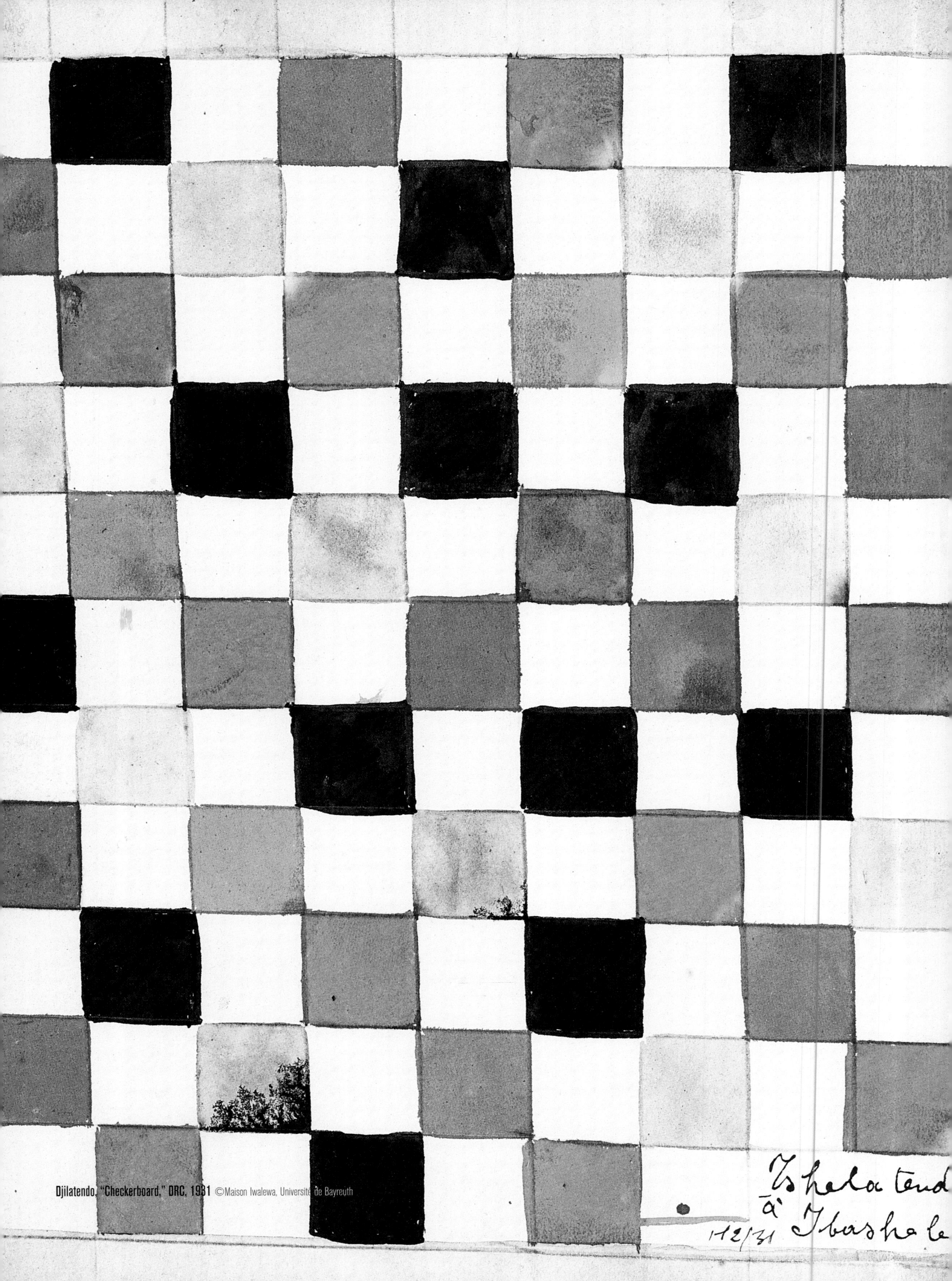

Djilatendo, "Checkerboard," DRC, 1931

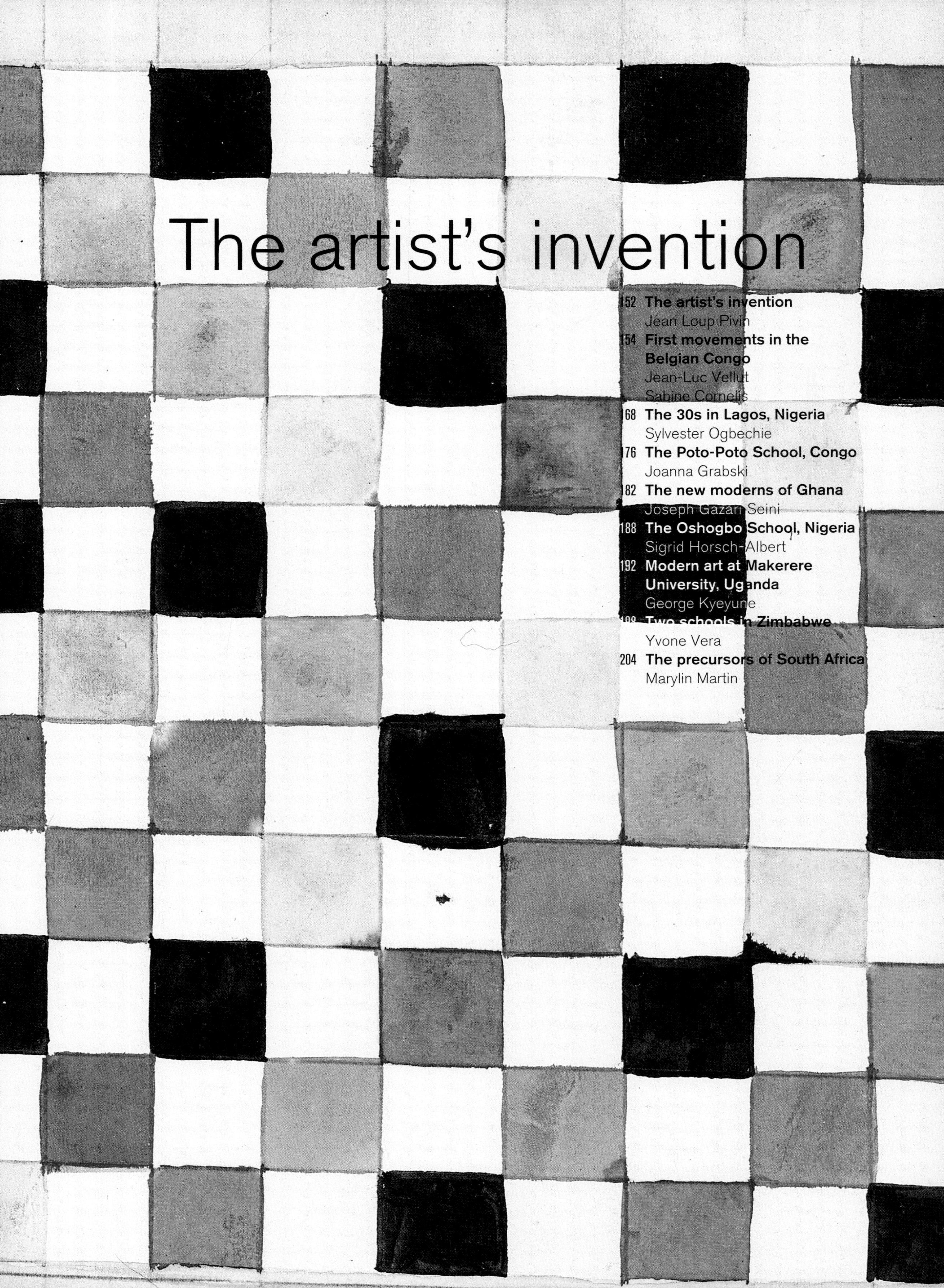

The artist's invention

THE ARTIST'S INVENTION
Jean Loup Pivin

Artistic experience was not invented in Africa in the 20th century under colonial influence; however, the "modern" artist's status did indeed develop at this time. Artistic experiences should be the focal point of such a reflection in order to better approach the artist in the current sense of the word.

Art as experience

What did those groups of men, painters and engravers who buried themselves deep within the caves of Europe and under the shelter of the rocks of Africa want to express? They did not live in these caves or shelters. They merely passed through them to draw or engrave portraits that remained mostly hidden. Did they intend to express another side of themselves to the world through the rite of drawing and engraving, as is done with singing? These prehistoric men drew figures using techniques and representations that do not appear to be from another time. The certain, precise and serene or tormented stroke is there, without any possibility of progress. There is no evolutionary pattern in art – as in love.

And what if art were nothing more than this experience? And what if humans only understood the world through this experience that, depending on its intensity and correspondence with our place in the world, would become art. Art as an experience for the person producing it cannot be the same as for the person contemplating it. Like the person standing at the edge of a night club dance floor, the observer cannot feel what the dancer feels, even if he understands, even if he feels what the dancer is expressing. Art is not communication, art is communion. Art is an experience that can only be understood by the person who has already lived it. "As long as I have not loved, all of the love stories I am told cannot explain to me what love is." As long as one has not experienced art as another approach to reality, all observations – including this one – will remain futile.

The artistic act is not concerned with communicating the finished image. Its intention touches upon what is implied at the very moment the image is produced, which may or may not be perceived by the observer. Emotions do not come from the image. They come from what remains of the experience of producing the image.

Marie Odile Briot used to say that painting is only a necessity for the artist. It is a way of saying that different expressions are only necessary for those who practice them. Producing forms is not a hobby, but a means of existing, of being a part of the world. Joseph Beuys' remark "Everyone is an artist" can only be interpreted if doing is simply being. We will not be covering the historical and cultural distance that separates the alleged practices of pre-historic European and African arts from those of the current different African civilizations. However, the different artistic practices of traditional societies certainly have little in common with current modern African and Western practices, except for the artist's full involvement, whatever his experience. It is in this context that the invention of the African artist is evoked.

Inventing the artist

The sudden emergence of the concept of fine arts onto the African artistic landscape has somewhat upset the picture. Admittedly, there were masters, schools, and trends in the days of ritual statuary, but the individual was not celebrated. The Western principal of art for art's sake, of the artist focused on himself, only took root on the Black continent in the first half of the twentieth century. Artists began to reinvent themselves beginning with the first aquarellists, who were confronted with Western esthetic quality, then with schools and workshops, which, at the end of the 20s, began to flourish on African soil, thanks to Western artists, patrons or instructors: Charles Combes (Bingerville, Ivory Coast, 1923), Georges Thiry (DRC/formerly Zaire, 1926), Kenneth Murray (Nigeria, 1927), H.V. Meyerowitz (Achimota, Ghana, 1937), Margaret Trowell (Kampala, Uganda, 1937), Reverend Paterson (Zimbabwe/formerly Southern

Rhodesia, 1939), Brother Marc-Stanislas (Gombe Matadi, DRC/formerly Zaire, 1943), Tom Blomfield (Zimbabwe/formerly Southern Rhodesia, 1943), Pierre Romain Desfossé (Lubumbashi, DRC/formerly Zaire, 1943/1944), Jean-Pierre Greenlaw (Sudan, 1946), Maurice Alhadeff (DRC/formerly Zaire, 1948-1950), Laurent Moonens (Lubumbashi, DRC/formerly Zaire, 1951), Mac Ewen (Salisbury, Zimbabwe/formerly Southern Rhodesia, 1957) Pierre Lods (Poto-Poto, Congo, 1951 and Dakar, Senegal, 1961), Ulli Beier and Suzanne Wenger (Oshogbo, 1963), Albert Botbol (Abidjan, 1966).

The originators of these schools brought various methods with them. There were those who encouraged their students' "authenticity" and those who, sometimes sub-consciously, guided them towards a type of production. This diversity in approaches gave birth to different esthetic trends, some of which are still seen as references.

The artist, in the current sense of the word, is an individual devoted to his art, which he will draw partially from his inspiration, "the genius," and partially from a critical relationship with the world of forms surrounding him. This new artist is confronted with imported and colonial cultures, with new ways of life. The experience's framework then changes, as occurred with European art a few centuries before. The artist leaves behind the path of traditional ritual, spirituality and collective orders in order to face a blank page, solitude and a market. The traditional artist is not, however, neglected, but is instead relegated to the rank of artisan, of a producer who is something of a "sorcerer," depending on the destination of the works to be produced. Was the lack of recognition of individual talents in pre-colonial societies fortuitous? For all that, the symbolic and commercial value of the signature could not, of course, have the same meaning.

Once the artist was invented under his Western name, he had to be given a formal specificity and a market.

Almost all first individual experiences revolve around art for the expatriate, a decorative art with pleasant features. The first workshops and schools led to the debate over the relationship with traditional forms and, for some, with the spirit of African forms: the spiritual world. However, everything unfolded without any actual involvement of the artists in the theoretical debate until the years surrounding the independence movements.

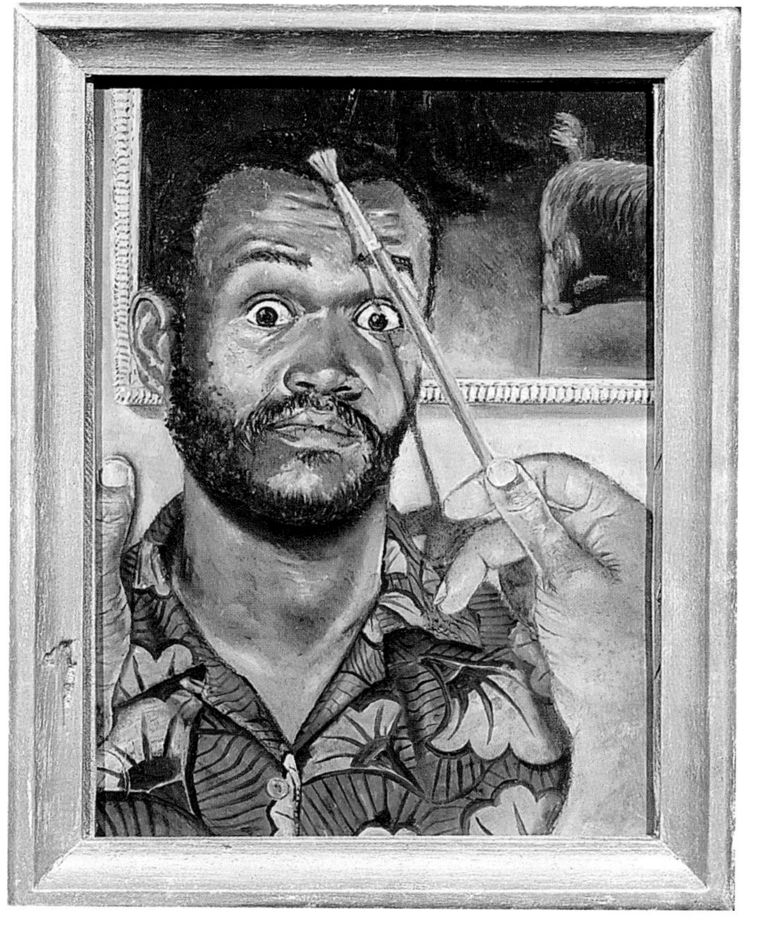

Trigo Paula (born in 1950), "Self-Portrait," Congo, 1986
oil on canvas, 60x57 cm.

First movements in the Belgian Congo

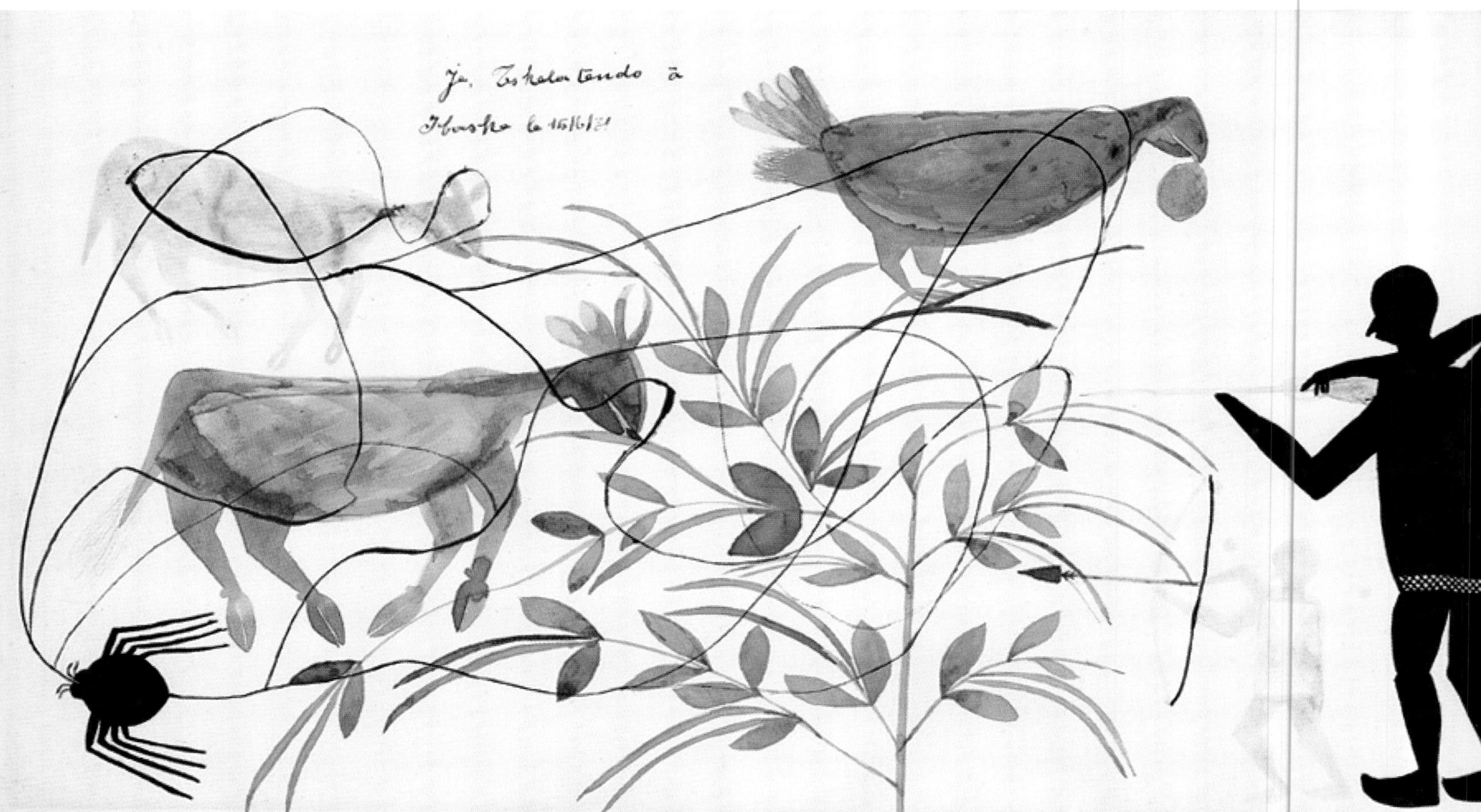

Djilatendo, "Hunting Scene," 1931

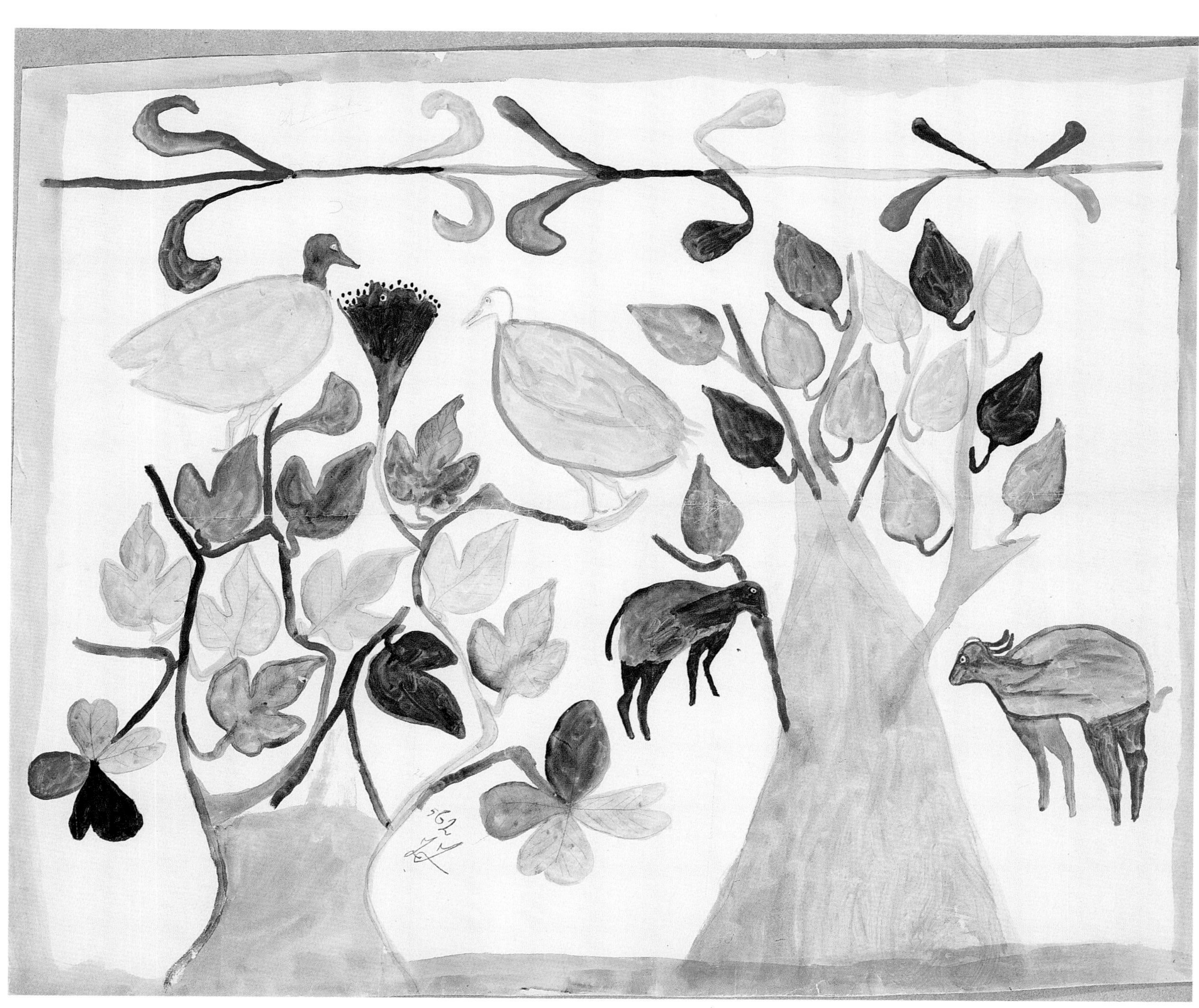

Albert Lubaki, c. 1930-1936

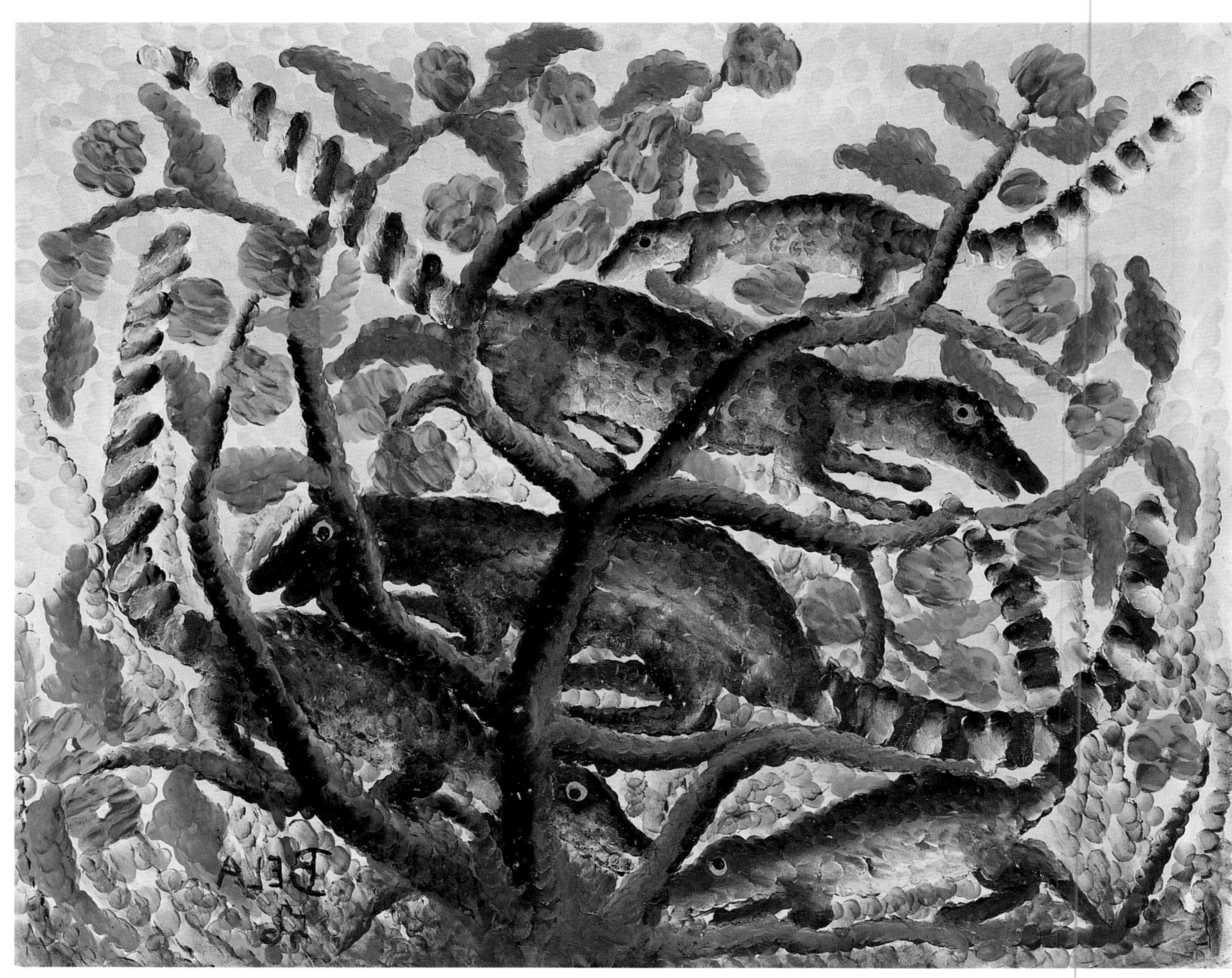

Bela, 1956

©Maison Iwalewa, Université de Bayreuth

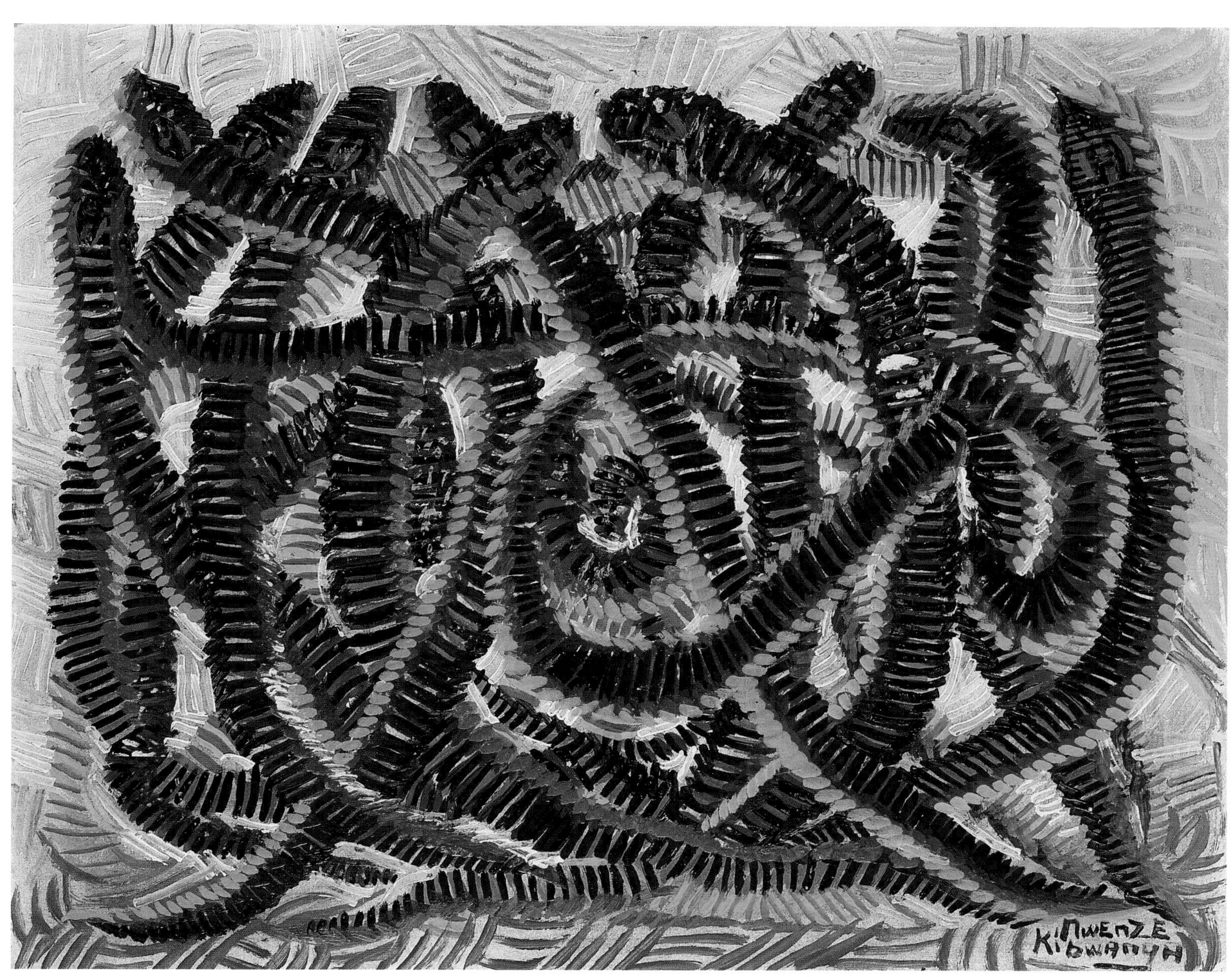

Mwenze Kibwanga (born in 1925), 1955

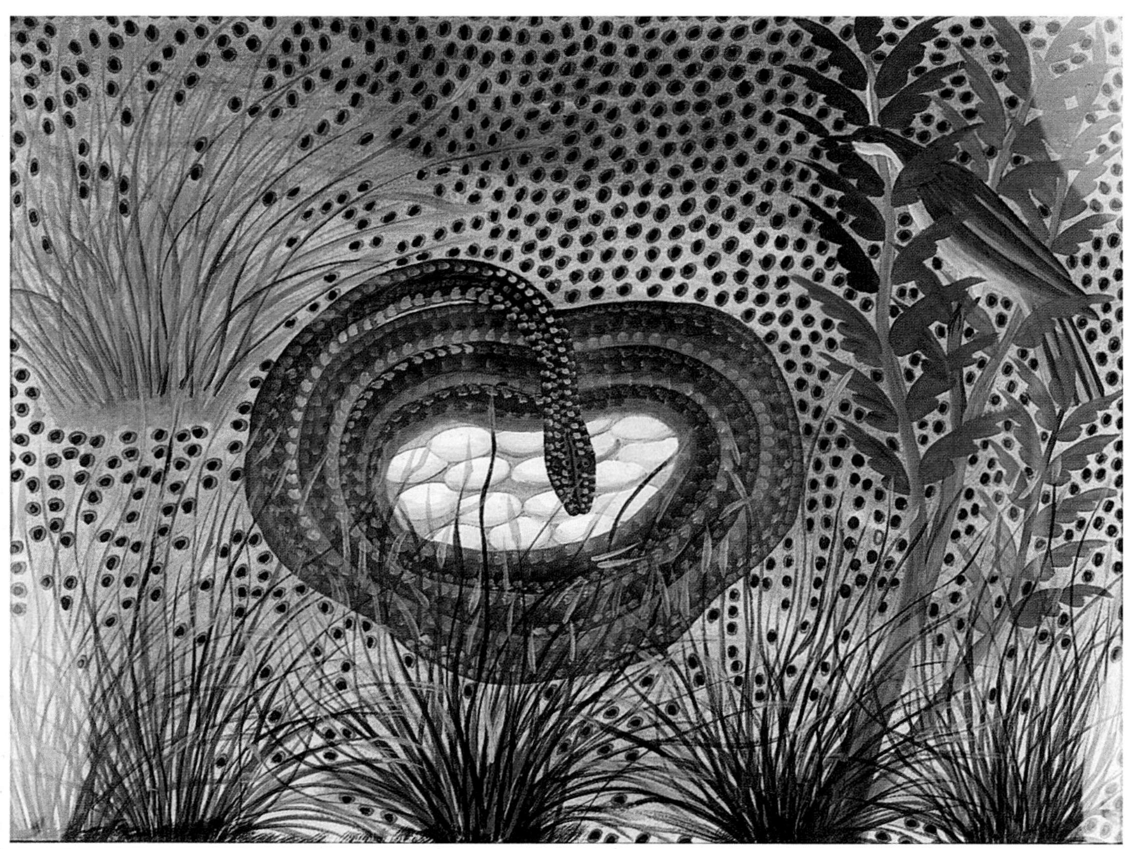

Pili-Pili Mulongoy (born in 1914), "Serpent brooding eggs," c. 1950
oil on paper, 50 x 60 cm
©MRAC, Tervuren

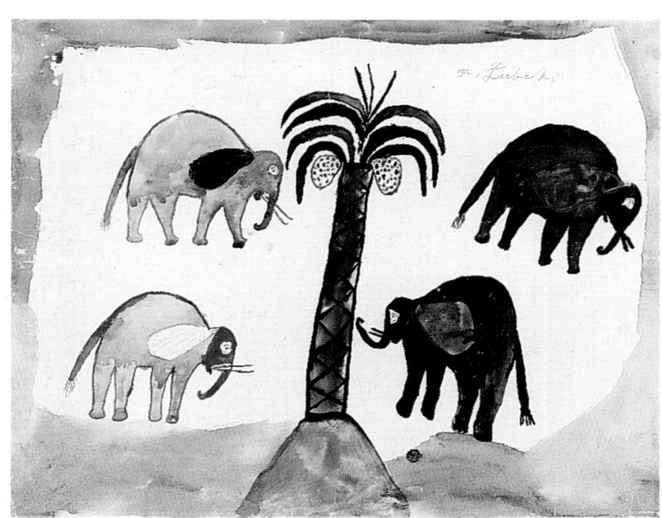

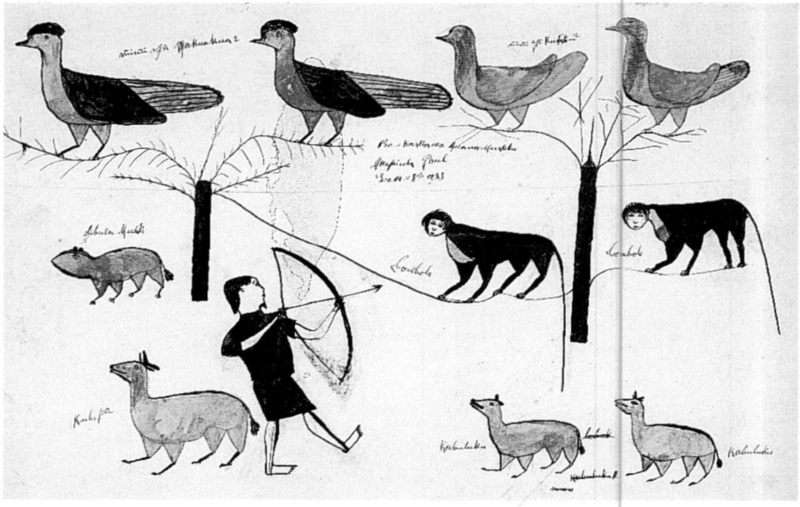

down:
Albert Lubaki, 1930
©Maison Iwalewa, Université de Bayreuth

Paul Mampinda, "Hunting for Two Monkeys," 1933
ink and watercolors, 32.5 x 50.5 cm
©MRAC, Tervuren

facing page:
Mode Muntu (1940-1985), "African Therapy"
oil on canvas, 58 x 45 cm
©Antoine Calmette-L. Albaret

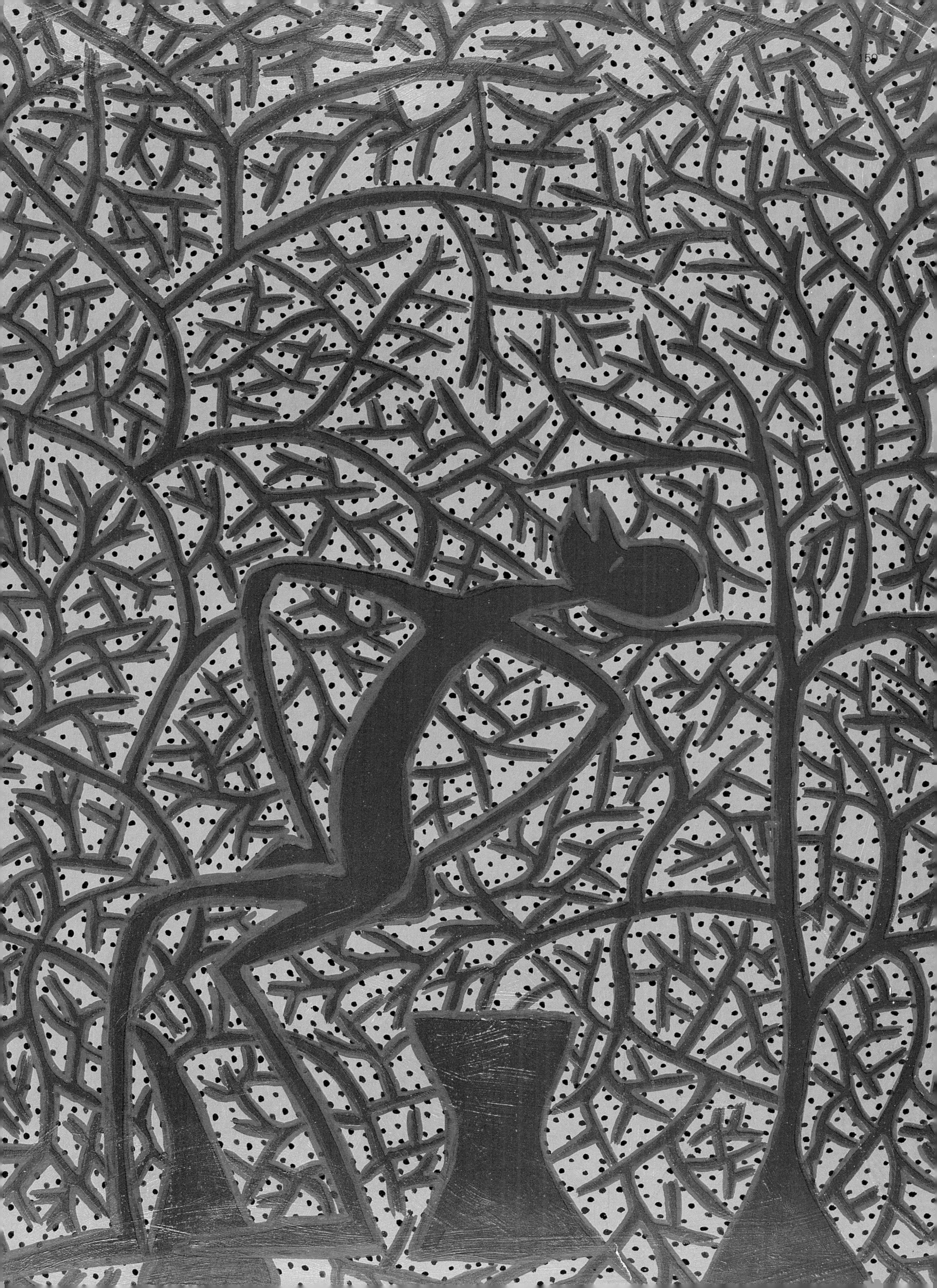

COLONIAL KITSCH
Jean-Luc Vellut

The entrance of European images into Africa and, conversely, the introduction of African representations onto the European scene, bring us back to the initial direct or indirect contacts between the African and European worlds. For the western part of Central Africa, these encounters and exchanges could be seen starting in the 16th century. The production of images underwent quite a boom in Europe as of the last third of the 19th century and the entrance of Europeans into Africa at this time was accompanied by a decisive quantitative change. Henceforth, Western travelers went to Africa carrying photographs, cameras, comics, magazines, postcards, portraits, and reproductions of paintings. They left the region with their bags overflowing with crafts, sculpted objects, fabrics and metallurgical productions. An objects market developed in Africa at the beginning of the colonial period, the ramifications of which could be felt elsewhere in the West, from its sites in Congo and Belgium.

From then on, several paths were set up. The paths of inventories and classifications of African material culture brought together sociologists and ethnologists who were, very early on, concerned with maintaining the integrity of the primitive cultures described as having traditions set in the reproduction of ancient models. During this same time, the concern with scientific classification and analysis gave way to less practical than esthetic criteria. This is how the notion of African art began to spread in the 1900s, even though it long collided with pervading skepticism. In 1923, Congo, a magazine of the Belgian Ministry of the Colonies, ridiculed the concept of Black Art, but this was already, at the time, a rearguard action.

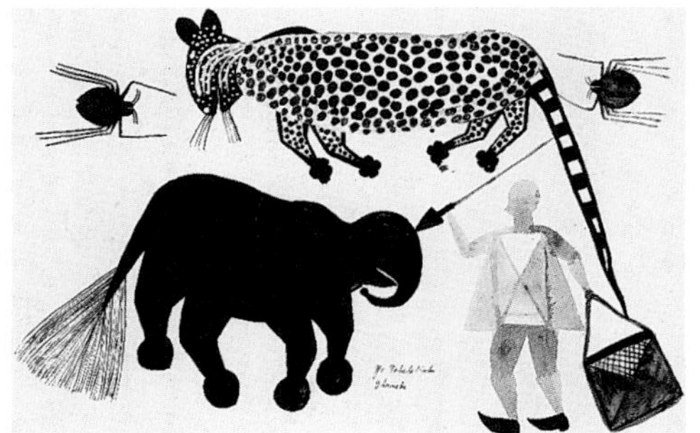

Djilatendo, 1930

©Maison Iwalewa, Université de Bayreuth

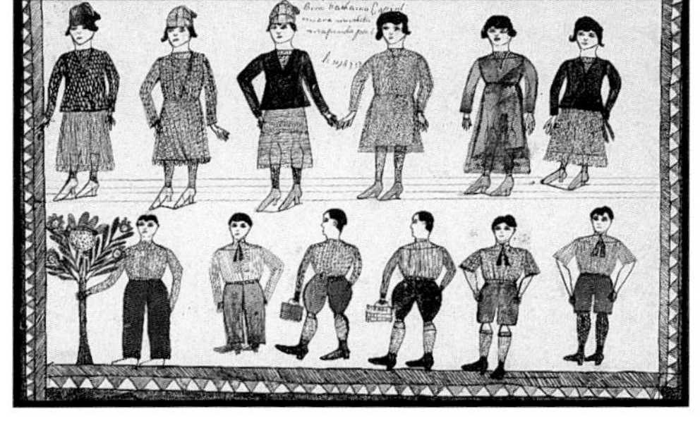

Paul Mampinda, "European People," 1933

ink and watercolors, 32.5 x 50 cm

©MRAC, Tervuren

Sculpture was, at this time, the royal path along which the North Atlantic, European and American world learned about African culture. The interpretation of objects was not, however, without problems.

There was often a great temptation to grant European consideration the power to decide not only what was acceptable based on Western esthetic experience, but also to define what the African soul should be, to claim to express the questions that Africa was asking. The answers provided were unavoidably riddled with concerns inherited from the history of thought and European sensibilities.

Other paths developed simultaneously and contributed to fitting African representations and decors into Western horizons. They were opened and explored by enthusiasts of the beauty and revival of artistic creation. A great tradition was represented by avant-garde artists or enthusiasts, whereas enthusiasts of exotic décors had a more modest and dense tradition. A colonial kitsch found its place in the intimacy of homes where the décor was responsible for announcing the owner's openness to the vast world.

The distinction between these two paths continues to fuel discussions in Europe today, as can be seen in the debates surrounding First Art. Should precedence be given to esthetic quality or should placing productions of African arts and crafts in a context be privileged? These European debates should not lose sight of the reverse movement, the movement of appropriation by Africa of images and representations borrowed from the West, of artistic techniques and new methods of expression.

Unlike the colonists, the first African visitors to Europe returned home laden with curious or useful objects and products. In this context, the production of images quickly took off in Africa itself. This is how the photographer became one of the first artisans to open workshops to service modern urban life. In Boma, the capital city of Leopoldian Congo, the first professional photographer in the colony was a Nigerian national, Herzekiah Shanu (deceased in 1905). Specializing in group scenes of budding urban life and in individual portraits, he set up, in his workshop, a stage, a set, fabric furniture, and a concept of the fashion and pose to be assumed by the subjects: a set of parameters aimed at building an ideal representation of Africans in modern life.

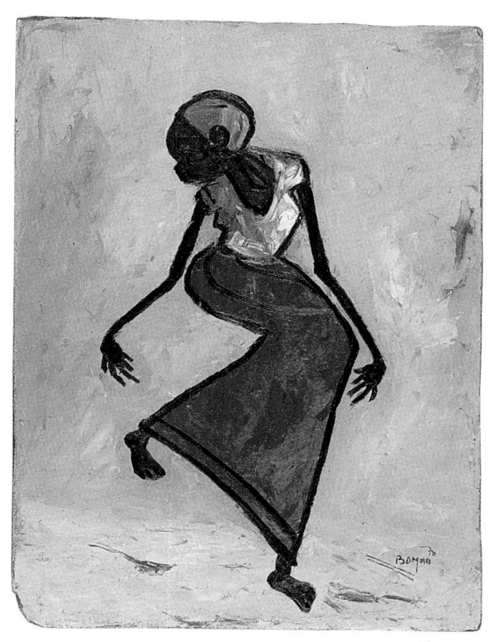

Bomolo, "Dancer," 1970
oil on panel, 61 x 82 cm
©MRAC, Tervuren

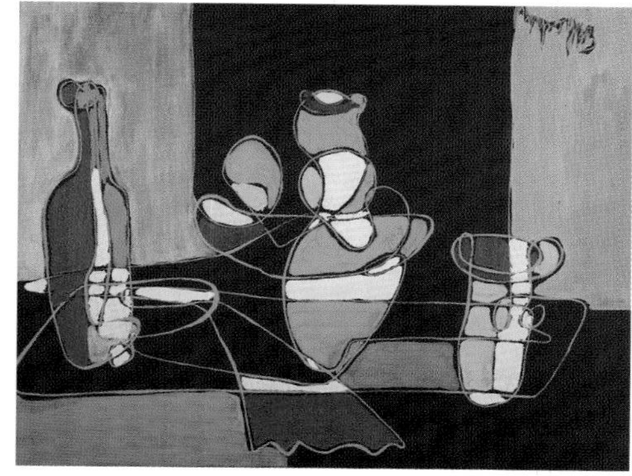

Pierre-Victor Mpoy (Mpoyo, born in 1937), "Still Life," 1963
gouache on paper, 50 x 65 cm
©MRAC, Tervuren

This art form was a certain money maker and, during the inter-war period, traveling photographers moved through the villages of the Congo with a dismantlable set and a stage model to be respected. A spin-off tradition, namely of portraits on canvas or paper, also developed as painting techniques on mobile mediums became more popular.

The decisive step here was to enable the transfer of techniques for wall painting or for making decorative wood or ivory sculptures onto paper or canvas. While a new African architecture incorporating European components (structures, doors, windows) was taking shape in the first urban or semi-urban centers along the modern roadways, images also began to appear on outer walls. These decorations were part of ancient traditions perhaps related to cave art. They replaced ancient graphics with symbolic characters, episodes or instruments used, if necessary, as commercial signs. The purpose of these decorations was, like the colonial kitsch or the Negro fetish in Europe, to announce the owner's openness to the modern world.

Individual itineraries

It was in this world of mirrors and borrowings that the colonial market and taste accepted the first individual African artists in Africa and in Europe. Unlike the traditional African artist, whose anonymity was never betrayed, these artists were producers who take root in the universe of artists with a known name. A convergence between esthetic feelings and individual itineraries explains this entrance of the modern African artist working in modern African décor onto the art and decorative art scene in Africa and Europe.

Included among the individual itineraries that have reached us are those of a few producers of sculpted ivory, of images on walls or of water colors on paper working in the mining region of the Katanga Hinterland or in the relatively mixed context of small industrial or stripped centers along the Kasai railroad. The two regions illustrate this semi-urbanized world where a small imagery market developed, aimed at a few Congolese or European enthusiasts.

One well-known meeting is the one held between two folk artists, Albert Lubaki and Djilatendo, with Georges Thiry (often known by the pseudonym Dulonge).

The itineraries of each of these actors are not completely known. It is thanks to Thiry alone that we have rare information about them. Through Thiry, we have learnt that Lubaki was a native of Lower Congo who settled in Kabinda, in Eastern Kasai, and that he was in close relations with the mining pool of industrial Katanga.
This was how we discovered Lubaki, working as an artisan and designer with wood or ivory, a small merchant of "native curiosities." Djilatendo was another of Thiry's "discoveries," who he met, this time, in Kasai, where this artist was covering walls with decorative geometric patterns or scenes inspired by the world of fables or of daily life. Djilatendo incorporated the representation of striking innovations of the modern world, of quick movement (bicycles, airplanes, etc.), of European furniture, and of objects from everyday life (bottles, pipes, etc.) into his work, and structured it around a written commentary. This form had continued success and is found in folk painting in the 70s and afterwards, together with moralistic comments on history and current times.
These themes were encouraged by Georges Thiry, a representative figure of these patrons-entrepreneurs that haunt the history of artistic productions of modern Africa. Thiry, a low-ranking colonial agent in Bukama in 1926-28 and then in Mweka in 1929-31, helped the artists he discovered by providing them with materials, paper and colors, by encouraging the artists and making suggestions, and by purchasing their works.

Thiry is partially responsible for the guidance given to this made-to-order production and his own concerns played an important role in it. Influenced by readings pierced with surreal esthetics, Thiry has left behind inventories of colorful Prévert-like characters and décors that embodied the semi-urban culture of the colonial Congo from 1929-1930.

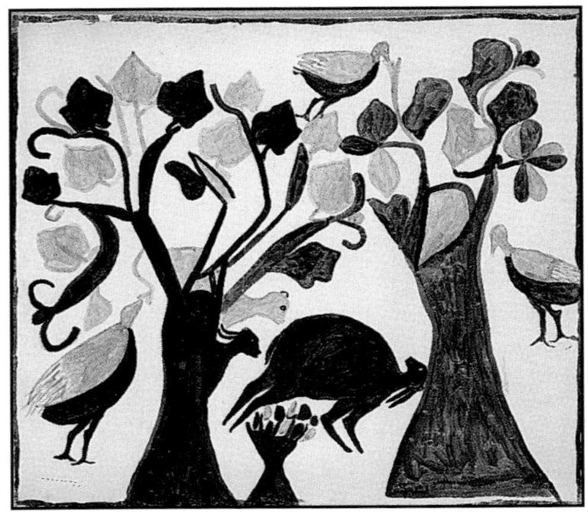

Albert Lubaki, c.a. 1930-1936

©Maison Iwalewa, Université de Bayreuth

Thiry himself made a few sketches illustrating the shady world of the ports, roads and urban centers of Congo as he saw them through the lenses of a fan of jazz and of those Negro décors he had already explored in Europe. He had a premonition about the trend, and therefore the market value of the representations of urban culture of modern Africa. In this respect, the instructions he gave artists are characteristic. He sought, above all else, to capture an African vision of the modern world, its modes of transportation, its characters, men and women, and of the marvelous crowded world of the Congo's tales and fables.

The market for this production of print manufacturers, as they were called at the time, only took off, however, following a new meeting: a meeting between Thiry and Gaston-Denys Périer, an esthete, man of letters and employee at the Ministry of the Colonies. Périer, a selfless person and a bit of an eccentric who knew many people on the Brussels scene, was one of the first to understand that an esthetic colonial space was awakening. In 1920-1930, he was the tireless artisan who introduced African décors onto the European horizon. He also saw this as an opportunity to introduce European esthetic designs and representations onto the African continent.

In 1929, Thiry, an enthusiast and a merchant, was able to exhibit a collection of watercolors produced by Congolese print manufacturers, using the format of the time, with the help of Périer. The opportunity arose when a large exhibit of Primitive and Folk Art was organized at the new Fine Arts Museum of Brussels. Entrusted to the best French and Belgian folk artists, the exhibit was devoted to the "history of the workers and little people of days gone by, whose lives historians had overlooked." Modern Congolese painting made its first appearance in Europe through folk art, next to Belgian masks or Java batiks, and not within the context of Black art. At that time, Congolese cartoons received only a lukewarm reception.[1] Some watercolors did, however, make it to Geneva, where another pioneer, Eugène Pittard, exhibited them at the city's Museum of Ethnography. Another exhibit took place in Paris, where ambiguities and rumors regarding the actual identity of the artists were spreading. It legitimized the expression of folk art given to these productions. The Museum of Tervuren did not, however, give the exhibit the same welcome. The institution did indeed acquire a few Congolese watercolors in 1930, but they were banished into collections, beyond the public eye. At that time, an Africanism of strict observance that maintained an absolute separation between tradition and metis art prevailed at the museum. This art was then confined to the ranks of degenerate art by scholarly anthropology. There are known cases of this in 1930s Europe, where a similar approach was taken with expressionist art that based itself on primitive esthetics.[2]

Not without ambiguity, Thiry broke with the set roles in which African art was evolving in the West. After the initial attempts, the exhibits soon began to multiply in Belgium and abroad. One step was the production of a collection of tales and fables written by a Congolese author, Badibanga, and illustrated by Djilatendo.[3] This was how modern Africa also entered the world of European publishing. Despite the initial reluctance, on several levels the consideration of artistic productions from modern Africa was becoming an actuality, but still evolving outside the main institutions.[4]
This entry onto the international scene was not without ambiguities, which can be seen from the start. Georges Thiry, in opening up the path to Western patrons who later sought to guide the production of Congolese folk artists, did indeed encourage "his" artists in a certain type of production that corresponded to what he felt was the African artistic genius, namely the sense of décor and taste for conjuring up types (rather than individualities). The dream announced was that of an innocent look cast by Africa on Europe. At the same time, the sketches and water colors signed by Thirty himself were indicative of the central spot that the white world, colored by eroticism, occupied in his ecstatic vision of the black world.

Despite the suggestions that he lavished on artists, Thiry was only partially

[1] In a provocative approach for the time, G.-D. Périer illustrated a collection of his essays with traditional Congolese art frames and crafts, and with sketches done by Dulonge and Lubaki: G.-D. Périer, Nègreries et Curiosités congolaises, Brussels, L'Églantine, 1930.

[2] P. Van Schuylenbergh and F. Morimont, Rencontres artistiques Beligique-Congo, 1920-1950, in: Enquêtes et Documents d'Histoire africaine (Louvain-la-Neuve), 12, 1995.

[3] L'Éléphant qui marche sur des oeufs, Brussels, L'Églantine, 1931. A German version was published by the University of Beirut in 1987.

[4] A Brussels Café, La Fleur en papier Doré (which still exists on rue des Alexiens, 26) but also certain African art exhibits reported by J.-L. Vellut in: La naissance de la peinture contemporaine en Afrique centrale, 1930-1970, Tervuren, Royal Museum of Central Africa, 1992, p. 5-11.

followed. Djilatendo, for example, undoubtedly the most original creator, preferred to structure artists' visions around fables, silhouettes and symbolic instruments of modern life. Mobility is an important part of this, with its airplanes and bicycles. This did not, however, prevent Denys-Périer from also developing a fantastical Africa. Standing before the productions of Lubaki and Djilatendo, he would rejoice that he finally had access to the African soul and not only to production units or medicalized bodies omnipresent in colonial discourse. But he too was overwhelmed with ecstatic feelings and dreamt "of Negro accents (...), mysterious hieroglyphs that undoubtedly resembled the writings of ancient Egypt." All décors, fables and images, provided that they were produced by a full-fledged Negro, were qualified as an invention of Africa.[5]

[5] "Nègre cent pour cent," according to the expression of Carlo Rim (1929), organizer of the Congolese watercolor exhibit held in Paris in 1931. Quoted by J. Cornet, et al., 60 ans de peinture au Zaïre, Brussels, Associated Art Publishers, 1989, p. 23. At this time, Carlo Rim, the pseudonym of Jean Richard, was the director of the Parisian magazine Jazz. The theme of the invention of Africa was explored by Anthony Appiah and Valentin Mudimbe.

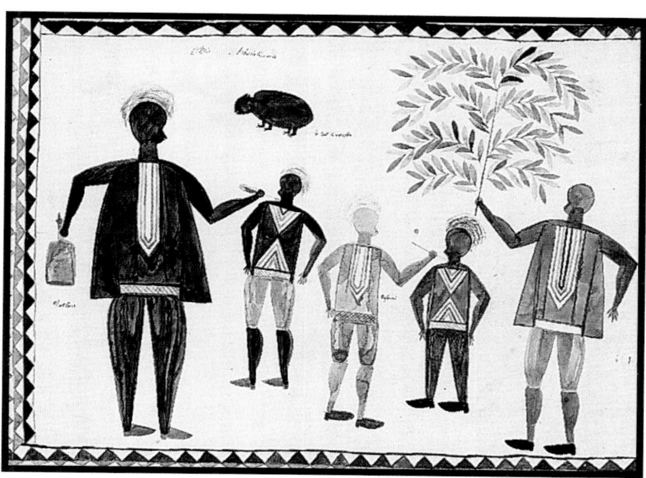

Djilatendo, 1937

©Maison Iwalewa, Université de Bayreuth

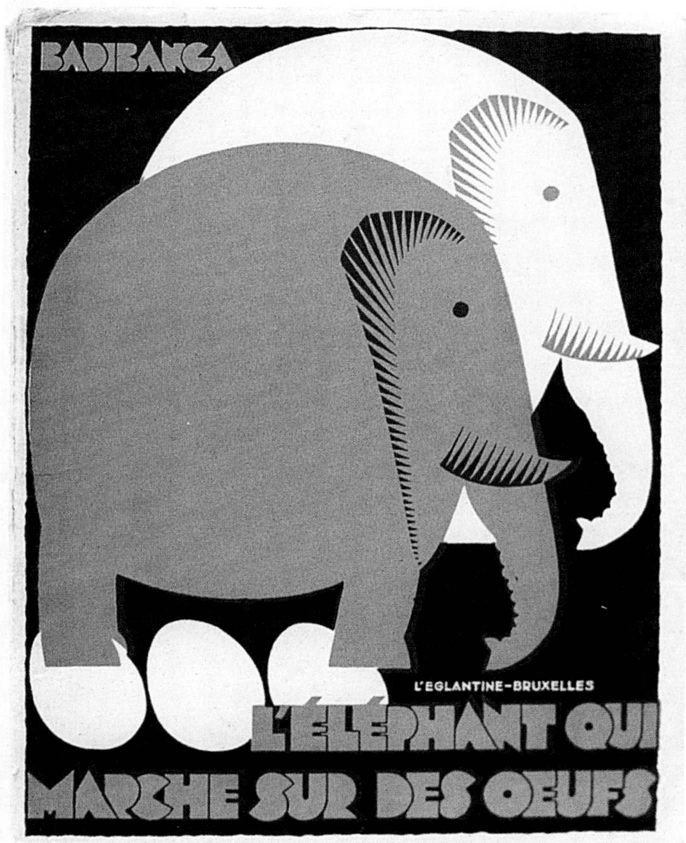

Cover of "L'éléphant qui marche sur des œufs,"
texts by Badibanga, illustrations by Djilatendo
L'Églantine Publishing House, Brussels, 1931

©Revue Noire

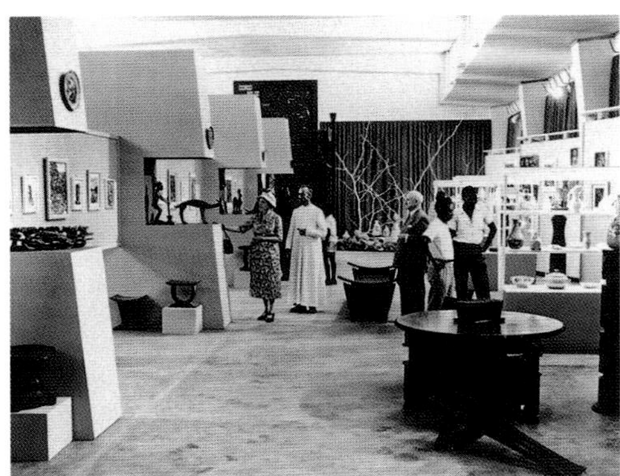

Brother Marc during an exhibit at the Saint-Luc School, c. 1950

©MRAC, Tervuren

BIRTH OF ACADEMICISM
Sabine Cornelis

During the inter-war period, the private cultural initiatives organized in the Belgian Colony focused, above all, on the idea of protecting "native" art, which had to be safeguarded, at all costs, from European influence. These initiatives encouraged quality artisan production in several workshops in the Colony and led to certain measures to protect Congolese heritage. In 1935, the Commission for the Protection of the Arts and Native Trades (C.O.P.A.M.I.), headquartered at the Ministry of the Colonies in Brussels, was created in the metropolis. In 1939, a decree was passed regarding the protection of sites, monuments and native art productions. A "Craft House," designed as an art focus, right in the heart of "native" ground, where artisans could work while drawing inspiration from models reproduced on photographs or in publications, was opened in the Congo capital city prior to World War II. Finally, the first Museum of the Colony, the "Native Life Museum" was inaugurated in Leopoldville in 1936, at a site lent by the textile company Utexleo. It had a "Sales Office," where objects of Congolese art from various craft centers around the Colony were offered. All of these efforts were related to traditional art trades.[1] Easel painting was overlooked, with the exception of a few precise experiments dealing with paper painting.

In the Congo, intellectual life experienced a remarkable development in the colonial environment during World War II. New magazines, especially cultural magazines, gave intellectuals the opportunity to express themselves. Discussions on "native" art progressively adapted to the new directions emerging in the Colony. In the 40s and early 50s, a few new artistic components helped to speed up the process that had begun during the previous periods. This process inevitably led Congolese art towards "modern" art.

The debate surrounding the new Congolese art

Congolese art began to transform in the Belgian colony after World War II. This was the case with painting in particular, which developed in urban centers. Self-taught painters moved through the large cities and sold their works on café patios. This moneymaking painting, intended to brighten up the homes of the colonists, was criticized because it was considered to be a clumsy copy of the works produced by European painters of questionable talent. But, in the 40s, this spontaneous art also got the colonial intelligentsia thinking. Is it not, after all, fruitless to want to confine African art to its past and classicism? Should one not accept that "native art" must follow new paths? The principal enthusiasts of Congolese art in the Colony, in the Congo and in Belgium, fell into a heated debate over how to direct this changing Congolese art. Following the example of film director André Scohy, most of them admitted that stubbornly confining artists to "art workshops," where ancient forms were repeated, would lead to "stifling the future of Congolese art, right from its inception." But the issue remained whether this Congolese art should be left to find its path freely or whether it needed Western guides to supervise it or to make it follow academic paths.[2] A few voices could be heard in the late 40s, especially among the "civilized,"[3] asking teachers and art schools to offer art education. Hesitation remained in the air: could European works be shown to the African artist? And if so, which ones? Should classic or modern works be shown?

While discussions, searches and gropings into the colonial cultural world regarding the future of Congolese art were taking place, branches of art education were being created in the Colony's two large urban centers. One branch responded to the aspirations of those who wished for the intervention of a spiritual "master" who would guarantee a certain freedom in how they worked. The other, a more structured branch, would give rise to the academies.

[1] Arts et métiers indigènes dans la province de Léopoldville, 9, November 1938, p.3 ; Official Gazette of the Belgian Congo, no. 1, 15/1/1939, p. 677-686; Une visite au Musée de la Vie Indigène à Léopoldville in Brousse, no. 3-4, 1946, no page numbering; S. CORNELIS, Élements pour une approche historique des arts plastiques européens et africains non traditionnels au Congo belge (1940-1947) et leur situation dans le contexte culturel de la Colonie in Revue des Archéologues et Historiens d'Art de Louvain, 31, 1998, p.143-156.

[2] S. Cornelis, op.cit; A. Scohy, Réflexions... sur l'évolution de l'Art Congolais in Brousse, no. 2-4, 1948, p.18-20; 7 Propositions sur la jeune peinture congolaise in Jeune Afrique, no. 5, March 1949, p.5-7; Libres propos sur l'Art nègre in Jeune Afrique, no. 5, March 1949, p.21-28; Notre enquête sur l'art nègre de demain in Bulletin de l'Union des Femmes coloniales, no. 128, January 1950, p. 9-10; G.-D. Perier, UNESCO et l'Art du Congo in Brousse, no. 3-4, 1947, p.6-7.

[3] A.R. Bolamba, editor in chief of the newspaper for the "civilized" La Voix du Congolais, Albert Mongita in La Voix du Congolais, no. 22, January 1948.

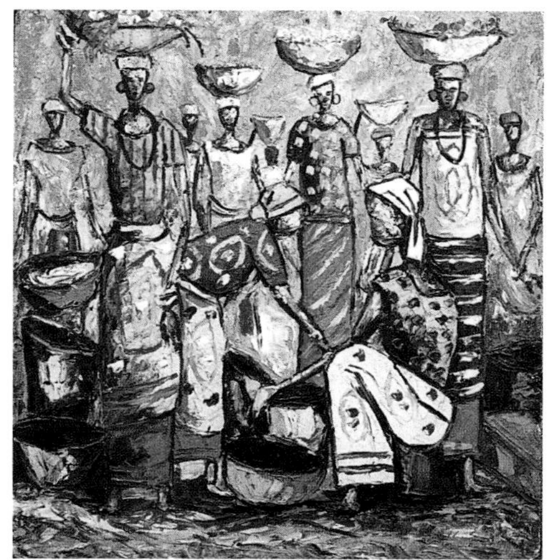

Louis Koyongonda (born in 1918)

©Revue Noire

Albert Mongita (born in 1916), "Village View"

oil on panel, 79 x 80.2 cm

©MRAC, Tervuren

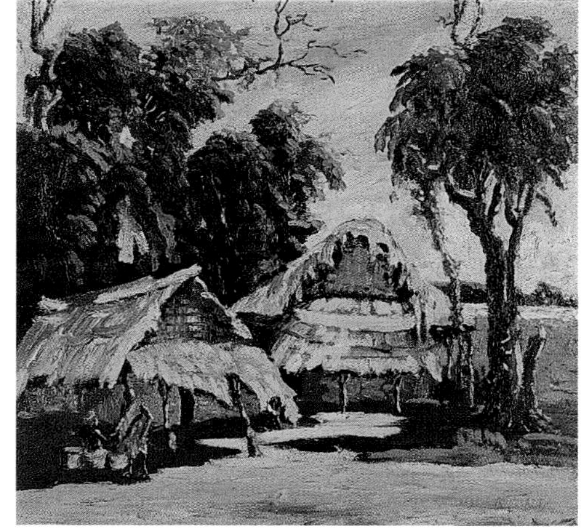

The self-taught painters of Stanley-Pool

From among the large number of self-taught painters wandering around Leopoldville on the eve of the 1950s emerged a small group of artists (Mongita, Bata, Kiabelua, Nkusu, Dombe, Demuko, Koyongonda) who André Scohy labeled the "School of Stanley-Pool." These independent painters received a few technical pointers from the Belgian artist Laurent Moonens before he moved to Elizabethville, where he created an academy. Of this group, Albert Mongita was the most famous and most appreciated in the colonial milieu. Albert Mongita was a man of the theater and radio, and also a painter. He drew inspiration for his paintings from the colonial painter Marques, held in very high esteem by the Europeans in the Congo, which ensured him success and enabled him to sell approximately ten paintings per month. Some people, such as André Scohy, actually criticized his gift and accused him of wallowing in "chromo style." According to Scohy, the Mongita "case" illustrated the drama of the talented artist "torn between the tendency to create and the ease of producing."

Exchanges, still exceptional at the time, began between Belgian painting in the Congo and Congolese painting, yet remained, despite everything, very compartmentalized. Mongita and Kiabelua, another young self-taught artist described as "naïve," attended the exhibit of the Belgian expressionist painter Maurice Van Essche in Leopoldville. Mongita left the exhibit very disappointed, feeling that Van Essche did not know how to paint. Kiabelua, on the other hand, while less talented than Mongita, from a technical point of view, was amazed. The notion of encounters and exchanges had already been championed by the magistrate and man of letters Joseph-Marie Jadot just after the war, when he proposed turning the three Belgian Congo museums (Leopoldville, Elizabethville and Kabgaie) into centers for study, popularization and documentation for black artists and "those who guide them"; however, this notion remained in the embryonic stages. A group of "civilized natives" visited the second Mongita exhibit in Leopoldville in 1950, which was an effective way of drawing attention to painting. There was talk of creating a meeting place for local artists, where seminars could be held. This would be a genuine "conservatory of African arts." André Scohy proposed a meeting between the groups of Congolese painters and exhibits in Leopoldville and in Elizabethville to foster these artistic relationships. Finally, of note is the appearance of "art biennials" in the Belgian Congo in the 1940s.[4] As we can see, Leopoldville became a fertile place, where innovative projects took off.

Art schools in urban centers

The two large art education centers in the Colony originated at the junction of the craft workshops that had opened in the 30s and the art school as such. Brother Marc in Gombe-Matadi and Pierre Romain-Desfossés in Elizabethville initially shared the same desire to create good artisans who could live from their art, both in Leopoldville and in Elizabethville. This was also the perspective of Laurent Moonens at the Elizabethville Academy in 1951.

The Saint-Luc School (Leopoldville)

In 1933, the Vicar General of the Brothers of the Christian Schools, while visiting the Congo, recommended the creation of a drawing school in the Colony. Brother Marc-Stanislas, commonly called "Brother Marc," an artist and former student of Saint-Luc School in Liège, arrived in the Congo in 1939. The first Saint-Luc School was inaugurated in Gombe-Matadi during the summer of 1943. The full course of study there lasted seven years. After four years of middle courses, the candidate would receive a sculptor-decorator diploma. This was truly a school of applied arts. The statuary sculptor diploma could be obtained after three additional years in the advanced course. Jacob Winenguane obtained the first decorator artist diploma in Gombe-Matadi in 1948. Saint-Luc School was set up in Leopoldville near the "native housing development" in 1949. This private initiative later received the status of an official school.

[4] A. Scohy, Libre propos sur un peintre Congolais. Albert Mongita in Jeune Afrique, no. 3, June 1948, p. 36-39; A. Scohy, op.cit. in Jeune Afrique, no. 5, March 1949, p. 5-7; A. Scohy, Où en est la jeune peinture congolaise ? in Jeune Afrique, no. 12, July-September 1950, p.21-22; J.-M. Jadot, La Colonisation belge du Congo et l'Art nègre in Institut Royal Colonial Belge, Bulletin des Séances, XVII, 1946, I, Brussels, 1946, p. 233-256, 289-290. J.-M. Jadot pleads for the State to resume private initiatives for "Black Art" and to create museums; J. Maquet-Tombu, Les possibilités artistiques des centres extra-coutumiers in La Femme et le Congo, no. 157, April 1957, p. 17-18; A.R. Bolamba, La seconde exposition du Peintre Mongita in La Voix du Congolais, no. 52, July 1950; J. Maquet-Tombu, Manifestations artistiques à Léopoldville in La Femme et le Congo, no. 155, October 1956, p. 10-11; J. Vanden Bossche, La Biennale des Arts de la Province de Léopoldville in Brousse, no. 10, 1957, p. 11-19.

Nzita (born in 1929), "Players"
oil on panel, 38 x 48 cm
©Antoine Calmette-L.Albaret

A painting section, involving seven years of training, was added on to the former sculpture class. The system was identical: in the middle course, the students were guided towards painting and the decoration of buildings. The most talented students continued in the advanced section where they did easel painting. The structure of the courses at Saint-Luc School made it possible to combine applied arts and art as such. Brother Marc initially sought to reconcile the forms and spirit of the traditional arts of Central Africa with art education as it is practiced in the West, while denying his students access to Western art history, which was an obvious challenge. However, in 1957 Brother Marc's school was renamed the Fine Arts Academy and its courses were more obviously guided towards international modern art.[5]

The Alhadeff Workshops (Leopoldville)

Pierre-Romain Desfossés at the Elizabethville workshop (Lumumbashi), c. 1950 ©MRAC, Tervuren

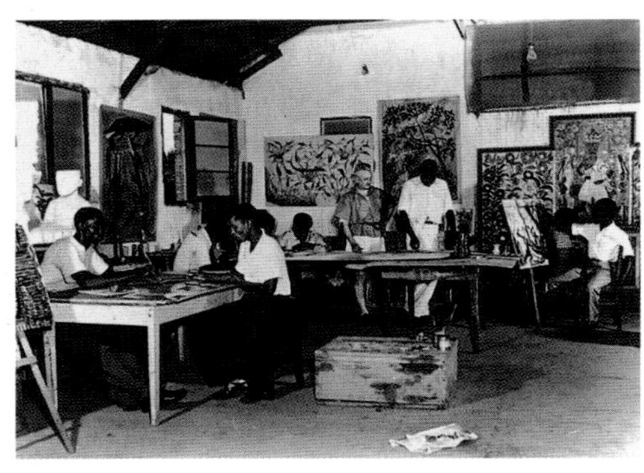

Businessman Maurice Alhadeff supported a series of artists, painters and sculptors outside any official framework, and enabled them to live from their art. Bomolo, Massamba, Kanza, Monene, Futa, Bazungula and Koyongonda were among these artists. Scorning taboos and hesitations that led other "friends" of Congolese art to question what should or should not be done to be able to "live," "re-emerge" or "regenerate oneself," Maurice Alhadeff did not hesitate to show reproductions of Van Gogh and Picasso to youths seeking his support. Alhadeff also provided work for ivory workers and had them sculpt large teeth. The savings he provided for them enabled them to avoid delving into the manufacture of trinkets to ensure their livelihood.[6] The Alhadeff workshop painters originated a type of repetitive painting with bold colors applied with a knife. This is a Congolese variant of what is usually called "airport art."

The Pierre Romain-Desfossés Workshop (Elizabethville)

The French painter Pierre Romain-Desfossés arrived in Elizabethville towards the end of the war. He settled there among his relics and African art collections and devoted himself to promoting "native" art. In 1947, he founded a workshop whose first items had been in the works since 1946. Pierre Romain-Desfossés was not a fan of academic learning as it was practiced in Leopoldville. According to him, the workshop was a place where young artists could find material and benefit from the advice of a "master." Obvious talents, such as Pilipili, Bela, Mwenze Kibwanga, Ilunga, Kaballa and many others, expressed themselves fairly freely in his workshop. They used a technique that was rather unconventional: some would paint lying down, others with their fingers, and others on an easel. While Desfossés' objective was initially to provide training in applied and decorative arts, a more in-depth analysis of his emulators' works produces symbols. It is, however, clear that Pierre Romain-Desfossés' personal painting influenced his disciples and guided them in how they worked. He urged them, for example, to use tales as a source of inspiration for their paintings. He encouraged Mwenze Kibwanga to abandon the portrait and pick up a more traditional theme. This master-disciple relationship between Pierre Romain-Desfossés and his students continued after his death. The "master" had taken all of the necessary steps for his students to be able to continue to work without "squandering" their financial resources and without giving in to the ease of painting in accordance with Western tastes.[7]

Academy of Fine Arts and Art Trades (Elizabethville)

In 1951, Laurent Moonens created an Academy of Fine Arts and Art Trades in Elizabethville. Shortly afterwards, the Academy was transformed into an official school and given the name Official Academy of Fine Arts of Elizabethville. More than one link would be established between the Academy of Fine Arts of Laurent Moonens and the workshop of Pierre Romain-Desfossés. Upon his arrival in the Congo, Laurent Moonens visited his predecessor's workshop, which, perhaps, left certain traces in how he worked with his students. The Moonens school appeared to be a compromise between academic education and "free" work.

[5] P. Davister, Le Frère Marc forme de jeunes artistes congolais qui s'efforceront de régénérer l'art indigène in Le courrier d'Afrique, 15-16/10/1949, reproduced in the archives of Guebels, MRAC, noinv. 69.14.113 (file 154); press release from Congopresse reproduced in the archives of Guebels, MRAC, Noinv. 69.14.187, file no. 249 ; J.-A. Cornet, La peinture à Kinshasa in J.-A. Cornet et al, 60 ans de peinture au Zaïre, Brussels, 1989, p. 109-203, J. Maquet-Tombu, op.cit. in La Femme et le Congo, no. 157, April 1957, p. 17-18.

[6] J. Maquet-Tombu, op.cit., 1957 ; J. Vanden Bossche, op.cit., 1957.

[7] Badi-Banga Ne-Mwine, Contribution à l'étude historique de l'art plastique zaïrois moderne (fin xve siècle-1975), Kinshasa, 1977, p. 36.

His purpose was to provide technical support while respecting individual inspiration. He wanted to encourage personalities to bloom. It was with this lesson that Mwembia, Amisi, Kabongo and Kamba graduated from his academy. Of all of his students, the most original and promising was Mode.

Laurent Moonens shared Desfossés' desire to enable students to make a living. He was, therefore, generally interested in applied arts. Architecture, advertising and ceramics classes could be found alongside his sculpture and painting classes. The style of certain paintings recalls the Desfossés workshop, such as those of Muvuma, for example. It should also be noted that, upon Pierre Romain-Desfossés' death in 1954, his workshop was taken over by Moonens, who installed it in a separate section of the academy (section D). One of Moonens' important innovations was organizing mixed courses in which European and Congolese students could work together, except in sculpture and painting classes, for which Blacks and Whites were separated.[8]

In highlighting the interest of colonial discussion on contemporary African art and the particularly engaging context of first experiences and first art schools in the former Belgian Congo, one must also mention a restriction: the main actors of this contemporary art, the African creators themselves, were excluded from the initial debate. The European masters and thinkers chose the terms according to which the new Congolese art could be structured.

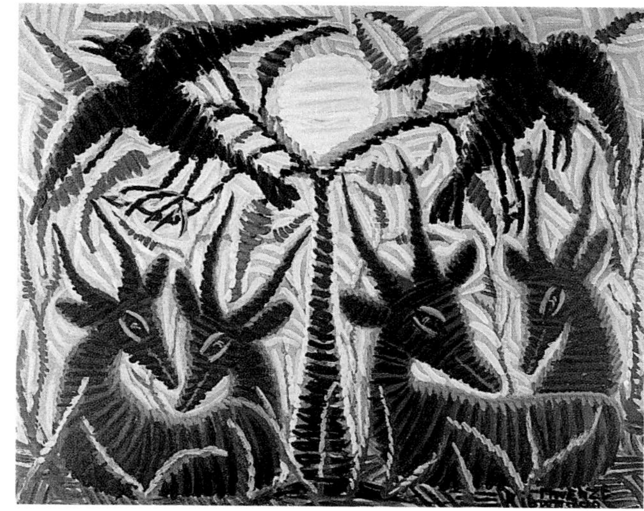

Mwenze Kibwanga (born in 1925), "Pale Moon," c. 1956
oil on paper, 49.9 x 60 cm
©MRAC, Tervuren

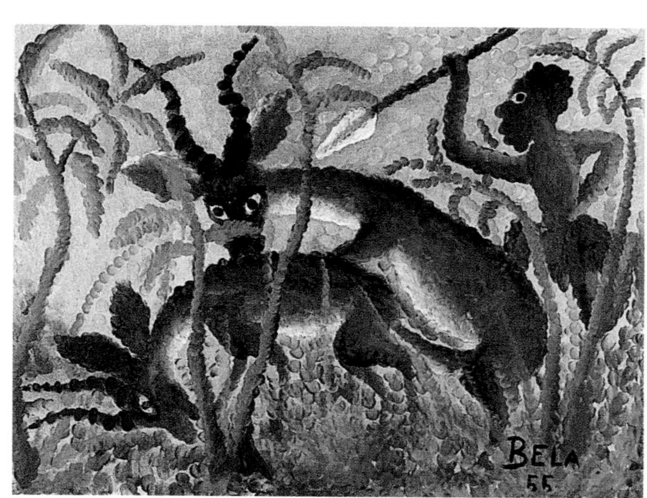

Bela, "Hunting Scene," 1955
oil on paper, 63 x 75 cm
©MRAC, Tervuren

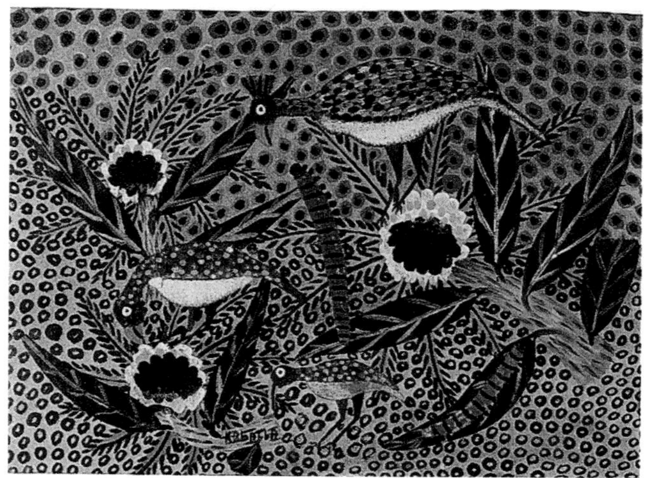

Sylvestre Kaballa (born in 1920), "Birds and Flowers"
oil on paper, 33 x 44 cm
©MRAC, Tervuren

[8] Copy of the archives of Laurent Moonens, MRAC, noinv. 97.46

The 30s in Lagos, Nigeria

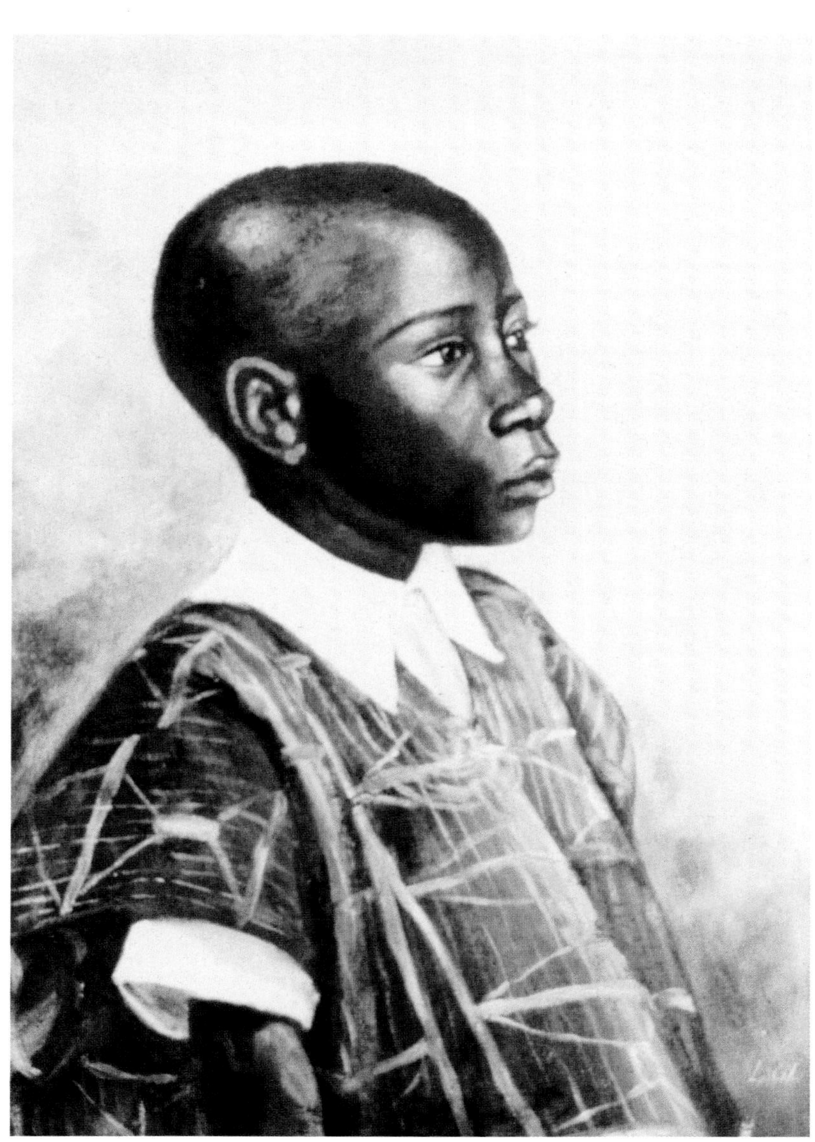

left:

Akinola Lasekan (1916-1974), "Young Haoussa"

facing page:

Ben Enwonwu (1918-1994), "Twins," 1978

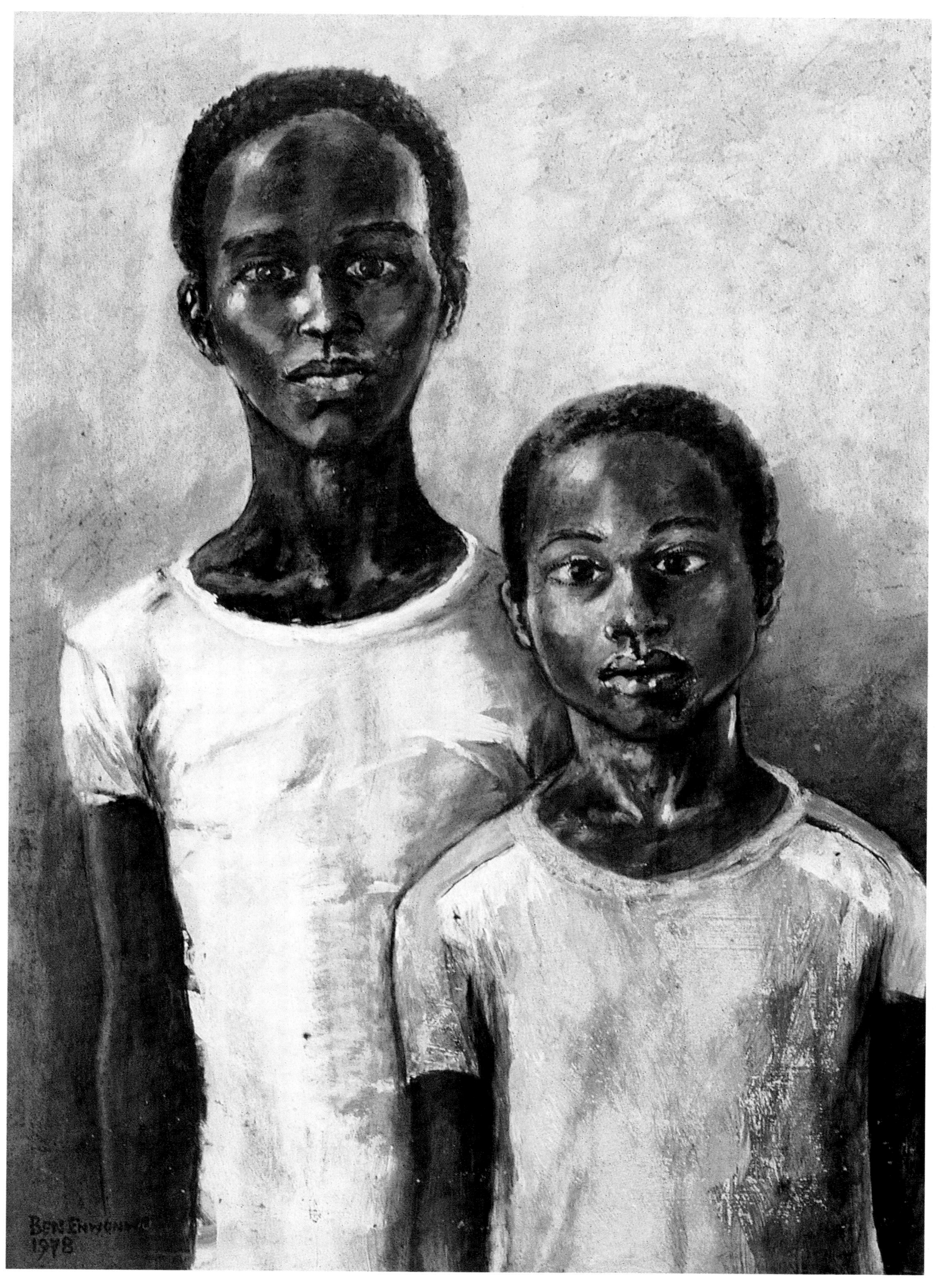
BEN ENWONWU
1978

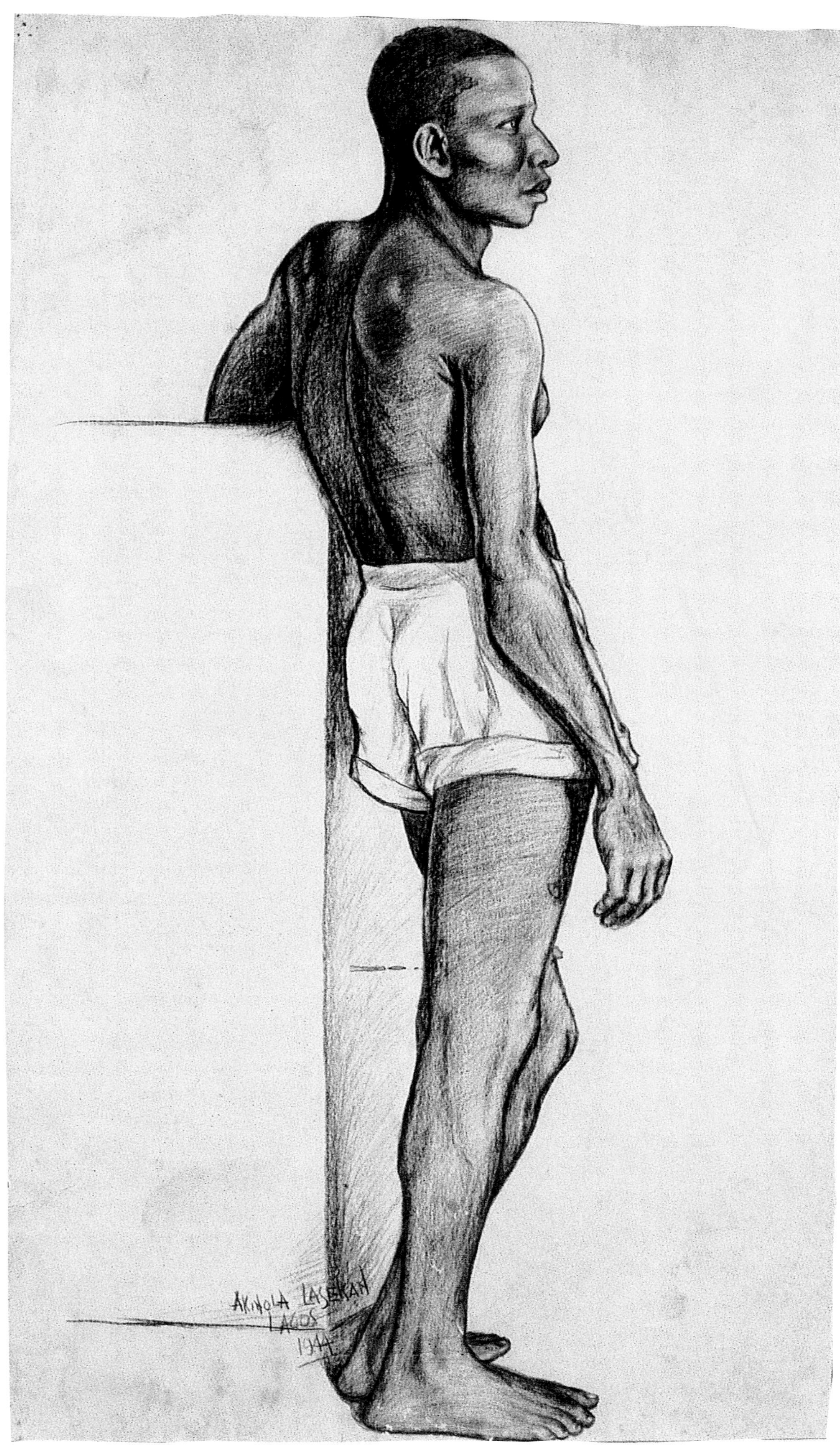

Akinola Lasekan (1916-1974), "Yoruba man," 1944
©National Gallery of Modern Art, Lagos

ONABOLU, LASEKAN AND THE MURRAY SCHOOL

Sylvester Obgechie

Modern Nigerian art was born of cultural interactions engendered by modernization processes during a colonial period that began early in the 20th century. It consists of those structures of art production and patronage that emerged in Nigeria with the introduction of European systems of representation and from its beginnings, modern Nigerian art engendered a distinct space of practice and a distinctive cadre of practitioners. The historical background to British colonization of Nigeria indicates that in the metropolitan areas like Lagos in which the presence and impact of the new colonial order was most evident, decades of interaction between European and Africans enabled the development of mutually comprehensible visual and verbal languages. Thus, the colonial order that was planted on this existing base had diverse heritage, as did the new forms of visual culture that it engendered. The history of modern Nigerian art reflects indigenous attempts to appropriate this visual culture and in that sense, it is a narrative about the constitution of Nigerian society under the systemic regime of colonization.

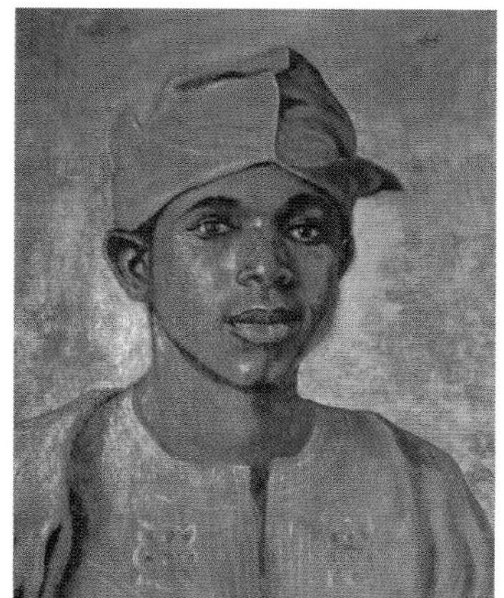

Akinola Lasekan (1916-1974), c.a. 1950, "Self-portrait," oil on canvas ©National Gallery of Modern Art, Lagos

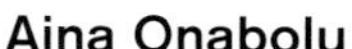

Aina Onabolu

Aina Onabolu (1882-1963) was the first Nigerian associated with formal training in European techniques of art production (specifically painting) and is thus the pioneer of modern Nigerian art. The European visual tradition that Onabolu appropriated through his training and subsequent practice favored pictorial verisimilitude and was as yet not a common mode of expression among Africans of that era. Verisimilitude in painting, (marked by the advent of easel painting tradition), was an indicator of wider changes in Nigerian societies during the colonial period. This mode of expression was not new to Nigerian art; naturalistic traditions of sculpture in Ife and Benin attest to this tendency in indigenous Nigerian art prior to the colonial incursion. However, the conceptual and cosmological models underpinning the imported European tradition differed from indigenous responses to art and culture in Nigerian societies. Onabolu's adoption of easel painting thus introduced a new context of practice and new forms of production to Nigerian art.

Aina Onabolu, born on September 13, 1882 to Ijebu Yoruba parents in Ijebu-Ode began his primary education in 1889 and taught himself to draw by copying illustrations from photographs, European textbooks and trade literature. He completed his primary education in 1895 and moved to Lagos where he lived with J.K. Randle, a friend of his father, political activist and medical practitioner who served as his guardian and mentor while Onabolu attended secondary school. Proximity to this well-connected political activist and nationalist placed Onabolu at the hub of upper echelon society in Lagos where he established connections with the families of future clients. In this favorable environment the budding artist produced portraits, landscapes and representations of daily life and developed his understanding of European visual culture. Onabolu's first art exhibition took place in 1901 at Randle's house and featured drawings, still life, landscapes, and portraits. This was the first exhibition of art by a modern Nigerian artist.

Onabolu completed his secondary education in 1900 and took up employment with the Colonial Marine and Customs Department in Lagos while operating as an artist in his spare time. His 1906 Portrait of Mrs. Spencer Savage reveals his skills as a watercolor painter and the portrait genre within which Onabolu based most of his mature practice reflects the middle-class culture in which he operated in Lagos. The representation of Mrs. Savage fits into a process of class identification fostered by this group. By 1911, Onabolu had become famous as a portrait painter and was receiving commissions to produce portraits that were presented to visiting dignitaries by the Nigerian colonial administration.

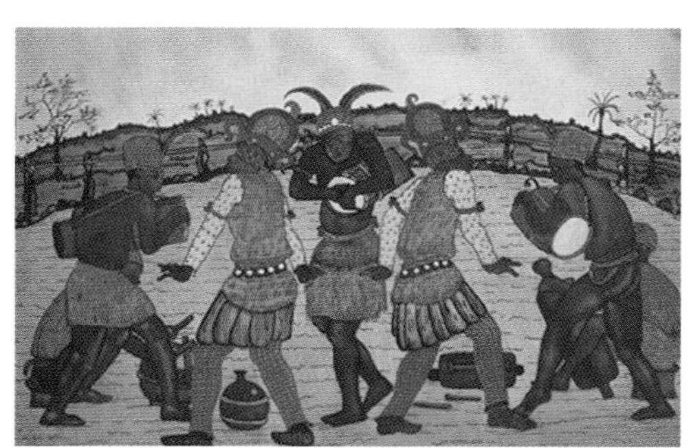

C. C. Ibeto, 1937, "Awka Dancers," watercolor
©Nigeria Magazine

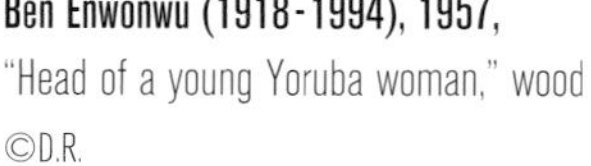

Ben Enwonwu (1918-1994), 1957,
"Head of a young Yoruba woman," wood
©D.R.

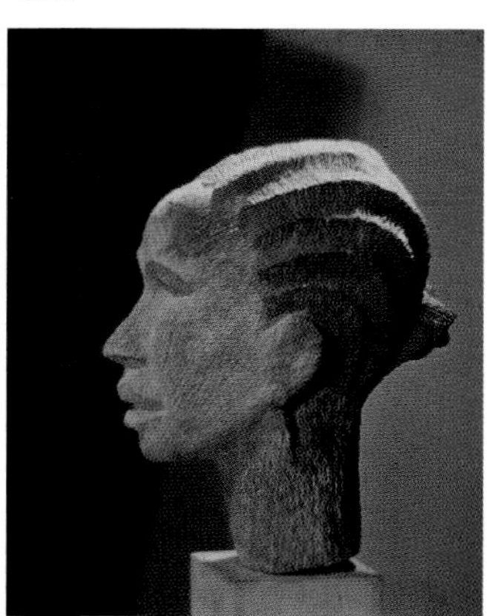

In 1920, Onabolu traveled to London for formal training at St. John's Wood School of Art from which he obtained a diploma in Fine Arts from in 1922. He also studied at the Academie Julian in Paris before returning to Nigeria where the colonial office formally appointed him to teach art on a part-time basis in Lagos secondary schools. Onabolu introduced art into the curriculum of these institutions although his efforts met with resistance from colonial administrators. He also petitioned the Colonial Nigerian Department of Education to develop a plan for art education in 1923 and establish tertiary institutions of art training. In response to Onabolu's demands, the Colonial government appointed K. C. Murray as Art Supervisor to the Colonial Department of Education in 1927. Onabolu practiced as a professional artist and taught art at different institutions in Lagos until his death in 1963. His adherence to classical academic techniques of naturalistic representation eventually developed into a major formalistic direction in modern Nigerian art. His practice as a modern Nigerian artist achieved the constitution of a social space in which notions of art and identity were filtered through the complex processes of Nigerian modernization.

Akinola Lasekan

Lasekan (1916-1974) belongs to the second-generation pioneers of modern Nigerian art and his practice can be interpreted within the initial tradition of pictorial naturalism that Onabolu introduced to modern Nigerian art. However, where Onabolu mainly focused on portrait painting, Lasekan created compositions based on Yoruba culture. He developed a broad genre whose subject matter consisted mainly of representations of immediate environmental realities: vendors, market scenes, landscapes and representations of social and cultural activities. Lasekan was a member of a new, upwardly mobile political generation, in contrast to Onabolu's associations with a conservative Nigerian elite. Partly in criticism of this conservative class, but more in reaction to the intolerable conditions of colonialism, Lasekan became a political cartoonist (the first in Nigeria) and contributed his political views as well as portraits of notable protagonists to the nationalist struggle for Nigerian independence between 1950 and 1960. He allied himself with Nigerian nationalists such as Nnamdi Azikiwe (who published Lasekan's cartoons in his newspaper, the West African Pilot) and was very popular in British West Africa for the biting satire of his cartoons.

Akinola Lasekan was born S. A. Oladetimi in Owo in June 1916 and he changed his name to Akinola Lasekan in 1941. He attended St. Patrick's Central School, Owo from 1925 to 1932 where he showed an aptitude for drawing at an early age.

Lasekan graduated from primary school in 1932 and received a standard-six certificate, which was then the minimal certification of competency in reading and writing. Lasekan arrived Lagos in 1935 and secured his first job as a textile designer with the Compagnie Française-Africaine Occidental (CFAO) where he learned how to manipulate the medium of watercolor. After a year with CFAO, Lasekan quit this job and took up employment with the Church Missionary Society (CMS) Bookshop in 1936. The management of the CMS Bookshop at this time was interested in art and encouraged the young artist by including some items it commissioned from him in the bookshop's stock of trade goods. Lasekan's products included illustrations of Bible stories, Christmas cards, calendars, and paintings. In keeping with the religious orientation of his missionary employers, Lasekan's illustrations mostly featured biblical narratives, which were printed as greeting cards and sold widely.

In 1940, Lasekan quit his job and with Justus Akeredolu, an artist and his colleague at CMS, opened an art studio in Lagos where he produced portraits and landscapes (mainly in watercolor) and some commercial art in the form of sign writing and lithography. Between 1935 and 1936, Lasekan took correspondence courses in art and received diplomas from Normal House, England and Washington School of Art. Now self-employed and practicing as an artist, he began to give lessons in drawing and painting. In 1941, he published his first book of cartoons and became a part-time art instructor in Lagos secondary schools.

He eventually established a correspondence school of art and counted among his students Uche Okeke, an influential Nigerian artist of the postcolonial period. In late 1943, Lasekan took up the oil medium and produced the first in a series of narrative paintings that culminated in detailed portraits of Nigerians of different ethnic groups. His narrative paintings focused on themes from Yoruba history and subjects from Yoruba folklore. He also held academic positions at the department of Fine Art of the University of Nigeria and the Institute of African Studies of the University of Ife (now Obafemi Awolowo University) where he remained until his death in 1974.

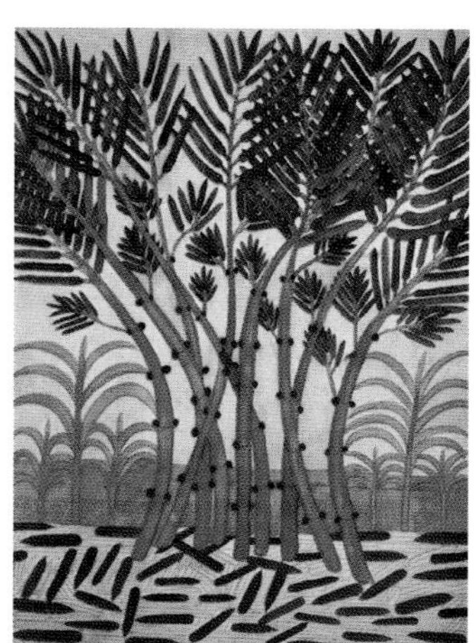

Ibrahim Uthman, 1936, "Bambo," watercolor
©Nigeria Magazine

In addition to his multiple practices as an artist, Lasekan published many instructional books on art and influenced a whole generation of aspiring artists by providing them with a pedagogical structure within which to educate themselves in strategies of pictorial representation. If one factors in his tenure as a faculty member of two prestigious Nigerian Universities, it becomes obvious that Lasekan exerted as much influence on the subsequent development of modern Nigerian art as any other major individual in the history of this tradition.

Ben Enwonwu (1918-1994), 1937, "Palm trees," watercolor
©Nigeria Magazine

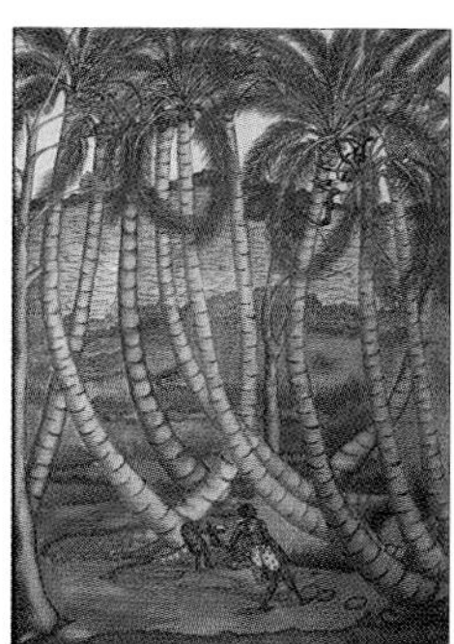

Kenneth C. Murray and the Murray Group

Kenneth C. Murray (1902-1972) was recruited by the colonial Nigerian government in 1926 as an education officer to implement the colonial government's program for formal art education in Nigerian schools. Murray asserted the need for modern Nigerian artists to utilize aspects of their indigenous art traditions as a means of defining a new cultural identity but he eschewed facile mimicry of historical styles and attitudes. He created a curriculum based on these ideas and selected five pioneer students to implement his new programs. The students were Ben Enwonwu, C. C. Ibeto, Uthman Ibrahim, D. K. Nnachy and A. P. Umana. Murray provided these students with instruction in art from 1933 to 1936 and subsequently organized an exhibition of their works in 1937 at the Zwemmer Gallery in London, marking the first international presentation of modern Nigerian art from the new colonial art education program. Murray's curriculum (hence his teaching methods) was designed to produce a crop of art teachers who would then introduce art education to Nigerian schools.

Murray's impact on the constitution of practice and discourse in modern Nigerian art stems from his subversion of Onabolu's Eurocentric orientation. He produced the first evaluations of indigenous aesthetics in relation to modern Nigerian art and theorized this new space of practice through the works of his students. He also encouraged his pioneer students to avail themselves of Nigeria's indigenous heritage in their practice as artists. This recourse to tradition as a conceptual framework for contemporary production engendered the Synthesis concept in modern Nigerian art. Murray's theories on culture and art education were central to the evolution of many conceptual frameworks for the practice and criticism of modern Nigerian art. More importantly, the museums he established became important sites for the rediscovery of indigenous art traditions by young Nigerian artists in the late colonial and postcolonial periods.

However, Murray's students were severely limited by the ambiguity of their training and as they were absorbed into the colonial bureaucracy as art teachers, their works stagnated. Of these five pioneer students, only Ben Enwonwu emerged as a serious artist because of an earlier training in indigenous Igbo traditions of sculpture and his later formal education in European art traditions at the University of London. He was thus the principal representative of the notion of modern Nigerian art that Murray enunciated through the practice of his students. Murray subsequently refracted his interpretation of theories of modernity in Nigerian art through Enwonwu's artistic practice since his integration of indigenous aesthetics and European modes of symbolic communication made him the ideal subject of Murray's concept of synthesis.

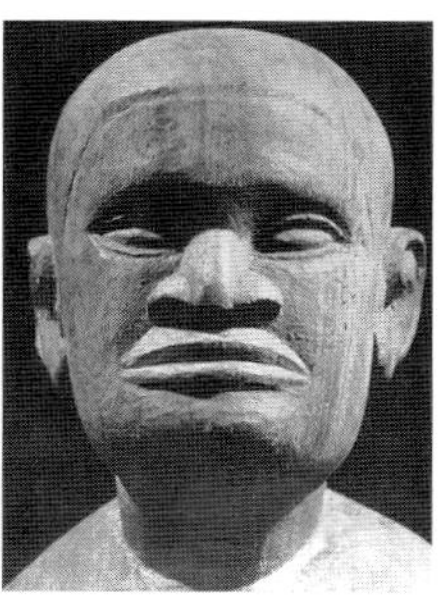

A. P. Umana, 1937, "Head," wood

Ben Enwonwu

Benedict Chukwukadibia Enwonwu (1918-1994) was one of the most significant African artists of the 20th century. Born in Nigeria at the onset of its colonial occupation by Britain, Enwonwu's career was framed by unique historical and cultural factors; his art encompassed the major aesthetic traditions and conceptual structures that comprise the diverse heritage of modern Nigerian art. These include the indigenous aesthetic traditions of Nigeria (his father was an Igbo sculptor) and the European modes of symbolic communication appropriated by indigenous artists during the colonial period. His career, which extended from the beginnings of modern Nigerian art to the postcolonial period, straddled the colonial and postcolonial discourses of African culture in the 20th century.

Enwonwu moved between Nigeria and London all his life but despite Nigeria's colonial culture and his access to the upper echelons of British society (Queen Elizabeth II was one of his patrons), he maintained identification with his Onitsha Igbo origins and asserted his identity as an African. In the colonial culture in which his career originated, and the postcolonial context in which it ended, his affirmation of these identities inserted him into the fractious politics of African nationalism and the struggle of African artists and intellectuals against different forms of European imperialism. In response to such political and intellectual imperatives, Enwonwu invented a unique visual language whose conceptual formats and ideological assertions provided a structure against which many significant modern Nigerian artists defined themselves in the colonial and postcolonial periods. This legacy above all makes Enwonwu a pivotal figure to the development of modern Nigerian and African art. His death in 1994 marked the passage of the last great pioneer of modern Nigerian art.

The Poto-Poto School, Congo

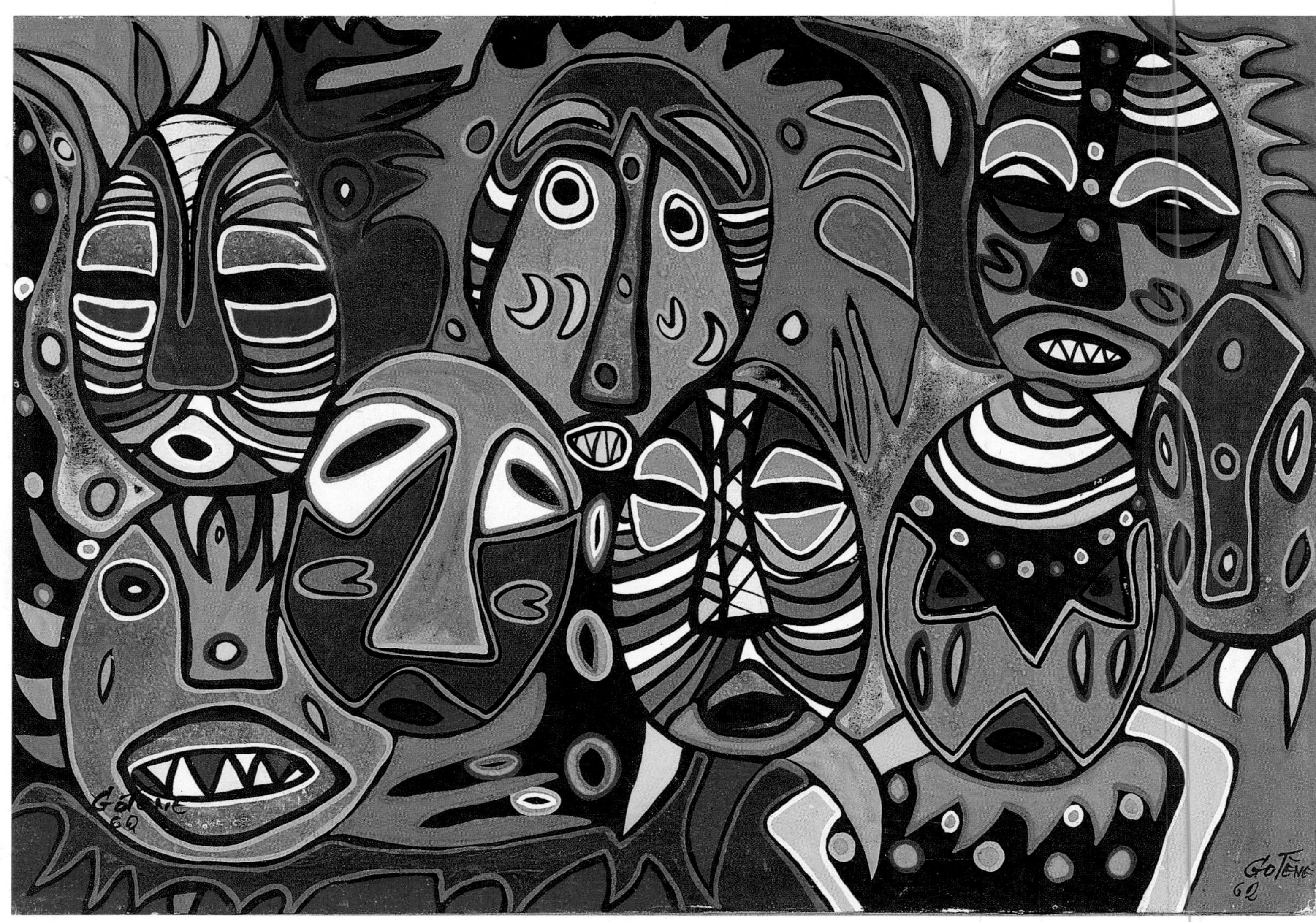

Marcel Gotène (born in 1939), "Kebe kebe Masks," c.a. 1955
gouache on canvas, 55 x 60 cm.

facing page:
François Thango (1936-1981)
oil on canvas, 88 x 92 cm.

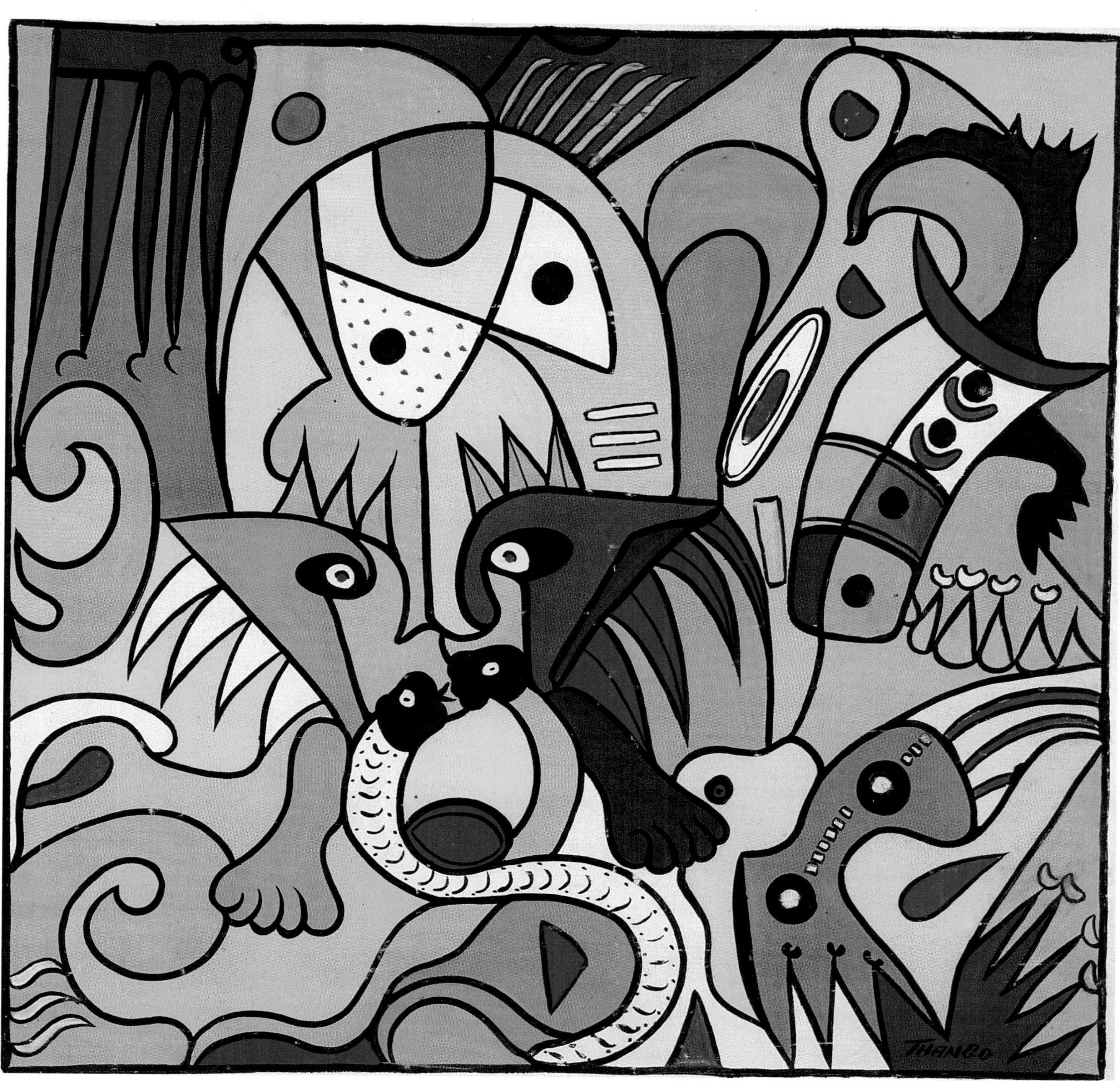
THANGO

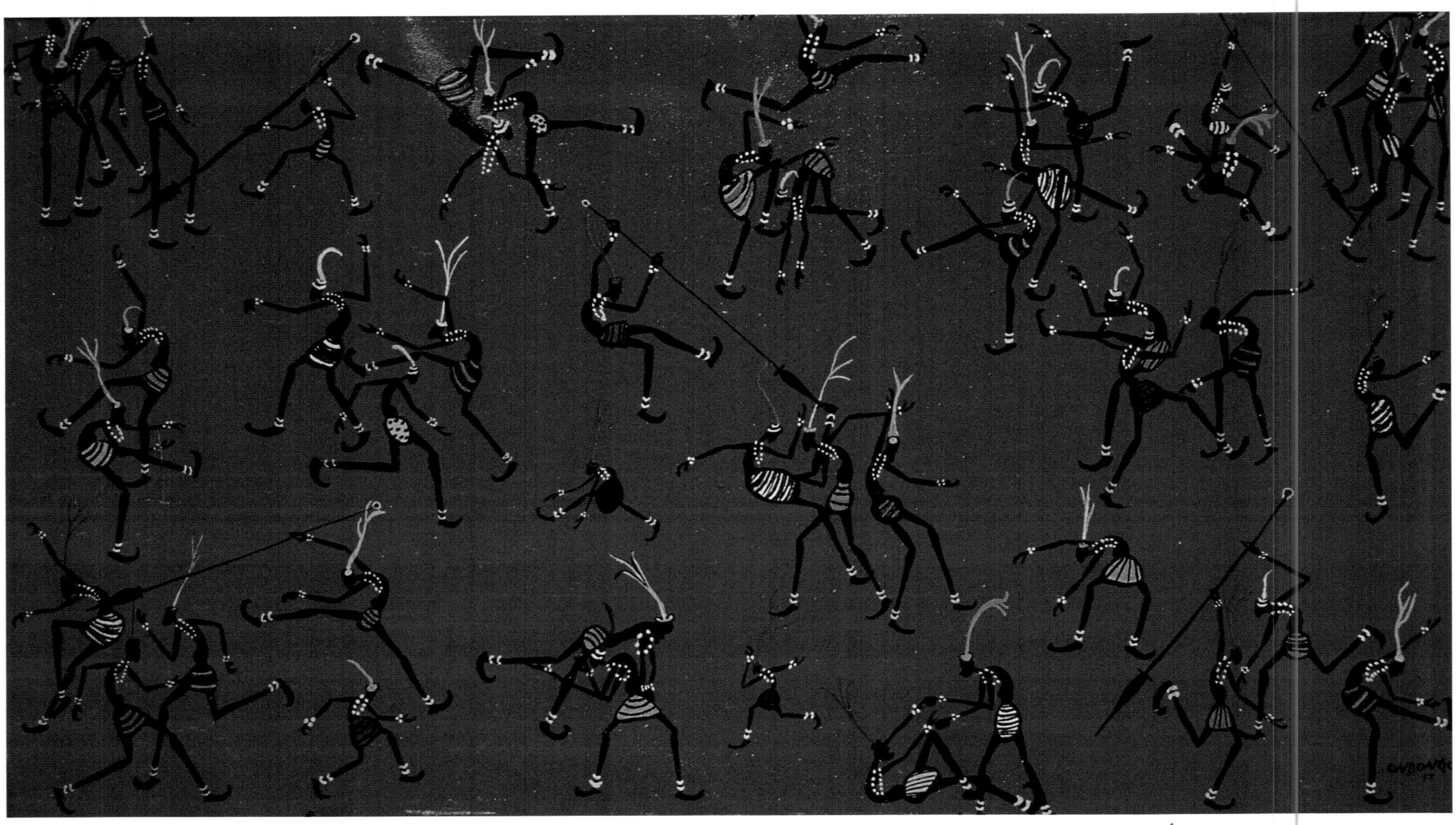

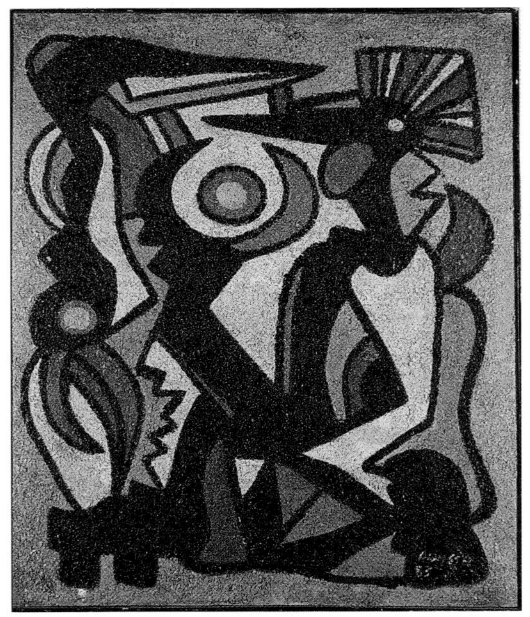

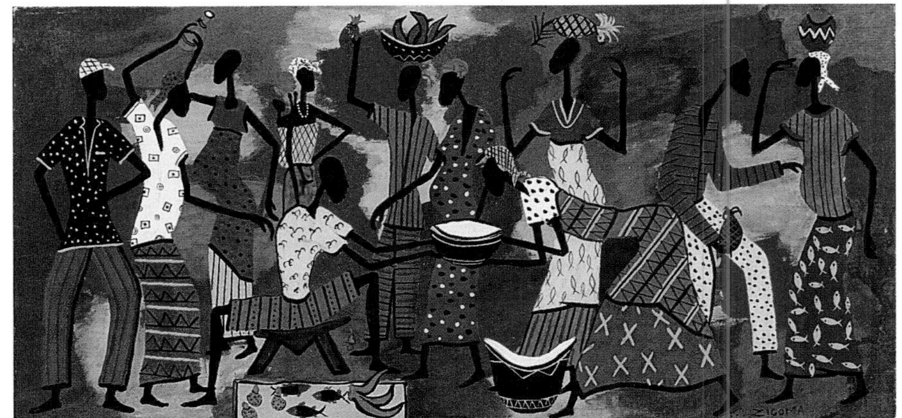

Nicolas Ondongo (born in 1933), "Warriors fighting"
oil in canvas, 67 x 114 cm
coll. Musées Nationaux du Congo ©Antoine Calmette-ADEIAO

Ouassa (born in 1936), "The Bird and the Prayer," c.a. 1955
mixed technique on canvas, 126 x 106 cm.
coll. Musées Nationaux du Congo ©Antoine Calmette-ADEIAO

Jacques Zigoma (1936-1987), "Return to the Market," c.a. 1955
oil on canvas, 36 x 74 cm, coll. MAAO ©Antoine Calmette-ADEIAO

PIERRE LODS AND THE POTO-POTO SCHOOL

Joanna Grabski

During the colonial period in Africa, European expatriates across the continent established art schools intended to provide local artists with work space, materials, and the opportunity to produce modern art. Of the art schools, the Poto-Poto School of Painting in Brazzaville, Congo is certainly one of the most significant due in large part to its multi-decade history and wide-ranging influence.

Pierre Lods and students

©Pierre Verger

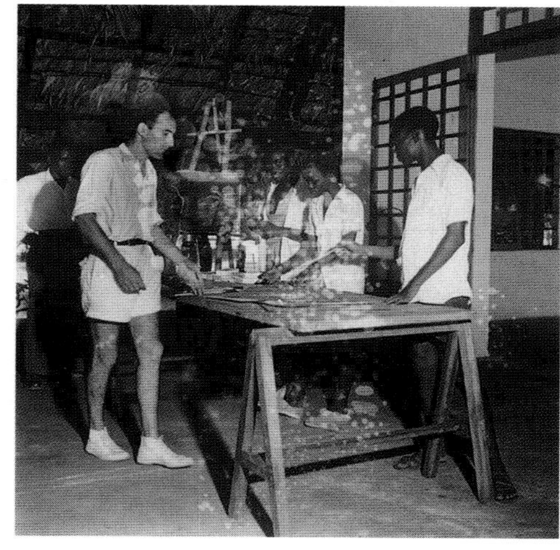

The school was founded by Pierre Lods, a French expatriate painter and math teacher, who had lived in Brazzaville for nearly ten years. A profound admirer of beauty and human creativity, Lods is remembered as a impassioned man who was fascinated by life and typically preferred to spend his time immersed in Congo's local culture. Although he did not intend to establish an art school during his tenure in Brazzaville, he founded the Poto-Poto School of Painting after stumbling upon his domestic employee using his oil paints and brushes. About the encounter, Lods wrote : "In my studio at Poto-Poto I employed an African boy called Ossali, who showed a very lively interest in my painting. One day he suddenly failed to turn up ; the day after he was still missing. I noticed that a few tubes of oil paint and some brushes had also disappeared and I decided to go and call on him at his own home. There I found him painting on an old nautical map ; he rapidly covered the yellowing paper with silhouettes of turquoise birds. Ossali painted with all the superb purity and simplicity of line that is found in African art. It was a revelation to me – an artist taking his bow."[1]

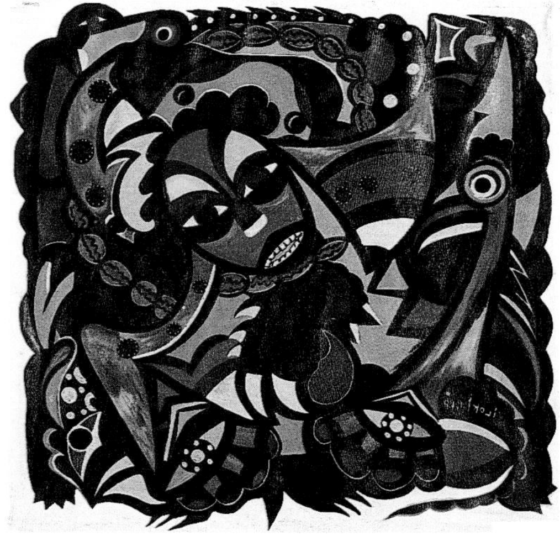

François Iloki (born in 1934), "The mask"
oil on canvas, 73x74 cm.
©Musées Nationaux du Congo

Lods was so impressed by what he had witnessed of Ossali's creative talents that he proposed plans for an art school in Brazzaville's Poto-Poto neighborhood. After securing the French government's financial assistance, he opened the school in 1951 with approximately ten painters, including Ossali, Ondongo, Zigoma, and Ouassa. Lods was known to recruit students through casual conversations with them in the streets of the neighborhood. Typically, these individuals had no previous experience with the materials and methods of art making. Lods positioned his own role as that of a watchful bystander observing and assisting a new art form blossom into existence. The school was premised on his conviction that being an artist was a "state of spirit" and art making was an act of self-expression rather than the depiction of the visible world or elucidation of an intellectual discourse. That is, artists were born rather than made at art school and what they created derived from what they knew intuitively as artists and as Africans. Based on what he had observed with Ossali and others, he anticipated that each artist's inherent creativity and internal vision would sufficiently drive his productions. In keeping with this philosophy, the school was conceived of as a space where the artist's personality could develop freely without the intervention of academic instruction.

Lods' pedagogical approach, described by his former students as laissez faire, offers a striking comparison to that advanced in other African art schools where artists received instruction in the techniques and methods of academic painting. By contrast, the Poto-Poto artists were provided with materials such as paper, canvas, brushes and paint, but offered no formal instruction. Neither a technical understanding of materials nor a mastery of formal elements was deemed necessary for the artists were to express themselves freely, intuitively, and spontaneously. Lods did not offer formal training because he viewed it as both an imposition which could block the artists' internal vision and a constraint which could hinder the artists' creativity. Although he did not cultivate among the artists familiarity with European subject matter and academic techniques, he occasionally suggested which colors were most suitable for a particular style of painting.

The practice of art making at the school was inscribed not only by ideas regarding the inherent creativity of the African artist, but also with valuations about the authenticity of the artist's production.

[1] in "African art, the years since 1920," Quoted in Marshall Mount, p. 84.

For Lods, modern art was to represent African tales, legends, and traditions using modern media. He believed that the artists should turn to their own environment, making use of their Congolese artistic heritage and cultural knowledge for inspiration and subject matter. To further inspire the artists, he surrounded them with masks and sculptures from central Africa and occasionally read proverbs, legends, and poems dealing with Africa. Similarly, Lods encouraged the artists to paint with the medium of gouache because he believed it most resembled the colors used traditionally for decorating murals, coloring woodcarvings, and painting bodies. Thematically and formally, the paintings created in this environment were considered to represent a pure and authentic African genre. Lods described them as "transposing in paint the character of great traditional masks."[2]

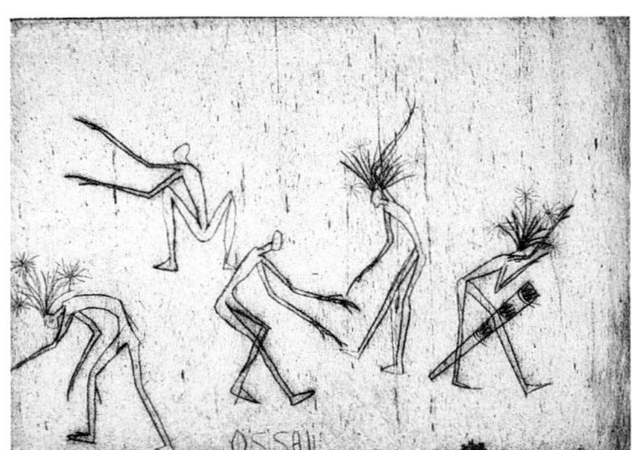

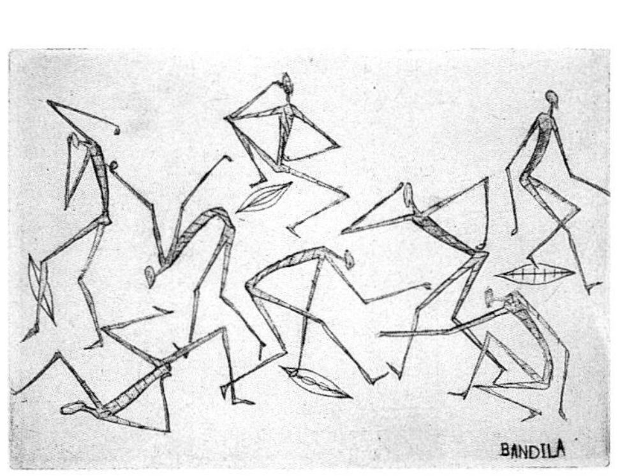

Ossali, "Lower Congo Dancer"
Bandila, "Snake Dancer"
Two prints on copper, 1955
coll. ADEIAO. ©Antoine Calmette

The early works constituting this genre depict masquerade performances, market scenes, and images of drumming, hunting, and dancing. Of the paintings created during the school's early years, two of the most ubiquitous are market scenes and images referring to the kebe-kebe masquerade, a dance performed during Kuyu and Mbosi initiation ceremonies in northern Congo. Although the so-called Poto-Poto style has become synonymous with mass-produced and repetitious scenes of a generic Africa, a great diversity of formal expression exists among the works created during this early period. A comparison of either market scenes or kebe-kebe images by Jacques Zigoma and François Thango exemplify the diversity of styles articulated within this genre. Their renderings diverge in compositional strategies as well as the interpretation of formal elements. The variety of formal expression not only points to the aesthetic choices of the individual artists, it also reveals the premium placed on authoring an individual style.

Despite what is characterized as his laissez-faire approach, Lods did encourage artists to develop their own œuvre by authoring a specialized pictural vocabulary and developing a well-affirmed artistic personality. He was known to employ a subtle pedagogy in which students identified and expanded upon a specific thematic element in their work in order to develop their oeuvre. The oeuvre was to be diverse yet unified and recognizable, but not repetitious or mass-produced. Above all, every artist's oeuvre was to be original. The emphasis on originality relates to the assumption that artists were authoring specialized themes inspired by their internal visions. Thus, authorship and ownership of subjects and styles are tightly woven together. As the expression of an internal vision, art was something the artists carried with them, something that they discovered spontaneously and that belonged to them alone as individuals.

As for the artists' motivation in joining the school, financial profit undoubtedly played an important role. While the school received partial funding from the French colonial administration in Africa, it functioned as a cooperative which divided the profit from a painting's sale equally between the artist and the school. Considering that the majority of Lods' students were not otherwise employed and had no primary school education, the promise of financial reward from the sale of their works was surely enticing. Additionally, the French government also provided the artists with scholarship money as an incentive to participate in the school. During the school's early years, the works were purchased by French colonial administrators and other Europeans living in Congo. While Lods was at the school, the artists enjoyed regular local and international exhibitions. After their first exhibitions in Brazzaville, they had shows in South Africa in 1953, New York in 1954, Germany in 1956, as well as Switzerland and France in 1957. In 1961, Lods accepted President Senghor's invitation to teach at the École des Arts du Senegal in Dakar. Although he had initially hoped to divide his time between Dakar and Brazzavile, Lods never returned to the Poto-Poto School. At this point, the Poto-Poto artists' international exhibitions became less frequent and their works became more commercialized due to the artists' interaction with European tourists and former students who mass-produced popular Poto-Poto themes.

[2] Hossman, p.36.

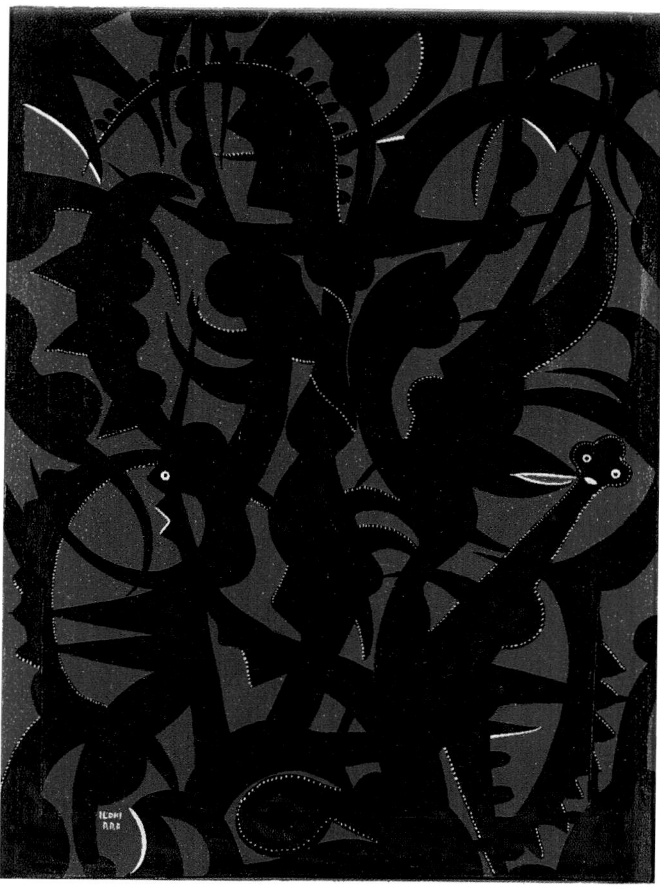

François Iloki (born in 1934)

François Thango (1936-1981)

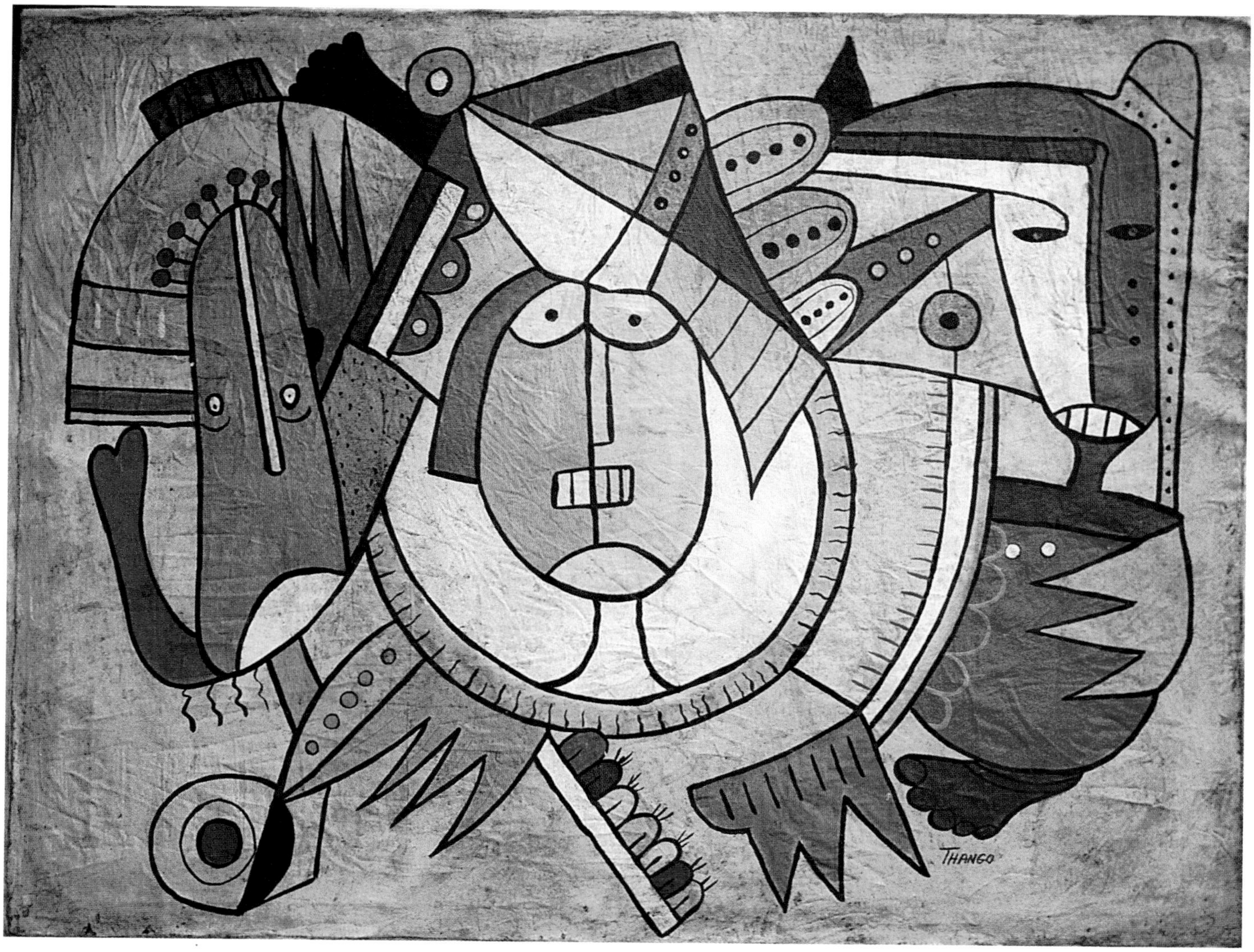

The new moderns in Ghana

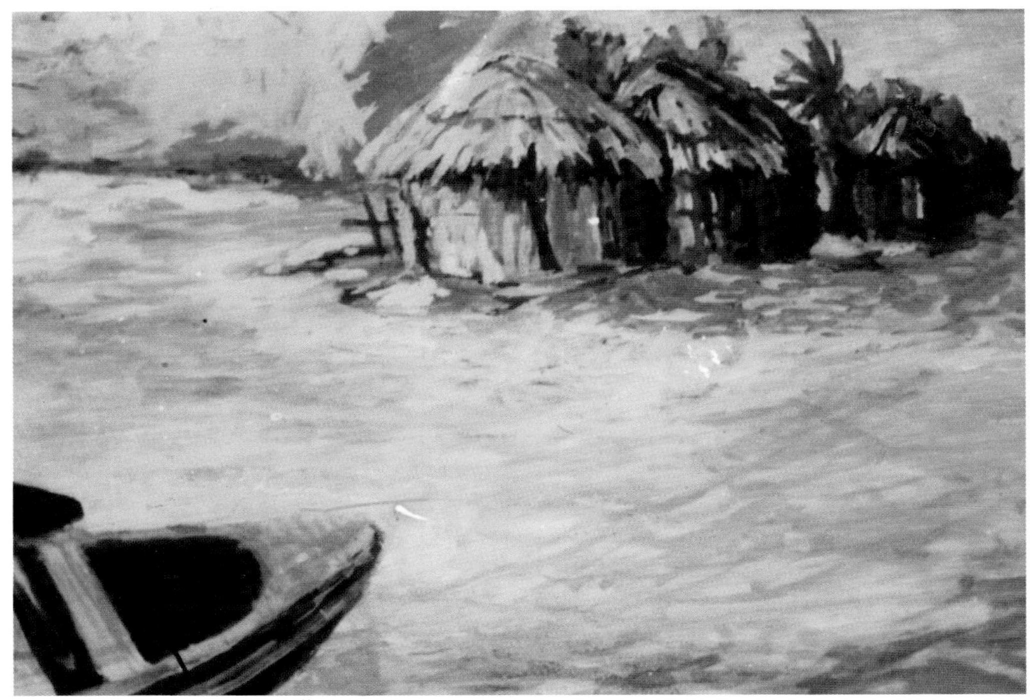

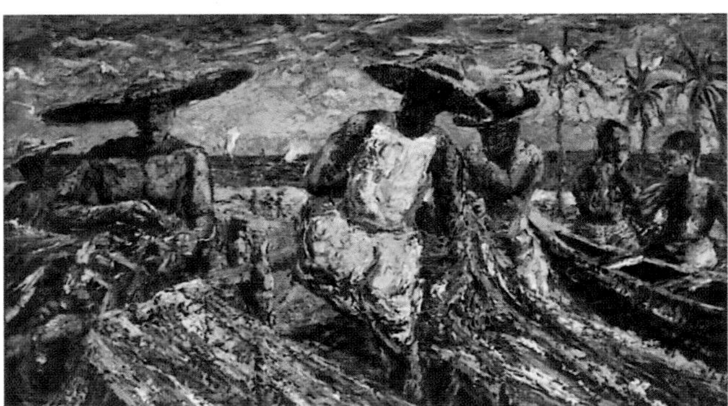

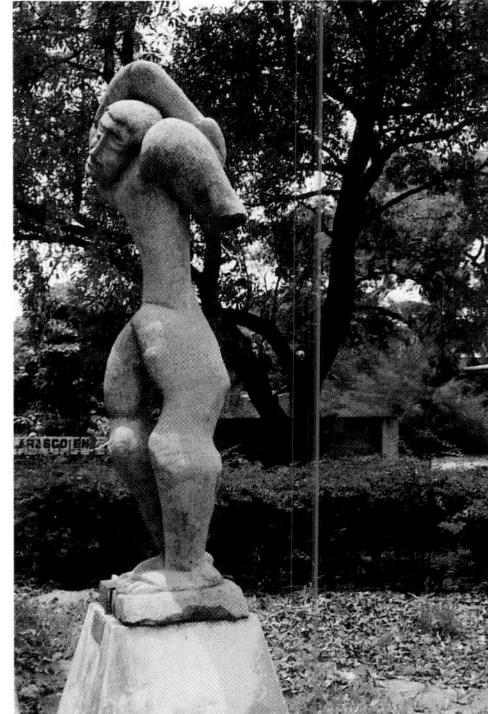

Oku Ampofo (1908-1998), "The struggling man"
©National Museum of Accra, Ghana

Ernest Victor Asihene (born in 1916), "Village scene"
©National Museum of Accra, Ghana

Albert Osabu Bartimeus (born in 1927), "Preparing for the Deep"
©National Museum of Accra, Ghana

facing page:
Oku Ampofo (1908-1998), "Eagle tale," 1964
©Elsbeth Court

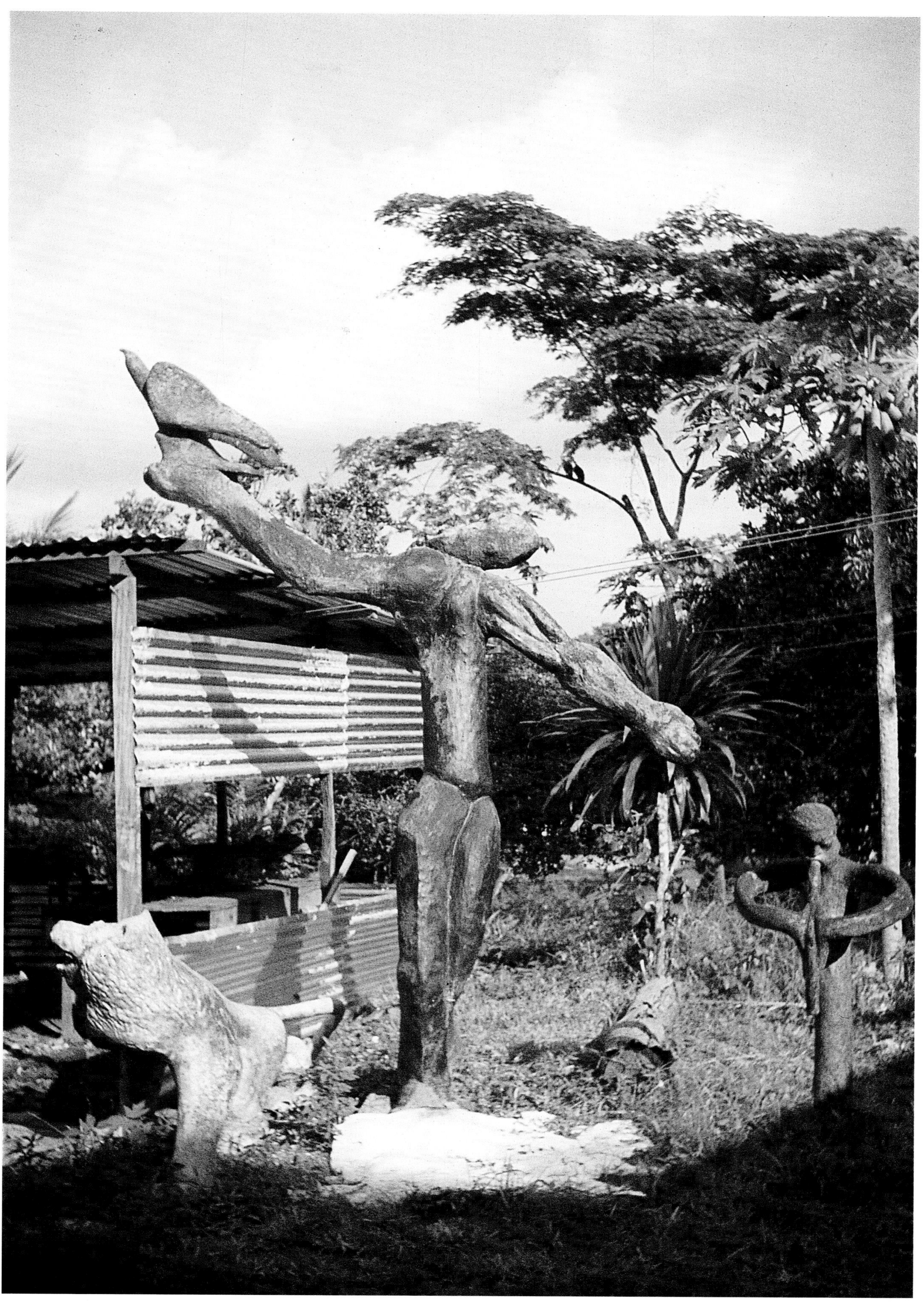

THE NEW MODERNS IN GHANA

Joseph Gazari Seini

Towards the end of the ninetieth century and the early years of the twentieth century, Ghanians found direction in artistic expression based on European artistic principles, especially in painting. With the opening of the Achimota School in 1924, art in the Gold Coast went through some drastic changes. The two most important personalities who where responsible of these changes where G. Stevens and H. V. Meyerovitz, both art and craft teachers of the school. With the advice of Stevens, the first art and craft teacher, a course was planned leading up to the "revise of art syllabus for tropical dependencies." The most ambitious work of the early days was the illustrations by teachers-in-training under Stevens' inspiration for publication by the Oxford Press of Rattray's Ashanti folk tales. Of these illustration, Sir William Rothenstein said: *"The result of Mr. Stevens' short stay in Achimota show a vitality, a happy enjoyment of nature which survive in the young African... The African had preserved his strong sense of pattern: do not let us weaken it by putting before the young, the dreary outline of charms, jugs and candle sticks which are still to be found as examples to be copied in Indian elementary schools."* (Vieta Kojo)

One area in which Achimota distinguished itself apart from the arts generally was the social as well as the public relations. During the early years, arts and crafts courses earned enviable reputation. They consisted of drawing and painting and such crafts as metalwork, woodwork, clay modelling, weaving and bookbinding. The high standard attained in this area was due to the enthusiasm of the College Council in promoting teaching and research in the subject and of the recruited to handle it. The keenness of the authorities was shown in the high priority attached to the expression of the Arts Block.

In 1934 a new Art Block was completed and this promoted the teaching of the subject in a significant way. Achimota was lucky in having another good instructor in the person of H. V. Meyerovitz in 1936. He was a most outstanding art supervisor Achimota employed in these early years. The three year specialist course was already being run. Inspired by Meyerovitz, it was decided to base the course on traditional arts. For this reason, local traditional artists were recruited to teach the pupils and art classes went on excursions to traditional art exhibitions.

Meyerovitz was a trained art teacher and an artist with previous African experience who soon after his appointment took steps to improve the standards in the school. During his first term, he and his wife – herself a sculptor, a trained teacher and later an anthropologist -, were sent by the college authorities on a tour through West Africa to collect information about local African art and craft and to make contact wit local African craftsmen and others. Meyerovitz threw himself with the energy of genius into the organisation of the Arts and Crafts Departments.
During his tour of the country, Meyerovitz discovered that crafts which Rattray has seen flourishing ten years before had disappeared and craft guilds themselves dying out. He noticed that something should be done to save the remnant. The one way he could do it was that modern techniques must be added to ancient skills and the traditional craftsmanship, and all on strictly business lines.
Proposals embodying these ideas were enthusiastically approved by the Colonial Office Advisor Committee and later by the 1938 Inspectors of the college.
Meyerovitz was a teacher who wanted his students to portray African culture in their work and not to imitate foreign styles. Records show that he got a student dismissed because he did not desist from imitating foreign styles.

His influence is to be seen in much of the art teaching in Ghana to this day not least in the Achimota Art School itself – relocated at the University of Science and Technology in Kumasi in 1951 – under the inspiring direction of his most distinguished pupil, Kofi Antubam.

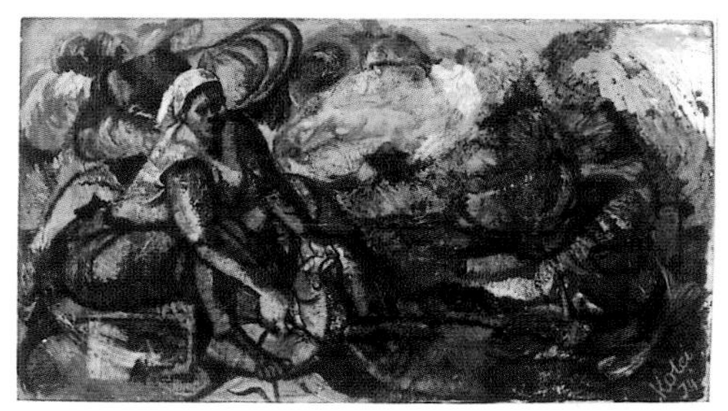

Amon Kotei (born in 1915), "The weight of thought"

©National Museum of Accra, Ghana

Oku Ampofo (1908-1998)

Oku Ampofo was born in 1908. From Mfantsipim School he entered the University of London in 1929 having passed the Matriculation examinations. He qualified as a member of the Royal College of Surgerons in 1939 after his practical training (internship) at Castleford, a village near Yorkshire. There after he took short courses in Stockholm and Liverpool school of Tropical Medicine. In the University of Edinburg, inspite of the rigours of the medical course, he managed to take night classes in sculpture at the Norman Forest Studio at Haymarket. He explained the functionality of art object thus: "It was not just enough to bring healing to the sick, equally important is the need to create objects of art and to satisfy the aesthetic sensibility and bring what Piato will call nourishment of the soul." (Kojo Vieta).

He returned to Ghana in 1940 and tried to achieve the nourishment of the soul first through his own handiwork and secondly by organising people in the artistic field. He is credited with founding the first ever society of artists in the Gold Coast and the National Commission on Culture has its roots in the efforts of Ampofo.

Ampofo was an outstanding physician and medical researcher who made tremendous contribution to research into plant medicine in Ghana. He succeeded in making inestimable contribution to the advancement of art and enrichment of the cultural life in Ghana. He was not only a skilful general practitioner but also a highly cultural social leader, a philanthropist and a humanist. He died in 1998 at the age of 89.

Amon Kotei (born in 1915)

Amon Kotei was born in 1915 in Labadi. He was one of the first art students of the Achimota College. He further studied drawing, painting and lithography art work at the London School of Printing and Graphic Arts from 1949 to 1952. He worked with the Ghana Publishing Corporation as a commercial artist. His works depict scenes of daily activities such as cocking, selling of fish, tomatoes, etc. Kotei is credited for his designing of the Ghana's Coat of Arms and the emblem of the Pan African Writers Association.

He often uses colour indiscriminately by combining impressionistic and expressionistic elements, especially when treating human beings. Even human beings treated realistically are usually rendered with multicolour tones of blues, yellows and reds regardless of whether the figures are nude of clothed. Amon Kotei has persistently held on to the use of palette knife exclusively for oil painting. With the hard edge of the palette knife, he amazingly captures the soft touch of his full body pulpy women. Using the brush for watercolor and palette knife for the oil medium, he usually explores genre scenes involving the activities of women. He treats landscapes and other themes but his favourite subject matter has been women who are wear traditional clothes.

At the age of 85 Kotei is one of the prominent longest living Ghanian painters. He has consistently maintained his style of painting, described as "Amon Kotei Waterfall of Colours."

Ernest Victor Asihene (born in 1916)

Born in 1916, Asihene is one of the most experienced practising artists in Ghana. Trained as a teacher of arts and crafts at Achimota College, he proceeded to obtain the National Diploma in Design and a Graduate Art Teachers' Diploma from the Goldsmiths College of the London University in 1952. He gained admission into the precious artists' professional association as a fellow of the Royal Society of Artists in 1958.

He was appointed cultural attaché to Ghana's mission in the US, the United Kingdom and in Italy from 1959 to 1960. He made a study tour of art institutions of higher education in Switzerland, Germany, Italy, Britain, Czechoslovakia, India and Japan.

In 1960 he was appointed staff University of Science and Technology in Kumasi, promoted professor of art, Dean of the College of Art and Head of the department of painting, sculpture and design. In his role as a dean, he gave art studies in this country some directions that have survived to the present; building bridges between corporate patrons

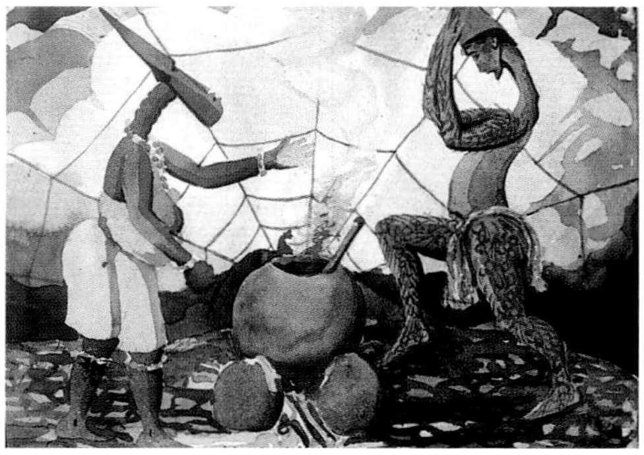

Ernest Victor Asihene (born in 1916), "Pot of beans," 1949

©National Museum of Accra, Ghana

and academic and undertaking public works of art. He was elected Pro-Vice Chancellor of UST in 1976.

Kofi Antubam (1922-1964)

Kofi Antubam was born in 1922 in Wassaw-Amanfi. On a pastoral mission in 1936, the Reverend Fr. Alan John Knight, chanced upon Antubam modelling and introduced him to the Governor of the Gold Coast Sir Arnold Hudson, who asked Kofi to make a bust of him in clay. The perfect tree dimensional effigy amazed the Governor who invited him to Accra and asked him to do some modelling at the forthcoming agricultural an general exhibition. The Governor drew the attention of H. V. Meyerovitz, the art master of the Achimota college, to the boy's works. Kofi Antubam got the " Principle scholarship " for specialist art and craft course at the Achimota college and spent two years at the Goldsmiths College University of London from 1948 to 1950 with a scholarship from the Gold Coast Government. Kofi Antubam was membership of the Artists International Association of London and fellowship of the Royal Authority Institute of the UK and Ireland.

On his return to Gold Coast in 1946, he thought at Tamale Government Middle Boarding school and at the Kumasi Government Boys school. From 1952, he though art at the Achimota college.
Kofi Antubam was fortunate as a painter in having a sense of mission to have recorded Ghanian customs and traditions for posterity. His works are based on intellectual and philosophical approach to art based on his study of the conceptual basis of African art. He saw beauty expressed in the characteristic Akan Akuaba dolls with oval shaped heads, ringed necks calm majestic repose and rounded hips and rumps. Antubam believed that art was vital only when it reflected the values and ideas of society. To him art should be applied to utility object such as panel of doors, stools, ect. Hence the artist must combine his virtues with the skills of a craftsman. His works range from book illustrations and state emblems to sculptures and murals and he wrote and lectured widely in Ghana. One of his achievements for Ghana was the carving of the state of chair of the president of the first republic, Osagyefo Dr. Kwame Nkrumah. Kofi Antubam died in 1964 at the age of 42.

Vincent Akwete Kofi (1923-1974)

Vincent Akwete Kofi was born in 1923 in Odumasi Krobo. He was trained at the Achimota College of Art and at The Royal College of Art in London where he gained ARCA in 1955. He was awarded an USA government grant to study sculpture and history of primitive art at Columbia University. In 1961 he was appointed the head of the art and craft department at Specialist Training College. In 1969 he was appointed senior lecturer and the head of the sculpture department in the College of art, University of Science and Technology in Kumasi, the post he held until his death in 1974.

Albert Osabu Bartimeus (born in 1927)

Albert Osabu Bartimeus was born in 1927 in Teshie, a suburb of Accra. He was trained at the Presbyterian Training College. He entered the UST in Kumasi in 1952 where he undertook a three-year course in art. He taught at Krobo Training College from 1955 to 1961 after which he worked with the Art Council of Ghana as the Eastern Regional Representative from April 1961 to June 1969.
Bartimeus's works portray the daily activities of the people – the market places, the beaches and festivities.

The Akwapim Six Art Society

This society was formed by art lovers and trained artists under the presidency of Oku Ampofo. The name Akwapim Six is indicative that the group was originally formed by only six people. It was made up oil/water colour painters, sculptors, potters, wood carver and engravers. Members' efforts were always exerted towards the complete independence and in developing their personalities in their perspective individuality of art expressions. The society exhibited annually with the Ghana Institute of Art and Culture.

By 10th December 1963 the membership was twelve. There were four associate members who were all trained art and craft specialists who had had their training courses at the UST in Kumasi. Except Oku Ampofo, president and founder of the society who was a self made artist, the rest were trained art and craft specialists. The joint exhibitions expressed the conscious pride of a group of people that had always considered art as the finest medium of communication between nations. Their art had sprung from the same creative force that is common to all artists of the world although far from perfect at that stage of its development it was closely related to the life and spirit of the people.

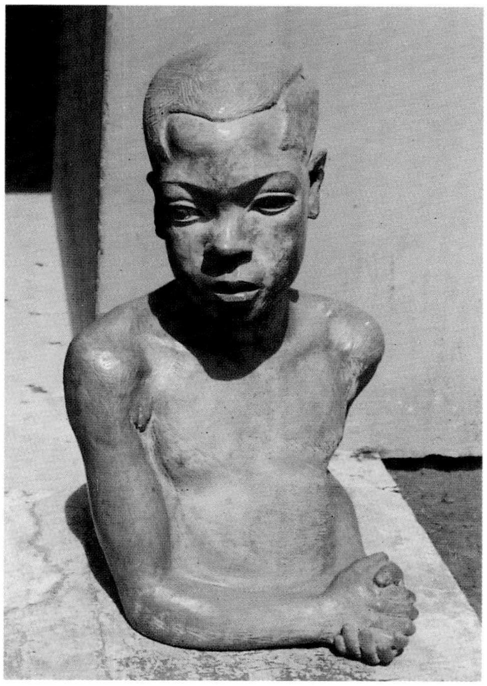

Kofi Antubam (1922-1964), "Kwabena, my son"

The Ghana Society of Artists

The Ghana Society of Artists was the product of a spontaneous action of a few artists in Ghana who were inspired by their desire "to free their country in the arts." Founded in April 1955 it remained as the only nation-wide society of artists in Ghana for many years. The society aimed at creating and maintaining interest in art and crafts. It did this by organising conferences for artists, craft men and art teachers in Ghana from time to time for them to exchange ideas. In such conferences prominent personalities in the art field were invited to give lecture on specific art subjects. As a society, it arranged temporary exhibitions for its members as well.

The society sought co-operation with all bodies in Ghana such as the Ghana Arts Council, Foreign embassies, the British Council etc. Art in the Gold Coast at the time was fraught with many problems, most of which could not be solved by the young artist unaided. Unlike his more fortunate and advanced European counterpart, the young Gold Coast artist had little access either to classes under experts after he had left school or to books which combined a comprehensive study of the Gold Coast aesthetic with critical analyses of his rapidly changing social environment.

The Oshogbo School, Nigeria

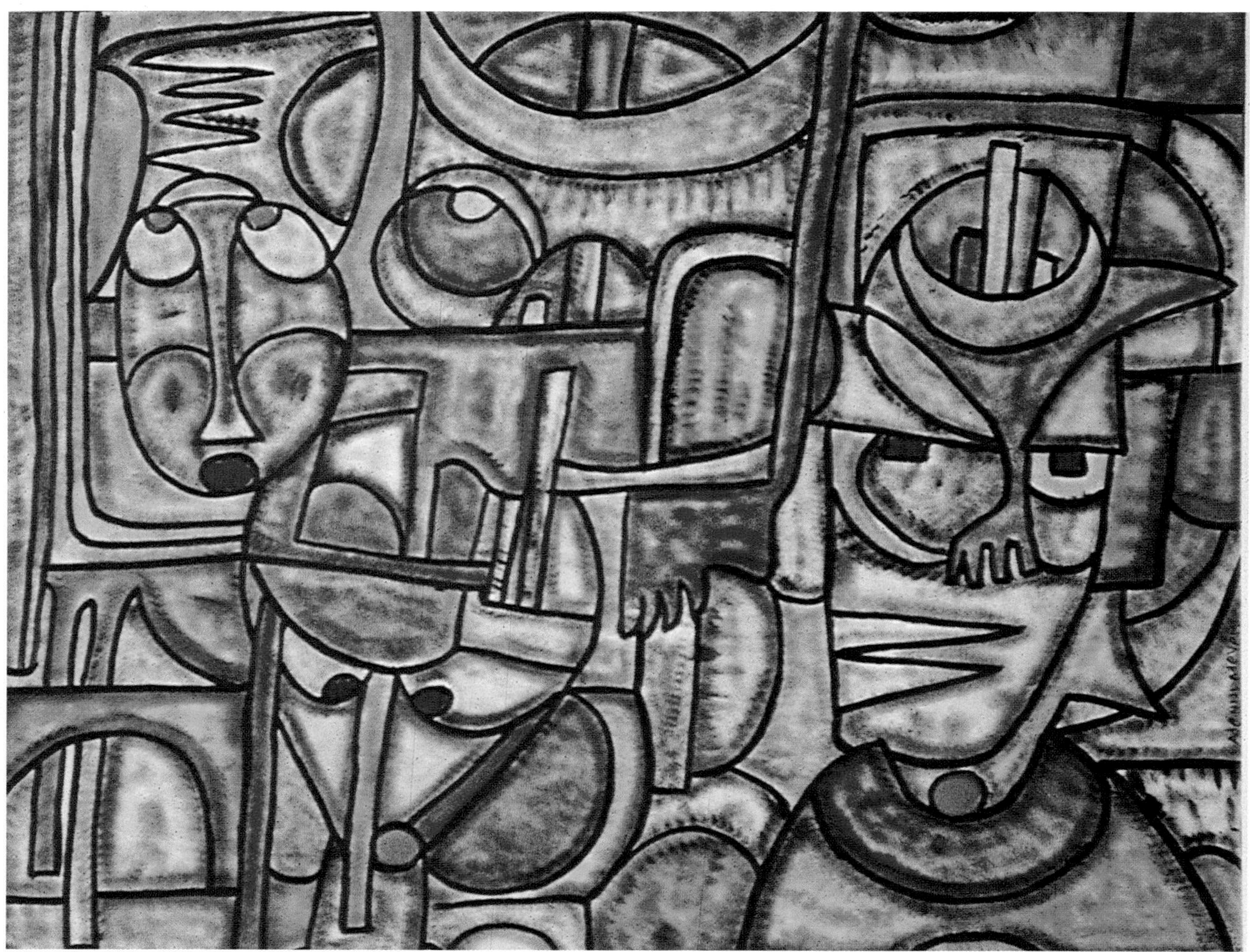

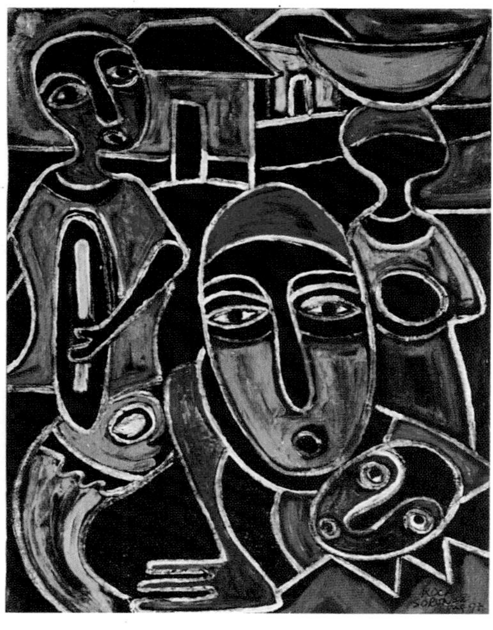

above:
R. Ogundele ©Revue Noire

left:
Adedayo ©Revue Noire

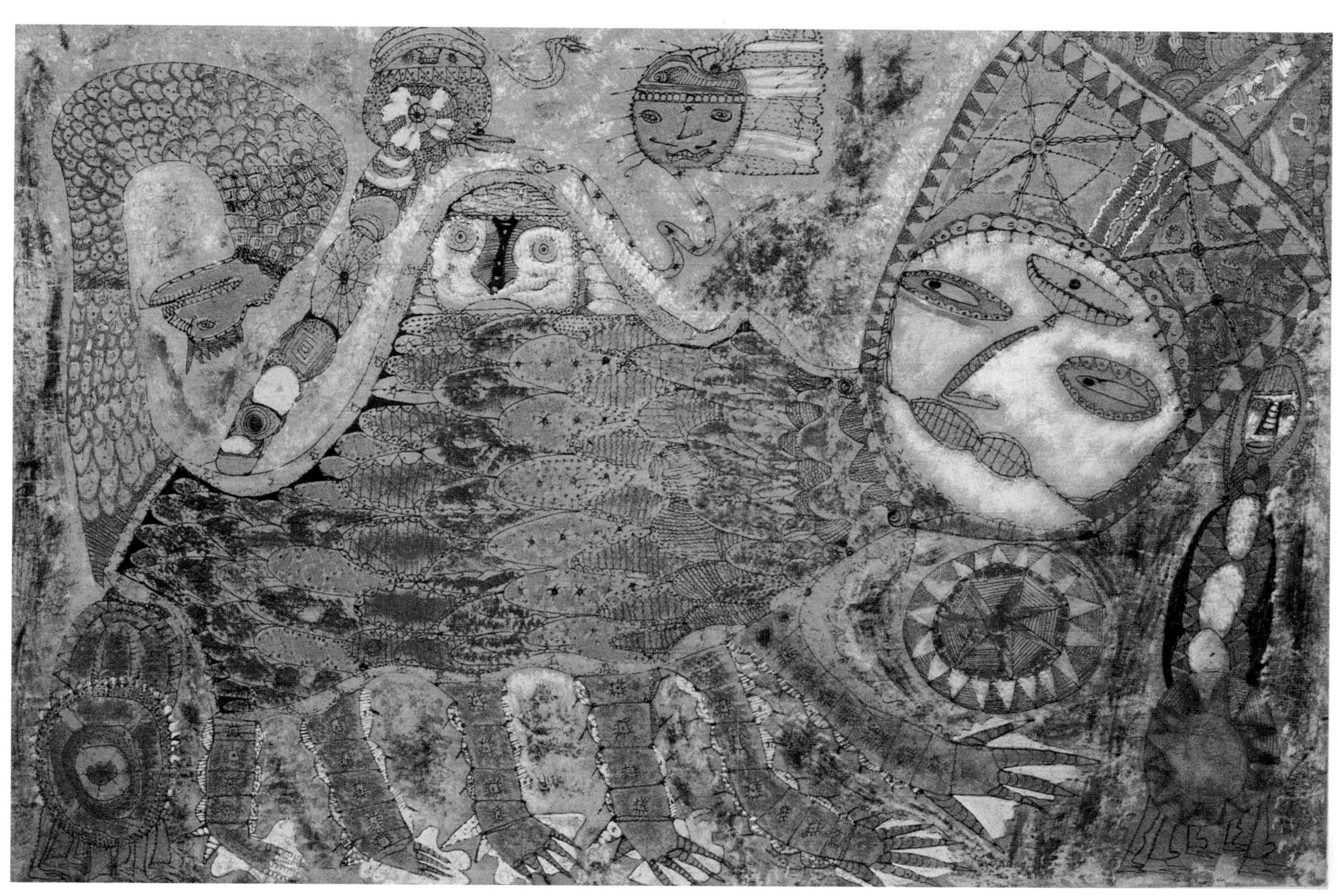

Twin Seven Seven (born in 1944), "Devils Dog," 1964
gouache, 73,5 x 113,8 cm.

OSHOGBO: HISTORY OF A SCHOOL
Sigrid Horsch-Albert

Oshogbo, a city in southwestern Nigeria, today a commercial and agricultural center, was already a relatively prosperous provincial city in the 50s. The city's image was marked by traditional regional clay houses, two-story houses and the villas of wealthy families in the Brazilian baroque style. Oshogbo, not far from Ifé, the former religious center of the Yoruba, is now, above all, known for its sacred forest and artists from the Oshogbo school. Susanne Wenger was the person primarily responsible for the development and conservation of the sacred forest. The Oshogbo school owes its global recognition to the initiative and commitment of Ulli Beier.

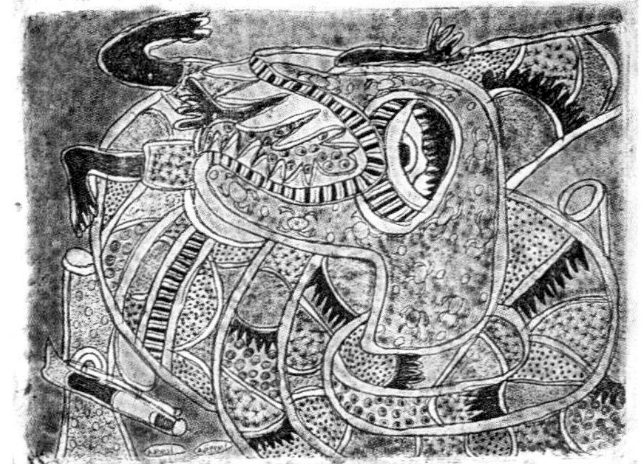

R. Ogundele ©Revue Noire

Ulli Beier, the son of a Jewish doctor, was born in Pomerania in 1922. The family emigrated to British-governed Palestine in 1933. During his boarding school years, Beier studied English, German and history, then phonetics in London in 1948. During a trip to Paris in 1950, he met Susanne Wenger, born in Grasse in 1915. She had been educated at the school of decorative arts, a graphic arts teaching and research institution, and at the Vienna Academy of Fine Arts. During World War II, she was considered a "degenerate" artist and forbidden to work. She therefore delved into reading about ancient religions and distant countries.

Kola Sorunke ©Revue Noire

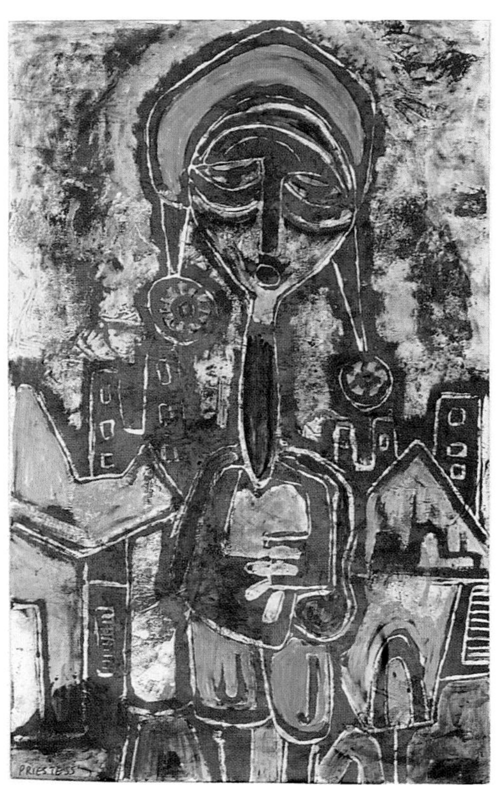

After marrying, Susanne Wenger and Ulli Beier left for Africa in 1950, where Ulli taught phonetics at the University of Ibadan. Since the couple was suffering from the discrimination that the Europeans inflicted upon the African population, Ulli Beier decided to teach in private continuing studies institutions. He traveled a great deal, discovered countries and people from nearby places. Early in 1951, Susanne Wenger contracted pulmonary tuberculosis and remained bedridden for fourteen months. During this period, she discovered the Yoruba civilization through anthropological works. Wenger met the High Priest Ajagemo when the couple moved to Ede in 1952. Her initiation into the Obatala cult, which took several years, wore her out physically and morally.

The couple settled in Oshogbo in 1958. Ulli Beier gave seminars on literature and civilization, organized workshops and exhibits, published magazines and critiques on artists he had discovered and their works. Susanne Wenger was busy trying to understand art as a living religion in honor of the gods.

Duro Lapido arrived in the city at the same time as the couple. In March 1962, the Oshogbo Club Mbari Mbayo and the "Popular Bar" were opened up in his home as a cultural center. In the summer of 1962, Ulli Beier organized at Lapido's home a workshop headed by the architect of the time, Julian Beinart, and painter Denis Williams. Theater actors from the Duro Lapido troop and young unemployed men from the neighborhood took part. Jacob Afolabi showed very promising talent. One year later, Rufus Ogundele stood out from among the participants of a workshop headed, once again, by Denis Williams in collaboration with Jacob Lawrence.

J. Afolabi and R. Ogundele were still active in the art field when Georgina Beier, then Georgina Bats, arrived in Oshogbo in 1963. Georgina Beier, born in London in 1938, had interrupted her art studies for financial reasons and was in the process of setting up a workshop in Oshogbo at that time. In 1964, she headed, together with graphics art specialist Ru van Rossem, a workshop in town, known today as the Oshogbo School, which produced artists such as Muraina Oyelami, Adebisi Fabunmi, Jimoh Buraimoh, Twins Seven Seven and Tijani Mayakiri. The latter, who had just basic education, survived thanks to small temporary jobs, and had never been confronted with representational art. Over the next few years, they acquired various artistic techniques and were trained through constant contact with artists. Not only was Georgina Beier a teacher for a short period of time, but she was also a colleague and a contact always ready to listen. This generated not only interest and reciprocal exchanges, but also great similarities with the initial pictorial style. It was only

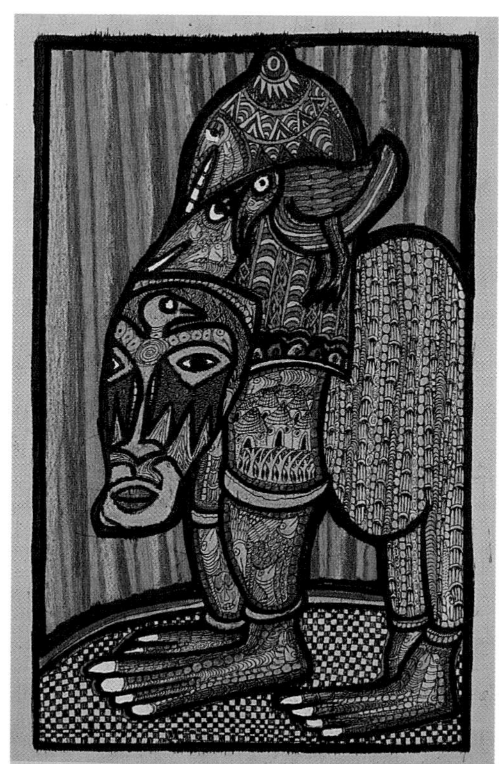

Twin Seven Seven (born in 1944) ©Revue Noire

after some time that the works began to differ and that painters began to discover new materials (for example, Fabunmi discovered wool and Buraimoh discovered glass beads).

The good relationships between Ulli Beier and the creditors ensured the subsistence of the artists and the acquisition of working material.

The first exhibit of the Oshogbo School in Lagos in 1965 gained it some respect. The exhibits that followed in Europe and the United States contributed to a global recognition of this group of artists.

During this time, a circle of artists was also forming around Susanne Wenger in Oshogbo. They asked for help from the Oshun priests in the 60s when the Oshogbo Oshun coffer was being rebuilt. An increase in the followers of Islam and Christianity had reduced people's interest in the Yoruba divinities: their coffers were abandoned. The peasants who extended their fields were threatening the sacred forest, as were the land speculators and the government, who wanted to divide it into lots and replace them with plantations.

The lack of money to acquire material and manpower forced Susanne Wenger to sell her own works and search for financial backers. Thanks to its commitment, the Department of Antiquities finally declared the sacred forest a national cultural asset.

When the time came to restore the forest, only two painters, Ojewale Amoo and his friend Laani, were available. They once again erected the enclosure wall and adorned it with decorative figures made by them. Adebisi Akanji became the closest collaborator on this project. He was a bricklayer and Ulli Beier discovered him in Ibadan in 1961, during a competition at an exhibit where he had created cement figures resembling the décor of "Brazilian houses."

The sculptors Buraimoh Gbadarnoshi and Kasali Akangbe participated in the restoration and arrangement of the sacred forest. Gbadamoshi's figures stood out in particular due to their closed attitude, and fixed and hypnotic stare, whereas the sculptures of Akangbe are more delicately worked and have expressionist traits. Akangbe also made the structure for Susanne Wenger's figures. Raiuyu Abeshu, Lamidi Ariusa, Kasall Oladepo, Issac Ojo Fjana and Sangodare also took part. While work was being done on the sacred forest, Susanne Wenger also found time for painting and batik. In 1967, she initiated some artists into her circle during a workshop. Among these artists was her "eldest son," on whom the Shango priest, Sangodare, bestowed a special honor.

In addition to Akanji, Asiru Olatunde, a qualified blacksmith, stood out as one of the first "modern" artists of Oshogbo. Weakened by illness, Olatunde was forced to devote himself to making jewelry. In 1961, he had already been discovered by Ulli Beier and Susanne Wenger and encouraged to produce large works. Since then, he has been telling stories, such as the battle of Fulani or the creation of Oshogbo, on repoussé aluminum or copper boards.

Modern art at Makerere University, Uganda

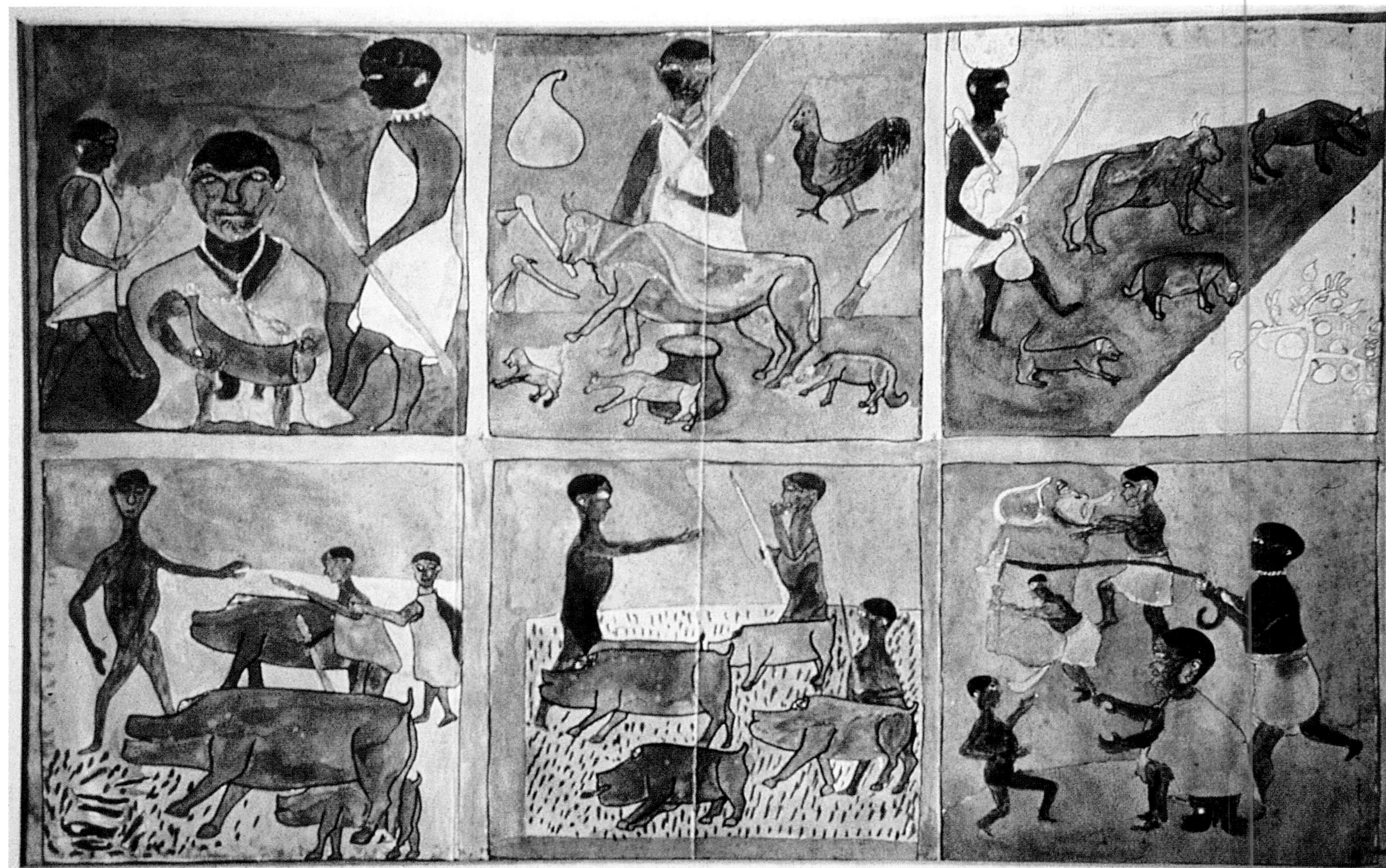

above:
Mukamba, "The Prodigal Son," Kenya, 1920

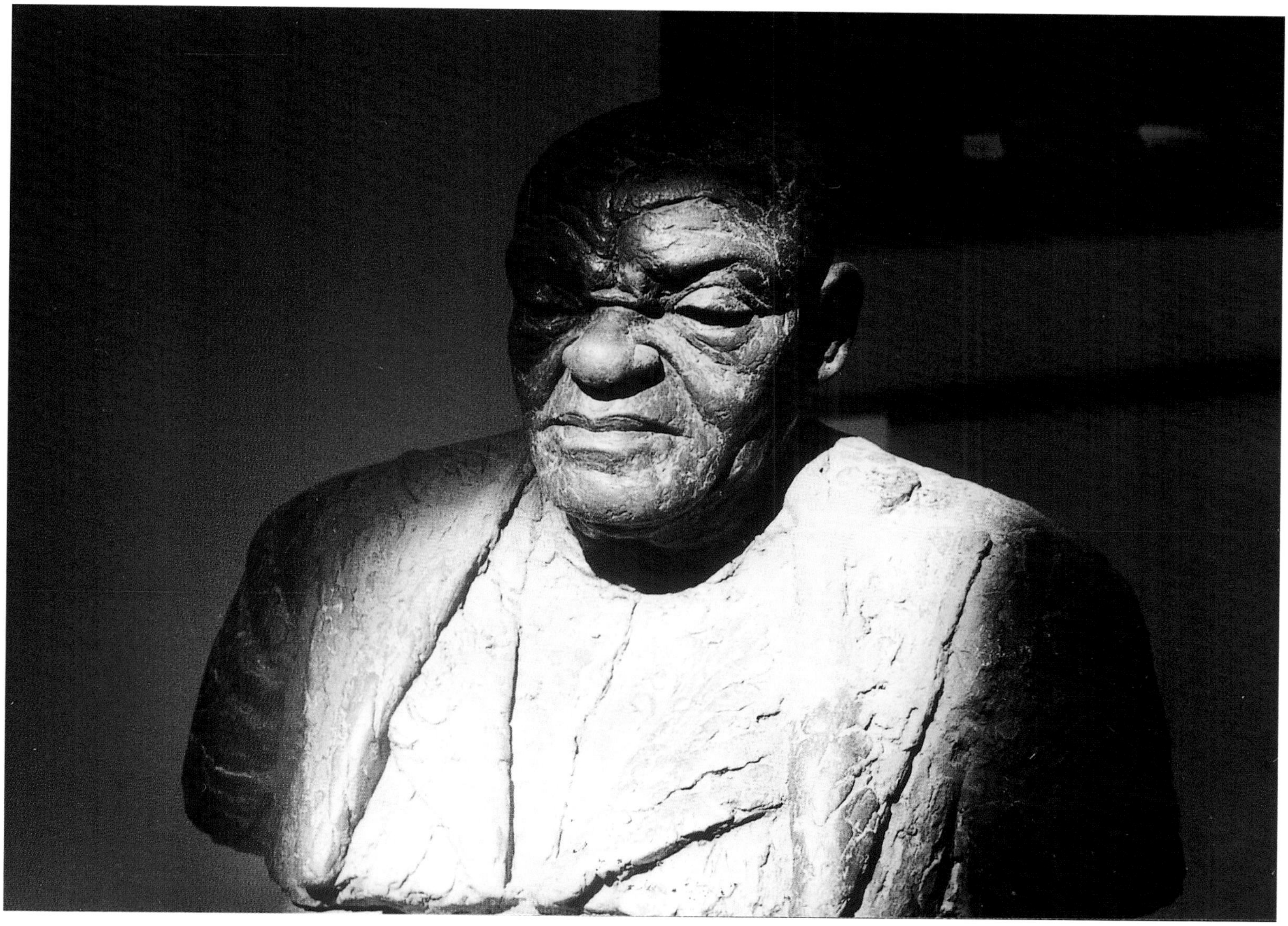

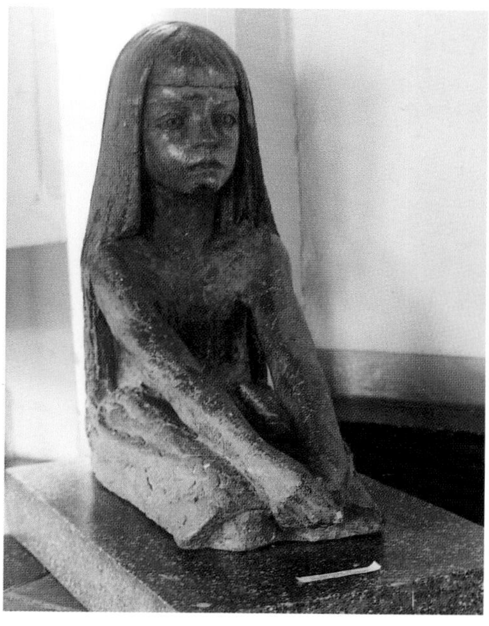

above:

Gregory Maloba (born in 1922), "Portrait of Hans Mukasa," Kenya, c.a. 1940 ©George Kyeyune

left:

Gregory Maloba, "The Young," Kenya, c.a. 1945
©Sunanda Sanyal

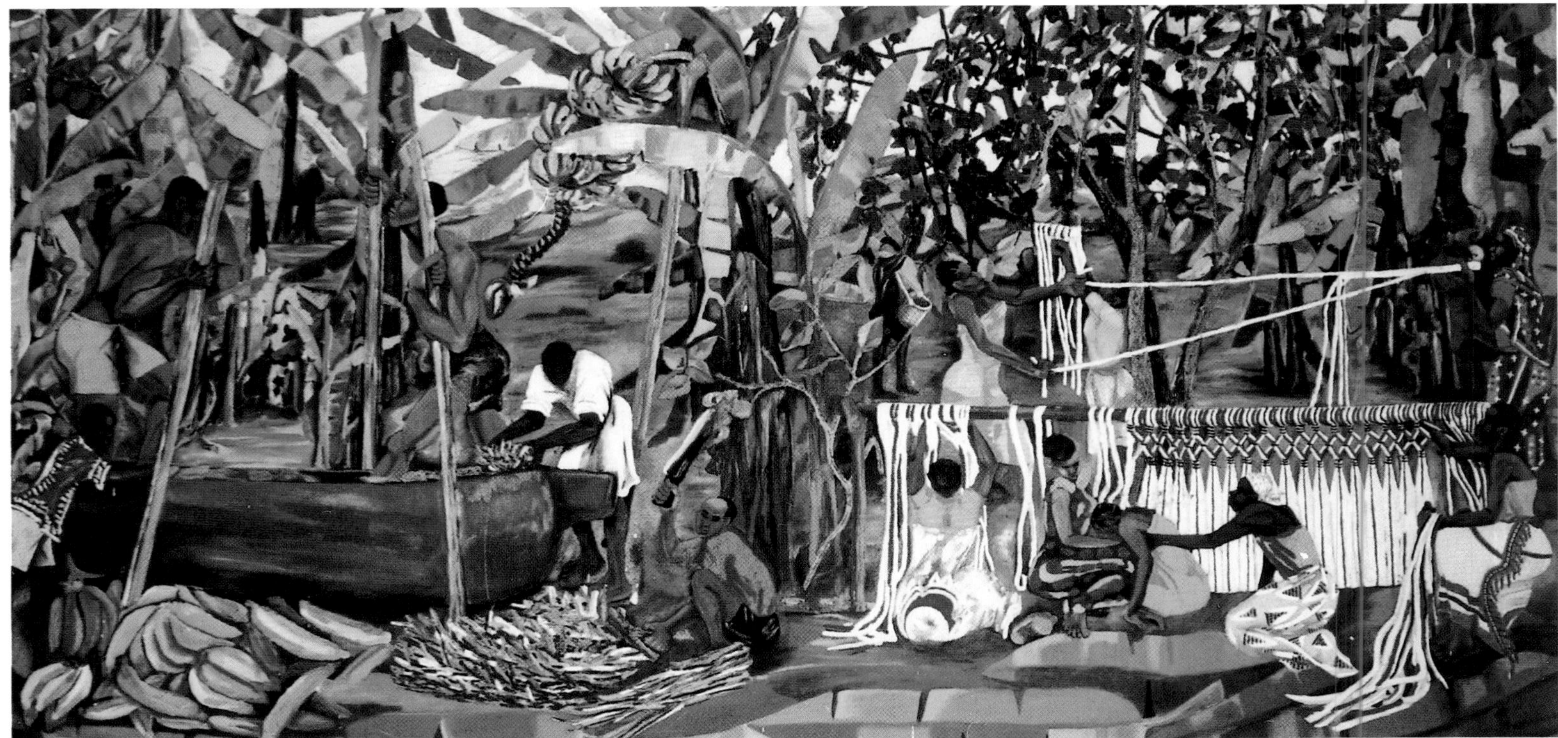

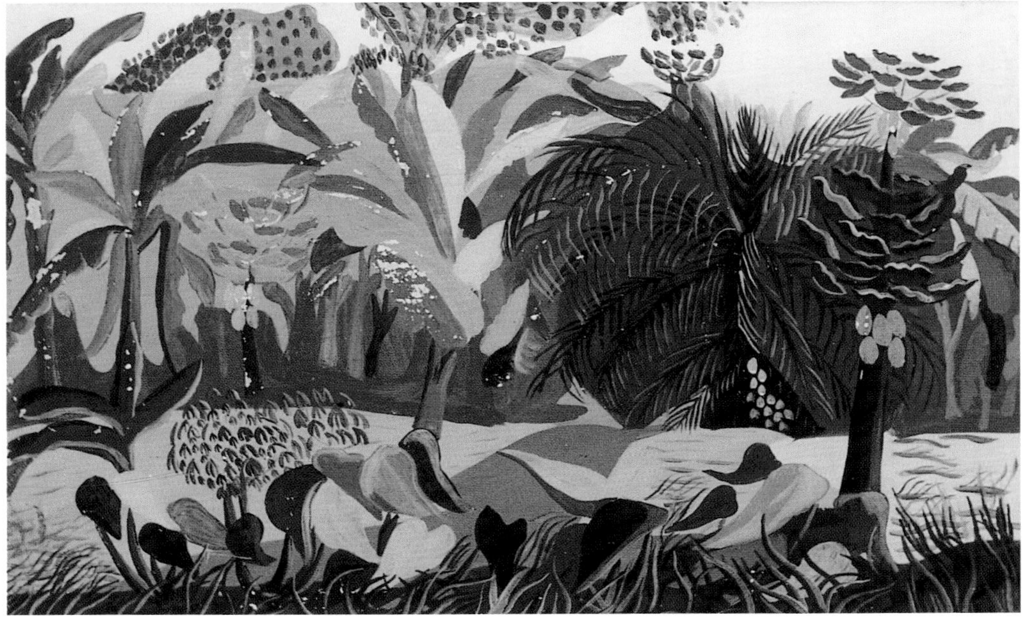

above:

Sam Ntiro (1923-1993), "Chagga life," Tanzanie, c.a. 1960

©Sunanda Sanyal

left:

Francis Musango (born in 1932), "Forest," Kenya, 1958

©George Kyeyune

MODERN ART AT MAKERERE UNIVERSITY, UGANDA

George Kyeyune

About fifty five years ago, a new movement of visual arts was born at Makerere University in the political and social circumstances least suspected to be supportive and propelling.[1] Because the East African region was in general lacking in pictorial art, the early scholars in African art always neglected it in favour of West Africa whose pictorial art traditions were by comparison far richer, when studying the changes and innovations in contemporary African art.[2] Yet it was in ornamental and performing arts, where East Africa was particularly rich, that the initial stimulus to develop a modern genre originated.[3] Over the years a unique and dynamic community of artist at Makerere and beyond has developed expressing in their work the different issues and ethos of the community. Their adaptability to changing circumstances has attracted scholarly attention in the recent past.

The origins of Makerere University

Like in other parts of Africa, formal education in East Africa was initiated by missionaries. In Uganda the colonial administration was too preoccupied with administrative and security questions to be bothered with the provision of Education until the years following the end of World War I when it developed a special interest on realisation of particular limitations in the Missionary Schools. The missionaries, whose focus was on literacy and spiritual, had not proved particularly innovative in adapting their education systems to the local needs. On the recommendation of Phelps-Stokes' commission,[4] Government followed a new policy of "education adaptation." Its implementation resulted into the setting up of Makerere College in 1921, as an institution for higher levers of technical and professional training, which were lacking in Mission Schools. Makerere's position therefore inevitably governed the aims and standards in Missionary Schools for entry to it. In 1929, in the Dar es Salaam Conference of Directors of Education, it was accepted that higher education for Africans of the East African Territories should be centred at Makerere.[5] By 1940 Makerere had taken on an ambitious plan to train Africans for the civil service to replace the Asians and Europeans who had proved to be too expensive to employ during the financially tight 1930s.[6] As a result the kind of education provided both in Missionary schools and at Makerere at this stage produced an educated African who adopted a negative attitude towards his cultural tradition.

The birth of Makerere Art School

By 1930s education opportunities were still limited to missionary established schools. In spite of the fact that strong cultural traditions continued to survive, very little effort was made to build aspects of these in the education system, until 1937 when Margaret Trowell attempted to develop a modern pictorial genre inspired by indigenous expression. A British teacher and painter, Trowell studied Fine Art at Slade school (1924-26) where strict academic art of observation was rife. Under Marion Richardson, Trowell pursued a course in art education also at London University, whose content (in contrast to the Slade) encouraged freedom of expression and the development of creative energies.[7] This philosophy had a profound influence on Trowell enabling her to appreciate the strength and sincerity inherent in African art upon which she expanded and modified through out her teaching career in Europe and Africa.

Following the appointment of Dr. Hugh Trowell (Mrs. Trowell's husband) to the colonial medical service the couple arrived in Kenya in 1929. For the next six years they lived in Kenya, mostly among the Kamba where Mrs. Trowell engaged herself in the study and collection of local decorative arts which enabled her to assimilate the African reflections of life guaranteed by the vitality of the art forms with which she came into contact. This involvement was a good preparation for Mrs. Trowell's career fulfilment in Uganda over the next twenty years. In contrast to Kenya, schools in Uganda had been founded at an earlier date. In addition, the priorities

1 During the 1950s Universities proliferated in Africa, modelled on those in Britain. In Uganda Makerere College developed as a regional centre for Higher Education in East Africa. Because the School of Fine Art flourished within the administrative and academic structures of Makerere, the idea that independent minded artists could emerge from such an environment was thought to be barely possible particularly for those who maintained a belief in imperial hegemony.

2 Johanna Agthe, 1990. Wezeichen. Signs; Art from East Africa 1974-89. Frankfurt, 67.

3 Although very few examples of pictorial art are known to exist in East Africa, those that are available, reveal that visual arts which was spiritually based has been part of peoples rives Uganda, for more than 500. They include the Luzira pottery Sculpture and the Nyero Rock Paintings.

4 In 1911, Miss Caroline Phelps Stokes of USA established a fund known as Phelps Stokes Fund, whose objectives included the education of Africans in America and in Africa. A commission under Dr. Jesse Jones was appointed to survey education in Africa which came to be known as the Phelps "Stokes commission." In 1923 it carried out its work in Uganda and recommended that Education facilities must be enlarged and better adapted to the needs of the local people

5 Margaret Macpherson, 1964, They build for the future; A Chronicle of Makerere University College 1922-1962. Cambridge, 13.

6 Hugh Dinwiddy and Michael Twaddle, 1982, Article - The crisis at Makerere, Uganda Now, 197.

7 For more information on Mrs. Trowell's Education in UK, see Elsbeth J. Court in her Article, Margaret Trowell and The Development of Art Education In East Africa. 1985, Art Education, 36.

Gregory Maloba (born in 1922), "Death," Kenya

©George Kyeyune

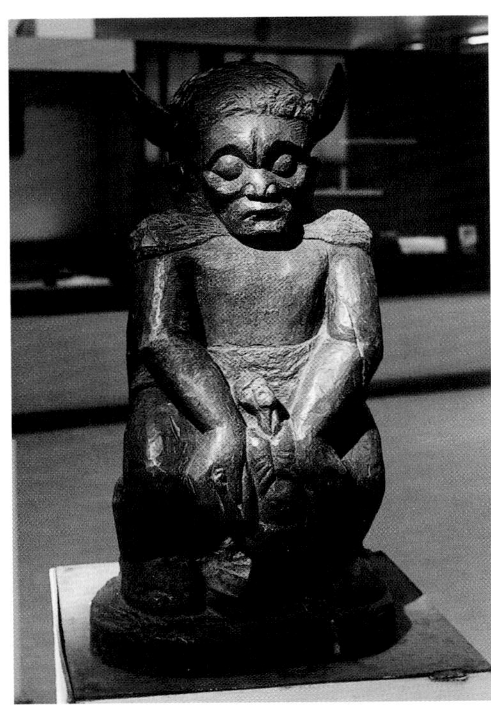

of the Uganda protectorate were more directed toward the encouragement of African development than those of White settler-oriented. Trowell continued her project of collecting and studying cultural objects during her time in Uganda, deepening further her insight and interest in the indigenous cultural expressions.

In 1937 she offered to start experimental art classes at Makerere and the Principal agreed, but for lack of facilities at the college, instructions started on the veranda of her residence at Mulago hill. Although Trowell's students were drawn from a diversity of cultural backgrounds, they nevertheless were unified by their formation in the mission schools and also by the prevailing attitude where people saw "academic" training as a safe way to the acquisition of statue. This problematises the issue of implementation of Trowell's philosophy of adaptation, which stressed the desirability of building on existing traditional motifs to develop a modem genre. How did her students respond to this attitude? Further more, given Trowell's strong spiritual base in Christianity, how was her passion for indigenous arts negotiated in her teaching?

As the region lacked a history of pictorial tradition, Trowell encouraged a narrative approach to painting supported with reproductions of Western and Asian art as well as those of indigenous African carvings.[8] By adopting Marion Richardson's imaging method in which the teacher's essential task is that of stimulation, Trowell's first students produced journalistic descriptive paintings which were fresh and delightful, emanating from a wealth of observed and remembered detail. However her principal iconographical reference, the Bible came to the fore, filtering in her students' work of the fifties. As Ssengendo observes, Africanised compositions of Christian themes such as the oil mural panels of Elimo Njau at Fort Hall chapel and the mural religious themes by Musangogwantamu (and his group) at Lubaga Cathedral, were common during this period.[9]

Following the success of the informal classes which resulted into an exhibition in Kampala, the Governor of Uganda Sir Philip Mitchell was compelled to support the planning of a larger exhibition in 1939 at the imperial institute in London which was complemented by the Ugandan material culture collected by Mrs. Trowell. This (material culture) bolstered the Museum collection of which she was the curator from 1939-1945. When in 1944 her art courses were officially incorporated in the college, the Museum now sharing premises with the art school, having been relocated from old Kampala hill, became an additional influence to her teaching. At this stage art was being offered as an optional minor and later an optional major in the College Higher Arts Certificate Course.

Two of Trowell's students, Gregory Maloba, a sculptor from Kenya and Sam Ntiro a painter from Tanzania, became her assistants in 1944. Together with Elimo Njau, a painter also from Tanzania, as well as Trowell's direct student, the trio became artists of notable distinction of the first generation of artists whose influence begun in the 1940s the early days of "contemporary" art in East Africa. Both Maloba and Ntiro received higher training in UK in the 1950s. However unlike Maloba who became deeply influenced by Western academic training, Ntiro remained largely unaffected. M. Mount describes his work as being related to that of typical early Trowell students.[10]

1949 and 1950 were the years of entering into special relationship with London University and this offered opportunities for adapting a curriculum within the standard and scope of London degrees. The School of Fine art was at this stage still offering a three year certificate which carried far less prestige and earning capacity. Art was ruled out as a subject for intermediate or degree, because London University had no place for it in any degree course.[11] Without a degree, the art school must wither.[12] For Trowell however, the exclusion from the degree structure was a blessing in disguise, for it presented the school the opportunity to develop an art education while preserving its freedom from London examinations, which might well have drowned the creativity of its students

[8] Margaret Trowell 19. . . African Tapestry, Faber and Faber, London.

[9] Ssengendo Pilkington, in his unpublished paper on: The birth and Growth of East African Modem Art at Makerere University. 19. . .

[10] Marsall W. Mount, 1973, African Art, The years since I920. Indiana University, 98.

[11] Margaret Macpherson, 1964; They build for the Future. A Chronicle of Makerere University College. Cambridge, 57.

[12] The new Principal, Bernard de Bunsen became Trowell's ally at this critical time when the School of Fine Art was being threatened with an impending closure. Bernard was sympathetic and supportive of Trowell's Education Project which sought to maintain what was best in the local traditions.

based on African materials and ideas.

Through linking with Slade School, an agreement was reached where Makerere was to decide the content, while Slade School would act as external examiners thus asserting an adequate standard of work. The award of the first diplomas in 1957 following the completion of a four year course of study,[13] also marked the retirement of Mrs. Trowell. Trowell created a formal infrastructure where art was not only part of the curriculum in schools but also institutionalised in a University structure. With four volumes of influential books; Tribal crafts of Uganda (1953), Classical African Sculpture (1954), African design (1960) and African Art (1970), made the most of her nearly three decades in East Africa.

Sam Ntiro (1923-1993), Tanzania, end of the 1950's

[13] At this stage the school awarded two different qualifications; the three years' art teachers' certificate for junior and intermediate secondary schools and the four year Diploma in Fine Art Course which could be followed by a one year Diploma Course in the Faculty of Education. Students specialised in painting and drawing, sculpture and pottery, textile and graphic design, together with some study of History of Art.

Two schools in Zimbabwe

The debate surrounding the authenticity of the creation of sculptors called Shonas, which some see as being too commercial, cannot hide the artistic reality proposed by generations of artists. The esthetic mould resembling the abstraction of the early 20th century provided by the initiators Frank McEwen and Tom Blomefield in the framework of types of outdoor schools on sites with a strong traditional and spiritual identity, launched this formal production intended for the whole world. Reverend Ned Paterson, in turn, created another tradition. These two forms of intervention on African talents recall the projection that well-wishing expatriate Europeans may have on and their own vision of the different African cultures and what they can contribute to the world.

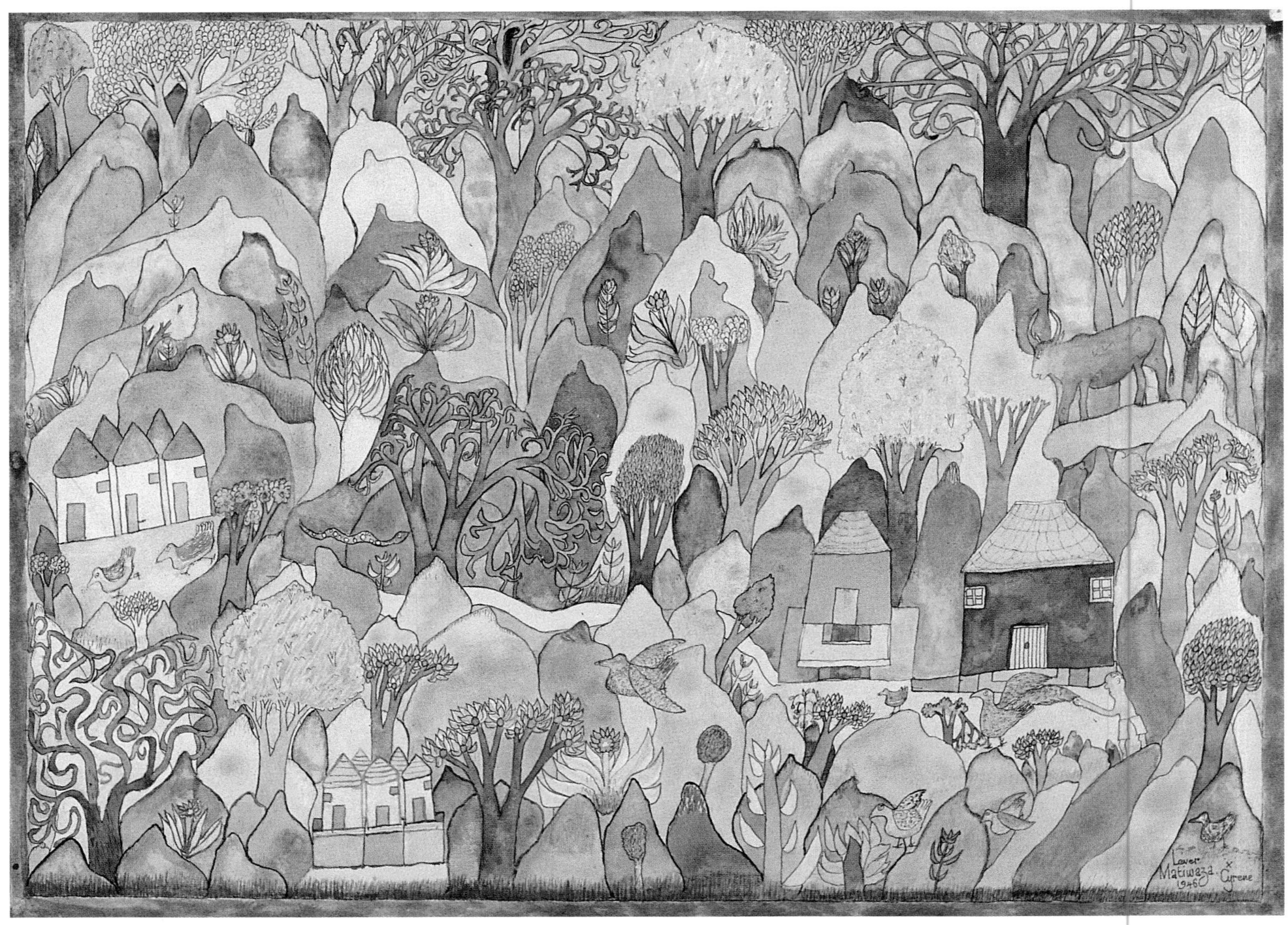

Lever Matiwasa, "The first day of spring," Cyrene, 1946

facing page: **John Masena, "Design for a village," Cyrene, 1945**

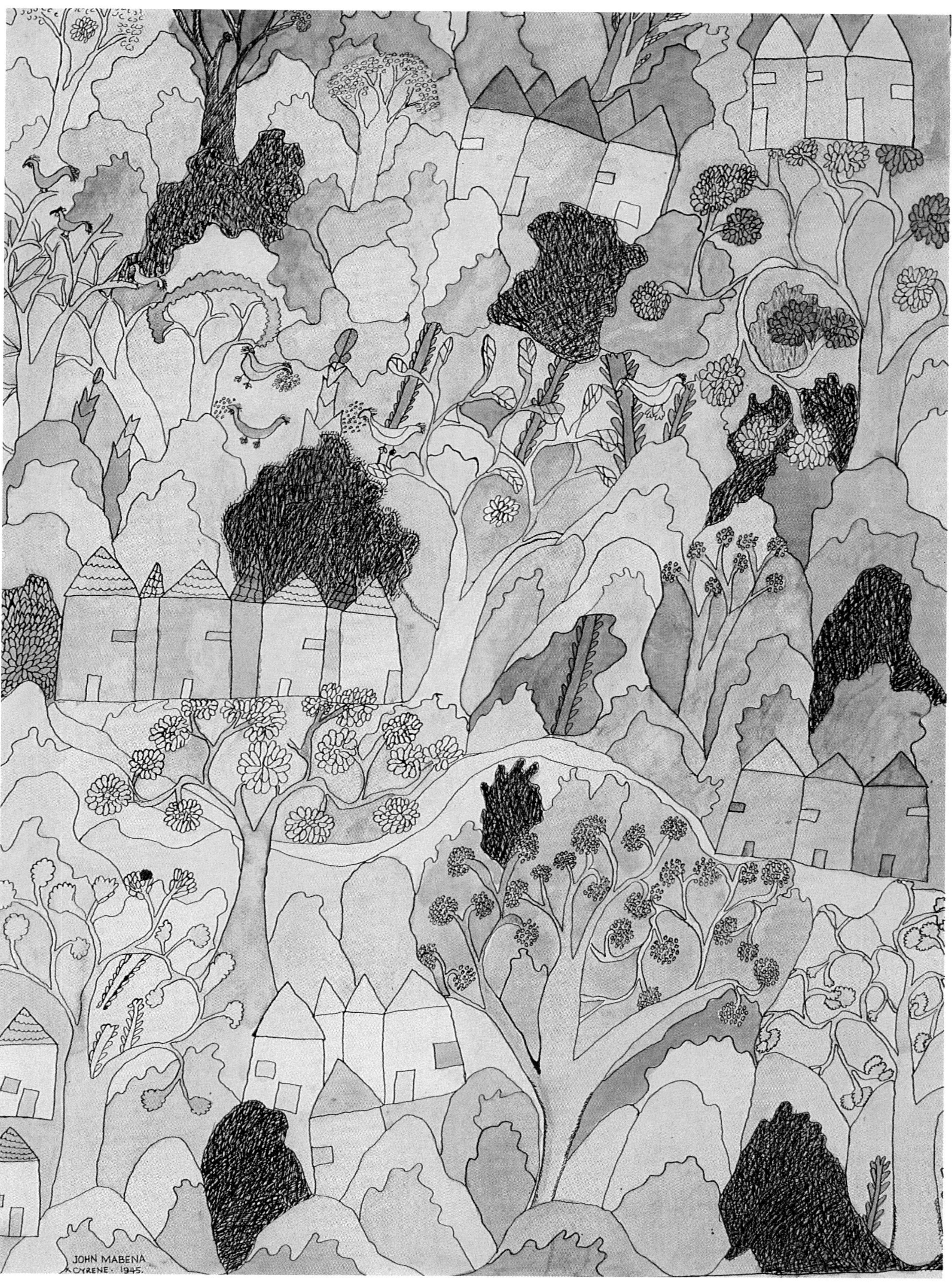
JOHN MABENA
CYRENE · 1945.

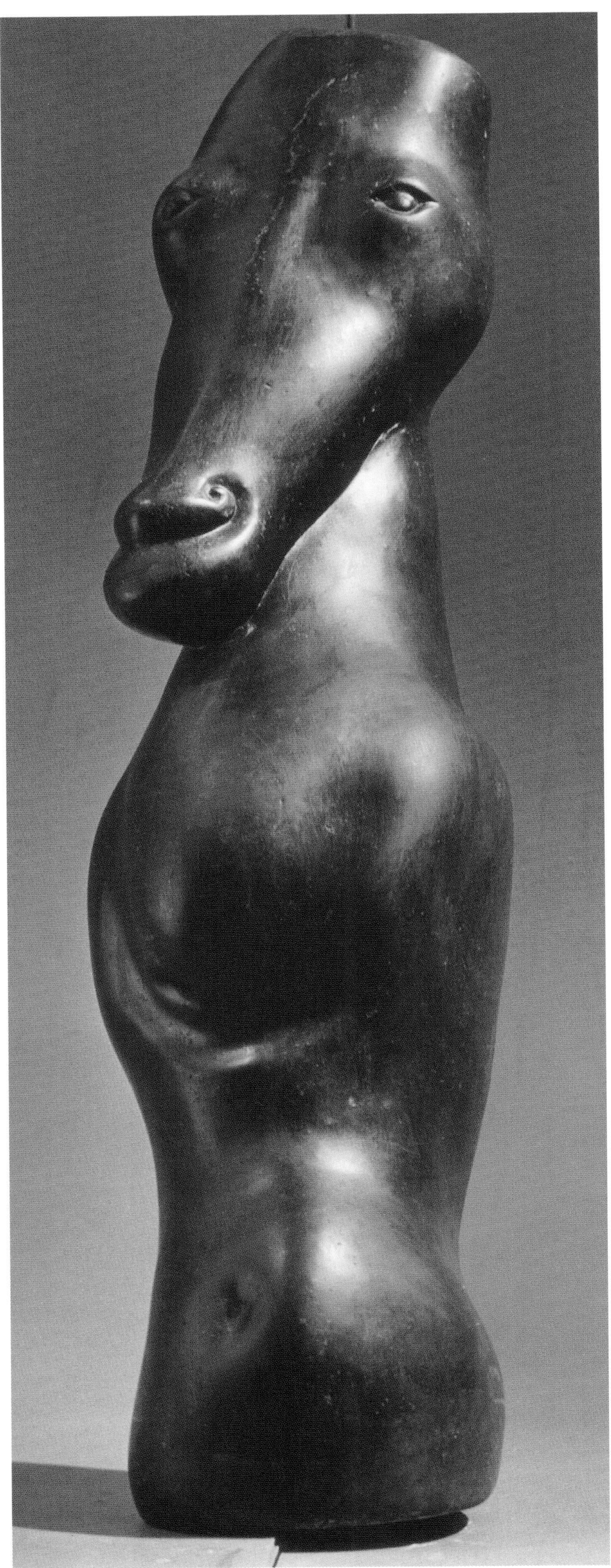

Moses Masaya (1947-1996), "Gentle spirit horse," 1972
black serpentine, h. 89 cm

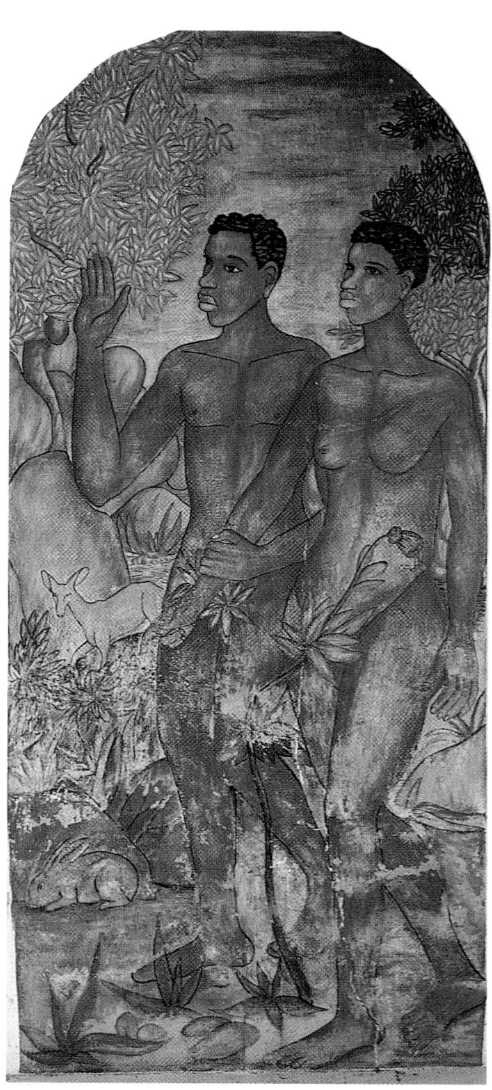

Fresco, Cyrene Mission, c.a. 1940

ZIMBABWE: TWO SCHOOLS OF "AUTHENTICITY"

Yvone Vera

Ned Paterson, Frank McEwen, and Tom Blomefield are the most visible early figures in the history of art and artists in Zimbabwe. Taken together they form a complex but telling tapestry full of ideological idiosyncrasy, deft negotiation, romantic zeal and simple creative will. Reverend Ned Paterson, a Scottish priest and teacher, demonstrated the most anxiety of influence. He claimed that he was not shaping the way Africans painted or drew, unlike McEwen or Blomefield, who led their pupils towards a "spiritual" West African art seen as "bogus" in the Rhodesian context.

Paterson held that what was produced at his centre Cyrene Mission, situated 20 km from Bulawayo, rose from "natural" forces, and that it went through the stages of world art history. African boys came to art "from below" while European boys were smothered by the art images in their homes and everywhere else. Paterson made dozens of books to illustrate his theories - in each, the different stages between the successive Cyrene classes; the differences between Shona and Ndebele; the difference between the art of boys and girls. At the time he distributed these to institutions throughout the world, he had more influence than McEwen and Blomefield, but he never matched their commercial success.

Reverend Ned Paterson

In 1938, Edward Paget, who was Bishop of Mashonaland, had invited Paterson to start a school for Africans. The students would consist of delinquents needing reform: Paterson differed and preferred to set up a school instead. In 1940, Cyrene Mission opened. Agriculture, carpentry and crafts were envisaged.
The now famous Cyrene Chapel consists of indigenous images of biblical scenes; Mary Magdalene and St. Peter; the Madonna and Child is depicted as an African Mother, the wise man ethnic chiefs with ankle bracelets and all the accouterments of African life. Inside the chapel "The Last Judgment" by John Mhlaba, "Christ Commissioning the Disciples" by Joseph Ndlovu. Livingston Sango's "Consider the Lilies" and the story of the Prodigal Son are depicted as narrative within the African landscape and family life - heaven manifests itself in the balancing rocks akin to the famous Matopo hills nearby. These murals were commenced in 1941 and ended in 1948. In 1999 through the teamwork of Canon J. Fenwick and architect John Knight,, Cyrene Chapel was refurbished, and now incorporates new work by Matebeleland artists, plus a protective verandah to preserve the old work along the rondavel.

In 1946 a first exhibition of Cyrene work was held at the City Hall. It consisted of large paintings and carvings in stucco, wood and stone. Six boys painted throughout the run of the exhibition, creating novelty and interest among shocked onlookers. 80 notebooks resulted. The exhibition went to Harare and South Africa. In 1947 Cyrene art showed in London, and was on permanent display in Livingstone Airport in Zambia.

Among the boys of Cyrene were many who were handicapped, Sam Songo among them. He set to carving. Songo became a teacher at Mzilikazi Art School, in Bulawayo. Livingstone Sango became the first black taxidermist in the region and worked till his retirement at the Museum and Monuments. Adomech Moyo, another handicapped boy, became the first African teacher of occupational therapy in Southern Africa. Richard Rachidi, from Malawi, became the first qualified teacher of art from his country. Many artists emerged from the Cyrene School and its presence had a remarkable influence.

Cyrene art possesses a recognisable style reminiscent of Persian art. There were two sort of pictures, the large on tinted paper in "powder color," very decorative, and the water color drawings. Paterson's diaries comment: "There was no hurry and no trains to catch so that a particular boy might put as many as 20,000 leaves on a tree of his own imagining and in colors as he saw in the veld round him."

Paterson left Cyrene in 1953 for Harare where he became of influence. He was placed in Chirodzo where again art was taught to boys, however, now urban city Africans, eager to paint scenes of political violence. The stoning of one of the political figures, Sithole, was depicted. The ferment of revolutionary politics was a major atmosphere and reference. Paterson moved to Highfield, at a new art centre, with 2000 pupils. Here, the boys seemed to learn about distance, and to "approximate" perspective, and depict houses in three dimensions. In 1965 Paterson was asked to train girls and found them to have a gentle sensitivity. Even if the subject was hunting, for the girls, the dogs and hunters were in arrested motion. The human figure static.

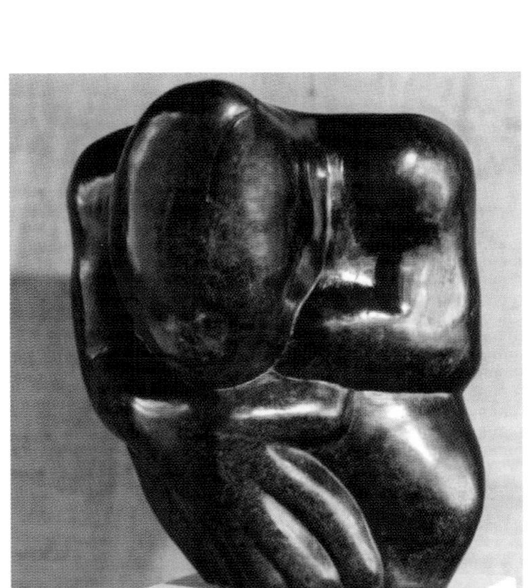

Bernard Takawira (1945-1997), "Man turning into an eagle," 1981
black serpentine, h.49 cm
©National Gallery of Zimbabwe

There was carving in serpentine and stone. Soapstone came from the Eastern Highlands of Nyanga.

Frank McEwen

Frank McEwen was invited from the United Kingdom in 1954 by the Southern Rhodesian Government to advise on the building of a gallery of modern art. The Rhodes National Gallery was opened in 1957 by the Queen Mother. In this same year, an exhibition entitled "From Rembrandt to Picasso" was staged. It became one of the most modern buildings to house a gallery in Africa. McEwen became the first Director and worked to influence art development, and began a Workshop School. The National Gallery Workshop School facilitated training and gestation of ideas, provided financial and material support, and explored individual ability.

The artists who emerged included Charles Fernando, Thomas Mukorobgwa and Joseph Ndandarika who moved from painting to experimenting with stone. Steatite, a soft stone, was used. Shona mythology figured prominently as a resource for creativity. "Shona Sculpture" became key, though now hotly contested among critics in terms of its constraints, regionalism, exoticism, and artificial primitivism, mysticism, and a constructed naivete. This classification erased the individualism of the artists, though it worked immensely for marketing purposes. A decentralised creative space, "Vukutu" in Inyanga, a cultural centre, was soon established by McEwen. Artists worked in open spaces in the mountains. A prestigious list emerged that boasts Sylvester Mubayi, Moses Masaya, John Takawira, Bernard Takawira, Nicholas Mukomberanwa and Moses Masaya. Joram Mariga, and agriculturist, influenced artists to be known later as the "Nyanga Group." Here, at Vukutu, were traditional graves, here were ancestors, here were unusual rock formations intimating spirits.

McEwen exhibitions from Vukutu were shown in Musee d'Art Moderne in Paris (1970), Musee Rodin (1971), Institute of Contemporary Art in London (1972). Shona Sculpture was viewed as "a myriad spectacle of form, color, substance and line." The viewer was said to be miraculously filled with an "intangible quality" emanating from its "non-verbal communication" (African Arts, 1972, U.S.A).

In 1965, Rhodesia declared unilateral Independence from British rule. McEwen was blacklisted, accused of inciting national pride and fostering criticism of government. He stressed kinship and social integrity of African belief systems and practices, and sought their expression in art. He resigned in 1973 due to political pressures. Through catalogues that provided commentary and reflection, through workshops, McEwen had brought critical attention to art practice in Rhodesia and attempted a consistent thoroughness in his approach.

Tom Blomefield

McEwen assisted in founding the Tengenenge Art Centre, though Tengenenge developed under the direct auspices of Tom Blomefield, its director, who came to Rhodesia in 1946. In 1966, he founded Tengenenge situated 150 km North of Harare where over 120 sculptures are based. From the beginning, it was dynamic in its holistic approach in linking social relations and art development. Entire families live in an equilibrium of creativity. Located in Zimbabwe's Horseshoe block, a tobacco area, and amidst the Msasa trees,

Tengenenge is an ideal and separate enclave of sculptural activity where libation ceremonies are performed to appease the ancestors, to foster creativity, to sustain a spiritual heritage.

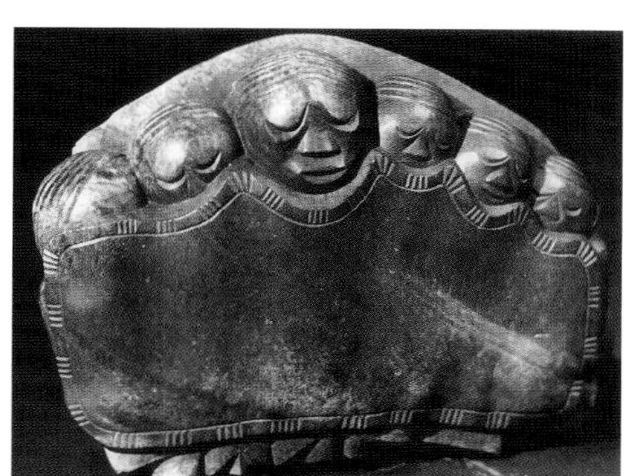

Nicolas Mukomberanwa (born in 1940), "Sleeping family," 1963
red and black serpentine, L. 42,5 cm
©National Gallery of Zimbabwe

Crispen Chakanyuka, a pupil of Joram Mariga of the Vukutu school, showed Blomefield the vast resource of sculpting rock. With tools made from farm implements, Blomefield provided food rations and space, and the villagers came eagerly to explore. Among the major artists discovered were Wazi Maicolo, Bernard Matemera, Henri Munyaradzi, Josia Manzi, Fanizani Akuda, Amali Malolo, Ephraim Chaurika, Sylvester Mubayi, Luigi Purumelo and Lemon Moses. McEwen had Thomas Mukorobgwa as on informant spiritual knowledge. Work was sold at the National Gallery, however in 1969 Tengenenge broke decisively from the National Gallery due to differences regarding distribution.

During the second "Chimurenga" the armed struggle of the 70's, the farm was sold due to insurmountable tensions and financial boycotts which strained resources. Blomfield lost his property but retained the art community. Once Tengenenge was surrounded by guerrillas and had to position itself as of no political affiliation, but only as a sculpture centre. However, few artists returned after the war, but since 1980, Zimbabwe's independence, the dealership of Roy Guthrie has improved matters, as he had also sustained galleries in Harare through which art activity continued during the war. Celia Winter-Irvin helped to keep Tengenenge still running, together with Blomefield. Tengenenge remains an institution separate and remarkable.

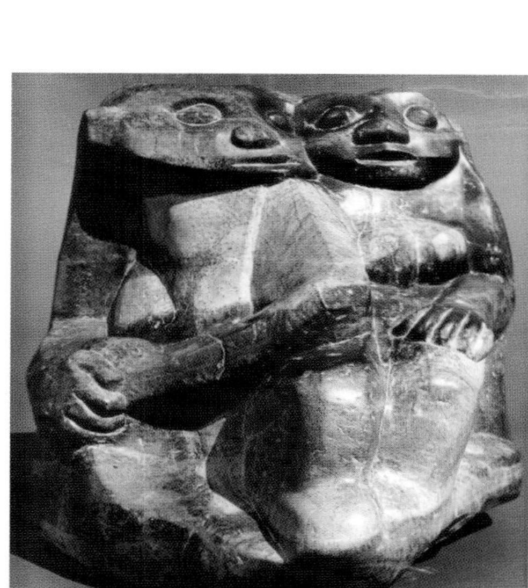

Joseph Ndandarika (born in 1940), "Lovers," 1972
red and grey serpentine, h. 56 cm
©National Gallery of Zimbabwe

The figures of Ned Paterson, Frank McEwen and Tom Blomefield combine in the invention of a tradition of art in Zimbabwe.

The precursors of South Africa

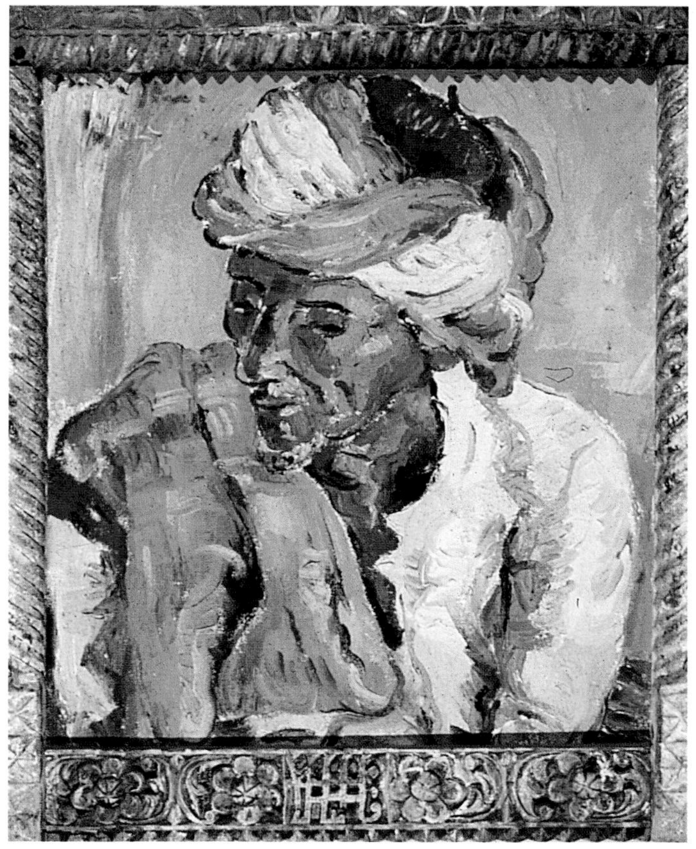

Ernest Mancoba (born in 1904), "Ancestor," 1969
oil on canvas, 92.3 x 60 cm.

facing page:
George Pemba (born in 1912), "I am sorry Madam," 1945
watercolor, 36.4 x 27.9 cm.

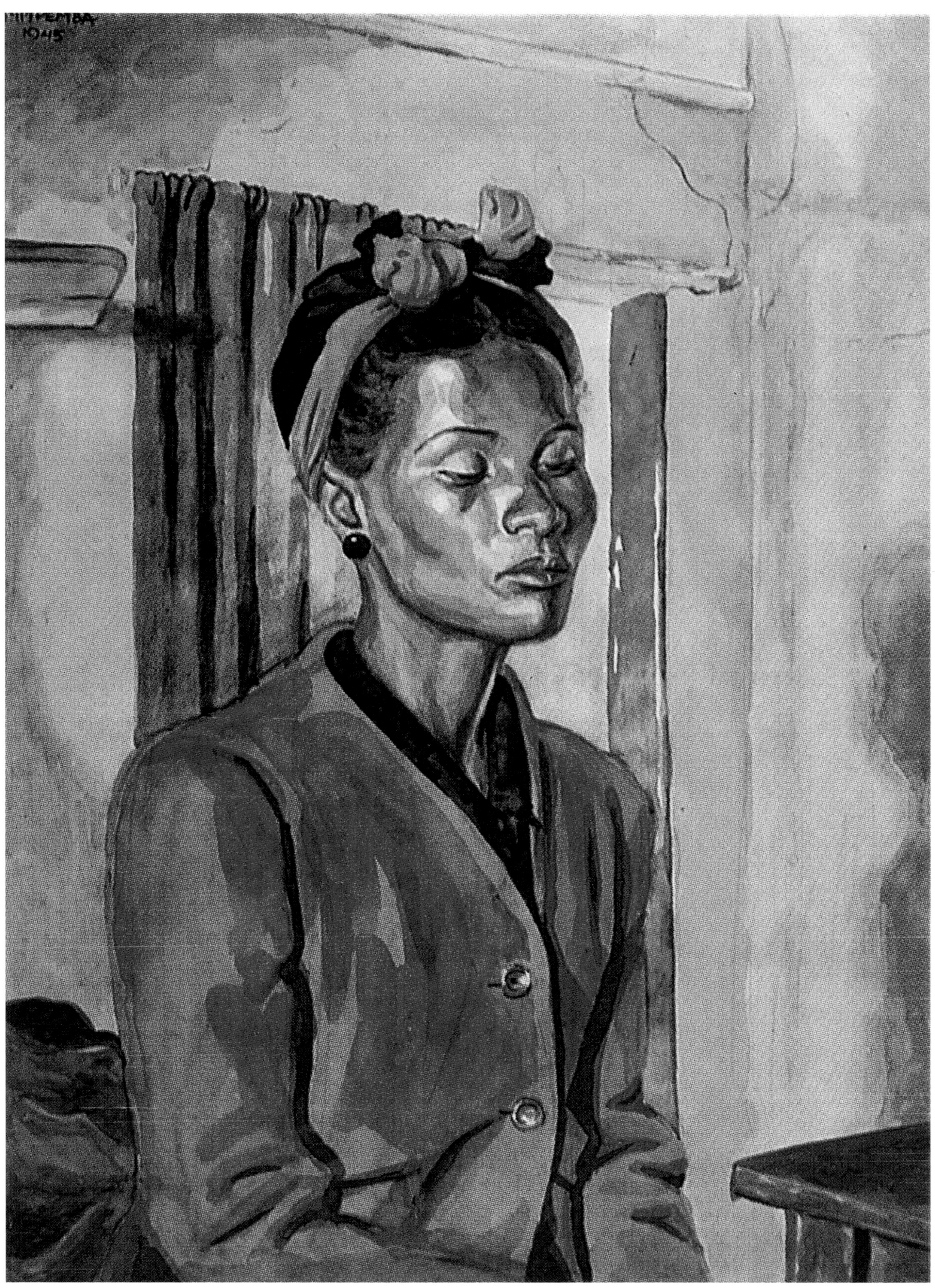

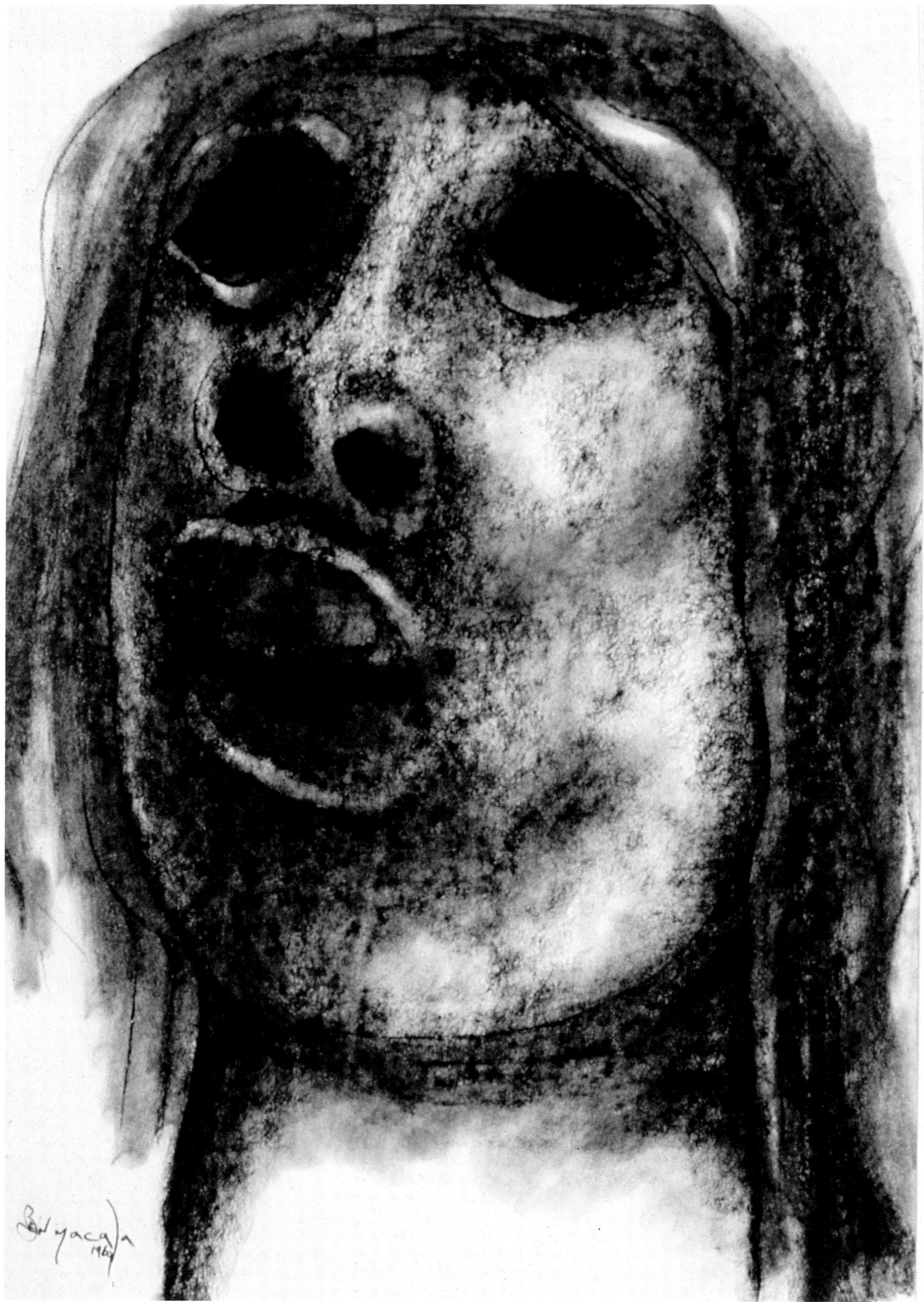

THE PRECURSORS OF SOUTH AFRICA

Marylin Martin

The precursors of twentieth century black art, who emerged from the rural and urban areas in South Africa during the 1920s and 1930s had different experiences, aspirations and educational opportunities, but they also had a great deal in common: they retained an histori-cal connection with traditional life, they were exposed to cultural, religious and educational influences from Europe and they were subjected to white-controlled capitalism. Many moved between the country and the city, often being forced to seek menial employment in order to survive. As the century progressed, material conditions changed - there were new forms of patronage and a white market for curios and artworks was added to the community-based market for functional and ritualistic objects. The notion of the individual artist took root.

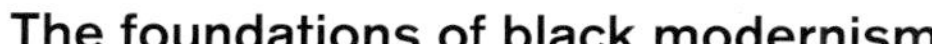

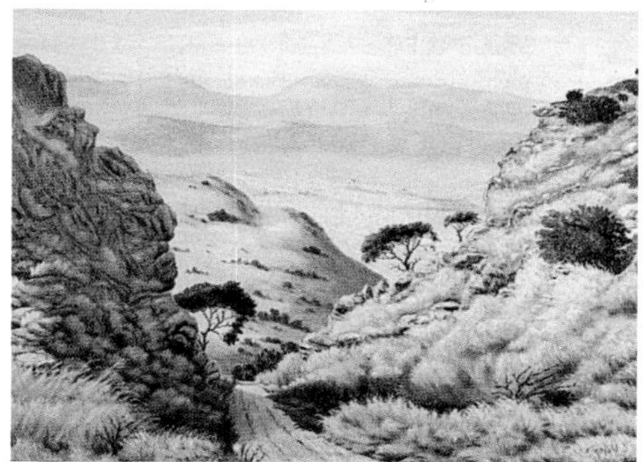

John Mohl (1903-1985), "Magaliesberg Mid-winter"
oil on wood, 62,5x86,8 cm.

The foundations of black modernism

Patronage and commissions were certainly forthcoming for the pioneers of black modernism, but this support was accompanied by a prescriptiveness that was to reverberate throughout the art world and market until recently. If Africans were to occupy themselves with the fine arts, their art should reflect "native" con-cerns and subjects. This was coupled with the conviction that black artists did not require any kind of tuition, because of their natural ability to make art, an ability that should not be tainted by out-side influence. Sculptor Samuel Makoanyane (1909-1944) was instructed and monitored by his patron C. G. Damant:

"About this time he produced a few fig-ures modelled from Europeans... They excited some interest because the like-nesses were very good, but I felt constrained to advise Samuel against this type of work, pointing out to him that, to really establish himself, he should produce models of his own people, in their various daily occupations... I lectured him continually on the desirability of turn-ing out likenesses of the men and women he saw about him, in his village and in the fields. I was certain that there would be a constant and growing demand for this and I was proved entirely correct. Samuel saw the point and followed the advice; he ceased to make any more European figures and settled down to making various types of Basuto, for which he became known far and wide."

John Koenakeefe Mohl (1903-1985) studied art at the Düsseldorf Kunst-Akademie in Germany in the 1920s and was a great and influential easel painter. He worked in oils and painted landscapes that revealed a strong sense of place and history and he rejected the prescriptiveness based on race.
Mohl was once approached by a white admirer and advised not to concentrate on landscape painting but to paint figures of his people in poverty and mis-ery. Landscape, he was advised, had become a field where Europeans had specialised and they had advanced very far in perfecting its painting. In a humble voice and manner humbler still, he smil-ingly replied: "But I am an African, and when God made Africa, he also created beautiful landscapes for Africans to admire and paint."

Mohl and Gerhard Bhengu (1910-1990) loved drawing as children and this was encouraged by sensitive school inspec-tors. But Bhengu, who became a fine painter of portraits and landscape, was denied the opportunity of acquiring formal art training by Professor O. J. P. Oxley, head of the Department of Fine Art at the Natal Technical College in Durban, who advised strongly against it.
Milwa Mnyaluza (George) Pemba (1912-) was told by white friends not to go overseas, as ."..I'd get mixed up with the wrong people and communists and come back frustrated." In 1931 he received about two weeks of tuition in water-colour painting from Ethyl Smythe who taught at the University College of Fort Hare. Six years later, he learned more water-colour technique from Professor Austin Winter-Moore at the Art School of Rhodes University College in Grahamstown. The two brief periods of instruction contributed greatly to Pemba becoming a superb painter in water-colour, as well as his knowledge of linear perspective and sound draughtsmanship.

facing page:
Benjamin Macala (born in 1939), "Head," 1969
charcoal, 68,5x48,4 cm.

Ironically he was dissuaded from exploiting his talent in the medium by Gérard Sekoto (1913-1993), whom he met in Cape Town in c.1941. Sekoto told him that water-colour was "too delicate" and "English" a medium and encouraged him to use oils. Pemba's early water-colour portraits and landscapes remain among the most superb examples in the medium in South Africa.[1]

The aspirations of many of the black precursors of modernism in South Africa were to paint in a European fashion and there were whites who supported art training for black artists, but they were in the minority and the situation was exacerbated by policies that kept black education separate and distinct. The emphasis was to be on "practical" education, on usefulness and the crafts. The arts/crafts distinction, which continues to this day, was entrenched - between the years 1920 to 1950 - by the South African Academy exhibitions and the classification and cataloguing of works made in wood and clay as "native art" or craft. Sekoto's work, created in oil paint or other media associated with the western tradition, was classified and exhibited as art.[2] Museums played a significant role in keeping the barriers firmly in place. Most of the work from the period under discussion is not to be found in art museums but in cultural history and natural history museums, as well as in private collections. The first work by a black South African artist was acquired by the South African National Gallery in 1964, Sekoto's Street Scene. Painted in Sophiatown, probably before 1942, the work is characteristic of Sekoto's depictions of the everyday lives and activities of people. The colour is vibrant and applied in varied, dynamic brush strokes that define volume, space and movement.

The foundations of black modernism in South Africa had been laid by the 1940s. Artists like Job Kekana (1916-1995), Ernest Mancoba (1904-), Mohl and Sekoto were very much drawn to Europe and its artistic traditions and went in search of experience, education and training. Sekoto left for Paris in 1947 and, except for a year spent in Senegal (1966), he never saw the continent again. Sekoto had no formal art training; neither did Mancoba, but the latter obtained a Bachelor of Arts degree in 1937 from the University of South Africa. He was awarded a bursary and a loan each of 100 pounds by the Bantu Welfare Trust to continue his studies in. Mancoba developed an enduring love for African sculpture and wished for the cultural experiences of Africa and the West to co-ordinate, both to become " *... richer by the exchange, and bring human beings together for a fellow understanding and a fellow living together, which would be progressive for our country.*"[3] In Europe he moved ahead of most of his contemporaries, black and white, and became a co-founder of the radical European avant-garde group, CoBrA, (an acronym for the capital cities Copenhagen, Brussels, Amsterdam of the founder members) in 1948.

White artists and the quest of an African Idiom

Throughout the history of art in colonial and post-colonial South Africa, British, European and later American models and standards would exert a strong influence, with many artists pursuing studies abroad. Among white artists the quest for an idiom that was identifiably local or African commenced in the 1930s and developed side-by-side with attempts to maintain international links and emulate international trends and styles. The regeneration of early 20th century European art, indeed the very emergence of modernism, was partly owing to artists seeking purity and authenticity through non-western cultures and ëprimitivismí. For the few white artists in South Africa, who were aware of the ancient artistic traditions of the African continent, the objects often only held ethnological interest and value.

Pioneers like Hugo Naudé (1869-1941) and Strat Caldecott (1886-1929) looked to French Impressionism to explore and capture the distinctive light and colour of the landscape and to shift the emphasis from recording details to the quality of paint application. Others were fascinated by the life and customs of the indigenous peoples, but did not necessarily understand the artistic merit of the artefacts or their potential for a

[1] Van Rooyen, B., "Leading Black Artists Exhibit at City Gallery," Pretoria News, 18 March 1992, p. 15 cited by Nolte, J., "Sources and Style in the Oil Paintings of George Milwa Mnyaluza Pemba" in the catalogue of the Pemba Retrospective Exhibition held at the South African National Gallery, 27 April -28 July 1996, p. 35.

[2] The South African Academy was established in 1920 under the auspices of the Transvaal Institute of South African Architects and in co-operation with the Transvaal Art Society from 1939. Exhibitions were held in the Selbourne Hall from 1920 to 1941, in the Duncan Hall in 1942, and at the Johannesburg Art Gallery between 1944 and 1950 (Sack 1988: 14).

[3] Mancoba in conversation with Alex Laird, Paris, May 1993; quoted in Miles, E. (1994: 15).

Samuel Makoanyane (1909-1944)
"Mother with Child," c.a. 1940
fired clay, 9 cm.
©South African Museum

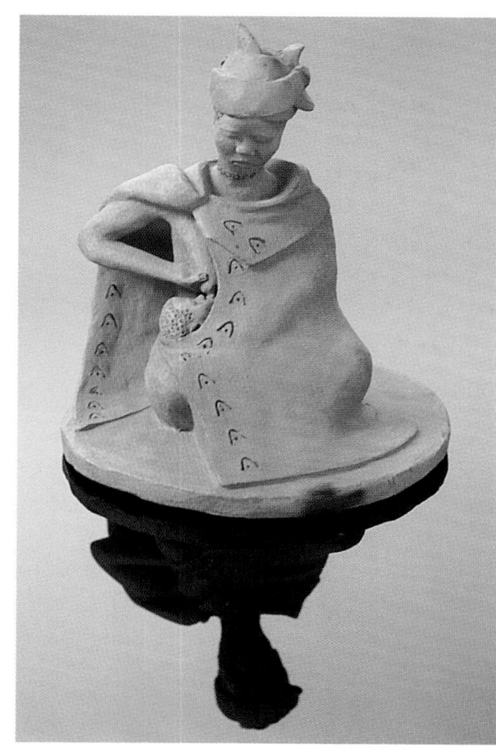

renewal of their own art. J. H. Pierneef (1886-1957) had recognised the aesthetic merit of rock art before 1920, but this had no direct influence on his unique, vaguely cubist, representation of the South African landscape. Irma Stern (1894-1966) painted powerful portraits of African people and included the objects she collected on her travels in her still lifes, her style remaining an intensely personal interpretation of German Expressionism. Her life and work reveal a desire to identify with the continent of Africa while keeping a foothold in the wider world.

In 1933 Walter Battiss (1906-1982) visited a San shelter where, for the first time, he saw rock paintings, as opposed to the petroglyphs (rock engravings) that he knew as a child. In 1938 he wrote of San painting "*... this is where we move from ... this is our beginning ....*"[4] In the same year he went to Europe and from that time Batiss would bring about a synthesis of influences as he searched for new expressive possibilities. In the process he became a truly individualistic artist and a forerunner of the cultural interaction that emerged forcefully in the 1980s. Alexis Preller (1911-1975) was similarly influenced by forces from both Africa and Europe, but his emphasis was on recreating ritual and myth in idyllic, surrealistic settings.

Dissatisfied with the general staleness and amateurism of South African art on the one hand, and a stifling academic orientation, dominated by the British tradition, on the other, Battiss and Preller formed the New Group with other young artists in 1938. With Gregoire Boonzaier (1909-), Freida Lock (1902-1962) and Terence McCaw (1913-1978) they organised exhibitions and lectures in order to educate the public, which was deeply conservative, and to raise awareness about trends and developments abroad. The New Group was active until 1954 and drew other members. Artistically and politically progressive artists such as Hanns Ludwig Katz (1892-1940) and Harry Trevor (1922-1970), who created intensely expressionistic paintings, were relegated to the radical fringe. The variety and vitality of South African art was given a boost with the arrival of artists from Western and Eastern Europe during and after World War II, for example Katz, Lippy Lipshitz (1903-1980), Edouardo Villa (1920-) and Armando Baldinelli (1908-).

The Polly Street Art Centre

The National Party came into power in 1948 and as apartheid ideology was developed, legislated and implemented, teaching was increasingly confined to specific racial groups. At the end of the 1950s even the "open" universities were closed to black artists and at the time there were no art departments at universities created to cater for black students. The exception was the South African Native College in Alice in the Eastern Cape, now known as the University of Fort Hare. Black art education was left to public and private initiatives outside the formal, official structures and was therefore vulnerable to the vicissitudes of funding and individual commitment. Mohl was the first black artist who worked and exhibited as a professional artist in Sophiatown and Soweto; he was also the first who offered art classes in his "White Studio" in Sophiatown.

In 1948 the Johannesburg Local Committee for Non-European Adult Education was formed and the following year a hall was obtained in Polly Street from the Johannesburg City Council and a Cultural Recreation Officer appointed. But it was only after Cecil Skotnes (1926-) was employed in this position that the Polly Street Art Centre emerged as the first large-scale urban art centre in South Africa.[5] Over the next ten years it developed into a place where artists learned how to draw, paint and sculpt; where practical and theoretical discussions took place; where apprenticeships and partnerships were arranged; where white artists could engage with their black compatriots and could share their skills as volunteer teachers. Although the centre never offered more than a workshop situation with a weekly class, for black artists it served as a professional art school.[6]

Skotnes augmented the limited resources with donations from companies and gained the confidence of

[4] Battiss, W. quoted in Schoonraad, M., Batiss and Prehistoric Rock Art, in Skawran & Macnamara (1985: 41)

[5] Rankin, E., "Teaching and Learning Skotnes at Polly Street" in Harmsen (1996: 75).

[6] Polly Street is today remembered as a centre for visual arts. It is important to note that, from its inception, it was to be a place for education and recreation. It featured an extensive music section, a collection of musical instruments and library. There were courses for school pupils, there were choirs and bands, and classes in boxing, judo and ballroom dancing. Skotnes as "director" of the centre, was not only an art master but had wide responsibilities. (Harmsen 1996: 67).

artists, churches and commercial galleries. He organised exhibitions and enlisted the support of the white art community, the press and radio. The extraordinary work done in Polly Street led to commissions from the church and the Johannesburg City Council, as well as interest from foreign buyers. Lifelong creative and teaching careers were established. The discrepancies in the experiences and between black and white artists at this time were glaring: most white artists could enjoy three to four years training, without having to be pressurised by commercial considerations; black artists had to learn quickly, develop a marketable style and make a living. Time, space and money constraints to some degree dictated the nature and direction of the workshops and classes at the Polly Street Art Centre - water-colour and terracotta rather than oils, bronze casting and wood carving. What to teach was also an issue. While the students worked from observation, according to European methods, and sound technical training was important, Skotnes encouraged individual vision, expression and style, steered clear of any prescriptiveness and was concerned about imposing too much, thereby "destroying something."[7]

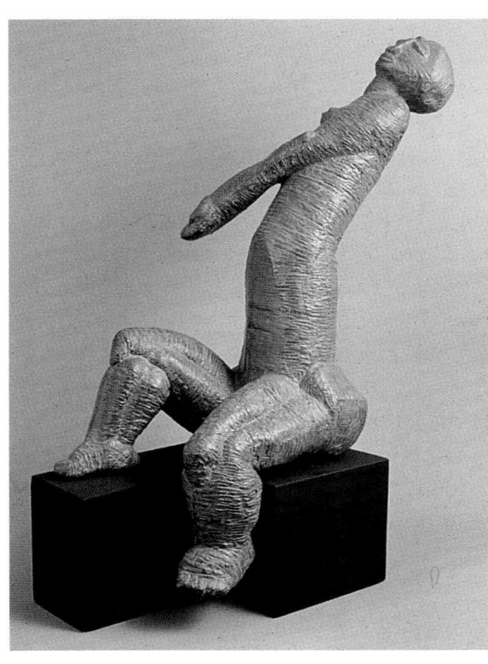

Sydney Kumalo (1935-1988), "Seated Woman," 1961
bronze, 56 cm.
©South African National Gallery

Something was being forged rather than destroyed - some of South Africa"s greatest black artistic talents, and two distinct approaches and styles. The prototype for what was later to be dubbed "Township Art" had been created by Gerard Sekoto prior to 1949. Now, at Polly Street, Ephraim Ngatane (19138-1971) and Durant Sihlali (1935-) used the medium of water-colour to reveal the realities and experiences of life in the mushrooming townships on the outskirts of Johannesburg and Pretoria. Benjamin Macala (1939-) and Leonard Matsoso (1950-) developed intensely expressionistic approaches to depicting myth and reality in their drawings. The second stream that emerged, and that for many characterise the production at Polly Street, was the influence of African art. At the time, the art of the continent was neither accessible nor valued in South Africa and the students had little or no knowledge of its material culture. Skotnes "discovered" African art in 1953 through Egon Guenther, a German jeweller and promoter of African art, who introduced him to the work of Willie Baumeister and Rudolf Scharpf, German artists who found their inspiration in the art of Africa. As an artist and teacher Skotnes started investigating and using a vocabulary that combined the figurative conventions of African sculpture with Cubist and Expressionist idioms. Sydney Kumalo (1935-1988), Ezrom Legae (1937-1999) and Lucas Sithole (1931-1994) developed distinctive interpretations of this synthesis of Africa and the West in their sculptures. Kumalo's bronze Seated woman (1964) reveals his characteristic stylisation of some physical features, while others are distorted and exaggerated. Sithole preferred wood and saw in broken trunks and branches analogies with life and with humanity, and with the spirits and the secrets of the African continent that he could capture and convey.

The policy of separate development was closing in on the city of Johannesburg, the West Rand Bantu Administration Board taking over control of the affairs of black people from the City Council. The people were being removed from the city, and in 1960 Polly Street was closed down and replaced by the Jubilee Centre, which also did not survive. Skotnes resigned in 1965 to focus on his own career as an artist. A few facilities were provided in the townships, for example the Mofolo Art Centre in Soweto and the Katlehong Art Centre and the need for a place of activity and debate in the city was to some extent fulfilled by the independent cultural venue, Dorkay House. In a country where people were being moved and separated by force, the Polly Street Art Centre had built bridges that would link and sustain communication and exchange for a long time to come.

7 Skotnes interviewed by Lucy Alexander and Sack, April 1988 and cited by Sack (1988: 11).

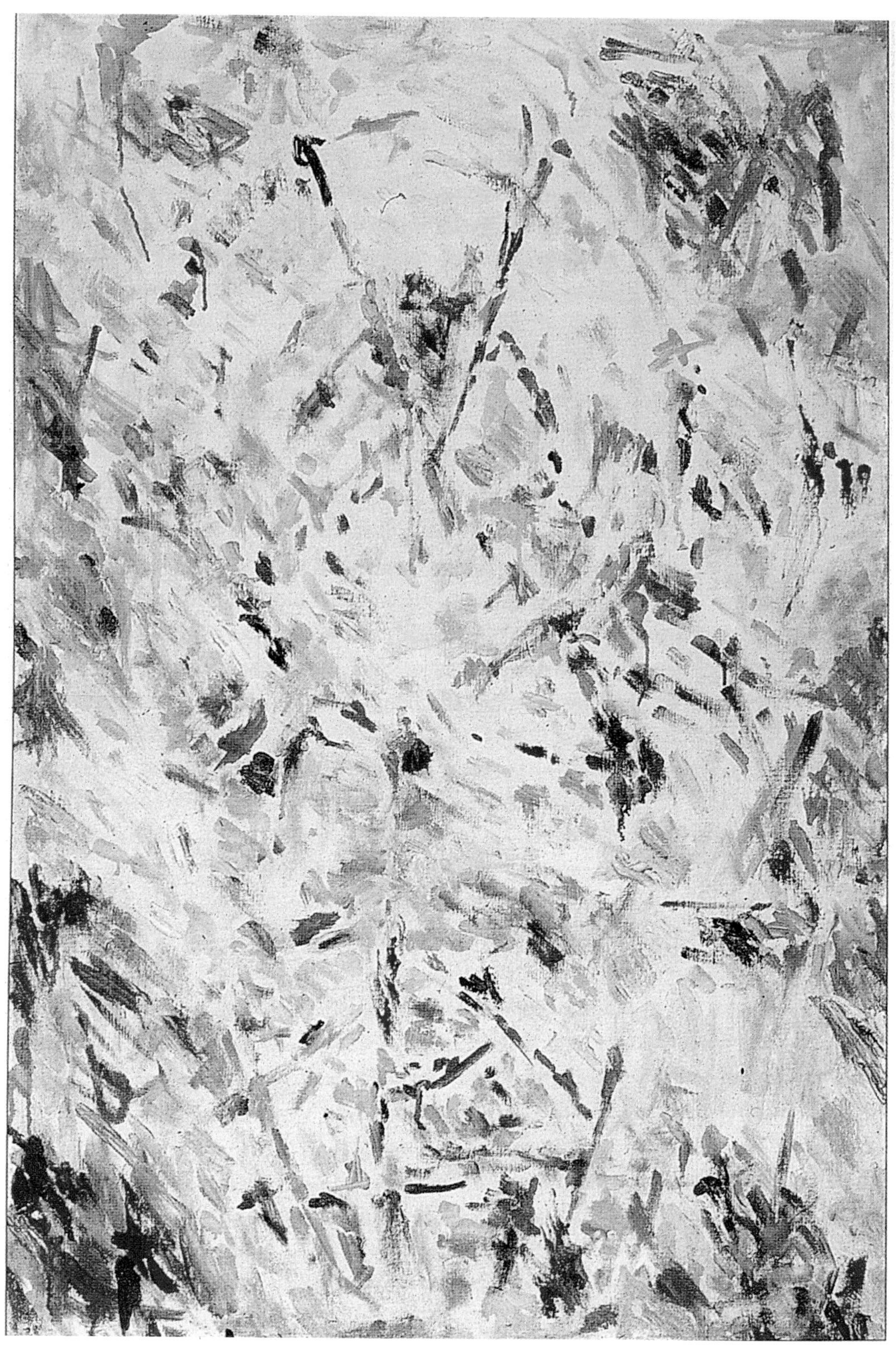

Irma Stern (1894-1966), "The golden shawl," 1945
oil on canvas, 65,5x56 cm.

facing page: **In the spirit of Kamba Luesa, RDC** ©D.R.

Rebirth and identities

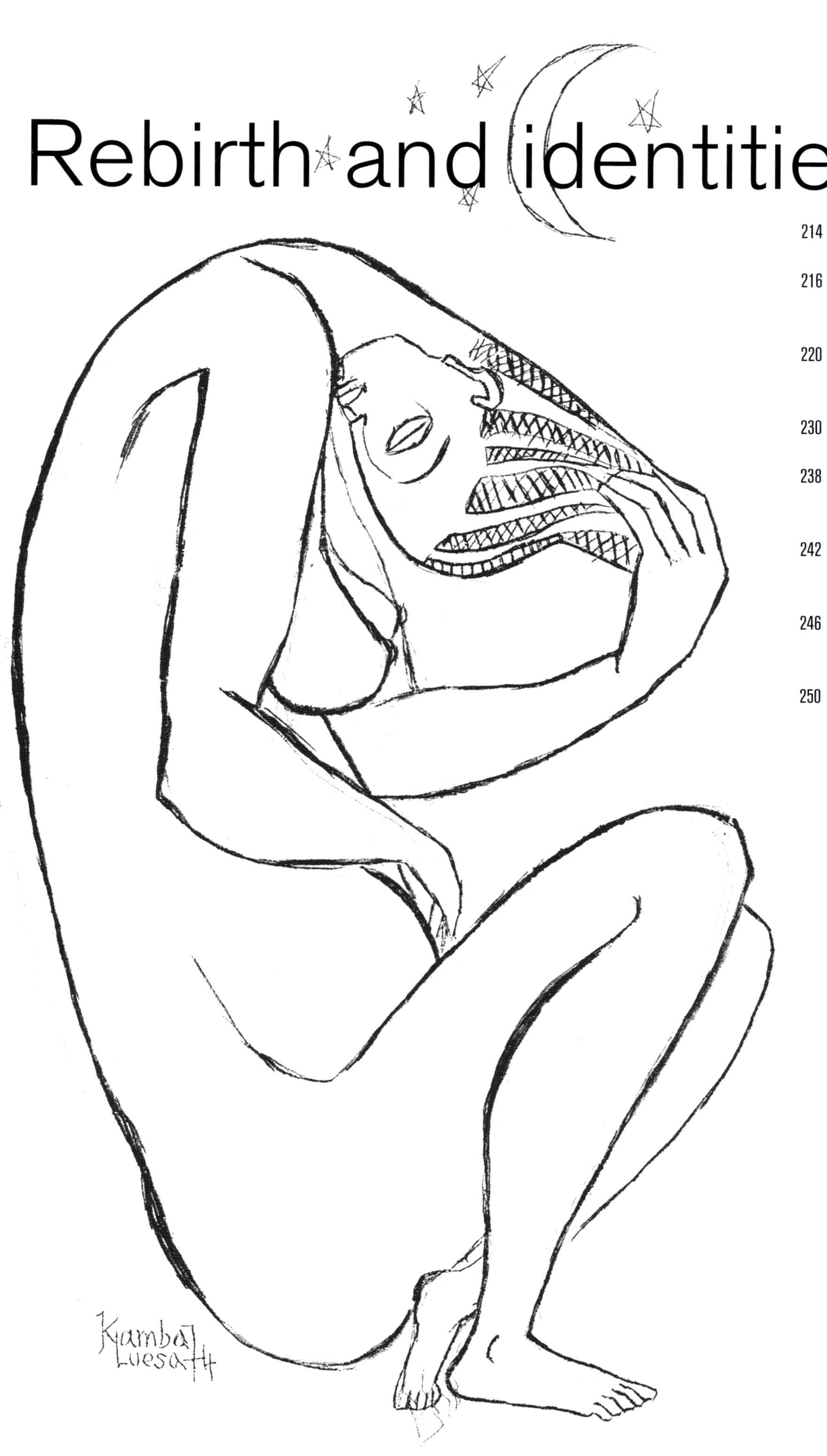

THE DAYDREAM OF A NEW AFRICA

Jean Loup Pivin

During the wave of independence movements in the 1960s, when the affirmation of differences in heritage and a return to cultural sources were strongly asserted in all discussions on esthetics relating to heritage, the desire for modernity appeared in every field: clothing, architecture and social behaviors. Set against a backdrop of rumba or the African twist, stovepipe pants or the mini-skirt, a Jimmy-Hendrix-type afro or hair puffed out in a smooth, teased and sprayed bun, the liberated Africa of the 1960s sang about its attachment to the world and its era. The new man, now free to enter the modern age and benefit from the world's riches, regardless of where they originated, prevailed over ancient man and his traditions. The discourse on slave and colonial plundering was focused more on preventing people from making their own way towards modernity, rather than on the need to return to societies of old. The promotion of Black culture and African identity, the pause sign of which would be the First International Festival of Black Arts, was in line with its time: the heritage was there to be reinvented. Universal thought advocated at this time felt that Western scientific and technological discoveries had been acquired and that it was up to Africa to make its contemporary contribution.

Kamba Luesa (1944-1995), "Silhouette," DRC, 1974
mixed media on paper, 51 x 30 cm
©Antoine Calmette-L. Albaret

Each Republic's government had a duty to be modern while maintaining its attachment to tradition. However, more concrete and glass buildings were built based on international models than museums. Apart from reviving the museum-type structures left behind by the colonizers, no new project saw the light of day during the first two decades following independence. There were no new collecting campaigns other than the Niamey eco-museum. There was even, in a few exceptional cases, institutionalized plundering, such as in the Guinea of Sékou Touré. A new state could not be both invented, often based on a totally artificial carving of borders, without true cultural unity. and have the cultural and heritage identities of each of the civilizations that comprise the new country defended without upsetting the new national units. For Houphouët-Boigny, the cause was clear: no action during the thirty years of his rule against the symbol of the national museum. All of the national riches were devoted to creating the image of a modern country. No political risk was taken that could awaken identity-related movements. The national unity of the State was based on its future and not its past. Almost no country escaped this mistrust of heritage, regardless of the discourse used. In socialist countries, the new states formed new men. All traces of the past had to be incidental and disappear. This was the case during the early days of the rule of Kérékou in Benin, in the late 1970s. He destroyed, using spectacular means, a few Voodoo temples (the resistance of the populations put an immediate stop to this initiative). The modern State, the new country, the new man, from liberal or socialist countries – all on the geopolitical chessboard of the great powers – was the only claim initially widely shared by the populations.
Socialist experiences, which were too unlike the traditional structures, all crumbled and gave way to fairly flexible liberalism with traditional powers. The head of State became the monarch and had his princely vassals. The State was a monarchy wearing a republican mask, in which the different populations that comprised each country finally found their way. Knowing that the mostly poor modern States had only little to offer their populations, enthusiasm quickly turned to mistrust or fear, as was the case during the colonial times or, further back, as in the times of the pre-colonial kingdoms and empires.

In this greatly ambiguous context, while the esthetics were inspired by tradition, although sometimes rejected by Professor Blanc, they did not delve beyond the sacred field of Western art. Regardless of the inspiration, this art was intended for galleries, the homes of the new bourgeois, the foreign market, and even ordered by the public, as can be seen on a larger scale in Senegal and the former Zaire. There is no disputing the function of art in society and its connection with traditional functions. Sometimes a sculptor would be taken out of traditional production and introduced into contemporary production, but things would never go any further. And this was the major problem of the new African man.

In socialist countries, art had to become social and useful to society. In Mali, artists had to contribute to the large-scale sanitation battles, and to moral and political messages. Art for art's sake was opposed, but individual talent was recognized. Students were sent to Eastern countries, to Cuba and to the Soviet Union, in order to better prepare themselves to adapt the academism taught in the local context. Sometimes professors from friendly countries went to teach in Africa. The arrival on the Black continent of a certain number of Caribbean, and particularly Haitian intellectuals and artists, who were convinced that Africa was experiencing the inspiring independence that Haiti had experienced over a century and a half prior, was a marginal, yet symbolic phenomenon of the early 1960s. Sometimes, after having passed through Moscow, the Caribbean natives who had settled in Africa played an important role. The Black Caribbean Group from Ivory Coast was more formal and its influence was felt until the end of the century. As in politics and popular cultural movements, artistic movements fully espoused the new functions of art, and material and architectural heritage was banished and sometimes even physically abandoned. Some have even dared to assert, while the discourse on African identity flourished through the entire continent, that the African cultural revolution was more harmful to its material heritage than Mao's Chinese Cultural Revolution because it allowed cultural plundering to intensify and permitted traditional architectures to crumble or be crushed under the double action of demographic explosion and the desire to belong to the world and its "international" forms.

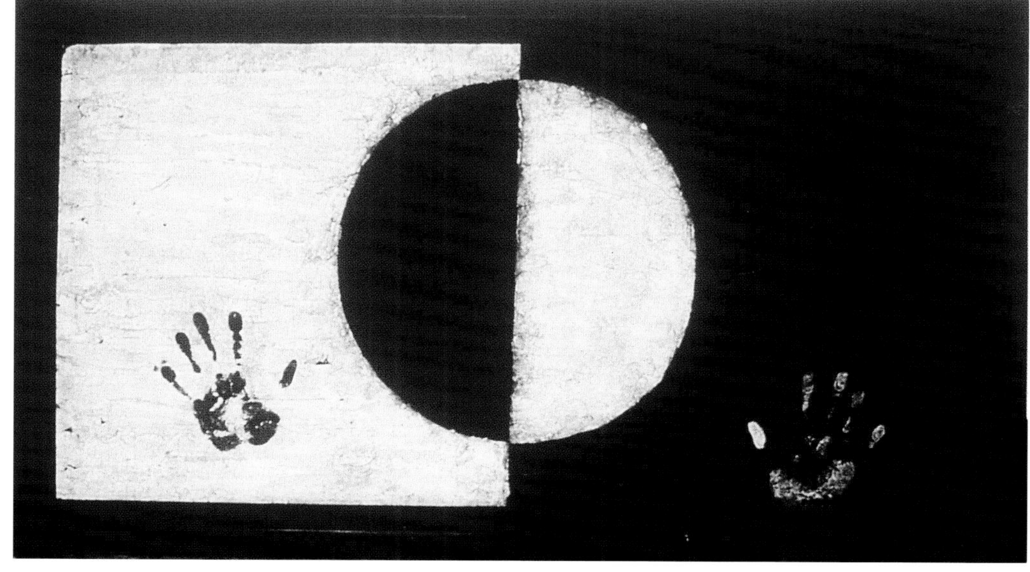

Erhabor Emokpae (1934-1984),
"The battle between Life and Death," Nigeria, 1962
oil on panel, 61 x 122 cm ©D.R.

THE INDEPENDENCE MOVEMENTS: A BIRTH MORE THAN A REBIRTH

Elikia M'Bokolo

The African independence era was both long and short. It was long because, from a strictly historical point of view, in extreme cases, it took fifty years. The beginnings can actually be placed in the mid-1930s, with the exemplary battle of the Negus Haïlé Sélassié and the Ethiopian people against the invasion of fascist Italy (1935-1941). It is known that the Negus, who became a genuine living myth, would play an important role in the surge of independence movements and in the continent's first attempts at unification, which led to the creation of the OAU (Organization of African Unity) twenty years later (1963). As for the liberation process, it was only completed in the last quarter of the 20th century, with the independence of the Portuguese colonies (1974-1975), followed by the independence of Zimbabwe (1980) and of Namibia (1990). Many people feel that, although South Africa proclaimed itself a Republic in 1961, it was only the liberation of Nelson Mandela (1990) and the dismantling of apartheid that finally put an end to the pernicious effects of an ancient colonization led by the Dutch in the 17th century and extended by the British into the 19th century.

However, in the minds of Africans, decolonization was a very short process, as is the case in heroic and founding times. It occurred in 1960, *annus mirabilis* par excellence, and during the years surrounding it: 1957, the independence of Ghana, the first country in Black Africa to regain its sovereignty; 1958, the independence of Guinea, acquired when, alone among the French colonies, Guinea voted "no" to the referendum in which General de Gaulle proposed a "Community" format; 1961, the independence of Tanganyika, followed by the independence of Rwanda, Burundi and Uganda (1962), Kenya (1963) and Zambia (1964). However, the reason everyone focuses on 1960 is because this was the year when seventeen African countries acquired international sovereignty all at once: the colonies of French Equatorial Africa and of French West Africa, plus Cameroon, Nigeria, Togo and Belgian Congo (DRC).

This was the time when, in a relatively spontaneous move, choirs of women celebrated Kwame Nkrumah in Ghana and Ahmed Sékou Touré in Guinea, where the South African singer Myriam Makeba sang to the entire world the praises of "Uhuru" (Freedom), and when the Congolese national Joseph Kabasele made all of Africa dance to the rhythm of his unforgettable "Independence Cha Cha." The perspective of a glorious future and the legitimate pride of having defeated the colonizers were thus being celebrated. African independence was truly obtained because Africans wanted it and because they put everything in motion to achieve it. Very few colonizers, if any, saw this solution at this time. At the end of the Second World War, the English were anticipating at least 30 years to emancipate the Gold Coast (Ghana), their "most advanced" colony, and much longer for the other territories. At the Brazzaville Conference, held in 1944, General de Gaulle and the free French pushed aside any idea of independence and even of self-government for the African territories, and it was only around 1956-1958 that they resigned themselves. Finally, the Belgians were shocked, in 1956, by the boldness of Jef Van Bilsen, in their opinion an inspired teacher, because he proposed a 30-year plan to decolonize the Congo. It was actually the determination of the Africans that triumphed over the colonizers' opposition to change.

For Africa, independence was a birth rather than a rebirth. Everything actually changed and had to be rebuilt. Apparently nothing, or almost nothing, remained of the former Africa. The independence movements initially devised a new political geography, a geography that was not conceived or desired by the Africans, because it was developed from the diplomatic calculations of the European States, from their conflicts and from the arrangements concluded between them following the Berlin Conference (1884-1885). Throughout the 1950s and 1960s, one of the main debates among African political elites and intellectuals focused on maintaining or dismantling colonial borders, which, in the end, were kept as they were.

Adept at "dividing to rule," certain colonial officers devised projects intended to set future independent African States on the road to division. In the case of France, the Defferre framework law, passed in 1956, established each of the French West Africa and French Equatorial Africa territories as an autonomous unit, intended to become a sovereign State, whereas the centralizing structures of the two federations constituted a good base for the grouping together of African States. Similarly, certain Belgian colonizers thought to break up Congo and, in particular, to separate from it the rich province of Katanga, a producer of copper and strategic metals. On the other hand, the only time the colonizers promoted a federal idea was in order to block the African emancipation movement. This was how the English instituted, in 1953, the Central African Federation, which grouped together Southern Rhodesia (Zimbabwe), Northern Rhodesia (Zambia) and Nyassaland (Malawi). The goal was quite clearly to give power, within this vast space, to the European colonists of Rhodesia, known for their racism and their admiration of the apartheid system. It was only in 1961 that the public service was equally accessible to all "races" of the Federation. We should not forget that several African leaders became part of this divisionary strategy, refusing, as stated by Félix Houphouët-Boigny, to see their country "become the cash cow" of the large federal groups.

However, in all parts of the continent, the loudest voices were opposed to this "balkanization." Kwame Nkrumah, who had become the Prime Minister of Ghana, had campaigned for the pan-African cause in the United States of America and in England, and became the champion of active solidarity among the nationalist parties. This was a first step towards the actual unification of the continent. The "Congress of All African Peoples," held in Accra in December 1958, accelerated the emancipation movement throughout the continent. Almost simultaneously, in the more restricted framework of the French colonies, the African Regrouping Congress, held in Cotonou in September 1958, defended the principles of federalism, in particular through Léopold Sédar Senghor. From the time of his return from Accra in December 1958 until his assassination in January 1961, Patrice Lumumba defended the integrity of Congo and pan-Africanism with the same vigor. It was also with this spirit that Julius Nyerere of Tanganyika attempted to show that, in his own words, "African nationalism has no meaning and may even become dangerous if it does not follow the ideals of pan-Africanism."

Across the continent, what emerged from these debates was a sort of compromise. The large federations – F.E.A., F.W.A. and the Central African Federation – ruptured, but the more extensive colonies, such as Nigeria and Congo (Kinshasa), where risks of "balkanization" existed, were able to maintain their integrity. The battle to come was, thus, to group together the former colonies, which had become sovereign States.

This problem of territoriality covered another issue: identity. This problem occurred because the colonial territories had been carved out using a straight line, without any consideration for their content or long-term viability. African leaders therefore had in their hands a heritage that was poisoned both on the human and on the economic level. Their entirely extroverted economies were aimed at fulfilling the needs of the colonizing countries in raw materials. The former merchant networks and relays that included African economic spaces had been abolished or were seriously weakened. On the human level, apart from a very small number of countries, such as Burundi, Botswana, Rwanda or Swaziland, none of the new States corresponded to a former, pre-colonial political unit, where inhabitants would become assimilated and learn to live together. All of the colonial borders cut into the living flesh of peoples having a relative cultural kinship in the same way that they dismantled constituted States elsewhere. Thus, for example, the colonizers transferred to Africa the principle, used in Europe, based on which rivers constitute ideal borders. However, this principle became absurd in Africa where rivers have always been places of passage, life spaces, supports of civilization rather than boundaries. Similarly, constituted States were often mercilessly torn apart when sovereigns committed acts of resistance against the colonizers. The colonizers replaced fluid traditional relationships between individuals and groups with a rigidity laden with consequences. In colonial taxonomy, tribal and ethnic nomenclatures are charged with conflicts between peoples that colonial power and so-called scientific discourse of ethnography has organized into a hierarchy and declared relentlessly different, and fatally confined to recurring secular wars. Was colonization not justified by, among other things, the need to put an end to these conflicts?

With the voluntarism that characterized all of his options, Kwame Nkrumah had founded a principle shared by all freedom fighters of his generation: "Take the political kingdom and the rest will follow." The heads of the new States quickly realized that nothing "follows." After the battle remained the task of building. For everyone, the urgency lay in building a national identity while upholding the memory of past battles and victories, shaping a common philosophy and counteracting vague separatist desires related to tribalism and regionalism. This is why, throughout Africa, culture – that irreplaceable glue that brings and binds peoples together – was constantly at the center of the discussions, concerns and practices of the States and its citizens.

facing page:
Iba N'Diaye (born in 1928), "Choir Child," Senegal, 1965
oil on wood, 79,5x180 cm.

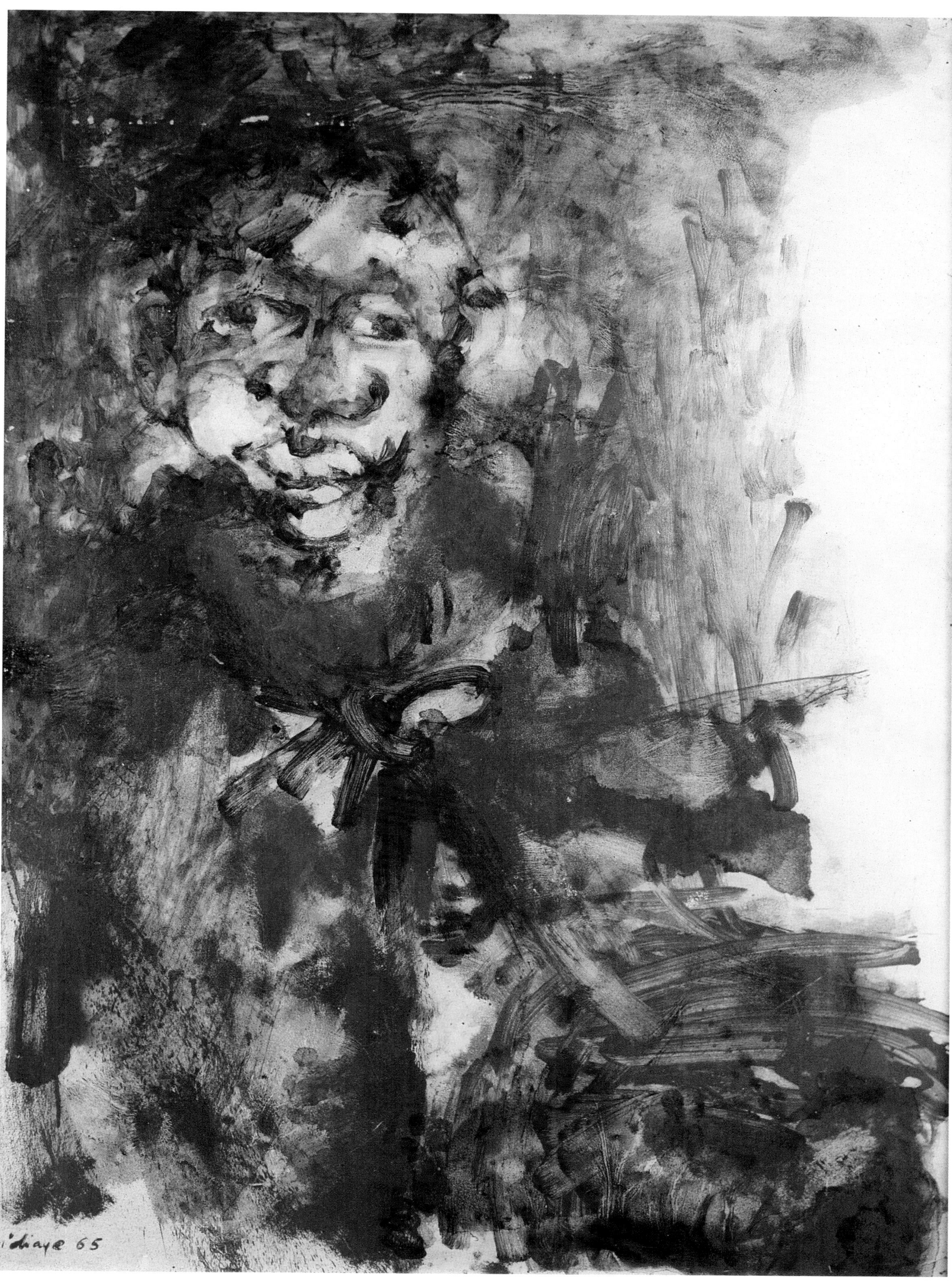

The 1st International Festival of Black Arts Dakar, Senegal, 1966

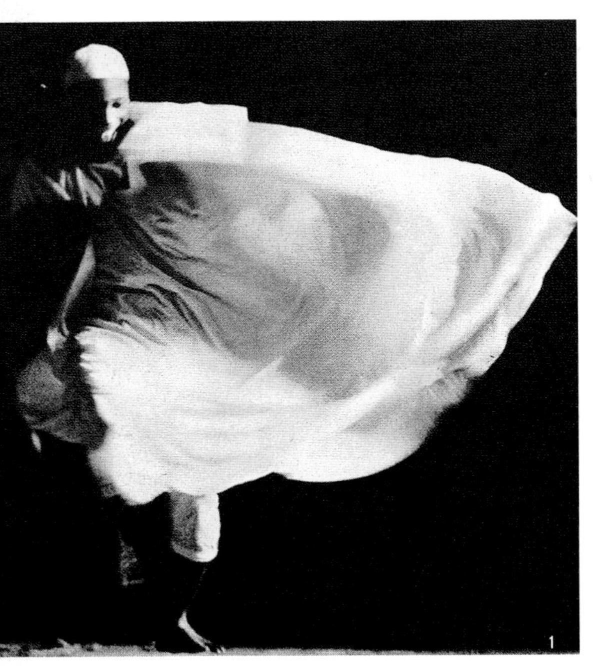
1

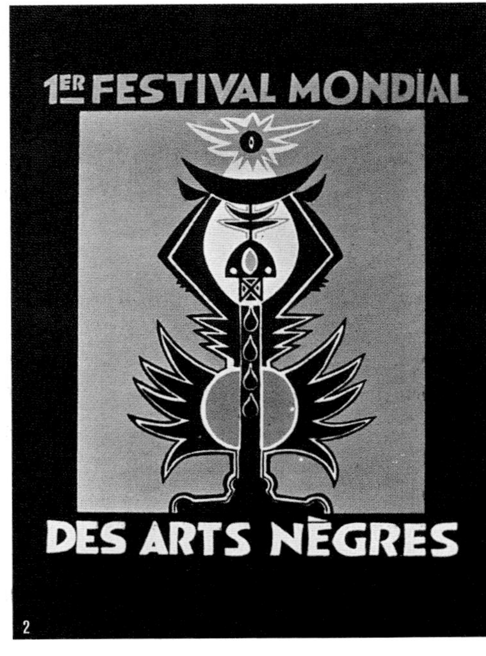

2

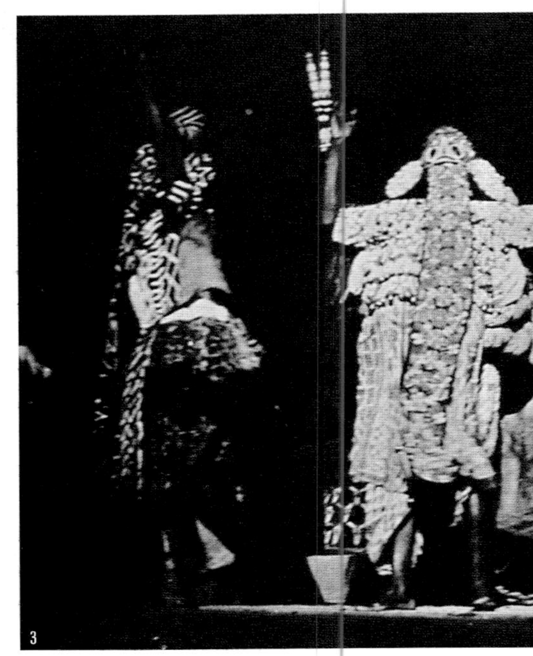
3

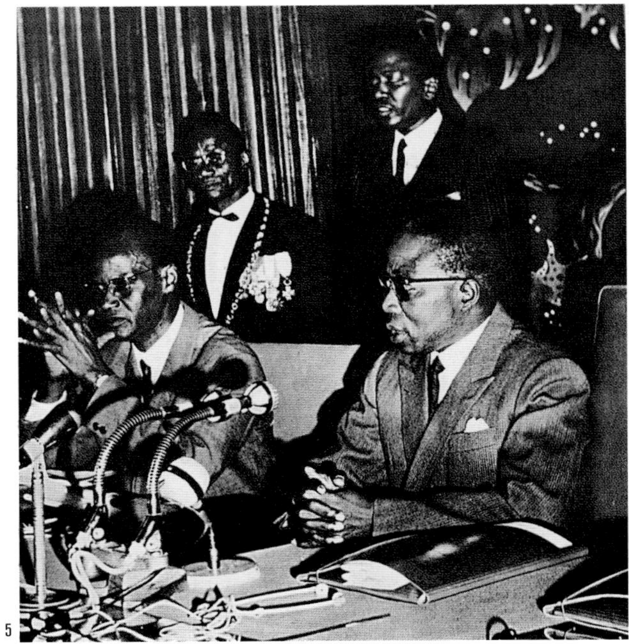
5

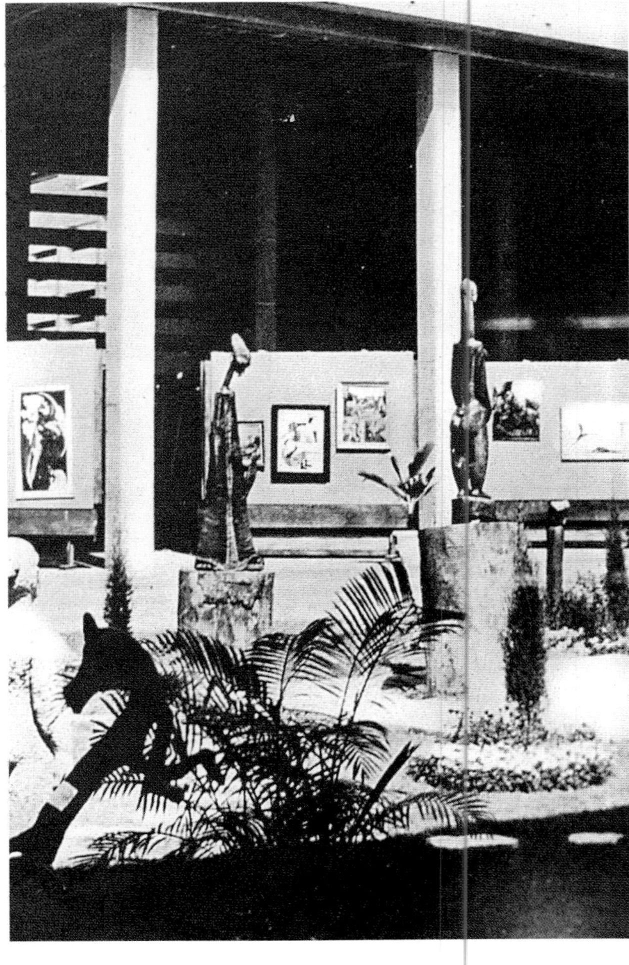

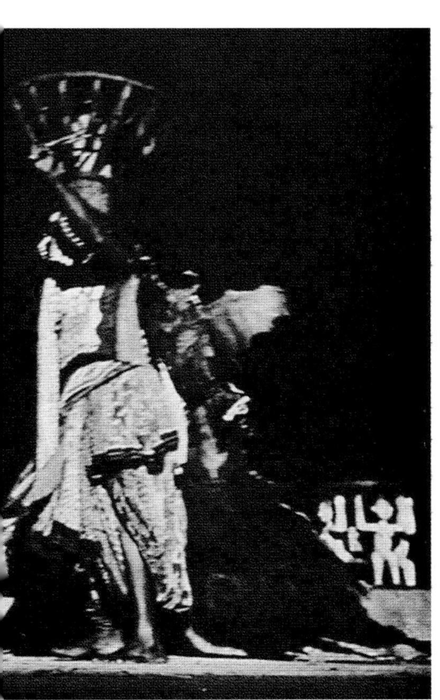

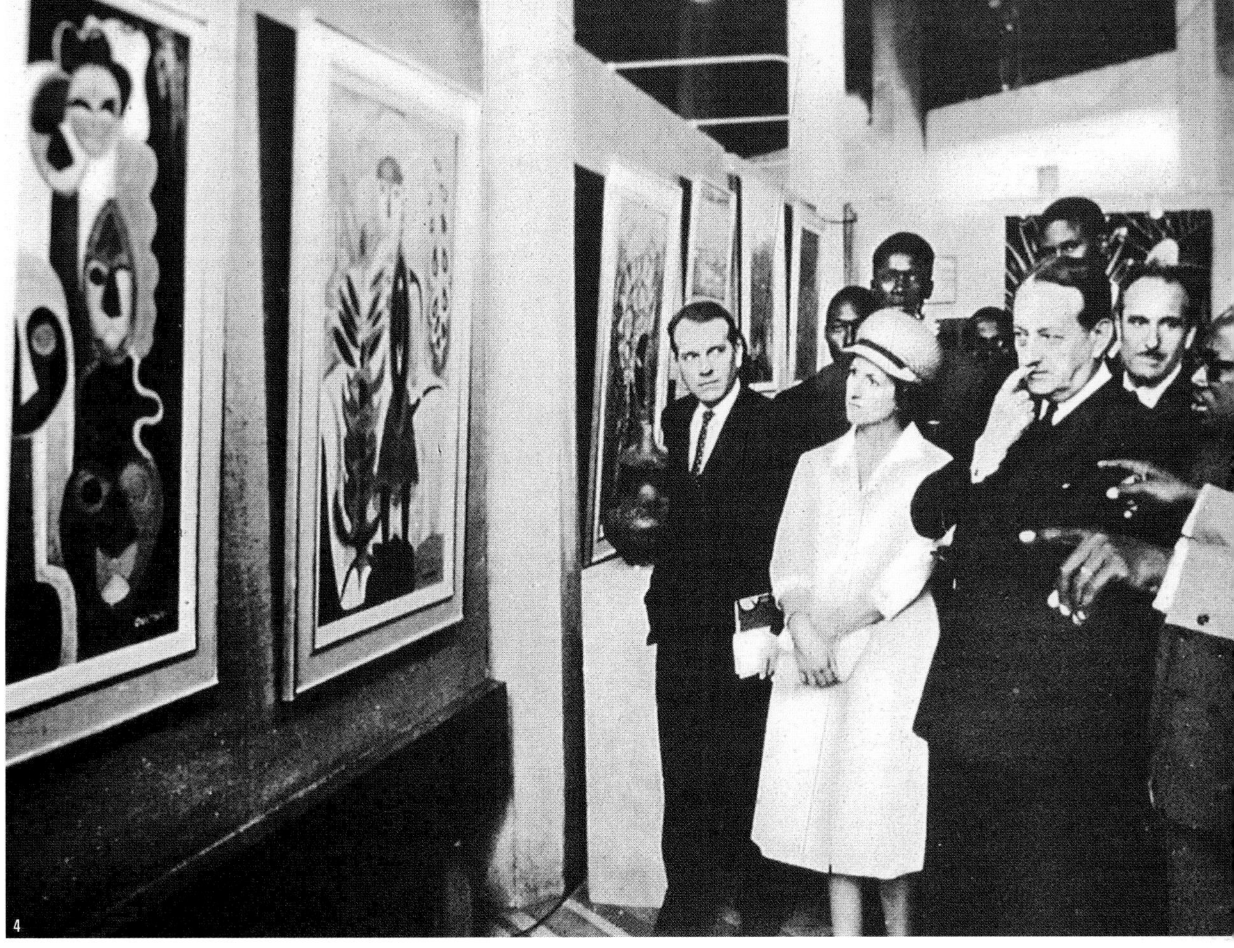

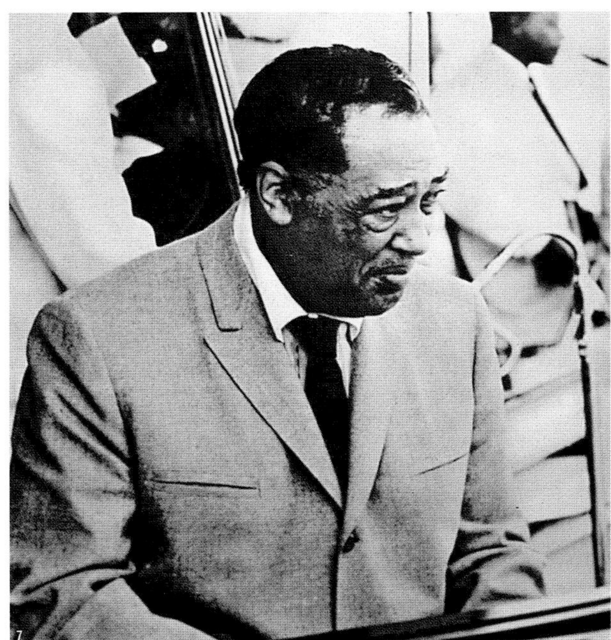

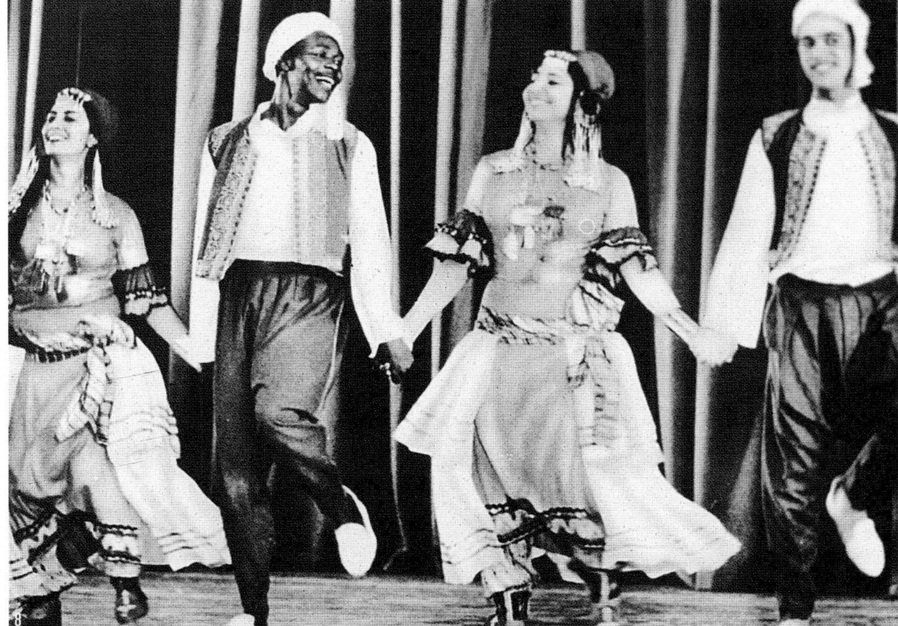

1. Dancer with the Mali National Troop ©Studio Renaudeau
2. Festival poster
3. The Cameroon troop ©Service Info Sénégal
4. from right to left: painter Iba N'Diaye, President L.S. Senghor, André Malraux, Mrs. Senghor, Pierre Lods, and Abdou Diouf (behind Malraux) ©Dakar Matin
5. President Léopold Sédar Senghor and Alioune Diop at the festival inauguration ©Dakar Matin
6. "Trends and Confrontations" exhibit ©Studio Renaudeau
7. Duke Ellington and his orchestra in concert at the Dakar stadium ©Studio Renaudeau
8. Troop of the United Arab Republic ©Studio Renaudeau

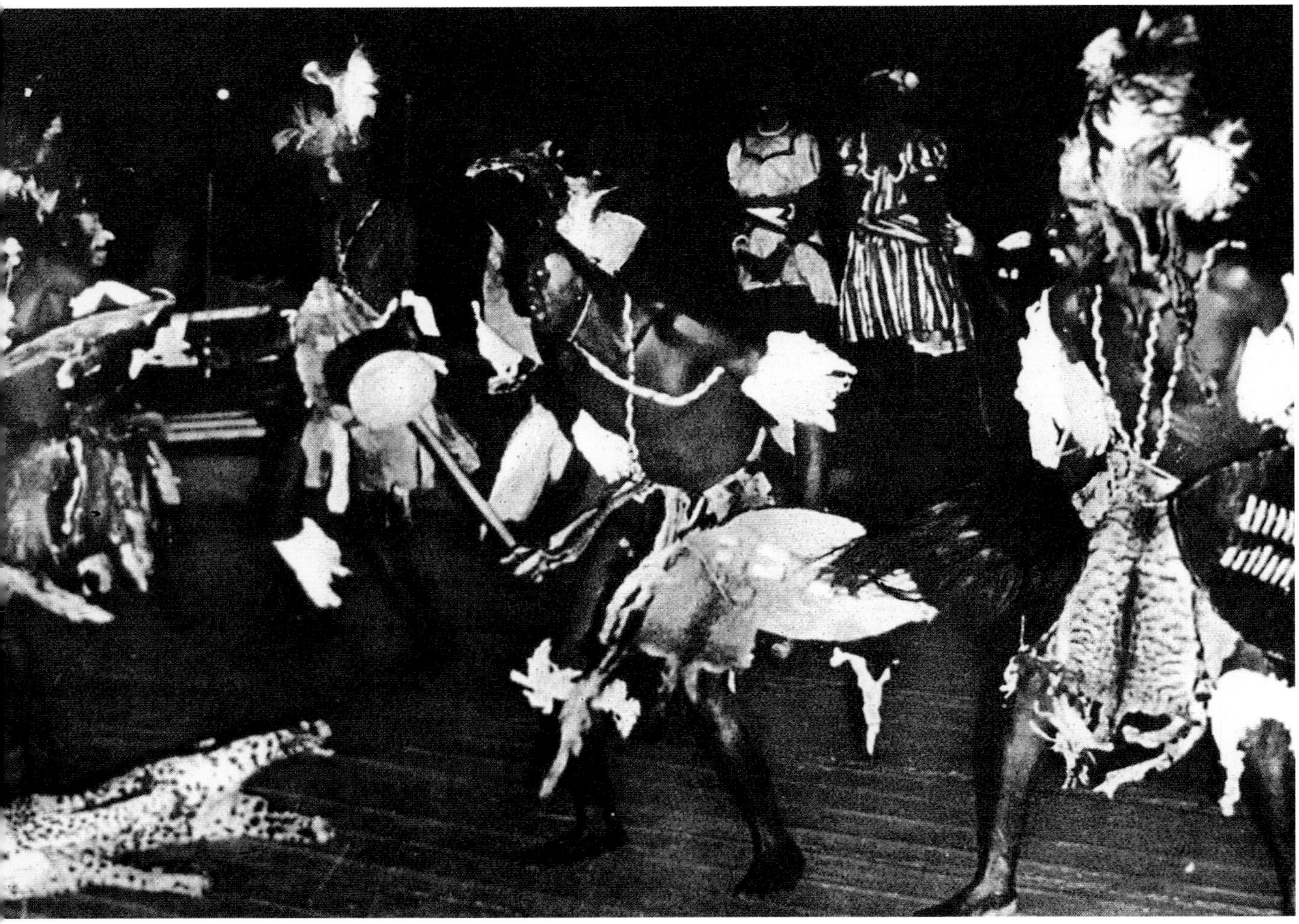

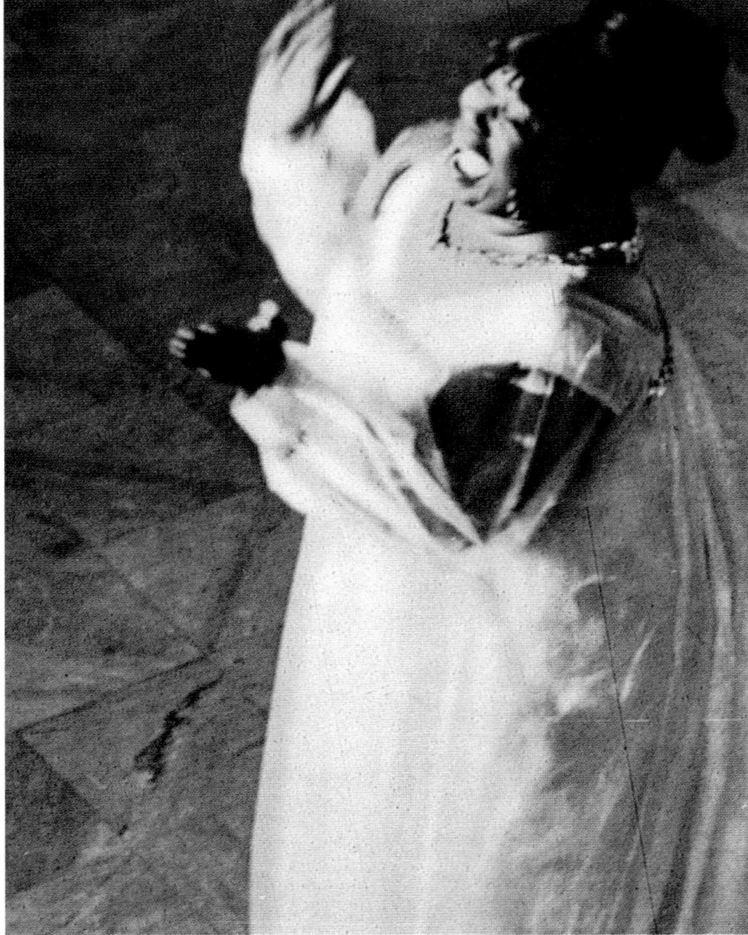

above:
The Zambia Troop ©Service Info Sénégal

left:
The recital of Marion Williams in the Dakar cathedral
©Sauvageot

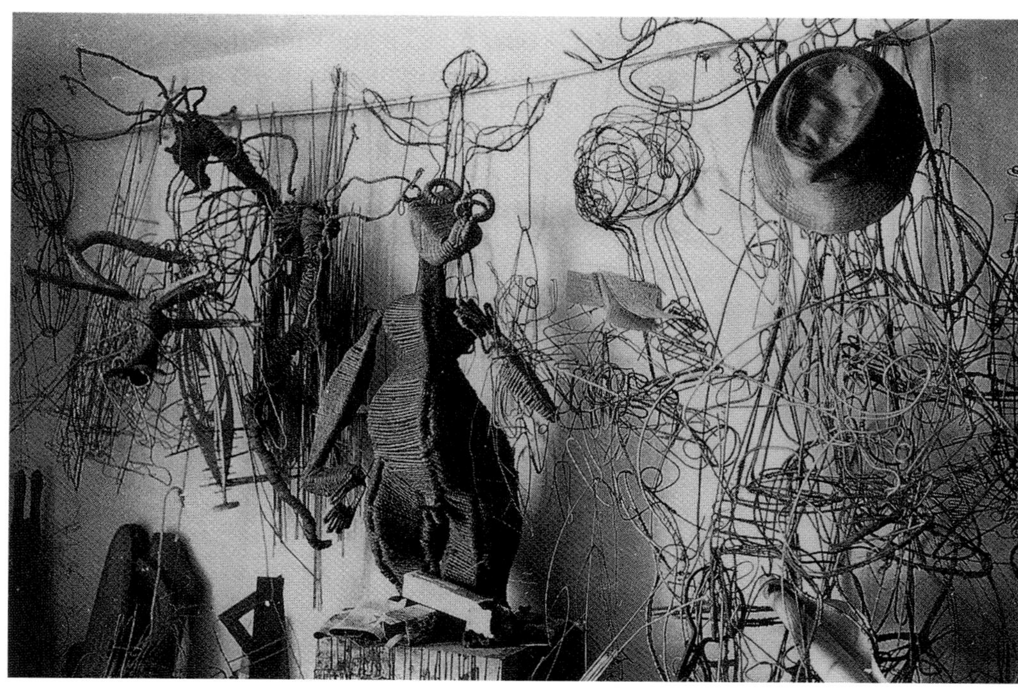

Christian Lattier

(1925-1978)

Christian Lattier was born in Ivory Coast in 1925. He graduated from the École des Beaux-Arts of St-Étienne and of Paris. In 1953, he discovered iron wire and twine. "I presented works using twine because I wanted to develop a sort of evolution." Upon his return to Ivory Coast in 1962, he became a teacher at the École des Beaux-Arts of Abidjan while continuing his research into plastic. "If I had worked with wood, I would have been accused of copying my ancestors. If I had carved stone, I would have been shunned for copying the white man. So, I had to find something new."[1] Lattier produced amazing sculptures using rope and iron, with the rope-work concealing the underlying iron frames. In this way he created monumental works using religious and historical themes, representations of masks, animal sculptures or characters and humorous figures. Some of his works include: "Mask," "The Three Ages of Ivory Coast" and the famous "Panther in Cord," which earned him the Jury Grand Prize at the First Festival of Black Arts in Dakar in 1966. Christian Lattier died in Abidjan in 1978.

1 Yacouba Konaté "Christian Lattier: le sculpteur aux mains nues," Ed. Sepia, 1993.

The workshop of Christian Lattier, Abidjan, Ivory Coast, in 1978
©Renaudeau/UNESCO

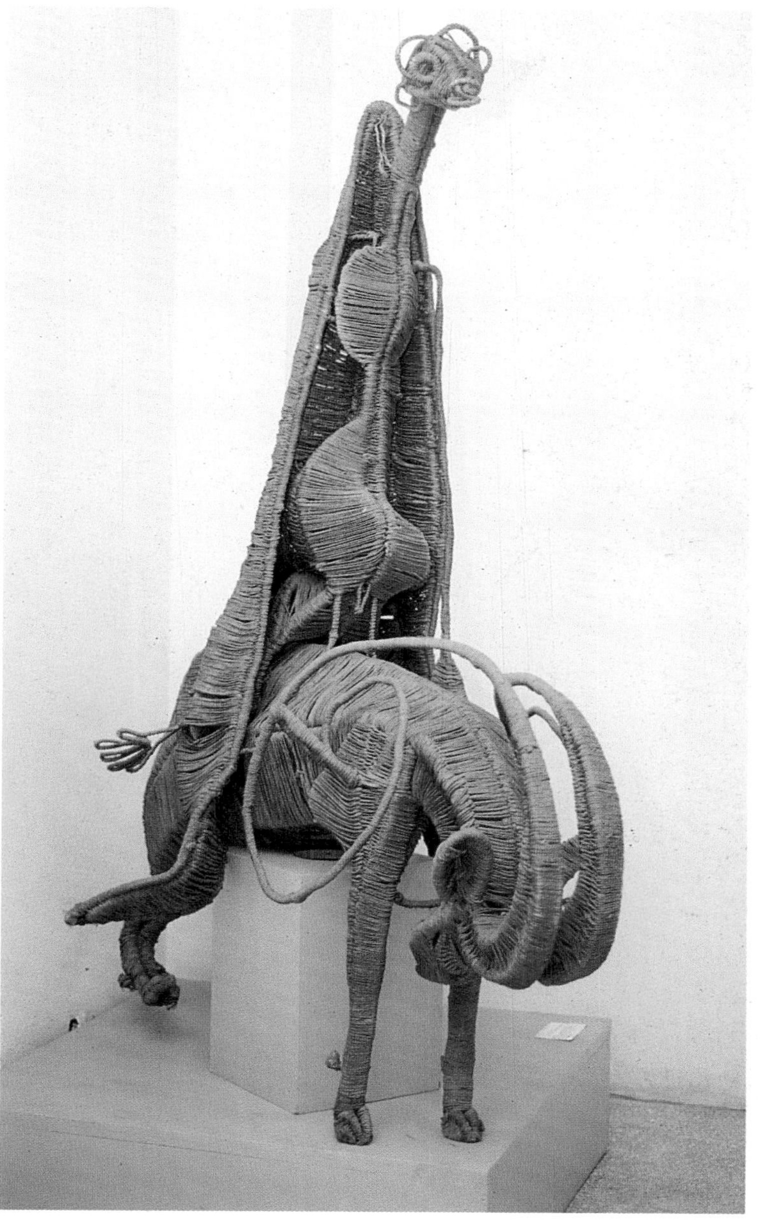

right:
"The Ram," 1965
©D.R.

THE FIRST INTERNATIONAL FESTIVAL OF BLACK ARTS

Ousmane Sow Huchard

"That we answer present
at the rebirth of the world.
Like the sourdough needed
for white flour.
For who will teach rhythm
to the defunct world of machines
and canons?"
Léopold Sédar Senghor

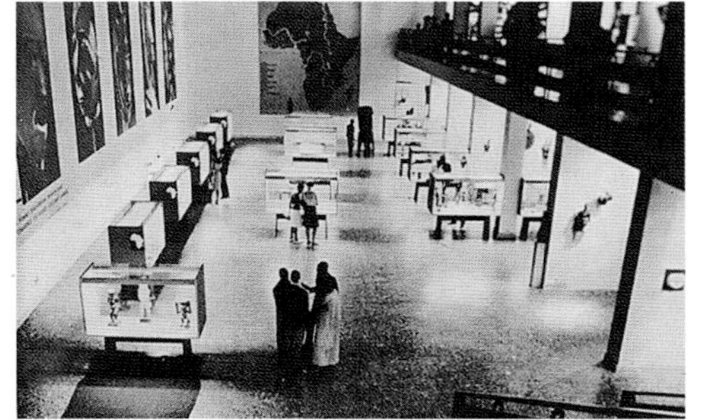

The Black Arts exhibit at the Musée Dynamique ©Dakar Matin

For poet-President Léopold Sédar Senghor, Senegal, by agreeing to organize the First International Festival of Black Arts, was taking on tremendous and heavy responsibilities before all of the members of the Black World, in the period following the accession of most African countries to international sovereignty. During the inaugural ceremony of the Estates General of Negritude on March 31, 1966 in Dakar, André Malraux, the French Minister of Cultural Affairs, honored the boldness of the African Cultural Society, which grouped together the originators of the event: "Here we are, making History..." he said in an almost theatrical lyrical flight of fancy. "For the first time, a head of State is taking into his perishable hands the spiritual destiny of a continent."

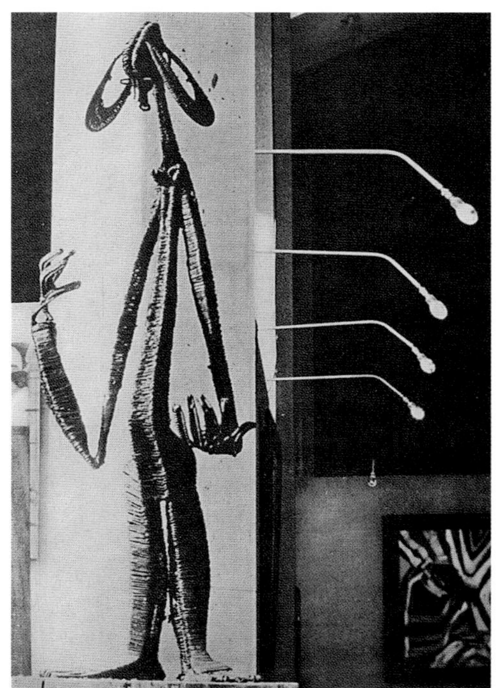

A sculpture by Christian Lattier at the "Trends and Confrontations" exhibit at the 1st International Festival of Black Arts
©Dakar Matin

Were the Senegalese people, through the diversity of their ethnic and social-professional components, truly conscious of the issues at stake in their country? This question, which continuously haunted this poet and President from the initial planning of the event, drove him to undertake an educational exercise to share, with his compatriots and close friends and family members, his concerns some ten days prior to the start of the event by broadcasting a message over the airwaves on March 19, 1966: *"What is, first and foremost, the meaning of the First International Festival of Black Arts? In order to properly answer this question, one must first be aware of this fact being developed, before our very eyes, by us and despite us, by a civilization that embraces all continents, all races, and all peoples of the Earth. The progress of science, the development of methods of transportation and information (today he would probably say "of communication"), the exchanges of people, goods and ensuing ideas have resulted, in this second half of the 20th century, in the fact that people are no longer strangers. We are thrown together. This leads to the imperialistic greed of some and the resistance of others, and to tensions and conflicts. However, despite the hatred and wars, we must enter into talks, negotiate and organize together, among people, our region, our continent and our planet Earth. Therefore, by us and despite us, a Universal Civilization has been developing since the start of the 20th century, in which each continent, each race and each people make a positive contribution.*
Negritude is all of the values of civilization specific to the Black world, which must enter, and which have been entering, for the past sixty years, as components, as fertile elements into the Universal Civilization. The purpose of the First International Festival of Black Arts is, quite specifically, to show, with the riches of traditional Black art, the participation of Negritude in Universal Civilization."

Various reference objects of Black African civilizations have been questioned and interpreted in other contexts. At the beginning of the 20th century, these questions had more serious implications on the esthetic level upon encountering Black art and European artists of the time. These artists, who established the new direction of Western art, never turned their backs on the fertile dialogue they had had with these Black art objects. Henri Matisse (1869-1954), a Fauvist who flirted with Cubism, clearly emphasizes this:
"*I often visited Gertrude Stein at rue de Fleurus. On my way, I would always walk past an antique shop. One day, I noticed a small wood-sculpted Negro head in the shop window. It reminded me of the huge red porphyry heads in the Egyptian collections at the Louvre. I got the impression that the methods for writing forms were the same in the two civilizations, even though they were quite foreign to each other. I therefore bought this head for a few francs and took it to Gertrude Stein's home. Picasso was there and he was quite impressed. We spoke about it for a long while and this*

was how we all became interested in Black art. An interest that we more or less expressed in our paintings… It was a time for new acquisitions. Since we were still somewhat unfamiliar with ourselves, we did not feel the need to protect ourselves from foreign influences, because they could only enrich us and make us more demanding vis-à-vis our own methods of expression. Fauvism, the glorification of color, the precision of drawing due to Cubism, visits to the Louvre and exotic influences through the ethnographic museum at the old Trocadero, are all things that shaped the landscape in which we lived and traveled, and from which we have all come. It was a time of artistic cosmogony."[1]

It was from this time that Black art, with its legendary, even original modernity, forced the hand of Western modernity and contributed to the development of "universal modernity," on which was based the dialogue of the civilizations that progressively advocated humanists from all walks of life, gathered on the banks of the Seine, after World War II.

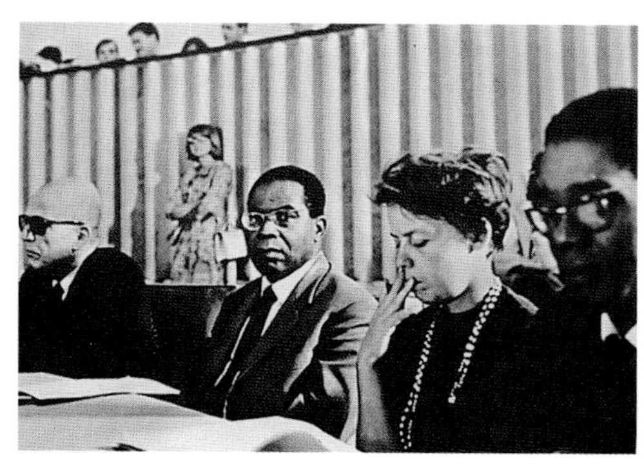

from left to right:
Michel Leiris, Aimé Césaire, Geneviève Galame-Griaule, M. Obama
©Studio Bracher

The creation of African Presence by Alioune Diop and his circle of friends in Paris in 1947, and the birth of the African Cultural Society at the same time, was a decisive turning point in the mobilization of Black and European intellectuals in a great humanist undertaking to redeem Black civilizations. Therefore, following the invention of the word "Negritude" by Aimé Césaire in his "Cahiers du retour au pays natal" in 1939, the word "Negro" (which comes from the Latin word niger, meaning black) also had to be redeemed. This task had already been begun in 1929 by Dr. Jean Price-Mars, the Haitian author of "Ainsi parla l'oncle," in order to present this term to all the Black people of the world as a term of nobility and to exorcise it of all of the soiled verbal connotations given to it since the slavery era, while keeping in mind the psychological block that persisted among Anglophone Blacks in relation to the use of this word.

The 1st Congress of Black Writers and Artists organized at the Sorbonne by African Presence in 1959 was the first step in this great mobilization. How else can one interpret Picasso's spontaneous gesture of drawing and offering the poster for this major gathering to the African Cultural Society than as an expression of a firm commitment behind a noble idea and as a significant way, in the eyes of the entire world, to positively respond to the call of Black humanists and to give a symbolic presence to this historic event.

In December 1959, the Executive Council of the Franco-African Community met in St-Louis, Senegal under the effective presidency of General de Gaulle. This Community helped to accelerate the accession to independence, in 1960, of most of the countries of French-speaking Africa. The idea to have a large gathering of artists and intellectuals from the Black world, together with their works, which was developed during the 1st Congress at the Sorbonne in 1959, actually took form when Léopold Sédar Senghor, after becoming the President of the Republic of Senegal, offered his country's capital city to host the event in the form of an International Festival of Black Arts.

The organization of this First International Festival of Black Arts was then given to an Association created in 1963 and presided over by Alioune Diop, with Aimé Césaire and Jean Mazel acting as Vice-President and Advisor, respectively. This association set up an organization committee supported by seven commissioners[2] through an agreement with the Senegalese State. Decree No. 64-784/PR/ENC of November 18, 1964 created an Interdepartmental Committee for the Festival, whose mission was to define the major options, formulate the financing plan and decide on the State's financial and material participation.

While the Organization Committee was laying the groundwork in Dakar, the African Cultural Society's Arts Committee was granted the large task of preparing the festival's symposium around the theme: "Purpose and meaning of Black art in the lives of the people and for the people." It was in this perspective that an international pre-symposium was held at UNESCO in

[1] Henri Matisse, Écrits et propos sur l'art, Paris, Hermann, 1972: 121; entretien avec Tériade: découverte de l'art nègre.

[2] Alexandre Adande, Minister of Justice of Dahomey: General Commissioner; Reverend Engelbert Mveng, Lecturer at the Federal University of Yaoundé in Cameroon; Salif Diop, Liaison Secretary for the Festival; Georges Henri Rivière, Chief Curator of the Musée des Arts et Traditions; Jacqueline Delange, Head of the Department of Black Africa at the Musée de l'homme; Pierre Meauze, Head of the Black Africa Section at the Musée des Arts africains et Océaniens; Jean Gabus, Director of the Ethnographic Museum and the Ethnology Institute of Neuchatel, consultant for Black art exhibits.

Paris on December 5 and 6. This pre-symposium was attended by almost all of the world's specialists renown for their knowledge and skills in Black Art. This approach of providing open and free speech was first and foremost aimed at being objective, as emphasized by Reverend Engelbert Mveng of Cameroon:
"*For many long centuries, you look at it (Africa), turn around it, weigh it with the scale of your scientific methods, analyze it in a laboratory and among yourselves, communicate in a secret language, with scholarly epithets that buzz around its ears. Africa is aware that we are speaking about it, but it has difficulty even hearing its name through the thick forest of foreign terms. Today, it turns towards you and asks: "What are you saying about me?" It asks you: "Show me my own face cut up into frames, sketches and paintings so that I may discover myself in the mirror of your eyes. For how can I speak of my beauty without ever seeing myself from a distance?*"[3]

For the canvassing work on the continent, Reverend E. Mveng explained the approach of the African commissioners, launched on the heels of the most significant reference objects in Black Art:
"*Africa, as you know, was formerly a country rich in sources of culture. These sources have not completely dried up. Entirely conscious of the drama that emptied the young African generation of its cultural soul, we did not intend to form, using different parts, a dream Africa differing from the actual Africa. We have examined the latter and it is still standing (...) We do not want to be poor parents, consumers of civilizations.*"

And this is why he stated in Dakar that, "Africa would be responsible for speaking for itself, to its own children and to the people of all countries." Thus the Organization Committee definitively convened the Estates General of Negritude, called the First International Festival of Black Arts, in Dakar, from April 1 to 24, 1966.

The official opening ceremony for the event, marked by the beginning of the international symposium, took place on March 30, 1966, in the presence of numerous international leading experts from the world of art and culture, high government, diplomatic, parliamentary and scientific authorities, members of the Festival's Association, in an atmosphere filled with solemnity and emotion.[4]
Following the address of Alioune Diop, President of the Festival's Association, officially inaugurating the event, the poet and President Léopold Sédar Senghor spoke. His long-awaited address ended on the following note:
"*In order to dialogue with others, to participate in the common work of those men of conscience and will who are rising up around the world, in order to bring new values to the symbiosis of the complementary values through which the Universal Civilization is defined, we, Negroes, must be ourselves in our dignity, in our regained identity. (...) Once again, the problem is posed in terms of complementarity, dialogue and exchange, and not of opposition or racial hatred. How, in fact, can we, Negroes, reject the scientific and technical discoveries of European and North American peoples, thanks to which man is being transformed along with nature. Ladies and Gentlemen, you are, as researchers and teachers, artists and writers, the true humanists of contemporary times. Because Senegal has chosen to be part of the dialogue and exchange, Senegal wants to be your second nation. He hope, in any case, that the great dialogue that is being established here today, will serve to build the Earth and to fulfil mankind.*"

It was then the turn of André Malraux, the representative of France, the primary partner and financial supporter of the event, to make the fourth speech of this inaugural ceremony. He was able, states Mazel: "*from the first words, to send a collective emotional shiver through the assembly and cause thundering applause.*" Malraux first spoke of Black Art, of its characters and its priceless contributions to global esthetics. He also spoke, of course, about culture and African artistic heritage:
"*What we call culture is that mysterious force of things much older and much more profound than we, and which are our greatest aids in the modern world, against the power of the dream factories.*

[3] Engelbert Mveng (1967) Signification africaine de l'art, in 1st International Festival of Black Arts, Symposium on Black Art, volume I, Ed. Présence africaine, p.8.

[4] Jean Mazel, Présence du Monde noir, Robert Laffont, Coll. "Les Énigmes de l'Univers," 1975, pp.253-254

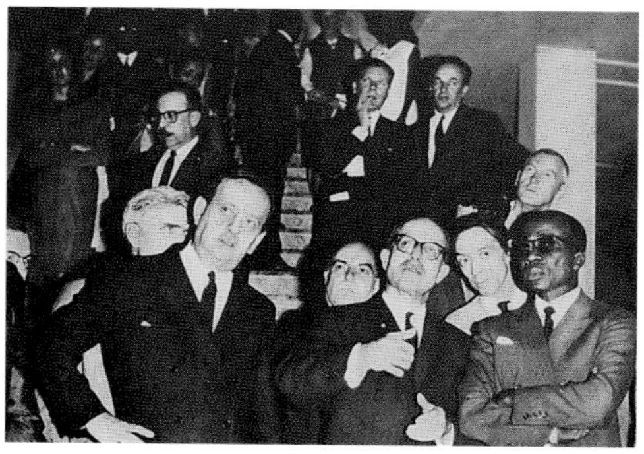

From left to right:
André Malraux, Pr Jean Gabus and President L.S. Senghor
©Studio Bracher

That is why each African country needs its own heritage, Africa's heritage, and to create its own global heritage. (...) It has been said: let us try to rediscover the African soul that designed masks. Through it we will reach the African people. Ladies and Gentlemen, I don't believe this. What once made the masks, like what once made the cathedrals, is lost forever. But this country is the heir of its masks and can say: I have with them a relationship that nobody else has. And when I look at them and ask them about their lesson from the past, I know that they are speaking directly to me. (...) Gather in your hands everything that was Africa, but take it knowing that you are in a metamorphosis. (...) Africa is strong enough to create its own cultural domain, a domain of the present and of the past, with the sole condition that it dare try. There is nothing more to it." "*My country (France) was twice or three times fairly great: when it tried to teach freedom. Ladies and Gentlemen, I would like to conclude by repeating its old message in the domain of the spirit: may Africa conquer its freedom.*"

The First International Festival of Black Arts could begin.

Picasso did not want to miss this First International Festival of Black Arts. Therefore, he offered one of his paintings, painted in 1965 and entitled "Head of a bearded man," to the Festival's French Association. The painting was displayed at the Court House in the same area as the "Trends and Confrontations" exhibit, and was donated for a raffle draw at the cost of CFA francs 1000 per ticket. It was won by the bearer of ticket No. 0280 during the draw held on the evening of the Festival's Closing Gala.

The "Hall of Lost Steps" at the Dakar Court House was specially converted to house the "Trends and Confrontations" exhibit of the contemporary works of art sent by the participating countries for the event. Of course, Black artists from Brazil, France, Haiti, the United Kingdom, Trinidad and Tobago, the United States and Canada presented their works next to artists from the continent, thus giving the exhibit an intercontinental flare. In total, about 800 works of varying techniques (painting, sculpture, carving, drawing, tapestry, illustration, models and drafts of original decorating works) were put on display in a space measuring about 2,500 m^2 and naturally lit by an open-sky "atrium" and complementary artificial lighting for the works placed at a distance from the skylight.

Through this first major gathering, African intellectuals were convinced, and they said so, that Africa had just proven to the rest of the world that traditional Black art, which already had a respectable side among Europeans since the beginning of the 20th century, had created a "contemporary Art," an "Art of Today," a living symbol of the dynamism of the various African artistic sources. This new art advocated a new type of relationship with its society. An art that is created to be exhibited in galleries, museums and private homes. An art for individual delight, an art for speaking, of course, to the new sensitivities ensuing from the urbanization and westernization of African elites and housing developments. An art that people called "critics" claim the right to judge, thereby making creations from the creations, and who have even made a career of this. We are, thus, according to the concepts or criteria of modernity or contemporaneousness to which one refers, in the presence of a plurality of readings and discussions on the same works, which, of course, lead to incomprehension and misunderstandings.

Fred Zeller, President of the Fédération Française des Beaux-Arts (French Federation of Fine Arts), confided in a Unité Africaine journalist for a long time.[5] "*As a general rule, while we find, in this exhibit, paintings that reflect the daily lives of people living in cities and towns, we also find ourselves in the presence of an African art that seeks itself. (...) There are, for example, many abstract paintings and, in my opinion, if you remove the names of the African artists and replace them with the names of French, American or Polish artists, there would hardly be any difference, because it is not a typically African painting. (...) I think that this is serious.*
(...) About fifteen truly interesting paintings caught my eye that can be said to

[5] Interview conducted by Aly Dioum in L'Unité Africaine, no. 199, of April 28, 1966, p.1 and 13.

be truly African and done with great talent. (...) Papa Ibra Tall, Iba N'Diaye and especially Ibou Diouf. I particularly appreciated the latter because he is precisely one of those people who, in their work, are the most heavily influenced by African realities. His works always contain extremely pretty colors and we see elusive figures in them that call to mind the richly colored and brocaded dresses of Black women walking down the street or dancing."

One cannot help but emphasize the contradictory ideas in Zeller's comments, especially the parallel between Iba N'Diaye and "a truly African inspiration of painting" or other rantings of this type.

On the morning of April 25, at the closing ceremony, the National Commissioner, Souleymane Sidibé, was able to declare to the world: *"The First International Festival of Black Arts had met its goals. It revealed the Negro to himself, it established the meaning and scope of his value, of his role and of his responsibility at the global level. It placed emphasis on the unity of Black Art in its diversity. The entire world resounded, and will resound for a long time, very profound echoes from encountering this Negritude. Senegal is happy to have had this heavy, yet thrilling responsibility."*
himself, it established the meaning and scope of his value, of his role and of his responsibility at the global level. It placed emphasis on the unity of Black Art in its diversity. The entire world resounded, and will resound for a long time, very profound echoes from encountering this Negritude. Senegal is happy to have had this heavy, yet thrilling responsibility."

PROGRAM AND HONORS

1. Award winners

- Grand Prize for Painting: Franck Bowling from British Guyana
- Grand Prize for Sculpture: Agnaldo Dos Santos from Brazil
- Grand Prize for Illustration and Carving: Williams Majors from the U.S.A.
- Grand Prize for Applied Art: to the makers of wicker baskets in Burundi
- Prize for Drawing: Sola Mahomey from Gambia and Ouassa from Congo-Brazzaville
- Prize for Tapestry Drawings: to the painter Ibou Diouf from Senegal
- Grand Prize for Contemporary Plastic Art: Christian Lattier, sculptor from Ivory Coast

Note: Special Honor to Iba N'Diaye for all of his work.

2. Music

- Traditional Music and Songs from Black Africa: Central African Music, gathered by Charles Duvelle
- Record of Christian African Religious Music: the Martyrs of Uganda
- Record of Christian African-American Religious Music: Mahalia Jackson from the U.S.A.
- Jazz Record: Louis Armstrong from the U.S.A.

3. Film

- Fiction Feature Film: Sembène Ousmane from Senegal, for "La Noire de"
- Fiction Short Feature: Ababacar Samb from Senegal, for "Et la neige n'était plus"
- Best Black Actor: Ivan Dixon
- Best Black Actress: Abey Lincoln

4. Literature

- Poetry

French: Chicaya U'Tamsi from Congo for "Epitome"
English: Robert Hayden from the U.S.A. for "Ballad of Remembrance"

- Novel

French: Sembène Ousmane from Senegal for "Vehi Ciosane"
English: James Ngugi from Kenya for "Weep not Child"

- Essay

French: Dominique Traoré from Mali for "Médecine et magie africaine"
English: Eldred Jones from Sierra Leone for "Othello's Countrymen"

- Art

French: Jacques Maquet from Belgium for "Les Civilisations africaines"
English: William Fagg from England for "Nigerian Images"

- Social Sciences

French: not awarded
English: Kenneth Clak from the U.S.A. for "Dark Ghetto"

- News Story

French: Hélène Tournaire and Robert Bouteau from France for "Le Livre noir du Congo"
English: Nelson Mandela from South Africa for "No easy walk to freedom"

- Theater

French: not awarded
English: Wole Soyinka from Nigeria, for "The Road"

- Special Jury Prize awarded to the Black author who has most influenced Black thought in the 20th century: Professor Cheikh Anta Diop from Senegal for "Nations Nègres et Cultures."

THE CONTEMPORARY ART EXHIBIT: "TRENDS AND CONFRONTATIONS"

Burundi
- artisans

Cameroon
- Moumbé Massangong (sculptor)
- Jacques Bengono (photographer)
- Jean Konko (sculptor)

Congo Brazzaville
- Artist group from the Poto-Poto School

Congo Kinshasa
- Mwenze Luc Kibwanga (painter)
- Célestin Kulumb (painter)
- Ferdinand Mbende (sculptor)
- Victor Binkoko (sculptor)
- Laurent Zoao (sculptor)
- Thomas Kinkita (sculptor)
- Jérémie Kikabakanga (sculptor)
- Ignace Bamba (sculptor)
- Emile Mokengo (sculptor)
- Adam Ngoie (sculptor)
- Albert Caude Nduku (painter)
- Julien Ndawu (painter)
- Joseph Matutadidi (sculptor)
- Séverin Ngamokuba (painter)
- Benjamin Mensah (sculptor)
- Donatien Wuma (sculptor)
- Daniel Bakala (sculptor)
- Édouard Gouveia (painter)
- Antoine Liujindula (sculptor)
- Placide Mpane (sculptor)
- Célestin Ntshiama (sculptor)
- Donatien Wuma (sculptor)
- Moussa Diouf (painter)
- Ignace Mankana (sculptor)
- Albert Muaka (sculptor)
- Jean Mukeba (sculptor)
- Basile Nzibu (painter)
- Benoît Babanzanga (painter)
- Victor Zowa (painter)
- Albert Ngusso (painter)
- Zéphérin Mazamba (painter)
- Joseph Mukaku (coppersmith)

Ivory Coast
- Yao Célestin Dogand (painter)
- Jean Mathieu Gensin (painter)
- Gnakpa Daple (sculptor)
- Louis Laouchez (sculptor)
- Christian Lattier (sculptor)
- Marcel Sarrazin (draftsman)
- Seri Luc (sculptor)
- Sogono Kouassi (sculptor)

Dahomey (Benin)
- Christian Zahoncou Mewu (painter)
- Armand Pascal Aniambossou (painter)
- Léonard Leleye (painter)
- Arthur Lishou (painter)
- Maurice Nicomède (painter)

Egypt (United Arab Republic)
- Ingi Aflatone (painter)
- Taheyya Halim (painter)
- Gazebeyya Serry (painter)
- Gamal Mahmoud (painter)
- Ahmed Sada (painter)
- Refaat Ahmed (painter)
- Sayed Abdel Zassoul (painter)
- Salah Taher (painter)
- Abdel H amid El Dawakhly (painter)
- Abdel Wahab Morsy (painter)
- Mohamed Hassanein Aly (painter)
- Adam H. Henein (sculptor)
- Anwar Abdel Mawla (sculptor)
- Mahmoud Mokhtar (sculptor)
- El Hussein Fawzy (engraver)
- Omar El Nagdy (engraver)
- Abdel El Nagdy (engraver)
- Abdel Ghani El Dibawy (maquette of the Grand Temple of Abou Simbel)
- Fouad Abdel Hamid (illustrator)

Ethiopia
- Afework Tekle (painter)
- Lemma Guya (painter)
- Ale Felege Selam (painter)
- Gebre Kristos Desta (painter)
- Bekele Stifanos (painter)
- Girma Gabre Mikael (painter)
- Skunder Boghossian (painter)
- Zawdu Bekele (painter)
- Ajecowerk Békélé (painter)
- Gebre Christophe (painter)
- Gélie Christophe Sesta (painter)
- Corebe Christophe Sesta (painter)

Gabon
- Louis Sorko
- Marc Mambingo
- Marcel Njondo
- Vay Vasky
- Mengue Salomon (sculptor)
- Daniel Abaa (sculptor)
- Obololam (sculptor)
- Théophile Tembangoye (sculptor)
- Georges Zoundou (sculptor)
- Gaston Lingwala (sculptor)
- Mukagni Cécilien (sculptor)
- Antoine Ndongobiang (sculptor)
- Pierre Clavier Burobu (sculptor)
- Faustin Moussoumba (sculptor)
- Jérôme Tsamba (sculptor)
- Élysée Matambo (sculptor)
- Masala Philénion (sculptor)
- Mabiala Étienne (sculptor)
- Bikendi Gabriel (sculptor)

Gambia
- Salla Mohamed (painter)

Ghana
- Seth Anku (painter)
- Kofi Antubam (painter)
- Kobina Asmash (painter)
- A.O. Bartimeus (painter)
- J.C.O. Okeyere (sculptor)
- W.C. Owusu (sculptor)
- Yapaga (sculptor)
- Kofi Va (sculptor)
- Oku Assyofo (sculptor)
- P.K. Ampah (sculptor)
- Oku Ampofo (sculptor)
- Anthony Ampah (sculptor)
- Daniel Cobblah (sculptor)
- Owusu Dartey (sculptor)

Haute-Volta (Burkina Faso)
- Jean-Pierre Bassoley (artisan, bronze lost wax technique)
- André Campaoré (artisan, bronze lost wax technique)
- Derme Issaka (artisan, bronze lost wax technique)
- Derme Kassoum (artisan, bronze lost wax technique)
- Derme Moumouni (artisan, bronze lost wax technique)
- Derme Ramane (artisan, bronze lost wax technique)
- Touré Billa (artisan, bronze lost wax technique)

Liberia
- Alfred Martin (sculptor)
- R. Vahnja Richards (sculptor)
- Neah Soudan (painter)
- Francs Cooper (painter)
- Emennuel Erskine (painter)
- R. Joseph W. Bailey (jeweler)
- R. Vahnadja Richards (sculptor)
- Cecil Marrin (painter)
- Samuel Walker (painter)
- Jordin (painter)
- Rebeca Jolison (painter)
- Edward J. Roye (painter)

Madagascar
- Madeleine Razanadranaivo (painter)
- Hélène Razanatefy (painter)
- Fidèle Raharinosy (painter)

Mali
- Bouba Keïta (painter)
- Salif Kondé (painter)
- Mamadou Somé Coulibaly (painter)

Morocco
- Ben (painter)

Mauritania
- El Hadji Adama Sylla
- Majhtar Cissé (mosaicist, gilder, binder)

Niger (no information)

Nigeria
- Demas Nwoko (sculptor)
- O. Osadebe (painter)
- Ben Aye (sculptor)
- Erhabor Emokpae (painter)
- Afi Ekouf (painter)
- Nma W. Udosen (painter)
- Ukpo Eze (painter)
- Félix Idukor (sculptor)
- Yusuf Grillo (painter)
- Bruce Onobrakpeya (painter)
- Félix Idehen (sculptor)
- J.D. Akeredolu (sculptor)
- Uche Okeke (painter)
- E. O. Nwagbara (painter)
- Jérôme Elaiho (painter)

Senegal
- Amamdou Niang (painter)
- Papa Sidy Diop (painter)
- Amadou Seydou (painter)
- Ousmane Wade (painter)
- Ibou Diouf (painter)
- Alpha Walid Diallo (painter)
- Bocar Pathé Diong (painter)
- Papa Ibra Tall (painter)
- Seydou Barry (painter)
- Mor Faye (painter)
- Iba N'Diaye (painter)

Sierra Leone
(no information)

Sudan
- Ibrahim El Salahi (leader of the delegation)

Togo
- John Agboli (painter)
- Paul Ahyi (painter, sculptor, architect)
- Augustin Ayayi Amah (painter)
- Emmanuel Dabla (painter)
- Raymond Dalakena K. (painter)
- Damien Gbegnon (painter)
- Délia Hunze (painter)
- Martin Sallah (painter)
- Lazare Togbonou Fogne (painter)

Tchad
- T. Sammuel (painter)
- N. Adom (painter)
- A. Fadoul (painter)
- M.A. Elias (painter)
- A. Dafoul (painter)
- A. Nagassoum (painter)

Zambie (no information)

Members of the International Jury
- Mr. N'Zekwu, Nigerian Magazine
- Pierre Spir, Connaissance des Arts
- Georges Boudailles, Lettres Françaises
- Michel Cohil Lacoste, Le Monde
- Ulli Beier, University of Ibadan (Nigeria)
- Mr. Nounow, Accra National Museum
- Aimé Césaire, Writer, Deputy Mayor of Fort-de-France
- Mr. Patrick Waldberg, Paris
- Bernard Dadier, Director of Arts et Lettres from Ivory Coast
- Alfred Barr, MOMA, New York
- M. M. C. Crowder, University of Fourabé in Freetown, Sierra Leone

Cultural policy in Senegal

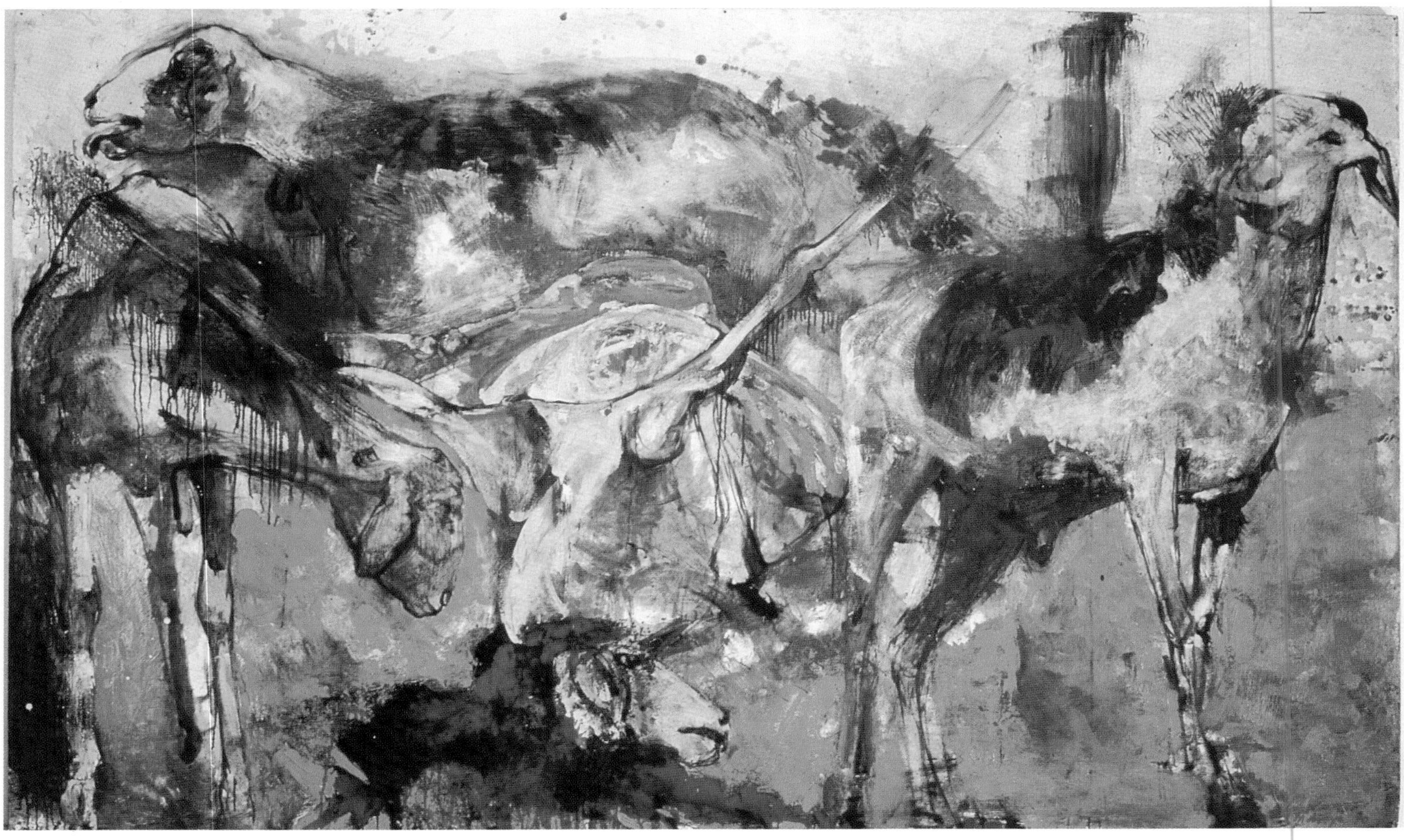

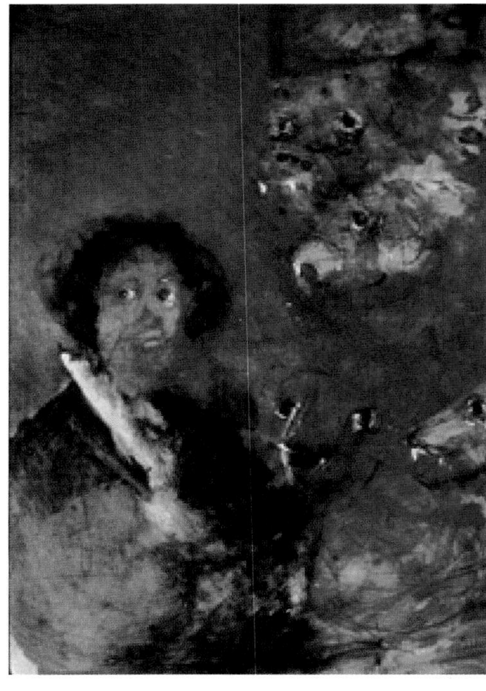

Iba N'Diaye (born in 1928), "Tabaski, whose turn is it?," 1970
oil on canvas, 150x250 cm.

"Jean de Peraja bothered by dogs," 1985-86
oil on canvas, 163x130 cm.
©D.R.

facing page:
Amadou Bâ (born in 1945), "The Cow," 1979
acrylic on canvas, 88x126 cm
©Revue Noire

Papa Ibra Tall (born in 1928), "The Dwarf's Calabash," 1978
tapestry, 350x250 cm.
©D.R.

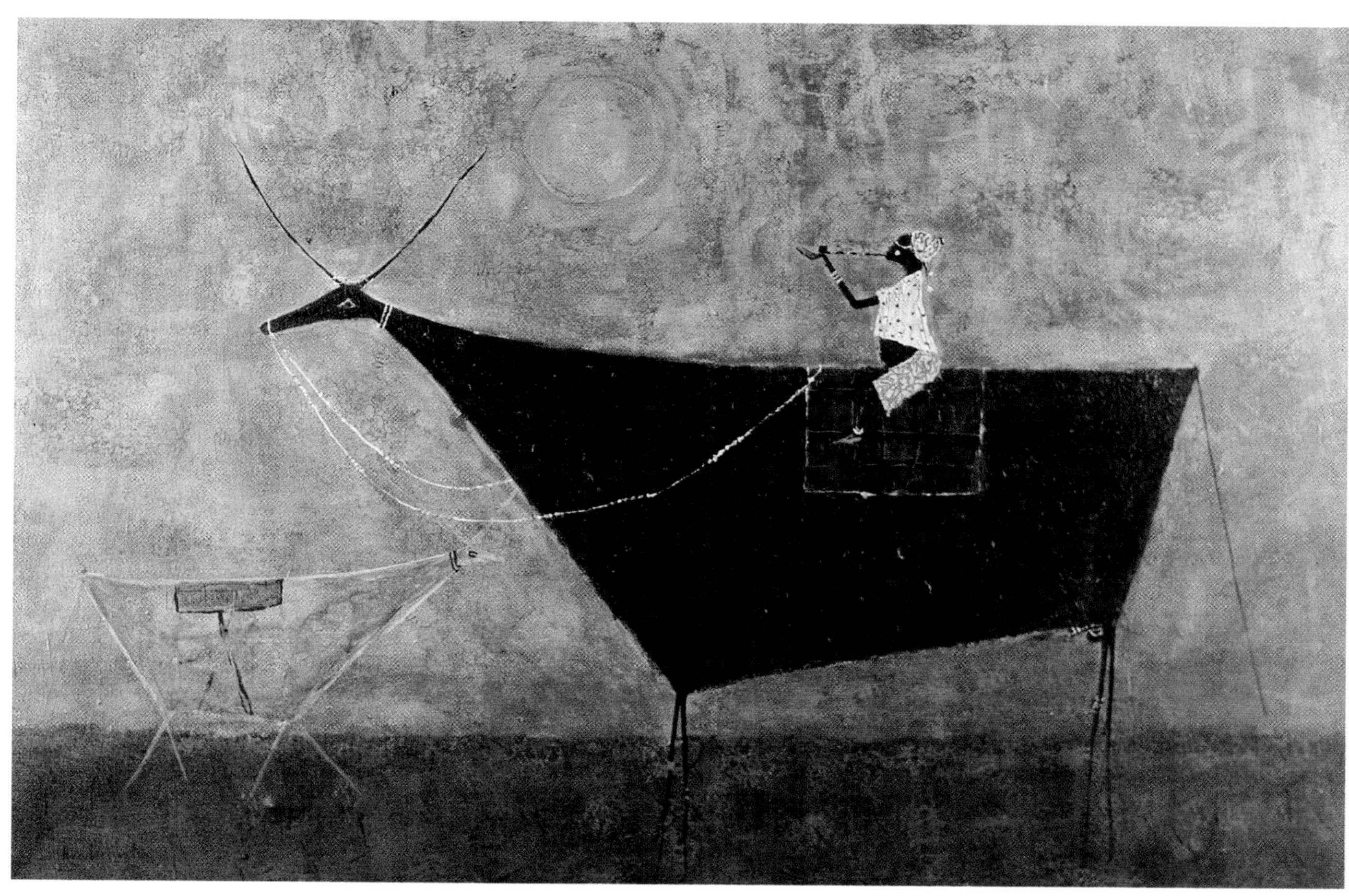

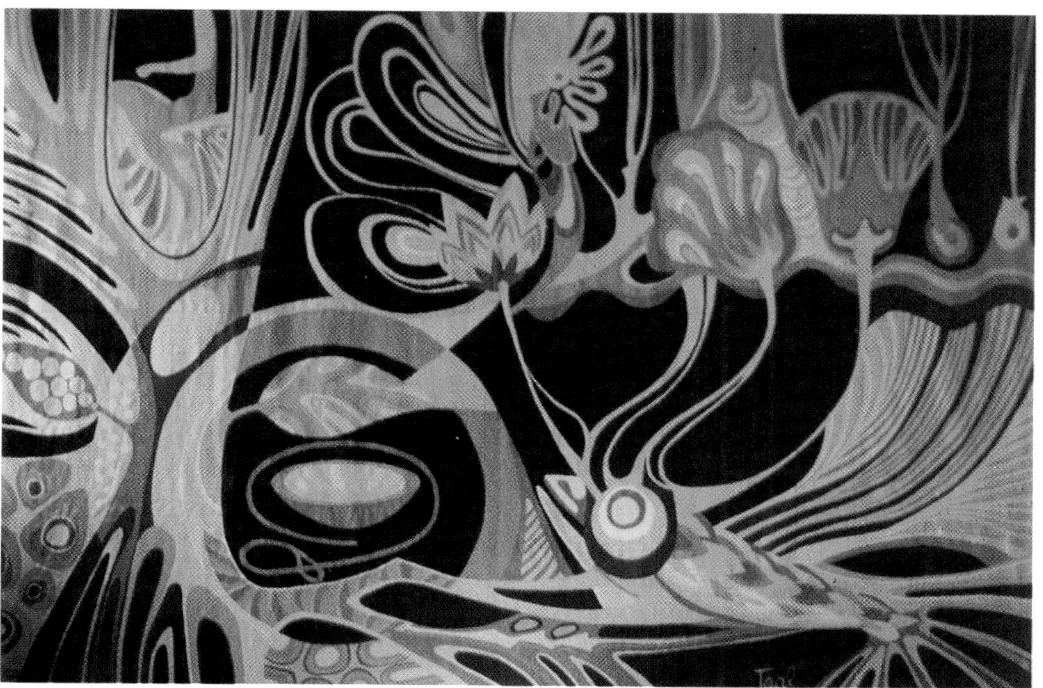

CULTURAL POLICY IN SENEGAL

Marie-Hélène Boisdur de Toffol

The accession of a country to independence is a sign that its aspirations have been confirmed in writing. Crucial political, economic, social and also cultural issues need resolving. Major issues crop up, such as the fight against acculturation, the illustration of values, links to be established between tradition and modernity.

A national art developed in Senegal during the first years of independence. The rebirth of plastic arts in Senegal is due to the important place given to culture in the country's general development program. During the 1960s and 1970s, the arrangement of new infrastructures, the creation of supports for cultural action, such as the Institut National des Arts, the Musée Dynamique, the Manufacture de Tapisserie de Thiès, the Théâtre National Daniel Sorano, had a decisive role. To this was, of course, added the role of Léopold Sédar Senghor as patron of the arts and as theoretician. This permitted him to organize the First International Festival of Black Arts in Dakar in 1966, with exhibits bringing together eminent artists from the African continent and from the Diaspora.

Negritude

The term Negritude, particularly questioned in the early days of the independence movements, appeared for the first time in the 30s, in the writings of young West Indian and African intellectuals studying in Paris. The prologue took shape in the sole issue of the magazine "Légitime défense," in June 1932. The co-authors of this magazine were seeking to reassert the value of the Black man and to become associated with the progressive movements of the time. "Légitime défense" proclaimed its solidarity with both the surrealist movement and with the 3rd International. The "étudiant noir," founded by Léopold Sédar Senghor, Léon-Gontran Damas, and Aimé Césaire looked into the theoretical research on the actions to be taken. Léon-Gontran Damas, a Guyanese poet, stated, during an interview with D. Racine (see L.G. Damas "L'homme et l'œuvre" D. Racine Présence Africaine), with respect to this magazine, that "there were three goals: first, we sought to redeem the Black race and deliver it from the pejorative term of "Negro"; we then wanted to denounce the colonial system, especially the principle on which it was based, namely assimilation through education, the alienation of individuals and of their depersonalization (...) This was supposed to lead to the freedom of the African continent, to the emancipation of the colonized peoples and to the birth of a new era of dialogue and understanding of different values and civilizations."

Aimé Césaire, a poet and writer from Martinique, was a very avid activist for the involvement of intellectuals from the Black world. "It is up to the poets, artists, writers and men of culture, who are exposed every day to suffering and desires for justice, to memories and hope, to establish these large reserves of faith, these large silos of strength, from which people may draw the courage to assume and force the hand of the future themselves during critical moments. Our duty to our Black writers and artists is to re-establish the double continuity ruptured by colonialism: continuity with the world and continuity with ourselves."

Léopold Sédar Senghor introduced and developed his concept of Negritude in the artistic, political and economic domains: "Objectively, Negritude is a fact and a culture. It is a set of economic, political, intellectual, moral, artistic and social values, not only of the people of Black Africa, but also of the Black minorities in America, Asia and Oceania. Subjectively, Negritude is the acceptance of this fact of civilization and its perspective projection into the history to be pursued and the Black civilization to be reborn and achieved. This is, in brief, the duty that the militants of Negritude have set for themselves, namely to assume the values of civilization of the Black world, to update them and enrich them, as needed, with foreign contributions, in order to make them live through and for oneself, but also to make them live by and for others, thereby involving the contribution of new Negroes in the Universal Civilization."

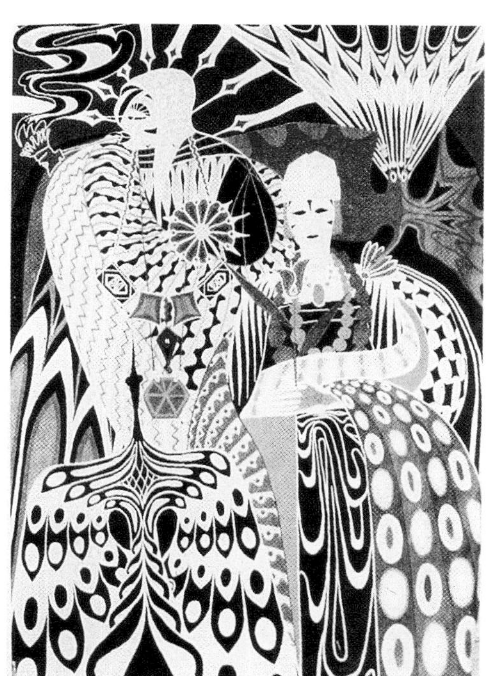

Papa Ibra Tall (born in 1928), "Royal couple," 1965
wool tapestry, 222x155 cm
©D.R.

The artist's commitment

From that moment onward, it was not surprising to see that a privileged share was reserved for artistic creation in the cultural policy of Senegal. The goal was to restore the pre-eminent position of artists-artisans in society. The artist had to be committed and conscious of his role. The goals of his production were major and plural on a national and global scale. Within the country, art contributed to the cultural development of the population. It fought against acculturation. Art was directed at the entire population. Through its presence, it enabled links to be restored between art and life, which are very strong in the traditional arts of sub-Saharan Africa. In rehabilitating traditional arts, by referring to them, the artist is restoring the population's taste for esthetics and themes from the past. But he must respond to new aspirations. Cheick Anta Diop mentioned in this respect: "An artist who deliberately turns his eyes towards the past and basks in a pure and simple evocation of this past lives apart from the needs of his era (…). Art must always reflect the art of one's era, i.e. it must serve the needs of the society that begot the artist. Therefore, the new direction of our art must result, whether we want it to or not, from examining the most representative needs of the African people in their current state."

Art must re-establish the feeling of community, of an ethnic community with its themes and specific values, but above all of a national community, because the various groups now had to live within a nation with vaster geographical and political outlines. The pan-African community and the vast community of Black populations, namely those in the West Indies and the United States, were questioned. This community had to be viewed as dynamic, moving and turned towards the future. In the name of humanism, Senegalese art was presented as the spokesperson of the "genius" of the Black peoples. It was propaganda art in the noble sense of the word and had a quest. It claimed its place in the "Universal Civilization" and was involved in the actions of the human community.

A national art

Léopold Sédar Senghor wondered about the esthetics of the future arts. Four plastic artists worked with him in exploring and promoting African Art. Iba N'Diaye, a theoretician and plastic artist trained, mainly in France, before the independence movements, proposed, within the Plastic Arts Section of the Arts School, a varied and comparative approach to art. Papa Ibra Tall created the "Black Plastic Arts Research Workshop," which referred, more systematically, to the Black cultural heritage. Alpha Woualid Diallo, a self-taught artist, established a link between visual realism and popular styles. Pierre Lods, called in 1961, based himself on the notion of Free Workshops already experimented with at the Art Center of Poto-Poto in Brazzaville, Congo, in order to develop students' creativity.

Symbolism and spirituality

The esthetics that were born out of this work were plural, but based on certain premises. Being Black, according to theoreticians of Negritude, is first and foremost a way of existing in the world, comprised of emotion, participation, symbolism, and gathering of forces. The works of Senegalese artists are a reaffirmation of a relationship between man and nature that is not a relationship of domination, but rather a relationship based on communication and, more generally, the expression of an emphatic relationship in the world, from which originated "the cosmic desire of our works" according to Papa Ibra Tall. In fact, certain themes of contemporary works recall the constants of African spiritualism, ancient cosmogonies, and the myths of origin. This can be used to interpret certain works of Amadou Ba, born in the Matam region in 1945, to Ayniam Thibaye, a student in the Black plastic arts research section of the National Arts School in Dakar, or of Papa Ibra Tall himself.

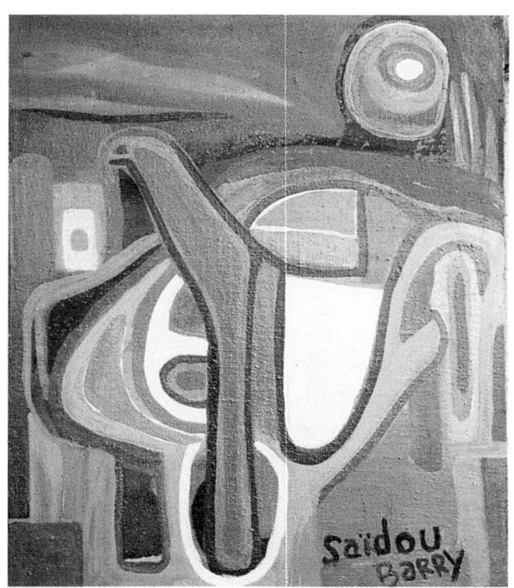

Saïdou Barry (born in 1943), 1970

©Revue Noire

Ibou Diouf (born in 1943), "Silence," 1970

©Revue Noire

Rhythms

Senegalese artists also referred to the structural aspects of traditional objects of art that emphasized the pre-eminence of rhythm. In view of Western art, presented as an "art of discussion," theoreticians of Negritude described traditional African art as the art of "rhythm." Each detail of the stylized work had its own rhythm and became integrated by polyphonic and polyrhythmic arrangements, all unified in the work. Out of loyalty to these specific choices of traditional sub-Saharan arts, Senegalese artists most often preferred not to refer to visual realism, but preferred, instead, the coded game of plastic signs and symbols to express the visible and the invisible as well. Traditional Africa "teaches us that it is possible to go beyond the real, and that religion, like art, conveys this wonder that Kiekegaard called the passion of the possible," wrote Papa Iba Tall. Such that ancient masks and sculptures are often evoked by contemporary painters. Boubacar Coulibaly, born in Dakar in 1944, a student in the Black plastic arts research section of the National Arts School in Dakar, proposed a series of paintings called "Masks" using this method.

Realism

These choices are, however, qualified. Senegalese artists did not always want to conform to traditional Black symbolism and stylization because they did not have the same relationships with beings and things that the ancient artists had. As a result, the work of Cheick Diop, born in Rufisque in 1918, was traditional in its technique and approach, but not in the esthetics developed. With respect to tradition, he favored the approach of referring to oral literature. For example, he would question old witnesses of the lives of historic characters of Senegal, such as Lat Dior, before representing them. He used the ancestral lost wax technique, but his bronze statues were rather realistic. Alpha Woualid Diallo, born in Rufisque in 1927, also specialized in evoking great historical moments and battles using a realistic approach.

Plural components

As with structural complexities, colors and materials can also be adapted to a contemporary context and the "specificity of the message." In an essay on "the cultural policy in Senegal" (Unesco 1973), M. S. M'Bengue wrote in this respect: "As far back as we can go in its history, Senegal has always appeared as a land of culture and encounter (…) In spreading animism and paganism, Islam and Christianity brought about a new dimension, without erasing the old African base, which today is expressed through original symbolism. It is this uniqueness that has been used since 1960 to promote the cultural policy of Senegal." Themes and esthetics may, therefore, refer to Islam. Representations of "Mosques," of scenes of religious life, the focus of Amadou Bamba, the founder of the Mourides brotherhood, appear in works on easel and in tapestries of Senegalese artists. As with themes, techniques and esthetics may also rise out of contact with the West. Léopold Sédar Senghor stated, in this respect, during a speech made at the inaugural session of the Committee of Studies for the Development of African Culture held on June 15, 1962: "The goal is not to renounce contributions from Europe. Europe offers us time-tested methods and techniques. What we have to do, using these methods and techniques, is "return to the sources," discover the sources gushing with Negritude, to channel them and, using new techniques, water our land so that future crops will grow."

Refusal of primitivism

Iba Ndiaye, who very early on participated in national and international events promoting Black Arts, worked on this issue. Besides tradition-related themes, such as the "Ramb" (ancestral spirits from Wolof mythology), he questioned the "screams of the continent," sacrifices, social and political violence, and exclusions. He was also interested in the world of the Black Diaspora and devoted many pieces of work to Jazz. Islam is evoked through the "Tabaski" series, with a slipping from the theme of animal sacrifice towards human sacrifice. The "Tabaski" are implicit references to the political and economic situations being experienced by Africa, but also to the situation of those oppressed around the world. His gestural style is expressionist by choice. At the time of the "New African Works" exhibit (1969), Iba N'Diaye wrote: "In my opinion, it is in rejecting all compromise with this well-meaning "primitivism" that we often expect of artists and in enriching their technical experience and their esthetic culture through contact with creators from other continents, while recognizing the traditional African plastic art that is part of the universal heritage (...) that the artists of the new Africa will help their fellow citizens (...)."

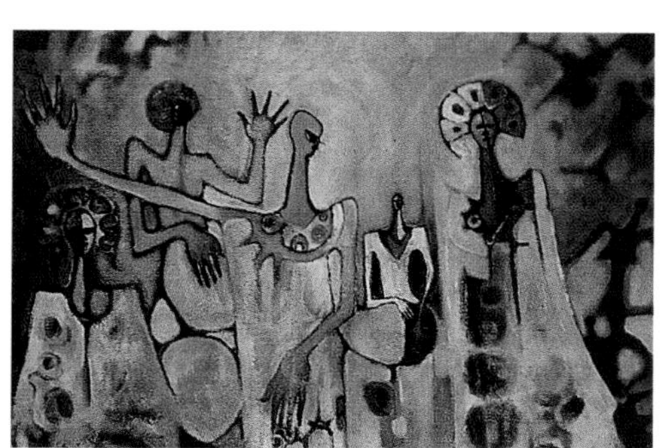

Bocar Pathé Diong (born in 1946), "Xawaré," c.a. 1965
oil on canvas
©Revue Noire

Mural art

The example of the activities of the Manufacture de Thiès, founded in 1966, is symbolic. The purpose of this establishment was "the interpretation, in the form of tapestry works, of the creative expression of Black artists, in general, and of Senegalese artists, in particular." Using these actions, Papa Ibra Tall insisted on the particularly important scope of mural art. He referred, for example, to the mural art of the American Black communities: "They create immense frescoes for the people. Authentic revolutionary ghetto poetry is splashed on gables and building facades. We are convinced that it is through decorative and monumental art that we will achieve the ideal of all democratic civilizations: making art into a bath for the people, an ideal being achieved by old Africa." After being trained in traditional weaving techniques and Western tapestry (fiber artists, for example, took courses at Gobelins and Aubusson in France) the artisans of the Manufacture made a large number of tapestries based on cartoons of young Senegalese painters and artists from various African countries. The themes restate local and universal community values. African values and social structures are expressed through plastic by Ibou Diouf, born in Tivavouane in 1943, a student at the National Arts School in Senegal from 1961 to 1966, or by Boubacar Diallo, born in St-Louis in 1949. Universal themes are evoked, such as "the bird of dreams" or "freedom" by Modou Dieng, born in Dakar in 1945, a student in the Black plastic arts research section and cartoon painter with the Manufacture de Tapisseries de Thiès. Through the State's sponsorship, these works were then placed in public venues, administrative buildings and embassies. Tapestries were offered to foreigners, bodies and States. They were also exhibited pursuant to cultural agreements made by Senegal with various African, European and American countries. These exhibits, whether or not combined with exhibits of paintings, renew the desire to address the entire global community through assertion and sharing. Each person must become entrenched with the values of his race, continent and nation in order to exist and to open up to other continents and nations, and to blossom.

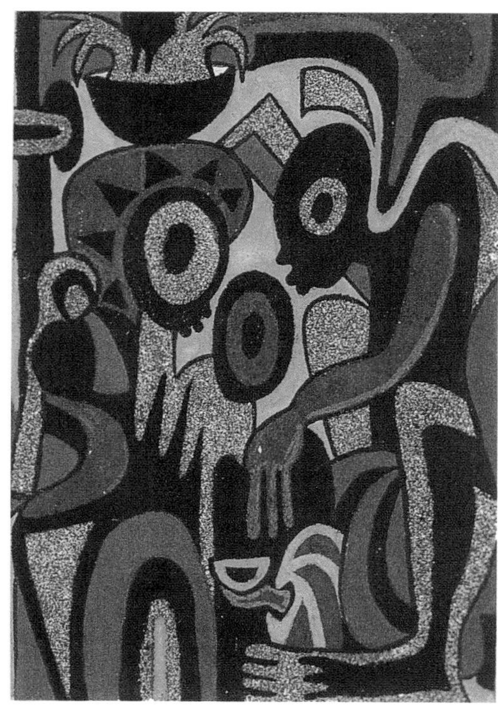

Boubacar Goudiaby (born in 1944), "Offering," 1969
collage on plywood
©D.R.

Social art, useful art?

In "Orphée Noir," Sartre appears to repeat the message: "Negritude is the content of the poem. It is the poem, a mysterious and open, undecipherable and suggestive thing of the world. It is the poet himself." Others have disputed the issues and modalities of this experience (see Adotevi "Négritude et négrologues"). But time and ideological modifications do not erase what came before.

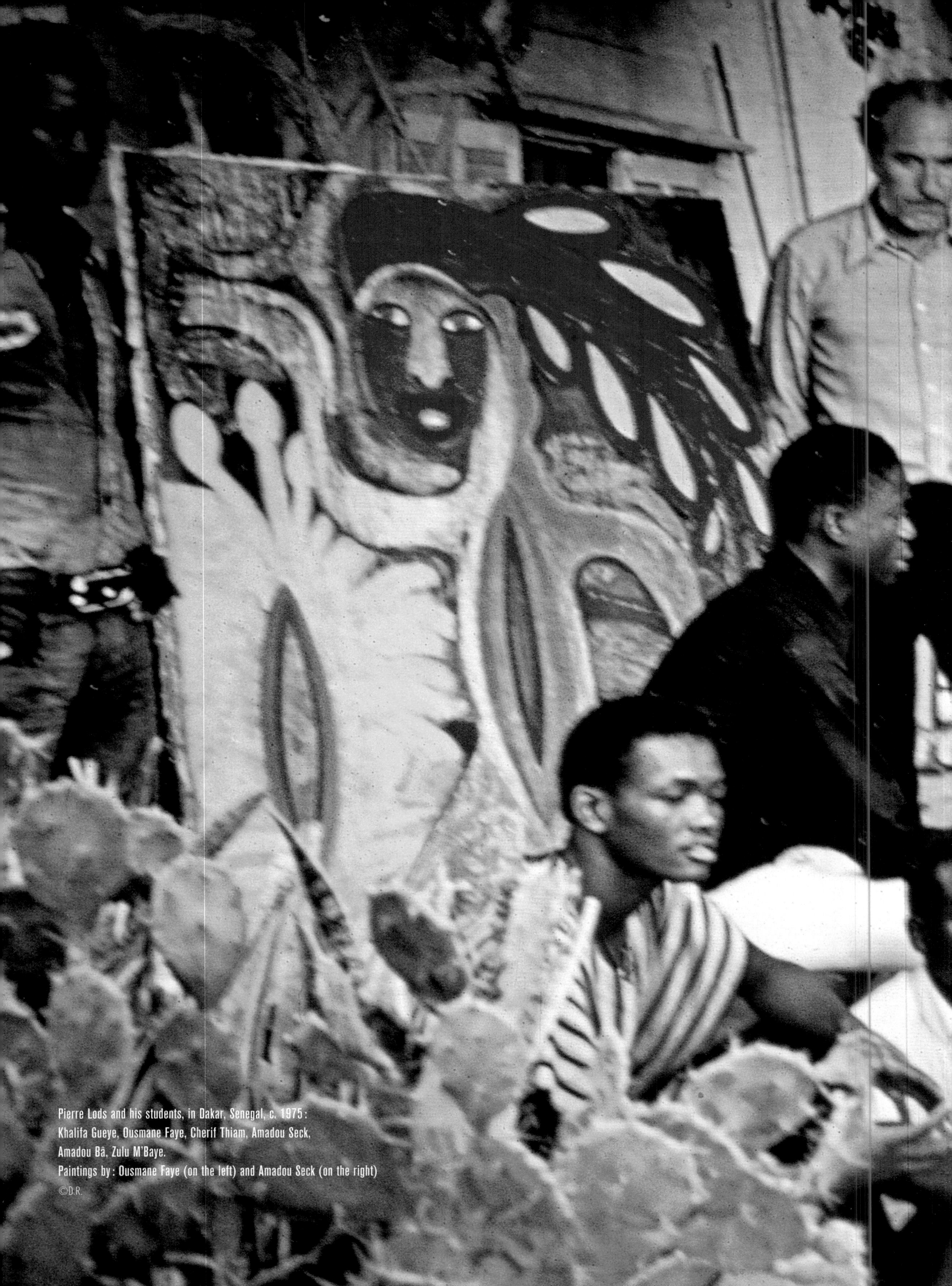

Pierre Lods and his students, in Dakar, Senegal, c. 1975:
Khalifa Gueye, Ousmane Faye, Cherif Thiam, Amadou Seck,
Amadou Bâ, Zulu M'Baye.
Paintings by: Ousmane Faye (on the left) and Amadou Seck (on the right)

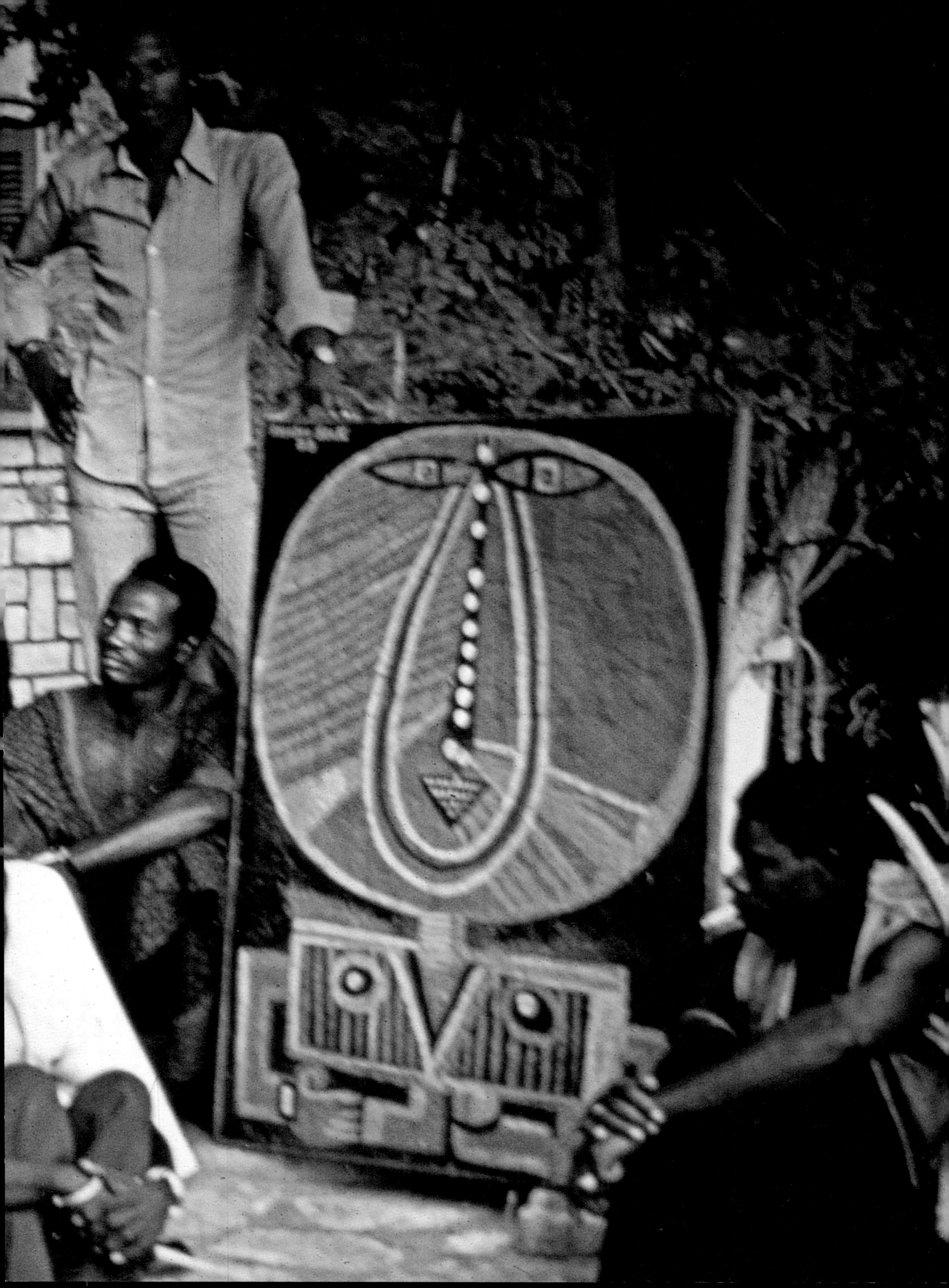

The Black Caribbean School and the Vohou-Vohou Movement

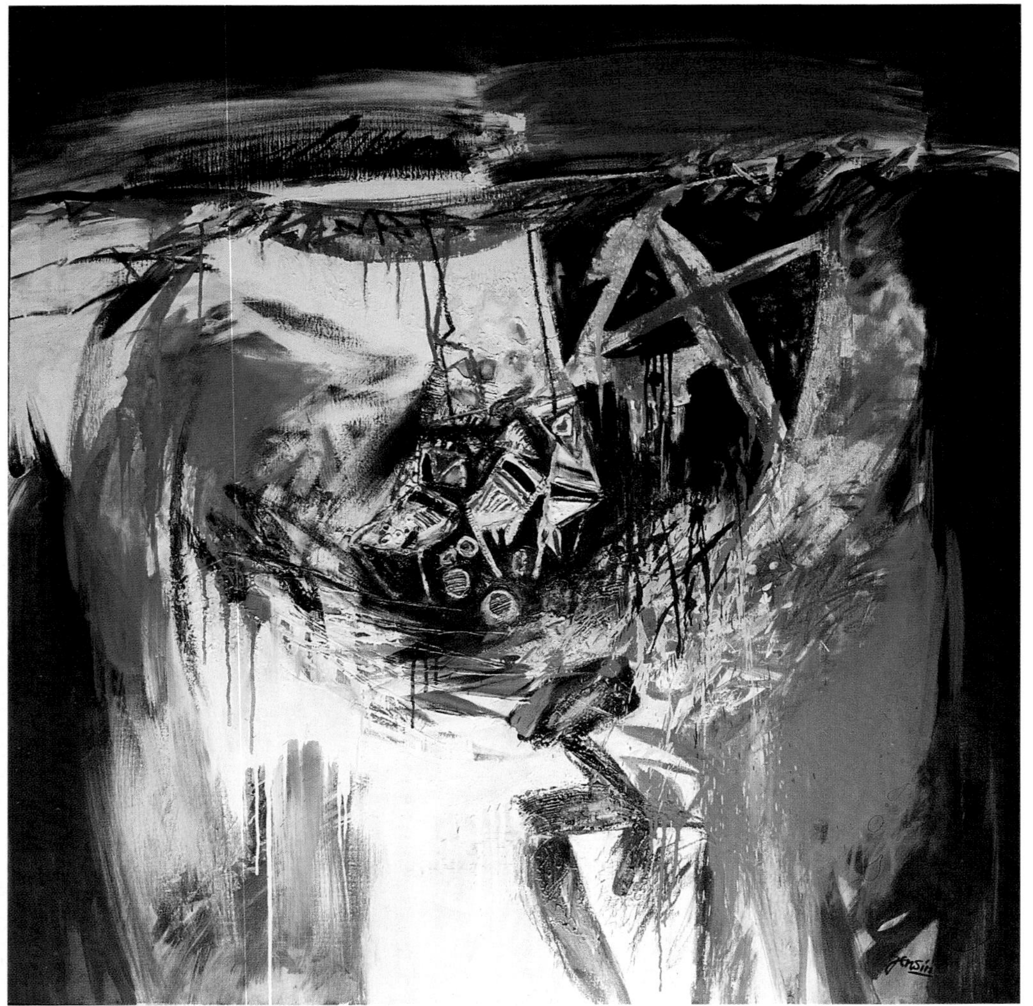

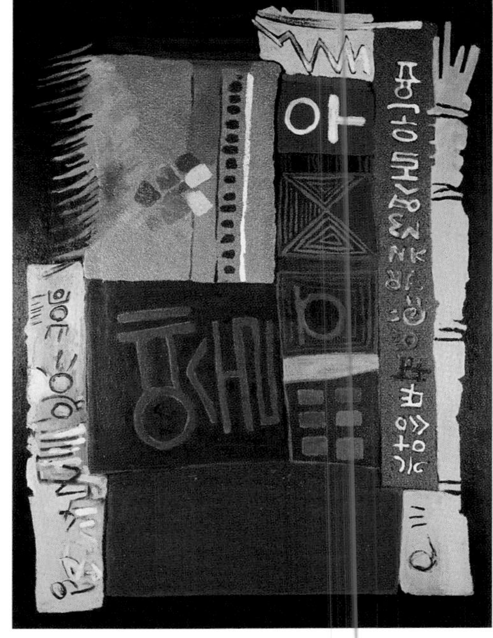

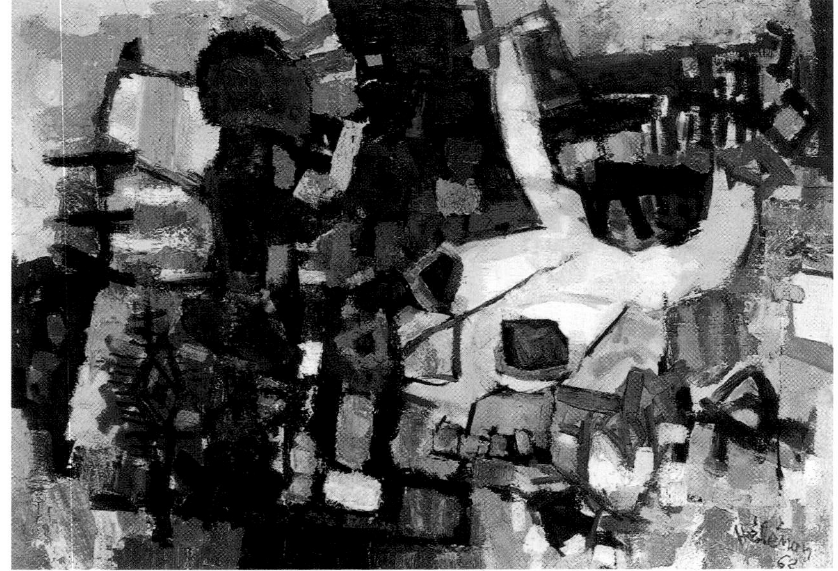

Jean Gensin (born in 1934), c.a. 1960
©D.R.

N'Guessan Kra (born in 1954), 1990
©Revue Noire

Serge Hélénon (born in 1934), "Cow's Skull," 1962
oil on canvas, 73x100 cm
©D.R.

facing page:
Théodore Koudougnon (born in 1951)
©Revue Noire

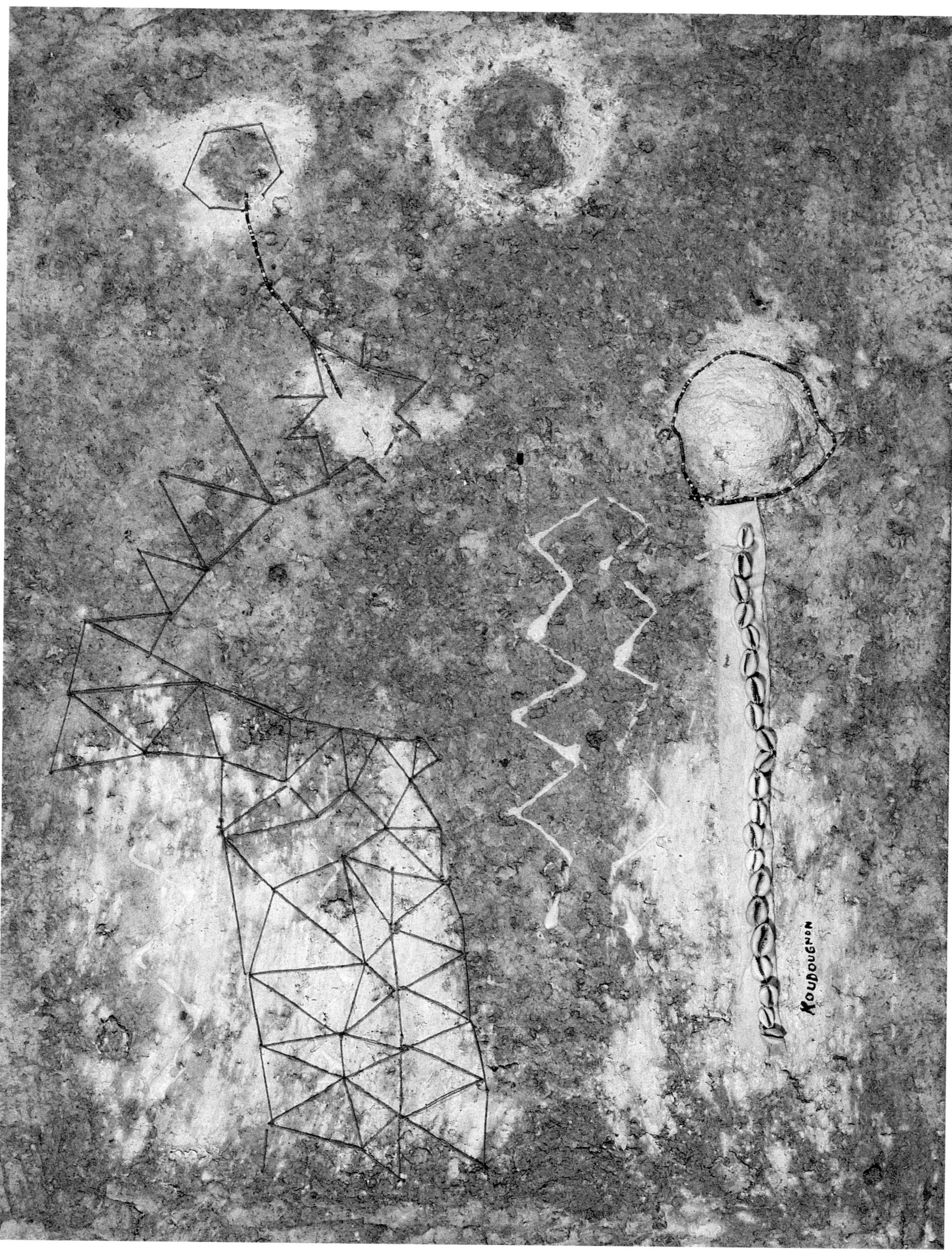
KOUDOUGNON

THE BLACK CARIBBEAN SCHOOL AND THE VOHOU-VOHOU MOVEMENT
Marie-Hélène Boisdur de Toffol

The École des Beaux-Arts of Abidjan was founded in 1962. It was born out of a restructuring and regrouping of different institutions: plastic arts were previously studied in Ivory Coast at two private art centers. One artist, M. Holms, taught drawing in the administrative district of the plateau and Charles Combes (1891-1968), a French sculptor who had been living in Ivory Coast since 1923, founded a sculpture workshop in Bingerville. In 1962, this workshop became a sculpture school attached to the École des Beaux-Arts. The drawing courses used locals from the Institut National des Arts in Cocody from the time it was built in the mid-60s. In the early 70s, the École des Beaux-Arts of Abidjan became the École Nationale Supérieure des Beaux Arts (ENSBA).

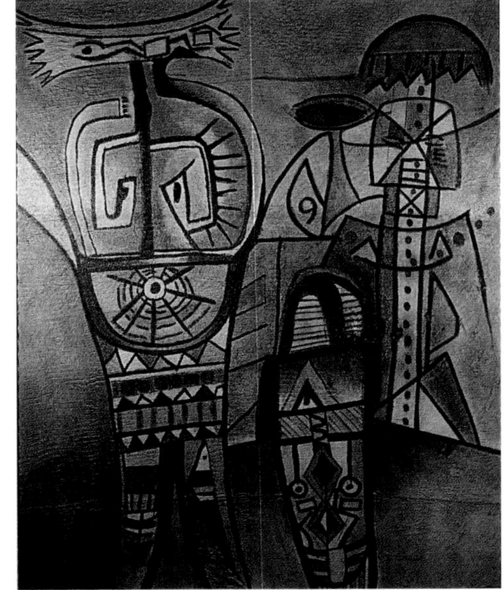

Youssouf Bath (born in 1949), c.a. 1985

©Revue Noire

The Black Caribbean group was formed in Abidjan in the late 60s. It did not have a style and was not a school per se; instead it had a state of mind. This movement was "a progressive trend of official art, (...) it was the expression of heartbreak, of an awareness due to the invasion of a foreign culture, an awareness whose legitimacy is later confirmed by the isolation of certain artists upon attending European art schools, where numerous prejudices widely contribute to their rejection of African culture" states James Oura, a plastic artist and theoretician from Ivory Coast. This group was the fruit of the joint reflections of three artists, Jean Gensin, Louis Laouchez and Serge Hélénon, West Indian painters and instructors.

Serge Hélénon and Louis Laouchez were both born in Martinique in 1934 and graduated from the École des Arts Décoratifs of Nice. Sensitive to the theories of Negritude, their desire to identify and promote their distant roots led them to Africa. In 1964, they found themselves in Bamako, Mali, and then in Ivory Coast, where, with Jean Gensin, they became instructors at the Institut National des Arts of Abidjan. In order to distance themselves from academic methods, these artists encouraged their painting workshop students to use new materials and to work with new concepts. The thinking process was based on a few premises, and advocated, in particular, a return to African elements by using and organizing forms, colors and materials.

This interest in traditional arts was not specific to Ivory Coast: *"Whether it be in Ivory Coast, Senegal or Gabon, artists had been rekindling their interest in the great history of African art for several decades. Around 1970, the new generation painters brought with them paintings done in their respective countries with mediums frequently used by their ancestors: mat work on a thick, worn piece of fabric, ochre or brown in color, made using the woody part of trees, namely the beaten bark called Tapa. Into this rough medium they painted, trimmed, sewed, and incorporated materials found on site: undyed or printed fabrics, cowries, ropes, threads, lianas, bamboos and colored earth. These painters used natural colors taken from different types of clay, powders and plants. All of these materials, with which they had been familiar since childhood, were used to make pottery, masks, costumes for festivals and ceremonies, and were later transformed into signs, tattoos, scarifications, graffiti on personal works, works driven by the very spirit of the country and of its ancestral traditions."*[1]

Heterogeneous materials
The assembly of heterogeneous materials, each with their own surface qualities and poetic and symbolic resonance, is one of the permanent features. The tapa contributes its roughness and history. It was once used to make clothing and ritual fabrics. Vegetable fibers were used for their flexibility and fluidity. The calabash contributes its rigidity and its light, shiny patina. Sand, earth and gravel bring to mind the ground, architecture and pottery. Wood evokes not only trees, but also frameworks, sculptures and masks. Works made using these materials are structured by alternating bumpy and heterogeneous surfaces. "That is all Vohou-Vohou" states a student in the Architecture Section of the School of

[1] M. Yankel, instructor at the École Nationale Supérieure des Beaux Arts of Paris, in the text presenting the exhibit "African Art, Sculptures of Yesterday – Painting of Today"

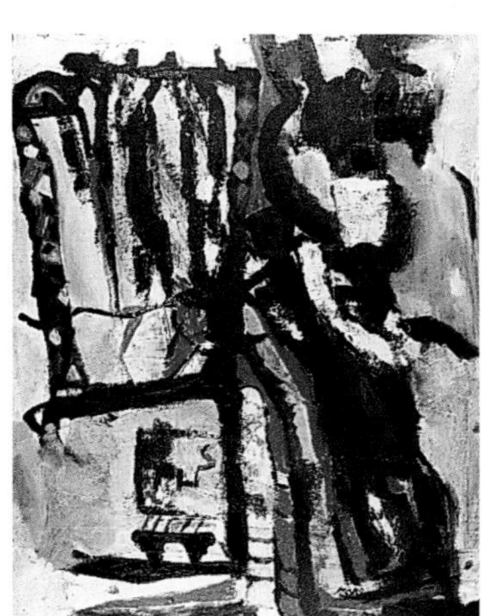

Mathilde Moro (born in 1958), 1986

©Revue Noire

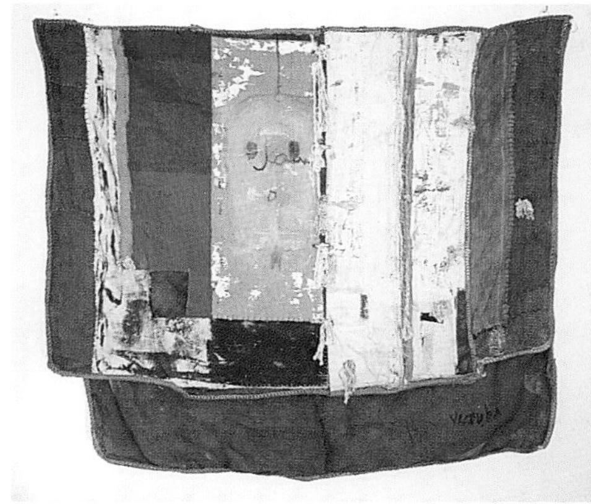

Yacouba Touré (born in 1830)

©Revue Noire

Abidjan, in a critical tone, in the early 70s. This is a term in the Gouro language, an ethnic group from central Ivory Coast. It expresses the idea of a confused and mixed whole. However, many works of traditional societies use associated heterogeneous materials. "Vohou-Vohou" says the healer as well, as he digs out the plants he will use to prepare ointments or upon applying various materials on the patient's body to ward off evil spirits. The word therefore refers to magical practices. Part of a plastic artist's research leads him into the field usually reserved for animist religious acts. This movement is based on the use of raw materials; however, the use of these materials is not solely formal. Artists want to speak about how they feel, about how they fit into the social setting and about what is essential to them, namely their culture.

Signs and symbols

Colorful harmonies were born of these practices. Shades of ochre, black, white and red dominate due to the importance of natural, organic or mineral materials. Beaten tree bark, line fiber, raffia, cotton, clay, gravel, ash, colored earth, ground cola, natural pigments, bird feathers, fish scales, all add shades of color. Oil paint in a tube, printed or dyed fabrics are added when greater polychromy is desired. The patterns are often derived from traditional abstract or representational patterns. African statuary is understood as a dictionary of forms and signs that artists have found necessary to question. Reinvention and reinterpretation then follows. As a result, we find silhouettes of Senufo or Baule statuettes and Dan or We mask profiles. Artists also refer to objects, pottery, jewels, weights for weighing gold and traditional fabrics for symbolic signs and tribal graphic designs. The forms are sometimes merely abstract. Approaches with more universal connotations are associated to this research into African traditions. This leads to an outlook on the history of mankind with allusions to the initial gestures that produced signs, paintings and prehistoric sculptures. These works therefore take us back to the origins of man.

"Working the material, which is fundamental for me, is part of a profound ritual taking me back to the origins of man. Gluing, scratching, sewing…marking the medium to indicate a presence." (N. Guessan Kra)

Rhythms and vibrations

We are in the presence of a specific manner of composing art. Plastic organizations are based on the search for rhythms and vibrations. Lines of force are drawn, ruptures mark the boundaries of masses and we read the paintings as we would painted fabrics, fragments of landscapes or village maps. The work's plan is asserted using geophysics. The first artists producing collage and assembly art were Dosso, N'Guessan Kra, Youssouf Bath, Kouakou, Yacouba, Meledge, Aboueu, Diamande, Théodore Koudognon, Oliko, Ozoua, and Louguet Zemblé Zégé. Grouped together under the name Vohou-Vohou, they organized many more events and exhibits in the 1970s and 1980s. A little later on, the second generation became more diversified, especially through its return to canvas painting.

Period of structuring in Makerere, Uganda

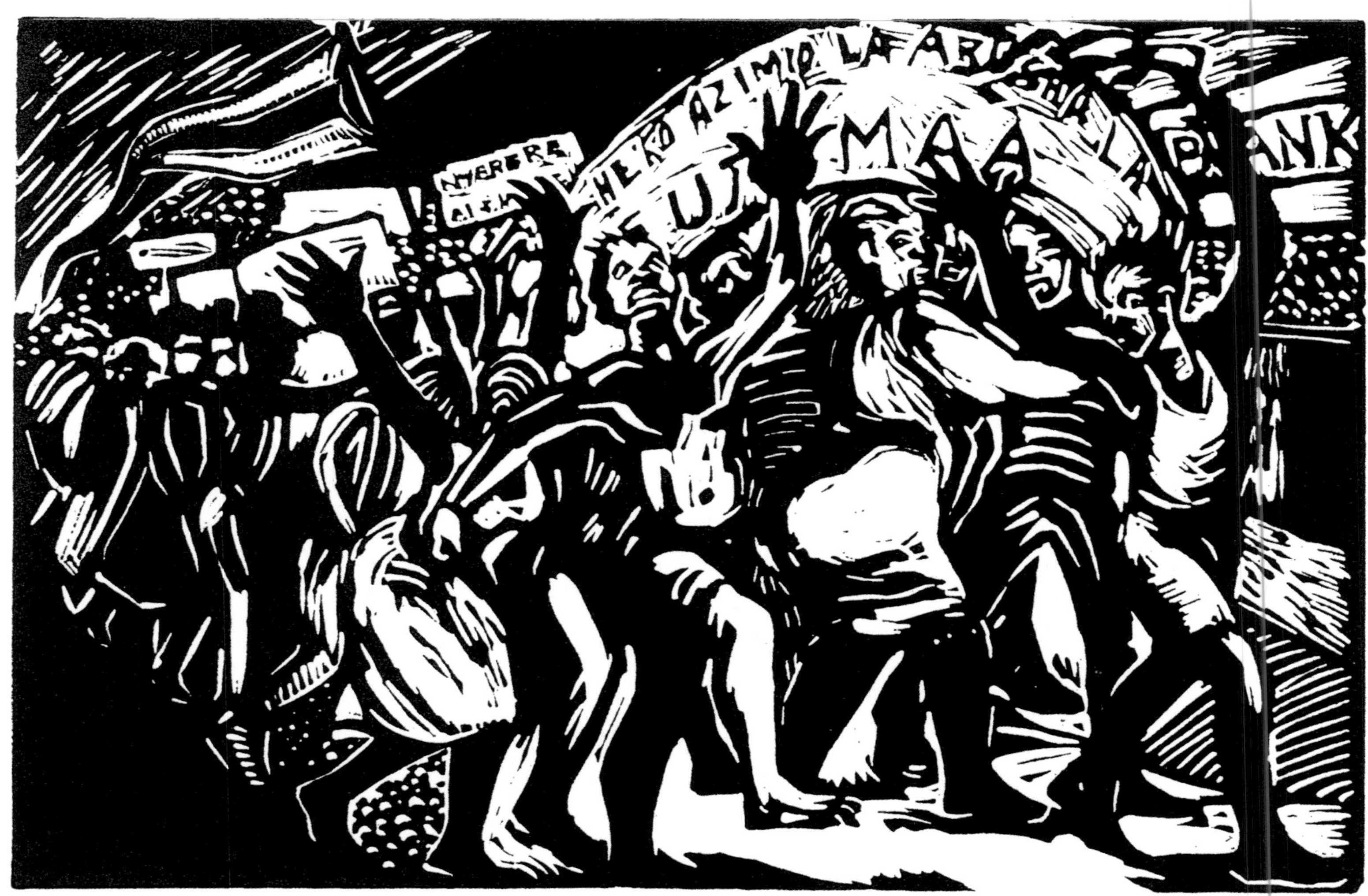

Francis Kiure Msangi (born in 1937), "Ujamaa," Tanzania, 1967

facing page:

Jonathan Kingdon, "Portrait of a bishop," Uganda, 1967

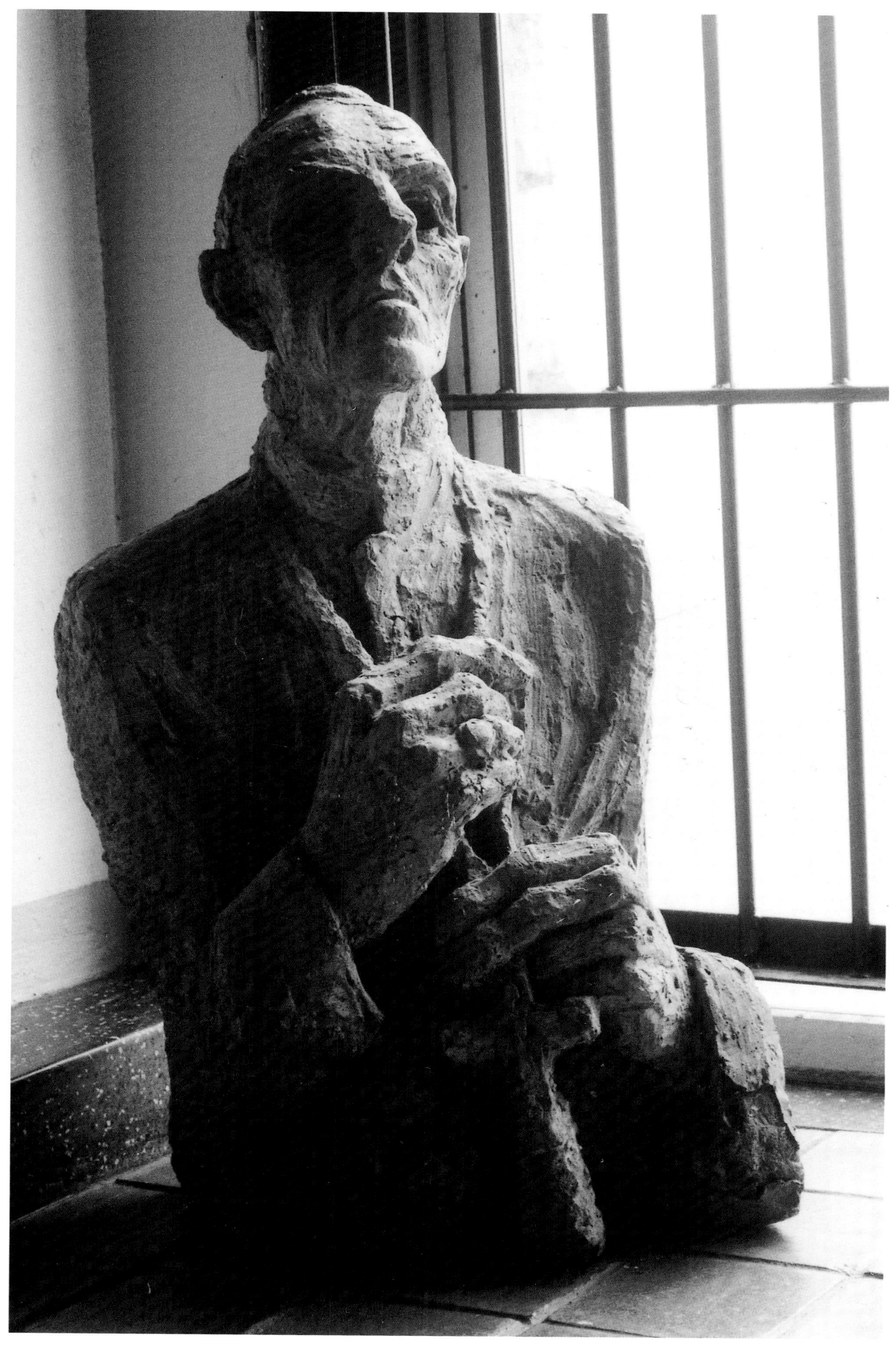

Mark Mutayaba, Uganda, 1967
©Elsbeth Court

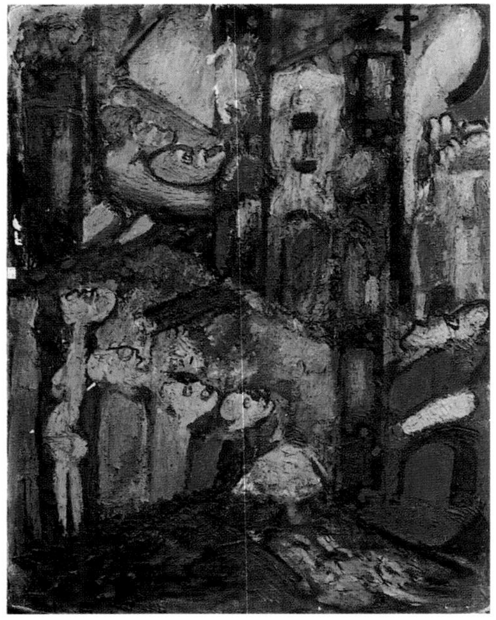

Kefa Ssempangi (born in 1944), "Golgotha," Uganda, 1969
oil on wood
©Sunanda Sanyal

MAKERERE ART SCHOOL, UGANDA: THE PERIOD OF FORMALISATION

George Kyeyune

In the decade (1960-70) during which the countries of Sub-Saharan Africa gained independence, it is hardly surprising that the concept of "decolonisation of the African mind" should be a major subject of scholarly attention. In the various departments of Makerere University, students and lecturers were writing very vigorously about this as well as the Africisation of the curriculum.[1] At Makerere Art school the reverse was happening. Mrs. Trowell's successor, Cecil Todd was exposing his students to a lot more western art including a wide range of modern styles. Todd, formerly a professor at the Rhodes University South Africa, was appointed in 1958 by the inter-university council of the Commonwealth Universities, to head the school and his commitment was to give it a formal professional standing through instilling a high lever of technical skills. He paid little attention to what Trowell had done, which sometimes brought him into conflict with some artists in the school, whose ideas of Africanisation he opposed. For instance, in the expansion of his diverse staff to include new members like Jonathan Kingdon, Ali Darwish, Taj Ahmad, Michael Adams, and later Theresa Musoke and Geraldine Roberts, Elimo Njau was not invited back despite his first class diploma, while Sam Ntiro, Trowell's appointee, was dismissed.[2]

Through G. Maloba (a survivor form Trowell's staff) and J. Kingdon's influence, however, students were encouraged to be free to approach any subject they wished, drawing on their own skills and sensitivities reflecting the heady climate of Uhuru (independence). Kingdon writes, "Gregory and I were the principal advocates of an East African social perspective in contrast to the more scholarstic detached views of Cecil Todd."[3] Even within these seemingly wide ranging opinions in training, some students such as Eli Kyeyune left without finishing their degrees, because they were opposed to what they considered an insufficiently Africanised curriculum. Kyeyune after his dismissal from the school made a success of his painting career when he joined Elimo Njau at his newly founded Paa ya Paa Cultural Centre in the early 60s in Nairobi.

Intellectual discussions in art materialised in the two volumes of "Roho" magazine, in 1961 and 1962, edited by Kingdon. The printing of Roho celebrated the school's latest venture of the introduction of the graphic design section which made it (Roho) the first colour publication in East Africa. Roho in 1964 dissolved itself into "Transition" Magazine which was culturally broader to cover literary and political issues. Todd's major projects included the construction of Makerere Art Gallery (a further land mark in the celebration of western modernism) funded by the Gulbenkian Foundation and during his time the first PhD in the school of fine art was awarded.

Although the school was developing into one of Makerere's most distinguished faculties, its necessity was still often questioned by the members of the academic community. But for the firm ideals and the strong character of its staff, the school developed a sense of identity and nationalism. Since for most colonials art was still regarded as a dispensable luxury, Makerere Art School took on a dutiful responsibility becoming the only serious choice for professional training in the region. Important graduates during this time include, George Kakooza, Theresa Musoke, Mugalula Mukiibi, Pilkington Ssengendo, Ignatius Sserulyo, Nobert Kaggwa and Kefa Ssempangi from Uganda, Kiure Msangi from Tanzania, Louis Mwaniki and Elkana Ongessa from Kenya, Henry Tayali from Zambia, Petson Lombe from Malawi and several others. In their work, the effect of Todd's direction and echoes of Maloba and Kingdon's ideas are apparent.
Kefa Ssempangi for example examines the ambivalence of the Ugandan belief system, that is indigenous versus Christianity. His collages are highly individual, a primordial vision that hang on to his early rural childhood, with resonances of "native" healing processes.
On the other hand Kakooza's sculptures are elongated figures, with severely

[1] Hugh Dinwidday and Michael Twaddle, 1988; Crisis at Makerere-Uganda Now, James Currey. 198

[2] Sydney Littlefield Kasfir, 1999: Contemporary African Art; Thames and Hudson, London 147.

[3] Quoted from Jonathan Kingdon's conversation with Wanjiku Nyacae on "Makerere Art School, Kampala," Seven Stories about modern Art in Africa. 281.

[4] Compare with Margaret Macpherson: They build for the future, 1964. Cambridge 136. Also with, Sydney L. Kasfir: Contemporary African Art, 1999, Thames and Hudson, 149

attenuated arms and legs which are then abstracted into geometric shapes. His work is more closely related to Giacometti and not his teacher Maloba.

Although during the late 50s and the 60s, artists enjoyed a modest patronage from government, private parastatals and individuals, for most if not all, as well as their protégés among the students, the Nommo (National) gallery in Kampala provided the needed access to patrons and audience.[4]

In subject master and style, Todd's era is associated with modern prototypes. The inclusion and engaging of culturally derived subjects in the work of this period can be assumed to have been handed clown from Trowell's period whose legacy expressed an East African cultural empathy.

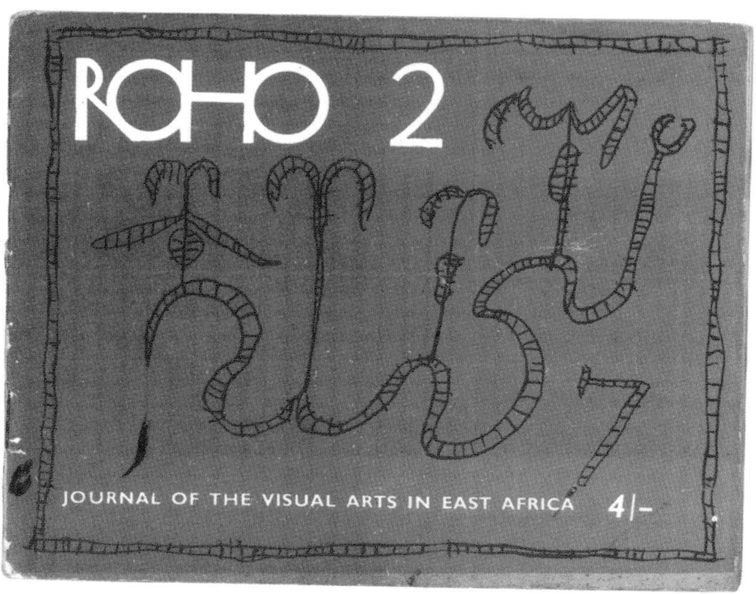

above:
Magazine Roho, n°2, June 1962
©D.R.

down:
Magazine Roho, n°1, June 1961
text and illustration by Elimo Njau (born in 1932), Tanzania
©D.R.

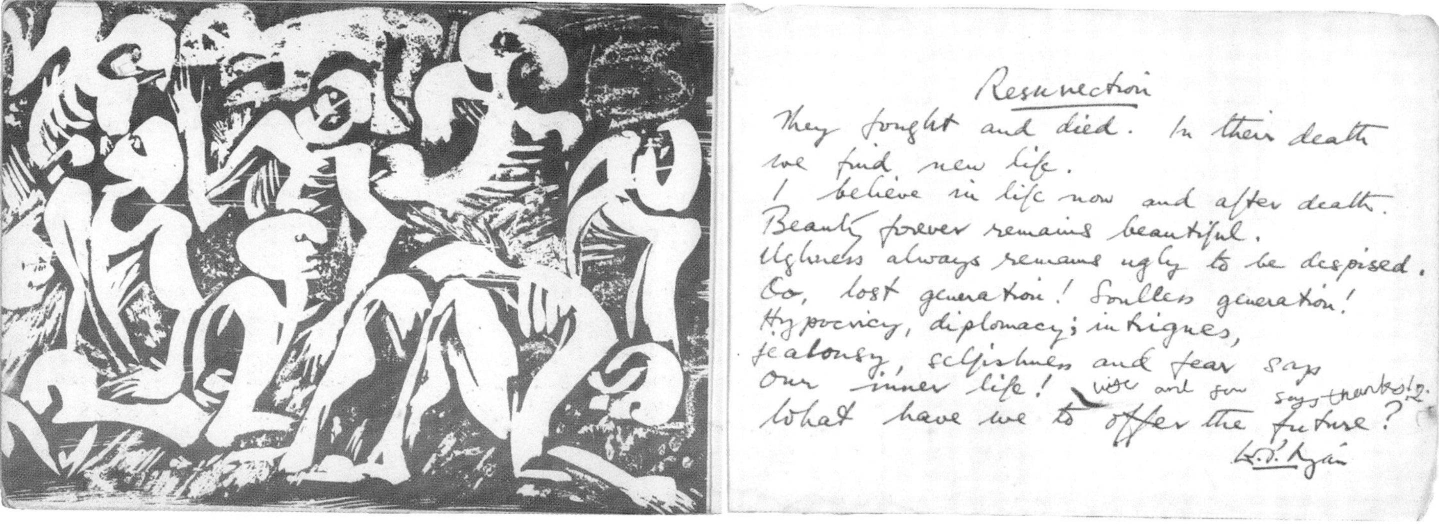

Resurrection

They fought and died. In their death
we find new life.
I believe in life now and after death.
Beauty forever remains beautiful.
Ugliness always remains ugly to be despised.
Oh, lost generation! Soulless generation!
Hypocricy, diplomacy; intrigues,
jealousy, selfishness and fear says
Our inner life!
What have we to offer the future?

Zaria Art Society and the Uli Movement, Nigeria

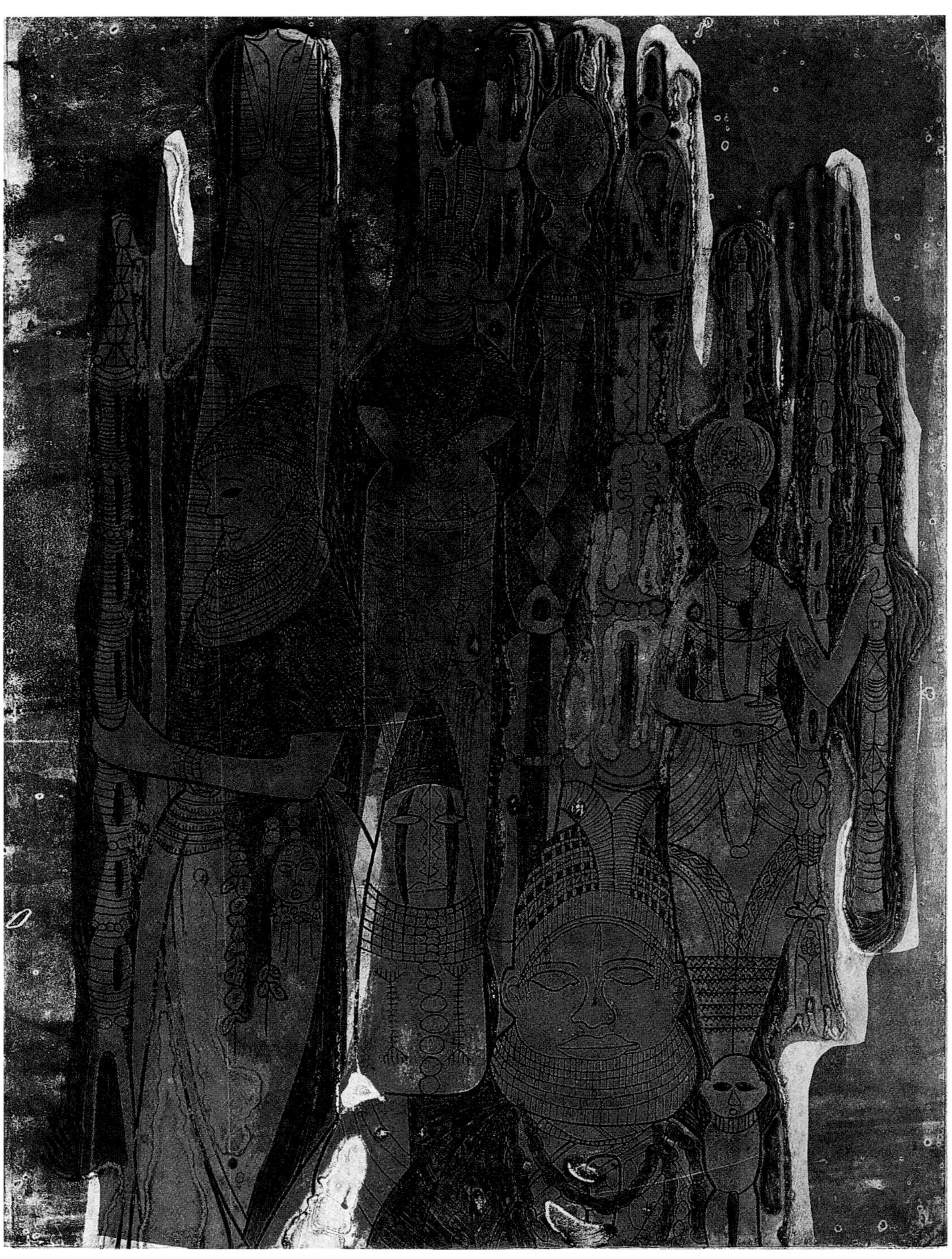

Bruce Onobrakpeya (born in 1932), "Ekassa," 1980"
etching

ZARIA ART SOCIETY AND THE ULI MOVEMENT, NIGERIA

Sylvester Ogbechie

The Zaria Art Society: 1958-1962

The postcolonial period saw a revision of ideologies in modern Nigerian art as a new crop of younger artists directed their attention to issues of nation building and cultural identity. In Nigerian art institutions, demands for a reconfiguration of teaching methods, subject matter and the racial configuration of teaching staff led to a rejection of the standard British curriculum and a call for a contemporary art practice based on interrogation of indigenous aesthetics. In 1958, some students at the Nigeria College of Arts, Science and Technology (NCAST) formed the Zaria Art Society as a forum to reflect on the role of indigenous cultures on modern Nigerian art in the postcolonial period especially as this affected their training and practice as artists.

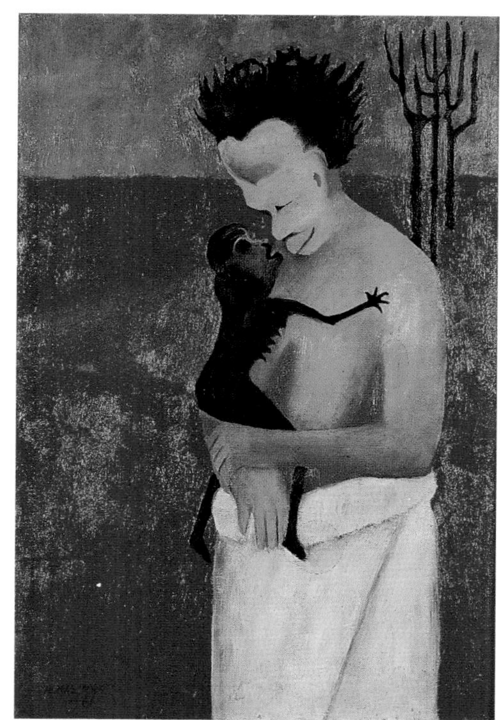

Demas Nwoko (born in 1935), "Folly," c.a. 1960
gouache
©Nigeria Magazine

The Zaria Art Society comprised of Uche Okeke, Yusuf Grillo, Demas Nwoko, Bruce Onobrakpeya, Simon Obiekezie Okeke (d. 1968), Ogbonnaya E. Nwagbara, William Olaosebikan, Felix N. Ekeada, Oseloka O. Osadebe, E. Okechukwu Odita and Jimoh Akolo. The group developed into a formal organization under the patronage of Clara Ugbodaga Ngu (a painting instructor) and Patrick George, chair of the department of Fine Art.

The curriculum at NCAST was based on the Goldsmiths School of Art (London) curriculum and its emphasis on forms of expression anchored on the academic model replicated a dedication to art studies based on European classical traditions. In fact, principal instructors at NCAST like Patrick H. George, the chair, were appointed by the Colonial Office to oversee the development of the NCAST Fine Art department along these lines. There would eventually be much criticism of this curriculum by both students in the institution (the Zaria Art Society's claim to rebellion hinges on their critique of the curriculum's subject matter and aesthetic orientation) and by prominent Nigerian artists like Ben Enwonwu.

As a conceptual framework for their critique of the colonial education's Eurocentric orientation, the Zaria Art Society formulated the ideology of Natural Synthesis, which advocated a natural, unforced and unconscious synthesis of European media and techniques with forms, styles and contents derived from indigenous Nigerian cultures. Members were encouraged to investigate indigenous aesthetics, styles and media and utilize their findings in their attempts to develop individual styles of expression. Given the diverse origins of the students involved in this organization, indigenous heritage varied widely and their utilization generated highly individual techniques and forms for the artists.

Uche Okeke turned to Igbo Uli body painting tradition for inspiration in keeping with his earlier involvement in studies of Igbo cultural traditions. His formulations created the basis for a broad revival of Uli aesthetics in contemporary Nigerian art especially among his students at the University of Nigeria where he became an instructor and administrator.

Simon Obiekezie Okeke created monumental watercolors with all the weight and illusion of sculpture using images of archetypal females as leitmotif in obvious deference to the Negritude ideology prevalent at that time. These experiments continued until his death in 1971.

Bruce Onobrakpeya practiced as a painter until he attended a workshop in printmaking at the 1962 Mbari Ibadan where he met the printmaker Ru Van Rossem who instructed him in printmaking techniques. Onobrakpeya's subsequent career as a printmaker cemented his reputation as he welded indigenous Nigerian visual traditions into a syncretic and expressive modern form. He also contributed an invention to this medium: the plastocast technique that he discovered accidentally when he spilled acid on a copper plate and was fascinated by the resulting deep etched grooves it created. Onobrakpeya is currently the most renowned African printmaker.

Demas Nwoko's investigations engendered a revival of Nok terracotta techniques for sculpture and he produced a significant body of work in

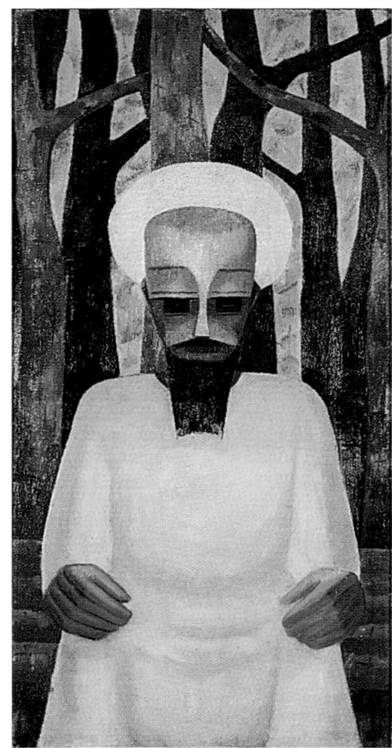

Uche Okeke (born in 1933), "Christ," 1961

©Maison Iwalewa, Université de Bayreuth

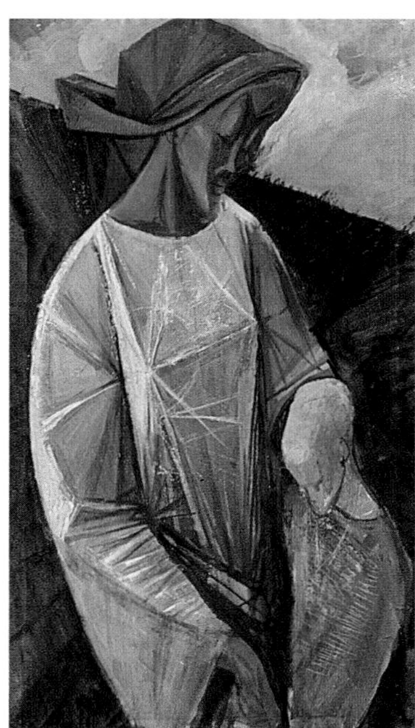

Yusuf Grillo (born in 1934), "Mother and child," 1974

©Amaize Ojeikere

this medium in addition to the broad range of his art and design interests. He designed several notable structures in his practice as an architect and was also involved with stage design for the theater, furniture design, and painting. Yusuf Grillo developed a highly formal visual structure for his paintings based on cubist forms and the blue and indigo color scheme of indigenous Yoruba textiles. His works focus on Yoruba life and culture in the context of a changing social structure while Jimoh Akolo chronicled the same themes with focus on northern Nigerian culture.

The Zarianists have been credited with creating a significant paradigm shift in modern Nigerian art because their interrogation of critical paradigms in art education enhanced the search for a theoretical basis for modern Nigerian art thus expanding the discourse instituted by Aina Onabolu at the inception of this practice. However, their ideology of Natural Synthesis antedated in the artworks and aesthetic philosophy of Ben Enwonwu, can be seen in the context of a broad international movement by colonized societies questioning and rejecting their dependence on the tropes and cultures of the colonizer.

The students who formed the Zaria Art Society in 1958 enrolled at NCAST between 1956 and 1958 and the Society disbanded in 1962 as its members graduated. Subsequently, their careers pursued independent paths although Uche Okeke, Demas Nwoko and Bruce Onobrakpeya remained very close and collaborated on many projects. All of them became influential artists, teachers and art administrators who helped shape the direction of postcolonial Nigerian art through their vast influence on art students in Nigerian art schools.

Uli Movement in the Nsukka School

The Uli Revivalist Movement of the Nsukka School came into being as an institutional manifestation of Uche Okeke's paradigm of Natural Synthesis following his appointment to the University of Nigeria as head of its art department in 1970. In the wake of a civil war (1967-1970) that left many parts of Eastern Nigeria devastated, Okeke's paradigm, which had earlier been directed towards articulating a national culture, was reconfigured into a militant affirmation of Igbo ethnic identity. He expanded his study of the Igbo Uli painting tradition, begun as a member of the 1958-1962 Zaria Art Society, into a broad investigation into Igbo cultural identity in a fractious post-war political context. The art that ensued from his work and those of his students in this institution (collectively known as the Nsukka School) evolved into the most potent aesthetic and ideological practice of modern Nigerian art in the 20th century.

Uli is an art form that was practiced among the Igbo of South Eastern Nigeria. The term (Uli) refers both to the indigo dye obtained from several species of plants from the genus Rothmania, and also to the body and mural painting traditions that utilize this dye to create complex symbolic forms abstracted from natural and cosmological archetypes. The design motifs and symbols used in traditional Uli painting are very organic and overall, have a fiercely linear character. Traditional Uli design sets up a taut dialogue between forms (its motifs) and space in compositions that employ space itself as a principal element of design.

Uche Okeke's contemporary adaptation of Uli sought to internalize the essence of the tradition through an understanding of its symbolic form and aesthetic paradigms. His stylistic innovations occupy one end of a continuum that includes markedly varied responses to the same aesthetic principles by other artists involved in the Uli revivalist movement. As his students moved out from their base at the University of Nigeria, the neo-Uli paradigm moved with them and underwent major transformations engendered by variations in media, cultural background, and other related factors. In addition to the Uli motifs and symbols that formed their core indigenous archetype, Nsukka artists have also investigated other indigenous art traditions like Nsibidi and through the pedagogy of the sculptor El Anatsui, Ghanaian Ewe Adinkra symbols and motifs. These investigations proceed upon a sound knowledge of European

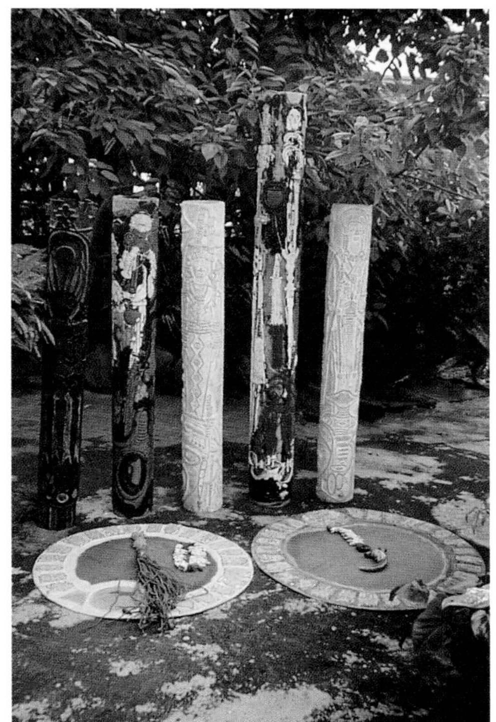

Bruce Onoprakpeya (born in 1932), "Shrine set"
305x305x183 cm

modernism, its techniques and strategies of representation. The influences on their art are thus varied and very eclectic.

Some of the principal artists of the Uli revivalist movement include Obiora Udechukwu who trained under Uche Okeke and in turn has trained two generations of Nsukka artists including Tayo Adenaike, Olu Oguibe and Marcia Kure. Although male artists dominate the contemporary Uli movement, the Nsukka School has produced some female artists with equally compelling styles and international reputations. In addition to Kure, these female artists include Ndidi Dike, a sculptor of renown, and Chinwe Uwatse, a painter. Other female artists in this movement like Ada Udechukwu, have also made significant contributions in textile design although this by no means indicate a curricular bias to these subjects by Nsukka female art students.

In addition to its obvious artistic orientation, the Nsukka Uli movement also encompasses a critical tradition engendered by the reflexiveness that artists, critics and art historians involved in this movement have brought to bear on their own works. The art historian, Ola Oloidi, who introduced a very rigorous critical style to the Nsukka School, mostly instigated this focus on art criticism. His assertions on the uses of art criticism, (refracted through his own critical engagements) demarcated between art journalism and art criticism in Nigerian art and encouraged a orientation to the latter among critics like Sylvester Ogbechie, Chika Okeke, and Kris Ikwuemezi who emerged from the Nsukka School.

In 1986, the AKA group brought together 13 significant artists involved in the Uli movement for yearly exhibitions of their works. The catalogs of these exhibitions provided scholarly assessments of Uli aesthetics and its implications for contemporary art practice while tracing the evolution of individual styles among the artists whose mediums include painting, sculpture, metalwork, textiles and ceramics design. These exhibitions helped direct international attention to the Uli movement. Subsequently, many artists involved with this movement participated in international exhibitions and in 1991, the Smithsonian Institution devoted an exhibition to their works accompanied by a book that chronicled the history of the Uli movement in Nigerian art. The Nsukka School has been very influential in the development of modern Nigerian art and continues to be a relevant force in African art through the international practice of its artists and critics.

Continuity and conflict in South Africa

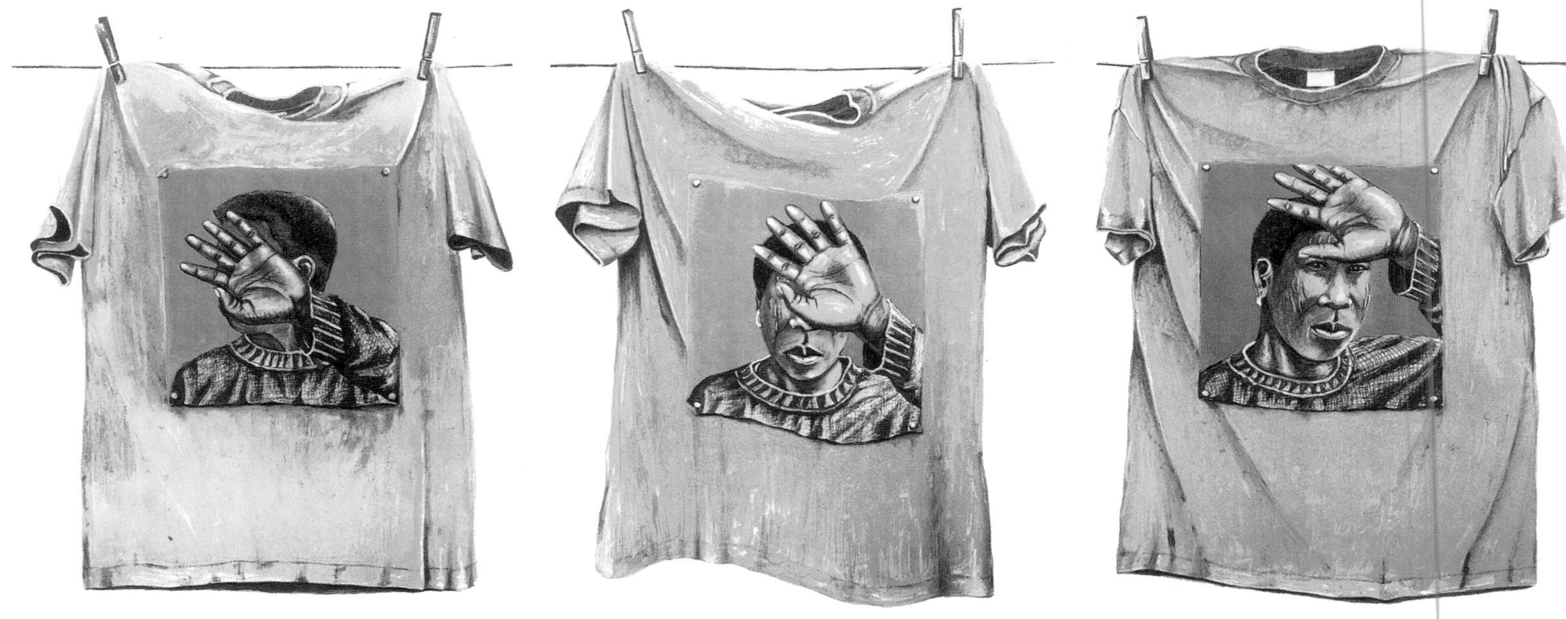

above:

Thembinkosi Goniwe, "XXX (Washing line series)," 1997

lithograph and oil pastels

facing page:

Doc Seoka (born in 1922), "Portrait of Madifukwana Muhala," 1984

wood

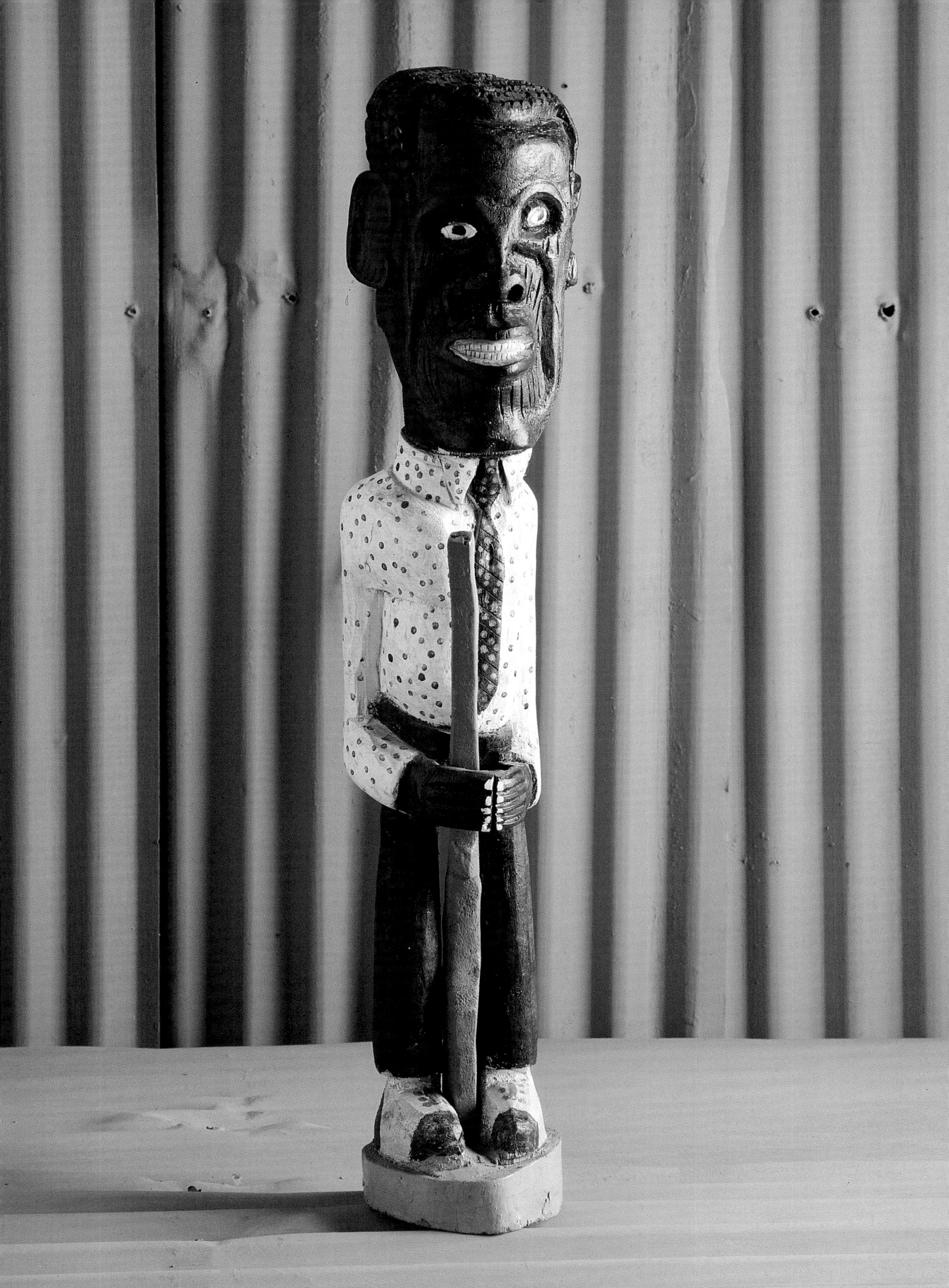

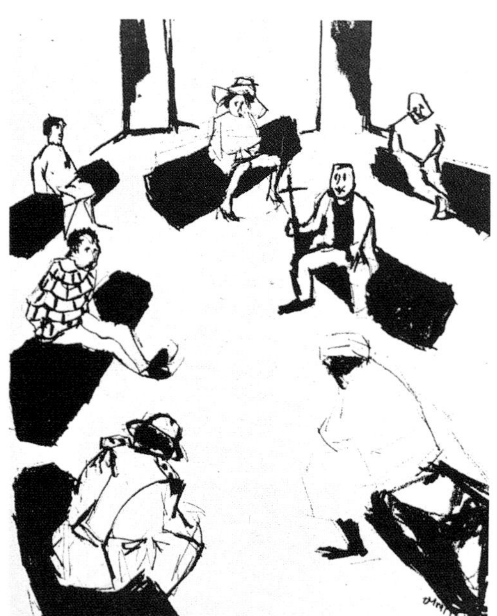

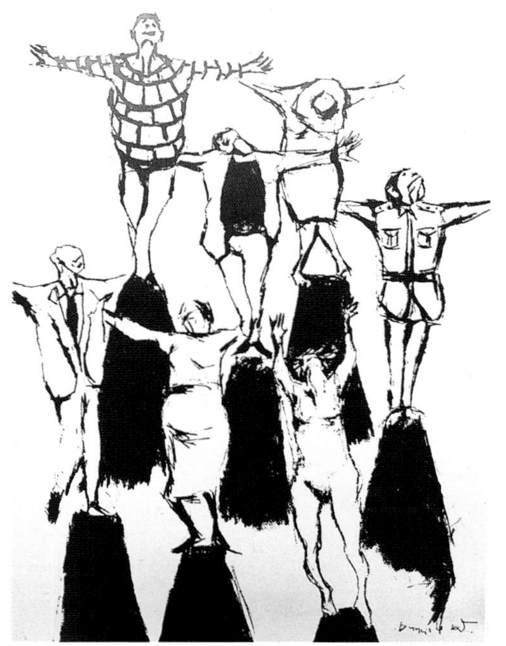

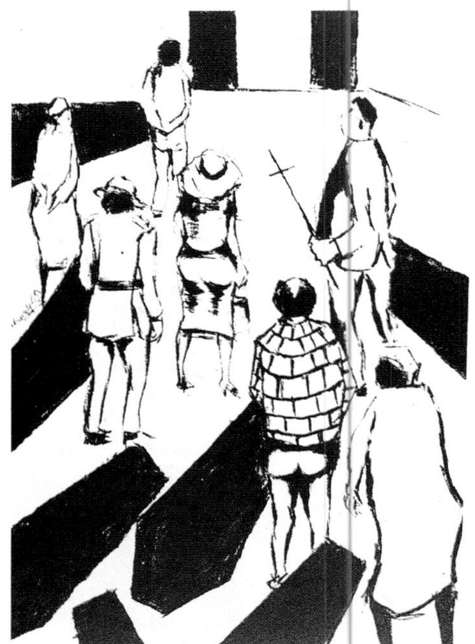

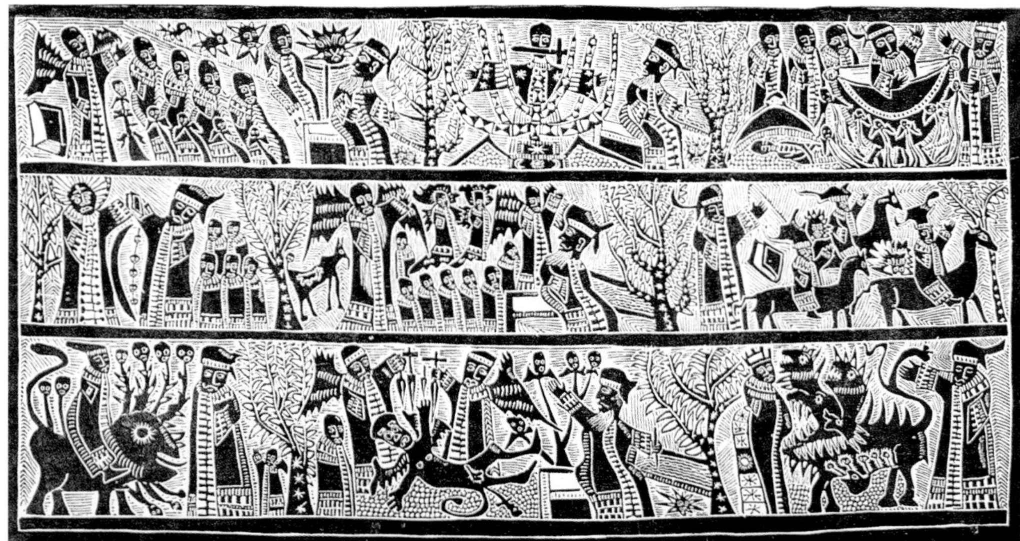

top:
Dumile Feni (1939-1991), "The Resurrection," 1965
crayon, 53,3x37,9 cm

above:
Azaria Mbatha (born in 1941), "The Revalation of Saint Jean," 1965
linogravure, 37,6x68 cm

facing page:
Cecil Skotnes (born in 1926), "Shaka kills the leopard," 1973
woodcut, 44,5x28 cm

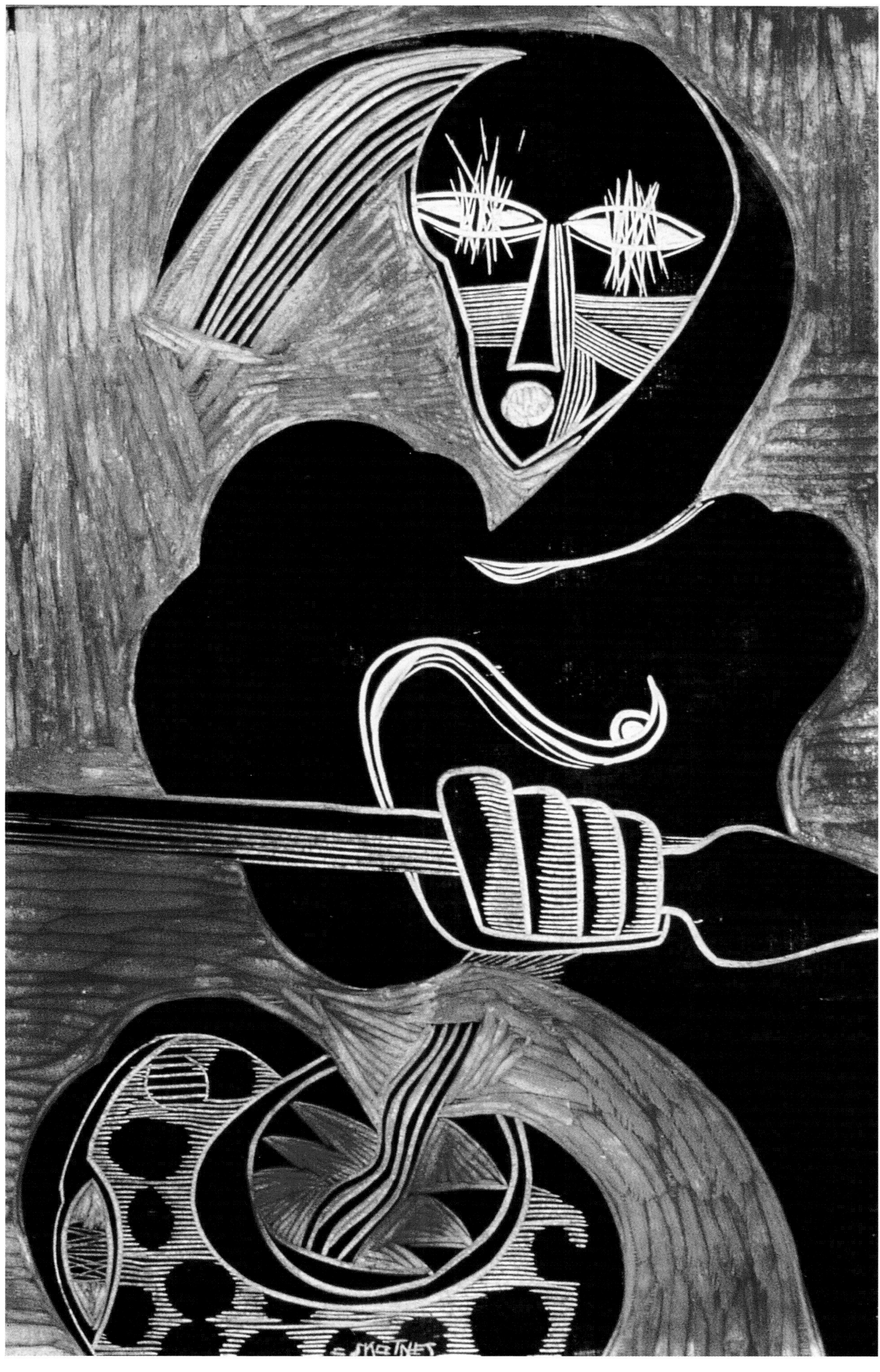

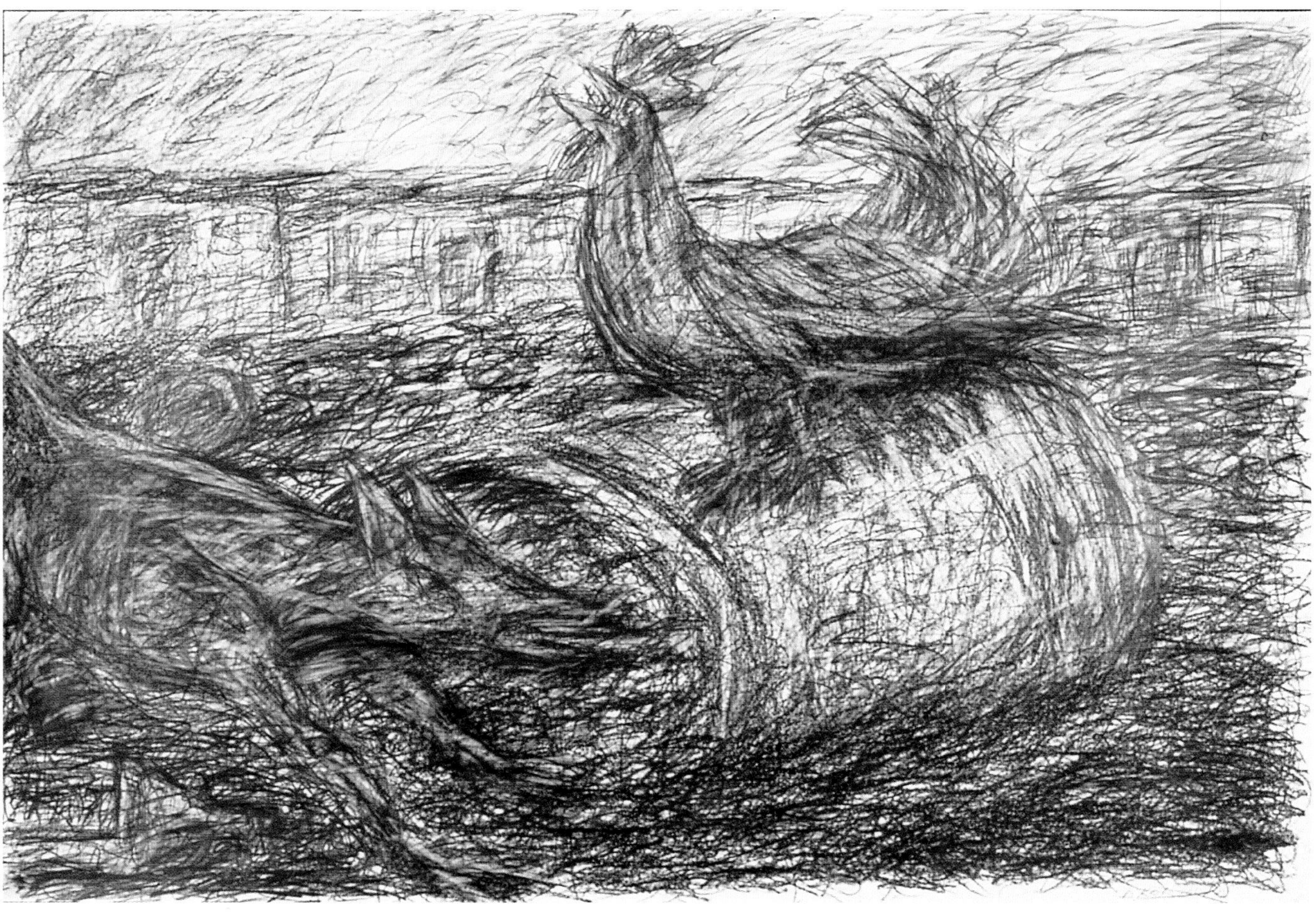

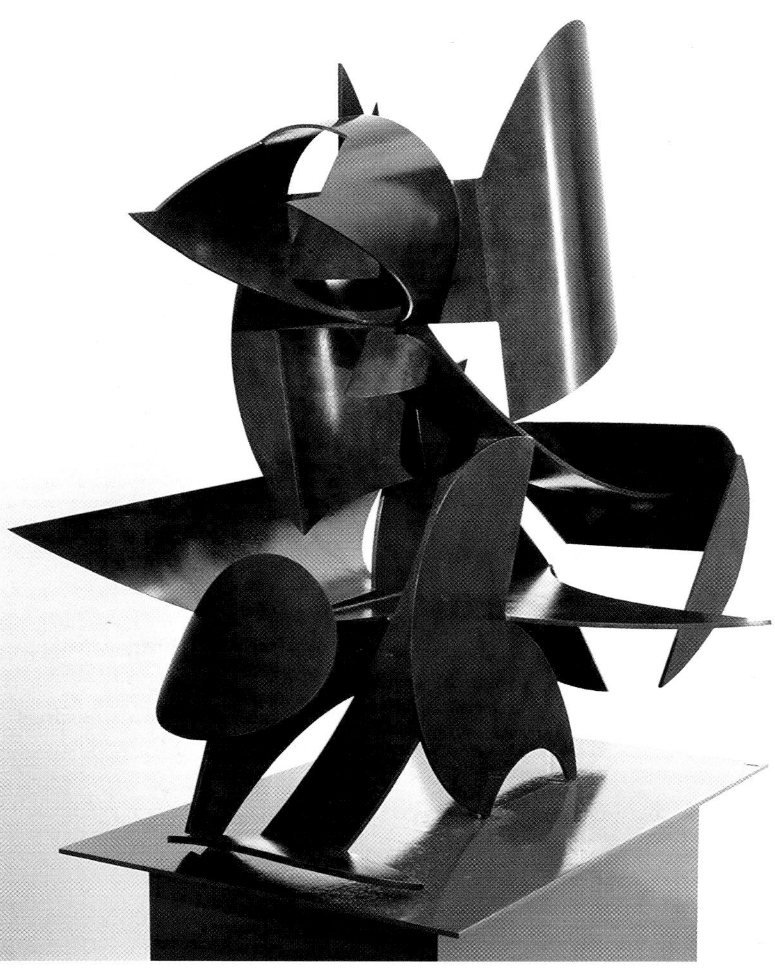

top:
David Koloane (born in 1938), "Made in S.A."
pencil

left:
Edouardo Villa (born in 1920), "African Chief," 1963
metal, h. 91 cm

CONTINUITY AND CONFLICT IN SOUTH AFRICA

Marylin Martin

Notions of separation and segregation lay at the heart of apartheid ideology and legislation and commonalities and similarities that had evolved over centuries were forcefully denied, negated and opposed. The cities, towns and spaces South Africans inhabit are the landscapes of apartheid. Divisions between town and township, black and white, rich and poor were created, with buffer strips to ensure effective separation. During the 1960s and 1970s the grip of apartheid laws continued to tighten, making movement for black people, and access to communication, facilities and education, increasingly difficult. For South African visual artists it was a time of continuity, conflict and new, alternative training initiatives.

The Rorke's Drift Art Centre

Another art centre that was to influence the course of black South African art was established in 1962- the Evangelical Lutheran Church Art and Craft Centre at Rorke's Drift in Natal. Rorke's Drift is situated in the heart of rural Africa, yet it was started by Swedish teachers Peder and Ulla Gowenius and staffed by white Americans and South Africans. Training was offered in fine art and crafts with clear differentiation with regard to gender: weaving and fabric painting were done by women (the designs sometimes generated by men); ceramics were created by men and women, but the latter used the traditional coil method, while men employed the kick-wheel; fine art was the preserve of men, with a few exceptions. There was a preference for "useful" arts that could generate money for the Centre. Yet there was a constant interaction and exchange of ideas and imagery between men and women working in the different media that proved advantageous for the overall production at Rorke's Drift.

Some extraordinary talents emerged under these unusual circumstances: Allina Ndebele (1939-) became a master weaver of international repute; Azaria Mbatha (1941-) John Muafangejo (1943-1987) and Cyprian Shilakoe (1946-1972) count among the great printmakers in the history of South African art. Mbatha and Muafangejo chose the lino technique for their biblical stories and renderings of their experiences, while Shilakoe preferred the softer, tonally subtle medium of etching and aquatint for his richly symbolic images of personal anguish the suffering of his people. A younger generation entered Rorke's Drift during the 1970s and became prominent artists, teachers and contributors to the flourishing of contemporary art. For various reasons, probably mostly financial, the fine art school was closed in 1982. The craft section continues to produce work that is dominated by a "Rorke's Drift style" that clearly misses the creative stimulation that artists had brought to the project.

The Amadlozi Group

In the white art world the quest for an idiom that was identifiably local would continue and would conflict or develop side by side with attempts to maintain international links by emulating overseas styles such as Abstract Expressionism, Pop Art, Op Art, Hard Edge painting and Assemblage. In 1963 the notion of an African identity was given particular focus and attention with the formation of the Amadlozi Group (amadlozi is a Zulu word meaning "spirit of our ancestors"). Egon Guenther, founder of the Group, recognised the "Africanness" apparent in Cecil Skotnes' wood engravings and prints, in the paintings of Cecily Sash (1925-) and Giuseppe Cattaneo (1929-) and in the sculptures of Sydney Kumalo and Edouardo Villa. Technically and stylistically their art was European, iconographically their sources were African. The group did not last long.

The Michaelis School of Fine Art

The 1970s and 1980s saw the establishment of a number of art centres that provided fertile ground for the growth and flowering of black art.[1] From the 1970s the Michaelis School of Fine Art of the University of Cape Town began to play a role, not only in educating art students, but also in influencing and challenging values – both inside the

[1] The list is impressive: Johannesburg Art Foundation (1972); Katlehong Art Centre (1977); Community Arts Project, Cape Town (1977); Fuba Academy, Johannesburg (1978); Nyanga Arts Centre (1979); Mofolo Art Centre, Soweto (1970s); African Institute of Art, Funda Centre, Soweto (1983); Community Arts Workshop, Durban (1983); Alexandra Arts Centre (1986) (Sack 1988: 25). The Johannesburg Art Foundation, Katlehong Art Centre, Community Arts Project, Fuba and Funda are still operative.

university and within the broader socio-political context. Students were transgressing the social and aesthetic norms of the day and they were moving from the private into the public domain. A number of artists were detained or imprisoned for political activity or went into exile. After the student uprising in Soweto in 1976, there was an eruption of independent, alternative, oppositional initiatives in Cape Town: this included the constitution of cultural workers' organisations such as The Visual Arts Group, the Cultural Workers' Congress and the Community Arts Project (Cap). Cap became a powerful player on the cultural-political map of the Western Cape, producing posters and banners for organisations and events, and providing a forum for political and cultural debate. It follows that the most important conference on art of the decade would be held in Cape Town, at the Michaelis School of Fine Arts in July 1979.

Ezrom Legae (1937-1999), "Waiting"
bronze
©D.R.

Art, culture and politics

In 1980 the cultural and academic boycott was instituted by the United Nations. It was conceived as an important aspect of a strategy for the total isolation of the minority regime in South Africa and formed part of a package of mandatory sanctions against the country. It lasted for ten years and had a profound effect on the scope and quality of productions and exhibitions offered in the country. Artists were denied exposure to other cultures and other creative people, as well as opportunities to work outside the country. The cultural isolation created a widespread sense of cultural inferiority among performers and audiences alike, but it played a part in bringing about the political negotiating process, and it forced artists, academics, art and museum administrators and dealers to re-assess candidly their roles and functions against the background of a rapidly changing socio-political landscape in general and the cultural boycott in particular. It made creative people sit up and take note of what "others" around them were doing. Questions were raised around the didactic and propagandistic functions of art, the artist's accountability to society and right to freedom of expression.

The relationship between art, culture and politics in South Africa has been close for a long time. Prior to the 1994 democratic elections, culture was used both as a basis for apartheid and as a site for liberation. Art was used as a weapon for political struggle, both inside and outside the country. But political art, in the form of direct and unambiguous comment on militarism, the security forces and the repressive Pretoria regime, only emerged in the 1960s and 1970s. Dumile Feni (1939-1991), who died in exile, was a great exponent of the art of drawing. He chronicled the disillusion and despair of black South Africans in his intensely expressionistic drawings and sculptures. Some artists started working towards finding the most appropriate technical, formal and expressive solutions for engaging the real political and societal questions of their time and their place; others continued to believe in art as a validation of individuality and a generator of the sublime; many remained primarily interested in following the swing of the international pendulum from figuration to abstraction, from realism to conceptualism.

Boundaries between art forms

Partly as a result of a post-modern emphasis on contextualism, and partly because of the political, economic, academic and artistic isolation that gathered momentum during the 1980s, a number of artists engaged in art that reflected their own environment. This resulted in increased cross-pollination and cross-over of cultures and contributed to the erosion of boundaries between art forms. Karel Nel (1955-) created cerebral and mystical drawings in which he included beadwork, dolls and African sculptures, in which he divined the dialogue between metaphysics and contemporary physics, between ancient ritual and space-age technology. Jackson Hlungwani (1923-) spent 30 years building a stone palace to the glory of God, a "New Jerusalem" in which he lived, preached and sculpted until he started moving between his village and Johannesburg. His Tsonga background and Christian beliefs meet in the monumental fish, angels, biblical figures and crucifixes that he carves, and the images from books and magazines that he

collects are a powerful source of information and reference.
Dissatisfaction with the sculptural means and methods of the International Style led Andries Botha (1952-) to explore the distinctly African materials of wattle and thatching grass and to transfer traditional Zulu skills to his own concerns and concepts.
Abstract styles had made their appearance in South Africa during the 1950s. Initially only one black artist saw abstraction as a means of incorporating his African heritage and his urban experience into drawing and painting. Louis Maqhubela (1939-) had studied at the Polly Street Art Centre and in the late 1960s, after a trip to Paris and London, started making abstract paintings. The Thupelo Workshops, initiated in Johannesburg in 1985 by David Koloane (1938-) and Bill Ainslie (1934-1989), concentrated on abstract approaches to painting. The aim was to widen the scope of artists who were disadvantaged by apartheid by providing spaces, facilities, materials and environments for interaction, and the opportunity of working freely on a large scale. White academics were outraged that black artists should paint in an abstract expressionistic manner, and the work produced was negated and criticised amidst accusations of American imperialism.[2] Today the workshops continue and the record of the artists' resilience and independence stands. Koloane, Kagiso Pat Mautloa (1952-), Sam Nhlengethwa (1955-) and Durant Sihlali have consistently stimulated and encouraged a process of redefining black art making, of defying colonialist stereotypes and challenging market demands and prescriptiveness.
Interestingly, Sihlali was a student at Polly Street, while Mautloa, recognised as one of South Africa's foremost artists, is a product of the "alternative" training system – Jubilee Centre (1969), Mofolo Art Centre (1970), Rorke's Drift Art Centre (1979) and the Thupelo Workshops. His work Reconstruction takes us into the next decade.
The stage was set for the release of Nelson Mandela and the unbanning of the liberation movements in February 1990. This would have profound effects on South African society and culture.

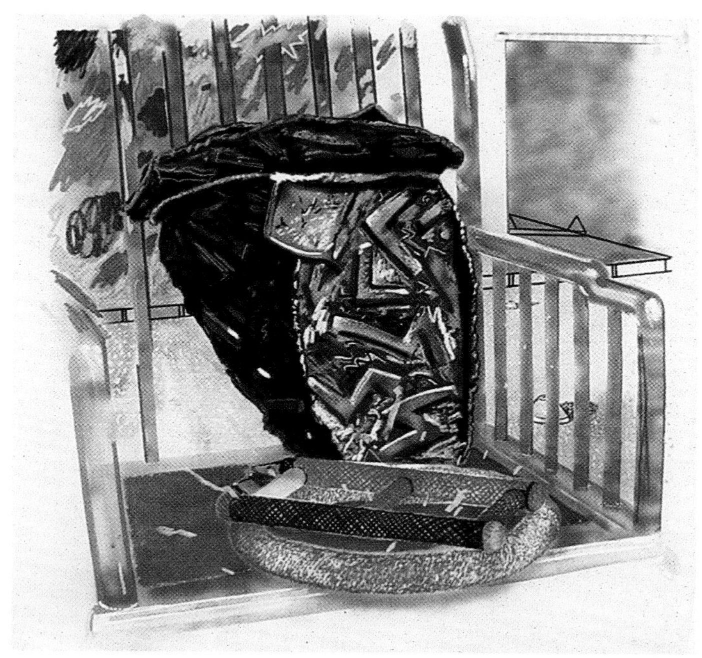

Karel Nel (born in 1955), "Arii Matamoe"
pastels
©South African National Gallery

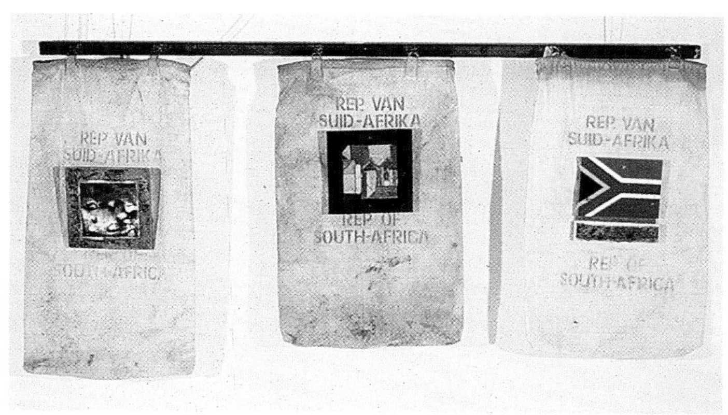

Kagiso Paul Mautloa (born in 1952), "Reconstruction," 1995
mixed techniques, 131x237 cm
©South African National Gallery

[2] See Martin, M. 1991. "Is There a Place for Black Abstract Painters in South Africa?" in de arte 44: pp. 25-29.

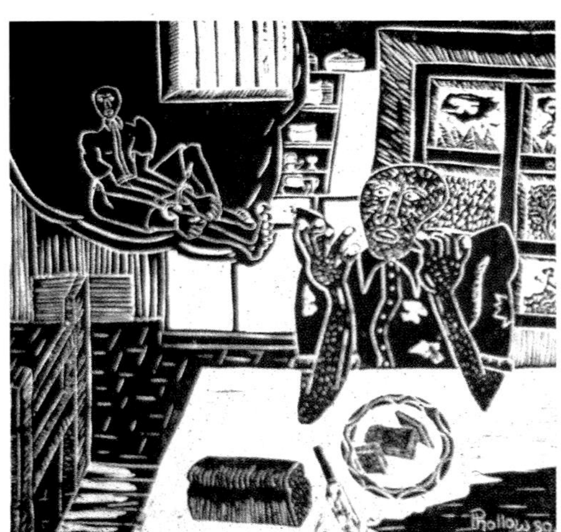

Patrick Hollow, "Thinking," 1980
paint on linoleum
©Gavin Younge

ART IN THE TOWNSHIPS
Gavin Younge

"Township art" came into use, and drew its framing power from the fact that, up until 1994, African people were prohibited from living anywhere other than in a declared black area. All important towns were declared "white" and several "black" townships were created around each town or city. This insistence on separation applied to rich and poor alike. No one was exempt from the scopic regime of their skin colour. No one was rich enough not to be black. . Up until the 1980s, townships were sealed spatial entities. Access roads, and physical layout all reinforced this sense of separation. This created a situation where almost all art produced by Africans was, in effect, produced in a township. When an early generation of African artists – Gerard Sekoto, Dumile Feni, George Pemba, and Gladys Mgudlandlu, among them – began showing their works publicly, audiences were astonished at the subject matter, as well as the painterly and graphic attributes of the works. These works passed through the closed physical and mental borders sealing the townships, and projected an authoritative text for outsiders.

This process of "revealing" that which is hidden continued into the 1970s and 1980s. Television coverage of events after the 1976 uprising began to take over this role, and young artists such as Robert Siwangaza and the Hollow brothers brought a more psychological emphasis to bear on these township scenes. Sydney and Patrick Hollow were involved in the Nyanga Art Centre[1] since its inception in 1979. Its trajectory, from hopeful and enthusiastic beginnings to its fitful demise after 1992, demonstrate how tenuous all such initiatives were. In the face of official neglect (attempts from the town council to buy a library and learning circle, failed), and pathetic private sponsorship, it is no wonder that people like Mteto Mwongwana, one of the most active members, lost heart.

Consequently "township art" is an art scripted by the state. Full of scopic regimes of influx control, "pass books," "administration boards," mielie boards, meat boards, and state-run beerhalls, "township art" is nonetheless, an art of devious delight. Musicians, kids playing in the street, the happy throng, sometimes a heavily stylized face. Dumile, Sam Nhlengethwa, Nat Mokgotsi to name three artists, without in any way accepting township life, have all produced images of the township which reach into people's minds in places all over the world. It is not folk art. Their realism is not passive or calculated as a style. There is no satire or reflective mimesis with the tradition of, say, Honoré Daumier. Instead, their works match the perception of what should be seen, because that is what they know. In this sense, their art is an art of telling stories well. In Xhosa, they say masibaliselane.

"Doctor" Phuthuma Seoka

Take the extraordinary images of "Doctor" Phuthuma Seoka. Are these gallant, striding dandies approbations of the apartheid era, or are they an expression of recoil? Following Gayyatri Chakravorty Spivak,[2] has Seoka learned to speak in forms acceptable to the architects of the migrant labour system? We can ask what these images "mean." For Seoka they were a means to earn a living. In other words he saw himself as a professional artist, "I like these things because they give me money to buy food, to build my house."[3] But they also inhabit another zone.
This is the liminal zone of memory and not acquiescence. Seoka spent his working life in a cycle of having a job, and not having a job. Like many black South Africans with limited access to schooling, his "occupation" could have been listed as "work seeker." In re-rendering elements of this hopeful army Seoka crafted images beyond absorption by state institutions. To begin with, like Johannes Maswanganyi, he found a black audience. His early works, like the portrait of Madifukwana Muhala, the headman of the next village, were commissioned by members of his (separate by law) community.

Helen Sebidi

Helen Sebidi uses exaggeration as a pictorial tensioning device. Her painting

1 Other important art centres are, or were; Polly Street in downtown Johannesburg, active in the 50s and 60s, ELC Art and Craft Centre "Rorke's Drift" in the Natal Midlands, active from the early 60s, Kathlehong Art Centre near Germiston on the East Rand, active from the mid 70s, Funda Centre in Soweto, active since the 80s, The Open School in mid-town Johannesburg, active during the 70s, Community Arts Project in Salt River Cape Town, active since 1977 and still running strongly, Dakawa in Grahamstown, relocated from Tanzania in 1992. Other centres included the Alexandra Art Centre in Alexandra, Johannesburg.

2 Gayatri Chakravorty Spivak, 1988, "Can the Subaltern Speak?," in Lawrence Grossberg (ed.), Marxism and the Interpretation of Culture, Macmillan.

3 Gavin Younge (Dir), 1990, Sixpence a Door, BetaCamSP, 54 mins, Les Films du Village, Paris.

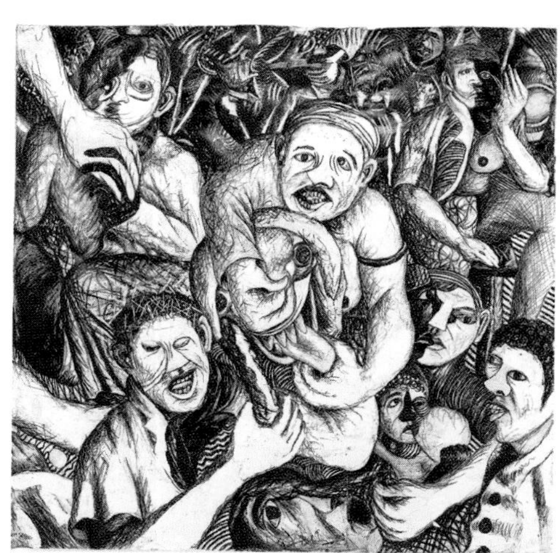

Helen Sedibi (born in 1943), "Tears of Africa," 1990
charcoal, collage in paper, 200x200 cm.
©D.R.

MookaMedi wa juanong (Modern president), takes up the issue of African tribal authority and points to the unresolved issues of the traditional, signified by the cow-hide shield, and the foreign. This last attribute is signaled by mere "book learning," and to a certain degree, by the form of the message – acrylic paint. The pattern of ethnicity and ascribed power, so important to an understanding of the violence in South Africa, promotes a reading of terror and incomprehension in the torn halves of Sebidi's portraits. Surely, they seem to ask, class antagonisms would have directed greater fury at the "oppressor" than fellow petitioners for relief?

Thembinkosi Alfred Goniwe

Working closely along themes of conflict between the old and the new, between "tradition" and "non-traditionalists" are two artists who have studied for Masters degrees in Fine Art at University; Mgcineni Sobopha and Thembinkosi Alfred Goniwe. Their specific focus is on the ritualized aspects of circumcision and scarification, and the part that these "traditional" practices play in framing male identity (in the case of circumcision) and female identity (in the case of female identity). In his thesis Goniwe explores the conflict between "traditional" and "non-traditional" social processes. He gives evidence of young Xhosa women[4] who, on gaining adulthood in a large city such as Cape Town, do not see the value of their facial scars in a contemporary world marked by different value systems of "beauty." Goniwe relates this discomfit to the part that the camera lens has played, through popular magazines and light television entertainment, in determining which stereotype is "modern," and thus good, and which stereotype is "ethnic" and therefore less valued.

Goniwe interrogates this expectation in a series of large inkjet prints that emulate glossy magazines aimed at the black bourgeoisie and growing young black elite. Called Face Value, the series parodies four different such magazines; Bona, Pace, Thandi, and Drum. Substituting the normal chic young model with an equally chic abakweta (young male initiate, his face painted with ash). The cover of "Drum" bears such racy titles as "Why I left the ritual seclusion – injured novice tells all" and "Horror treatments of the killer sangomas."

Goniwe's triptych entitled XXX (the three Xs hint at the missing surname bestowed upon Africans by economic slavery), bears a hand drawn likeness of an actual woman who had been scarred by her grandmother at the age of six. The cuts, known as ukuchaza/ukubhaca (eponymous with the clan name bhaca) were made in an attempt to ensure the bearer's good health. Today the woman laments the scars. Not only do they not conform with contemporary mores regarding female beauty, they also hark back to a superstitious past. The woman's likeness (Goniwe identifies her as Nikiwe) is shown on the front of photo-lithographed T-shirts. The choice of this reference is important. T-shirts have gained a special, almost fatal significance in South Africa. T-shirts are the banners and badges of the formerly disenfranchised majority. The slogans which adorned these vote-catching acoutrements , also served as beacons declaring the political party affiliation of the wearer. Both free hand-out and manifesto, T-shirts "marked" the wearer. To wear the wrong T-shirt, say that of Inkatha in a PAC or ANC section of a township (or vice-versa) could lead to death or a severe beating. In the face of non-existent office organization, these were the membership "cards."

The link between vision and violence, between emblem and the sign in search of its signified other, find form in the substrate of his imagery and in the confidence of Goniwe's new archetypes. His model's gaze counters that of the presumed Western viewer's with a beguiling equanimity. Goniwe posits a seamless whole. He also adds that Masibaliselane means more than "telling stories." He says it means telling stories to one another, or telling each other stories. So whereas "township art" was a message which passed through the closed boundaries of separation and was directed mainly at an incredulous white audience, contemporary black imagery speaks to white and black viewerships alike. On occasion these stories are about loss, death and displacement. At other times they interrogate notions of the body, identity.

[4] Thembinkosi Alfred Goniwe, 1998, "Scarification in a contemporary urban setting," in Artworks in Progress – Yearbook of the Staff of the Michealis School of Fine Art, University of Cape Town, Vol 4, 18.

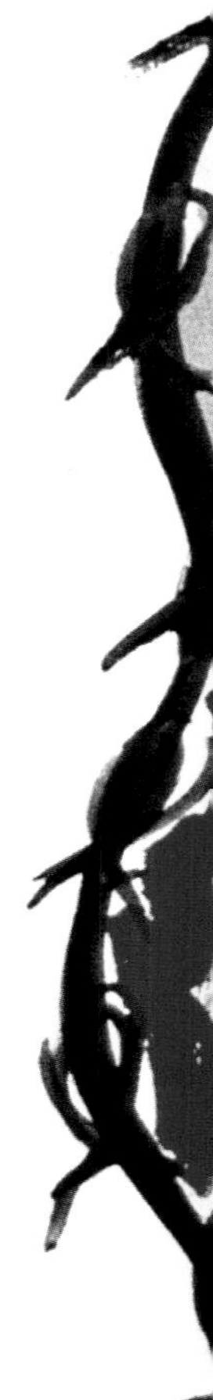

Modibo Franky Diallo, Mali ©Revue Noire

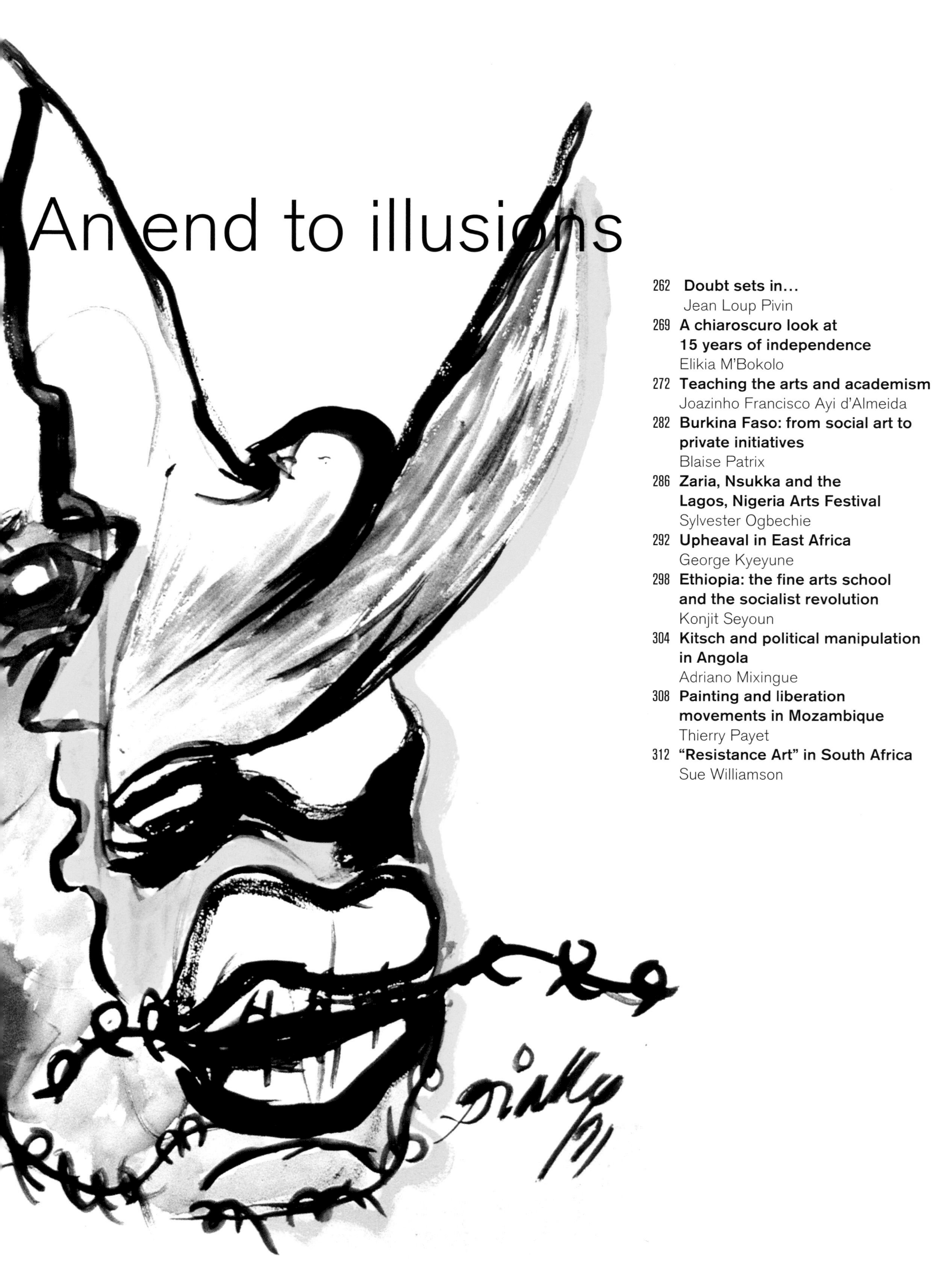

An end to illusions

Doubt sets in...

Jean Loup Pivin

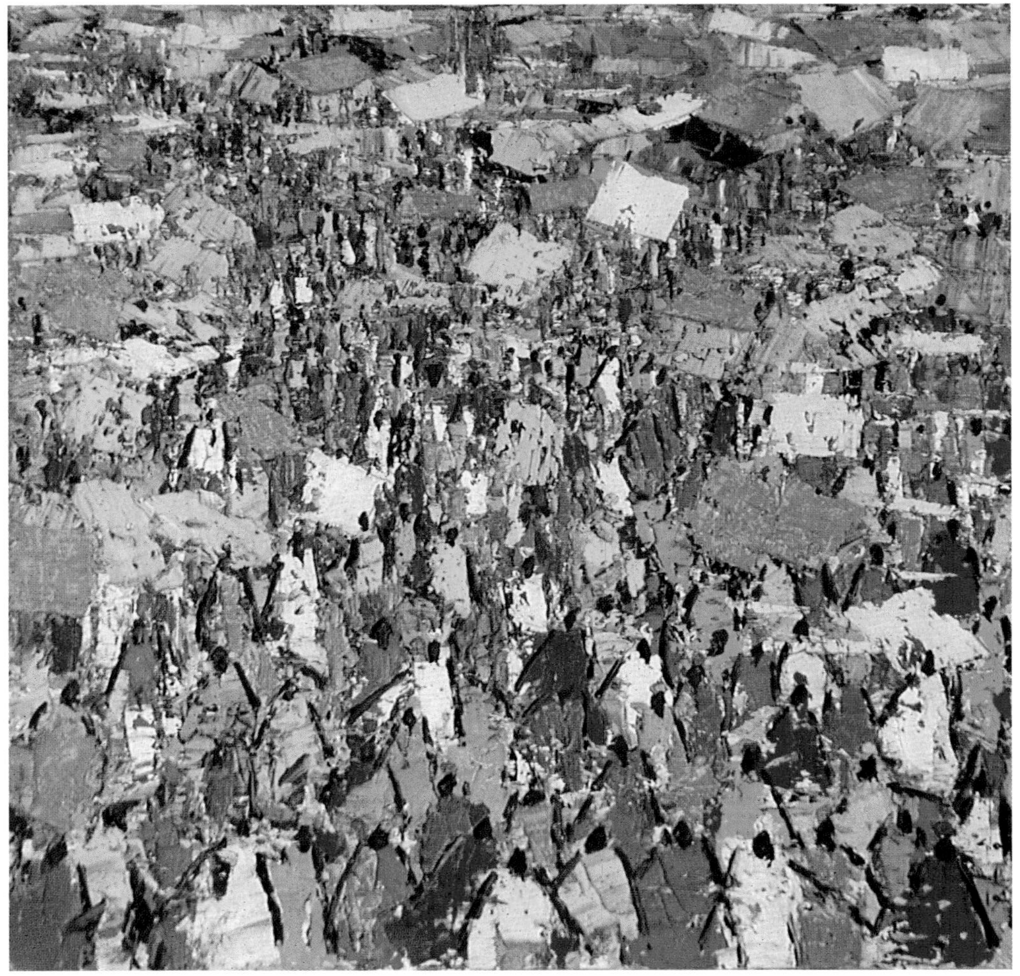

Ablade Glover (born in 1934), "Market scene," Ghana, 1996,
102,5x102,5 cm
©Revue Noire

facing page:
Kré M'Baye (born in 1949), "Untitled," Senegal, 1986
oil on canvas, 89x108 cm ©Bouna Medoune Seye/Revue Noire

Ibrahima Kébé (born in 1955), Senegal
©Bouna Medoune Seye/Revue Noire

No one was fighting for the new collective man anymore in the independent countries in the late 70s. Everyone was fighting to be a new man himself, in his own way. While the shortcomings of the modern African states were the result of all of the international mono-information on the continent, countries were being built without the enthusiasm of the 1960s. The last independence movements occurred in the Portuguese-speaking countries in the mid 1970s. What remained were the South African apartheid countries, and these were finally freed in the 1990s. The Lagos Arts Festival in 1977, an extension of the International Festival of Black Arts in Dakar, eleven years later, appears to be the end of the pan-Africanism of the early days. Dictatorships and military powers fell out of touch with their societies. The Sankara episode appeared as no more than the last incident in the history of the collective utopias. Africa was no longer a geopolitical fact, but rather an economic stake in the case of a few countries rich in oil and raw materials.

The ever-chanted words of a free and prosperous Africa, inventive and proud of itself, collided with all of the economic, political, social, health and educational realities. People were becoming poorer, the health and education systems were deteriorating, the political regimes were arrogantly taking refuge in misadministration and investments were becoming rarer. Few countries would escape. The economic emigration of the early 70s was coupled in the 80s and 90s with cultural emigration: the elites abandoned Africa. During this time, cities developed at head-spinning rates and the cultural

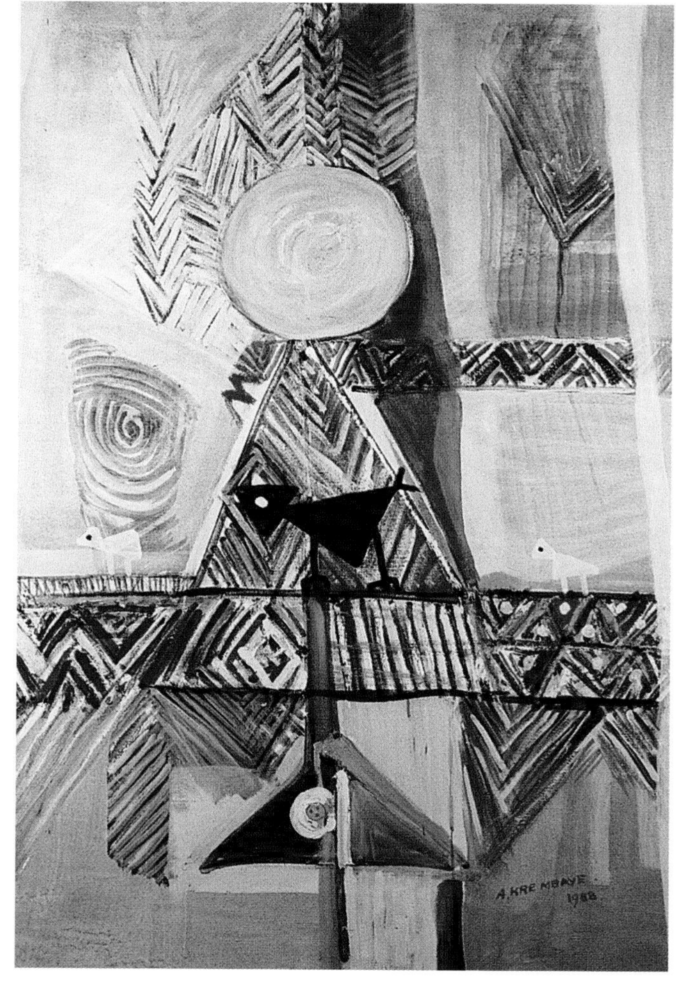

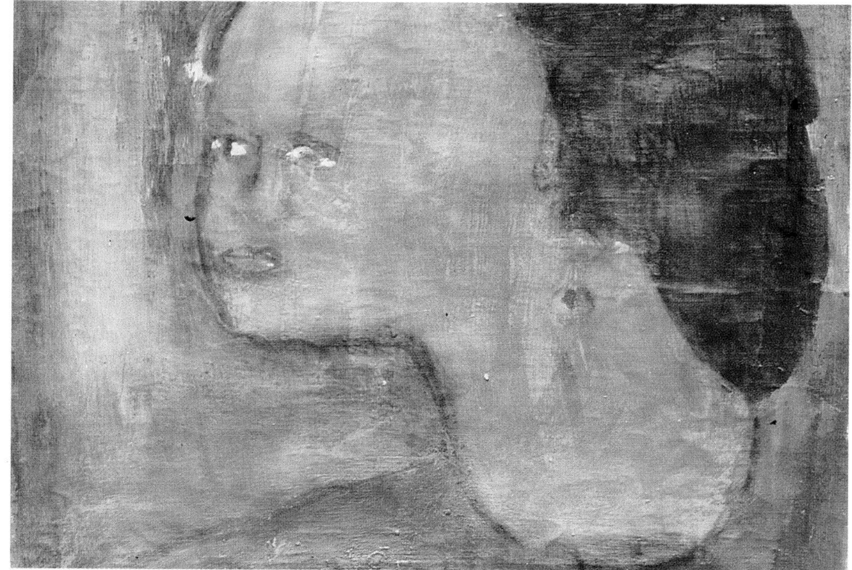

revolution of the 1960s changed due to the facts and in light of increased global media entering the homes of people at all levels of society. This led to a profound alteration among those societies that were now building themselves, for better or worse, based on the international urban model. In fact, everything appeared to be diving into complete chaos, hence the notion of a rebirth in the 1990s. While the torments affecting almost all of the states persisted, signs of an end to the "depression" only appeared at the turn of the century. Africa proclaimed itself loud and clear through its musical expressions and fashion, but it was only in the 80s that the continent developed its collective and individual, public and private talents and initiatives. African pride has been expressed through the flagship talents of stylist Chris Seydou, singers Youssou N'dour and Salif Keïta, and through companies, especially computer firms such as those in Cameroon. And this without mentioning the economic importance of the "informal sector," which means nothing in a country where formalism – solely administrative and fiscal – does not exist: activities and initiatives exist, and that is what counts. These years of disillusion and doubt created inner and unformulatable conflicts in the minds of each citizen. The artist's conflict is probably the most symbolic, because the very nature of his own production is at stake.

Invisible artistic conflict

Artistic conflict is found in the symbolic framework of the modern city. However, visible conflict did not take place. It is as though two parallel paths were drawn: one commissioned by traditional national demand, that follows its course, and the

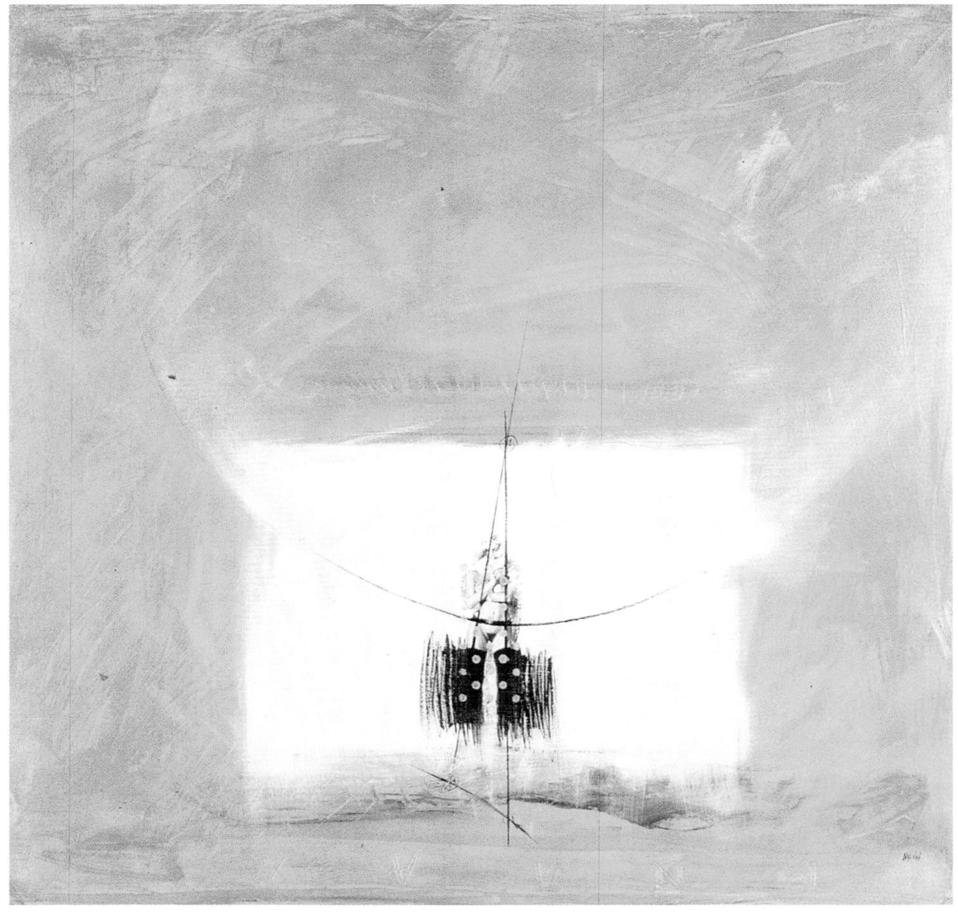

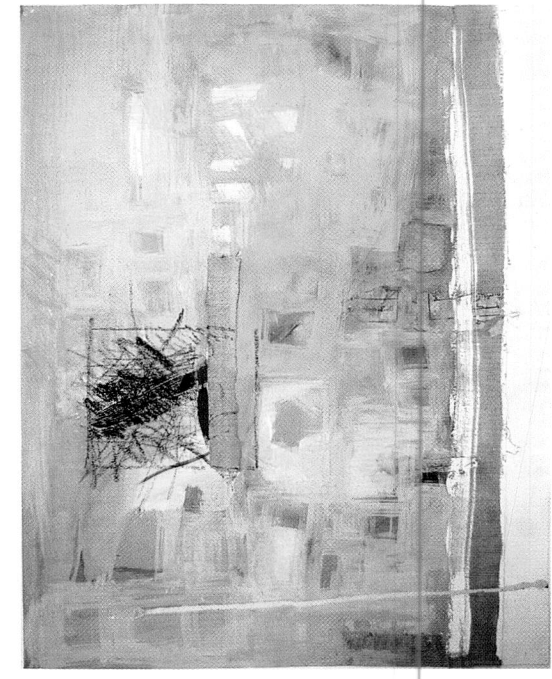

David Nal Vad (born in 1954), "The Quadrature of the circle," Gabon, 1998
oil on canvas, 98x97 cm ©D.R.

Moussa Diop Samba Laye (born in 1949), Senegal, 1992
©Bouna Medoune Seye/Revue Noire

Mor Faye (1947-1985), "Caricature of President, A. D.," Senegal, 1984
gouache on paper, 50x63 cm
©Revue Noire

other commissioned by the new bourgeois class, national leaders, expatriates, travelers and foreign tourists (most often of European and American origin). The conflict does, however, exist, in people's minds. While the contemporary African artist sees himself as an artist first and as an African artist second, the artist in Africa wants to move beyond the expected codes of his fixed cultural membership. Conflict is thus expressed as a mere rejection or an incorporation of heritage on a medium, through a technique, an inspiration of the very object of his difference. Could this be a contradiction? Probably not, but the artist is cunning and skilled at responding to demand without adhering to it, thereby giving priority to the expression of new forms without killing the expected narration and imagery. The mental conflict remains whole. It could be assimilated to the forms that cover daily behaviors. First of all, there is the costume, despite the official fashions of the "abat-coast" in the former Zaire or of Faso Danfani in Burkina. Secondly, there is the house and its furniture, despite the building experience obtained with stabilized soil. And last, but not least, the relationship with the extended family, whose pressing obligations are being increasingly set aside. None of these signs misrepresents the mental conflict confronting each artist, whoever he may be. The internationalization of lifestyles has become an obvious fact that must coexist with what many people feel is only a cultural heritage and not a fact to be perpetuated. Reinvention yes, but not perpetuation.

This type of conflict, without a clear voice and image, leads to tensions and refusals. However, seen from the outside, an entire production appears to reveal a

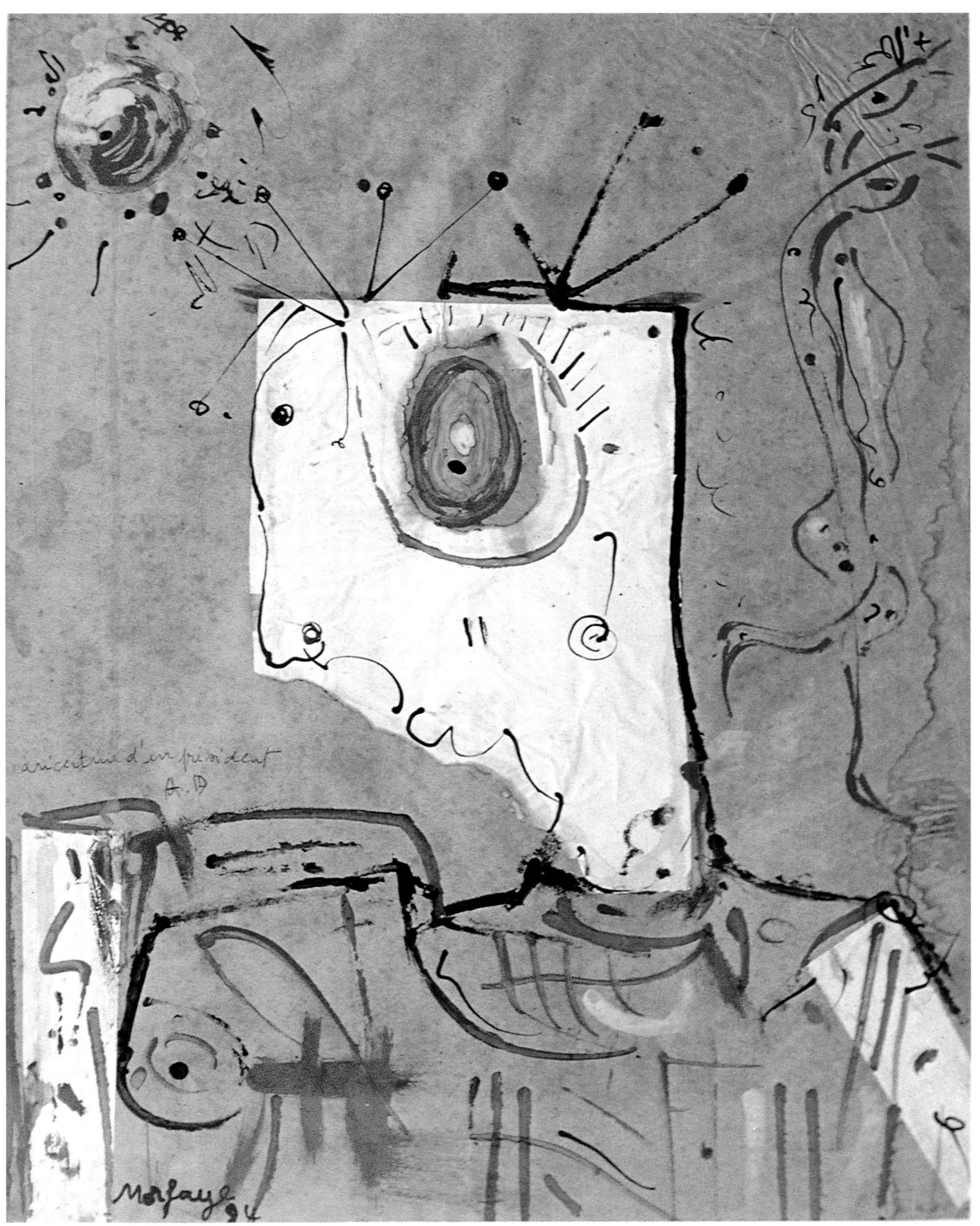
aricature d'un président
A.D

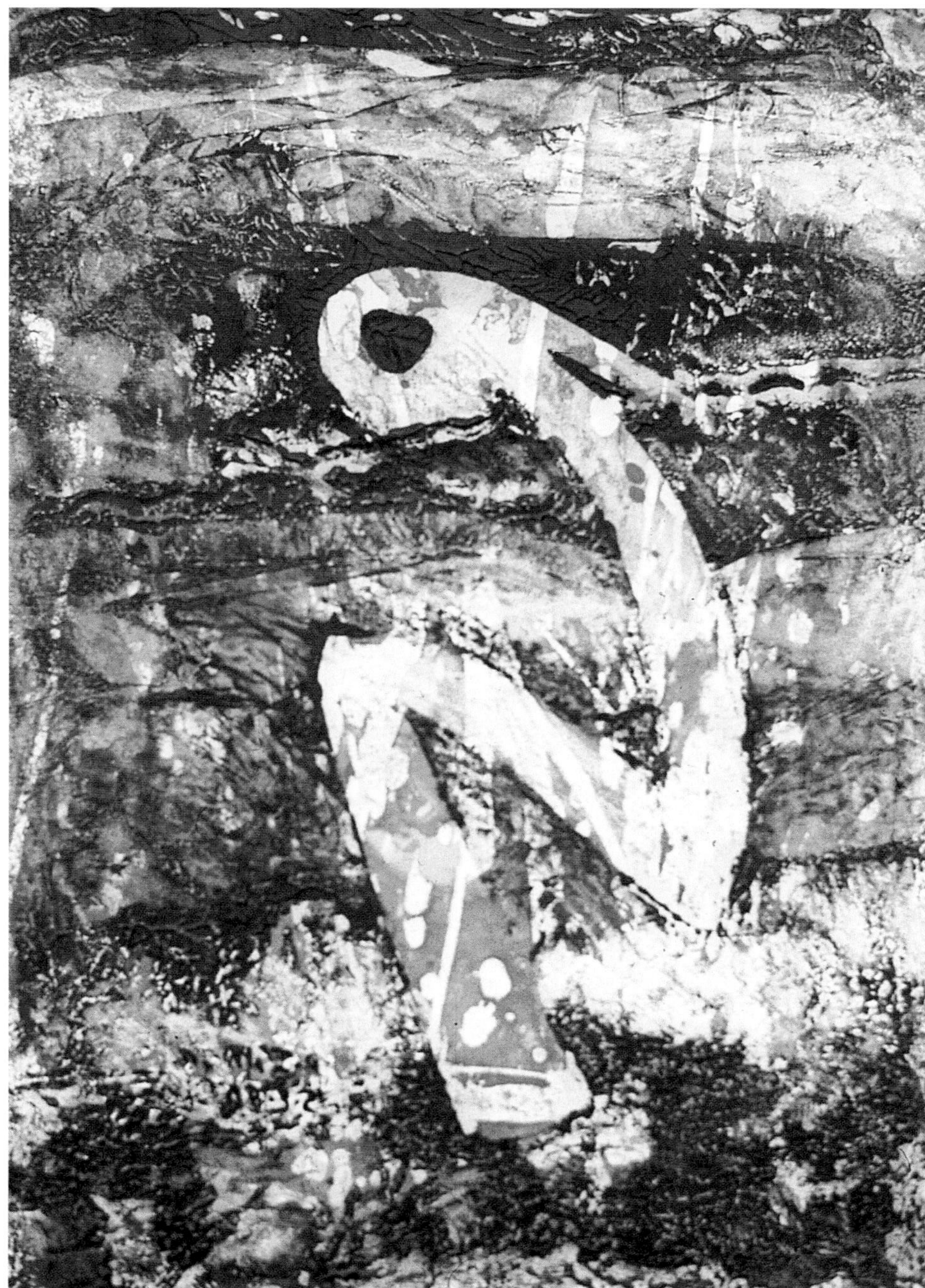

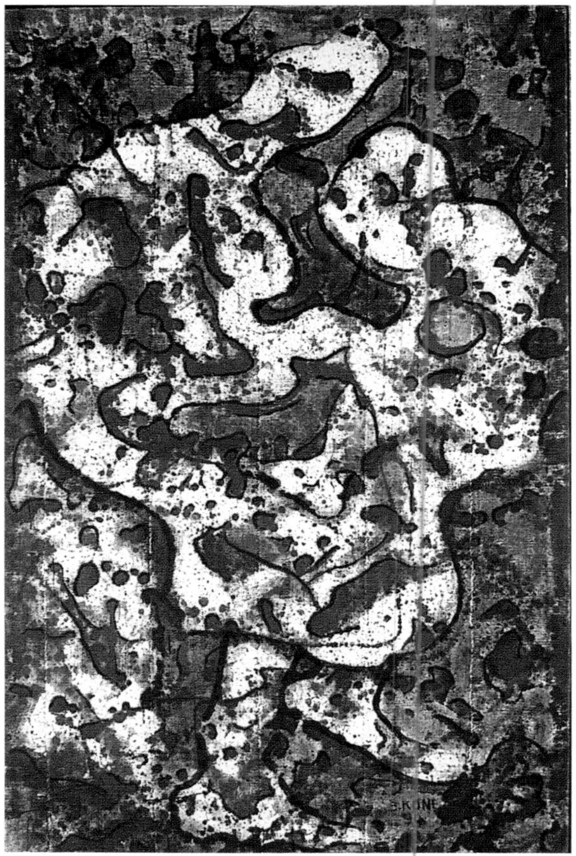

tame face that may be perceived as being "behind" the international movements of the rich countries. Resistance is much stronger than it appears. From the beginning, conflict, like many other initiatory signs, has been portrayed with violent features, an out-of-scale design and an excessively heavy paste.

The end of a teaching method

"You are going to be taught perspective. It is a base that will enable you to then be free to do whatever you want." These were the words of a French teacher from the National Arts Institute of Bamako for over fifteen years to his Mali students in the 1970s and 1980s. Neither the administration nor his Malian colleagues, however, ever spoke a contradictory word, as they were partisans of this method. The bases for learning art in almost all Fine Arts Schools in Africa first start with an academic education, whether or not the teachers are European. The formal production of generations of artists could not help but be influenced by this, despite systematic discussions on heritage and traditional practices. "This led to us painting a mask using perspective."

Although some institutions (the Dakar and Oshogbo Schools) sought to change the teaching method at one point or another, they always returned to the values on which Western art was founded (including modern art), because all of the schools were founded by artists and instructors educated in France. No real work was done with those who produced traditional forms. No observation from the traditional educational system was transferred into the public educational system. This deficiency was a benefit in that it allowed traditional production to

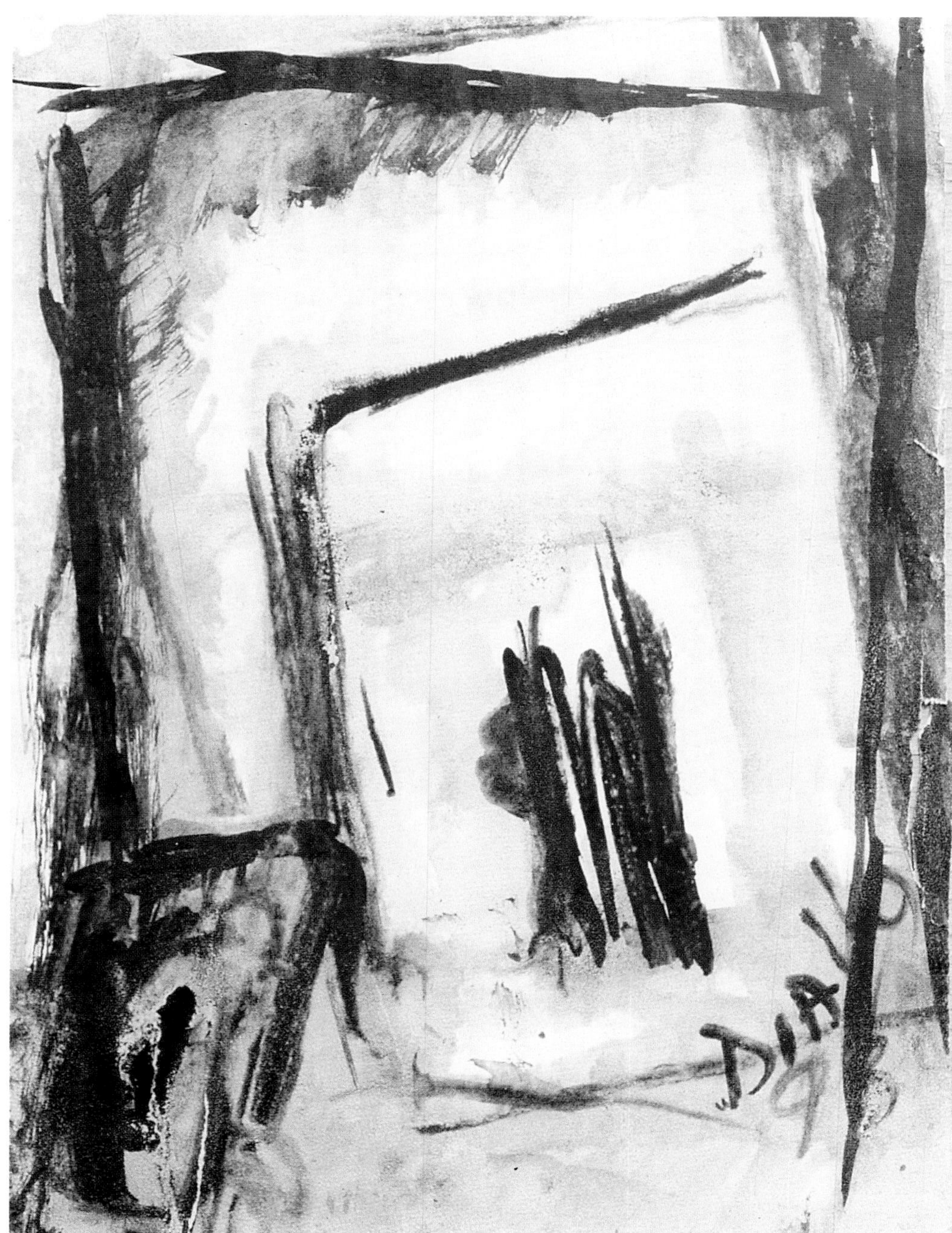

Ismaël Diabaté (born in 1945), "Nokoya," Mali, 1989
oil on paper, 29,5 x 21 cm ©Revue Noire.

Ibrahima Koné (born in 1963), Mali, 1995
©Revue Noire

facing page:
Modibo Franky Diallo (born in 1954), Mali, 1996
©Revue Noire

continue while artistic expression based on so-called "international" criteria developed alongside, in an almost absolutely airtight environment, regardless of the subject being dealt with: from the water carrier to the celebration of the anti-colonial battle and, later on, the anti-apartheid battle.
Education remained academic despite all attempts made. The connection with the tradition of ritual arts was most often formal and void of meaning. The 20th century enabled art and the status of the modern artist to develop in a modern social and cultural environment, where deculturation was great and where the reconquest of an ideal identity was often illusory beneath the straddle of economic and cultural globalization. The media and the movement of humans and of ideas put an end to the Africa of old. Education in Africa at the turn of the 3rd millennium is on the brink of bankruptcy. A new start will probably take place through a revolution in techniques and the digital culture, through an investment in all artistic and formal expressions, and not through an academism renewed a thousand times, of which the West is trying to rid itself.

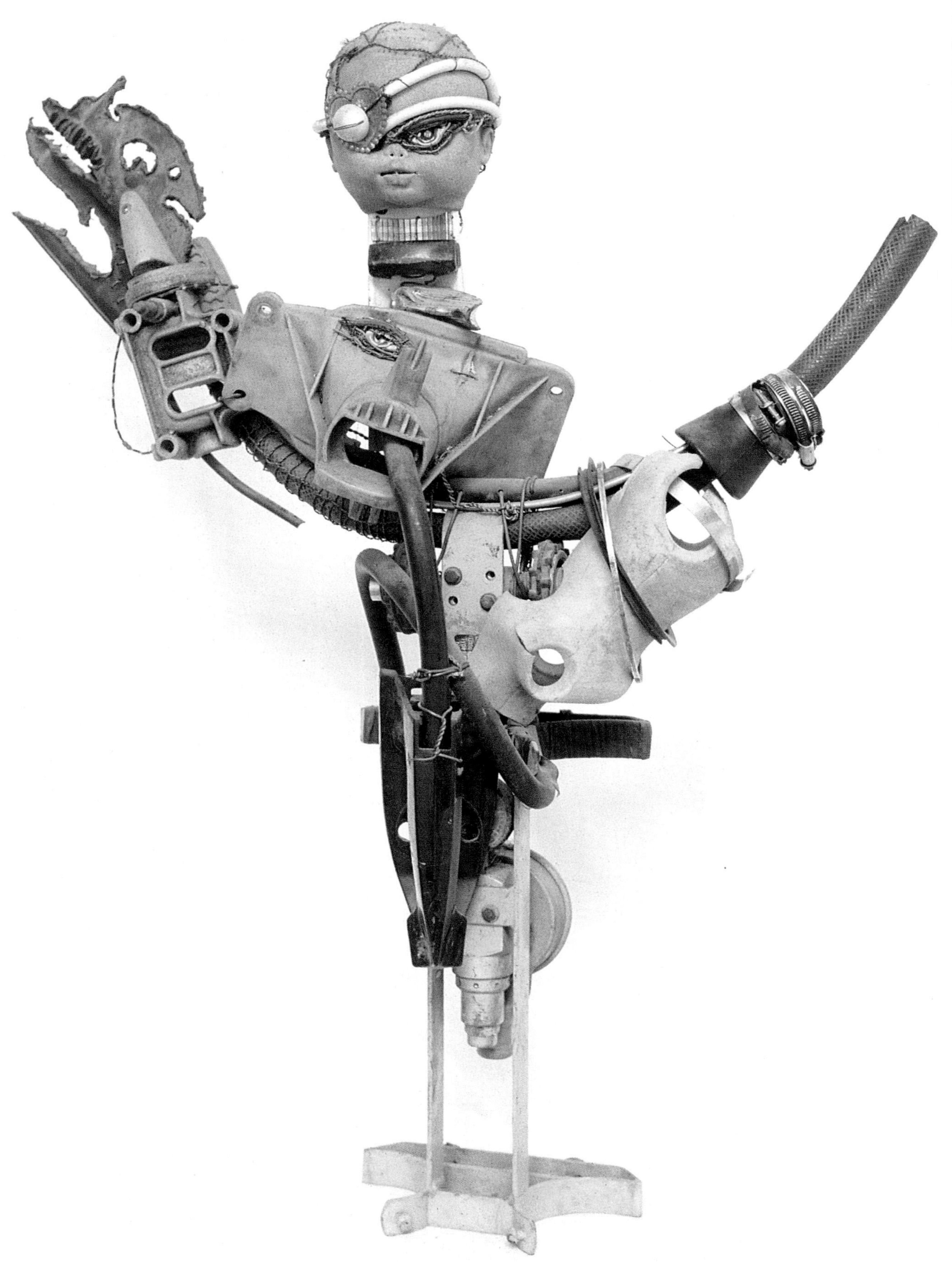

Joseph Francis Sumégné (born in 1951), "Doll," Cameroon, 1995

A CHIAROSCURO LOOK AT 15 YEARS OF INDEPENDENCE

Elikia M'Bokolo

Slogans are convenient, but often misleading. From the days following the independence movements, especially outside Africa, images of the continent were fixed in everyone's minds and memories, and rash comments about Africa began to fill newspapers and periodicals: images of crises, wars and misery; preconceived notions according to which Africa had once and for all missed the boat towards modernity and development. Nothing could be less certain and everything is much more complicated. The crucial issue of African unity is a good illustration of the advancement and blocking processes that characterize the new independent Africa. Although Africans may have strived for unity, various attempts to achieve it have often been compromised by the egoism of the States, the short-sightedness of certain leaders and the tactics of the major powers, who fear the idea of having to confront a united Africa.

First, in West Africa, the memory of the former States, chiefdoms, kingdoms, and empires that colonization sought to erase, and the pragmatism consisting of starting with the existing structure (French West Africa) in order to build the future one (United Africa or United West Africa) led to the development of the Federation of Mali project. This project consisted of restoring the former Malian empire, a multi-ethnic unit, extending from Senegal to Niger, from the desert to the Sudanese savannah. This empire was a powerful, prosperous and envied State in the Western and Muslim world in the Middle Ages. Senegal championed the idea by proposing that Dahomey (Benin), Upper Volta (Burkina Faso) and Sudan (Mali) join this new grouping. Shortly after its birth, the Federation of Mali was already defunct. This was partly because several of the States approached to be members (Upper Volta and Dahomey) joined the competing grouping of the Entente Council that had just been formed by Ivory Coast and Niger, and also because the antagonism between Senegal and Sudan, and especially between the two executive officers, Léopold Sédar Senghor from Senegal, and Modibo Keita from Sudan, continued to intensify. In June 1960, one year after its official proclamation and without ever truly seeing the light of day, the Federation broke up and Sudan kept the name of the former Malian empire.

Although less ambitious, the unity projects in East Africa were more effective. At the instigation of Julius Nyerere and of Tom Mboya, a pan-African movement formed, requesting that the former English colonies accede to independence together under a Federal State. Nyerere even proposed delaying Tanganyika's independence day and recognizing Jomo Kenyatta from Kenya as the President of the new grouping. However, the English did everything they could to disperse the dates of accession to sovereignty (between December 1962 and December 1963) and limited the margin of maneuverability of the new States by having them sign neo-colonist type "cooperation" and "assistance" agreements. Despite all of this, the determination and insistence of Julius Nyerere enabled the formation of a new State, Tanzania, in 1964, which was a merger of Tanganyika and Zanzibar. All through the 1960s and 1970s, Tanzania, and its capital city Dar es Salam, became poles where the Black African intellectual elite would gather and a privileged place of refuge and training for southern African liberation movements.

Across the continent, the unification process appeared to be even more confused. The cold war was no stranger to these difficulties, like the initial crises with which independent Africa was faced. Although the former States of the Franco-African Community were grouped in the A.M.U. (African and Malagasy Union, 1961), which was very close to the French government, Africa was forced to take part in the crisis of the former Belgian Congo (assassination of Prime Minister Patrice Lumumba, secession of the rich provinces of Katanga and Kasai, intervention of the U.N.'s peacekeepers, mutual accusations of intervention by the United States and the U.S.S.R.). Two sides then emerged and would clash until the OAU was created. On one side were the "moderates" from the Monrovia Group, the largest (21 States that attended the Monrovia Conference held May 8-12, 1961), lined along the western countries, who opposed revolutionary plotting, condemned "the political integration of sovereign African States," declared themselves in favor of the "unity of aspirations and of action" and advocated the creation of an inter-African consultative organization. On the other side were the "radicals" or "revolutionaries" of the Casablanca Group (6 States that attended the Casablanca Conference held January 3-7, 1963), who were in favor of a united Congo and the political heirs of Lumumba, who defended an effective unity, if needed, such as Kwame Nkrumah, in the form of a continental State.

Once in Addis Ababa (May 14-21, 1963) to sign the Organization of African Unity Charter, the African States could only agree on one compromise. The "moderates" obtained confirmation of the principles of non-interference, cooperation, and consultation between the heads of State and, shortly afterwards, the proclamation of inviolability of the borders established under colonization. The "radicals" imposed the acceptance of unfailing support to "freedom fighters," especially in southern Africa and in the Portuguese colonies. In theory, this support appeared, in most cases, to be effective, because it greatly contributed to the independence of territories where a retrograde colonialism refused any perspective of emancipation (Guinea-Bissau, Angola and Mozambique, Zimbabwe and Namibia). But on more serious and complex issues, the OAU was helpless and the African States divided. In view of the war opposing Nigeria to one of its regions, Biafra (1967-1970), most of the States condemned the secession of Biafra in the name of territorial integrity, whereas a small calculated number supported Biafra, a symbol, in their eyes, of a bullied nation (Ivory Coast, Gabon, Tanzania). Even the unanimously condemned regime of apartheid contributed to dividing independent Africa because, from 1970, Ivory Coast, soon followed by Gabon, chose to "dialogue" with Pretoria. Apparent since the early 60s, the disenchantment was, therefore, quite real, but it did not prevent Africans from acting, creating, thinking and preparing the paths for the future.

During the fever of the Glorious Thirties, the African States began to dream of "development," a fetish word in the 60s and early 70s. At the same time, the generally unequal partition of more or less abundant resources, depending on the country, provoked social movements everywhere and a hardening of the regimes in place. From about 1963 to 1968, Africa was the privileged terrain of military coups, uprisings and (real or imaginary) plots.

With respect to appearances and ideological references, divides began to appear between at least three types of regimes. Some openly declared themselves to be "scientific socialist" and "Marxist" regimes. This was the case of the former Portuguese colonies, where anti-colonial guerillas, controlled by Marxists, assumed power following the collapse of the Salazar dictatorship in 1974, and of countries where a "revolution," or coup d'etat later proclaimed a "revolution," had overthrown pro-Western regimes (Benin, Congo, Madagascar, Ethiopia). Most of the regimes, making themselves out to be "pragmatic," invoked economic liberalism and praised the economic successes of the West. Others, stating that they were "neither right, left nor center," as in the case of Mobutu Sese Seko, declared themselves to be "authentically African."

In fact, apart from declarations of faith, the various regimes had widely identical structural characteristics and socio-political practices: maintaining income economies inherited from colonization and founded on the export of agricultural raw materials and minerals, with oil being the last on the scene; single-party dictatorships, often replaced by the cult of personality of the State's head, proclaimed "father of the nation"; wealth management of the State, involving massive misappropriations of public funds and sometimes degenerating into a genuine system – kleptocracy. The West actually remained the master of the alliance game, even though certain States grappling with civil war received arms and logistical support from the USSR, from popular European democracies (Ethiopia) and from Cuba (Angola).

Finally, it was on the cultural level that Africa showed itself to be the most inventive and the cities were undoubtedly the most fertile crucible of this creativity. Since the State powers had deserted the cultural sector, so-called low-profit, private, individual or collective initiatives took over. Intellectuals, isolated artists and cultural groups of all types invested in the area of music, scientific and philosophical thought or literary creation, and the plastic arts sector. With the collapse of colonization and the limits it imposed, memory began to expand, posing new questions and searching to build, for the long-term, coherence for Africa's future. The origins of humanity, the Pharaoh and Abyssinian past, the former kingdoms and empires, the slave trade and the resistances to colonization were incorporated in the most recent evolutions and have composed a much more complex past than was often believed, and has offered new generations new reasons to hope.

Teaching the arts and academism

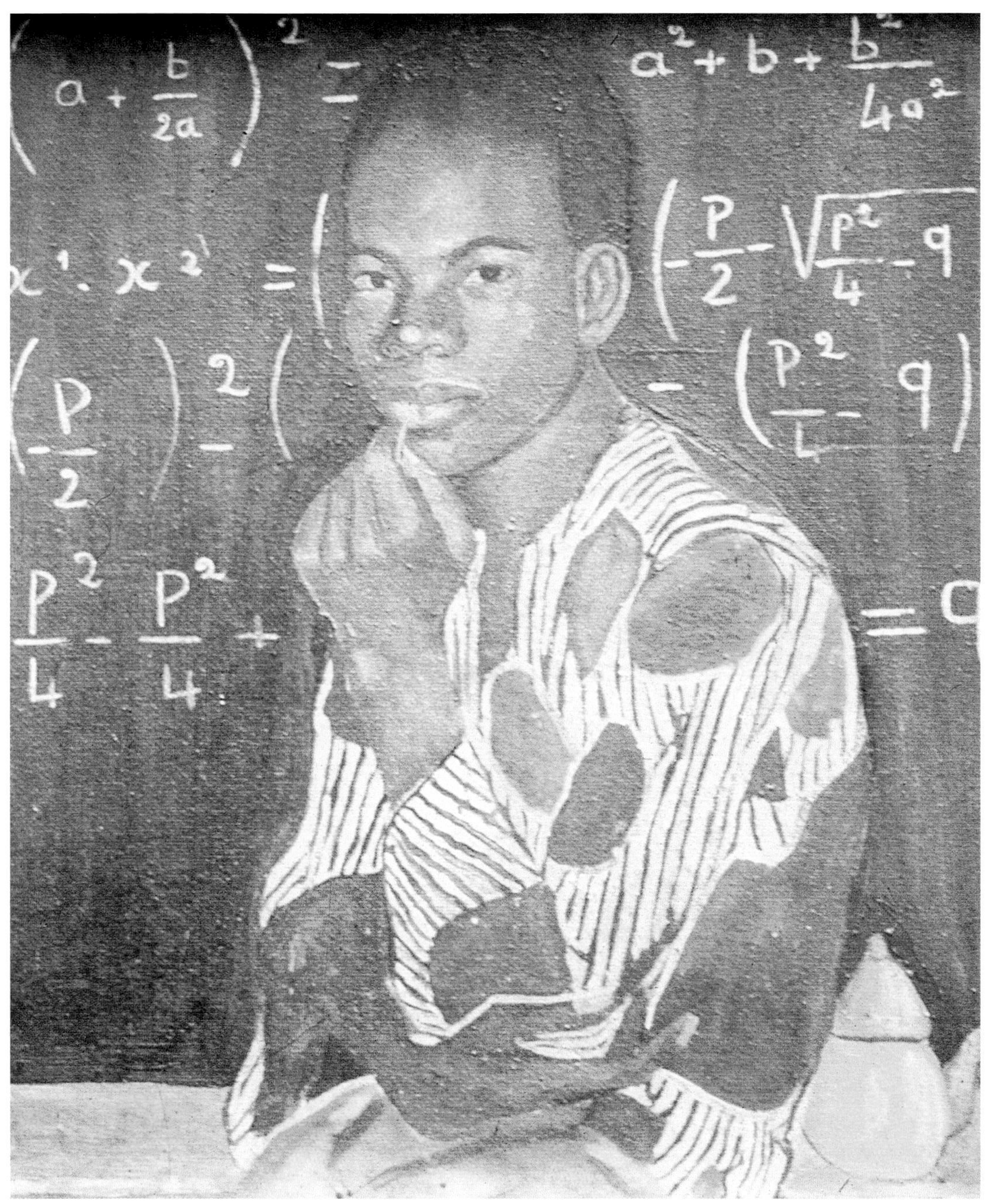

Mamadou Somé Coulibaly, "The Mathematician," Mali, 1968
oil on canvas, 70x50 cm
©Revue Noire

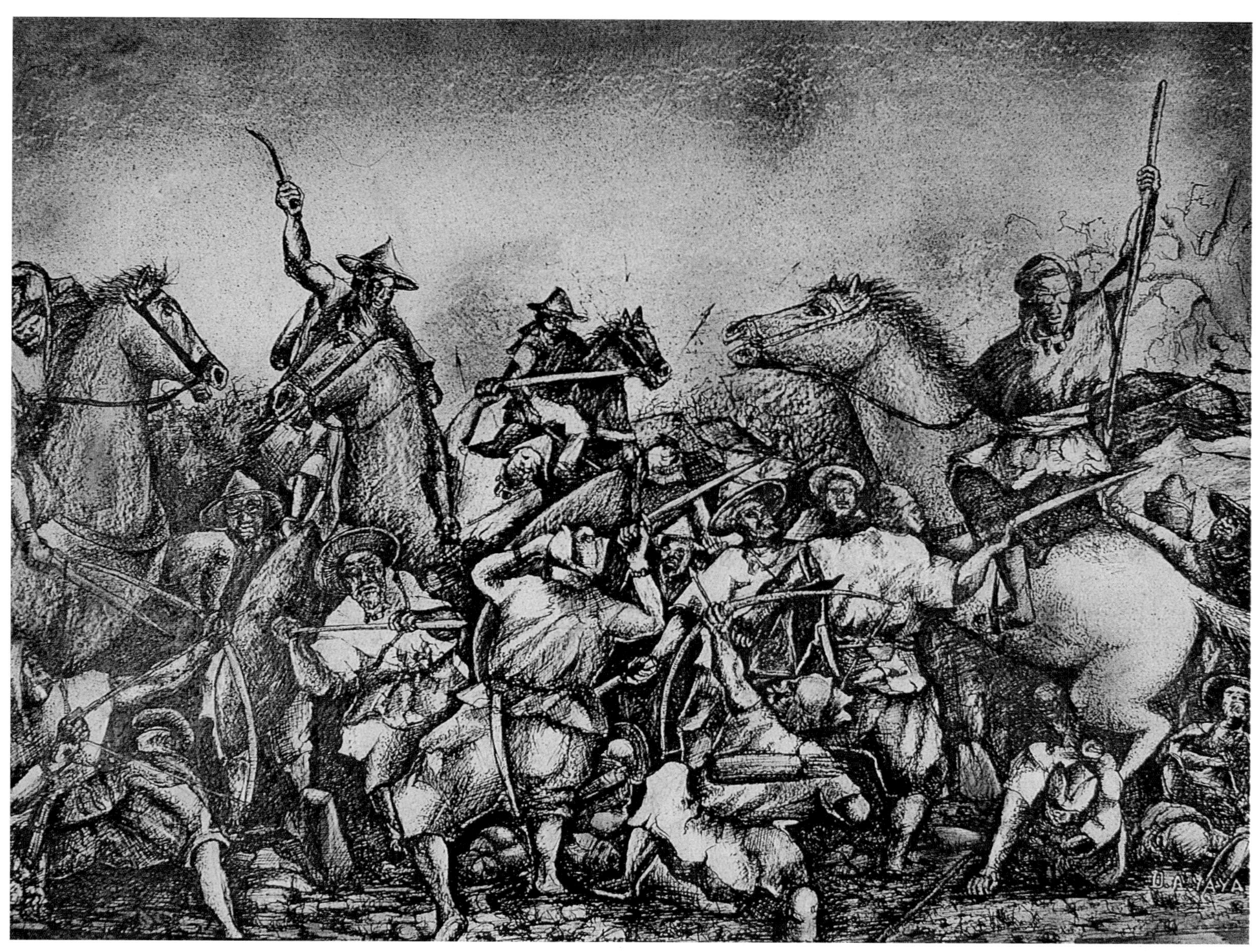

Alpha Yaya Diarra (born in 1934), "Battle Scene," Mali
oil on canvas

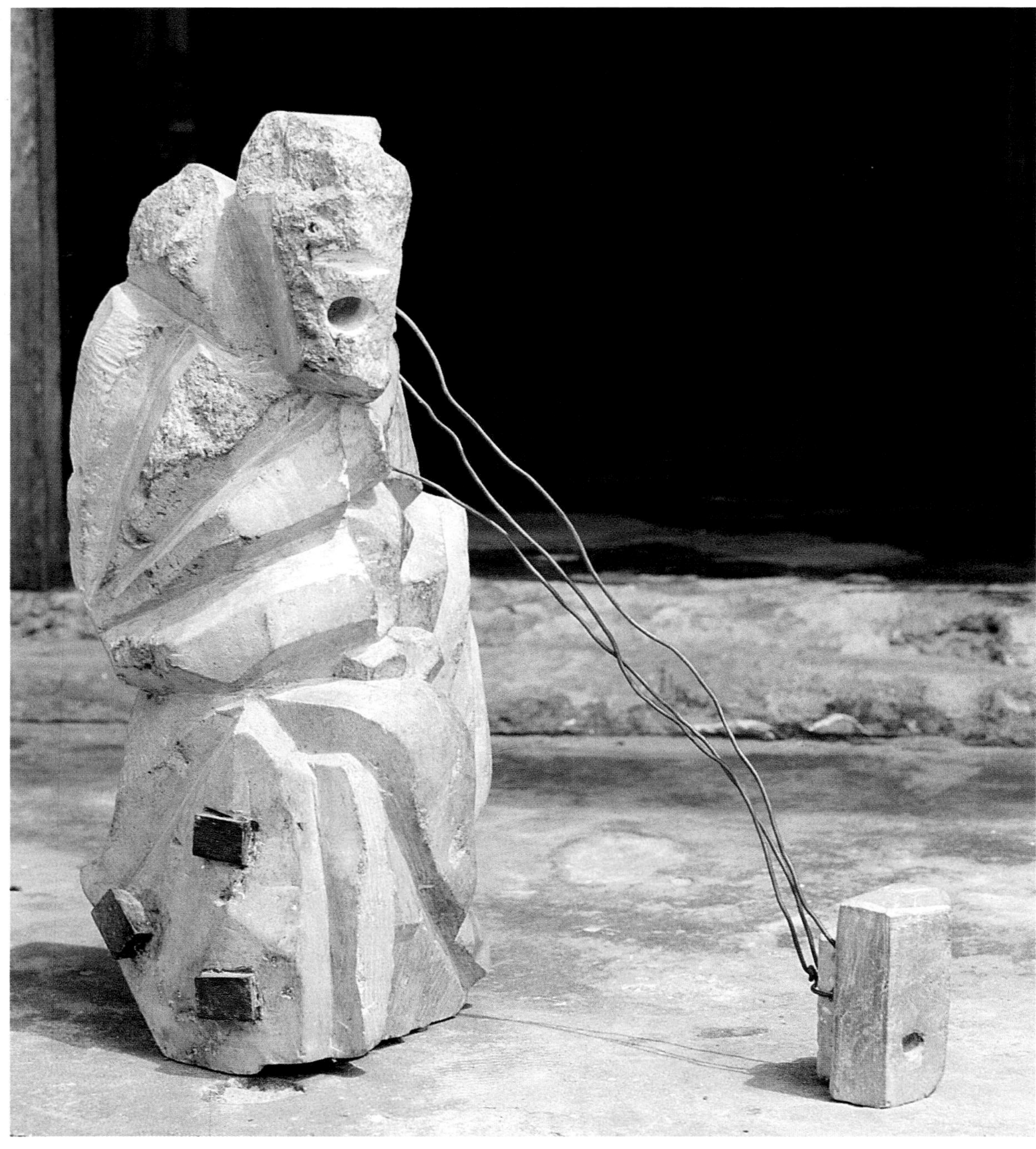

Antonio Pépin (born in 1956), "Citharist," Gabon, 1990

©Revue Noire

facing page:

Djibril André Diop (born in 1953), Senegal, 1991

©Revue Noire

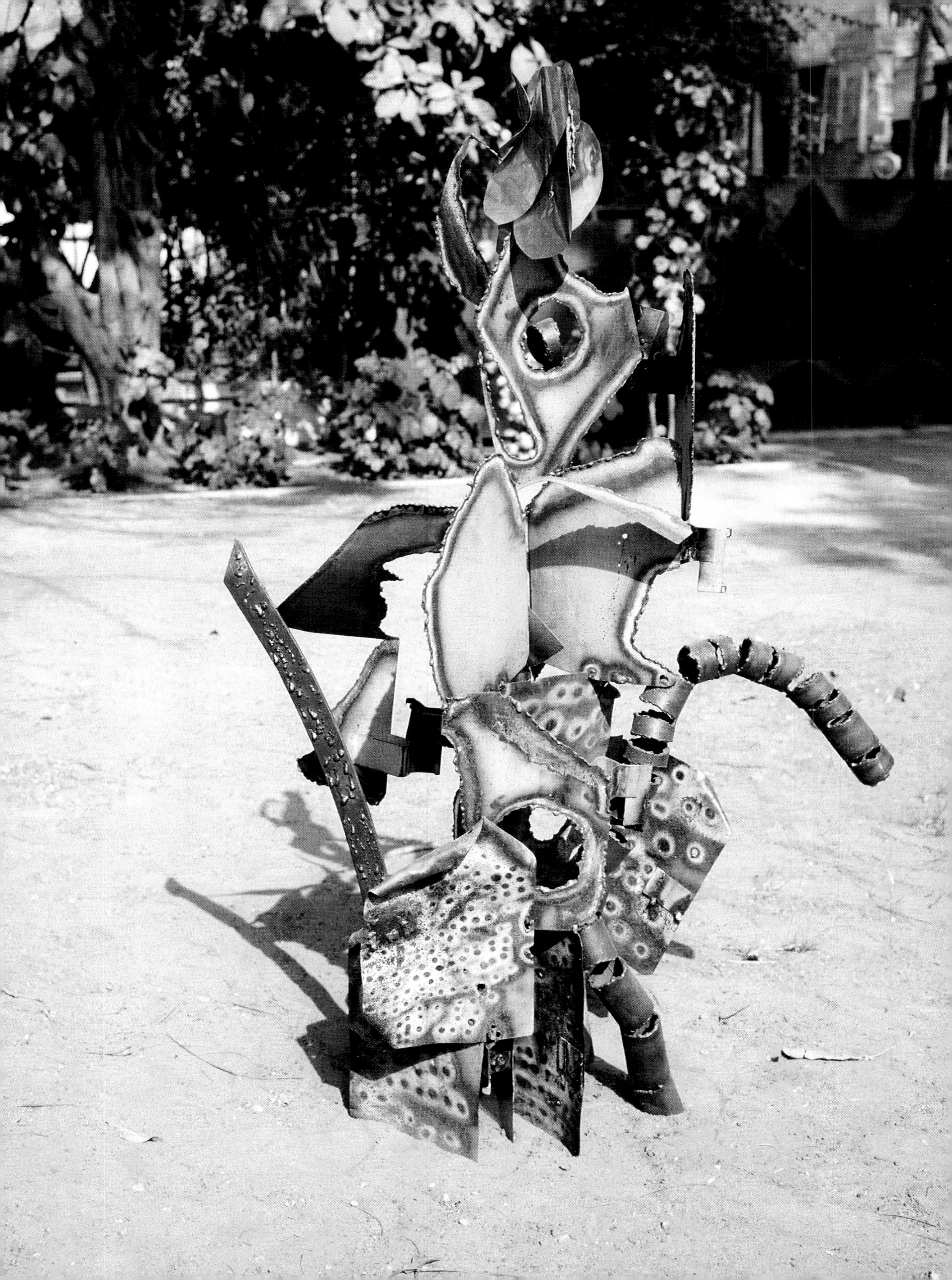

TEACHING THE ARTS IN SEARCH OF THEIR PATHS

Joazinho Francisco Ayi d'Almeida

The state of artistic education in the 80s was indicative of the degree of interest granted to this discipline by makers of cultural policies in Africa. And this weak interest was based on the symbolic and economic results they obtained from it. Brewing with the relative revival currently perceptible in visual creation in Africa, the 80s were first and foremost years of crisis. Following the historic period of the independence movement, a period that mobilized forces of energy and a stream of illusions regarding the recovery and reconstruction of an African identity, the initial process slowly broke down. These illusions were filled with the impulse to "draw up the inventory of the treasures of African cultural heritage and to retake speech, their hermeneutics."[1] These illusions were the basis for the establishment of art schools in several countries such as Ivory Coast, Mali and Gabon, to name but a few.

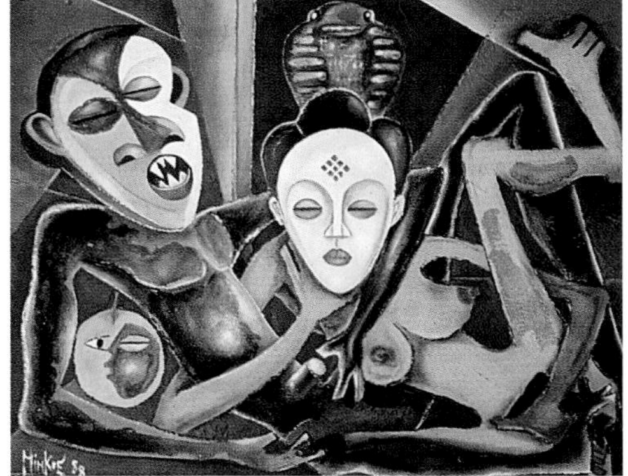

Marcellin Minkoe Minzé (born in 1953), Gabon, 1988

The forces died down because true artistic process is not based solely on abstract ideological discourse. It is nourished by its link to society, develops according to the logic of the art trade and based on the relationship between artists and their public, and the existence of those whose mission is to make art work known and appreciated. However, the ideological illusion was based on short-sightedness.

The recent inventory of art education institutions in Africa drawn up by Culture and Development[2] reveals a situation characterized by a few common traits and a contrast between Southern Africa and West Africa or Central Africa. Even in West Africa, deep-rooted differences exist between countries such as Nigeria and Ghana, where art education has developed within universities, and French-speaking countries, such as Benin, Niger and Togo, which do not have art schools. In Nigeria, for example, the art education begun in the 50s enabled the establishment of an artistic milieu rich in quantity and quality, even if the initial impetus was impeded by a lack of means.

Elsewhere, whether in Senegal or Ivory Coast, in Gabon or Mali, the desire to have an "inventory of the country's heritage and to retake speech" gave way, paradoxically, to educational structures largely modeled on the Western example with respect to their general image and curriculum. Did the excessively present Western reference make the mission impossible for a generation still affected by colonial traumatism? These two reasons are perhaps responsible for the impasse into which art education was drawn in several countries. To these can be added the lack of teachers and appropriate materials, as well as a weak interest from public powers in a discipline perceived as minor or even "non-indigenous."

But what were the causes of the impasse in art education? Although an entire generation sought to "take back the floor" or "wash its eyes," few artists south of the Sahara, with some exceptions, truly attempted their hand at an esthetic investigation in order to draw up an inventory, analyze their visual heritage, discover their plastic rules and shed light on their features, not in order to reproduce them with systematic mimeticism, but to gain from them a singular plastic energy and force.
The result of this incoherence was that art education and the confined artistic milieu it produced went into crisis. The criteria and missions of schools torn between training teachers and training artists were jumbled, causing the fossilization of an educational system out of step with society's movement as it produced its own signs and created other art teaching alternatives. Schools were "imprisoned" without proper means to open up students to the international art movement. All of this was worsened by the lack of teachers, the rupture with the local cultural milieu – museums, film, music or arts in general – or with society as it continued to spontaneously produce new forms and practices, in particular in the field of daily objects (fabrics, hairstyles, commercial visual production, etc.).

However, all crises are followed by a new impetus. Thus, in the 80s, a revival took place, the results of which we are

[1] E. Mveng, "Les problématiques d'une esthétique négro-africaine," in Littérature et esthétique négro-africaines, Ilena symposium, Ed. NEA, Abidjan 1979

[2] Médianes No. 14/15, Fall 1999

currently coming to understand. Throughout Africa, whether in South Africa, Zimbabwe, Namibia, Senegal, Cameroon or Togo, a new generation of artists decided to react. By updating the old traditional educational practice once again, some people, such as Kossi Assou in Togo, created their own place of work and training. In Cameroon, Doual'art, the Goethe Institute and the Natema Foundation (P. Kenfack) offered training times in the form of workshops, while official training courses were provided by the department of "art and archeology" of the University of Yaounde and the Institute of Art Education of Mbalmayo.

But it was above all in South Africa, where social and political turmoil nourished a cultural and artistic process extended to the liberation movement, that community workshops of artists proliferated. These contributed to training an entire generation of artists in all disciplines while academic education structures were being built.

More significant and fertile was the phenomenon of artist residences arising from the sphere of influence of the Triangle network of international workshops. Based in the USA, Canada and the United Kingdom,[3] the principle of this network was initially picked up by painter David Koloane in South Africa. Thupelo, the workshop he set up in Johannesburg, was aimed at bringing artists from southern Africa together. Corresponding to the needs of openness and exchange felt by African plastic artists, the principle and outline of this type of encounter and training was adopted throughout the continent, whether in Zimbabwe, with Pachipemwe, in Namibia, with Tulipamwe, or in Senegal, with Tenq, the Huit Facettes workshops, or in Togo with Ewole, for example.

According to Robert Loder, one of the originators of the Triangle workshops, this type of creation and learning "*became pertinent in Africa because it (the workshop) seemed to provide the African artist with a way to work that was not didactic but instead rather stimulating by introducing artists to influences from other regions of Africa and, to a lesser extent, from Europe and the United States.*"[4] Paradoxically, these workshops, which were not specific eras of education, were, however, moments filled with artistic enrichment through experimentation with new materials and techniques and the introduction to other artists, and brought about different approaches, techniques and thought processes. Far from being a panacea, the formula used by the temporary workshops provided African artists with certain benefits. This formula is, in the current state of academic education, more dynamic and alive, more adapted to the artistic needs and issues of new generations. This is a flexible, inexpensive and rather effective formula. Examined in the light of the identity issue, the workshop provided fruitful education. Based on exchange, it enables artists to experiment with approaches, esthetics and various tools, and offers participants the opportunity to find their path and uniqueness. It, therefore, seems absurd to compare the exogenous – endogenous aspect of the techniques because "endogenous creation does not exclude exchange, but enriches its terms."[5]

However, my intention is not to compare formal and informal education, but rather to emphasize that an informal movement existed at the same time as the formal training process and gave vigor, depth, openness and modernity back to African artistic creation.

Other artistic training or teaching approaches should also be mentioned. There is the new method that, following the example of the Olorun Foundation in Burkina Faso, tends to offer a logistic structure welcoming artists who have come to explore or experiment with work techniques. There is, above all, the important traditional trend of apprenticeship structures in the local, ethnic or religious context, such as the Guelede sculptors from Benin in Nigeria, whose creations and forms sometimes migrate beyond the system for which they were created. Finally, there are the urban painting workshops, where a certain know-how is passed along to a creative trend that is very much in sync with the society and

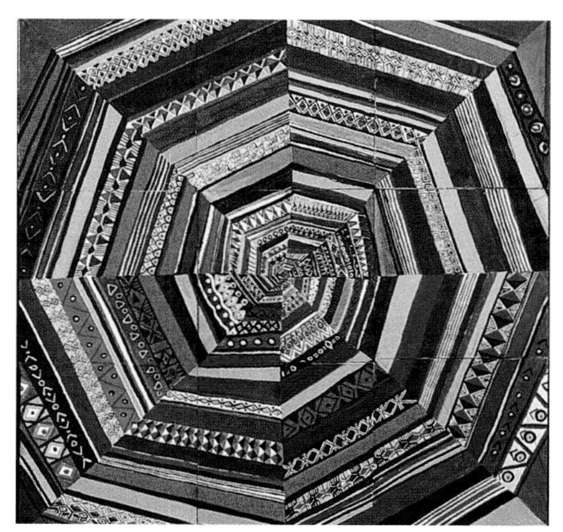

Boubacar Boureima (born in 1950), Niger
©Revue Noire

3 Network originally established by artist Anthony Caro and contemporary art collector Robert Loder

4 Robert Loder, "Workshops en Afrique," Médianes No. 14/15, Fall 1999

5 François-Noël Simoneau, "Échanges, échanges," Médianes No. 14/15, Fall 1999

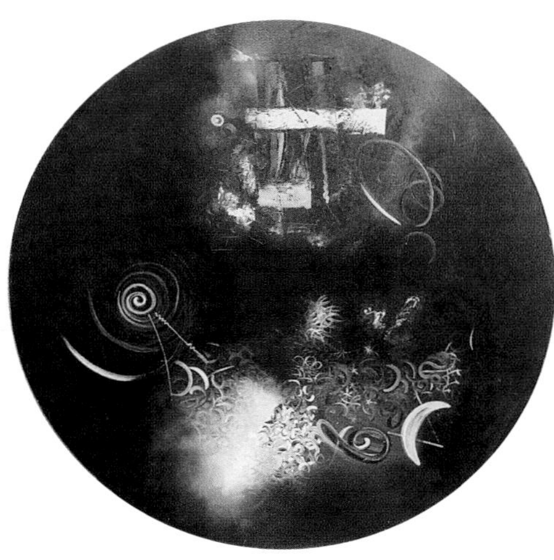

Souleymane Keïta (born in 1947), "Tutsi Massacre ," Senegal, 1990

©Bouna Medoune Seye/Revue Noire

producer of images this society requests, understands and socializes.

Thus, the crisis freed up energies that contributed to a certain reconnection of Africa with the universal movement of forms. This opening also drew attention to the diversity of African creation and showed the diversity of its traditional, modern, formal or informal sources. Although the professional training of artists is essentially the focus of the official course of study, it is not the only one. This professional training is done by following different formal and informal courses of study.

What is therefore important is to know whether these courses of study meet the artists' educational needs, and whether they meet society's artistic issues at this stage in history. What have we actually lost by ignoring the techniques and know-how of the traditional "artists" in the official course of study?
Initiatives to reform and re-energize the official course of study remain necessary. Other forms of artistic education must be invented.

These should be based on African modernity, extracting forms and works from national enclosures, imposing an autonomous definition of art and its criteria in relation to ideological positions. In brief, an African modernity must be invented that is not an identical copy of contemporary art processes, but which is based on a syncretism that combines the memories and visual cultures of Africa with all of the artistic techniques, mediums and means of the universal movement of forms. For the real issue does not reside in the origin of technique, but, fundamentally, in the artistic individuality used by technique and its uniqueness.

Another fundamental issue is raised: the ability of official art schools to become open places offering artists in training the ability to discover, explore and invent forms by soliciting all the aspects of modern art. A change in how education is approached is required.

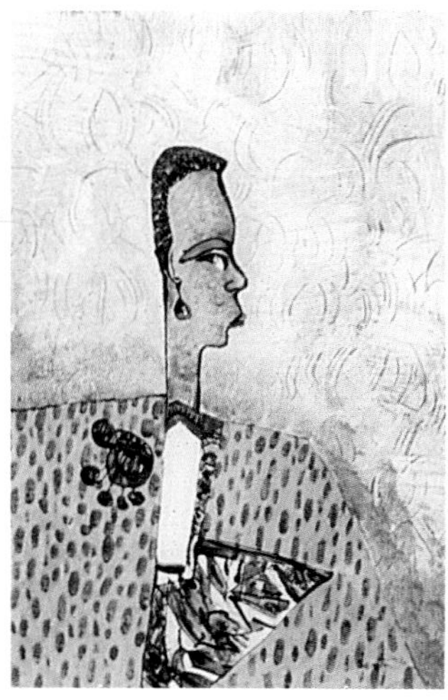

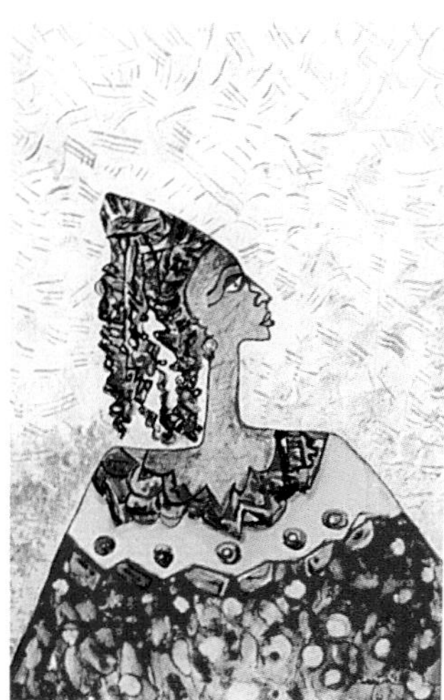

Serigne N'Diaye (born in 1953), Senegal

©Bouna Medoune Seye/Revue Noire

facing page:
Atelier de Pascal Kenfack (born in 1950), Cameroon, 1993

©Revue Noire

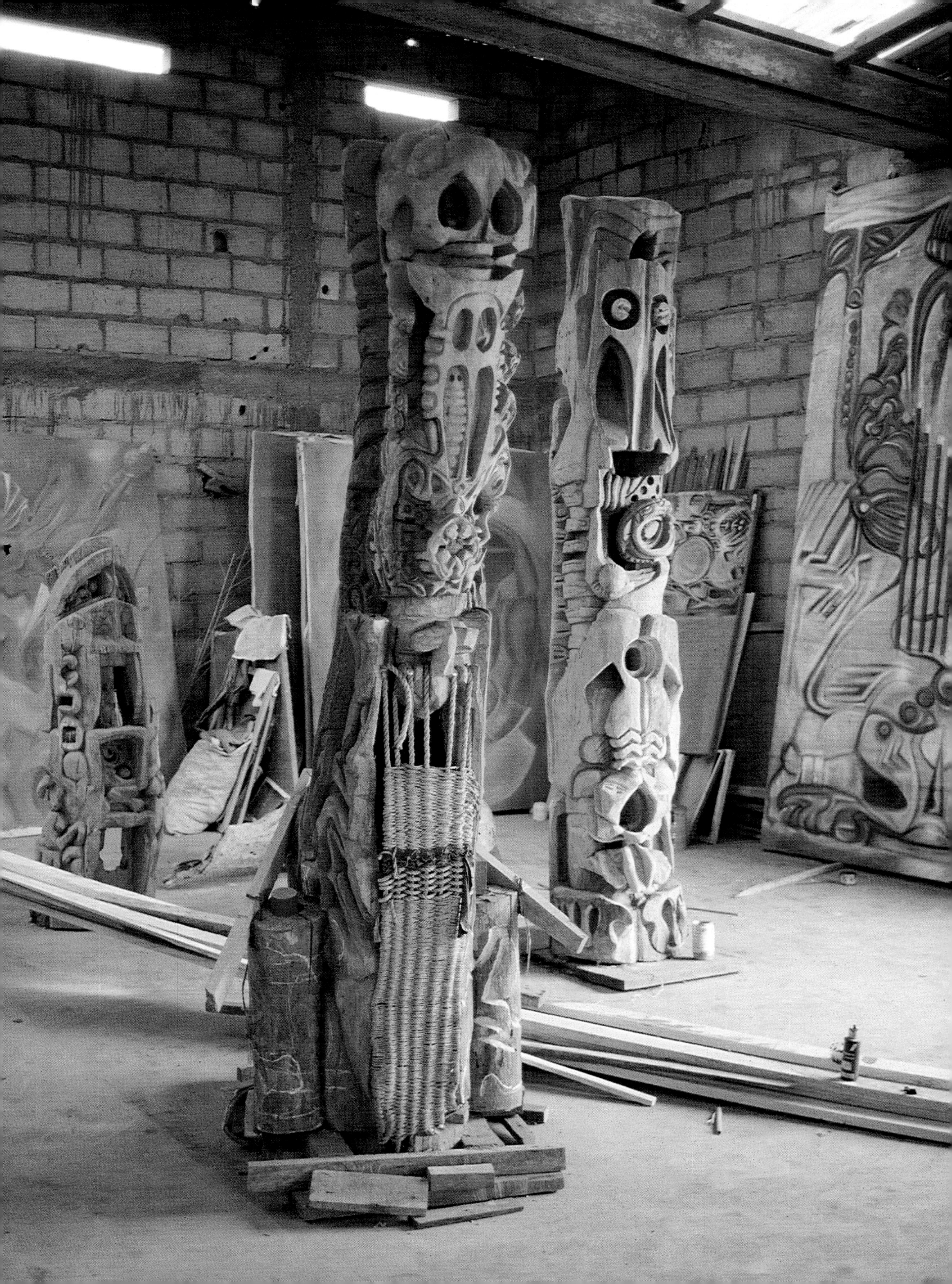

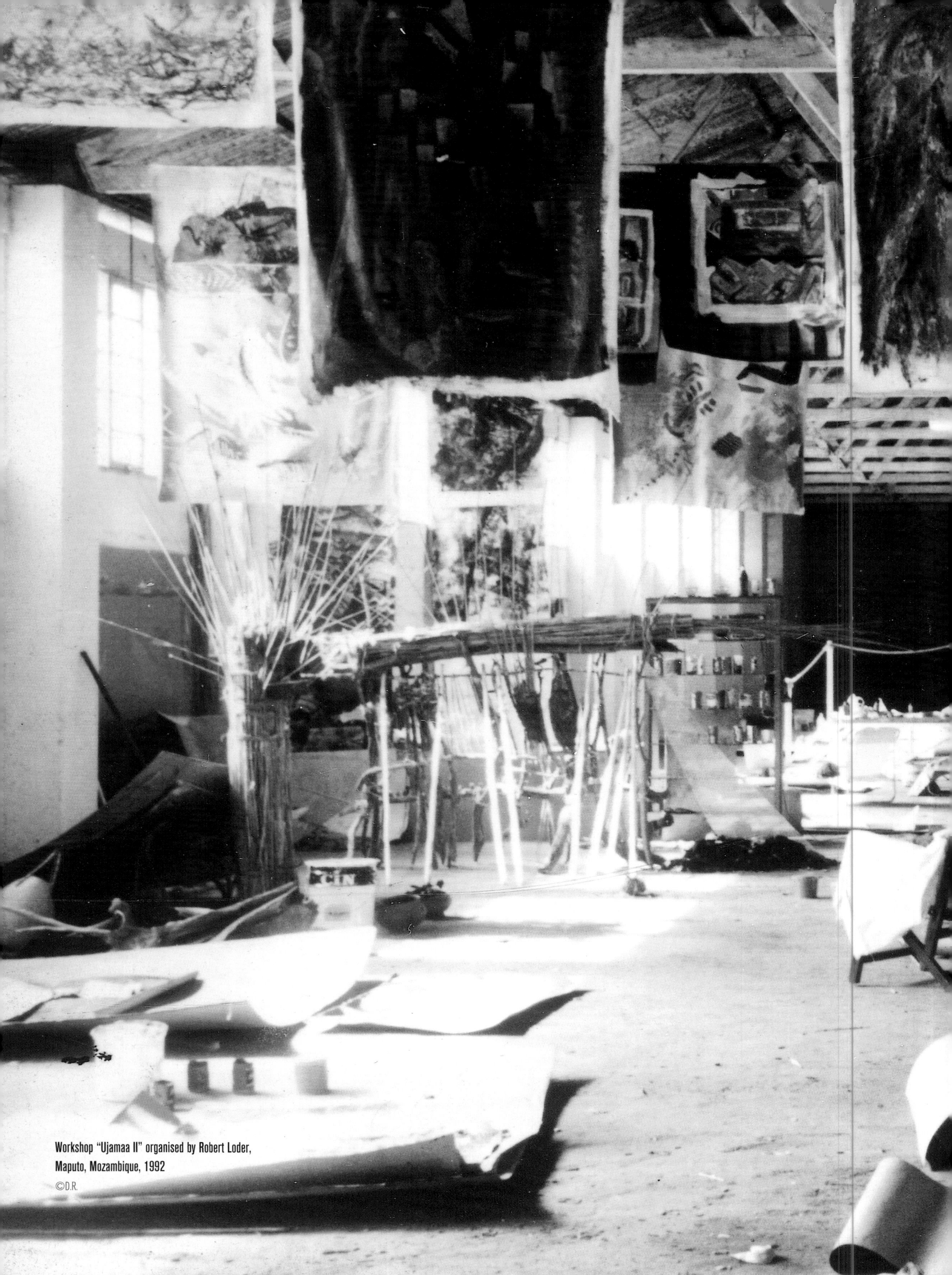

Workshop “Ujamaa II” organised by Robert Loder, Maputo, Mozambique, 1992

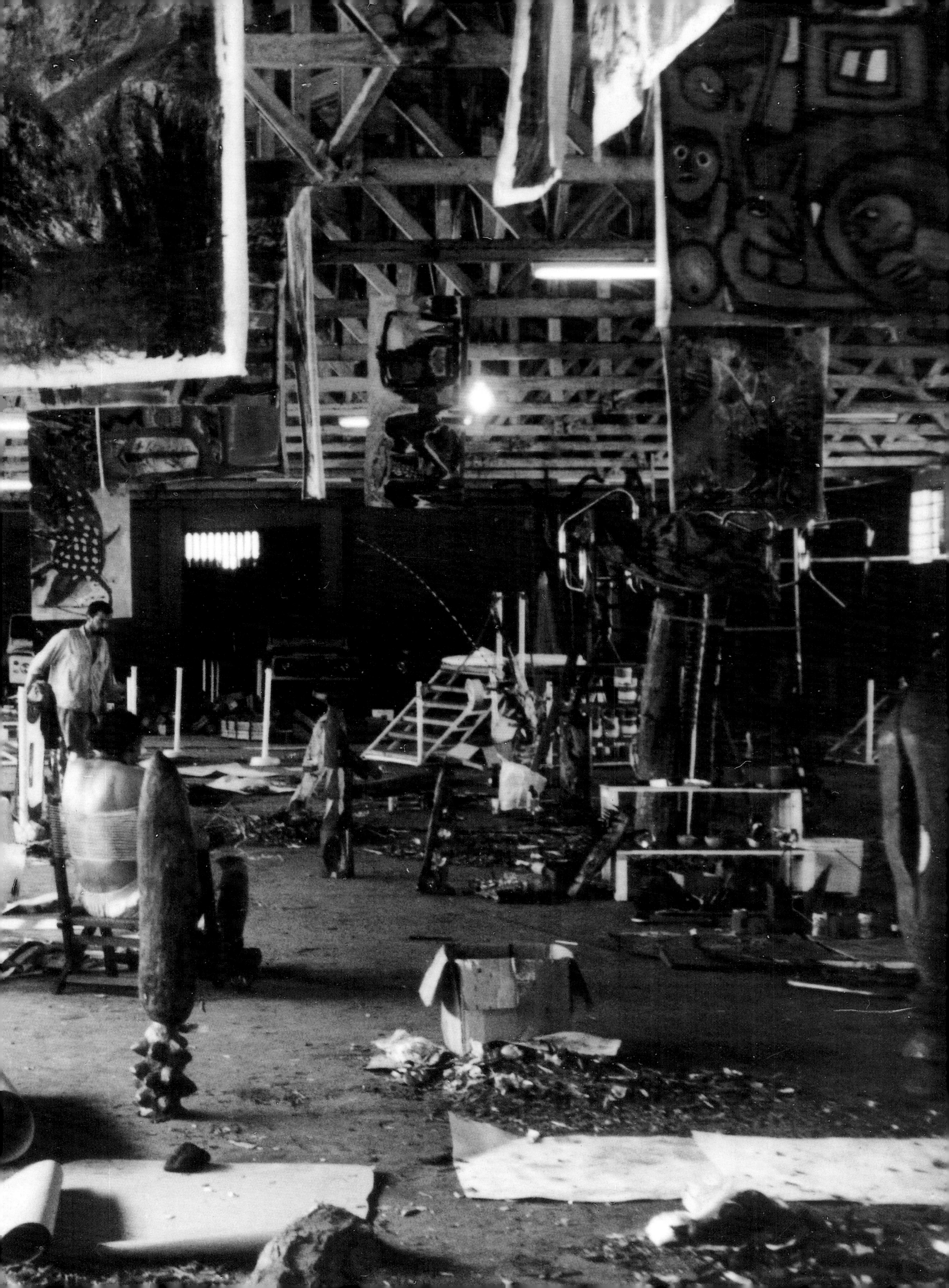

Burkina Faso: from social art to private initiatives

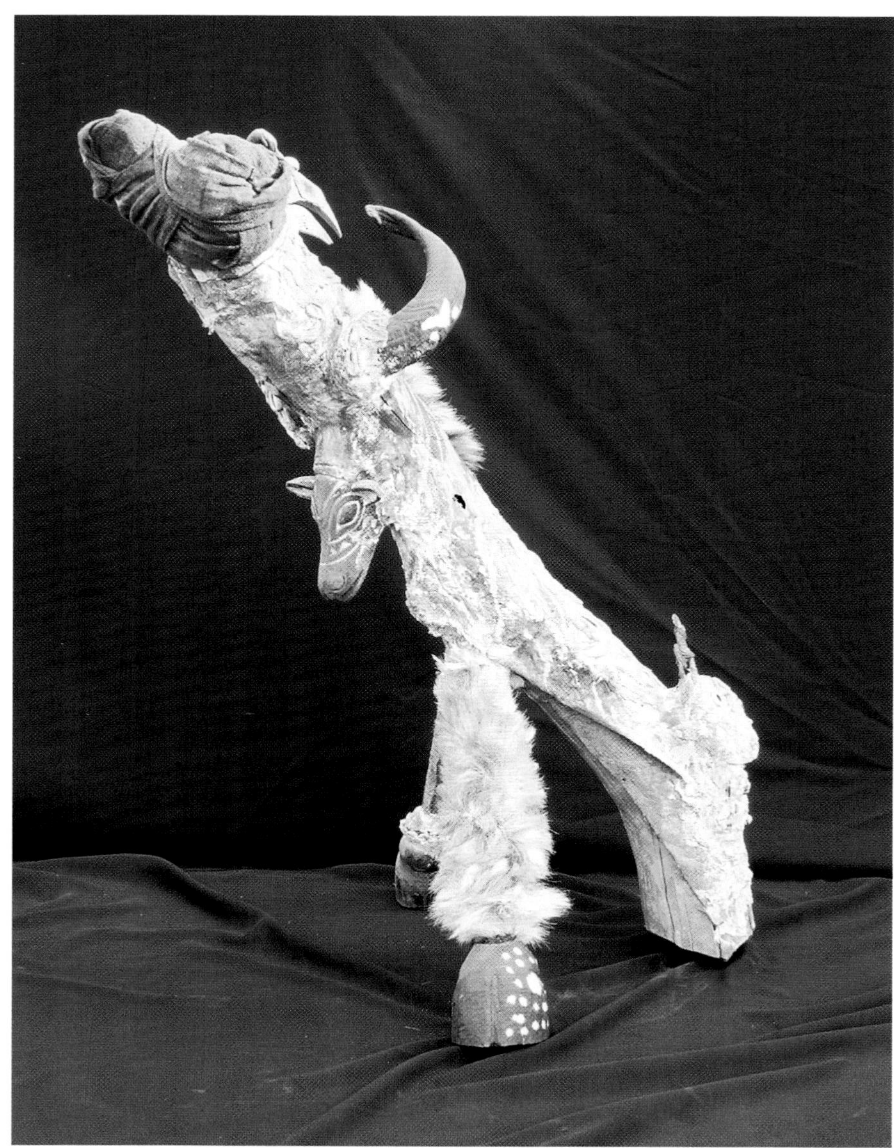

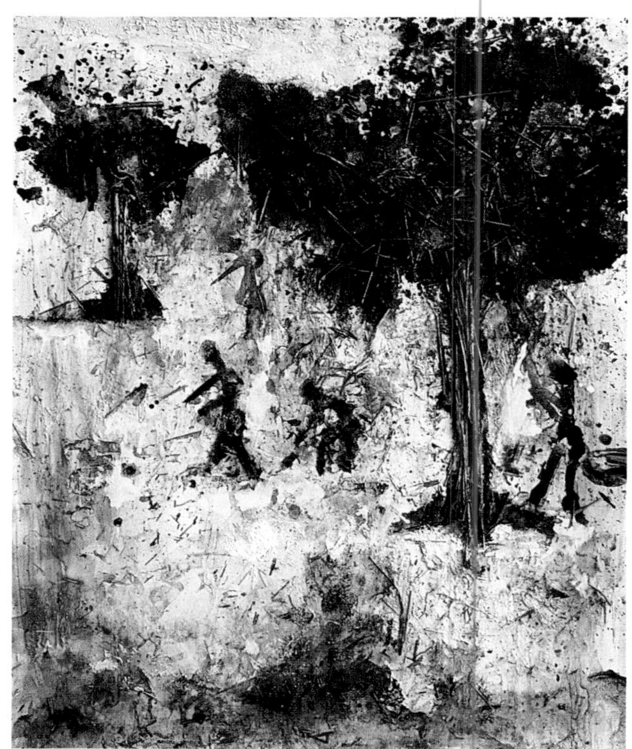

Siriki Ky (born in 1953)
©Revue Noire

Jean-Didier Yanogo (born in 1967)
©Revue Noire

USEFUL ART AND SANKARA

Blaise Patrix

In Burkina Faso, perpetuation of a cultural symbiosis combining the esthetic influences from the region within the Mossi melting pot explains the little interest raised by attempts by missionaries and African artists to develop a competitive spirit. The invitation extended by Moro Naba, the Mossi emperor, to the Derme family, Songhai bronze casters from the Bandiagara region, to assume the prestigious duty of royal jeweler, gave rise to ornamental art. The production of jewels, weapon pommels and trappings became enriched by the techniques of potters in 1915 and provided a statuary that also interested the colonists.
In overthrowing the colonial and aristocratic powers, independence dethroned art of its exemplary role. Insensibly, the meaning of identity became blurred, the prestigious gave way to the rational, and the honorary was confined to being symbolic. The notion of culture newly adopted by a power deemed republican and democratic was perceived in its educational dimension to be used as a didactic tool. The national needed to be built, the popular masses needed to be taught civil consciousness, the political messages needed to be promoted and the cultural portfolio was vacillating between "national education" and "youth and sports."

Artistic creativity was deemed a bit of a folly in view of the imperatives of development. Self-consciousness was compromised. In a feudal-like system, during national festivals, "artists," or rather "creative artisans," as a publication of the ACCT called them in 1977, went as a delegation to the Presidential Palace to offer a useless piece of work. Out of desperation, souvenirs were spread at the feet of cooperants leaving on vacation. In 1968, the state created the National Center for the Craft Industry, a place dedicated to American volunteers for progress. One of them showed Noufou Ouedraogo the batik technique learned in Indonesia. Noufou Ouedraogo is now teaching in Burkina and in the sub-region. The country currently has over 400 batik artists. The name National Center of Arts and Crafts (CNAA), given to the project in 1980, shows the confusion that has prevailed to date concerning artistic professions. It is headed by one of the three students trained at a fine arts school in Europe. The interns that I trained, in 1982, to use the materials available on site are unanimous: they will become building painters or civil servants because "there is no future in artistic professions." Stagnant at a time when everything appears to be evolving elsewhere, the mind resigns itself to fatalism.

Revolutionary determinism set out to conquer the future

On August 4, 1983, a putsch led by captains ousted the previous military power whose actions were deemed elitist and corrupt. The members of this putsch were about thirty years old and were surrounded by executives from their generation who, like themselves, had been educated in communist countries and who created the National Revolution Council (CNR), headed by Captain Thomas Sankara.
From the outset, the CNR urged everyone to take their place in order to set up an active development policy working for the people. Accordingly, and at the sustained level of military training, actions came together aimed at streamlining public services and at giving the entire nation a sense of responsibility. Revolution Defense Committees were set up and were given ideological training and weapons to bear. The country's name and flag were changed.

"The revolution expects our artists to know how to describe reality, produce living images out of it, express these images in melodious tones, while informing our people of the righteous voice leading them to a better future" (Thomas Sankara). This quotation from the brand new head of state set the tone for cultural policy until 1987. Less authoritative and more ludic than Mao Tse Tung's thought, which required artists to "...become a powerful army to unite and educate the people...," it still, however, allocated artists to their media-conscious utility. Art was restored to its central place in the heart of a cultural activity whose educational functions were renewed. The Burkinabé Copyright Office was established.

A national seminar organized on this theme in 1985 defined the major goals: the achievement of a national identity and ideological awareness. The National Culture Weeks established in 1983 expanded culture to include its sociological scope by adding "clothing art," "culinary art" and "hair art" to the usual disciplines of "stage art" and "plastic arts." As of 1986, the event was enriched by the presence of "tradi-practitioners." The major watchwords of the revolution provided the themes for plastic art competitions geared towards participants coming from all over the country. The prevailing works were initially put on tour then kept by the national museum. Lougué Kou, a state nurse trained in Japan on graphic techniques, was entrusted with promoting public health awareness. The program for starting up primary health centers in all villages throughout Burkina Faso made his posters a fixture on the national landscape. In order to obtain objective realism, cooperation was requested from Cuba to teach classical drawing at the People's Academy of Arts. Sign-painting artisans were asked to paint awareness posters. Humorous drawings and comic strips appeared in newspapers. In 1986, the creation of the Institute of Black Peoples extended the quest for an identity to the Diaspora. A series of monumental sculptures were also ordered by the state at this time.

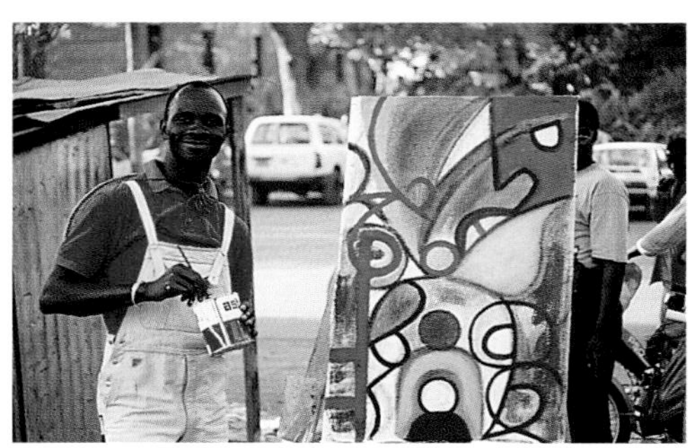

Fernand Noukouni
©Revue Noire

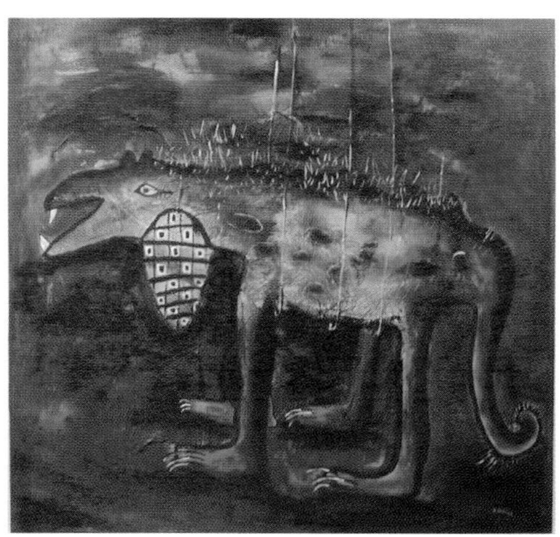

Suzanne Ouedraogo (born in 1973), "Bestiary n°1," 1999
150x150 cm ©Revue Noire

Happy to feel useful and stimulated by the enthusiastic spirit of a government that did not hesitate to "jazz up" an orchestra to have the people dance during the new national festival, the workshop masters became excited and united, and expanded their skills. Guy Compaoré and Tasséré Guiré, educated at the Fine Arts School of Rome, sculpted monuments in welded sheet metal and concrete. In 1984, Ky Siriky returned to Ivory Coast where he was raised, and took classes at the Fine Arts School of Abidjan. He initiated the monumental cast iron technique by co-signing a work with Ali Nikiema.
In 1987, the First International Craft Fair of Ouagadougou (SIAO) was launched. It presented traditional crafts, furniture creations and original painted and sculpted objects and works. Burkina became, with its President's charisma, a focus of media attention.

However, the speeches were sprinkled with contradictions. Just as the rejuvenation of power contravened the call to respect a heritage based on oligarchy, so to the instruction "to use art as a speaker for the revolution" and the call to "liberate the creative spirit" were not compatible. The alternative would be to participate in the process where exclusion and creators deprived of their critical duty were relegated to the position of representatives. Converted to reason, the mad were no longer entitled to stand up to the king. The discomfort of this frustration and latent conflict was not unlike the dissension that would soon shake the solidarity of the leaders and end in well-known tragic extremes.

Decentralization and professionalism

The new government restored democracy in the country in 1991, after fifteen years of military dictatorship. Economic entrepreneurs, frightened by talk of redistribution of riches, had to be reassured and production had to be revived. The self-confidence and sense of responsibility stimulated by the previous regime bore fruit. Beyond the perpetuation of the actions begun, cultural policy guided the identity issue towards the encounter between heritage and modernity, and promoted the decentralization and professionalization of the cultural initiative. Consequently, cultural engineering courses were extended to the private sector, the Symposium on grained sculpture of Laongo and the Cultural Resources and Development Center (CRDC) were subsidized, and the Support Program for Decentralized Cultural Initiatives (PSIC) was launched.

Ouag'art

Four courses organized by the French cultural center, from 1993 to 1998, were enthusiastically greeted by the rising generation, whose ambition had already been stimulated by the residence of artist Brahim Injaï (Guinea Bissau) in 1992. Like the strict teachings of sculptor Henri Georges Vidal, François Kiené, designer of objects and furniture, and As Mbengue, painter from Senegal, assisted in putting an end to the feeling of poverty covering the so-called "developing country" by making use of recovery materials. Better than anyone else, As, with his generosity, jubilation and perseverance, hit home: there is no problem, everyone is getting by, and, day and night, the creative mind is being freed once and for all! Things were being done that nobody thought possible. All that was left to be done was to make a living from this activity in order to get past the stage of punctual event. I guided the Ouag'art, which was entrusted to me the following year, towards making contact, towards the industrial suppliers of materials, and towards the public, by putting files together, searching for a sponsor and making a model of the monumental project. The internship began with the organization and stage design of an exhibit whose hook was renewed each week by newly produced works. This resulted in strong sponsorship from the country's First Lady, in the national television station being at the preview, and in coverage by the entire press, and it led to certain artists making, in one month, the equivalent of a year's wages.

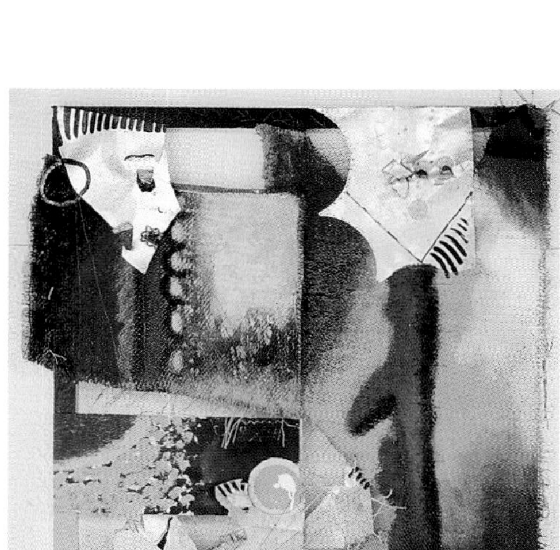

Ali Kéré (born in 1960)

©Revue Noire

Olorun and its after-effects

Created in 1995 by an enthusiast fan, the Olorun Foundation got on the right track and built its experience "on-the-job." An old bar, transformed into a workshop, was used as a springboard or example. A workshop invited artists such as Soly Cissé (Senegal) or Sokey Edorh (Togo). Exhibits were organized in the United States, France and on site. Painters Jean-Didier Yanogo, Paul-Marie Kabré, Fernand Noukouni, Suzanne Ouedraogo, Samadoulougou, Christophe Sawadogo and sculptors Saliou Traoré and Allassane Drabo passed through this hug of activity, which, since then, has been devoting itself more specifically to the production of "design" crafts. Two art galleries opened: the Farafina gallery, which exhibits the first works of Takité Kambou, and the Zaka gallery, which has given opportunities to Sambo Boly, Michel Sam and Doo+. The latter come from the distant periphery called "the village." Their approach to modernity, laden with identity-related consciousness, calls out to the contemporary art centers. Their presence explained how "useful art" came to be.

Zaria, Nsukka and the Lagos, Nigeria Arts Festival

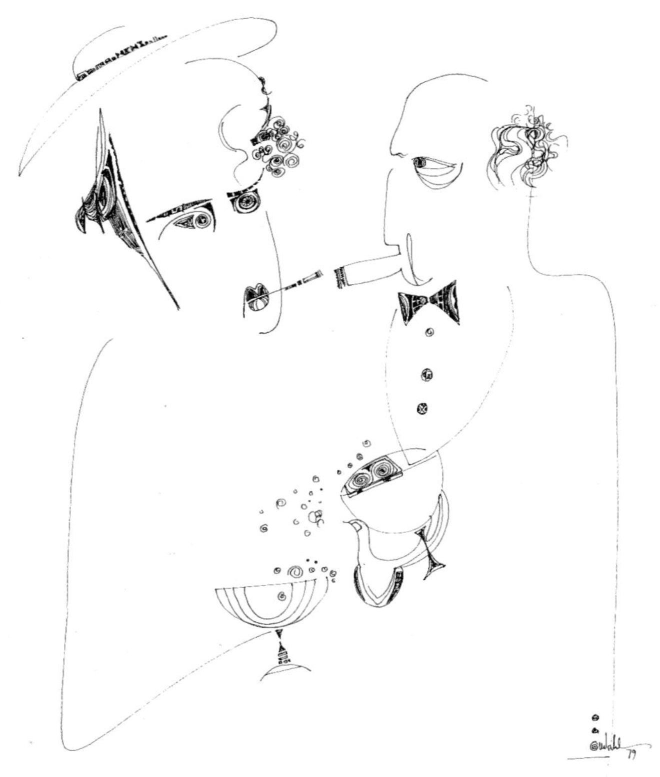

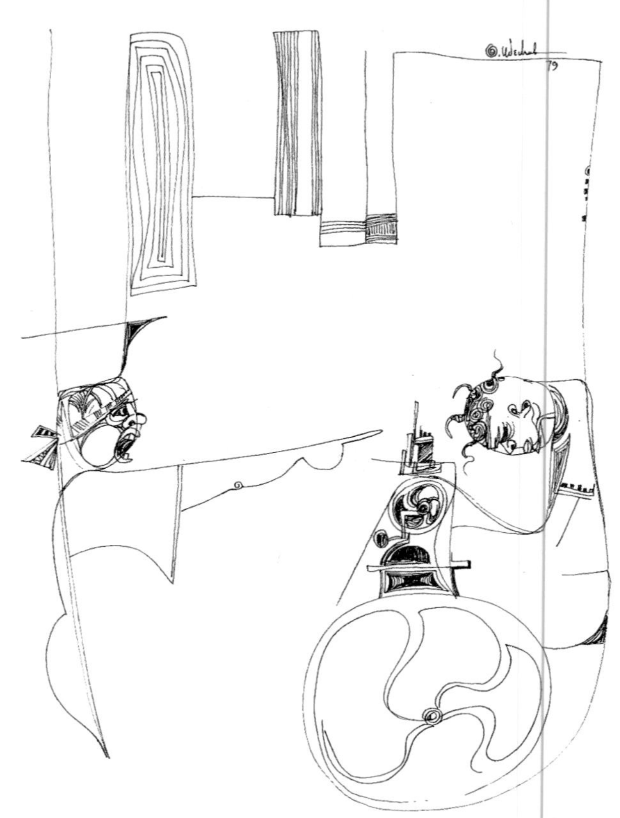

Obiora Udechukwu, "Diplomats," 1979
India ink on paper

Obiora Udechukwu, "Burden," 1979
India ink on paper

facing page:
Jacob Jari (born in 1960), 1993

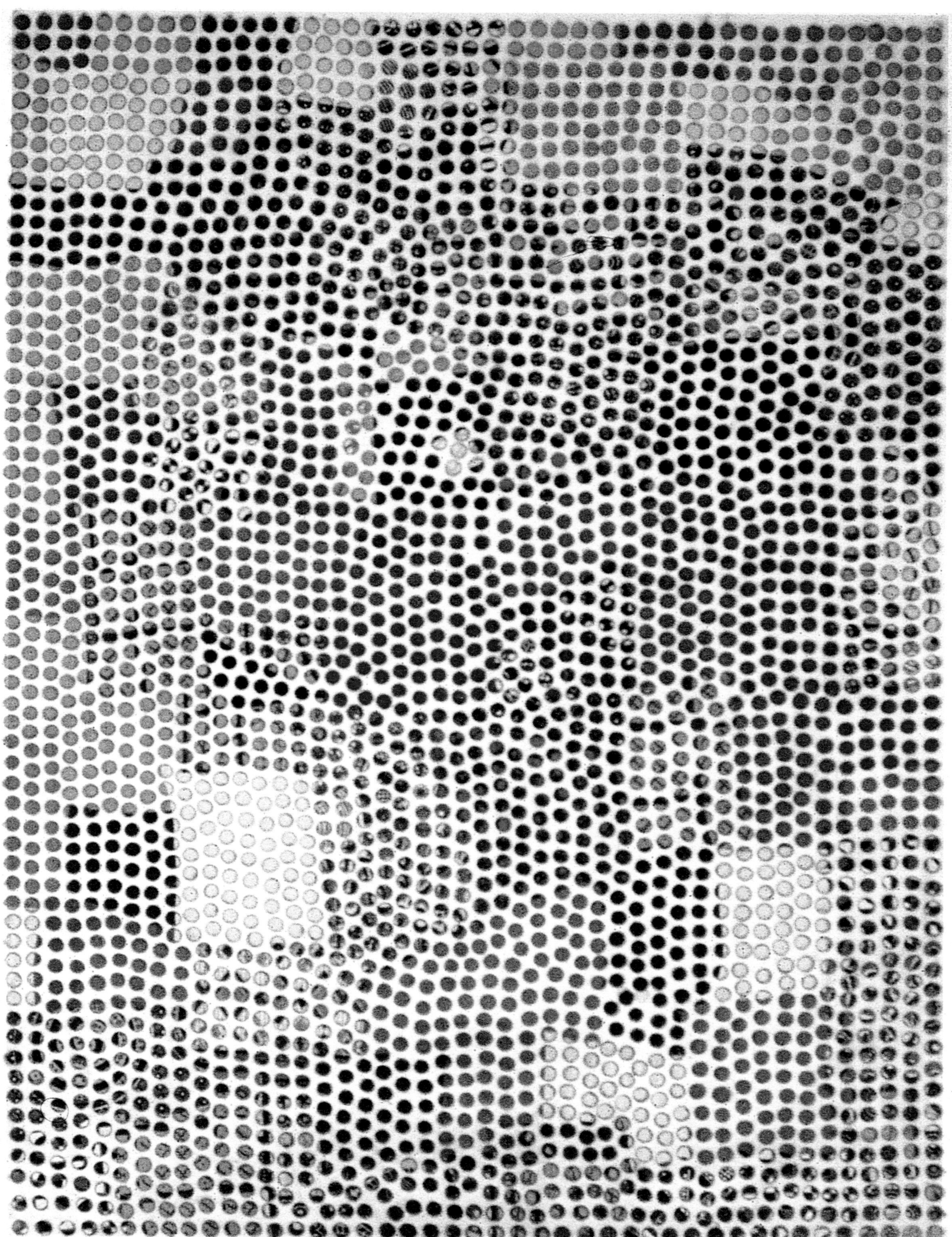

Ndidi Dike, "The spirit of African art," 1994
wood, 85 x 250 cm
©D.R.

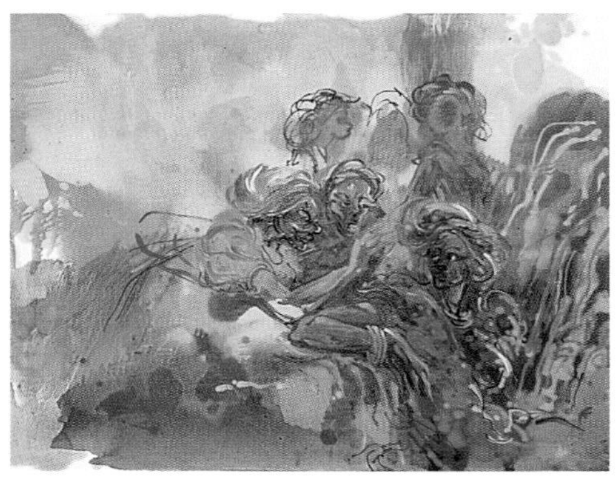

Ganiyu Odutokun (born in 1946), 1994
©Whitechapel Art Gallery

ART SCHOOLS IN NIGERIA: ZARIA AND NSUKKA

Sylvester Ogbechie

Zaria

The origin of the Nigerian College of Art, Science and Technology (NCAST) Zaria dates from 1943 when the British Secretary of State for the Colonies appointed a commission under the chairmanship of Rt. Hon. Walter Elliot to consider the issue of higher education in West Africa. The Colonial Office expressed the view that there was need for the provision of facilities, other than those which come within the scope of a university, for education beyond the school certificate program. The College began operations in 1953 at Ibadan with art courses as part of the curriculum. This program was later transferred in 1955 to NCAST Zaria where the institution was relocated.

The art department of NCAST (later renamed Ahmadu Bello University) was one of the new tertiary levels of art training in Nigeria and its staff in 1956 was mainly composed of British and European teachers with the exception of Clara Etso Ugbodaga, a female Nigerian painter and mosaic artist. The head of department, Patrick Herbert George, was an instructor in Painting and Drawing at the Slade (1949 - 1955) from where he was appointed by the Colonial Office to oversee the development of the NCAST Fine Arts department from 1956 to 1960. Eric Taylor who was the Senior Lecturer in charge of the studio programs and Vincent Butler who taught sculpture were both graduates of Goldsmiths College of the University of London. The other lecturers included Clifford Frith, Diana Madgett, Mrs. A. S. Laurenson, G. E. Todd, and P. J. De Monchaux, a graduate of the Slade who also taught briefly in London before securing employment at Zaria. The curriculum at NCAST was based on the Goldsmiths School of Art's and was dedicated to art studies based on European classical traditions. NCAST attracted a diversified body of students whose population was fairly large for the period with at least 336 students by December 1958.

The institution became a full University after Nigeria's independence by which time most its largely European faculty was replaced by Nigerians who by 1988 included Ganiyu Oduntokun, a master formalist whose lyrical style and synthesis of European, Islamic and Nigerian aesthetic traditions influenced a generation of postcolonial Zaria students. The paradigm of Natural Synthesis promulgated at this institution in 1958 by members of the Zaria Art Society has since been codified into a recognizable style in modern Nigerian art. Their tradition of critical engagement continued with the formation of The Eye Society in 1989 which brought together influential Zaria art instructors like Odutokun, Jacob Jari, Toni Okpe, Jerry Buhari and Matt Ehizele to interrogate the artistic climate of Nigeria following the harsh economic downturn of the 1980s. These artists now define the direction of art at Zaria and their solutions to conceptual and formalistic issues reflect an enduring spirit of critical engagement.

Nsukka

The Department of Fine Arts of the University of Nigeria was established in 1961, one year after the institution was founded through the direct intervention of Dr. Nnamdi Azikiwe, first President of Nigeria and Chairman of the University Provisional Council. Azikiwe also recruited the initial faculty of the new program by soliciting prominent Nigerian artists of that era like Ben Enwonwu and Akinola Lasekan to lend their considerable expertise towards the development of this institution. Lasekan and Margaret Dunlap, an American (and first chair of the department) accepted his invitation; together, they constituted the pioneer faculty of the department which began operation in the 1961/62 academic year with a class of five students all of whom graduated in 1965. In the 1962/63 academic year, Robert J. Pfister joined the Department as its chair and recruited O. O. Esedebe and E. Okechukwu Odita.

Between 1963 and 1965, P. D. Abaye and Anthony Nkememena were recruited and Mrs. J. Pfister came on board as a part-time instructor. A. O. Morah joined the department in 1965 when Lasekan became the head of department (he would resign his post in 1966) and in the 1966/67 academic year, V. C. Amaefuna, N. W. Udosen, F. Oluigbo, and I. T. Clark became new additions. In all, this faculty graduated thirteen students before the Nigerian civil war (1967-1970) engulfed the fledgling institution and forced its closure (along with the University) until 1970.

Before 1967, the aesthetic orientation of the Department generally tended towards an academic style directed to achieving Azikiwe's goal of humanistic ethos and Pan-Africanist affirmation. The devastated campus (with its largely Igbo population) that resumed operations in 1970 was more concerned with issues of ethnic identity in the context of a contentious political existence. Uche Okeke, who was appointed in 1970 to lead the program, changed its conceptual focus from the formalist aesthetics of the prewar era to one based on interrogations of indigenous aesthetics. His earlier experiments with Igbo Uli motifs became a source material for subsequent practice and engendered what came to be known as the Nsukka School.
In addition to Uche Okeke, instructors like Chike Aniakor and V. C. Amaefuna helped shape the first generation of Nsukka neo-Uli artists among whom Obiora Udechukwu emerged as the most influential. El Anatsui, a Ghanaian sculptor who was recruited in 1975, introduced a unique and influential style of sculpture to this institution. The combined effort of these instructors and the art historian Ola Oloidi fostered three generations of Nsukka artists and critics whose practice brought the department immense international acclaim.

From 1970 to 1990, the Nsukka School refracted art practice through contemporary interpretations of the Igbo Uli art tradition. While many students at the institution still mine this indigenous art for aesthetic concepts, a profound paradigm shift has occurred as their attention turned to the international arena of art practice where new technologies of art production orient them towards other conceptual frameworks. For these younger students, the Uli ideal has already attained historical status but its underlying spirit of conceptual and aesthetic excellence continues to guide their interrogation of local and international culture.

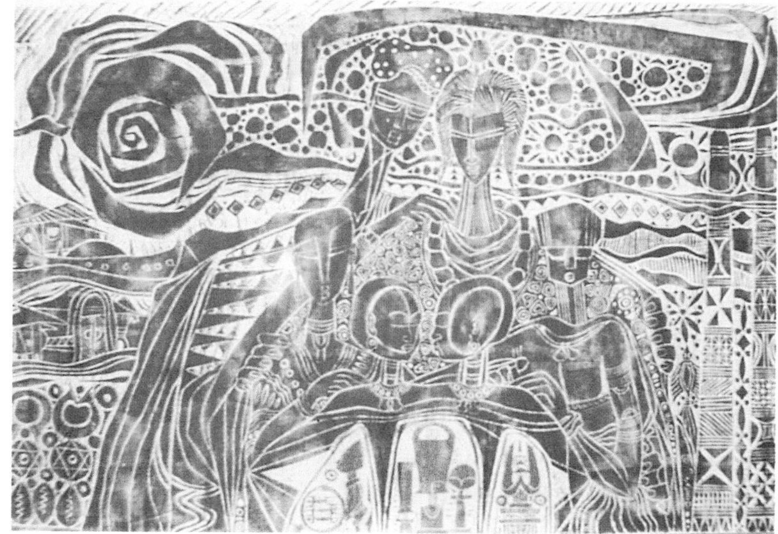

Tayo Quyaye
©D.R.

LAGOS ART FESTIVAL
Sylvester Ogbechie

The 2nd World Black Festival of Arts and Culture (FESTAC 77) was a vast display of African creativity for the continent and its Diaspora populations through international exhibitions of dance, drama, literature, architecture and the visual arts. 17000 artists from 56 countries participated in events that spanned several weeks in two major Nigerian cities, Lagos and Kaduna, and included related programs at several venues. FESTAC built upon antecedents like the 1966 Festival of Negro Arts in Dakar, Senegal convened by Léopold Sédar Senghor as a forum to reflect on the role and function of African arts and culture in the postcolonial aspirations of African nations and in international discourses of cultural practice.

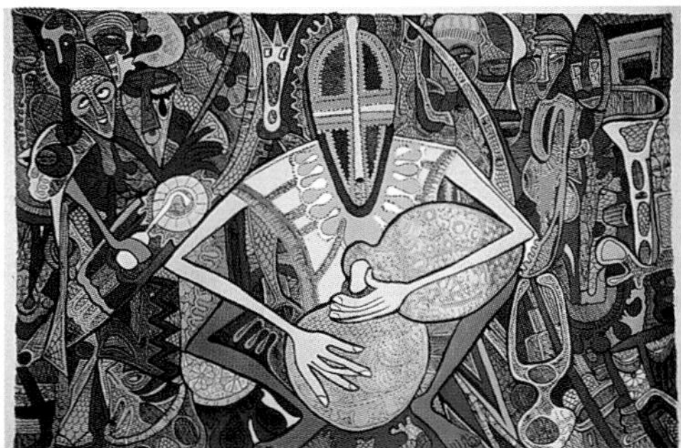

Emmanuel Ekong Ekefrey (born in 1952)

The organizers of the Dakar festival hoped that such gatherings would be a regular affair, hosted by different African nations as a means of engendering a unity of purpose in African cultural affairs. However, the intervening years between 1966 and 1977 was fraught with political unrest for several African nations whose resources were thus diverted to propagating or resolving different forms of conflict. Nigeria hosted FESTAC in a decade in which revenues from its massive oil reserves boosted the country's economy. Infrastructure preparations for the festival necessitated the construction of a city to house the cast of international delegates that visited the country for the event. In addition, the government constructed a national theater that provided a physical and conceptual focus for the festival.

Kolade Oshinowo

The arts exhibitions held in Lagos in 1977 showcased pride in Black culture through a vast conglomeration of contemporary expressions that reflected a continuity of the plastic arts tradition and was fairly representative of black arts worldwide. The patron of the exhibition, Nigerian Head of State General Olusegun Obasanjo expressed the hope that myriad manifestations of African cultural practice at FESTAC would hasten the abandonment of the "museum approach" that interprets African culture only in terms of prehistoric objects displayed in European museums. Rather, he hoped African culture would be studied as a living thing that portrays the ethos of black people and reflects ways in which Black African cultural heritage can co-exist with the cultural values of other peoples without much conflict. FESTAC, in this sense, would showcase the contributions of African peoples to universal currents of thought in culture and the arts.

Nigeria, the host nation, held separate displays of visual arts at two locations. The principal exhibition of contemporary Nigerian art, titled the Nigerian National Exhibition, also took place from January to February 1977 and was explicitly convened in connection with FESTAC 77 at the Lagos State Cultural Center. The second show titled Exhibition of Contemporary Nigerian Art took place from January 24-February 19 at the National Center for Arts and Culture (also in Lagos) under the aegis of the National Council for Arts and Culture. Its 30-page catalogue provided biographical details of participating artists and paid homage to Nigerian collectors for their contributions to the development of modern Nigerian art.

The Nigerian art historian Ola Oloidi reviewed the national exhibition in light of it mandate to provide symbolic, therapeutic and patriotic images of African culture. He criticized some of the artworks for elevating aesthetic impact above relevant content and noted that the many of the artists failed to use their representation of quotidian experiences as political instruments capable of stimulating intellectual and cultural pride. Oloidi castigated the plethora of genre paintings in this exhibition as insincere works that did not respond to FESTAC's call for the reinvigoration of Black patriotism. He felt that Nigerian artists should reflect social issues in their art and that the exhibition, although successful, did not provide enough innovation to ensure the nation's spiritual and national evolution.

The above criticism raised valid concerns since one of the stated goals of the

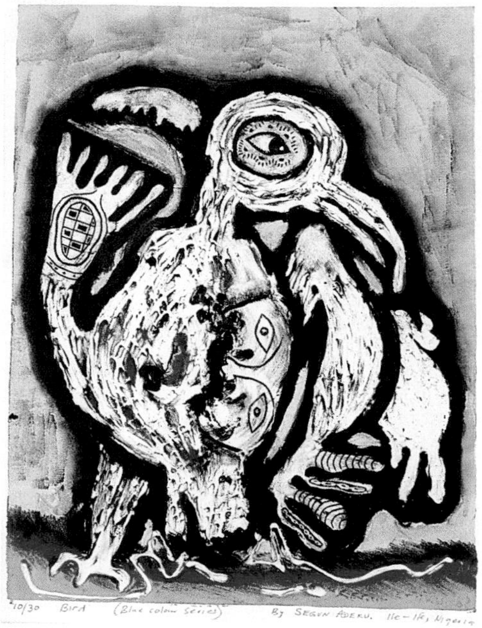

Segun Adeku
©Revue Noire

exhibition was to rekindle an interest in the African past and prescribe directions for its future. The Nationalist movement that brought about the end of colonial rule in many parts of Africa by 1960s used the ideology of Pan-Africanism as a tool to organize African colonial subjects. This ideology advocated political and cultural action for the emancipation of African and peoples of African descent. However, while it was easy to formulate a political response to colonial domination and the desire for political freedom, it was more difficult to formulate a cultural response to the Eurocentric modes of symbolic communication imposed on colonized African populations. In this context, the question of how to rehabilitate Africa's past and engender pride in African culture became a contentious issue and the notion of African culture itself became a battleground of contesting ideologies. These raised questions about the nature of African culture in the past and in the postcolonial era, the issue of authenticity in African culture, and the need to reject European cultural domination while appropriating from it certain forms of cultural practice.

The ideology of Negritude was arguably the most influential among the various interpretations of Pan-Africanism that were proffered by African intellectuals as viable modes of cultural practice in the postcolonial period. Léopold Sédar Senghor, Negritude's chief theorist, defined it as the "sum of the cultural values of the black world" that engenders an active presence for black people in the cultural and political affairs of the human race. Negritude ideology underpinned the 1966 Dakar festival and its influence remained evident at FESTAC where calls for an affirmation of Black cultural pride was filtered through Negritude inflected images and its largely apolitical aesthetics. As Oloidi rightly noted, such apolitical focus quickly resolves itself into a glorification of the past through genre images rather than focus on contemporary social and political issues through art.

Despite the above criticism, the Lagos art festival impacted positively on subsequent artistic practice in Nigeria since it provided a forum for interrogating the influence of Negritude ideology on postcolonial African culture. In the wake of this exhibition, a more rigorous and politically engaged attitude to art practice emerged in modern Nigerian art with a stronger focus on investigations of indigenous aesthetics. Although this new orientation would eventually be criticized for fostering affirmations of militant ethnicity, the art movements it engendered rescued modern Nigerian art from an incipient parochialism.

Upheaval in East Africa

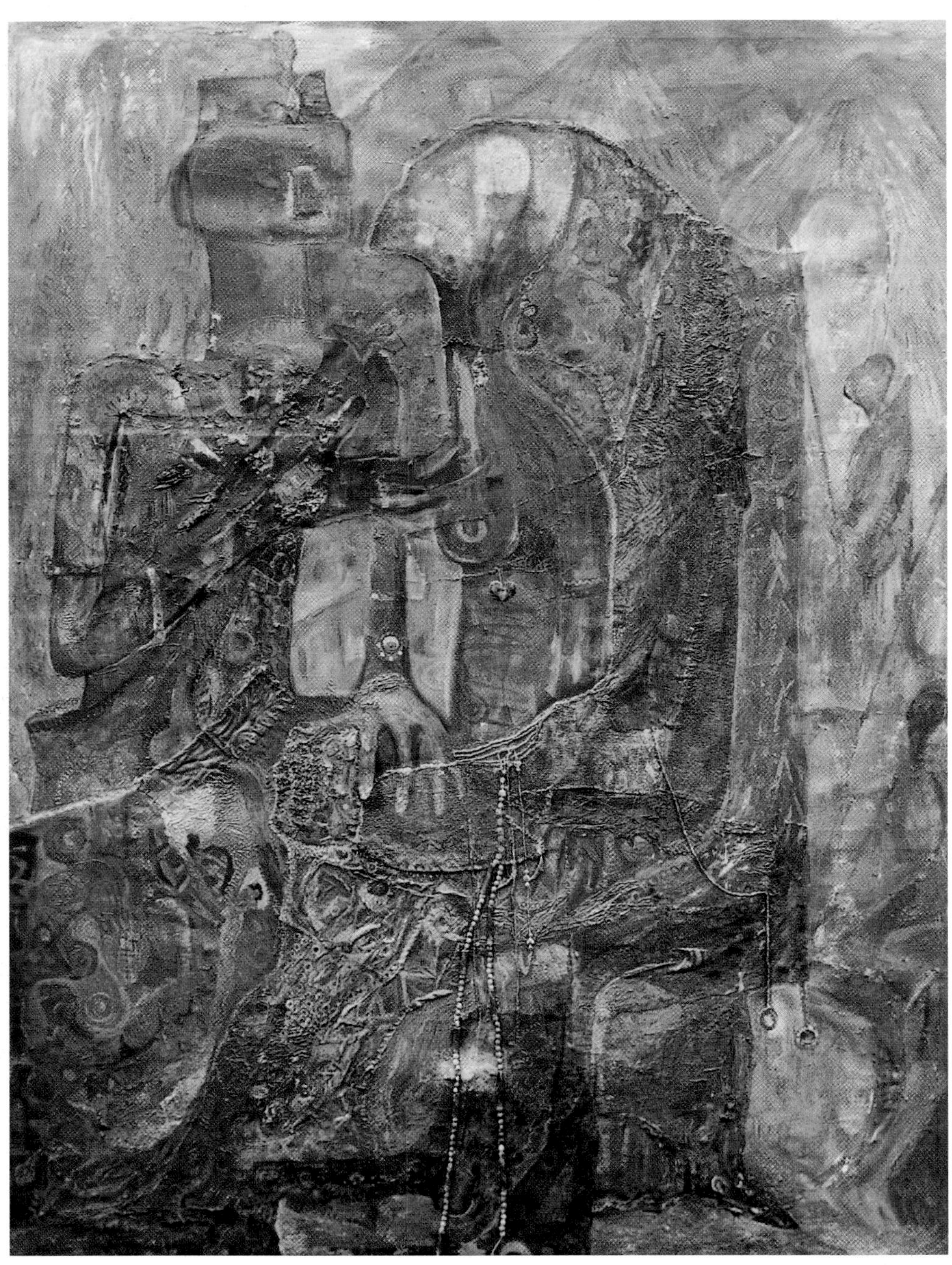

Pilkington Ssengendo (born in 1942), "King and Queen," Uganda, 1998
60x100 cm
©George Kyeyune

facing page:
Francis Nnaggenda (born in 1936), "War victim," Uganda, 1990
h. 3 m.
©George Kyeyune

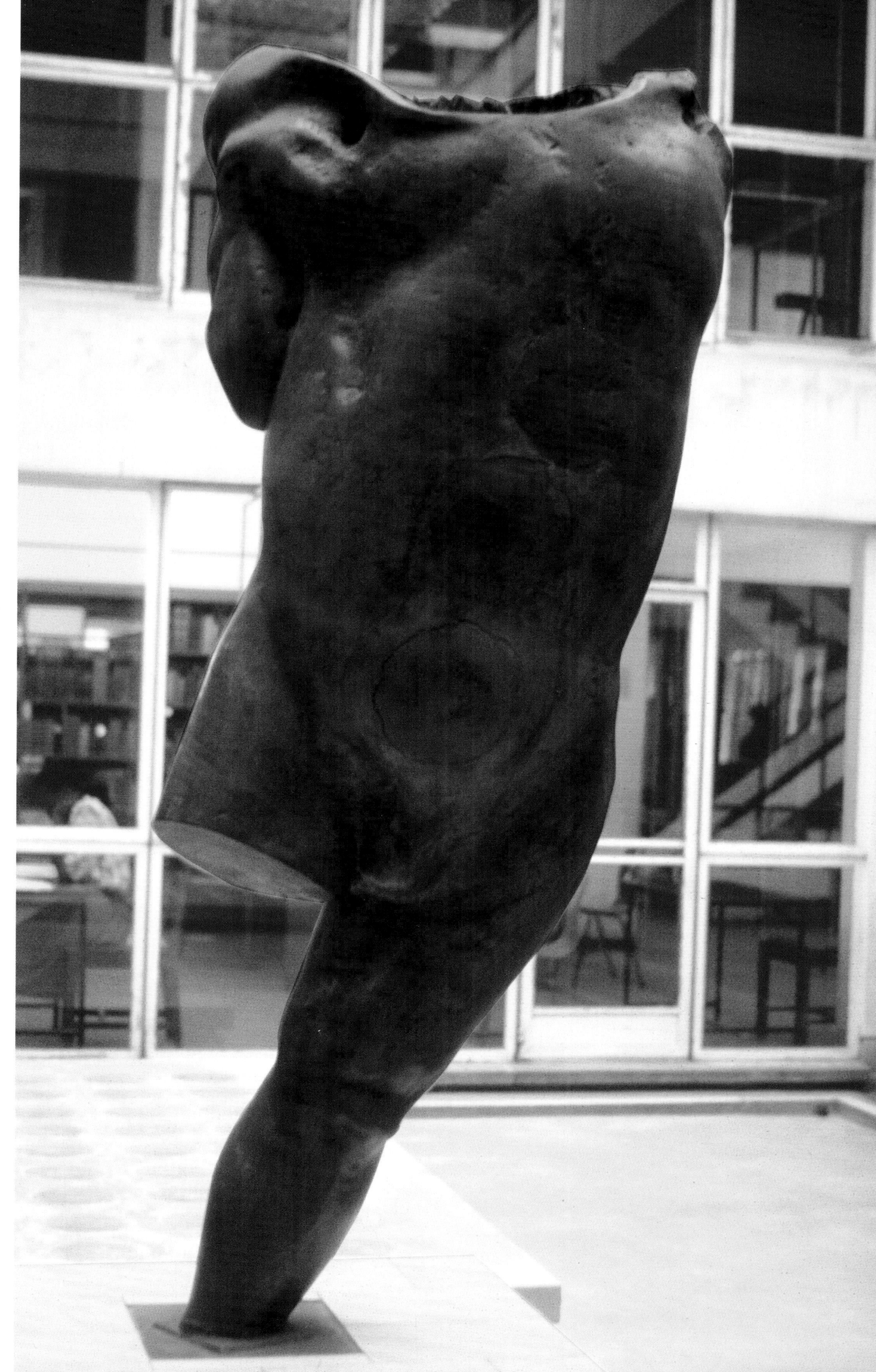

MAKERERE ART SCHOOL: THE PERIOD OF SURVIVAL
George Kyeyune

Elkana O. Ongessa, Kenya, 1995
©UNESCO/photo Claude Michel

In the 70s and early 80s, the euphoric confident and cosmopolitan culture of Makerere which characterised the 1960s was quickly degraded under Amin and later Obote II's years of blood stained politics (1971-79) and (l980-86). The break up of the Federal University of East Africa in 1970 and the simultaneous break up of the East African Community pushed Makerere further in an era of sustained decay and as its constituent part, it was inevitable that the art school would be affected. While Ugandan students continued to be admitted in Nairobi and Dar es Salaam Universities for courses which were not offered at Makerere, fear of brutal regimes became a real obstacle for the admission of foreign students to Makerere during this period.

Cecil Todd retired in 1970 and was succeeded by J. Kingdon and then Ali Darwish, the first East Africans to head the school. These and more of Makerere Art School staff fled the country as the political conditions became unbearable. As a result, the school was forced to recruit its recent BA graduates such as, Mpagi F., Ocitti S. etc. Although Amin was suspicious of the loyalty of educated people, he respected the art school. Both Amin and Obote possessed a natural and deep rooted understanding of the importance of art as an instrument of propaganda. By keeping both regimes supplied with symbols, medals, coats of arms, the school remained open.

On the occasion of the 1975 OAU summit in Kampala for example, Amin ordered from the school the production of textile fabric design based on African motifs with a dominating portrait of his, festooned with medals, to stress his military achievements, while I. Sserulyo was commissioned to paint a mural about the story of bark cloth making in Uganda as a glorification of the country's past high technological attainment. No artists were set aside as official employees by either of the two governments. Although the support and interest from both regimes was considerable these could not sustain the artistic production. Nommo Gallery which by this time had completely decayed mainly due to a combination of mismanagement and reduced Government funding, was no longer suitable for serious art shows. Artists therefore looked for markets in centres outside Uganda such as Nairobi.

With the cordial and symbiotic relationship, which prevailed between the school and the regimes not withstanding however, (and this seemed to be an exclusive preserve of the Art School within the Makerere Academe), artists produced work disguised in biblical and mythical imagery, which criticised, protested, and expressed emotions of concern to society. Paintings became increasingly darker in expression of fear and agony.[1]

In Francis Nnaggenda's sculpture, The War Victim, strong feelings which express resistance of spirit to the experience of destruction, particular to this period are strongly evident.[2] At a professional level, Nnaggenda's career bore the brunt of his colleagues' denigration. Trained in Germany in the 60s, taught at Nairobi University Kenya and later Indiana University USA in the 1970s, Nnaggenda absorbed several foreign experiences and with the years of turmoil at home he brings together the elements of conflict. To arrive at this he combines various types of wood with prefabricated metal and paint, sometimes with marks of the chisel still in evidence. Kasfir described him as an experimental sculptor.[3] In the early eighties, Nnaggenda's approach as well as his work, were made to feel as unfit in teaching models laid clown by Todd, which were being followed at Makerere Art School at the time. Yet his influence has been most considerable, permeating the works of his protégés some of whom have developed his ideas further on, sometimes with indistinguishable traces. For Lilian Nabulime, for example, roots of trees are her preferred medium: they are not just suitable materials for her figurative sculptures, but they are equally seen as metaphor for perseverance.

[1] Adapted from the interview Wanjiku Nyacae had with Fabian Mpagi former Makerere Art student during the 70s and Francis Nnaggenda a Sculpture Professor at Makerere Art School Since the late 1970s - in the Catalogue, Seven Stories p273 and 274 respectively.

[2] ibid.

[3] Sydney L. Kasfi, in her article on Nnaggenda, addresses the conflicts that present a challenge to today's artists. She cites another; "Widespread belief in witch craft, in which now supposedly a Christian country, poses endless riddles and ambiguities for the sensitive artist responsive to his environment." Drawing attention to the difference between the works of Nnaggenda and other African sculptors, who consciously adapt African classical forms, she points out that, "There is no anthropological self-consciousness in Nnaggenda's work."

George Kakooza (1936-1982), "Saint-Francis," Uganda
h. 4,80 m.
©George Kyeyune

Recovery and new directions

Following the end of civil war in 1986, which brought Y. K. Museveni into political power, there has been an improvement in Uganda's political climate, stimulating not only business and commerce but also renewal of academic excellence. Currently Makerere University is engaged in a massive training of its staff to acquire a minimum level of a PhD . At the school of Fine Art where PhD qualifications have hitherto existed only in the department of Art History, there is a frantic effort to create them in studio practice.

If the internal tensions prevalent in the Art School in 1980s raised emotions, these have become an essential ingredient to reflect on the important events in its (school's) training role since its inception. With the extensive interrogation of the somewhat didactic differences and similarities contained in the legacies of Trowell and Todd, a wide range of options and possibilities have been opened, offering a rich base for research. Because expressing of subjects which reflect political repression had become less relevant, the school's teaching agenda shifted more to investigating formal issues and local materials. Looking back in time, Ssengendo's (staff member) painting, for example explores the role of bark cloth and its decorative function among the Ugandan cultures. At the same mode, several post graduate researches are exploring material culture and folklore from their own social backgrounds. Maria Naita, for instance, is translating body ornamentation among the Karamojong to enhance the strength of her sculpture based on female figures, – not unlike the natural synthesis developed by the Uli painters at Zaria University, Nigeria.[4]

In its effort to increase its participation in public life, the school is engaged in numerous outreach programmes. In pottery for example, an extant indigenous tradition, in which Uganda is particularly reputable, Bruno Sserunkuuma has carried out extensive technical analysis of local clays. His consultancy has benefited several local posters, (particularly in clay body formulations), in the suburbs of Kampala.

The last decade has witnessed more participation of Makerere staff in major international exhibitions, such as, Africa 95 in London and the Southern African Biennale in Johannesburg, 1995, besides attending international artists workshops and getting involved in exchanges with overseas universities. This has rustled into the School Fresh Air from Outside, supplanting the unbidden "in house" style which had developed during the years of seclusion. Rose Kirumira for example spent a spell at D'Anza College in the USA, (1997), while, Bella Feldman (1990) from California USA, and Roger Palmer (1999) from Glasgow Scotland, conducted studio workshops at Makerere. In the last two cases above, emphasis in teaching was laid upon all aspects of life however ordinary as content and materials for art.

Through workshops and all other such sources, ideas have been canvassed to feed into the ongoing restructuring process of the curriculum, bearing the shifting social conditions of the country in mind. In this project, old units like photography and textile design have been reinstated under graphics and design section and together with ceramics, they now form the department of industrial design. Sculpture and Painting departments too have undergone extensive internal expansion and reorganisation. In addition, students learn about commerce. With such, major changes and achievements, the school which had hitherto ambiguously existed between a Department and Faculty, was in 1994 promoted to faculty statue and to reflect its expanded considerations and engagements, its nomenclature changed from, the Margaret Trowell School of Fine Art to The Margaret Trowell School of Industrial and Fine Arts. The combined effect of the country's improved political conditions with that of Makerere's expanding academic programmes, foreign students have been attracted back and the School of Fine Art has had a fair share in this dream.

However, while of Government's call to increase students intake (including private students) has been well implemented, the school's physical infrastructure has remained unchanged.

[4] See Uche Okeke, 1995 article on natural synthesis, in the Seven Stories about Modem Art in Africa, 208-211

This puts a strain on both lecture and storage space and to some extent the quality of teaching. One method to raise funds is through selling selected students' work at the end of annual exhibitions. It is hoped that with the money realised, expansion of physical space as well as more purchase of essential studio equipment will be possible. Prices are deliberately kept very low as a strategy to improve the engagement of art to the public. In the same spirit, Makerere Art School lecturers now hold a yearly exhibition of their own work, known as "Different But One" which has become an inspiration to students as well as offering the necessary critical debates in art.

Today, Makerere Art School is taking advantage of the wider access to current theory, practice and techniques from the diverse local and world cultures, while it is committed to recapture its own prominence on the world cultural stage.

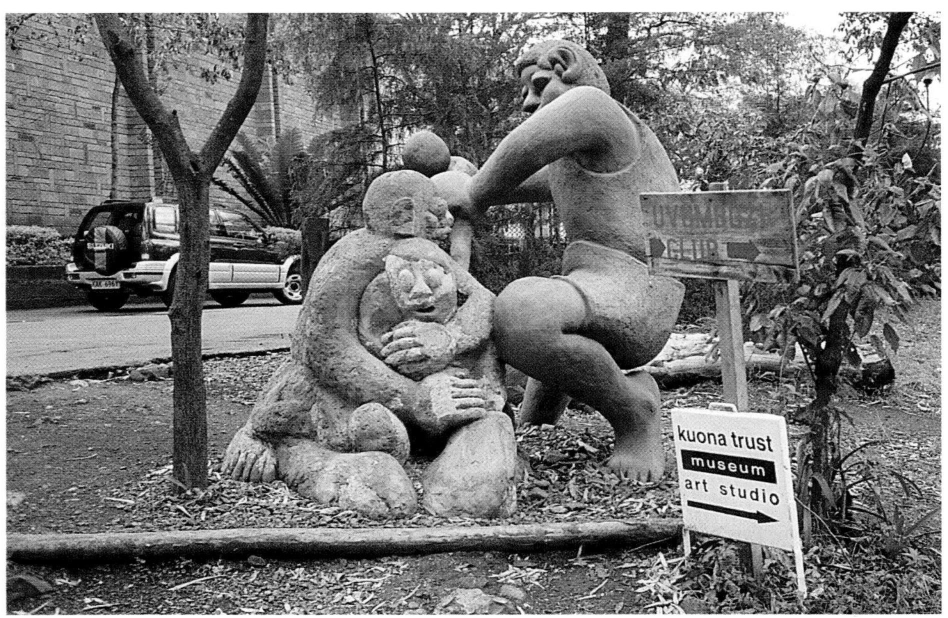

Kuona Trust Center, sculpture by Samuel Wanjau's son, Nairobi, Kenya ©Elsbeth Court

ART TRAINING IN KENYA AND TANZANIA

Sunanda K. Sanyal

Academic art training in both Kenya and Tanzania is largely indebted to the Art School of Uganda's Makerere University, the first art school in East Africa. Founded in 1937 by Margaret Trowell, an English artist and educator, this institution trained the first generation of formally trained East African artists. Some of these individuals later took up teaching positions in Kenya and Tanzania.

Kenya has received the least state funding in East Africa for promotion of art education. The Department of Design at the University College of Nairobi was established in 1966, with the sculptor Gregory Maloba, an early Makerere student, serving as its head. The following year it became the Department of Design and Architecture, while the Department of Art and Design Education was founded at nearby Kenyatta University. Both African and expatriate instructors at these two Nairobi institutions made valiant efforts to train art teachers and artists in a time when art hardly even had a peripheral status in Kenya's elementary school curriculum. At Kenyatta, Tanzanian painter and Makerere graduate Elimo Njau, Czech ceramist and sculptor Frank Foit, painter Ursula Rauta, and printmakers Terry Hirst and Elphas Webbo were among the early teachers. Later, Louis Mwaniki and Kiure Francis Msangi, two younger Makerereans with farther training in the West, also joined the staff.

From the sixties through the mid-seventies, artists in Kenya, as anywhere else in Africa, faced the formidable challenge of legitimating their discipline and forging their professional identities in a young nation state with no local precedents of formal art training. Amidst various intellectual debates of the period, students and teachers in the two Kenyan Art Schools explored numerous technical and conceptual possibilities in search for contemporary artistic expressions in a changing urban milieu. Students were encouraged as much to draw from cross-cultural sources, as to look into their indigenous roots. Student research on regional visual traditions not only informed and enriched contemporary art, but brought Kenya's cultural diversity to the attention of a wider audience. This social consciousness of Kenyan artists later bore fruit in various cultural movements, such as the short-lived efforts of the group named Sisi Kwa Sisi under the leadership of the prominent artist-sociologist Etale Sukuro. Denouncing urban exhibition spaces and elite clientele, this group took their art and theatre to rural Kenya. The strong political content of many of their works often caused serious controversies.

Kenya, however, is the only country in East Africa where self-taught artists currently overshadow those with art school training. Though Elimo Njau's Paa Ya Paa Art Centre has provided an alternative space for experimental shows and workshops, especially for the latter since the early seventies, representation of self-taught artists by high-profile Nairobi galleries like Watatu to serve a large tourist clientele has made careers of art school graduates increasingly uncertain. The only place where the two groups work together is at the ongoing workshop of the Kuona Trust, which is housed at Nairobi's National Museum.

The scenario in Tanzania has been significantly different. Initially, the Dar es Salaam campus of the University of East Africa (founded in 1961) offered theatre courses, while Makerere taught art. Formal art training in Tanzania began only with the foundation of the University of Dar es Salaam later in that decade. Though adverse economic conditions and socialist policies in Tanzania since 1961 have largely resisted a free market and autonomous enterprises, unlike in Kenya, here both formally trained artists and the traditional carvers have usually received the limited government resources. Painter Sam Ntiro, a contemporary of Gregory Maloba at Makerere, was the first artist to head the cultural wing of the Tanzanian government. Both he and Elias Jengo, a younger Makererean who later became the head of the Art Department at the University, have been instrumental in painting public murals on government commissions. Kibo Art Gallery, on the other hand, is one of the oldest autonomous cultural enterprises in the country. Founded in 1964 by Elimo Njau in his home district of Moshi, Kibo organized the first show of the Community of East African Artists, a group representing contemporary artists from all over East Africa. The establishment now exists without its past fervor.

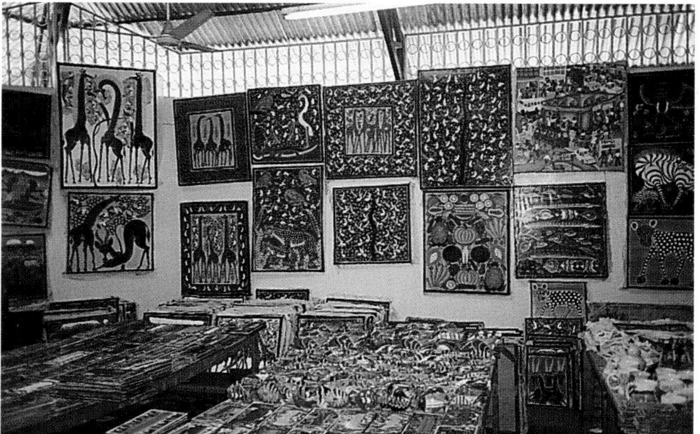

Tinga Tinga workshop, Dar-es-Salam, Tanzania

©Elsbeth Court

Ethiopia: the fine arts school and the socialist revolution

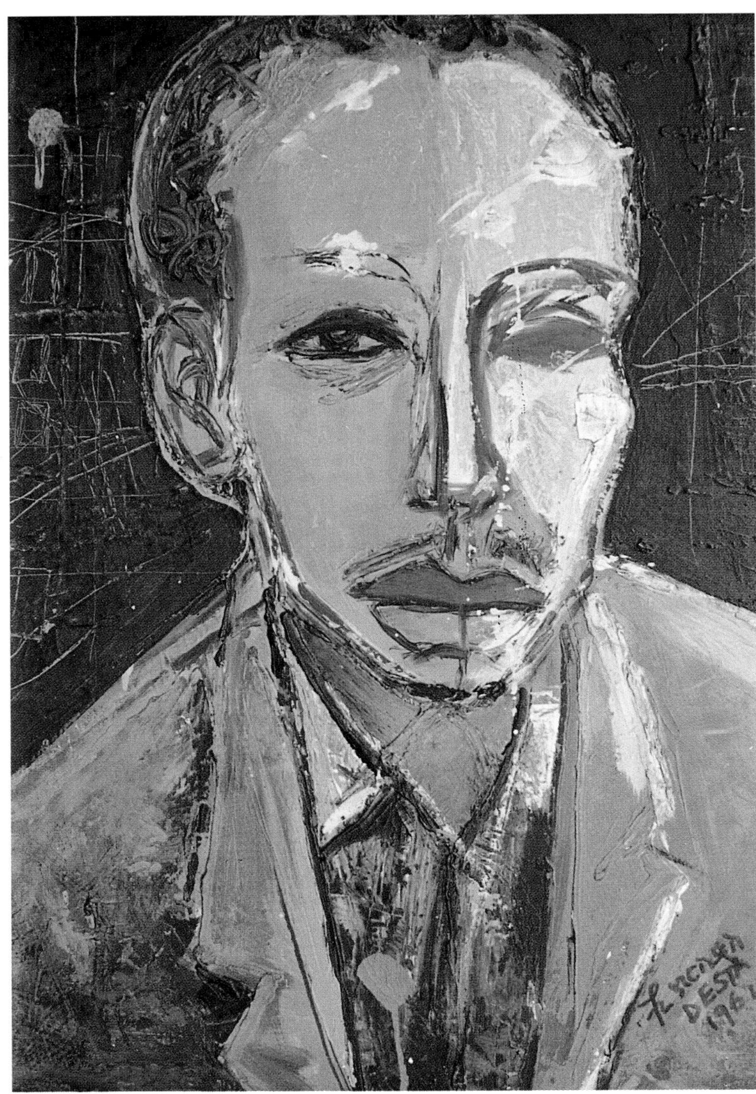

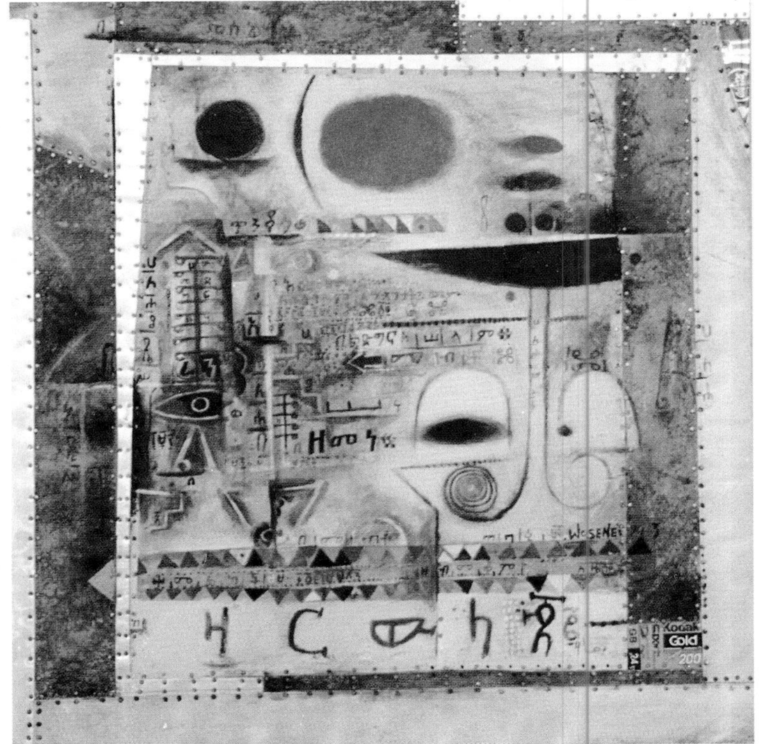

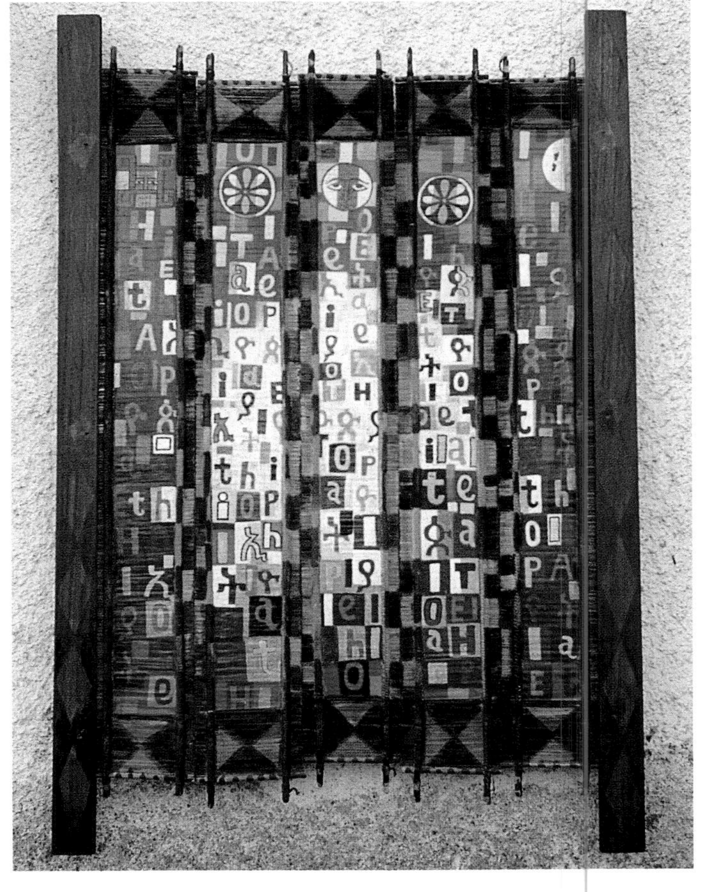

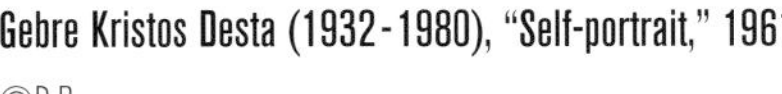

Gebre Kristos Desta (1932-1980), "Self-portrait," 1961
©D.R.

top:
Wosone Kosrof (born in 1950), 1994
©Geta Mekonnen

right:
Zerihun Yetmgeta (born in 1940), "Magic scrolls," 1992
©Revue Noire

facing page:
Skunder Boghossian (born in 1937), "Equilibrium," 1994
©D.R.

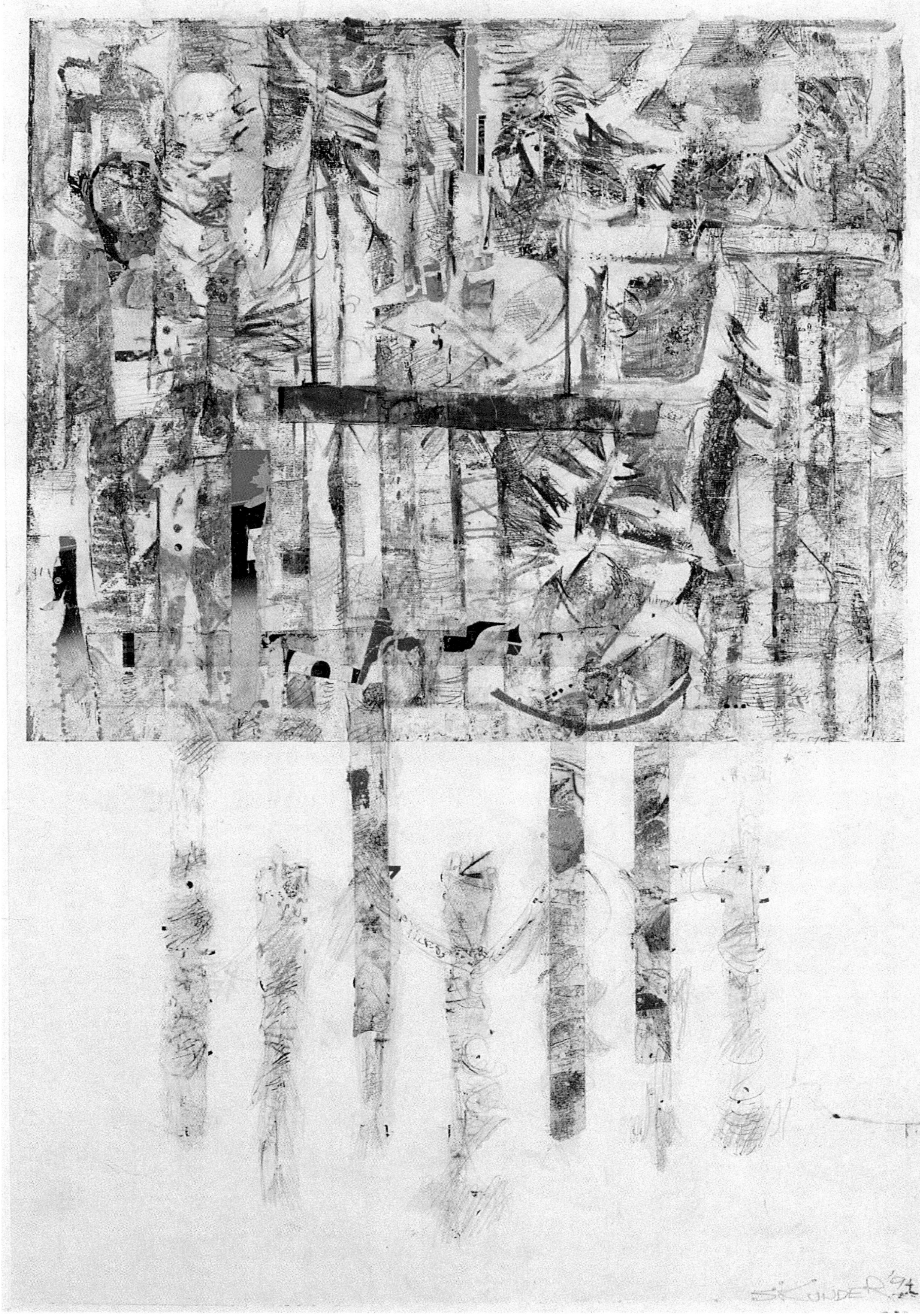
SKUNDER '94

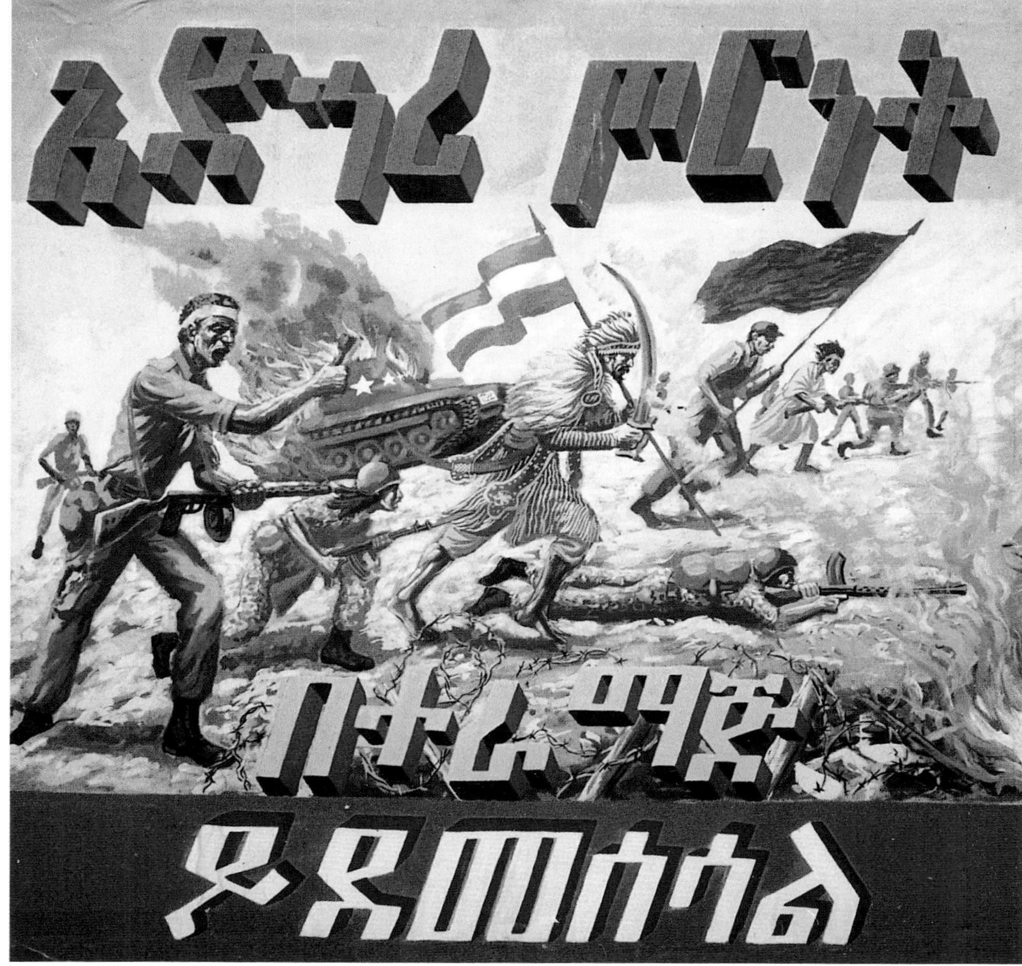

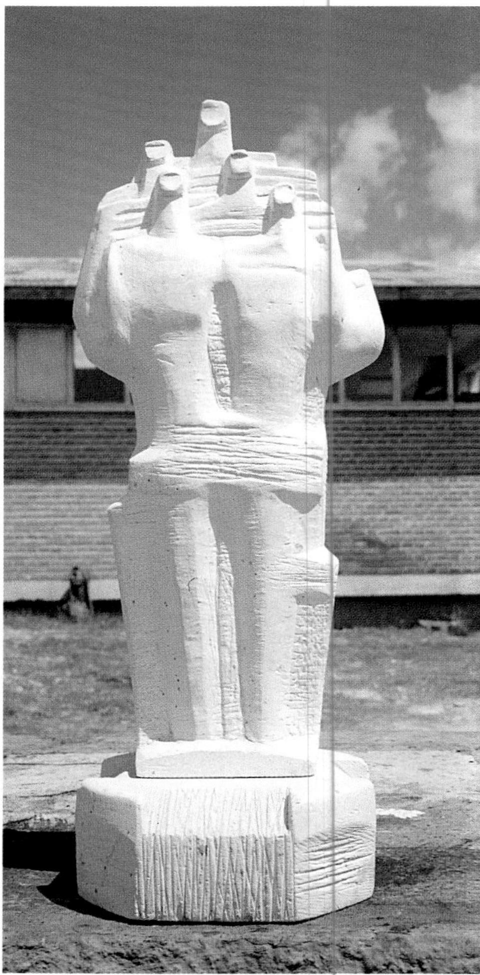

Poster made by students of the Fine Arts School, "Reactionary war will be crushed by progressives," c.a. 1980
©Alula Pankhurst

right:
Tadesse Belaineh (born in 1943)
©Revue Noire

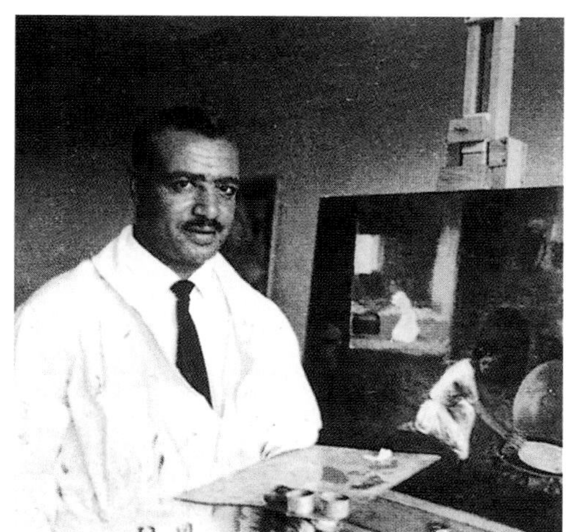

Ale Felege Selam (born in 1929) c. 1960
©D.R.

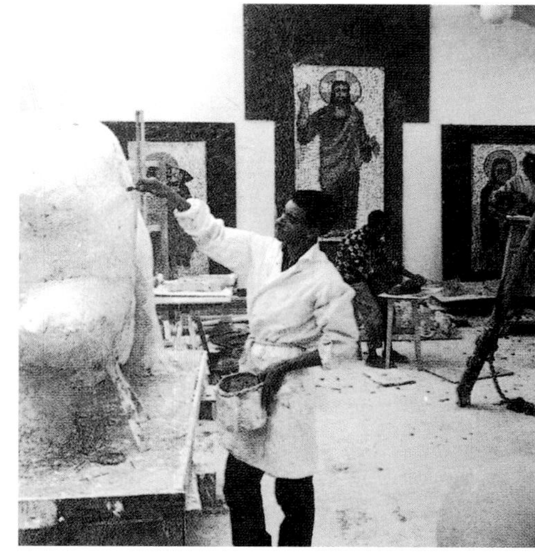

Student at L'ecole des Beaux-Arts, c.a. 1960
©D.R.

THE ADDIS ABEBA FINE ARTS SCHOOL AND THE ETHIOPIAN SOCIALIST REVOLUTION

Konjit Seyoum

The teaching of art education in Ethiopia began in an embryonic form from the 1930s. Emperor Menelik, an advocate of modern education, sent some students abroad to study. Among these, were Aleqa Elias Hailu and Aleqa Merawi who were sent to France to study painting and illustrating manuscripts. Afewerk Gebreyessus (1868-1947) studied at the Accademia di Belle Arti and Collegio Internazionale of Turin and also worked in Naples between 1894 and 1912, and Tessema Eshete (1877-1965) was sent to Germany from 1908 to 1910. The Ministry of Education was established in 1930 and in 1932 the elementary school curriculum included art classes. Three artists played key roles in the modernization and institutionalization of art education. Abebe Woldegiorgis (1897-1967) spent eighteen years in France where he studied and worked as a sculptor. In the early forties he attempted to open up a small art school with 15 students enrolled. Agegnehu Ingida (1906-1950) was one of the first individuals who attempted to start up a separate art school. Zerihun Dominik (1911) established the Prince Sahle Selassie Art School, funded by the Ministry of Education. In all these preliminary schools a significant departure from traditional art was the introduction of the notion of perspective. The students depicted the daily life that surrounded them and also painted portraits.
In terms of an emergence of a distinct tradition of modern Ethiopian art, however, activities began in earnest in the mid fifties, after the return from abroad of young Ethiopian artists. Four prominent painters Afewerk Tekle, Ale Felege Selam, Skunder Bogossian and Gebre Kristos Desta had a dramatic impact on the role and status of the artist, the development of art education, and views about subject matters to be addressed and the importance of art in Ethiopia.

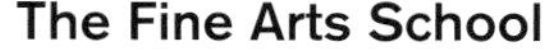

The Fine Arts School

The credit for establishing the Addis Ababa Fine Arts School, goes to Ale Felege Selam, born in 1929 in Shewa. He came from an artistic family, and was sent in 1949 to the United States of America for higher education. He studied at the Chicago Art Institute (1949-1954). Upon his return he set up an informal art school for high school students at his residence. At the end of the training, he organized a fund-raising exhibition inviting the Royal Family and dignitaries. Soon he was able to collect enough money to start up the Addis Ababa School of Fine Arts. The building, designed by an English architect was inaugurated by Emperor Haile Selassie on the occasion of his birthday on the 24th of July 1958. That same year in September, the School started its activities registering 60 students. The course was a five-year diploma program.

Felege Selam, who was the founder of the School, also became the director. Since there were no formally trained teachers apart from himself who could cater for the school's needs for instructors, Felege Selam initially had to rely on the help of a few foreigners who happened to be residing in Ethiopia at the time. The Austrian Herbert Seiler taught drawing and sculpture, and the English woman Mrs. Hassler taught composition in painting and also served as the secretary of the school. Soon after, the Germans Peter Roenparge and Ebba Detenberg joined the school consecutively. The first taught commercial art while the latter was in charge of painting. In 1963, a German graphic artist by the name Karl Heinz Hansen Bahia was employed. He introduced wood cut techniques which were until then an unknown form of art in the country. One of the best students in mastering the wood cutting technique was Zerihun Yetmgeta who was even assigned to teach the lower classes when Bahia left in 1966, until the American Wendy Kindred took over the Department in 1967. In addition, Vincenzo Fumo was hired to teach painting. By then the curriculum included fundamentals of drawing, painting, anatomy, perspective, commercial design, modeling, history of art, lettering, art education and English. The students were encouraged to depict their surroundings as well as produce folkloric and patriotic scenes in their paintings and sculptures.

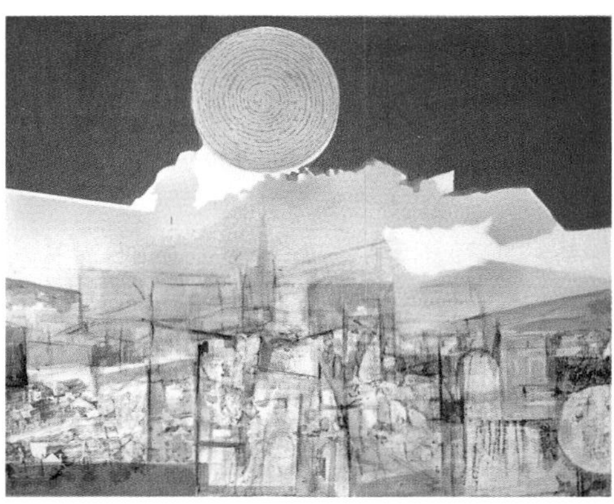

Abdurahman M. Sherif (born in 1935)
©Revue Noire

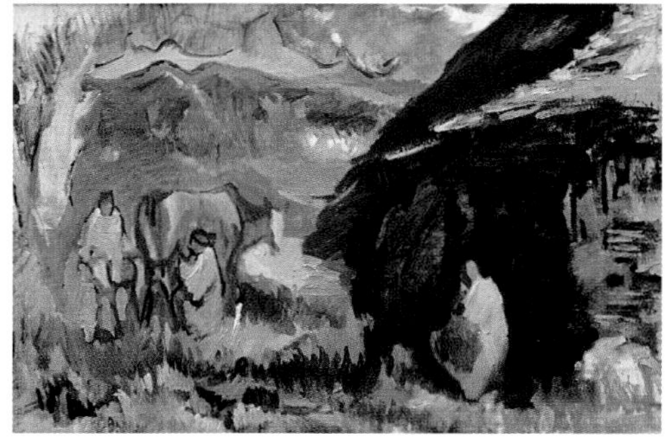

Worku Mamo (born in 1935)
©Revue Noire

Significant changes in the development of modern Ethiopian art began in the 1960s. Gebre Kristos Desta was employed by the Fine Arts School to teach painting. He became responsible for introducing non figurative art and brought significant changes in the ways students viewed art. Gebre Kristos was awarded the Best Teacher of the Year Award in 1971. His teaching career lasted until 1975. Skunder Bogossian, who spent ten years in England and France joined the school. Skunder, who was involved in the Négritude movement while in Paris, was very much influenced by his own country's historical monuments and religious paintings. He encouraged his students to adopt an experimental approach and also to make use of local materials. Although Skunder's involvement with the Art School was short (1966-1969), his impact on the students was considerable. Both Gebre Kristos and Skunder had a considerable influence on students of the time many of whom developed themes and techniques they learnt from these influential figures. Among the artists who studied under them were Achamyeleh Debela, Yohannes Gedamu, Zerihun Yetmgeta, Desta Hagos, Girmay Hiwet, and Wossene Kosrof. The kind of art works produced at the time were no longer simply attempts to depict the artist's surroundings in a strictly realistic or photographic manner. Subjects relating to the social, economic and political context of the time also began to be taken into consideration.

Artistic fervor

Artists who became concerned with changing the role and status of art in the society formed the first Ethiopian Artists' Association with the support of the Ministry of Education in 1960 with Afewerk Tekle as its president. Afewerk Tekle (b.1932) studied at the Slade School of Fine Arts in London (1947-1953). A versatile and prolific artist, Afewerk is well-known for his majestic 50 square meters stained glass executed between 1959 and 1961 for the entrance of Africa Hall in Addis Ababa, the headquarters of the United Nations Economic Commission for Africa. The aims of the association were to develop as well as promote Ethiopian art at national and international levels, to support artists in their artistic endeavors, to create a linkage with art institutions and artists outside the country, to set up a permanent exhibition venue as well as to organize travelling exhibitions within the country, and finally to publish art books with artists biographies. Although the objectives of the association were laudable, the association failed to live up to its ambitions.
In the meantime students at the art school formed the United Ethiopian Artists Association in 1961 with Hailu Tsighe as its chairman. Later on young artists also started to organize themselves in groups to stage exhibitions. One of the popular groups in the sixties was "The Vegetable Market Area Artists" whose members were Skunder Bogossian, Endale Haile Selassie, Tewodros Tighe Markos and Zerihun Yetmgeta. Then came " The Young Artists Group " (Ashenafi Wolde Yessus, Berhe Temeliso, Desta Hagos, Mamo Hiruy and Tadesse Ghile). The "Sixteen Young Artists Association" whose founding members included Tibebe Terffa and Teshome Bekele was established in 1971. The cultural and artistic activities of the pre-revolution period were constantly documented by newspapers and magazines. Contributors of such articles were prominent writers, poets and historians. The flourishing artistic scene in Addis was a reflection of, and contributed to, the prevailing sense of optimism and experimentation.

The socialist revolution

Following the 1974 revolution in which Ethiopia underwent significant changes after embracing the socialist ideology, art became largely an instrument of propaganda. Hence, the modern experimental artistic fervor that had started to thrive in the sixties came to a sudden halt and artists were expected to concentrate on depicting images of socialist Ethiopia. With the prevailing view that art should serve the cause of the revolution, artists were required to depict realistic revolutionary themes and to document and glorify for posterity the achievement of the revolution and the struggle of the masses. Russian and Chinese style propaganda art was adopted as models, and for the first time, poster art became popular, leading to a new trend in graph-

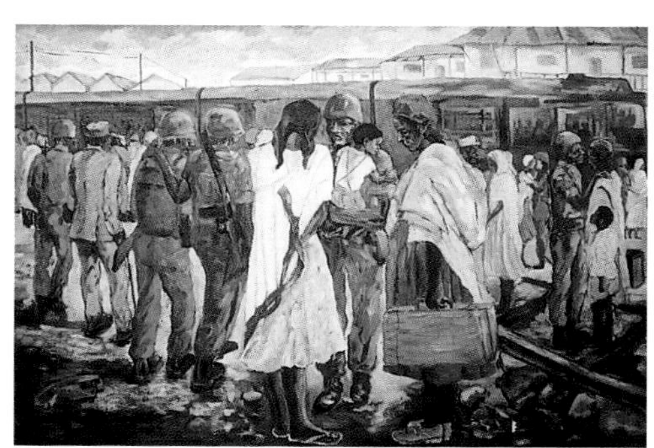

Girma Tilahun, "Farewell," 1979
oil on canvas, 200x140 cm.
©Alula Pankhurst

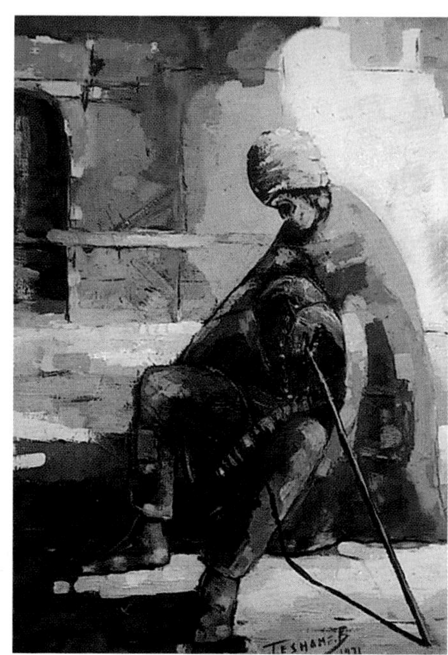

Teshome Bekele, "The Prayer," 1972
oil on panel, 45x64 cm.
©Alula Pankhurst

ics and mural art. Attacks on the pre-revolution regime, emphasis on the importance of class struggle and devotion to the Motherland were subjects constantly treated. Life size portraits of the leader, Mengistu Haile Mariam, and of international socialist leaders became common in Revolution squares around the country.
National and international political events and holidays such as the Revolution Day and May Day led to the mass production of painted slogans and posters to be used in the towns and the country at large. Such events were organized by the Ethiopian Workers' Party, and other government and mass organizations.

The Addis Ababa Fine Arts School went through a significant transformation. In 1974, Abdurahman Sherif succeeded Ale Felege Selam and became the director, a post he occupied until the change of regime in 1991. There were no graduates in 1975 and 1976 as the students of the third, fourth and fifth years were sent to the countryside to participate in the national Development through Cooperation Campaign. By 1977, all the school's instructors were Ethiopian. In 1978, a Graphic Arts Department was opened, and a Mural Arts Department was established. Although in theory the students were free in their choice of theme for graduation works, the subjects were, however, expected to be coherent with the socialist ideology. Battle scenes, victorious soldiers returning home, epic paintings with historic figures and heroes set in idealized landscapes, factory workers peasants and emancipated women became prominent in diploma works.
The trend of sending students for training in Eastern Block countries, which had started in imperial times, continued under the socialist period. Students who received their Masters of Fine Arts in the Soviet Union included Mezgebu Tessema, Tadesse Mesfin, Bekele Mekonen and Ashenafi Kebede. Getachew Yosef and Melaku Ayele studied in the German Democratic Republic while Mulugeta Tafesse and Tadesse Teshome studied in Bulgaria. Upon their return some joined the Addis Ababa Fine Arts School, such as Mezgebu Tessema, Bekele Mekonen and Getachew Yosef, while others later on became government employees like Eshetu Tiruneh working in the Ministry of Culture, and Tadesse Teshome in the Ministry of Education. A few remained abroad, such as Mulugeta Tafesse, who currently resides and works in Belgium, and Ashenafi Kebede, who lives in Finland.

A new Ethiopian Artists Association was established in 1975, the main duty of the members being to serve their Motherland and the Revolution. The association also aimed at overcoming shortage of art materials and exhibition spaces and improving the artists' working conditions and environment. However, apart from the full political recognition the association was able to obtain from the government, it did not have the means and the support it needed to fulfil its objectives. At the time, individual art exhibitions were no longer encouraged and it was the duty of mass organizations and local institutions to organize group art exhibitions. The City Hall at the Addis Ababa Municipality, which had played an important role in the organization of art exhibitions during the sixties, was no longer active during the revolution days, and, in 1976, the National Gallery of Ethiopia was founded within the same municipality premises. Gebre Kristos Desta was appointed as its Director. The few private art galleries that had sprouted in the sixties no longer existed (Belvedere Art Gallery closed down in 1975) and foreign cultural institutes such the Alliance Française, and the German and Italian Cultural Institutes became instrumental in the promotion of contemporary Ethiopian art.

During the last years of the Derg Regime, two major group art exhibitions took place at the National Museum. By the time these exhibitions were held, the tone of the revolution had mellowed and there seemed to be more freedom and space for personal expression through the arts. For instance, of the works featured in the 1990 exhibition, very few directly treated revolutionary and patriotic themes. By the time of 1991 exhibition, just before the final collapse of the Derg, there were hardly any representations of revolutionary themes.
With the end of this period, artists are able to experiment in their art freely and the young generations will have to face the challenges ahead.

Kitsch and political manipulation in Angola

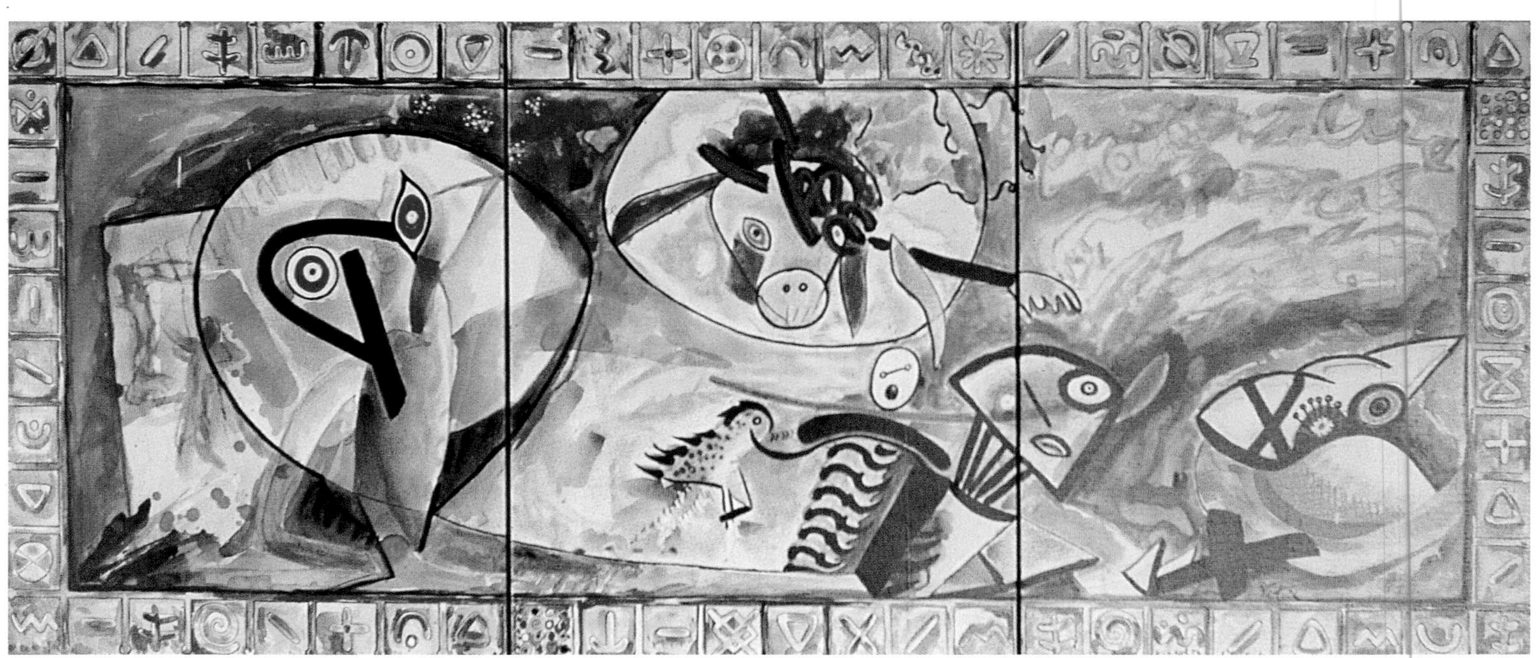

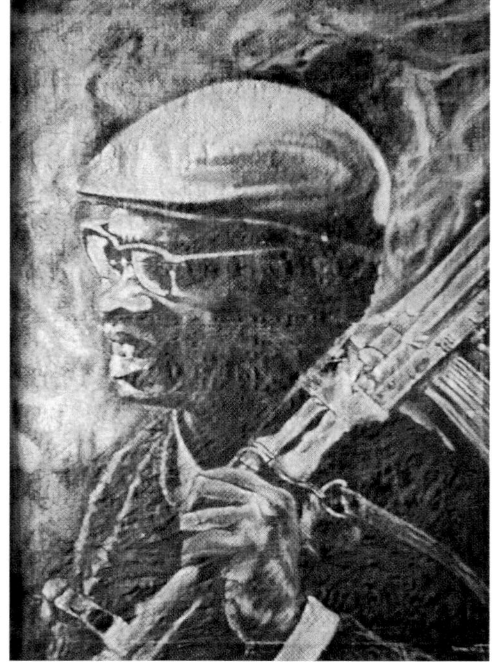

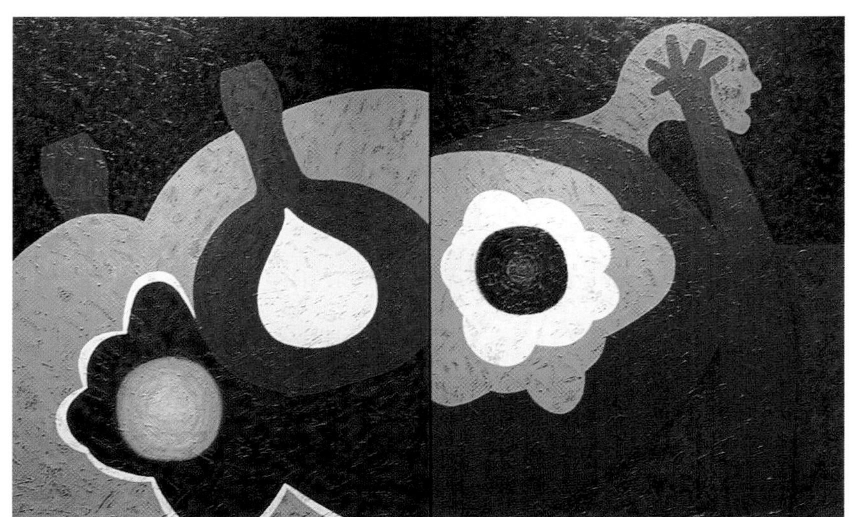

top:
Victor Emmanuel Texeira (aka Viteix, 1940-1993)
left:
Thomas Vista (born in 1940)
Telmo Vaz Pereira (born in 1949)

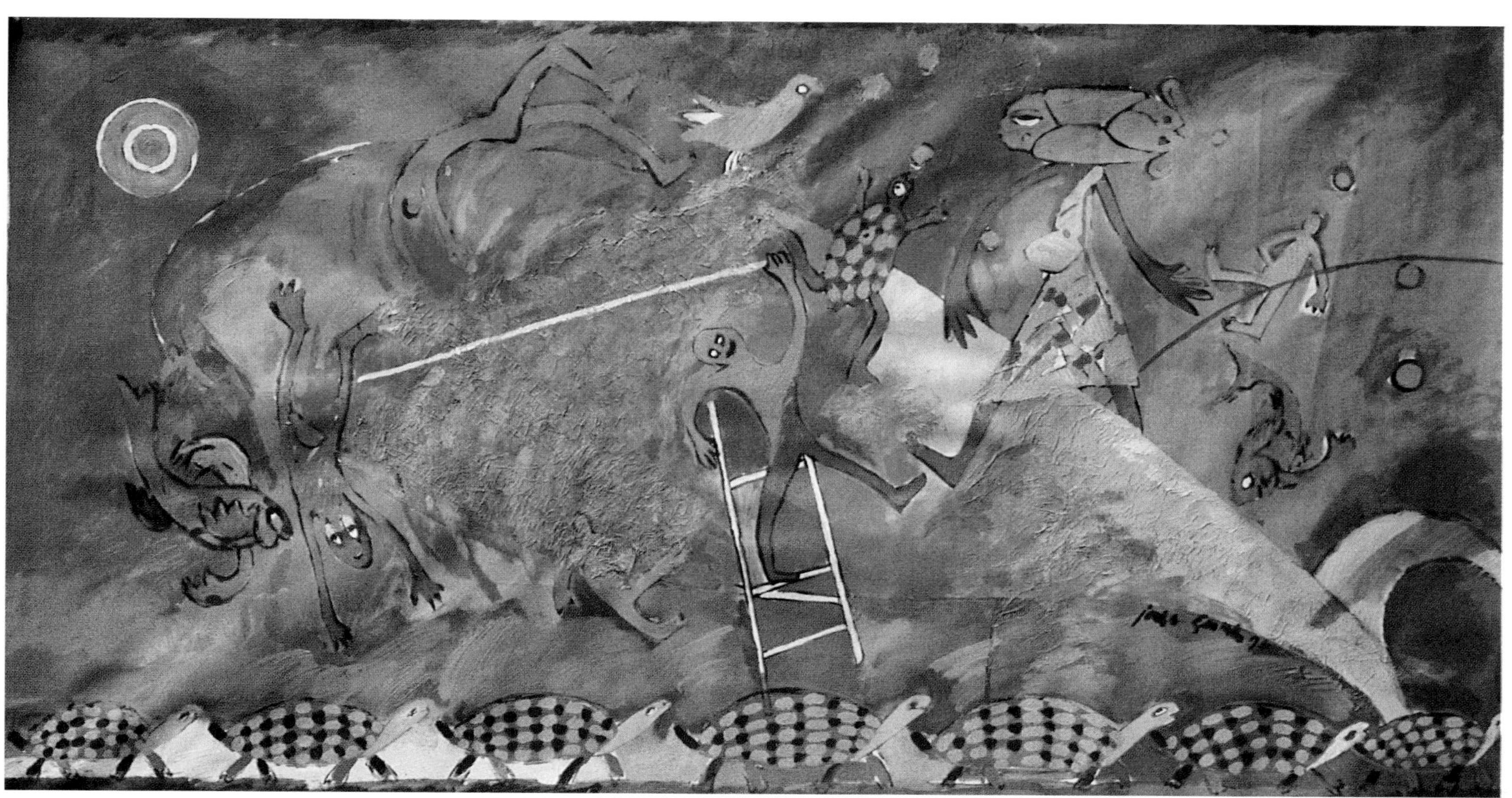

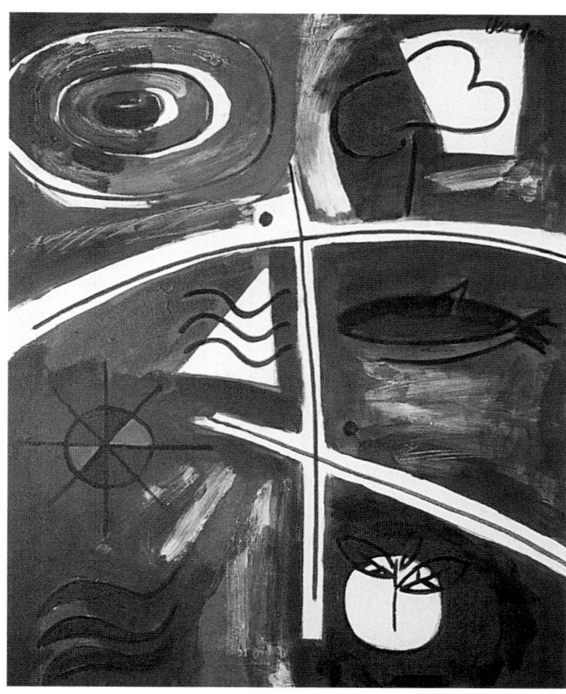

Jorge Gumbe (born in 1959)
Francisco Van Dúnen (born in 1959)

KITSCH AND POLITICAL MANIPULATION IN ANGOLA
Adriano Mixinge

The forerunners of modern art in Angola have inherited, in their way and rather belatedly, from the esthetics of European Renaissance and from the late 19th century-early 20th century Renaissance. Coming from several European countries – essentially the Netherlands, Italy, France, Belgium and Portugal – these artists painted portraits of the kings of Angola (especially the portrait of Queen Nzinga Mbandi) using the canons of beauty of the Mannerist era or by representing them realistically (such as Queen Nhacatolo of Los Luenoas, for example). They also sought to capture the characteristics and customs of the different ethnolinguistic groups of Angola. Basing themselves on cubism, expressionism and surrealism, they rejected the models, themes and modes of representation specific to colonial esthetics, by attempting to establish artistic codes aimed at building a new canon of beauty and post-colonial esthetics.

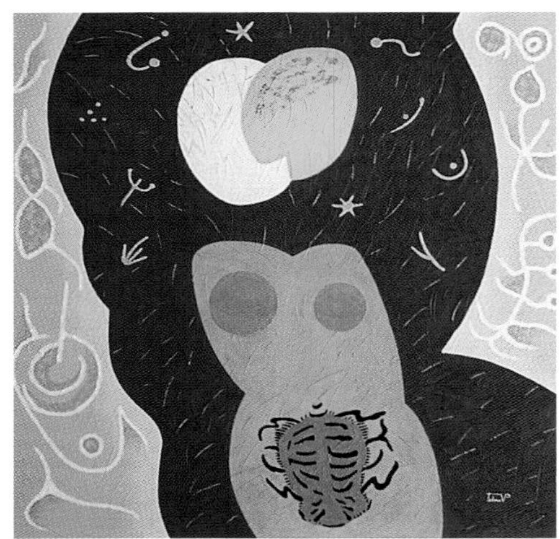

Telmo Vaz Pereira (born in 1949)

"Vamos descubrir Angola" (Let's discover Angola) is a name and a slogan that originated from the dynamic exchange of ideas between Angolan writers and intellectuals in the 40s and 50s. In the beginning, the movement was a declaration in a project to save identities in order to resist the Portuguese policy of assimilation that had already wreaked havoc. With the independence of the country in 1975, the knowledge of the various peoples of Angola made it possible to speed up the Nation project. Therefore, plastic arts, as structural and (re)inventive icons of both cultural memory and collective conscience, had and continue to have an important role to play. Jorge Gumbe, Francisco Van Dunem (Van), Masongui Afonso and others have worked to artistically recreate the icons, forms and concepts subjacent to the respective Cokwe and Bakonga cultures. Antonio Ole traveled to the province of Luanda-Norte, in the Cokwe land, in order to study their wall painting, ceramic decoration and sand drawings.

Independence was a catalyst of Angola's spirit of discovery. Unaware of the most interesting Russian artists (from Kandinsky to Malevitch), Angolan plastic artists, the majority of whom, at this time, did not have any academic training at fine arts schools, took part in the triumphalist euphoria of the national liberation movements through representations in poor taste (kitsch) and through their subordination to the manipulation of temporality (Jean Godefroy Bidima), which is defended by utopian thought. Between 1974 and 1980, the influence of artistic propaganda productions from Eastern European countries was, without a doubt, one of the saddest and most ludicrous eras in the history of Angolan plastic arts.

Angolan plastic arts were not involved in legitimizing the political powers or the propaganda for or against the war. In the 70s, through posters and wall paintings, art assisted in disclosing the program outlines of the various liberation movements. The National Union of Plastic Arts (UNAP) worked, from 1977, for the ideology defended by the MPLA, whereas Zavarra, according to the testimony of Honorio Van-Dunen, put his artwork at the service of UNITA and the Savimbi cult of personality.
Although incomplete and given the era, In the War, a painting done by Victor Manuel Teixeira (Viteix) in 1976 is probably one of the most heterodox approximations on the war in Angola. This is due, on the one hand, to how it represents the war and, on the other hand, to the plastic solution retained, namely the remote angle with a so-called "socialist realism" that could be found in caricature form in the wall paintings at the time.

Save for a few exceptions, such as Sallo Sally, who, among others, studied at the Academy of Fine Arts of Moscow and devised an individual mythology distant from socialist realism and close to the pictorial design of De Chirico, the influence from the Eastern block had a disastrous overall influence on Angolan artistic and literary productions. And although this influence should not be forgotten, it should be rightfully recognized that it did not contribute to elevating the esthetic taste of the people exposed to it.

Victor Emmanuel Texeira (aka Viteix, 1940-1993)

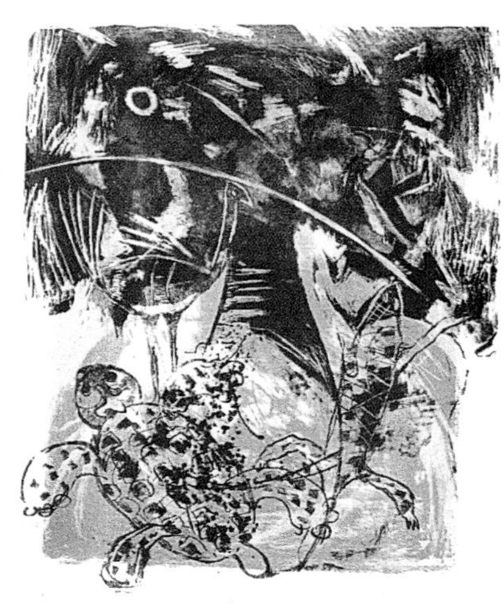

Jorge Gumbe (born in 1959)

Viteix: reality and myth

With works and exhibits scattered around the world (from Harare to Paris, from Oporto to Havana, and from Dakar to Venice), and with a life and work that place him between reality and myth, Victor Manuel Teixeira (Viteix) is, along with Albano Neves e Sousa and Antonio Ole, one of the three biggest and best known references of contemporary Angolan art. Viteix was born in Luanda in 1940 and was associated his entire life with the upper-crust district of the Ingombotas, a neighborhood of assimilated white, mixed and black bourgeois who succeeded in integrating the public service.

An insatiable creator, Viteix obtained a solid academic education between 1973 and 1983, at which time he completed his bachelor's and master's degrees at the Ecole des Beaux-Arts of Paris, and his doctorate in esthetics at the University of Paris VII. His thesis was entitled "*Plastic Arts Theory and Practice: from tradition to the new expression. Not only was Viteix in Paris. Paris was always in Viteix because*" he did everything, or almost everything. He was a construction worker, cook, graphic artist, teacher, head of a cleaning team, driver, bar employee and art student."[1]

Taking advantage of the lessons of bohemian life (lots of jazz, whisky and good food), as is appropriate for urban heroes of modernity, and of the possibilities that national independence in 1975 opened up for Angolan culture, Viteix, as a founding member and President of the National Union of Plastic Arts (UNAP), made seminars, workshops, and plastic arts exhibits more dynamic, and also held conferences on art and crafts in Angola. This gained him membership in the International Association of Arts Critics and allowed him to leave, as an activist, commissioner and theoretician, a set of practical and conceptual references in the history of Angolan plastic arts over the past thirty years.

Viteix strove to save all of the iconography of the rock painting, wall painting, ceramics and sculptures done by the various Angolan ethnolinguistic groups (very well documented, in particular, in the texts of Carlos Ervedosa, Marie-Louise Batin, José Redinha, and Father Carlos Estermann) and erected, starting with the founding icons, an artistic work in which tradition and contemporaneousness are constantly in dialogue and all of the myths they recreate or reinvent are presented "framed" by signs he appropriated. He used several techniques in his work, such as painting, engraving and pencils. He even produced a series of painted banquettes that he presented, in 1986, at the second biennial of Havana, Cuba.

He criticized all forms of mediocrity and provincialism, was an ardent defender of education for plastic artists, was supported by the authorities, was a friend of Geronimo Belo, was the master of Jorge Gumbe and of Francisco Van Dunen (Van), and was studied by Alfred Margarido, who said about him: "Viteix, like other Angolan painters, was at the delicate crossroads imposed on him by both history and his personality. He was a creator who was attentive to his specific world, an Angolan without renouncing the forms that marked the dynamic evolution of his own history."[2] José Lunaidno Viera said about Viteix's works: "*I warn the air travelers of this universe about the work of Viteix. They will not be limited to seeing the visible elements that are at the source of his paintings. They will also see what comes from the magma of esthetic and Angolan consciousness, and what is ritually spewed in these dreams that are his exhibited paintings*."[3] Victor Manuel Teixeira (Viteix) died in Luanda on May 10, 1993.

[1] in Viteix. Texte de Geronimo Belo no seu livro Feijoada., 1st Edition, Luanda, 1998. p.120.

[2] in A Pintura Angolana Universal de Viteix, Paris, October 1985.

[3] in Artes plasticas angolanas, exhibition catalogue, Lubango, 1989.

Painting and liberation movements in Mozambique

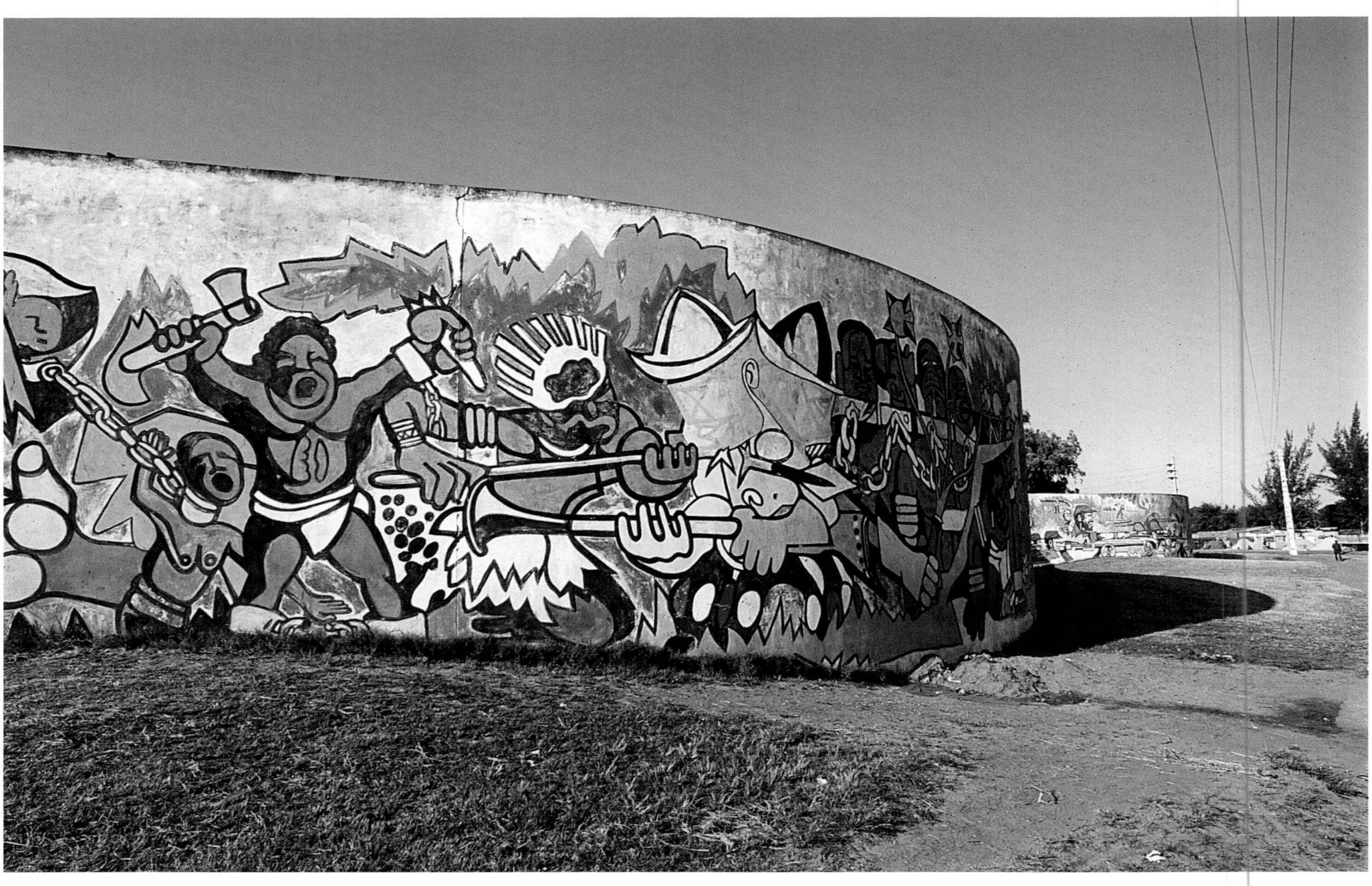

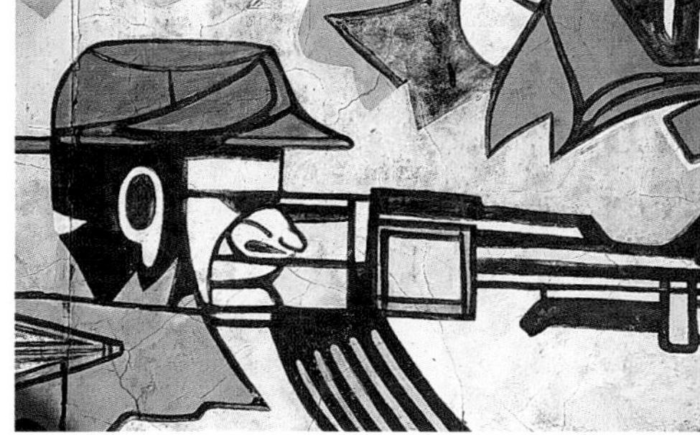

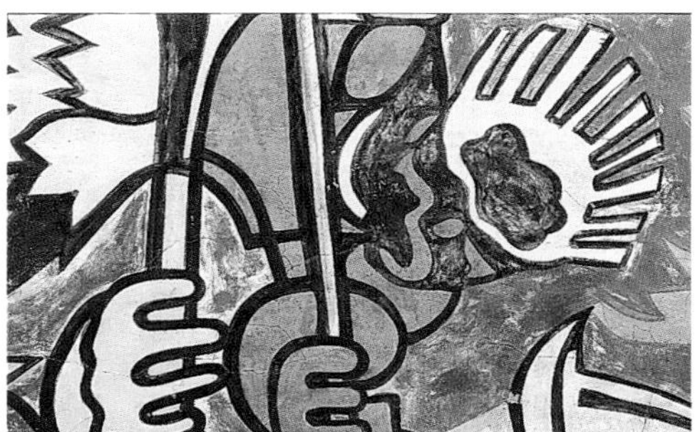

The Wall of the Heroes Square
collective work done in part by Malangatana and Shikhani
©Thierry Payet

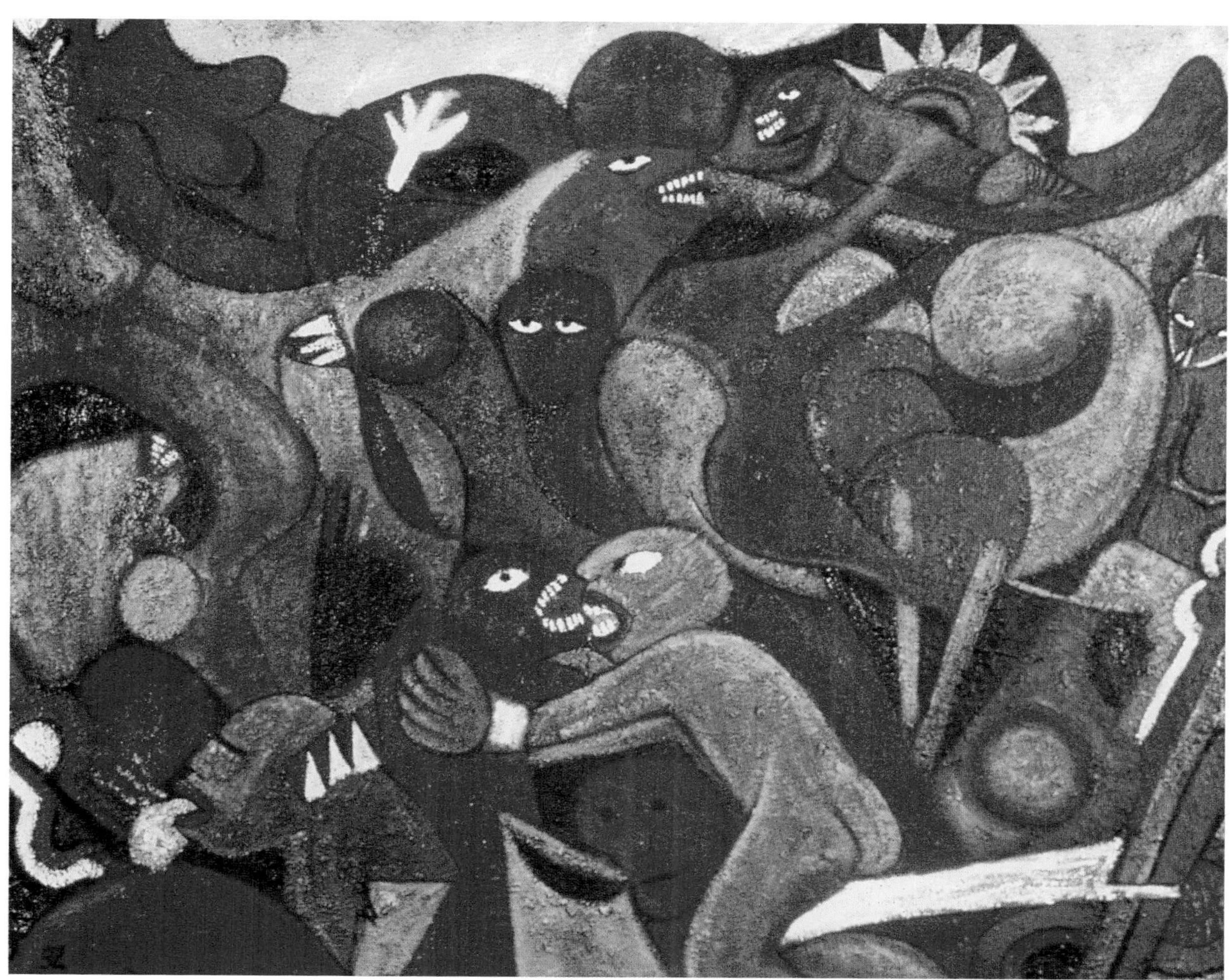

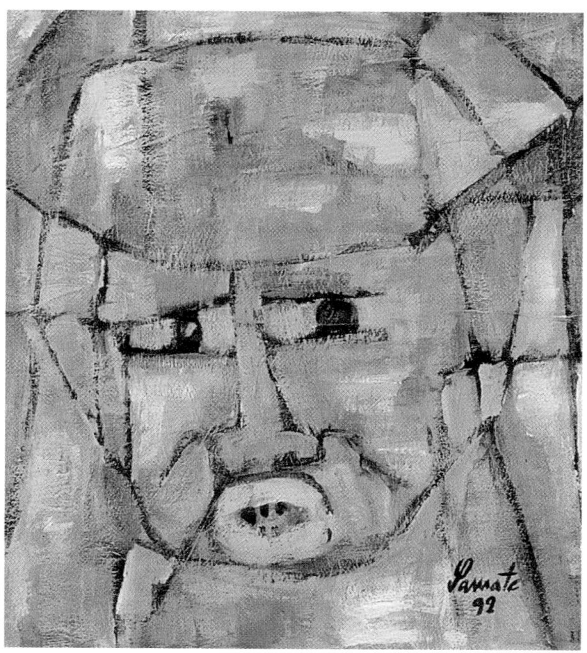

top:

Valente Ngwenya Malangatana (born in 1936), 1992

©Revue Noire

left:

Samate, 1992

©Revue Noire

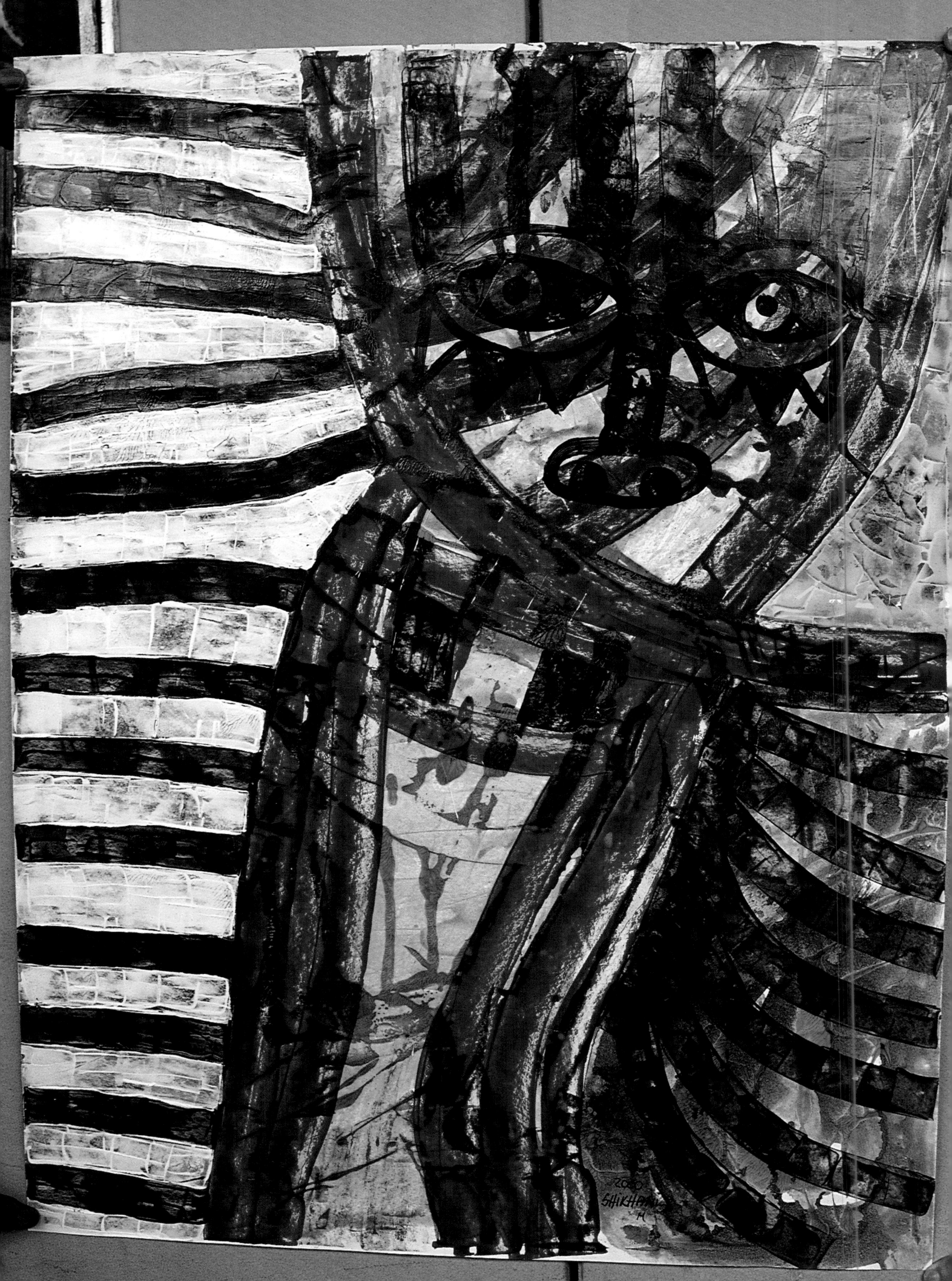
2000

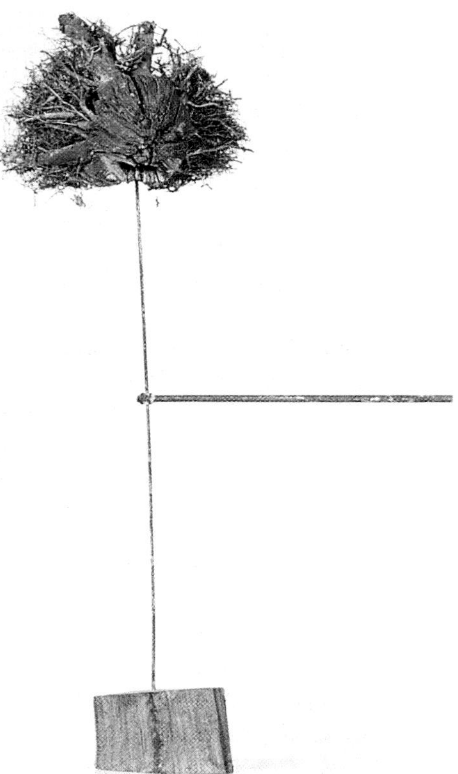

Alberto Chissano (born in 1935)
©CFF

A SHORT HISTORY OF MOZAMBIQUE
Thierry Payet

Art in Mozambique began to change in 1936 with the foundation of the Nucleo de Arte by artists of Portuguese origin, such as Frederico Ayres, an impressionist, Jacob Estavao and Vasco Campira. The "Nucleus of All Types of Art," a gathering place for intellectuals and artists, would be the laboratory for all artistic expressions.

In 1958, an academic painting course was set up where "Pancho," a Portuguese architect and painter, encouraged a young painter named Malangatana. Albert Chissano, a jack-of-all-trades around the Nucleo, was given wood scraps and Lobo Fernandes trained Shikani in painting and sculpture. These three men marked the beginnings of Black painting and sculpture in Mozambique. The painter Antonio Quadros built a ceramic kiln and contributed to developing esthetics with a social purpose.

In 1962, intellectuals from the Nucleo joined Frelimo.[1] Bertina Lopes, Malangatana and "Pancho" refused to attend the Sao Paulo biennial event in 1963 representatives of Portugal. Art was used in the fight for independence and the political police tried to contain the claims against the authorities. There were numerous exhibits. With their oblique titles, the painting sometimes had to be read between the lines, leading some to dub this the camouflage period.

With the independence of Mozambique in 1975, the socialist Frelimo party developed a system of propaganda under the influence of its information director José Freire, a painter and graphic artist. The former "camouflaged" artists were placed at the forefront and the mural technique (wall painting) developed at the instigation of the Chileans and Bolivians. The Nucleo de Arte lost all of its centralizing role. All that was left was the ceramic process of Victor Souza. In this context, with the Nucleo de Arte being adrift, the State invested in Musart (art museum) in 1977 and founded the National School of Visual Arts (ENAV) in 1983. During a basic three-year level, students are introduced to painting, visual communication, design, photography and drawing. Intermediary levels, completed over two and a half years, provide a second diploma and a more direct link to the professional world.

History dictated the influences. In the 80s, over 50% of teachers were Cuban, Portuguese and Russian. So were the styles. Today, trends have changed. Only the three fundamental disciplines (graphic art, textile and ceramics, which gave a new twist to creations) are practiced by foreigners, but not for long. The ENAV generally gives students a desire to look elsewhere in order to complete their artistic training. Exchanges and workshops are organized with foreign countries on a regular basis: universities and fine arts schools in Oporto, in Natal in South Africa, and in Holland.

A revival began to take place in the late 90s: following a major reorganization, the Nucleo de Arte has become a meeting place for painters, the Musart is organizing a biennial event and free expression has its infrastructures.

facing page:
Shikhani (born in1939), "O mocho," 2000
oil on canvas, 80x60 cm
©CFF

[1] Mozambique Liberation Front

“Resistance Art” in South Africa

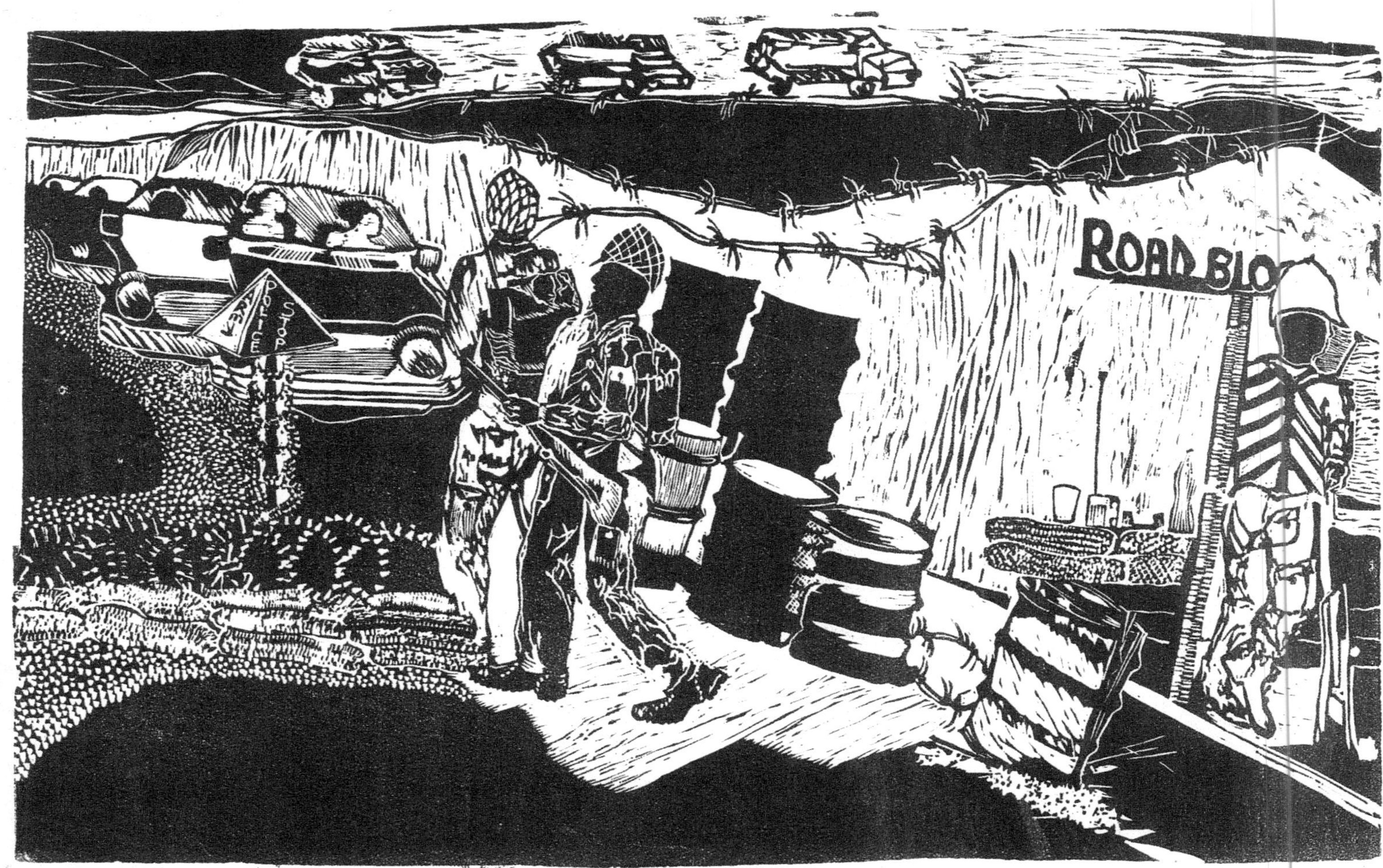

Bongiwe Dhlomo, “The sate of the 80’s, Roadblock,” 1988
30x50 cm.

facing page:
Paul Stopforth (born in 1945), “George Botha,” 1977
plaster and wax, actual size

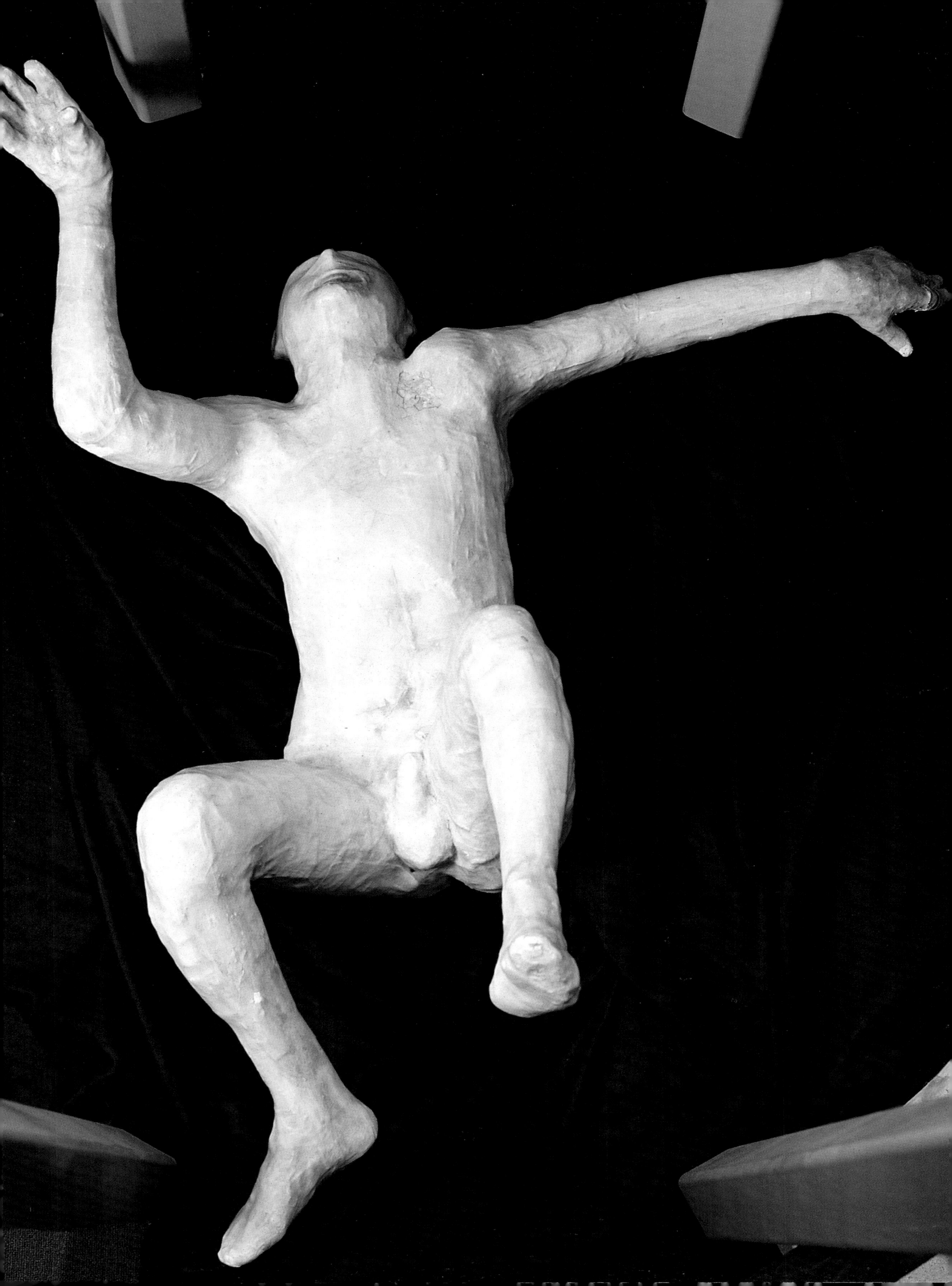

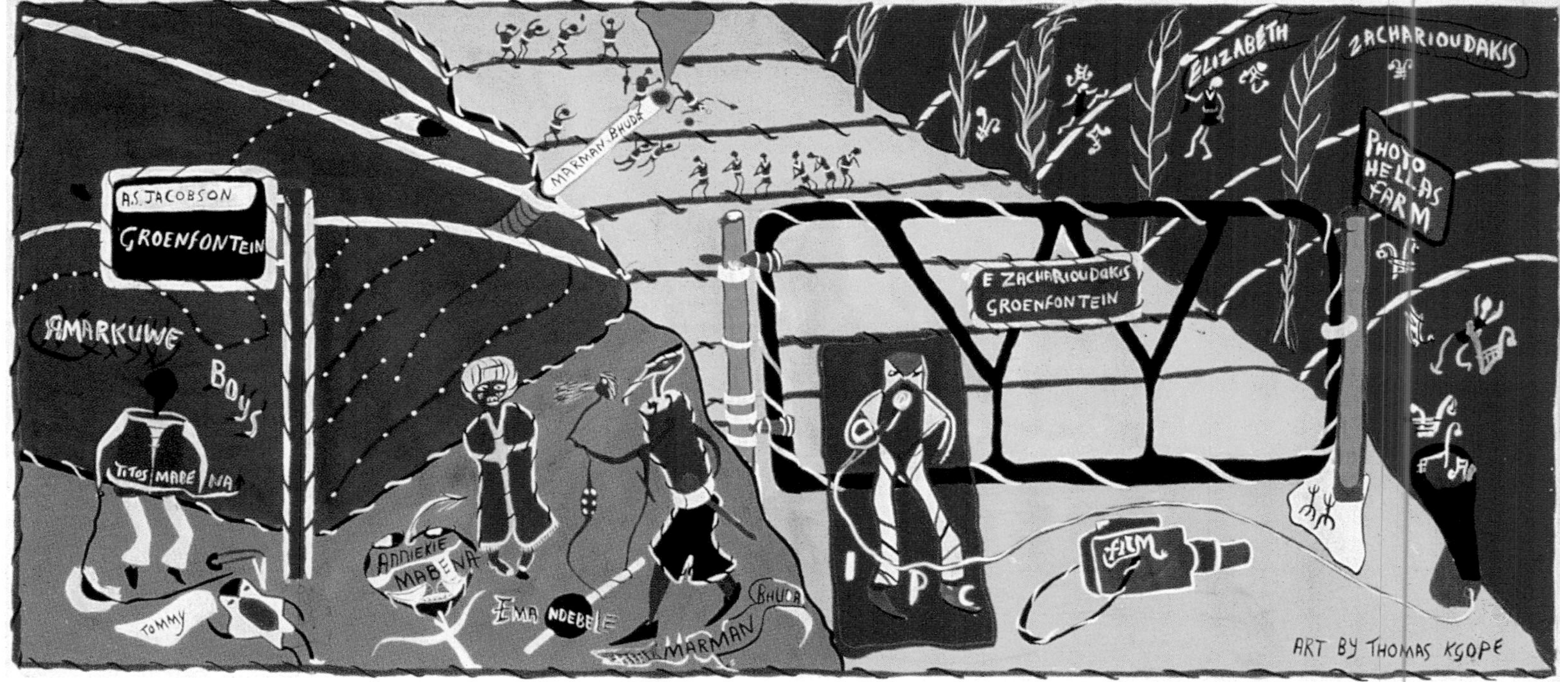

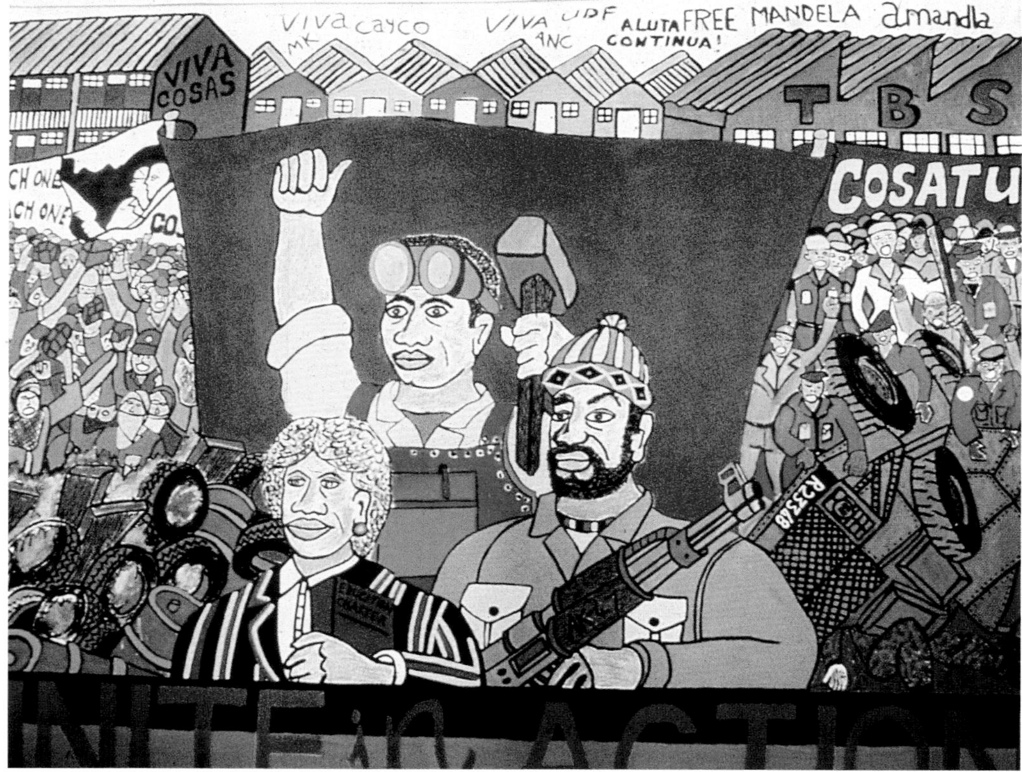

Thomas Gkope (born in 1954), "Groenfotein"
©Nathalie Knight Gallery

Collective banner
©Sue Williamson

facing page:
John Muafangejo (1943-1987), "A woman is milking a cow," 1981
©Maison Iwalewa, Université de Bayreuth

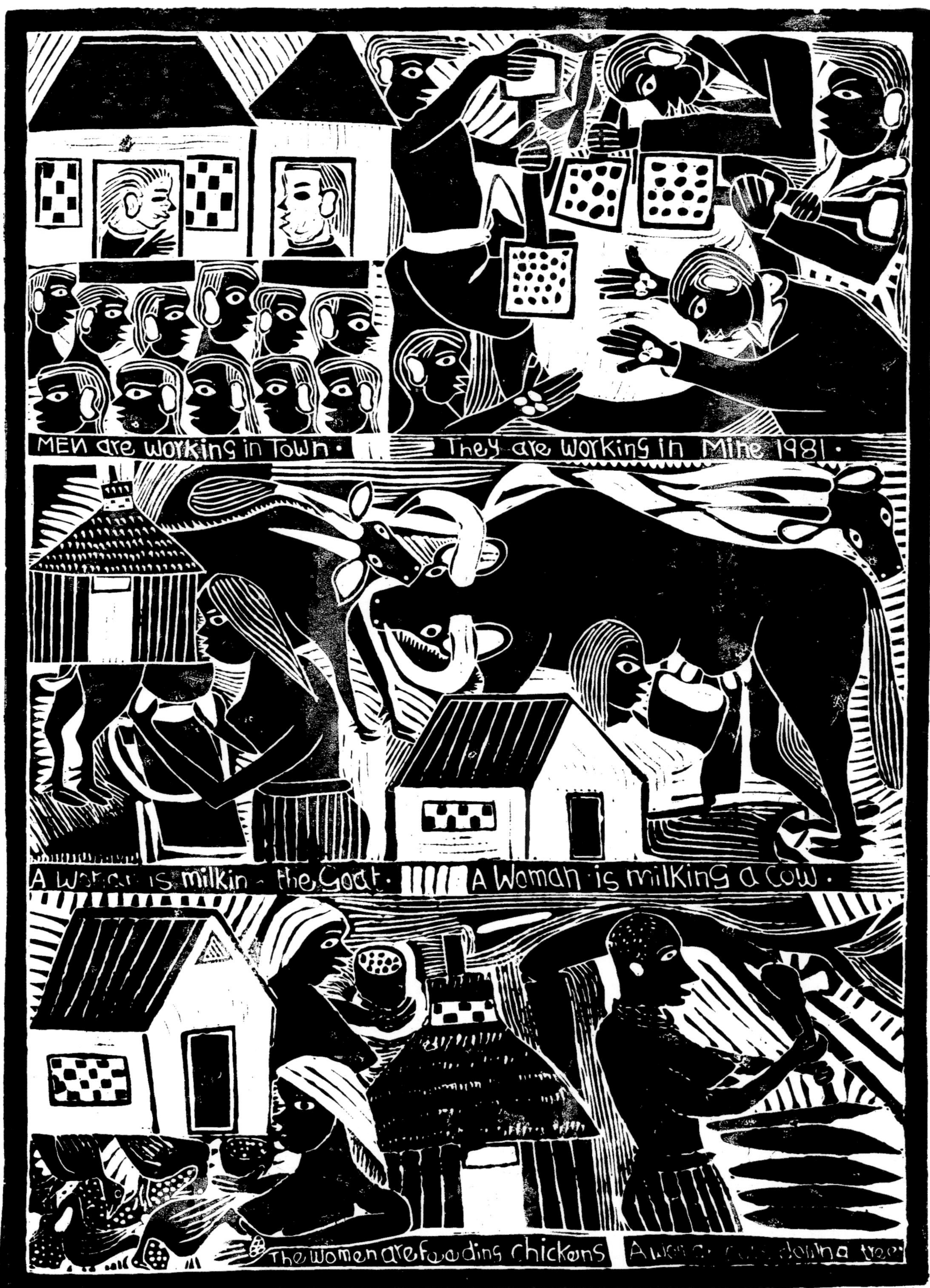
MEN are working in Town ·
They are working in Mine 1981 ·
A Woman is milking a cow ·
The women are feeding chickens
35/150
1981

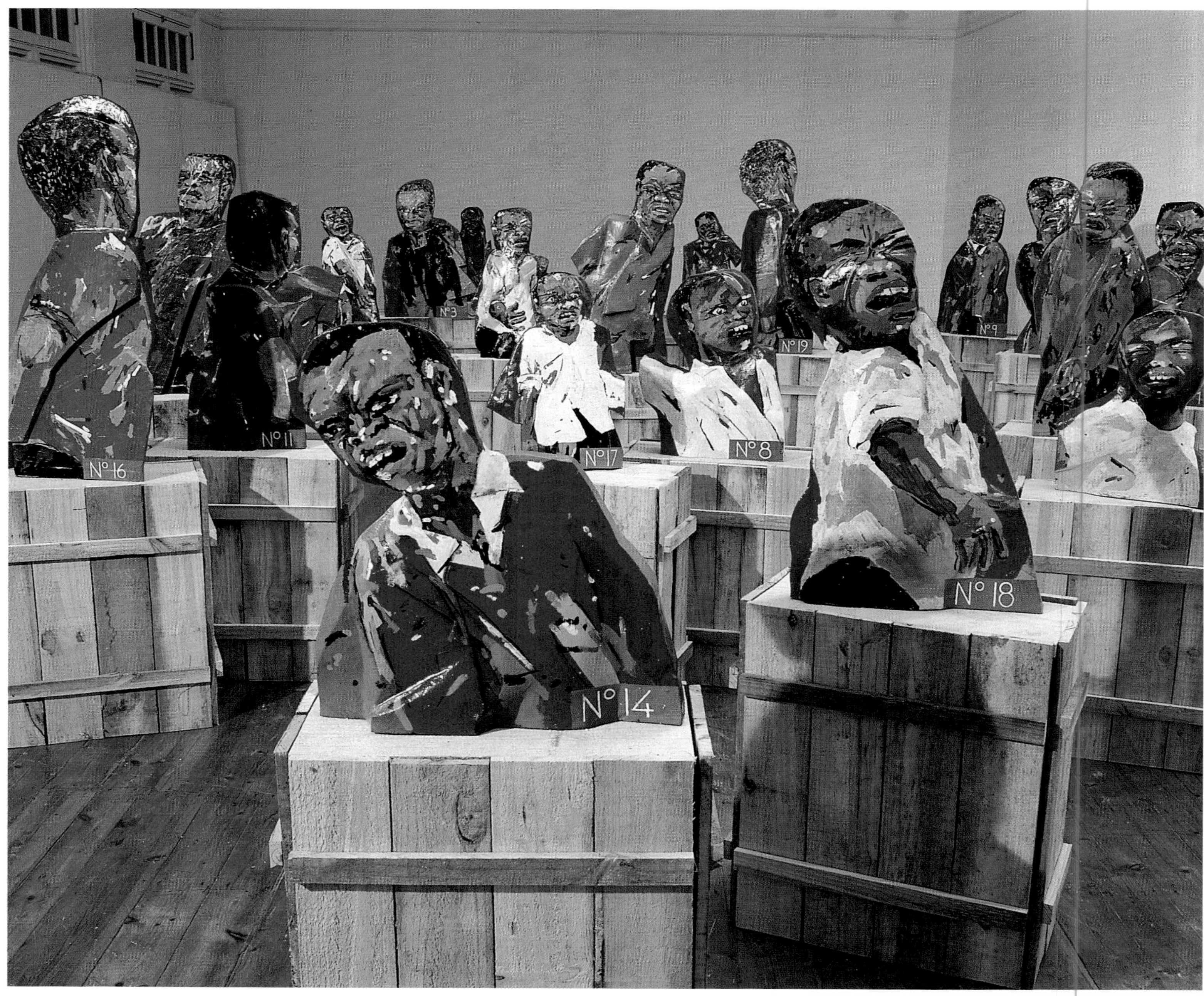

Kevin Brand (born in 1953), "19 boys running," 1988
wood, polystyrene and paper

"RESISTANCE ART" IN SOUTH AFRICA
Sue Williamson

It is said that the hour before dawn is always the darkest, and so it was in South Africa in the second half of the eighties, a time when the repressive power of the apartheid state had never seemed stronger. The "hour before dawn" quote was often given from political platforms as popular leaders attempted to assure their followers that the longed-for freedom from political and economic domination, although so impossible to imagine, would indeed come. This period of intense political activity, matched by a series of States of Emergency imposed by the Nationalist government, also marked the peak of the movement which came to be known as "resistance art."

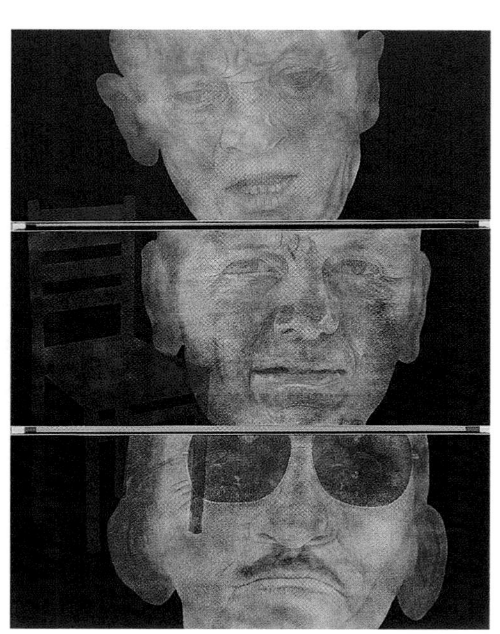

Paul Stopforth (born in 1945), "The interrogators," 1979

Those who actively opposed the state came to understand that it was necessary to voice that opposition in as many different ways as possible. Thus messages calling for freedom and appealing for unity appeared on walls, on T-shirts, posters, banners and murals; cultural activity was seen as an integral part of the struggle, and those engaged in the arts – writers, playwrights, musicians and visual artists – were often referred to as "cultural workers." In a 1986 speech, writer Menan du Plessis had this to say: "*At the mass rallies and funerals, during our assemblies and on our marches, we've been stirred, sometimes profoundly moved, heartened and inspired by the popular culture of resistance. It is not the morally self-conscious art of liberal protest, nor is it the defiant art of outrage, it is the diverse, complex, extraordinarily rich art of resistance. It is rooted directly in the context of struggle. It seems inconceivable that any of these living forms of art could be isolated from their directly political context and placed up on a stage, behind footlights, or mounted on the walls of a picture gallery.*"

Even though Du Plessis' definition of the culture of resistance seems to exclude the studio production of the country's visual artists, many of the country's leading artists were making work which engaged either directly or more subtly with social issues. In the intervening years, it is all of this work too which is now understood to fall into the category of "resistance art."

At this point, it is important to look back, and consider how this culture of resistance germinated and grew. Certainly there was little sign of it in the passive first half of the seventies, a period in which gold kept the country's economy in fine shape, the rand was worth more than the dollar, the African National Congress and the Pan African Congress had been banned into outward silence, the country's most popular leaders had been incarcerated in Robben Island for the past fifteen years, and the power of the state seemed impregnable. Viewers walking round the country's art museums and galleries at the time would have overwhelmingly taken away with them an impression of colonialism: of genre and landscape and figure painting, or of pastiches of modernist trends popular overseas. In the streets, the police ruled, rounding up all those black persons whose passbooks showed some unfortunate irregularity. On the surface, the State was in control, and if there was an occasional Free Nelson Mandela scrawled on a wall, it could go ignored.

It was the youth that pointed the way forward. In 1976, rebelling against having to study in school in the hated language of the oppressor, Afrikaans, the school children of Soweto demonstrated on the streets. The demonstration was met with gunfire. The picture of Hector Peterson, the first youth to die in this battle, went around the world, and has remained an icon of the struggle ever since. There is no doubt that Soweto in 1976 and all of the subsequent uprisings around the country presented a sharp wake-up call to whites and blacks alike, shaking them out of apathy.

The year 1976 marked the birth of a whole host of new organisations committed to change, and various disciplines, too, were forced to consider their role or non-role, in the bringing about of a more equitable and democratic

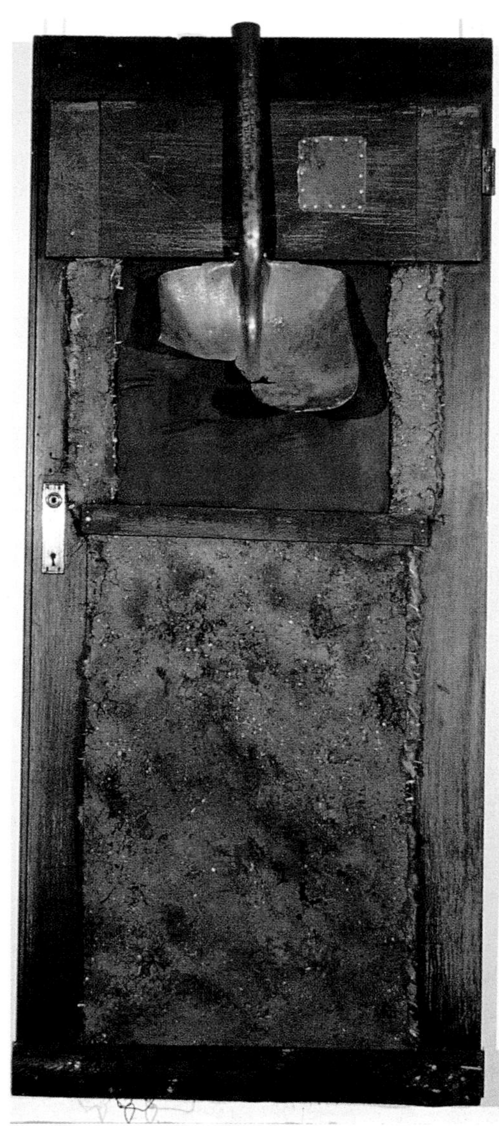

Lucas Seage (born in 1956), "Found object"
©South African National Gallery

society. A certain amount of cynicism amongst black artists and activists greeted this sudden soul searching: were whites only being brought into awareness when their own safety was in question? There were few black artists present at a conference hosted by the University of Cape Town in July 1979, entitled "The State of Art in South Africa." Cliff Bestall's conference poster showed an artist's hand painting a rainbow above a gloomy landscape of heavily burdened figures. The metaphor of the blinkered artist who ignored social reality to paint landscape was apt. For many of the white artists in the audience, the conference marked the beginning of a political activism, and the conference culminated in the signing of a pledge to no longer allow their art to be sent overseas to represent South Africa on international art biennials and exhibitions until all state funded art institutions were open to black as well as white students. No longer would it seem that artists were giving the apartheid regime their cooperation. It was a gesture that would pre-figure the international cultural boycott of South Africa, which still lay in the future.

If "The State of Art in South Africa," held as it was in white-dominated academia, was notable for the lack of black artists, a second conference, held as part of an art festival conveniently just outside the borders of the country – in Gaborone, Botswana – had an attendance which was considerably more representative. Exiles like Gavin Jantjes were able to fly in from overseas to present papers, and in South Africa, buses left from Cape Town and Johannesburg to carry participants. It was now 1982, and the title of the conference was "Art Towards Social Development and Change in South Africa." The theme was "culture and resistance" and the festival had as an aim "to serve as an indication of the current direction of committed art in South Africa" and to encourage "cultural workers to be part and parcel of the communities from which they come." This conference might be said to mark the true shift of general consciousness in the way art could be used as a vehicle for change.

Of course, up to this time, a handful of artists had already been making overtly political work. One thinks of Thami Mnyele, Ezrom Legae. As Lucas Seage was to say in a 1981 interview with David Koloane, himself a socially engaged artist of note, "I try to crack the apartheid system, even if it is a tiny, tiny little crack I manage to make. My message is directed to the man in the street, hence I use symbols he can easily identify with – such as a reference book, a Bible, chains, a primus stove." Seage's Found Object, a low, steel "bed" with a nail roughened surface, a bible chained to the head, and a rolled blanket stands as a metaphor for the degrading working conditions of the vast army of migrant labourers who kept the country's gold mines in production.

For it was not only the State which kept discriminatory controls in place. Big business, often purporting to espouse fair employment practice, in fact used apartheid and job discrimination to pay low wages and offer little, if any, job security to their black workers. Gavin Younge, now Head of the Department of Fine Art at the University of Cape Town, used his work to take one such company to task.

Afrox was a company which manufactured gases and welding equipment, which sponsored a yearly competition for metal sculpture. In 1979, Younge's abstract piece, To the Dark Rising, won the annual Afrox prize for metal sculpture. Younge knew that a black artist had never won this prize. He also knew that the fledgling Community Art Project, set up in an old building in Cape Town to provide a space where young black artists could get art tuition, had approached Afrox for a donation of welding equipment and had been rejected. Younge decided to use his R2000 prize to make a piece which commented on the poor working conditions and inadequate wages Afrox paid its workers. Workmen's Compensation was a sculpture of three steel wheelbarrows, containing battered enamel mugs, plates and worn shoes collected by Young from the Afrox workers. So furious was Afrox, that the planned catalogue for the award show was never printed, and the prize was never again awarded.

Working in the same period was the painter and sculptor Paul Stopforth, whose work in the late seventies and early eighties focussed on the subject of the victims of torture at the hands of the police. Worked in wire, plaster and gauze, Stopforth's life-size sculptures were of naked figures in tortured poses of suffering: cringing, waiting to be assaulted, hooded, trussed, handcuffed and strung from a pole – or like George Botha (1977) having met his death "falling down stairs" while in police hands.

One might have imagined that work as explicit as this would draw a reaction from a State which sought to exercise control over every aspect of its citizens' lives, to the point where at times it was not even possible to discover the names of those who had been detained. Yet ... "*It is part of the contradiction of this country,*" wrote art critic Anne Pogrund,[1] "*that at a time when the treatment of detainees is arousing acute anxiety, it should be possible for an artist to hold an exhibition depicting torture during interrogation. It is astonishing that such a public protest should pass without much response, positive or negative, from anyone.*"

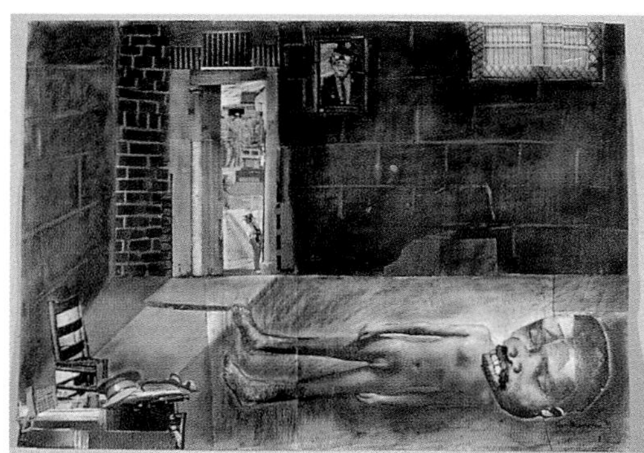

Sam Nhlegthgwa (born in 1955), "The death of Steve Biko," 1990

©D.R.

Stopforth himself made this comment on his work: "*I want to make and spread an image as real as possible for the time now. I want to bring the facts home to those willing to look. My figures parallel something that we can't be witness to. We can't refuse to accept that these things happen.*"

In 1979 Stopforth completed his triptych The Interrogators, three horizontal close-ups of the faces of the policemen responsible for the death of Black Consciousness leader Steve Biko. In the background is the ominously simple shape of a wooden chair. Worked in graphite and floor wax, the piece has a dull metallic sheen. Now in the collection of the South African National Gallery, the piece can be seen on the touring show, "Liberated Voices: Contemporary Art from South Africa," which opened at the Museum for African Art in New York in September 1999.

Once such work moved out of the "safe" or semi-hidden confines of the local galleries however, it became more threatening to the State. In 1981, two years after the conference pledge not to support overseas exhibitions channeled through the government, Stopforth decided to confront the State in a different way. As one of six artists invited to send work to the Valparaiso Biennial International Exhibition in Chile, Stopforth submitted two small graphite drawings of damaged hands and feet. The titles: Steve Biko and We Do It. After viewing Stopforth's work, the State stepped in, sending a letter which read in part: "*The works chosen made political statements, While the department did not want to interfere with the autonomy or artists, it decided, after discussion with interested parties, that it was not the way of the department to promote and finance such works overseas.*"

Although it seemed strange at the time that while the State was quick to ban T-shirts, posters, books, plays and all manner of relatively innocuous publications, (famously, the children's classic tale of a horse, Black Beauty), work in galleries seemed to escape the censors' ire. In retrospect, one can only draw the conclusion that the State considered fine art to be unimportant, peripheral, catering to an effete minority.

This conclusion was borne out by the fact that on several occasions paintings that were turned into posters or postcards would quite quickly find their way on to the "banned for distribution" list which came out in the weekly Government Gazette.

Resistance art would take many forms. Some work, like Stopforth's, was extremely direct, as was the art of Durban artist Sfiso Ka Mkame, with his pastels worked in sgrafitto technique, revealing little cameos of death and violence in such pieces as Homage to the Mothers and Letters to God (1988).

[1] Rand Daily Mail of September 9, 1978.

There was Michael Goldberg's Monument to the Nationalists (1978) – a filing cabinet with four drawers, one for each of the Nationalist prime ministers to have held power since 1948, holding the legislative acts which had most strongly and stringently enforced the policies of apartheid. Printed on the top was "This monument commemorates leaders of the Nationalist government, their legislation regarding the separate development of races and all that has come of it." There was Kevin Brand's 19 boys running (1988), an installation of 19 figurative sculptures in wood, polystyrene and paint, in which the top halves of the boys are rendered expressionistically, their faces stretched with fear, but the lower half of each body is a wooden crate. The piece commemorated a shameful massacre of mourners in a funeral procession by the police in Uitenhage, and small town in the Eastern Cape, in 1985. There were the strongly graphic linocuts showing township incidents and police confrontations by such artists as Bongiwe Dhlomo, and the brothers Patrick and Sidney Holo.

Other work was more coded. Mmakgabo Helen Sebidi, who took classes at the Johannesburg Art Foundation, captured the disruptions caused to African culture and family life by apartheid in her large pastel and collage pieces which show a seething mass of figures fighting for physical and psychic space, every inch of the paper covered. William Kentridge's work of that period, in pieces such as The Boating Party (1985), in his trademark charcoal and pastel, showed the life of the genteel being played out against strange interruptions, like burning tyres. Penny Siopis in her "History Painting" series laid questions of patriarchy and colonialism open for examination, and Jane Alexander gave expression to a sick and maladjusted society with sculptures like The Butcher Boys (1985). This piece has become the most popular in the collection of the South African National Gallery, and few who see it can remain unmoved by the three "boys," naked life size figures seated on a bench, horns on their heads, and their faces mashed into bestial features.

But perhaps the most popular aspect of resistance art was the way this manifested itself in black townships throughout the country. Murals were painted on public walls. Under threat of imminent demolition, the Crossroads squatter camp near Cape Town persuaded a paint manufacturer to give the community enough brightly coloured paint for residents to paint their corrugated iron shacks in defiantly brilliant colours, part of a sustained campaign which eventually led to the camp being spared.

And then there were the peace parks. These came into being in the last months of 1985 in townships around Johannesburg and Pretoria, not only a direct response to repression but also an assertion of pride in community. Following the declaration of the first state of emergency in July 1985, essential services normally provided by the authorities like the removal of refuse from the townships had broken down. Residents were dumping their rubbish on street corners and in open spaces. Youth committees decided to take action. "*They can kill us and detain us, but they can never remove from us the pride of caring for our environment,*" said Luckyboy Zulu, a 15-year-old peace park worker. Groups of youths requisitioned the family's tools, persuaded graders to move mounds of rubbish, collected money from motorists for paint. Environmentalists donated trees and shrubs, and soon what had once been foul smelling dumping grounds, soon became well constructed and laid out parks, with sculptures assembled from tree trunks, old bicycles, car tyres, and then painted. The movement spread, and younger children created little "Gardens of Eden" and sculptures appeared on street corners.

The peace parks were not to last long. The names given to the parks, Oliver Tambo Park in White City, Nelson Mandela and Steve Biko Park in Mohlakeng and Sisulu Park in Orland West made it clear to the police that the youth committees were reaffirming their political beliefs. The security forces were sent in to systematically destroy the parks, using the pretext that they were being used as sites to hide caches of arms.

Shortlived the peace parks may have been, but the creative energy, the determination not to give in to oppression and the belief in freedom could not be so easily suppressed. The factors which eventually led to the Nationalist government announcing the freeing of Nelson Mandela and the unbanning of the African National Congress in February 1990 were many and varied, but the role played by the movement of cultural resistance, even if it was a minor one, cannot be denied.

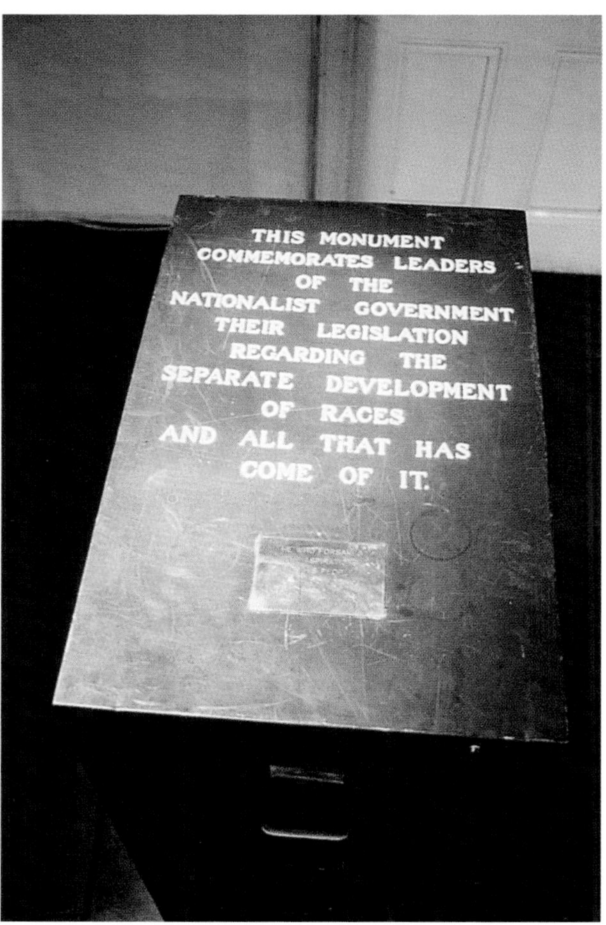

Michael Goldberg (born in 1952),
"Monument to the Nationalists," 1978
h. 160 cm ©Anna Zeminski

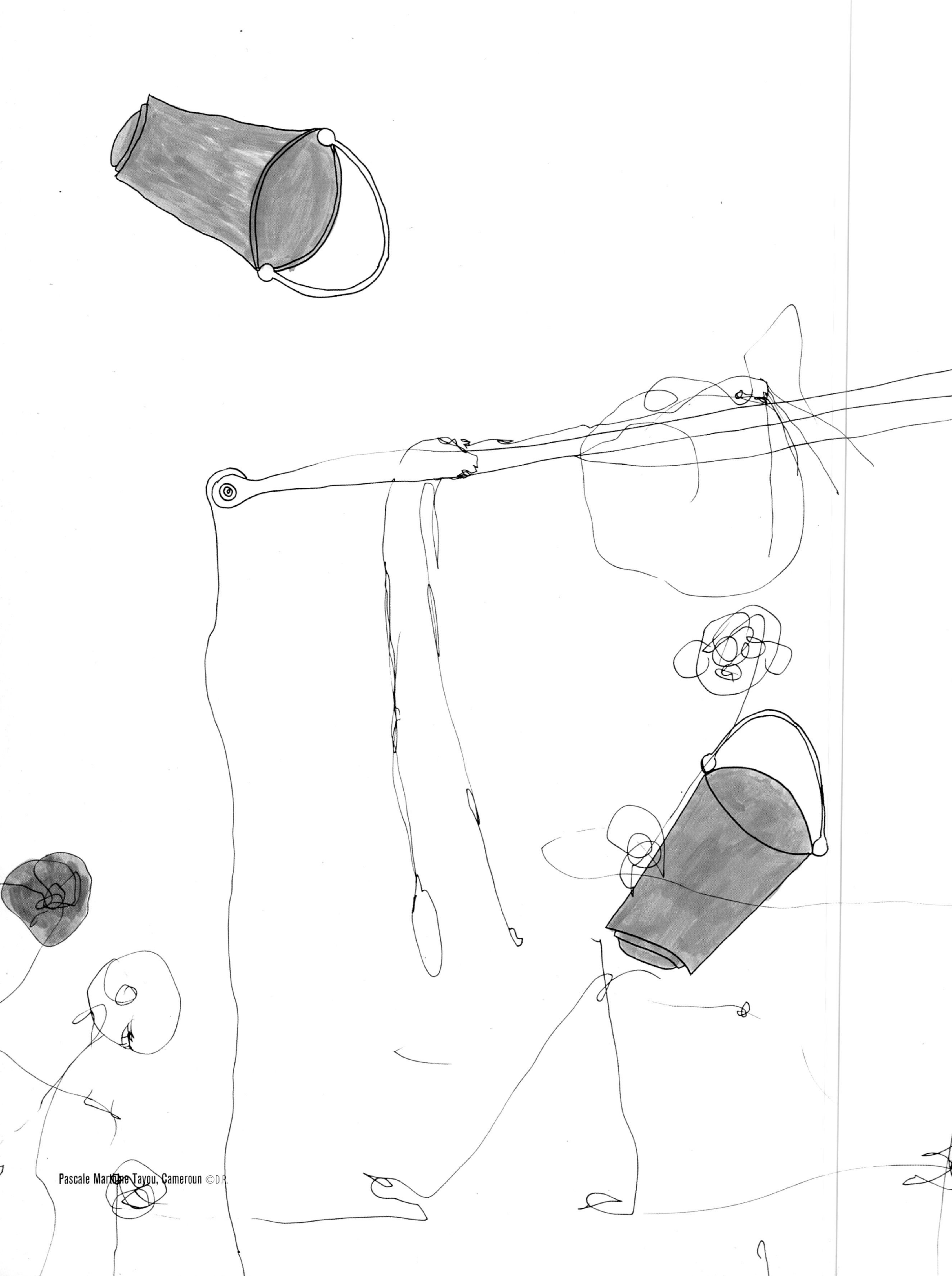

Pascale Martine Tayou, Cameroun ©D.R.

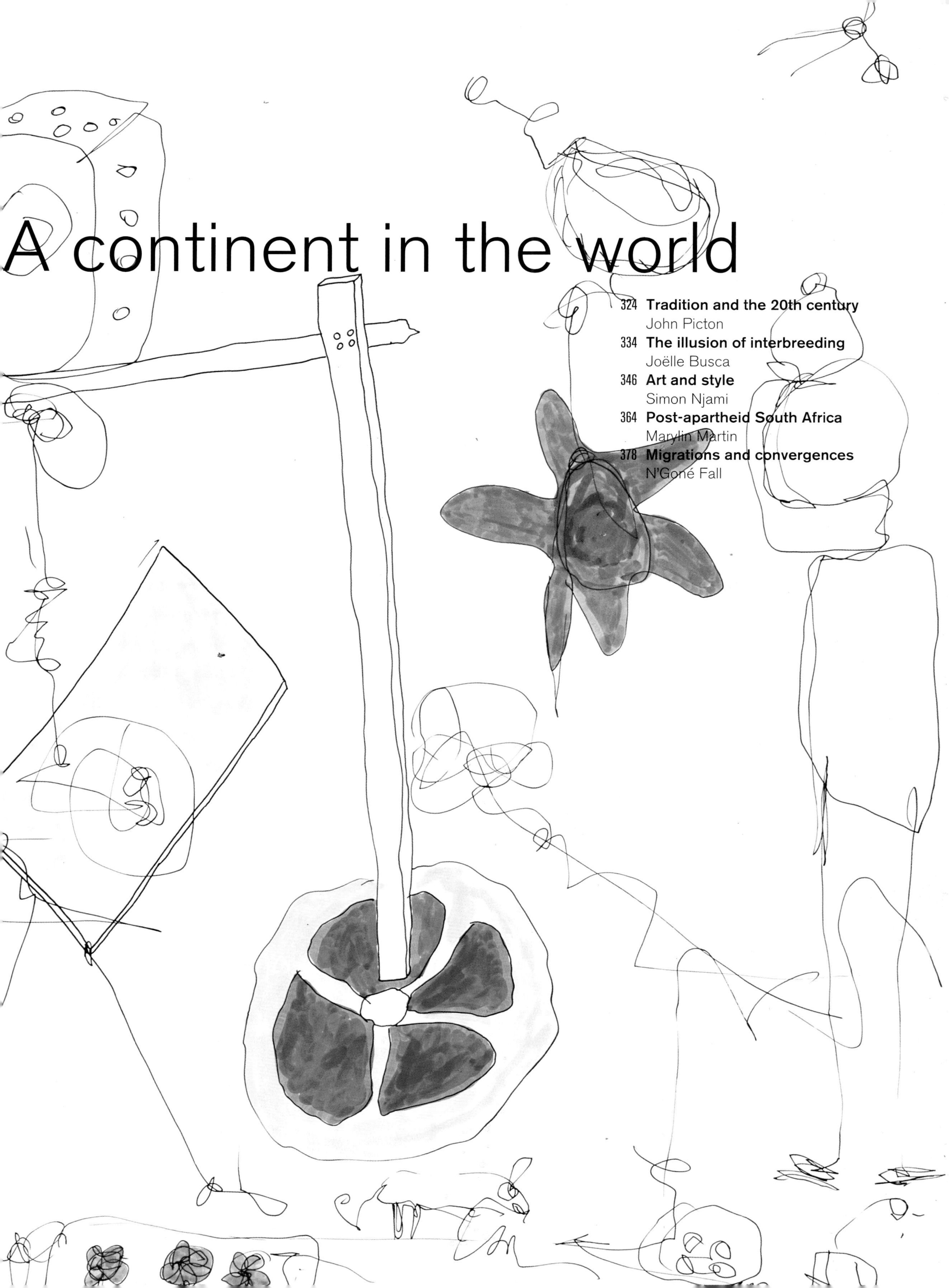

A continent in the world

Tradition and the 20th century

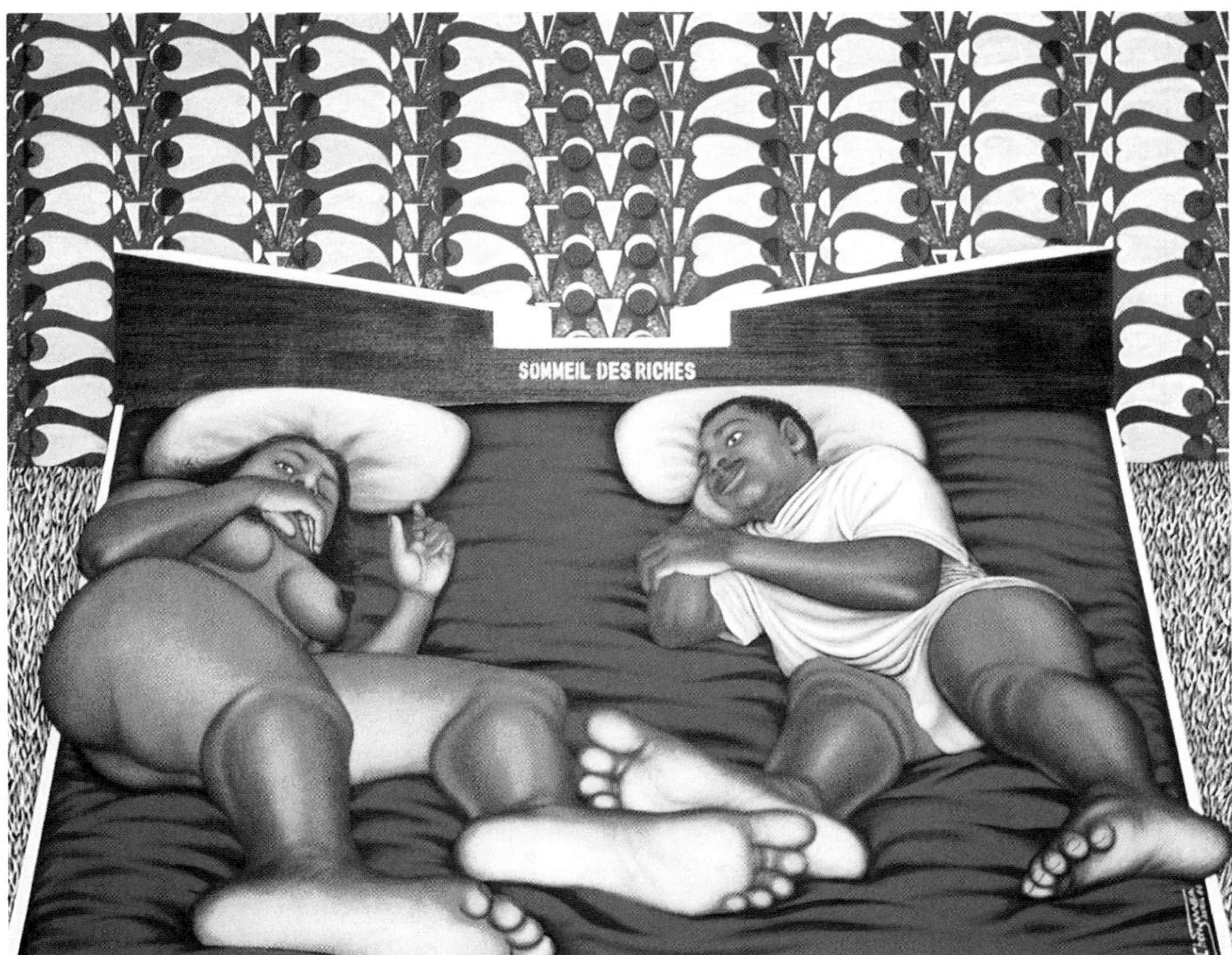

Chéri Samba

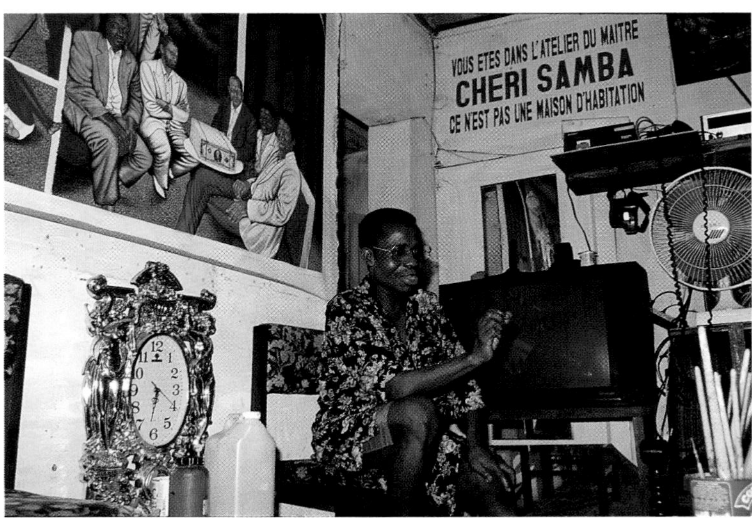

Chéri Samba was born in Lower Congo in 1956. He settled in Kinshasa where he started as an assistant in a working class painter's workshop. He has been taking part in numerous exhibits abroad since 1982. He defines his career in three stages: selling to colored people, selling to Blacks and Whites, selling to non-colored people. His unfinished paintings show his unique technique. Once the tile composition or composition by production is in place, Chéri Samba applies the shading and bistre of the skin. "Is it me or my painting that is working class?"

"The Sleep of the Rich," 1996

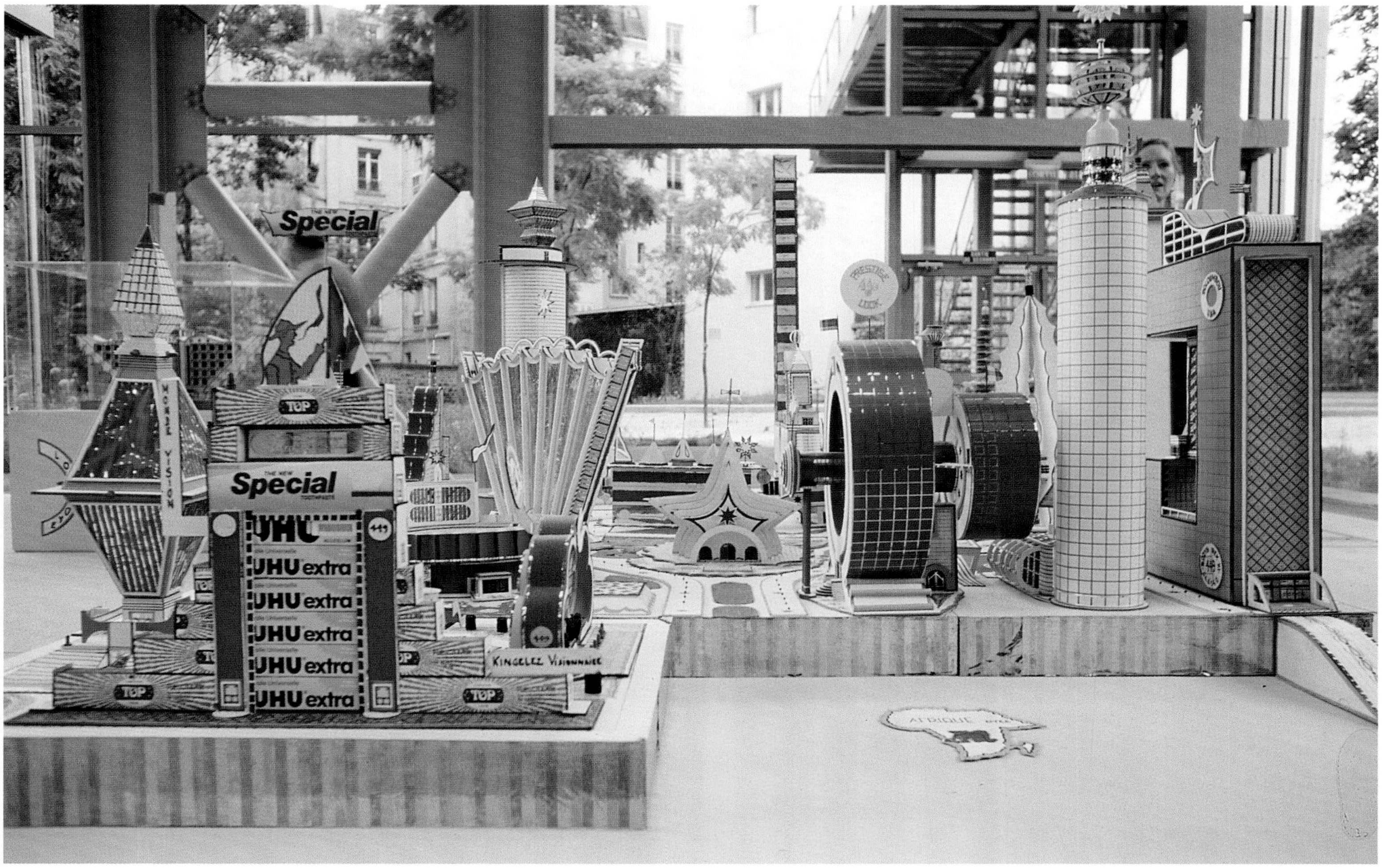

Bodys Isek Kingelez

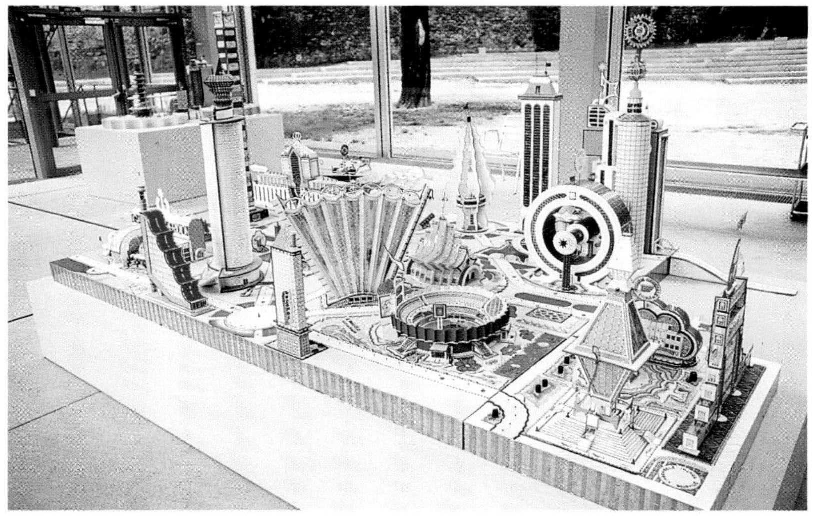

Bodys Isek Kingelez was born in the DRC in 1948. This architect-layout artist and visionary creator of modern cities has produced social projects, futuristic cities with a concern for detail and surprising work on space. Nothing is left to chance and Kingelez puzzles through his unexpected concept of a dream Africa composed of skyscrapers, monumental fountains and brightly colored architectonic buildings, as if to recall that his city, Kinshasa, is also a kaleidoscope, a symbol of celebration and pleasure.

"Third Millenium City," Fondation Cartier, Paris

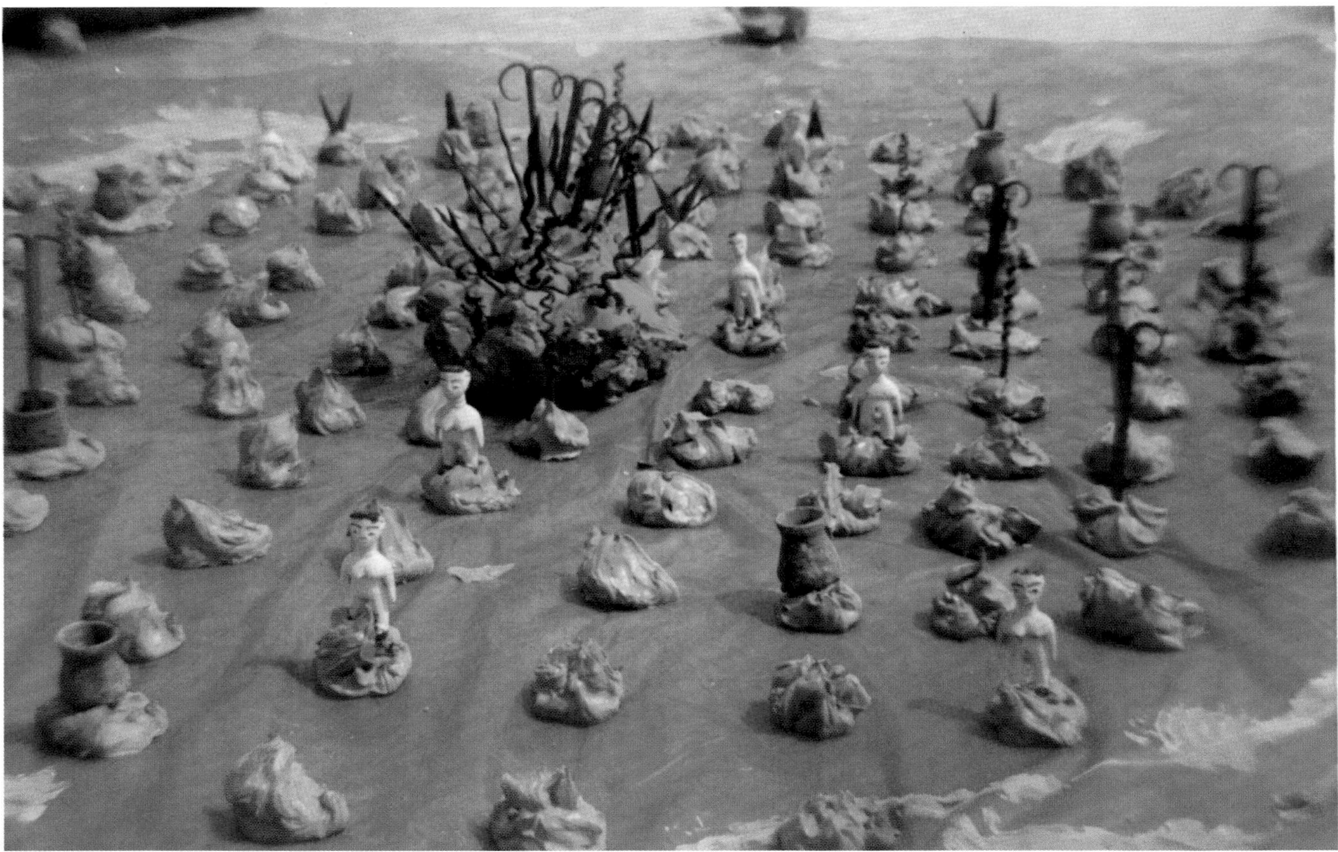

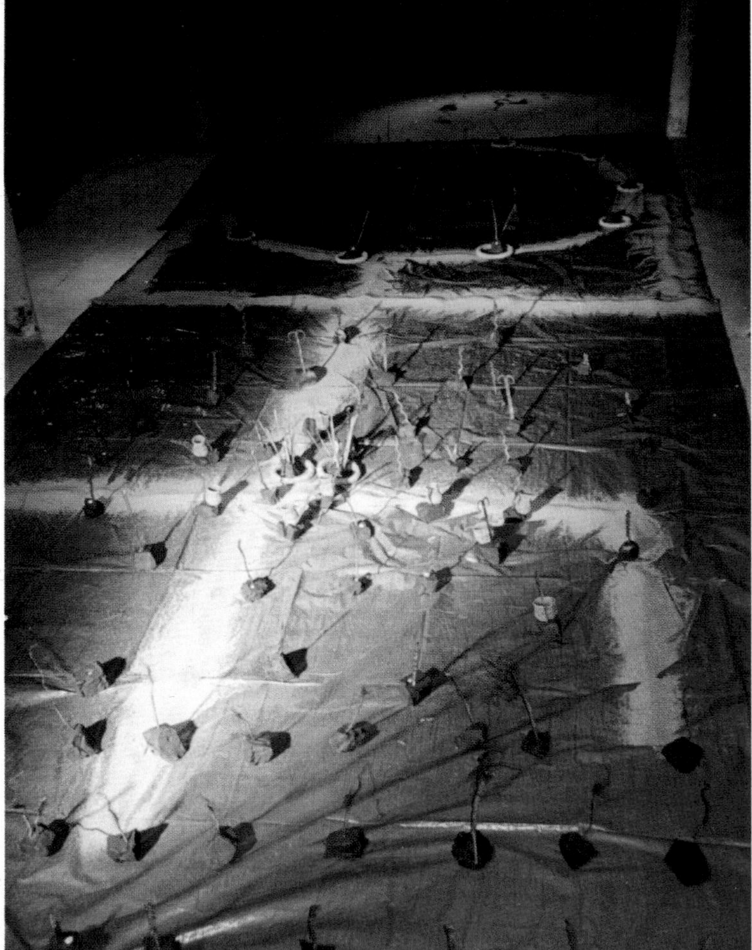

Sokey Edorh

This painter and sculptor was born in Togo in 1955. Sokey Edorh studied philosophy at the University of Lomé from 1984-86 and spent some time at the École des Beaux-Arts of Bordeaux in 1989-90, before returning to Togo.
His work, which is traditional through the use of earth and materials from the African continent, is usually based on symbols and signs used throughout Africa. Each year he visits countries and villages in order to obtain new signs and learn how to interpret them so as to better integrate them into his work. He is attached to the major trends that shake an often conventional plastic modernity and seeks, through his desire to write, a necessity that runs through all of his work.

Pume

Pume lives in Kinshasa. This self-taught artist was born in the DRC in 1967. His fascination with cinematographic projection equipment and its precise mechanics led him to delve into creation. He named his artistic concept Bylex, a "philosophy" characterized by the presence of tiles (symbol of balance). This unclassifiable artist develops his theories in work that is part design and part sculpture.

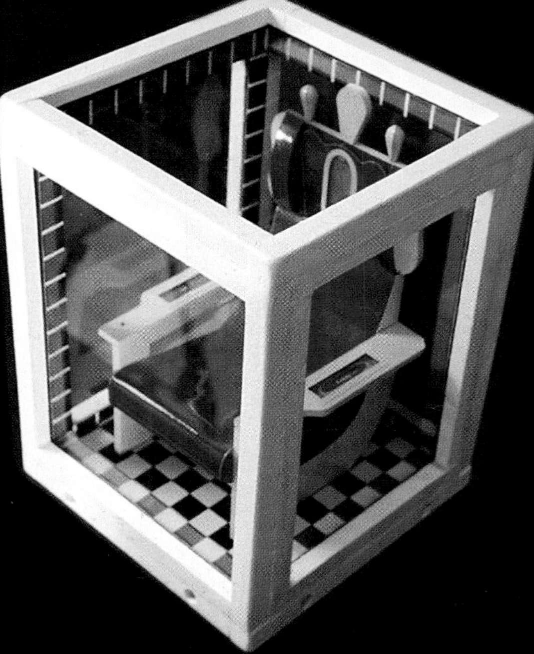

top:
"Byl Statue," 1994

"Byl Chair," 1994

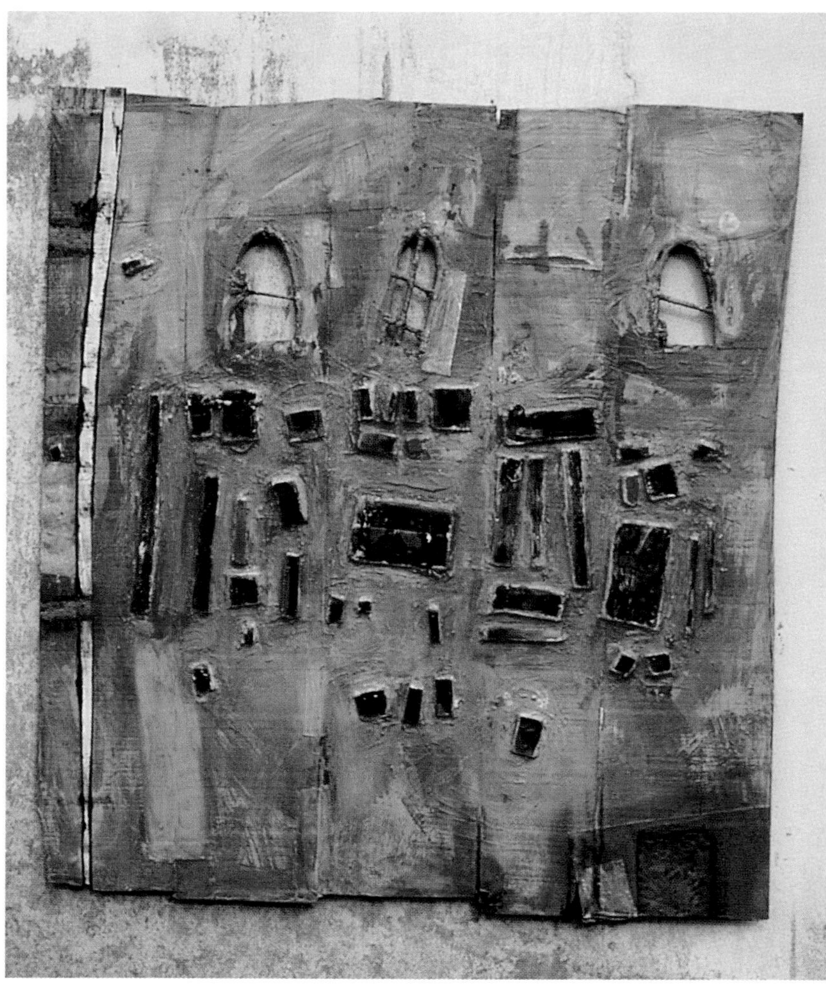

Tiébéna Dagnogoi

Born in Roubaix in 1963, Tiébéna Dagnogoi currently lives in Ivory Coast. Before delving into wood sculpture, he devoted himself to interior design and painting. He uses all types of materials (earth, metal, beads, ropes, all kinds of pigments) for his preferred theme, filled with meanings and symbols: the door.

"Facade," 1997
mixed media, 175x152 cm
©Revue Noire

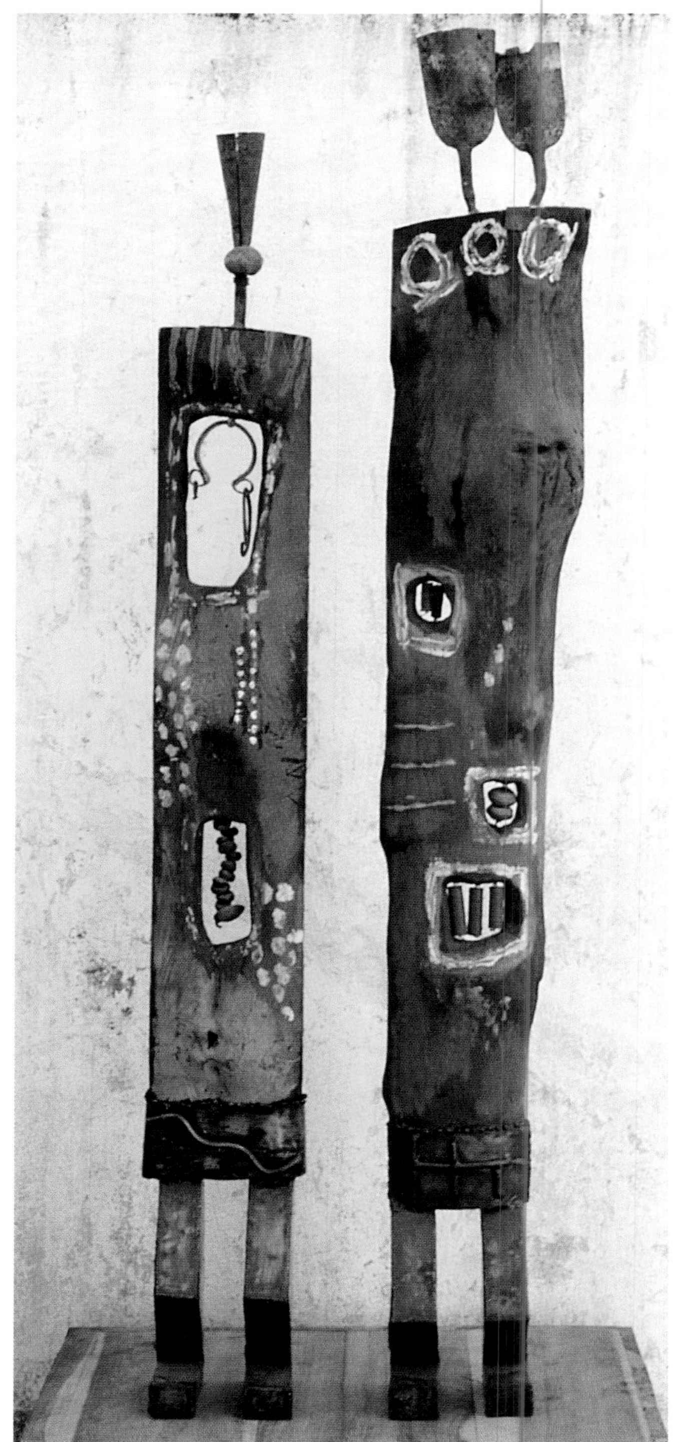

Kouas

As a painter and sculptor, Dominique Kouas Gnonnou, a Benin native, dedicates his work to anonymous artists of past centuries. As an artist by duty, he feels that he has a mission: to uphold the memory of the dead. Old pieces of wood, baked clay incorporated in copper, the influence of metals recall the Assins (commemorative altars representing the spirit of elders) and are all transformed into totems or doormen. The traditional colors of the Guelede masks, omnipresent in his paintings, refer to the sacred curtains of the ancient Benin palaces.

"The Guardians of the Temple," 1995 ©Revue Noire

TRADITION AND THE 20TH CENTURY

John Picton

The idea or sense of tradition is fundamental to any understanding of visual practice in Africa. Equally, the idea of "traditional art" has proved fundamentally pernicious in its capacity to mask the realities of this practice, especially in its international reception. When used as a quick reference to practices inherited from the past, it might seem innocuous enough, but when "traditional" then serves to identify an authentic 'Africa' it has ideological implications that place it alongside words such as "primitive" and "tribal."

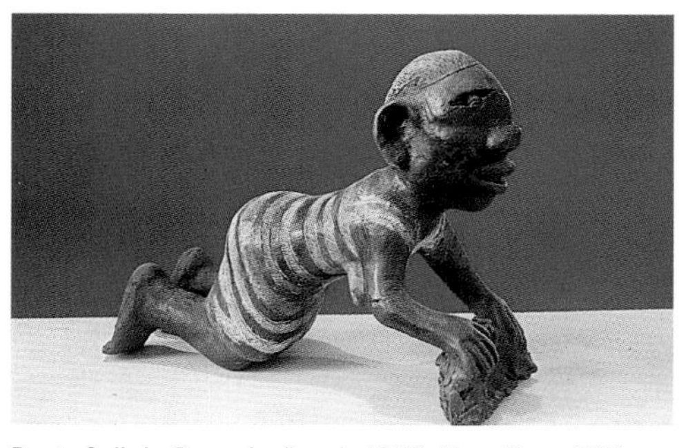

Renata Sadimba Passemba (born in 1954), Mozambique, 1994

©Troels

Tradition, i.e. the handing on of social practice, is fundamental to any social environment, in Africa as elsewhere; but the processes of that handing on necessarily entail possibilities for change and development. Extant practices may of course be replicated with minimal alteration (though some small measure of incremental development is always more-or-less inevitable); or, in the context of that handing on, new elements may be grafted more obviously on to extant practices; and, of course, from time to time, and for complex reasons, extant practices cease, perhaps to be replaced by new forms. These possibilities have always been present in the transfer of art from one place or generation to another, in Africa as elsewhere.

What matters art-historically is that we document this relationship between past and present; as also the manner in which artists do or do not draw upon a sense of tradition, and/or on the forms of particular traditions; and the manner in which artists interpret the past in the context of present concerns; and the facts and circumstances of the demise of traditions of visual practice, and the birth of others; and the complex factors which enable and/or govern these possibilities. To put it another way, we should concern ourselves, first, with what people do, and, then, with what they say about what they do; and our understanding must be informed by the assessment of local agency in reckoning with the possibilities available to artists in the circumstances in which he and she find themselves. The inception of complex local modernities in Africa defines a period from about 1850 that is also marked by the demise of the Atlantic slave trade and the imposition of colonial government, this accompanied almost immediately by the rise of independence movements; and, sooner or later, colonial rule was replaced by the independent states of modern Africa. This is, of course, a time of rapid change and development in all areas of social practice, including the visual arts; but it has been possible for this to be overlooked as if somehow "inauthentic." On the other hand, it is also possible to over-emphasize the impact of change. The real surprise subsists in the extraordinary diversity of current practice; and it is only in that current and contemporary context that we can assess, first, how much remains intact and, second, how much has changed bearing in mind that external influences will have been domesticated within local African terms.

Masquerade, for example, in many parts of West and Central Africa has a now-proven resilience and adaptability. So too have hand-loom textile production and resist-dyeing, and the arts of royal and chiefly ceremonial; and these arts inform a modern fashion industry, as they have also informed the development of an African photography which is the very first of the modern arts in Africa.

In due course other new techniques and forms in sculpture and architecture, graphics and textile printing, painting and printmaking would develop, entailing complex questions of identity and difference in art, as in all areas of social practice. Whether we are considering arts that are now of the past, or extant traditions inherited from the past, or, indeed, new traditions that turn away from the past, we can never understand those questions as long as writing about "African art," and the institutions that define an African art world internationally, remain fractured within a simple binary contrast between "primitive/tribal/traditional" on the one hand and all the new technical means (i.e. photography, painting, printmaking, etc) on the other. This contrast inevitably carries implications of authenticity that are as false as the con-

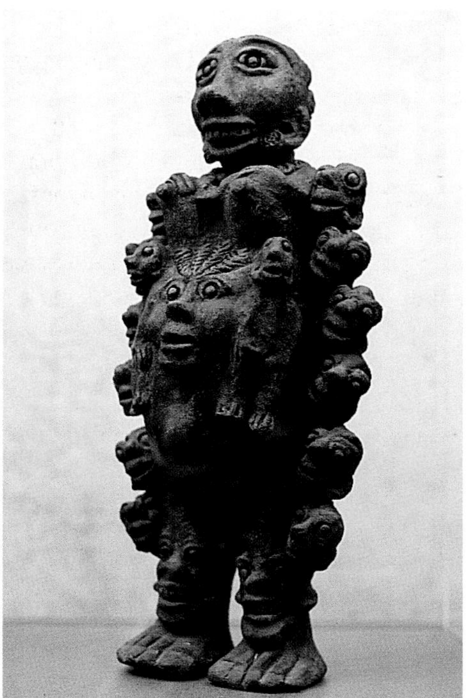

Seyni Awa Camara (born in 1945), "Mask of people," Senegal, 1989
h.48 cm ©Revue Noire

Calixte & Théodore Dakpogan (born in 1958 and 1956), Benin, 1994
©Revue Noire

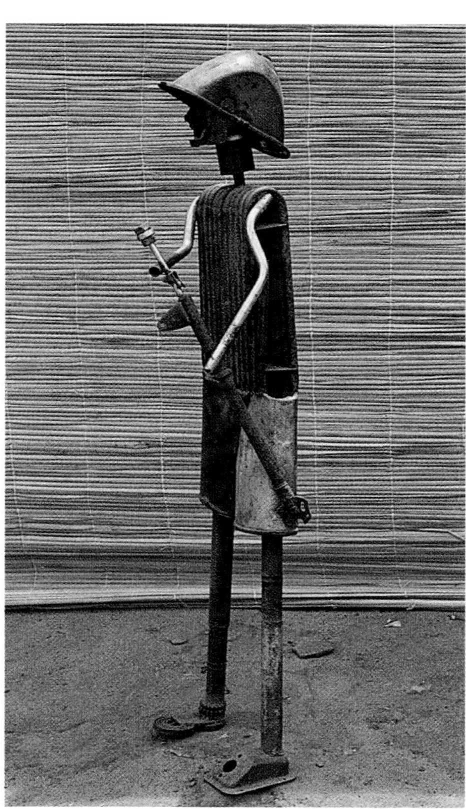

trast itself is false.
Of course, there was a time when African art was a kind of footnote to the history of modernism in European art. Because of an atavistic search for renewal via the "primitive," whether located in Africa, the South Seas, Central Asia, Europe, ancient Greece, or ancient Iberia, African sculpture was labeled "primitive" even as its unique three-dimensionality was recognized. For African sculptors had effectively invented sculpture in the round; but they were none-the-less seen in Europe at the lower end of an evolutionary ladder that the anthropology of the 19th century had misappropriated from Darwinian theory.

West African ivory sculptures had been present in European collections from the late 15th century (the so-called Afro-Portuguese ivories). By the 19th century these were often assumed to have come from India and it was only subsequent research that reconnected these works to the wider field of African material that was now beginning to enter the museums of Europe and America. Nevertheless, because of the accidents of colonial history, those artists in Paris at a crucial turning point in the formal developments of European art really only had a very limited selection of material available to them, the generally rather schematic work coming from French Equatorial Africa. Primitivist modernisms in Britain and Germany took somewhat different shapes because of the rather different kinds of sculpture from Kuba, Benin City and the grasslands of Cameroon; but, whichever the source, already by the time Picasso revealed his notorious Demoiselles local photographers could be found throughout Africa; and in Lagos a 15-year-old Aina Onabolu was perhaps beginning to think through his future career as the pioneer artist and art educator of modern Africa.

The "primitivism" that informed European modernism thus depended not only upon a misappropriated zoological paradigm, but also on what one can call the collectible-artifact view of African art. There were three elements to this. First, the 18th-19th century notion of Fine Art as painting and sculpture was taken for granted, and it was assumed that what mattered as art in Europe mattered there too. Secondly, as the new generation of 20th century anthropologists pioneered first first-hand field research, they rejected any interest in visual and material practice together with the zoological paradigm of their predecessors, in favor of an interest in basic patterns of social structure. Although now in a position to correct previous misunderstandings, anthropology had moved on, and uniformed views of African art in early 20th-century Europe were left intact. Thirdly, while all manner of things were now arriving in the ethnographic departments of European museums, they were easily fitted in to the taken-for-granted ready-made categories of "craft" (the pots, the textiles, etc) and "art" (i.e. sculpture; for painting was assumed not to exist: rock painting was the province of archaeologists while the rich traditions of mural painting and body art had to wait until the advent of good quality cheap color photography made their "collection" possible).

The collaboration between ethnographic museums and artists, collectors and critics, confirmed a connoisseurship that has remained in place within the dominant art world of Europe and America throughout most of the 20th century, as recently celebrated in Africa, The Art of a Continent at the Royal Academy in London 1995. It was as if all the research during the period since the countries of Africa had gained their independence had not happened. Within this art world, the supposed essential values of an authentic Africa as embodied in forms and institutions described as "tribal" or, indeed, "traditional" were confirmed by the Ethnographic Present mode of writing (i.e. a reconstruction of the past from the evidence of current practice as if that past were indeed still current). Yet these terms, and the Ethnographic Present, while avoiding a now untenable cultural-evolutionary ladder, because of their ahistoricity served to confirm the authenticity of a once "timeless" Africa that had been spoiled by missionaries or education or industrialization or whatever. Yet this was no more than the imaginary of those who would keep Africa out of the century to which the rest of the world belongs; and whereas the "tribe" was a

Gérard Quenum (born in 1971), Benin
©D.R.

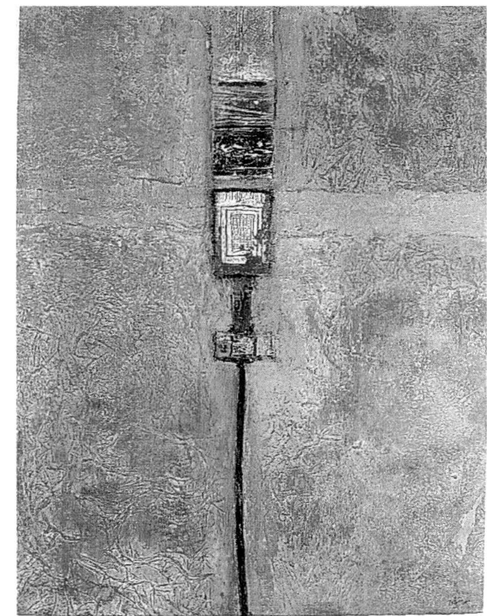

Tchif (born in 1973), Benin
©D.R.

colonial misreading of the processes of negotiating identity and difference, so the "traditional" was a post-colonial misreading of the temporal status of tradition.

Now, of course, it would be utterly foolish if we did not celebrate the extraordinary genius of countless African sculptors; but it would have been as foolish had we not worked to write back in to the account all those other artists, working in other mediums of practice; and in this context it is possible to identify five directions in research and writing:
- the masquerade, festival and performance contexts of particular sculptural traditions;
- the manner in which the sculptural traditions inherited from the past have developed to ensure a continuing social relevance;
- forms which hitherto had been overlooked: textiles, pottery, the personal arts, women's arts;
- the development of the art and artists emerging through the modern institutions of art education;
- the new forms of urban or "popular" culture, significant material that cannot be ignored despite a European and American tendency to play up the wilder aspects (the figurative coffins of coastal Ghana, the seemingly naive realism of urban sign painters) thereby effectively inventing and privileging a Neo-Primitivism that is a mere parody of the reality in which these arts subsist.

The first three of these were of course acceptable within the dominant art world, while the fourth was excluded, thereby effectively creating an alternative (and politically more radical, but financially underfunded) African art world. The necessary research has been initiated, however, mostly within universities, though without that wider raft of interest, as supplied by museums, galleries and salerooms. Nevertheless, it has been possible slowly to open up a wider view of African art internationally by studying the developments of the 20th century. (The publication of this material was pioneered by Ulli Beier in Contemporary Art in Africa, 1963, soon followed by the archaeologist of ancient Ife, Frank Willett, in his ever-popular African Art, 1971 [revised ed 1993], and leading via Fosu 1986, to Revue Noire, Elliot 1990, Agthe 1990, Deliss 1995, Ottenburg 1997, Oguibe & Enwezor 1999, and Kasfir 1999.) For this is an art that frequently engages with the past by drawing upon its forms or by illustrating mythic events and folk tales. Current issues and problems are thereby addressed by reference to that past. These are artists thinking through their cultural inheritance and presenting an interpretation of its relevance to the present. Of course, I write with the "Zaria rebels" particularly in mind, that group of artists in Nigeria who were concerned to celebrate both ethnicity and nationality at the time of Independence. I realize that in other countries, most obviously South Africa, other conditions apply; but the argument has wider relevance, because this is an art that has transgressed the "Africa" of monied connoisseurship and museum ethnography by offering an interpretive trajectory of its own. Yet, with the obvious exception of archaeological material, most of the art from Africa, whatever its medium and form, is of the period since 1850. Whether an object represents a tradition of practice inherited from the past or not, almost everything we can see in the collections of Europe and America is contemporary with the modern period, as usually defined.

In Europe and America, as all too often in Africa also, there are no major public collections of this work; but things have changed and are continuing to do so. The late Sylvia Williams, the former director of National Museum of African Art in Washington DC, insisted upon her curators collecting across the entire range of African material, with a particular thrust towards the new developments of the 20th century from all parts of the continent; and a curatorial post for modern African art has recently been opened. No other museum in America or Europe has so comprehensive a collection, although the Museum fur Volkerkunde, Frankfurt am Main, has substantial holdings of recent East African work, the British Museum has acquired work by Sokari Douglas Camp, and by Magdalene Odundo, and the personal collection of modern Zimbabwe sculpture of the late Frank McEwen, but it has yet to purchase material from the

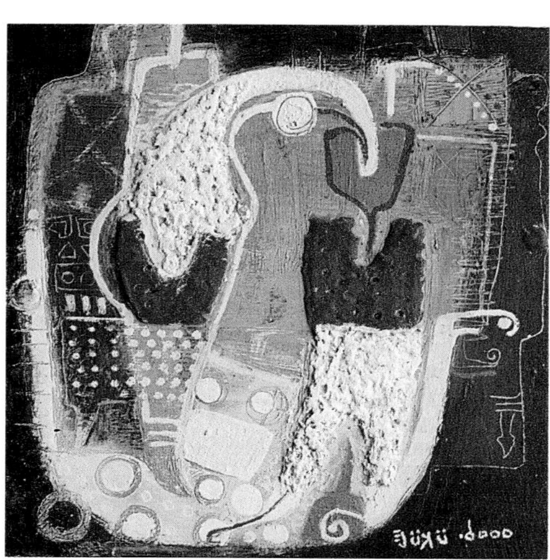

Ernest Dükü, "Who is crazy for who?," Ivory Coast,
©D.R.

Ndary Lô (born in 1961), 1999, Senegal
Biennal of Dakar 2000
©Revue Noire

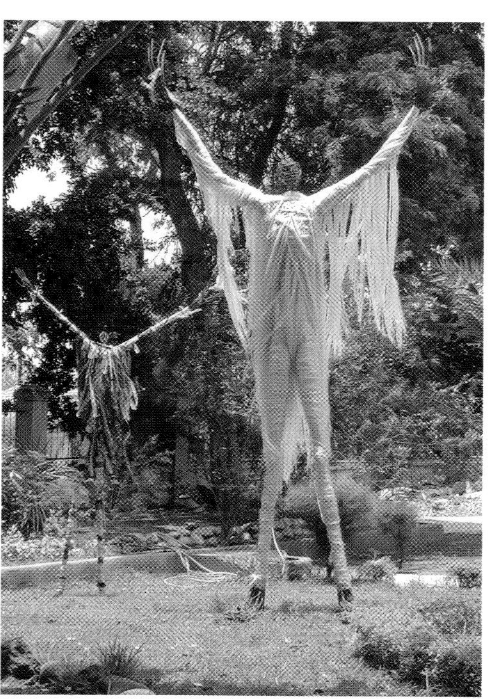

rich traditions of printmaking in Nigeria or South Africa. Rosemary Miles of the Victoria and Albert Museum, however, has been putting together a small but well-chosen collection of prints and drawing alongside its holdings of Black British material. Meanwhile, in London, the October Gallery and Art First Gallery have continuing programmes of contemporary art that includes Africa, the Gasworks Studios in Vauxhall offers residencies to artists from Africa, and the Horniman Museum has commenced a programme of contemporary exhibitions to complement their renewed ethnographic display.

Also among the more recent developments has been the willingness of the auction houses to sell 20th-century African art, which they had hitherto classified as having no commercial value. In June 1999 the contemporary art department of Sotheby's held its first sale of African material, and although it included a number of works by such major figures as David Koloane, Willie Bester, Cheri Samba, Frederic Bruly Bouabre, and Seydou Keita, much of the rest was just the kind of thing that gives "contemporary" African art a bad name. The reason for this is to be found in the peculiar status of that fifth direction of research and writing referred to earlier, concerning the makers of new forms of urban or "popular" arts. For a time, this work with its naive realism and wild imagery had become the acceptable face of a modern African art within the dominant art world, thereby privileging a supposed neo-primitivist expressionism and, as, a result, occluding its informed assessment.

This interpretation was given some authority by the extraordinary if now notorious Magiciens de la Terre exhibition at the Pompidou Center in 1989, when the African artists selected were proclaimed as self-taught visionaries, free of the constraints of the art academy. This material was seen by the Swiss photographer Jean Christophe Pigozzi who immediately wanted to buy it all. This he could not do as the material was already owned by others, so he asked the curator to make him another collection like it, and some of the collection that resulted was exhibited in the Canary Islands as Africa Hoy in 1991, and as Out of Africa at the Saatchi Gallery in London in 1992. Since then, Pigozzi's collection has been developed to include more overtly modernist figures such as Koloane and Keita even though his neo-primitivist preference has remained; and it was part of this collection that was for auction at Sotheby's in June 1999.

The problem here is that the basis for the collection and its interpretation is faulty. The artists represented in these three exhibitions were, with one exception (Bruly, truly a visionary) the products of a well-structured and tightly controlled apprenticeship system: the naive realism simply comes from copying advertisements. Moreover, the blatant imagery can sometimes be attributed to an attempt to fulfill the neo-primitivist expectations of a European patronage. Of course, some fine artists have emerged, Chéri Samba for example, but naive self-taught visionaries they are not; and their misappropriation as the acceptable face of a contemporary African art was the cause of great annoyance amongst that wider community of artists whose academic training had given them precisely that freedom to dream mistakenly attributed to the sign painters.

Also in 1991, the New York exhibition Africa Explores was an attempt to overcome this fractured view of the contemporary that had developed by including aspects of the full range of visual production. It was a brave attempt, vitiated, it seemed to me, first by a somewhat naive structuring of the work on show according to ready-made categories of the curator's invention ("traditional," "new functional," etc.), and second by the sheer impossibility of the enterprise itself given the diversity of current production. We saw fine work, but perhaps we learned only that we shall make better progress by concentrating our efforts upon detailed studies of particular places rather than attempting to "stitch up" an entire continent.

However, in September 2000, a second auction of modern African art was held in London, this time at Bonhams. The material was evidently drawn from several sources, as a result of which the range of work offered for sale was much better balanced including, indeed, a selection of rarely seen work by the very first sub-Saharan African artist to gain an international reputation, Ben Enwonwu. The National Museum for African Art in Washington, D.C. continued to register its interest by purchasing one of his paintings and one also by the Tanzanian painter Sam Nitro. In contrast, the British Museum was noted for its absence. This seemed like a small measure of progress towards establishing the proper international reception of 20th-century African art, and as such a fitting, if temporary, conclusion to this essay.

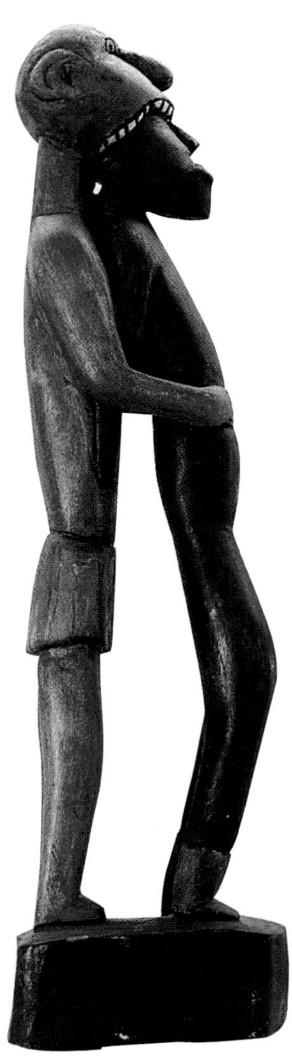

Zephania Tshuma (born in 1932), Zimbabwe

The illusion of interbreeding

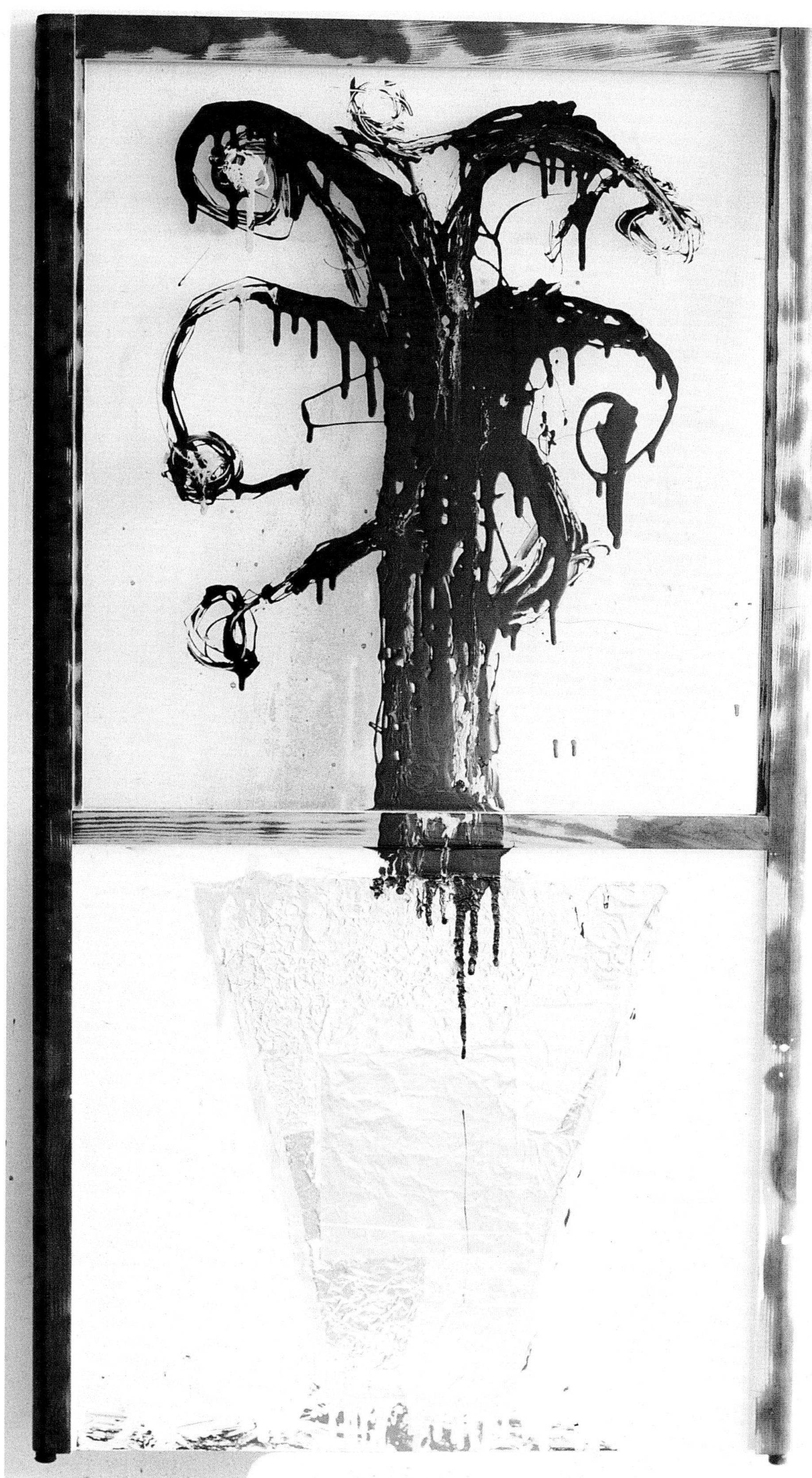

Bili Bidjocka

Bili Bidjocka was born in Cameroon in 1962. He has been living in Paris since 1974, where, after dance and theater, he enrolled at the Fine Arts School. For the past few years, he has considered art as an enigma. The answers provided by his teachers at the Fine Arts School, those certainties engraved in students' minds, have long been deemed insufficient. His confrontation with market laws, with history and with his own Africanity have all been elements that have forced him to look at art concepts in a new light. After trying his hand at painting, he moved towards doing stage productions and directing. His plays work like puzzles, enigmas throughout which he asks the essential question about the meaning and purpose of creation.

"Still Life"
80x160 cm

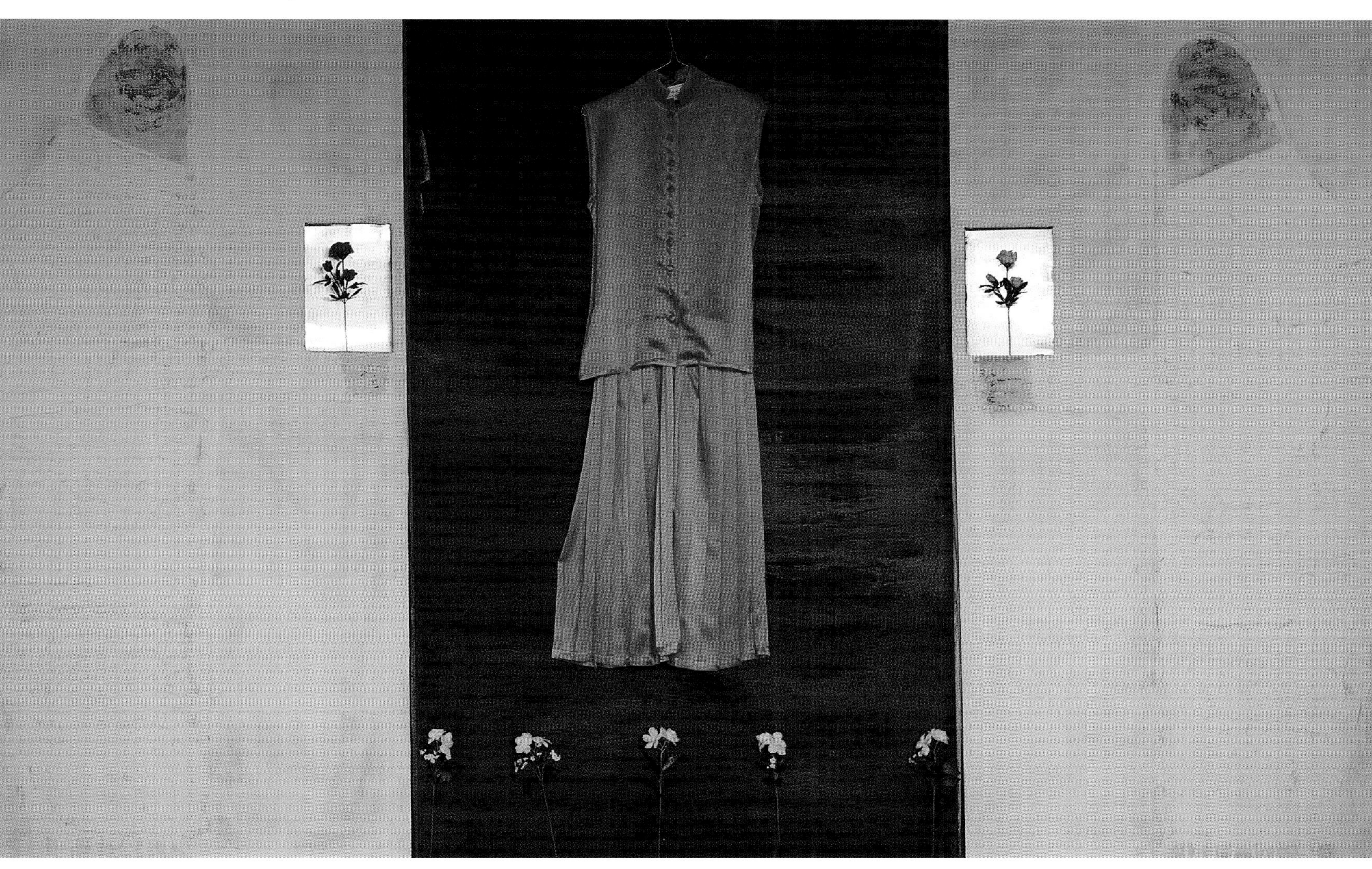

"Two monks making advances to a missing woman"
tryptic, 100x100x100x200 cm

Abdoulaye Konaté

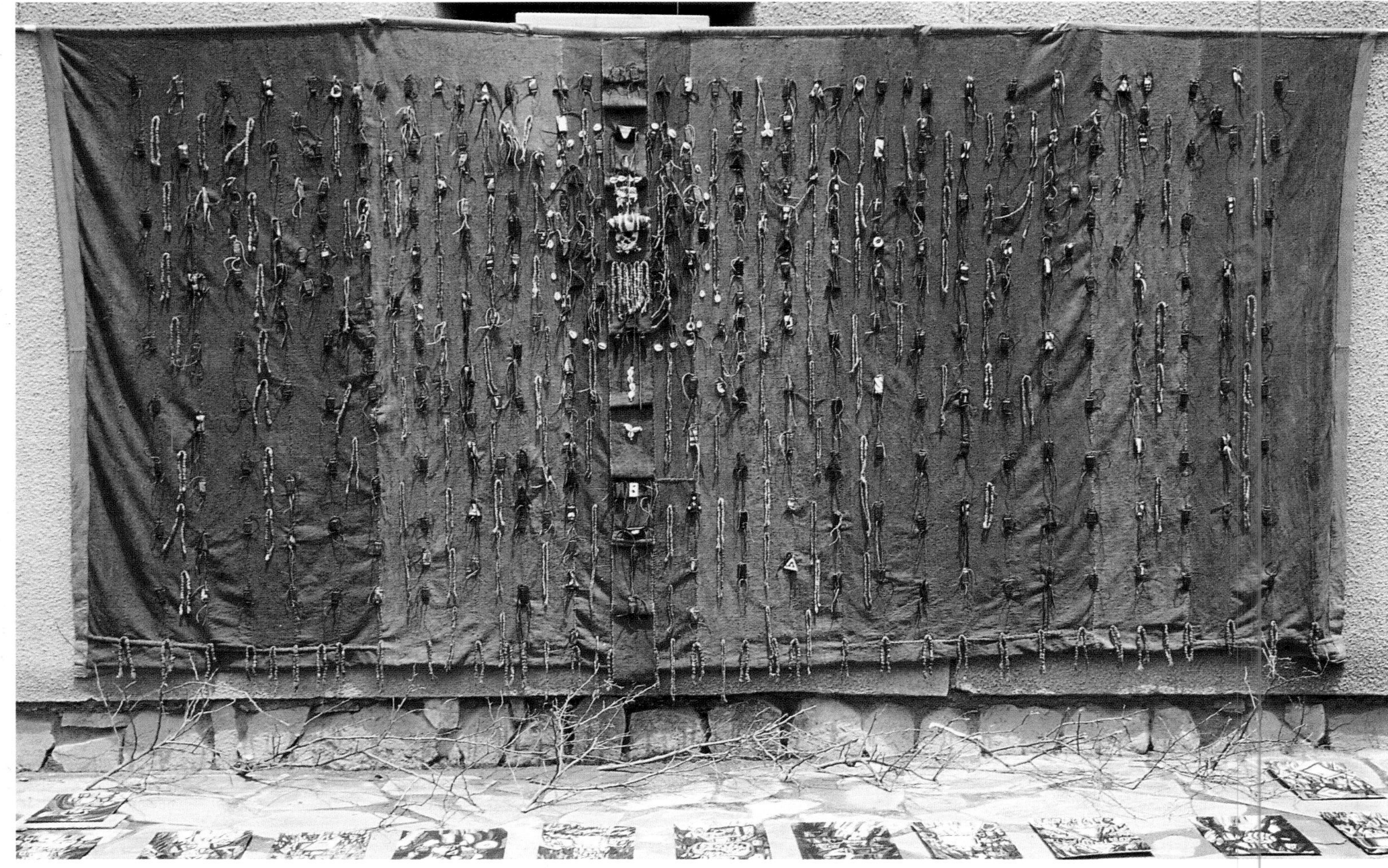

Abdoulaye Konaté was born in Mali in 1953. After studying at the Institut National des Arts of Mali, he went to the Institut Supérieur des Arts of Havana, Cuba. Upon his return to Mali, he became a graphic artist, then managed exhibits at the National Museum. In his work as a plastic artist, he mixes the signs and symbols of secret Malian societies on large raw cotton canvases, dyed with added elements (pieces of fabric, grigri, cowry beads). Concepts of productions take part in societal themes such as student revolts, Malian hunters or the Rwanda genocide.

"Hommage to the hunters of Mandé," 1994
800 x 200 cm.
©Alioune Bâ/Revue Noire

"Struggle against the VIH," 1995
400 x 200 x 120 cm.
©Alioune Bâ/Revue Noire

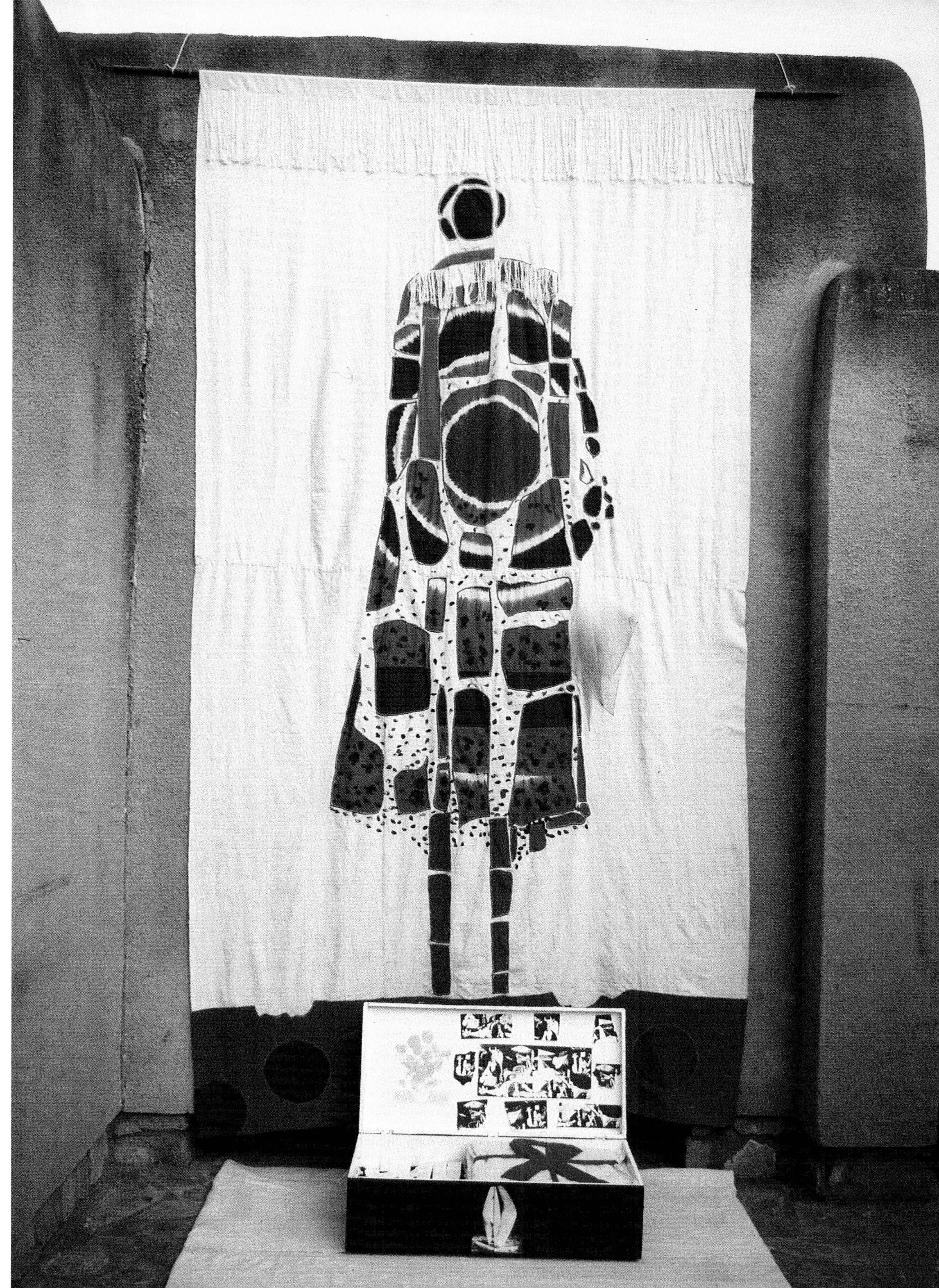

Sokari Douglas Camp

Sokari Douglas Camp was born in Nigeria in 1958. She graduated from the California College of Arts and Crafts in Oakland, USA, and from the Royal College of Art in London. Through her sculptures, she breathes new life into the characters of the ritual festivals in the Kalabari region of Nigeria. Living in London, she defies taboos, transcends the sacred and the secret with modern tools. Her mechanical "machines" are a concentration of Western technology and African spirituality, where the sounds and movements of her animated objects are mixed together.

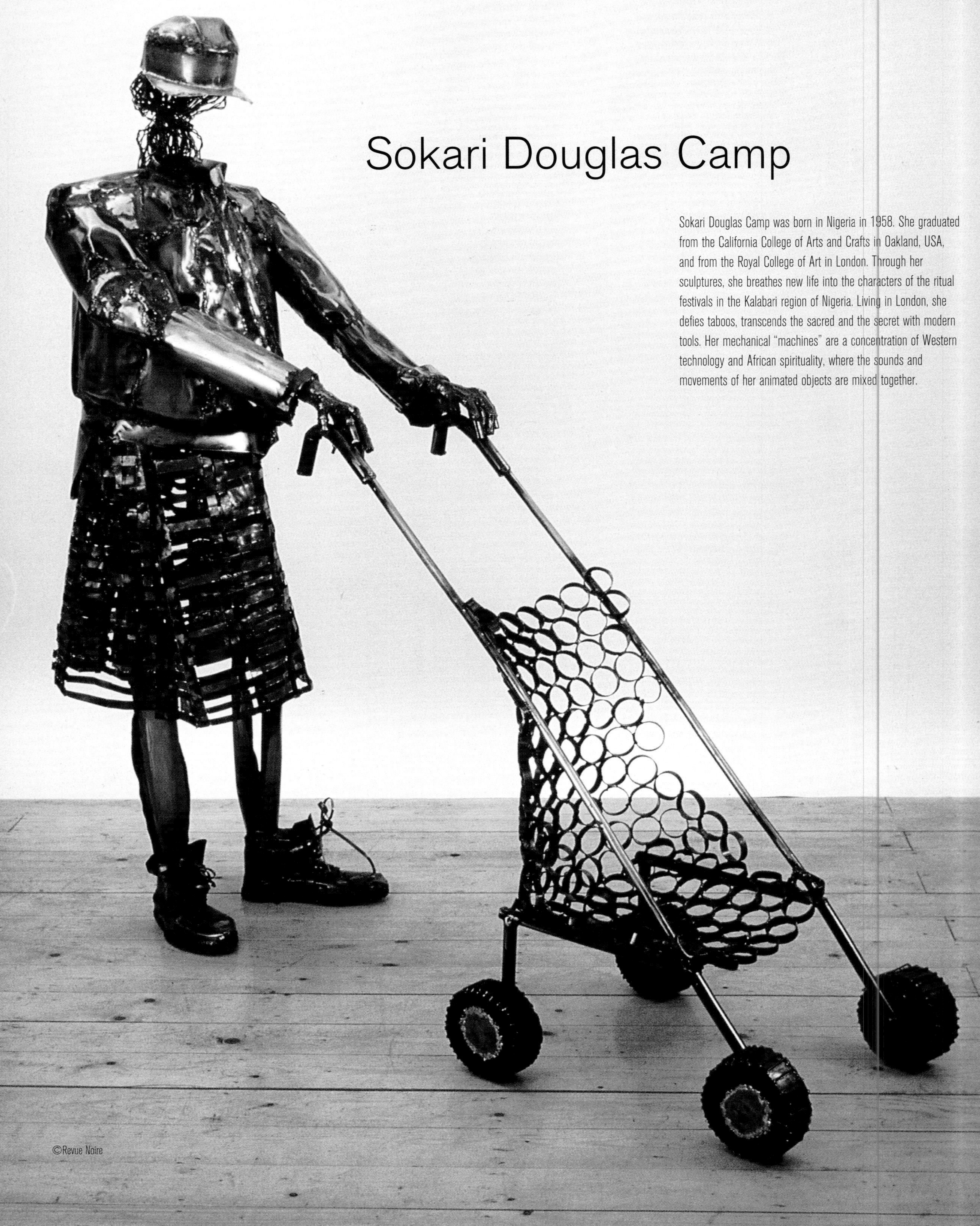

Owusu-Ankomah

Born in Ghana in 1956, Owusu-Ankomah studied at the College of Arts in Accra. He was exiled in Germany in 1986. His large, brightly colored paintings almost systematically represent silhouettes of naked men, covered with signs or scarifications. Using a mystical approach, it is not the savage man that is naked, but rather the individual freed of all of his certainties. The creation of his paintings is done guided by a transparency, a search for kinetic effects or the decomposition of light.

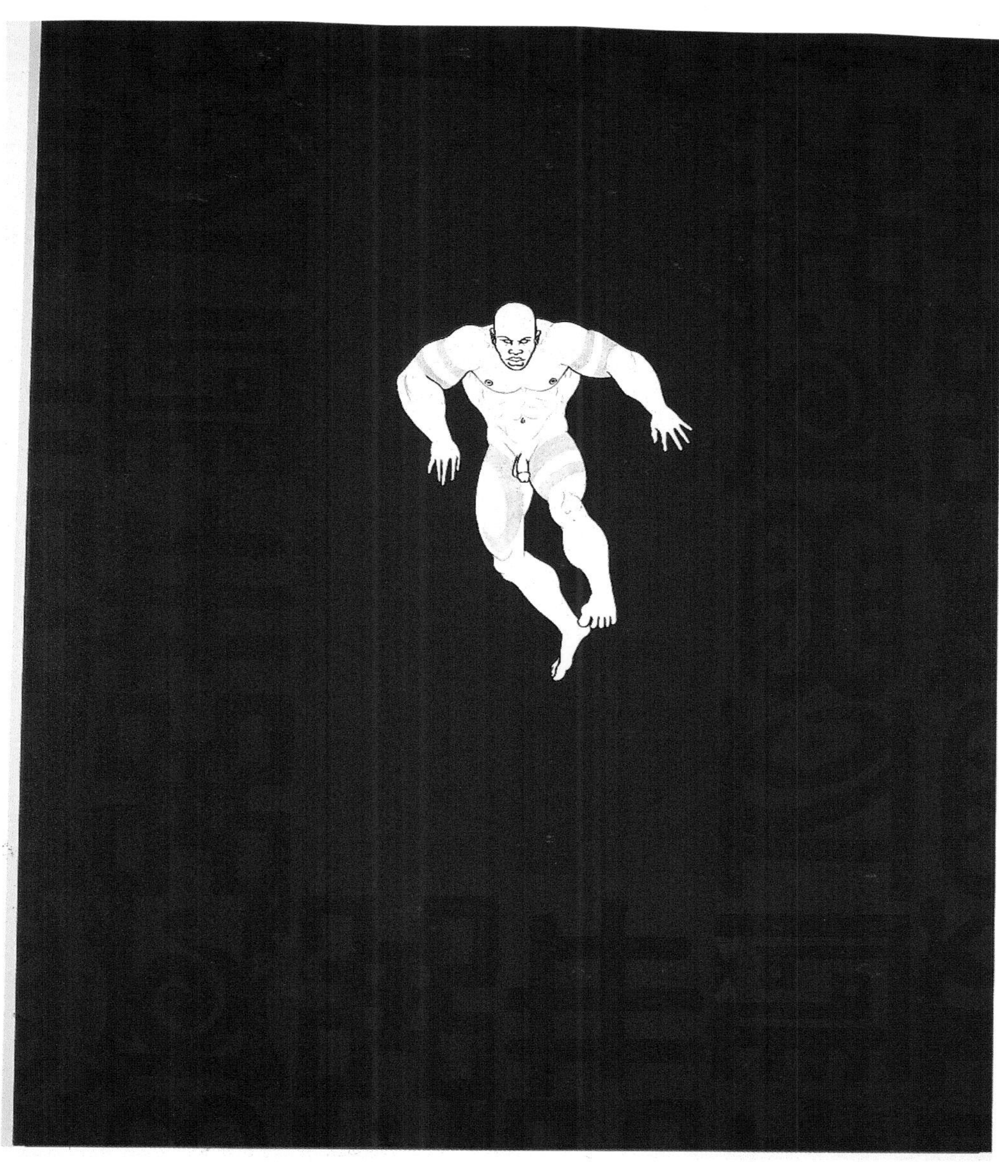

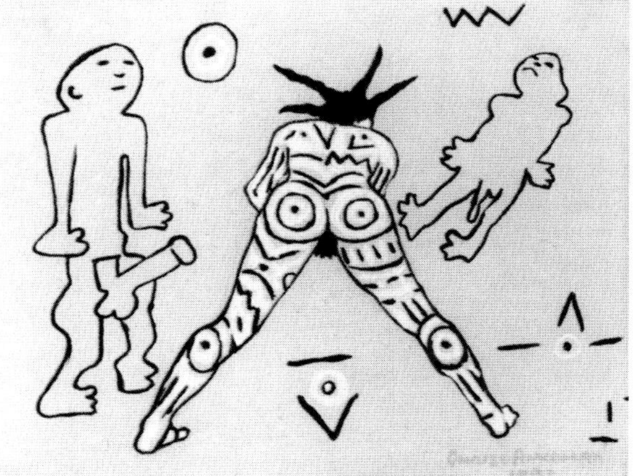

"Captive hero," 1997
180x150 cm.
©D.R.

"Erotica 1," 1993
24x30 cm.
©D.R.

THE GENDER OF AFRICAN ANGELS OR THE ILLUSION OF INTERBREEDING
Joëlle Busca

He is obviously an angel. Naked and with wings attached to his back. He does not, however, have that evanescent expression of an ephebe or the chubby look of an infant, suspended incredulously in mid-air.
Instead, this angel has a triangular-shaped face, with well-defined features, huge eyes, a mischievous mouth, a very well proportioned nose, and an Iroquois-style crest. Swaying in a discreetly human and – the context demands it – a terribly conciliatory gesture, he prepares to hide this virile limb that discredits his wings.
An Edo saltcellar from the 16th century, the fruit of the delicate and talented work of the inhabitants of Ivory Coast from the ancient kingdom of Benin. It was commissioned by the Portuguese and, without distorting them, combines an entire range of decorative figures and elements both identifiable and already melted into a work of art. Let me use Ezio Bassani's[1] explanations: knights dressed in a baroque style, heavily armored and armed in the European way, with Bini designs of tracery and diamond shapes, strips of granules inspired by Manueline architecture, leaf-shaped horse ears, etc. It is a garden of vastly diverse esthetic signs.
The Renaissance period also introduced Europe to meticulously worked ivory. This material was not unknown on the continent at this time, when backers are curious, political relations are harmonious, trade is fruitful, there are fair exchanges between ambassadors and goods, and plastic solutions intermingle.
African artists would adorn objects of typical European functionalism with figures characteristic of their perception of the Portuguese, and, in return, European backers would accept this expressive game within limits marked by the notorious sexualization of the angel, which still maintained its role of link between two worlds.
We should see this work of art for what it is: an artist's consent to a foreign request, still peaceful at the time.
The systemized colonization that would follow, and the cultural upheavals that ensued, led to African artists being seen as skilled workers, at best, and artisans reduced to reproducing the same artifacts ad aeternam, at worst.
The introduction of materials, techniques, forms and demand imposed a production that was quite often artistic only in name. This included a series of Shona sculptures in Zimbabwe, the abusive use of the Mali Bogolan, street painters in the Democratic Republic of Congo or epigones from the Paris School in West Africa.
Although a few particularly gifted figures appeared, they were exceptions, and included a surprising plastic trip, a fascinating connection between the sculptures of Henry Munyaradzi, the "Tambula Man," from 1971, and pre-Columbian figures. The Zimbabwean sculptor was initiated at the workshops of the Frank McEwen School in Salisbury, Harare, who was himself influenced by the statuary style of Henry Moore. The latter, confronted with a taste for Mayan sculpture, found, in this sculpture, the inspiration for formal solutions that migrated until the era of this great sculptor Henry Munyaradzi.

Lisbon inaugurated a new subway station for the 1998 Universal Exposition. Its promoters invited some ten artists from all over the world to design a permanent work based on the unifying theme of the oceans, mostly in the form of ceramic wall panels. Abdoulaye Konaté designed a sea in the background, filled with fish, from which emerge, like unreal mermaids, three musical birds, appearing both limpid and deafening. These were splendidly universal beings, not established in any particular place and speaking a language understood by all.
At a time when he intended to express the universal, Abdoulaye Konaté rediscovered the crucial figures of his work from the 80s. He forgot the heavy, evocative symbolism of the installations and recalled the period when he was studying in Cuba, where, after the National Institute of Art (1972-1976) in Bamako, he came to develop himself as a painter (1978-1985). There, he discovered a language, culture, landscape, art history, art histories and

Aboudramane (born in 1961), Ivory Coast
©Revue Noire

[1] Receptacles - Dapper Museum - 1997 - p.258 and 261

Colleen Madamombe (born in 1964), "Traditional greetings," Zimbabwe, 1998

©Peter Fernandes

heterogeneous practices.

He painted forests of man-birds, musicians with human, animal, and plant shapes all at once. He then proceeded with the metaphoric replacement of the face of the musician, who had become a bird and calabash. At the same time, the image that was a bird and a calabash disguised itself as a musician's musical instrument. He summoned the mythical hornbill and metamorphosed it into a fabulous bestiary. He borrowed poetics from the marvelous real world of Alejo Carpentier. Combining magic and reality, the image emerged with a happy dramatic quality and the transformation of clement nature to the point of altering its components in order to perfect its interrelationship with humans. A baroque-type fantasy and reality, an osmosis between different worlds.

In three gouaches from 1987, the human face is divided into profiles resembling Tyi-Wara crests, the antelope heads of that initiatory Bamana society that reveres the sacred values of agrarian fertility, mixing the cubist method of the portraits of Wifredo Lam and the more realistic profiles of a 1942 painting titled "Your own life."

In Cuba, he discovered the work of one of the greatest painters of modern times: Wifredo Lam. For Abdoulaye Konaté, this work represented an extremely solid base on which to construct his own building and a springboard from which to launch himself. He made discoveries and worked. He admired his elder's work as the invention of a formal and graphic grammar, as a lesson in freedom and respect for classical forms, whether or not Western. The knowledge gained from African geometric art, cubism, negritude, surrealism, occultism, Chinese philosophy, the New York avant-garde movement of the 40s, Cobra and the Paris School flooded him like an already established echo of his artistic concerns. What affects him in Wifredo Lam's work is this spirit of independence towards anatomy, the recourse to an unobstructed analogy of the literal nature of quotations, the obstinacy of obvious ties, the power of surpassing oneself, the lesson of formal liberation and the dynamism of the compositions.

The Cuban painter was familiar with the African traditions still enduring in the West Indies, such as Haitian voodoo, the struggle against Francoism or Hitlerism, modernity, and a heterogeneous family history. André Breton attributed to him a path leading from the primitive to modernity, unlike the path taken by Pablo Picasso.

Wifredo Lam destabilized the distinctions between atavistic and composite culture established by Edouard Glissant. He shattered the negativity of the atavistic concept and shifted the place and limits of the composite. He was also a man from the West Indies, Europe, Asia and Africa. His origins could not be traced back to the bottom of a slave boat. He was not a man condemned by birth into exile. He was born in Cuba and lived here and there. He passed through different places without wreaking havoc. None of the words relating to the idea of interbreeding applied to Wifredo Lam. He truly filled this idea dear to Edouard Glissant with a diversity that protects and perpetuates, with the power of archipelago-based thought, with constantly changing relationships between people, and with the absence of fear of the world. He produced an esthetic of the Relationship, a visual metaphor of connection. It would be absolutely wrong to justify Wifredo Lam's work based on his family origins and travels. And according to Ulrich Krempel,[2] he himself would not want this.

He had a prodigious mastery of the pictorial surface, developed and gave life to images through very sound drawing and color. It was above all his desire, talent and imagination that produced this work. His career was a labyrinth of encounters between beings, objects, paintings and texts. He used mainly poetry, and his work was a vibrant poetry of the universe, if one does not attempt to fruitlessly decode the origin of the different signs. He found his own solutions to bring his worlds together.

He sought to "communicate a psychic state"[3] by painting the artistic process, because art undergoes perpetual change.

Wifredo Lam and Abdoulaye Konaté both have rich traditions. They have the ability to sublimate forms, signs and symbols that have already been around the block. Abdoulaye Konaté took over from

[2] Ulrich Krempel - Wifredo Lam - Lelong Gallery - 1988 - p.13

[3] Max Pol Foucher - Wifredo Lam - Editions Cercle d'art 1976 - p.198

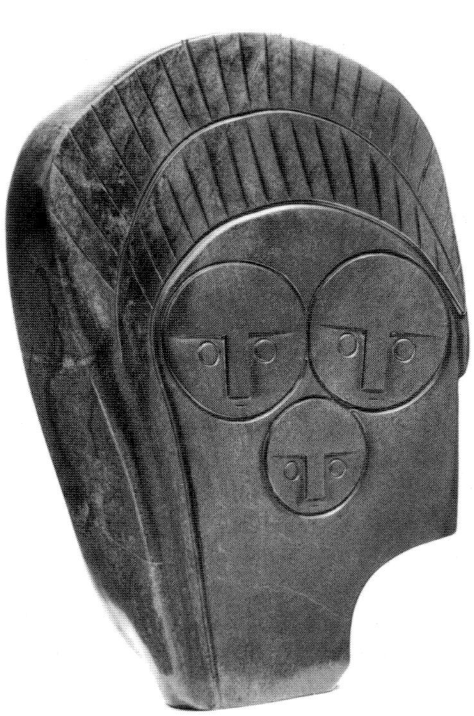

Henry Munyaradzi (born in 1931), "Family under a Palm Tree," 1996
©Peter Fernandes

Wifredo Lam and has succeeded in capturing an echo that can be understood by both the painter and the African, and that is in line with historical, continental, pictorial, ethic and formal continuity.

The word interbreeding in inappropriate for restoring the richness of exchanges specific to artistic practice.
The issue of interbreeding in art must be addressed in an absolutely radical manner. The common antonym to all words relating to this notion is purity, and this is enough to absolutely eliminate this concept from the artistic field. It is a convenient metaphor because it is vague.[4] There is no need to spend one more moment on this postcolonial and postmodern rhetoric.

Interbreeding does not exist because there is no certainty that the artist's identity will be revealed prior to his creation. Identity does not establish a fate. In order to move towards freedom, a concept inherent in artistic creation, identity-related markers must be overcome and limits must be tested against the desire to exhaust and to master it after having delved into every corner of its territory, where violence is obvious. Purity is a fantastical vision that assumes that the "Other" is completely separated from an "I" that is inaccessible by nature. Interbreeding is confused with reality. If we were to qualify all art as impure and just move on to the works, we would still be as far away from what is called "cultural interbreeding," which leads to a prescriptive and soothing international culture of merely postmodernism that continues to produce eclectic and powerless works, a hodgepodge of remains, with, as its sole outlook, the "déjà vu" inherent in the "everything has already been done."

The question "is art miscible" appears to be groundless, unless one advocates an authenticity not subject to disruption. There are fundamental dynamics at play in creation that push aside all ideas of absolute coherence: a heraclitism, an irrepressible desire for movement. A work occurs at a moment in social, political, personal, subjective history, a moment in the history of art, forms and ideas, if we consider that the time of images is not linear. The true continuity of a History with a composite and polysemous nature resides in the uncertain, in metamorphosis and precariousness.
If the world is none other than the "great perpetual swing," according to Michel de Montaigne, namely an eternal swing, something both fastened and forced to move back and forth, subjecting it, in whole or in divided fields, to being sorted in order to locate, isolate and name elements that may establish a taxonomy, is as delicate as it is vain, because that would simply mean referring each sign to a pure and microcosmic home among cohorts of criteria for belonging or exclusion. If I were to refer to a philosopher, it would be Jacques Derrida and his configuration of hospitality.

A determinist reading of the genesis of the works and events of the artistic world is not enough to understand their plan and meaning. If a work must be interpreted in the context of the local art in which it was created, we should not forget to include it in a vast whole, a global artistic space. The world offers an inexhaustible collection of all types of signs from which everyone and anyone may freely draw. Let us first look at the theory according to which art is impossible outside a planetary point of view, not as a globalized and standardized idiom, but as a potentiality, an openness that breaks with stereotypes, a movement and renewal of the terms of debate, an unforeseeable configuration of combinations, no synthesis or renunciation, just dynamism.

Three artistic strategies are foreseeable. Assimilation calls for adhesion to the dominant international model, the world culture. The exclusive claim of an original specificity transforms artists into standard-bearers of their original culture. The last attitude is autonomy. Artists free themselves from local circumstances and a hegemonic model in order to gain access to sovereign esthetics subject to the contradictory forces of standardization and ultra-individual appropriation. We move from the sociological influence to an esthetic position, from anthropological study to the analysis of works, from a

[4] Serge Gruzinski - La pensée métisse - Fayard - 1999

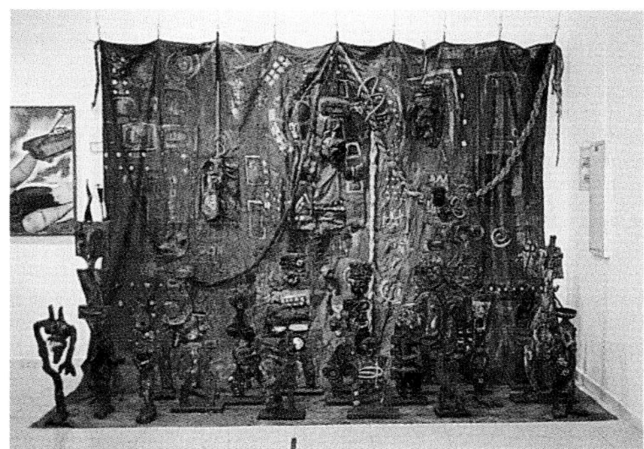

Dominique Zinkpe (born in 1969), "A Question of Identity," 1997, Benin
©Ananias Léki Dago

Hervé Yamguen (born in 1971), Cameroon, 2000
acrylic on canvas, 60x81 cm.
©Olivier Percheron/Doual'Art

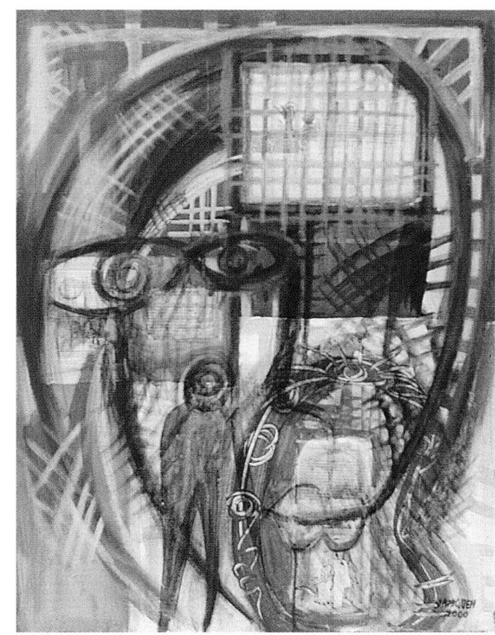

local and/or dominated undertaking to a universal adventure that includes the entire possible future of all plastic forms. The universal prohibits treating local culture in the way the colonizer considers conquered peoples, namely as natives, small things confined to a very small territory. The author is the predominant figure who discovers the world for the spectator and for himself. He organizes and hosts operations of change and erosion between various esthetic economies.

To whom do the dresses of Bili Bidjocka belong? Formal African atavism, the sublime Amratian-style Egyptian predynastic statuette (5000-4000 B.C.) that now welcomes visitors to the African rooms at the Louvre, is very close. Many Fang, Mumuye, Igbo or Mossi statues contain these unfailing qualities, these hieratic forms and the smoothness of caryatids. I could, with the same success, find analogies in "Women From Antiquity," which Anselm Kiefer included in his last exhibit at the Yvon Lambert Gallery (Paris, December 1999). A similar rapture was carried out on hordes of headless, timeless, theatrical, anonymous, yet real beings. For the spectator, the same feeling of ruin unites them. The silhouette, more so than the body, is a stencil of contemporary art. Where does Bili Bidjocka find his dresses? What is African in his works? From a long and remarkable stylistic and metaphoric work ensues a completely new work of art that breaks with all stereotypes of African and contemporary art. It frees the spectator's outlook because he is spared the climb, because a new world is delivered to him through a universal standard.

Theodor W. Adorno and Marx Horkheimer[5] define mass culture as a fabric of stereotypes, i.e. capable of taking up, by neutralizing them, ideas such as the idea of Creolization, and making them into a Benetton-like advertising slogan that makes the clothing industry out to be a project to humanize humanity.[6] Instrumentalized as a planetary means of communication, art is irresistibly drawn to cultural anthropology. Therefore, all that matters is the existence, as such, of a visual content – regardless of its qualitative nature – capable of moving about and being present everywhere at the same time. Global communication and the acceptance of the pluralism of artistic identity appeared at the same time. Was this by chance or out of necessity? However, minds do not open up as quickly as the information highways.

Cultural confrontation existed as soon as two "strangers" met. Thinking about the world in this light means including movement, withdrawal and reception within an egalitarian view of cultures, of their right to exist in their diversity, and to participate, despite not only their content, but also their different structures, in the common heritage of humanity. This is not referred to as a standardization or abolition of barriers, but it stands against iconic internationalism. Peter Brook built his theater on the idea that no human or culture holds the entire truth. By discovering spiritual ties everywhere, man submits his artistic practice to this friendship.

Kwesi Owusu-Ankomah paints bodies of naked men and Adinkra symbols. In 1986, Keith Haring, in a performance entitled "Coffee table," covered an entire room and his whitened body with abstract and hazardous signs. He was naked, perched on his coffee table, in a fighting stance. Enter Paul Klee, international decoration and parody. The artist from Ghana reveals the metaphoric and sensitive presence of his culture of origin in his work, whereas the hero of the New York stage, through similar types of signs, is ironic about the primitive-type quest of our advanced societies. But, together, they state the primordial importance of body marking.
Creation in an individual affair nourished by the world, without any debarment.

Toni Negri positions what he calls the Empire's counterattack (postcolonial (ethnic) cleansing, in politically correct language) between advertising and meteorology[7] and I fear that art, relatively speaking, is headed for a similar fate.

The question imperiously asked by liberal society, at a time when art is suffering from a lack of definition, from a proliferating and distorting hybridization, in which its identity is painfully confronted

5 Theodor W. Adorno - Marx Horkheimer - La dialectique de la raison - Fragments philosophiques - 1994
6 Paolo Landi - Oui, nous sommes des précurseurs - Le Monde - 29 mars 2000
7 Point d'ironie - No. 13 - June 1999

Kan-Sy (born in 1961), 1994, Senegal
©Bouna Medoune Seye/Revue Noire

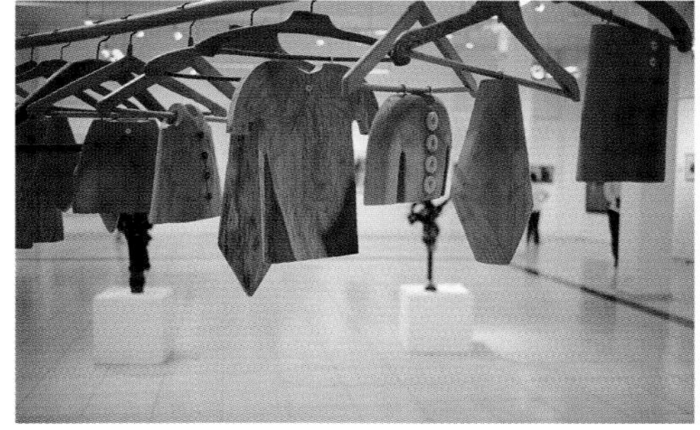

Barthélémy Toguo Tamokoné (born in 1967), "Wardrobe," 1997, Cameroon
©Ananias Léki Dago/Revue Noire

with contemporaneousness, appears to be terribly trivial: what does plastic art have to offer the world? Works? Events? Amusement parks? The proliferation of large-scale social events (biennials, universal expositions, etc.) has led the transformation of artistic facts into a technical, logistical and financial performance, where ludic and relational aspects are privileges. These international events mobilize budgets and technical means that keep African artists at bay from the onset. When they have access to such exhibits, they are displayed as a concept by ethnologists or scenic artists of the context, prisoners between alibis and instruments, but never considered as contemporary artists.
The multiplication of art centers that could guarantee independence and non-submission to an unequivocal doctrine, the replacement of an imperial and irremovable doctrine in favor of networks whose characteristics are recognized by mobility, the absence of hierarchy, encounters, and incessant communication, are done for the benefit of the spectator and the compulsory presence of signs recognizable by the largest number.

Interbreeding may be what the Western spectator accepts and encourages by deviance from the canon. That is, the production of a certain number of exotic, folkloric signs, on a globally legible background medium that does not place the spectator out of place, in matter or in manner. It should provide a deliciously surprising effect, not a defeat, in spite of the most elementary ethic rules, in favor of mimetic practices, literal appropriations and pretences of authenticity.

Sokari Douglas Camp is fully aware of the aura that surrounds the blacksmith in numerous African cultures, and the artist in the West. And his wives, as they push along baby strollers, know everything about Pablo Picasso, the sculptor. This aura skillfully mixes techniques, subjects, forms and materials coming alternatively or jointly from Africa and/or Europe. The Kalabari dancers may be animated by an engine and supermarket carts can be strengthened by African-style welding, because we are dealing with works of art. The ideal African artist would be the nomadic artist, the political refugee born in Kinshasa, living between his workshops in New York and Amsterdam, entirely devoured by his constituent problems of identity and exposed/hidden works at the specialized "Camouflage" gallery in Brussels. Admirably alone, to the point of being paranoid. Can the art of insult be labeled camouflage? The camouflage of what, art or Africanity? Who is being disguised? What is the coding, for blurring what? Unless it is a war, and works and artists must be hidden from the enemy. These are apparently cruel but real dilemmas for certain people, for artists whose only creative resort is their cultural difference, which for them is a situation of tension, precariousness and instability.

Barthélémy Toguo offers spectators a cock and bull voyage into a "Spiral Land" (Migrators – ARC – Musée d'art moderne de la ville de Paris – 1999) inspired by the absurdity of mental, relational and territorial borders. The artistic identity of this Cameroon native living in Germany is based on the movement and passage of limits. He acts as both subject and narrator of a work described as interactive, ecological and communicational. This exclusively identity-related project constitutes an esthetic impasse and places the artist in a dramatic setting with an African outline, filled with social and moral anecdotes. All daily events feed his creative process. He incessantly recombines and works his productions in different situations, mixing together the past, present and future, like a Fluxus movement, in which he plays the role of transmitter, mediator and receiver. A supplier of images without any hierarchy ("Labyrinth Process" 1999), he is the one who, when faced with unknown signals, is able to establish self-defense strategies that appear as communication actions. As the originator of operations of "Transit" – the title of a series of performances – he decides upon the conditions for passing the borders, by making things particularly difficult for customs agents who want to open the massive wooden suitcases and check their content. He questions access, art and social life codes and brings together very different realities. He places himself in a no-man's land where he manages to bring together many different worlds.

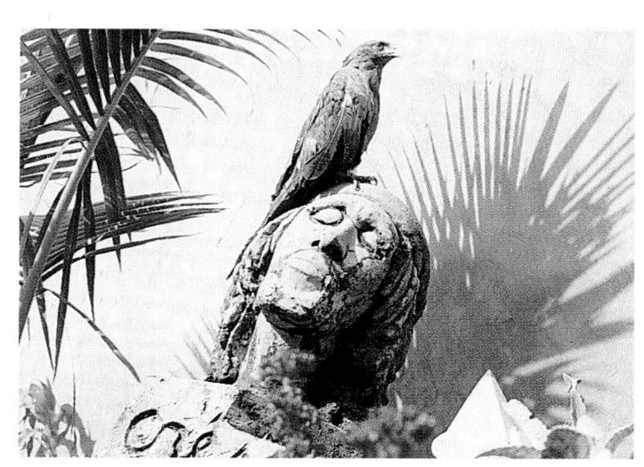

Babacar Sedikh Traoré (born in 1956), Senegal

©Bouna Medoune Seye/Revue Noire

Today, African plastic arts are not experiencing a great collective utopia. Most artistic activity in Africa appears in the form of false localism, worldism conditioned by a Western outlook, and suffering from delays and repetitions. Must one choose between cautious markets and liberal capitalism, and the politically correct refuge of postcolonial ethnology, seen as the only place where differences and identity can exist? No. Esthetics and geopolitics are not destined to agree.

Art, no matter which field of art, whether spatial or temporal, is a permanent transit of challenges and crossroads: encounters, divisions, games, unpredictability, grafts, overlapping, shifts, movements, muddling, borrowings, at the risk of deception, repetition, weariness, rejection, crushing, blundering, accidents, inextricability, theft. It is a zapping or patch-work, in favor of new forms and contents, masterpieces, under which lies a powerful link to ancient conceptual and iconographic sites, coupled with an intense relationship with a maximum number of various cultural areas, in order to open up horizons of freedom to art. Interbreeding is merely an agreement, a submission to a diktat. The ethics that state that artists are independent and open is the sole basis for evaluation and spares the confusion between artists and doers.

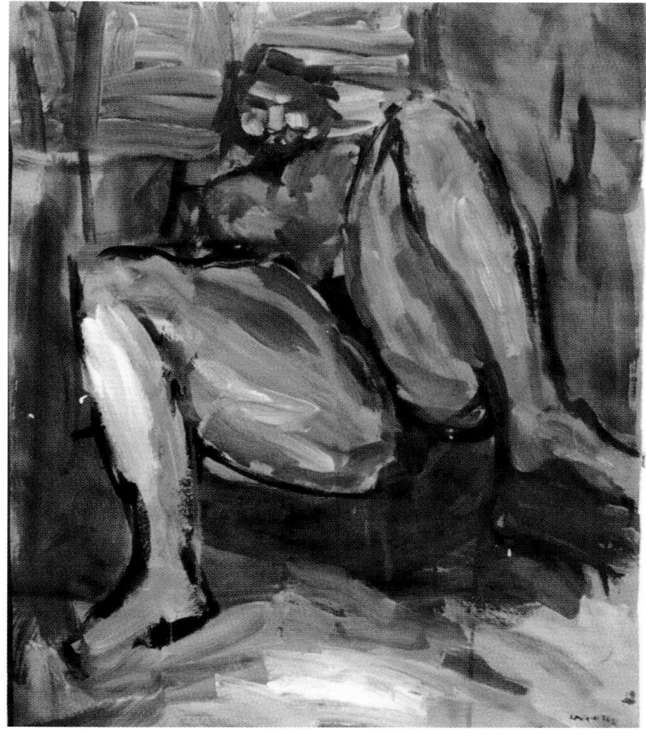

Luis Mecque (1966-1998) , "Nude," 1997, Zimbabwe

©Alan Allen

Art and style

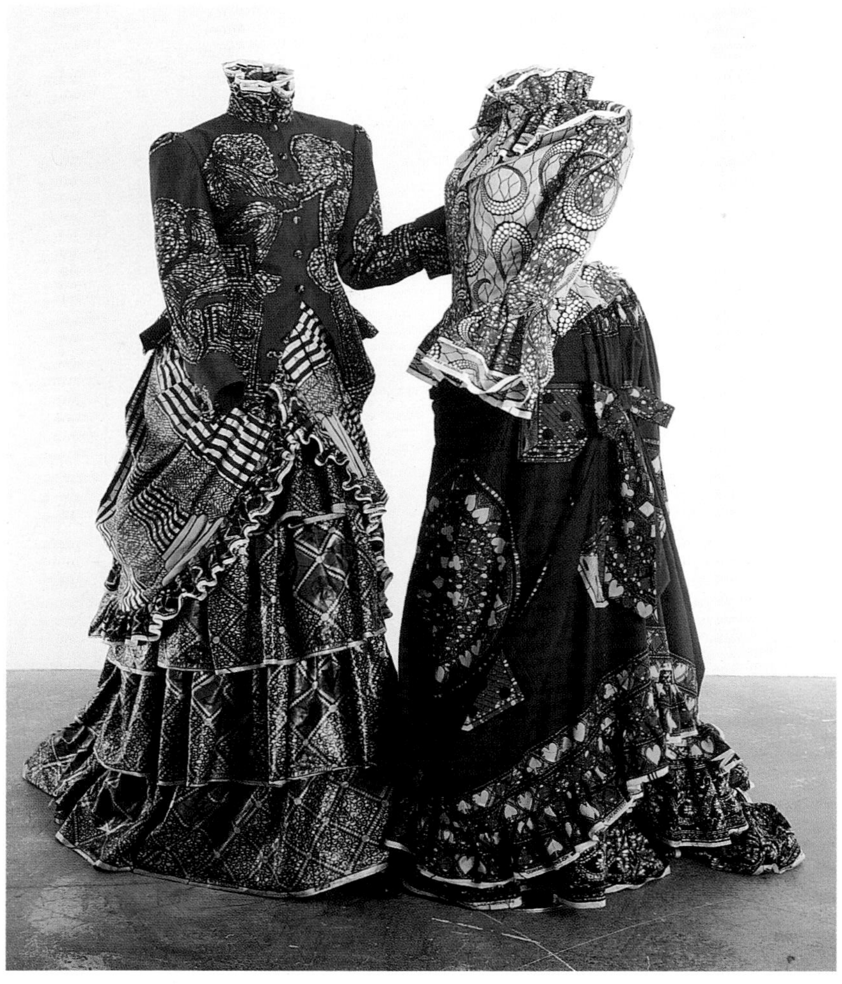

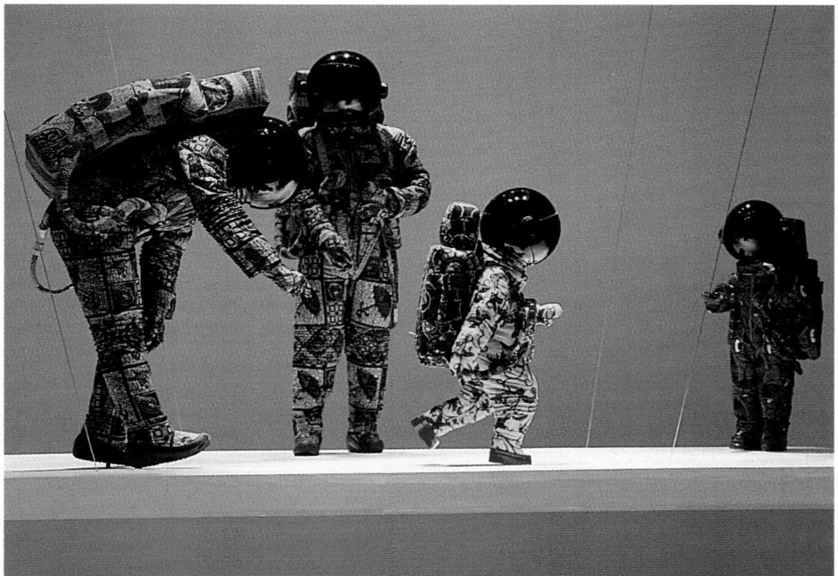

Yinka Shonibare

Yinka Shonibare was born to Nigerian parents in England in 1962. In his work (photographs and productions) he uses humor to explore the archetypes of Victorian England by using Dutch fabric (wax), a popular symbol of African identity.

Models, dandies, cosmonauts and extraterrestrials covered in wax remind us of our own vision of modernity through the prism of History. Shonibare pushes the notion of cultural identity to extremes through the use and juxtaposition of images and frames of Africa and the West.

"Gay Victorians," 1999
wax, 165x63,5x106,5 cm / 165x73,5x109 cm.
©Stephen White, courtesy Stephen Friedman Gallery

"Vacation," 2000
wax, 152,5x61x61 cm / 152,5x61x61 cm
101,6x61x61 cm / 101,6x61x61 cm
coll. Hanz Bogatzke ©Stephen White, courtesy Stephen Friedman Gallery

facing page:
"The swing (In the fashion of Fragonard)," 2001
wax, mannequin, swing, leaves
c.a. 330x350x220 cm.
©Stephen White, courtesy Stephen Friedman Gallery

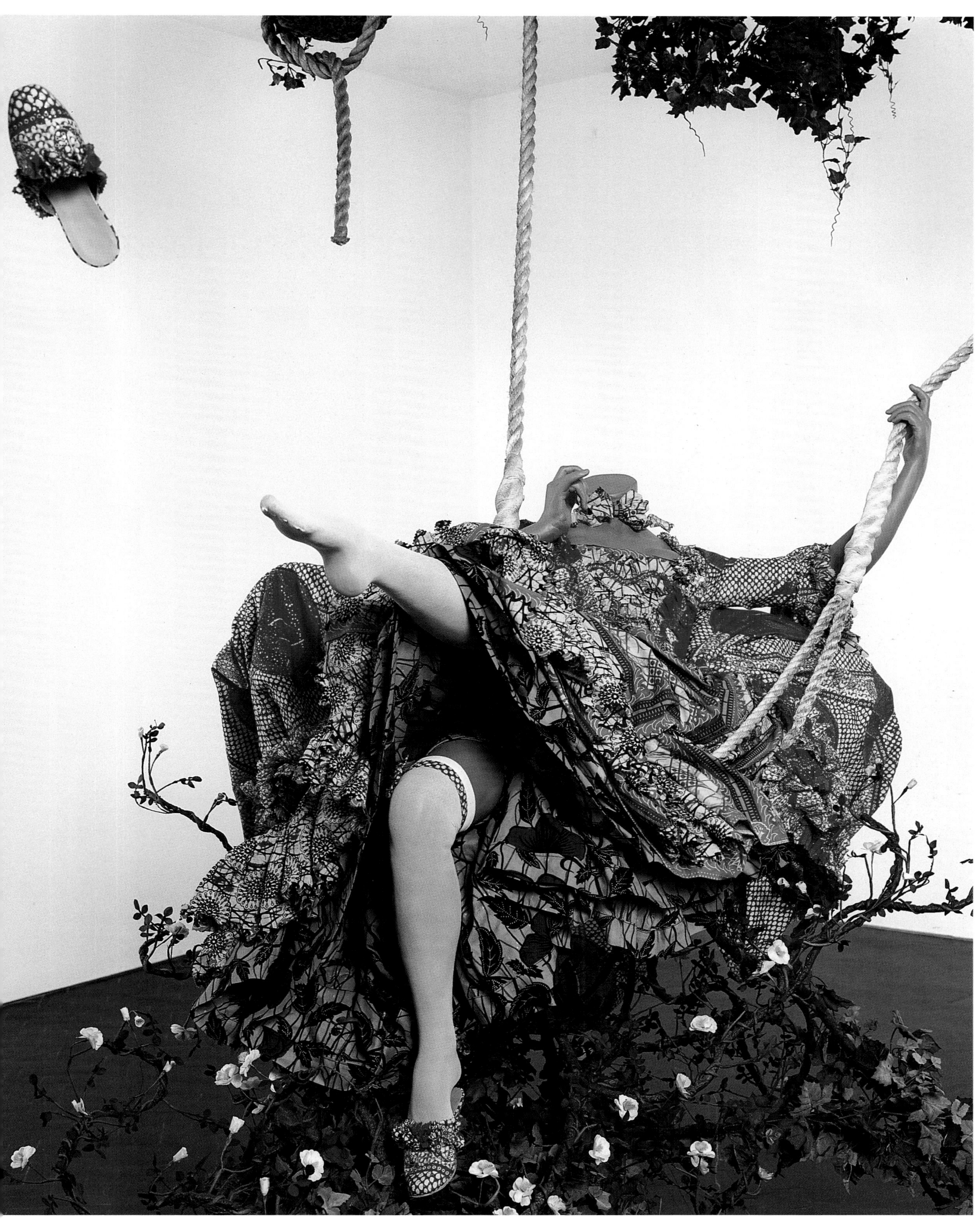

Fernando Alvim Faria

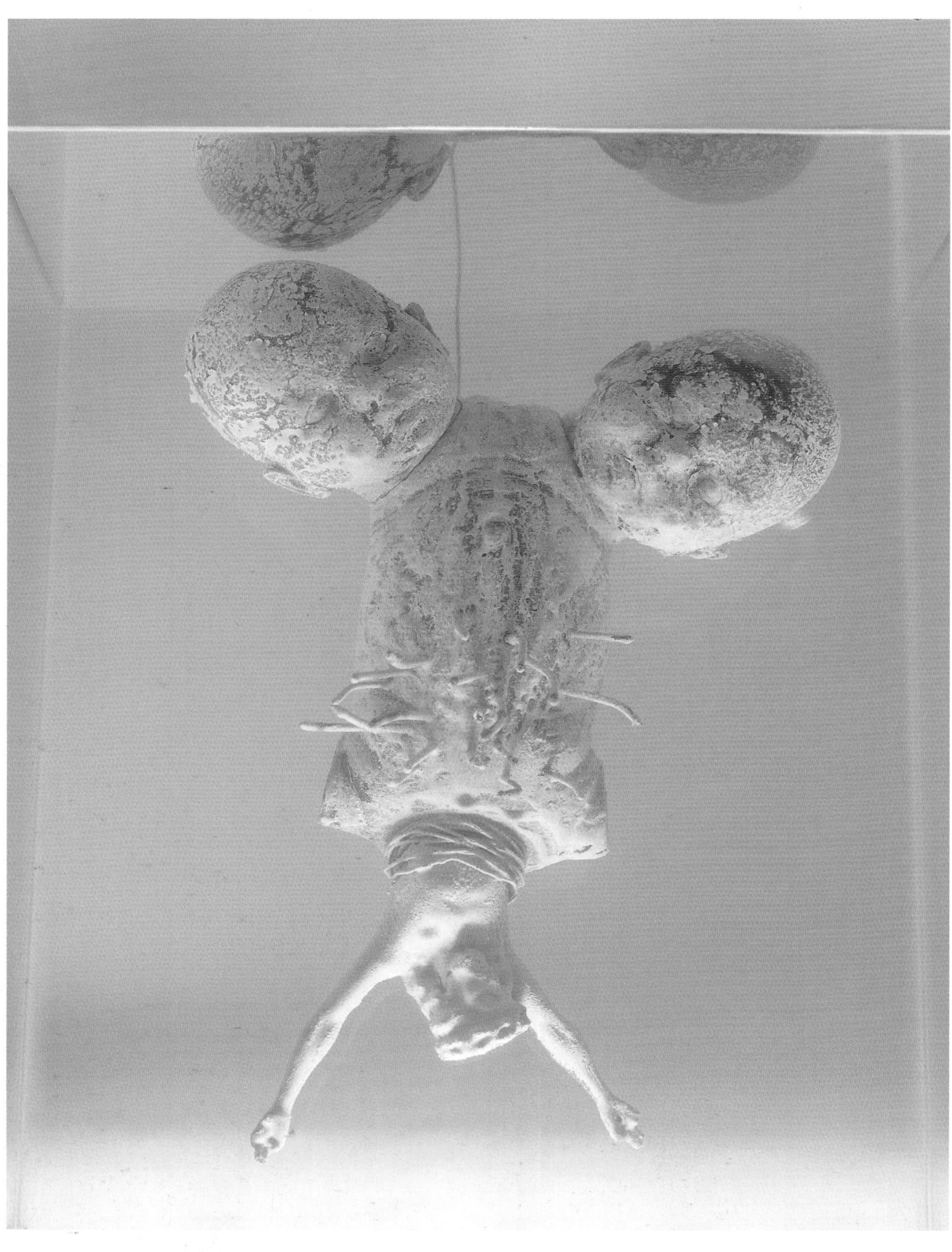

"Detail of Difumbe," 1998
©Roger Wooldridge

facing page:
"Amnesia," 1998
©Roger Wooldridge

Fernando Alvim Faria, a self-taught artist born in Luanda in 1963, had the ambition, through his pictorial work from the late 80s and early 90s, to obtain and recycle the texts from the graffiti on the walls of Luanda neighborhoods. He was able to gather them by inventing a writing style filled with popular slang and several languages (Kimbundu, Portuguese and English) and combining them in an indistinct and ambiguous cocktail of multiple allusions to the sociopolitical and cultural realities of Angola.
Basing himself on various multimedia facilities, and with his project Memórias Intimas Marcas (Intimate Marks of Memories), begun in 1997, Alvim has attempted to examine the war issue and its consequences on the cultural memory of the people, by visiting, together with the South African artist Gavin Younge and the Cuban Carlos Garaicoa, the historical town of Kuito Kuanavale, the stage of one of the most unforgettable and bloody battles of the Angola war.

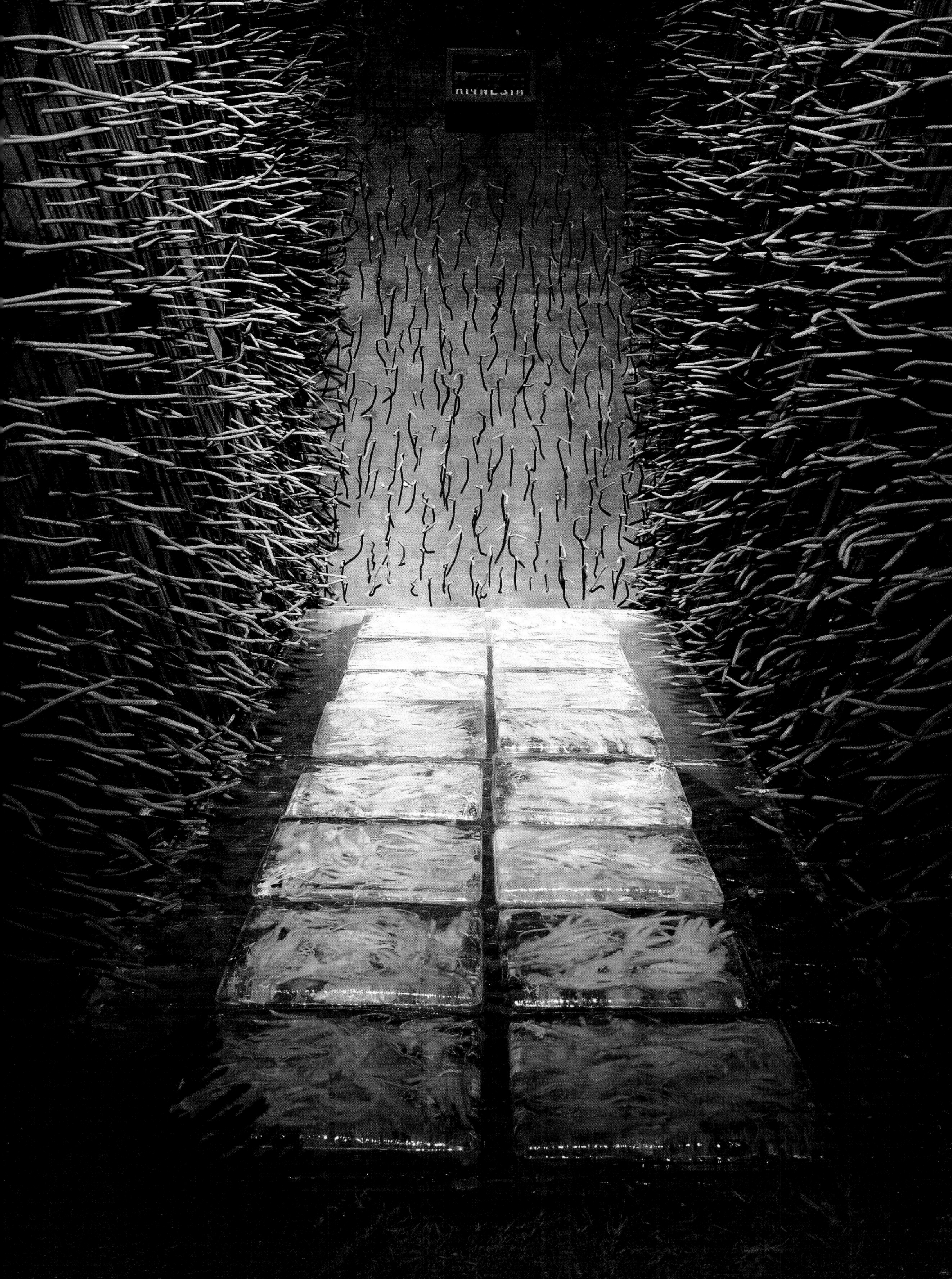
AMNESIA

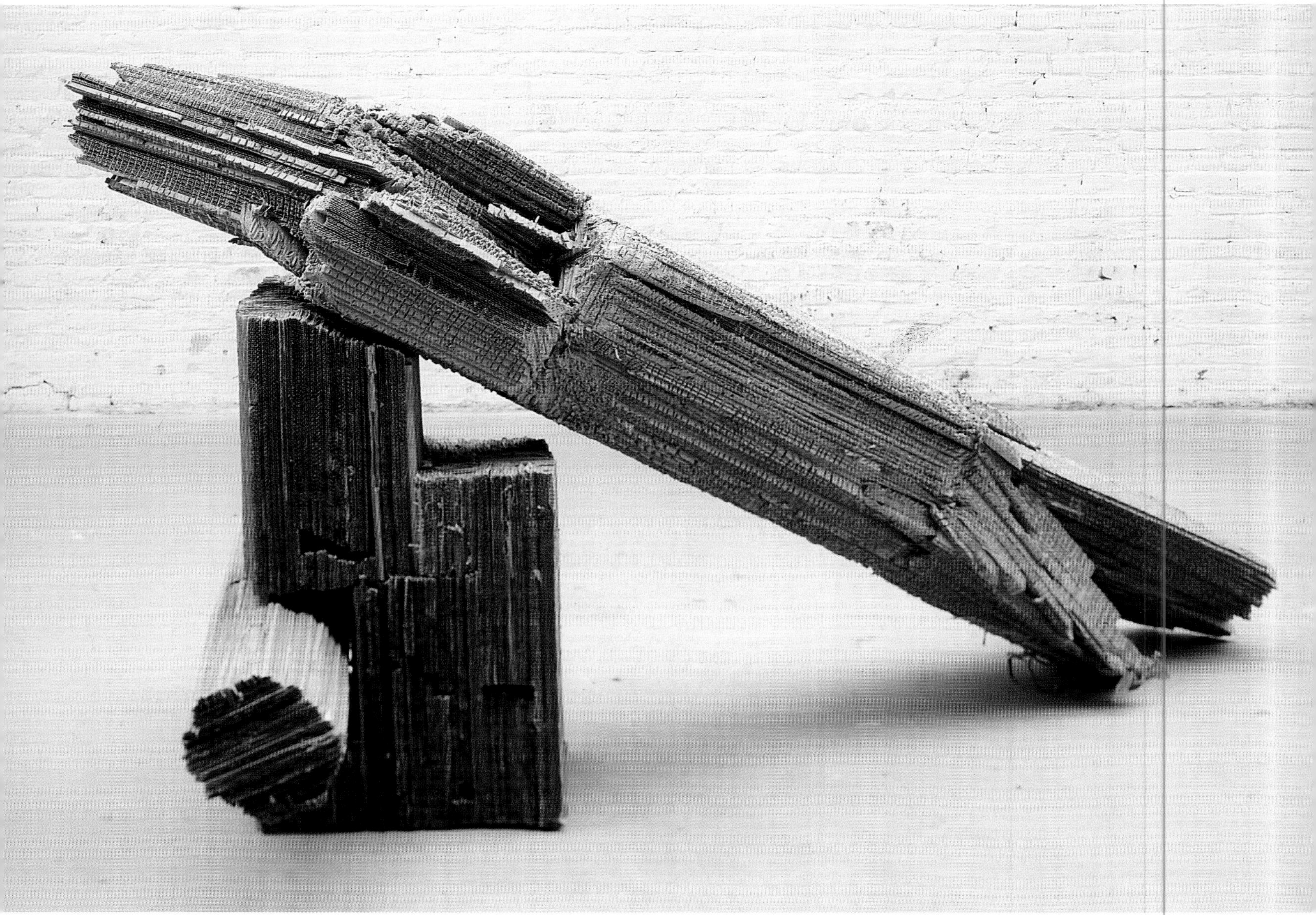

Gaby Nzekwu

Gaby Nzekwu was born in Nigeria in 1956. He has been living in Lille, in northern France, since 1981, after having spent some time in England. As an architect and plastic artist, he creates productions for medical (psychiatric hospitals) and academic environments. He is very involved in the cultural and social life of his adopted city, far from the effects of fashion, cynics and easy concepts. He works with cardboard, to which he gives an impressionable density and a remarkable hieratic force.

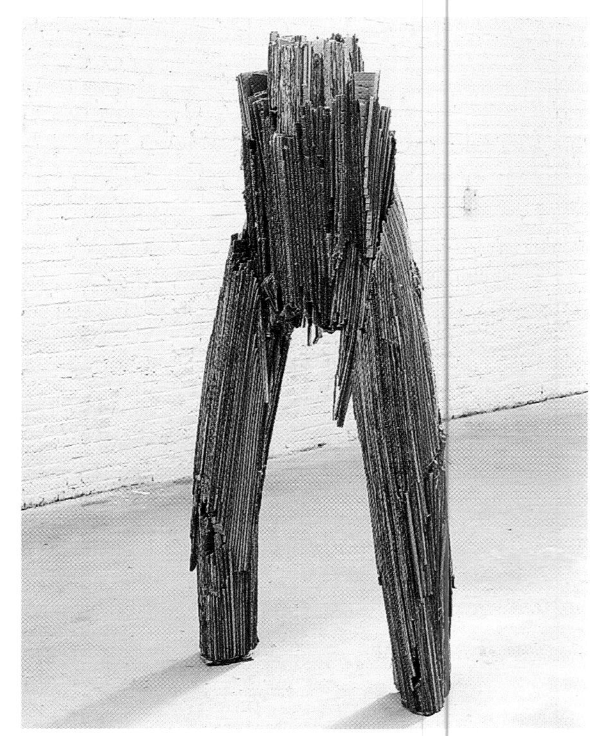

Cardboard, mixed media
©D.R.

Jems Robert Koko Bi

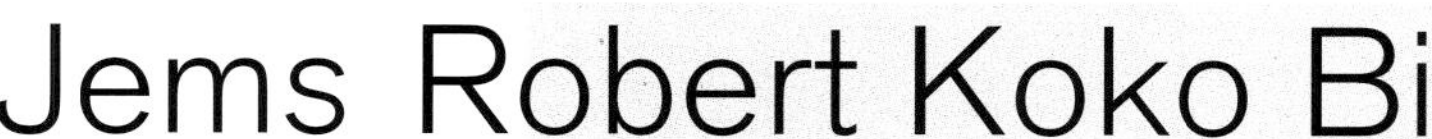

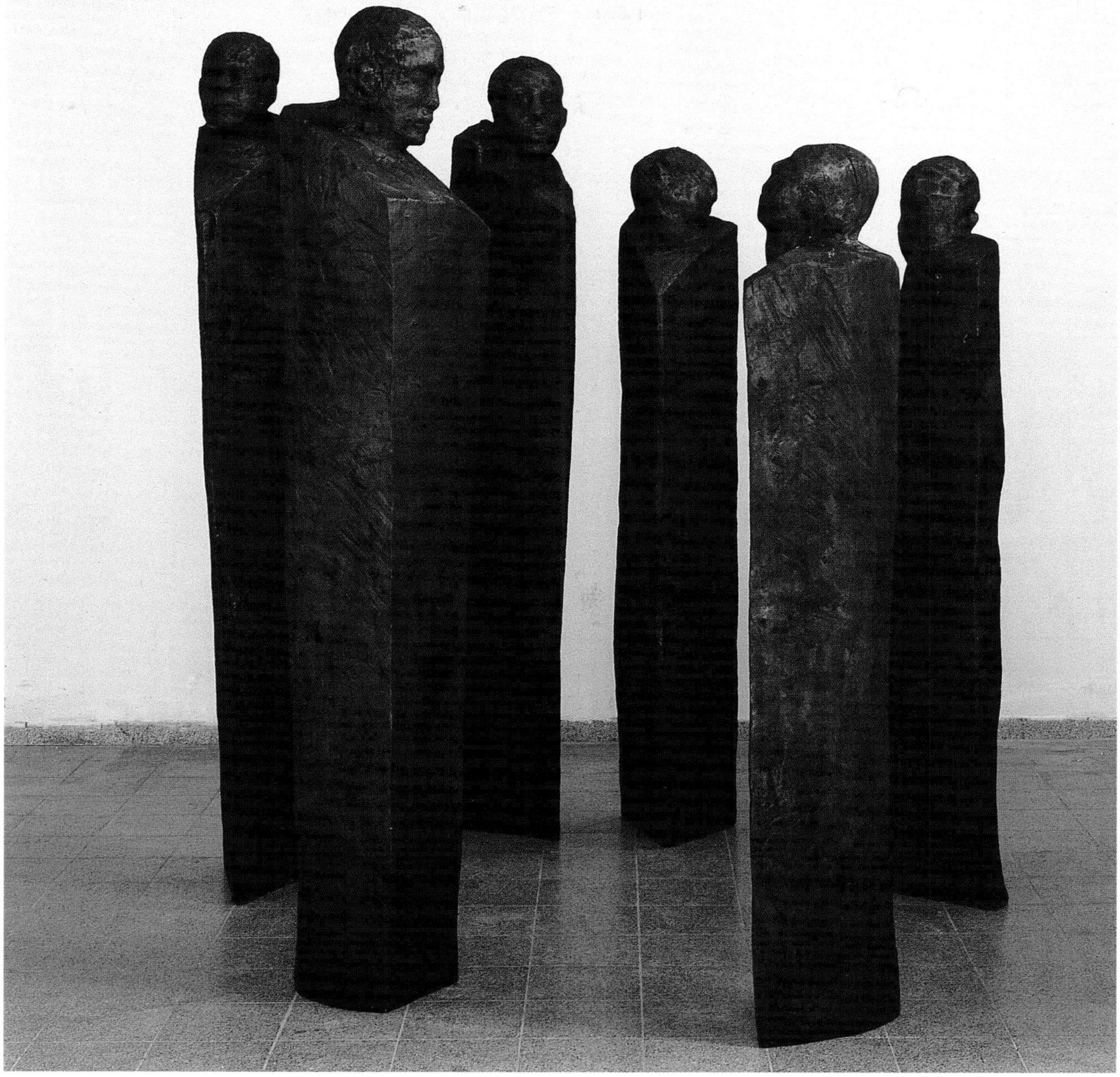

Jems Robert Koko Bi was born in Ivory Coast in 1966. He graduated in 1997 from the Institut National des Arts of Abidjan, and then settled in Germany, where he attended the Art Academy of Düsseldorf. As a sculptor, he works with raw or burnt wood. His latest series, enigmatic heads, are a symbolic representation of Africans of the Diaspora. Through this work, Koko Bi wants to give a face – filled with serenity – to a tragic moment in history.

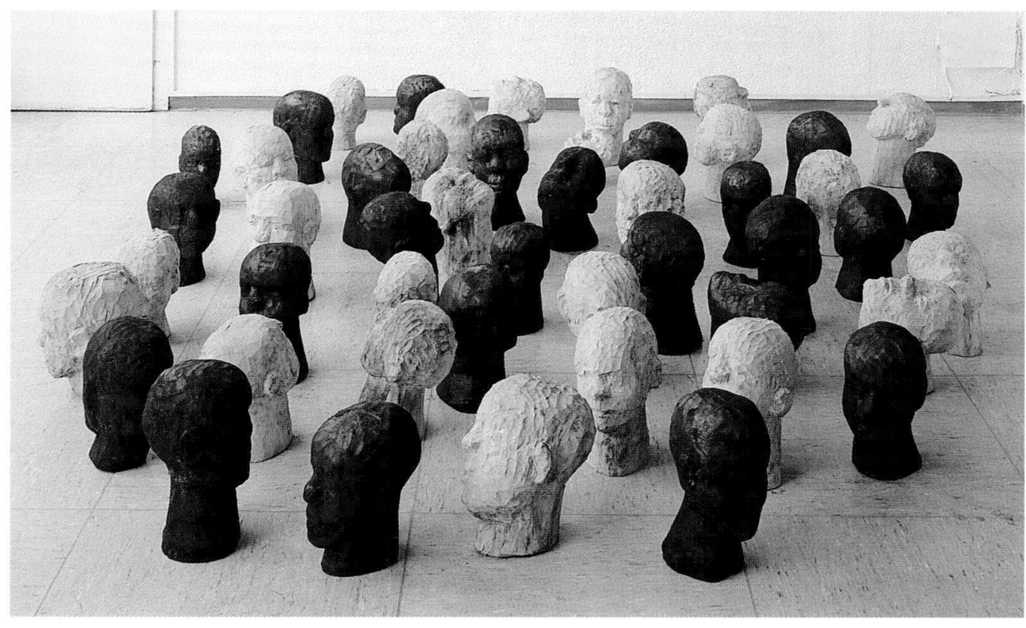

top:
"Diaspora," 1999
burnt poplar wood, 250x180x180 cm
©D.R.

right:
"The children of Gorée," 2000
poplar wood, 34x210x250 cm
©D.R.

Pascale Marthine Tayou

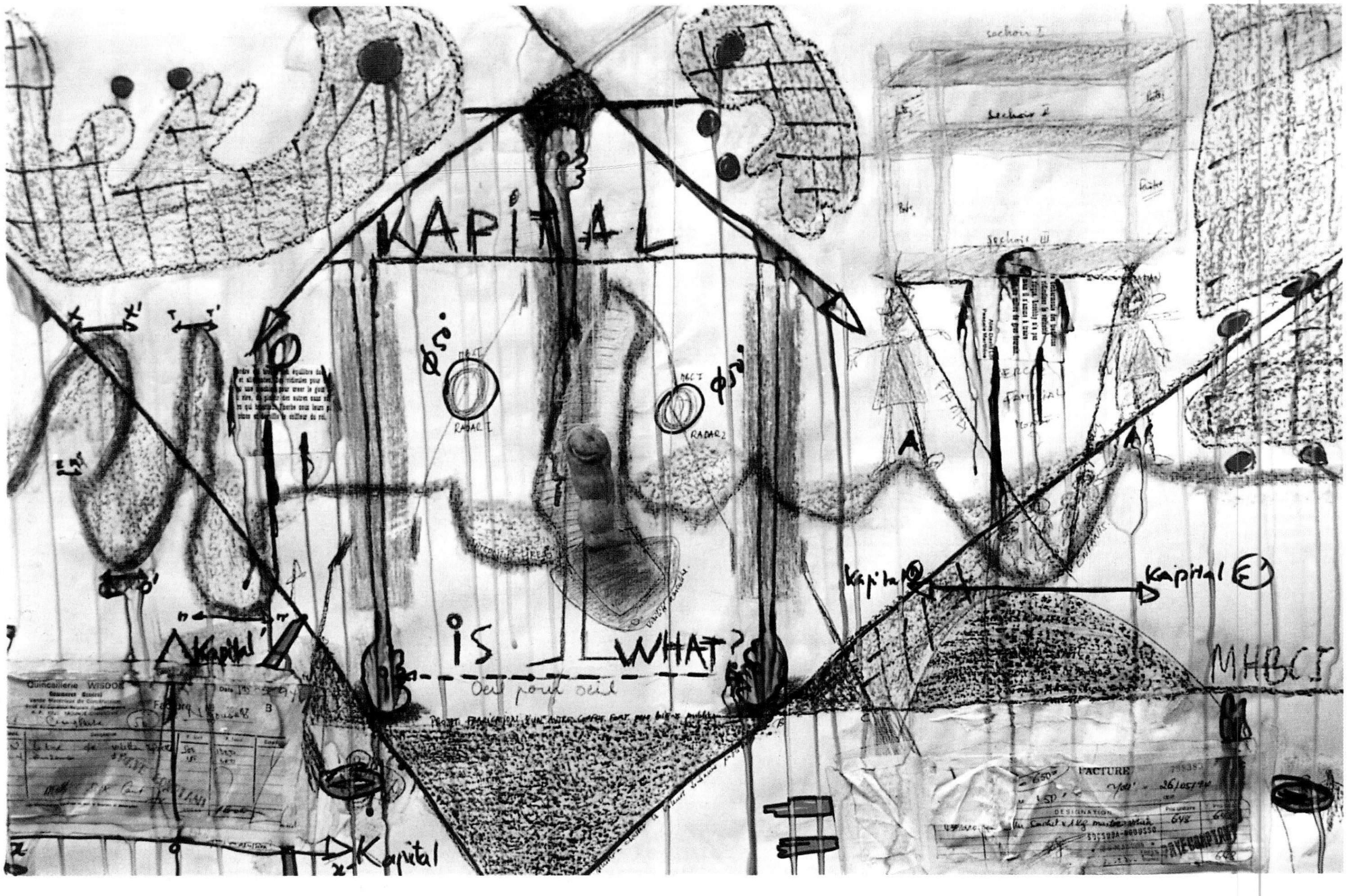

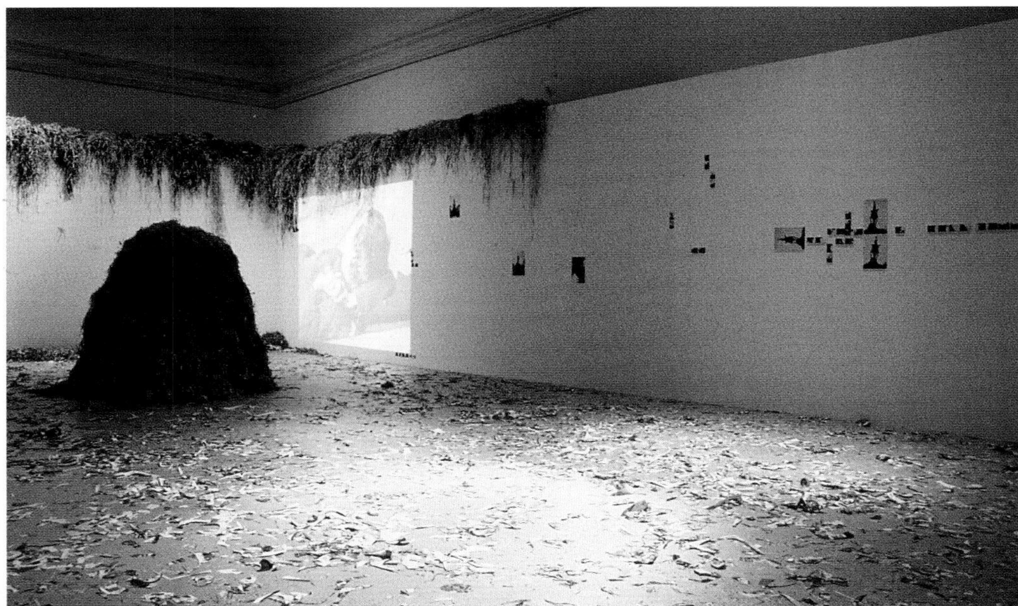

Pascale Marthine Tayou was born in Cameroon in 1967. After living in Paris for a while, he chose Brussels as his base to travel the world. Like a soccer ball, Tayou's art waits to be kicked and for its forms, which refer to nothing more than the present time, to be played with. These works are not born out of a surrealist or revolutionary theory, but rather tap directly into reality, without any prior reasoning other than intuition about the world.

top:
"Untitled," 1996 ©D.R.

left:
"Connecting cities," 2000 ©Anna Kleberg

facing page:
"SIDA Series," 1993 ©Revue Noire

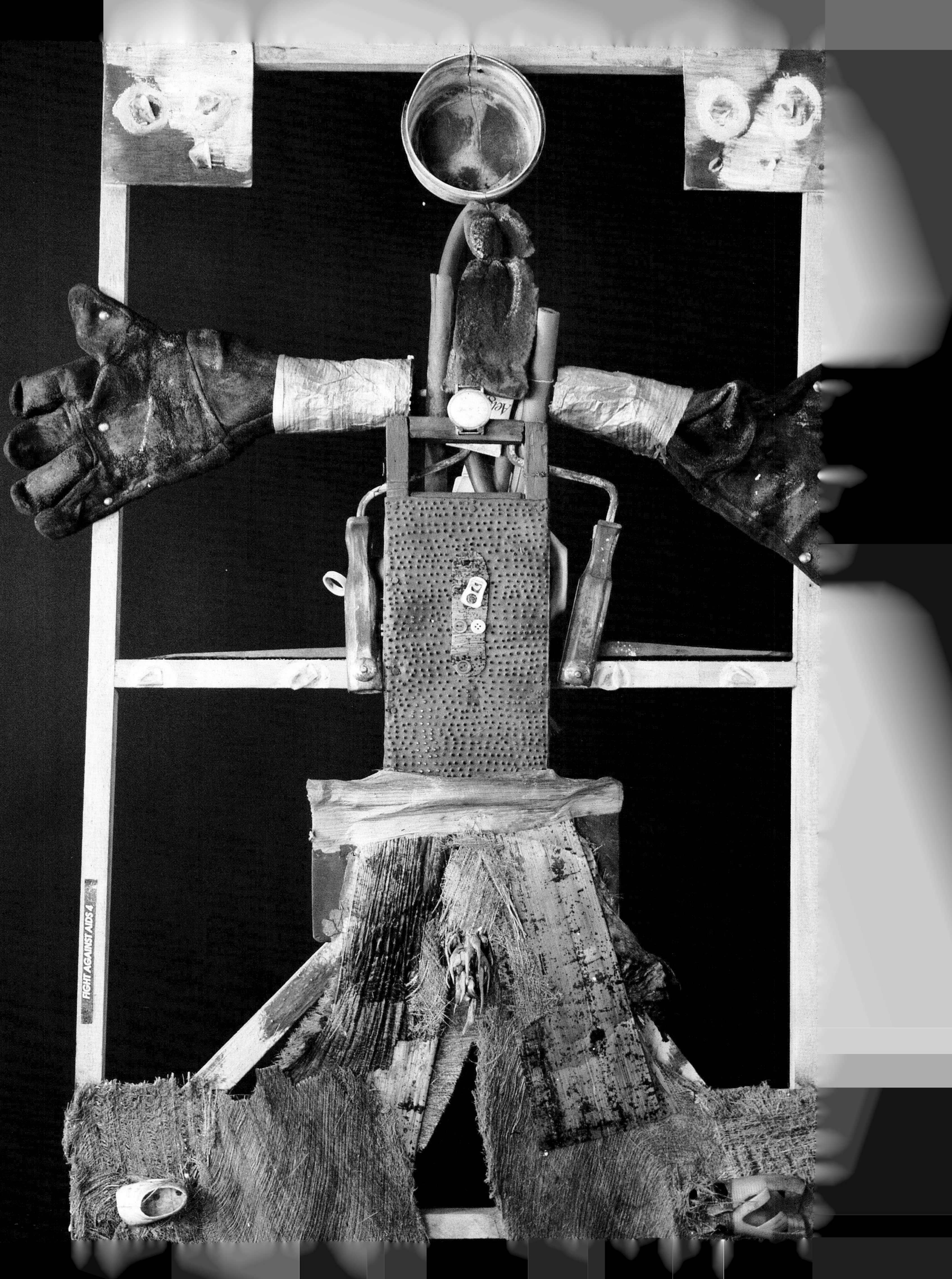
FIGHT AGAINST AIDS 4

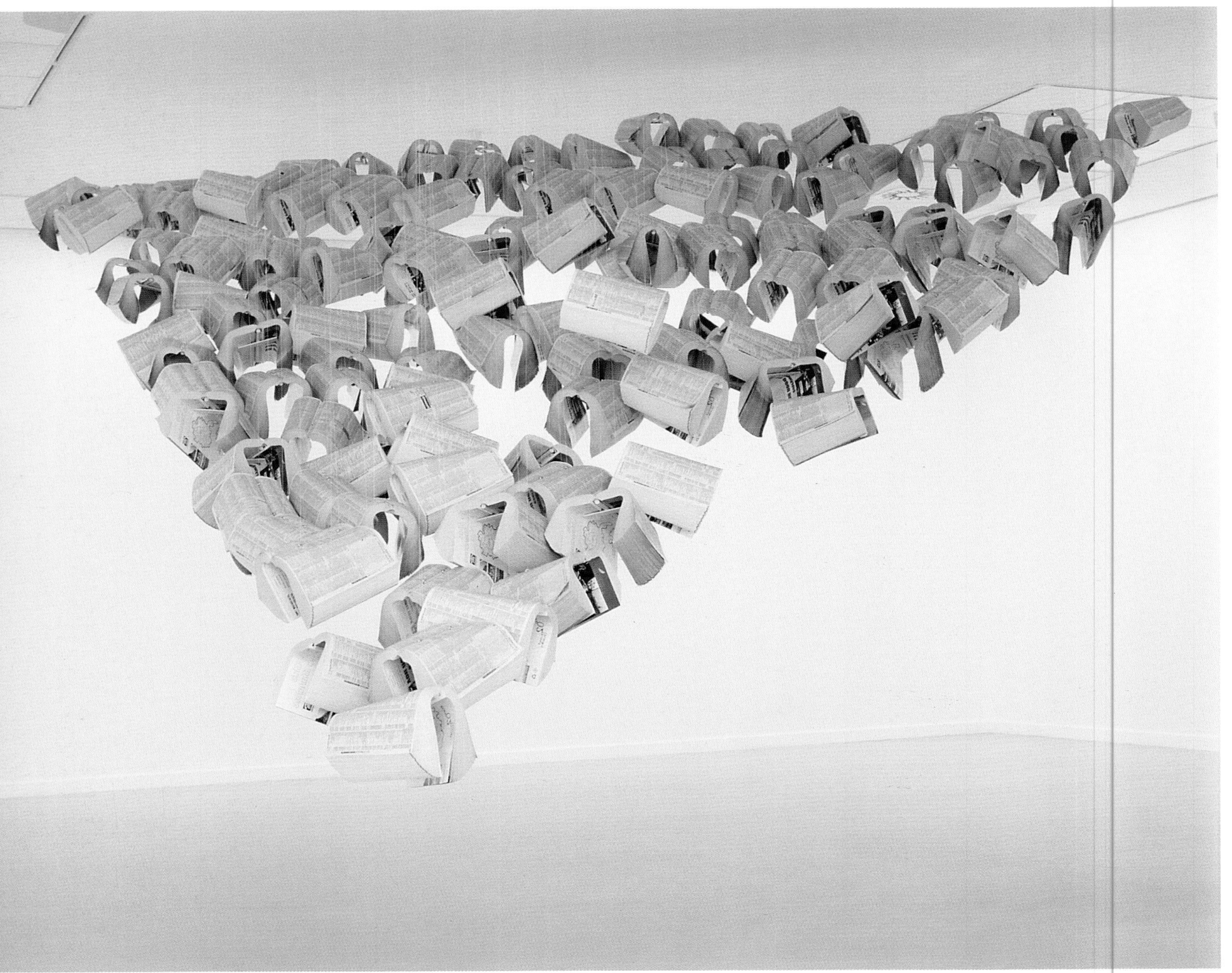

Aimé Ntakiyica

Aimé Ntakiyica was born in Burundi in 1960. He graduated from the Académie Royale des Beaux-Arts of Brussels in 1985, and he was a senior lecturer at the Academy of Fine Arts of Kinshasa in the DRC before returning to Belgium in 1994. During these nomadic times, when artists, especially those from the African continent, lugged their experiences and dreams to the four corners of the Earth, Ntakiyica has resolved to adopt his status as an "uprooted" person and transform what could appear as a weakness. "The World is My Home," a production presented at the Musée d'art moderne in Paris in 2000, illustrates the desire of this new generation of artists to transcend both physical and cultural borders.

"Verba volent, scripta manent ," 2000

Amouzou-Glikpa

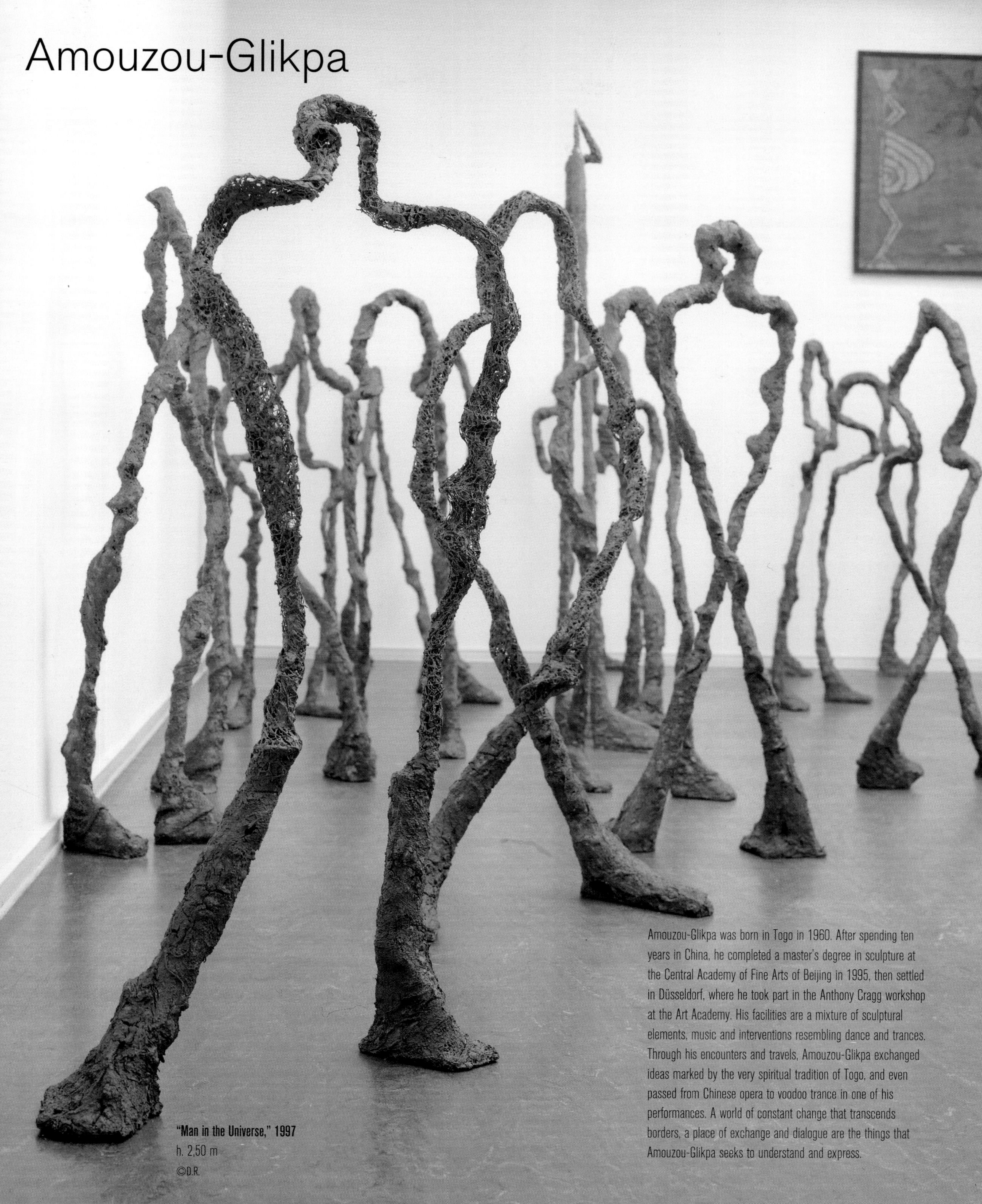

"Man in the Universe," 1997
h. 2,50 m
©D.R.

Amouzou-Glikpa was born in Togo in 1960. After spending ten years in China, he completed a master's degree in sculpture at the Central Academy of Fine Arts of Beijing in 1995, then settled in Düsseldorf, where he took part in the Anthony Cragg workshop at the Art Academy. His facilities are a mixture of sculptural elements, music and interventions resembling dance and trances. Through his encounters and travels, Amouzou-Glikpa exchanged ideas marked by the very spiritual tradition of Togo, and even passed from Chinese opera to voodoo trance in one of his performances. A world of constant change that transcends borders, a place of exchange and dialogue are the things that Amouzou-Glikpa seeks to understand and express.

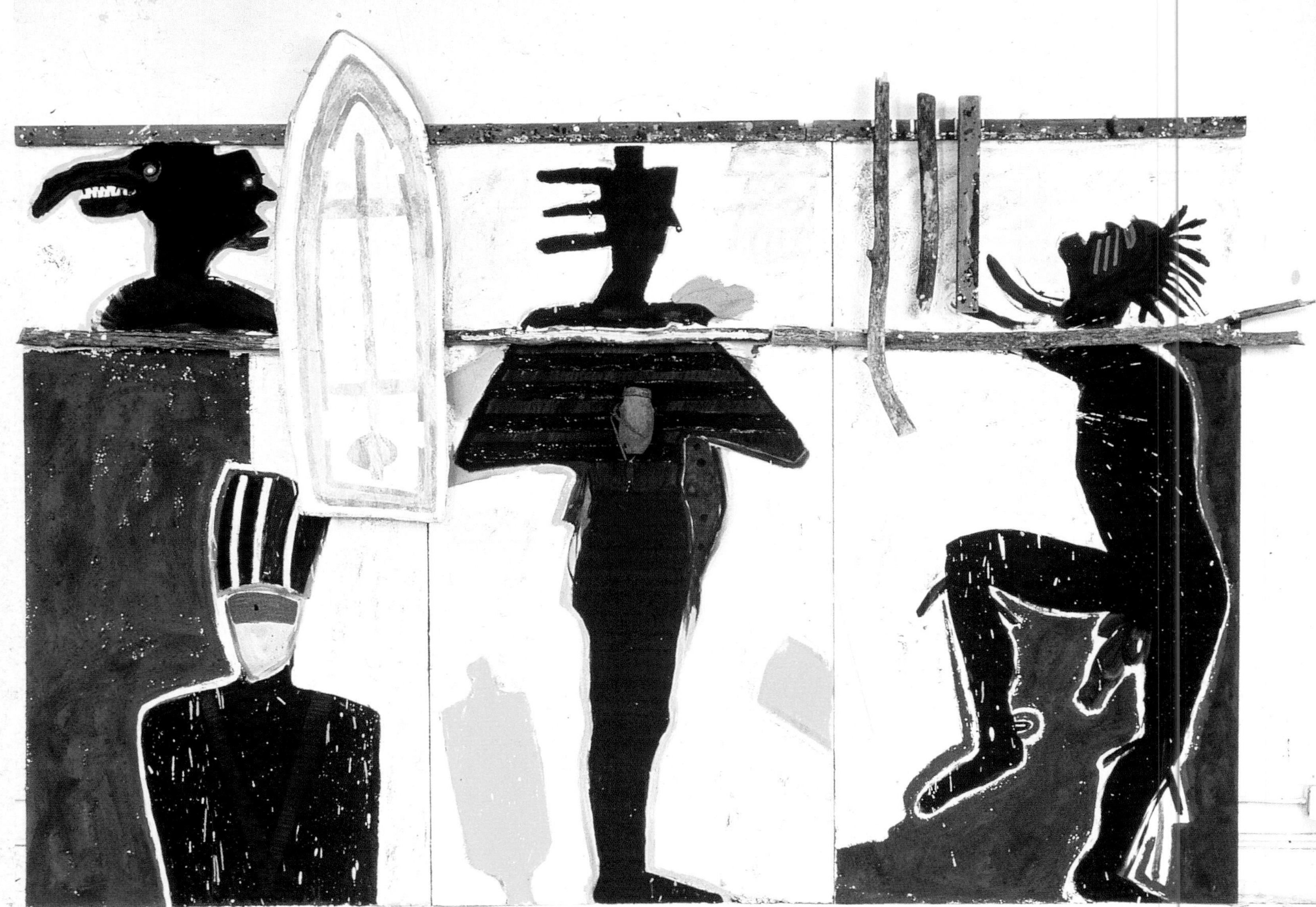

Ouattara

Ouattara was born in Ivory Cost in 1957. "I did not attend the Fine Arts School of Abidjan. When I was young, I was initiated – I don't know if you can call it teaching – by my mother and grandparents. Every person has a talent, and mine was art. In this initiation, the vision of things is rather cosmic. You travel and you meet people." By mixing blues, browns and reds with pieces of wood, skulls and all types of objects that suddenly make the once underlying animist dimension of his work emerge, Ouattara slowly moved from intangible to tangible painting. He lives in New York, in the USA.

"Trance of the Shaman," 1990
tryptic, acrylic, pigments, sand and wood on canvas, 291x390 cm.

Mickaël Bethe Selassié

Mickaël Bethe Selassié was born in Ethiopia in 1951. In 1971, he settled in Paris, where he specialized in physics and chemistry. In the early 80s, he decided to devote himself to art using his material of choice, papier-mâché. "In the beginning, paper was a tree. For me, working with papier-mâché symbolizes rebuilding a forest." With their totem-like forms and evocative titles (menhir, initiatory voyage, the Magus, tabernacle, transportation of remains) his brightly painted sculptures convey the artist's spiritual quest.

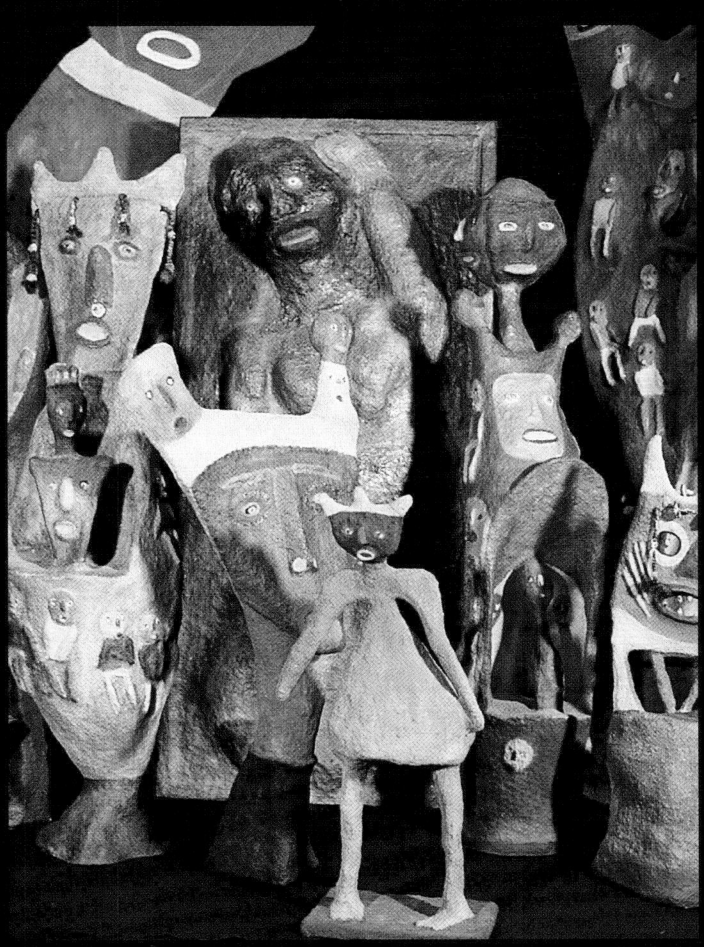

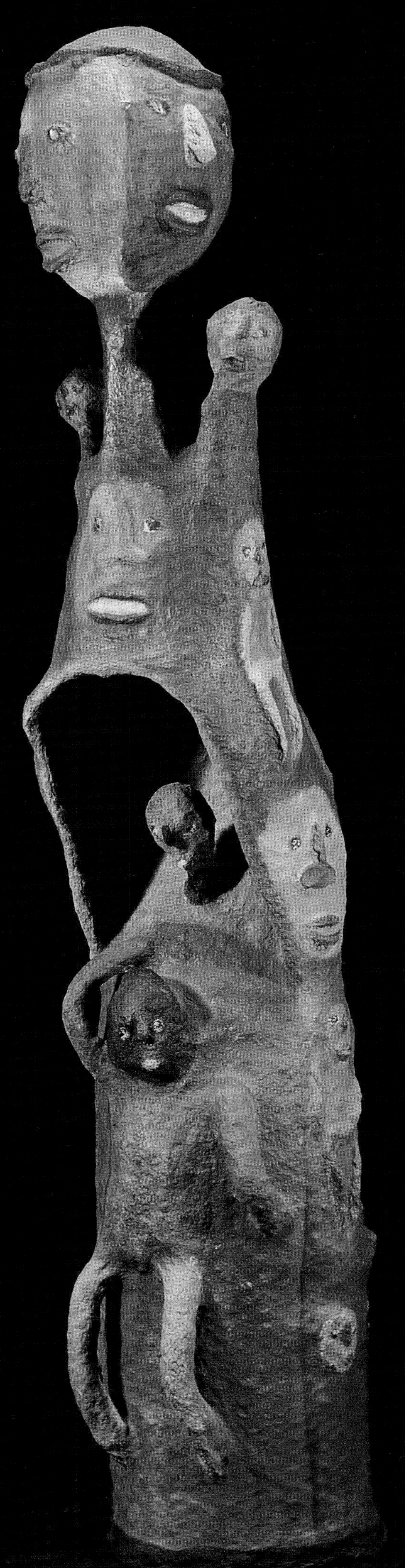

Moshekwa Langa

Born in Bakenberg, South Africa in 1975, Langa lives and works in Amsterdam. He dreams of a world that cannot exist. A miniature, abstract world that we could change at will. Its intimate cartography, when it is not recalling the virgin and soiled space of his own country, when it does not reproduce the dream contours of a very personal history, ploughs through the fields of utopia and recreation. Moshekwa Langa plays hard and his compositions take us back to the disclosed memories of a very old child who, however, has not forgotten the very nature of childhood and play.

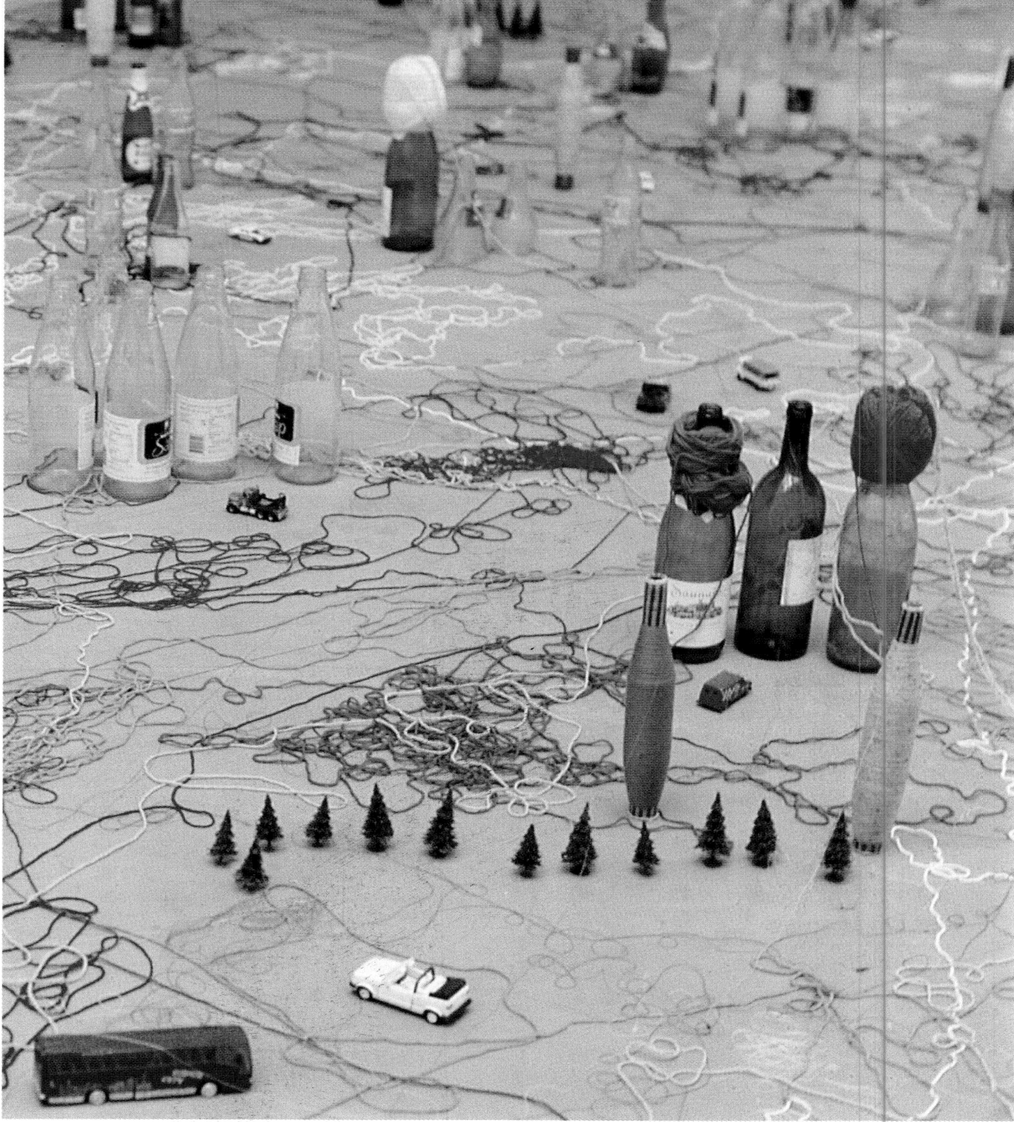

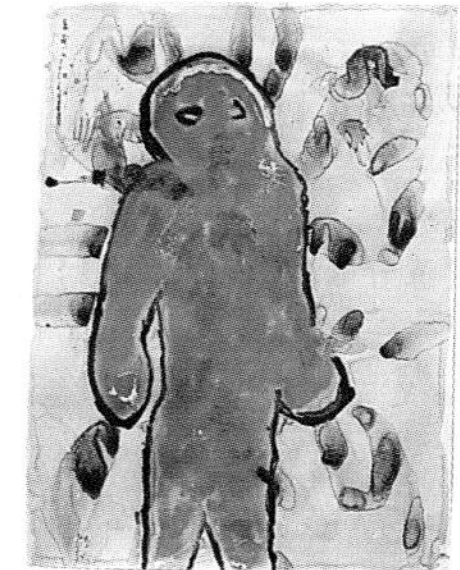

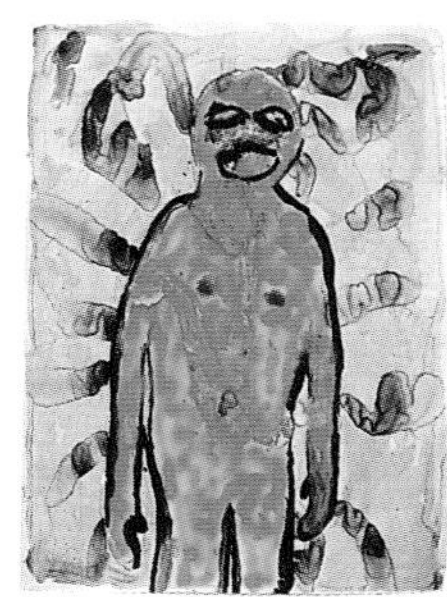

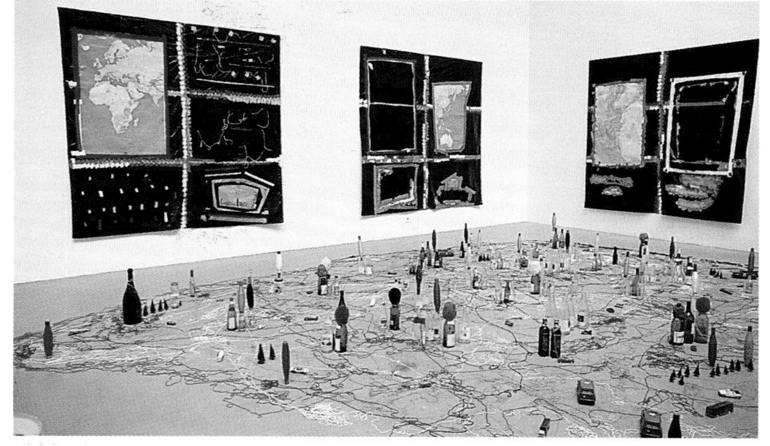

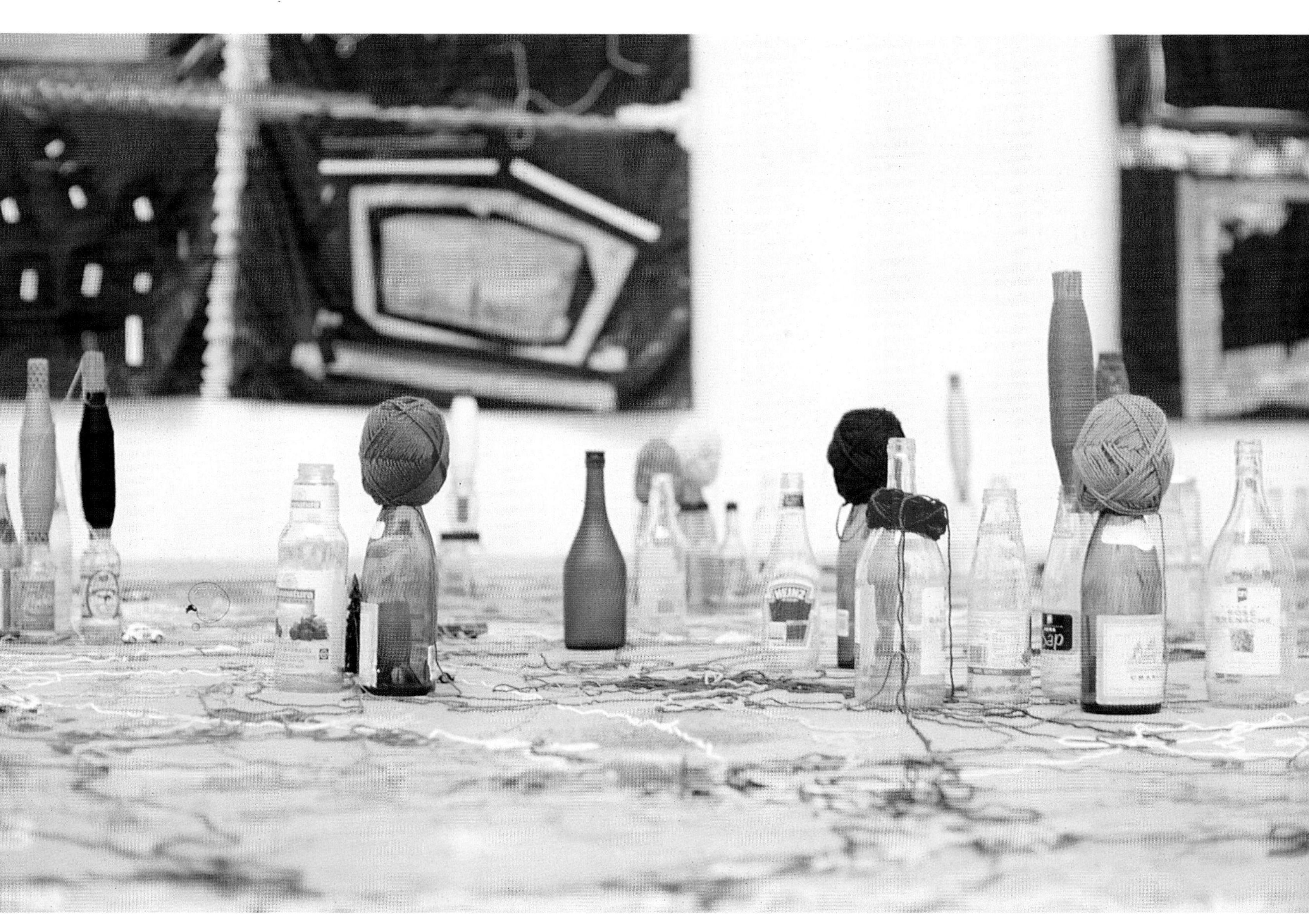

Paris, 2001 ©Revue Noire

Amadou Sow (born in 1951)

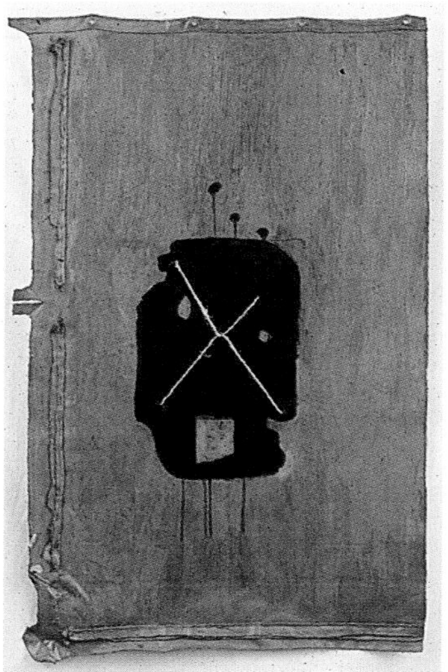

William Sagna (born in 1950), "Tombouctou," Senegal

ART AND STYLE

Simon Njami

The history of the perception of contemporary African creation is recent. It has only been included in global debate for barely ten years. The issue no longer appears to be to prove the existence of a creation whose artists have exhibited at all international events. Rather, the issue appears to be today how to exhibit these artists. Who should exhibit them? From what point of view? And what are we actually dealing with?

The issue currently under debate among curators of French ethnology museums in relation to the presidential project to bring together all so-called first art collections in the same place also includes a larger issue on African art by highlighting this unavoidable mix between ethnology and creation whenever the black continent is involved. We act as if the past and future of art around the world should undergo Western sanctification, which alone would provide it with its raison d'être. This is an attitude that, far from considering creation for what it is, confines us to falling into the trappings of comparative analysis, of the debate on strategies and policies that overlooks dealing with objects and their purpose.
Unlike so-called primitive or first art, contemporary African art remains an art without a market, a vague domain governed by outlooks bound to be exogenous, by quarrels among schools, by disputes between Ancients and Moderns, whose stakes go beyond the simple framework of artistic creation. Why does this specific outlook, or rather this lack of outlook, still persist today?

Anonymity and ethnography

The first major symposiums organized with the clear purpose of crushing myths and exploring a new approach occurred in the early 90s at the Center for African Art in New York and at the Kunstsammlung Nordrhein-Westfalen of Düsseldorf. These events revealed that the way in which contemporary African art is dealt with in the West, how it is marred by misunderstanding that sometimes borders on maliciousness, as if African art, had it been born in this 21st century, corresponded to specific interpretation grids that could only be construed following an in-depth analysis of the civilization and history of the people concerned.

This approach inevitably leads to the intellectual discourse of the colonial years, based on the argument according to which universalism – namely civilization – could only be conceived in a narrow framework of European nations. This is how an impassible border was established between how European artistic production and the production of other peoples was considered. Europe granted itself a monopoly on the power to be a judge because it had the means to impose its universalistic vision on the rest of the world. And its most precious tool was ethnology. Henceforth, these primitive tribes and all of their productions became objects of study. It is on this outlook, which has survived until now, that African creation is dependent.

In fact, Suzan Vogel, who in 1991 exhibited Africa Explores the Twentieth Century in New York, illustrated, in a scathing manner, the position defended by advocates of the ethnological approach to art. Although, for the first time, Africa was considered for what it is on such a large scale, the exhibit was, however, no more than a poor inventory whose sole thread was ethnology. The only tangible and questionable contribution of this experience was a new classification that resembles the classification devised by Pierre Gaudibert a few years earlier in his book on contemporary African art. But, in her defense, Suzan Vogel was not entirely fooled by the result of her work: "*Like most summary work, mine ended with warnings and qualifications, such as, for example, the understanding that there are numerous exceptions to the trends I described and the acute discomfort of knowing that the information on which I based my theories is only partial and that my conclusions are taken from things than remain widely unknown.*"

The global village

The case of Magiciens de la Terre (the Magicians of the Earth) is a bit atypical. By reintegrating Africa and its creators, Jean-Hubert Martin established a solidarity between the black continent and the rest of the world. Magiciens de la Terre, a title with mystical beauty, was designed to show the most striking creations of the world, because, as stated by Martin: "We usually use the word "magic" to describe the deep and inexplicable influence of art." However, this statement also led to problems with definition and approach because, although Vogel was guilty of too much contextualization, it could be said that decontextualization was the major weakness of Jean-Hubert Martin's exhibit.

Ass Mbengue (born in 1959), Senegal

©Revue Noire

Jean-Hubert Martin's desire was undoubtedly misinterpreted by those for whom Magiciens de la Terre would become a founding myth. A new approach would then lead exhibit commissioners to search for the authentic Africa and create someone new who did not recognize himself in the discourse of which he had suddenly become the target. Coffins became sculptures and wall paintings were affixed to canvas. The principle of decontextualization then became the credo for a series of exhibits, in a setting of complete confusion. The museum that served as a telluric center, as an extraterritorial and sacred place, and all references were abandoned to create an environment that would make this or that peasant "contemporary."

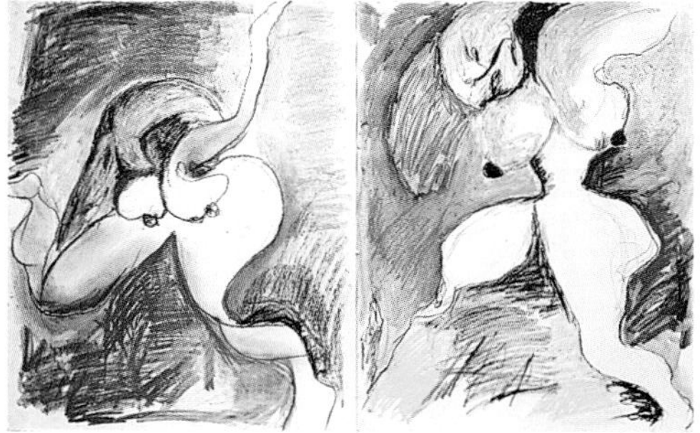

Braïma Injaï (born in 1964), Guinea Bissau

©Revue Noire

Although in the 80s the debate on contemporary African creation was limited to a circle of academics based mainly in Europe and the United States, who defined this issue as a study of civilizations, the 90s witnessed a quantitative and qualitative explosion in this field. Specialists were joined by historians and contemporary art curators, whose training and leanings would give thought a boon by finally sparking debates that would go to the very heart of what contemporary African art could be. Divergent approaches, whether those based on a third-world sensitivity or a dualistic debate opposing the so-called Periphery in the old Center, multiplied remarks and created those conflicts without which no valid thought could be pursued.

There is undeniably a need for reference points, to create a language that can be understood by as many people as possible. The classification appeared to be the ideal solution, for a certain time. The method that would enable the creation of a history and would give a past, albeit invented, to artists who were difficult to place on the international scale, was clearly an attempt to create a framework in which these artists could identify themselves and based on which they could yearn for their own existence. It was important to create the conditions for a genuine discussion that would do away with the temptations of exoticism and paternalism that until then had prevailed and that, sometimes, bordered on contempt. This led to splits and to the integration (if only parsimoniously) of African artists in the major international events of Venice and Kassel. The start-up of the Dakar biennial in the early 90s arrived just in time to play the role of reference point. A few years later, the Johannesburg biennial was launched, but was only around for two editions. In Africa and Europe, an awareness of the risks of categorization began to guide curators' and commissioners' choices. For her exhibit Seven Stories About Modern Art in Africa (London, 1995), Clementine Deliss had chosen the historical approach in seven points on the continent. Suites Africaines (Paris 1997) attempted to address interdisciplinarity by tearing down the barriers between the different forms of esthetics and by bringing together, under the same roof, film, plastic arts, literature, music and dance. Otro Pais (Las Palmas, Barcelona, 1994) and Die Andere Reise (Krems 1995) brought together the black world from Africa to the West Indies. More recently, with The Short Century (Munich 2001), Okwui Enwezor tried to address the political conflicts that shook Africa during the gravest period surrounding the independence movements, whereas Salah Hassan and Olu Oguibe tried to impose Africa in Venice with their Authentic/Eccentric. The same concern of avoiding the traps of accepted ideas and easy notions could be found at each of these exhibits.

In the world

The history of the past few centuries has drastically changed the traditional structures of colonized countries. Africa is no longer the immobile continent deaf to the movement of the world. As a result, the ruptures occurring there are not exclusively turned towards the continent, but are addressed to the entire world. The mere shifting caused by conflicting histories has cast the African artist into an unexplored space that he must invent, in a new syncretism that reinterprets the benefits without seeking to classify or name them.

What, for example, differentiates Cameroon artists Pascale Marthine Tayou and Pascal Kenfack? There is, of course, the fact that one has a high idea of the artist while the other claims that he is not one. Although, in the 60s, the affirmation of a flamboyant and proud Africanism and of an ethnic and political position were necessary, and although the idea of Africa could not be considered without a certain notion of grandeur, times have changed and these extreme demonstrations are no longer acceptable. On the other hand, as ignorant victims of this complex unconscious that condemned them to subordinate their work to what they had learned in European schools, artists from the 60s could not conceive that a serious artist had not studied, like themselves, at a Fine Arts School. Today, among the ten most famous African artists in the world, few have had a classical education. The young generations, unlike their elders, have nothing more to prove. Or, at least the questions facing them are completely different.

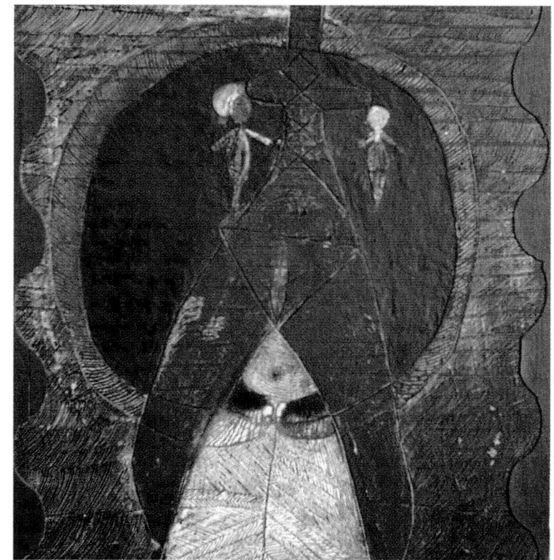

Afi Nayo (born in 1969), Togo

©Revue Noire

Africa has always been considered a closed physical space. However, today, Africa has become a metaphor. A corner of the world that artists lug about with them wherever they go. Their Africa is mythical and sometimes impalpable. Playing hide-and-go-seek with accepted ideas, they cloud the issues. The new generation of African artists has certainly kissed goodbye a romanticism that no longer concerns it. But it is confronted with identity-related problems of an entirely different nature than merely belonging to the African continent.

The lost paradise exists only in the back of our minds. It is no longer a place on earth that intimately refers us to our unique and special condition while giving us the feeling of belonging to a whole that surpasses us, a whole of which we are the invisible architects. We are confined to thinking about ourselves no longer as a reference to a fixed and obsolete identity, but as protean beings, with multiple and changing identities. The nomadism revealed by Roberta Smith has become our only territory. How do we move from secular settlement to evolution in spaces that can no longer be included on any existing map? It is this hallucinatory map that Moshekwa Langa long tried to fix, as if to redefine himself before losing himself in another place. Leaving a South Africa in the process of reconstructing itself, where even the ancient certainty of the color of one's skin was no longer a guarantee against schizophrenia, the artist embarked on this imaginary treasure hunt with the sole goal of looking for the being he though he was in a former life. A life before a nuclear catastrophe rehashed, in deformed bits and pieces, by his memory.

A few years ago, Aimé Ntakiyica nurtured an obsessional passion for the sacred forests he reduced to the most forced abstraction. His refined works could not show, but did allow one to feel, that which could not be said or shown. Today, he proclaims loud and strong "the world is my home," as if the era of the obvious were over and with its decline the chaos that Malraux called metamorphosis had settled in. This metamorphosis has been consumed. Work today does not consist of attempting to unravel the interwoven threads that are at the basis of all creation, but of attempting to make out its meaning. And the fact that we each carry in us a portion of this meaning forces us into a life of joyous and fertile solitude. It is with this type of solitude that contemporary artists, and perhaps Africans more than others, are faced with today, in the image of young South African Tracey Rose, whose violent and poetic videos and performances do not mask the anguish of being unknown.

It is time to completely put into perspective all of the experiences that have marked these last few years and that may form the basis for a discourse free of any overly simplistic reference. The necessary synthesis of the past and projection onto the future are a problem. We grope around in the dark, we experiment and search, and action overtakes thought or, at least, thought develops as action occurs. Critics, historians and artists become one and the same entity whose destinies are inseparable.

While understanding the paintings of the Sistine Chapel and the Dogon masks does not require any knowledge per se, the contemporary world functions on other modes. And these modes depend on each person's intimate experience. The basis for the proximity of certain artists today is precisely this community of experiences that enables them to speak the same language and to try to respond to the same questions with different solutions. Today, we have multiple identities whose many parameters we have not finished exploring.

The only certainty is that contemporary African artists are familiar with this bittersweet happiness. The bitterness of a world that does not quite correspond to the world of their dreams. Bitterness towards a history whose truthfulness is questioned. Bitterness towards their forgetful and unpredictable memory. Bitterness in view of the schizophrenic quartering of their souls. And sweetness. The sweetness of being and living in the here and now. The sweetness of experiencing this gift of ubiquity without which there is no art or artist. The sweetness of being able to reconstruct the world according to their desires. The sweetness of knowing that the world finally belongs to them as it does to everyone else, and that this world, in the future, will be what they helped it to become. It begins there, with this initial emotion, like a new birth, with this special vibration that gives meaning to our actions.

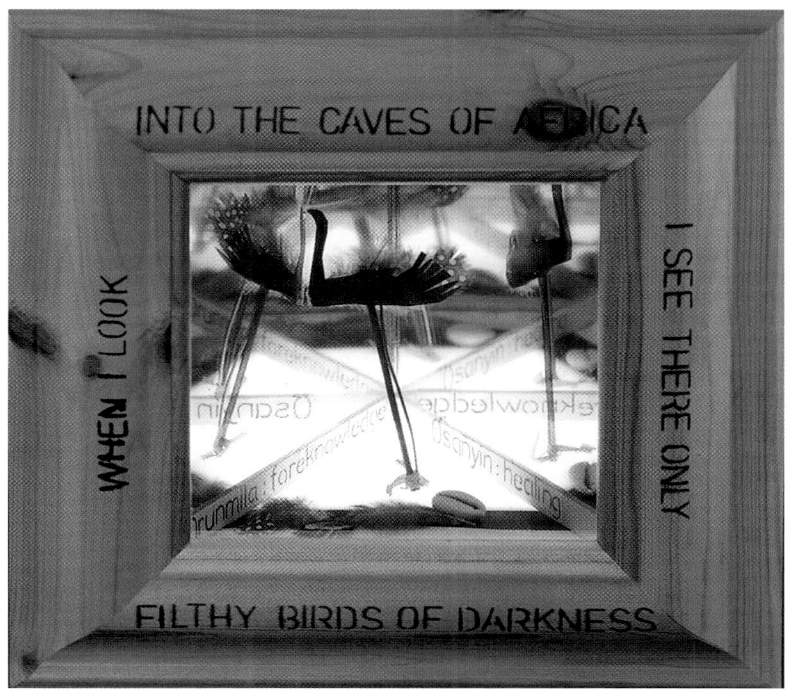

Folake Shoga, "The glass of Showcase," Nigeria
©D.R.

Post-apartheid South Africa

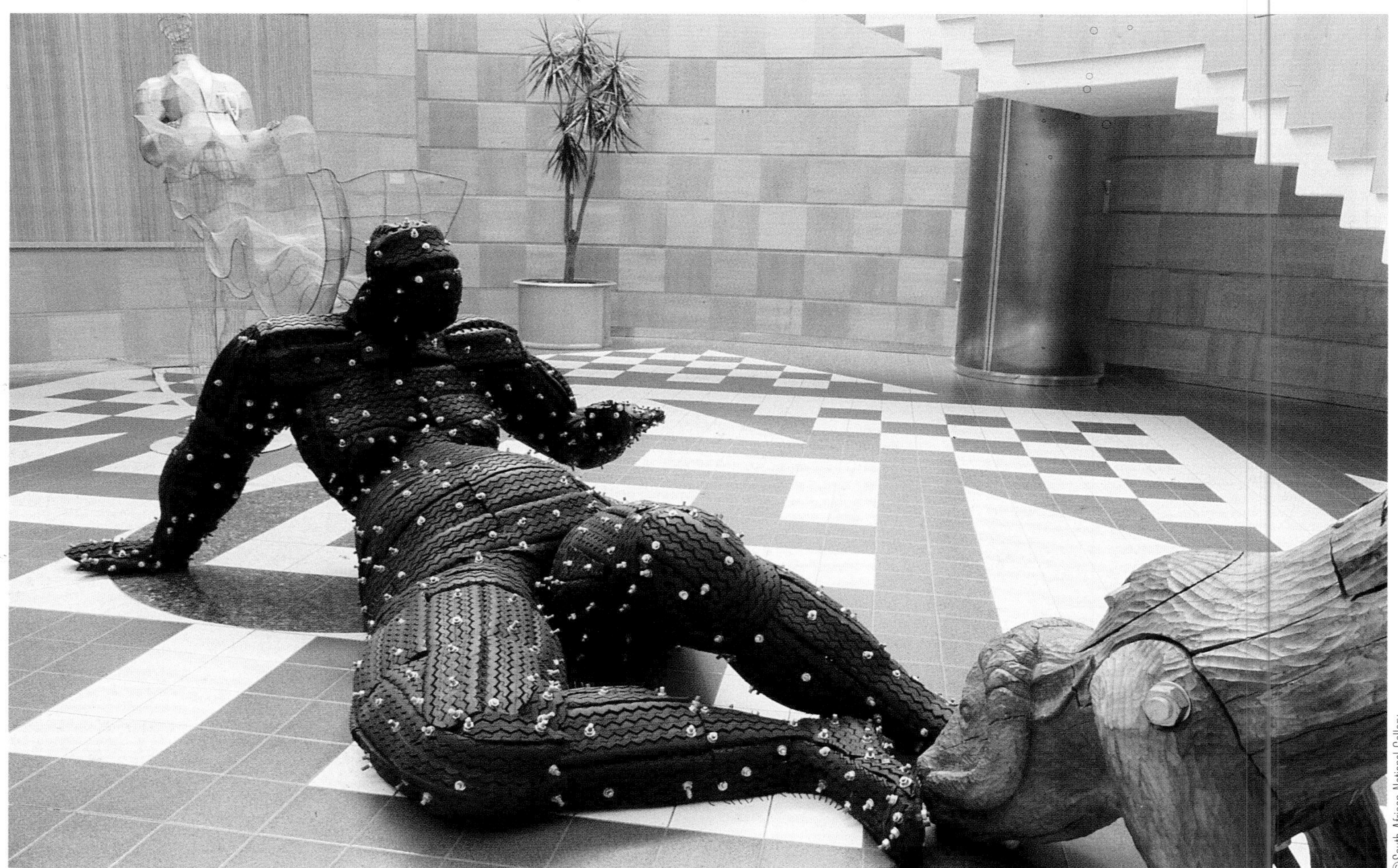

Andries Botha

Born in Durban in 1952, Andries Botha began sculpting in 1971 at the Natal University in Pietermaritzburg, where he obtained a Fine Arts Degree in 1976.

Botha uses a combination of natural and industrial materials, such as grass and acacia, plastic, wire, metal and rubber. He uses a wide range of techniques, often combining those derived from traditional African methods and those from modern assemblies. Botha's monumental sculptures are, as he calls them, "spiritual vehicles" that reflect the meditation on "the dilemma of South African life." They also explore encounters between the male and female psyche.

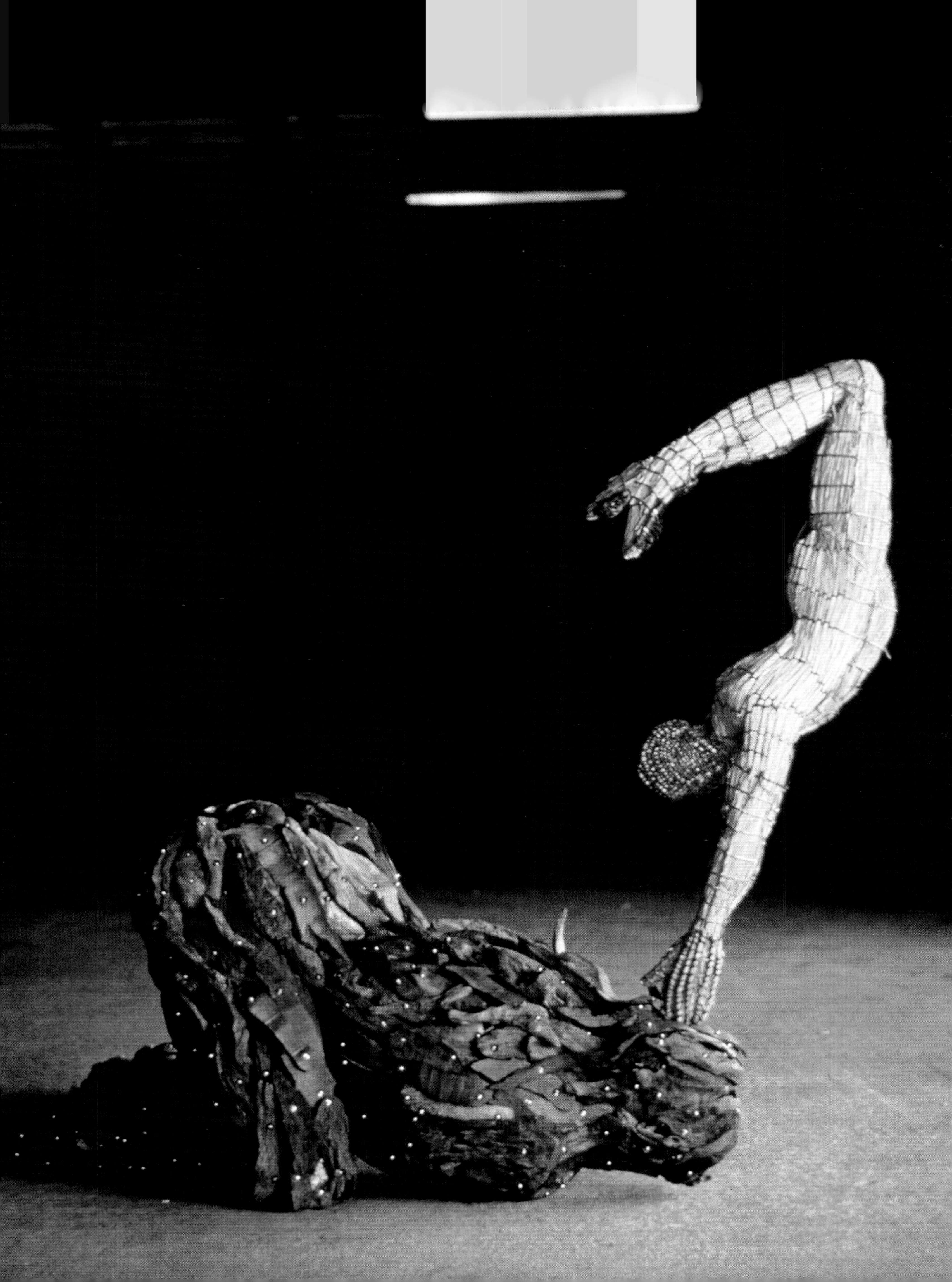

Willie Bester

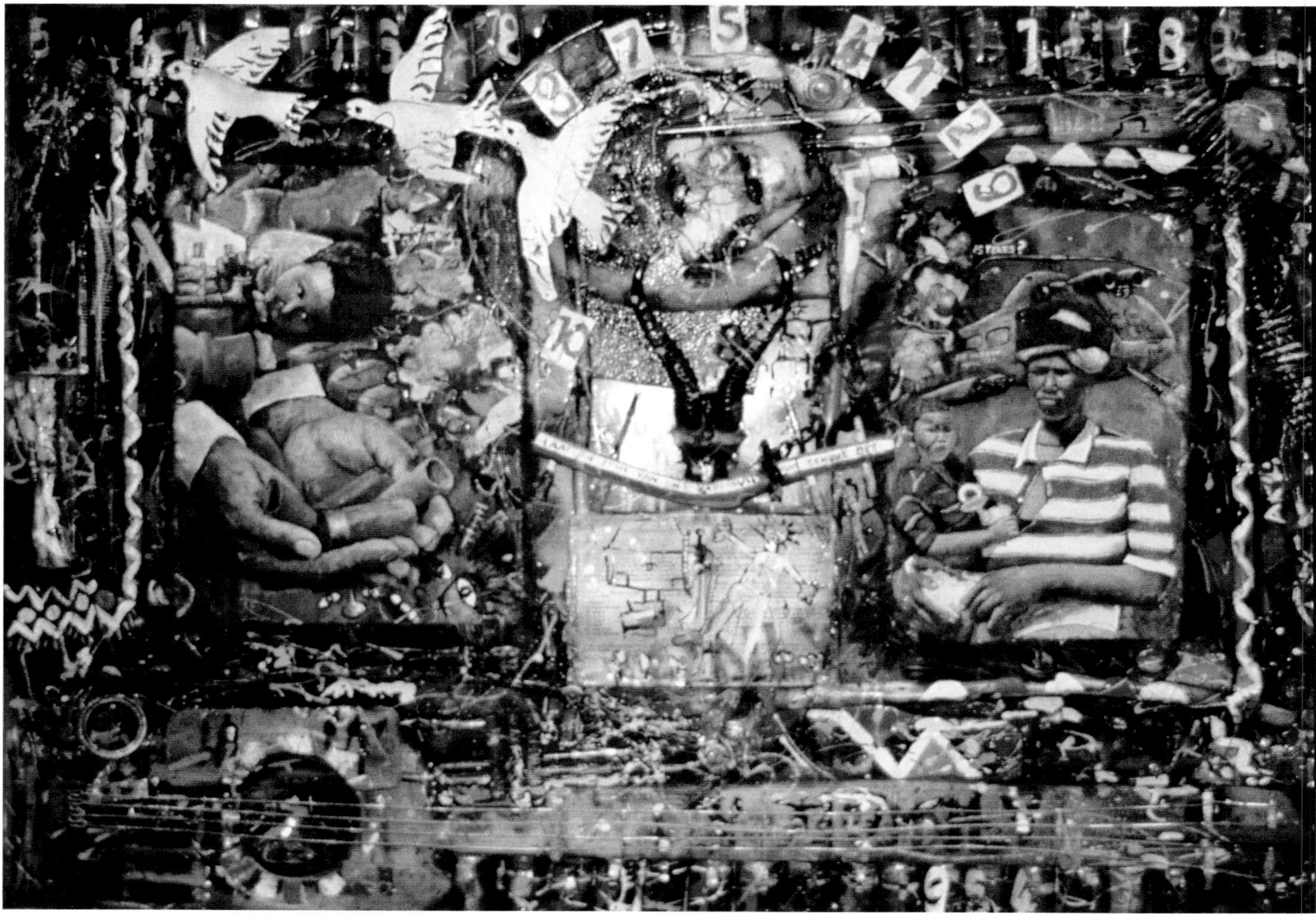

Willie Bester was born in Cape Town in 1956 and is a self-taught artist. In 1980, he took part in the Community Arts Project. His archeological approach, his treatment of the townships between an archeological site and a public dump (license plates, cans, wire) where agents and victims of apartheid stand side by side in relief paintings led him to create brightly colored sculpture-assemblages.

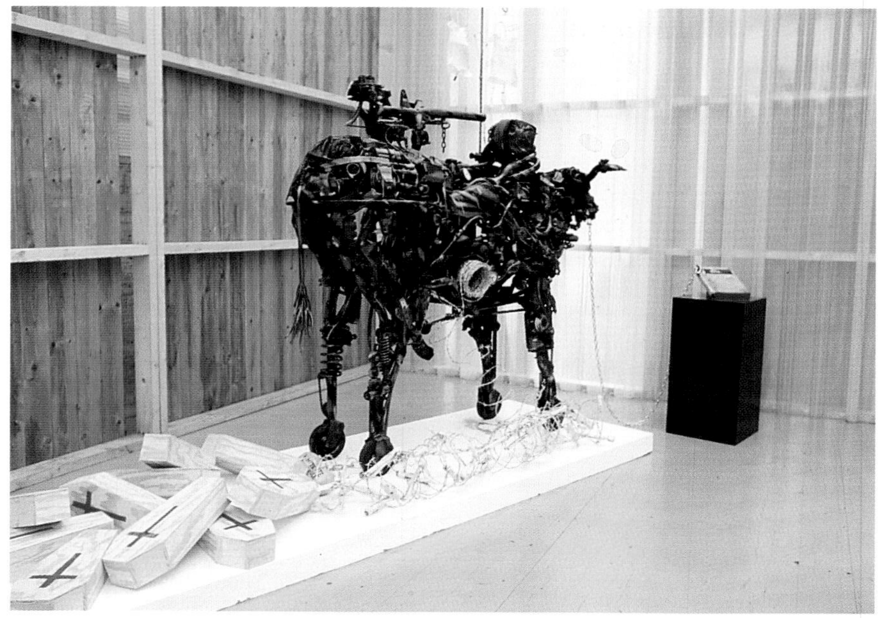

"Transition," 1993, 92 x 152 cm ©D.R.
50th Anniversary of the United Nations, 1995 ©Revue Noire

Bernadette Searle

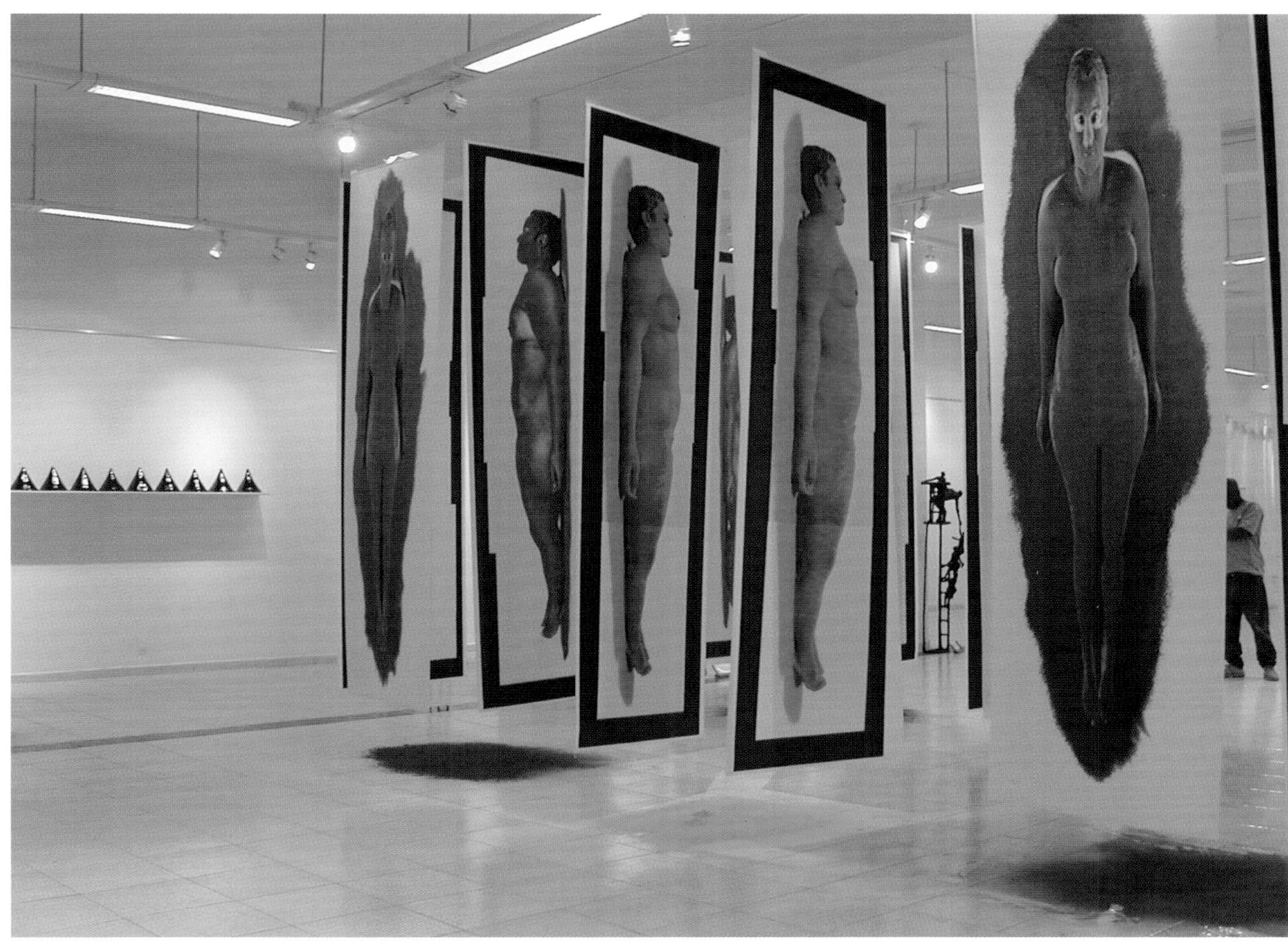

Bernadette Searle was born in 1964. Her productions, which display life-size photographs of herself covered with spices and pigments, deal with the identity and racial classification of South African apartheid. A representation of the battle between the individual, his community and the visible traces of prohibited interbreeding. Using her own body enables her to explore the cultural and sexual identity of the African woman and informs us of her social status.

Dak'Art, Biennial of Dakar, 2000 ©Revue Noire

William Kentridge

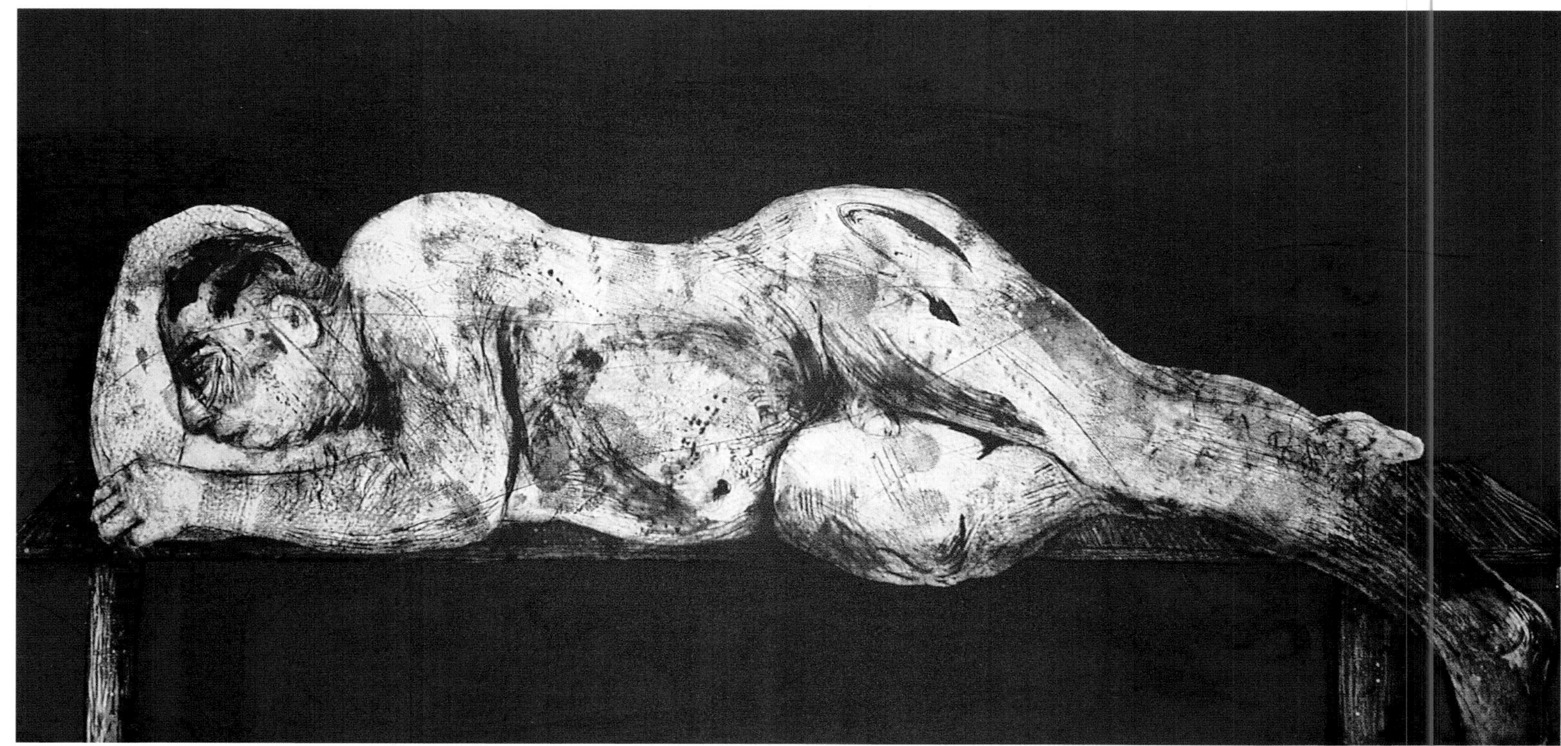

"I have been unable to escape Johannesburg. The four houses I have lived in, my school, studio, have all been within three kilometers of each other. And in the end all my work is rooted in this rather desperate provincial city. I have never tried to make illustrations of apartheid, but the drawings and films are certainly spawned by and feed off the brutalized society left in its wake. I am interested in a political art, that is to say an art of ambiguity, contradiction, uncompleted gestures, and uncertain endings. An art (and a politics) in which optimism is kept in check and nihilism at bay."

William Kentridge was born in 1955 in Johannesburg. He majored in Political Science and African Studies at the University of Witwatersrand in Johannesburg. He also studied mime and theater in Paris.

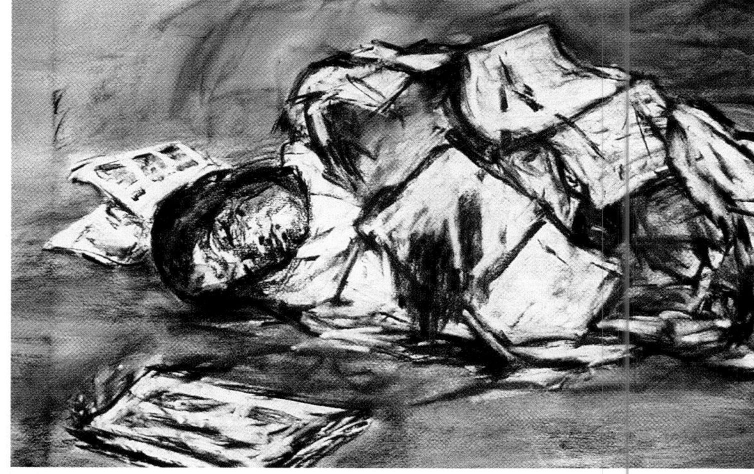

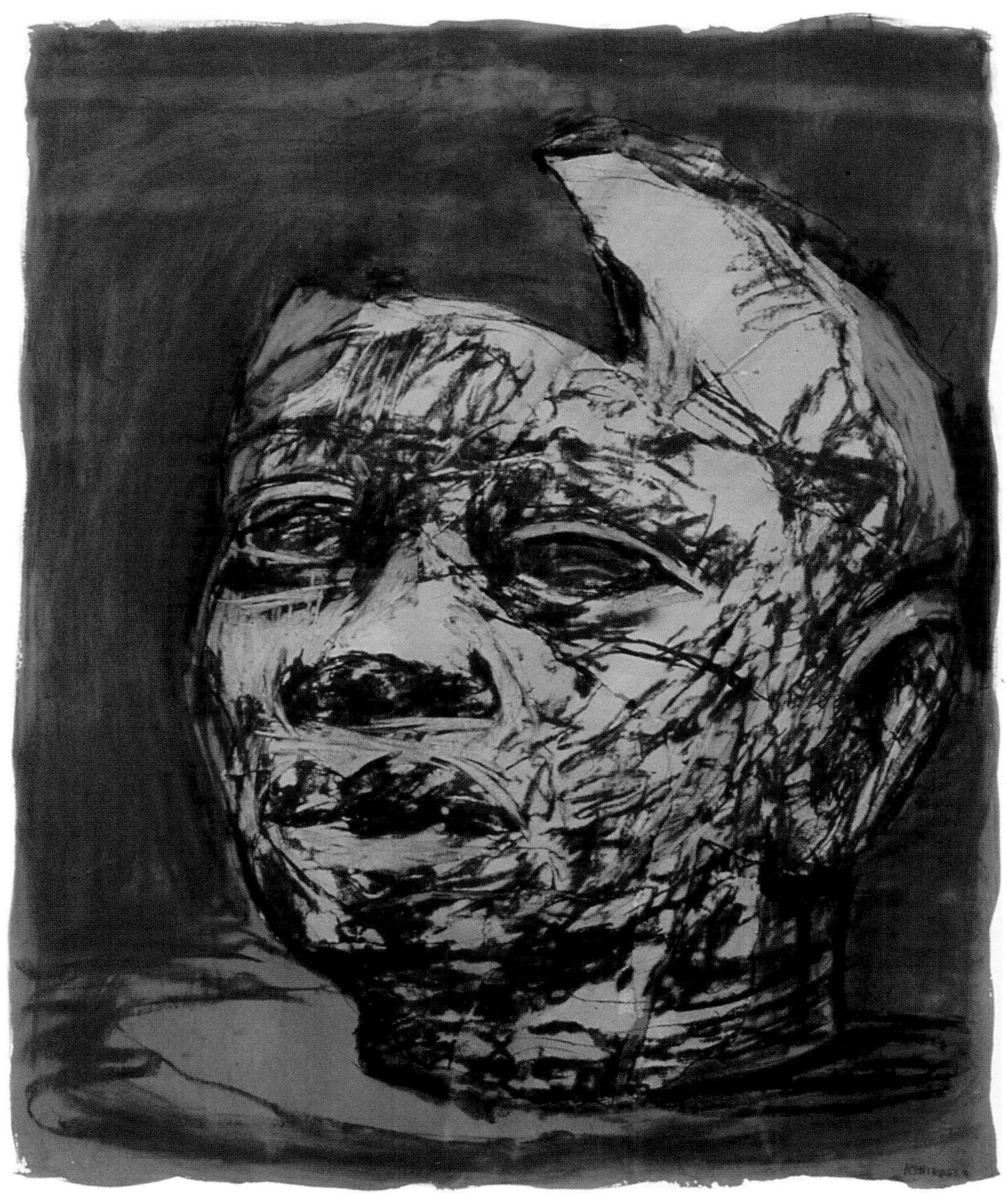

"Large untitled head," 1991, gouache and charcoal on paper

Gavin Younge

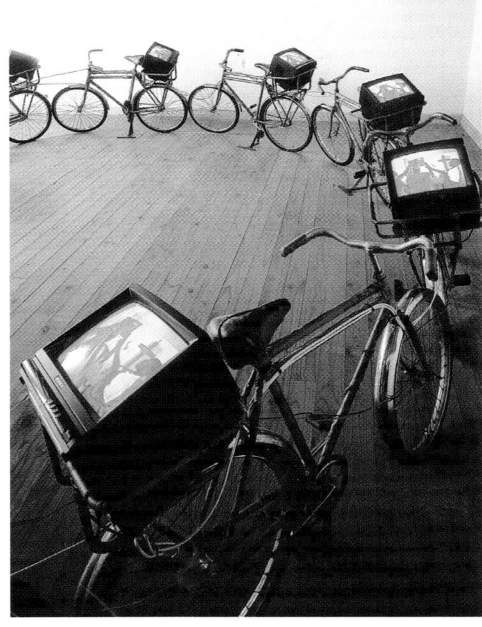

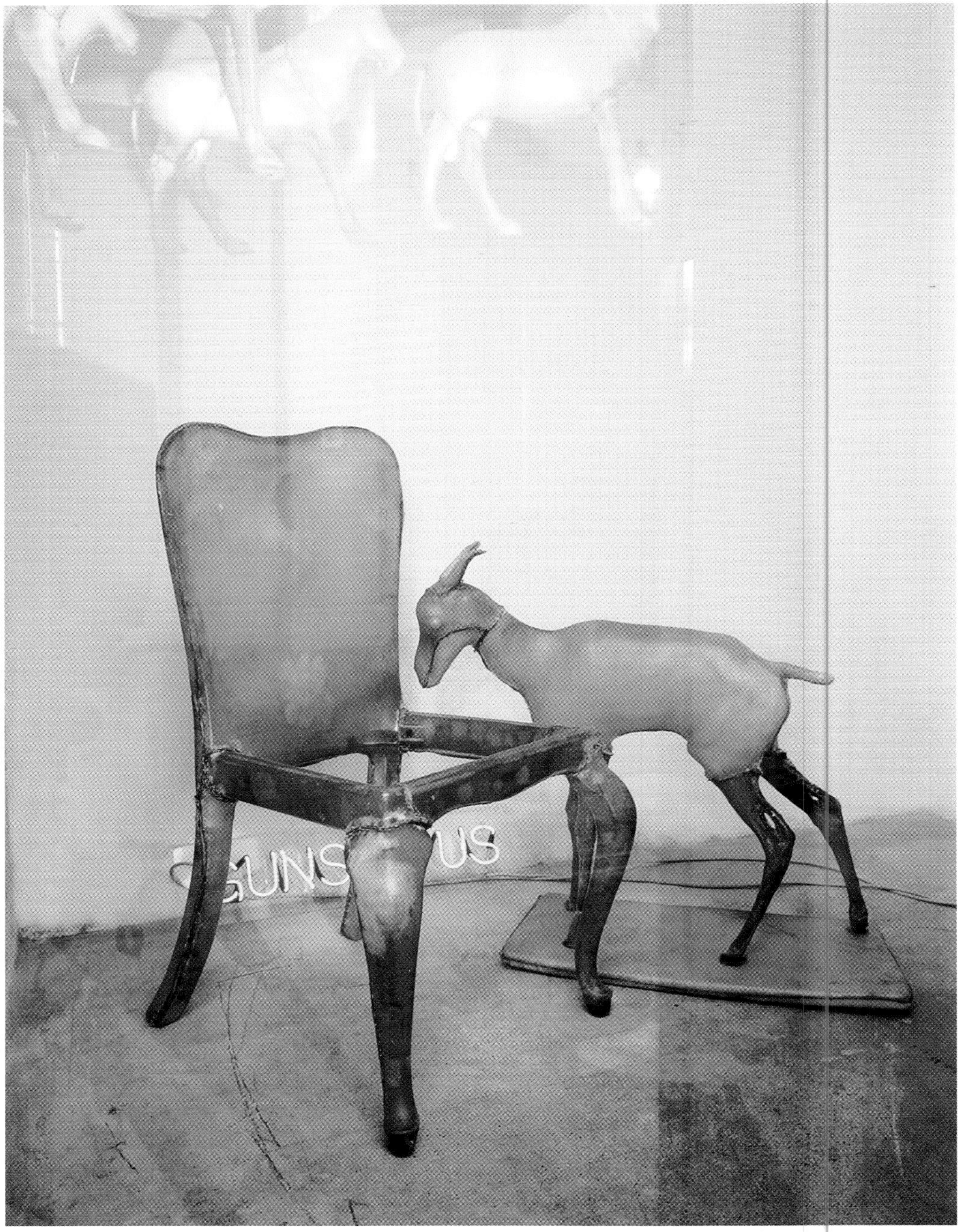

Gavin Younge was born in Zimbabwe in 1947. A sculptor, he is currently the director of the Michaelis School of Fine Art in Cape Town.

Through his works, he portrays the condition of South Africa's changing landscape. Between the new laws on quotas and the concern of maintaining a fragile balance, the South African transition is a series of small persistent injuries. And these injuries are stitched up by Gavin. He uses skin, a metaphor for the envelope that protects and conceals. Mannequins inflated to bursting capacity with stitched up skin (cradle), blankets of newspapers imprisoned by stretched skin (shroud), his work reflects this duality between the visible and the hidden. It carries the memory of a collective trauma.

"Favourite Forces," 1997, installation vidéo ©D.R.
"Guns-R-Us," 1997 ©D.R.

Sue Williamson

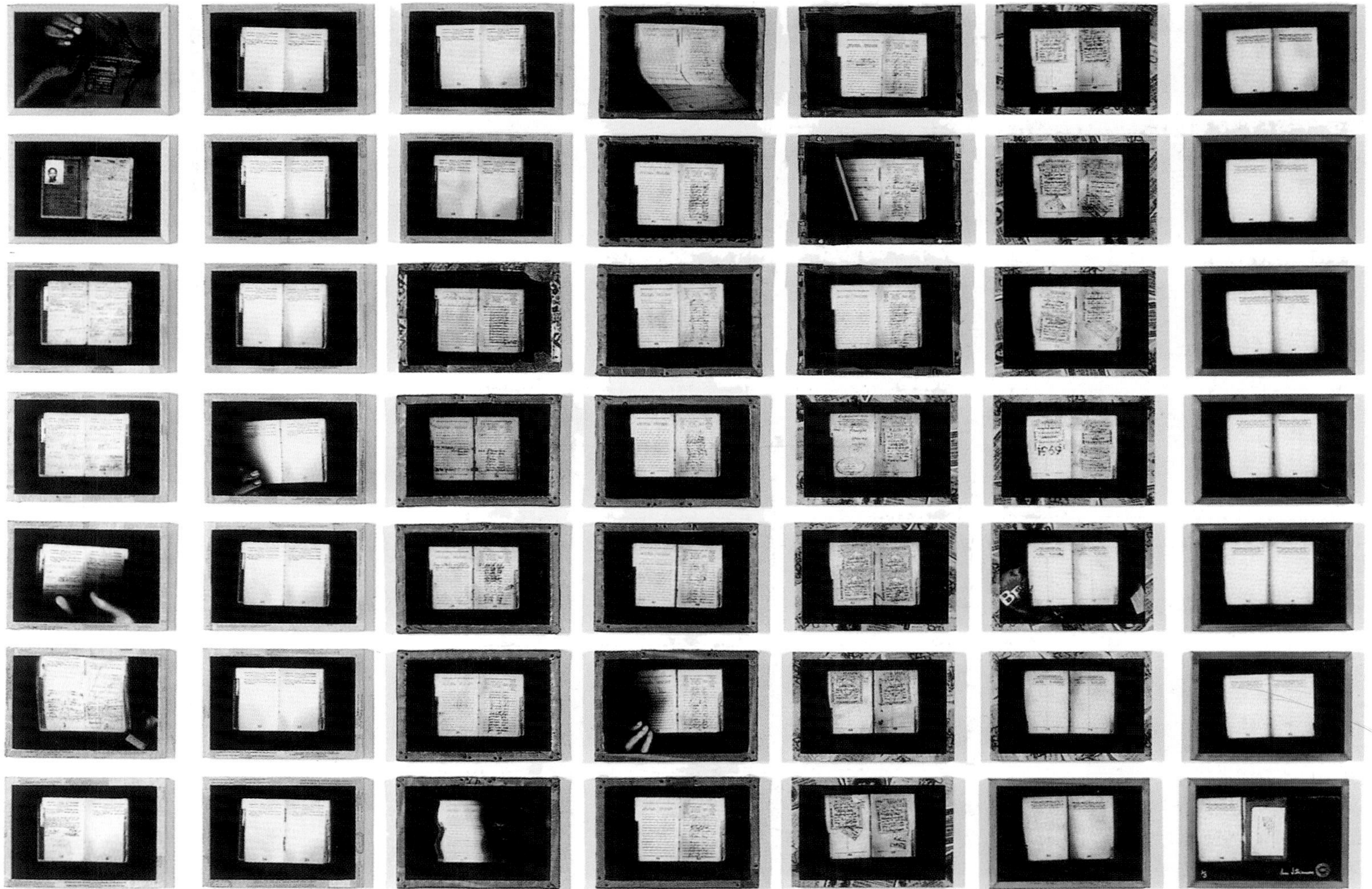

Sue Williamson, born in 1941, studied at the Art Student League of New York and at the Michaelis School of Fine Arts of Cape Town.

"I spent seven days in August 1977 watching the absolute demolition of 2000 houses in Modderdam, a community of squatters settled just on the outskirts of Cape Town, by state agents equipped with bulldozers covered by police officers. The cold brutality I witnessed had a profound effect on my life. I became involved in community actions and this undertaking is reflected in my artistic work. The time I spent at Crossroads (another squatters' center) made me realize that people were hanging mainly family photographs on their walls, usually in brightly colored hand-painted frames."

Sue Williamson continues to explore the painful memory of apartheid in her work.

"For Thirty Years Next to his Heart," 1990 ©D.R.

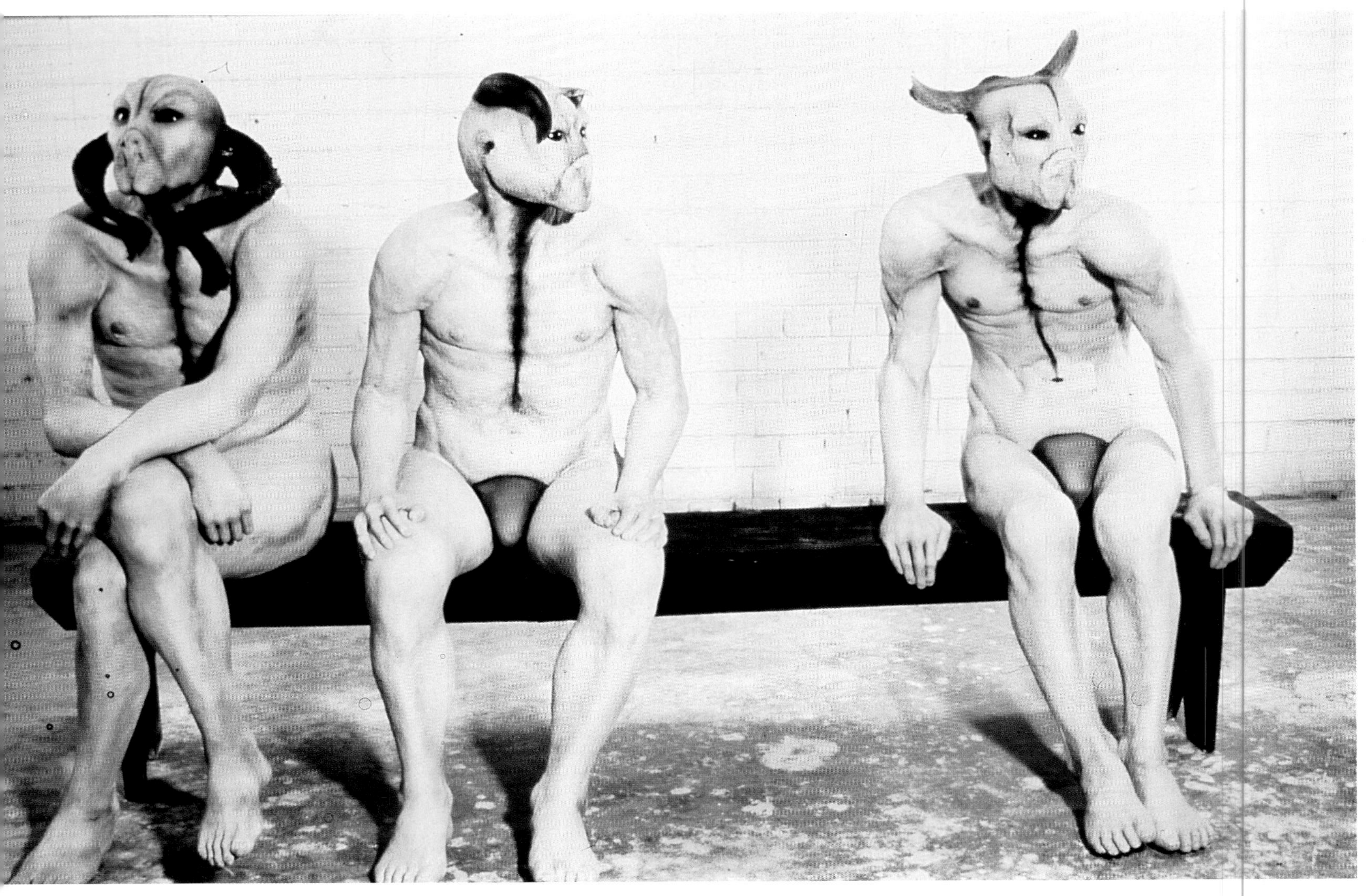

Jane Alexander

Jane Alexander, born in 1959, graduated from the Fine Arts School of the University of the Witwatersrand in Johannesburg. The horrible thing about belonging to a sick society is that one cannot escape the illness. When in the presence of the supernatural universe of Jane Alexander's life-size sculptures, this truth is immediately obvious. One is not so much looking at a work of art, but rather suddenly confronted with the macabre aspect of one's own life.

"One of the reasons I work in a realistic manner is that I don't really feel like explaining what I do," says Alexander. "What I am trying to communicate is communicated easier, I think, through this realism. People may have their own interpretation and if it differs from my idea, that's o.k."

"Butcher boys," 1985 ©South African National Gallery
"Black Madonna" ©D.R.

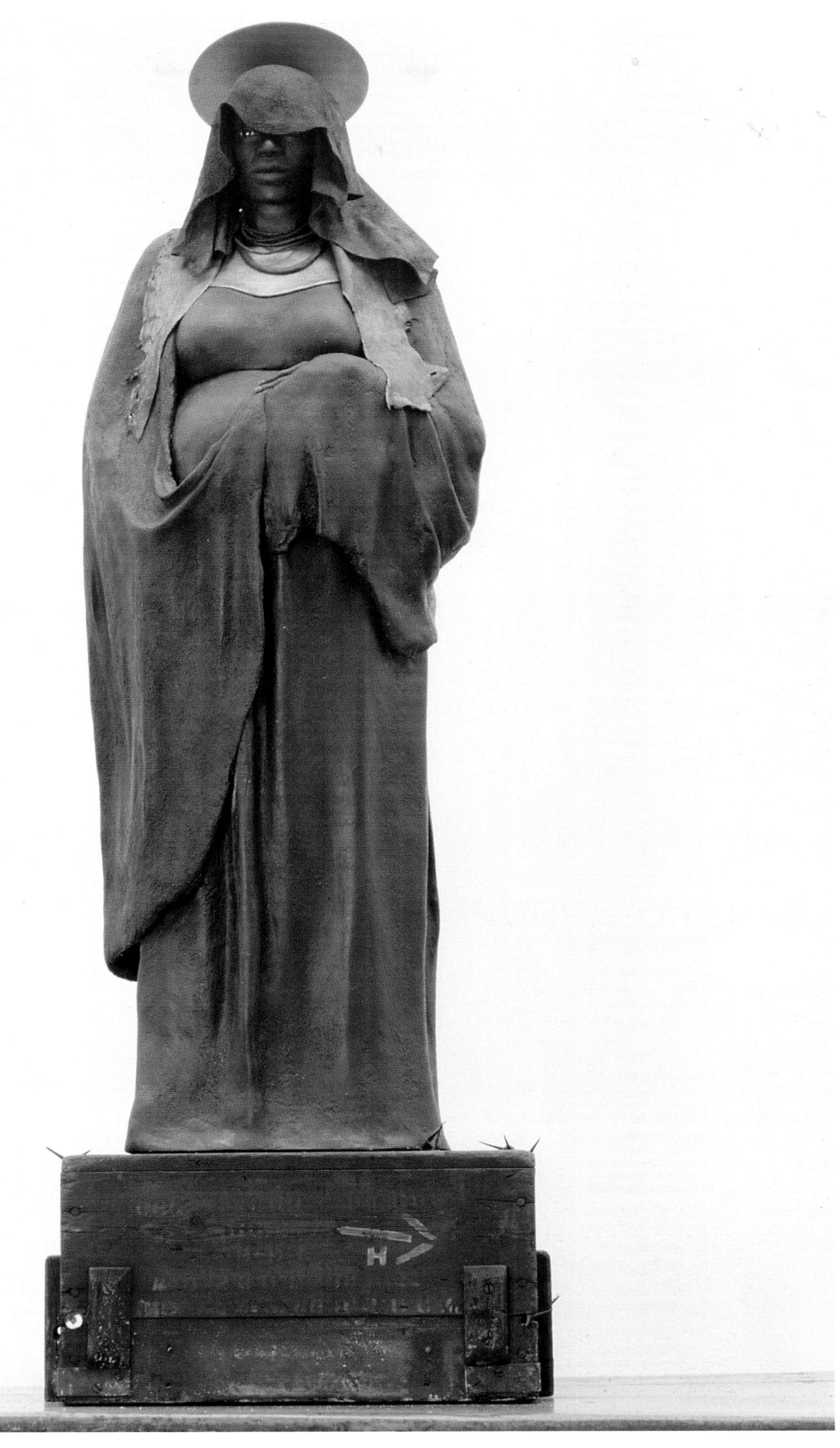

POST-APARTHEID SOUTH AFRICA

Marylin Martin

The 1980s saw the production of an extraordinary body of work that was stimulated and fired by opposition to the apartheid regime and made in the face of adversity. Much of this work was shown on the first major exhibition of contemporary South African art that was organized by David Elliot at the Museum of Modern Art in Oxford, England, in 1990 and subsequently seen at the South African National Gallery. With the release of Nelson Mandela and the unbanning of the liberation movements in the same year, the cultural and academic boycott was rapidly eroded. Since the first democratic elections were held in April 1994, artists have participated in numerous exhibitions throughout the world, as well as in art festivals and biennials. South African art has been the subject of articles in many and divergent publications and catalogues and two biennials were organized in Johannesburg in 1995 and 1997.

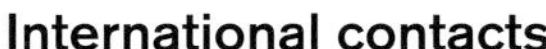

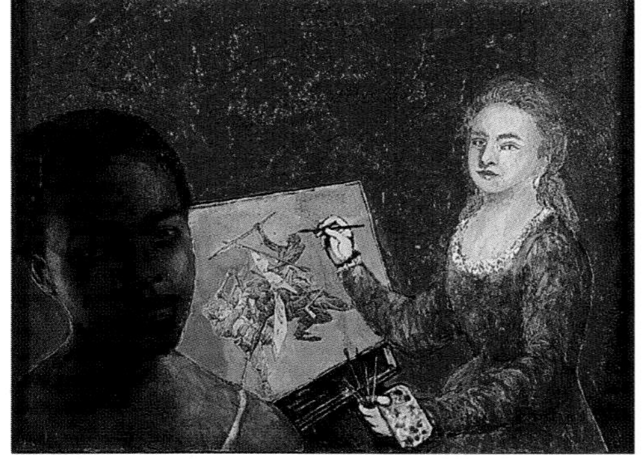

Penny Siopsis (born in 1953), 1990

©Revue Noire

International contacts

Externally new challenges and opportunities were presenting themselves. International exposure has proved to be a liberating factor for some artists, who are engaging in the critical language of contemporary art at the highest level, while for others it is often limiting. The latter applies mostly to artists who come from disadvantage and deprivation and who have difficulty coming to terms with the culture shock that travel brings. Overseas they are celebrated; when they return home the reality of their lives is unchanged. Because the new and unknown are so seductive, and the international art market so competitive and demanding, a great deal of focus of aesthetic production and debate has shifted abroad, leaving many South Africans out of the picture. South African artists and curators had to learn to deal with (and at times be at odds with) the stream of international curators and culture-mongers, who came looking for inspiration and new work. Some were open to influence and discussion, others came with "shopping lists" and tried to call the shots. Through international contact we are witnessing the introduction of new expressive vehicles such as installation, video and performance art and public, site-specific works.

The situation inside South Africa

Internally, entry into the international community brought much soul-searching about the position and meaning of South African art and artists in the international arena. South African society was moving from confrontation and opposition to reconciliation, from resistance to reconstruction. There were calls that political considerations be put aside and that artists find themes, images and metaphors for the new, democratic society, that they embrace the plenitude and beauty of life. Ironically, this cry was going up at the very moment that Americans wanted political art: "*If in the eighties it became fashionable to embrace pastiche and appropriation, make work that referenced the art world or art history, the most visible pressure in the early nineties has been to make political art.*" There was indeed a real crisis in the ranks of artists for whom resistance to apartheid was the prime, or only, source of stimulation and inspiration. Writers, dramatists and photographers were particularly disorientated and affected. Some artists believe that the international mainstream offers the only route of confronting and engaging the art community (and the curators) abroad, while others have reassessed and rejected Western styles, methods and norms; they seek their inspiration in the kinship – or dissimilarity – between Western concepts, traditions of thought and training and the experience of living in Africa. There is a turning inward as artists explore more personal narratives and dramas, as they investigate identity, sexual and gender politics and roles.

The legacies and ravages of colonialism and apartheid are slow to retreat and a number of artists are occupied with unraveling the past. The 150th anniversary of the abolition of slavery was commemorated in 1998 and the profound evil of apartheid has been shockingly brought to consciousness by the work of the Truth and Reconciliation Commission (TRC). The TRC was creat-

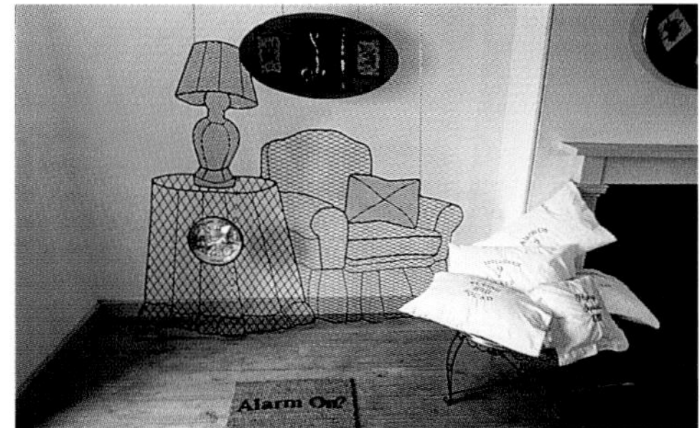

Lise Brice, "Make your home a castle," 1995

©South African National Gallery

ed to record the pain of the past and cleanse the wounds in a series of public hearings, so that healing may take place and give rise to reconstruction and a more just future. Many have, however, criticized the TRC as having been born of political compromise and therefore being no more than a means of subverting the rule of law. Victims have not received reparation. Sue Williamson's (1941-) work Can't Forget, Can't Remember on CD-ROM involves the viewer in testimonies through the direction and manipulation of the imagery and sound track.

Abortion, the death penalty, illiteracy, mass unemployment and poverty, land ownership and restitution, lack of basic services and education, unbridled criminal violence, financial fraud, corruption, rampant capitalism, international drug dealing, growing xenophobia, individual and collective racism and the devastating effect of HIV/Aids on South Africa are raised and discussed every day. Heroes and heroines of the struggle for political liberation are shown to have feet of clay, and cynicism and disillusionment are the order of the day. Poet Sandile Dikeni bemoans the conviction of theft of "the people's poet" Mzwakhe Mbuli and former clergyman and African National Congress (ANC) leader Allan Boesak. They were the "star acts" at the launch of the United Democratic Front (UDF) in Mitchell's Plain, Cape Town in 1983, and participated in the establishment of an order in which the positive aspects of human nature were to be upheld. Dikeni maintains that ."..the falls or deaths of icons denote the ends of eras and the crumbling of particular value systems" and sees "the emergence of a dominant culture that has chosen for itself greed, as the single defining characteristic of this day and times."[1]

The Africus Johannesburg Biennale
One of the most important factors in the entry and acceptance of South African artists in the international arena was the first Africus Johannesburg Biennale held in 1995; the second event (1997) established the country as a major venue on the African continent for the interchange of ideas and discourse on contemporary art. It brought numerous artists, curators, critics, journalists, dealers, collectors and visitors to Johannesburg and to Cape Town where two exhibitions took place. It was taken for granted that a third biennial would follow. To date this has not happened. Why? The reasons are varied and controversial; suffice it to say that the main contributing factor was that the cash-strapped Greater Johannesburg Metropolitan Council decided, without consultation, to pull the plug by closing the biennial overnight on 30 November, when the original closing date was 18 January 1998. This display of philistinism and irresponsibility shocked the art community and public alike, and interested parties and stakeholders rallied to the Africus Institute's call to save the Biennale – and save face. They succeeded in turning the crisis around, but the loss of faith and the termination of key contracts mitigated forcefully against a third Biennale.

Arts and culture policy

What happened in Johannesburg needs to be understood within the bigger picture of arts and culture policy in post-apartheid South Africa. In August 1995 the Minister of the new Department of Arts, Culture, Science and Technology (DACST) initiated a long and democratic process with a view to creating policies and structures for arts, culture and heritage. An Arts and Culture Task Group (ACTAG) was formed and the work culminated in the publication of a White Paper in 1996. Gradually the vision and proposals contained in this document were implemented. In 1997 the National Arts Council (NAC), a channel for public funds to the arts, came into being. In the same year, Business Arts South Africa (Basa) was launched, with the mission to promote and to encourage sustainable partnerships between the private sector and the artist, to their mutual benefit and to that of the community at large. The Cultural Industries Growth Strategy (CIGS) focuses on the production of cultural products for commercial purposes. Restructuring of the former Performing Arts Councils is ongoing and national museums are being brought in line with the new political dispensation.

The initiatives by DACST speak of politi-

[1] "top of the times," Cape Times, 1 April 1999, p. 2.

cal will and commitment and most policies are strong and transformative. And yet there is a long shadow between vision and reality, a shadow that relates to the capacity of government and its departments to deliver and the broader social and economic context in which action has to occur. The macro-economic policy, known as the Growth, Employment and Redistribution (GEAR) strategy is not addressing the inherited inequities of the apartheid system, let along transforming them. Lack of adequate funding threatens the growth and sustainability of the arts, culture and heritage sectors, where many are facing unprecedented crises. The situation is fuelled by individuals and organizations struggling and competing for power and resources. Sadly, for the majority of black artists nothing has changed – they still have no access to education, facilities or even basic materials.

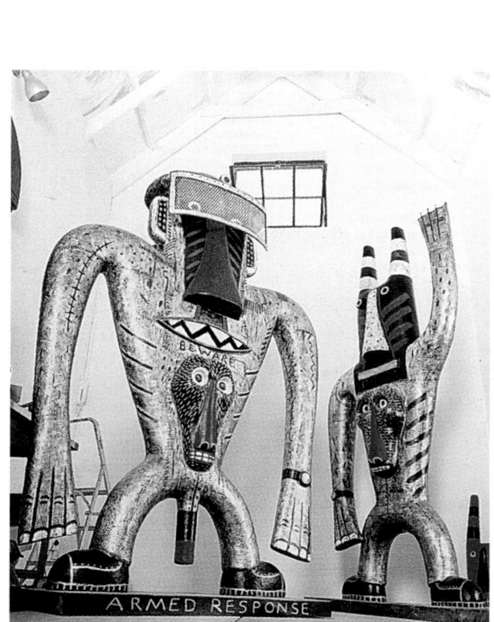

Norman Catherine (born in 1949), "Armed response," 1999
©D.R.

History, identity, memory

The South African experience is made more complex and contradictory within the context of unprecedented technological acceleration and the international discourse around globalism and tradition, multiculturalism and fundamentalism, modernity and atavism. How are visual artists reacting and responding to the challenges and possibilities? There has been a move away from resistance art, where there was no doubt about the identity and nature of the apartheid enemy, to concerns that are infinitely more diversified, ambivalent, unpredictable and contentious. History, identity and memory are central to the enquiry. The haunting land and city-scapes in William Kentridge's (1955-) drawn, animated films form the constant and constantly changing background against which human stories of growth, change, exploitation and pain are told. His many talents have found expression in animated films and related drawings, plays with puppets and opera. In the year 2000 Kentridge is the most internationally renowned of all South African artists. Informed by German Expressionism of the 1920s and 1930s, Kentridge's work is specific to South African history, incidents, experiences and states of mind; yet it finds multiple echoes in the world outside.

Penny Siopis (1953-) has expressed her concern with history, memory and otherness in works that range from the "History Paintings" of the late 1980s to those in which mechanically reproduced images are manipulated and encoded with new meaning and emotions, from assemblages built up of a variety of found objects to videos dealing with personal and political issues. Berni Searle's (1964-) installations, that include life-size photographs of herself covered in spices, as well as actual spices and pigments, deal with identity and apartheid racial classification. Senzeni Marasela (1977-) was born a year after the Soweto uprisings. Using images from press photographs for her embroideries and etched mirrors, she reclaims a history of which she has a sense, but no personal experience. Artists are confronting the socio-political questions of South Africa in 2000 in different ways. Much of Lisa Brice's (1968-) work is fuelled by the escalation of crime and the concomitant threat to personal safety in contemporary South Africa. In her installation Make Your Home Your Castle, she used domestic imagery – beautifully crafted wire furniture, embroidered cloths and pillows, a doormat and burglar bars – to carry shocking messages of suburban angst and security paranoia. The Butcher Boys (1985-86) by Jane Alexander (1959-) was the only South African work selected for the exhibition "Identity and Alterity" curated by Jean Clair for the 1995 Venice Biennale. In a recent series of sculptures and photomontages, entitled "Bom Boys" and "Lucky Girls," Alexander continues to raise questions about power relations between victims and perpetrators, but they are now rooted in urban violence, alienation and deprivation. These masked street children are at the same time pitiable and terrifying. Kay Hassan (1956-) approaches city life from the vantage point of the influx of people and their movements, their possessions and dispossession, their locations and dislocation. The titles of Norman Catherine's (1949-) gigantic sculptures, created in 1999 – In Sheep's Clothing, Armed Response, and Sentry I – capture some of the pre-occupations of South Africans. Simultaneously futuristic and primitive, these theriomorphic beasts utter dark, fearsome sounds as the viewer approaches them – harbingers of a society that lacks coherence, one that faces the danger of regressing.

Confronting the agonies of the past, healing the damage and the wounds, probing racism and resisting official intolerance to criticism on the one hand, and celebrating and exploring the liberation of the imagination on the other, are matters of personal choice. Some artists will remain activists while others will seek inspiration and redemption in beauty and optimism. They can neither be compelled nor coerced to tow any line, political or aesthetic – they are the visionaries who inform and invigorate the present and who shape the future.

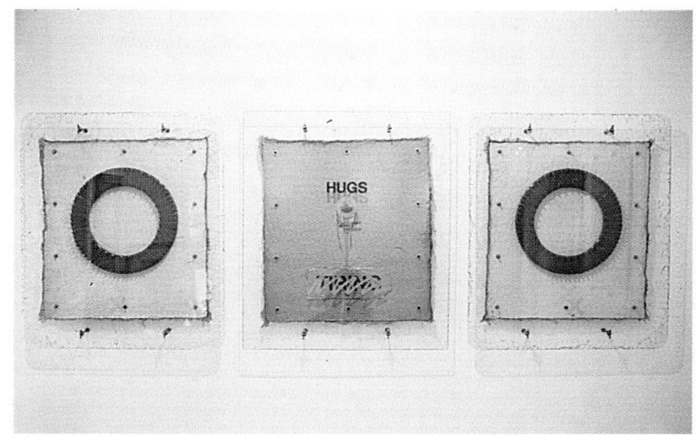

Alan Alborough (born in 1964), "Noughts"

Migrations and convergences

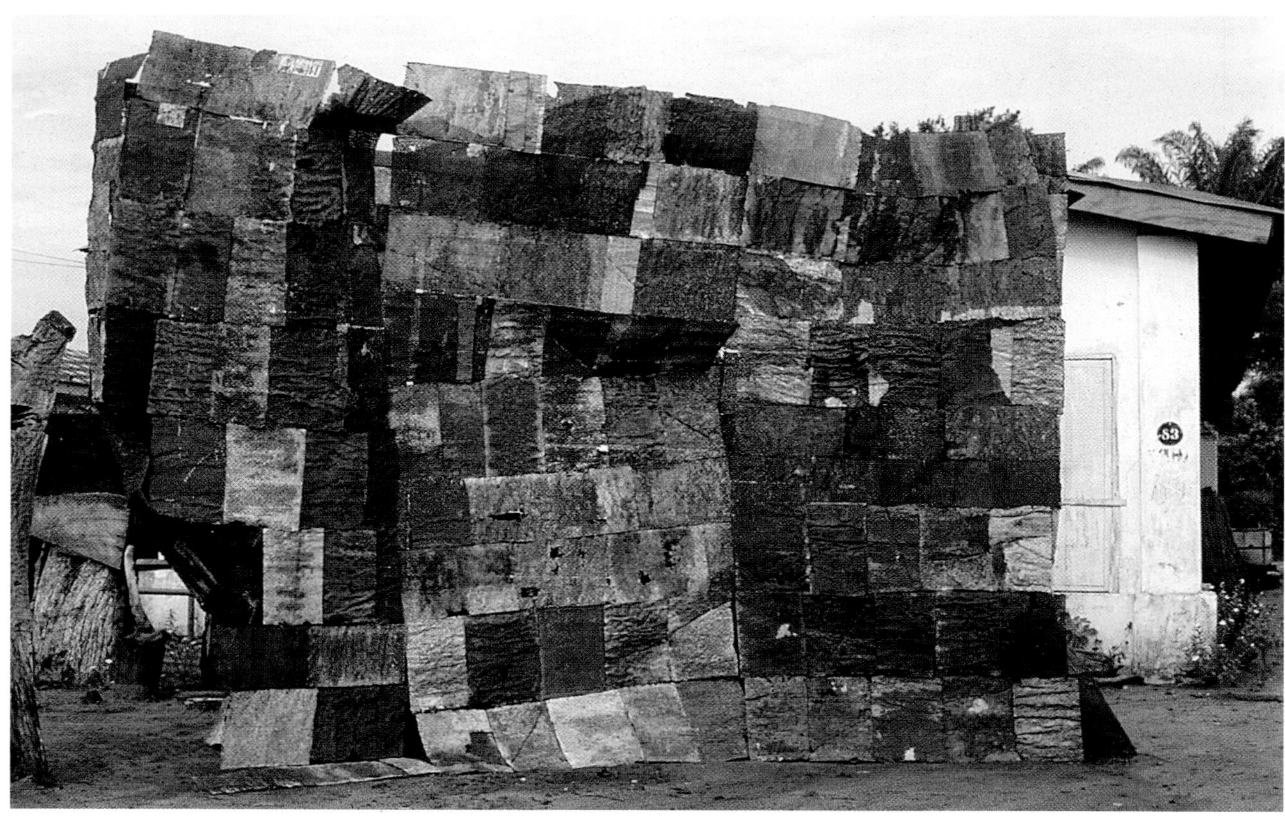

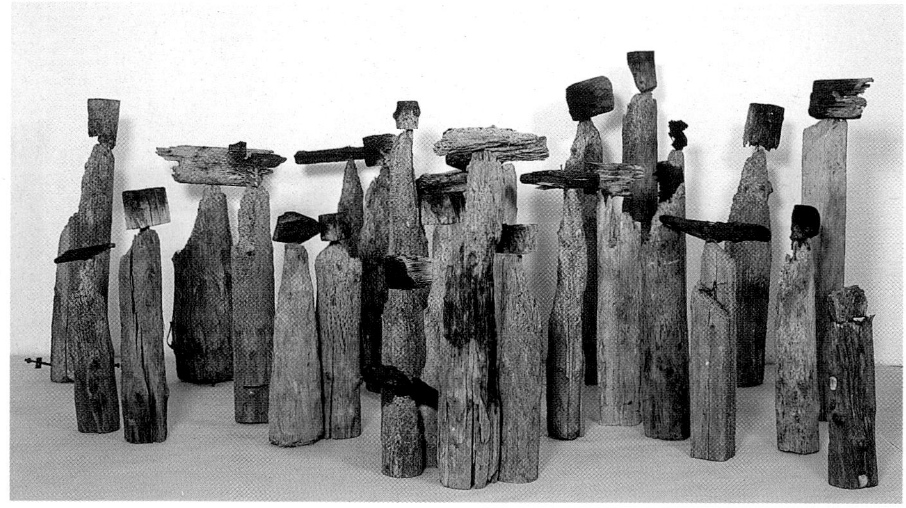

"Crumbling wall," 2000
h. 4 m
©Revue Noire

"Aqua's surviving children," 1996
h. 165 cm
©October Gallery

El Anatsui

In 1975, sculptor El Anatsui, born in Ghana in 1944, was appointed professor at the Fine Arts Department of the University of Nigeria in Nsukka, where he can still be found today. The sculptures of Anatsui refer to African esthetic traditions. The Uli esthetics of the African rebirth practices at the School of Nsukka benefited from Anatsui's approach: use of Ghanaian Adinkra patterns, Ewe techniques with ceramic art and the visual structure of striped woven fabrics. Anatsui's unusual technique (he sculpts partially charred burnt wood panels, metal pieces and found objects that he organizes in productions) and the proliferation of symbolic images in his sculpture allow us to "read" his work, as if we had a text before our eyes. His sculptures concentrate on the history of Africa (especially its colonial past) and the relationships of his history with the transgressions of contemporary existence on the continent.

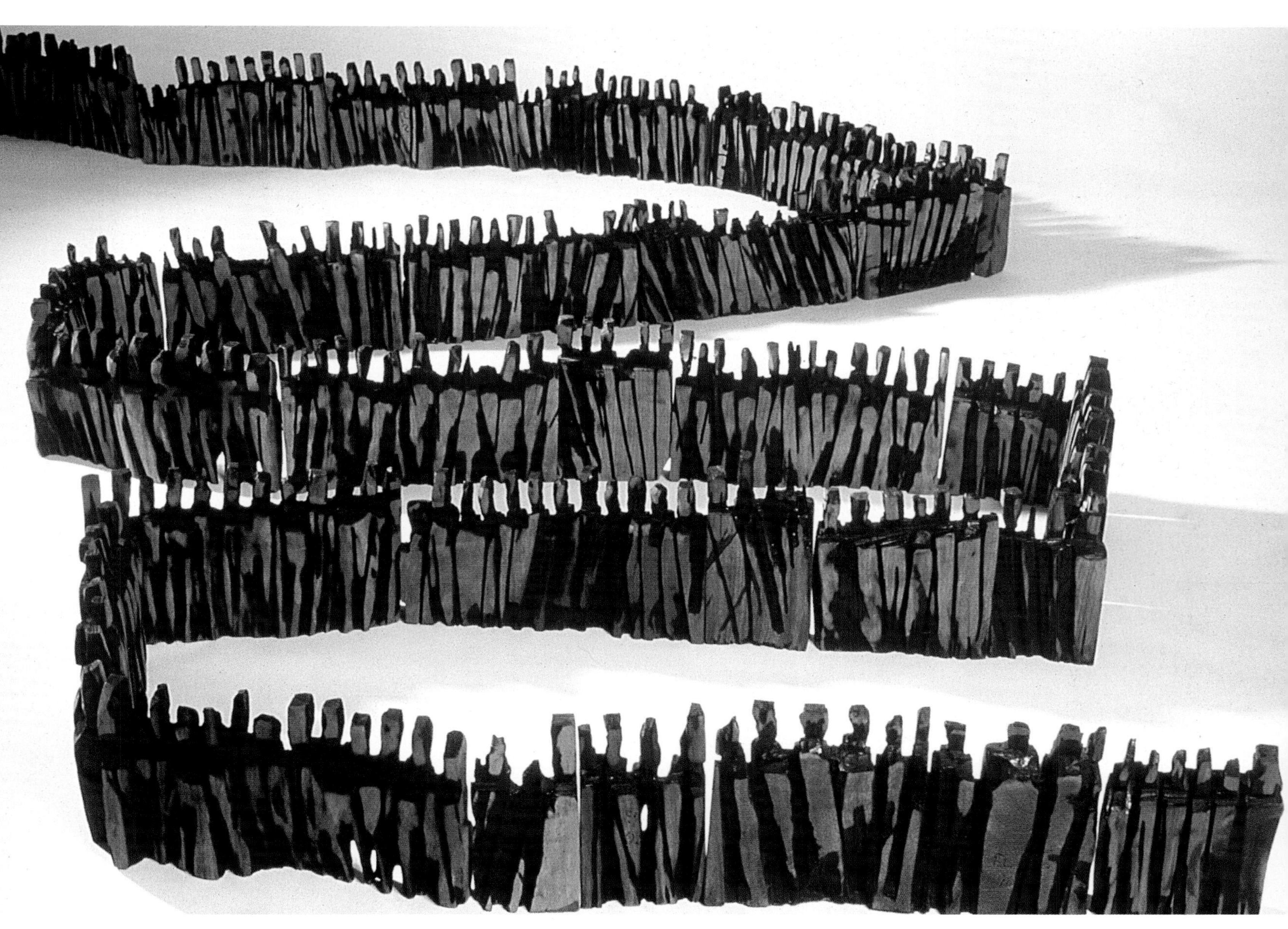

"Visa Line," 1992
wood, h. 20 cm

Moustapha Dimé

Born in Louga in 1952, Moustapha Dimé died in Saint-Louis, Senegal in July 1998.

"I experienced several "circumcisions" in my life: the relationships I had with sculpture, with others and with myself are decisive passages. New values were added on as I gained new experiences. For example, in May 68, I was studying sculpture and that radicalized my work. In the 70s, the sculptor was considered an artisan and not a social player. There were no references to allow me to move forward. At school, the West was the reference for academic art education.

I don't like the word "recovery." I am not going to dig through garbage bins and dumps. I feel the need to invest myself in the expressive means that certain materials offer me and that I use to say what I want to say. I am looking for harmony between things and materials. That is all I am interested in, nothing else."

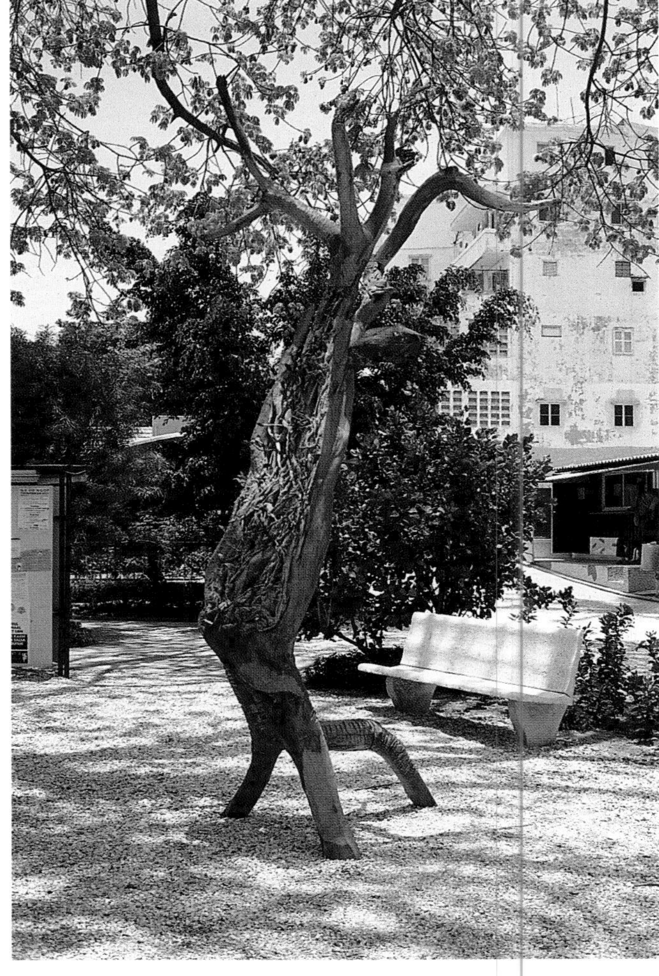

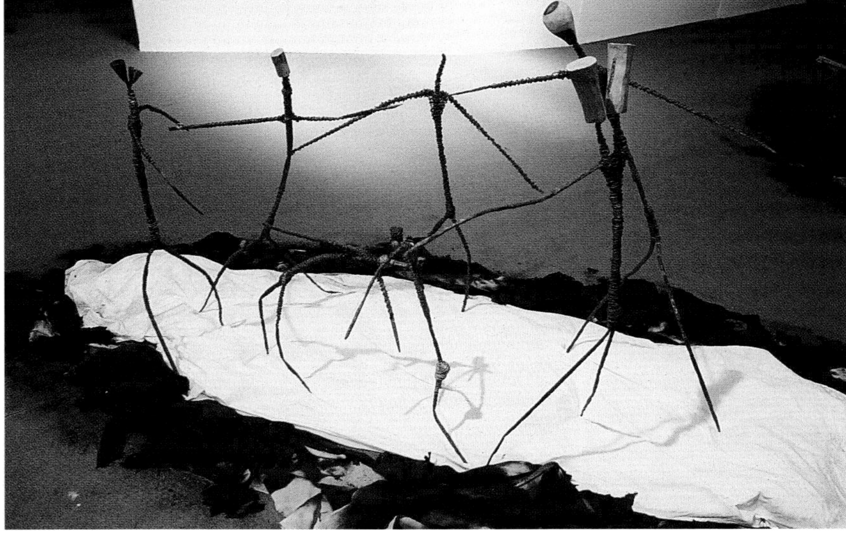

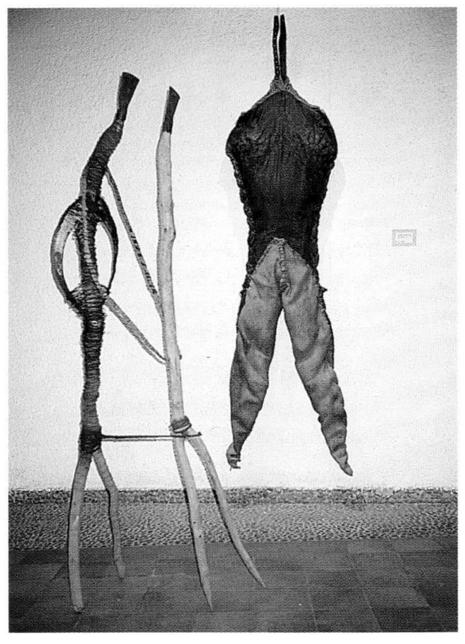

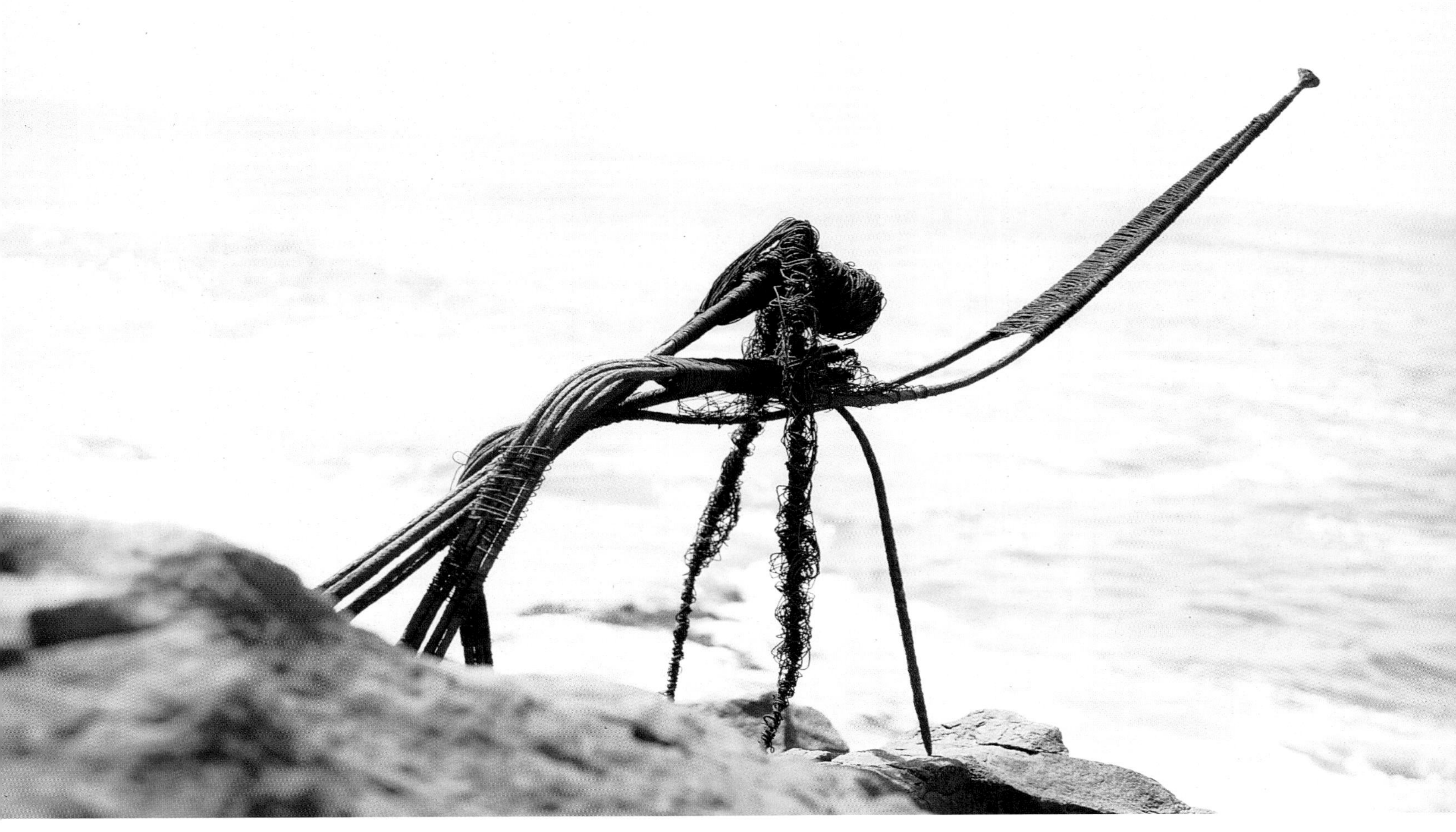

facing page:
"The Circle," 1996
©Revue Noire

above:
"AIDS," 1996
©Bouna Medoune Seye/Revue Noire

António Ole

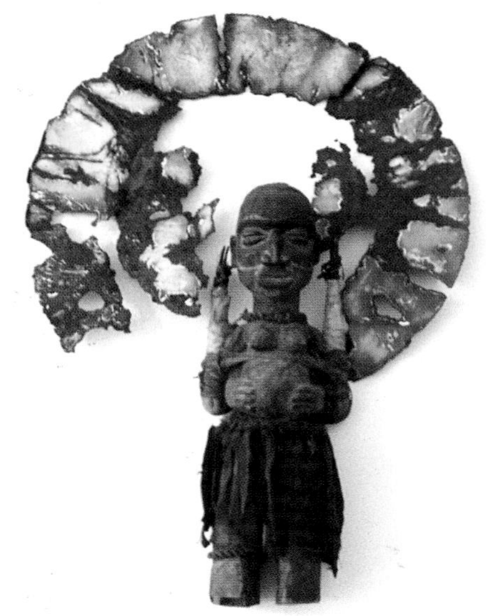

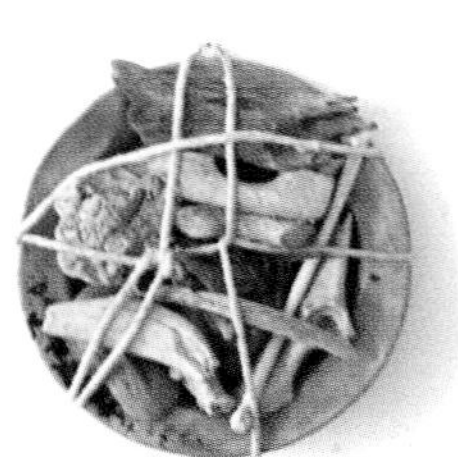

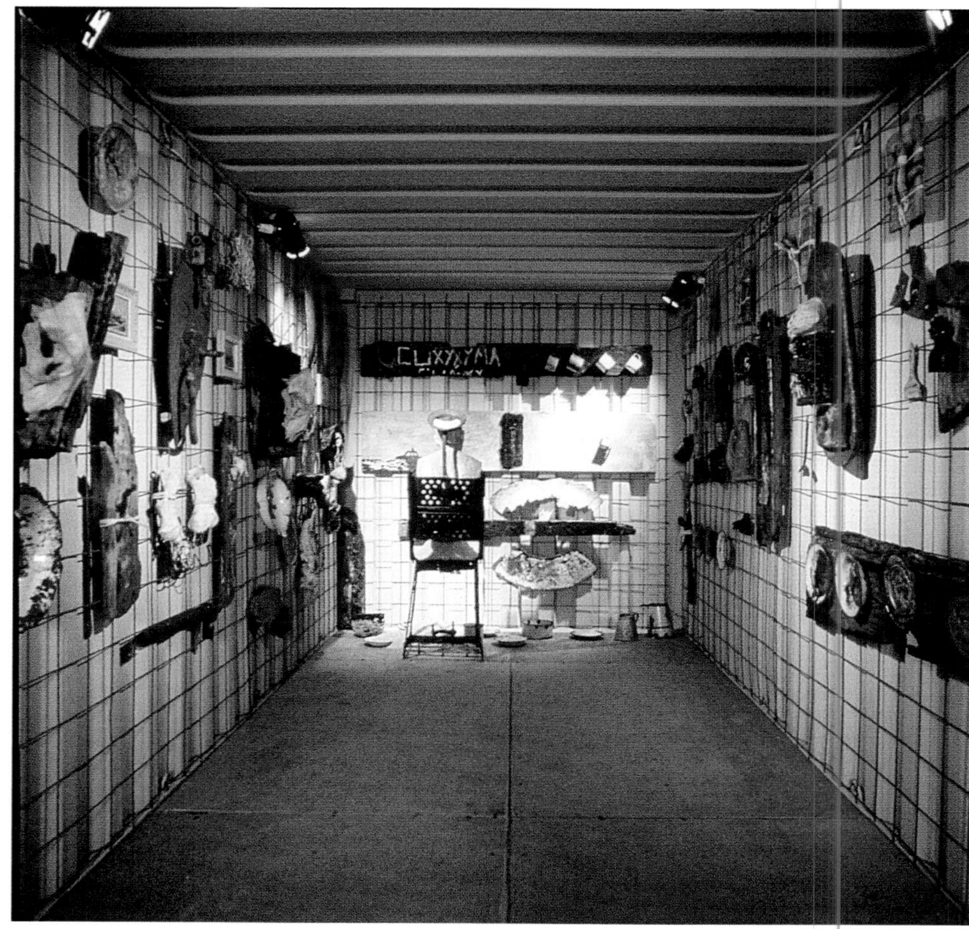

António Ole was born in Angola in 1951. This self-taught artist began painting at age 16 and today navigates among several expressions: painting, sculpture, video and photography. Deeply marked by his country's turbulent trajectory, he draws inspiration from reminiscences of Angolan history. Colonial letters, old anonymous portraits, film extracts, rusty utensils, mannequins gagged with gas masks – a reflection of imminent catastrophe – show a common aborted adventure where the past, present and future confront each other.

Small sculptures and heteroclite objects each tell a dramatic story. Behind the malaise that emerges from these facilities is hidden a man who stands as a parapet of a drifting society. A series of tragic "beacons" that disintegrate in view of the capital city's amnesia and that he is patiently reviving.

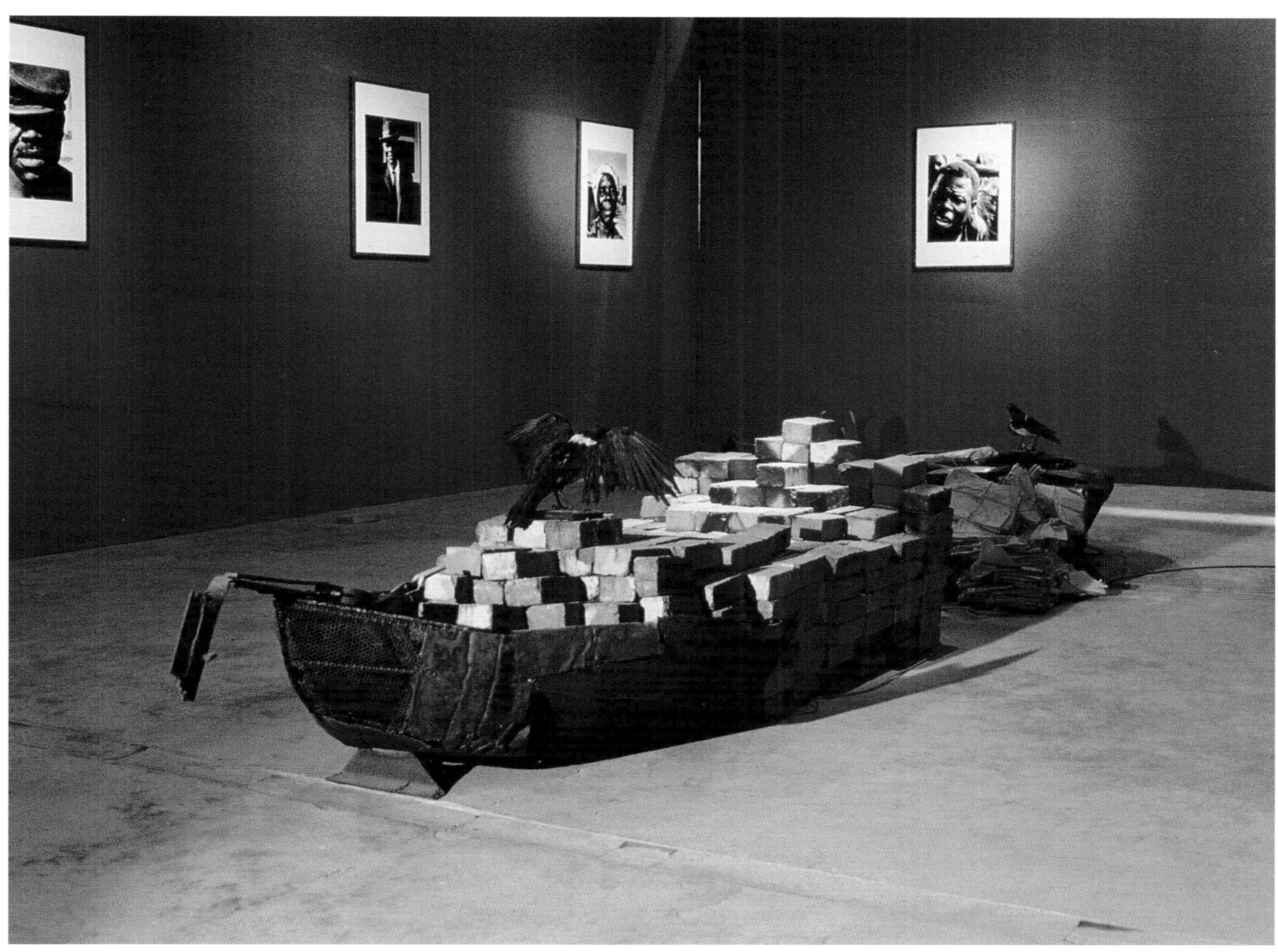

facing page:
"Margem da zona limite," The Biennial of Dakar, 1998
©Revue Noire

"Deep South," 1996
©Roberto Fontana

this page:
"Margem da zona limite," Johannesburg Biennial, 1995
©Jean Brundrit

Serigne M'Baye Camara

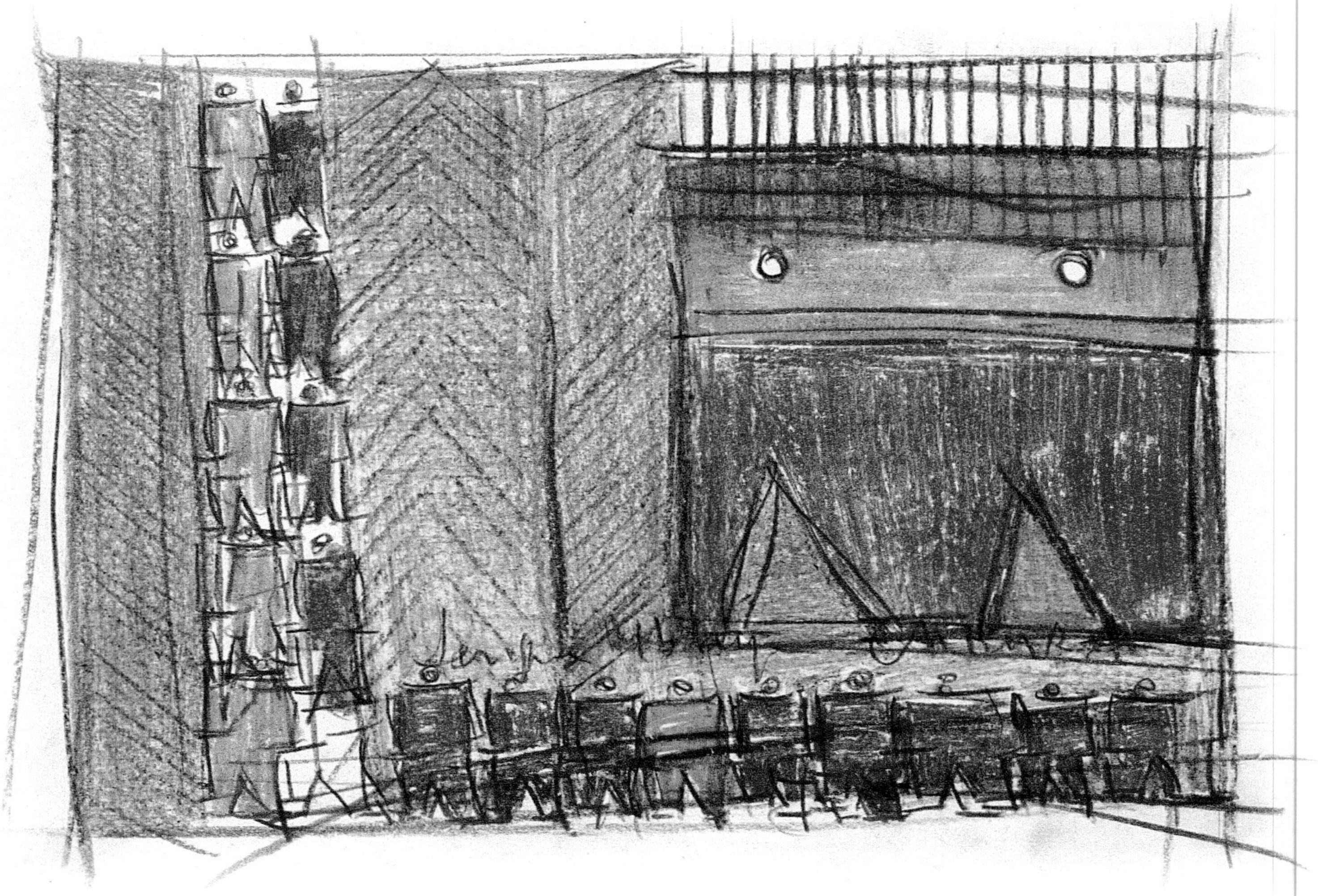

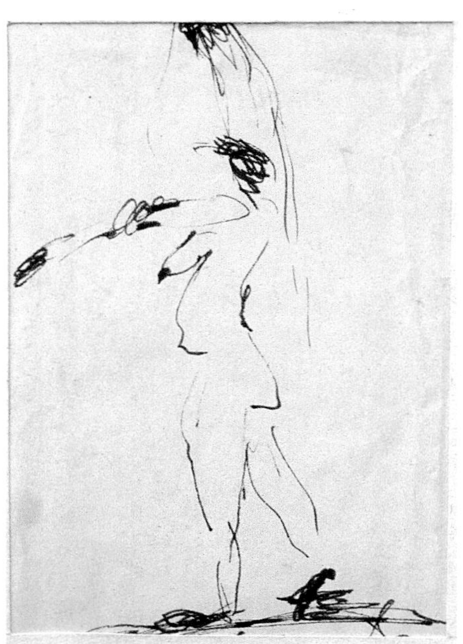

Serigne M'Baye Camara was born in Senegal in 1948. From 1972 to 1977, he was at the Fine Arts School of Dakar and then the École Supérieure de Cachan in France. He works his paintings using the Supports Surfaces artists' method, without a frame, by cutting up, overlapping and repeating elements such as friezes, patterns, lines, color spots and anthropomorphic silhouettes. His simple combinations lead, however, to complex worlds in chromatic ranges limited to one or two shades. A virtual and poetic calligraphy on an eternal search.

Kofi Setordji

Kofi Setordji, a sculptor and painter, was born in Ghana in 1957. After teaching himself graphic art and producing very commercial work, he began to train at the studios of the Ghanaian sculptor Saka Acquaye in 1984.

He was very affected by the images of Rwanda and decided, in 1997, to produce a creation-production on the theme of genocide. "Art is therapy. In order to master the creativity I need, my anger must become positive by striking on metal or stone. If I work with earth, the bad feelings subside."

In using all types of materials and mediums, Genocide portrays the victims, accused, judges and witnesses, and gives the eyes an essential place. Only the eyes "speak" when faced with suffering or death. Genocide is a multidimensional work through its ensemble of sculptures, paintings and a universe of sounds. In it man, in the spiral of life and death, is no longer quite sure when he is a spectator and when he is a player.

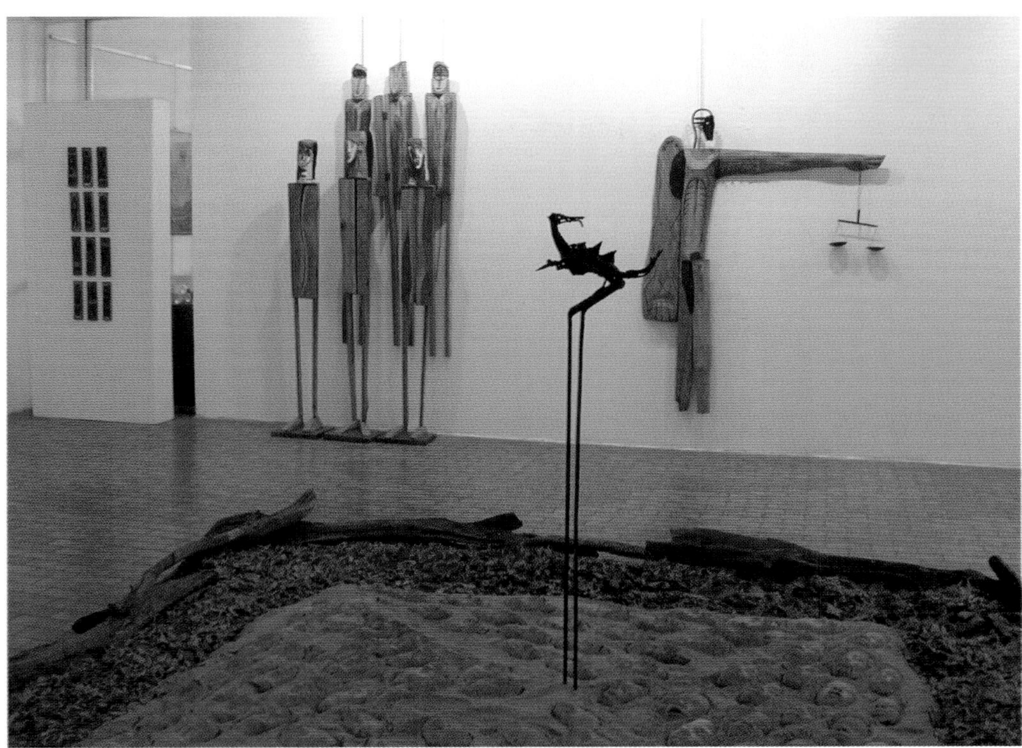

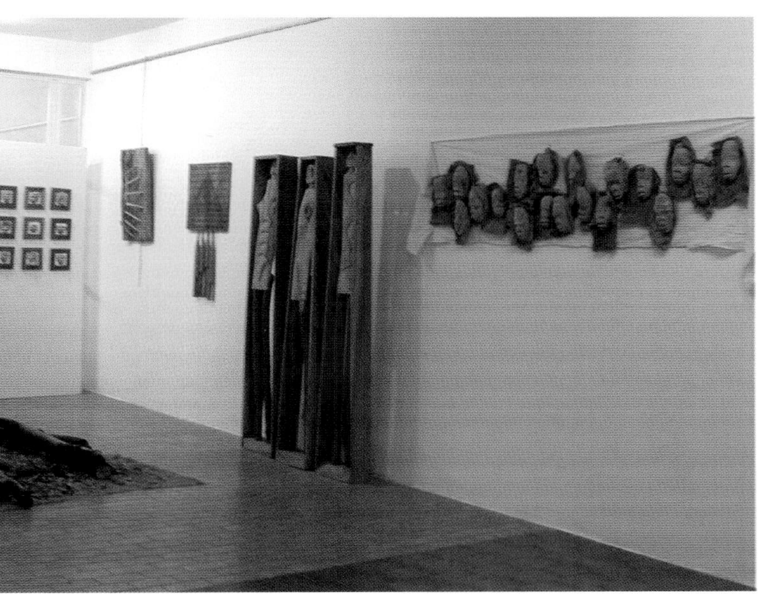

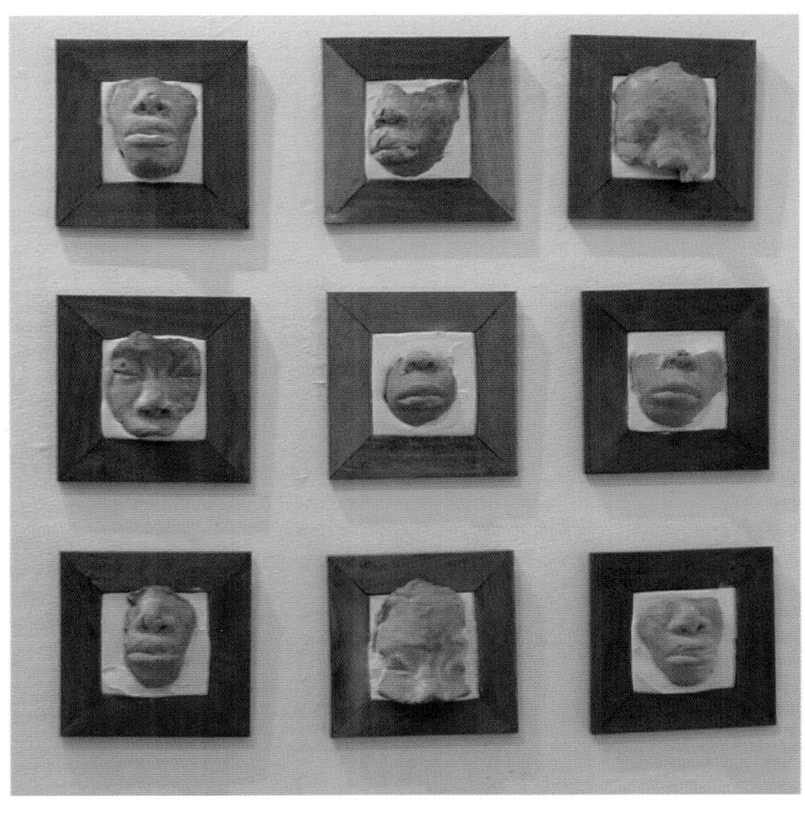

"Rwanda, homage to victims", The Biennial of Dakar, 2000

Viyé Diba

Viyé Diba was born in Senegal in 1954. He graduated from the Fine Arts School of Dakar and the École Pilote International d'Art of Nice. Today he teaches at the Fine Arts School of Senegal. Diba has been questioning his work for some ten years. From his initial paintings, with a central character moving amidst bright colors, he now seeks abstraction. The character is no more than a silhouette and matter takes a predominant place: strips of cotton, pieces of animal hide, mysterious sewn pockets, bits of wood. Without turning it into a technique, he produces countless paintings and recently had a turning point with a living "play" combining men with painted bodies who whisper, an actor who chants psalms, paintings and sacrifice altars, all in the dark. Diba wants to get back in touch with the old tradition of "dialoguing" and transforms the spectator into a future initiate.

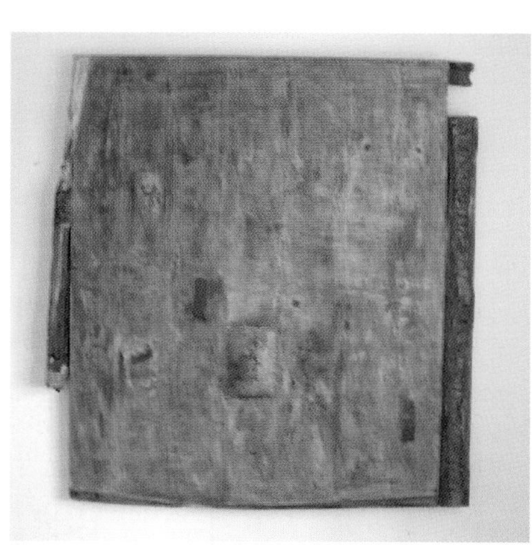

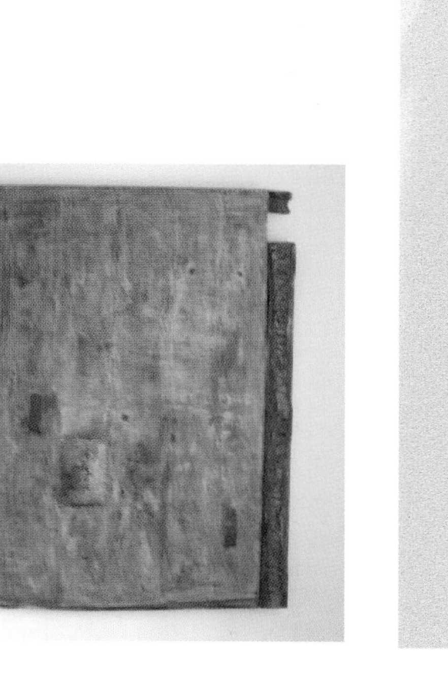

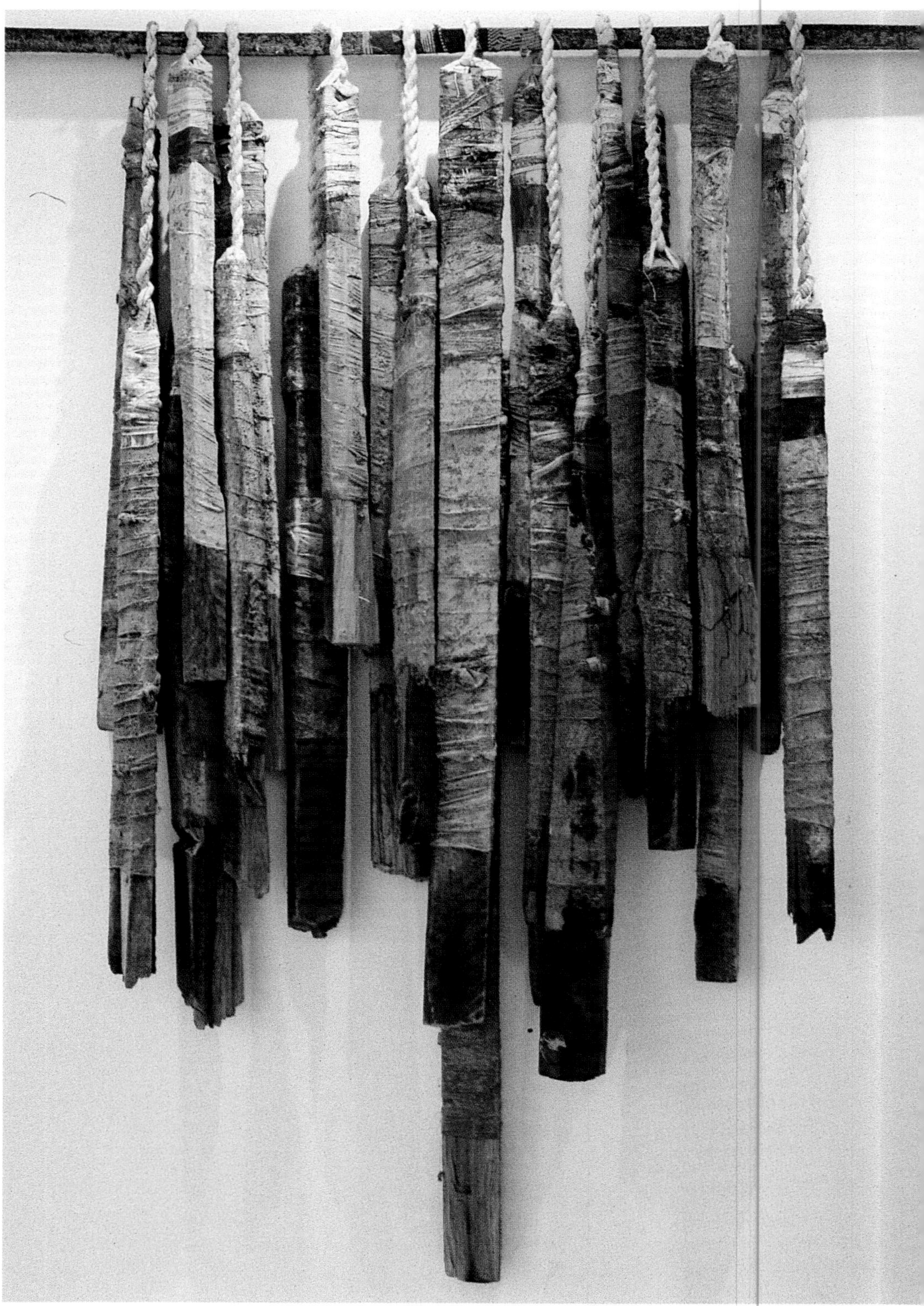

left: ©Revue Noire
right: ©Ananias Léki Dago/Revue Noire

Amahiguere Dolo

Amahiguere Dolo was born in Mali in 1955. He began sculpting at a very young age, gathering pieces of wood hauled by the river. From these stumps or roots, he makes forms, beasts, bodies and faces appear that draw heavily on Dogon mythology. Using the smallest bump or accident on the wood, he develops a vocabulary of powerful and sensual forms.

Following his studies at the National Art Institute of Bamako and a position at the Gao Museum, he settled in Ségou to work exclusively on his art. His practice is above all personal, almost secretive and cabbalistic. His works were only shown for the first time in 1988, in Spain, Mali and France.

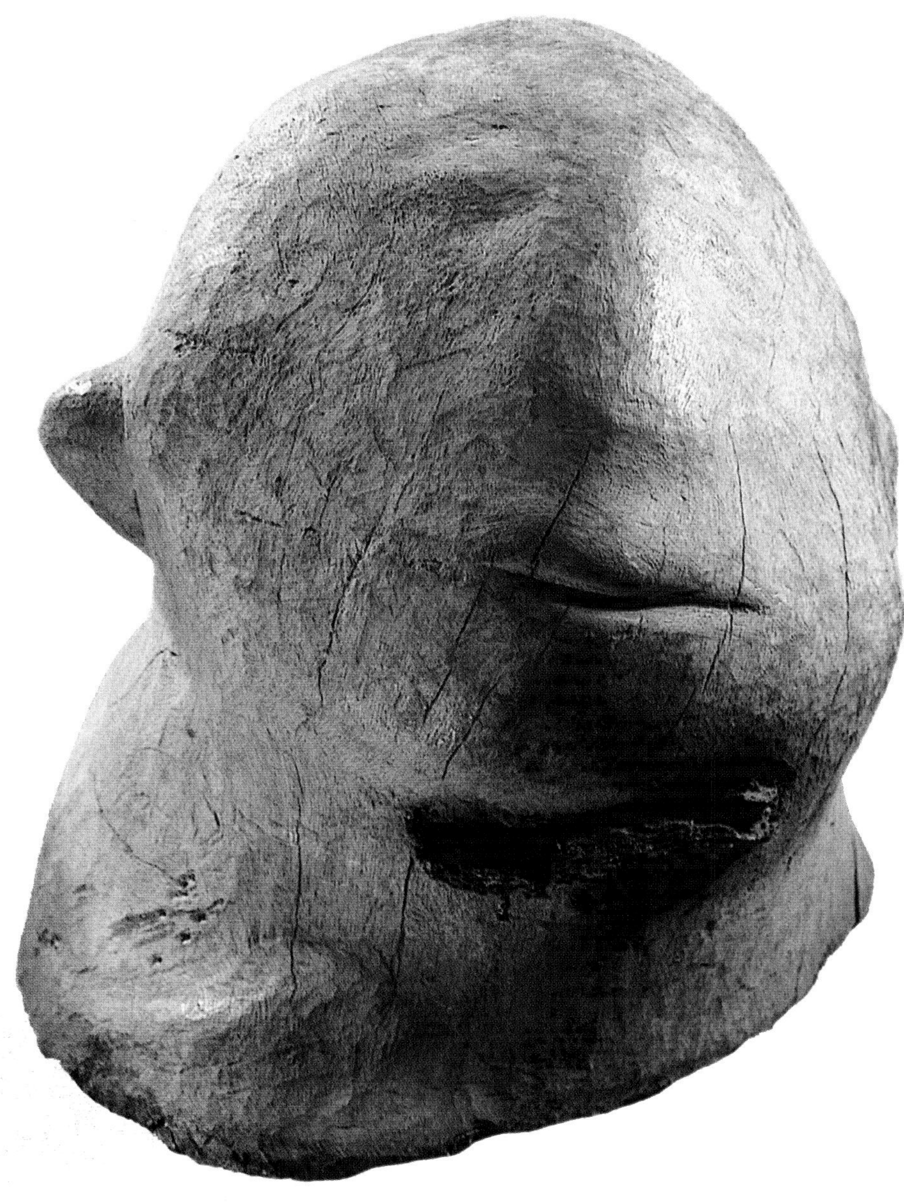

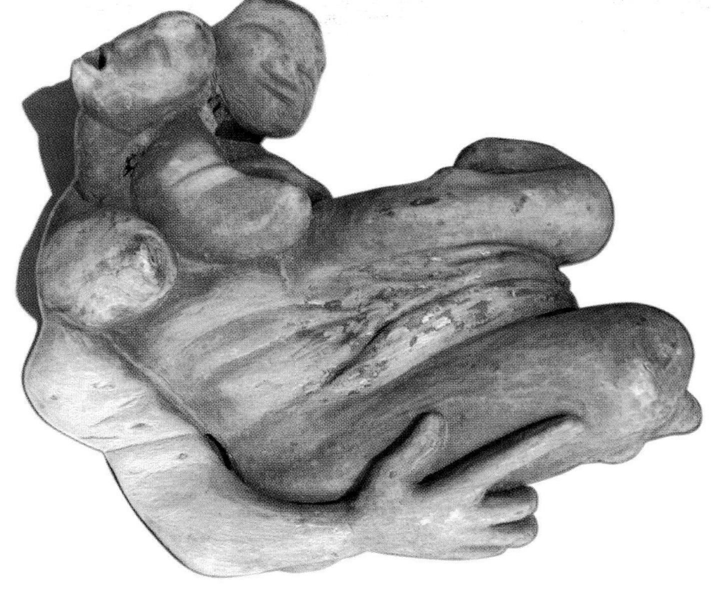

"Iné-Kouh"
wood, H. 50 cm
©Éditions de l'Œil

"Yana koub leyè, spirit of water"
wood, H. 60 / L. 53 cm
©Éditions de l'Œil

Berry Bickle

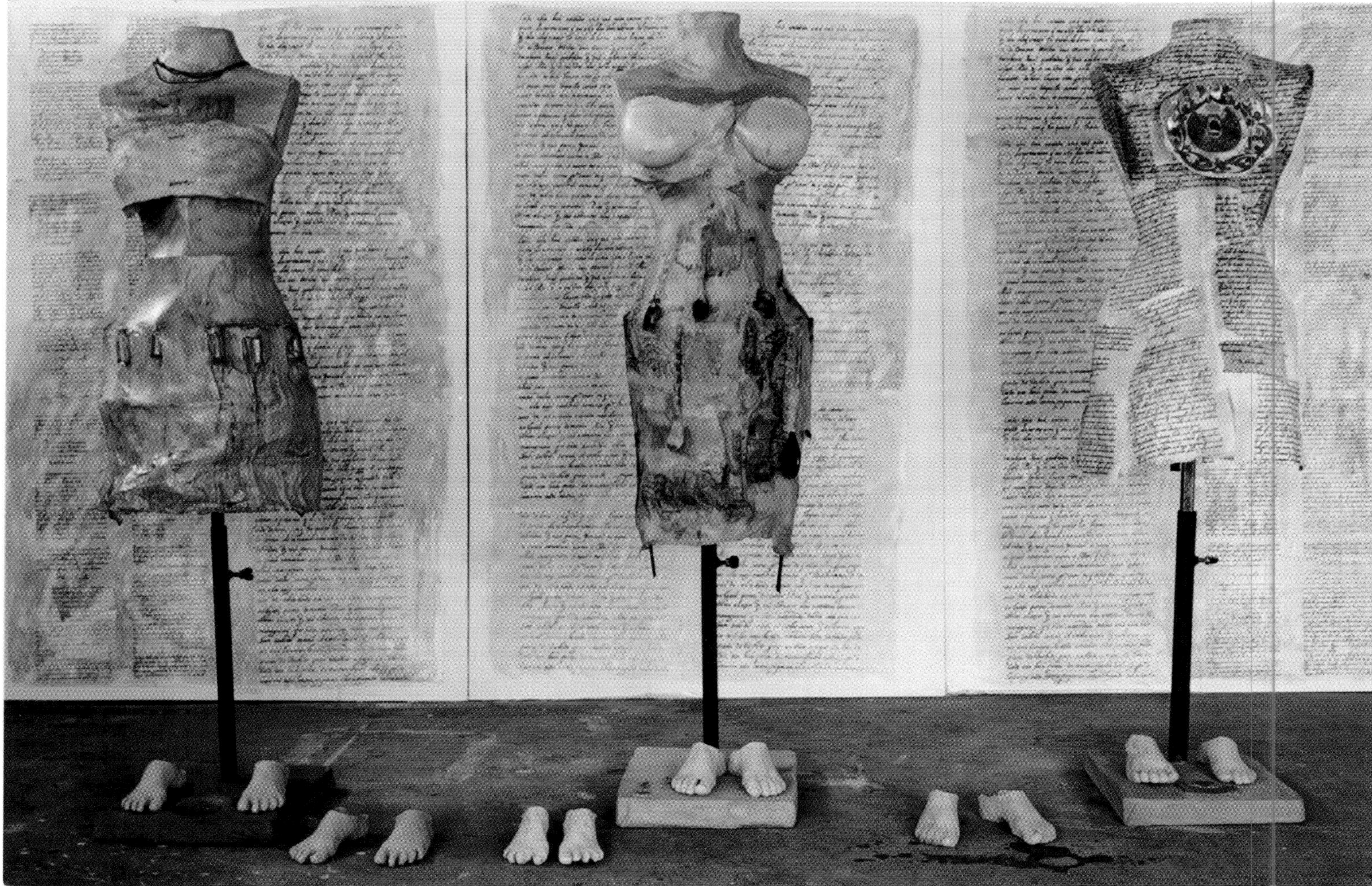

Berry Bickle was born in Zimbabwe in 1959. After pursuing art studies in South Africa, she returned to Harare in Zimbabwe. In her work, she questions the primitive elements, allows proverbs to speak, awakens memories and continuously commits herself as if to exorcise the sorrow, pain and anguish of a divided society. This white woman was born in this country that changed its name when she was twenty years old. Berry Bickle's productions disturb as much as the injuries that the country no longer knows how to heal.

"The children of this world are in their generation wiser than the children of the light"
180 x 360 x 130 cm

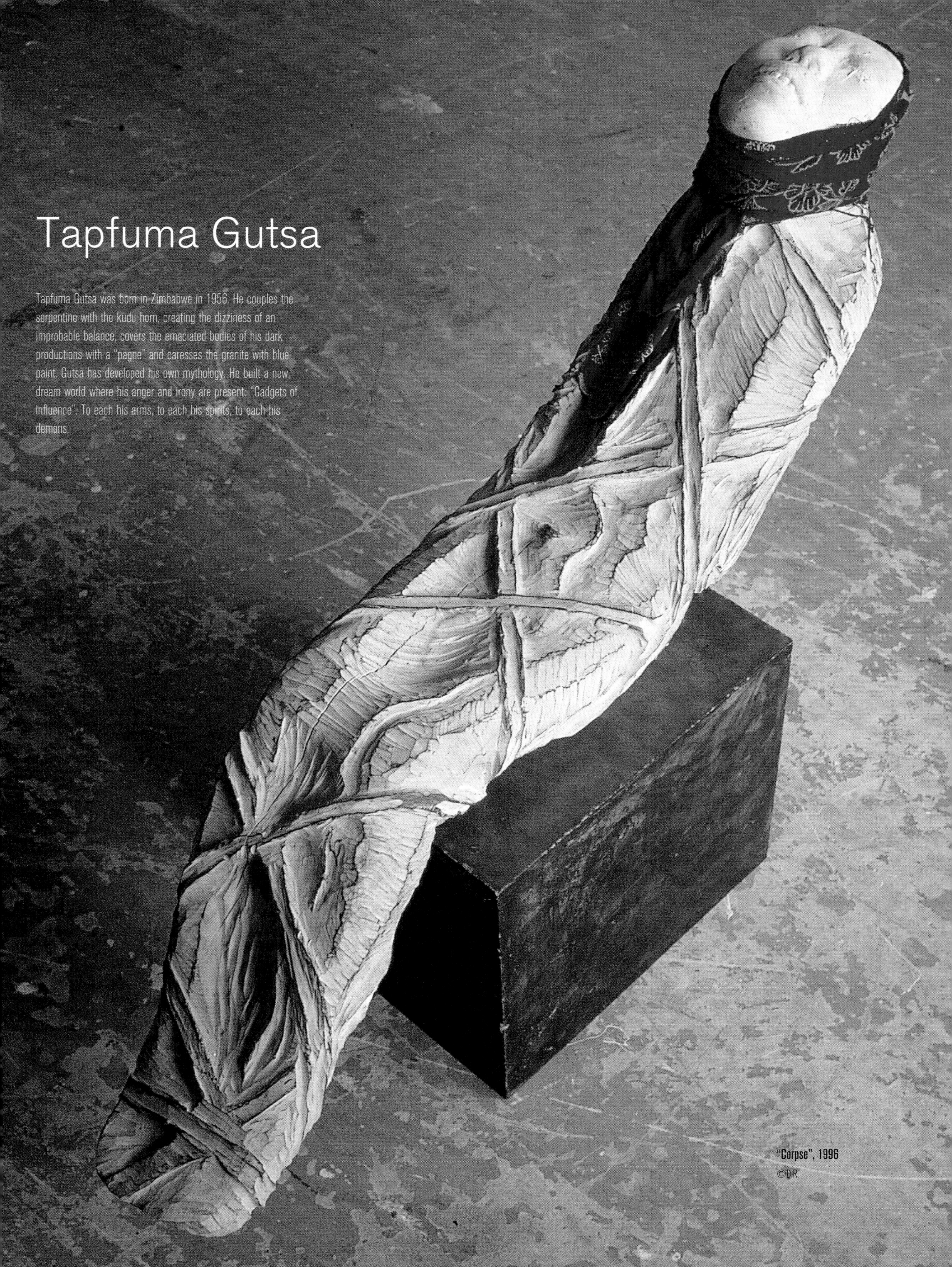

Tapfuma Gutsa

Tapfuma Gutsa was born in Zimbabwe in 1956. He couples the serpentine with the kudu horn, creating the dizziness of an improbable balance, covers the emaciated bodies of his dark productions with a "pagne" and caresses the granite with blue paint. Gutsa has developed his own mythology. He built a new, dream world where his anger and irony are present: "Gadgets of influence". To each his arms, to each his spirits, to each his demons.

"Corpse", 1996

El Hadj Sy

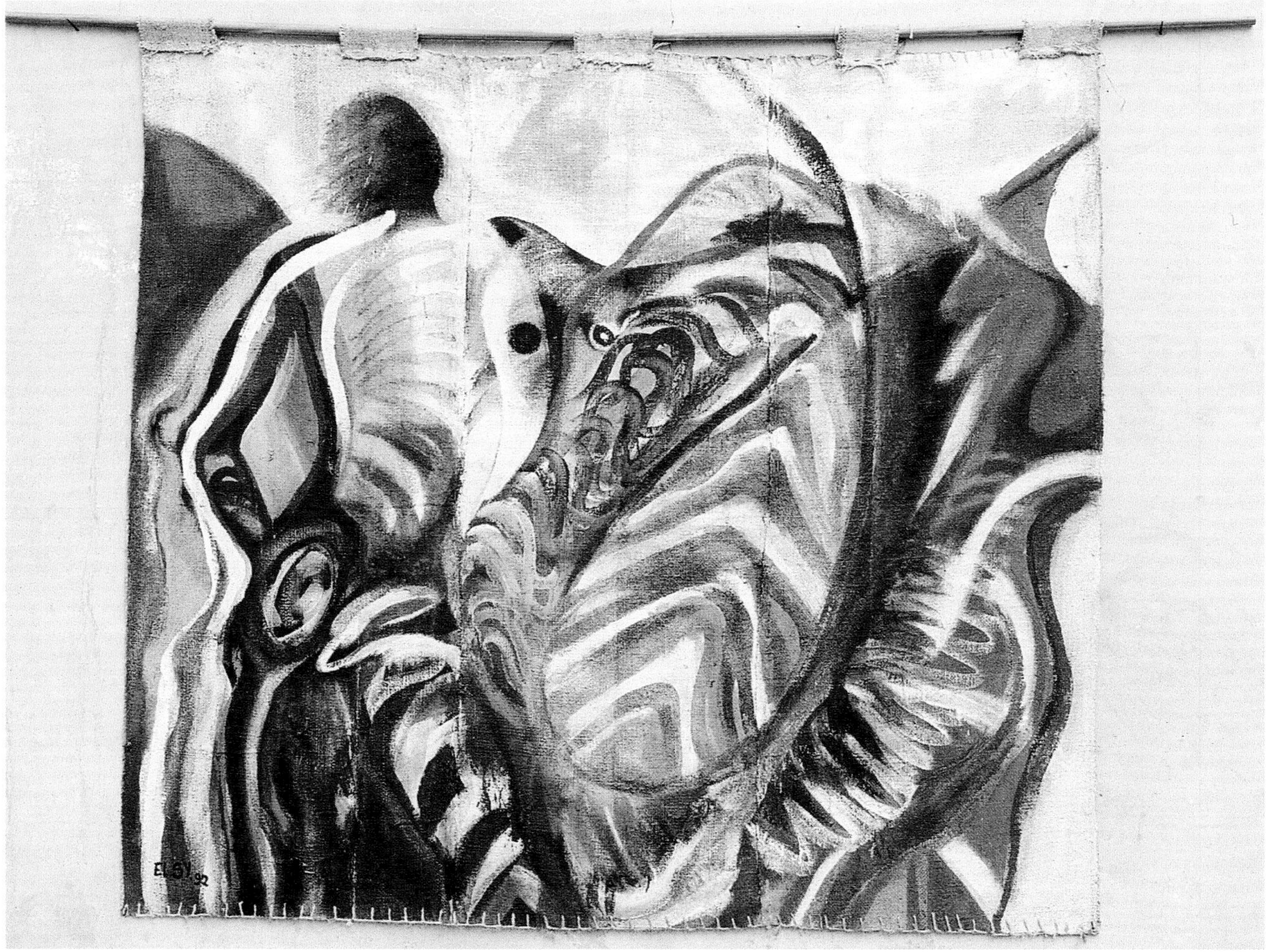

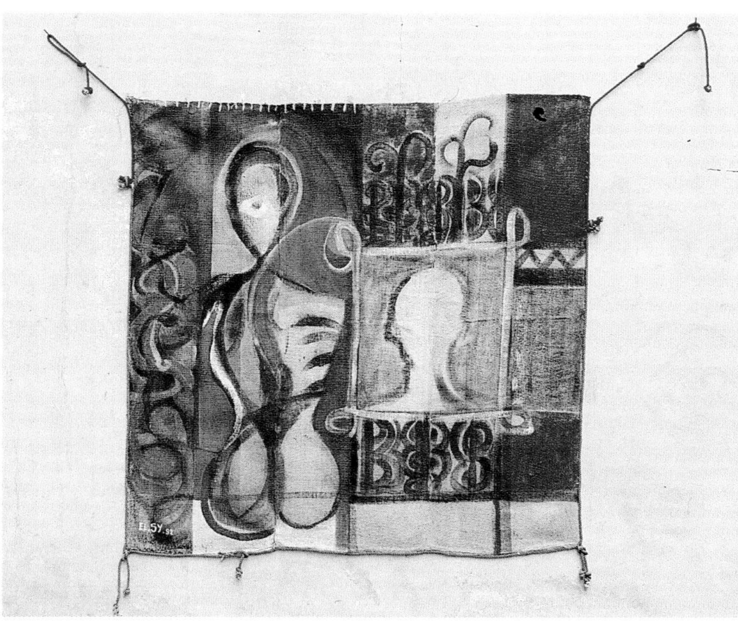

El Sy was born in Senegal in 1954. He graduated from the Fine Arts School of Dakar in 1977, and was long involved in the defense and promotion of Senegalese artists.
Cardboard, canvas and rice bags streaming past, silhouettes painted using large strokes, this virtuosity sometimes masks El Sy's true quest. He does not want to be trapped in any sort of style and be prisoner of a stereotyped image of his work. He is also a photographer, a man of the theater and a writer. His last work, the large-scale reconstitution of a Senegalese village, marks a break in his plastic and formal research.

Joël Mpah Dooh

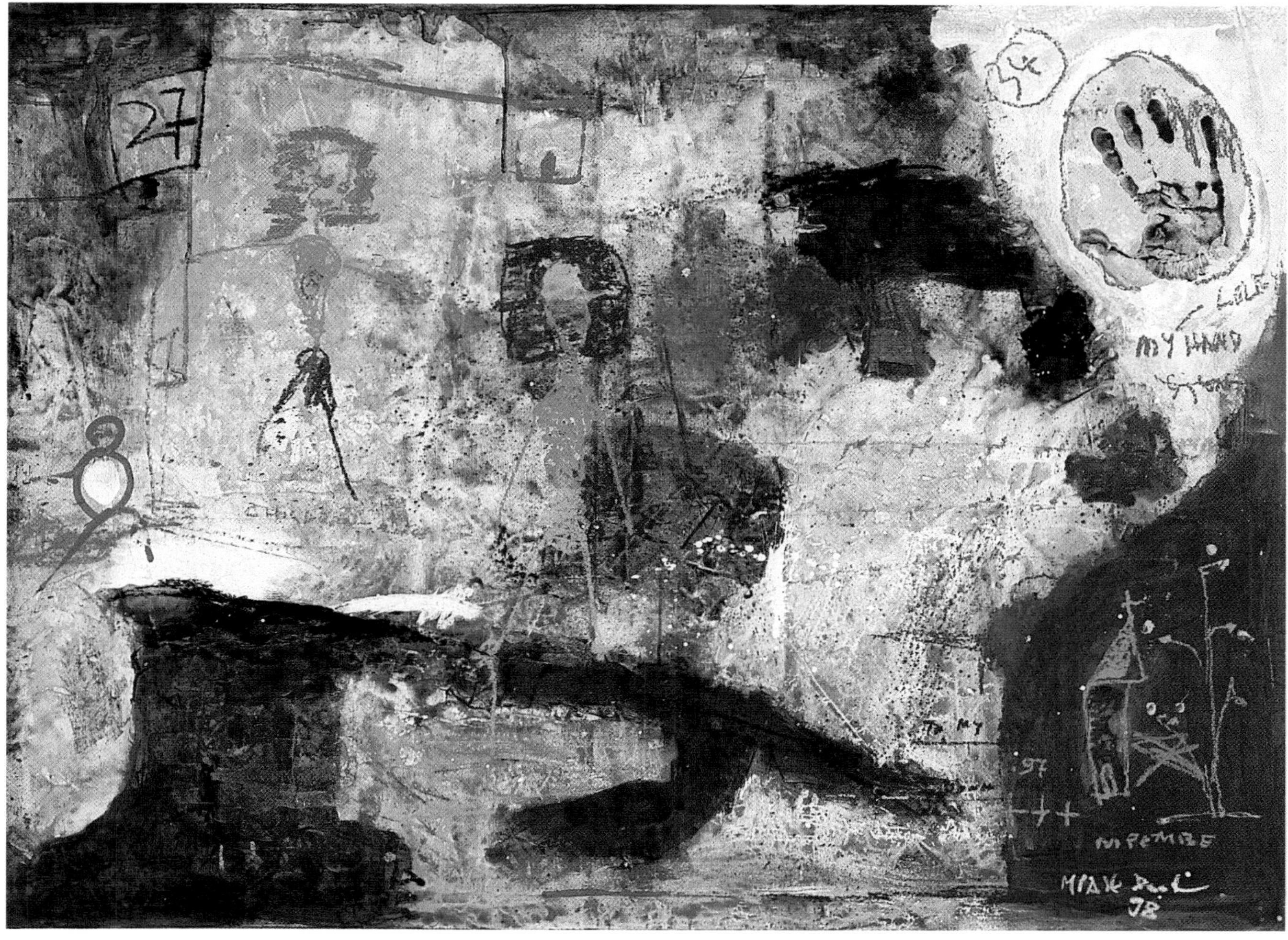

Born in Douala in 1956, Mpah Dooh took courses at the Conservatoire Municipal des Beaux-Arts of Amiens (France). His first meetings with the public in 1988 encouraged him to pursue his vocation. Rejecting all formal esthetic approaches, he quickly found his own language. Straying from a moralistic attitude, he has become a witness to an environment that torments and obsesses him.

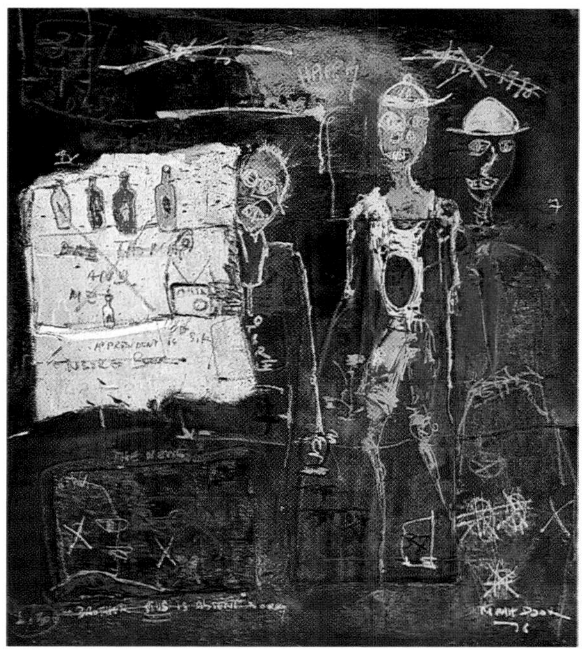

top:
Untitled, 1998
146x120 cm ©Galerie MAM

bottom:
Untitled, 1998
110x96 cm ©Galerie MAM

Ousmane Sow

Ousmane Sow was born in Senegal in 1935. This self-taught artist began sculpting in 1983 using a personal technique that incorporates glue residue, plastic straw, burlap and clay cloth. He has produced monumental series rendering homage to different peoples of Africa, such as the Nouba, the Massai, the Zulu, the Fulani, and, lastly, in 1998, the Battle of Little Big Horn in the United States. Each series required about 3 years of work. The strength emitted from the modeled bodies (sometimes repainted) and from the expressive faces reminds us that Ousmane Sow worked as a physical therapist before devoting himself to art.

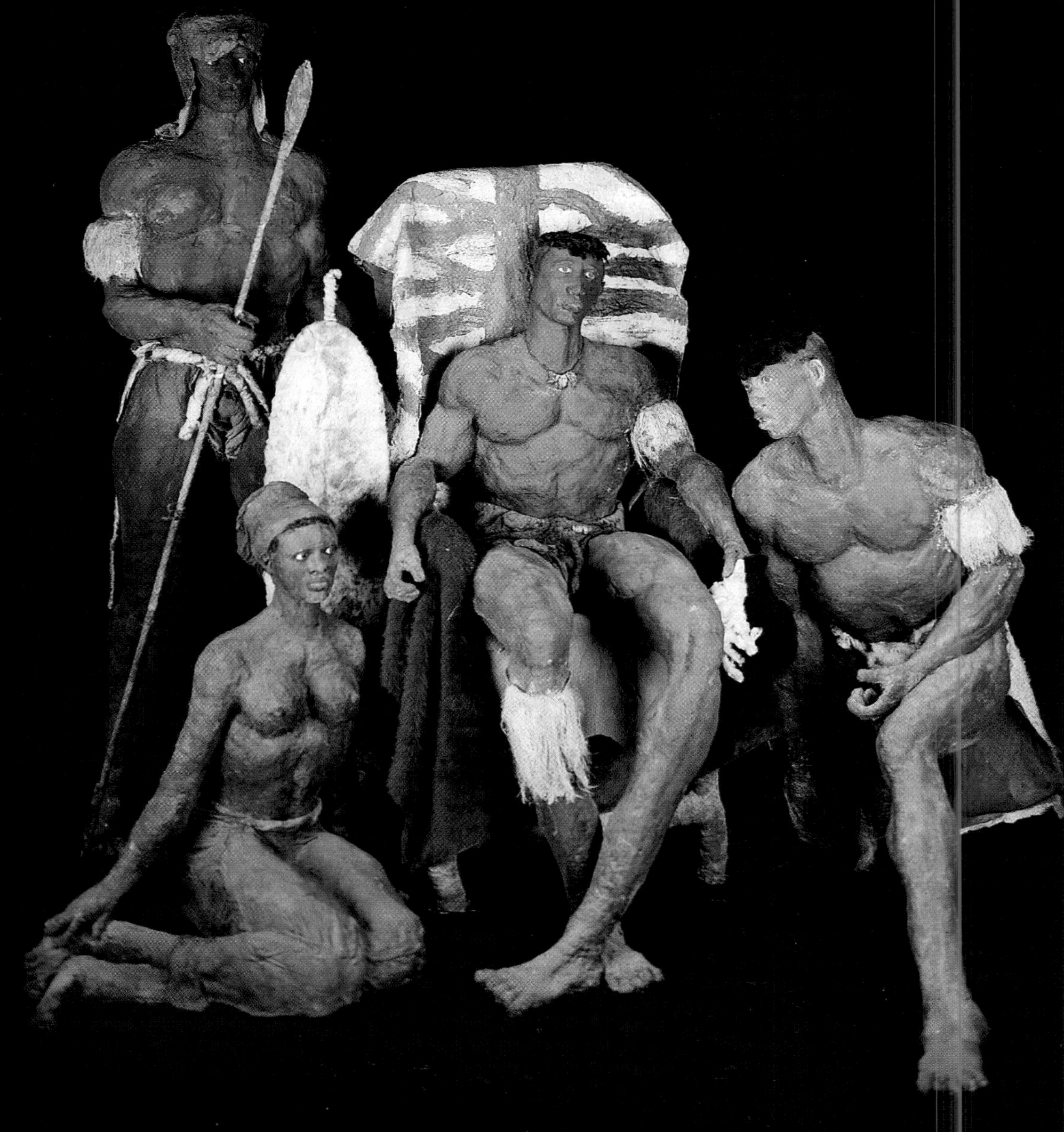

The Zulus

©Jean-Marc Tingaud/Revue Noire

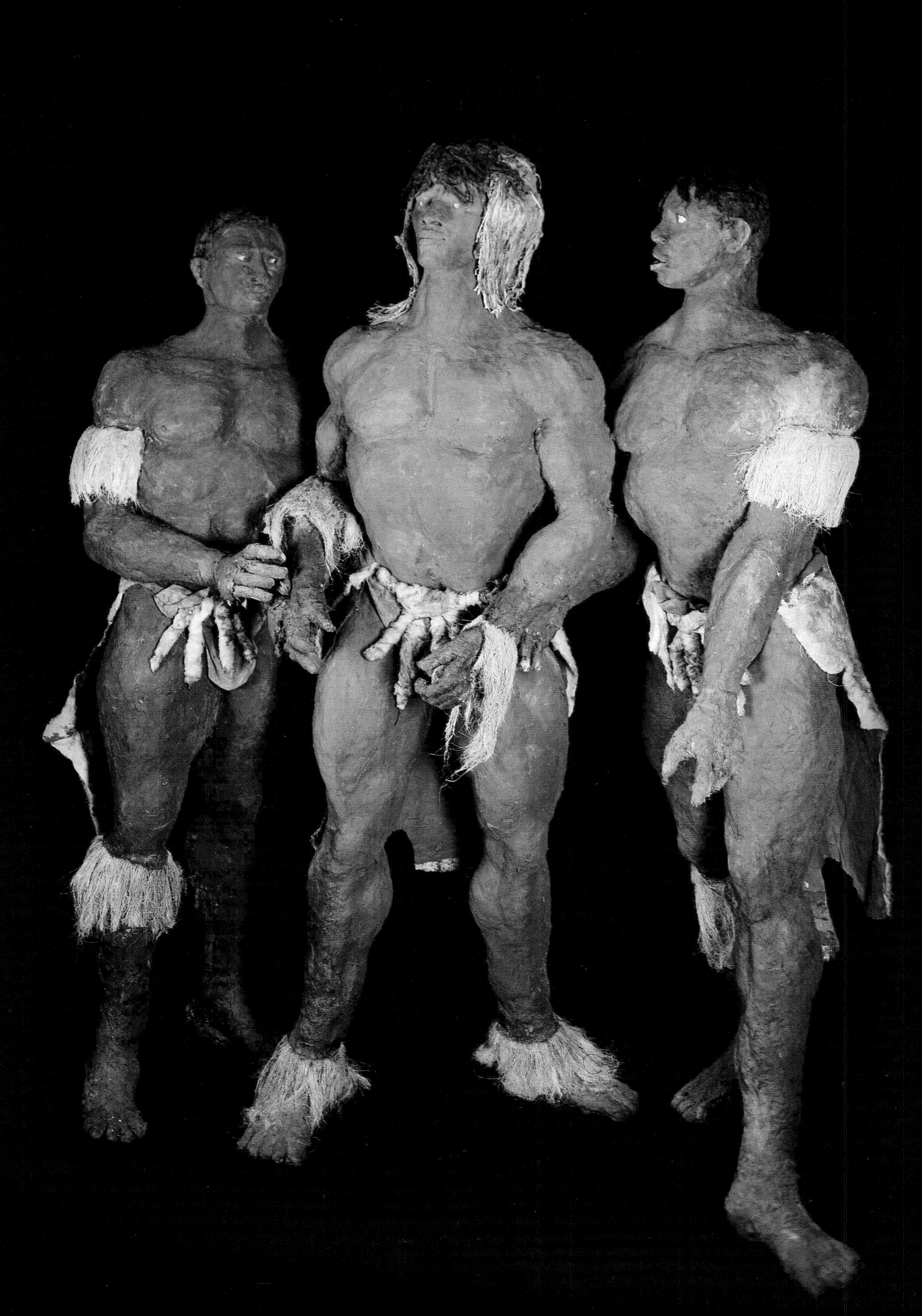

MIGRATIONS AND CONVERGENCES
N'Goné Fall

About ten years ago, contemporary African art was truly opening its doors to the general public in the West. This belated "revelation" would lead one to believe that this art developed out of nowhere in the late 80s. Albert Lubaki, Djilatendo and many others sunk into oblivion once their patrons left Africa. The African art theories and movements of the 50s and 60s barely went beyond their regional borders, receiving a significant echo in the North. The failure of the academic educational systems of the 80s and the ensuing challenges it faced did not make the front page of trade newspapers. Today, thousands of unclassifiable individuals are producing creations on the continent: artists, artisans, prophets, visionaries, con artists. In addition to the passion for "first arts" and folk art, a new generation of African artists has found its place in the closed circle of museums (of contemporary art and not of ethnography), of the international art market, of critics and of exhibition board members. However, the notions of contextualization and decontextualization still accompany African art analysis: the Lyons 2000 Biennial requested the blessing of ethnologists and certain critics continue to refer to sociologists.
The African artistic production of the 90s, the fruit of mutations and hybrid references, raises many questions about its relationship with modernity, a modernity that, because it is not Western modernity, does not seem to be rooted in any historical continuity. Lack of curiosity or of reference points?

Fodé Camara (born in 1958), Senegal

A world of collages
With the new forms of communication, the phenomena of rise and decline have picked up speed. *http//:* is the new magical access code that opens countless windows on unknown horizons. The euphoria of the Great Discoveries, over one century later, is now experienced using a mouse and a cold screen: amateur explorers travel through thousands of pixels and find each other through clicks, double clicks and downloading.

Today's world consists of a freely accessible intercontinental image bank. Diverting or obtaining another image (culture) is not an illusory hymn to interbreeding, but a way of affirming that one belongs to the collective movement of creation. That Christian Dior produces a Massai line of jewelry is normal. That Michael Jackson dances with Zulu warriors is also normal. That rap resembles the staccato prose of the Senegalese Griots or that Playboy pin-ups inevitably have callipygian forms resembling a Hottentot Venus are all images that suggest that the world is no more than a vast collage. The "pure" icon and "authentic" culture that produced it no longer exist. Only the model and thought have given in to the bulimia of our collective subconscious: free consumption, free re-appropriation. And that also holds true for an African artist who inspires and receives inspiration here or elsewhere.

Apart from a few workshops, the Dakar Art Biennial or the (short-lived) Johannesburg Biennial, there are few opportunities for meetings and confrontations in sub-Saharan Africa. Excluded from international debates on the specificity of contemporary art, on the fringes of the fashions that inundate the Western art market (performances and conceptual productions, video), mostly deprived of the democratic tool that is the Internet,[1] in Africa, artists invent their own esthetic codes, without any feeling of inferiority. Magazines, videos and advertising slogans provide them with a perversion of artistic references on the "heritages of humanity," detached from the image of the creator implanted in an unchanging and eternal Africa. The Black continent is not a mythical land and, today, masks are used both to honor the gods and to lure the tourist. These artists are not messengers from the hereafter, and their concerns do not differ in the least from those of their peers. War, love, death, great myths, urban violence and the complexity of contemporary societies remain the universal themes of choice. Whether they use bronze or cardboard, plastic or wood, oil on canvas or graffiti, the representational or the abstract, Mona Lisa or a Kota reliquary, all are normal since

[1] The internet revolution presupposes an infrastructure, a wired network and reasonable communications costs that are still barely accessible in the "less advanced countries", despite the proliferation of cyber cafés.

these artists are contemporaries in a world of collages. And only certain typical African objects could convince an uninformed eye that these creators are not the voice of the world.

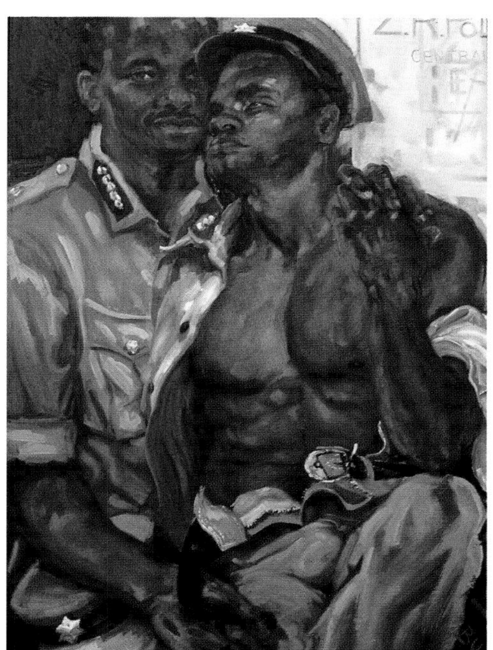

Bulelwa Madekurozwa (born in 1972), "Sunday Afternoon", Zimbabwe

©Delta Gallery

An end to the pseudo "recovery movement"

António Ole, Moustapha Dimé, Abdoulaye Konaté, Joël Mpah Dooh, Berry Bickle, Tapfuma Gutsa, Kofi Setorji, Viyé Diba, Serigne Mbaye Camara, Amahiguere Dolo, Romuald Hazoumé, Sokey Edorh, Ousmane Sow and El Anatsui are among those artists who, despite their participation in major international events, have chosen to remain in Africa.

Although they use materials from their city (bits of wood spewed forth by the sea, scraps from consumer society, charcoal, earth, bones, strips of cotton), breathing new life into objects in no way constitutes an "act-manifesto-theory" on their part. Considering them to be members of the same artistic movement, the peculiar artists of an "art for the poor," denotes a persistent attitude by certain analysts desperately searching to classify African art trends in, at the very least, hazardous terms: neo-primitive, naive, academic (Western imitation), recovery, etc. According to this logic, because he recovers and compresses old objects, French artist Arman is also a member of this family of "recovery-men," who share the same practice, the same approach, the same theories. The exercise of contextualization has its limits and the "colonial kitsch" outlook is dead.

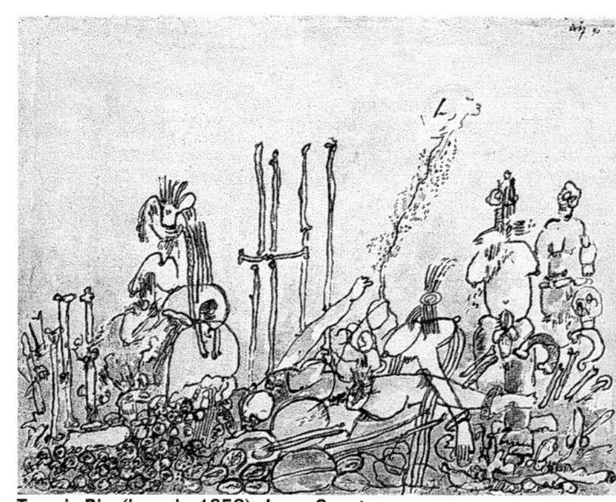

Tamsir Dia (born in 1950), Ivory Coast

©Revue Noire

These artists, witnesses of the impasse among Fine Arts schools, want to break with the dependency on products imported at prohibitive prices, and to resume a dialogue with the African public that has died down since the establishment of workshops and the first art schools in the 30s. The search for an adapted language, through the hybridization of different forms of expression (sculpture, painting, chanting, dancing, text), has led them to delve into the essence of their African culture and not into its superficial forms. Viyé Diba put on a performance at the Dakar 2000 Biennial that combined altars, paintings, sculptures, a musician, moaning men covered in soil, and he himself sitting in a suit, silent. Initiation rite? Vault of a secret society? The public, moving into this lair plunged in absolute darkness, becomes one of the components of this event, lasting only a few hours. An ephemeral act to undoubtedly state that art is also a communion. A communion that Berry Bickle reproduces when she places the vital elements of Zimbabwe on iron plates: salt, soil, ashes, indigo. These symbols of life (the soil that nourishes and the salt that preserves) and death (ashes from the dead and the blue sky that welcomes them) await the promise of better days on the trays of the scale. These codes, accessible to members of the same culture, transform a work of art into allegories of a shared memory. This desire to witness and banish the fading memory is also visible in the works of Kofi Setorji and António Ole. "Homage to the victims of Rwanda" by Setorji is a production comprised of a mass grave of charred bodies, immure faces and frozen ghosts. Plaster, soil, ashes and wood. An oppressive, macabre and direct atmosphere: in Rwanda, laughter died one morning in 1994. In "Margem da Zona Limite" (the banks of the border zone), Ole exorcises the demons of a fratricidal war that plunged Angola into black humor-like madness: "we have nothing more to eat since we have eaten all of the dead." Extracts from movies, photographs, one-legged models wearing gas masks, rusty utensils and miscellaneous objects (war scraps) meticulously set out, recount the suicidal path of a country where public places have been used as graves. Electric shock therapy for a tragic fate, Angolans perceive this production as a warning against amnesia. And when Moustapha Dimé "exhibits" old Koranic wooden annals alongside a dance of silhouettes in rusty iron, it is not to shock the religious Muslim community, but perhaps to state that art, even when its sacred aura is destroyed, does not kill the spirit of the rite.

This "revival" is neither a nostalgic return to the past (spiritual function of an artist-artisan) nor a "social art" movement as occurred during the independence movements. These creators do not seek to enlighten the people or generously

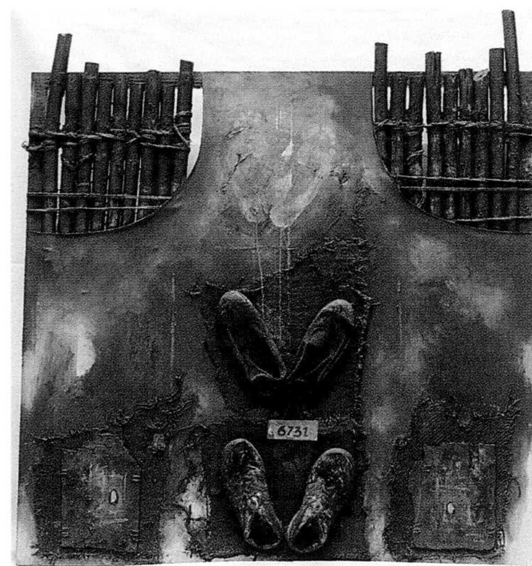

Hervé Youmbi (born in 1973), "6731", 2000
mixed techniques
©Olivier Percheron/Doual'Art

Soly Cissé (born in 1969), "Witnesses of Sorrow", Senegal
Dakar's Biennial 2000,
©Revue Noire

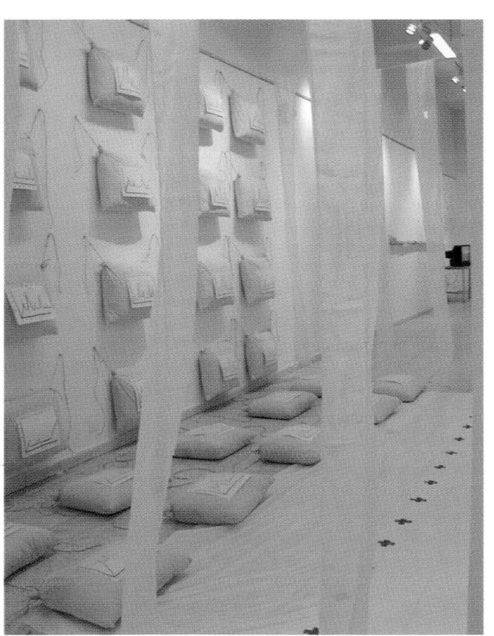

educate the masses. For these artists living in Africa, the first mirror is African and sometimes the Western gallery owner or art critic who has a hedged interpretation of their works.

The Dakar Biennial

Although there was some hesitation surrounding the first Dak'Art in 1992, the Dakar Pan-African Arts Biennial has, nonetheless, become a showcase with a public and international jury. The different opinions of artists living in Africa and the West, journalists, gallery owners, museum directors and art critics regarding contemporary African creation are not always convergent and the debate surrounding the function of this platform is far from being closed. Should preference be given to trends that have proven themselves in the West in order to please dealers, even if it means diverting the local public? Should the exclusive productions of the entire continent be put on display for the sake of quotas, at the risk of confining artists into a ghetto for specialists? Or should the selection be opened up to the entire world (e.g. Cairo or Johannesburg) and the event transformed into a hybrid appendix of the Havana Biennial (less the myth of the location)?

Dak'Art was born out of the desire of artists and the Senegalese state (which is the only owner) to display the artistic production of a continent still poorly perceived, to index the evolution of trends and to allow (finally!) artists to come together and exhibit their creations to all sensibilities. This exercise also consists in removing the exotic aspect of this art and in reminding people – as if this were needed – that there will always be many forms of expression in Africa and that they can also resemble those in Europe, America or Asia, and so creating, there as well, a world of mosaics and collages.

With its self-taught artists and graduates, its established artists and discoveries of young talent, acrylics on canvas and conceptual productions, Dak'Art blurs (thank goodness) reference points and unravels accepted ideas. Trying to satisfy everyone sometimes sows discord in people's minds. What is contemporary African art? What should it look like? Is a performance reminiscent of traditional rituals or the imitation of a Western method? Should art be beautiful and pleasant to look at? Do we need to understand an artist's approach in order to become immersed in his work? All of these recurrent questions were also asked by art magazine directors from the five continents in Paris, in October 2000, during the "L'art dans le monde" conference that accompanied the exhibition of the same name, without, necessarily finding answers. Tackling contemporary creation is an exercise that brings about the same outlooks, whether or not this art has been produced in Africa.

Art without borders

Although the idea that African artists should live on the continent in order to experience osmosis with their creation still has supporters today, many of them have abolished both the physical and formal borders of an art exclusively stamped "Africa." Fernando Alvim, Aimé Ntakiyica, Moshekwa Langa, Bili Bidjocka, Michaël Bethe Sélassie, Gabi Nzweku, Ouattara, Afi Nayo, Sokey Edorh, Amouzou-Glikpa, Miguel Petchkovsky, Otobong Nkanga and Pascale Marthine Tayou live in Paris, Brussels, Amsterdam and New York. Nomad artists? Citizens of the world? They see themselves as syncretic beings, penetrated by different world art trends. Apparently freed from the debates to which their elders were subject, they do not, however, renounce their origins. Poorly understood, vacillating between belonging and not belonging, their creation is a disturbing game of hide-and-seek.

Amouzou-Glikpa does not hesitate to mix Chinese opera and voodoo trance in a sculpture where the I Ching and the Fa stand face-to-face: spiritualities come to life in an abstract, stateless work. Esthetics and thought work for the artist whose creations feed off of all of the flavors of the world. African sensuality and American kitsch confront each other in the work of Otobong Nkanga. The envy of a perfect body (sublimated by model Naomi Campbell) and the dependency on cosmetic products are the pretext for

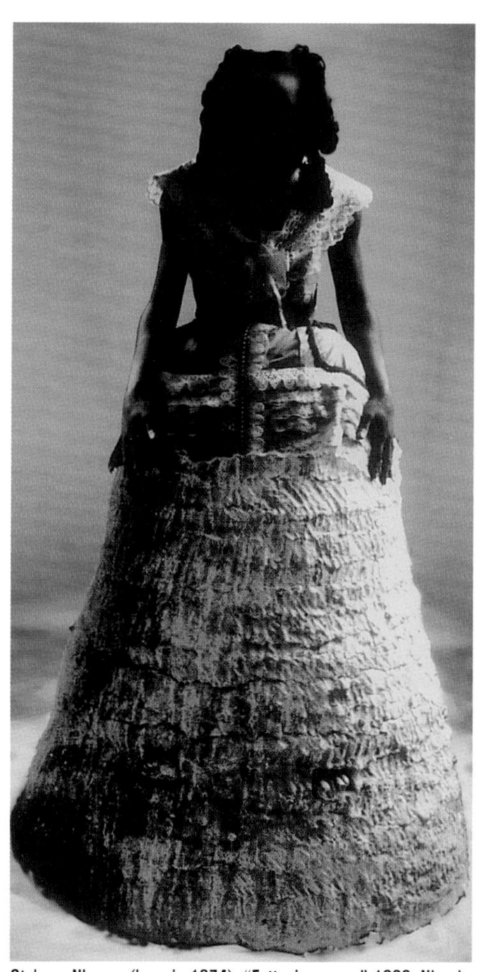

Otobong Nkanga (born in 1974), "Fattening room," 1999, Nigeria
17TH Century costume, skirt made of earth

a performance of bodies that move in sequences with geometric, acidulous and intoxicating lines. Contrast, imprisonment, obsessions. Sculptures, productions and photographs refer to the ambiguous image of the Black woman: nourishing mother or sexual fantasy? Provocation and perversion in the works of Yinka Shonibare and Pascale Marthine Tayou. Looking at the exotic approach from behind, through a re-appropriation of frames, it appears as if the South is calling out to the North. In the work of Shonibare, the Victorian dandy (a symbol of the British Empire) is black and wax crinoline dresses clothe headless models. Tayou proposes the itinerary of an old taxi: from Brussels to Douala then Lyons, the fondness of Africans for used articles is represented by an ageless skeleton that recounts its life on video. The quest for recognition is sometimes done using forceps, because this new generation wants to quash the power of the unilateral outlook.

Sedentary, nomads and migrants, these artists all contribute, through their relationships with the African public and the international art world, a new element to the debate on the redefinition of models. And despite the interference caused by their verbose references, their quests are actually the same as those of all of today's contemporary artists. A quest for meaning, references, self-definition and culture in a world where physical and virtual migrations will always produce unexpected cultural convergences.

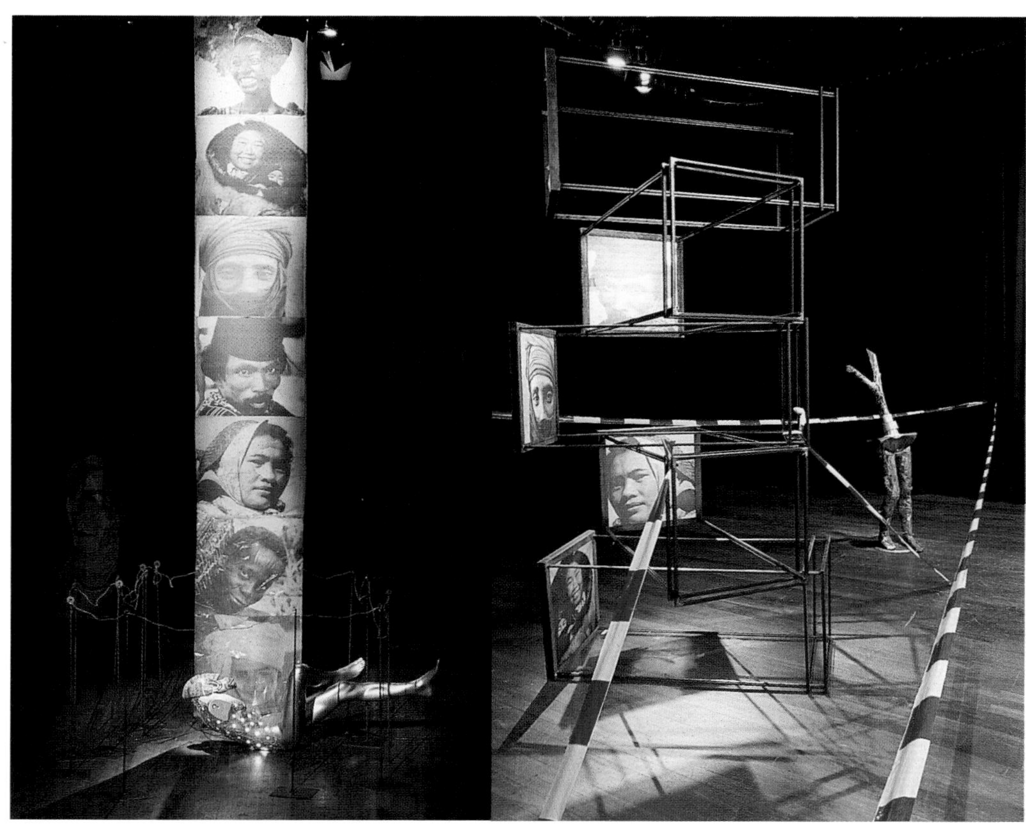

Miguel Petchkovsky (born in 1956), "Confinement nomadism," "Urban minorities," Angola

A chronology of African art events

1920

• Aina Onabolu exhibits his portraits in Nigeria before leaving for England.

1923

• Charles Combes, a French artist, opens a sculpture workshop in Bingerville, Ivory Coast.

1924

• Nana Bonju, a Ghanaian artist, exhibits in London.

• Creation of the Art Department at Achimota College in Ghana, with G. A. Stevens acting as director.

1926

• Georges Thiry, a Belgian poet, meets and encourages Albert Lubaki in Belgian Congo.

1927

• Exhibit of works of students from the Gold Coast (Ghana) at the London Imperial Institute. Commissioner G.A. Stevens, art teacher at Achimota School, Ghana.

• Kenneth Murray introduces art education in Nigerian secondary schools.

1929

• **Sept. – Oct.:** Exhibition of 163 watercolors by Albert Lubaki (Belgian Congo) at the inauguration of the Palais des Beaux-Arts of Brussels. Commissioner Georges Thiry.

• **Dec.:** Exhibition of 121 watercolors by Albert Lubaki at the ethnography museum of Geneva.

1930

• Art is part of the curriculum of elementary and secondary schools in Sudan.

1931

• Colonial exhibition at Vincennes. Presentation of Black mural watercolors at the Belgian pavilion.

• Exhibition of Djilatendo and Permeke (Belgian Congo), Magritte, Delvaux at the Centaure Gallery in Brussels.

• Publication of the story book "L'éléphant qui marche sur des œufs". Text by Badibanga, illustrations by Djilatendo. Publisher l'Eglantine, Brussels.

• **Nov. 18 - 30:** Exhibition of watercolors by Albert Lubaki at the Charles Auguste-Girard Gallery in Paris.

• **Oct. 1 – Dec. 31:** Exhibition of 8 watercolors by Djilatendo and 12 by Albert Lubaki at the Prima Mostra Internazionale d'Arte Coloniale in Rome.

1932

• Shimeles Kabtimer and Zerihun Dominique, Ethiopian painters, set the stage for the techniques and theories of modern Ethiopian art.

• The Ethiopian Ministry of Education establishes a Department of Plastic Arts and offers studios to artists who decorate the Ethiopian Parliament.

• The Menelik II and Teferi Makonnen schools offer academic art classes in Addis Ababa, Ethiopia.

1935

• Creation, by the governor of the colony of Belgian Congo, of the "Commission for the Protection of Indigenous Arts and Trades" and the "Friends of Indigenous Art Association", which publishes the magazine Brousse.

1936

• Inauguration of the Musée de la Vie Indigène in Leopoldville (Kinshasa, Belgian Congo). First exhibit of sacred art.

• Abebe Wolde Giorgis, an Ethiopian student at the École des Beaux-Arts, exhibits in Paris in the 30s.

• A plastic arts association organizes an exhibit in Sudan.

1937

• Exhibition of 5 Nigerian artists, including Ben Enwonwu, at the Zwemmer Gallery, London. Commissioner Kenneth Murray, a teacher at the Murray School of Art in Nigeria.

• German sculptor H.V. Meyerowitz heads the Art Department at Achimota College in Ghana.

• Margaret Trowell creates the School of Arts in Kampala, Uganda.

1938

• Ben Enwonwu, a Nigerian artist, exhibits in London and Glasgow.

1939

• Exhibition of works by Ugandan students entitled "Painting and Indigenous Crafts", at the Imperial Institute, London. Commissioner Margaret Trowell, their teacher.

• The Cyrene Mission creates an art center for Southern Africa in Southern Rhodesia (Zimbabwe) at the instigation of Reverend Edward Paterson.

• In "Cahier d'un retour au pays natal", Martinique native Aimé Césaire "invents" the word Negritude.

1940

• Akinola Lasekan, a Nigerian artist, publishes "Nigeria in Cartoons", in which he denounces colonial racism.

1941

• Agegnehu Engeda, an Ethiopian painter, opens an art school with 15 students in Addis Ababa, Ethiopia.

1943

• Brother Marc Wallendo opens the Gombe-Matadi center in Middle Congo (Belgian Congo). Sculpture and drawing classes.

1945

• Oku Ampofo, a Ghanaian artist, organizes the first exhibition of young artists in Ghana: Neo-African Art.

• Zerihun Dominique, an Ethiopian artist, heads the Sahle Selassie Art School in Addis Ababa.

Publication in Brazzaville of the book "Gutemberg dans la brousse", illustrations by Bela (student of Desfossés)

1946

• Pierre Romain-Desfossés, an amateur French painter, creates the "Union Africaine des Arts et Lettres" and the Hangard, an indigenous art workshop in Elisabethville (Lubumbashi, Belgian Congo).

• Jean-Pierre Greenlaw founds the School of Design of the Gordon Memorial College in Khartoum, Sudan.

1947

• Creation of the newspaper Présence Africaine by Senegalese writer Alioune Diop in Paris.

• Exhibition of the works of Ugandan students at the Imperial Institute, London. Commissioner Margaret Trowell, their teacher.

• Exhibition of the works of students of the Cyrene Mission of Rhodesia (Zimbabwe), London.

1948

• "Contemporary African Art" exhibition (Nigeria), at the Camden Arts Centre, London.

• Art classes at Yaba Technical College in Lagos, Nigeria.

• Laurent Moonens, a Belgian painter, founds the Stanley-Pool School, in Léopoldville (Kinshasa, Belgian Congo).

• Contemporary Colonial Art exhibition in Antwerp, Belgium.

1949

• Exhibitions of the works of students from Hangard (Belgian Congo) in New York.

• The Gombe-Matadi Center is transferred to Leopoldville, Belgian Congo.

• **Dec. 17 – Jan. 5:** Ilunga, Bela, Pilipili, Kaballa and Nkulu (Belgian Congo) exhibit at the Séminaire des Arts, Palais des Beaux-Arts of Brussels.

1950

• The Congolese students of Laurent Moonens (Albert Mongita, Dom, Koyongonda and Lekumbe) exhibit in Rome.

• Ben Enwonwu exhibits in the USA.

1951

• Exhibitions of the works of students from Hangard (Belgian Congo), University of Philadelphia.

• Pierre Lods creates the Poto-Poto school (African art center), Brazzaville, Congo.

• Laurent Moonens creates the Académie des Beaux-Arts et Métiers d'Art of Elisabethville (Lubumbashi, Belgian Congo).

• The School of Design becomes the College of Fine and Applied Arts at the Khartoum Technical Institute in Sudan.

1952

• Creation of the College of Art at the University of Sciences and Technology, Kumasi, Ghana.

• Italian missionaries found the Ecole Céramique de Giheta in Burundi. In 1967, it becomes the technical secondary art school.

1953

• Classes at the department of art and engraving at a secondary school in Ibadan, Nigeria.

• The students of the Poto-Poto school (Congo) exhibit in South Africa and New York in 1954, in Germany in 1956, and in Switzerland and France in 1957.

1954

• Hangard is annexed to the Académie des Beaux-Arts of Lubumbashi in Belgian Congo.

1955

• Creation of the African Cultural Society in Paris.

• Opening of the Department of Fine Arts at the University of Zaria, Nigeria.

• Ale Felege Selam, a graduate of the Chicago Art Institute in 1954, opens a school with 35 students in Addis Ababa, Ethiopia.

• Biennial of Congolese Art in Kassaï.

• Creation of the Akwapim 6 group by Oku Ampofo and of the Ghana Society of Artists by Kofi Antubam.

1956

• Exhibition of young Congolese painters at the Palais des Beaux-Arts of Brussels.

1957

• Creation of the American Society of African Culture (AMSAC), which published the quarterly magazine African Forum from 1965 to 1967 and organized exhibitions in the United States.

• Creation of the National Museum of Ghana.

• Hailé Selassie creates the Fine Art School of Addis Ababa. Ale Felege Selam, director, is the only Ethiopian instructor.

• The Gombe-Matadi center, which had become the Saint-Luc school, becomes the Académie des Beaux-Arts in Belgian Congo.

• Rolf Italiaander exhibits 131 oil paintings, gouaches, drawings and watercolors from his personal collection at the Stedelijk Museum in Amsterdam, at the Gemeente Museum in The Hague and at the Museum of Volkenkunde in Rotterdam. Title: Negro Art from Central Africa (French Equatorial Africa, Uganda, Belgian Congo, Congo, Ethiopia).

1958

• Creation of the Zaria Art Society in Nigeria. President Uche Okeke.

• Foundation of the Maison des Arts in Dakar, Senegal.

• Felelo Nsuku, Bela, Pilipili, Mwenze, Kaballa, Masamba (Belgian Congo), Marcel Gotène, Thango (Congo) take part in the World Exposition of Brussels.

1959

• Conference of Black Writers and Artists organized by Présence Africaine at the Sorbonne University, Paris.

1960

• Opening of the Department of Fine Arts in Yaba and Ibadan, Nigeria.

• Traveling exhibition in Germany at the Kunst aus Zentralafrika, organized by the German Africa Society. Contemporary and traditional art from Ghana, Nigeria and Belgian Congo.

1961

• Creation of the College of Fine Arts of Nsukka in Nigeria.

• Collection from the workshops of Maurice Alhadeff (patron of the arts in Kinshasa, DRC) travels throughout the USA.

• The Maison des Arts becomes the École des Arts du Sénégal, headed by painters Iba N'Diaye, Papa Ibra Tall and Pierre Lods.

• The Poto-Poto school in Congo (founded by Pierre Lods) is taken over by Nicolas Ondogo, a student of Lods.

• Creation of the Mbari Club in Ibadan, Nigeria by Ulli Beier.

• Ben Enwonwu produces a piece of art for the headquarters of the London Daily Mirror newspaper in England.

1962

• First International Congress of African Culture (ICAC), Salisbury, Rhodesia, supervised by Frank McEwen. Three exhibitions took place: African, New African, Neo-African. Participation of Kofi Antubam (Ghana), Malangatana (Mozambique), Ben Enwonwu (Nigeria), Workshop school (Rhodesia), Makerere Art School (Uganda).

• Yaba and Ibadan in Nigéria become Faculties of Art.

• Creation of the Oshogbo Center in Nigeria. Exhibition "Art from the Commonwealth" with stone sculptures from Rhodesia (Zimbabwe), at the Commonwealth Institute, London.

• Works by students from the Makerere School of Uganda: "Let the Children Paint" exhibition. Travels to Munich, Mannheim, Frankfort, Hanover and Hamburg, organized by Dr Friedrich Vogel.

1963

• Creation of the Federal Society of Arts and Humanities, Nigeria.

• Creation of the Mbari Club in Munich, which, one year later, becomes Orpheus Africanus. Organization of exhibitions in Germany.

• "New Art from Rhodesia" exhibition, Commonwealth Institute, London.

1964

• Creation of the Society of Nigerian Artist, Nigeria.

• International pre-symposium on the theme "Function and meaning of Black art in the lives of people and for the people", organized by the African Cultural Society at UNESCO, Paris.

• Exhibition of 220 paintings by African children, Munich Stademuseum.

1965

• Creation in London of the monthly publication Cultural Events in Africa: announcement and reports of exhibitions in England and Africa. "New Art from Rhodesia" exhibition, Commonwealth Arts Festival, South Bank Centre, London.

• Exhibition of Oku Ampofo at the Union Carbide Building, New York.

• Creation of the Manufacture Nationale des Arts Décoratifs of Senegal, headed by painter Papa Ibra Tall.

1966

• First International Festival of Black Arts in Dakar, Senegal.

• Creation of the Musée Dynamique of Senegal.

• Creation of the Institut National des Arts in Abidjan, Ivory Coast by Albert Botbol.

• Tom Blomefield founds the Tengenenge Art Centre in Zimbabwe.

• Exhibition of African art (including contemporary art) from the Harmon Foundation collection, Commercial Museum, Philadelphia Civic Center, USA.

1967

• "Contemporary African Art" exhibition with the Oshogbo group, El Salahi from Sudan and Skunder Boghossian from Ethiopia at the Transcription Centre, London.

• Montreal World Fair, participation of Masamba, Ndamvu Tsiku Pezo (Belgian Congo).

• Creation of the African Arts journal in the United States..

1968

• Mpoyo (Belgian Congo) attends the 34th Venice International Biennial.

1969

• Pan-African Festival of Cultures of Algiers.

• "Contemporary African Art" exhibition. 90 artistes from 12 African countries at the Camden Arts Centre, London.

• Exhibition of works from the Oshogbo School, Otis Art Institute, Los Angeles.

1970

• Makonde Sculpture exhibition at the Grosvenor Gallery, London.

• Exhibition of contemporary sculptures of the Vukutu (Zimbabwe) at the Musée d'Art Moderne, Paris.

• Gabon: founded in 1959, the artisan section of the technical high school becomes the CENAM (Centre national d'art et de manufacture) (National center for art and manufacture) and, in 1983, the ENAM.

1971

• Exhibition of contemporary sculptures by the Shonas of Africa (Zimbabwe), Musée Rodin, Paris.

1972

• Exhibition of contemporary sculptures by the Shonas of Africa (Zimbabwe), Institute of Contemporary Art, London and Museum of Modern Art, New York.

• Contemporary Nigerian Art exhibition, Africa Centre, London.

1973

• Special Conference of the International Association of Art Critics (IAAC) in Kinshasa, DRC.

1974

• Art Sénégalais d'Aujourd'hui exhibition, Grand Palais, Paris, then touring in the USA.

• Contemporary Makonde Sculpture exhibition, Commonwealth Institute Art Gallery, London.

1977

• FESTAC, the Second World Black Festival of Arts and Culture in Lagos, Nigeria. 17,000 participants from 56 countries.

• African Contemporary Art exhibition, 45 artists from 15 countries at Howard University in Washington, DC.

1978

• Birth of the Crystalist Manifesto in Sudan by Kamala Ibrahim Ishaq, Muhammad Hamid Shaddad and Nayla Al Tayib.

1979

• Modern Kunst aus Afrika Horizonte exhibition, Staatliche Kunsthalle.

1982

• Culture & Resistance; conferences and exhibitions in Gaborone, Botswana.

• Arts in Africa exhibition, Commonwealth Institute, London.

1984

• Contemporary African Art exhibition, Albert Gordon Gallery, New York

• Sanaa exhibition: Contemporary Art from East Africa, Commonwealth Institute, London.

• Havana Biennial, first African attendance.

• Tributaries exhibition, Johannesburg. Tour in Germany.

1985

• The Art that Survives exhibition, Uganda 1960s-1980s, Africa Centre, London.

1986

• From Two Worlds exhibition, Whitechapel Gallery, London.

1987

• Modern Art from Mozambique exhibition, Africa Centre, London.
• Ethnicolor, Cirque d'hivers, Paris.

1988

• Art Contemporain Arabe exhibition with the participation of Sudan, the Institut du Monde Arabe, Paris.
• Contemporary Art from Western Africa exhibition – The Oshogbo School, Zamana Gallery, London.
• Contemporary Stone Sculpture from Zimbabwe exhibition, Barbican Centre, London.

1989

• Magiciens de la Terre exhibition, Centre Georges Pompidou, Paris.
• Makonde exhibition: wooden sculpture from East Africa from the Malde Collection, Museum of Modern Art, Oxford.
• The Other Story exhibition: Afro-Asian Artists in Post-War Britain, Hayward Gallery, London.
• Art/Images in Southern Africa exhibition, Kulturhuset, Stockholm.

1990

• Exposition Contemporary Stone Carving from Zimbabwe, Yorkshire Sculpture Parck.
• Contemporary African Artists exhibition: Changing Tradition at Studio Museum, Harlem, New York.
• Lotte or the Transformation of the Object exhibition, Academy of Fine Arts, Vienna.
• Art from the Frontline exhibition, Glasgow Art Gallery.
• Art from South Africa exhibition, Museum of Modern Art, Oxford.

1991

• Africa Explorers exhibition, Center for African Art, New York.
• Venice Biennial: presentation of the Contemporary African Artists exhibition from the Harlem Studio Museum.
• Art Sur Vie exhibition, contemporary art from Senegal, Grande Arche de la Défense, Paris.
• Signs of the Time exhibition: New Art from Africa, Museum Für Völkerkunde, Frankfort.
• Africa Hoy exhibition, Centro Atlantico de Arte Moderno, Las Palmas.
• Congo/Zaïre: Thango de Brazza à Kin exhibition, Musée des Arts d'Afrique et d'Océanie, Paris.
• A Grain of Wheat exhibition, Commonwealth Institute, London.
• Ny Africa exhibition, Copenhagen.
• 60 ans de Peinture Zaïroise exhibition, Brussels & New Museum for Contemporary Art and Center for African Art in New York.
• Revue Noire Magazine, a tri-annual publication, is founded in Paris.

1992

• Dak'Art, 1st Art Biennial of Dakar, Senegal.
• Kassel Documenta with Mo Edoga (Nigeria) and Ousmane Sow (Senegal).
• Out of Africa exhibition (Africa Hoy), Saatchi Gallery, London.
• Seville World Exposition with 9 artists from Mozambique.
• Les Peintres du Grand Atelier (Kin) and les Peintres de Lubumbashi at Maastricht.
• La Naissance de la Peinture Contemporaine en Afrique Centrale 1930-1970 exhibition, Musée Royale d'Afrique Centrale de Tervuren, Brussels.

1993

• Venice Biennial, presentation of Fusion: West African Artists at the Venice Biennial (Museum for African Art, NY 93).

1994

• Otro Pais, Escalas Africanas, Centro Atlantico de Arte Moderno exhibition, Las Palmas.
• Rencontres Africaines exhibition, Institut du Monde Arabe, Paris.
• Seen/Unseen exhibition, African artists of London, Bluecoat Gallery, Liverpool.
• Un Art d'Afrique du Sud exhibition, La Défense, Paris.
• 5th Havana Biennial.
• Nka, journal of contemporary african art, a biennial, is founded in New York.

1995

• Seven Stories about Modern Art in Africa exhibition, Africa 95, London..
• Die Andere Reise exhibition, Krems.
• 1st Biennial of Kwangju, South Korea. Participation of Pascale Marthine Tayou, Cameroon.
• An Inside Story: African art of our time exhibition, Stagaya Museum, Japan.
• Les artistes africains et le Sida multimedia exhibition, Cotonou, Benin, then the Dakar Biennial in 1996.
• Africus, 1st Biennial of Johannesburg, South Africa.

1996

• Neue Kunst Aus Africa exhibition, Berlin.
• 2nd Art Biennial of Dakar, Senegal
• Colours: Contemporary Art from South Africa exhibition, Haus der Kulturen der Welt, Berlin.

1997

• Suites Africaines multimedia exhibition, Couvent des Cordeliers, Paris.
• 2nd Biennial of Kwangju, Korea.
• 6th Havana Biennial.
• Santa Fe Biennial, USA.
• Images of Other Cultures exhibition, Setagaya Museum, Japan.
• Islas-Islands exhibition, Centro Atlantico de Arte Moderno, Canary Islands and tour in Spain.
• Africus, 2nd Biennial of Johannesburg, South Africa.
• Die Anderen Modernen, Haus der Kulturen der Welt, Berlin.

1998

• 3rd Art Biennial of Dakar, Senegal.
• 23rd Sao Paulo Biennial.
• 7th der Kleinplastik Triennial
• Transatlántico, Centro Atlántico, de Arte Moderno exhibition, Canary Islands

1999

• South Meets West exhibition, Ghana then in Kunsthalle and at the Musée Historique de Berne in Switzerland, Spring 2000.
• Liberated voices: Contemporary Art from South Africa, Museum for African Arts, New York
• (Trans)Africa: trafique exhibition, Gand, Belgium

2000

• 4th Art Biennial of Dakar, Senegal.
• L'Afrique à Jour exhibition, Lille, France.
• Sao Paulo Biennial.
• Havana Biennial.
• L'art dans le monde exhibition, Pont Alexandre iii, Paris.
• Le Temps de l'Afrique exhibition, Centro Atlantico de Arte Moderno, Canary Islands.

2001

• The Short Century: Independence & Liberated Movements in Africa multimedia exhibition, Munich, Germany.
• Authentic/Eccentric: Africa in and out of Africa exhibition, Venice Biennial.
• Africas: The Artist and the City exhibition, Barcelona.

Biographies of the authors

Francisco d'Almeida

An associate professor at the Senghor University in Alexandria, Egypt, Francisco d'Almeida is a general representative of the association Culture et Développement. He has organized different seminars on the situation of contemporary art in Africa, as well as the Taxi-Colors event. He lives in Grenoble, France.

Marie-Hélène Boisdur de Toffol

With a Ph.D. in visual arts, specializing in art ethnology, Marie-Hélène Boisdur de Toffol is a lecturer at the Université de Paris I Sorbonne-UFR (department of training and research) in visual arts and art sciences. She has written articles for the Société Africaine d'Édition, the magazines Esthétique, Afrique Contemporaine and the journal of the ADEIAO.

Joëlle Busca

A doctor of philosophy and an art critic, Joëlle Busca wrote her doctoral thesis on 20th century African art and its impact on mentalities and societies. She is the author of many articles on contemporary African art and lives in Paris.

Sabine Cornelis

A Ph.D. in archeology and art history (Université Catholique de Louvain), Sabine Cornelis is the senior assistant at the Musée Royal d'Afrique Centrale (Tervuren, Belgium), where she works in the department of the history of Belgian presence abroad. Her work deals with the colonial and cultural history of Congo Kinshasa and, in particular, the birth of contemporary art in the Congo.

Elsbeth Court

Elsbeth Court is a researcher specializing in art education issues in Africa at the School of Oriental and African Studies (SOAS) of London. She spent 17 years in East Africa and has written numerous works and conferences on the history of modern art in Africa. She lives in London.

N'Goné Fall

Architect, Pepsi girl and managing editor of Revue Noire in Paris.

Étienne Féau

Curator of the Musée des Arts d'Afrique et d'Oceanie (MAAO), Étienne Féau also teaches African art history at the École du Louvre in Paris and is an associate professor at Senghor University in Alexandria, Egypt.

Till Förster

A researcher and art historian, Till Förester is the director of the research unit of Iwalewa Haus, Universitat Bayreuth in Germany. He has written numerous works, mainly on art in Nigeria.

Joseph Gazari Seini

An art historian, Joseph Gazari Seini is a curator at the National Museum in Ghana.

Joanna Grabski

Joanna Grabski is writing a doctoral thesis on modern art in Senegal at Indiana University in the USA. She has done research on the work of Pierre Lods in the Congo and in Senegal.

Sigrid Horsch-Albert

Sigrid Horsch-Albert is a researcher at the Iwalewa Haus, Universitat Bayreuth in Germany.

Bennetta Jules-Rosette

Bennetta Jules-Rosette is a professor of sociology at the University of California at San Diego and coordinator of study programs in African and African-American research. She undertook various studies on contemporary art and African literature, has written many books and is a consultant for the magazine African Arts.

George Kyeyune

A Ugandan and a graduate of the School of Fine Arts of Makerere in Uganda, George Kyeyune was a lecturer at the University of Makerere from 1990 to 1999. He is currently working on a doctorate on contemporary Ugandan art at the School of Oriental and African Studies (SOAS) in London.

Alexandra Loumpet-Galitzine

An archeologist, Alexandra Loumpet-Galitzine teaches in the department of art and archeology at the University of Yaounde I in Cameroon. She was deputy director of the operation for the inventory of museographical heritage of Cameroon, jointly responsible for the creation of the Musée National du Cameroun and for the inventory, creation and opening of the Musée du Palais des rois Bamun in Foumban (West Cameroon).

Marylin Martin

The director of the South African National Gallery (SANG) in Cape Town, South Africa, Marylin Martin has been a commissioner for many exhibitions in Africa and abroad. She was notably responsible for the selection of South African photographs for the traveling exhibition "Africa by Africans" (Revue Noire). She lives in Cape Town.

Elikia M'Bokolo

Elikia M'Bokolo is an historian and teaches at the École des Hautes Études en Sciences Sociales (HEESS) in Paris. He is one of the authors of the book "Anthology of African Photography", Ed. Revue Noire, 1998. He lives in Paris.

Adriano Mixinge

An historian and art critic, Adriano Mixinge headed the department of scientific research at the National Museum of Anthropology in Luanda, Angola. A commissioner for numerous exhibitions in Angola, Spain and South Africa, he is a consultant in the cultural department of the Angolan Embassy in Spain. He has written numerous works on African art and the evolution of plastic arts in Angola. He lives in Madrid.

Simon Njami

Writer, commissioner for exhibitions and co-founder of Revue Noire in Paris.

Sylvester Ogbechie

An assistant professor of art history at Pomona College in California, USA, Sylvester Ogbechie is writing a thesis on the history of art in Nigeria and has written numerous essays on the subject. He lives in the USA.

Richard Pankhurst

An historian, Richard Pankhurst founded the Institute of Ethiopian Studies in Addis Ababa, Ethiopia, where he has been living for the past 30 years. The author of numerous works on art, photography and culture in Ethiopia, he is one of the authors of the book "Anthology of African Photography", Ed. Revue Noire, 1998.

Blaise Patrix

A plastic artist, Blaise Patrix spent 17 years in Burkina Faso and is at the source of the artistic vocation of numerous artists of this country. Having witnessed the evolution of art in Burkina, he is preparing a collection of texts on the subject. He lives in Dakar, Senegal.

Thierry Payet

A photographer, Thierry Payet was a plastic arts consultant for the French cultural centers in Dakar and Djibouti.

John Picton

Is an associate professor at the School of Oriental and African Studies (SOAS) of London University. He has written numerous works on the history and sociology of African art, especially in the south of Nigeria. He lives in London.

Jean Loup Pivin

Architect, director of the Bureau d'Ingénierie Culturel de la Fête et du Loisir (BICFL) and co-founder of Revue Noire, of which he is the editor of publications.

Sunanda K. Sanyal

Sunanda K. Sanyal has a Ph.D. in the history of 19th century African art and Western art from Emory University in the USA. A commissioner for exhibitions and the author of numerous articles on African art (M. Trowell and the School of Makerere, and art in East Africa, in particular), he teaches and gives conferences at the Art Institute of Boston at Lesley University and at Tufts University, USA.

Konjit Seyoum

Is Ethiopian, has a degree in art history, and is the director of the Asni Gallery (contemporary Ethiopian art) in Addis Ababa, Ethiopia, where she lives.

Ousmane Sow Huchard

Former director of the Musée Dynamique in Dakar, Senegal, Ousmane Sow Huchard is the Scientific Commissioner of the Dakar Biennial and the director of the cultural engineering firm CIWARA in Dakar, where he lives.

Yvone Vera

She teaches history and is the director of the National Gallery of Bulawayo, Zimbabwe.

Jean-Luc Vellut

A professor in the history department of the Université Catholique de Louvain, Jean-Luc Vellut taught at the Universities of Kinshasa and Lubumbashi in the Congo for many years. He has published articles on the cultural and social history of Central Africa between the 18th and 20th centuries. He lives in Brussels.

Sue Williamson

A plastic artist known for her productions on the contemporary history of South Africa, and an anti-apartheid militant during the 1980s, Sue Williamson is the author of "Resistance Art in South Africa", 1989, and "Art in South Africa: the Future Present", 1996. Sue Williamson edits the South African contemporary art internet magazine "Artthob", which she created in 1997. She lives in Cape Town, South Africa.

Gaving Younge

A plastic artist and anti-apartheid militant from the very beginning, Gavin Younge is the director of the Michaëlis School of Fine Arts in Cape Town, South Africa. He has been a commissioner for exhibitions and is an author, notably of the book "Art of the South Africa Township". He lives in Cape Town.

Bibliography

1. Traditional arts, History, Archeology, Decorative arts

Books

- APOLLINAIRE Guillaume and GUILLAUME Paul, *Sculptures Nègres*, Paris,1917.
- BAQUÉ Philippe, *Un nouvel or noir: pillage des œuvres d'art en Afrique*, Paris-Mediterranean, documents, Paris, 1999.
- BASTIN Marie-Louise, *La sculpture Tshokwé*, A&F. Chaffin, Meudon, 1982.
- BASTIN Marie-Louise, *Introduction aux Arts de l'Afrique Noire*, Arnouville,1984.
- BAUMANN H. and WESTERMANN D., *Les peuples et les civilisations de l'Afrique*, Paris, 1948.
- BEN-AMOS Paula, *L'art du Bénin*, Rive Gauche Productions, Paris, 1978.
- BRAIN R., *The decorated body*, Harper & Row, New York, 1979.
- BURAUD G., *Les masques*, essai, Seuil, Paris, 1948.
- BUXTON, *The Abyssinians*, London, 1970.
- CAILLOIS Roger, preface, *Masques*, Musée Guimet, Paris, 1959.
- CATON-THOMPSON G., *The Zimbabwe culture: ruins & reactions*, Cass library of African studies, *African Prehistory*, n°1, London, 1931, (new edition 1971).
- CHOJNACKI S., *"Short Introduction to Ethiopian Painting"*, Journal of Ethiopian Studies, 1964.
- CHOJNACKI S., *Notes on Art in Ethiopia in the 15th and early 16th century*, Journal of Ethiopian Studies, T VIII, 1970.
- CHOJNACKI S., *Ethiopia, the Christian Art of an African Nation*, Salem, Mass, 1978.
- CHOJNACKI S., *Major Themes in Ethiopian Painting. Indigenous Developments, the Influence of Foreign Models and their Adaptation from the 13th to the 19th Century*, Wiesbaden, 1983.
- CLOUZOT Henri and LEVEL André, *L'Art Nègre, Sculptures Africaines et Océaniennes*, Librairie de France, Paris, 1926.
- COQUET Michèle, *Textiles africains*, Adam Biro, Paris, 1993.
- COLE Herbert, *Icons, ideals and power in the Art of Africa*, National Museum of African Art, Smithsonian Institution, Washington DC / London, 1989.
- *Colloque sur l'art nègre*, First International Festival of Black Arts, 2 vol, Dakar, 1966.
- CORNEVIN Marianne, *Archéologie Africaine*, Maisonneuve et Larose, Paris, 1993.
- CORNEVIN Marianne, *Secrets du continent noir révélés à l'archéologie*, Maisonneuve et Larose, Paris, 1998.
- COURTNEY-CLARKE Margaret, *Ndebele, the art of an african tribe*, Rizzoli, New York, 1986.
- COURTNEY-CLARKE Margaret, *Tableaux d'Afrique, l'art mural des femmes de l'ouest*, Arthaud, 1990.
- COURTNEY-CLARKE Margaret, *Ndebele, L'art d'une tribu d'Afrique du Sud*, Arthaud, 1992.
- DARKOWSKA Olenka, *l'Afrique Noire en marionnettes*, Unima, Charleville-Mézières, 1988.
- DE GRUNNE Bernard (under the direction of), *Mains de maîtres, à la découverte des sculpteurs d'Afrique*, Espace Culturel BBL, Brussels, 2001.
- DELANGE J. and LEIRIS Michel, *Arts et peuples de l'Afrique Noire, la création plastique*, Gallimard, Paris, 1967.
- DUCHÂTEAU Armand, *Bénin, trésor royal*, collection of the Museum für Völkerkunde de Vienne, Fondation Dapper, Paris, 1990.
- EINSTEIN Carl, *Neger Plastik*, München,1920. (French translation, 1922: *La Sculpture Africaine*, Crès, Paris).
- FAGG William, *Tribes and forms in African Art*, London, Methuen, 1965.
- FAGG William, *Nok terracottas*, The Nigerian Museum & Ethnographica Ltd, Lagos & London, 1973.
- FAGG William, *Masques d'Afrique*, Nathan, Paris, 1980.
- FAGG William, *Yoruba beadwork*, Rizzoli, New York, 1980.
- FAÏK-NZUJI Clémentine, *Symboles graphiques en Afrique Noire*, Karthala-Ciltade, Paris, 1992.
- FÉAU Étienne and JOUBERT Hélène, *L'art africain, tableaux choisis*, Éditions Scala, Paris, 1996.
- FÉLIX M., *Kipinga*, Fred Jahn, München, 1991.
- FISCHER Angela, *Fastueuse Afrique*, Chêne, Paris, 1984.
- FOSU K., *20th Century Art of Africa*, Zaria, 1986.
- FROBENIUS Léo, *L'Art Africain*, Cahiers d'Art n°5, Paris, 1930.
- GABUS Jean, *Art nègre, recherche de ses fonctions et dimensions*, Neuchâtel, 1967.
- GALLOIS-DUQUETTE Danielle, *Dynamique de l'art Bidyogo*, Instituto de Investigaçao Cientifica Tropical, Lisbonne, 1983.
- GERSTER G., *Churches in Rock: Early Christian Art in Ethiopia*, London, 1970.
- GILLON W., *A short history of African Art*, Penguin Book, London, 1984.
- GRIAULE Marcel, *Silhouettes et grafittis abyssins*, Paris, 1933.
- GRIAULE Marcel, *Masques Dogon*, Institut d'Ethnologie, Paris, 1938.
- HENZE P., *Aspects of Ethiopian Art from Ancient Aksum to the 20th Century*, London, 1993.
- *Historique de l'IFAN*, in Notes Africaines, april 1961, trimestriel n°90, 1961.
- HUET M., Laude J. and Paudrat J-L., *Danses d'Afrique*, Chêne, Paris, 1978.
- HUET M. and Savary CL., *Danses d'Afrique*, Chêne, Paris, 1994.
- JEWELL Rebecca, *African Designs*, British Museum Pattern Books, London, 1994.
- KERCHACHE J., PAUDRAT J-L. and STEPHAN L., *l'Art Africain*, Mazenod, Paris, 1988.
- KERCHACHE Jacques, (under the direction of), *Sculptures Afrique, Asie, Océanie, Amériques*, Galerie des Arts Premiers, Louvre, Pavillon des Sessions, R.M.N, Paris, 2000.
- KI-ZERBO Joseph, *Histoire de l'Afrique Noire*, Hattier, Paris, 1978.
- KJERSMEIER C., *Centres des style de la sculpture nègre africaine* (4 vol), 1935-38, Paris. (New edition New York, 1967).
- *L'Art Nègre*, special issue of *Présence Africaine*, n°10-11, Paris 1951.
- LAUDE Jean, *Les arts de l'Afrique Noire*, Horizons de France, Paris, 1966.
- LEBEUF Jean-Paul, *Archéologie Tchadienne: les Sao du Cameroun et du Tchad*, Hermann, Paris, 1962.
- LELOUP Hélène, *Statuaire Dogon*, éditions Amez, Strasbourg, 1994.
- LE MOAL Guy, *Les Bobo: nature et fonction des masques*, ORSTOM, coll. Travaux et Documents, n°121, Paris, 1980.
- LEROY J., *Ethiopian Painting in the Late Middle Ages and under the Gondar Dynasty*, London, 1967.
- *Major Themes in Ethiopian Painting Indigenous Developments, the Influence of Foreign Models and their Adaptation from the 13th to the 19th Century*, Wiesbaden, 1983.
- MAQUET Jacques, Afrique, *Les civilisations noires*, Horizons de France, Paris, 1962.
- MAUNY Raymond, *Les siècles obscurs de l'Afrique noire*, Fayard, coll. Résurrection du passé, Paris, 1970.
- MEYER Laure, *Objets africains, vie quotidienne, rites, arts de cour*, Terrail, Paris, 1994.
- MURDOCK G.P., *Africa: its peoples and their culture history*, New York, 1959.
- MVENG Engelbert, *L'art d'Afrique Noire: liturgie cosmique et langage religieux*, CLE, Yaoundé, 1974.
- NEYT François, *La grande statuaire Hemba du Zaïre*, Institut Supérieur d'Archéologie et d'Histoire de l'Art, Louvain-la-Neuve, 1977.
- NIANGORAN-BOUAH Georges, *L'univers des poids à peser l'or*, N.E.A, 3 tomes, Abidjan, 1984-85-87.
- PANKHURST Richard, *Some Notes for a History of Ethiopian Secular Art*, Ethiopia Observer, 1966.
- PANKHURST R., *Ethiopian Manuscript Illustrations: Some Aspects of the Artist's Craft as Revealed in Seventeenth and Eighteenth Century Bindings in the British Library*, Azania, 1984.
- PERROIS Louis, *La statuaire fan, Gabon*, ORSTOM, Collection Mémoires, n°59, Paris, 1972.
- PICTON John and MACK John, *African Textiles, looms, weaving & design*, British Museum, London, 1979.
- PLANT P., *Painter's Pattern Book*, Mekelle, Tigre Province, Ethiopia, Ethiopia Observer, 1973.
- PLASCHKE Dieter and ZIRNGIBL Manfred A., *Afrikanische Schielde, African Shields*, Panterra, München, 1992.
- PRICE Sally, *Primitive Art in Civilized Places*, The University of Chicago Press, Chicago/London, 1989.
- *Primitivisme dans l'art du xxe siècle (Le)*, under the direction of W. Rubbin, Flammarion, Paris, 1987.
- Royal Asiatic Society, *Proceedings of the First International Conference on the History of Ethiopian Art*, London, 1989.
- SÉDAR SENGHOR Léopold, *Liberté 1, Négritude et Humanisme*, Seuil, Paris, 1964.
- SCHAEDLER Karl-Ferdinand, *Le tissage en Afrique au sud du Sahara*, Panterra-Verlag, Munich, 1987.
- SIEBER Roy, *African furniture & household objets*, The American Federation of Arts, New York, Indiana University Press, Bloomington, London, 1980.
- TARDITS Claude, *Le royaume Bamoun*, Armand Colin, Paris, 1980.
- *Textiles of Africa*, edited by Dale Idiens & K.G. Pontins, the Pasold Research Fund LTD, Bath, 1980.
- TROWELL Margaret, *African Design*, Faber & Faber, London, 1960.
- VAN DER SLEEN W.G.N, *A handbook on beads*, Association internationale pour l'histoire du verre, Librairie Halvart, Liège, 1973.
- VANSINA Jan, *Art history in Africa*, Longman, London & New York, 1984.
- VOGEL Susan, *L'art Baoulé: du visible et de l'invisible*, Adam Biro, Paris, 1999.
- WILLETT Frank, *Ifé, une civilisation africaine*, Jardin des Arts, Tallandier, 1971.
- ZIRNGIBL Manfred A., *Seltene Afrikanische Kurzwaffen, rare african short weapons* (Engl.

& French. translation), Verlag Morsak, Grafenau RFA, 1983.

Exhibition catalogues

- *Africa, the art of a continent*, London, Royal Academy of Arts, 1995.
- *African textiles & decorative arts*, Sieber Roy, MOMA, New York, 1972.
- *Afrikanische Keramik,Traditionelle Handwerskunst Südlich der Sahara*, edited by Arnulf Stössel, Hirmer Verlag & Staatliches Museum für Völkerkunde, Munich, 1984.
- *Ama Ndebele, signals of colour from South Africa*, Berlin, Haus der Kulturen der Welt, 1991.
- *Arts d'Afrique*, Musée Dapper, Gallimard, Paris, 2000.
- *Art of African textiles (The), technology, tradition & lurex*, Barbican Art Gallery, London, 1995.
- *Art Nègre : sources, évolution, expansion*, First International Festival of Black Arts, Dakar-Paris, 1966.
- *Au fil de la parole*, Musée Dapper, Paris, 1995.
- *Batéké, peintres et sculpteurs d'Afrique centrale*, RMN, Paris, 1998.
- *Beauté fatale, armes d'Afrique centrale*, Crédit communal, Brussels, 1992.
- *Corps sculptés, corps parés, corps masqués, chefs-d'œuvre de Côte d'Ivoire*, Galeries nationales du Grand-Palais, Paris, 1989.
- *Dessins Bamum (Les)*, exhibition catalogue, Musée d'Arts Africains, Océaniens et Amérindiens, Musées de Marseille, Skira, 1998.
- *Face of the Spirits, masks from the Zaïre Basin*, Etnografisch Museum, Antwerpen, 1993.
- *Images from Bamun*, German Colonial Photography at the court of King Njoya, Cameroon, West-Africa, National Museum of African Art, Smithsonian, Washington, 1988.
- *Masques et mascarades*, Musée de la Civilisation, éditions Fides, Québec, 1984.
- *Middle Art* (Augustin Okoye), Beier Ulli, Berlin, Maison des Cultures du Monde, 1990.
- *Milwa Mnyaluza Pemba George Retrospective Exhibition*, South African National Gallery, 1996.
- *Neglected Tradition Towards a New History of South African Art (1930-1988) (The)*, Johannesburg Art Gallery, Johannesburg 1988.
- *Neue Kunst aus Afrika*, Maison des Cultures du Monde, Berlin, 1996.
- *Parole du fleuve (La), harpes d'Afrique centrale*, Musée de la Musique, Cité de la Musique, 1999.
- *Planète des masques, œuvres majeures de la Communauté française de Belgique et du Musée international du Carnaval et du masque Binche*, preface by Claude Lévi-Strauss, Communauté française de Belgique, Ministère de la Culture et des Affaires Sociales, Brussels, 1995.
- *Potter's art in Africa (The)*, Fagg William and Picton John, British Museum, London, 1970.
- *Power of the hand : african arms and armour (The)*, Spring Christopher, Museum of Mankind, London, 1996.
- *Rois sculpteurs (Les), art et pouvoir au Grassland camerounais*, legs Pierre Harter, R.M.N, MAAO, Paris, 1993.
- *Sculptures Africaines dans les collections publiques Françaises*, Orangerie, Paris, 1972.
- *Sièges Africains*, Prestel-R.M.N, Paris, 1994.
- *Smashing pots, feats of clay from Africa*, Barley Nigel, Museum of Mankind, British Museum, London, 1994.
- *Sura Dji : visages et racines du Zaïre*, Musée des Arts Décoratifs, Paris, 1982.
- *Tellem textiles, archaeological finds from burial caves in Mali's Bandiagara cliff*, Bolland R., Bedaux R. and Boser-Sarivaxévanis R., Tropenmuseum-Amsterdam, Rijksmuseum voor Volkenkunde-Leiden, Institut des Sciences Humaines-Musée national-Bamako, 1991.
- *Trésors de l'ancien Nigeria*, Galeries nationales du Grand-Palais, AFAA, Paris, 1984.
- *Trésors d'Afrique, Musée de Tervuren*, Musée Royal de l'Afrique Centrale, Tervuren, 1995.
- *Vallées du Niger*, M.A.A.O, R.M.N, Paris, 1993.

2. Architecture and African Villages

- *Architectures de terre (Des)*, Centre Georges-Pompidou, CCI, 1981.
- BEDAUX Roger, VAN DER WAALS J.D., *Djenné, une ville millénaire au Mali*, Leiden-Gand, 1994.
- DENYER Susan, *African traditional architecture*, Heinemann, London, 1978.
- DOMIAN Sergio, *Architecture soudanaise, vitalité d'une tradition urbaine et monumentale, Mali/Côte-d'Ivoire/BurkinaFaso/Ghana*, L'Harmattan, Paris, 1989.
- ELA Jean-Marc, *La ville en Afrique*, Khartala, Paris, 1989.
- GARDI René, *Maisons africaines : l'art traditionnel de bâtir en Afrique occidentale*, Elsevier-Sequoia, Paris, 1974.
- MAAS Pierre and Mommersteeg Geert, *Djenné, chef-d'œuvre architectural*, Institut Royal des Tropiques-Amsterdam, Université de Technologie-Eindhoven, Inst. des Sciences Humaines-Musée national-Bamako, 1992.
- RONCAYOLO M. and Paquot T., *Villes et civilisation urbaine, XVIIIe-XXe siècles*, Larousse, Paris, 1992.
- SOULILOU Jacques (under the direction of), *Rives Coloniales*, architectures de St-Louis à Douala, Parenthèses-Orstorm, Paris.

3. Plastic Arts

Books

- ADÉAGBO Georges, *Conversations avec Muriel Bloch*, Éd. Au figuré, le Quartier, Paris, 1998.
- ADLER Peter and Barnard Nicholas, *Asafo! African Flags of the Fante*, Thames & Hudson, London, 1993.
- ALEXANDER Lucy, *Art in South Africa since 1900*, AA Balkema, Cape Town, 1962.
- ALEXANDER Lucy and COHEN Evelyn, *150 South African Paintings, Past and Present*, Struikhof Publishers, Cape Town, 1990.
- *Anthologie des Arts Plastiques Contemporains au Sénégal*, Museum für Völkerkunde, Frankfurt am Main, 1989.
- ASHRAF Jamal and Williamson Sue, *Art in South Africa*, David Philip, Cape Town, 1996.
- BECKER C., *The Subversive Imagination Artists*, Society, & Social Responsibility, New York and London, Routledge, 1994.
- BEIER Ulli, *Art in Nigeria 1960*, Cambridge 1960.
- BEIER Ulli, *Contemporary art in Africa*, London, 1968.
- BERMAN Esmé, *Art & Artists of South Africa, An Illustrated biographical dictionary and historical survey of painters, sculptors and graphic artists since 1875*, AA Balkema, Cape Town, 1983.
- BIANCHI Paolo, *Afrika-Iwalewa*, Kunstforum 122, Rupprichteroth, Editions Bechtloff, 1993.
- BRULY BOUABRÉ Frédéric, *La grande vérité, Les astres africains:* éditions Braus, Heildelberg, 1993.
- BRULY BOUABRÉ Frédéric, *Domin et Zézé, Légende*, Hazan/Revue Noire, Paris, 1994.
- CORNET Joseph-Aurélien, DE CNODDER Remi, TOEBOSCH Wim, *60 ans de peinture au Zaïre*, Les Editeurs d'Art Associés, Brussels, 1989.
- COLE H. M. and ROSS D.H., *The Arts of Ghana*, Los Angeles, 1977.
- COUZENS T., *The New Africans: A Study of the Life and Work of H. I. E. Dhlomo*, Raven Press, Johannesburg, 1985.
- DAMANT C.G., *Samuel Makoanyane*, Morija Sesuto Book Depot, Basutoland, 1951.
- De Jager Ej, *Images of Man, Contemporary South African Black Art and Artists*, Fort Hare University Press, 1992.
- DEVERDUN René, *Jérôme Ramedane, peintre centrafricain*, Sépia, Paris, 1995.
- EDWARD Lucie-Smith, *Race, Sex, and Gender in Contemporary Art*, Harry N. Abrams, New York, 1994.
- ELLIOT David and al, *Art from South Africa*, London, 1990.
- FABIAN Johannes, *Remembering the Present. Painting and Popular History in Zaire*, Berkeley University, Los Angeles, 1996.
- FÖRSTER Till, *Schildermalerei oder urban art? Postmoderne Interpretationen in der afrikanischen Kunst*, Paideuma, 1996.
- FRANSEN Hans, *Three Centuries of South African Art, Fine Art, Architecture, Applied Arts*, AD. Donker, Johannesburg, 1982.
- GAUDIBERT Pierre, *Un pop'art d'Afrique noire?*, Silex nº23, "Expressions d'Afrique", Grenoble, 1982.
- GAUDIBERT Pierre, *Art Africain contemporain*, Cercle d'Art, Paris, 1991. (New edition 1994).
- *Image and Form – Prints, Drawings and sculpture from southern Africa and Nigeria*, School of Oriental and African Studies, London, 1997.
- JEWSIEWICKI Bogumil, *Chéri Samba, The Hybridity of Art*, Contemporary African Artists Series, Esther A. Dagan, Montreal, 1995.
- JOUANNAIS Jean-Yves (under the direction of), *Un art contemporain d'Arique du Sud*, Éditions Plume, Paris, 1994.
- JULES-ROSETTE Benetta, *The Messages of Tourist Art, An African Semiotic System in Comparative Perspective*, Indiana University, Thomas A.Sebeok, Bloomington, 1984.
- KONATÉ Yacouba, *Christian Lattier, le sculpteur aux mains nues*, Sépia, Saint-Maur, 1993.
- LEVINSOHN Rhoda, *Treasures in Transition, Art and Craft of Southern Africa*, Delta Book, Johannesburg, 1984.
- LITTLEFIELD-KASFIR Sidney, *Contemporary African Art*, Thames & Hudson, London, 2000.
- MAGNIN André and SOULILLOU Jacques, *Contemporary Art of Africa*, Harry N. Abrams, New York, 1996.
- MILES E., *Lifeline out of Africa, The Art of Ernest Mancoba*, Human & Rousseau, Cape Town, 1994.
- MILES E., *Land and Lives a story of early black artists*, Human & Rousseau, Cape Town, 1997.
- MOUNT M. W., *African Art : the years since 1920*, Indiana University Press, 1973.
- NETTLETON Anitra and HAMMOND-TOOKE David, *African Art in Southern Africa/From Tradition to Township*, Johannesburg, 1989.
- NDOMBASI Kufimba Bamba, and NTEMO Musangi, *Anthologie des sculpteurs et peintres zaïrois contemporains*, Nathan, Paris, 1987.
- OGUIBE Olu and ENWEZOR Okwui, *Reading the Contemporary, African Art from Theory to the Marketplace*, Institute of International Visual Arts, 1999.

- OTTENBERG Simon *New Traditions from Nigeria, Seven Artists of the Nsukka Group*, Smithsonian Institution, Washington, 1997.
- PICTON John, *Image and Form: prints, drawings and sculpture from southern Africa and Nigeria*, London, 1997.
- PICTON John et al. *El Anatsui, A sculpted history of Africa*, Saffron Books, London, 1998.
- PICTON J and LAW J. (under the direction of), *Cross Currents: contemporary art practice in South Africa*, Millfiled School, Somerset, 2000.
- RENAUDEAU Michel and STROBEL Michèle, *Peintures sous verre du Sénégal*, Nathan, NEA, Paris/Dakar, 1984.
- *Sculptures en ciment du Nigeria de S.J. Akpan et A.O. Akpan*, AFAA, Paris, 1985.
- *Sculptures contemporaines du Zimbabwe*, MAAO, ADEIAO, Paris, 1990.
- SENDEGEYA Peter-Claver, *Anthologie des sculpteurs et peintres contemporains*, ACCT, Nathan, Paris, 1989.
- *Set setal: des murs qui parlent... Nouvelle culture urbaine à Dakar*, Enda, Dakar, 1991.
- SHAW Th., Brincard and DEDIEU M., *Treasures of a popular art: Paintings on glass from Sénégal*, The African-American Institute of New York, 1986.
- SILLERY, *Art pictural zaïrois*, Éditions du Septentrion, Québec, 1992.
- *Souleymane Keita, La représentation de l'inconnu*, Sépia-NEAS, Saint-Maur, 1994.
- SOW HUCHARD Ousmane, *Viyé Diba, Plasticien de l'environnement*, Sépia/NEAS, Saint-Maur, 1994.
- *Sow Ousmane, sculptures*, Ed. Revue Noire, Paris 1995.
- SYLLA Abdou, *Arts plastiques et État au Sénégal*, Dakar, IFAN-CAD, 1998.
- VOGEL Susan, *African Explores, 20th Century African Art*, The Center for African Art, New York/Munich, Prestel, 1991.
- WILLIAMSON Sue, *Resistance Art in South Africa*, David Philip, Johannesburg, 1989.
- WINTER-IRVING Celia, *Contemporary Stone Sculpture in Zimbabwe, Context, Content and Form*, Craftsman House, Sydney, 1993.
- YOUNGE Gavin, *Art of the South African Townships*, Thames & Hudson, London,1988.
- *Zimbabwe, Témoins de la Terre, Passé et Présent*, Musée royal de l'Afrique centrale, Geert G. Bourgois, Tervuren, 1997.

Exhibition catalogues

- AGTHE Johanna and MUNDT Christina, *Signs of the Time, New Art from Africa*, Museum für Völkerkunde, Frankfurt,1991.
- *Africa, Vibrant New Art from a Dynamic Continent*, Tobu Museum of Art, Tokyo, 1998.
- *Africas: The artist and the city, a journey and an exhibition*, Actar A, Consortium of the centre de culture contemporània de Barcelona, Barcelona, 2001.
- *Africa Hoy*, Centro Atlantico de Arte Moderno, Las Palmas de Gran Canaria, 1991.
- *Africus: Johannesburg Biennale*, Transtional Metropolitan Council, Johannesburg, 1995.
- *António Ole, retrospectiva 1967-1997*, Centre culturel portugais, Insitut Camões, 1997.
- *Art et Traditions du Congo*, MAAO, ADEIAO, Paris, 1987.
- *Art From The Frontline, Contemporary Art from Southern Africa*, Frontline States and Karia Press, London, 1990.
- *Art pour l'Afrique*, MAAO, ADEIAO, Paris, 1988.
- *Arts sénégalais d'aujourd'hui*, Lassaigne J., *Le Journal des grandes expositions*, Galeries nationales du Grand Palais, Paris, 1974.
- *Art sur Vie, Art contemporain du Sénégal*, Ministère de la Coopération et du développement, la Grande Arche, Paris, 1990.
- *Andere Reise (Die), The other journey, Afrika und die Diaspora*, Holzhausen, Vienne, 1996.
- *Anderen Modernen (Die)*, Zeitgenössische kunst aus afrika asien und lateinamerica, Éditions Braus, Berlin, 1997.
- BEIER Ulli, Middle Art (Augustin Okoye), *Mein Leben, Middle Art*, Berlin, Maison des Cultures du Monde, Stutgart, 1990.
- *Beyound the Borders, Kwangju Biennale*, 1995.
- BIAZIN Clément-Marie, Laude Jean, *Esquisses pour une encyclopédie biazine*, Tiers Mondes, Arts Majeurs, MAAO, Paris, 1994.
- *Biennale Internationale des arts, Dakar 1992*, Beaux-Arts Magazine, Paris, 1992.
- *Big City, Artists from Africa*, Serpentine Gallery, London, 1995.
- *Bogolan et arts Graphiques du Mali*, Musée national des arts africains et océanies, ADEIAO, Paris, 1990.
- *Bomoi Mobimba, Toute la Vie, 7 artistes zaïrois, Collection Lucien Bilinelli*, Palais des Beaux-Arts, Charleroi, 1996.
- *Chéri Samba*, MAAO-Hazan, Paris, 1996.
- *Contemporary African Artists: Changing Tradition*, The Studio Museum of Harlem, New York, 1990.
- *Contemporary South African Art 1985-1995, from the South African National Gallery Permanent Collection*, Emma Bedford, 1997.
- *Contemporary South African Art, The Gencor Collection*, Jonathan Ball Publishers, Johannesburg, 1997.
- *Dak'Art 96*, Biennale de l'Art Africain Contemporain, Cimaise Paris, April 1996.
- *Dak'Art 98*, Biennale de l'Art Africain Contemporain, Cimaise Paris, April 1998.
- *Dak'Art 2000, Biennale de l'art africain contemporain*, Cimaise Paris, May 2000.
- Deliss Clémentine and al, *Seven Stories about Modern Art in Africa*, London, 1995.
- *Dessins Bamun (Les)*, Musée d'Arts Africains Océaniens et Amérindiens, Milan/Skira, Marseille, 1997.
- *Dialogues de paix*, AFAA, Paris, 1995.
- *Every Day, 11th Biennale of Sysdney*, Jo Spark and Jonathan Watkins, Sydney, 1998.
- *Galerie des cinq continents (La)*, MAAO, R.M.N, Paris, 1995.
- *Home and the World: Architectural Sculpture by Two Contemporary African Artists*, The Museum for African Art, New York, Prestel, Munich, 1993.
- *Iba N' Diaye, un peintre, un humaniste*, Staaliches Museum für Völkerkunde, Munich, 1987.
- *Images of other cultures, Re-viewing Ethnographic Collections of the British Museum and the National Museum of Ethnology*, Kenji Yoshida and John Mack, Osaka, 1997.
- *I was Lonelyness, The Complete Graphic Works Old John Muafangefo, A Catalogue Raisonné 1968-1987*, Levinson (Orde), Struik Winchester, Cape Town, 1992.
- *Kenya Art Panorama*, Centre Culturel Français, Nairobi, 1992.
- *Le roi Salomon et les maîtres du regard, art et médecine en Éthiopie*, RMN, Paris, 1992.
- *Les Toiles du sud et d'ailleurs, dix jeunes plasticiens francophones exposent*, éditions ACCT, Paris, 1991.
- *Liberated Voices, Contemporary Art from South Africa*, The Museum for African Art, New York/Munich, Prestel, 1999.
- *Lumière noire, Art Contemporain*, Centre d'Art de Tanlay, 1997.
- McEvilley Thomas, *Fusion: West African Artists At The Venice Biennale*, The Museum For African Art, New York,1993.
- *Magiciens de la Terre (Les)*, Centre Beaubourg-La Villette, Paris, 1989.
- *Magiciens de la Terre (Les)*, Cahiers du Musée national d'art moderne, Centre Georges-Pompidou, nº28, Paris, été 1989.
- *Milwa Mnyaluza Pemba George*, Retrospective Exhibition, South African National Gallery, Cape Town, 1996.
- *Moustapha Dimé*, Association pour la Promotion des Arts, Paris, 1999.
- *Mozambique! Exhibition Workshop Programmes*, Kerstin Danielsson, The Culture House, Stockholm, 1987.
- *Neglected Tradition Towards a New History of South African Art (1930-1988)*, Johannesburg Art Gallery, Johannesburg, 1988.
- *Neue Kunst aus Afrika*, Afrikanische gegenwartskunst aus der sammlung Gunter Peus, Katholische Akademie, Hamburg, 1984.
- *Neue Kunst aus Afrika*, Haus der kulturen der welt, Editions Braus, Berlin, 1996.
- *9 Artistas de Moçambique*, Commissariat général du Mozambique pour l'Exposition Universelle de Séville, Séville, 1992.
- *Osaka Triennale'90, The International Triennale Competition of Painting*, Osaka Foundation of Culture, Osaka, 1990.
- *Otro pais, escalas africanas*, Centro Atlantico de Arte Moderno, Las Palmas de Gran Canaria, Tabapress S.A, Las Palmas, 1994.
- *Peintures Populaires du sénégal, "Souwerew"*, Musée national des Arts Africains et Océaniens, ADEIAO, Paris, 1987.
- *Persons and Pictures, the modernist eye in Africa*, Newtown Galleries, Johannesburg, 1995.
- *Published privately in conjunction with the "Cecil Skotnes Retrospective"* at the South African National Gallery, Harmsen F., Cecil Skotnes, Cape Town, 1996.
- *Rencontres africaines*, Institut du Monde Arabe, Paris, 1994.
- SACK S., *The Neglected Tradition Towards a New History of South African Art (1930-1988)*, Johannesburg Art Gallery, Johannesburg 1989.
- *South Meets West*, National Museum of Ghana, Accra, Kunsthalle, Bern, 1999.
- *Tiempo de Africa (El)*, Centre Atlantique d'Art Moderne, Espagne, 2000.
- *TRUCE: Echoes of Art in an Age of Endless Conclusions*, Janine Sieja, Site Santa Fe, 1997.
- SECRETAN T, *Going into Darkness, fantasy coffins from Africa*, London, 1995. (Édition française, Paris, 1994)
- *Suites Africaines*, Couvent des Cordeliers, La Revue Noire, Paris, 1997.
- *Zeitgenössische Skulptur Europa Afrika, 7.Triennale der Kleinplastik*, Ostfildern-Ruit, Cantz, 1998.

Periodicals

- *Arts d'Afrique Noire* renamed *Arts Premiers*, Arnouville, France.
- *African Arts*, Center of African Studies, UCLA, Los Angeles, USA.
- *Objets et Mondes*, Musée de l'Homme, Paris, France.
- *Journal de la Société des Africanistes*, Paris, France.
- *NKA, journal of contemporary african art*, New York, USA.
- *Revue Noire*, Paris, France.

Index of artists cited

• Bold numbers indicate illustrated works.
• List of the participants in the 1st World Festival of Black Arts in Dakar, in 1966: p. 229

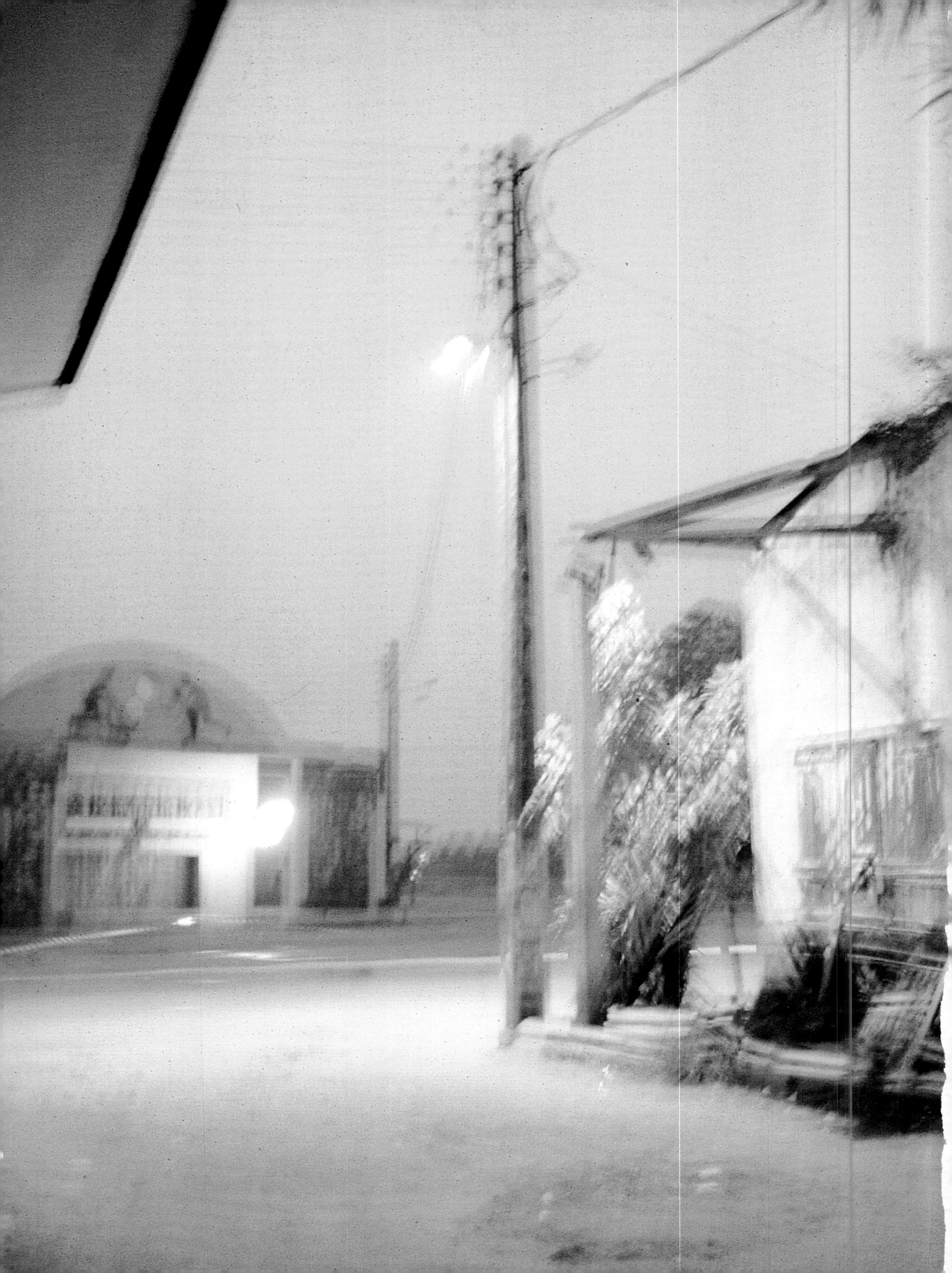